Cooking Light®

ANNUAL RECIPES 2006

Oxmoor House®

Our Favorite Recipes

Not all recipes are created equal. At *Cooking Light*®, only those that have passed muster with our Test Kitchens staff and food editors—not an easy crowd to please—make it onto the pages of our magazine. We rigorously test each recipe, often two or three times, to ensure not only that they're healthy and reliable, but also that they taste as good as they possibly can. So which of our recipes are our favorites? They're the ones readers keep calling and writing about, the ones our staff whip up for their own families and friends. They're not always the ones that rated the highest, but they're the dishes that are definitely the most memorable.

◀ **Garlic Flatbreads with Smoked Mozzarella and Tomato Vinaigrette** (*page 296*):

Tapas, or small-plate dining, is gaining popularity for the variety and excitement it can provide to meals. Smoked mozzarella gives this appetizer a distinctive appeal.

◀ **Country Lima Beans** (*page 165*):

Humble ingredients combine to make this side dish a flavorful and homey addition to your plate.

◀ **Carrot Sheet Cake with Cream Cheese Frosting** (*page 123*):

Moist, rich, and lightly spiced, this carrot cake is so delicious you'll never miss the extra calories.

◀ **Easy Schnitzel** (*page 273*):

Ready to become a family favorite, chicken makes this dish not only lighter than the original veal version, but also a snap to prepare.

◀ **Chicken and Broccoli Casserole** (*page 298*):

Here's a lightened version of a classic. Enjoy the delightful combination of chicken and broccoli in a creamy sauce.

◀ **Apple Brown Betty** (*page 45*):

In this variation of the rustic dessert, two types of apples ensure that it's not too sweet or tart—the perfect warm and fruity complement to any meal.

◀ **Cilantro-Serrano Pesto with Grilled Chicken and Penne** (*page 20*):

Authentic Texas accents of cilantro, pecans, and Mexican cheese are prominent in this colorful pasta.

▲ **Roasted Chicken with Onions, Potatoes, and Gravy** (page 165): For a complete meal, pair this succulent chicken with a green vegetable and dinner rolls.

◄ **French-Style Stuffed Eggs** (page 74):

Often served warm in France, these eggs showcase ham, green onions, and herbs.

◄ **Smoky Tomato Salsa** (page 216):

Smoked tomatoes and jalapeño pepper blend beautifully with garlic and lime in this salsa.

◄ **Herbed Chicken Breasts with Tomatillo Salsa and Queso Fresco** (page 25):

Citrus, tomatillos, and fresh herbs brighten this wintertime dish.

◄ **Beet and Leek Salad with Peanut Dressing** (page 67):

This simple salad features hearty roasted beets, mild leeks, and a zesty peanut dressing.

◄ **Lemon Drop Liqueur** (page 209):

Homemade lemon-flavored liqueur mixes well with sparkling water for a light, refreshing spritzer. Or serve it straight up as a fruity martini.

◄ **Blueberry-Lemon Coffee Cake** (page 186):

Blueberries and lemon are a natural match. They come together nicely in this fruit-filled snack cake with a nutty hint of almond paste.

◄ **Hand-Hacked Pot Stickers** (page 310):

Tasty bundles full of shrimp, pork, cabbage, and spinach provide a pop of Asian flavor in your mouth.

◄ **Lemon Meringue Baked Alaska** (page 252):

What could be better than a refreshing lemon ice cream pie topped with a toasty meringue? This is a surefire summer treat.

▲ **Polenta Cake with Late-Summer Berries** *(page 226)*:

The grilled polenta cake offsets the vibrant collection of seasonal berries for a dessert that will satisfy any sweet tooth.

▲ **Lemon-Mint Bulgur Risotto with Garlic Shrimp** *(page 49)*:

Mint makes this risotto an ideal foil for the garlic-infused shrimp. Although chewy bulgur grains separate in tabbouleh, they stick together when cooked as a risotto.

▲ **Roast Pork Loin with Savory Fennel Bread Pudding** *(page 47)*:

Savory bread pudding adds flair to this tender pork roast for an effect that's equally satisfying and comforting.

▲ **Sautéed Scallops with Parsley and Garlic** *(page 213)*:

The secret to perfectly browned scallops is patience. Serve these simply seasoned scallops with gourmet greens.

Our Year at *Cooking Light*®

As editor in chief of *Cooking Light*, my own life is sometimes a laboratory of sorts for the magazine's stories and recipes. By my reckoning, I spent the last year making at least 300 breakfasts, lunches, and dinners. (Vacations, eating out, and family visits might whittle down that figure, but not by much.) That's a lot of cooking, and a lot of recipes. Yet I know I'm not alone; every reader of *Cooking Light* has the same steady need for new ideas for fresh menus. The quickest solution: this edition of *Cooking Light Annual Recipes*. Whatever you have facing you—be it a fast family dinner, a posh dinner party, or a holiday buffet—the magazine's staff and I hope you'll find help here.

As you can imagine, producing the country's top healthy living and epicurean magazine kept us busy in 2005. Here are some of the things we've enjoyed working on this year:

- Our "Cooking Class" series explored the many ways Americans learn to cook, from college classes to culinary vacations.
- Nationally and internationally renowned chefs—including Mark Bittman, Brian Glover, and Lise Stern—contributed their creativity to our "Inspired Vegetarian" column.
- The perennial popularity of Cooking Light Supper Clubs across the United States inspired a new array of stories in our September issue, which was full of party ideas and menus.
- The rousing response to our signature "Holiday Cookbook" encouraged us to move it to November. This year's edition is bigger and even better, featuring lots of great ideas for entertaining and gift giving.
- We continued to polish our readers' favorite columns. "Dinner Tonight" renders complete menus in about 30 minutes. And "Superfast" still delivers healthful recipes that are ready in less than 20 minutes—prep time included.

It was a busy year, to be sure. The happy result is that if you like to eat smart, be fit, and live well, this is the book for you. On behalf of all my *Cooking Light* colleagues, I hope you enjoy this new, recipe-packed edition of *Cooking Light Annual Recipes*.

Very truly yours,

Mary Kay Culpepper

Editor in Chief

contents

©2005 by Oxmoor House, Inc.
Book Division of Southern Progress Corporation
P.O. Box 2262, Birmingham, Alabama 35201-2262

ISBN: 0-8487-3012-7
ISSN: 1091-3645

Printed in the United States of America
First printing 2005

Be sure to check with your health-care provider before making any changes in your diet.

Oxmoor House, Inc.
Editor in Chief: Nancy Fitzpatrick Wyatt
Executive Editor: Katherine M. Eakin
Copy Chief: Allison Long Lowery

Cooking Light Annual Recipes 2006
Editor: Heather Averett
Copy Editor: Jacqueline B. Giovanelli
Editorial Assistants: Brigette Gaucher, Jessica Dorsey Kohls
Publishing Systems Administrator: Rick Tucker
Director of Production: Laura Lockhart
Production Manager: Greg A. Amason
Production Assistant: Faye Porter Bonner

Contributors:
Designer: Carol Damsky
Indexer: Mary Ann Laurens
Editorial Interns: Rachel Quinlivan, Mary Catherine Shamblin

To order additional publications, call 1-800-765-6400, or visit **oxmoorhouse.com**

Cover: *Mango Rice Salad with Grilled Shrimp* (page 192)
Page 1: *Streusel-Topped Key Lime Squares* (page 191)

Cooking Light®
Editor in Chief: Mary Kay Culpepper
Executive Editor: Billy R. Sims
Art Director: Susan Waldrip Dendy
Managing Editor: Maelynn Cheung
Senior Food Editor: Alison Mann Ashton
Senior Editor: Anamary Pelayo
Projects Editor: Mary Simpson Creel, M.S., R.D.
Associate Food Editors: Timothy Q. Cebula, Ann Taylor Pittman
Assistant Food Editor: Kathy C. Kitchens, R.D.
Assistant Editor: Cindy Hatcher
Contributing Beauty Editor: Lauren McCann
Test Kitchens Director: Vanessa Taylor Johnson
Food Stylist: Kellie Gerber Kelley
Assistant Food Stylist: M. Kathleen Kanen
Test Kitchens Professionals: Sam Brannock, Kathryn Conrad, Mary H. Drennen, Jan Jacks Moon, Tiffany Vickers, Mike Wilson
Assistant Art Director: Maya Metz Logue
Senior Designer: Fernande Bondarenko
Designer: J. Shay McNamee
Assistant Designer: Brigette Mayer
Senior Photographers: Becky Luigart-Stayner, Randy Mayor
Senior Photo Stylist: Cindy Barr
Photo Stylists: Melanie J. Clarke, Jan Gautro
Digital Photo Stylist: Jan A. Smith
Studio Assistant: Celine Chenoweth
Copy Chief: Maria Parker Hopkins
Senior Copy Editor: Susan Roberts
Copy Editor: Tara Trenary
Copy Researcher: Johannah Paiva
Production Manager: Liz Rhoades
Production Editors: Joanne McCrary Brasseal, Hazel R. Eddins
Administrative Coordinator: Carol D. Johnson
Office Manager: Rita K. Jackson
Editorial Assistants: Melissa Hoover, Brandy Rushing
Correspondence Editor: Michelle Gibson Daniels
Interns: Rachel Cardina, Marie Hegler, Emily Self

CookingLight.com
Editor: Jennifer Middleton
Online Producer: Abigail Masters

Congratulations! As a buyer of *Cooking Light Annual Recipes* 2005, you have exclusive access to the *Cooking Light* Web site on America Online. Simply go to www.cookinglight.com. When prompted, log on with this Web site access code: CLAR3222

Effective until December 31, 2006

In Search of the Perfect Food

We asked nine nutrition authorities to share their "perfect foods" choices. Here are some of the recipes they recommend along with the reasons why (page 8).

Melon, Berry, and Pear Salad with Cayenne-Lemon-Mint Syrup

This simple fruit salad takes its cue from Kelly Brownell. It's full of flavor and nutrients.

SYRUP:
- ⅓ cup sugar
- ⅓ cup water
- ¼ cup fresh lemon juice
- 3 tablespoons honey
- ½ teaspoon ground red pepper
- ¼ cup chopped fresh mint
- 1 tablespoon grated lemon rind

SALAD:
- 6 cups (1-inch) cubed cantaloupe
- 6 cups (1-inch) cubed honeydew melon
- 2 cups fresh blueberries
- 2 cups quartered fresh strawberries
- 1½ cups (½-inch) cubed ripe pear (about 2 medium)
- 1 cup fresh blackberries
- 1 tablespoon chopped fresh mint
- ⅛ teaspoon freshly ground black pepper

1. To prepare syrup, combine first 5 ingredients in a small saucepan. Bring to a boil; cook 3 minutes or until mixture is slightly syrupy. Remove from heat; stir in ¼ cup mint and rind. Let stand 30 minutes. Strain syrup through a sieve into a bowl; discard solids.
2. To prepare salad, combine cantaloupe and remaining 7 ingredients in a large bowl. Add syrup; toss gently to coat. Cover and refrigerate 2 hours, stirring occasionally. Yield: 10 servings (serving size: about 1½ cups).

CALORIES 168 (4% from fat); FAT 0.7g (sat 0.1g, mono 0.1g, poly 0.3g); PROTEIN 2.3g; CARB 42.6g; FIBER 3.1g; CHOL 0mg; IRON 0.8mg; SODIUM 37mg; CALC 33mg

MAKE AHEAD

Three-Grain Breakfast Cereal with Walnuts and Dried Fruit

Jane Brody loves a variety of cereals. Serve with yogurt or milk, and top with fresh fruit.

- ½ cup maple syrup
- ⅓ cup honey
- 3 tablespoons canola oil
- 1½ tablespoons vanilla extract
- 4½ cups regular oats
- 1 cup uncooked quick-cooking barley
- ¾ cup chopped walnuts or pecans
- ½ cup wheat germ
- 1 teaspoon ground cinnamon
- ¼ teaspoon ground nutmeg
- Cooking spray
- 1 (7-ounce) package dried mixed fruit, chopped (such as Sun-Maid brand)

1. Preheat oven to 325°.
2. Combine first 4 ingredients, stirring with a whisk.
3. Combine oats and next 5 ingredients in a large bowl. Add syrup mixture; stir well to coat. Spread oat mixture evenly onto a jelly-roll pan coated with cooking spray. Bake at 325° for 30 minutes or until browned, stirring every 10 minutes. Stir in dried fruit. Cool completely. Yield: 24 servings (serving size: ⅓ cup).
NOTE: Store in an airtight container up to 5 days.

CALORIES 185 (28% from fat); FAT 5.8g (sat 0.6g, mono 1.7g, poly 2.8g); PROTEIN 4.5g; CARB 31.3g; FIBER 4g; CHOL 0mg; IRON 1.6mg; SODIUM 4mg; CALC 24mg

Frisée, Baby Spinach, and Golden Beet Salad

(pictured on page 23)

This salad of greens, beets, and goat cheese would please Walter Willett's palate.

- ¾ pound golden beets
- 1 cup cranberry juice cocktail
- ⅓ cup sweetened dried cranberries
- 3 tablespoons sugar
- 2 tablespoons raspberry vinegar
- 1 tablespoon minced shallots
- ¼ teaspoon salt
- ¼ teaspoon freshly ground black pepper
- 1 tablespoon walnut oil
- 4 cups frisée or radicchio
- 4 cups baby spinach
- ½ cup (2 ounces) crumbled soft (log-style) goat cheese

1. Preheat oven to 400°.
2. Wrap each beet in foil. Bake at 400° for 1½ hours or until tender. Discard foil; cool beets 30 minutes. Trim off roots, and rub off skins. Cut beets into ⅛-inch-thick slices.
3. Combine cranberry juice, cranberries, sugar, and vinegar in a small saucepan. Bring to a boil; cook 11 minutes or until thick. Remove from heat. Stir in shallots, salt, and pepper. Gradually add oil, stirring with a whisk.
4. Combine lettuce and spinach in a large bowl. Add cranberry mixture; toss to coat. Add beets; toss gently to combine. Divide salad evenly among 6 plates. Top each salad with 4 teaspoons cheese. Yield: 6 servings.

CALORIES 175 (28% from fat); FAT 5.4g (sat 2.2g, mono 1.2g, poly 1.6g); PROTEIN 4.2g; CARB 28.7g; FIBER 3.3g; CHOL 7mg; IRON 1.7mg; SODIUM 214mg; CALC 74mg

Bowled Over by Fruit Salad

"A perfect food for me is fruit salad. I make it using cantaloupe, blueberries, strawberries, pears, and dried cranberries. It's low in calories and fat, and high in phytochemicals, antioxidants, fiber, and other vitamins essential for good health. Fruit also leaves you feeling fuller longer, which can help with weight maintenance. The other benefit is that you can find fruit almost year-round."
—Kelly Brownell, Ph.D., director of the Yale Center for Eating and Weight Disorders

Breakfast Salad

"Four or five kinds of cereals are my perfect foods—whole-grain corn puffs, Cheerios, shredded wheat, Bran Buds, corn bran, or oat squares—with 10 ounces of 'half-percent' milk. I mix skim and 1 percent milk because I like the taste better than pure skim. I top off the cereal with pineapple, raisins, bananas, or strawberries—whatever is in season—and always walnuts. You can call it my breakfast salad."
—Jane Brody, longtime personal-health columnist for the *New York Times* and author of *Jane Brody's Nutrition Book*

Salad Days

"I have a perfect dish. It's a salad that includes greens like baby spinach and green lettuce, almonds, modest amounts of a flavorful cheese like chèvre, a seasonal fruit like grapes, and perhaps an olive oil and vinegar dressing. The greens and fruit provide fiber and many vitamins and phytochemicals. The nuts provide healthy fats and more vitamins in a crunchy and tasty form, and the small amount of cheese delivers great flavor and some calcium. The dressing adds more healthy fats, energy, and antioxidants."
—Walter Willett, M.D., professor of epidemiology and nutrition at the Harvard School of Public Health and author of *Eat, Drink, and Be Healthy*

Blueberries—A Pint of Cure

"Blueberries are just packed with antioxidants and phytochemicals—and they taste great. You can find them year-round in supermarkets. They may be a hedge against Alzheimer's and colon cancer, plus they help fight the aging process. As a doctor, I'm always looking for foods that work for your health and are delicious to eat. These berries deliver on both fronts."
—Sanjay Gupta, M.D., senior medical correspondent for CNN

Hooked on Tuna

"I love tuna. I eat as much of it as I can. It's a lean source of protein, has heart-friendly omega-3 fatty acids, and is low in calories."
—Marianne J. Legato, M.D., founder of The Partnership for Women's Health at Columbia University and author of *Eve's Rib: The New Science of Gender-Specific Medicine and How It Can Save Your Life*

Souping Up Supper

"My perfect food is a perfect meal—vegetable soup using V8 juice (the spicy kind) and water as a base with a mixture of vegetables, especially corn, lima beans, tomatoes, green peas, carrots, and other veggies I have on hand. I'll add a dash of cayenne (ground red) pepper, garlic powder, white pepper, and a small piece of cinnamon stick that is left in the soup only for a short while. I go heavy on herbs like basil and rosemary, and might add some chopped chicken or diced stew beef for flavor. It's a one-pot meal, easy to make, tastes great, and delivers several servings of vegetables, as well as phytochemicals, vitamins, and fiber in a single bowl."
—Vivian W. Pinn, M.D., director of the Office of Research on Women's Health, National Institutes of Health

Rewarding Raspberries

"I love to eat raspberries straight—no sugar, perhaps with some low-fat frozen yogurt for dessert or paired with blueberries when they're in season. I also put them on my cereal in the morning and just snack on them during the day. Raspberries are a storehouse of fiber, antioxidants, vitamin C, folic acid, and potassium."
—Susan Laramee, M.S., R.D., president of the American Dietetic Association

Talking Tofu

"My favorite foods are red wine and dark chocolate. My perfect food is tofu, made from soybeans. I combine it with dark chocolate to make a tasty pudding. That's the great thing about tofu—mix it with anything and it magically takes on the taste of those foods you can't live without."
—Susan Love, M.D., medical director of the Susan Love, M.D., Breast Cancer Foundation and author of *Dr. Susan Love's Menopause and Hormone Book*

Health by Chocolate

"Here's a bit of a curveball: high-quality dark chocolate. I'm talking Belgian or French chocolate with no ingredients other than cocoa or chocolate liqueur, cocoa butter, and sugar, and maybe tiny amounts of flavoring like vanilla. It's a portable, highly concentrated source of nutrition. The dark kind usually has lower amounts of sugar compared with milk chocolate, and most of the saturated fat comes in the form of stearic acid, which is converted in the body to oleic acid—the main fatty acid in heart-healthy olive oil. Plus, it has antioxidants. All of which are good for heart health."
—Andrew Weil, M.D., author of *The Healthy Kitchen*

Chicken with Blueberry-Ginger Chutney

Sanjay Gupta would approve of this recipe that's loaded with blueberries. The chutney can be served warm, chilled, or at room temperature. Make it first, and chill while the chicken marinates, or prepare the chutney when the chicken is almost done marinating. Compared to fresh, frozen blueberries take about five minutes longer to cook and thicken because they release additional water.

CHUTNEY:
- 2 cups fresh or frozen blueberries
- ⅓ cup packed brown sugar
- ⅓ cup finely chopped onion
- ¼ cup golden raisins
- 3 tablespoons cider vinegar
- 1½ teaspoons grated peeled fresh ginger
- ¼ teaspoon salt
- ¼ teaspoon ground cinnamon
- ⅛ teaspoon crushed red pepper
- Dash of ground cloves
- 1 garlic clove, minced

CHICKEN:
- 1½ tablespoons olive oil
- ¾ teaspoon dried basil
- ¾ teaspoon dried oregano
- 6 (6-ounce) skinless, boneless chicken breast halves
- 3 garlic cloves, minced
- ¾ teaspoon salt
- ¼ teaspoon freshly ground black pepper

1. To prepare chutney, combine first 11 ingredients in a medium saucepan; bring to a boil. Reduce heat to medium-low, and simmer 25 minutes or until thick, stirring occasionally.
2. To prepare chicken, combine oil, basil, oregano, chicken, and 3 minced garlic cloves in a large heavy-duty zip-top plastic bag; seal. Marinate in refrigerator 2 hours, turning occasionally. Remove chicken from bag. Discard marinade. Sprinkle ¾ teaspoon salt and black pepper evenly over chicken.
3. Heat a large grill pan over medium-high heat. Cook chicken 5 minutes on each side or until done. Serve with chutney. Yield: 6 servings (serving size: 1 chicken breast half and about ¼ cup chutney).

CALORIES 321 (16% from fat); FAT 5.7g (sat 1.1g, mono 3g, poly 0.9g); PROTEIN 40.2g; CARB 26.9g; FIBER 1.9g; CHOL 99mg; IRON 2.1mg; SODIUM 511mg; CALC 51mg

Grilled Tuna Sandwiches with Onions, Bell Peppers, and Chile-Cilantro Mayonnaise

The tangy citrus quality of the mayonnaise pairs well with the grilled tuna—a favorite of Marianne Legato. Red bell peppers are a good source of the antioxidant beta-carotene, and the amount of bell peppers in just one sandwich delivers almost a whole day's requirement for vitamin C. When the weather is nice, prepare this on the grill.

- 6 tablespoons low-fat mayonnaise
- 2 tablespoons chopped fresh cilantro
- 1 teaspoon ground ancho chile pepper
- 1 teaspoon grated lime rind
- 1 teaspoon fresh lime juice
- ¼ teaspoon ground chipotle chile pepper
- 5 teaspoons olive oil, divided
- 4 (¼-inch-thick) slices Oso Sweet or other sweet onion
- 1 red bell pepper, seeded and quartered
- ½ teaspoon salt, divided
- 4 (5-ounce) tuna steaks (about ¾ inch thick)
- ¼ teaspoon ground cumin
- ¼ teaspoon freshly ground black pepper
- 4 (2-ounce) sandwich buns
- 4 red leaf lettuce leaves

1. Heat a grill pan over medium-high heat.
2. Combine first 6 ingredients in a small bowl.
3. Brush 3 teaspoons oil evenly over onion and bell pepper; sprinkle with ¼ teaspoon salt. Place onion and bell pepper on grill pan; cook 3½ minutes on each side or until tender. Remove from pan; keep warm.
4. Brush 2 teaspoons oil evenly over tuna; sprinkle with ¼ teaspoon salt, cumin, and black pepper. Place tuna on grill pan; cook 3½ minutes on each side or until medium-rare or desired degree of doneness.
5. Split buns horizontally. Spread mayonnaise mixture evenly over cut sides of buns. Top bottom half of each bun with 1 lettuce leaf, 1 bell pepper quarter, 1 onion slice, and 1 tuna steak. Cover with top halves of buns. Yield: 4 servings (serving size: 1 sandwich).

CALORIES 434 (24% from fat); FAT 11.7g (sat 1.8g, mono 5.8g, poly 1.6g); PROTEIN 38.9g; CARB 41.8g; FIBER 3.4g; CHOL 64mg; IRON 3.4mg; SODIUM 888mg; CALC 119mg

Chilled Vegetable Basil Soup with Vegetable Confetti

To make a spicier starter soup, use a spicy or hot variety of tomato or vegetable juice. For the best texture and freshest flavor, don't stir in the zucchini and remaining ingredients until just before serving. Vivian Pinn will approve.

- 2 teaspoons olive oil
- ½ teaspoon fennel seeds
- 2 garlic cloves, minced
- 1 (46-ounce) can no-salt-added tomato juice
- 1 cup basil leaves
- 1 teaspoon hot pepper sauce (such as Tabasco)
- ¼ teaspoon salt
- 1 cup finely chopped zucchini
- 1 cup finely chopped cucumber
- 1 cup halved cherry tomatoes
- ½ cup chopped green onions
- ¼ cup chopped fresh basil

1. Heat oil in a large saucepan over medium heat. Add fennel and garlic; cook 1 minute, stirring frequently. Add juice; bring to a boil. Reduce heat; simmer 2 minutes. Remove from heat; stir in basil, hot pepper sauce, and salt. Cover and chill 6 hours. Strain mixture through a sieve into a bowl; discard solids. Stir in zucchini and remaining ingredients. Serve immediately. Yield: 6 servings (serving size: about 1 cup).

CALORIES 69 (25% from fat); FAT 1.9g (sat 0.3g, mono 1.2g, poly 0.3g); PROTEIN 2.7g; CARB 12.9g; FIBER 2.2g; CHOL 0mg; IRON 1.7mg; SODIUM 130mg; CALC 54mg

Raspberry-Mango Crisp

Hearty, traditional fruit crisp gets a touch of island flair, now that mangoes and Susan Laramee's preferred fruit, raspberries, can be found year-round. This juicy and colorful dessert will brighten a winter day.

FILLING:

    4   cups raspberries
    3   cups chopped peeled mango
        (about 3)
    ⅓   cup packed light brown sugar
    1   tablespoon all-purpose flour
    ½   teaspoon vanilla extract
    ¼   teaspoon ground ginger
    ⅛   teaspoon ground cardamom
    Cooking spray

TOPPING:

    ½   cup all-purpose flour
    ¾   cup regular oats
    ½   cup packed light brown sugar
    ½   teaspoon ground cinnamon
    ¼   cup chilled butter, cut into
        small pieces

1. Preheat oven to 400°.
2. To prepare filling, combine first 7 ingredients. Spoon into an 11 x 7-inch baking dish coated with cooking spray.
3. To prepare topping, lightly spoon ½ cup flour into a dry measuring cup; level with a knife. Combine ½ cup flour, oats, ½ cup sugar, and cinnamon in a medium bowl. Add butter to oat mixture; cut in butter with a pastry blender or 2 knives until mixture resembles coarse meal. Sprinkle topping evenly over filling. Bake at 400° for 25 minutes or until bubbly and lightly browned. Yield: 8 servings.

CALORIES 279 (22% from fat); FAT 6.9g (sat 3.8g, mono 1.7g, poly 0.8g); PROTEIN 3.5g; CARB 53.6g; FIBER 6.6g; CHOL 15mg; IRON 1.8mg; SODIUM 51mg; CALC 52mg

Ma Po Tofu

This simple Chinese stir-fry uses tofu, the food touted by Susan Love. In addition to its potential health benefits for women, the soy in tofu may help protect against prostate cancer. Depending on how much chili garlic sauce you use, you can customize the heat in this mix of lean ground pork, tofu, and Asian spices. Add a side of chilled melon and a cold glass of dry riesling for a satisfying supper.

    1   (1-pound) package reduced-fat
        firm tofu, cut into 6 slices
    ½   cup fat-free, less-sodium chicken
        broth
    2   tablespoons low-sodium soy sauce
    1   tablespoon oyster sauce
    1   tablespoon cornstarch
    1   to 2 teaspoons chili garlic sauce
        (such as Lee Kum Kee)
    4   ounces lean ground pork
    1   tablespoon grated peeled fresh
        ginger
    3   garlic cloves, minced
    2   cups hot cooked long-grain
        brown rice
    ⅓   cup chopped green onions

1. Place tofu slices on several layers of paper towels; cover with additional paper towels. Place a dinner plate on top of covered tofu; let stand 30 minutes. Remove plate; discard paper towels. Cut tofu slices into ½-inch cubes.
2. Combine broth and next 4 ingredients, stirring with a whisk.
3. Heat a large nonstick skillet over medium-high heat. Add pork; cook 4 minutes or until done, stirring to crumble. Add ginger and garlic; cook 1 minute, stirring constantly. Add tofu; cook 4 minutes or until golden, stirring frequently. Add broth mixture to pan. Bring to a boil; cook 1 minute or until thick. Remove from heat.
4. Serve tofu mixture over rice. Sprinkle with onions. Yield: 4 servings (serving size: ½ cup rice, about ⅔ cup tofu mixture, and about 1 tablespoon onions).

CALORIES 290 (26% from fat); FAT 8.4g (sat 1.9g, mono 2.5g, poly 3.3g); PROTEIN 21.5g; CARB 32.5g; FIBER 4.6g; CHOL 21mg; IRON 2.8mg; SODIUM 390mg; CALC 72mg

Shrimp with Mole Poblano

This recipe features Andrew Weil's "perfect" food: dark chocolate. Store the mole poblano, covered, in the refrigerator up to three days, or freeze up to two months.

    2   pounds large shrimp, peeled and
        deveined
    1   tablespoon olive oil
    ½   teaspoon salt
    ¼   teaspoon freshly ground black pepper
    2   cups Mole Poblano

1. Heat a grill pan over medium-high heat.
2. Pat shrimp dry with paper towels. Combine shrimp, oil, salt, and pepper. Thread shrimp onto 6 (8-inch) skewers. Place skewers on grill pan; cook 2 minutes on each side or until done. Serve with Mole Poblano. Yield: 6 servings (serving size: 1 skewer and ⅓ cup Mole Poblano).

(Totals include ⅓ cup Mole Poblano per serving) CALORIES 230 (25% from fat); FAT 6.5g (sat 1.5g, mono 2.1g, poly 1.2g); PROTEIN 32g; CARB 10.1g; FIBER 1.3g; CHOL 230mg; IRON 3.7mg; SODIUM 556mg; CALC 79mg

MAKE AHEAD • FREEZABLE

MOLE POBLANO:

If needed, add more water during the final 18 minutes of cooking to achieve the desired consistency.

    2   ancho chiles, seeded
    2   mulato chiles, seeded
    1   pasilla chile, seeded
    2   plum tomatoes
    2   (6-inch) corn tortillas
    1   (14-ounce) can fat-free,
        less-sodium chicken broth
    Cooking spray
    ½   cup chopped onion
    1   soft black plantain, cut into
        ¼-inch slices
    ¼   cup sliced almonds
    4   garlic cloves, chopped
    1   tablespoon unsweetened cocoa
    ¼   teaspoon ground cumin
    ¼   teaspoon ground cinnamon
    ⅛   teaspoon ground cloves
    1¼ cups water, divided
    2   ounces dark chocolate, chopped
    1   tablespoon fresh lime juice
    ¾   teaspoon salt

1. Heat a large nonstick skillet over medium-high heat. Add ancho, mulato, and pasilla chiles; cook 1 minute on each side. Place chiles in a medium bowl; cover with hot water. Let stand at room temperature 30 minutes; drain.

2. While chiles soak, place tomatoes in pan, and cook 6 minutes, browning on all sides. Remove from pan. Add tortillas to pan, and cook 1½ minutes on each side or until browned. Place drained chiles, tomatoes, tortillas, and broth in a blender; process until smooth.

3. Heat pan over medium-high heat. Coat pan with cooking spray. Add onion, and sauté 3 minutes. Add plantain, and sauté 3 minutes or until browned. Add almonds and garlic; sauté 1 minute. Stir in cocoa, cumin, cinnamon, and cloves; sauté 15 seconds. Place onion mixture and ¼ cup water in blender with chile mixture; process until smooth.

4. Place chile mixture, 1 cup water, and chocolate in pan; cook over medium heat, partially covered, 18 minutes, stirring occasionally. Remove from heat. Stir in lime juice and salt. Yield: 4 cups (serving size: ⅓ cup).

CALORIES 80 (30% from fat); FAT 2.7g (sat 1.1g, mono 0.7g, poly 0.4g); PROTEIN 1.9g; CARB 13.8g; FIBER 1.8g; CHOL 0mg; IRON 0.6mg; SODIUM 219mg; CALC 23mg

WINE NOTE: The complex flavors of moles are a big challenge when it comes to wine. Fruity but dry rieslings work well. These have crisp acidity to counterbalance a mole's intense flavor, plus a touch of fruitiness that plays perfectly off the chiles. A great example: Chateau Ste. Michelle Riesling Cold Creek Vineyard 2003 from Washington's Columbia Valley ($17).

Chocolate contributes richness without adding sweetness to mole, a traditional Mexican sauce.

The French Connection

A Maryland doctoral student did her homework to devise a stellar onion soup.

When our Test Kitchens staff tested this recipe for French Onion Soup, they were delighted by its richness and praised its authenticity. But the reader who submitted it, Jennifer Dabbs Sciubba, doesn't pretend to be a French cook (she actually comes from a line of Southern cooks). She was certain, though, she had what it took to make a great version of the classic soup. And after her research and recipe development, we agree.

French Onion Soup

(pictured on page 21)

Allowing the soup to simmer for a couple of hours tenderizes each piece of onion until it's perfectly infused with the broth.

    2 teaspoons olive oil
    4 cups thinly vertically sliced Walla Walla or other sweet onion
    4 cups thinly vertically sliced red onion
    ½ teaspoon sugar
    ½ teaspoon freshly ground black pepper
    ¼ teaspoon salt
    ¼ cup dry white wine
    8 cups less-sodium beef broth
    ¼ teaspoon chopped fresh thyme
    8 (1-ounce) slices French bread, cut into 1-inch cubes
    8 (1-ounce) slices reduced-fat, reduced-sodium Swiss cheese (such as Alpine Lace)

1. Heat oil in a Dutch oven over medium-high heat. Add onions to pan; sauté 5 minutes or until tender. Stir in sugar, pepper, and salt. Reduce heat to medium; cook 20 minutes, stirring frequently. Increase heat to medium-high, and sauté 5 minutes or until onion is golden brown. Stir in wine, and cook 1 minute. Add broth and thyme; bring to a boil. Cover, reduce heat, and simmer 2 hours.

2. Preheat broiler.

3. Place bread in a single layer on a baking sheet; broil 2 minutes or until toasted, turning after 1 minute.

4. Place 8 ovenproof bowls on a jelly-roll pan. Ladle 1 cup soup into each bowl. Divide bread evenly among bowls; top each serving with 1 cheese slice. Broil 3 minutes or until cheese begins to brown. Yield: 8 servings.

CALORIES 290 (30% from fat); FAT 9.6g (sat 4.8g, mono 1.9g, poly 0.7g); PROTEIN 16.8g; CARB 33.4g; FIBER 3.1g; CHOL 20mg; IRON 1.6mg; SODIUM 359mg; CALC 317mg

MAKE AHEAD
Hearty, Healthful Lentil Stew

"This recipe is a variation of my mother's lentil dish from her native Italy."
—Lucille Rothen, Morristown, New Jersey

    1   tablespoon olive oil
    1¼   cups chopped onion
    1   cup chopped celery
    ¾   cup chopped carrot
    1   garlic clove, sliced
    4   cups fat-free, less-sodium chicken broth
    1   cup water
    1   (28-ounce) can crushed tomatoes, undrained
    1   cup dried lentils
    ¾   cup instant brown rice
    ½   teaspoon crushed red pepper
    ¼   teaspoon salt
    ¼   teaspoon black pepper

1. Heat oil in a small Dutch oven over medium-high heat. Add onion, celery, carrot, and garlic to pan; sauté 8 minutes or until tender. Add broth, water, and tomatoes; bring to a boil. Stir in lentils; simmer 25 minutes, stirring occasionally. Stir in rice; simmer 20 minutes, stirring occasionally. Stir in red pepper, salt, and black pepper. Yield: 6 servings (serving size: 1⅓ cups).

CALORIES 292 (11% from fat); FAT 3.6g (sat 0.4g, mono 1.8g, poly 0.6g); PROTEIN 15.5g; CARB 52.3g; FIBER 14.7g; CHOL 0mg; IRON 5.2mg; SODIUM 605mg; CALC 95mg

Tortilla Soup

"I like Mexican spices and came up with this simple chicken soup recipe. My husband enjoys the flavors, and I love how quick it is to make."

—Laura Sozio, Charlotte, North Carolina

Cooking spray
2 garlic cloves, minced
3 cups fat-free, less-sodium chicken broth
1½ cups chopped cooked chicken breast
1 cup water
1 tablespoon chili powder
1 tablespoon ground cumin
1 (10-ounce) can diced tomatoes and green chiles, undrained
½ cup fat-free baked tortilla chips, crushed
¼ cup (1 ounce) shredded Monterey Jack cheese
¼ cup chopped fresh cilantro
¼ cup diced peeled avocado
4 lime wedges

1. Heat a large saucepan over medium-high heat. Coat pan with cooking spray. Add garlic; sauté 1 minute. Add broth and next 5 ingredients; bring to a boil. Reduce heat; simmer 15 minutes. Ladle soup into 4 bowls; top each with 2 tablespoons chips, 1 tablespoon cheese, 1 tablespoon cilantro, and 1 tablespoon avocado. Serve with lime wedges. Yield: 4 servings (serving size: 1½ cups soup).

CALORIES 207 (32% from fat); FAT 7.4g (sat 2.4g, mono 2.8g, poly 1.2g); PROTEIN 22.3g; CARB 12.6g; FIBER 3g; CHOL 51mg; IRON 1.9mg; SODIUM 804mg; CALC 112mg

Wheat Berry-Black Bean Soup

"I often make a big pot of soup for my husband's colleagues since they are enthusiastic 'guinea pigs' for my culinary adventures."

—Beth Easter, Watertown, Massachusetts

1 tablespoon olive oil
4 cups chopped onion
1¾ cups chopped carrot
1 cup chopped celery
3 garlic cloves, minced
½ cup uncooked wheat berries (hard winter wheat)
4⅓ cups water, divided
2 (14-ounce) cans fat-free, less-sodium chicken broth
½ cup sun-dried tomatoes, packed without oil, chopped
2 teaspoons ground cumin
2 (15-ounce) cans black beans, rinsed and drained
1 (7-ounce) can chipotle chiles in adobo sauce
1 tablespoon tomato paste

1. Heat oil in a Dutch oven over medium-high heat. Add onion, carrot, celery, and garlic; sauté 15 minutes or until tender. Stir in wheat berries; sauté 2 minutes. Add 4 cups water and broth; bring to a boil. Partially cover, reduce heat, and simmer 1 hour.
2. Stir in sun-dried tomatoes, cumin, and beans. Remove 1½ teaspoons adobo sauce from can of chipotle chiles; reserve remaining chipotle chiles and adobo sauce for another use. Add adobo sauce to onion mixture; simmer 30 minutes or until wheat berries are tender. Combine ⅓ cup water and tomato paste in a bowl, stirring with a whisk. Stir tomato paste mixture into onion mixture. Simmer 15 minutes. Yield: 8 servings (serving size: 1 cup).

CALORIES 215 (14% from fat); FAT 3.4g (sat 0.3g, mono 1.3g, poly 1.1g); PROTEIN 10.5g; CARB 36.4g; FIBER 9.9g; CHOL 0mg; IRON 3.5mg; SODIUM 704mg; CALC 80mg

Jane's Vegetarian Chili

"My mother, Jane Stevens, has been making the best-tasting vegetarian chili for years. She says it's a takeoff of her mom's recipe and thinks the Worcestershire gives it its unique flavor."

—Melissa Ohlson, Kalamazoo, Michigan

1 tablespoon olive oil
2 cups chopped onion
3 garlic cloves, minced
4 cups water, divided
2 tablespoons sugar
2 tablespoons chili powder
2 tablespoons Worcestershire sauce
2 (14.5-ounce) cans diced tomatoes, undrained
1 (15½-ounce) can chickpeas (garbanzo beans), rinsed and drained
1 (15-ounce) can black beans, rinsed and drained
1 (15-ounce) can kidney beans, rinsed and drained
1 (16-ounce) can cannellini beans or other white beans, rinsed and drained
1 (6-ounce) can tomato paste
½ cup (2 ounces) reduced-fat shredded Cheddar cheese, (optional)

1. Heat oil in a large Dutch oven over medium-high heat. Add onion and garlic; sauté 3 minutes or until tender. Stir in 3 cups water and next 8 ingredients.
2. Combine 1 cup water and tomato paste in a bowl, stirring with a whisk until blended. Stir tomato paste mixture into bean mixture. Bring to a boil; reduce heat, and simmer 5 minutes or until thoroughly heated. Ladle chili into bowls. Top with cheese, if desired. Yield: 8 servings (serving size: 1½ cups chili).

CALORIES 276 (11% from fat); FAT 3.5g (sat 0.3g, mono 1.3g, poly 1g); PROTEIN 12.7g; CARB 49.7g; FIBER 14.7g; CHOL 0mg; IRON 4.2mg; SODIUM 587mg; CALC 107mg

Seafood Chowder

"My family eats a lot of fish, and I devised this chowder recipe to use with any leftovers. I serve it as a main course with salad and bread."

—Claire Strom, Fargo, North Dakota

2½ cups (½-inch) cubed peeled baking potato
2 cups finely chopped onion
1 cup water
2 teaspoons chicken-flavored bouillon granules
2 teaspoons Worcestershire sauce
½ teaspoon dried thyme
¼ teaspoon freshly ground black pepper
1 (8-ounce) bottle clam juice
2 tablespoons all-purpose flour
1½ cups 1% low-fat milk, divided
1 (12-ounce) can evaporated fat-free milk
1½ pounds grouper or other firm white fish fillets, cut into ½-inch pieces
12 medium shrimp, peeled, deveined, and halved lengthwise (about 6 ounces)

1. Combine first 8 ingredients in a Dutch oven; bring to a boil. Cover, reduce heat, and simmer 15 minutes or until potatoes are tender.
2. Place flour in a large bowl; gradually add ¼ cup 1% milk, stirring with a whisk until smooth. Stir in 1¼ cups 1% milk. Add evaporated milk to flour mixture. Stir milk mixture into potato mixture, and increase heat to medium-high. Cook 5 minutes or until slightly thick, stirring frequently. Add fish; cook 4 minutes. Stir in shrimp; cook 6 minutes or until shrimp are done. Serve chowder immediately. Yield: 8 servings (serving size: 1¼ cups).

CALORIES 231 (8% from fat); FAT 2g (sat 0.7g, mono 0.4g, poly 0.5g); PROTEIN 27.3g; CARB 24.9g; FIBER 1.1g; CHOL 67mg; IRON 2.3mg; SODIUM 525mg; CALC 234mg

Broccoli Soup

"This appetizer soup has been adapted from a recipe in a Junior League cookbook."

—Jane Pekelder, Grand Rapids, Michigan

6 cups small broccoli florets
2 cups fat-free, less-sodium chicken broth
¼ cup chopped onion
2 cups 2% reduced-fat milk
2 tablespoons all-purpose flour
1 tablespoon fresh lemon juice
2 teaspoons butter
½ teaspoon salt
⅛ teaspoon black pepper
Dash of ground mace

1. Combine first 3 ingredients in a large saucepan; bring to a boil. Cover, reduce heat, and simmer 10 minutes. Place half of broccoli mixture in a blender; process until smooth. Pour puréed mixture into a bowl. Repeat procedure with remaining broccoli mixture. Return puréed mixture to pan.
2. Combine milk and flour, stirring with a whisk until well blended; add to broccoli mixture. Cook over medium heat 3 minutes or until mixture begins to thicken, stirring frequently. Add lemon juice, butter, salt, pepper, and mace, stirring until butter melts. Yield: 6 servings (serving size: 1 cup).

CALORIES 91 (31% from fat); FAT 3.1g (sat 1.8g, mono 0.8g, poly 0.2g); PROTEIN 6.2g; CARB 10.8g; FIBER 2.3g; CHOL 10mg; IRON 0.8mg; SODIUM 418mg; CALC 136mg

inspired vegetarian

Homemade Takeout

These fast dishes let you savor ethnic fare without leaving home.

One of the reasons many folks like takeout, beyond its convenience, is that they love the flavors—Asian, Italian, Mexican—that may not be part of their everyday repertoire. But these dishes are really not difficult to cook once you stock up on a few ingredients.

Three-Cheese Veggie Pizza

Use this recipe as a template, and vary the cheeses and vegetables to make your own creations. Allow the pizza to stand five minutes before slicing to allow any liquid on top time to be reabsorbed into the toppings so the crust won't get soggy.

2 teaspoons olive oil
¼ teaspoon freshly ground black pepper
2 garlic cloves, minced
1 (8-ounce) package presliced mushrooms
1 cup marinara sauce
1 (1-pound) Italian cheese-flavored pizza crust (such as Boboli)
½ cup (2 ounces) shredded part-skim mozzarella cheese
½ cup (2 ounces) shredded fontina cheese
¼ cup (1 ounce) grated fresh Parmesan cheese
¾ cup sliced bottled roasted red bell peppers
1 tablespoon capers, rinsed and drained
4 drained canned artichoke hearts, thinly sliced

1. Preheat oven to 500°.
2. Heat 2 teaspoons olive oil in a large nonstick skillet over medium-high heat. Add black pepper, minced garlic, and mushrooms, and sauté 5 minutes or until mushrooms are tender and most of liquid evaporates.
3. Spread sauce over pizza crust, leaving a ½-inch border, and top with mushroom mixture. Sprinkle evenly with mozzarella, fontina, and Parmesan cheeses. Top with roasted red bell peppers, 1 tablespoon capers, and artichokes. Bake at 500° for 10 minutes or until cheese melts and begins to brown. Let pizza stand 5 minutes before slicing. Yield: 6 servings (serving size: 1 slice).

CALORIES 345 (30% from fat); FAT 11.5g (sat 5.4g, mono 4.1g, poly 1.1g); PROTEIN 17g; CARB 42.2g; FIBER 1.6g; CHOL 19mg; IRON 3.2mg; SODIUM 860mg; CALC 393mg

STAFF FAVORITE
Yang Chow Fried Rice

Here is a vegetarian version of the classic Chinese dish that traditionally includes shrimp and ham.

2 tablespoons canola oil, divided
4 large eggs, lightly beaten and divided
¼ teaspoon freshly ground black pepper, divided
Dash of salt
1¾ cups thinly sliced green onions, divided
2 teaspoons grated peeled fresh ginger
2 garlic cloves, minced
5 cups cooked short-grain rice, chilled
¼ cup low-sodium soy sauce
½ teaspoon salt
1 (10-ounce) package frozen green peas, thawed
3 tablespoons chopped fresh cilantro

1. Heat 2 teaspoons oil in a large nonstick skillet over medium-high heat. Add half of eggs; swirl to coat bottom of pan evenly. Sprinkle with ⅛ teaspoon pepper and dash of salt; cook 3 minutes or until egg is done. Remove egg from pan; thinly slice, and set aside.

2. Wipe pan clean with a paper towel. Heat 4 teaspoons oil in pan over medium-high heat. Add 1 cup onions, ginger, and garlic; stir-fry 30 seconds. Add remaining eggs and rice; stir-fry 3 minutes. Stir in half of egg strips, ¾ cup onions, ⅛ teaspoon pepper, soy sauce, ½ teaspoon salt, and peas; cook 30 seconds, stirring well to combine. Top with remaining egg strips and cilantro. Yield: 6 servings (serving size: about 1 cup).

CALORIES 348 (22% from fat); FAT 8.5g (sat 1.5g, mono 4.1g, poly 2g); PROTEIN 11g; CARB 55g; FIBER 4.9g; CHOL 141mg; IRON 3.9mg; SODIUM 683mg; CALC 34mg

Buddha's Delight with Tofu, Broccoli, and Water Chestnuts

This simple version of a popular Chinese take-out dish will work with just about any vegetable.

3 tablespoons low-sodium soy sauce
1 tablespoon dark sesame oil
1 tablespoon rice vinegar
1 teaspoon sugar
1 (14-ounce) package water-packed extra-firm tofu, drained and cut into 1-inch cubes
5 cups small broccoli florets
1½ cups (¼-inch) diagonally sliced carrot
½ cup peeled chopped broccoli stems
2 tablespoons canola oil
1½ cups sliced green onions
1 tablespoon grated peeled fresh ginger
2 garlic cloves, minced
1 cup snow peas, trimmed
1 (14-ounce) can whole baby corn, drained
1 (8-ounce) can sliced water chestnuts, drained
½ cup vegetable broth
1 tablespoon cornstarch
½ teaspoon salt
4 cups hot cooked short-grain rice

1. Combine first 5 ingredients, tossing to coat; cover and marinate in refrigerator 1 hour. Drain in a colander over a bowl, reserving marinade.

2. Cook broccoli florets, carrot, and broccoli stems in boiling water 1½ minutes; drain. Plunge into ice water. Drain.

3. Heat canola oil in a wok or large nonstick skillet over medium-high heat. Add tofu; stir-fry 5 minutes or until lightly browned on all sides. Stir in onions, ginger, and garlic; stir-fry 30 seconds. Stir in broccoli mixture, snow peas, corn, and water chestnuts; stir-fry 1 minute. Combine broth and cornstarch, stirring with a whisk. Add cornstarch mixture, reserved marinade, and salt to pan; bring to a boil. Cook 2½ minutes or until slightly thick, stirring constantly. Serve over rice. Yield: 6 servings (serving size: about 1⅓ cups stir-fry and ⅔ cup rice).

CALORIES 378 (28% from fat); FAT 11.6g (sat 1.6g, mono 4.7g, poly 4.7g); PROTEIN 15.8g; CARB 55.9g; FIBER 9.3g; CHOL 0mg; IRON 4.4mg; SODIUM 698mg; CALC 129mg

QUICK & EASY
Portobello Mushroom Fajitas

Portobello mushrooms and red onions make a meaty fajita filling with satisfying, pungent flavors. If you can't find queso fresco, crumbled feta cheese is a good substitute.

1 tablespoon olive oil
4 cups (½-inch-thick) slices portobello mushrooms (about 8 ounces)
1 cup vertically sliced red onion
1 cup (¼-inch-thick) green bell pepper strips
2 garlic cloves, minced
3 tablespoons chopped fresh cilantro
1 tablespoon fresh lime juice
¼ teaspoon salt
¼ teaspoon freshly ground black pepper
1 serrano chile, minced
12 (6-inch) flour tortillas
1 cup (4 ounces) crumbled queso fresco
¾ cup salsa verde

1. Heat oil in a large nonstick skillet over medium-high heat. Add mushrooms;

sauté 5 minutes or until almost tender. Add onion, bell pepper, and garlic. Reduce heat to medium, and cook 4 minutes or until bell pepper is crisp-tender, stirring frequently. Remove from heat; stir in cilantro, lime juice, salt, black pepper, and chile.

2. Warm tortillas according to package directions. Spoon about ¼ cup mushroom mixture down center of each tortilla; top each tortilla with 4 teaspoons cheese and 1 tablespoon salsa. Roll up. Yield: 4 servings (serving size: 3 fajitas).

CALORIES 437 (26% from fat); FAT 12.7g (sat 3.6g, mono 6.8g, poly 1.5g); PROTEIN 13.8g; CARB 65.9g; FIBER 4.9g; CHOL 9mg; IRON 3.9mg; SODIUM 792mg; CALC 219mg

Pinto Bean Nachos

Garlic and cumin-infused refried beans top freshly baked tortilla chips, which are sturdy and hold up well under the assortment of toppings. You can use black beans in place of pinto beans, if you prefer. If the bean mixture is too thick, stir in a little hot water.

12 (6-inch) corn tortillas, quartered
    Cooking spray
 1 tablespoon canola oil
 2 teaspoons ground cumin
 1 teaspoon chili powder
 2 garlic cloves, minced
 2 (15-ounce) cans pinto beans, undrained
 1 cup (4 ounces) crumbled queso fresco
 1 cup bottled salsa
 1 cup diced peeled avocado
 6 tablespoons chopped fresh cilantro

1. Preheat oven to 425°.
2. Arrange half of tortilla wedges in a single layer on a large baking sheet; lightly coat wedges with cooking spray. Bake at 425° for 8 minutes or until crisp. Repeat procedure with remaining tortilla wedges and cooking spray.
3. Heat oil in a medium saucepan over medium-high heat. Add cumin, chili powder, and garlic; cook 30 seconds,

stirring constantly. Add pinto beans, and bring to a boil, stirring frequently. Reduce heat to medium, and simmer 10 minutes. Partially mash bean mixture with a potato masher until slightly thick. Place 8 chips on each of 6 plates. Spoon about ½ cup bean mixture evenly over tortilla chips on each plate; top each serving with about 2½ tablespoons queso fresco, 2½ tablespoons salsa, and 2½ tablespoons avocado. Sprinkle each serving with 1 tablespoon cilantro. Yield: 6 servings.

CALORIES 344 (27% from fat); FAT 10.5g (sat 2.2g, mono 4.8g, poly 2.3g); PROTEIN 13.5g; CARB 52.4g; FIBER 11.7g; CHOL 6mg; IRON 3.9mg; SODIUM 723mg; CALC 232mg

dinner tonight

Better Beans

Canned beans are a handy start to many quick and satisfying winter suppers.

Beans Menu 1
serves 4

White Bean and Sausage Ragoût with Tomatoes, Kale, and Zucchini

Garlic-rosemary bruschetta*

Green salad with bottled low-fat vinaigrette

*Cut a 4-ounce baguette into ¼-inch slices; broil 3 minutes or until golden brown. Cut 1 peeled garlic clove in half; rub cut sides of garlic clove and a sprig of rosemary over bread. Brush with 2 teaspoons olive oil; sprinkle with ¼ teaspoon salt and ⅛ teaspoon freshly ground black pepper.

Game Plan

1. Chop vegetables and sausage for ragoût.
2. While ragoût simmers:
   • Prepare bruschetta
   • Toss salad

White Bean and Sausage Ragoût with Tomatoes, Kale, and Zucchini

Chock-full of vegetables, this colorful ragoût warms up a chilly winter evening.

TOTAL TIME: 35 MINUTES

QUICK TIP: Look for bags of trimmed and washed kale at the supermarket.

 1 tablespoon olive oil
 ½ cup chopped onion
 2 (4-ounce) links chicken sausage, cut into ½-inch slices
 1 zucchini, quartered and cut into ½-inch slices (about 2 cups)
 3 garlic cloves, peeled and crushed
 6 cups chopped trimmed kale (about ½ pound)
 ½ cup water
 ¼ teaspoon salt
 ¼ teaspoon freshly ground black pepper
 2 (16-ounce) cans cannellini beans or other white beans, rinsed and drained
 1 (14.5-ounce) can diced tomatoes, undrained

1. Heat oil in a large skillet over medium-high heat. Add onion and sausage; sauté 4 minutes or until sausage is browned. Add zucchini and garlic; cook 2 minutes. Add kale and remaining ingredients; bring to a boil. Cover, reduce heat, and simmer 10 minutes or until thoroughly heated. Serve immediately. Yield: 4 servings (serving size: 1¾ cups).

CALORIES 467 (20% from fat); FAT 10.2g (sat 2.3g, mono 4.6g, poly 2.5g); PROTEIN 28.5g; CARB 71.8g; FIBER 15.4g; CHOL 42mg; IRON 8.8mg; SODIUM 764mg; CALC 370mg

Beans Menu 2

serves 4

Pasta with Chickpeas and Garlic Sauce

Broccoli rabe with garlic*

Chocolate sorbet

*Heat 1 tablespoon extravirgin olive oil in a skillet over medium heat. Add 2 crushed peeled garlic cloves; cook 30 seconds or until garlic is fragrant. Add 1½ pounds cleaned and trimmed broccoli rabe, tossing to coat. Reduce heat to medium-low. Add ¼ cup water; cover and cook 9 minutes or until tender, stirring occasionally. Toss with 2 teaspoons lemon juice, ¼ teaspoon salt, and ⅛ teaspoon black pepper.

Game Plan

1. While oil heats for garlic:
   • Boil water for pasta
2. While chickpeas simmer:
   • Cook pasta
   • Prepare broccoli rabe
   • Halve tomatoes
   • Juice lemon

Pasta with Chickpeas and Garlic Sauce

Puréed chickpeas make a hearty pasta sauce. To make this a vegetarian meal, use vegetable broth in place of chicken broth.

TOTAL TIME: 28 MINUTES

    2   teaspoons olive oil
    2   garlic cloves, peeled and crushed
    ¾   teaspoon kosher salt
    ¼   teaspoon crushed red pepper
    1   (15.5-ounce) can chickpeas
        (garbanzo beans), rinsed and
        drained
    1   (14-ounce) can fat-free,
        less-sodium chicken broth
 1½   cups uncooked medium seashell
        pasta (about 6 ounces)
    ½   cup grape tomatoes, halved
    2   garlic cloves, minced
    1   tablespoon minced fresh parsley
    1   tablespoon fresh lemon juice
    3   tablespoons shredded Parmigiano-
        Reggiano cheese

1. Heat oil in a medium saucepan over medium heat. Add crushed garlic; sauté 1 minute. Add salt, pepper, chickpeas, and broth; bring to a boil. Cover, reduce heat, and simmer 15 minutes.
2. While garlic mixture simmers, cook pasta in boiling water 9 minutes, omitting salt and fat; drain well.
3. Place chickpea mixture in a food processor, and process until smooth. Combine chickpea mixture, pasta, tomatoes, minced garlic, parsley, and lemon juice; toss well. Sprinkle with cheese. Serve immediately. Yield: 4 servings (serving size: 1 cup pasta and 2¼ teaspoons cheese).

CALORIES 333 (24% from fat); FAT 9g (sat 1.6g, mono 3.2g, poly 2.7g); PROTEIN 13.6g; CARB 57.3g; FIBER 6.6g; CHOL 3mg; IRON 3.3mg; SODIUM 808mg; CALC 92mg

Beans Menu 3

serves 4

Southwest Pinto Bean Burgers with Chipotle Mayonnaise

Stewed onions*

Prepared coleslaw tossed with bottled vinaigrette and queso fresco or goat cheese

*Heat 1 tablespoon olive oil in a large skillet over medium-low heat. Add 3 cups thinly sliced onions; cook over medium-low heat 10 minutes or until soft and browned. Add 1 tablespoon sugar, 1 tablespoon barbecue sauce, and 1 tablespoon cider vinegar. Cook 30 seconds or until liquid evaporates. Sprinkle with ¼ teaspoon salt and ⅛ teaspoon black pepper.

Game Plan

1. While onions cook:
   • Combine ingredients for burgers
2. While burger patties refrigerate:
   • Prepare Chipotle Mayonnaise
   •Toss coleslaw with dressing and cheese

Southwest Pinto Bean Burgers with Chipotle Mayonnaise

TOTAL TIME: 43 MINUTES

BURGERS:

    ½   cup diced onion
    ½   cup dry breadcrumbs
    ¼   cup chopped fresh cilantro
    2   tablespoons minced seeded
        jalapeño pepper
    2   tablespoons reduced-fat sour cream
    1   teaspoon hot pepper sauce
    ½   teaspoon ground cumin
    ¼   teaspoon freshly ground black pepper
    ⅛   teaspoon salt
    1   large egg, lightly beaten
    1   (15-ounce) can pinto beans, rinsed
        and drained
    1   (8¾-ounce) can no-salt-added
        whole-kernel corn, drained

CHIPOTLE MAYONNAISE:

    ¼   cup low-fat mayonnaise
    1   teaspoon canned minced chipotle
        chile in adobo sauce

REMAINING INGREDIENTS:

    1   tablespoon canola oil
    4   (1½-ounce) whole wheat
        hamburger buns, toasted
    4   romaine lettuce leaves

1. To prepare burgers, combine first 10 ingredients in a large bowl. Add pinto beans and corn; partially mash with a fork. Divide bean mixture into 4 equal portions, shaping each into a 3½-inch patty, and refrigerate 10 minutes.
2. To prepare chipotle mayonnaise, combine mayonnaise and chipotle in a small bowl; set aside.
3. Heat oil in a large nonstick skillet over medium-high heat. Add patties to pan, and cook 4 minutes on each side or until thoroughly heated. Place patties on bottom halves of buns; top each patty with 1 tablespoon mayonnaise, 1 lettuce leaf, and top half of bun. Yield: 4 servings.

CALORIES 411 (23% from fat); FAT 10.7g (sat 1.9g, mono 3.2g, poly 3.2g); PROTEIN 15.2g; CARB 63.1g; FIBER 9.1g; CHOL 57mg; IRON 3.9mg; SODIUM 837mg; CALC 153mg

Cross-Country Ski Picnic

After a fresh snow, a sortie with family and friends offers sublime rewards and a fun meal on the go.

MAKE AHEAD
Maple-Almond Granola

This granola makes an ideal snack when skiing (or hiking or snowshoeing). Serve leftovers with yogurt or milk for breakfast the next morning.

```
4   cups regular oats
¼   cup slivered almonds
1½  teaspoons ground
      cinnamon
¼   teaspoon salt
⅓   cup water
⅓   cup honey
⅓   cup maple syrup
2   tablespoons brown
      sugar
2   tablespoons canola oil
Cooking spray
1   cup minced dried apricots
1   cup raisins
```

1. Preheat oven to 325°.

2. Combine first 4 ingredients in a large bowl.

3. Combine water, honey, syrup, sugar, and oil in a small saucepan; bring to a boil. Pour over oat mixture; toss to coat. Spread oat mixture on a jelly-roll pan coated with cooking spray. Bake at 325° for 35 minutes or until golden, stirring every 10 minutes. Place in a large bowl; stir in apricots and raisins. Cool completely. Yield: 6 cups (serving size: ¼ cup).

NOTE: Store in an airtight container up to 1 week.

CALORIES 129 (20% from fat); FAT 2.8g (sat 0.3g, mono 1.4g, poly 0.7g); PROTEIN 2.7g; CARB 25.7g; FIBER 1.9g; CHOL 0mg; IRON 1.2mg; SODIUM 28mg; CALC 20mg

Beef and Barley Soup

Lamb may be used in place of beef stew meat, if desired. Use 1 pound of boneless lamb leg, cut into 1-inch pieces.

```
Cooking spray
2   pounds beef stew meat, trimmed
      and cut into 1-inch pieces
2   teaspoons canola oil
2   cups chopped leek (about
      4 medium)
2   cups chopped carrot
4   garlic cloves, minced
6   cups water
1½  teaspoons salt
1   teaspoon dried thyme
½   teaspoon freshly ground black
      pepper
4   bay leaves
2   (14-ounce) cans less-sodium beef
      broth
1   cup uncooked pearl barley
```

1. Heat a large Dutch oven over medium-high heat. Coat pan with cooking spray. Add half of beef; cook 5 minutes, browning on all sides. Remove from pan. Repeat procedure with remaining beef.

2. Heat oil in pan over medium-high heat. Add leek, carrot, and garlic; sauté 4 minutes or until lightly browned. Return beef to pan. Add water and next 5 ingredients; bring to a boil. Cover, reduce heat, and simmer 1 hour. Add barley; cook 30 minutes or until beef and barley are tender. Remove and discard bay leaves. Yield: 8 servings (serving size: 1½ cups).

CALORIES 308 (30% from fat); FAT 10.1g (sat 3.3g, mono 4.4g, poly 0.9g); PROTEIN 26.9g; CARB 26.7g; FIBER 5.4g; CHOL 71mg; IRON 4.1mg; SODIUM 548mg; CALC 48mg

Rosemary Focaccia

The rosemary steeps in boiling water; be sure to let the mixture cool to 100° to 110° before adding the yeast so the dough will rise correctly.

```
1¼  cups boiling water
3   tablespoons chopped fresh
      rosemary, divided
1   tablespoon honey
1   package dry yeast (about 2¼
      teaspoons)
3¾  cups all-purpose flour,
      divided
¼   cup olive oil, divided
1   teaspoon salt
Cooking spray
1   teaspoon water
1   large egg yolk
1   teaspoon sea salt or kosher salt
```

1. Combine boiling water, 1 teaspoon rosemary, and honey in a large bowl; cool to 100° to 110°. Sprinkle yeast over honey mixture; let stand 5 minutes. Lightly spoon flour into dry measuring cups; level with a knife. Add 3¼ cups flour, 2 tablespoons oil, and 1 teaspoon salt to honey mixture, stirring to form a soft dough. Turn dough out onto a floured surface. Knead until smooth and elastic (about 10 minutes); add enough of remaining flour, 1 tablespoon at a
Continued

time, to prevent dough from sticking to hands (dough will feel sticky).

2. Place dough in a large bowl coated with cooking spray, turning to coat top. Cover and let rise in a warm place (85°), free from drafts, 45 minutes or until doubled in size. (Gently press two fingers into dough. If indentation remains, dough has risen enough.) Punch dough down. Pat dough into a 14 x 12-inch rectangle on a baking sheet coated with cooking spray. Cover and let rise 20 minutes or until doubled in size.

3. Preheat oven to 350°.

4. Uncover dough. Make indentations in top of dough using handle of a wooden spoon or your fingertips. Combine 1 tablespoon oil, 1 teaspoon water, and egg yolk; brush over dough. Drizzle with 1 tablespoon oil; sprinkle with 8 teaspoons rosemary and sea salt.

5. Bake at 350° for 25 minutes or until lightly browned. Remove from pan; cool on a wire rack. Yield: 14 servings.

CALORIES 166 (25% from fat); FAT 4.6g (sat 0.7g, mono 3g, poly 0.6g); PROTEIN 3.9g; CARB 27.1g; FIBER 1.1g; CHOL 15mg; IRON 1.7mg; SODIUM 335mg; CALC 9mg

Fudgy Mocha-Toffee Brownies

Coffee and toffee give these rich chocolate brownies a unique twist, and they're perfect with tea or hot cider. If they haven't all been gobbled up, store leftover brownies in an airtight container up to one week, or wrap tightly in aluminum foil and freeze up to four months.

Cooking spray
2 tablespoons instant coffee granules
¼ cup hot water
¼ cup butter
¼ cup semisweet chocolate chips
1½ cups all-purpose flour
1⅓ cups sugar
½ cup unsweetened cocoa
1 teaspoon baking powder
½ teaspoon salt
1 teaspoon vanilla extract
2 large eggs, lightly beaten
¼ cup toffee chips

1. Preheat oven to 350°.

2. Coat bottom of a 9-inch square baking pan with cooking spray.

3. Combine coffee and hot water, stirring until coffee dissolves.

4. Combine butter and chocolate chips in a small microwave-safe bowl. Microwave at HIGH 1 minute or until butter melts; stir until chocolate is smooth.

5. Lightly spoon flour into dry measuring cups; level with a knife. Combine flour, sugar, cocoa, baking powder, and salt in a large bowl, stirring with a whisk. Combine coffee mixture, butter mixture, vanilla, and eggs in a medium bowl, stirring with a whisk. Add coffee mixture to flour mixture; stir just until combined. Spread evenly into prepared pan. Sprinkle evenly with toffee chips. Bake at 350° for 22 minutes. Cool on a wire rack. Yield: 20 servings.

CALORIES 145 (30% from fat); FAT 4.8g (sat 2.4g, mono 1.8g, poly 0.3g); PROTEIN 2.2g; CARB 24.9g; FIBER 1.1g; CHOL 30mg; IRON 0.9mg; SODIUM 121mg; CALC 23mg

Hungarian Venison Stew

If you can't find venison, this recipe is good with beef stew meat. Pungent all-spice and juniper berries lend the stew spicy, complex flavor; be sure to remove the berries and bay leaf before pouring the stew into a thermos. We found this tasted good with white or red wine.

¼ cup all-purpose flour
1½ teaspoons salt, divided
½ teaspoon freshly ground black pepper, divided
2 pounds venison, cut into 1-inch cubes
2 tablespoons butter
2 cups chopped onion
2 teaspoons minced garlic
2 cups dry white wine or fruity red wine
2 tablespoons sugar
1 tablespoon sweet Hungarian paprika
1 teaspoon ground red pepper
8 juniper berries
2 whole allspice berries
1 bay leaf

1. Preheat oven to 300°.

2. Lightly spoon flour into a dry measuring cup; level with a knife. Combine flour, ½ teaspoon salt, and ¼ teaspoon black pepper in a large zip-top plastic bag. Add venison; seal and shake to coat. Remove venison from bag; discard remaining flour mixture.

3. Melt butter in an ovenproof Dutch oven over medium-high heat. Add venison, onion, and garlic; sauté 5 minutes, browning venison on all sides. Add wine, scraping pan to loosen browned bits. Add 1 teaspoon salt, ¼ teaspoon black pepper, sugar, and remaining ingredients to pan; bring to a boil.

4. Cover and bake at 300° for 3 hours or until venison is tender. Remove and discard berries and bay leaf before serving. Yield: 8 servings (serving size: about ¾ cup).

CALORIES 212 (25% from fat); FAT 5.8g (sat 2.6g, mono 2g, poly 0.8g); PROTEIN 27.1g; CARB 11.9g; FIBER 1.1g; CHOL 104mg; IRON 4.6mg; SODIUM 527mg; CALC 24mg

Cornmeal-Cheddar Muffins

Use Monterey Jack cheese with jalapeño peppers to add a bit of heat. Sprinkling cheese on the top before baking gives the muffins a nice crust. These are a delicious accompaniment to either Beef and Barley Soup (recipe on page 17) or Hungarian Venison Stew (recipe at left). Store cooked muffins in an airtight container up to two days.

1¾ cups all-purpose flour
¼ cup yellow cornmeal
1½ teaspoons baking powder
¼ teaspoon baking soda
¼ teaspoon salt
⅛ teaspoon ground red pepper
3 tablespoons chilled unsalted butter, cut into small pieces
⅓ cup (about 1½ ounces) shredded reduced-fat Cheddar cheese, divided
1 cup fat-free buttermilk
¼ cup water
1 large egg, lightly beaten
Cooking spray

1. Preheat oven to 350°.

2. Lightly spoon flour into dry measuring cups; level with a knife. Combine

flour and next 5 ingredients in a large bowl, stirring with a whisk. Cut in butter with a pastry blender or 2 knives until mixture resembles coarse meal. Stir in 3 tablespoons cheese. Combine buttermilk, water, and egg, stirring with a whisk. Add buttermilk mixture to flour mixture; stir just until moistened.

3. Divide batter evenly among 10 muffin cups coated with cooking spray. Sprinkle batter evenly with remaining cheese. Bake at 350° for 30 minutes or until muffins spring back when touched lightly in center. Cool muffins completely on a wire rack. Yield: 10 servings (serving size: 1 muffin).

NOTE: Place in heavy-duty zip-top plastic bags, and freeze up to 3 months.

CALORIES 151 (30% from fat); FAT 5g (sat 2.8g, mono 1.2g, poly 0.3g); PROTEIN 5g; CARB 20.9g; FIBER 0.9g; CHOL 34mg; IRON 1.1mg; SODIUM 247mg; CALC 99mg

---

MAKE AHEAD
Fig Bars

For a nonalcoholic version, omit the port and increase the orange juice to 1 cup. Store leftover bars in an airtight container.

    1   (8-ounce) package dried figs or
        1¾ cups chopped figs
    ½   cup port wine
    ½   cup orange juice
    1   cup all-purpose flour
    1½ cups quick-cooking oats
    ⅔   cup packed light brown sugar
    ½   teaspoon ground cinnamon
    6   tablespoons chilled butter, cut
        into small pieces
    1   large egg white
Cooking spray

1. Remove stems from figs; discard stems. Coarsely chop figs. Combine figs, wine, and juice in a medium saucepan; bring to a boil over medium heat. Reduce heat, and simmer, uncovered, until figs are tender and most of liquid is absorbed (about 20 minutes). Remove from heat. Cool slightly. Place fig mixture in a food processor; process until smooth. Spoon into a bowl; cool completely.

2. Preheat oven to 350°.

3. Lightly spoon flour into a dry measuring cup; level with a knife. Place flour, oats, sugar, and cinnamon in a food processor; process until oats are finely ground. Add butter; process until mixture resembles coarse meal. Add egg white; pulse to combine. Firmly press half of crumb mixture into an 8-inch square pan coated with cooking spray. Spread fig mixture over crumb mixture. Sprinkle with remaining crumb mixture; press gently. Bake at 350° for 25 minutes. Cool completely on a wire rack. Yield: 25 servings.

CALORIES 112 (26% from fat); FAT 3.2g (sat 1.5g, mono 1.2g, poly 0.3g); PROTEIN 1.7g; CARB 19.5g; FIBER 1.5g; CHOL 7mg; IRON 0.8mg; SODIUM 25mg; CALC 25mg

---

enlightened cook

Life on the Range

Following a visit to Texas Hill Country, an adventurous food lover swapped stilettos for cowboy boots.

Paula Disbrowe traded her New York City life for ranch life in January 2002. She and her fiancé, David Norman, now run Hart and Hind, an emerging fitness ranch 90 miles west of San Antonio in Rio Frio, Texas. Because many guests come to Hart and Hind to jump-start a fitness program, or just cinch their belt a bit tighter when they leave, Paula cooks with inherently healthful ingredients and keeps everything on the light side.

The menu is influenced by the Hill Country's bounty and multicultural heritage. The food is healthy but hearty, so guests have enough energy to climb the canyon trails each day. The cowboy mystique is revealed through a campfire breakfast (buttermilk biscuits cooked in a Dutch oven under coals, homemade turkey sausage with marjoram from Paula's garden, and scrambled eggs with green chiles). This area also has deep Czech and German roots, so she serves sausage (the best lean venison sausage from a local purveyor) with a fennel and cabbage slaw.

Carrot Habanero Soup

Piercing the habanero pepper and letting it steep in the cooking liquid (then disposing of the chile) infuses the soup with pleasant heat. If you like your soup hotter, seed and chop the habanero, and sauté it with the vegetables.

    1   tablespoon olive oil
    1   cup thinly sliced leek (about 1 large)
    ½   cup chopped onion
    1   pound carrots, chopped
    1   whole habanero pepper
    1   tablespoon minced peeled fresh
         ginger
    1   garlic clove, minced
    ¼   cup dry white wine
    3½   cups water
    1   cup chopped peeled sweet potato
    ¼   cup fresh orange juice
    ½   teaspoon ground coriander
    1   tablespoon honey
    ½   teaspoon salt
    5   tablespoons plain low-fat yogurt
Chopped fresh cilantro leaves
    (optional)

1. Heat oil in a Dutch oven over medium-high heat. Add leek, onion, and carrots; sauté 7 minutes or until tender. Pierce habanero several times with a knife. Add habanero, ginger, and garlic to pan; sauté 2 minutes. Stir in wine, scraping pan to loosen browned bits. Add water and sweet potato; bring to a boil. Partially cover, reduce heat, and simmer 30 minutes or until tender. Stir in orange juice and coriander. Remove and discard habanero.

2. Place half of carrot mixture in a blender; process until smooth. Pour puréed mixture into a medium bowl; repeat procedure with remaining carrot mixture. Press carrot mixture, in batches, through a large fine sieve into pan; discard solids. Stir honey and salt into carrot mixture; cook over medium heat 5 minutes or until thoroughly heated. Ladle into bowls; top with yogurt. Garnish with cilantro leaves, if desired. Yield: 5 servings (serving size: 1 cup soup and 1 tablespoon yogurt).

CALORIES 119 (20% from fat); FAT 2.8g (sat 0.5g, mono 1.7g, poly 0.4g); PROTEIN 2.4g; CARB 20.9g; FIBER 3.7g; CHOL 1mg; IRON 0.9mg; SODIUM 269mg; CALC 75mg

Cilantro-Serrano Pesto with Grilled Chicken and Penne

This pesto incorporates ingredients Disbrowe finds on the ranch: cilantro and pecans. *Cotija* is an aged Mexican cheese available in many supermarkets and in any Latin grocery. Substitute Parmesan if you can't find cotija. If the sauce is too thick, thin it with a little hot cooking water from the pasta.

1½ cups fresh cilantro
½ cup fresh mint
½ cup cotija cheese
3 tablespoons toasted pecan halves
1 teaspoon kosher salt
2 garlic cloves
1 serrano chile, seeded and sliced
2 tablespoons extravirgin olive oil
2 teaspoons sherry vinegar
⅛ teaspoon freshly ground black pepper
¾ pound skinless, boneless chicken breast
Cooking spray
6 cups hot cooked penne pasta (about 3 ounces uncooked)
2 cups cherry tomatoes, halved

1. Place first 7 ingredients in a food processor; process until well blended. With processor on, slowly pour oil through food chute; process until well blended. Place pesto in a large bowl; stir in vinegar and pepper.
2. Heat a grill pan over medium-high heat. Coat chicken with cooking spray. Add chicken to pan; cook 5 minutes on each side or until done. Cut chicken into bite-size pieces. Add chicken, pasta, and tomatoes to pesto; toss to combine. Yield: 6 cups (serving size: 1 cup).

CALORIES 429 (29% from fat); FAT 13.8g (sat 3.5g, mono 6.5g, poly 1.9g); PROTEIN 28.2g; CARB 47.1g; FIBER 2.4g; CHOL 60mg; IRON 11.5mg; SODIUM 492mg; CALC 104mg

Quinoa Salad with Vegetables and Tomatillo Vinaigrette

Quinoa, a high-protein grain, combines with crisp, colorful vegetables and tart vinaigrette for a delicious main-dish salad. Creamy *queso anejo* balances the tartness of the dressing. *Queso blanco* or *ricotta salata* are good substitutes.

¾ cup coarsely chopped onion (about ½ medium)
½ cup chopped fresh cilantro
3 tablespoons fresh lime juice
1½ tablespoons extravirgin olive oil
1½ teaspoons Champagne vinegar
½ teaspoon salt
Dash of freshly ground black pepper
½ pound tomatillos (about 4 medium), husked and quartered
½ serrano chile, minced
1 garlic clove, minced
3 cups water
2 cups uncooked quinoa (about ¾ pound)
1 cup thinly sliced peeled English cucumber
4 large radishes, halved and thinly sliced
1 small red bell pepper, thinly sliced
½ cup (2 ounces) queso anejo, crumbled
2 tablespoons chopped fresh parsley

1. Place first 10 ingredients in a blender or food processor, and process until smooth. Set aside.
2. Place 3 cups water in a large saucepan over medium-high heat, and bring to a boil. Stir in quinoa; cover, reduce heat, and simmer 15 minutes or until water is absorbed. Transfer to a large bowl. Drizzle with tomatillo mixture; stir well. Cool.
3. Add cucumber, radish, and bell pepper to cooled quinoa mixture; toss gently to combine. Place salad on each of 6 plates; top with cheese and parsley. Yield: 6 servings (serving size: 1 cup salad, about 1½ tablespoons cheese, and 1 teaspoon parsley).

CALORIES 311 (28% from fat); FAT 10g (sat 2.7g, mono 4.3g, poly 2g); PROTEIN 10.6g; CARB 46.9g; FIBER 5.1g; CHOL 10mg; IRON 5.9mg; SODIUM 325mg; CALC 120mg

Mexican Lentil Soup with Roasted Garlic

This is a hearty soup with deep, subtle flavors. Serve with a green salad, crusty bread, and a cold Mexican beer. If you can find fresh *epazote*, a pungent herb available in Latin markets and some supermarkets, use it in place of the parsley.

1 whole garlic head
2 tablespoons plus 1 teaspoon olive oil, divided
2 cups chopped onion (about 1 large)
1½ cups chopped peeled carrot (about 2 medium)
1 cup chopped celery (about 2 stalks)
8 cups fat-free, less-sodium chicken broth
2 cups black lentils, rinsed
½ cup chopped fresh parsley
2 fresh bay leaves
1 teaspoon ground cumin
½ teaspoon ground coriander
1½ teaspoons hot pepper sauce
¼ teaspoon freshly ground black pepper
1 teaspoon sherry vinegar

1. Preheat oven to 325°.
2. Remove white papery skin from garlic head (do not peel or separate cloves). Rub 1 teaspoon oil over garlic head, and wrap in foil. Bake at 325° for 1 hour; cool 10 minutes. Separate cloves; squeeze to extract garlic pulp. Discard skins.
3. Heat 2 tablespoons oil in a Dutch oven over medium-high heat. Add onion, carrot, and celery; sauté 5 minutes or until softened. Stir in broth, lentils, parsley, and bay leaves; bring to a boil. Cover, reduce heat, and simmer 25 minutes or until lentils are tender.
4. Remove and discard bay leaves. Place 2 cups lentil mixture and garlic pulp in a blender or food processor; add cumin, coriander, pepper sauce, and pepper. Process until smooth. Return puréed mixture to pot; stir well. Stir in vinegar. Yield: 6 servings (serving size: about 1⅓ cups).

CALORIES 325 (17% from fat); FAT 6.2g (sat 0.8g, mono 4g, poly 0.9g); PROTEIN 23.1g; CARB 45.7g; FIBER 21.6g; CHOL 0mg; IRON 6.5mg; SODIUM 657mg; CALC 74mg

French Onion Soup, page 11

Thai Fish Sauce and Lime Chicken,
page 30

Coconut-Cranberry Muffins,
page 28

Frisée, Baby Spinach, and Golden Beet Salad,
page 7

Peach Salad with Cumin Dressing, facing page

Forcing Spring

Although it may still be chilly outside, these lively ingredients can transform the season.

When the charm of snow-covered lawns and windowpanes framed with frost has worn thin, and eager eyes scan the ground for the first tiny crocuses peeking through the ground, ambitious gardeners know they can bring a bit of spring cheer inside with forced bulbs. And in similar mode you can brighten a winter-weary palate and add a bit of color to your menus with ingredients that mimic spring.

QUICK & EASY
Peach Salad with Cumin Dressing
(pictured on facing page)

Thaw the peaches and pat them dry with paper towels to remove excess moisture. Frozen berries, which are good in cooked or puréed applications, don't have the same consistency as fresh. Pairing a small amount of fresh berries with the frozen peaches makes this taste like a fresh fruit salad.

- 2 cups sliced frozen peaches, thawed
- 1 cup thinly sliced seeded peeled cucumber
- ½ teaspoon grated lemon rind
- 1 tablespoon fresh lemon juice
- 2 teaspoons minced fresh mint
- 2 teaspoons honey
- ¾ teaspoon cumin seeds, toasted and crushed
- ½ teaspoon salt
- ¼ teaspoon freshly ground black pepper
- ½ cup fresh raspberries

1. Combine first 6 ingredients in a large bowl, tossing gently. Combine cumin, salt, and pepper; sprinkle over peach mixture. Add raspberries, and toss gently to combine. Serve immediately. Yield: 4 servings (serving size: ¾ cup).

CALORIES 144 (3% from fat); FAT 0.4g (sat 0g, mono 0.1g, poly 0.2g); PROTEIN 1.4g; CARB 36.3g; FIBER 3.7g; CHOL 0mg; IRON 1.1mg; SODIUM 307mg; CALC 21mg

---

STAFF FAVORITE
Herbed Chicken Breasts with Tomatillo Salsa and Queso Fresco

Queso fresco is a Mexican cheese that's mild, crumbly, and a bit salty. It's a wonderful topping for the tangy sauce.

SALSA:
- 2 quarts water
- ½ pound tomatillos (about 10 small), husks and stems removed
- 1 garlic clove
- ½ to 1 serrano chile
- ½ cup chopped fresh cilantro
- ¼ cup coarsely chopped onion
- 1 teaspoon fresh lime juice
- ¼ teaspoon salt

CHICKEN:
- 3 (1-ounce) slices white bread
- 4 (6-ounce) skinless, boneless chicken breast halves
- ½ teaspoon salt
- ½ teaspoon ground cumin
- ¼ teaspoon ground red pepper
- 1 large egg, lightly beaten
- 1 tablespoon olive oil
- ½ cup (2 ounces) crumbled queso fresco
- Cilantro sprigs (optional)
- Lime wedges (optional)

1. Preheat oven to 350°.
2. To prepare salsa, bring water to a boil. Add tomatillos, garlic, and chile; cook 7 minutes. Drain and rinse with cold water. Combine tomatillos mixture, chopped cilantro, onion, lime juice, and ¼ teaspoon salt in a food processor or blender; pulse 4 or 5 times or until coarsely chopped. Set aside.
3. To prepare chicken, place bread in a food processor, and pulse 10 times or until coarse crumbs measure 1½ cups. Arrange crumbs on a baking sheet; bake at 350° for 3 minutes or until lightly browned. Cool completely.
4. Place each chicken breast half between 2 sheets of heavy-duty plastic wrap; pound to ½-inch thickness using a meat mallet or rolling pin. Combine ½ teaspoon salt, cumin, and red pepper; sprinkle evenly over chicken.
5. Place breadcrumbs in a shallow dish. Place egg in another shallow dish. Dip chicken in egg; dredge in breadcrumbs.
6. Heat oil in a large nonstick skillet over medium-high heat. Add chicken; cook 4 minutes on each side or until done. Top chicken with salsa, and sprinkle with queso fresco cheese. Garnish with cilantro sprigs and lime wedges, if desired. Yield: 4 servings (serving size: 1 chicken breast half, ¼ cup salsa, and 2 tablespoons cheese).

CALORIES 364 (26% from fat); FAT 10.7g (sat 3.2g, mono 4.5g, poly 1.6g); PROTEIN 47.1g; CARB 17.7g; FIBER 2g; CHOL 162mg; IRON 3mg; SODIUM 770mg; CALC 169mg

---

Plant an Indoor Herb Garden

You can enjoy fresh flavor during the cold of winter by growing herbs indoors. Buy small plants at the supermarket or nursery. Or use a ready-to-go indoor herb garden. Indoor herb plants thrive with at least five hours of daylight in a south- or west-facing window. Don't overwater—let them dry out a bit between watering. Give them a periodic boost with plant food.

QUICK & EASY
Linguine with Basil-Pea Cream

Frozen peas are cooked in a broth mixture, and half are puréed to create a creamy sauce. If the tossed pasta is thick, add a little pasta cooking water to thin the sauce.

       3   tablespoons butter, divided
       ½   cup chopped leek
    1½   cups fat-free, less-sodium chicken broth, divided
       2   (10-ounce) packages frozen green peas
       1   cup fresh basil leaves
       1   tablespoon extravirgin olive oil
       2   (8-ounce) packages presliced mushrooms
       2   garlic cloves, minced
       6   cups hot cooked linguine (about 12 ounces uncooked pasta)
    1¼   teaspoons salt
       ¼   teaspoon freshly ground black pepper
       ¼   cup chopped fresh basil

1. Melt 1 tablespoon butter in a large nonstick skillet over medium heat. Add leek; cook 3 minutes, stirring frequently.

Stir in ¾ cup broth and peas; bring to a boil. Partially cover, reduce heat, and simmer 5 minutes. Place 1½ cups pea mixture, ¾ cup broth, 1 cup basil leaves, and oil in a blender, and process until smooth. Place puréed pea mixture in a large bowl. Stir in remaining pea mixture.
2. Melt 2 tablespoons butter in pan over medium-high heat. Add mushrooms and garlic; sauté 6 minutes or until mushrooms are tender. Stir mushroom mixture, pasta, salt, and pepper into pea mixture. Sprinkle 2 teaspoons chopped basil over each serving. Yield: 6 servings (serving size: about 1⅓ cups pasta).

CALORIES 383 (22% from fat); FAT 9.5g (sat 4.1g, mono 3.3g, poly 1.1g); PROTEIN 15.7g; CARB 59.8g; FIBER 6.8g; CHOL 15mg; IRON 4.5mg; SODIUM 759mg; CALC 55mg

QUICK & EASY
Lime-Scented Orange Roughy and Spinach

Cooking *en papillote* (in parchment) helps the citrus rind and juice lend aroma and flavor to the spinach and fish. To make the packets for the fish and spinach, we use heavy-duty foil because it's easy to find and handle.

       1   tablespoon olive oil
       1   cup thinly sliced carrot
       2   garlic cloves, minced
       ½   teaspoon salt, divided
       1   (10-ounce) package fresh baby spinach
       ⅓   cup sliced green onions
       ¼   cup mirin (sweet rice wine)
       1   teaspoon grated lime rind
       3   tablespoons fresh lime juice
       1   teaspoon grated peeled fresh ginger
       4   (6-ounce) orange roughy fillets
       ¼   teaspoon freshly ground black pepper
       4   lime wedges

1. Preheat oven to 400°.
2. Heat oil in a large nonstick skillet over medium-high heat. Add carrot; sauté 2 minutes or until tender. Add garlic; sauté 15 seconds. Add ¼ teaspoon salt and spinach; sauté 2 minutes or until spinach wilts.
3. Combine ¼ teaspoon salt, green onions, and next 4 ingredients.
4. Fold 4 (16 x 12-inch) sheets heavy-duty foil in half lengthwise. Open foil; place about ½ cup spinach mixture in center of each foil sheet. Top each with 1 fillet. Drizzle mirin mixture evenly over fillets; sprinkle evenly with black pepper. Fold foil over fillets; tightly seal edges. Place foil packets in a single layer on a jelly-roll pan. Bake at 400° for 20 minutes or until fish flakes easily when tested with a fork. Serve with lime wedges. Yield: 4 servings.

CALORIES 221 (20% from fat); FAT 4.9g (sat 0.5g, mono 3.3g, poly 0.4g); PROTEIN 27.6g; CARB 13.3g; FIBER 3.4g; CHOL 34mg; IRON 2.5mg; SODIUM 470mg; CALC 138mg

Raspberry-Chocolate Soufflés

These pink and chocolate-brown individual desserts are a great recipe for the soufflé novice. To coat the insides of the ramekins with sugar, divide the sugar evenly, or place all 2½ tablespoons sugar in one ramekin. Tilt the ramekin to coat evenly with sugar, and pour all remaining sugar into another ramekin; repeat until all are coated.

          Cooking spray
    2½   tablespoons sugar
       ½   cup 1% low-fat milk, divided
       1   (10-ounce) bag frozen unsweetened raspberries, thawed
       2   large egg yolks
       1   tablespoon cornstarch
       4   large egg whites
       ⅓   cup sugar
       2   ounces semisweet chocolate, chopped

1. Preheat oven to 400°.
2. Coat 6 (6-ounce) ramekins or custard cups with cooking spray. Divide 2½ tablespoons sugar evenly among ramekins, and turn to coat insides of ramekins with sugar.
3. Combine 6 tablespoons milk and raspberries in a blender or food processor;

process until smooth. Strain raspberry mixture through a sieve into a large bowl, pressing with back of a spoon to remove as much liquid as possible. Discard solids. Add egg yolks to raspberry mixture; stir with a whisk until smooth. Combine 2 tablespoons milk and cornstarch, stirring with a whisk. Add cornstarch mixture to raspberry mixture; stir well.

4. Place egg whites in a large bowl; beat with a mixer at high speed until soft peaks form. Gradually add ⅓ cup sugar, 1 tablespoon at a time, beating until stiff peaks form. Gently stir one-fourth of egg white mixture into raspberry mixture; gently fold in remaining egg white mixture. Fold in chocolate just until combined. Spoon mixture into prepared ramekins, and place ramekins on a baking sheet.

5. Bake at 400° for 14 minutes or until soufflés are puffed and lightly browned. Serve immediately. Yield: 6 servings (serving size: 1 soufflé).

CALORIES 195 (21% from fat); FAT 4.6g (sat 2.3g, mono 1.7g, poly 0.4g); PROTEIN 4.7g; CARB 36g; FIBER 1.5g; CHOL 69mg; IRON 0.8mg; SODIUM 51mg; CALC 43mg

---

Shrimp and Rice Salad with Cilantro-Lemon Dressing

If making this salad a day ahead, wait until serving to toss in the cilantro.

- 10 cups hot water
- 1 (3½-ounce) bag boil-in-bag long-grain rice
- 1½ pounds large shrimp, peeled and deveined
- ¾ cup finely chopped poblano chile (about 1 medium)
- ½ cup fresh cilantro, coarsely chopped
- ¼ cup fresh lemon juice
- ¾ teaspoon salt
- ¼ teaspoon freshly ground black pepper
- ⅛ teaspoon ground red pepper
- 2 tablespoons extravirgin olive oil
- 4 lemon wedges

1. Bring water to a boil in a large Dutch oven. Add bag of rice; cook 5 minutes. Add shrimp; return to a boil. Cook 5 minutes or until shrimp are done. Drain bag of rice and shrimp; rinse with cold water. Drain.

2. Combine poblano and next 5 ingredients in a large bowl. Open bag of rice. Add rice and shrimp to poblano mixture; toss gently to combine. Drizzle with oil, and toss gently to coat. Serve with lemon wedges. Yield: 4 servings (serving size: 1½ cups).

CALORIES 348 (26% from fat); FAT 10g (sat 1.5g, mono 5.8g, poly 1.8g); PROTEIN 37g; CARB 25.1g; FIBER 0.4g; CHOL 259mg; IRON 5.2mg; SODIUM 715mg; CALC 108mg

---

Strawberry-Cabernet Sauce

This deep-red sauce is good served warm, at room temperature, or chilled over ice cream or pound cake. Use a good cabernet in the sauce. To save their flavorful juice, place thawed berries in a measuring cup, and cut with kitchen shears.

- ¾ cup plus 1 tablespoon cabernet sauvignon or other dry red wine, divided
- ¼ cup packed brown sugar
- ½ teaspoon vanilla extract
- 1 (10-ounce) bag frozen strawberries, thawed and divided
- ½ teaspoon fresh lemon juice

1. Combine ¾ cup wine and sugar in a small saucepan; bring to a boil over medium-high heat. Cook until reduced to ⅓ cup (about 4 minutes). Remove from heat. Place wine mixture, vanilla, and half of strawberries in a blender or food processor; process until smooth. Spoon puréed strawberry mixture into a large bowl.

2. Coarsely chop remaining strawberries. Add chopped strawberries, 1 tablespoon wine, and lemon juice to puréed strawberry mixture; stir to combine. Yield: 9 servings (serving size: about 3 tablespoons).

CALORIES 50 (0% from fat); FAT 0g; PROTEIN 0.2g; CARB 9.2g; FIBER 0.1g; CHOL 0mg; IRON 0.4mg; SODIUM 4mg; CALC 12mg

---

Chicken Salad with Peas and Fresh Herb Vinaigrette

Fresh parsley and thyme in the vinaigrette and sweet frozen peas in the chicken salad render a lighter flavor than the traditional mayonnaise-based chicken salads.

- ½ cup fresh parsley
- ½ cup chopped green onions
- 3 tablespoons rice vinegar
- 1 tablespoon stone-ground mustard
- 2 teaspoons extravirgin olive oil
- 1 to 2 teaspoons chopped fresh thyme
- 1 teaspoon sugar
- ¼ teaspoon salt
- 1 garlic clove
- 1½ cups chopped cooked chicken breast
- ¾ cup chopped celery
- 1 (10-ounce) package frozen green peas, thawed
- 2 tablespoons sliced almonds, toasted

1. Combine first 9 ingredients in a food processor; process until smooth. Combine parsley mixture, chicken, celery, and peas in a large bowl, tossing well. Sprinkle with almonds. Yield: 4 servings (serving size: 1 cup).

CALORIES 209 (29% from fat); FAT 6.8g (sat 1.1g, mono 3.8g, poly 1.3g); PROTEIN 21.8g; CARB 14.8g; FIBER 4.9g; CHOL 45mg; IRON 2.7mg; SODIUM 364mg; CALC 70mg

Citrus, frozen fruit, tomatillos, frozen peas, and fresh herbs brighten the flavor of wintertime dishes.

Coconut Milk

To add depth and subtle taste to breads, stir-fries, and soups, reach into your cupboard for this surprisingly versatile ingredient.

Spicy Coconut Soup with Spinach and Shrimp

Curry paste and crushed red pepper give this soup a double dose of heat.

Cooking spray
⅔ cup chopped onion
½ cup chopped red bell pepper
2 garlic cloves, minced
1½ teaspoons red curry paste
¼ teaspoon crushed red pepper
2 (14-ounce) cans fat-free, less-sodium chicken broth
1 (14-ounce) can light coconut milk
1 pound medium shrimp, peeled and deveined
6 cups torn spinach

1. Heat a medium saucepan over medium-high heat. Coat pan with cooking spray. Add onion, bell pepper, and garlic; sauté 4 minutes. Add curry paste and red pepper; cook 1 minute, stirring constantly. Stir in broth and coconut milk; bring to a boil. Reduce heat, and simmer, uncovered, 20 minutes, stirring occasionally. Add shrimp; cook 4 minutes or until shrimp are done. Stir in spinach; cook 2 minutes or until spinach wilts. Yield: 6 servings (serving size: about ¾ cup).

CALORIES 145 (30% from fat); FAT 4.8g (sat 3.2g, mono 0.3g, poly 0.6g); PROTEIN 18.7g; CARB 7.8g; FIBER 1.5g; CHOL 115mg; IRON 3.3mg; SODIUM 384mg; CALC 84mg

Five More Great Uses for Coconut Milk

1. Stir into coffee, especially iced coffee.
2. Use to braise bone-in chicken pieces.
3. Replace dairy milk for rice pudding.
4. Use in smoothies or milk shakes.
5. Add to mashed sweet potatoes.

QUICK & EASY
Coconut Milk Punch

Milk punch is an American cocktail of rum, whiskey, or brandy combined with milk and sugar; a version made with brandy is a classic brunch offering in New Orleans.

⅓ cup bourbon
3 tablespoons sugar
1 (14-ounce) can light coconut milk
Crushed ice
⅛ teaspoon grated nutmeg

1. Combine first 3 ingredients in a small pitcher; stir until sugar dissolves. Serve over crushed ice; sprinkle evenly with nutmeg. Yield: 4 servings (serving size: about ½ cup).

CALORIES 140 (30% from fat); FAT 4.7g (sat 4.4g, mono 0g, poly 0g); PROTEIN 1.2g; CARB 12.9g; FIBER 0g; CHOL 0mg; IRON 0.4mg; SODIUM 24mg; CALC 0mg

QUICK & EASY • MAKE AHEAD
Coconut-Cranberry Muffins

(pictured on page 23)

Coconut milk gives these muffins a little more sweetness and a slightly denser texture than cakelike muffins. Use any other dried fruit you like in place of the cranberries—dried currants or chopped dried apricots work well.

2 cups all-purpose flour
⅔ cup sugar
2 teaspoons baking powder
¼ teaspoon salt
1 cup sweetened dried cranberries
⅔ cup light coconut milk
¼ cup butter, melted
1 teaspoon grated lemon rind
½ teaspoon vanilla extract
1 large egg, lightly beaten
2 teaspoons sugar

1. Preheat oven to 400°.
2. Lightly spoon flour into dry measuring cups; level with a knife. Combine flour and next 3 ingredients in a medium bowl, stirring with a whisk. Stir in cranberries; make a well in center of mixture. Combine coconut milk and next 4 ingredients, stirring well with a whisk. Add to flour mixture, stirring just until moist.
3. Place 12 muffin cup liners in muffin cups. Spoon batter into lined cups. Sprinkle evenly with 2 teaspoons sugar. Bake at 400° for 20 minutes or until muffins spring back when touched lightly in center. Remove muffins from pans immediately; place on a wire rack. Yield: 1 dozen (serving size: 1 muffin).

CALORIES 200 (23% from fat); FAT 5.1g (sat 2.7g, mono 1.7g, poly 0.3g); PROTEIN 2.9g; CARB 36.1g; FIBER 1.1g; CHOL 28mg; IRON 1.2mg; SODIUM 167mg; CALC 52mg

Oven-Fried Coconut Chicken

The marinade infuses dark-meat chicken with a light coconut flavor; flaked coconut heightens the nutty taste. Find panko in your supermarket's ethnic food aisle.

1 tablespoon fresh lime juice
1 tablespoon hot pepper sauce
1 (14-ounce) can light coconut milk
4 (4-ounce) chicken thighs, skinned
4 (4-ounce) chicken drumsticks, skinned
¾ cup panko (Japanese breadcrumbs)
½ cup flaked sweetened coconut
½ teaspoon salt
¼ teaspoon freshly ground black pepper
Cooking spray

1. Combine first 3 ingredients in a large zip-top plastic bag. Add chicken to bag; seal. Marinate in refrigerator 1½ hours, turning bag occasionally.
2. Preheat oven to 400°.
3. Combine panko, flaked coconut, salt, and black pepper in a shallow dish. Remove chicken from bag; discard marinade. Dredge chicken, 1 piece at a time, in panko mixture. Place chicken on a baking sheet lined with parchment paper. Lightly coat chicken with cooking spray. Bake at 400° for 30 minutes or until golden brown. Carefully turn chicken over; bake an additional 30 minutes or until done. Yield: 4 servings (serving size: 1 thigh and 1 drumstick).

CALORIES 256 (30% from fat); FAT 8.6g (sat 4.4g, mono 1.6g, poly 1.2g); PROTEIN 27.7g; CARB 15.6g; FIBER 0.8g; CHOL 103mg; IRON 1.6mg; SODIUM 464mg; CALC 18mg

Coconut Rice with Beef Stir-Fry

Fragrant jasmine rice cooks in a combination of coconut milk and water to become soft and slightly creamy—a fitting foil to the spicy stir-fry.

RICE:

    1 cup water
    ¼ teaspoon salt
    Dash of ground red pepper
    1 (14-ounce) can light coconut
       milk
    1 cup uncooked jasmine rice

STIR-FRY:

    1 teaspoon dark sesame oil,
       divided
    1 (1-pound) flank steak, trimmed
       and thinly sliced across the grain
    1 cup vertically sliced onion
    1 cup red bell pepper strips
    3 cups sliced bok choy
    2 tablespoons chopped fresh
       cilantro
    1 tablespoon chili garlic sauce (such
       as Lee Kum Kee)
    ¼ teaspoon salt
    ¼ teaspoon freshly ground black
       pepper
    4 lime wedges

1. To prepare rice, bring first 4 ingredients to a boil in a medium saucepan; stir in rice. Cover, reduce heat, and simmer 15 minutes or until liquid is absorbed.
2. To prepare stir-fry, heat ½ teaspoon oil in a large nonstick skillet over medium-high heat. Add half of beef; stir-fry 4 minutes or until done. Remove from pan; cover and keep warm. Repeat procedure with ½ teaspoon oil and remaining beef.
3. Add onion and bell pepper to pan; stir-fry 5 minutes. Add bok choy; stir-fry 3 minutes or until vegetables are tender. Add beef, cilantro, chili garlic sauce, ¼ teaspoon salt, and black pepper; cook 2 minutes or until thoroughly heated. Serve with rice and lime wedges. Yield: 4 servings (serving size: 1¼ cups stir-fry, about ¾ cup rice, and 1 lime wedge).

CALORIES 416 (28% from fat); FAT 13.1g (sat 7.5g, mono 3.2g, poly 0.9g); PROTEIN 28.3g; CARB 46.5g; FIBER 1.7g; CHOL 45mg; IRON 4.7mg; SODIUM 561mg; CALC 90mg

A Rediscovered Favorite

Long-forgotten salmon croquettes get a needed update.

Karen Lagnese of Silver Spring, Maryland, found a recipe for salmon croquettes. She couldn't justify preparing it because it was high in calories and fat. So we stepped in, revised the recipe, and gave Karen a new version that's even better than the original.

Salmon Croquettes with Rémoulade

RÉMOULADE:

    ⅓ cup plain fat-free yogurt
    1½ tablespoons low-fat mayonnaise
    2 teaspoons chopped fresh
       parsley
    2 teaspoons chopped green onions
    2 teaspoons whole-grain Dijon
       mustard
    1 teaspoon capers
    ¼ teaspoon dried tarragon
    ⅛ teaspoon freshly ground black
       pepper
    Dash of hot pepper sauce

CROQUETTES:

    ⅓ cup plain fat-free yogurt
    1 tablespoon whole-grain Dijon
       mustard
    2 large egg whites
    Cooking spray
    ½ cup chopped onion
    ½ cup chopped celery
    1 cup crushed saltine crackers
       (about 15 crackers), divided
    ¼ teaspoon dried tarragon
    ⅛ teaspoon freshly ground black
       pepper
    2 (6-ounce) cans pink salmon,
       skinless, boneless, and drained
       (such as Bumble Bee)
    2¼ cups grated carrot
    4 teaspoons butter
    Tarragon sprigs (optional)

1. To prepare rémoulade, combine first 9 ingredients in a bowl; cover and chill.
2. To prepare croquettes, combine ⅓ cup yogurt, 1 tablespoon mustard, and egg whites in a bowl. Set aside.
3. Heat a nonstick skillet over medium-high heat. Coat pan with cooking spray. Add ½ cup onion and celery; cook 4 minutes or until tender. Cool slightly. Combine onion mixture, yogurt mixture, ½ cup crackers, ¼ teaspoon dried tarragon, ⅛ teaspoon pepper, and salmon in a bowl; toss gently. Cover and chill 10 minutes. Divide salmon mixture into 8 equal portions, shaping each into a ½-inch-thick patty. Coat patties evenly with ½ cup crackers. Cover and chill 20 minutes.
4. Combine carrot and ¼ cup rémoulade in a bowl (reserve remaining sauce); toss gently to coat.
5. Melt butter in a large nonstick skillet over medium-high heat. Add patties; reduce heat to medium. Cook 4 minutes on each side or until lightly browned. Serve croquettes with carrot salad and remaining sauce. Garnish with tarragon sprigs, if desired. Yield: 4 servings (serving size: 2 croquettes, 1 tablespoon sauce, and about ½ cup carrot salad).

CALORIES 273 (30% from fat); FAT 9.1g (sat 3g, mono 2.6g, poly 1.6g); PROTEIN 24.6g; CARB 26.7g; FIBER 3.2g; CHOL 43mg; IRON 1.1mg; SODIUM 743mg; CALC 91mg

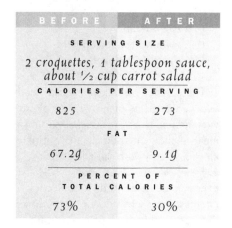

BEFORE	AFTER
SERVING SIZE	
2 croquettes, 1 tablespoon sauce, about ½ cup carrot salad	
CALORIES PER SERVING	
825	273
FAT	
67.2g	9.1g
PERCENT OF TOTAL CALORIES	
73%	30%

Chicken with 8 Simple Sauces

The procedure is the same—sauté chicken and deglaze the pan—but the recipes yield very different results. Whip up one of these variations tonight.

QUICK & EASY
Chicken with Provençal Sauce

Herbes de Provence, a heady combination of dried basil, thyme, marjoram, rosemary, lavender, and sage, is a classic French seasoning. Try it in other Mediterranean dishes, such as pasta sauce or baked black olives. Serve with roasted potato wedges.

- 4 (6-ounce) skinless, boneless chicken breast halves
- ¼ teaspoon salt
- ¼ teaspoon freshly ground black pepper
- 1½ tablespoons olive oil
- 1 garlic clove, minced
- 1 cup fat-free, less-sodium chicken broth
- 1½ teaspoons dried herbes de Provence
- 1 teaspoon butter
- 1 teaspoon fresh lemon juice
- Thyme sprigs (optional)

1. Place each chicken breast half between 2 sheets of heavy-duty plastic wrap; pound to ½-inch thickness using a meat mallet or rolling pin. Sprinkle chicken evenly with salt and pepper.
2. Heat oil in a large nonstick skillet over medium heat. Add chicken; cook 6 minutes on each side or until done. Remove chicken from pan; keep warm.
3. Add garlic to pan; cook 1 minute, stirring constantly. Add broth and herbes de Provence; bring to a boil, scraping pan to loosen browned bits. Cook until broth mixture is reduced to ½ cup (about 3 minutes). Remove from heat; add butter and lemon juice, stirring until butter melts. Serve sauce over chicken. Garnish with thyme sprigs, if desired. Yield: 4 servings (serving size: 1 chicken breast half and about 2 tablespoons sauce).

CALORIES 248 (30% from fat); FAT 8.2g (sat 1.8g, mono 4.5g, poly 1g); PROTEIN 40.2g; CARB 1g; FIBER 0.3g; CHOL 101mg; IRON 1.5mg; SODIUM 376mg; CALC 32mg

QUICK & EASY
Thai Fish Sauce and Lime Chicken
(pictured on page 22)

Sweetened chili sauce is found in Asian markets; it's often served alongside egg rolls. A similar condiment available in most grocery stores is called Thai sweet red chile dipping sauce. Serve this chicken with white rice.

- 4 (6-ounce) skinless, boneless chicken breast halves
- ¼ teaspoon salt
- 1 tablespoon canola oil
- 1 cup fat-free, less-sodium chicken broth
- 3 tablespoons sweetened chili sauce
- 2 teaspoons fish sauce
- ¼ cup fresh lime juice
- 1 teaspoon creamy peanut butter
- 2 tablespoons chopped roasted peanuts
- Lime wedges (optional)

1. Place each chicken breast half between 2 sheets of heavy-duty plastic wrap; pound to ½-inch thickness using a meat mallet or rolling pin. Sprinkle chicken evenly with salt.
2. Heat oil in a large nonstick skillet over medium heat. Add chicken; cook 6 minutes on each side or until done. Remove chicken from pan; keep warm.
3. Add broth, chili sauce, and fish sauce to pan; bring to a boil, scraping pan to loosen browned bits. Cook until broth mixture is reduced to ⅔ cup (about 4 minutes). Remove from heat; add lime juice and peanut butter, stirring until smooth. Serve sauce over chicken; sprinkle with peanuts. Garnish with lime wedges, if desired. Yield: 4 servings (serving size: 1 chicken breast half, about 3 tablespoons sauce, and 1½ teaspoons peanuts).

CALORIES 296 (26% from fat); FAT 8.5g (sat 1.7g, mono 3.6g, poly 2.4g); PROTEIN 41.8g; CARB 12.1g; FIBER 0.6g; CHOL 99mg; IRON 1.4mg; SODIUM 649mg; CALC 25mg

QUICK & EASY
Mexican Chicken with Almond-Chile Cream

Look for ground ancho chile pepper in the spice section. If you can't find it, substitute 1½ teaspoons regular chili powder and ½ teaspoon ground chipotle chile pepper. Crema Mexicana is similar to crème fraîche but has a thinner consistency and sweeter flavor. Slice the chicken and serve with flour tortillas and a tossed salad.

- 3 tablespoons sliced almonds
- 2 teaspoons ground ancho chile pepper
- 4 (6-ounce) skinless, boneless chicken breast halves
- ¼ teaspoon salt, divided
- ¼ teaspoon freshly ground black pepper
- 2 teaspoons butter
- 1 teaspoon canola oil
- 1 garlic clove, minced
- 1 cup fat-free, less-sodium chicken broth
- 2 tablespoons crema Mexicana
- Cilantro sprigs (optional)

1. Combine almonds and chile pepper in a blender or food processor; process until mixture resembles coarse meal.
2. Place each chicken breast half between 2 sheets of heavy-duty plastic wrap; pound to ½-inch thickness using a

meat mallet or rolling pin. Sprinkle with ⅛ teaspoon salt and black pepper.

3. Heat butter and oil in a large nonstick skillet over medium heat. Add chicken; cook 6 minutes on each side or until done. Remove chicken from pan; keep warm.

4. Add garlic to pan; cook 1 minute, stirring constantly. Add almond mixture, ⅛ teaspoon salt, and broth; bring to a boil, scraping pan to loosen browned bits. Cook until broth mixture is reduced to ½ cup (about 3 minutes). Remove from heat. Stir in crema Mexicana. Serve sauce over chicken. Garnish with cilantro, if desired. Yield: 4 servings (serving size: 1 chicken breast half and 2 tablespoons sauce).

CALORIES 269 (30% from fat); FAT 8.9g (sat 2.8g, mono 3.1g, poly 1.4g); PROTEIN 41.3g; CARB 2.8g; FIBER 1.2g; CHOL 109mg; IRON 1.4mg; SODIUM 387mg; CALC 35mg

QUICK & EASY
Chicken with Goat Cheese Sauce

To create the smoothest sauce, use soft goat cheese and serve immediately. Pluck the tiny leaves of a thyme sprig to get 1 teaspoon of leaves for the sauce.

- 4 (6-ounce) skinless, boneless chicken breast halves
- ¼ teaspoon salt
- ¼ teaspoon freshly ground black pepper
- 1 tablespoon canola oil
- 2 tablespoons dry white wine
- 1 cup fat-free, less-sodium chicken broth
- 4 thyme sprigs
- ¼ cup (2 ounces) soft (log-style) goat cheese
- 1 teaspoon fresh thyme leaves

1. Place each chicken breast half between 2 sheets of heavy-duty plastic wrap; pound to ½-inch thickness using a meat mallet or rolling pin. Sprinkle chicken evenly with salt and pepper.

2. Heat oil in a large nonstick skillet over medium heat. Add chicken; cook 6 minutes on each side or until done. Remove chicken from pan; keep warm.

3. Add wine to pan; bring to a boil,

Quick Chicken Tips

1. *Place the breasts between plastic wrap, and pound to a ½-inch thickness so they cook quickly and evenly.*

2. *To tell if the chicken is done, pierce it with a fork. If the juices run clear, it is done.*

3. *After adding liquid to the pan, scrape the bottom to loosen the browned bits and add flavor to the sauce.*

4. *Pour the sauce into a measuring cup to be sure that it has reduced enough.*

scraping pan to loosen browned bits. Cook until mixture is reduced to 1 tablespoon (about 1 minute). Add broth and thyme sprigs; cook until mixture is reduced to ½ cup (about 5 minutes). Remove from heat; discard thyme sprigs.

4. Add cheese to pan; stir with a whisk until smooth. Serve sauce over chicken; sprinkle with thyme leaves. Yield: 4 servings (serving size: 1 chicken breast half and about 3 tablespoons sauce).

CALORIES 267 (29% from fat); FAT 8.6g (sat 2.9g, mono 3.3g, poly 1.6g); PROTEIN 42.7g; CARB 0.6g; FIBER 0.1g; CHOL 105mg; IRON 1.6mg; SODIUM 421mg; CALC 41mg

WINE NOTE: Goat cheese is an ideal partner for sauvignon blanc. Both goat cheese and the sauvignon blanc have clean, fresh, tangy, earthy flavors, so the food and wine mirror each other. A perfect sauvignon blanc for the flavor: Tin Roof Sauvignon Blanc from the North Coast of California—about $9.

Trim the fat and any small pieces attached to the breast before cooking.

Chicken with Cider and Bacon Sauce

    4 (6-ounce) skinless, boneless
       chicken breast halves
    ¼ teaspoon salt
    ¼ teaspoon freshly ground black
       pepper
    2 bacon slices, chopped
    ¼ cup minced fresh onion
    ¾ cup unsweetened apple cider
    ½ cup fat-free, less-sodium chicken
       broth

1. Place each chicken breast half between 2 sheets of heavy-duty plastic wrap; pound to ½-inch thickness using a meat mallet or rolling pin. Sprinkle chicken evenly with salt and pepper.
2. Cook bacon in a large nonstick skillet over medium heat until crisp. Remove bacon from pan. Add chicken to drippings in pan; cook 6 minutes on each side or until done. Remove chicken from pan; keep warm.
3. Add onion to pan; cook 2 minutes or until tender, stirring constantly. Add cider and broth; bring to a boil, scraping pan to loosen browned bits. Cook until broth mixture is reduced to ½ cup (about 5 minutes). Stir in cooked bacon; serve sauce over chicken. Yield: 4 servings (serving size: 1 chicken breast half and about 2 tablespoons sauce).

CALORIES 269 (24% from fat); FAT 7.2g (sat 2.3g, mono 2.8g, poly 1g); PROTEIN 41.1g; CARB 6.9g; FIBER 0.2g; CHOL 106mg; IRON 1.3mg; SODIUM 412mg; CALC 22mg

Chicken with Sun-Dried Tomato Sauce

    1 (8-ounce) jar oil-packed sun-dried
       tomato halves
    4 (6-ounce) skinless, boneless
       chicken breast halves
    ¼ teaspoon salt, divided
    ¼ teaspoon freshly ground black
       pepper
    1 cup fat-free, less-sodium chicken
       broth
    1 teaspoon dried oregano
    ½ teaspoon balsamic vinegar

1. Drain sun-dried tomatoes in a sieve over a bowl, reserving oil. Set aside 1½ tablespoons reserved oil to cook chicken. Finely chop ¼ cup tomatoes; set aside for sauce. Place remaining oil and tomatoes in sun-dried tomato jar; reserve for another use.
2. Place each chicken breast half between 2 sheets of heavy-duty plastic wrap; pound to ½-inch thickness using a meat mallet or rolling pin. Sprinkle chicken evenly with ⅛ teaspoon salt and pepper.
3. Heat 1½ tablespoons reserved oil in a large nonstick skillet over medium heat. Add chicken; cook 6 minutes on each side or until done. Remove chicken from pan; keep warm.
4. Add chopped sun-dried tomatoes, ⅛ teaspoon salt, broth, oregano, and vinegar; bring to a boil, scraping pan to loosen browned bits. Cook until broth mixture is reduced to ½ cup (about 3 minutes). Serve sauce over chicken. Yield: 4 servings (serving size: 1 chicken breast half and 2 tablespoons sauce).

CALORIES 254 (29% from fat); FAT 8.2g (sat 1.4g, mono 4.9g, poly 1.1g); PROTEIN 40.4g; CARB 2.3g; FIBER 0.6g; CHOL 99mg; IRON 1.7mg; SODIUM 387mg; CALC 29mg

Pollo con Mojo de Ajo

The name of this recipe, translated from Spanish, is "Chicken with Garlic Sauce." A squeeze of lime juice brightens its flavor.

    4 (6-ounce) skinless, boneless
       chicken breast halves
    ¼ teaspoon salt
    ¼ teaspoon freshly ground black
       pepper
    1 tablespoon canola oil
    1 tablespoon butter
    4 garlic cloves, thinly sliced
    ¾ cup fat-free, less-sodium chicken
       broth
    2 teaspoons fresh lime juice
    1 tablespoon minced fresh
       cilantro
    4 lime wedges

1. Place each chicken breast half between 2 sheets of heavy-duty plastic wrap; pound to ½-inch thickness using a meat mallet or rolling pin. Sprinkle chicken evenly with salt and pepper.
2. Heat oil in a large nonstick skillet over medium heat. Add chicken; cook 6 minutes on each side or until done. Remove chicken from pan; keep warm.
3. Melt butter in pan over medium-low heat. Add garlic; cook 1 minute (do not brown). Add broth; bring to a boil, scraping pan to loosen browned bits. Cook until broth mixture is reduced to ½ cup (about 4 minutes). Remove from heat; stir in lime juice. Serve sauce over chicken; sprinkle with cilantro. Serve with lime wedges. Yield: 4 servings (serving size: 1 chicken breast half, about 2 tablespoons sauce, 1½ teaspoons cilantro, and 1 lime wedge).

CALORIES 253 (30% from fat); FAT 8.5g (sat 2.6g, mono 3.3g, poly 1.6g); PROTEIN 40.1g; CARB 1.6g; FIBER 0.1g; CHOL 106mg; IRON 1.3mg; SODIUM 361mg; CALC 26mg

Chicken with Barbecue-Bourbon Sauce

    4 (6-ounce) skinless, boneless
       chicken breast halves
    ¼ teaspoon salt
    ¼ teaspoon freshly ground black
       pepper
    1 tablespoon canola oil
    1 tablespoon butter
    ⅓ cup minced shallots
    ¼ cup bourbon
    ¾ cup fat-free, less-sodium chicken
       broth
    2 teaspoons tomato-based barbecue
       sauce

1. Place each chicken breast half between 2 sheets of heavy-duty plastic wrap; pound to ½-inch thickness using a meat mallet or rolling pin. Sprinkle chicken evenly with salt and pepper.
2. Heat oil and butter in a large nonstick skillet over medium heat. Add chicken; cook 6 minutes on each side or until done. Remove chicken from pan; keep warm.
3. Add shallots to pan; cook 1 minute, stirring constantly. Add bourbon to pan; bring to a boil, scraping pan to loosen browned bits. Cook until bourbon

mixture is reduced to 2 tablespoons (about 5 minutes). Add broth and barbecue sauce; cook until broth mixture is reduced to ½ cup (about 3 minutes). Serve sauce over chicken. Yield: 4 servings (serving size: 1 chicken breast half and 2 tablespoons sauce).

CALORIES 294 (26% from fat); FAT 8.4g (sat 2.6g, mono 3.3g, poly 1.7g); PROTEIN 40.3g; CARB 2.9g; FIBER 0.2g; CHOL 106mg; IRON 1.5mg; SODIUM 384mg; CALC 26mg

lunch box chronicles

Ham It Up

Bake a succulent ham for dinner, and use the leftovers in portable salads, sandwiches, and wraps.

Here, we offer a basic recipe for baked ham half, the most common cut offered in supermarkets. Prepare it for dinner one night, and serve with simple sides, such as steamed broccoli and mashed potatoes. Use the remaining meat in any of the following tasty dishes, all of which can be made a day ahead, transport well, and can be served cold or at room temperature.

MAKE AHEAD
Simple Baked Ham

This basic recipe yields a fine ham to serve for breakfast or dinner. Because the seasonings are mild, leftovers are at home in a variety of dishes. Soaking the ham in water draws out some of the sodium so the ham won't taste too salty.

   1 (8-pound) 33%-less-sodium smoked, fully cooked ham half
   2 teaspoons whole cloves
 Cooking spray
   2 cups apple juice, divided
   2 tablespoons dark brown sugar
   1 tablespoon Dijon mustard

1. Place ham in a large Dutch oven or stockpot. Cover with water to 2 inches above ham; cover and refrigerate 24 hours.

Drain; rinse well with warm water. Drain.
2. Preheat oven to 325°.
3. Trim fat and rind from ham. Score outside of ham in a diamond pattern; stud with cloves. Place ham, skin side down, on rack of a broiler pan coated with cooking spray. Place rack in pan; pour 1 cup apple juice over ham. Cover ham loosely with foil. Bake at 325° for 2½ hours, basting occasionally with remaining 1 cup apple juice.
4. Remove ham from oven (do not turn oven off); uncover ham. Combine sugar and mustard; brush over ham. Bake, uncovered, at 325° for 30 minutes or until a thermometer inserted into thickest portion registers 140°. Place ham on a cutting board; cover and let stand 10 minutes before slicing. Yield: 26 servings (serving size: about 3 ounces).

CALORIES 130 (44% from fat); FAT 6.3g (sat 2.1g, mono 3g, poly 0.7g); PROTEIN 14.6g; CARB 3.5g; FIBER 0g; CHOL 52mg; IRON 0.8mg; SODIUM 819mg; CALC 2mg

QUICK & EASY • MAKE AHEAD
German-Style Potato Salad with Ham

Ham takes the place of bacon in this version of the classic.

   2 pounds small red potatoes
   1 cup finely chopped Simple Baked Ham (about 5 ounces) (recipe at left)
   1 cup finely chopped celery
   ⅔ cup finely chopped green bell pepper
   ⅔ cup finely chopped red onion
   ⅓ cup white wine vinegar
   1 tablespoon olive oil
   ½ teaspoon salt
   ¼ teaspoon freshly ground black pepper
   ⅓ cup chopped fresh parsley

1. Place potatoes in a large Dutch oven; cover with water. Bring to a boil; reduce heat, and simmer 10 minutes or until tender. Drain and cool slightly. Cut potatoes into quarters; place in a large bowl. Add Simple Baked Ham and next

7 ingredients. Toss gently to combine. Sprinkle with parsley. Serve chilled or at room temperature. Yield: 4 servings (serving size: about 2 cups).

CALORIES 270 (22% from fat); FAT 6.5g (sat 1.4g, mono 3.8g, poly 0.8g); PROTEIN 11.2g; CARB 42.6g; FIBER 4.9g; CHOL 22mg; IRON 2.7mg; SODIUM 680mg; CALC 52mg

MAKE AHEAD
Ham and Four Bean Salad

 1½ cups finely chopped Simple Baked Ham (about 8 ounces) (recipe at left)
 1½ cups chopped green onions
   1 (16-ounce) can lima beans, rinsed and drained
   1 (15½-ounce) can chickpeas (garbanzo beans), rinsed and drained
   1 (15-ounce) can red kidney beans, rinsed and drained
   1 (15-ounce) can black beans, rinsed and drained
   ½ cup cider vinegar
   1 teaspoon sugar
   1 teaspoon extravirgin olive oil
   ½ teaspoon ground cumin
   ⅛ teaspoon salt
   ⅛ teaspoon freshly ground black pepper

1. Combine first 6 ingredients in a large bowl.
2. Combine vinegar and remaining 5 ingredients, stirring with a whisk. Drizzle over bean mixture; toss gently to coat. Cover and chill at least 2 hours. Toss gently before serving. Yield: 6 servings (serving size: 1 cup).

CALORIES 264 (17% from fat); FAT 5.1g (sat 1.1g, mono 2.3g, poly 1.2g); PROTEIN 16.7g; CARB 39.1g; FIBER 11.9g; CHOL 23mg; IRON 3.5mg; SODIUM 892mg; CALC 62mg

QUICK & EASY

Ham and Bacon Cobb Wraps

¼ cup low-fat mayonnaise
1 tablespoon crumbled blue cheese
6 (8-inch) fat-free flour tortillas
3 cups thinly sliced Simple Baked Ham (about 1 pound) (recipe on page 33)
2 cups chopped romaine lettuce
2 cups thinly sliced plum tomato (about 5 tomatoes)
½ cup thinly vertically sliced red onion
4 bacon slices, cooked and crumbled

1. Combine mayonnaise and cheese; spread evenly over tortillas. Arrange ½ cup Simple Baked Ham on each tortilla; top each tortilla with ⅓ cup lettuce and ⅓ cup tomato. Divide onion and bacon evenly among tortillas. Roll up. Yield: 6 servings (serving size: 1 wrap).

CALORIES 244 (24% from fat); FAT 6.5g (sat 2g, mono 2.5g, poly 0.7g); PROTEIN 13.7g; CARB 32.6g; FIBER 2.3g; CHOL 34mg; IRON 1.9mg; SODIUM 1,005mg; CALC 23mg

MAKE AHEAD

Corn and Cherry Tomato Salad with Ham

If fresh corn is hard to find, 2½ cups frozen corn kernels will work just as well. If using frozen, thaw and combine with the other ingredients—there's no need to cook it.

⅓ cup cider vinegar
1 teaspoon olive oil
¼ teaspoon salt
¼ teaspoon freshly ground black pepper
¼ teaspoon dried Italian seasoning
5 ears shucked corn
1½ cups finely chopped Simple Baked Ham (about 8 ounces) (recipe on page 33)
½ cup finely chopped Walla Walla or other sweet onion
¼ cup finely chopped green bell pepper
1 (12-ounce) container cherry tomatoes, halved
¼ cup chopped fresh basil

1. Combine first 5 ingredients, stirring with a whisk; set aside.
2. Cook corn in boiling water 8 minutes. Drain and plunge corn into ice water; drain. Cut kernels from ears of corn; discard cobs. Place corn in a large bowl; add Simple Baked Ham, onion, bell pepper, and tomatoes. Drizzle with vinegar mixture; toss to coat. Sprinkle with basil. Cover and chill. Yield: 4 servings (serving size: 1 cup).

CALORIES 224 (28% from fat); FAT 6.9g (sat 1.8g, mono 3.3g, poly 1.3g); PROTEIN 14.6g; CARB 30.9g; FIBER 4.7g; CHOL 35mg; IRON 1.7mg; SODIUM 722mg; CALC 25mg

QUICK & EASY • MAKE AHEAD

Mediterranean Vegetable Salad with Ham

Eat the salad with pitas on the side, or spoon into pita halves to eat as a sandwich. But pack the salad and pita separately so the bread doesn't become soggy.

⅓ cup fresh lemon juice (about 3 lemons)
2 teaspoons extravirgin olive oil
½ teaspoon dried oregano
¼ teaspoon Greek seasoning blend
¼ teaspoon freshly ground black pepper
2 cups halved cherry tomatoes
1 cup red bell pepper strips
1 cup green bell pepper strips
1 cup finely chopped Simple Baked Ham (about 5 ounces) (recipe on page 33)
¼ cup (1 ounce) crumbled feta cheese
2 tablespoons sliced ripe olives
1 English cucumber, halved lengthwise and sliced (about 2½ cups)
4 (6-inch) pitas, cut in half

1. Combine first 5 ingredients in a large bowl, stirring with a whisk. Add tomatoes and next 6 ingredients; toss well to combine. Serve with pitas. Yield: 4 servings (serving size: 1 cup salad and 2 pita halves).

CALORIES 310 (25% from fat); FAT 8.5g (sat 2.8g, mono 3.8g, poly 1.1g); PROTEIN 14.6g; CARB 45.2g; FIBER 3.4g; CHOL 30mg; IRON 3mg; SODIUM 814mg; CALC 125mg

QUICK & EASY

Pimiento-Ham Sandwiches

A big batch of this versatile spread keeps up to five days in the refrigerator. Besides making great sandwiches, it's a nice dip with crackers. It can also fill a wrap sandwich made from honey-wheat tortillas and shredded lettuce. If you crave a kick, add up to 1 teaspoon of hot pepper sauce to the spread.

2 cups Pimiento-Ham Spread
12 (1-ounce) slices white or sourdough bread

1. Spread about ⅓ cup Pimiento-Ham Spread on each of 6 bread slices; top with remaining bread slices. Yield: 6 servings (serving size: 1 sandwich).

CALORIES 277 (30% from fat); FAT 9.1g (sat 4.9g, mono 2.5g, poly 0.3g); PROTEIN 15.6g; CARB 33.3g; FIBER 1.6g; CHOL 30mg; IRON 1.9mg; SODIUM 793mg; CALC 321mg

PIMIENTO-HAM SPREAD:

- 4 cups (16 ounces) shredded reduced-fat extrasharp Cheddar cheese
- 1 cup diced Simple Baked Ham (about 5 ounces) (recipe on page 33)
- ⅔ cup fat-free mayonnaise
- ¼ cup finely chopped Walla Walla or other sweet onion
- 1 (4-ounce) jar diced pimiento, drained

1. Combine all ingredients in a large bowl; stir well. Cover; chill. Yield: about 4½ cups (serving size: about ⅓ cup).

CALORIES 130 (55% from fat); FAT 8g (sat 4.9g, mono 2.5g, poly 0.3g); PROTEIN 9.9g; CARB 3.8g; FIBER 0.4g; CHOL 30mg; IRON 0.3mg; SODIUM 464mg; CALC 231mg

---

Pesto-Flavored Ham and Pasta Salad

- 1 pound uncooked small seashell pasta
- ⅓ cup red wine vinegar
- 1 tablespoon sugar
- 2 teaspoons extravirgin olive oil
- 1 teaspoon Dijon mustard
- ½ teaspoon salt
- ½ teaspoon freshly ground black pepper
- 1 garlic clove, minced
- 1 cup (4 ounces) preshredded Parmesan cheese
- 1 cup diced Simple Baked Ham (about 5 ounces) (recipe on page 33)
- ¾ cup chopped fresh basil
- ¼ cup pine nuts, toasted

1. Prepare pasta according to package directions, omitting salt and fat. Drain; place in a large bowl.
2. Combine vinegar and next 6 ingredients. Add cheese, ham, basil, and pine nuts to pasta; toss gently to combine. Drizzle with vinegar mixture; toss to coat. Cover and chill. Yield: 8 servings (serving size: 1 cup).

CALORIES 328 (27% from fat); FAT 10g (sat 3.3g, mono 3.4g, poly 2.2g); PROTEIN 15.5g; CARB 43.6g; FIBER 2.2g; CHOL 20mg; IRON 2.7mg; SODIUM 582mg; CALC 187mg

---

simple suppers

Dinner in a Hurry

Speedy meals come to the rescue on busy days.

Simple Suppers Pantry

Flour tortillas • Dry breadcrumbs Potatoes • Onions • Garlic • Olive oil Balsamic vinegar • Sun-dried tomatoes (oil- and dry-packed) • Tomato paste Canned beans • Bottled roasted red peppers • Fat-free, less-sodium chicken broth • Pasta (in several shapes)

Stove-Top Macaroni and Cheese with Roasted Tomatoes

In Step 4, the macaroni mixture is cooked over medium-low heat so the cheese won't become stringy and the sauce grainy.

- 3 cups halved cherry tomatoes
- Cooking spray
- ¼ teaspoon black pepper
- 3 ounces sourdough bread, torn into pieces
- 1 teaspoon butter, melted
- 12 ounces large elbow macaroni
- 2 cups (8 ounces) shredded extrasharp Cheddar cheese
- ¼ cup egg substitute
- 1½ teaspoons kosher salt
- ¼ teaspoon ground red pepper
- 1 (12-ounce) can evaporated low-fat milk

1. Preheat oven to 375°.
2. Place tomatoes in a 13 x 9-inch baking dish coated with cooking spray. Sprinkle with black pepper. Bake at 375° for 30 minutes or until browned, stirring occasionally.
3. While tomatoes cook, place bread in a food processor; pulse 2 times or until crumbly. Toss crumbs with melted butter.

Sprinkle crumbs on a baking sheet, and bake at 375° for 12 minutes or until golden, stirring frequently.
4. Cook macaroni in boiling water 7 minutes; drain. Return macaroni to pan; place over medium-low heat. Add cheese and remaining 4 ingredients; cook 4 minutes or until cheese melts, stirring constantly. Stir in tomatoes. Sprinkle each serving with about 3 tablespoons breadcrumbs. Yield: 8 servings (serving size: 1 cup).

CALORIES 357 (29% from fat); FAT 11.4g (sat 6.6g, mono 3.1g, poly 0.8g); PROTEIN 18.1g; CARB 45.2g; FIBER 2g; CHOL 33mg; IRON 2.7mg; SODIUM 669mg; CALC 350mg

---

Greek-Flavored Turkey Burgers

Bursts of feta cheese, red onion, and fresh mint add spark to these flavorful burgers.

- 1 large egg white
- 1 cup chopped red onion
- ¾ cup chopped fresh mint
- ½ cup dry breadcrumbs
- ⅓ cup (about 1½ ounces) crumbled feta cheese
- 2 tablespoons fresh lemon juice
- 1 teaspoon dried dill
- 1 pound ground turkey
- Cooking spray
- 4 (1½-ounce) hamburger buns, split
- 1 (7-ounce) bottle roasted red bell peppers, drained and cut into 1-inch strips

1. Place egg white in a large bowl; lightly beat with a whisk. Add onion and next 6 ingredients; stir well. Divide turkey mixture into 4 equal portions, shaping each into a ½-inch-thick patty.
2. Heat a large nonstick skillet over medium-high heat. Coat pan with cooking spray. Add patties to pan; cook 8 minutes on each side or until done.
3. Place patties on bottom halves of buns. Divide peppers evenly among burgers; cover with top halves of buns. Yield: 4 servings (serving size: 1 burger).
NOTE: To freeze extra servings, wrap each uncooked patty individually first in
Continued

plastic wrap and then in heavy-duty aluminum foil. Freeze up to 2 months. To serve, thaw patties completely in refrigerator, and then cook and serve as directed.

CALORIES 426 (33% from fat); FAT 15.7g (sat 5.7g, mono 5.5g, poly 3.2g); PROTEIN 30.5g; CARB 40g; FIBER 2.8g; CHOL 101mg; IRON 4.5mg; SODIUM 790mg; CALC 177mg

Ham, Spinach, and Sun-Dried Tomato Calzones

Refrigerated pizza dough makes this entrée easy to put together. Spoon warmed bottled marinara sauce over the calzones before serving, or serve the sauce on the side.

    1   cup part-skim ricotta
    ¾   cup (3 ounces) shredded
        part-skim mozzarella cheese
    ¼   cup (1 ounce) grated Parmesan
        cheese
    1   teaspoon dried basil
    ½   teaspoon fennel seed, crushed
    ¼   teaspoon black pepper
    1   (10-ounce) package frozen
        chopped spinach, thawed,
        drained, and squeezed dry
    3   ounces lean ham, chopped
    6   oil-packed sun-dried tomato
        halves, drained and chopped
    1   (13.8-ounce) can refrigerated
        pizza crust dough
    Cooking spray

1. Preheat oven to 450°.
2. Combine first 9 ingredients.
3. Divide dough evenly into 5 pieces; pat each dough piece into a 5-inch circle. Spoon about ½ cup spinach mixture onto half of each circle, leaving a ½-inch border. Fold dough over filling until edges almost meet. For each calzone, bring bottom edge over top edge; crimp with fingers to form a rim. Place calzones on a baking sheet coated with cooking spray. Bake at 450° for 14 minutes or until browned. Yield: 5 servings (serving size: 1 calzone).

CALORIES 356 (32% from fat); FAT 12.5g (sat 5.6g, mono 4g, poly 1.5g); PROTEIN 25.2g; CARB 44.3g; FIBER 3.2g; CHOL 37mg; IRON 3.6mg; SODIUM 967mg; CALC 497mg

Chicken Sausage and Provolone Penne Bake

Change the flavors in this dish by choosing different versions of the chicken sausage.

    1   pound uncooked penne
        (tube-shaped pasta)
    1   tablespoon olive oil
    1½ cups chopped onion
    ¾   cup chopped red bell
        pepper
    1   (12-ounce) package sweet
        basil and pine nut chicken
        sausage (such as Gerhard's),
        halved lengthwise and cut
        crosswise into ½-inch-thick
        slices
    2   garlic cloves, minced
    1   tablespoon tomato paste
    1   tablespoon balsamic
        vinegar
    ½   teaspoon salt
    ¼   teaspoon dried oregano
    ¼   teaspoon crushed red pepper
    3   (14.5-ounce) cans diced tomatoes,
        undrained
    Cooking spray
    1   cup (4 ounces) shredded sharp
        provolone cheese
    1   cup (4 ounces) grated fresh
        Parmesan cheese

1. Cook pasta according to package directions, omitting salt and fat.
2. Preheat oven to 350°.
3. Heat oil in a large nonstick skillet over medium-high heat. Add onion, bell pepper, sausage, and garlic; sauté 5 minutes or until sausage is browned. Add tomato paste and next 5 ingredients; cover, reduce heat, and simmer 15 minutes.
4. Combine pasta and tomato mixture; spoon into a 13 x 9-inch baking dish coated with cooking spray. Sprinkle with cheeses. Bake at 350° for 25 minutes or until bubbly. Yield: 8 servings (serving size: 1½ cups).

CALORIES 453 (30% from fat); FAT 15.3g (sat 6.6g, mono 5.7g, poly 2.1g); PROTEIN 24.4g; CARB 55.3g; FIBER 4.6g; CHOL 56mg; IRON 2.1mg; SODIUM 954mg; CALC 319mg

Black Bean Burritos with Avocado

    ½   cup diced peeled avocado
    1   tablespoon fresh lime juice
    1   teaspoon olive oil
    2   garlic cloves, minced
    ¼   cup water
    2   teaspoons ground cumin
    2   (15-ounce) cans black beans,
        drained
    4   (10-inch) flour tortillas
    6   tablespoons fat-free sour cream
    6   tablespoons bottled salsa

1. Combine avocado and lime juice, tossing to coat.
2. Heat oil in a medium saucepan over medium-high heat. Add garlic; sauté 1 minute. Stir in water, cumin, and beans. Reduce heat to medium; simmer 3 minutes or until thoroughly heated, stirring occasionally. Warm tortillas according to package directions. Spoon ¼ cup bean mixture onto each tortilla. Top with 1½ tablespoons sour cream, 1½ tablespoons salsa, and 2 tablespoons avocado; roll up. Yield: 4 servings (serving size: 1 burrito).

CALORIES 424 (23% from fat); FAT 10.7g (sat 2.1g, mono 5.3g, poly 2.2g); PROTEIN 15.7g; CARB 65g; FIBER 11g; CHOL 2mg; IRON 5.6mg; SODIUM 931mg; CALC 178mg

Flank Steak Wrap with Caramelized Onions and Blue Cheese

You can also use large flour tortillas in place of lavash.

    ½   teaspoon salt
    ½   teaspoon black pepper
    2   garlic cloves, minced
    1   (1-pound) flank steak,
        trimmed
    Cooking spray
    6   cups vertically sliced onion (about
        3 medium onions)
    ½   cup (2 ounces) crumbled blue
        cheese
    ¼   cup fat-free mayonnaise
    2   (20-inch) lavash, cut in half

1. Combine first 3 ingredients; rub evenly over steak. Cover and chill 2 hours.

2. Preheat broiler.

3. Place steak on a broiler pan coated with cooking spray; broil 7 minutes on each side or until done. Cut steak diagonally across grain into thin slices.

4. While steak cooks, heat a large nonstick skillet over medium-high heat. Coat pan with cooking spray. Add onion to pan; cover and cook 10 minutes or until golden brown, stirring frequently.

5. Combine cheese and mayonnaise; spread 2 tablespoons on each lavash half. Top each with 3 ounces steak and ½ cup onion; roll up. Yield: 4 servings.

CALORIES 450 (30% from fat); FAT 14.9g (sat 7g, mono 5g, poly 0.5g); PROTEIN 29.8g; CARB 47.9g; FIBER 3.5g; CHOL 62mg; IRON 4.4mg; SODIUM 940mg; CALC 153mg

Rice with Mushrooms and Shrimp

Lemon juice and rind add a bright accent.

1 cup uncooked basmati rice
1 tablespoon olive oil
½ cup chopped onion
1 cup chopped carrot
4 garlic cloves, minced
1½ cups chopped mushrooms
½ cup chopped bottled roasted red bell peppers
½ cup fat-free, less-sodium chicken broth
½ teaspoon salt
¼ teaspoon black pepper
1½ pounds medium shrimp, peeled and deveined
¼ cup minced fresh chives
1½ teaspoons grated lemon rind
2 tablespoons fresh lemon juice
2 teaspoons capers

1. Cook rice according to package directions, omitting salt and fat.

2. Heat oil in a large nonstick skillet over medium-high heat. Add onion, and sauté 3 minutes. Add carrot and garlic; sauté 3 minutes. Add mushrooms; sauté 3 minutes. Stir in bell pepper, broth, salt,

pepper, and shrimp. Cover, reduce heat to medium, and cook 3 minutes or until shrimp are done. Stir in rice, chives, and remaining ingredients. Cook 3 minutes or until thoroughly heated, stirring constantly. Yield: 4 servings (serving size: about 1¾ cups).

CALORIES 438 (14% from fat); FAT 6.7g (sat 1.1g, mono 2.9g, poly 1.6g); PROTEIN 40g; CARB 56.6g; FIBER 3.6g; CHOL 259mg; IRON 6.4mg; SODIUM 733mg; CALC 116mg

Braised Herb Chicken Thighs with Potatoes

Choose red skin potatoes that are similar in size so they'll be done at the same time.

2 tablespoons all-purpose flour
2 teaspoons paprika
1 teaspoon salt
1 teaspoon dried thyme
1 teaspoon dried oregano
½ teaspoon black pepper
8 chicken thighs (about 2 pounds), skinned
1 teaspoon olive oil
1½ cups (2-inch-thick) slices carrot
1 large onion, cut into 8 wedges
1½ cups fat-free, less-sodium chicken broth
½ cup dry white wine
1½ pounds small red potatoes, quartered

1. Combine first 6 ingredients in a large zip-top plastic bag. Add chicken; seal bag, and shake to coat.

2. Heat oil in a Dutch oven over medium heat. Add chicken and remaining flour mixture to pan; cook 3 minutes on each side or until lightly browned. Add carrot and onion; cook 3 minutes, stirring frequently. Add broth, wine, and potatoes; bring to a boil. Reduce heat, and simmer 35 minutes or until chicken is done and vegetables are tender. Yield: 4 servings (serving size: 2 thighs and about 1⅓ cups vegetable mixture).

CALORIES 467 (29% from fat); FAT 14.9g (sat 3.9g, mono 5.9g, poly 3.4g); PROTEIN 37.2g; CARB 40g; FIBER 5.7g; CHOL 115mg; IRON 4.4mg; SODIUM 887mg; CALC 71mg

Broccoli and Cheese-Stuffed Potatoes

Round out the meal with a garden salad, soup, or half a sandwich.

2 baking potatoes (about 1¾ pounds)
2 bacon slices
1 cup broccoli florets
1 cup presliced mushrooms
½ cup chopped onion
1 teaspoon bottled minced garlic
½ cup (2 ounces) shredded reduced-fat Swiss cheese
¼ cup fat-free sour cream
2 tablespoons fat-free milk
½ teaspoon black pepper
⅛ teaspoon salt

1. Preheat oven to 450°.

2. Pierce potatoes with a fork; arrange on paper towels in microwave oven. Microwave at HIGH 16 minutes or until done, turning and rearranging potatoes after 8 minutes. Let stand 5 minutes.

3. While potatoes cook, cook bacon in a large nonstick skillet over medium heat until crisp. Remove bacon from pan; reserve 1 teaspoon drippings in pan. Crumble bacon; set aside. Add broccoli, mushrooms, onion, and garlic to drippings in pan; cook 7 minutes or until tender, stirring frequently. Remove pan from heat.

4. Cut each potato in half lengthwise; scoop out pulp, leaving ¼-inch-thick shells. Combine potato pulp, onion mixture, cheese, and remaining 4 ingredients; divide evenly among shells.

5. Bake at 450° for 8 minutes or until potatoes are thoroughly heated. Sprinkle with reserved bacon. Yield: 4 servings (serving size: 1 potato half).

CALORIES 245 (22% from fat); FAT 5.9g (sat 3.1g, mono 1.3g, poly 0.3g); PROTEIN 12.5g; CARB 42.3g; FIBER 5.3g; CHOL 17mg; IRON 2.1mg; SODIUM 408mg; CALC 297mg

Tune in, Learn to Cook

Meet Graham Kerr, one of the pioneers of TV food shows that have shown a generation how to cook.

The road to culinary knowledge is varied and constantly changing, from cookbooks and moms to television and the Internet. Our cooking class columns in this book will explore the most influential ways Americans learn to cook and the effect each has had on how we consider—and prepare food. We start off the year with Graham Kerr and TV food shows.

No one got us more hooked on TV cooking than Graham Kerr, with his hit PBS show The Galloping Gourmet, which began in 1969 and spanned 470 episodes over three years and is still in reruns. Kerr's pot-rattling, wine-sipping panache had 200 million people in 38 countries tuned in to his show. Here are tips from Kerr on how to reinvent classic recipes. Included are some new favorites, as well as a few standbys.

Crab Cakes on Mixed Greens with Peanut Vinaigrette

CRAB CAKES:
1 cup plain fat-free yogurt
¼ cup finely chopped Walla Walla or other sweet onion
¼ cup finely chopped celery
¼ cup finely chopped red bell pepper
¼ cup chopped fresh parsley
2 tablespoons egg substitute
1 tablespoon fresh lemon juice
1 teaspoon paprika
1 teaspoon prepared horseradish
½ teaspoon dried thyme
¼ teaspoon salt
20 unsalted saltine crackers, finely crushed
1 pound lump crabmeat, shell pieces removed
2 teaspoons olive oil, divided

SALAD:
¼ cup rice vinegar
1 tablespoon creamy peanut butter
1 teaspoon olive oil
½ teaspoon brown sugar
¼ teaspoon dry mustard
1 garlic clove, crushed
Dash of ground red pepper
3 cups gourmet salad greens
3 cups trimmed watercress

1. To prepare crab cakes, place a small sieve or colander in a 2-quart glass measure or medium bowl. Line colander with 4 layers of cheesecloth, allowing cheesecloth to extend over sides. Spoon yogurt into colander. Cover loosely with plastic wrap; refrigerate 12 hours. Spoon yogurt cheese into a bowl; discard liquid.
2. Combine yogurt cheese, onion, and next 10 ingredients. Add crab; stir just until blended. Divide mixture into 12 equal portions, shaping each into a ½-inch-thick patty. Heat 1 teaspoon oil in a large nonstick skillet over medium-high heat. Add 6 patties; cook 3 minutes on each side or until lightly browned. Remove from pan; cover and keep warm. Repeat procedure with 1 teaspoon oil and 6 patties.
3. To prepare salad, combine vinegar and next 6 ingredients, stirring with a whisk. Place greens and watercress in a large bowl. Drizzle with vinaigrette; toss well to coat. Arrange about 1 cup salad on each of 4 plates; top each serving with 3 crab cakes. Yield: 4 servings.
NOTE: You can also use a quick-drain method for the yogurt. Spread yogurt onto several layers of paper towels, and cover with more paper towels. Let stand 5 minutes, and scrape into a bowl. Quick-drained yogurt isn't as thick as yogurt that's drained overnight, so start

with a little bit less to ensure the crab mixture won't become too watery.

CALORIES 286 (30% from fat); FAT 9.6g (sat 1.7g, mono 4.8g, poly 2.1g); PROTEIN 30.1g; CARB 19.9g; FIBER 2.4g; CHOL 114mg; IRON 3.3mg; SODIUM 670mg; CALC 267mg

How to Quick-Drain Yogurt

Spread yogurt onto several layers of paper towels, and cover with more paper towels. Let stand 5 minutes, and scrape into a bowl.

Falafel Pitas with Goat Cheese Sauce

These baked chickpea patties are much leaner than traditional falafel.

FALAFEL:
1 cup dried chickpeas (garbanzo beans)
½ cup chopped green onions
½ cup chopped fresh parsley
1 teaspoon baking powder
1 teaspoon ground coriander
1 teaspoon ground cumin
½ teaspoon salt
¼ teaspoon baking soda
¼ teaspoon freshly ground black pepper
¼ teaspoon ground red pepper
1 (6-inch) whole wheat pita, torn into large pieces
2 garlic cloves, chopped
3 large egg whites
Cooking spray

RELISH:

- 2 cups chopped seeded plum tomato
- 1 cup chopped seeded English cucumber
- ¼ cup chopped green onions
- 1 tablespoon chopped fresh parsley
- 1 tablespoon fresh lemon juice
- 1 serrano chile, minced

SAUCE:

- 1 cup plain low-fat yogurt
- ¼ cup (2 ounces) soft (log-style) goat cheese
- ⅛ teaspoon salt
- 1 small garlic clove, minced

REMAINING INGREDIENT:

- 4 (6-inch) whole wheat pitas, halved

1. To prepare falafel, sort and wash chickpeas, and place in a large bowl. Cover with water to 2 inches above beans; cover and let stand 8 hours or overnight. Drain.

2. Preheat oven to 350°.

3. Combine chickpeas ½ cup onions, and next 10 ingredients in a food processor; pulse 8 to 10 times or until finely chopped. Spoon mixture into a bowl. Add egg whites to chickpea mixture, and stir well. Let stand 15 minutes. Divide mixture into 16 equal portions, shaping each into a ½-inch-thick patty. Place patties on a baking sheet coated with cooking spray. Bake at 350° for 10 minutes or until lightly browned.

4. To prepare relish, combine tomato and next 5 ingredients.

5. To prepare sauce, combine yogurt and next 3 ingredients, stirring with a whisk until smooth.

6. Place 2 falafel patties in each pita half; spoon about ⅓ cup relish and 2½ tablespoons sauce into each pita half. Serve immediately. Yield: 4 servings (serving size: 2 stuffed pita halves).

CALORIES 450 (17% from fat); FAT 8.7g (sat 3.3g, mono 1.8g, poly 2.1g); PROTEIN 24.9g; CARB 72.3g; FIBER 14.9g; CHOL 10mg; IRON 6.2mg; SODIUM 997mg; CALC 315mg

---

Breakfast for Four Menu
serves 4

This filling meal is great for lazy weekend mornings. The hash browns are a cinch to prepare when you start with refrigerated shredded potatoes.

McKerr Muffins

Spicy hash browns*

Orange juice and coffee

*Heat 1 tablespoon canola oil in a large nonstick skillet over medium-high heat. Add ⅔ cup chopped onion; sauté 3 minutes. Add 3 minced garlic cloves; sauté 1 minute. Add 1 (1-pound, 4 ounce) package refrigerated shredded hash browns (such as Simply Potatoes); cook 20 minutes or until lightly browned, stirring occasionally. Sprinkle with ½ teaspoon salt, ½ teaspoon chipotle chile powder, and ¼ teaspoon ground red pepper; toss to combine.

QUICK & EASY
McKerr Muffins

Egg substitute is a fat- and cholesterol-free alternative to whole eggs for many applications, but it needs to be cooked gently, with little stirring, to produce light, fluffy scrambled eggs. This is a whole new twist on a breakfast standard—lemon- and dill-flavored mushrooms enliven the egg-topped English muffins.

- 4 (2½-inch) mushroom caps
- Cooking spray
- 2 teaspoons fresh lemon juice
- ½ teaspoon chopped fresh dill
- ⅛ teaspoon ground red pepper
- 1 teaspoon butter
- 1½ cups egg substitute
- 2 whole wheat English muffins, split and toasted
- 4 (1-ounce) slices Canadian bacon
- 4 (1-ounce) slices part-skim mozzarella cheese
- 1 tablespoon finely chopped green onions

1. Heat a medium nonstick skillet over medium heat. Remove stems from mushrooms; discard stems. Coat pan with cooking spray. Add mushroom caps to pan, stem sides up. Pour ½ teaspoon lemon juice into each cap. Sprinkle evenly with dill and pepper. Cook 6 minutes or until mushrooms are browned. Turn mushrooms over; cook 1 minute. Remove from pan; cover and keep warm.

2. Wipe pan with a paper towel. Melt butter in pan over medium heat. Add egg substitute; allow to set about 30 seconds. Gently scrape cooked part of egg substitute to center of pan with a rubber spatula; continue gently scraping occasionally until egg substitute is set (about 3 minutes). Remove from heat.

3. Preheat broiler.

4. Arrange muffin halves, cut sides up, on a baking sheet. Top each muffin half with 1 Canadian bacon slice, about ⅓ cup scrambled egg substitute, and 1 mushroom cap, stem side down. Gently press mushroom cap down. Top each mushroom cap with 1 cheese slice. Broil 1½ minutes or until cheese melts. Sprinkle with green onions, and serve immediately. Yield: 4 servings (serving size: 1 topped muffin half).

CALORIES 241 (30% from fat); FAT 8g (sat 4.2g, mono 2.6g, poly 0.7g); PROTEIN 25.2g; CARB 17.4g; FIBER 2.6g; CHOL 32mg; IRON 2.9mg; SODIUM 843mg; CALC 328mg

How to Prepare Mushrooms

Add mushroom caps to pan, stem sides up. Pour ½ teaspoon lemon juice into each cap. Sprinkle evenly with dill and pepper. Cook 6 minutes or until mushrooms are browned. Turn mushrooms over; cook 1 minute. Remove from pan; cover and keep warm.

New England Boiled Dinner

Defatting the cooking liquid is an easy step that removes a good bit of fat from this classic one-dish meal. Store the extra strained vegetable cooking liquid in airtight containers in the freezer, if desired, and use it to flavor soups, sauces, or rice.

2½ pounds cured corned beef brisket, trimmed
½ teaspoon black peppercorns
½ teaspoon mustard seeds
4 whole cloves
4 whole allspice
4 bay leaves
3 cups thinly sliced carrot (about 1 pound)
2½ cups peeled (4 x ½-inch) strips rutabaga (about 12 ounces)
2¼ cups thinly sliced parsnips (about 12 ounces)
½ cup frozen pearl onions
16 small red potatoes, halved (about 2 pounds)
1 small head green cabbage, cut into 8 wedges

1. Place beef in a large Dutch oven. Add peppercorns, mustard seeds, cloves, allspice, and bay leaves. Cover with water to 2 inches above beef; bring to a boil. Reduce heat; partially cover. Simmer 2 hours or until beef is tender. Remove beef from pan.
2. Strain cooking liquid through a sieve into a large bowl, reserving cooking liquid; discard solids. Place 1 large heavy-duty zip-top plastic bag inside each of 2 bowls. Pour reserved cooking liquid into bags; let stand 10 minutes (fat will rise to top). Seal bags; carefully snip off 1 bottom corner of 1 bag. Drain liquid into pan, stopping before fat layer reaches opening; discard fat. Repeat procedure with second bag. Add beef, carrot, and next 4 ingredients to pan; bring to a boil over high heat. Reduce heat to medium, and simmer 5 minutes. Arrange cabbage on top; cover, reduce heat, and simmer 15 minutes or until cabbage is tender.
3. Remove beef from pan; cut across grain into 16 slices. Strain vegetable mixture through a sieve into a large bowl; reserve vegetable mixture and cooking liquid. Place 1 cabbage wedge, 1½ cups vegetable mixture, and 2 beef slices into 8 large soup bowls. Pour ½ cup reserved liquid over each serving; reserve remaining liquid for another use. Yield: 8 servings.

CALORIES 337 (36% from fat); FAT 13.3g (sat 4.1g, mono 6.2g, poly 0.7g); PROTEIN 17.5g; CARB 38.5g; FIBER 6.4g; CHOL 46mg; IRON 3.5mg; SODIUM 951mg; CALC 110mg

Chicken Caesar Salad

Use drained yogurt as the foundation for a creamy, low-fat Caesar salad dressing. Store the remaining spice blend in an airtight container; it's also good on pork chops, pork tenderloin, or beef tenderloin steaks. If you don't have a spice or coffee grinder, use a mortar and pestle.

DRESSING:
1 cup plain low-fat yogurt
1½ tablespoons water
1½ tablespoons Dijon mustard
1½ teaspoons balsamic vinegar
1 garlic clove, crushed

CROUTONS:
2 cups (1-inch) cubed whole wheat bread (about 4 [1-ounce] slices)
Olive oil-flavored cooking spray
¼ teaspoon Italian Spice Blend
⅛ teaspoon freshly ground black pepper
Dash of salt

CHICKEN:
1 pound skinless, boneless chicken breast
1 teaspoon Italian Spice Blend
¼ teaspoon salt
¼ teaspoon freshly ground black pepper

REMAINING INGREDIENTS:
6 cups sliced romaine lettuce
3 cups trimmed watercress (about 1 large bunch)
¼ cup (1 ounce) grated fresh Parmesan cheese
Freshly ground black pepper (optional)

1. To prepare dressing, place a colander in a 2-quart glass measure or medium bowl. Line colander with 4 layers of cheesecloth, allowing cheesecloth to extend over sides. Spoon yogurt into colander. Cover loosely with plastic wrap; refrigerate 12 hours. Spoon yogurt cheese into a bowl; discard liquid. Combine yogurt cheese, 1½ tablespoons water, mustard, vinegar, and garlic; stir well. Set dressing aside.
2. Preheat oven to 350°.
3. To prepare croutons, arrange bread cubes in a single layer on a jelly-roll pan. Lightly coat bread cubes with cooking spray. Sprinkle evenly with ¼ teaspoon Italian Spice Blend, ⅛ teaspoon pepper, and dash of salt; toss well to coat. Bake at 350° for 15 minutes or until lightly browned; set aside.
4. To prepare chicken, heat a large non-stick skillet over medium-high heat. Rub chicken with 1 teaspoon Italian Spice Blend, ¼ teaspoon salt, and ¼ teaspoon pepper. Coat skillet with cooking spray. Place chicken in pan; cook 4 minutes on each side or until done. Remove chicken from pan; cool slightly. Cut chicken across grain into thin slices.
5. To assemble salad, combine croutons, lettuce, and watercress in a large bowl. Drizzle with dressing; toss well to coat. Place 2 cups salad on each of 4 plates. Divide sliced chicken evenly among salads, and sprinkle each serving with 1 tablespoon Parmesan cheese. Sprinkle with additional pepper, if desired. Yield: 4 servings.

(Totals include 1¼ teaspoons Italian Spice Blend) CALORIES 277 (17% from fat); FAT 5.3g (sat 1.9g, mono 1.6g, poly 0.9g); PROTEIN 35.6g; CARB 22g; FIBER 3.8g; CHOL 71mg; IRON 3.1mg; SODIUM 706mg; CALC 244mg

ITALIAN SPICE BLEND:
2 teaspoons dried oregano
1 teaspoon dried basil
1 teaspoon dried mint
1 teaspoon dried rubbed sage
½ teaspoon fennel seeds
½ teaspoon dried rosemary

1. Place all ingredients in a clean spice or coffee grinder; process until finely ground. Store in an airtight container. Yield: 1½ tablespoons.

CALORIES 23 (20% from fat); FAT 0.5g (sat 0.1g, mono 0.1g, poly 0.1g); PROTEIN 1g; CARB 3.9g; FIBER 2.7g; CHOL 0mg; IRON 3.1mg; SODIUM 5mg; CALC 105mg

MAKE AHEAD

Key Lime Tart

Before pasteurized egg whites were widely available, meringues were made with raw egg whites, which required extended baking to reach the recommended safe temperature. Using a pasteurized product reduces the baking time to just long enough for the meringue to become a beautiful golden brown.

CRUST:
- ¾ cup cake flour
- ½ teaspoon sugar
- Dash of salt
- 2 tablespoons chilled butter, cut into small pieces
- 1 tablespoon olive oil
- 2 tablespoons ice water
- ½ teaspoon cider vinegar

FILLING:
- 4 teaspoons grated lime rind
- ½ cup fresh lime juice (about 4 limes)
- 4 large pasteurized egg yolks
- 1 (14-ounce) can fat-free sweetened condensed milk

MERINGUE:
- ¼ teaspoon cream of tartar
- 3 large pasteurized egg whites
- ¼ cup sugar
- ¼ teaspoon vanilla extract

1. To prepare crust, lightly spoon flour into a dry measuring cup; level with a knife. Place flour, ½ teaspoon sugar, and salt in a food processor; pulse 2 times or until combined. Add butter and oil; pulse 5 times or until mixture resembles coarse meal. Drizzle flour mixture with water and vinegar; pulse 10 times or just until combined. Gently press mixture into a 3-inch circle on plastic wrap; cover and chill 30 minutes.

2. Preheat oven to 425°.

3. Slightly overlap 2 sheets of plastic wrap on a slightly damp surface. Unwrap and place chilled dough on plastic wrap. Cover with 2 additional sheets of overlapping plastic wrap. Roll dough, still covered, into a 10-inch circle. Remove top plastic wrap. Fit dough, plastic wrap side up, into a 9-inch round removable-bottom tart pan. Remove remaining plastic wrap. Press dough against bottom and sides of pan. Pierce bottom of dough with a fork. Line bottom of dough with a piece of parchment paper; arrange pie weights on paper. Bake at 425° for 16 minutes or until edge is lightly browned. Remove pie weights and parchment paper; bake an additional 5 minutes or until bottom of crust is lightly browned. Cool on a wire rack.

4. Reduce oven temperature to 350°.

5. To prepare filling, combine rind, juice, egg yolks, and milk, stirring with a whisk until well blended. Pour into prepared crust. Bake at 350° for 15 minutes or until set. Remove tart from oven; place on a wire rack.

6. Increase oven temperature to 425°.

7. To prepare meringue, place cream of tartar and egg whites in a large bowl; beat with a mixer at high speed until foamy. Add ¼ cup sugar, 1 tablespoon at a time, beating until stiff peaks form; beat in vanilla. Spread meringue evenly over filling, sealing to edge of crust. Make peaks with back of a spoon. Bake at 425° for 4 minutes or until golden brown. Serve chilled or at room temperature. Yield: 8 servings (serving size: 1 piece).

CALORIES 287 (22% from fat); FAT 7g (sat 2.5g, mono 3.4g, poly 0.7g); PROTEIN 8.2g; CARB 48.1g; FIBER 0.4g; CHOL 113mg; IRON 1.3mg; SODIUM 118mg; CALC 157mg

Roasted Chicken with Pineapple-Curry Sauce

Cooking the chicken breast side down ensures the lean breast meat stays moist and doesn't overcook. The sauce recreates the taste of a high-fat coconut milk version but is made with creamy yogurt cheese as a base.

- 1 cup plain low-fat yogurt
- ⅓ cup diagonally sliced peeled fresh lemongrass
- 6 garlic cloves, chopped
- 1 (4-inch) piece peeled fresh ginger, thinly sliced
- 1 (5-pound) roasting chicken
- ¾ teaspoon salt
- Cooking spray
- 1½ cups water
- 1 teaspoon olive oil
- ¾ cup finely chopped Walla Walla or other sweet onion
- 1 tablespoon curry powder
- 1 tablespoon thinly sliced peeled fresh lemongrass
- 1 tablespoon grated peeled fresh ginger
- 2 garlic cloves, minced
- ¾ cup fat-free, less-sodium chicken broth
- ¼ cup thawed pineapple-orange juice concentrate, undiluted
- 1 tablespoon fish sauce
- ⅛ teaspoon coconut extract

1. Place a colander in a 2-quart glass measure or medium bowl. Line colander with 4 layers of cheesecloth, allowing cheesecloth to extend over sides. Spoon yogurt into colander. Cover loosely with plastic wrap; refrigerate 12 hours. Spoon yogurt cheese into a medium bowl; discard liquid. Refrigerate yogurt cheese.

2. Preheat oven to 350°.

3. Combine ⅓ cup lemongrass, 6 garlic cloves, and sliced ginger. Remove and discard giblets and neck from chicken. Rinse chicken with cold water; pat dry. Trim excess fat. Spoon lemongrass mixture into body cavity. Starting at neck cavity, loosen skin from breast and drumsticks by inserting fingers, gently pushing between skin and meat; rub salt under loosened skin. Lift wing tips up and over back; tuck under chicken. Place chicken, breast side down, on a rack coated with cooking spray. Pour water into a shallow roasting pan; place rack in pan. Bake at 350° for 1 hour and 55 minutes or until a thermometer inserted in meaty part of thigh registers 180°. Cover chicken loosely with foil; let stand 10 minutes. Discard skin. Reserve drippings in pan.

Continued

4. Heat oil in a medium saucepan over medium heat. Add onion and curry; cook 5 minutes, stirring frequently. Stir in 1 tablespoon lemongrass, 1 tablespoon ginger, and 2 garlic cloves; cook 1 minute, stirring frequently. Stir in broth and concentrate; bring to a boil. Reduce heat; simmer 3 minutes. Strain mixture through a sieve into a bowl; discard solids.

5. Stir fish sauce and coconut extract into yogurt cheese. Gradually add hot pineapple sauce, stirring constantly with a whisk. Cover and keep warm.

6. Place a heavy-duty zip-top plastic bag inside a 2-cup glass measure. Pour pan drippings into bag; let stand 10 minutes (fat will rise to the top). Seal bag; carefully snip off 1 bottom corner of bag. Drain drippings into yogurt mixture, stopping before fat layer reaches opening; discard fat. Stir well. Serve chicken with pineapple-curry sauce. Yield: 6 servings (serving size: about 4 ounces chicken and about 1/3 cup sauce).

CALORIES 260 (21% from fat); FAT 6.2g (sat 1.5g, mono 2.2g, poly 1.4g); PROTEIN 41.4g; CARB 7.2g; FIBER 0.5g; CHOL 126mg; IRON 2.4mg; SODIUM 738mg; CALC 68m

MAKE AHEAD
Lamb Shanks Pipérade

3 (1-pound) lamb shanks, trimmed
1/2 teaspoon salt, divided
1/4 teaspoon freshly ground black
     pepper, divided
Cooking spray
1 1/2 cups water, divided
1 teaspoon olive oil
3 cups chopped red bell pepper
2 cups chopped onion
2 teaspoons dried thyme
1/8 teaspoon ground cloves
3 garlic cloves, minced
1/2 cup tomato paste
2 cups dry red wine
1 1/2 cups (1/2-inch-thick) sliced celery
1/2 teaspoon crushed red pepper
1 tablespoon water
2 teaspoons cornstarch

1. Preheat oven to 350°.
2. Sprinkle lamb with 1/4 teaspoon salt and 1/8 teaspoon black pepper. Place lamb in a shallow roasting pan coated with cooking spray. Add 1/2 cup water. Bake at 350° for 1 hour and 15 minutes. Remove lamb from oven; cool slightly. Remove meat from bones, and chop; discard bones, fat, and gristle. Add 1 cup water to roasting pan, scraping pan to loosen browned bits. Place a zip-top plastic bag inside a 2-cup glass measure. Pour drippings into bag; let stand 10 minutes (fat will rise to the top). Seal bag; carefully snip off 1 bottom corner of bag. Drain drippings into a bowl, stopping before fat layer reaches opening; discard fat. Reserve lamb broth.

3. Heat oil in a large nonstick skillet over medium-high heat. Add bell pepper and onion; sauté 1 minute. Stir in thyme, cloves, and garlic; sauté 1 1/2 minutes. Add tomato paste; cook 5 minutes or until paste begins to brown, stirring constantly. Stir in 1/4 teaspoon salt, 1/8 teaspoon black pepper, wine, celery, and crushed red pepper. Bring to a boil; cover, reduce heat, and simmer 30 minutes.

4. Combine 1 tablespoon water and cornstarch; stir with a whisk. Add lamb, reserved lamb broth, and cornstarch mixture to bell pepper mixture. Bring to a boil; cook 1 minute or until thick. Stir occasionally. Yield: 6 servings (serving size: 1 1/3 cups).

CALORIES 331 (38% from fat); FAT 14g (sat 5.4g, mono 6.1g, poly 1.1g); PROTEIN 32.6g; CARB 18.3g; FIBER 3.8g; CHOL 102mg; IRON 3.7mg; SODIUM 321mg; CALC 55mg

superfast

. . . And Ready in Just About 20 Minutes

These recipes offer plenty of variety, and you'll be in and out of the kitchen in no time.

QUICK & EASY
Italian Eggs over Spinach and Polenta

Look for the polenta in the refrigerated produce section.

1 (16-ounce) tube of polenta, cut
   into 12 slices
Cooking spray
2 cups fat-free tomato-basil pasta
   sauce
1 (6-ounce) package fresh baby
   spinach
4 large eggs
1/2 cup (2 ounces) shredded Asiago
     cheese

1. Preheat broiler.
2. Arrange polenta slices on a baking sheet coated with cooking spray. Coat tops of polenta with cooking spray. Broil 3 minutes or until thoroughly heated.
3. While polenta heats, bring sauce to a simmer in a large nonstick skillet over medium-high heat. Stir in spinach; cover and cook 1 minute or until spinach wilts. Stir to combine. Make 4 indentations in top of spinach mixture using back of a wooden spoon. Break 1 egg into each indentation. Cover, reduce heat, and simmer 5 minutes or until eggs are desired degree of doneness. Sprinkle with cheese. Place 3 polenta slices on each of 4 plates; top each serving with one-fourth of spinach mixture and 1 egg. Yield: 4 servings.

CALORIES 264 (30% from fat); FAT 8.8g (sat 4g, mono 2.9g, poly 0.9g); PROTEIN 15.4g; CARB 29.4g; FIBER 2.9g; CHOL 224mg; IRON 3.2mg; SODIUM 780mg; CALC 238mg

MAKE AHEAD
Mussels in Herbed Tomato Broth

Buy fresh mussels, and use them within a day. Choose tightly closed shells, or those that are slightly open and snap shut when tapped. Serve with crusty bread.

4 basil leaves
4 fresh oregano sprigs
2 1/2 cups chopped plum tomato
       (about 1 pound)
1/8 teaspoon black pepper
1 small lemon, sliced
2 pounds small mussels, scrubbed
   and debearded
1 1/2 cups fat-free, less-sodium chicken
       broth
1/4 cup dry white wine

1. Place basil and oregano in a large saucepan; top with tomato, pepper, and lemon. Arrange mussels over lemon; pour broth and wine over mussels. Cover, bring to a boil, and cook 3 minutes or until shells open. Remove from heat; discard any unopened shells. Yield: 2 servings (serving size: about 1½ cups).

CALORIES 297 (19% from fat); FAT 6.4g (sat 1.2g, mono 1.4g, poly 1.8g); PROTEIN 32.6g; CARB 23.1g; FIBER 3.4g; CHOL 67mg; IRON 11mg; SODIUM 999mg; CALC 110mg

How to Scrub and Debeard Mussels

1. *When ready to cook, scrub the mussel to remove any sand or dirt on the shell. Holding it under cool water, scrub the mussel's shell with a stiff-bristled brush, such as those used for cleaning vegetables.*

2. *Next, debeard to remove the byssal threads (or beard), which connect the mussel to rocks or piling in the sea. Grab the fibers with your fingers, and pull them out, tugging toward the hinged point of the shell.*

QUICK & EASY
Grilled Sausage, Onion, and Pepper Sandwiches

The balsamic vinegar adds a sweetness that pairs nicely with Italian spices in the sausage. This recipe calls for a lot of onions; be sure to stir them frequently in the pan so they cook evenly. The filling for the sandwich is also good over egg noodles.

  Cooking spray
  4 cups thinly sliced Oso Sweet or other sweet onion
  4 (4-ounce) turkey Italian sausage links, halved lengthwise
  3 tablespoons balsamic vinegar
  1 (7-ounce) bottle roasted red bell peppers, drained and thinly sliced
  ¼ teaspoon black pepper
  1 (8-ounce) French bread baguette, halved lengthwise

1. Heat a large grill pan over medium-high heat. Coat pan with cooking spray. Add onion and sausage; cook 1 minute. Sprinkle with vinegar; cook 14 minutes or until sausage is done, turning sausage and onions frequently. Add bell peppers; cook 1 minute. Sprinkle with black pepper. Arrange sausage mixture evenly over bottom half of bread; top with top half. Cut into 5 sandwiches. Yield: 5 servings (serving size: 1 sandwich).

CALORIES 388 (26% from fat); FAT 11.4g (sat 3.2g, mono 4.5g, poly 3.3g); PROTEIN 23.4g; CARB 48.2g; FIBER 6.1g; CHOL 76mg; IRON 3.3mg; SODIUM 900mg; CALC 121mg

QUICK & EASY
Chicken-Chile Tostadas

  1 tablespoon olive oil
  1 cup chopped onion
  1 teaspoon bottled minced garlic
  ½ teaspoon ground cumin
  ½ teaspoon ground chipotle chile pepper
  ¼ teaspoon ground cinnamon
  1 pound ground chicken breast
  ½ cup bottled fat-free salsa
  ¼ cup water
  ½ teaspoon salt
  2 tablespoons chopped fresh cilantro

  1 teaspoon lime juice
  4 (6-inch) corn tortillas
  1 cup shredded iceberg lettuce
  1 cup (4 ounces) preshredded reduced-fat Mexican cheese blend or Cheddar cheese
  ¼ cup reduced-fat sour cream

1. Preheat oven to 400°.
2. Heat oil in a large nonstick skillet over medium-high heat. Add onion and garlic; sauté 2 minutes or until onion begins to soften. Add cumin, chipotle, and cinnamon; cook 30 seconds, stirring constantly. Add chicken; cook 4 minutes or until chicken is done, stirring to crumble. Add salsa, water, and salt; cook 3 minutes or until mixture begins to thicken. Stir in cilantro and lime juice; remove from heat.
3. While chicken cooks, place tortillas directly on oven rack; bake at 400° for 5 minutes or until slightly crisp. Place 1 tortilla on each of 4 plates; top each tortilla with ¼ cup lettuce, ¾ cup chicken mixture, ¼ cup cheese, and 1 tablespoon sour cream. Yield: 4 servings.

CALORIES 341 (24% from fat); FAT 11.6g (sat 5.2g, mono 3g, poly 0.9g); PROTEIN 35.9g; CARB 21.7g; FIBER 2.6g; CHOL 86mg; IRON 1.6mg; SODIUM 751mg; CALC 296mg

QUICK & EASY
Pork Tenderloin with Ginger-Soy Sauce

Serve over steamed white rice with sugar snap peas.

  1 teaspoon canola oil
  1 (1-pound) pork tenderloin, trimmed and cut crosswise into 8 pieces
  ¼ teaspoon salt
  ¼ teaspoon black pepper
  ¼ cup water
  2 tablespoons rice vinegar
  1 tablespoon water
  1 tablespoon low-sodium soy sauce
  1 tablespoon bottled minced fresh ginger
  1 teaspoon sugar
  ½ teaspoon dark sesame oil
  ¼ cup chopped green onions

Continued

1. Heat canola oil in a large nonstick skillet over medium-high heat.

2. Flatten each piece of pork to 1-inch thickness with fingertips; sprinkle pork with salt and pepper. Add pork to pan; cook 5 minutes on each side. Remove pork from pan; keep warm.

3. Add ¼ cup water to pan, scraping to loosen browned bits. Add vinegar and next 5 ingredients to pan; cook over medium-low heat 2 minutes. Stir in onions; serve sauce over pork. Yield: 4 servings (serving size: about 3 ounces pork and about 1 tablespoon sauce).

CALORIES 165 (31% from fat); FAT 5.6g (sat 1.6g, mono 2.2g, poly 1.3g); PROTEIN 24.1g; CARB 3.1g; FIBER 0.4g; CHOL 74mg; IRON 1.6mg; SODIUM 338mg; CALC 8mg

Warm Tortellini and Cherry Tomato Salad

You can also try this with chicken or mushroom tortellini or cheese ravioli.

    2 (9-ounce) packages fresh cheese
       tortellini
 1½ cups (1½-inch-long) slices fresh
       asparagus (about 1 pound)
    3 tablespoons red wine vinegar
    1 tablespoon balsamic vinegar
    1 tablespoon extravirgin olive oil
   ¼ teaspoon black pepper
    4 cups trimmed arugula
 1½ cups halved cherry tomatoes
   ¾ cup (3 ounces) grated fresh
       Parmesan cheese
   ½ cup thinly sliced red onion
   ⅓ cup thinly sliced fresh basil
    1 (14-ounce) can artichoke hearts,
       drained and quartered

1. Cook pasta according to package directions; omit salt and fat. Add asparagus during last 2 minutes of cook time. Drain.

2. While pasta cooks, combine vinegars, oil, and pepper in a large bowl, stirring with a whisk. Add pasta mixture, arugula, and remaining ingredients; toss to coat. Yield: 6 servings (serving size: 1½ cups).

CALORIES 403 (26% from fat); FAT 11.6g (sat 5.7g, mono 4.4g, poly 0.6g); PROTEIN 21.7g; CARB 52.4g; FIBER 7.9g; CHOL 50mg; IRON 1.9mg; SODIUM 725mg; CALC 415mg

Shrimp and Avocado Salad with Creole Sauce

To save time, purchase cooked peeled shrimp from the grocery store. Serve with crisp crackers or warm bread.

   ½ cup low-fat mayonnaise
   ¼ cup sliced red onion
    2 tablespoons fresh lemon juice
    2 tablespoons Creole mustard
    1 tablespoon chopped fresh flat-leaf
       parsley
    1 teaspoon bottled minced
       garlic
   ¼ teaspoon ground red pepper
   ⅛ teaspoon paprika
    8 cups torn Boston lettuce (about
       4 small heads)
 1½ pounds cooked peeled and
       deveined large shrimp
   ½ peeled avocado, thinly sliced

1. Combine first 8 ingredients in a large bowl. Add lettuce and shrimp to bowl; toss well to coat. Place about 2 cups salad on each of 4 plates; arrange one-fourth of avocado slices around each serving. Yield: 4 servings.

CALORIES 280 (26% from fat); FAT 8g (sat 1.2g, mono 3.3g, poly 2.4g); PROTEIN 37.7g; CARB 14.1g; FIBER 2.6g; CHOL 332mg; IRON 6mg; SODIUM 753mg; CALC 109mg

Thai Basil Beef with Rice Noodles

    8 cups water
    1 pound flank steak, trimmed
   ¼ teaspoon salt
 1½ cups 1½-inch-long slices fresh
       asparagus (about 1 pound)
    4 ounces wide rice stick noodles
       (bánh pho)
    1 tablespoon sugar
    3 tablespoons fresh lime juice
    1 tablespoon fish sauce
   ½ teaspoon Thai red curry paste
    1 cup cherry tomatoes, halved
   ½ cup thinly sliced fresh basil

1. Heat a large grill pan over medium-high heat.

2. While pan heats, bring water to a boil in a large saucepan.

3. Add steak to grill pan; grill 5 minutes on each side or until desired degree of doneness. Sprinkle steak with salt. Cut steak across grain into thin slices.

4. While steak cooks, add asparagus to boiling water; cook 2 minutes. Remove asparagus with a slotted spoon. Add noodles to boiling water; cook 3 minutes or until done. Drain; rinse well. Cut noodles into smaller pieces; place in medium bowl.

5. While noodles cook, combine sugar, lime juice, fish sauce, and curry paste in a large bowl. Add half of lime mixture to noodles; toss to coat. Add steak, asparagus, tomatoes, and basil to remaining lime mixture in large bowl; toss to combine. Serve steak mixture over noodles. Yield: 4 servings (serving size: ½ cup noodles and 1 cup steak mixture).

CALORIES 328 (24% from fat); FAT 8.6g (sat 3.6g, mono 3.4g, poly 0.4g); PROTEIN 26.1g; CARB 34.9g; FIBER 3.6g; CHOL 54mg; IRON 3.2mg; SODIUM 615mg; CALC 50mg

Orange Sweet-and-Sour Chicken Thighs with Bell Peppers

If you're not a fan of dark-meat chicken, use chicken breast instead.

    1 (3½-ounce) bag boil-in-bag
       long-grain rice
 1½ tablespoons canola oil, divided
    1 pound skinless, boneless chicken
       thighs
   ¼ teaspoon salt
    1 cup orange juice
    3 tablespoons low-sodium soy
       sauce
    2 tablespoons honey
    2 tablespoons rice vinegar
    1 tablespoon cornstarch
    1 cup chopped onion
    1 teaspoon bottled minced
       garlic
    1 teaspoon bottled minced fresh
       ginger
    1 green bell pepper, cut into ¼-inch
       strips
    1 red bell pepper, cut into ¼-inch
       strips

1. Cook rice according to package directions, omitting salt and fat.
2. While rice cooks, heat 1 tablespoon oil in a large nonstick skillet over medium-high heat. Sprinkle chicken with salt. Add chicken to pan, and cook 3 minutes on each side or until done. Remove chicken from pan, and cut into thin strips.
3. While chicken cooks, combine orange juice and next 4 ingredients, stirring with a whisk.
4. Add 1½ teaspoons oil to pan. Add onion, garlic, and ginger; sauté 1 minute. Add bell pepper strips, and sauté 2 minutes. Add orange juice mixture, and bring to a boil. Reduce heat, and simmer 1 minute. Add chicken to pan; cook 1 minute or until thoroughly heated. Serve over rice. Yield: 4 servings (serving size: ¾ cup rice and 1¼ cups chicken mixture).

CALORIES 382 (23% from fat); FAT 9.9g (sat 1.5g, mono 4.5g, poly 2.7g); PROTEIN 26.5g; CARB 45.9g; FIBER 1.9g; CHOL 94mg; IRON 2.4mg; SODIUM 705mg; CALC 38mg

technique

Daily Bread

Creative techniques from around the world show you how to use every crumb of a leftover loaf.

Use a Hearty Loaf

We call for day-old Italian or French bread in these recipes, but you can use any type of hearty, rustic bread with a large crumb—ciabatta or sourdough boules, for example. (Avoid using soft white or sweet enriched breads, which aren't substantial enough to hold up in these dishes.) When large chunks are called for, peasant rounds work nicely. Long loaves are easier to cut into slices. The bottom line: Aside from the exceptions noted above, take a cue from the Italians and use whatever you have on hand.

Spaghetti with Anchovies and Breadcrumbs

The breadcrumbs can be made ahead and stored in the refrigerator up to two days.

BREADCRUMBS:
- 1 ounce day-old Italian or French bread, torn into large pieces
- 1 tablespoon extravirgin olive oil
- 1½ teaspoons minced garlic
- 1 tablespoon minced fresh parsley
- ¼ teaspoon freshly ground black pepper

PASTA:
- 1 pound uncooked spaghetti
- 1 tablespoon extravirgin olive oil
- 1½ teaspoons minced garlic
- ½ teaspoon salt
- ½ to ¾ teaspoon crushed red pepper
- ¼ teaspoon freshly ground black pepper
- 3 canned anchovy fillets, minced
- ½ cup fat-free, less-sodium chicken broth
- ½ cup (2 ounces) grated fresh Parmesan cheese

1. Preheat oven to 450°.
2. To prepare breadcrumbs, place bread in a food processor; pulse 10 times or until coarse crumbs measure 1 cup. Place breadcrumbs in an even layer on a jelly-roll pan; bake at 450° for 4 minutes or until lightly toasted.
3. Heat 1 tablespoon oil in a large nonstick skillet over medium heat. Add breadcrumbs and 1½ teaspoons garlic; cook 2 minutes or until breadcrumbs are lightly browned. Place breadcrumb mixture in a bowl. Add parsley and ¼ teaspoon black pepper.
4. To prepare pasta, cook pasta according to package directions, omitting salt and fat. Drain.
5. Heat 1 tablespoon oil in pan over medium heat. Combine 1½ teaspoons garlic and next 4 ingredients in a small bowl; mash with a fork. Add anchovy mixture to pan; cook 1 minute. Stir in broth; cook 1 minute. Add pasta; toss well. Add cheese; toss well. Place on a large serving platter; sprinkle with breadcrumbs. Serve immediately. Yield: 6 servings (serving size: 1⅓ cups).

CALORIES 385 (21% from fat); FAT 8.8g (sat 2.5g, mono 4.4g, poly 1.2g); PROTEIN 14.8g; CARB 60.4g; FIBER 2.1g; CHOL 10mg; IRON 3.4mg; SODIUM 501mg; CALC 138mg

STAFF FAVORITE
Apple Brown Betty

- 2 cups sliced peeled Granny Smith apple (about ¾ pound)
- 2 cups sliced peeled Rome apple (about ¾ pound)
- 1 tablespoon fresh lemon juice
- ¼ cup granulated sugar
- ½ teaspoon ground cinnamon
- ¼ teaspoon ground nutmeg
- ¼ cup 1% low-fat milk
- 1 tablespoon molasses
- 1 teaspoon vanilla extract
- 2 ounces day-old Italian or French bread, torn into ½-inch pieces
- Cooking spray
- ½ cup all-purpose flour
- ¼ cup packed brown sugar
- ¼ cup chilled butter, cut into small pieces

1. Preheat oven to 350°.
2. Combine first 3 ingredients in a large bowl. Sprinkle apple mixture with granulated sugar, cinnamon, and nutmeg; toss well. Combine milk, molasses, and vanilla in a medium bowl. Add bread to milk mixture; toss to combine. Add bread mixture to apple mixture; toss to combine. Spoon bread mixture into an 8-inch square baking dish coated with cooking spray.
3. Lightly spoon flour into a dry measuring cup; level with a knife. Combine flour and brown sugar; cut in chilled butter using a pastry blender or 2 knives until mixture resembles small pebbles. Sprinkle brown sugar mixture over apple mixture. Bake at 350° for 40 minutes or until golden and bubbly. Serve warm. Yield: 6 servings.

CALORIES 256 (30% from fat); FAT 8.4g (sat 4.9g, mono 2.3g, poly 0.5g); PROTEIN 2.4g; CARB 44.1g; FIBER 2g; CHOL 21mg; IRON 1.2mg; SODIUM 139mg; CALC 47mg

Cranberry and Chestnut Dressing

Bottled chestnuts are available year-round at the site www.chefshop.com. Shield the dish with foil at the end of baking if it's getting too brown.

Cooking spray
1   cup chopped onion
¾   cup chopped pancetta (about 5 ounces)
3   garlic cloves, minced
¼   cup dry white wine
1   cup dried cranberries
½   cup coarsely chopped bottled chestnuts
1   tablespoon chopped fresh sage
¼   teaspoon salt
¼   teaspoon freshly ground black pepper
8   ounces day-old Italian or French bread, torn into 1-inch pieces
2¼ cups fat-free, less-sodium chicken broth

1. Preheat oven to 400°.
2. Heat a large nonstick skillet over medium heat. Coat pan with cooking spray. Add onion, pancetta, and garlic; cook 8 minutes or until onion is tender and pancetta is browned, stirring frequently. Stir in wine; cook until liquid evaporates, scraping pan to loosen browned bits. Remove from heat.
3. Add cranberries, chestnuts, sage, salt, and pepper to pancetta mixture; stir until combined. Combine pancetta mixture and bread in a large bowl. Pour broth over bread mixture; toss to combine. Spoon into an 11 x 7-inch baking dish coated with cooking spray.
4. Bake at 400° for 30 minutes or until golden brown. Yield: 8 servings.

CALORIES 220 (28% from fat); FAT 6.9g (sat 2.6g, mono 2.7g, poly 0.8g); PROTEIN 6.2g; CARB 34.2g; FIBER 3.1g; CHOL 13mg; IRON 0.8mg; SODIUM 635mg; CALC 28mg

Creole Banana Bread Puddings with Caramel Sauce

This recipe incorporates the flavors of the classic New Orleans dessert Bananas Foster with the ease of a bread pudding.

¼   cup packed brown sugar
1   tablespoon butter
2   tablespoons water
¼   cup bourbon
2   cups sliced bananas
½   cup 1% low-fat milk
¼   cup granulated sugar
¼   cup whipping cream
¼   teaspoon vanilla extract
⅛   teaspoon ground nutmeg
3   large eggs, lightly beaten
6   ounces day-old Italian or French bread, torn into 1-inch pieces
Cooking spray
¼   cup fat-free caramel topping

1. Combine first 3 ingredients in a small saucepan; cook over medium heat 4 minutes or until mixture is thick. Add bourbon; cook until mixture is reduced to ¼ cup (about 5 minutes). Remove from heat. Add sliced bananas; toss gently. Spoon banana mixture into a bowl; set aside.
2. Combine milk and next 5 ingredients in a large bowl, stirring well with a whisk. Add bread; stir to combine. Divide bread mixture evenly among 6 (8-ounce) ramekins coated with cooking spray. Divide banana mixture evenly over bread mixture. Place ramekins on a small baking sheet. Cover and chill 30 minutes.
3. Preheat oven to 375°.
4. Uncover and bake at 375° for 25 minutes or until set. Drizzle caramel topping evenly over bread puddings. Yield: 6 servings.

CALORIES 332 (25% from fat); FAT 9.2g (sat 4.5g, mono 2.6g, poly 0.6g); PROTEIN 6.8g; CARB 52.6g; FIBER 2.7g; CHOL 125mg; IRON 1.4mg; SODIUM 249mg; CALC 77mg

---

Premature Aging

To prepare these recipes with fresh bread, you'll have to dry the loaf first. Preheat the oven to 350°, break the bread as directed in the recipe, and toast in a single layer on a baking sheet until lightly toasted—10 to 15 minutes.

MAKE AHEAD
Bacon, Onion, and Fontina Strata

5   cups chopped Oso Sweet or other sweet onion
¼   cup water
2½ cups fat-free milk
1   cup egg substitute
2   teaspoons Dijon mustard
¼   teaspoon salt
¼   teaspoon freshly ground black pepper
5   slices bacon, cooked and crumbled
10 ounces day-old Italian or French bread, torn into 1-inch pieces
Cooking spray
1   cup (4 ounces) shredded fontina cheese, divided

1. Heat a large nonstick skillet over medium heat. Add onion; sauté 10 minutes or until onion begins to brown. Add water; cover, reduce heat to low, and simmer 25 minutes, stirring occasionally. Uncover and simmer 30 minutes or until liquid almost evaporates. Cool.
2. Combine milk, egg substitute, mustard, salt, and pepper in a large bowl, stirring with a whisk. Stir in onion and bacon. Add bread; toss gently to coat.
3. Arrange half of bread mixture in an 11 x 7-inch baking dish coated with cooking spray. Sprinkle with ½ cup cheese. Top with remaining bread mixture. Cover and chill overnight.
4. Preheat oven to 350°.
5. Uncover strata. Bake at 350° for 25 minutes. Sprinkle with ½ cup cheese; bake an additional 20 minutes or until browned. Let stand 10 minutes before serving. Yield: 8 servings.

CALORIES 257 (27% from fat); FAT 7.6g (sat 3.6g, mono 2.3g, poly 1g); PROTEIN 14.8g; CARB 32.6g; FIBER 2.4g; CHOL 22mg; IRON 1.9mg; SODIUM 614mg; CALC 236mg

---

Day-old bread can be turned into breadcrumbs to top a pasta or serve as the base for a sweet-and-savory dressing.

Roast Pork Loin with Savory Fennel Bread Pudding

The bread pudding is similar in texture to a soufflé or stuffing. The pork and bread pudding both need to be baked at 350°, so put the bread pudding into bake first; then add the pork after about 30 minutes. To ensure that both the pork and the pudding brown evenly, switch pans on the oven racks once during baking. Serve with a green salad.

- 1 cup sugar
- 8 cups water
- ¼ cup kosher salt
- 1 (2-pound) pork loin
- 1 teaspoon olive oil
- 3 cups thinly sliced fennel (about 1 large bulb)
- 2 cups thinly sliced onion
- 4 garlic cloves, minced and divided
- 2 (14-ounce) cans fat-free, less-sodium chicken broth, divided
- ½ teaspoon freshly ground black pepper, divided
- 8 ounces French bread or other firm white bread, torn into 1-inch pieces
- ¼ cup (1 ounce) shredded fontina cheese
    Cooking spray
- 1 tablespoon ground fennel seeds

1. Combine sugar, water, and salt in a large bowl, stirring until sugar and salt dissolve. Add pork; cover and brine 2 hours to overnight in refrigerator.
2. Preheat oven to 350°.
3. Heat oil in a large nonstick skillet over medium heat. Add sliced fennel, onion, and 2 garlic cloves; cook until golden brown (about 20 minutes), stirring frequently. Add ¼ cup broth; cook until liquid evaporates, scraping pan to loosen browned bits. Stir in ¼ teaspoon pepper. Add remaining broth; bring to a boil. Remove from heat.
4. Combine bread and fennel mixture. Stir in cheese. Spoon mixture into an 11 x 7-inch baking dish coated with cooking spray. Bake at 350° for 1 hour and 10 minutes or until golden brown.

5. While bread pudding bakes, rinse pork and pat dry. Combine fennel seeds, 2 garlic cloves, and ¼ teaspoon pepper; rub evenly over pork.
6. Heat a large ovenproof skillet over medium-high heat. Coat pan with cooking spray. Add pork to pan; cook 5 minutes, browning on all sides. Place skillet in oven; bake at 350° for 40 minutes or until a thermometer registers 140° (slightly pink). Let stand 10 minutes before serving. Serve bread pudding with pork. Yield: 8 servings (serving size: about 3 ounces pork and about ½ cup bread pudding).

CALORIES 316 (30% from fat); FAT 10.6g (sat 3.8g, mono 4.6g, poly 1g); PROTEIN 28.2g; CARB 25.8g; FIBER 3.1g; CHOL 68mg; IRON 2.4mg; SODIUM 790mg; CALC 97mg

Sausage and Mushroom Strata

- 8 ounces hot turkey Italian sausage
- 1 cup chopped onion
- 1 (16-ounce) package presliced mushrooms
- 2 cups 1% low-fat milk
- 1 tablespoon Dijon mustard
- ½ teaspoon salt
- ½ teaspoon dry mustard
- ¼ teaspoon freshly ground black pepper
- 5 large eggs
- 12 ounces day-old Italian or French bread, diagonally cut into ½-inch-thick slices, divided
    Cooking spray
- ½ cup (2 ounces) grated fresh Parmesan cheese, divided

1. Remove casings from sausage. Cook sausage in a large nonstick skillet over medium heat until browned; stir to crumble. Remove from pan. Add onion and mushrooms to pan; cook 5 minutes or until onion is tender and moisture evaporates. Remove from heat. Add sausage; stir to combine.
2. Combine milk and next 5 ingredients in a medium bowl, stirring with a whisk.
3. Arrange half of bread in a 13 x 9-inch baking dish coated with cooking spray. Spoon half of sausage mixture evenly over bread; sprinkle with ¼ cup cheese. Top with remaining bread. Spoon remaining sausage mixture over bread; sprinkle with remaining ¼ cup cheese. Pour egg mixture evenly over bread mixture. Cover and chill overnight.
4. Preheat oven to 350°.
5. Uncover and bake at 350° for 35 minutes or until browned. Let stand 10 minutes before serving. Yield: 8 servings.

CALORIES 279 (31% from fat); FAT 9.6g (sat 3.3g, mono 3.2g, poly 1.7g); PROTEIN 18.8g; CARB 29.6g; FIBER 2.3g; CHOL 163mg; IRON 2.1mg; SODIUM 777mg; CALC 188mg

Spanish Garlic Soup

This simple soup uses ingredients most Spanish cooks have on hand—garlic, eggs, broth, smoked paprika, and olive oil.

- 1 teaspoon olive oil
- ½ cup chopped garlic
- 4 cups water
- 3 cups fat-free, less-sodium chicken broth
- 2 cups (1-inch) pieces stale peasant bread
- ½ teaspoon Spanish smoked paprika
- ⅛ teaspoon salt
- 2 large eggs, beaten

1. Heat oil in a large saucepan over medium heat. Add garlic; sauté 4 minutes or until lightly browned. Add water and broth; bring to a boil. Reduce heat, and simmer 25 minutes or until garlic is tender. Add bread, paprika, and salt, stirring to break up bread pieces. Gradually add eggs, stirring constantly to form long threads. Yield: 8 servings (serving size: 1 cup).

CALORIES 84 (30% from fat); FAT 2.8g (sat 0.7g, mono 1.3g, poly 0.5g); PROTEIN 5.1g; CARB 9.3g; FIBER 0.5g; CHOL 71mg; IRON 0.9mg; SODIUM 367mg; CALC 47mg

Ribollita

This traditional Italian soup is better made the day before and reheated.

2½   tablespoons extravirgin olive oil, divided
 1   cup sliced carrots
 1   cup chopped onion
 ½   cup sliced celery
 ½   teaspoon dried thyme
 4   garlic cloves, minced
 3   cups chopped Swiss chard
 3   cups chopped kale
 3   cups water
 3   cups fat-free, less-sodium chicken broth
 ¼   cup canned tomato purée
 1   teaspoon sugar
 ¼   teaspoon salt
 ¼   teaspoon ground red pepper
 1   (14.5-ounce) can diced tomatoes
 1   (19-ounce) can cannellini beans, rinsed and drained
12   ounces day-old Italian or French bread, torn into 1-inch pieces

1. Heat 1½ teaspoons oil in a Dutch oven over medium heat. Add carrots and next 4 ingredients; cook 5 minutes or until onion is tender, stirring frequently. Add chard and next 8 ingredients; stir to combine. Bring to a boil; reduce heat, and simmer 45 minutes.

2. Place ⅓ cup beans in a bowl; mash with a fork until smooth. Add mashed beans, remaining beans, and bread to soup; cook 5 minutes or until thoroughly heated. Ladle soup into bowls. Drizzle remaining oil over soup. Yield: 8 servings (serving size: 1½ cups soup and ¾ teaspoon oil).

CALORIES 235 (14% from fat); FAT 3.6g (sat 0.6g, mono 1.5g, poly 1.2g); PROTEIN 9.3g; CARB 41.9g; FIBER 6.6g; CHOL 0mg; IRON 3.5mg; SODIUM 715mg; CALC 126mg

Zinfandel-Braised Beef Brisket with Onions and Potatoes

When it's cold outside, count on the richness of Zinfandel-Braised Beef Brisket with Onions and Potatoes to comfort you inside.

Zinfandel-Braised Beef Brisket with Onions and Potatoes

As this dish (which requires minimal preparation) bakes in the oven, you will have time to set the table, prepare dessert, and enjoy a glass of zinfandel. Thanks to its distinctive fruitiness, it's the wine of choice to season the beef and vegetables as they braise.

 2   cups zinfandel or other fruity dry red wine
 ½   cup fat-free, less-sodium chicken broth
 ¼   cup tomato paste
 1   (2½-pound) beef brisket, trimmed
 2   teaspoons salt, divided
 ½   teaspoon freshly ground black pepper, divided
Cooking spray
 8   cups sliced Walla Walla or other sweet onion (about 4 medium)
 2   tablespoons sugar
1¼   teaspoons dried thyme, divided
 6   garlic cloves, thinly sliced
 2   carrots, peeled and cut into ½-inch-thick slices
 2   celery stalks, cut into ½-inch-thick slices
1½   pounds small red potatoes, cut into quarters
1½   teaspoons extravirgin olive oil
 1   teaspoon dried oregano
 ¼   teaspoon ground red pepper
Chopped fresh parsley

1. Preheat oven to 325°.

2. Combine first 3 ingredients, stirring with a whisk.

3. Heat a large Dutch oven over medium-high heat. Sprinkle beef with ¾ teaspoon salt and ¼ teaspoon black pepper. Coat pan with cooking spray. Add beef to pan; cook 8 minutes, browning on all sides. Remove beef from pan; cover and set aside.

4. Add ½ teaspoon salt, ¼ teaspoon black pepper, onion, sugar, and 1 teaspoon thyme to pan. Cook 20 minutes or until onions are tender and golden brown, stirring occasionally. Add garlic, carrots, and celery; cook 5 minutes, stirring occasionally. Place beef on top of onion mixture; pour wine mixture over beef. Cover and place in oven.

5. Bake at 325° for 1 hour and 45 minutes.

6. While beef mixture cooks, place potatoes in a large bowl. Add ¾ teaspoon salt, ¼ teaspoon thyme, oil, oregano, and red pepper; toss to coat. Arrange in a single layer on a jelly-roll pan coated with cooking spray.

7. Remove beef from oven; turn beef over. Place potatoes on lower rack in oven. Cover beef; return to oven. Bake potatoes and beef at 325° for 45 minutes or until beef is tender. Remove beef from oven; cover and keep warm. Increase oven temperature to 425°. Place potatoes on middle rack in oven; bake at 425° for 15 minutes or until crisp and edges are browned.

8. Remove beef from pan; cut across grain into thin slices. Serve with onion mixture and potatoes. Sprinkle with parsley. Yield: 8 servings (serving size: about 3 ounces beef, ¾ cup onion mixture, and ½ cup potatoes).

CALORIES 342 (25% from fat); FAT 9.5g (sat 3.1g, mono 4.6g, poly 0.5g); PROTEIN 27.2g; CARB 34.4g; FIBER 4.7g; CHOL 70mg; IRON 3.5mg; SODIUM 619mg; CALC 67mg

Rethinking Risotto

Risottos can be made with ingredients other than rice. Stir up a creamy dish with barley, bulgur, or pasta.

Sage Risotto with Fresh Mozzarella and Prosciutto

- 2 (14-ounce) cans fat-free, less-sodium chicken broth
- 1 tablespoon butter
- 1 cup finely chopped leek
- 2 garlic cloves, minced
- 1¼ cups Arborio rice
- ¼ teaspoon salt
- ½ cup dry white wine
- 1½ to 2 tablespoons finely chopped fresh sage
- 1 cup (4 ounces) finely chopped fresh mozzarella cheese
- 2 ounces prosciutto, chopped (about ⅓ cup)
- ¼ teaspoon freshly ground black pepper
- Sage sprigs (optional)

1. Bring broth to a simmer (do not boil). Keep warm over low heat.
2. Melt butter in a medium sauté pan over medium heat. Add leek and garlic; cook 3 minutes, stirring frequently. Add rice and salt; cook 1 minute, stirring constantly. Stir in wine; cook 2 minutes or until liquid is nearly absorbed, stirring constantly. Add broth, ½ cup at a time, stirring frequently until each portion is absorbed before adding the next (about 20 minutes total). Stir in chopped sage, and cook 2 minutes. Remove from heat; stir in mozzarella. Spoon 1 cup risotto into each of 4 bowls; top each serving with about 1½ tablespoons prosciutto. Sprinkle with black pepper. Garnish with sage sprigs, if desired. Yield: 4 servings.

CALORIES 443 (25% from fat); FAT 12.3g (sat 7g, mono 3g, poly 1g); PROTEIN 18.8g; CARB 59.6g; FIBER 1.4g; CHOL 43mg; IRON 1.3mg; SODIUM 863mg; CALC 193mg

Quinoa and Onion Risotto with Crème Fraîche and Hazelnuts

- 1½ cups uncooked quinoa
- 6 cups water
- 1 teaspoon salt
- 2 thyme sprigs
- 1 bay leaf
- 1 teaspoon butter
- 1½ cups finely chopped Oso Sweet or other sweet onion
- 2 tablespoons white wine vinegar
- 3 tablespoons crème fraîche
- 3 tablespoons chopped hazelnuts, toasted

1. Place quinoa in a fine sieve; place sieve in a large bowl. Cover quinoa with water. Using your hands, rub grains together 30 seconds; rinse and drain. Repeat procedure twice. Drain well.
2. Combine 6 cups water, salt, thyme, and bay leaf in a large saucepan; bring to a simmer over medium heat. Cover and cook 5 minutes; discard thyme and bay leaf. Keep warm over low heat.
3. Melt butter in a medium sauté pan over medium heat. Add onion, and cook 10 minutes, stirring frequently. Add quinoa; cook 2 minutes, stirring constantly. Add warm seasoned water, ½ cup at a time, stirring frequently until each portion is absorbed before adding the next (about 30 minutes total). Stir in vinegar. Spoon ⅔ cup risotto into each of 6 small bowls or plates; top each serving with 1½ teaspoons crème fraîche. Sprinkle each serving with 1½ teaspoons hazelnuts. Yield: 6 servings.

CALORIES 245 (29% from fat); FAT 8g (sat 2.5g, mono 3.3g, poly 1.5g); PROTEIN 7.3g; CARB 37.4g; FIBER 4.3g; CHOL 8mg; IRON 4.3mg; SODIUM 413mg; CALC 61mg

Lemon-Mint Bulgur Risotto with Garlic Shrimp

The strong mint flavor makes this risotto a great foil for the garlic-infused shrimp. Although chewy bulgur grains separate in tabbouleh, they stick together when cooked as a risotto.

- 3 cups water
- 1 teaspoon salt, divided
- 2 tablespoons olive oil, divided
- ¾ cup finely chopped green onions
- 1 cup uncooked bulgur
- 4 cups torn spinach
- ⅓ cup chopped fresh mint
- 1 tablespoon grated lemon rind
- 2 tablespoons fresh lemon juice
- 4 garlic cloves, minced
- ¼ teaspoon freshly ground black pepper
- 1 pound medium shrimp, peeled and deveined
- Lemon wedges (optional)

1. Combine water and ¾ teaspoon salt in a medium saucepan; bring to a simmer (do not boil). Keep warm over low heat.
2. Heat 1 tablespoon oil in a medium sauté pan over medium heat. Add green onions; cook 1 minute, stirring constantly. Add bulgur; cook 2 minutes, stirring constantly. Add warm salted water, ½ cup at a time, stirring frequently until each portion is absorbed before adding the next (about 20 minutes total). Remove from heat. Add spinach, mint, rind, and juice; stir until spinach wilts. Keep warm.
3. Heat 1 tablespoon oil in a medium nonstick skillet over medium-high heat. Add garlic; sauté 30 seconds. Add ¼ teaspoon salt, pepper, and shrimp; sauté 2 minutes or until shrimp are done. Spoon risotto into each of 4 small bowls, and arrange shrimp over risotto. Garnish with lemon wedges, if desired. Yield: 4 servings (serving size: about ¾ cup risotto and about 3 ounces shrimp).

CALORIES 321 (26% from fat); FAT 9.4g (sat 1.4g, mono 5.3g, poly 1.6g); PROTEIN 28.9g; CARB 32.3g; FIBER 8.2g; CHOL 172mg; IRON 4.9mg; SODIUM 789mg; CALC 132mg

Pasta Risotto with Fennel

The entire fennel plant is used in this recipe, so purchase one with fresh-looking fronds. The bulb adds flavor, while the feathery green fronds finish the dish. The wine is added with a broth to keep more of the wine flavor and balance the licorice hint from the fennel.

    2   tablespoons butter, divided
    2   cups chopped fennel bulb
    1   cup thinly sliced leek (about 2 large)
    1   teaspoon fennel seeds
    ¼   teaspoon salt
    3   cups fat-free, less-sodium
        chicken broth
    1   cup dry white wine
 1¼   cups uncooked orzo (about
        8 ounces rice-shaped pasta)
    ¼   cup (1 ounce) grated pecorino
        Romano cheese
    2   tablespoons chopped fennel
        fronds
    ¼   teaspoon freshly ground black
        pepper

1. Melt 1 tablespoon butter in a large nonstick skillet over medium heat. Add fennel bulb, leek, and fennel seeds; cook 2 minutes, stirring frequently. Stir in salt. Cover and cook 12 minutes or until fennel is tender, stirring occasionally. Set aside.
2. Combine broth and wine; bring to a simmer in a large saucepan (do not boil). Keep warm over low heat (mixture will look curdled).
3. Melt 1 tablespoon butter in a medium sauté pan over medium heat. Add orzo; cook 2 minutes, stirring constantly. Add broth mixture, ½ cup at a time, stirring frequently until each portion is absorbed before adding the next (about 17 minutes total). Stir in leek mixture; cook 2 minutes. Remove from heat; stir in cheese, fennel fronds, and pepper. Yield: 4 servings (serving size: about 1 cup).

CALORIES 366 (22% from fat); FAT 9.1g (sat 4.7g, mono 2.1g, poly 0.7g); PROTEIN 12.7g; CARB 48.9g; FIBER 5.5g; CHOL 21mg; IRON 3.7mg; SODIUM 660mg; CALC 172mg

Lobster and Corn Risotto

STOCK:

    1   (2-pound) lobster, cooked
    3   cups water
    2   cups chopped onion
    2   celery stalks, chopped
    2   (8-ounce) bottles clam juice

RISOTTO:

    1   tablespoon butter
    ¾   cup finely chopped onion
    2   garlic cloves, minced
 1¼   cups Arborio rice
    ½   cup dry white wine
    ½   teaspoon salt
    1   cup fresh corn kernels
    ½   cup (2 ounces) shredded
        Monterey Jack cheese
    ⅓   cup chopped green onions
    1   tablespoon fresh lemon juice

1. To prepare stock, remove meat from cooked lobster tail and claws. Chop meat; chill. Place lobster shell in a large zip-top plastic bag. Coarsely crush shell using a meat mallet or rolling pin. Place crushed shell in a large saucepan; add 3 cups water, 2 cups onion, celery, and clam juice. Bring to a simmer over medium heat. Cover and cook 20 minutes. Strain shell mixture through a sieve into a bowl, reserving stock (about 3 cups); discard solids. Place stock in a large saucepan; keep warm over low heat.
2. To prepare risotto, melt butter in a medium sauté pan over medium heat. Add ¾ cup onion and garlic; cook 3 minutes or until tender, stirring frequently. Add rice; cook 2 minutes, stirring constantly. Add wine and salt; cook 2 minutes or until liquid is nearly absorbed, stirring constantly. Add stock, ½ cup at a time, stirring frequently until each portion is absorbed before adding the next (about 25 minutes total). Stir in reserved lobster meat and corn; cook 2 minutes or until heated. Remove from heat; stir in cheese, green onions, and lemon juice. Yield: 4 servings (serving size: 1¼ cups).

CALORIES 450 (18% from fat); FAT 9g (sat 4.8g, mono 2.5g, poly 0.9g); PROTEIN 23g; CARB 63.9g; FIBER 3.9g; CHOL 68mg; IRON 4.2mg; SODIUM 769mg; CALC 169mg

The Risotto Technique

1. Bring cooking liquid to a simmer. Keep the liquid hot so the risotto stays at a simmer with each addition. Cold ingredients slow the release of starch.
2. Sauté aromatic vegetables in oil or butter to provide a taste foundation on which to build the risotto.
3. Add grain. Sautéing the grain infuses it with flavors from the vegetables and allows the risotto to boil quickly when the first liquid is added.
4. Add wine before any other cooking liquid to allow the alcohol to cook out. Since wine is a primary ingredient in most of these recipes, use one that's good enough to drink; avoid "cooking wines."
5. Begin stirring as you add the wine, and continue stirring frequently until the wine is absorbed. This jostles the starch out of the grain.
6. Slowly add hot cooking liquid. Allow only a veil of liquid to cover the grain and ensure the stirring properly agitates the grain (causing it to release its starch), and to keep the cooking time down.
7. Add remaining ingredients such as meat, fish, or vegetables in the last few minutes to keep them intact.

MAKE AHEAD
Orange-Vanilla Risotto Pudding

Milk gives this risotto the consistency of rice pudding. To prevent a skin from forming, cover the warm milk.

    4   cups 1% low-fat milk
 1¼   cups water
    ½   cup sugar
    1   (2-inch) piece vanilla bean, split
        lengthwise
    ¾   cup Arborio rice
    ¼   teaspoon salt
    2   teaspoons grated orange rind
    2   tablespoons fresh orange juice
    1   tablespoon fresh lemon juice

1. Combine first 3 ingredients in a large saucepan. Scrape seeds from vanilla bean; stir seeds and bean into milk mixture. Bring to a simmer (do not boil). Cover and keep warm over low heat.
2. Place rice in a medium sauté pan over medium heat; cook 3 minutes, stirring constantly. Stir in salt. Add milk mixture, ½ cup at a time, stirring frequently until each portion is absorbed before adding the next (about 45 minutes). Remove from heat; stir in rind and juices. Remove vanilla bean, and discard. Chill risotto at least 3 hours before serving. Yield: 7 servings (serving size: ½ cup).

CALORIES 204 (9% from fat); FAT 2g (sat 1.1g, mono 0.5g, poly 0.3g); PROTEIN 7g; CARB 40.2g; FIBER 0.4g; CHOL 6mg; IRON 0.2mg; SODIUM 156mg; CALC 176mg

Orzotto with Radicchio and Bacon

Serve this immediately since the hot barley turns the radicchio brown.

    1¼ cups water
    2 (14-ounce) cans fat-free,
       less-sodium chicken broth
    4 bacon slices
    1 cup finely chopped red onion
    1 cup uncooked pearl barley
    ½ cup dry white wine
    ⅛ teaspoon salt
    3 cups chopped radicchio
    ½ cup (2 ounces) grated Parmigiano-
       Reggiano cheese
    ¼ teaspoon freshly ground black
       pepper

1. Combine water and broth; bring to a simmer in a large saucepan (do not boil). Keep warm over low heat.
2. Cook bacon in a Dutch oven over medium heat until crisp. Remove bacon from pan, reserving 2 teaspoons drippings in pan. Crumble bacon; set aside.
3. Return pan to medium heat. Add red onion; sauté 3 minutes. Add barley; cook 2 minutes, stirring constantly. Add wine and salt; cook 2 minutes or until liquid is nearly absorbed, stirring constantly. Add broth mixture, ½ cup at a time, stirring until each portion is absorbed before

adding the next (about 45 minutes total). Stir in bacon; cook 2 minutes. Remove from heat; stir in radicchio, cheese, and pepper. Serve immediately. Yield: 4 servings (serving size: 1½ cups).

CALORIES 317 (19% from fat); FAT 6.8g (sat 3.2g, mono 2.5g, poly 0.8g); PROTEIN 14.5g; CARB 45.2g; FIBER 8.8g; CHOL 13mg; IRON 1.9mg; SODIUM 754mg; CALC 171mg

Bulgur Risotto with Roasted Garlic and Butternut Squash

Slightly chewy bulgur contrasts beautifully with the tender roasted squash and garlic.

    3 cups (¾-inch) cubed peeled
       butternut squash (about 1¼
       pounds)
    8 garlic cloves, unpeeled
    4 teaspoons olive oil, divided
    5 cups water
    1 teaspoon salt
    1½ cups uncooked bulgur
    ½ cup dry white wine
    1 tablespoon chopped fresh
       parsley
    1 teaspoon chopped fresh sage
    ¾ cup (3 ounces) grated Parmigiano-
       Reggiano cheese

1. Preheat oven to 400°.
2. Combine squash and garlic in a shallow roasting pan. Drizzle with 2 teaspoons oil, tossing gently to coat. Bake at 400° for 20 minutes or until squash is tender, stirring once. Cool 10 minutes. Peel garlic cloves; chop, and discard skins.
3. Combine water and salt in a medium saucepan, and bring to a simmer (do not boil). Keep warm over low heat.
4. Heat 2 teaspoons oil in a medium sauté pan over medium heat. Add bulgur; cook 2 minutes, stirring constantly. Add wine; cook 2 minutes or until liquid is nearly absorbed, stirring constantly. Add warm salted water, ½ cup at a time, stirring frequently until each portion is absorbed before adding the next (about 27 minutes total). Stir in squash and garlic; cook 3 minutes or until thoroughly heated. Remove from heat; stir in parsley

and sage. Sprinkle each serving with cheese. Yield: 6 servings (serving size: 1 cup risotto and 2 tablespoons cheese).

CALORIES 243 (24% from fat); FAT 6.6g (sat 2.4g, mono 3.2g, poly 0.6g); PROTEIN 9.5g; CARB 36.7g; FIBER 8.9g; CHOL 8mg; IRON 1.7mg; SODIUM 590mg; CALC 198mg

Steel-Cut Oat Risotto with Chicken, Red Peppers, and Manchego

Steel-cut oats are whole-oat groats that have been cut into pieces to cook quickly. Find them on the cereal aisle in the supermarket labeled "steel-cut Irish oatmeal." Do not substitute quick-cooking Irish oatmeal or American-style rolled oats.

    2 (14-ounce) cans fat-free,
       less-sodium chicken broth
    2 teaspoons olive oil
    ¾ cup finely chopped onion
    1 large red bell pepper, chopped
    1¼ cups steel-cut oats
    ½ cup dry white wine
    1 cup chopped cooked dark-meat
       chicken
    ½ cup (2 ounces) shredded
       Manchego cheese
    1 teaspoon chopped fresh
       rosemary
    ½ teaspoon salt

1. Bring broth to a simmer in a medium saucepan (do not boil). Keep warm.
2. Heat oil in a medium sauté pan over medium heat. Add onion and pepper; sauté 5 minutes. Add oats; cook 2 minutes, stirring constantly. Stir in wine; cook 2 minutes or until nearly absorbed, stirring constantly. Add broth, ½ cup at a time, stirring until each portion is absorbed before adding the next (about 20 minutes). Stir in chicken, cheese, rosemary, and salt. Yield: 4 servings (serving size: 1 cup).

CALORIES 419 (30% from fat); FAT 14g (sat 4.4g, mono 5.1g, poly 2.2g); PROTEIN 23.3g; CARB 43.2g; FIBER 7.6g; CHOL 48mg; IRON 3.1mg; SODIUM 774mg; CALC 143mg

One Smart Cookie

A young baking enthusiast updates a classic treat.

With cookbooks being her idea of a good read, it's no surprise that Lauren Harwick often has food on her mind. "I like creating recipes off the top of my head," she says. Her recipe for chocolate chip cookies is an example. Harwick, 20, is a sophomore majoring in liberal arts at Western Washington University in Bellingham. She says baking is her passion, and after college, she wants to attend culinary school. In fact, this is Harwick's second time to appear in *Cooking Light Annual Recipes*. Her recipe for Snickerdoodle cookies was in *Cooking Light Annual Recipes 2004*.

MAKE AHEAD
Lauren's Chocolate Chip Cookies

Look for grain-sweetened chocolate chips in health-food stores.

  3   tablespoons canola oil
2½   tablespoons light-colored corn syrup
  ¾   cup packed brown sugar
  ½   cup granulated sugar
1½   teaspoons vanilla extract
  3   large egg whites, lightly beaten
1¼   cups all-purpose flour
1¼   cups whole wheat pastry flour
  1   teaspoon baking soda
  ½   teaspoon salt
  1   cup grain-sweetened chocolate chips (such as Sunspire)
Cooking spray

1. Combine oil and syrup in a large bowl; stir with a whisk. Add sugars; stir with a whisk until well blended. Stir in vanilla and egg whites.
2. Lightly spoon flours into dry measuring cups; level with a knife. Combine flours, baking soda, and salt; stir with a whisk. Add flour mixture to sugar mixture, stirring until well combined. Stir in chips; cover and chill 1 hour.
3. Preheat oven to 375°.
4. Drop dough by level tablespoons 2 inches apart onto baking sheets coated with cooking spray. Bake at 375° for 8 minutes or until almost set. Cool on pans 2 minutes or until firm. Remove from pans; cool on wire racks. Yield: 44 servings (serving size: 1 cookie).

CALORIES 74 (22% from fat); FAT 1.8g (sat 0.5g, mono 0.6g, poly 0.3g); PROTEIN 1.3g; CARB 13.7g; FIBER 0.7g; CHOL 0mg; IRON 0.4mg; SODIUM 62mg; CALC 5mg

FREEZABLE
Tomato Florentine Soup

"I had this soup at a favorite lunch spot near where I attended law school in Manhattan. I searched for a recipe but couldn't find one, so I made my own. The result is delicious and tastes exactly like the one I had in the city."
—Kathleen Scannell Graham, Harwich, Massachusetts

  1   tablespoon olive oil
2¼   cups finely chopped onion
  ⅔   cup chopped celery
  3   garlic cloves, minced
  1   cup water
  2   (14-ounce) cans fat-free, less-sodium chicken broth
  1   (14.5-ounce) can diced tomatoes, undrained
  1   (8-ounce) can no-salt-added tomato sauce
  ⅔   cup uncooked small seashell pasta
  2   cups bagged prewashed spinach
  ¼   teaspoon freshly ground black pepper
  ⅛   teaspoon salt
  ¼   cup (1 ounce) grated fresh Parmesan cheese

1. Heat oil in a small Dutch oven over medium heat. Add onion and celery; cook 7 minutes or until tender, stirring frequently. Stir in garlic; cook 1 minute. Add water, broth, tomatoes, and tomato sauce. Bring to a simmer; cook 25 minutes, stirring occasionally. Stir in pasta; cook 8 minutes. Add spinach; cook 2 minutes or until spinach wilts and pasta is done. Stir in pepper and salt. Ladle soup into each of 4 bowls; top with cheese. Yield: 4 servings (serving size: 1¾ cups soup and 1 tablespoon cheese).

CALORIES 211 (23% from fat); FAT 5.4g (sat 1.4g, mono 3g, poly 0.7g); PROTEIN 9.5g; CARB 32g; FIBER 4.7g; CHOL 4mg; IRON 2mg; SODIUM 713mg; CALC 131mg

QUICK & EASY
Pappardelle with Smoked Salmon

"This is a recipe I created for my husband and me. It's great for a quick work-night meal with a salad of spinach, thinly sliced sweet onion, and pine nuts."
—Karlette Warner, Palo Alto, California

  ½   pound uncooked pappardelle (wide ribbon pasta) or fettuccine
  1   teaspoon butter
  2   cups chopped Oso Sweet or other sweet onion
  1   cup fat-free, less-sodium chicken broth
  ½   cup (4 ounces) ⅓-less-fat cream cheese, cubed
  ½   cup chopped plum tomato
  1   (10-ounce) package frozen petite green peas, thawed
  1   (4-ounce) smoked salmon fillet, skinned and cut into small pieces
  ½   teaspoon dried dill
  ¼   teaspoon salt
  ¼   teaspoon freshly ground black pepper

1. Cook pasta according to package directions; omit salt and fat. Drain. Keep warm.
2. Melt butter in a large nonstick skillet over medium-high heat. Add onion; sauté 4 minutes or until tender. Add broth and cheese; cook 4 minutes or until cheese melts, stirring frequently. Add tomato, peas, and salmon; cook 3 minutes or until thoroughly heated. Stir in dill, salt, and pepper.
3. Combine pasta and salmon mixture in a large bowl; toss gently. Yield: 6 servings (serving size: 1⅓ cups).

CALORIES 290 (23% from fat); FAT 7.4g (sat 3.7g, mono 2.1g, poly 0.5g); PROTEIN 15g; CARB 41.6g; FIBER 4.4g; CHOL 26mg; IRON 1.9mg; SODIUM 322mg; CALC 39mg

Salsa Picante

"I would never have believed that canned tomatoes could give you such an authentic and fresh-tasting salsa. It's sublime for dipping with baked tortilla chips and works well as a base for many Mexican dishes."

—Erin Renouf Mylroie, St. George, Utah

- 1 cup coarsely chopped onion
- 1 cup cilantro sprigs
- 1 jalapeño pepper, coarsely chopped
- 1 garlic clove, coarsely chopped
- 1 (14.5-ounce) can diced tomatoes, undrained
- 3 tablespoons fresh lime juice
- ¼ teaspoon salt
- 1 (14.5-ounce) can diced tomatoes, drained

1. Place first 5 ingredients in a food processor, and process until minced. Combine onion mixture, lime juice, salt, and drained tomatoes in a medium bowl; stir until well blended. Yield: 4 cups (serving size: ⅔ cup).

CALORIES 43 (2% from fat); FAT 0.1g (sat 0g, mono 0g, poly 0g); PROTEIN 1.5g; CARB 10.3g; FIBER 2.7g; CHOL 0mg; IRON 0.5mg; SODIUM 275mg; CALC 31mg

Breakfast Salad with Warm Pine Nuts

"I came up with this recipe while trying to jazz up our traditional Sunday waffles."

—Renata Perry, Austin, Texas

- 2 cups cubed Fuji apple (about ¾ pound)
- 1½ cups cubed Asian pear or ripe pear (about 1 medium)
- 1 cup coarsely chopped orange sections (about 1 large)
- ½ cup cubed peeled kiwifruit
- 1 tablespoon dried blueberries
- 1 tablespoon dried cranberries
- 1 tablespoon roasted sunflower seed kernels
- 1 tablespoon unsalted pumpkinseed kernels
- Cooking spray
- 2 tablespoons pine nuts

1. Combine first 8 ingredients in a medium bowl.
2. Heat a nonstick skillet over medium-high heat. Coat pan with cooking spray. Add pine nuts to pan; cook 3 minutes or until lightly browned, shaking pan frequently. Add pine nuts to salad; toss gently to combine. Serve immediately. Yield: 4 servings (serving size: 1 cup).

CALORIES 178 (28% from fat); FAT 5.5g (sat 0.5g, mono 1.3g, poly 2.6g); PROTEIN 2.8g; CARB 34.3g; FIBER 6.6g; CHOL 0mg; IRON 1mg; SODIUM 1mg; CALC 43mg

Sautéed Chicken with Penne Pasta

"We're big chicken eaters, and I'm always looking for new ways to make it. Don't leave out the olives—they really add to the flavor. Serve with good crisp bread to sop up the juices."

—Christine Wilcox, East Greenville, Pennsylvania

- 1 pound uncooked penne pasta
- 1 tablespoon olive oil
- 1 pound skinless, boneless chicken breast, cut into ½-inch pieces
- ¼ cup minced shallots
- 1 (8-ounce) package presliced mushrooms
- 1 garlic clove, minced
- 1 cup dry white wine
- 3 tablespoons chopped ripe olives
- 2 tablespoons chopped pitted green olives
- 1 (14.5-ounce) can diced tomatoes with balsamic vinegar, basil, and olive oil (such as Hunt's)
- 1 (14-ounce) can fat-free, less-sodium chicken broth
- ¼ cup (1 ounce) grated fresh Parmigiano-Reggiano cheese
- ⅛ teaspoon freshly ground black pepper

1. Cook pasta according to package directions, omitting salt and fat. Drain. Keep warm.
2. Heat oil in a large nonstick skillet over medium-high heat. Add chicken; sauté 2 minutes or until lightly browned. Remove chicken from pan; keep warm.

Add shallots, mushrooms, and garlic to pan; cover and cook 4 minutes. Stir in wine, olives, tomatoes, and broth; simmer, uncovered, 10 minutes. Return chicken to pan; cook 5 minutes. Remove from heat; add pasta, cheese, and pepper, tossing to combine. Yield: 6 servings (serving size: 2 cups).

CALORIES 489 (14% from fat); FAT 7.7g (sat 1.6g, mono 2.7g, poly 0.6g); PROTEIN 31.9g; CARB 65.4g; FIBER 3.1g; CHOL 46mg; IRON 3.7mg; SODIUM 570mg; CALC 78mg

culinary postcard

Home to Moloka`i

For Hawaiian-born novelist Lois-Ann Yamanaka, Grandma's comfort food is more than worth the trip.

Lois-Ann Yamanaka enjoys visiting her grandma on the small Hawaiian island, Moloka`i. "Moloka`i has been all about my grandmother since the day I was born there. Grandma is solace. Grandma is refuge. Grandma is comfort food from the moment of my arrival at her Kaunakakai house," Yamanaka says. Here are some of her favorite comfort foods.

Lomi Lomi Salmon

The popular luau dish is named for the Hawaiian words for rub, massage, or knead. Traditionally, the salt is rubbed onto the salmon, and the salmon, onions, and tomato are then massaged together by hand. We opted for a tidier preparation. Soaking the diced white onion mellows the flavor by taming its sharp bite.

- ¼ cup coarse sea salt
- 8 ounces salmon fillet
- ½ cup finely diced white onion
- 3 tablespoons finely chopped green onions
- 1 cup diced tomato
- 16 iceberg lettuce leaves

Continued

1. Place salt and fish in a large zip-top plastic bag; shake bag to coat fish evenly. Chill 8 hours or overnight.

2. Remove fish from bag; rinse well. Soak fish in ice water 2 hours, changing water every 30 minutes. Drain well. Pat fish dry with paper towels. Dice fish; place in a large bowl. Set aside.

3. Soak white onion in ice water 15 minutes. Drain well. Add diced onion, green onions, and diced tomato to fish; toss gently to combine. Spoon about 3 tablespoons fish mixture into each lettuce leaf. Yield: 4 servings (serving size: 4 filled lettuce leaves).

CALORIES 113 (37% from fat); FAT 4.6g (sat 1.1g, mono 1.9g, poly 1.2g); PROTEIN 13g; CARB 5.1g; FIBER 0.9g; CHOL 29mg; IRON 0.6mg; SODIUM 467mg; CALC 24mg

Poi

Look for taro in the produce department with other tubers, or order from www.melissas.com.

    2   quarts plus 1¼ cups water, divided
    1½ pounds taro root, unpeeled

1. Bring 2 quarts water to a boil in a medium saucepan. Add taro; cook 40 minutes or until tender. Drain; cool 15 minutes. Peel; discard skin. Roughly chop taro. Place taro and 1 cup water in a blender; process until smooth. Add ¼ cup water, 1 tablespoon at a time, until desired consistency. Yield: 3 cups (serving size: ¼ cup).

CALORIES 53 (0% from fat); FAT 0g; PROTEIN 0.4g; CARB 1.1g; FIBER 0.2g; CHOL 0mg; IRON 0.3mg; SODIUM 1mg; CALC 6mg

Like grits in the American South, Poi, is a bland side dish you serve plain and season with salt or pepper.

Poi Pointers

This Hawaiian national dish is made from taro root, a starchy tuber early Hawaiians brought with them from Polynesia. Poi is considered a traditional Hawaiian food because it was eaten before the cuisine was influenced by the Western world. Taro is boiled, peeled, and pounded into a paste (the white or pink flesh often turns purple when cooked). Here, we've let the blender take care of pounding. Water is added to reach the desired consistency—one-finger, two-finger, or three-finger—described by the number of fingers needed to scoop it up.

Hawaiian Bread

This famous bread is actually a Portuguese sweet bread. It's delicious toasted for breakfast or used to make sandwiches.

    1   (6-ounce) can pineapple juice
    1   package dry yeast (about
        2¼ teaspoons)
    3   cups all-purpose flour, divided
    ½   cup warm 2% reduced-fat milk
        (100° to 110°)
    ½   cup egg substitute
    ⅓   cup sugar
    ¼   cup butter, melted
    ½   teaspoon salt
    Cooking spray
    2   tablespoons all-purpose flour

1. Place juice in a medium microwave-safe bowl. Microwave at HIGH 45 seconds or until 100° to 110°. Dissolve yeast in warm juice; let stand 5 minutes.

2. Place yeast mixture in the bowl of a stand-up mixer fitted with a paddle attachment. Lightly spoon flour into dry measuring cups; level with a knife. Add 1 cup flour to yeast mixture; beat until combined. Add warm milk, egg substitute, sugar, butter, and salt, beating to combine. Beat in 2 cups flour, ½ cup at a time, until combined (dough will be very soft and sticky). Beat at medium-low

---

speed 2 minutes. Scrape down sides of bowl. Lightly coat sides of bowl with cooking spray.

3. Cover bowl with a damp towel. Let dough rise in a warm place (85°), free from drafts, 1 hour or until doubled in size. (Gently press two fingers into dough. If indentation remains, dough has risen enough.)

4. Preheat oven to 350°.

5. Coat 2 (8-inch) round pans with cooking spray; dust each pan with 1 tablespoon flour. Divide dough evenly between prepared pans. Cover and let rise in a warm place (85°), free from drafts, 45 minutes or until doubled in size. Bake at 350° for 30 minutes or until golden brown. Yield: 2 loaves, 12 servings per loaf (serving size: 1 slice).

CALORIES 98 (24% from fat); FAT 2.6g (sat 1.4g, mono 0.7g, poly 0.2g); PROTEIN 2.4g; CARB 16.1g; FIBER 0.5g; CHOL 23mg; IRON 0.9mg; SODIUM 71mg; CALC 12mg

Kimchi

This Korean salt-pickled cabbage dish is a very popular side in Hawaii. It can also be served on a *pupu*, or appetizer, platter.

    14 cups coarsely chopped napa
        (Chinese) cabbage (about 2 pounds)
    3   tablespoons salt
    1½ cups water
    1   cup coarsely chopped green
        onions
    4   teaspoons grated peeled fresh
        ginger
    1½ teaspoons crushed red pepper
    4   garlic cloves, minced

1. Place cabbage and salt in a large bowl, tossing gently to combine. Weigh down cabbage with another bowl. Let stand at room temperature 3 hours, tossing occasionally. Drain and rinse with cold water. Drain and squeeze dry.

2. Combine cabbage, water, and remaining ingredients. Cover and refrigerate at least 4 hours before serving. Yield: 8 servings (serving size: about ⅔ cup).

CALORIES 29 (3% from fat); FAT 0.1g (sat 0g, mono 0g, poly 0g); PROTEIN 1.8g; CARB 6g; FIBER 1.9g; CHOL 0mg; IRON 0.3mg; SODIUM 283mg; CALC 95mg

Oven Kalua Pork

This more accessible version of the classic slow-roasted pig enjoyed at luaus is cooked as a roast in a regular oven. It is typical to stir any reserved meat juice into the shredded pork. If you do, we recommend that you skim the fat first. Place a heavy-duty plastic bag into a measuring cup; pour collected juices into the bag. Let stand 10 minutes or until fat rises to the top. Using kitchen shears, snip a small portion of one bottom corner of the bag, and pour the juices over the shredded pork, stopping before you reach the fat layer.

4¼   pounds Boston Butt pork roast, trimmed
  2   tablespoons barbecue smoked seasoning (such as Hickory Liquid Smoke)
  ¾   teaspoon salt

1. Preheat oven to 275°.
2. Rub pork with liquid smoke. Wrap pork tightly in foil; place on a jelly-roll pan. Bake at 275° for 5 hours. Cool slightly. Remove pork from bone; discard bone. Shred meat with 2 forks. Combine shredded pork and salt in a large bowl, tossing well. Yield: 16 servings (serving size: about 3 ounces).

CALORIES 234 (44% from fat); FAT 11.5g (sat 3.9g, mono 5.5g, poly 1.1g); PROTEIN 30.5g; CARB 0g; FIBER 0g; CHOL 108mg; IRON 1.8mg; SODIUM 249mg; CALC 8mg

Tuna Poke

Be sure to use sushi-grade tuna for this fish salad because the fish is raw and isn't "cooked" with citrus juice, as in seviche.

  ¼   cup chopped green onions
  1   tablespoon low-sodium soy sauce
  ½   teaspoon grated peeled fresh ginger
1½   teaspoons peanut oil
  ½   teaspoon dark sesame oil
  ½   pound sushi-grade tuna, cut into ½-inch cubes
  1   garlic clove, minced
  2   cups (¼-inch-thick) diagonally cut slices peeled cucumber

1. Combine first 7 ingredients in a medium glass bowl. Cover and chill 2 hours. Serve tuna mixture over cucumber. Yield: 4 servings (serving size: ¼ cup tuna and ½ cup cucumber).

CALORIES 94 (28% from fat); FAT 2.9g (sat 0.5g, mono 1.1g, poly 0.9g); PROTEIN 13.9g; CARB 2.4g; FIBER 0.7g; CHOL 26mg; IRON 0.6mg; SODIUM 157mg; CALC 19mg

STAFF FAVORITE
Chicken and Pork Adobo

Depending on your preference, you can use another cut of pork or even all chicken thighs. This is a popular luau offering and is a national dish of the Philippines. Let your guests know that there are peppercorns in the sauce so they can avoid biting into them. The sauce has a strong vinegar flavor that is balanced by the pepper, soy sauce, and garlic.

      Cooking spray
  1   (1-pound) pork tenderloin, trimmed and cut into 2-inch pieces
  ⅓   cup low-sodium soy sauce
  ¼   cup water
  ½   teaspoon black peppercorns
1½   pounds skinless, boneless chicken thighs, cut into 2-inch pieces
  1   (14-ounce) can fat-free, less-sodium chicken broth
  1   (12-ounce) bottle rice vinegar
  8   garlic cloves, crushed
  1   bay leaf

1. Heat a large nonstick skillet over medium heat. Coat pan with cooking spray. Add pork pieces; cook 4 minutes, browning on all sides. Add soy sauce and remaining ingredients; bring to a boil. Cover, reduce heat, and simmer 1 hour. Uncover and increase heat to medium-high; simmer 20 minutes or until liquid is slightly syrupy. Discard bay leaf. Yield: 10 servings (serving size: about ½ cup).

CALORIES 154 (30% from fat); FAT 5.2g (sat 1.5g, mono 1.9g, poly 0.9g); PROTEIN 23.7g; CARB 1.7g; FIBER 0.3g; CHOL 86mg; IRON 1.5mg; SODIUM 428mg; CALC 17mg

Chicken Char Siu

This dish is typically made with baby back ribs. Skinless, boneless chicken thighs are a tender and tasty substitute with less fat.

  1   tablespoon grated peeled fresh ginger
  2   tablespoons low-sodium soy sauce
  2   tablespoons hoisin sauce
  1   tablespoon honey
  1   garlic clove, minced
1½   pounds skinless, boneless chicken thighs, cut into 18 strips
      Cooking spray

1. Combine first 6 ingredients; marinate in refrigerator 2 hours.
2. Preheat broiler.
3. Thread 1 chicken strip onto each of 18 (6-inch) skewers, reserving marinade. Place skewers on a broiler pan coated with cooking spray; broil 6 minutes. Turn skewers over; baste with reserved marinade. Broil 6 minutes or until done. Yield: 9 servings (serving size: 2 skewers).

CALORIES 108 (26% from fat); FAT 3.1g (sat 0.8g, mono 0.9g, poly 0.8g); PROTEIN 15.2g; CARB 4.1g; FIBER 0.1g; CHOL 63mg; IRON 0.9mg; SODIUM 241mg; CALC 10mg

Luau Lingo

This feast, originally called *aha'aina* or *pa'ina*, is a Hawaiian tradition to honor accomplishments. Today, Hawaiians throw luaus to celebrate weddings, graduations, and other big events—and to welcome visitors to the islands. There is dancing, singing, and food. The featured food at a luau is a whole pig (*puaa*) cooked in an underground oven (*imu*) or stone-lined pit. The pig is covered in banana, *ti*, or taro leaves, and buried for hours to roast. In Hawaiian, the taro leaves are called *lu'au*, giving the feast its current name. Oven Kalua Pork (recipe at left), Lomi Lomi Salmon (recipe on page 53), Poi (recipe on page 54), Chicken Char Siu (recipe above), and Chicken and Pork Adobo (recipe at left) are *Cooking Light*'s versions of traditional fare served at luaus.

Warm Asparagus Salad

Although hothouse-grown bundles are available year-round, spring is the natural season for asparagus.

Aficionados eagerly anticipate the year's first tender, bright-green stalks. Our Warm Asparagus Salad features fresh stalks drizzled with a delicate vinaigrette of extravirgin olive oil, fresh lemon juice, and grated lemon rind. The salad is finished with a garnish of twice-baked breadcrumbs tossed in browned butter that adds crispness and a pleasant nuttiness that complements the asparagus.

QUICK & EASY
Warm Asparagus Salad
(pictured on facing page)

2   ounces day-old French bread or other firm white bread, sliced
1   garlic clove, peeled and halved
1   tablespoon unsalted butter
1   tablespoon white wine vinegar
2   teaspoons extravirgin olive oil
1   teaspoon grated lemon rind
2   teaspoons fresh lemon juice
1   shallot, peeled and minced
¼   teaspoon salt
¼   teaspoon freshly ground black pepper
1   cup water
1½ pounds asparagus
1   teaspoon grated lemon rind (optional)

1. Preheat oven to 375°.
2. Place bread in a single layer on a baking sheet. Bake at 375° for 10 minutes or until toasted. Rub cut sides of garlic over one side of each bread slice. Place bread slices in a food processor; pulse 10 times or until bread is coarsely ground. Arrange breadcrumbs in a single layer on a baking sheet; bake at 375° for 5 minutes or until golden brown. Transfer breadcrumbs to a bowl.

3. Melt butter in a small saucepan over medium-high heat. Cook 1 to 2 minutes or until butter is lightly browned, shaking pan occasionally; remove from heat. Drizzle butter over toasted breadcrumbs; toss well to coat.
4. Combine vinegar and next 4 ingredients; stir well with a whisk. Stir in salt and pepper.
5. Bring water to a boil in a large skillet. Snap off tough ends of asparagus; add asparagus to pan. Cook 5 minutes or until tender, stirring constantly. Place asparagus on a serving platter. Drizzle with vinaigrette; top with breadcrumb mixture. Garnish with 1 teaspoon grated lemon rind, if desired. Serve immediately. Yield: 6 servings.

CALORIES 94 (36% from fat); FAT 3.8g (sat 1.3g, mono 2g, poly 0.4g); PROTEIN 4.1g; CARB 13.2g; FIBER 0.4g; CHOL 5mg; IRON 3mg; SODIUM 172mg; CALC 37mg

Back on the Table

A North Carolina reader's recipe for beef Stroganoff returns to the family fold.

Greg and Sue Weekes, of Cary, North Carolina, changed their attitudes about health and food when Greg learned his cholesterol was above the recommended range. Sue made a valiant effort to lighten their favorite meal—beef Stroganoff—by using less beef and substituting margarine for butter, but when the results didn't meet her expectations, she called on *Cooking Light* to help. Here's our revision.

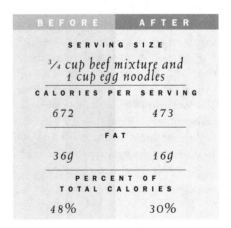

	BEFORE	AFTER
SERVING SIZE		
	¾ cup beef mixture and 1 cup egg noodles	
CALORIES PER SERVING		
	672	473
FAT		
	36g	16g
PERCENT OF TOTAL CALORIES		
	48%	30%

Beef Stroganoff

This classic Russian dish is easy to make; use frozen chopped onions and presliced mushrooms to speed preparation. To maintain a creamy consistency, be careful not to bring the sauce to a boil once you stir in the sour cream mixture. Serve with rice if you need a substitute for egg noodles.

1   (8-ounce) carton reduced-fat sour cream
3   tablespoons no-salt-added tomato paste
1   teaspoon Worcestershire sauce
½   cup all-purpose flour
1   teaspoon salt
⅛   teaspoon freshly ground black pepper
2   pounds boneless sirloin steak, cut into (2-inch) strips
1   tablespoon butter
½   cup chopped onion
1   (14-ounce) can less-sodium beef broth
2   cups sliced mushrooms
Chopped fresh parsley (optional)
8   cups cooked medium egg noodles (about 7 cups uncooked pasta)

1. Combine first 3 ingredients in a bowl. Set aside.
2. Lightly spoon flour into a dry measuring cup; level with a knife. Combine flour, salt, and pepper in a large zip-top plastic bag. Add beef; seal and shake to coat beef.
3. Melt butter in a large nonstick skillet over medium-high heat. Add onion; sauté 2 minutes or until tender. Add beef and flour mixture; sauté 3 minutes or until beef is browned. Gradually add broth, scraping pan to loosen browned bits. Add mushrooms; cover and cook 5 minutes or until mushrooms are tender. Reduce heat to low; gradually stir in sour cream mixture. Cook, uncovered, 1 minute or until heated (do not boil). Stir in parsley, if desired. Serve over egg noodles. Yield: 8 servings (serving size: ¾ cup beef mixture and 1 cup noodles).

CALORIES 473 (30% from fat); FAT 16g (sat 7g, mono 4.3g, poly 1.1g); PROTEIN 30.2g; CARB 50.6g; FIBER 2.6g; CHOL 129mg; IRON 5.7mg; SODIUM 417mg; CALC 81mg

Yellow Pepper Soup with Wild Mushroom Croutons, page 84

Warm Asparagus Salad, page 56

Strawberry Shortcake Jelly Roll,
page 77

Spring Risotto, page 75; Salmon with Fresh Sorrel Sauce, page 75; and Fresh Peas with Mint, page 76

Chunky Two-Bean and Beef Chili,
page 62

A Casual Chili Party

Place a pot of chili on the sideboard, surround it with simple make-ahead accompaniments, and this no-fuss buffet practically serves itself.

Chili Party Buffet Menu
serves 6

Garlicky Spinach Dip with Hearts of Palm

Southwestern Chili
or
Chunky Two-Bean and Beef Chili

Peanutty Cabbage-Apple Slaw with Raisins

Savory Two-Cheese Biscotti
or
Sour Cream, Cheddar, and Green Onion Drop Biscuits

Assorted chili toppings: sour cream, chopped green onions, chopped tomato, and shredded cheese

Toffee Blond Brownies

Assorted beers, soft drinks, and red wine

STAFF FAVORITE • MAKE AHEAD
Garlicky Spinach Dip with Hearts of Palm

With a delicate taste similar to an artichoke's, hearts of palm's smooth texture and ivory color add a nice touch to any meal. The edible core of a cabbage palm tree, hearts of palm are mostly found canned. After opening, store them in a nonmetal container filled with fresh water to preserve their flavor. Assemble the dip a day ahead and store, covered, in the refrigerator. Let stand at room temperature for 15 minutes before baking.

CHIPS:
22 (6-inch) corn tortillas, each cut into 8 wedges
Cooking spray
 1 teaspoon salt

DIP:
1¼ cups (5 ounces) shredded part-skim mozzarella cheese
 ½ cup (2 ounces) grated Asiago cheese, divided
 ½ cup fat-free sour cream
 1 tablespoon minced fresh garlic
 1 (14-ounce) can hearts of palm, drained and chopped
 1 (10-ounce) package frozen chopped spinach, thawed, drained, and squeezed dry
 1 (8-ounce) block fat-free cream cheese, softened
 1 (6.5-ounce) tub light garlic-and-herbs spreadable cheese (such as Alouette Light)

1. Preheat oven to 375°.
2. To prepare chips, arrange tortilla wedges in a single layer on baking sheets coated with cooking spray. Lightly coat wedges with cooking spray; sprinkle evenly with salt. Bake at 375° for 15 minutes or until wedges are crisp and lightly browned.
3. Reduce oven temperature to 350°.
4. To prepare dip, combine mozzarella, ¼ cup Asiago, sour cream, and remaining 5 ingredients, stirring until well blended. Spoon spinach mixture into a 1½-quart baking dish coated with cooking spray. Sprinkle with ¼ cup Asiago. Bake at 350° for 40 minutes or until bubbly and lightly browned. Serve warm with chips. Yield: 22 servings (serving size: about ¼ cup dip and 8 chips).

CALORIES 128 (30% from fat); FAT 4.3g (sat 2.4g, mono 0.6g, poly 0.4g); PROTEIN 6.9g; CARB 15.7g; FIBER 2.1g; CHOL 16mg; IRON 1.2mg; SODIUM 384mg; CALC 175mg

MAKE AHEAD • FREEZABLE
Southwestern Chili

Chili-style beef is coarse and makes chunkier chili than regular ground beef. When browning the beef, stir gently to avoid breaking it up into small pieces. Salsa verde, made with tomatillos, and masa harina, used to thicken the chili, will be in the Latin foods section of your supermarket. Mexican beer is a natural to use in and drink with this chili. Green onions, queso fresco, and sour cream are good condiment choices.

Cooking spray
 ¼ teaspoon salt
 ½ pound chili-style ground sirloin
 1 cup chopped onion
 1 cup chopped green onions
 ⅓ cup chopped green bell pepper
 ½ pound Cajun smoked sausage, chopped (such as Conecuh)
 1 tablespoon minced fresh garlic
 1 (12-ounce) bottle beer
 2 teaspoons chili powder
 ½ teaspoon ground chipotle chile pepper
 ¼ teaspoon ground cumin
 ¼ teaspoon ground coriander
 1 (28-ounce) can whole tomatoes, undrained and chopped
 1 (15-ounce) can dark red kidney beans, rinsed and drained
 1 (15-ounce) can yellow hominy, rinsed and drained
 1 (15-ounce) can garbanzo beans, rinsed and drained
 1 (7-ounce) can salsa verde (such as Herdez)
 2 tablespoons masa harina

1. Heat a large Dutch oven over medium-high heat. Coat pan with cooking spray. Add salt and beef to pan; cook 5 minutes or until browned, stirring gently. Remove from pan.
2. Add onion, green onions, bell pepper, and sausage to pan; sauté 5 minutes or until sausage is lightly browned. Add garlic; sauté 1 minute. Add beer, scraping pan to loosen browned bits. Return beef to pan. Stir in chili powder and next
Continued

8 ingredients; bring to a boil. Cover, reduce heat, and simmer 1 hour, stirring occasionally. Stir in masa; cook 30 minutes. Yield: 7 servings (serving size: about 1⅓ cups).

CALORIES 410 (33% from fat); FAT 15.2g (sat 5.2g, mono 6.2g, poly 1.7g); PROTEIN 20.6g; CARB 45g; FIBER 12.3g; CHOL 43mg; IRON 2.7mg; SODIUM 913mg; CALC 88mg

MAKE AHEAD • FREEZABLE
Chunky Two-Bean and Beef Chili

(pictured on page 60)

Garnish with Monterey Jack cheese, chopped onion, chopped cilantro, and chopped tomato.

  1   tablespoon canola oil, divided
      Cooking spray
1½   pounds beef stew meat
  ¾   teaspoon salt
1½   cups chopped onion
  ½   cup chopped green bell pepper
  1   tablespoon minced fresh garlic
  2   teaspoons finely chopped jalapeño pepper
  ⅔   cup Cabernet Sauvignon or dry red wine
  2   tablespoons tomato paste
1½   tablespoons brown sugar
1½   teaspoons ground ancho chile pepper
  1   teaspoon dried oregano
  1   teaspoon ground red pepper
  ½   teaspoon chili powder
  ¼   teaspoon ground cumin
  ¼   teaspoon ground coriander
  ⅛   teaspoon ground cinnamon
  1   (28-ounce) can whole tomatoes, undrained and chopped
  1   (15-ounce) can dark red kidney beans, rinsed and drained
  1   (15-ounce) can hot chili beans

1. Heat 1 teaspoon oil in a large Dutch oven coated with cooking spray over medium-high heat. Sprinkle beef with salt. Place half of beef in pan; sauté 8 minutes or until browned. Remove from pan. Repeat procedure with remaining beef; remove from pan.

2. Add 2 teaspoons oil, onion, and bell pepper to pan, and sauté 3 minutes. Add garlic and jalapeño; sauté 1 minute. Add wine, scraping pan to loosen browned bits. Return beef to pan.

3. Stir in tomato paste and remaining ingredients; bring to a boil. Cover, reduce heat, and simmer 1½ hours or until beef is tender, stirring occasionally. Yield: 6 servings (serving size: about 1⅓ cups).

CALORIES 390 (26% from fat); FAT 11.4g (sat 3.2g, mono 4.8g, poly 1.1g); PROTEIN 31.3g; CARB 37.5g; FIBER 10.1g; CHOL 71mg; IRON 5mg; SODIUM 825mg; CALC 94mg

WINE NOTE: Hearty, spicy dishes like this chili need a wine that's gutsy enough to stand up not just to the chili pepper, chile powder, cumin, and other spices, but also to the beans and beef. A juicy Australian shiraz is a great pick. Its mouth-filling, plush, almost syrupy softness is a great contrast to the beef and beans, and the wine's rich fruitiness cushions all that spice. There are loads of terrific Australian shirazes on the market at all price levels. The affordable Yalumba Shiraz 2003 (South Australia, $10) is priced right for chili.

QUICK & EASY • MAKE AHEAD
Peanutty Cabbage-Apple Slaw with Raisins

A small amount of roasted peanut oil gives this slaw a big hit of flavor with a minimum of fat. Any nut oil will work.

  ⅓   cup white balsamic or cider vinegar
  ¼   cup packed brown sugar
1½   tablespoons roasted peanut oil
  ½   teaspoon salt
  ¼   teaspoon crushed red pepper
  3   cups coarsely chopped Granny Smith apple
  ½   cup golden seedless raisins
  1   (16-ounce) package cabbage-and-carrot coleslaw

1. Combine first 5 ingredients, stirring with a whisk until sugar dissolves.

2. Combine apple, raisins, and coleslaw. Drizzle with vinaigrette; toss well to combine. Chill up to 3 hours. Yield: 8 servings (serving size: about 1 cup).

CALORIES 128 (20% from fat); FAT 2.9g (sat 0.5g, mono 1.2g, poly 0.9g); PROTEIN 1.2g; CARB 26.7g; FIBER 3.1g; CHOL 0mg; IRON 0.8mg; SODIUM 167mg; CALC 40mg

MAKE AHEAD
Savory Two-Cheese Biscotti

Savory biscotti are great for dipping into chili. Make these a couple days ahead, and store in an airtight container.

2¾   cups all-purpose flour
  ¾   cup (3 ounces) shredded extrasharp Cheddar cheese
  ½   cup (2 ounces) grated fresh Parmesan cheese
  2   teaspoons baking powder
  ¾   teaspoon salt
  ¼   teaspoon ground red pepper
  ¼   cup fat-free milk
  2   teaspoons olive oil
  3   large eggs, lightly beaten
      Cooking spray

1. Preheat oven to 350°.

2. Lightly spoon flour into dry measuring cups; level with a knife. Combine flour and next 5 ingredients in a large bowl. Combine milk, oil, and eggs; stir with a whisk. Add milk mixture to flour mixture, stirring until well blended (dough will be dry and crumbly). Turn out onto a lightly floured surface; knead 8 times. Divide dough in half. Shape each portion into an 8-inch-long roll. Place rolls, 6 inches apart, on a baking sheet coated with cooking spray; flatten to 1-inch thickness. Bake at 350° for 30 minutes. Remove from baking sheet; cool 10 minutes on a wire rack.

3. Reduce oven temperature to 325°.

4. Cut each roll diagonally into 12 (⅔-inch) slices. Place slices, cut sides down, on baking sheet. Bake at 325° for 10 minutes. Turn biscotti over; bake an additional 10 minutes (biscotti will be slightly soft in center but will harden as they cool). Remove from baking sheet; cool completely on wire rack. Yield: 2 dozen (serving size: 1 biscotto).

CALORIES 83 (30% from fat); FAT 2.8g (sat 1.5g, mono 0.5g, poly 0.1g); PROTEIN 3.9g; CARB 10.8g; FIBER 0.4g; CHOL 32mg; IRON 0.8mg; SODIUM 160mg; CALC 80mg

---

QUICK & EASY • MAKE AHEAD

Sour Cream, Cheddar, and Green Onion Drop Biscuits

Roll out these biscuits, or drop into 12 muffin tins and bake the same amount of time. These are best the same day they're baked, but you can store them in an airtight container up to two days. To warm them, wrap loosely in aluminum foil, and place in a 300° oven for five to 10 minutes.

   2 cups all-purpose flour
   1 tablespoon sugar
   2 teaspoons baking powder
   1 teaspoon salt
   ¼ teaspoon baking soda
   3 tablespoons chilled butter, cut into small pieces
   ¾ cup (3 ounces) shredded reduced-fat sharp Cheddar cheese
   ¼ cup finely chopped green onions
   1 cup fat-free buttermilk
   ½ cup fat-free sour cream
   Cooking spray

1. Preheat oven to 450°.
2. Lightly spoon flour into dry measuring cups; level with a knife. Combine flour and next 4 ingredients in a large bowl, stirring with a whisk. Cut in butter with a pastry blender or 2 knives until mixture resembles coarse meal. Add cheese and onions; toss well. Add buttermilk and sour cream; stir just until moist.
3. Drop dough by ¼ cupfuls onto a baking sheet coated with cooking spray. Bake at 450° for 15 minutes or until edges are brown. Remove biscuits from pan; cool on wire racks. Yield: 1 dozen (serving size: 1 biscuit).

CALORIES 146 (29% from fat); FAT 4.7g (sat 2.9g, mono 0.8g, poly 0.2g); PROTEIN 5.2g; CARB 20.1g; FIBER 0.7g; CHOL 14mg; IRON 1mg; SODIUM 406mg; CALC 134mg

---

MAKE AHEAD

Toffee Blond Brownies

The toffee bits melt during baking and give the thin, gooey brownies a crunchy topping.

   1 cup packed brown sugar
   ¼ cup butter, melted
   ¼ cup egg substitute
   2 teaspoons vanilla extract
   1 cup all-purpose flour
   ½ teaspoon baking powder
   ⅛ teaspoon salt
   Cooking spray
   ¼ cup toffee baking bits (such as Heath)

1. Preheat oven to 350°.
2. Combine first 4 ingredients in a large bowl; stir with a whisk. Lightly spoon flour into a dry measuring cup; level with a knife. Combine flour, baking powder, and salt. Add flour mixture to sugar mixture; stir just until moist. Spread batter in an 8-inch square baking pan coated with cooking spray. Sprinkle with toffee bits. Bake at 350° for 22 minutes or until a wooden pick inserted in center comes out almost clean. Cool in pan on a wire rack. Yield: 12 servings.
NOTE: Store, covered, up to 3 days.

CALORIES 168 (29% from fat); FAT 5.4g (sat 3.2g, mono 1.1g, poly 0.2g); PROTEIN 1.6g; CARB 28.4g; FIBER 0.3g; CHOL 14mg; IRON 1mg; SODIUM 120mg; CALC 31mg

---

enlightened traveler

Spring Break for Grown-Ups

Welcome the season with a trip to a terrific outdoor destination.

Take a trip to the Hyatt Regency Tamaya Resort and Spa in Santa Ana Pueblo, New Mexico, for spring break—or at least try this appetizer that's a resort favorite. In this recipe, Asian flavors spark locally made goat cheese. For the crispest rolls, be sure to serve immediately after baking.

Goat Cheese Spring Rolls with Asian Pear Salad

SALAD:
   2 cups sliced Asian pear or ripe pear
   ¼ cup chopped red bell pepper
   ¼ cup chopped red onion
   2 tablespoons rice vinegar
1½ tablespoons chopped fresh cilantro
   1 tablespoon maple syrup

SPRING ROLLS:
   1 tablespoon sesame oil
1½ cups matchstick-cut carrots
1½ cups vertically sliced red onion
1½ cups chopped green onions
1½ cups thinly sliced shiitake mushroom caps
1½ cups red bell pepper, cut into ¼-inch strips
   1 tablespoon low-sodium soy sauce
   1 tablespoon sweet red chile sauce
   ¼ cup (2 ounces) goat cheese, crumbled
   8 egg roll wrappers
   Cooking spray

1. To prepare salad, combine first 6 ingredients.
2. Preheat oven to 425°.
3. To prepare spring rolls, heat oil in a large nonstick skillet over medium-high heat. Add carrots and next 4 ingredients; sauté 3 minutes or until slightly tender. Remove from heat; stir in soy sauce and chile sauce. Cool 5 minutes. Stir in cheese.
4. Working with 1 egg roll wrapper at a time (cover remaining wrappers to prevent drying), spoon about ⅓ cup vegetable mixture into center of each wrapper. Fold lower right corner over vegetable mixture; fold lower left and top right corners over vegetable mixture. Moisten top left corner with water; roll up jelly-roll fashion. Coat spring rolls with cooking spray; place rolls, seam sides down, on a baking sheet. Bake at 425° for 18 minutes or until golden brown, turning after 9 minutes. Cut rolls crosswise at an angle; serve immediately with salad. Yield: 8 servings (serving size: 2 spring roll halves and ¼ cup salad).

CALORIES 171 (23% from fat); FAT 4.3g (sat 1.8g, mono 0.5g, poly 0.1g); PROTEIN 5.7g; CARB 30.3g; FIBER 3g; CHOL 6mg; IRON 1.5mg; SODIUM 267mg; CALC 53mg

Let's Go Fly a Kite

When sunny weather and warm days arrive, head outdoors for good food and some fun.

MAKE AHEAD

Mini Meatballs with Creamy Dill Dip

Prepare the meatballs and dip up to two days ahead, and chill separately until ready to serve. Dunk the meatballs into the creamy dip with toothpicks.

MEATBALLS:

1 cup finely chopped onion
¼ cup dry breadcrumbs
½ teaspoon kosher salt
½ teaspoon dill seeds
⅛ teaspoon freshly ground black pepper
1 pound ground round
1 large egg white, lightly beaten
Cooking spray

DIP:

⅔ cup fat-free sour cream
1 tablespoon chopped fresh dill
2 teaspoons minced garlic
¼ teaspoon kosher salt

1. To prepare meatballs, combine first 7 ingredients in a bowl; shape mixture into 32 (1-inch) meatballs. Heat a large nonstick skillet over medium-high heat. Coat pan with cooking spray. Add half of meatballs to pan; cook 8 minutes or until done, browning on all sides. Remove from pan; drain well on paper towels. Repeat procedure with remaining meatballs. Cover and chill.

2. To prepare dip, combine sour cream and remaining 3 ingredients; stir with a whisk. Cover and chill. Serve meatballs with dip. Yield: 8 servings (serving size: 4 meatballs and about 1 tablespoon dip).

CALORIES 76 (43% from fat); FAT 3.6g (sat 1.4g, mono 1.5g, poly 0.2g); PROTEIN 6.7g; CARB 3.7g; FIBER 0.3g; CHOL 20mg; IRON 0.6mg; SODIUM 136mg; CALC 29mg

MAKE AHEAD

Honey-Molasses Chicken Drumsticks

The zesty chicken and sauce will keep up to two days in the refrigerator.

2 tablespoons water
2 tablespoons honey
2 tablespoons balsamic vinegar
1 tablespoon brown sugar
1 tablespoon Dijon mustard
1 tablespoon molasses
1 teaspoon minced garlic
1 teaspoon olive oil
6 chicken drumsticks, skinned
½ teaspoon kosher salt
¼ teaspoon freshly ground black pepper

1. Combine first 7 ingredients, stirring with a whisk.

2. Heat oil in a large nonstick skillet over medium-high heat. Sprinkle chicken with salt and pepper. Add chicken to pan, browning on all sides. Add honey mixture to pan, turning chicken to coat. Reduce heat to medium-low. Cover and cook 15 minutes or until chicken is done, turning chicken every 5 minutes. Uncover and cook 1 minute or until mixture is thick and a mahogany color, and chicken is well coated. Remove from heat; cool 15 minutes. Cover and chill. Yield: 6 servings (serving size: 1 drumstick).

CALORIES 180 (36% from fat); FAT 7.2g (sat 1.8g, mono 3g, poly 1.6g); PROTEIN 16.7g; CARB 11.9g; FIBER 0.1g; CHOL 53mg; IRON 1.3mg; SODIUM 291mg; CALC 24mg

MAKE AHEAD

Brick Chicken Baguette Sandwiches

Weighing down the sandwich with a brick or other heavy object presses the filling together so it's easier to eat. Do this in the refrigerator or at the bottom of the cooler.

1 tablespoon finely chopped shallots
1 tablespoon fresh lemon juice
2 teaspoons freshly ground black pepper
2 teaspoons extravirgin olive oil
1 teaspoon chopped fresh thyme
¾ pound skinless, boneless chicken breast
¼ cup fat-free mayonnaise
1 teaspoon chopped fresh rosemary
2 garlic cloves, minced
¼ teaspoon kosher salt
Cooking spray
1 red bell pepper, halved lengthwise and seeded
2 (½-inch-thick) slices red onion
1 (16-ounce) loaf French bread, cut in half horizontally
4 (1-ounce) slices provolone cheese
1 cup sliced hearts of palm
1 cup arugula leaves

1. Combine first 5 ingredients in a large zip-top plastic bag. Add chicken to bag; seal. Marinate in refrigerator 3 hours, turning occasionally.

2. Prepare grill to medium-high heat.

3. Combine mayonnaise, rosemary, and garlic; set aside.

4. Remove chicken from bag, discarding marinade. Sprinkle chicken with salt. Place chicken on grill rack coated with cooking spray; grill 5 minutes on each side or until done. Remove chicken from grill. Place bell pepper and onion on grill rack coated with cooking spray; grill 6 minutes on each side or until slightly charred. Cut chicken diagonally across grain into thin slices. Separate onion into rings; cut bell pepper into thin strips.

5. Spread mayonnaise mixture evenly over cut sides of bread. Arrange cheese evenly over bottom half of bread. Arrange onion, bell pepper, and hearts of palm evenly over cheese; top with chicken and arugula. Place top half of bread over arugula. Cut filled baguette in half. Wrap each half tightly in plastic wrap. Place filled baguette halves in refrigerator; top with a cast-iron skillet or other heavy object. Let chill at least 2 hours. Cut each filled baguette half into 3 equal portions. Yield: 6 servings (serving size: 1 sandwich).

CALORIES 382 (24% from fat); FAT 10.1g (sat 4.2g, mono 3.6g, poly 1.1g); PROTEIN 25.9g; CARB 46.4g; FIBER 4.1g; CHOL 47mg; IRON 3.7mg; SODIUM 927mg; CALC 239mg

Roast Beef and Blue Cheese Wraps

If blue cheese seems too strongly flavored, try Havarti or Muenster cheese. Wrap these sandwiches tightly in plastic wrap, and store in the refrigerator up to one day.

- ¾ cup (3 ounces) crumbled blue cheese
- 2 tablespoons prepared horseradish
- 2 tablespoons low-fat mayonnaise
- ½ teaspoon freshly ground black pepper, divided
- 2 tablespoons sherry vinegar
- 1 tablespoon honey
- 1 garlic clove, minced
- 2 cups thinly sliced red cabbage
- ¼ cup thinly sliced celery
- ¼ cup thinly sliced fresh basil
- 3 (10-inch) flour tortillas
- ½ pound thinly sliced deli roast beef

1. Combine blue cheese, horseradish, mayonnaise, and ¼ teaspoon pepper. Combine 1 tablespoon cheese mixture, vinegar, honey, and garlic in a medium bowl. Add ¼ teaspoon pepper, cabbage, celery, and basil.

2. Warm tortillas according to package directions. Spread remaining cheese mixture evenly over tortillas. Divide beef and cabbage mixture evenly among tortillas; roll up. Cut each rolled tortilla in half crosswise. Yield: 6 servings (serving size: 1 wrap half).

CALORIES 241 (29% from fat); FAT 7.7g (sat 3.6g, mono 2.5g, poly 0.6g); PROTEIN 13.5g; CARB 29.5g; FIBER 2.1g; CHOL 24mg; IRON 2.1mg; SODIUM 725mg; CALC 143mg

Farfalle with Zucchini and Prosciutto

This light and brightly flavored pasta salad will keep up to two days in the refrigerator. The alcohol in the wine cooks away, so it's fine for kids to enjoy this dish, or you can use broth instead. Add cubed fresh mozzarella to any leftovers for a lunch to take to work.

- 1 tablespoon butter
- ¼ cup chopped onion
- 5 cups matchstick-cut zucchini (about 1 pound)
- ¼ cup dry white wine
- ¼ cup thinly sliced green onions
- ¼ cup reduced-fat sour cream
- 2 tablespoons extravirgin olive oil
- 1 teaspoon kosher salt
- ½ teaspoon grated lemon rind
- 1 teaspoon fresh lemon juice
- ½ teaspoon freshly ground black pepper
- 2 ounces prosciutto, cut into thin strips (about 1 cup)
- 7 cups cooked farfalle (about 1 pound uncooked bow tie pasta)

1. Melt butter in a large nonstick skillet over medium-high heat. Add onion; sauté 2 minutes or until brown. Add zucchini; sauté 2 minutes. Remove zucchini mixture from pan. Add wine to pan; cook until reduced to 1 tablespoon (about 1 minute), scraping pan to loosen browned bits. Combine wine reduction, green onions, and next 7 ingredients in a large bowl. Add zucchini and pasta; toss to coat. Yield: 10 servings (serving size: about 1 cup).

CALORIES 240 (24% from fat); FAT 6.3g (sat 2.1g, mono 2.5g, poly 0.4g); PROTEIN 9.2g; CARB 36.5g; FIBER 2.1g; CHOL 13mg; IRON 1.8mg; SODIUM 367mg; CALC 24mg

Sweet and Sour Slaw

This tangy, sweet, and crunchy slaw derives pleasant heat from the serrano chile.

- ½ cup white wine vinegar
- ⅓ cup sugar
- ¼ cup fresh orange juice
- 4 cups very thinly sliced green cabbage
- 4 cups very thinly sliced red cabbage
- ½ cup finely chopped red onion
- ½ teaspoon kosher salt
- 1 serrano chile, seeded and finely chopped

1. Combine first 3 ingredients in a small saucepan; cook over low heat 3 minutes or until sugar dissolves, stirring with a whisk. Chill.

2. Combine vinegar mixture, cabbages, onion, salt, and chile. Cover and chill. Toss gently before serving. Yield: 6 servings (serving size: about 1 cup).

CALORIES 85 (2% from fat); FAT 0.2g (sat 0g, mono 0g, poly 0.1g); PROTEIN 1.9g; CARB 20.9g; FIBER 2.6g; CHOL 0mg; IRON 1mg; SODIUM 186mg; CALC 59mg

MAKE AHEAD

Olive and Sun-Dried Tomato Tapenade Potatoes

These zesty potatoes are a great alternative to traditional potato salad. They're sure to be a hit at picnics or any potluck gathering. Vinegar and salt are added to the potatoes while they're slightly warm to heighten the flavor. The cook time for the potatoes will vary according to size, so it might take as long as 30 minutes for them to become tender. Start checking after 15 minutes to avoid overcooking.

    2 pounds small red potatoes
    2 tablespoons white wine vinegar
    ½ teaspoon kosher salt, divided
    ¼ cup oil-packed sun-dried tomato
       halves, drained and minced
    1 cup cherry tomatoes, halved
    ¼ cup pitted kalamata olives, minced
    2 tablespoons fresh basil, chopped
    1 tablespoon extravirgin olive oil
  1½ teaspoons minced garlic
    ¼ teaspoon freshly ground black
       pepper

1. Place potatoes in a large saucepan; cover with water. Bring to a boil. Reduce heat, and simmer 15 minutes or until tender; drain. Cool slightly; cut into 1½-inch chunks. Place in a large bowl; toss with vinegar and ¼ teaspoon salt. Cool completely.
2. Combine tomatoes, olives, basil, oil, and garlic. Add olive mixture, pepper, and ¼ teaspoon salt to potatoes; toss gently to combine. Yield: 6 servings (serving size: 1 cup).

CALORIES 140 (24% from fat); FAT 3.7g (sat 0.5g, mono 2.5g, poly 0.4g); PROTEIN 4g; CARB 22.3g; FIBER 4.4g; CHOL 0mg; IRON 1.4mg; SODIUM 225mg; CALC 19mg

MAKE AHEAD

Raspberry Cheesecake Bars

Line your pan with foil to easily remove and cut these bars. They're better if made the day before you serve them.

  1½ cups all-purpose flour
    ¾ teaspoon salt
  3½ tablespoons butter, melted
    1 cup packed brown sugar
  1½ teaspoons vanilla extract, divided
    3 large eggs, lightly beaten
    ½ cup granulated sugar
    ½ cup light sour cream
    1 teaspoon grated lemon rind
    1 tablespoon fresh lemon juice
    1 (8-ounce) package ⅓-less-fat
       cream cheese
  Cooking spray
  1½ cups fresh raspberries

1. Preheat oven to 350°.
2. Lightly spoon flour into dry measuring cups; level with a knife. Combine flour and salt, stirring with a whisk.
3. Combine butter, brown sugar, 1 teaspoon vanilla, and eggs in a medium bowl, stirring with a whisk until smooth. Add flour mixture to butter mixture; stir just until moist.
4. Place ½ teaspoon vanilla, granulated sugar, and next 4 ingredients in a large bowl; beat with a mixer at high speed until fluffy.
5. Line a 13 x 9-inch baking pan with foil that extends 1 inch beyond sides; coat foil with cooking spray. Spread half of batter into pan. Pour cream cheese mixture over batter in pan, and spread evenly over batter. Sprinkle with raspberries. Drop remaining batter by tablespoonfuls over raspberries. Swirl batter, cream cheese mixture, and raspberries together with a knife.
6. Bake at 350° for 35 minutes or until a wooden pick inserted in center comes out clean. Cool completely on a wire rack. Remove from pan by lifting foil. Remove foil; cut into 30 bar cookies. Yield: 30 servings (serving size: 1 cookie).

CALORIES 111 (32% from fat); FAT 4g (sat 2.3g, mono 1.1g, poly 0.2g); PROTEIN 2.3g; CARB 16.9g; FIBER 0.6g; CHOL 32mg; IRON 0.6mg; SODIUM 113mg; CALC 23mg

MAKE AHEAD

Green Bean Salad with Bacon

Mustard and honey emulsify and flavor a warm bacon vinaigrette that coats the beans thoroughly, even after the salad has chilled.

    2 pounds green beans, trimmed
    3 bacon slices
    2 tablespoons finely chopped
       shallots
    ¼ cup red wine vinegar
    1 tablespoon honey
    1 tablespoon Dijon mustard
    ½ teaspoon freshly ground black
       pepper
    ¼ teaspoon kosher salt

1. Cook beans in boiling water 5 minutes. Drain and plunge beans into ice water; drain. Place beans in a large bowl.
2. Cook bacon in a large nonstick skillet over medium heat until crisp. Remove bacon from pan, reserving 1 teaspoon drippings in pan. Crumble bacon; set aside. Add shallots to drippings in pan; cook 1½ minutes, stirring frequently. Add vinegar; cook 30 seconds, scraping pan to loosen browned bits. Drizzle mixture over beans.
3. Combine honey, mustard, pepper, and salt, stirring with a whisk. Pour over bean mixture; toss to coat. Sprinkle with crumbled bacon. Yield: 6 servings (serving size: about 1⅔ cups).

CALORIES 86 (24% from fat); FAT 2.3g (sat 0.7g, mono 0.7g, poly 0.2g); PROTEIN 3.3g; CARB 13.1g; FIBER 5.6g; CHOL 4mg; IRON 1mg; SODIUM 217mg; CALC 80mg

Easy Entertaining for Friends

Mix and match menus for casual good times.

The ultimate dinner party is one where your guests are nourished, but you have a chance to be nourished, too. Keeping it simple and small is the best way to ensure this happens.

Casual Get-Together Menu 1
serves 6

Beet and Leek Salad with Peanut Dressing

Thai Tomato Soup

Sweet Potato and Cashew Korma over Coconut Rice

Chocolate-Walnut-Cranberry Cake

WINE NOTE: For this menu inspired by the bold flavors of the southern hemisphere, try three sensational southern hemisphere wines. First, with the Thai Tomato Soup, try serving an Australian riesling. Very reasonably priced, Australian rieslings are bone dry, pure, and fresh with a crispness that balances Thai dishes perfectly. (Three top choices: Wynns, Grosset Polish Hill, and Peter Lehman.) The Sweet Potato and Cashew Korma has a terrific potential wine partner: an Australian sémillon/chardonnay blend. Australian sémillon, with flavors that hint of cashews and sweet potatoes, is just the ticket with chardonnay. Try Penfolds "Koonunga Hill" Sémillon Chardonnay 2002, about $11.

STAFF FAVORITE • MAKE AHEAD
Beet and Leek Salad with Peanut Dressing

The beets, leeks, and dressing can all be prepared and stored separately in the refrigerator up to two days in advance; just let them all come close to room temperature before serving. The dressing gets thicker as it stands, so add more water to thin it if necessary. To avoid staining your hands when rubbing the skins off the beets, wear gloves or rub the beets under running water.

    2   beets (about ¾ pound)
    Cooking spray
    4   cups thinly sliced leek (about
        1 pound)
    ½   teaspoon olive oil
    ½   teaspoon salt, divided
    ¼   cup water
    1   tablespoon fresh lime juice
    1   tablespoon creamy peanut butter
    1½ teaspoons minced peeled fresh
        ginger
    2   cups alfalfa sprouts

1. Preheat oven to 425°.
2. Leave root and 1 inch of stem on beets; scrub with a brush. Place beets on a small baking sheet coated with cooking spray. Bake at 425° for 1 hour or until tender when pierced with a fork. Cool. Trim off beet roots and stem; rub off skins. Cut each beet in half lengthwise; slice each beet half crosswise into ¼-inch-thick slices.
3. Combine leek, oil, and ¼ teaspoon salt on a baking sheet coated with cooking spray; toss well to coat. Bake at 425° for 15 minutes or until leek is tender and just beginning to brown; stir after 8 minutes.
4. Combine water, lime juice, peanut butter, ginger, and ¼ teaspoon salt, stirring well with a whisk until smooth.
5. Arrange ⅓ cup sprouts on each of 6 salad plates; divide beets and leek evenly among servings. Drizzle about 2 teaspoons dressing over each serving. Yield: 6 servings.

CALORIES 84 (23% from fat); FAT 2.1g (sat 0.4g, mono 1g, poly 0.5g); PROTEIN 2.9g; CARB 15.1g; FIBER 3.1g; CHOL 0mg; IRON 1.9mg; SODIUM 266mg; CALC 49mg

---

QUICK & EASY • MAKE AHEAD
Thai Tomato Soup

This soup goes well with each of our suggested menus, but it's also great with grilled cheese sandwiches. It takes less than 30 minutes to prepare and is made with pantry ingredients so you can enjoy it on the spur of the moment. Cook the soup up to two days before serving, and refrigerate it in an airtight container. Before serving, reheat gently over medium heat.

    1½ teaspoons canola oil
    1   cup chopped onion
    1½ tablespoons minced peeled fresh
        ginger
    2   garlic cloves, minced
    1½ cups water
    1   (28-ounce) can diced tomatoes,
        undrained
    2   teaspoons sugar
    1   teaspoon chile paste with
        garlic
    ¼   teaspoon salt
    ⅓   cup light coconut milk
    6   lime wedges

1. Heat oil in a large saucepan over medium-high heat. Add onion; sauté 5 minutes or until tender. Add ginger and garlic; sauté 2 minutes. Add water and tomatoes. Bring to a boil; reduce heat, and simmer 5 minutes. Stir in sugar, chile paste, and salt. Remove from heat; let stand 5 minutes.
2. Place half of tomato mixture in a blender; process until smooth. Pour puréed tomato mixture into a large bowl. Repeat procedure with remaining tomato mixture. Return puréed mixture to pan. Stir in coconut milk; cook over medium heat 2 minutes or until thoroughly heated. Serve with lime wedges. Yield: 6 servings (serving size: about ¾ cup).

CALORIES 64 (27% from fat); FAT 1.9g (sat 0.5g, mono 0.7g, poly 0.4g); PROTEIN 1.4g; CARB 11.6g; FIBER 2.5g; CHOL 0mg; IRON 0.5mg; SODIUM 284mg; CALC 29mg

Sweet Potato and Cashew Korma over Coconut Rice

Butternut squash can be used in place of sweet potatoes. Prepare and refrigerate the korma up to two days ahead, the rice up to one day ahead. Before serving, reheat both, separately, in the microwave.

RICE:

2¾ cups plus 2 tablespoons water
1 cup coconut milk
¾ teaspoon salt
1½ cups uncooked basmati rice

KORMA:

Cooking spray
1½ cups chopped onion
1 tablespoon minced peeled fresh ginger
2 teaspoons ground coriander
2 teaspoons garam masala
2 garlic cloves, minced
4 cups chopped peeled sweet potato
1 cup water
⅔ cup chopped plum tomato
¾ teaspoon salt
3 tablespoons finely chopped cilantro
1 teaspoon chile paste with garlic
1 (14-ounce) package reduced-fat water-packed firm tofu, drained and cut into ½-inch cubes
3 tablespoons plain fat-free yogurt
2 tablespoons finely chopped dry-roasted cashews

1. To prepare rice, bring first 3 ingredients to a boil in a medium saucepan. Stir in rice, and cook, uncovered, 5 minutes. Cover, reduce heat, and simmer 15 minutes or until liquid is absorbed. Remove from heat; let stand 10 minutes. Fluff with a fork before serving.
2. To prepare korma, while rice cooks, heat a Dutch oven over medium heat. Coat pan with cooking spray. Add onion; cook 7 minutes or until tender, stirring frequently. Add ginger, coriander, garam masala, and garlic; cook 2 minutes, stirring frequently. Add sweet potato, 1 cup water, tomato, and ¾ teaspoon salt. Bring to a boil; cover, reduce heat, and simmer 10 minutes or until

sweet potato is tender. Stir in cilantro, chile paste, and tofu. Serve korma over rice, and top with yogurt and cashews. Yield: 6 servings (serving size: 1 cup rice, 1 cup korma, 1½ teaspoons yogurt, and 1 teaspoon cashews).

CALORIES 426 (27% from fat); FAT 13g (sat 7.5g, mono 1.8g, poly 2.1g); PROTEIN 14.4g; CARB 64.5g; FIBER 6.8g; CHOL 0mg; IRON 5.3mg; SODIUM 634mg; CALC 114mg

Chocolate-Walnut-Cranberry Cake

MAKE-AHEAD TIP: Bake and completely cool the cake. Wrap in plastic wrap, and refrigerate up to two days, or wrap in plastic wrap and foil, and freeze up to one month. Bring to room temperature before serving.

1⅔ cups all-purpose flour
1½ cups sugar
¾ cup Dutch process cocoa
1½ teaspoons baking powder
½ teaspoon baking soda
½ teaspoon salt
1 cup applesauce
½ cup plain soy milk
¼ cup canola oil
1 cup sweetened dried cranberries
½ cup chopped walnuts, toasted
Cooking spray
1 tablespoon powdered sugar

1. Preheat oven to 350°.
2. Lightly spoon flour into dry measuring cups; level with a knife. Combine flour and next 5 ingredients in a large bowl, stirring with a whisk. Combine applesauce, milk, and oil; add to flour mixture, stirring just until moist. Stir in cranberries and walnuts. Spread into a 10-inch springform pan coated with cooking spray (batter will be thick).
3. Bake at 350° for 45 minutes or until edges begin to pull away from sides of pan. Cool on a wire rack. Sprinkle with powdered sugar. Yield: 12 servings (serving size: 1 slice).

CALORIES 295 (27% from fat); FAT 9g (sat 1.1g, mono 3.4g, poly 3.9g); PROTEIN 3.9g; CARB 53.7g; FIBER 3.4g; CHOL 0mg; IRON 2.2mg; SODIUM 214mg; CALC 48mg

---

Casual Get-Together Menu 2
serves 6

Romaine Salad with Creamy Dressing

Thai Tomato Soup

Spaghetti Squash with Edamame-Cilantro Pesto

Sweet Potato Pie

Romaine Salad with Creamy Dressing

Firm tofu is a creative stand-in for bread cubes when it comes to topping this salad. For the best results, use silken tofu for a creamy dressing and regular water-packed tofu for the "croutons." Prepare and chill the dressing up to three days ahead.

DRESSING:

¾ cup reduced-fat silken firm tofu
2 tablespoons fresh lemon juice
1 teaspoon low-sodium soy sauce
1 teaspoon Dijon mustard
¼ teaspoon salt
¼ teaspoon freshly ground black pepper
1 garlic clove, minced
2 tablespoons grated fresh Parmesan cheese

CROUTONS:

8 ounces reduced-fat water-packed firm tofu, drained and cut into ½-inch cubes
¼ teaspoon salt
¼ teaspoon freshly ground black pepper
Cooking spray

SALAD:

12 cups chopped romaine lettuce
2 cups halved cherry tomatoes
2 tablespoons grated fresh Parmesan cheese

1. To prepare dressing, place first 7 ingredients in a food processor; process until smooth. Spoon into a small bowl; stir in 2 tablespoons cheese.
2. To prepare croutons, press tofu

between paper towels until barely moist. Sprinkle tofu with ¼ teaspoon salt and ¼ teaspoon pepper. Heat a large non-stick skillet over medium-high heat. Coat pan with cooking spray. Add tofu; cook 10 minutes, browning on all sides.
3. To prepare salad, combine lettuce, tomatoes, croutons, and dressing in a large bowl; toss gently to coat. Sprinkle with 2 tablespoons cheese. Yield: 6 servings (serving size: about 2 cups).

CALORIES 93 (33% from fat); FAT 3.4g (sat 0.7g, mono 0.8g, poly 1.4g); PROTEIN 8.6g; CARB 8.9g; FIBER 3.4g; CHOL 3mg; IRON 2.2mg; SODIUM 330mg; CALC 103mg

---

"Pasta" Night Menu
serves 6

Delicate strands of spaghetti squash stand in for pasta in this easy meatless menu. Miniature panini are a welcome accompaniment and offer a nice change from garlic bread or cheese toast.

Spaghetti Squash with Edamame-Cilantro Pesto

Baguette panini*

Strawberry sorbet with vanilla wafer cookies

*Top each of 6 diagonally cut baguette slices with 2 tablespoons shredded provolone cheese, 2 thin slices plum tomato, and 3 arugula leaves. Top each with 1 diagonally cut baguette slice. Heat a large nonstick skillet over medium heat. Add panini to pan. Place a cast-iron or heavy skillet on top of panini; press gently to flatten. Cook 3 minutes on each side or until bread is lightly toasted (leave cast-iron skillet on panini while they cook).

Spaghetti Squash with Edamame-Cilantro Pesto

Prepare and chill the pesto up to two days ahead, and bring to room temperature before serving. Bake and chill the squash halves a day or two before; it's actually easier to remove the flesh when it's cold. Reheat the cold squash in the microwave. The unique pesto would also be good on a pizza with sun-dried tomatoes.

2 (2½-pound) spaghetti squash
Cooking spray
½ teaspoon salt, divided
1¼ cups chopped fresh cilantro
1 cup vegetable broth
1 tablespoon extravirgin olive oil
¼ teaspoon freshly ground black pepper
2 garlic cloves, minced
1 pound frozen shelled edamame (green soybeans), thawed
¼ cup (1 ounce) grated fresh Parmesan cheese

1. Preheat oven to 350°.
2. Cut each squash in half lengthwise; discard seeds. Place squash halves, cut sides down, on a baking sheet coated with cooking spray. Bake at 350° for 1 hour or until tender. Cool slightly. Scrape inside of squash with a fork to remove spaghettilike strands to measure about 8 cups. Place in a large bowl. Sprinkle with ¼ teaspoon salt; toss gently to combine. Cover squash, and keep warm.
3. Place ¼ teaspoon salt, cilantro, and next 5 ingredients in a food processor; pulse until coarsely chopped. Serve edamame pesto over squash; sprinkle with cheese. Yield: 6 servings (serving size: 1½ cups squash, ½ cup edamame pesto, and 2 teaspoons cheese).

CALORIES 233 (29% from fat); FAT 7.6g (sat 1.3g, mono 2.8g, poly 2.4g); PROTEIN 12.5g; CARB 31.3g; FIBER 8.8g; CHOL 3mg; IRON 3mg; SODIUM 533mg; CALC 182mg

---

Sweet Potato Pie

Bake pie up to two days ahead. Cool; cover with plastic wrap and chill. Reheat it for about 15 minutes at 325° to bring back its texture.

PASTRY:
1¼ cups all-purpose flour
2 tablespoons granulated sugar
½ teaspoon salt
5 tablespoons chilled butter, cut into small pieces
4 to 5 tablespoons ice water
Cooking spray

FILLING:
1 cup mashed cooked sweet potato
1 cup evaporated fat-free milk
¾ cup packed light brown sugar
2 tablespoons all-purpose flour
1 large egg white
½ cup 1% low-fat milk
1 tablespoon butter, melted
1 teaspoon vanilla extract
½ teaspoon ground cinnamon
¼ teaspoon ground nutmeg
Dash of salt

1. To prepare pastry, lightly spoon 1¼ cups flour into dry measuring cups; level with a knife. Place 1¼ cups flour, granulated sugar, and ½ teaspoon salt in a food processor. Process 10 seconds. Add butter; pulse 4 times or until mixture resembles coarse meal. Place flour mixture in a bowl. Sprinkle surface with ice water, 1 tablespoon at a time; toss with a fork until moist. Place pastry on a lightly floured surface; knead lightly 3 or 4 times. Gently press mixture into a 4-inch circle on plastic wrap; cover. Chill 30 minutes.
2. Slightly overlap 2 sheets of plastic wrap on a slightly damp surface. Unwrap and place dough on plastic wrap. Cover with 2 additional sheets of overlapping plastic wrap. Roll still covered, into an 11-inch circle. Place in freezer 5 minutes or until plastic wrap can be easily removed.
3. Preheat oven to 350°.
4. Remove top sheets of plastic wrap; fit dough, plastic wrap side up, into a 9-inch pie plate. Remove remaining plastic wrap. Fold edges under; flute. Line bottom of dough with a piece of foil coated with cooking spray; arrange pie weights or dried beans on foil. Bake at 350° for 15 minutes. Remove pie weights and foil; cool pastry on a wire rack.
5. To prepare filling, combine sweet potato and next 4 ingredients in a food processor; process until blended. Spoon into a large bowl. Add 1% milk and remaining 5 ingredients; stir well. Pour filling into pastry. Bake at 350° for 50 minutes or until a knife inserted in center comes out clean. Cool completely on wire rack. Yield: 8 servings (serving size: 1 wedge).

CALORIES 302 (27% from fat); FAT 9g (sat 5.6g, mono 2.3g, poly 0.5g); PROTEIN 6.2g; CARB 49.4g; FIBER 1.5g; CHOL 24mg; IRON 1.7mg; SODIUM 295mg; CALC 147mg

High-Flavor Supper

Prepare beef or pork tenderloin for a speedy, high-flavor supper.

High-Flavor Menu 1
serves 4

Pork Tenderloin Medallions with Chinese Ginger and Lemon Sauce

Stir-fried snow peas and green onions*

Steamed rice

*Heat 1 teaspoon peanut oil in a large nonstick skillet over medium-high heat. Add 1 teaspoon minced peeled fresh ginger; sauté 30 seconds. Add 2 cups snow peas; sauté 1 minute. Add ½ cup thinly sliced green onions; sauté 30 seconds. Add 2 tablespoons water; cook 30 seconds or until snow peas are tender, stirring constantly. Stir in ¼ teaspoon salt and ¼ teaspoon black pepper.

Game Plan

1. While rice cooks:
- Trim snow peas
- Mince ginger for pork and snow peas
- Chop green onions for pork and slice for snow peas
- Mince garlic for pork
- Grate rind and juice lemon for pork

2. Cook pork and sauce; keep warm.

3. Cook snow peas.

Pork Tenderloin Medallions with Chinese Ginger and Lemon Sauce

The cooking goes quickly in this stir-fry, so have all the ingredients prepped before you begin.

TOTAL TIME: 41 MINUTES

- ½ teaspoon salt
- ½ teaspoon five-spice powder
- ½ teaspoon freshly ground black pepper
- 1 (1-pound) pork tenderloin, trimmed and cut crosswise into ½-inch-thick slices
- Cooking spray
- 2 tablespoons chopped green onions
- 1 tablespoon minced peeled fresh ginger
- 1 garlic clove, minced
- ¼ cup dry sherry
- ¼ cup fat-free, less-sodium chicken broth
- 1 teaspoon grated lemon rind
- 3 tablespoons fresh lemon juice
- 1 tablespoon low-sodium soy sauce
- 2 teaspoons brown sugar
- 2 tablespoons water
- 1 teaspoon cornstarch
- ¼ cup chopped green onions

1. Combine first 3 ingredients, and rub evenly over pork.

2. Heat a large nonstick skillet over medium-high heat. Coat pan with cooking spray. Add pork to pan, and cook 1½ minutes on each side or until lightly browned. Remove pork from pan, and set aside.

3. Reduce heat to medium. Add 2 tablespoons onions, ginger, and garlic to pan; cook 2 minutes or until fragrant, stirring constantly. Combine sherry and next 5 ingredients in a small bowl. Add sherry mixture to pan; bring to a boil, scraping pan to loosen browned bits. Add pork to pan; cook 3 minutes or until pork is done. Remove pork from pan using a slotted spoon; reserve liquid in pan.

4. Combine water and cornstarch in a small bowl, stirring with a whisk. Add cornstarch mixture to pan, and bring to a boil. Cook 30 seconds or until slightly thick. Serve over pork. Sprinkle with ¼ cup green onions. Yield: 4 servings (serving size: 3 ounces pork, 2 tablespoons sauce, and 1 tablespoon green onions).

CALORIES 189 (30% from fat); FAT 6.2g (sat 2.1g, mono 2.8g, poly 0.7g); PROTEIN 24g; CARB 6.1g; FIBER 0.6g; CHOL 75mg; IRON 2mg; SODIUM 513mg; CALC 22mg

---

High-Flavor Menu 2
serves 4

Roasted Pork Tenderloin Medallions with Dried Cranberry Sauce

Quinoa with parsley and pine nuts*

Steamed broccoli

*Heat 1 teaspoon olive oil in a medium saucepan over medium-high heat. Add 1 cup plain quinoa. Cook 2 minutes or until golden brown, stirring frequently. Add 1 (14-ounce) can fat-free, less-sodium chicken broth; bring to a boil. Cover, reduce heat to medium-low, and simmer 15 minutes or until most of liquid is absorbed, stirring occasionally. Remove from heat; cover and let stand 5 minutes. Stir in 2 tablespoons chopped fresh parsley and 2 tablespoons toasted pine nuts.

Game Plan

1. While oven preheats:
- Start quinoa
- Combine herbs, salt, and pepper for pork
- Brown pork in skillet

2. While pork cooks in oven:
- Steam broccoli

3. While pork stands:
- Prepare sauce
- Stir parsley and nuts into quinoa

Roasted Pork Tenderloin Medallions with Dried Cranberry Sauce

A tablespoon of grape jelly helps thicken the tangy-sweet sauce. Tenderloin is lean and juicy when properly prepared. Use a meat thermometer to avoid overcooking.

TOTAL TIME: 42 MINUTES

QUICK TIP: To ensure the tenderloin roasts evenly, tuck the thin end under, and secure with kitchen twine or wooden skewers. Before slicing, allow meat to stand to keep in juiciness.

PORK:

- 1 teaspoon dried sage
- 1 teaspoon dried thyme
- ¾ teaspoon salt
- ½ teaspoon freshly ground black pepper
- 1 (1-pound) pork tenderloin, trimmed
- Cooking spray

SAUCE:

- 1 cup fat-free, less-sodium chicken broth
- 1 cup dried cranberries
- ½ cup cranberry juice cocktail (such as Ocean Spray)
- 1 tablespoon grape jelly

1. Preheat oven to 400°.

2. To prepare pork, combine first 4 ingredients; rub evenly over pork.

3. Heat a large ovenproof nonstick skillet over medium-high heat. Coat pan with cooking spray. Add pork; cook 4 minutes on each side or until browned. Place pan in oven; cook pork at 400° for 12 minutes or until a meat thermometer registers 160° (slightly pink). Place pork on a cutting board; keep warm.

4. To prepare sauce, add broth, cranberries, and juice to pan; bring to a boil, scraping pan to loosen browned bits. Stir in jelly; cook 8 minutes or until mixture is slightly thick, stirring occasionally. Cut pork into ½-inch slices. Serve with sauce. Yield: 4 servings (serving size: 3 ounces pork and ¼ cup sauce).

CALORIES 282 (20% from fat); FAT 6.3g (sat 2.2g, mono 2.8g, poly 0.7g); PROTEIN 24g; CARB 33.6g; FIBER 2.1g; CHOL 75mg; IRON 2.1mg; SODIUM 596mg; CALC 21mg

---

Get a high-flavor dinner on the table quickly with a beef or pork tenderloin.

High-Flavor Menu 3
serves 4

Fresh Herb-Coated Beef Tenderloin Steaks with Mushroom Gravy

Green peas and leeks*

Baked potatoes

*Melt 2 teaspoons butter in a medium nonstick skillet over medium heat. Add ½ cup thinly sliced leek (white part only); cover and cook 5 minutes or until tender. Add ¼ cup fat-free, less-sodium chicken broth and 1 (10-ounce) package frozen green peas. Cover and cook 10 minutes or until thoroughly heated. Stir in ¼ teaspoon salt and ¼ teaspoon black pepper.

Game Plan

1. While oven preheats:
- Microwave potatoes at HIGH 6 minutes
- Rub spices on steaks
- Wash and slice leeks

2. While steaks cook:
- Put potatoes in oven to bake (cook at 450° for 20 minutes or until done)
- Cook leeks
- Sauté mushrooms and garlic for gravy

3. While steaks rest:
- Add cornstarch mixture to thicken gravy
- Add peas to leeks

Fresh Herb-Coated Beef Tenderloin Steaks with Mushroom Gravy

TOTAL TIME: 43 MINUTES

BEEF:

- 1 teaspoon salt
- 1 teaspoon chopped fresh thyme
- 1 teaspoon chopped fresh rosemary
- ½ teaspoon freshly ground black pepper
- 4 garlic cloves, minced
- 4 (4-ounce) beef tenderloin steaks
- Cooking spray

GRAVY:

- 1 teaspoon olive oil
- ½ teaspoon chopped fresh thyme
- 1 (8-ounce) package presliced cremini mushrooms
- 4 garlic cloves, minced
- ½ cup fat-free, less-sodium chicken broth
- ½ cup white wine
- 1 tablespoon water
- 1 teaspoon cornstarch

1. Preheat oven to 450°.

2. To prepare beef, combine first 5 ingredients. Coat both sides of steaks with cooking spray, and rub steaks evenly with thyme mixture. Place steaks on rack of a broiler or roasting pan coated with cooking spray; bake at 450° for 8 minutes on each side or until desired degree of doneness. Remove from oven; keep warm.

3. To prepare gravy, heat oil in a large nonstick skillet over medium-high heat. Add ½ teaspoon thyme, mushrooms, and 4 garlic cloves; cook 5 minutes or until mushrooms are tender. Add broth and wine; bring to a boil. Cook until reduced to 1 cup (about 4 minutes).

4. Combine water and cornstarch in a small bowl, stirring with a whisk. Add cornstarch mixture to pan; bring to a boil. Cook 1 minute or until slightly thick, stirring constantly. Serve sauce with steaks. Yield: 4 servings (serving size: 1 steak and ¼ cup gravy).

CALORIES 202 (29% from fat); FAT 6.5g (sat 2.2g, mono 2.9g, poly 0.4g); PROTEIN 24.5g; CARB 6.3g; FIBER 0.7g; CHOL 52mg; IRON 2mg; SODIUM 692mg; CALC 44mg

High-Flavor Menu 4

serves 4

Beef Tenderloin Steaks with Creole Spice Rub

Corn Maquechoux*

Strawberries tossed with brown sugar and low-fat sour cream

*Melt 1 tablespoon butter in a large saucepan over medium heat. Add 1 cup chopped yellow or red bell peppers (or a combination), ½ cup finely chopped onion, and 2 minced garlic cloves. Cook 5 minutes or until vegetables are tender, stirring occasionally. Add 3 cups frozen corn kernels, 1 cup 1% low-fat milk, ¼ cup chopped fresh parsley, ¼ cup chopped green onions, ¼ teaspoon dried thyme, and ¼ teaspoon ground red pepper. Reduce heat, and simmer 15 minutes or until most of milk is absorbed. Stir in ¼ teaspoon salt, ¼ teaspoon black pepper, ⅛ teaspoon sugar, and a dash of hot pepper sauce.

Game Plan

1. Chop ingredients for Corn Maquechoux.

2. While Corn Maquechoux cooks:
• Prepare rub for steaks
• Preheat skillet for steaks
• Cook steaks

3. While steaks rest:
•Toss strawberries with sugar and sour cream

QUICK & EASY

Beef Tenderloin Steaks with Creole Spice Rub

The kicky spice rub for the steaks is easy to make, and the results are dynamite. The steaks need to stand for a few minutes after cooking to allow their juices to reabsorb. Corn Maquechoux (mock-SHOE) is a traditional Cajun side dish. You also can serve it as a chunky salsa over meat strips in soft tacos.

TOTAL TIME: 38 MINUTES

QUICK TIP: Make an extra batch of the Creole Spice Rub to use on chicken breasts, shrimp, or pork tenderloin another night.

CREOLE SPICE RUB:
  1 teaspoon dry mustard
  1 teaspoon garlic powder
  1 teaspoon ground sage
  1 teaspoon dried thyme
  ¾ teaspoon salt
  ½ teaspoon ground cumin
  ½ teaspoon ground red pepper
  ½ teaspoon freshly ground black pepper

REMAINING INGREDIENTS:
  4 (4-ounce) beef tenderloin steaks, trimmed (1 inch thick)
  Cooking spray

1. Combine first 8 ingredients; rub evenly over steaks.
2. Heat a large nonstick skillet over medium-high heat. Coat pan with cooking spray. Add steaks to pan; cook 4 minutes on each side or until desired degree of doneness. Remove from heat; let stand 5 minutes. Yield: 4 servings (serving size: 1 steak).

CALORIES 155 (35% from fat); FAT 6g (sat 2g, mono 2.2g, poly 0.4g); PROTEIN 22.8g; CARB 1.4g; FIBER 0.5g; CHOL 52mg; IRON 2.1mg; SODIUM 490mg; CALC 31mg

simple suppers

Noodle Bowls

Warm up your nights with satisfying, soupy meals.

Noodle bowls are traditional comfort food in Asia and Asian-American communities in the States. Made with steaming, ginger-infused broth; long noodles; and small pieces of meat, they're a simple affair, too. Though noodle bowls are typically thought of as Asian, our versions are inspired by different spots around the world, from Mexican Fideos con Frijoles to a down-home Ham, Collard Greens, and Egg Noodle Bowl. Canned broth and quick-cooking pasta make these meals easy to master. With each bite, you get a little of everything—vegetables, pasta, broth, and meat—all contained in one soothing bowl.

QUICK & EASY

Chorizo-Mussel Noodle Bowl

This recipe incorporates authentic Catalonian flavors, thanks to saffron and the smoked pork used in Spanish chorizo. Serve with a tossed green salad.

  6 ounces uncooked linguine
  Cooking spray
  1 cup chopped onion
  ½ cup chopped green bell pepper
  4 ounces Spanish chorizo sausage or turkey kielbasa, cut into ½-inch-thick slices
  3 garlic cloves, minced
  ¼ teaspoon saffron threads, crushed
  2 cups chopped plum tomatoes
  ½ cup dry white wine
  ¼ teaspoon freshly ground black pepper
  1 (14-ounce) can fat-free, less-sodium chicken broth
  2 pounds mussels, scrubbed and debearded (about 60 mussels)
  ⅓ cup chopped fresh parsley

1. Cook pasta according to package directions, omitting salt and fat. Drain.
2. While pasta cooks, heat a large nonstick skillet over medium-high heat. Coat pan with cooking spray. Add onion, bell pepper, sausage, and garlic to pan; sauté 3 minutes. Add saffron, and sauté 4 minutes or until sausage is browned. Stir in tomatoes; cook 2 minutes. Add wine, black pepper, and broth; bring to a boil. Add mussels; cover and cook 4 minutes or until mussels open. Remove from heat; discard any unopened shells. Stir in parsley. Serve mussel mixture over pasta. Yield: 4 servings (serving size: about 1½ cups mussel mixture and ¾ cup pasta).

CALORIES 482 (28% from fat); FAT 15.2g (sat 5g, mono 6.1g, poly 2g); PROTEIN 32.4g; CARB 49.1g; FIBER 3.9g; CHOL 65mg; IRON 8.7mg; SODIUM 936mg; CALC 82mg

Ham, Collard Greens, and Egg Noodle Bowl

To speed up the preparation of this Southern-style noodle bowl, cook the pasta and broth mixture at the same time. Spice it up with hot pepper sauce, if you wish, and serve it with corn bread.

3⅓ cups uncooked wide egg noodles (about 6 ounces)
1 tablespoon butter
2 cups diced reduced-sodium smoked ham (about 11 ounces)
1 cup chopped onion
½ cup chopped carrot
½ cup chopped celery
½ cup chopped red bell pepper
1 teaspoon dried oregano
½ teaspoon dried thyme
3 garlic cloves, minced
4 cups sliced collard greens, stems removed
2 tablespoons cider vinegar
3 cups fat-free, less-sodium chicken broth
¼ teaspoon freshly ground black pepper

1. Cook noodles according to package directions, omitting salt and fat. Drain.
2. Melt butter in a large Dutch oven over medium-high heat. Add ham; cook 8 minutes or until lightly browned, stirring frequently. Add onion and next 6 ingredients; cook 5 minutes or until vegetables are just tender, stirring frequently. Add collard greens; cook 1 minute, stirring constantly. Stir in vinegar; cook 1 minute. Stir in chicken broth; bring to a boil. Cover, reduce heat, and simmer 12 minutes. Stir in noodles and black pepper, and cook 1 minute or until thoroughly heated. Yield: 6 servings (serving size: about 1¼ cups).

CALORIES 270 (29% from fat); FAT 8.8g (sat 2.8g, mono 2.3g, poly 3g); PROTEIN 18.8g; CARB 29.4g; FIBER 3.5g; CHOL 76mg; IRON 2.1mg; SODIUM 999mg; CALC 76mg

Malaysian Noodle Soup with Chicken

The spicy broth is balanced by earthy mushrooms and delicate noodles. If overcooked, rice noodles become mushy.

4 ounces uncooked wide rice stick noodles (*banh pho*)
1 tablespoon canola oil
1 pound skinless, boneless chicken thighs, cut into ¼-inch-thick strips
2 tablespoons grated peeled fresh ginger
1 teaspoon ground cumin
¾ teaspoon fennel seeds, crushed
¼ teaspoon ground cinnamon
3 garlic cloves, minced
1 star anise
1½ cups thinly sliced shiitake mushroom caps
1 tablespoon Thai fish sauce
2 (14-ounce) cans fat-free, less-sodium chicken broth
¼ teaspoon freshly ground black pepper
¼ cup chopped green onions

1. Cook noodles according to package directions, omitting salt and fat. Drain.
2. Heat oil in a large Dutch oven over medium-high heat. Add chicken; cook 8 minutes or until browned, stirring constantly. Remove chicken from pan. Add ginger and next 5 ingredients to pan; cook 30 seconds, stirring constantly. Stir in chicken, mushrooms, fish sauce, and broth; bring to a boil. Reduce heat; simmer 12 minutes. Discard star anise. Stir in pepper. Place ¾ cup noodles into each of 4 bowls. Ladle 1 cup soup into each bowl; sprinkle each serving with 1 tablespoon onions. Yield: 4 servings.

CALORIES 343 (23% from fat); FAT 8.6g (sat 1.5g, mono 3.6g, poly 2.3g); PROTEIN 26.9g; CARB 37g; FIBER 3.2g; CHOL 94mg; IRON 2.3mg; SODIUM 788mg; CALC 46mg

Spicy Tofu Udon Noodle Bowl

The crunchy snow peas are a nice contrast to the tender tofu and the chewy bite of the noodles. Spaghetti is a good substitute if you can't find udon.

6 ounces uncooked udon noodles (thick, round fresh Japanese wheat noodles) or spaghetti
2 teaspoons canola oil
2 cups sliced mushrooms
3 cups fat-free, less-sodium chicken broth
2 cups snow peas, trimmed
2 tablespoons low-sodium soy sauce
1 tablespoon minced peeled fresh ginger
1 teaspoon brown sugar
2 garlic cloves, minced
1 serrano chile, sliced
1 cup light coconut milk
3 tablespoons fresh lime juice
1 teaspoon Sambal oelek (ground fresh chile paste)
1 (12.3-ounce) package lite firm silken tofu, cut into ½-inch cubes
½ cup chopped green onions
¼ cup chopped cilantro

1. Cook noodles according to package directions, omitting salt and fat. Drain.
2. Heat oil in a large saucepan over medium-high heat. Add mushrooms; sauté 3 minutes or until tender. Add broth and next 6 ingredients; bring to a boil. Cook 4 minutes. Stir in milk, lime juice, and Sambal oelek; reduce heat, and simmer 5 minutes. Add tofu; cook 5 minutes. Place about 1 cup noodles into each of 4 bowls. Ladle about 1¼ cups soup into each bowl; sprinkle each serving with 2 tablespoons green onions and 1 tablespoon cilantro. Yield: 4 servings.

CALORIES 321 (28% from fat); FAT 10.1g (sat 2.8g, mono 2.3g, poly 3g); PROTEIN 16.9g; CARB 39.2g; FIBER 4.6g; CHOL 0mg; IRON 3mg; SODIUM 863mg; CALC 77mg

Fideos con Frijoles

Fideos are very thin vermicelli noodles. They're broken into pieces and browned in the pan before being cooked in the soup. This procedure is typical of Mexico's *sopa seca*, in which the noodles absorb nearly all the broth and make a thick, almost dry, soup.

    1   tablespoon olive oil
    6   ounces vermicelli, broken into
        thirds
    1   cup chopped white onion
    3   garlic cloves, minced
    1   serrano chile, seeded and
        minced
    1   teaspoon ground cumin
    ¼   teaspoon ground chipotle chile
        pepper
    ½   teaspoon salt
    2   (14-ounce) cans fat-free,
        less-sodium chicken broth
    1   (15-ounce) can pinto beans,
        rinsed and drained
    1   cup chopped fresh tomato
    2   tablespoons chopped fresh
        cilantro
    ½   cup chopped green onions
    ½   cup (2 ounces) reduced-fat
        shredded Cheddar cheese

1. Heat oil in a large nonstick skillet over medium heat. Add pasta; cook 4 minutes or until brown, stirring frequently. Add white onion, garlic, and serrano; cook 1 minute or until fragrant, stirring constantly. Add cumin and ground chipotle chile; cook 30 seconds, stirring constantly.
2. Add salt, broth, and beans; increase heat to medium-high. Bring to a boil; reduce heat, and simmer 12 minutes or until pasta is done. Remove from heat; stir in tomato and cilantro. Ladle 1½ cups soup into each of 4 bowls; top each with 2 tablespoons green onions and 2 tablespoons cheese. Serve immediately. Yield: 4 servings.

CALORIES 371 (20% from fat); FAT 8.3g (sat 2.7g, mono 2.6g, poly 1.3g); PROTEIN 18g; CARB 55.9g; FIBER 9.7g; CHOL 10mg; IRON 3.5mg; SODIUM 758mg; CALC 172mg

Easter Celebration

Enjoy an elegant springtime dinner that is surprisingly simple to make.

Easter Menu
serves 8
French-Style Stuffed Eggs
or
Fava Bean Bruschetta
Salmon with Fresh Sorrel Sauce
New Potatoes with Balsamic and Shallot Butter
or
Spring Risotto
Fresh Peas with Mint
Greek Easter Bread
Chocolate Pots de Crème
or
Strawberry Shortcake Jelly Roll
Sparkling wine and ginger ale

French-Style Stuffed Eggs

If you plan to dye Easter eggs, cook extras for this dish. Stuffed eggs are often served warm in France, and this recipe is similar to one from the Périgord region.

    8   large eggs
    ⅓   cup minced reduced-fat ham
    1   tablespoon minced green onions
    1   tablespoon minced fresh parsley
    1   tablespoon low-fat mayonnaise
    1   teaspoon mustard
    ¼   teaspoon chopped fresh thyme
    ⅛   teaspoon salt
    ⅛   teaspoon freshly ground black
        pepper
    2   (1-ounce) slices white bread, torn
        into large pieces
        Cooking spray
        Fresh thyme leaves (optional)

1. Place eggs in a large saucepan. Cover with water to 1 inch above eggs; bring just to a boil. Remove from heat; cover and let stand 12 minutes. Drain and rinse with cold running water until cool.

2. Peel eggs; slice in half lengthwise. Remove yolks; discard 4 yolks. Place remaining 4 yolks in a medium bowl. Add ham and next 7 ingredients; stir until combined.
3. Place bread in a food processor; pulse 10 times or until coarse crumbs measure 1 cup.
4. Spoon about 1 teaspoon yolk mixture into each egg white half. Top each half with 1 tablespoon breadcrumbs. Coat breadcrumbs with cooking spray.
5. Preheat broiler.
6. Place eggs on a baking sheet; broil 1 minute or until breadcrumbs are toasted. Garnish with thyme leaves, if desired. Yield: 16 servings (serving size: 1 egg half).

CALORIES 38 (38% from fat); FAT 1.6g (sat 0.5g, mono 0.6g, poly 0.2g); PROTEIN 3.3g; CARB 2.3g; FIBER 0.1g; CHOL 54mg; IRON 0.4mg; SODIUM 127mg; CALC 14mg

Fava Bean Bruschetta

Favas are sometimes called broad beans or horse beans, and are most often used in Mediterranean foods. This bruschetta is a delicious way to showcase them. *Manchego viejo* cheese is aged and has a firm texture similar to Parmesan. If you can't find Manchego viejo, use Parmesan.

    2¼ pounds unshelled fava beans
    2   tablespoons extravirgin olive oil
    1   tablespoon chopped fresh tarragon
    1   tablespoon fresh lime juice
    ¼   teaspoon salt
    1   garlic clove, minced
    1   (1-pound) French bread baguette,
        cut into 32 slices
    ½   cup (2 ounces) shaved Manchego
        viejo cheese

1. Remove beans from pods; discard pods. Cook beans in boiling water 1 minute; rinse with cold water. Drain;

remove outer skins from beans. Discard skins. Place beans in a food processor. Add oil and next 4 ingredients; process until almost smooth. Spread about 1½ teaspoons bean mixture over each bread slice. Arrange cheese evenly over bread slices. Yield: 16 servings (serving size: 2 bruschetta).

CALORIES 115 (28% from fat); FAT 3.6g (sat 1g, mono 1.9g, poly 0.4g); PROTEIN 4.4g; CARB 16g; FIBER 1.2g; CHOL 3mg; IRON 0.9mg; SODIUM 268mg; CALC 64mg

Salmon with Fresh Sorrel Sauce

(pictured on page 59)

Sorrel is a tart, slightly sour spring herb. You can substitute watercress or arugula, if you'd like. The bread helps thicken the sorrel sauce for a consistency that is similar to pesto.

SAUCE:
- 1 cup coarsely chopped fresh parsley
- 1 cup chopped sorrel
- ⅔ cup water
- ½ cup chopped fresh chives
- ¼ cup coarsely chopped walnuts, toasted
- 1 tablespoon capers
- ½ teaspoon salt
- ¼ teaspoon freshly ground black pepper
- 2 garlic cloves, chopped
- 1 (1-ounce) slice white bread

FISH:
- 8 (6-ounce) salmon fillets (about 1 inch thick)
- ½ teaspoon salt
- ¼ teaspoon freshly ground black pepper
- Cooking spray

1. To prepare sauce, combine first 10 ingredients in a food processor; process until smooth.
2. Preheat broiler.
3. To prepare fish, sprinkle fish with ½ teaspoon salt and ¼ teaspoon pepper. Place fish on a broiler pan coated with cooking spray; broil 10 minutes or until

fish flakes easily when tested with a fork. Serve fish with sorrel sauce. Yield: 8 servings (serving size: 1 fillet and 2 tablespoons sorrel sauce).

CALORIES 315 (45% from fat); FAT 15.8g (sat 3.4g, mono 6.1g, poly 5g); PROTEIN 37.8g; CARB 3.8g; FIBER 1.2g; CHOL 87mg; IRON 1.8mg; SODIUM 437mg; CALC 53mg

Simple Entertaining for Eight Menu

serves 8

To get a jump start on this easy menu, make the butter mixture for the potatoes and the breadcrumbs for the chicken a day ahead.

Breaded chicken breasts*

New Potatoes with Balsamic and Shallot Butter

Steamed green beans

*Place 6 (1-ounce) bread slices in a food processor; pulse until coarse crumbs measure 3 cups. Spread on a baking sheet; bake at 350° for 10 minutes or until golden. Place each of 8 (6-ounce) chicken breasts between 2 sheets of plastic wrap; pound to ½-inch thickness. Sprinkle chicken with 1 teaspoon salt and ½ teaspoon black pepper. Beat 2 large eggs in a shallow bowl; dip each breast in egg, and dredge in breadcrumbs. Heat 1 tablespoon olive oil in a large nonstick skillet over medium-high heat. Add 4 breasts; cook 4 minutes on each side or until done. Repeat procedure with 1 tablespoon oil and remaining breasts.

New Potatoes with Balsamic and Shallot Butter

The butter can be made ahead, chilled, and tossed with the potatoes just before serving.

- ⅔ cup balsamic vinegar
- ⅓ cup butter, softened
- 3 tablespoons finely chopped shallots
- 2 teaspoons chopped fresh thyme
- ½ teaspoon salt, divided
- ⅛ teaspoon freshly ground black pepper
- 4 pounds small red potatoes
- 1½ tablespoons finely chopped fresh parsley

1. Bring vinegar to a boil in a small saucepan; reduce heat, and simmer until reduced to 2 tablespoons (about 10 minutes). Place in a medium bowl, and cool completely. Add butter, shallots, thyme, ¼ teaspoon salt, and pepper; stir well.
2. Place potatoes in a saucepan; cover with water. Bring to a boil; reduce heat, and simmer 20 minutes or until tender. Drain. Cut potatoes in half; place in a large bowl. Sprinkle with ¼ teaspoon salt. Add butter mixture and parsley; toss gently to coat. Serve immediately. Yield: 8 servings (serving size: 1¼ cups).

CALORIES 246 (29% from fat); FAT 7.9g (sat 4.9g, mono 2g, poly 0.4g); PROTEIN 4.6g; CARB 39.9g; FIBER 3.9g; CHOL 20mg; IRON 2mg; SODIUM 221mg; CALC 34mg

Spring Risotto

(pictured on page 59)

Fava beans must be shelled twice. First they're removed from their pods, then blanched, cooled slightly, and pinched to remove the outer skins. Fresh beans taste the best, but canned fava beans will also work when fresh are out of season. Look for sun-dried tomato paste with the other tomato products in the supermarket.

- 6 cups boiling water, divided
- 1 cup dried morels
- 2 pounds unshelled fava beans
- 5 cups fat-free, less-sodium chicken broth
- 1 tablespoon olive oil
- 2 cups thinly sliced leek (about 3 large)
- 2 garlic cloves, minced
- 2 cups Arborio rice
- 2 tablespoons sun-dried tomato paste
- 1 cup dry white wine
- ¾ teaspoon salt
- ½ teaspoon freshly ground black pepper
- ⅓ cup sliced green onions
- ¾ cup (3 ounces) finely grated fresh Romano cheese

1. Combine 3 cups boiling water and morels; cover and let stand 30 minutes. Drain; rinse with cold water. Drain and chop.
Continued

2. Remove beans from pods; discard pods. Place beans in a medium saucepan with 3 cups boiling water; cook 1 minute. Rinse with cold water. Drain; remove outer skins from beans. Discard skins.

3. Bring broth to a simmer in a medium saucepan (do not boil). Keep broth warm over low heat.

4. Heat oil in a large saucepan over medium-high heat. Add leek and garlic; sauté 2 minutes or until leek is tender. Add rice and tomato paste; cook 2 minutes, stirring constantly. Stir in wine, salt, and pepper; cook 1½ minutes or until liquid is absorbed. Stir in 1 cup broth; cook about 2½ minutes or until liquid is nearly absorbed, stirring constantly. Add remaining broth, 1 cup at a time, stirring constantly until each portion is absorbed before adding the next (about 20 minutes total). Stir in morels and beans; cook 30 seconds or until thoroughly heated. Stir in green onions. Sprinkle each serving with cheese. Yield: 8 servings (serving size: 1 cup risotto and 1½ tablespoons cheese).

CALORIES 238 (22% from fat); FAT 5.9g (sat 2.2g, mono 2.9g, poly 0.4g); PROTEIN 9.9g; CARB 29.7g; FIBER 1.6g; CHOL 11mg; IRON 2.6mg; SODIUM 648mg; CALC 135mg

QUICK & EASY
Fresh Peas with Mint
(pictured on page 59)

Look for pea pods that are plump, firm, and bright green. Store the pods in a plastic bag in the refrigerator up to 1 day, and shell just before cooking.

  1 tablespoon butter
  1 cup sliced green onions
  2 garlic cloves, minced
  4 cups shelled green peas (about 3½ pounds unshelled)
  1 cup water
  1 cup fat-free, less-sodium chicken broth
  1 tablespoon honey
  ½ teaspoon salt
  ¼ cup chopped fresh mint

1. Melt butter in a medium saucepan over medium-high heat. Add onions and garlic; sauté 1 minute. Add peas, water,

broth, honey, and salt; bring to a boil. Reduce heat, and simmer 12 minutes or until peas are tender. Remove from heat; stir in mint. Serve with a slotted spoon. Yield: 8 servings (serving size: ½ cup).

CALORIES 89 (17% from fat); FAT 1.7g (sat 1g, mono 0.4g, poly 0.2g); PROTEIN 4.4g; CARB 14.2g; FIBER 4.3g; CHOL 4mg; IRON 1.1mg; SODIUM 220mg; CALC 22mg

MAKE AHEAD
Greek Easter Bread

  1 teaspoon whole allspice
  1 (3-inch) cinnamon stick
  1 cup warm water (100° to 110°)
Dash of salt
Dash of sugar
  2 packages dry yeast (about 2¼ teaspoons each)
4¾ cups bread flour, divided
  ½ cup sugar
  3 tablespoons butter
  3 large eggs
  1 teaspoon salt
Cooking spray
  1 tablespoon water
  1 large egg yolk

1. Place allspice and cinnamon in a spice or coffee grinder; process until finely ground. Set aside.

2. Combine warm water, dash of salt, dash of sugar, and yeast in a large bowl, stirring with a whisk. Let stand 5 minutes. Lightly spoon flour into dry measuring cups; level with a knife. Add 1 cup flour to yeast mixture, stirring until well combined. Let stand 20 minutes.

3. Place ½ cup sugar and butter in a large bowl; beat with a mixer at medium speed until light and fluffy. Add eggs, 1 at a time, beating well after each addition. Stir in allspice mixture. Add yeast mixture to butter mixture; stir with a whisk until well combined. Stir in 1 teaspoon salt. Add 3½ cups flour, about 1 cup at a time, stirring until a soft dough forms. Turn dough out onto a floured surface. Knead until smooth and elastic (about 8 minutes); add enough remaining flour, 1 tablespoon at a time, to prevent dough from sticking to hands (dough will feel tacky).

4. Place dough in a large bowl coated with cooking spray, turning to coat top. Cover and let rise in a warm place (85°), free from drafts, 1 hour or until doubled in size. (Gently press 2 fingers into dough. If indentation remains, dough has risen enough.)

5. Divide dough into 3 equal portions, shaping each portion into a 14-inch-long rope. Place ropes lengthwise on a baking sheet coated with cooking spray (do not stretch); pinch ends together at one end to seal. Braid ropes; pinch loose ends to seal. Lightly coat dough with cooking spray. Cover and let rise 45 minutes or until doubled in size.

6. Preheat oven to 350°.

7. Combine 1 tablespoon water and egg yolk, stirring with a whisk. Uncover loaf, and brush half of yolk mixture over loaf. Let stand 5 minutes. Brush with remaining yolk mixture. Bake at 350° for 30 minutes or until loaf sounds hollow when tapped. Cool on a wire rack 20 minutes. Yield: 20 servings (serving size: 1 slice).

CALORIES 168 (18% from fat); FAT 3.3g (sat 1.5g, mono 0.9g, poly 0.4g); PROTEIN 5.3g; CARB 29.1g; FIBER 1.1g; CHOL 47mg; IRON 1.8mg; SODIUM 150mg; CALC 13mg

MAKE AHEAD
Chocolate Pots de Crème

Pots de crème are creamy custards served in tiny cups.

  2 large eggs
2½ cups fat-free milk
  ¾ cup sugar
  ¼ cup unsweetened cocoa
  ⅛ teaspoon salt
  1 teaspoon vanilla extract
  4 ounces semisweet or bittersweet chocolate, chopped

1. Preheat oven to 350°.

2. Place eggs in a medium bowl; stir with a whisk until eggs are lightly beaten.

3. Combine milk, sugar, cocoa, and salt in a medium saucepan over medium heat. Cook until sugar dissolves, stirring occasionally (about 3 minutes). Add vanilla and chocolate; stir until chocolate melts.

4. Gradually add ¼ cup hot milk mixture

to eggs, stirring constantly with a whisk. Add egg mixture to milk mixture in pan, stirring with a whisk to combine. Pour into 8 (4-ounce) ramekins. Place ramekins in a 13 x 9-inch baking pan; add hot water to pan to a depth of 1 inch. Bake at 350° for 35 minutes or until a knife inserted in center comes out clean. Remove ramekins from pan; cool completely on a wire rack. Chill 8 hours or overnight. Yield: 8 servings (serving size: 1 custard).

CALORIES 196 (36% from fat); FAT 7.8g (sat 3.7g, mono 2.7g, poly 0.4g); PROTEIN 5.7g; CARB 31.3g; FIBER 1.9g; CHOL 54mg; IRON 1mg; SODIUM 87mg; CALC 106mg

MAKE AHEAD

Strawberry Shortcake Jelly Roll

(pictured on page 58)

    4 cups sliced strawberries (about
         1½ pounds)
  ¾ cup sugar, divided
Cooking spray
  ⅔ cup all-purpose flour
    1 teaspoon baking powder
  ¼ teaspoon salt
    5 egg whites
    3 egg yolks
    2 teaspoons grated lemon rind
    1 teaspoon vanilla extract
    2 tablespoons powdered sugar
    1 (10-ounce) jar strawberry jam
  ½ cup whipping cream
Orange rind strips (optional)
Mint sprig (optional)

1. Combine strawberries and ¼ cup sugar in a medium bowl. Cover and chill 1 hour; stir occasionally.
2. Preheat oven to 400°.
3. Coat a 15 x 10-inch jelly-roll pan with cooking spray, and line bottom of pan with wax paper. Coat wax paper with cooking spray.
4. Lightly spoon flour into a dry measuring cup; level with a knife. Combine flour, baking powder, and salt, stirring with a whisk. Set aside.
5. Place ½ cup sugar, egg whites, and egg yolks in a large bowl; beat with a mixer at high speed until pale and fluffy (about 5 minutes). Stir in lemon rind and vanilla. Sift half of flour mixture over egg

How to Make a Jelly-Roll Cake

1. *While the cake is baking, lay a dry kitchen towel slightly larger than the pan on a flat surface, and dust the towel with a thin layer of powdered sugar. The sugar prevents the cake from sticking.*

2. *Remove the cake from the oven, and turn the pan over onto the towel, releasing the cake and wax paper. Slowly peel the wax paper from the cake. It's OK if a thin layer of cake remains on the paper.*

3. *Roll the towel and the cake together, pressing gently. Be sure to move slowly and carefully throughout the entire rolling process. The towel will end up coiled inside the cake.*

4. *Cool the cake on a wire rack, seam side down. After 1 hour, unroll and remove the towel. The cake will be slightly wavy. Carefully spread the filling as directed, and reroll the cake.*

mixture; fold in. Repeat procedure with remaining flour mixture. Spoon batter into prepared pan; spread evenly.
6. Bake at 400° for 10 minutes or until cake springs back when touched lightly in center. Loosen cake from sides of pan; turn out onto a dishtowel dusted with powdered sugar. Carefully peel off wax paper; cool cake 2 minutes. Starting at narrow end, roll up cake and towel together. Place, seam side down, on a wire rack; cool completely (about 1 hour). Unroll carefully; remove towel.

Spread jam over cake, leaving a ½-inch border. Reroll cake, and place, seam side down, on a platter. Cut into 8 slices.
7. Beat cream with a mixer at high speed until stiff peaks form. Serve strawberries and whipped cream with cake. Garnish with orange rind and mint sprig, if desired. Yield: 8 servings (serving size: 1 cake slice, about ½ cup berries, and about 2 tablespoons whipped cream).

CALORIES 318 (22% from fat); FAT 7.6g (sat 4.1g, mono 2.4g, poly 0.6g); PROTEIN 5.2g; CARB 59.3g; FIBER 2g; CHOL 97mg; IRON 1.1mg; SODIUM 179mg; CALC 69mg

Stealing the Show

Sides do more than just round out the meal.

If the chicken breasts, flank steak, or pork chops you're planning for tonight's dinner are a little ho-hum, give the meal a boost with an intriguing side dish. Don't be surprised if these snag the spotlight from your entrée.

Caramelized Onion-Stuffed Baked Potato

Baking the potato in the microwave makes this dish a snap to prepare. Fontina, mozzarella, or even Parmesan will work in this dish. Serve with filet mignon or flank steak.

- 2 baking potatoes (about 1½ pounds)
- ½ cup (2 ounces) shredded Gruyère cheese, divided
- 2 tablespoons reduced-fat sour cream
- ½ teaspoon salt
- ¼ teaspoon freshly ground black pepper
- 1½ teaspoons butter
- 2 cups vertically sliced red onion
- 2 teaspoons sugar
- 2 tablespoons dry sherry
- 1 teaspoon Worcestershire sauce
- ½ teaspoon dried thyme
- 1 garlic clove, minced

1. Pierce potatoes with a fork; arrange on paper towels in microwave oven. Microwave at HIGH 10 minutes or until done, rearranging potatoes after 5 minutes. Let stand 5 minutes.
2. Cut each potato in half lengthwise; scoop out pulp, leaving ¼-inch-thick shells. Combine potato pulp, ¼ cup cheese, sour cream, salt, and pepper. Spoon potato mixture evenly into shells.

3. Melt butter in a medium nonstick skillet over medium-high heat. Add onion and sugar; sauté 8 minutes or until browned. Stir in sherry, Worcestershire, thyme, and garlic; cook 1 minute or until liquid evaporates, scraping pan to loosen browned bits. Top each potato half with about 2 tablespoons onion mixture and 1 tablespoon cheese. Arrange stuffed potato halves on paper towels in microwave oven. Microwave at HIGH 1 minute or until thoroughly heated. Yield: 4 servings (serving size: 1 stuffed potato half).

CALORIES 238 (24% from fat); FAT 6.4g (sat 3.8g, mono 1.8g, poly 0.3g); PROTEIN 9.9g; CARB 40.7g; FIBER 5g; CHOL 21mg; IRON 1.7mg; SODIUM 375mg; CALC 192mg

MAKE AHEAD
Baked Fennel and Tomatoes with Herbs

Use fresh basil and oregano, if possible. Serve over chicken, pork tenderloin, or pasta for a Mediterranean accent.

- 1¾ cups chopped fennel bulb (about 1 pound)
- 1 cup halved cherry tomatoes
- ½ cup chopped onion
- ½ cup (1 x ½-inch) slices red bell pepper
- ½ cup (1 x ½-inch) slices yellow bell pepper
- 2 tablespoons dry white wine
- 1 tablespoon olive oil
- 1 tablespoon chopped fresh basil or 1 teaspoon dried basil
- 1½ teaspoons chopped fresh oregano or ½ teaspoon dried oregano
- ¼ teaspoon freshly ground black pepper
- ⅛ teaspoon salt
- 2 garlic cloves, crushed

1. Preheat oven to 350°.
2. Combine all ingredients in an 11 x 7-inch baking dish, stirring gently. Bake at 350° for 45 minutes or until fennel is tender, stirring occasionally. Yield: 4 servings (serving size: ½ cup).

CALORIES 99 (32% from fat); FAT 3.9g (sat 0.5g, mono 2.5g, poly 0.4g); PROTEIN 2.4g; CARB 14.9g; FIBER 5.1g; CHOL 0mg; IRON 1.3mg; SODIUM 138mg; CALC 72mg

MAKE AHEAD
Roasted Parsnip and Red Onion

Parsnips are at their peak in the fall and winter, but if you make this dish during another season, parboil them for four minutes before roasting.

- 6½ cups (1-inch-thick) slices peeled parsnip (about 1½ pounds)
- 1½ cups (1-inch-thick) slices red onion
- 2 tablespoons low-sodium soy sauce
- 1 tablespoon olive oil
- ⅛ teaspoon coarsely ground black pepper
- Cooking spray

1. Preheat oven to 425°.
2. Combine first 5 ingredients in a bowl, tossing gently to coat. Spoon onto a jelly-roll pan coated with cooking spray. Bake at 425° for 25 minutes or until tender, stirring occasionally. Yield: 6 servings (serving size: about 1 cup).

CALORIES 148 (17% from fat); FAT 2.8g (sat 0.4g, mono 2g, poly 0.3g); PROTEIN 2.5g; CARB 29.9g; FIBER 7.8g; CHOL 0mg; IRON 1.1mg; SODIUM 216mg; CALC 61mg

Black-Eyed Peas with Swiss Chard

This hearty, soupy side dish pairs nicely with chicken. Look for Swiss chard with other greens in the produce section.

- 1 pound Swiss chard
- 1½ cups dried black-eyed peas
- 1 teaspoon olive oil
- 1 cup finely chopped onion
- 1½ tablespoons tomato paste
- 2 garlic cloves, minced
- 2 cups fat-free, less-sodium chicken broth
- 1 cup (4 ounces) crumbled feta cheese
- 1 tablespoon chopped fresh oregano
- ¼ teaspoon salt
- ¼ teaspoon freshly ground black pepper
- ¼ cup fresh lemon juice

1. Wash chard thoroughly. Remove stems; chop. Slice leaves into 1-inch strips.

2. Place peas in a large Dutch oven; cover with water to 2 inches above beans. Bring to a boil; cook 5 minutes. Drain peas; set aside. Wipe pan with a paper towel.

3. Heat oil in pan over medium-high heat. Add onion; sauté 2 minutes. Add tomato paste and garlic; cook 1 minute, stirring constantly. Stir in peas and broth; bring to a boil. Cover, reduce heat, and simmer 20 minutes or until peas are tender. Stir in chard stems and cheese; cover and cook 4 minutes. Stir in chard leaves, oregano, salt, and pepper; cover and cook 2 minutes. Stir in lemon juice. Yield: 8 servings (serving size: ¾ cup).

CALORIES 177 (20% from fat); FAT 4.1g (sat 2.3g, mono 1.1g, poly 0.4g); PROTEIN 11.5g; CARB 25.1g; FIBER 4.8g; CHOL 13mg; IRON 3.8mg; SODIUM 463mg; CALC 142mg

Sweet Potatoes in Picante Sauce

Also known as *Picante de Papas*, this dish is often made in Latin American countries. Enjoy it with pork chops.

    1   tablespoon olive oil
    ½   cup minced celery
    ½   teaspoon crushed fennel seeds
    2   garlic cloves, minced
    ¾   cup finely chopped onion
    1   teaspoon salt
    ½   teaspoon ground turmeric
    ¼   teaspoon paprika
    1   dried red chile, crumbled (about ¼ ounce)
    6   cups (1½-inch) cubed peeled sweet potatoes (about 2 pounds)
    ½   cup water
    1   tablespoon chopped fresh cilantro

1. Heat oil in a Dutch oven over medium heat. Add celery, fennel, and garlic; cook 1 minute, stirring constantly. Add onion and next 4 ingredients; cook 10 minutes, stirring frequently. Add potato and water; bring to a boil. Cover, reduce heat, and simmer 35 minutes or until potato is tender. Sprinkle with cilantro. Yield: 10 servings (serving size: 1 cup).

CALORIES 105 (15% from fat); FAT 1.7g (sat 0.3g, mono 1g, poly 0.3g); PROTEIN 1.7g; CARB 21.5g; FIBER 3g; CHOL 0mg; IRON 0.7mg; SODIUM 252mg; CALC 26mg

MAKE AHEAD
Carrots with Ginger and Coriander Seeds

    4½ cups (½-inch-thick) slices carrot (about 2 pounds)
    ⅓   cup vegetable broth
    1   tablespoon julienne-cut peeled fresh ginger
    1   teaspoon crushed coriander seeds
    1   teaspoon brown sugar
    1   teaspoon melted butter
    ½   teaspoon salt
    ½   teaspoon freshly ground black pepper
    1   tablespoon chopped fresh parsley

1. Preheat oven to 375°.
2. Combine first 8 ingredients in a shallow 2-quart baking dish. Cover and bake at 375° for 1 hour or until tender, stirring occasionally. Sprinkle with parsley. Yield: 8 servings (serving size: ½ cup).

CALORIES 40 (16% from fat); FAT 0.7g (sat 0.3g, mono 0.2g, poly 0.1g); PROTEIN 0.9g; CARB 8.3g; FIBER 2.3g; CHOL 1mg; IRON 0.5mg; SODIUM 219mg; CALC 23mg

MAKE AHEAD
Roasted Ratatouille with Balsamic Vinegar

This dish nicely complements beef or chicken.

    1½ teaspoons chopped fresh cilantro
    ½   teaspoon Old Bay seasoning
    ½   teaspoon dried oregano
    ½   teaspoon dried thyme
    2   zucchini, halved crosswise and cut lengthwise into ¼-inch slices
    2   small onions, cut into ¼-inch slices
    1   (¾-pound) eggplant, peeled and cut crosswise into ¼-inch slices
    Cooking spray
    2   tablespoons balsamic vinegar
    ½   cup drained bottled roasted red bell peppers, cut into ¼-inch strips
    ¼   cup chopped fresh parsley
    ¼   cup coarsely chopped kalamata olives

1. Preheat oven to 425°.
2. Combine first 4 ingredients in a large heavy-duty zip-top plastic bag. Add zucchini, onions, and eggplant; seal and shake to coat. Arrange vegetables in a shallow roasting pan coated with cooking spray. Lightly coat vegetables with cooking spray. Bake at 425° for 20 minutes; drizzle with vinegar. Bake an additional 20 minutes or until vegetables are tender. Combine vegetables, peppers, parsley, and olives, tossing well. Yield: 4 servings (serving size: 1 cup).

CALORIES 91 (16% from fat); FAT 1.6g (sat 0.3g, mono 0.7g, poly 0.4g); PROTEIN 3.6g; CARB 18.3g; FIBER 5.8g; CHOL 0mg; IRON 1.9mg; SODIUM 271mg; CALC 62mg

Balsamic Succotash

If you have high-quality balsamic vinegar, use it to finish this dish. Serve with shrimp or fish.

    2   tablespoons butter
    1   cup chopped yellow onion
    1   garlic clove, minced
    2   cups frozen corn kernels
    ½   cup chopped red bell pepper
    1   teaspoon dried basil
    1   (10-ounce) package frozen baby lima beans
    ½   cup fat-free, less-sodium chicken broth
    ½   teaspoon sugar
    ½   teaspoon salt
    ⅛   teaspoon freshly ground black pepper
    1   tablespoon balsamic vinegar

1. Melt butter in a large nonstick skillet over medium heat. Add onion and garlic; cook 3 minutes or until onion softens, stirring occasionally. Add corn, bell pepper, basil, and beans; cook 4 minutes, stirring occasionally. Add broth, sugar, salt, and black pepper; cook 7 minutes or until liquid almost evaporates. Remove from heat, and stir in vinegar. Yield: 6 servings (serving size: ⅔ cup).

CALORIES 159 (29% from fat); FAT 5.4g (sat 2.9g, mono 1.7g, poly 0.4g); PROTEIN 5.1g; CARB 24.7g; FIBER 4.5g; CHOL 11mg; IRON 1.3mg; SODIUM 407mg; CALC 29mg

... And Ready in Just About 20 Minutes

QUICK & EASY
Sweet Hot Tofu

1 (3½-ounce) bag boil-in-bag long-grain rice
2 teaspoons canola oil
1 (14-ounce) package firm reduced-fat tofu, cut into 1-inch cubes
⅔ cup fat-free, less-sodium chicken broth
¼ cup hoisin sauce
1 tablespoon sherry
2 teaspoons low-sodium soy sauce
1 teaspoon cornstarch
1 teaspoon honey
½ teaspoon dark sesame oil
Dash of crushed red pepper
2 teaspoons bottled minced fresh ginger
2 teaspoons bottled minced garlic
⅓ cup thinly sliced green onions

1. Prepare rice according to package directions, omitting salt and fat.
2. Heat canola oil in a large nonstick skillet over medium-high heat. Add tofu, and sauté 5 minutes or until lightly browned. Remove from pan.
3. Combine broth and next 7 ingredients, stirring well with a whisk.
4. Add ginger, garlic, and onions to pan; sauté 30 seconds. Stir in broth mixture; cook 1 minute or until thickened, stirring constantly. Add tofu to pan; cook 30 seconds, stirring gently to coat. Spoon rice onto each of 4 plates; top each serving with tofu mixture. Yield: 4 servings (serving size: about ½ cup rice and about ½ cup tofu mixture).

CALORIES 275 (26% from fat); FAT 7.9g (sat 1g, mono 2.8g, poly 3.9g); PROTEIN 14.1g; CARB 36.1g; FIBER 3.2g; CHOL 0.5mg; IRON 2.6mg; SODIUM 425mg; CALC 55mg

QUICK & EASY
Red Bean Stew with Pasta

1 tablespoon olive oil
1½ cups presliced mushrooms
1 cup diced carrot
1½ cups water
¼ teaspoon black pepper
1 (15-ounce) can kidney beans, rinsed and drained
1 (14.5-ounce) can diced tomatoes, undrained
1 (14-ounce) can less-sodium beef broth
1 cup uncooked ditalini (about 4 ounces short tube-shaped pasta)
2 tablespoons commercial pesto
¼ cup (1 ounce) grated fresh Parmesan cheese

1. Heat oil in a Dutch oven over medium-high heat. Add mushrooms and carrot; sauté 4 minutes. Stir in water and next 4 ingredients. Cover; bring to a boil. Stir in pasta; cook, uncovered, 11 minutes or until pasta is done. Stir in pesto; sprinkle each serving with cheese. Yield: 4 servings (serving size: 1½ cups stew and 1 tablespoon cheese).

CALORIES 324 (28% from fat); FAT 10.2g (sat 2.3g, mono 4.7g, poly 1.7g); PROTEIN 15.2g; CARB 43.7g; FIBER 10.4g; CHOL 6mg; IRON 3.1mg; SODIUM 560mg; CALC 150mg

QUICK & EASY
Double-Bean Burritos

Serve these burritos with your favorite salsa for dipping.

1 (3½-ounce) bag boil-in-bag brown rice
1 cup chunky bottled salsa
1 (15-ounce) can black beans, rinsed and drained
6 (10-inch) flour tortillas
6 tablespoons bean dip (such as Frito Lay)
¾ cup (3 ounces) shredded Monterey Jack cheese with jalapeño peppers
1 avocado, peeled and cut into 6 slices
12 cilantro sprigs
6 lime wedges (optional)

1. Cook rice according to package directions, omitting salt and fat.
2. While rice cooks, combine salsa and beans in a small saucepan; cook over medium heat 5 minutes or until thoroughly heated. Stack tortillas; wrap in damp paper towels. Microwave at HIGH 25 seconds or until warm.
3. Spread 1 tablespoon bean dip over each tortilla; top each with ¼ cup rice, ⅓ cup bean mixture, 2 tablespoons cheese, 1 avocado slice, and 2 cilantro sprigs; roll up. Serve with lime wedges, if desired. Yield: 6 servings (serving size: 1 burrito).

CALORIES 503 (29% from fat); FAT 16.4g (sat 4.9g, mono 7.5g, poly 2g); PROTEIN 16.1g; CARB 72.9g; FIBER 7.7g; CHOL 18mg; IRON 4.1mg; SODIUM 905mg; CALC 211mg

QUICK & EASY
Duck with Olives and Couscous

1 cup water
¾ cup couscous
¼ teaspoon salt
1 tablespoon olive oil
4 (6-ounce) boneless duck breast halves, skinned
1¼ cups fat-free, less-sodium chicken broth
½ cup dry white wine
¼ cup minced shallots
1½ teaspoons tomato paste
1 teaspoon dried herbes de Provence
1 (3-inch) cinnamon stick
¼ cup chopped pitted green olives

1. Bring 1 cup water to a boil in a medium saucepan; gradually stir in couscous and salt. Remove from heat; cover and let stand 5 minutes. Fluff with a fork.
2. While couscous stands, heat oil in a large nonstick skillet over medium-high heat. Add duck; cook 3 minutes on each side or until browned. Combine broth and next 5 ingredients in a bowl, stirring with a whisk. Add broth mixture to pan. Cover, reduce heat, and simmer 3 minutes. Remove duck from pan; keep warm. Bring broth mixture to a boil; cook, uncovered, 2 minutes. Stir in olives; cook 1 minute. Discard cinnamon stick. Spoon about ½ cup couscous onto each

of 4 plates. Top each serving with 1 duck breast half and about ¼ cup sauce. Yield: 4 servings.

CALORIES 376 (28% from fat); FAT 11.7g (sat 2.9g, mono 5.2g, poly 1.4g); PROTEIN 38.3g; CARB 22.3g; FIBER 2g; CHOL 131mg; IRON 9mg; SODIUM 480mg; CALC 45mg

---

Speedy Weeknight Supper Menu
serves 4

Precooked bacon, bottled vinaigrette, and produce department convenience products help this meal come together in a flash.

Stuffed Portobello Mushrooms

Cobb-style salad*

Multigrain crackers

*Arrange 1 cup packaged romaine salad in each of 4 salad bowls. Top each serving with 1 tablespoon prechopped onion, 1 tablespoon crumbled precooked bacon, and 2 teaspoons crumbled blue cheese. Drizzle each serving with 1 tablespoon bottled low-fat balsamic vinaigrette.

QUICK & EASY
Stuffed Portobello Mushrooms

You can substitute freshly made coarse breadcrumbs, if necessary.

  4 (6-inch) portobello mushrooms, stems removed
Cooking spray
  1 cup chopped red tomato
  1 cup chopped yellow tomato
  1 cup panko (Japanese) breadcrumbs
  1 cup (4 ounces) preshredded part-skim mozzarella cheese
  ¼ cup chopped fresh chives
  ¼ teaspoon salt
  ¼ teaspoon black pepper

1. Preheat broiler.
2. Remove brown gills from undersides of mushrooms using a spoon; discard gills. Place mushrooms, gill sides down, on a foil-lined baking sheet coated with cooking spray. Broil mushrooms 5 minutes.
3. While mushrooms broil, combine tomatoes, breadcrumbs, cheese, and chives.

4. Turn mushrooms over, and sprinkle evenly with salt and pepper. Divide tomato mixture evenly among mushrooms. Broil 5 minutes or until cheese melts. Yield: 4 servings (serving size: 1 stuffed mushroom).

CALORIES 184 (26% from fat); FAT 5.3g (sat 2.9g, mono 1.3g, poly 0.2g); PROTEIN 12.6g; CARB 21.6g; FIBER 3.5g; CHOL 16mg; IRON 1.3mg; SODIUM 325mg; CALC 209mg

---

QUICK & EASY
Sesame-Orange Chicken

Ground sesame seeds thicken the sauce as it cooks. Serve with a salad and bread.

  2 tablespoons sesame seeds, toasted
  1 tablespoon grated orange rind
  ¼ teaspoon salt, divided
Dash of ground red pepper
  4 (6-ounce) skinless, boneless chicken breast halves
  2 teaspoons canola oil
  1 teaspoon butter
  1 cup fat-free, less-sodium chicken broth
  ⅓ cup orange juice
  1 tablespoon whipping cream

1. Combine sesame seeds, rind, ⅛ teaspoon salt, and pepper in a food processor; process until mixture resembles coarse meal.
2. Place each chicken breast half between 2 sheets of heavy-duty plastic wrap; pound to ¼-inch thickness using a meat mallet or rolling pin. Sprinkle chicken evenly with ⅛ teaspoon salt.
3. Heat oil and butter in a large nonstick skillet over medium heat until butter melts. Add chicken; cook 6 minutes on each side or until done. Remove chicken from pan; keep warm.
4. Add sesame mixture to pan, stirring with a whisk. Add broth, and bring to a boil, scraping pan to loosen browned bits. Cook broth mixture until reduced to ⅔ cup (about 3 minutes). Add orange juice and cream; cook 30 seconds, stirring constantly. Serve sauce over chicken. Yield: 4 servings (serving size: 1 chicken breast half and 3 tablespoons sauce).

CALORIES 271 (30% from fat); FAT 9.1g (sat 2.5g, mono 3.4g, poly 2.2g); PROTEIN 41.1g; CARB 4g; FIBER 0.7g; CHOL 106mg; IRON 1.9mg; SODIUM 377mg; CALC 70mg

---

QUICK & EASY
Spicy Asian Lettuce Wraps

Cooked, chopped shrimp or pork also work in these wraps.

  2½ ounces bean threads (cellophane noodles)
  ¼ cup minced fresh cilantro
  ¼ cup low-sodium soy sauce
  1 tablespoon chile paste with garlic
  2 teaspoons dark sesame oil
  2 cups chopped roasted skinless, boneless chicken
  12 large Boston or Romaine lettuce leaves

1. Cover bean threads with boiling water. Let stand 5 minutes or until softened. Drain and rinse with cool water. Chop noodles.
2. While bean threads soak, combine cilantro, soy sauce, chile paste, and oil in a large bowl, stirring with a whisk. Add noodles and chicken to soy sauce mixture; toss well to coat. Spoon about ⅓ cup chicken mixture down center of each lettuce leaf; roll up. Yield: 4 servings (serving size: 3 lettuce wraps).

CALORIES 213 (21% from fat); FAT 4.9g (sat 1g, mono 1.8g, poly 1.5g); PROTEIN 23.2g; CARB 18.3g; FIBER 0.7g; CHOL 60mg; IRON 1.7mg; SODIUM 641mg; CALC 31mg

---

QUICK & EASY
Cuban-Style Chicken

To save time, use drained canned pineapple tidbits in place of fresh fruit.

  ½ cup diced fresh pineapple
  2 tablespoons rice vinegar
  1 tablespoon orange marmalade
  1 (15-ounce) can black beans, rinsed and drained
  ¼ teaspoon ground red pepper, divided
  ½ teaspoon salt
  ½ teaspoon paprika
  4 (6-ounce) skinless, boneless chicken breast halves
Cooking spray
  ¼ cup chopped fresh cilantro

Continued

1. Combine first 4 ingredients in a medium saucepan; add ⅛ teaspoon pepper. Bring to a simmer over medium heat; cook 1 minute or until thoroughly heated. Keep warm.

2. Heat a large nonstick skillet over medium heat. Combine ⅛ teaspoon pepper, salt, and paprika, and sprinkle evenly over chicken. Coat chicken with cooking spray. Add chicken to pan; cook 5 minutes on each side or until done. Serve with bean mixture; sprinkle with cilantro. Yield: 4 servings (serving size: 1 chicken breast half, ½ cup bean mixture, and 1 tablespoon cilantro).

CALORIES 293 (8% from fat); FAT 2.7g (sat 0.6g, mono 0.5g, poly 0.5g); PROTEIN 45.2g; CARB 22.4g; FIBER 6.2g; CHOL 99mg; IRON 2.9mg; SODIUM 632mg; CALC 57mg

QUICK & EASY
Hoisin-Glazed Chicken Breasts

¼ cup hoisin sauce
1 tablespoon fresh lime juice
1 tablespoon low-sodium soy sauce
2 teaspoons bottled minced garlic
2 teaspoons dark sesame oil
¾ teaspoon bottled minced fresh ginger
Cooking spray
4 (6-ounce) skinless, boneless chicken breast halves
4 lime wedges

1. Preheat broiler.
2. Combine first 6 ingredients. Remove 2 tablespoons of hoisin mixture, and reserve to brush on cooked chicken. Line a shallow roasting pan with foil; coat foil with cooking spray. Place chicken on prepared pan. Brush 2 tablespoons of hoisin mixture evenly over chicken; broil 5 minutes. Turn chicken over; brush with 2 tablespoons of hoisin mixture. Broil 5 minutes or until chicken is done. Spoon reserved 2 tablespoons of hoisin mixture over cooked chicken. Serve with lime wedges. Yield: 4 servings (serving size: 1 breast half and 1 lime wedge).

CALORIES 249 (18% from fat); FAT 4.9g (sat 1g, mono 1.6g, poly 1.7g); PROTEIN 40.2g; CARB 8.4g; FIBER 0.5g; CHOL 99mg; IRON 1.4mg; SODIUM 520mg; CALC 26mg

Learning in Store

Gourmet emporiums across the country lure customers with hands-on cooking classes.

How times change. Cooking classes are now taught on culinary vacations and in the kitchens of the country's fanciest restaurants. Retail stores offer even more options. There are vegetable primers at Texas' Central Market stores, and cooking class date nights at the upscale Sur La Table cookware shops. Supermarkets, farmers' markets, wineries, department stores, and kitchenware shops are all settings for "continuing education" in the most delicious sense of the word. Whether you want a culinary diploma or simply dinner on the table in less than 15 minutes, there's a class to satisfy your curiosity and your palate. Here is a sampling of some recipes that are used at some of the Sur La Table cooking classes.

Roasted Duck with Roasted Fruit Compote

We call for frozen duck here because it's more widely available. If you can find fresh duck, the dish will taste even better. Serve with a simple tossed salad.

—Recipe by Dana Landry

DUCK:
1 (4-pound) frozen dressed domestic duck, thawed
½ teaspoon kosher salt, divided
¼ teaspoon freshly ground white pepper, divided
½ cup coarsely chopped celery
½ cup coarsely chopped carrot
1 small onion, quartered
1 garlic clove, minced
Cooking spray
1 orange, halved and seeded
⅔ cup dry red wine

COMPOTE:
1 cup pitted cherries
1½ teaspoons chopped fresh rosemary
1 peach, peeled and cut into 1-inch pieces
2 Bartlett or Anjou pears, peeled and cut into 1-inch pieces
2 Golden Delicious apples, peeled and cut into 1-inch pieces
2 tablespoons dry white wine

1. Preheat oven to 375°.
2. To prepare duck, rinse duck with cold water; pat dry. Sprinkle ¼ teaspoon salt and ⅛ teaspoon pepper in body cavity. Place celery, carrot, onion, and garlic in cavity; tie ends of legs together with string. Lift wing tips up and over back; tuck under duck. Place duck on rack of a broiler pan or roasting pan coated with cooking spray. Place rack in pan. Rub cut sides of orange halves over duck; pierce skin over breast several times with a fork. Bake at 375° for 1 hour and 45 minutes or until a thermometer registers 180°, basting every 30 minutes with red wine. Let stand 10 minutes. Discard skin; sprinkle duck with ¼ teaspoon salt and ⅛ teaspoon pepper. Cover; keep warm. Drain pan drippings.
3. Increase oven temperature to 475°.
4. To prepare compote, combine cherries and next 4 ingredients in bottom of roasting pan coated with cooking spray, tossing gently. Bake at 475° for 25 minutes or until very tender, stirring occasionally. Stir in 2 tablespoons white wine; bake an additional 5 minutes. Serve with duck. Yield: 4 servings (serving size: 4 ounces duck and about ¾ cup fruit sauce).

CALORIES 379 (31% from fat); FAT 13.4g (sat 4.8g, mono 4.2g, poly 1.7g); PROTEIN 28.5g; CARB 33g; FIBER 6.1g; CHOL 101mg; IRON 3.9mg; SODIUM 361mg; CALC 45mg

Roasted Tomato Salsa

—Recipe by Taji Marie

8   plum tomatoes, halved and seeded
3   garlic cloves, peeled
1   small white onion, peeled and
      quartered
1   jalapeño pepper, halved and
      seeded
Cooking spray
½   cup chopped fresh cilantro
3   tablespoons fresh lemon juice
½   teaspoon salt
⅛   teaspoon freshly ground black
      pepper

1. Preheat oven to 500°.
2. Place first 4 ingredients on a baking sheet coated with cooking spray. Bake at 500° for 20 minutes or until charred; stir occasionally. Remove from oven; cool.
3. Place vegetables in a food processor, and pulse 10 times or until chunky. Place in a medium bowl, and stir in cilantro and remaining ingredients. Cover and chill. Yield: 1½ cups (serving size: 3 tablespoons).
NOTE: Store, covered, in the refrigerator up to 3 days.

CALORIES 22 (12% from fat); FAT 0.3g (sat 0g, mono 0g, poly 0.1g); PROTEIN 0.8g; CARB 4.9g; FIBER 0.9g; CHOL 0mg; IRON 0.4mg; SODIUM 153mg; CALC 10mg

Rock Salt-Roasted Potatoes

—Recipe by Jason Vickers

1   (4-pound) box coarse food-grade
      rock salt
3   pounds small potatoes (about 24)
3   tablespoons extravirgin olive oil
1   tablespoon chopped fresh thyme
1   teaspoon freshly ground black
      pepper

1. Preheat oven to 350°.
2. Place ½-inch layer of rock salt in bottom of a shallow roasting pan. Arrange potatoes in a single layer on top of salt; pour remaining rock salt around and over potatoes. Bake at 350° for 50 minutes or

until tender. Remove from oven; let stand 10 minutes. Rub excess salt from potatoes. Combine oil, thyme, and pepper in a bowl. Add potatoes; toss gently to coat. Yield: 6 servings (serving size: 1 cup).

CALORIES 214 (29% from fat); FAT 6.8g (sat 0.9g, mono 5g, poly 0.7g); PROTEIN 6.2g; CARB 40.2g; FIBER 4.8g; CHOL 0mg; IRON 1.9mg; SODIUM 590mg; CALC 34mg

Pork Tenderloin with Dijon Cranberry Sauce

—Recipe by Christopher Green

PORK:
½   cup Dijon mustard
3   tablespoons chopped fresh tarragon
½   teaspoon freshly ground black
      pepper
2   (1-pound) pork tenderloins, trimmed
1   tablespoon olive oil

SAUCE:
1½   cups whole-berry cranberry sauce
2   teaspoons chopped fresh tarragon
2   teaspoons Dijon mustard
¼   teaspoon salt
⅛   teaspoon freshly ground black
      pepper

1. To prepare pork, combine first 3 ingredients in a large zip-top plastic bag. Add pork; seal and marinate in refrigerator 8 hours, turning bag occasionally.
2. Preheat oven to 400°.
3. Remove pork from bag; discard marinade.
4. Heat oil in a large ovenproof skillet over medium-high heat. Add pork; cook 4 minutes, browning on all sides. Place pan in oven; cook at 400° for 15 minutes or until thermometer registers 155°. Remove from heat; let stand 5 minutes. Cut pork into ¼-inch slices; keep warm.
5. To prepare sauce, combine cranberry sauce and remaining 4 ingredients in a small saucepan; cook over medium heat 5 minutes or until thoroughly heated, stirring occasionally. Serve sauce with pork. Yield: 8 servings (serving size: about 3 ounces pork and ¼ cup sauce).

CALORIES 248 (26% from fat); FAT 7.1g (sat 1.6g, mono 3.5g, poly 1g); PROTEIN 25g; CARB 21.6g; FIBER 1g; CHOL 74mg; IRON 1.9mg; SODIUM 552mg; CALC 34mg

Rosemary-Ginger Chicken

Chicken is a classic for roasting. In this version, start marinating the chicken at least two hours before cooking.

—Recipe by Gwen Ashley Walters

1   (3-pound) roasting chicken
3   tablespoons minced garlic
2   tablespoons chopped fresh
      rosemary
1   tablespoon chopped fresh parsley
1   tablespoon chopped fresh sage
1   tablespoon chopped fresh thyme
1   tablespoon olive oil
1   teaspoon kosher salt
1   teaspoon ground red pepper
1   teaspoon chopped peeled fresh
      ginger
1   teaspoon grated lemon rind
2   tablespoons fresh lemon juice
Cooking spray

1. Remove and discard giblets and neck from chicken. Rinse chicken with cold water, and pat dry. Trim excess fat. Place chicken, breast side down, on a cutting surface. Cut chicken in half lengthwise along backbone (do not cut through breastbone). Turn chicken over. Starting at neck cavity, loosen skin from breast and drumsticks by inserting fingers, gently pushing between skin and meat.
2. Combine garlic and next 10 ingredients. Rub garlic mixture under loosened skin and over surface of chicken. Cut a 1-inch slit in skin at bottom of each breast half; insert tips of drumsticks into slits. Place chicken in a large zip-top plastic bag; seal bag. Refrigerate at least 2 hours or up to 8 hours.
3. Preheat oven to 425°.
4. Place chicken, breast side up, on rack of a roasting pan coated with cooking spray. Add water to pan to a depth of ¼ inch. Place rack in pan. Bake at 425° for 40 minutes or until a thermometer inserted into meaty part of thigh registers 180°. Remove from oven; cover loosely with foil. Let stand 5 minutes, and discard skin. Yield: 4 servings (serving size: about 4 ounces).

CALORIES 151 (29% from fat); FAT 4.9g (sat 1g, mono 2.2g, poly 0.9g); PROTEIN 23.5g; CARB 2.3g; FIBER 0.5g; CHOL 74mg; IRON 1.6mg; SODIUM 322mg; CALC 27mg

Yellow Pepper Soup with Wild Mushroom Croutons

(pictured on page 57)

—Recipe by Taji Marie

SOUP:

6 large yellow bell peppers
Cooking spray
1½ teaspoons olive oil
1 cup chopped leek
1 cup finely chopped peeled baking potato
1 cup chopped carrot
2 teaspoons Hungarian sweet paprika
1 bay leaf
2 cups water
1 cup fat-free, less-sodium chicken broth
1½ teaspoons white balsamic vinegar
½ teaspoon salt
⅛ teaspoon freshly ground black pepper

CROUTONS:

1½ teaspoons olive oil
4 cups chopped mixed mushrooms (such as cremini, shiitake, button, and oyster)
2 tablespoons dry white wine
½ teaspoon chopped fresh thyme
2 garlic cloves, minced
2 tablespoons finely chopped parsley
2 tablespoons whipping cream
⅛ teaspoon salt
⅛ teaspoon freshly ground black pepper
1 (8-ounce) French bread baguette, cut into 12 slices

1. Preheat oven to 500°.
2. To prepare soup, place peppers on a jelly-roll pan. Lightly coat peppers with cooking spray. Bake at 500° for 30 minutes or until blackened on all sides, turning occasionally. Place peppers in a large zip-top plastic bag; seal. Let stand 20 minutes. Peel and discard skins. Cut in half lengthwise; discard membranes and seeds.
3. Heat 1½ teaspoons oil in a large saucepan over medium heat. Add leek, potato, and carrot; cook 5 minutes. Stir in paprika and bay leaf. Add water and broth; bring to a boil. Reduce heat; simmer 20 minutes or until vegetables are very tender. Stir in roasted pepper halves; simmer 5 minutes. Discard bay leaf. Stir in vinegar, ½ teaspoon salt, and ⅛ teaspoon black pepper.
4. Place half of bell pepper mixture in a blender. Remove center piece of blender lid (to allow steam to escape); secure blender lid on blender. Place a clean towel over opening in blender lid (to avoid spills). Process until smooth. Pour into a large bowl. Repeat procedure with remaining bell pepper mixture. Keep warm.
5. Preheat oven to 350°.
6. To prepare croutons, heat 1½ teaspoons oil in a large skillet over medium-high heat. Add mushrooms; reduce heat to medium. Stir in wine; cook 15 minutes or until liquid evaporates. Stir in thyme and garlic; cook 1 minute. Remove from heat, and stir in parsley, cream, ⅛ teaspoon salt, and ⅛ teaspoon black pepper.
7. Place bread on a baking sheet. Bake at 350° for 5 minutes or until toasted. Place 1 heaping tablespoon mushroom mixture on each crouton. Serve croutons with soup. Yield: 6 servings (serving size: 1 cup soup and 2 croutons).

CALORIES 244 (21% from fat); FAT 6.1g (sat 1.8g, mono 2.7g, poly 0.9g); PROTEIN 8.1g; CARB 41.5g; FIBER 6.5g; CHOL 7mg; IRON 2.5mg; SODIUM 588mg; CALC 68mg

Garlic and Onion Soup with Gruyère Toasts

—Recipe by Kathie Finn

SOUP:

1 whole garlic head
1½ tablespoons olive oil, divided
1 pound yellow onions, peeled and halved
½ pound shallots, peeled
½ pound Spanish onions, peeled and halved
½ teaspoon kosher salt
½ teaspoon freshly ground black pepper
Cooking spray
2 cups less-sodium beef broth
⅓ cup uncooked long-grain rice
2 cups fat-free, less-sodium chicken broth
¼ cup half-and-half

TOASTS:

½ cup (2 ounces) shredded Gruyère cheese
6 ounces French bread, cut into 12 slices

REMAINING INGREDIENT:

2 tablespoons chopped fresh chives

1. To prepare soup, preheat oven to 375°.
2. Remove white papery skin from garlic head (do not peel or separate cloves). Cut top third off head, and discard. Drizzle 1 teaspoon oil over cut side of garlic; wrap in foil. Bake at 375° for 50 minutes, cut side up, or until tender and cut side is lightly golden; cool 10 minutes. Separate cloves, and squeeze to extract pulp. Discard skins.
3. Increase oven temperature to 400°.
4. Combine 2 teaspoons oil, yellow onions, and next 4 ingredients; toss gently. Arrange on a jelly-roll pan coated with cooking spray. Bake at 400° for 30 minutes or until tender and golden brown. Remove from oven, and cool slightly. Coarsely chop onions and shallots.
5. Heat 1½ teaspoons oil in a large Dutch oven over medium heat. Add onions, shallots, and garlic; cook 10 minutes, stirring occasionally. Add beef broth and rice; bring to a boil. Cover, reduce heat, and simmer 15 minutes or until rice is tender. Add chicken broth, and cook 5 minutes or until thoroughly heated.
6. Place one-fourth broth mixture in a blender. Remove center piece of blender lid (to allow steam to escape); secure blender lid on blender. Place a clean towel over opening in blender lid (to avoid spills). Process until smooth. Pour puréed broth mixture into a large bowl. Repeat procedure in batches with remaining broth mixture. Stir in half-and-half.
7. To prepare toasts, preheat broiler.
8. Sprinkle cheese evenly over bread slices. Place bread slices on a baking sheet. Broil 5 minutes or until cheese melts and is lightly browned. Ladle soup into bowls; sprinkle with chives. Serve toasts with soup. Yield: 6 servings (serving size: 1 cup soup and 2 toasts).

CALORIES 298 (27% from fat); FAT 9g (sat 3.3g, mono 4.4g, poly 0.9g); PROTEIN 11.3g; CARB 43.3g; FIBER 3g; CHOL 15mg; IRON 2.2mg; SODIUM 550mg; CALC 185mg

april

Happy Hour

A retro-style cocktail supper combines the glamour of a bygone era with updated dishes for today's entertaining.

The late James Beard, considered by many to be the godfather of American cuisine, once noted that the cocktail party is "not a formal affair; it is as democratic as the subway." And Beard knew that better than anyone. Around 1940, he played a crucial role in making the cocktail party an American institution when he started his New York catering business and published his first cookbook, called *Hors d'Oeuvre and Canapés*. We've updated some of his recipes to create a selection of delicious appetizers that have nostalgic charm but still appeal to modern palates. And these recipes live up to Beard's timeless advice: "Nothing but the best is good enough for friends."

Cocktail Supper
serves 12

Eggplant Caponata

Creamy Mushroom Phyllo Triangles

Wrinkled Potatoes with Black Caviar

Marinated Shrimp

Mixed Vegetable Salad

Cognac-Marinated Beef Tenderloin Sandwiches with Horseradish Cream

Desserts

Coconut Biscotti

Spicy Meringue Kisses

Beverages

Classic Dry Martini

Old-Fashioned

Pineapple Margarita

MAKE AHEAD

Eggplant Caponata
(pictured on page 94)

Serve with sliced Italian bread or pita bread.

- ¼ cup golden raisins
- 6 cups diced peeled eggplant (about 1 pound)
- 1½ teaspoons salt
- 4 teaspoons olive oil, divided
- 1 cup chopped onion
- 2 garlic cloves, minced
- 1 cup diced seeded plum tomato
- ¼ cup sugar
- ¼ cup red wine vinegar
- ¼ cup chopped pitted kalamata olives
- 2 teaspoons capers
- ⅓ cup chopped fresh parsley

1. Place raisins in a small bowl; cover with hot water. Let stand 15 minutes; drain. Set aside.

2. Place eggplant in a colander; sprinkle with salt. Toss well. Drain 1 hour. Rinse well; pat dry with paper towels.

3. Heat 1 tablespoon oil in a large nonstick skillet over medium-high heat. Add eggplant; sauté 9 minutes or until well browned. Spoon eggplant into a large bowl; set aside.

4. Heat 1 teaspoon oil in pan over medium-high heat. Add onion; sauté 3 minutes or until golden. Add garlic; sauté 1 minute. Add tomato; sauté 2 minutes. Add tomato mixture to eggplant.

5. Return pan to heat. Add sugar and vinegar, stirring until sugar dissolves. Stir in raisins, olives, and capers. Add eggplant mixture, stirring to combine. Remove from heat; stir in parsley. Serve warm or at room temperature. Yield: 12 servings (serving size: ¼ cup).

NOTE: Caponata will keep in the refrigerator up to 5 days; bring to room temperature before serving.

CALORIES 59 (31% from fat); FAT 2g (sat 0.3g, mono 1.4g, poly 0.2g); PROTEIN 0.8g; CARB 10.8g; FIBER 1.5g; CHOL 0mg; IRON 0.5mg; SODIUM 141mg; CALC 14mg

---

STAFF FAVORITE • MAKE AHEAD
FREEZABLE

Creamy Mushroom Phyllo Triangles

This elegant appetizer takes a couple of hours to make, but you can do all the preparation ahead. Don't fold the triangles too tightly or the mixture will burst through the phyllo. Assemble and freeze up to two weeks before the party. Don't thaw the triangles before baking; just add seven minutes to the baking time.

- ¾ cup dried porcini mushrooms (about ¾ ounce)
- 1 pound button mushrooms
- 1 large onion, cut into 1-inch pieces (about 8 ounces)
- 2 tablespoons olive oil
- 1 teaspoon dried oregano
- ¾ teaspoon salt
- ½ teaspoon freshly ground black pepper
- ¼ teaspoon freshly grated nutmeg
- 6 ounces ⅓-less-fat cream cheese
- ½ cup finely chopped flat-leaf parsley
- 24 (18 x 14-inch) sheets frozen phyllo dough, thawed
- Olive oil-flavored cooking spray

Continued

1. Cover porcini mushrooms with boiling water in a bowl. Let stand 1 hour. Drain well; chop.

2. Place half of button mushrooms in a food processor; pulse 8 times or until finely chopped. Remove from processor. Repeat procedure with remaining button mushrooms. Add onion to processor; pulse 8 times or until finely chopped.

3. Heat oil in a large nonstick skillet over medium heat. Add onion; sauté 5 minutes. Add button mushrooms; cook until mushrooms are tender and liquid evaporates (about 10 minutes). Stir in porcini mushrooms, oregano, salt, pepper, and nutmeg; cook 2 minutes. Remove from heat. Add cheese; stir until cheese melts. Stir in parsley.

4. Preheat oven to 375°.

5. Place 1 phyllo sheet on a large cutting board or work surface (cover remaining phyllo to prevent drying). Cut sheet in half lengthwise; lightly coat with cooking spray. Fold each phyllo piece in half lengthwise to form 3½-inch-wide strips. Spoon a level tablespoon of mushroom mixture onto 1 short end of each strip, leaving a 1-inch border. Fold 1 corner over mixture, forming a triangle; continue folding back and forth into a triangle to end of strip. Repeat procedure with remaining phyllo, cooking spray, and mushroom mixture. Place triangles, seam side down, on baking sheets coated with cooking spray. Lightly coat tops of triangles with cooking spray.

6. Bake at 375° for 20 minutes or until golden. Serve warm. Yield: 48 triangles (serving size: 2 triangles).

CALORIES 49 (37% from fat); FAT 2g (sat 0.8g, mono 1g, poly 0.2g); PROTEIN 1.5g; CARB 6.2g; FIBER 0.5g; CHOL 3mg; IRON 0.6mg; SODIUM 97mg; CALC 7mg

Wrinkled Potatoes with Black Caviar

(pictured on page 94)

The potatoes are cooked in ¾ cup salt, which seems excessive, but they absorb very little. The salt seasons the spuds and helps create distinctively wrinkled skins.

    3   (8-ounce) cartons plain fat-free
        yogurt
    ¾   cup kosher salt
   24   small red potatoes (about 2¼ pounds)
    2   tablespoons caviar

1. Spoon yogurt onto several layers of heavy-duty paper towels; spread to ½-inch thickness. Cover with additional paper towels; let stand 5 minutes. Scrape into a bowl using a rubber spatula; cover and chill.

2. Place salt and potatoes in a saucepan. Cover with water; bring to a boil. Reduce heat, and simmer 20 minutes or until tender. Drain and return to pan. Cook 10 minutes over low heat, shaking pan frequently. Cool potatoes.

3. Cut a ¼-inch-deep X in top of each potato, squeezing each potato to reveal pulp. Top each potato with 1½ teaspoons drained yogurt and ¼ teaspoon caviar. Yield: 12 servings (serving size: 2 potatoes).

CALORIES 110 (5% from fat); FAT 0.6g (sat 0g, mono 0.2g, poly 0.1g); PROTEIN 7g; CARB 18.5g; FIBER 1.5g; CHOL 16mg; IRON 1.1mg; SODIUM 379mg; CALC 11mg

Cocktail Supper Countdown

Up to 2 weeks ahead:
• Assemble Creamy Mushroom Phyllo Triangles; place on a baking sheet and freeze. When completely frozen, transfer to heavy-duty zip-top freezer bags.

4 to 5 days ahead:
• Bake Coconut Biscotti; cool completely, and store in an airtight container at room temperature.
• Bake Spicy Meringue Kisses; cool completely, and store in an airtight container at room temperature.
• Prepare and refrigerate Eggplant Caponata.

2 days ahead:
• Marinate beef for Cognac-Marinated Beef Tenderloin Sandwiches with Horseradish Cream in refrigerator, turning the package once or twice a day.

1 day ahead:
• Prepare horseradish cream for Cognac-Marinated Beef Tenderloin Sandwiches with Horseradish Cream. Cover and chill.
• Stock up on ice, liquor, etc., for the bar.

Party day:
In the morning:
• Cook beef for Cognac-Marinated Beef Tenderloin Sandwiches with Horseradish Cream; chill until ready to serve. Slice before serving.
• Prepare Mixed Vegetable Salad.
• Drain yogurt for Wrinkled Potatoes with Black Caviar; cover and chill.

In the afternoon:
• Set the table; be sure to have enough salad plates for all guests.

2 hours before guests arrive:
• Squeeze and refrigerate lime juice for Pineapple Margarita.
• Marinate shrimp for Marinated Shrimp.

1 hour before guests arrive:
• Bake Creamy Mushroom Phyllo Triangles (if the pastries have been frozen, add 7 minutes to baking time).
• Prepare Marinated Shrimp; chill until ready to serve.
• Prepare Wrinkled Potatoes with Black Caviar.
• Prepare a dish of salt, and cut up limes and lemon rinds for cocktails.

30 minutes before guests arrive:
• Remove the horseradish cream for Cognac-Marinated Beef Tenderloin Sandwiches with Horseradish Cream from refrigerator.
• Remove Eggplant Caponata from refrigerator.

Marinated Shrimp

(pictured on page 94)

Ideal for a cocktail buffet, these shrimp are quite flavorful without any sauce. Serve with toothpicks.

¼ cup dry vermouth
2 tablespoons fresh lemon juice
2 tablespoons chopped fresh thyme
1 tablespoon chopped fresh marjoram
1 teaspoon salt
½ teaspoon hot pepper sauce (such as Tabasco)
36 large shrimp, peeled and deveined (about 1¾ pounds)
4 garlic cloves, minced
1 jalapeño pepper, finely chopped
2 tablespoons olive oil, divided

1. Combine first 9 ingredients in a large zip-top plastic bag. Marinate in refrigerator 30 minutes, turning occasionally.
2. Heat 1 tablespoon oil in a large non-stick skillet over medium-high heat. Add half of shrimp; cook 1½ minutes on each side or until done. Remove shrimp from pan. Repeat with 1 tablespoon oil and remaining shrimp. Yield: 12 servings (serving size: 3 shrimp).

CALORIES 101 (30% from fat); FAT 3.4g (sat 0.5g, mono 1.8g, poly 0.6g); PROTEIN 13.6g; CARB 2g; FIBER 0.2g; CHOL 101mg; IRON 1.8mg; SODIUM 199mg; CALC 41mg

Mixed Vegetable Salad

Unlike tossed greens, this salad is easy for guests to eat while standing.

MARINADE:
1 cup dry white wine
½ cup white wine vinegar
¼ cup fresh lemon juice
1 tablespoon olive oil
2 teaspoons sea salt
1 teaspoon sugar
1 teaspoon coriander seeds
1 teaspoon black peppercorns
¼ teaspoon crushed red pepper
5 garlic cloves, peeled and sliced
3 bay leaves
2 thyme sprigs

VEGETABLES:
4 quarts water
1 tablespoon sea salt
2 cups small cauliflower florets
1 cup (½-inch) slices carrot
1 cup (1-inch) cut green beans
2 cups chopped fennel bulb
2 cups coarsely chopped red onion
8 ounces button mushrooms, halved
1 tablespoon chopped fresh flat-leaf parsley

1. To prepare marinade, combine first 12 ingredients in a medium saucepan; bring to a boil. Cook until reduced to 1 cup (about 12 minutes). Cool; discard bay leaves and thyme.
2. To prepare vegetables, bring water and 1 tablespoon salt to a boil in a Dutch oven. Add cauliflower, carrot, and beans; cook 2 minutes. Add fennel, onion, and mushrooms; cook 3 minutes. Drain; rinse with cold water. Drain. Place vegetables in a large bowl. Pour marinade over vegetables; toss well to coat. Cover and chill 4 hours. Drain; sprinkle with parsley. Yield: 12 servings (serving size: about ¾ cup).

CALORIES 45 (16% from fat); FAT 0.8g (sat 0.1g, mono 0.4g, poly 0.1g); PROTEIN 1.7g; CARB 7.5g; FIBER 2.2g; CHOL 0mg; IRON 0.7mg; SODIUM 293mg; CALC 33mg

Cognac-Marinated Beef Tenderloin Sandwiches with Horseradish Cream

This is an updated version of James Beard's "cocktail hamburgers." You can marinate the beef two days before the party and mix the horseradish cream the day before. Assemble sandwiches, as we have; or have the beef on a platter, the rolls in a basket, and the horseradish cream in a bowl, and let your guests make their own.

CREAM:
½ cup reduced-fat sour cream
⅓ cup low-fat mayonnaise
2 tablespoons minced fresh chives
2 tablespoons prepared horseradish

TENDERLOIN:
1 (2½-pound) center-cut beef tenderloin, trimmed
⅓ cup finely chopped shallots
⅓ cup cognac
⅓ cup water
2 tablespoons minced fresh tarragon
2 teaspoons chopped fresh thyme
½ teaspoon freshly ground black pepper
2 garlic cloves, minced
1 teaspoon kosher salt
Cooking spray
30 (1½-ounce) sandwich rolls, cut in half horizontally

1. To prepare cream, combine first 4 ingredients. Cover and chill.
2. To prepare tenderloin, secure tenderloin at 1-inch intervals with twine. Combine tenderloin, shallots, and next 6 ingredients in a large zip-top plastic bag; seal. Shake to coat. Marinate in refrigerator at least 2 hours, turning bag occasionally.
3. Preheat oven to 450°.
4. Remove tenderloin from bag; discard marinade. Sprinkle tenderloin with salt. Place tenderloin in a shallow roasting pan coated with cooking spray. Bake at 450° for 40 minutes or until medium-rare or desired degree of doneness. Let stand 10 minutes before slicing. Cut tenderloin crosswise into thin slices. Spread 1½ teaspoons cream on bottom half of each roll; top each roll with about 1 ounce beef and top half of roll. Yield: 30 sandwiches (serving size: 1 sandwich).

CALORIES 198 (23% from fat); FAT 5.1g (sat 2.4g, mono 1.1g, poly 0.2g); PROTEIN 10.6g; CARB 26.3g; FIBER 1.1g; CHOL 21mg; IRON 2.7mg; SODIUM 385mg; CALC 71mg

Serve only the best cocktails and desserts to your friends.

A cocktail party is "not a formal affair; it is as democratic as the subway."

Spicy Meringue Kisses

If you don't have a piping bag and star tip, snip a corner from a large zip-top plastic bag, and use it to pipe meringue onto a baking sheet.

    2   large egg whites
    ⅛   teaspoon cream of tartar
    Dash of salt
    ¼   cup packed light brown sugar
    ¼   teaspoon ground cinnamon
    ¼   teaspoon ground ginger
    ¼   teaspoon vanilla extract
    Dash of ground black pepper
    Dash of ground cloves

1. Preheat oven to 225°.
2. Cover 2 large baking sheets with parchment paper; secure with masking tape.
3. Place egg whites, cream of tartar, and salt in a medium bowl; beat with a mixer at medium speed until soft peaks form. Increase speed to high; gradually add sugar, 1 tablespoon at a time, beating until stiff peaks form. Add cinnamon and remaining ingredients; beat just until blended.
4. Spoon batter into a pastry bag fitted with a large star tip. Pipe 60 mounds onto prepared baking sheets.
5. Bake meringues at 225° for 1½ hours. Turn oven off, and cool meringues in closed oven 1½ hours or until dry. Carefully remove meringues from paper. Yield: 5 dozen (serving size: 1 cookie).

CALORIES 4 (0% from fat); FAT 0g; PROTEIN 0.1g; CARB 0.9g; FIBER 0g; CHOL 0mg; IRON 0mg; SODIUM 5mg; CALC 1mg

Coconut Biscotti

Standing the cookies eliminates the traditional step of flipping them halfway through baking. Chocolate lovers can stir ½ cup mini chocolate chips into the batter or dip half of each cookie into melted chocolate.

    1½ cups all-purpose flour
    ¾   teaspoon baking powder
    ¼   teaspoon salt
    ¼   teaspoon baking soda
    ⅛   teaspoon grated whole nutmeg
    ¾   cup sugar
    1   teaspoon vanilla extract
    2   large eggs
    1   cup flaked sweetened coconut

1. Preheat oven to 300°.
2. Lightly spoon flour into dry measuring cups; level with a knife. Combine flour and next 4 ingredients. Place sugar, vanilla, and eggs in a large bowl; beat with a mixer at medium speed 2 minutes or until thick. Add flour mixture and coconut; stir to combine (dough will be very sticky). Turn dough out onto a heavily floured surface; knead lightly 7 or 8 times. Shape dough into a 15 x 3-inch roll. Place roll on a baking sheet lined with parchment paper, and pat to 1-inch thickness. Bake at 300° for 40 minutes or until roll is golden brown. Cool 5 minutes on a wire rack.
3. Cut roll diagonally into 20 (½-inch-thick) slices; stand slices upright on baking sheet. Bake 20 minutes (cookies will be slightly soft in center but will harden as they cool). Remove from baking sheet; cool completely on wire rack. Yield: 20 cookies (serving size: 1 biscotto).

CALORIES 90 (25% from fat); FAT 2.5g (sat 2.2g, mono 0.2g, poly 0.1g); PROTEIN 1.8g; CARB 15.3g; FIBER 0.6g; CHOL 21mg; IRON 0.5mg; SODIUM 87mg; CALC 13mg

The Well-Stocked Bar

We suggest three mixed drinks to offer your guests. It's hard to juggle more, unless you want to play bartender the whole time. A well-stocked bar should include the following:

- Ice-cold, top-quality vodka (keep in freezer)
- Kentucky bourbon, single-malt scotch, and tequila—all at room temperature—plus dry white French vermouth, dark and medium rums, tonic, bitters, and liqueurs
- Plenty of ice; bucket and tongs
- Red and white wines for guests who prefer wine
- Water, club soda, soft drinks, and fruit juices
- Metal cocktail shaker (to shake the Pineapple Margarita; use shaker container to stir the vodka, vermouth, and ice for the Classic Dry Martini)
- Strainer for martinis
- Appropriate glasses for martinis, Old-Fashioneds, highballs, and wine
- Olives and onions (for martinis), lemons (zest for martinis), and limes (rub on rims of glasses for margaritas)

Classic Dry Martini

Unlike James Bond's favorite cocktail, this version is stirred, not shaken. Chill vodka in the freezer so it's as cold as possible.

    Crushed ice
    6   tablespoons chilled vodka
    ½   teaspoon dry white vermouth
    1   (2-inch) strip lemon rind

1. Place crushed ice in a martini shaker. Add vodka and vermouth; stir.
2. Rub rim of a martini glass with inside of lemon rind. Twist rind, and drop into glass. Strain vodka mixture in shaker into glass. Serve immediately. Yield: 1 serving (serving size: about ⅓ cup).

CALORIES 228 (0% from fat); FAT 0g; PROTEIN 0g; CARB 0.3g; FIBER 0g; CHOL 0mg; IRON 0mg; SODIUM 1mg; CALC 0mg

Indian in origin, curry has traveled the world. These warm, saucy dishes reveal the distinct flavors of the countries that have adopted the vivid spice blend.

QUICK & EASY
Old-Fashioned

This is an adaptation of James Beard's formula for this American classic. Most people use bourbon, but it can also be made with rum or brandy. There is no garnish of maraschino cherry or orange because, as Beard wrote, "I loathe fruit salad . . . and all the decorations that usually accompany this simple drink."

- ½ teaspoon sugar
- 3 dashes bitters
- 1 (1-inch) strip lemon rind
- 6 tablespoons bourbon
- Crushed ice

1. Place sugar, bitters, and rind in a tall glass; crush with back of a spoon. Add bourbon; stir to combine. Fill glass with crushed ice. Yield: 1 serving (serving size: about ⅓ cup).

CALORIES 261 (0% from fat); FAT 0g; PROTEIN 0g; CARB 7g; FIBER 0.1g; CHOL 0mg; IRON 0mg; SODIUM 1mg; CALC 1mg

QUICK & EASY
Pineapple Margarita

The pineapple juice adds an extra dimension of Caribbean flavor. To serve in salt-rimmed glasses, rub a lime wedge around the rims of the glasses. Spread 1 teaspoon margarita or sea salt on a small plate. Place glass, rim side down, on salt; turn to coat rim.

- ½ cup tequila
- ½ cup pineapple juice
- 6 tablespoons fresh lime juice
- 3 tablespoons triple sec
- 2 teaspoons sugar
- Crushed ice
- Lime slices (optional)

1. Place first 5 ingredients in a cocktail shaker. Add ice; shake vigorously until blended. Garnish with lime slice, if desired. Yield: 2 servings (serving size: ¾ cup).

CALORIES 264 (0% from fat); FAT 0.1g (sat 0g, mono 0g, poly 0.1g); PROTEIN 0.4g; CARB 24.4g; FIBER 0.3g; CHOL 0mg; IRON 0.2mg; SODIUM 3mg; CALC 15mg

QUICK & EASY • MAKE AHEAD
Chickpea Curry with Yogurt

Whole milk yogurt contributes a silky, creamy texture to this mild vegetarian stew from India. Serve with steamed or sautéed spinach and Indian bread. Replicate *naan*, the Indian flatbread, by cooking flour tortillas in a grill pan or cast-iron skillet until blackened in spots. The cinnamon sticks and bay leaves are removed before the dish is served, but the cardamom pods are more difficult to fish out. Be careful as you eat not to bite into one.

- 2 teaspoons peanut oil
- 2 teaspoons cumin seeds
- 1 teaspoon coriander seeds
- 6 cardamom pods
- 2 bay leaves
- 2 (3-inch) cinnamon sticks
- 1½ cups chopped onion
- 2 tablespoons minced peeled fresh ginger
- 4 garlic cloves, minced
- 2 teaspoons garam masala
- 1 cup water
- ½ cup chopped plum tomato (about 1 large)
- ½ teaspoon salt
- 2 (15½-ounce) cans chickpeas (garbanzo beans), rinsed and drained
- 1 cup plain whole milk yogurt
- ½ cup chopped fresh cilantro

1. Heat oil in a large nonstick skillet over medium heat. Add cumin and next 4 ingredients; cook 30 seconds or until fragrant, stirring constantly. Add onion, and cook 2 minutes, stirring frequently. Add ginger and garlic; cook 30 seconds, stirring constantly. Stir in garam masala, and cook 10 seconds, stirring constantly. Stir in 1 cup water, tomato, salt, and chickpeas; bring to a simmer. Cook 5 minutes, stirring occasionally. Remove from heat; discard bay leaves and cinnamon sticks. Stir in yogurt and cilantro. Yield: 4 servings (serving size: 1 cup).

CALORIES 262 (28% from fat); FAT 8.2g (sat 1.7g, mono 3.1g, poly 2.9g); PROTEIN 10.2g; CARB 38.9g; FIBER 8.6g; CHOL 8mg; IRON 3.8mg; SODIUM 579mg; CALC 173mg

MAKE AHEAD
Rogan Josh

Originating in Kashmir in northern India, where various trade routes and political rivalries have played out, this mild, aromatic lamb curry uses seasonings reflective of its crossroad status. It takes on a characteristic red hue from the use of bright-colored spices. Serve inside a pita pocket or with toasted pita chips.

- 1½ teaspoons ground cumin
- 1½ teaspoons ground coriander
- 1 teaspoon ground ginger
- 1 teaspoon chili powder
- 1 teaspoon ground cinnamon
- ½ teaspoon salt
- ½ teaspoon ground turmeric
- ¼ teaspoon saffron threads
- ¼ teaspoon ground cloves
- 1½ pounds boneless leg of lamb, trimmed and cut into ½-inch cubes
- 1 teaspoon canola oil
- 1 cup less-sodium beef broth
- ½ cup low-fat yogurt
- ½ cup chopped fresh cilantro

1. Combine first 9 ingredients in a large zip-top plastic bag. Add lamb; seal and *Continued* shake to coat. Refrigerate 8 hours or overnight.

2. Heat oil in a large saucepan over medium-high heat. Add lamb mixture; cook 4 minutes, stirring constantly. Add broth, scraping pan to loosen browned bits; bring to a boil. Cover, reduce heat, and simmer 1 hour. Increase heat to medium-high; partially cover and cook 1 hour or until lamb is tender. Uncover and cook 5 minutes or until sauce thickens. Remove from heat; stir in yogurt and cilantro. Yield: 4 servings (serving size: about ⅔ cup).

CALORIES 193 (38% from fat); FAT 8.2g (sat 2.5g, mono 3.5g, poly 0.9g); PROTEIN 24g; CARB 4.8g; FIBER 1.5g; CHOL 67mg; IRON 2.6mg; SODIUM 396mg; CALC 90mg

Burmese Chicken Curry with Yellow Lentils
Kalapei Kyetharbin

Situated between India and China, Myanmar (formerly Burma) combines the food traditions of both countries it borders. This dish is evidence of those influences—yellow lentils, sometimes called *chana dal*, are common to Indian cooking, and this thick, comforting stew is often served over Chinese egg noodles (though basmati rice is also a good base). As with most curries, a frosty cold beer is a great match.

1½ cups dried yellow lentils
2 teaspoons ground cumin
2 teaspoons sweet paprika
2 teaspoons ground turmeric
¾ teaspoon salt
½ teaspoon ground nutmeg
¼ teaspoon ground cloves
1½ pounds skinless, boneless chicken thighs, cut into bite-size pieces
1 tablespoon canola oil
1 cup chopped onion
2¾ cups fat-free, less-sodium chicken broth
3 bay leaves

1. Place lentils in a large saucepan; cover with water to 2 inches above lentils. Bring to a boil over medium-high heat; cover, reduce heat, and simmer 25 minutes or until tender. Drain and set aside.

2. Combine cumin and next 5 ingredients in a large zip-top plastic bag. Add chicken; seal and shake to coat.

3. Heat oil in a large Dutch oven over medium-high heat. Add onion; sauté 3 minutes or until tender. Add mixture; sauté 4 minutes. Stir in broth, scraping pan to loosen browned bits. Add lentils and bay leaves; cover and simmer 30 minutes. Uncover and simmer 10 minutes. Discard bay leaves. Yield: 6 servings (serving size: about 1¼ cups).

CALORIES 344 (21% from fat); FAT 8.2g (sat 1.6g, mono 3.1g, poly 2.4g); PROTEIN 35.8g; CARB 31.9g; FIBER 6.3g; CHOL 94mg; IRON 5.3mg; SODIUM 576mg; CALC 50mg

Shrimp Vindaloo

Although most people know this fiery stew as an Indian dish, it actually was created in the Portuguese-Indian colony of Goa. The name comes from two of the curry's key ingredients—*vinho*, which refers to wine vinegar, and *alhos*, which means garlic. The original Goan version was not as spicy, but as India adopted the dish as its own, the seasonings became hotter. Vindaloos are often made with meat, but this seafood version is pleasantly light. Customize according to your preference—just go up or down on the ground red pepper to suit your taste. Serve over white or brown rice to cut the heat.

2 teaspoons minced peeled fresh ginger
½ teaspoon salt
½ teaspoon dry mustard
½ teaspoon ground coriander
½ teaspoon ground cumin
½ teaspoon ground turmeric
¼ to ½ teaspoon ground red pepper
¼ teaspoon ground cinnamon
⅛ teaspoon ground cloves
1 tablespoon red wine vinegar
1 tablespoon canola oil
1½ cups chopped onion
2 tablespoons minced peeled fresh ginger
3 garlic cloves, minced
1¼ cups fat-free, less-sodium chicken broth
2 tablespoons golden raisins, chopped
1 pound medium shrimp, peeled and deveined

1. Combine first 9 ingredients in a small bowl. Add vinegar, stirring to form a paste; set aside.

2. Heat oil in a large nonstick skillet over medium-high heat. Add onion, and sauté 2 minutes. Stir in 2 tablespoons ginger and garlic; sauté 20 seconds. Add spice paste; cook 30 seconds, stirring constantly. Stir in broth and raisins. Simmer, uncovered, 10 minutes. Add shrimp; cook 4 minutes or until shrimp are done, stirring occasionally. Yield: 4 servings (serving size: about ¾ cup).

CALORIES 208 (26% from fat); FAT 5.9g (sat 0.7g, mono 2.4g, poly 1.9g); PROTEIN 25.3g; CARB 12.5g; FIBER 1.9g; CHOL 127mg; IRON 3.4mg; SODIUM 607mg; CALC 87mg

Cape Malay Curry

Cape Malay curry is known for its combination of sweet and savory flavors—sweet spices, dried fruit (especially dried apricots), and savory seasonings. Though usually served with rice, this beef stew is also great over mashed potatoes or egg noodles.

1½ teaspoons ground turmeric
1½ teaspoons ground cumin
1½ teaspoons ground coriander
1½ teaspoons chili powder
¾ teaspoon ground cinnamon
½ teaspoon salt
2 teaspoons canola oil
2 cups chopped onion
1½ tablespoons minced peeled fresh ginger
2 bay leaves
1 garlic clove, minced
1 pound beef stew meat, cut into bite-size pieces
1¼ cups less-sodium beef broth
1 cup water
1 cup chopped green bell pepper (about 1 medium)
⅓ cup chopped dried apricots
⅓ cup apricot spread (such as Polaner All Fruit)
2 teaspoons red wine vinegar
¼ cup low-fat buttermilk

1. Combine first 6 ingredients in a small bowl, stirring well.

2. Heat oil in a Dutch oven over medium-high heat. Add spice mixture; cook 15 seconds, stirring constantly. Add onion; sauté 2 minutes. Add ginger, bay leaves, and garlic; sauté 15 seconds. Add beef; sauté 3 minutes. Add broth and next 5 ingredients; bring to a boil. Cover, reduce heat, and simmer 1½ hours. Uncover; discard bay leaves. Simmer 30 minutes or until beef is very tender. Remove from heat; stir in buttermilk. Yield: 4 servings (serving size: 1¼ cups).

CALORIES 349 (30% from fat); FAT 11.5g (sat 3.4g, mono 5.1g, poly 1.2g); PROTEIN 25.7g; CARB 35.3g; FIBER 3.9g; CHOL 71mg; IRON 4.3mg; SODIUM 396mg; CALC 77mg

Colombo Curry

This version uses pork tenderloin and sweet potatoes for similar flavors with more readily available ingredients. Uncooked rice is toasted and ground with the spices to thicken the stew as it cooks.

    2   tablespoons uncooked long-grain
        white rice
    2   teaspoons coriander seeds
    2   teaspoons cumin seeds
    2   teaspoons mustard seeds
    2   whole cloves
    2   teaspoons ground turmeric
    2   teaspoons ground fenugreek
    1   tablespoon canola oil
 1½   cups thinly sliced green onions
    ½   cup finely chopped shallots
    2   tablespoons minced peeled fresh
        ginger
    2   garlic cloves, minced
 1½   pounds pork tenderloin, trimmed
        and cut into ½-inch cubes
    3   cups (½-inch) cubed peeled sweet
        potato
    1   (14-ounce) can fat-free,
        less-sodium chicken broth
    1   tablespoon fresh lime juice
    ¾   teaspoon salt
    ½   teaspoon black pepper

1. Place rice in a small nonstick skillet; cook over medium-high heat 3 minutes or until lightly browned, stirring constantly. Add coriander, cumin, mustard seeds, and cloves; cook 30 seconds, stirring constantly. Add turmeric and fenugreek; cook 15 seconds, stirring constantly. Remove mixture from pan; let stand 5 minutes. Place in a spice or coffee grinder; process until finely ground.
2. Heat oil in a Dutch oven over medium-high heat. Add onions, shallots, ginger, and garlic; sauté 1½ minutes. Add pork; sauté 3 minutes. Add sweet potato; cook 1 minute, stirring frequently. Stir in broth; bring to a boil. Stir in ground rice mixture; cover, reduce heat, and simmer 15 minutes or until sweet potato is tender. Stir in lime juice, salt, and pepper. Yield: 6 servings (serving size: 1 cup).

CALORIES 288 (23% from fat); FAT 7.4g (sat 1.7g, mono 3.4g, poly 1.3g); PROTEIN 27.8g; CARB 27.2g; FIBER 4.4g; CHOL 74mg; IRON 4.1mg; SODIUM 491mg; CALC 70mg

Masaman Curry

Tamarind paste—found in Indian, Middle Eastern, and Asian markets—has a sweet-sour taste that's key to many curries; substitute 1½ teaspoons fresh lime juice plus ½ teaspoon molasses if you can't find it.

    1   teaspoon cumin seeds
    1   teaspoon coriander seeds
    ½   teaspoon ground cinnamon
    ½   teaspoon ground nutmeg
    3   large dried New Mexico chiles,
        halved lengthwise, seeded, and
        torn into large pieces
    2   cardamom pods
    2   tablespoons chopped peeled fresh
        lemongrass
    1   tablespoon chopped peeled fresh
        ginger
    3   garlic cloves, halved
    1   (14-ounce) can less-sodium beef
        broth, divided
    2   teaspoons peanut oil
    3   cups thinly vertically sliced onion
    1   pound boneless sirloin steak,
        trimmed and cut into 1-inch cubes
    1   cup water
    1   tablespoon tamarind paste
    ¾   teaspoon salt
    1   pound small white potatoes,
        halved
    ⅓   cup light coconut milk

1. Heat a large nonstick skillet over medium heat. Add first 6 ingredients; cook 2 minutes or until fragrant, stirring frequently. Remove from heat; cool 5 minutes. Place spice mixture in a food processor; add lemongrass, ginger, garlic, and ¼ cup broth. Process 1 minute, scraping sides occasionally; set aside.
2. Heat oil in a Dutch oven over medium heat. Add onion; cook 3 minutes or until tender, stirring occasionally. Stir in spice mixture; cook 1 minute, stirring constantly. Add beef, and cook 3 minutes, stirring frequently. Stir in remaining broth and water, scraping pan to loosen browned bits. Stir in tamarind paste, salt, and potatoes; bring to a simmer. Cover, reduce heat, and simmer 1 hour or until beef is very tender. Remove from heat; stir in coconut milk. Yield: 6 servings (serving size: about ¾ cup).

CALORIES 239 (27% from fat); FAT 7.2g (sat 2.7g, mono 2.8g, poly 0.8g); PROTEIN 19.3g; CARB 23.5g; FIBER 3.1g; CHOL 49mg; IRON 2.8mg; SODIUM 347mg; CALC 45mg

Homemade vs. Commercial

All these recipes derive distinct flavors from freshly made curry powders or pastes. We also tried the recipes using commercial versions, and the results were far less successful. The bottled powders and pastes we used were often less pungent, less aromatic, and less woody (because the various spice oils, including chile oils, had lost flavor over a period of time). The result was that everything was hot but not very fragrant. It doesn't take much time to prepare these blends from scratch, and the results are well worth it. You may discover that you have most of the ingredients on your spice rack already.

MAKE AHEAD

Cambodian Chicken Curry
Chicken Samlá

This is one of the most popular dishes in Cambodia. It's a soupy curry that's more aromatic and less spicy than curries found in other parts of Southeast Asia. It uses a substantial amount of fresh ginger and lemongrass for flavor and fragrance. Serve over rice to soak up the sauce.

½   cup thinly sliced peeled fresh ginger
¼   cup chopped peeled fresh lemongrass
1½ tablespoons shrimp sauce (such as Lee Kum Kee) or shrimp paste
1   tablespoon rice wine vinegar
1   teaspoon grated lime rind
½   teaspoon salt
½   teaspoon crushed red pepper
½   teaspoon ground turmeric
5   garlic cloves, halved
2   large shallots, peeled and quartered
    Cooking spray
6   (4-ounce) chicken drumsticks, skinned
6   (4-ounce) chicken thighs, skinned
1   cup fat-free, less-sodium chicken broth
¾   cup light coconut milk
1   teaspoon sugar
1   tablespoon fresh lime juice
    Lime wedges (optional)

1. Place first 10 ingredients in a food processor; process until minced, scraping sides of bowl occasionally.
2. Heat a large nonstick skillet over medium-high heat. Coat pan with cooking spray. Add ginger mixture; sauté 2 minutes. Add chicken; cook 2 minutes on each side. Add broth, coconut milk, and sugar, scraping pan to loosen browned bits; bring mixture to a boil. Cover, reduce heat, and simmer 45 minutes or until chicken is done.
3. Remove pan from heat. Remove chicken from pan, reserving liquid in pan; cool chicken slightly. Remove meat from bones, and discard bones. Place pan over medium heat. Stir in chicken and lime juice; cook 2 minutes or until thoroughly heated. Serve with lime wedges, if desired. Yield: 4 servings (serving size: 1½ cups).

CALORIES 299 (29% from fat); FAT 9.6g (sat 4g, mono 2.2g, poly 1.8g); PROTEIN 41.2g; CARB 11g; FIBER 1g; CHOL 159mg; IRON 3.3mg; SODIUM 871mg; CALC 65mg

Potato Roti Curry
(pictured on facing page)

This mild, soupy side dish hails from the Caribbean. While *roti* is traditional, whole wheat tortillas or pitas are great accompaniments for sopping up the liquid. Serve with lime wedges and rice.

2   teaspoons ground cumin
1½ teaspoons ground turmeric
1¼ teaspoons salt
1   teaspoon ground ginger
¼   teaspoon ground allspice
¼   teaspoon crushed red pepper
1   tablespoon canola oil
1½ cups chopped onion
4   garlic cloves, minced
4   cups (1-inch) cubed peeled Yukon gold potato (about 1½ pounds)
3   cups (1-inch) cubed peeled acorn squash (about ¾ pound)
1   cup chopped red bell pepper
2   cups water
½   cup light coconut milk
½   cup chopped fresh cilantro

1. Combine first 6 ingredients; set aside.
2. Heat oil in a large Dutch oven over medium heat. Add onion; cook 3 minutes or until tender, stirring frequently. Add garlic; cook 15 seconds, stirring constantly. Add spice mixture; cook 30 seconds, stirring constantly. Add potato, squash, and bell pepper, stirring to coat with spice mixture; cook 1 minute, stirring constantly. Stir in water and coconut milk, scraping pan to loosen browned bits; bring to a boil. Cover, reduce heat, and simmer 25 minutes or until potato is tender. Sprinkle with cilantro. Yield: 6 servings (serving size: about 1 cup).

CALORIES 183 (19% from fat); FAT 3.9g (sat 1.2g, mono 1.4g, poly 0.9g); PROTEIN 3.6g; CARB 36.2g; FIBER 4.1g; CHOL 0mg; IRON 1.7mg; SODIUM 510mg; CALC 56mg

Potato Roti Curry, page 92

From left: Eggplant Caponata, page 85,
Marinated Shrimp, page 87, and Wrinkled
Potatoes with Black Caviar, page 86

Grilled Vegetable Lasagna, page 120

Ricotta Cheesecake with Fresh
Berry Topping, page 110

Fruit Salad with Citrus-Mint Dressing,
page 97

More Potassium, Please

Abundant in many everyday foods, this important mineral helps keep blood pressure in check.

Here are recipes and a daily menu (page 100) to help you see how easy it is to add more potassium to your diet, with an emphasis on fresh fruits, vegetables, lean meats, and whole grains.

QUICK & EASY
Fruit Salad with Citrus-Mint Dressing
(pictured on facing page)

Serve this potassium-packed fruit salad (662 milligrams per serving) with breakfast or as a light dessert. Use a mini chopper to combine the dressing ingredients—it's the ideal size to blend the small amount of dressing for the salad.

    6   kiwifruit, peeled and each cut into
        8 wedges
    2   cups (1½-inch) cubes
        honeydew
    2   cups (1½-inch) cubes cantaloupe
    1   papaya, peeled and cut into
        1-inch chunks
    ½   teaspoon finely grated fresh
        orange peel
    2   tablespoons fresh orange
        juice
    1½ tablespoons fresh mint
    1   tablespoon sugar
    1   teaspoon fresh lime juice

1. Combine first 4 ingredients in a medium bowl.
2. Place grated peel and remaining 4 ingredients in a mini chopper or food processor; pulse until mint is finely chopped. Pour sugar mixture over fruit, and stir gently to coat. Yield: 6 servings (serving size: about 1⅓ cups).

CALORIES 120 (6% from fat); FAT 0.8g (sat 0.1g, mono 0g, poly 0.1g); PROTEIN 2.2g; CARB 29.4g; FIBER 3.5g; CHOL 0mg; IRON 0.9mg; SODIUM 21mg; CALC 55mg

QUICK & EASY • MAKE AHEAD
Multibean Salad

This is an updated take on a traditional three-bean salad. Soybeans are rich in potassium, and matched with other good vegetable sources, this is a side dish that can add 430 milligrams of the mineral to your next lunch.

    2   cups (½-inch) diagonally cut
        haricots verts (about 8 ounces)
    2   cups (½-inch) diagonally cut wax
        beans (about 8 ounces)
    1   cup frozen shelled edamame
        (green soybeans)
    1   cup grape or cherry tomatoes,
        halved
    ½   cup finely chopped orange bell
        pepper
    ½   cup thinly sliced red onion
    2   tablespoons sherry vinegar
    ½   teaspoon sugar
    ¼   teaspoon Dijon mustard
    2   teaspoons extravirgin olive oil
    ¼   cup chopped fresh parsley
    ¼   teaspoon salt
    ¼   teaspoon freshly ground
        black pepper

1. Steam first 3 ingredients, covered, 6 minutes or until haricots verts and wax beans are crisp-tender. Drain and plunge haricots verts and beans into ice water; drain. Combine beans, tomatoes, bell pepper, and onion in a large bowl.
2. Combine vinegar, sugar, and mustard, stirring with a whisk. Gradually add oil to vinegar mixture, stirring constantly with a whisk. Stir in parsley, salt, and black pepper. Drizzle vinaigrette over bean mixture; toss gently to coat. Yield: 6 servings (serving size: about 1 cup).

CALORIES 85 (29% from fat); FAT 2.7g (sat 0.2g, mono 1.1g, poly 0.2g); PROTEIN 4.4g; CARB 11g; FIBER 4g; CHOL 0mg; IRON 1.5mg; SODIUM 125mg; CALC 48mg

QUICK & EASY
Maple-Bourbon Glazed Salmon

This speedy recipe uses staple ingredients and provides 790 milligrams of potassium per serving—97 percent of it from the salmon.

    5   teaspoons fresh orange juice,
        divided
    1   tablespoon maple syrup
    1   teaspoon bourbon
    ⅛   teaspoon ground red pepper
    4   (6-ounce) salmon fillets
    Cooking spray
    ¼   teaspoon salt

1. Preheat broiler.
2. Combine 1 teaspoon juice, syrup, bourbon, and pepper, stirring with a whisk. Place salmon on a broiler pan coated with cooking spray. Brush syrup mixture evenly over salmon, and sprinkle with salt.
3. Broil salmon 5 minutes. Remove pan from oven; drizzle 1 teaspoon juice over each fillet. Broil 1 minute or until fish flakes easily when tested with a fork. Yield: 4 servings (serving size: 1 fillet).

CALORIES 291 (41% from fat); FAT 13.1g (sat 3.1g, mono 5.7g, poly 3.2g); PROTEIN 36.2g; CARB 4.1g; FIBER 0g; CHOL 87mg; IRON 0.7mg; SODIUM 228mg; CALC 25mg

Pan-Seared Grouper with Roasted Tomato Sauce

Most types of fish are high in potassium. Here, grouper, which provides 822 milligrams in a six-ounce serving, is paired with a potassium-rich sauce made of roasted tomatoes for an entrée with more than 1,300 milligrams of potassium per serving.

 1 red bell pepper, cut into 1-inch strips
12 plum tomatoes, halved lengthwise and cut into 1/2-inch slices
Cooking spray
 2 tablespoons olive oil, divided
3/4 teaspoon salt, divided
1/2 teaspoon dried Italian seasoning
 1 tablespoon red wine vinegar
1/4 teaspoon freshly ground black pepper
 5 basil leaves
 2 tablespoons all-purpose flour
 1 tablespoon cornmeal
 4 (6-ounce) grouper fillets (about 1 inch thick)
 2 tablespoons chopped fresh basil (optional)

1. Preheat oven to 350°.
2. Arrange bell pepper and tomato in a single layer on a jelly-roll pan coated with cooking spray; drizzle with 1 tablespoon oil. Sprinkle with 1/4 teaspoon salt and Italian seasoning; stir to coat. Bake at 350° for 40 minutes or until edges are lightly browned. Remove from oven.
3. Increase oven temperature to 400°.
4. Transfer tomato mixture to a food processor. Add 1/4 teaspoon salt, vinegar, black pepper, and basil leaves; process until smooth. Spoon tomato mixture into a bowl. Cover and keep warm.
5. Heat 1 tablespoon oil in a large ovenproof skillet over medium-high heat. Combine flour and cornmeal in a shallow dish. Sprinkle fish with 1/4 teaspoon salt; dredge in flour mixture. Add fish to pan; cook 3 minutes. Turn fish over; bake at 400° for 8 minutes or until fish flakes easily when tested with a fork. Serve fish with tomato sauce; garnish with chopped basil, if desired. Yield: 4 servings (serving size: 1 fillet and about 1/4 cup tomato sauce).

CALORIES 278 (29% from fat); FAT 9g (sat 1.4g, mono 5.4g, poly 1.5g); PROTEIN 35.4g; CARB 13.4g; FIBER 3g; CHOL 63mg; IRON 2.5mg; SODIUM 543mg; CALC 70mg

Avocado-Mango Salsa with Roasted Corn Chips

Avocado provides more than half of the 158 milligrams of potassium in each serving of this snack, which is also a good source of fiber and monounsaturated fat.

12 (6-inch) corn tortillas, each cut into 6 wedges
Cooking spray
1/4 teaspoon kosher salt, divided
1 1/4 cups chopped peeled avocado
 1 cup chopped peeled mango
 4 teaspoons fresh lime juice
 1 tablespoon finely chopped fresh cilantro
Cilantro sprigs (optional)

1. Preheat oven to 425°.
2. Arrange tortilla wedges in a single layer on baking sheets coated with cooking spray. Coat wedges with cooking spray; sprinkle 1/8 teaspoon salt over wedges. Bake at 425° for 8 minutes or until crisp.
3. Combine 1/8 teaspoon salt, avocado, and next 3 ingredients, tossing gently. Garnish with cilantro sprigs, if desired. Let stand 10 minutes. Serve with chips. Yield: 12 servings (serving size: about 3 tablespoons salsa and 6 chips).

CALORIES 92 (30% from fat); FAT 3.1g (sat 0.5g, mono 1.7g, poly 0.6g); PROTEIN 1.9g; CARB 15.8g; FIBER 2.4g; CHOL 0mg; IRON 0.6mg; SODIUM 83mg; CALC 49mg

Chocolate and Malt Pudding

Puddings are good sources of potassium because their main ingredient, milk, is potassium-rich. Both the malted milk powder and the chocolate add small amounts of the mineral to this creamy dessert, which has 539 milligrams of potassium in each serving. If you like strong malt flavor, you can increase the malt powder to one cup. This recipe earned our Test Kitchens highest rating.

2/3 cup malted milk powder
1/3 cup sugar
1/3 cup cornstarch
1/8 teaspoon salt
 4 cups 1% low-fat milk
1/3 cup semisweet chocolate chips
 1 teaspoon vanilla extract
 8 malted milk ball candies (such as Whoppers), crushed

1. Combine first 4 ingredients in a medium, heavy saucepan, stirring well with a whisk. Gradually add milk, stirring constantly with a whisk until well blended. Place pan over medium heat, and bring to a boil. Cook 1 minute or until thick, stirring constantly with a whisk. Remove from heat. Add chocolate chips, and stir until smooth. Stir in vanilla.
2. Pour pudding into a bowl; cover surface of pudding with plastic wrap. Chill. Remove plastic wrap; spoon 2/3 cup pudding into each of 6 bowls. Sprinkle each serving with 2 teaspoons crushed malted milk balls. Yield: 6 servings.

CALORIES 305 (18% from fat); FAT 6g (sat 3.5g, mono 1.3g, poly 0.2g); PROTEIN 8.3g; CARB 54.3g; FIBER 0.4g; CHOL 13mg; IRON 4.5mg; SODIUM 238mg; CALC 303mg

Flank Steak with Caramelized Onions and Balsamic Glaze

Both the steak and onions contribute a hefty dose of potassium to this entrée—766 milligrams in each serving. Serve with steamed broccoli or asparagus, and drizzle some of the glaze over the vegetable.

- ⅔ cup balsamic vinegar
- 1 tablespoon olive oil
- 6 cups vertically sliced onion (about 1½ pounds)
- ½ teaspoon salt, divided
- 1 (1-pound) flank steak, trimmed
- ¼ teaspoon freshly ground black pepper
- ¼ teaspoon dried thyme
- Cooking spray

1. Bring vinegar to a boil in a small, heavy saucepan. Reduce heat to medium; cook until reduced to ¼ cup (about 5 minutes). Remove from heat.
2. Heat oil in a large nonstick skillet over medium-high heat. Add onion, and sauté 10 minutes or until tender. Sprinkle with ¼ teaspoon salt; sauté 18 minutes or until onions are golden brown. Remove from heat.
3. Preheat broiler.
4. Sprinkle steak with ¼ teaspoon salt, pepper, and thyme. Place steak on a broiler pan coated with cooking spray; broil 6 minutes on each side or until desired degree of doneness. Cut steak diagonally across grain into thin slices. Serve steak over onions; drizzle with balsamic glaze. Yield: 4 servings (serving size: about 3 ounces steak, about ¼ cup onions, and about 1 tablespoon balsamic glaze).

WINE NOTE: Steak and caramelized onions are fabulous partners for numerous red wines. But the balsamic vinegar glaze presents a bit of a challenge since vinegar can make wine taste sharp. One variety stands up especially well to vinegar: syrah (also known as shiraz). Try Geyser Peak Winery's shiraz from California, which is dense and lip-smacking—a steal at $18.

CALORIES 317 (28% from fat); FAT 9.9g (sat 2.8g, mono 4.8g, poly 0.7g); PROTEIN 26.9g; CARB 30.6g; FIBER 3.4g; CHOL 37mg; IRON 2.7mg; SODIUM 375mg; CALC 95mg

---

MAKE AHEAD
Walnut-Crusted Potato and Blue Cheese Cakes

To avoid dirtying another dish, mash the potatoes in the same pot used to cook them. The cakes can be shaped a few hours ahead, covered, and chilled until you're ready to eat. After chilling, cook them in the pan for an extra minute to make sure the inside of the cakes are thoroughly heated. Two potato cakes have 761 milligrams of potassium.

- 2 pounds small red potatoes, halved
- 1 garlic clove, peeled
- ⅓ cup (about 1½ ounces) crumbled blue cheese
- ¼ cup 1% low-fat milk
- 1 tablespoon chopped fresh parsley
- ¾ teaspoon salt
- ¼ teaspoon freshly ground black pepper
- 3 tablespoons chopped walnuts
- 2 (1½-ounce) slices sourdough bread
- 1 tablespoon olive oil, divided

1. Place potato and garlic in a large saucepan; cover with water. Bring to a boil; reduce heat, and simmer 20 minutes or until tender. Drain. Return potato and garlic to pan. Add blue cheese and next 4 ingredients; mash with a potato masher to desired consistency. Cool slightly. Shape potato mixture into 12 (½-inch-thick) cakes; set aside.
2. Place walnuts and bread in a food processor; pulse 10 times or until coarse crumbs form. Place in a shallow bowl or pie plate. Dredge potato cakes in breadcrumb mixture.
3. Heat 1½ teaspoons oil in a large nonstick skillet over medium heat. Add 6 potato cakes, and cook 2 minutes on each side or until browned. Remove cakes from pan; cover and keep warm. Repeat procedure with 1½ teaspoons oil and 6 potato cakes. Yield: 6 servings (serving size: 2 potato cakes).

CALORIES 219 (30% from fat); FAT 7.4g (sat 2g, mono 2.6g, poly 2.2g); PROTEIN 6.7g; CARB 32.5g; FIBER 3.3g; CHOL 6mg; IRON 1.9mg; SODIUM 489mg; CALC 84mg

---

Best Sources of Potassium

1,000mg
- Avocado (1 cup)
- Baked potato (8 ounces with skin)
- Beet greens (¾ cup, cooked)
- Edamame (1 cup shelled, cooked)
- Lima beans (1 cup, cooked)
- Papaya (1 large)
- Sweet potato (1 cup, cooked)

750mg
- Plantains (1 cup, cooked)
- Salmon (6 ounces, raw)
- Tomato sauce (1 cup)
- Winter squash (1 cup, cooked)

500mg
- Banana (1 large)
- Beets (1 cup, cooked)
- Cantaloupe (1 cup)
- Dried apricots (12 halves)
- Dried figs (4)
- Orange juice (1 cup)
- Yogurt (1 cup plain low-fat)

250mg
- Broccoli (½ cup, cooked)
- Chicken breast (5 ounces, roasted)
- Dates (5 whole)
- Kiwifruit (1)
- Mango (1)
- Milk (1 cup)
- Nectarine (1)
- Orange (1 medium)
- Peanut butter (2 tablespoons)
- Peanuts (1 ounce, about ¼ cup)
- Pear (1 large)
- Raisins (¼ cup)
- Strawberries (1 cup)
- Zucchini (½ cup, cooked)

Potassium Adds Up

This example of a daily menu shows how recipes that accompany this story, along with other foods, can provide your recommended potassium intake of 4,700 mg.

		Calories	Fat(g)	Potassium(mg)	Sodium(mg)
breakfast	Fruit Salad with Citrus-Mint Dressing (page 97)	120	0.8	**662**	21
	Coffee (1 cup)	9	1.8	**114**	2
	Bran muffin	154	4.2	**300**	224
	2% milk (¾ cup)	91	3.5	**283**	91
lunch	Turkey Sandwich:				
	Whole-grain bread (2 ounces)	142	2.2	**116**	276
	Turkey breast (2 ounces)	77	0.4	**166**	29
	Swiss cheese (1 ounce)	107	7.8	**31**	74
	1 romaine lettuce leaf	2	0	**25**	1
	2 tomato slices (½ inch thick)	10	0.1	**128**	3
	1 red onion slice (⅛ inch thick)	6	0	**20**	0
	Fat-free mayonnaise (1 tablespoon)	13	0	**8**	126
	Multibean Salad (page 97)	85	2.7	**430**	125
	Iced tea (1 cup)	2	0	**88**	7
	Apple (1 medium)	72	0.2	**148**	1
snack	Avocado-Mango Salsa with Roasted Corn Chips (page 98)	92	3.1	**158**	83
dinner	Flank Steak with Caramelized Onions and Balsamic Glaze (page 99)	317	9.9	**766**	375
	Walnut-Crusted Potato and Blue Cheese Cakes (page 99)	219	7.4	**761**	489
	Broccoli (½ cup)	22	0.3	**253**	21
	Red wine (4 ounces)	82	0	**127**	6
dessert	Chocolate and Malt Pudding (page 98)	305	6	**539**	238
	Totals	**1,927**	**50.4 (24%)**	**5,123**	**2,192**

Spicy Squash Stew

Most vegetables contain small amounts of potassium, but winter vegetables like squash and parsnips have particularly high amounts. This stew gains 203 milligrams of potassium from the butternut squash and 62 milligrams from the parsnips. The ingredient list is long, but most are easy-to-measure spices. Canned chickpeas and frozen lima beans help keep the cooking time short.

1½ tablespoons canola oil
1½ cups coarsely chopped onion
4 garlic cloves, minced
½ teaspoon salt, divided
1 tablespoon curry powder
1 tablespoon ground cumin
½ teaspoon ground coriander
½ teaspoon ground cinnamon
¼ teaspoon ground red pepper
4 cups (1-inch) cubed peeled butternut squash
1¾ cups less-sodium vegetable broth (such as Swanson Certified Organic)
1 cup chopped parsnip (about 2 medium)
1 (14.5-ounce) can diced tomatoes, undrained
1 cup frozen lima beans, thawed
1 cup canned chickpeas, drained
2 cups fresh baby spinach
1 cup light coconut milk
¼ cup chopped fresh cilantro
1 tablespoon fresh lime juice

1. Heat oil in a Dutch oven over medium-high heat. Add onion; sauté 4 minutes or until tender. Add garlic and ¼ teaspoon salt, and sauté 1 minute. Add curry powder and next 4 ingredients; cook 2 minutes, stirring constantly. Stir in squash, broth, parsnip, and tomatoes; bring to a boil. Cover, reduce heat, and simmer 15 minutes or until squash is slightly tender, stirring occasionally.

2. Stir in ¼ teaspoon salt, lima beans, and chickpeas. Uncover and simmer 8 minutes or until vegetables are tender, stirring occasionally. Add spinach and coconut milk; cook 2 minutes or until thoroughly heated, stirring frequently. Remove from heat. Stir in cilantro and juice. Serve immediately. Yield: 8 servings (serving size: about 1 cup).

CALORIES 167 (29% from fat); FAT 5.4g (sat 1.7g, mono 1.9g, poly 1.3g); PROTEIN 5.2g; CARB 27.2g; FIBER 6.3g; CHOL 0mg; IRON 2.4mg; SODIUM 419mg; CALC 77mg

Chipotle Corn and Two-Bean Chili

This hearty chili has more than 1,170 milligrams of potassium per serving.

1 pound ground round
1 teaspoon canola oil
1½ cups chopped onion
2 garlic cloves, minced
1 tablespoon chili powder
1 tablespoon ground cumin
2 teaspoons minced fresh oregano
¾ teaspoon salt
1½ cups frozen whole-kernel corn
2 (14.5-ounce) cans no-salt-added diced tomatoes, undrained
1 cup coarsely chopped zucchini
1 cup water
1 tablespoon finely chopped canned chipotle chile in adobo sauce
1 (15-ounce) can kidney beans, rinsed and drained
1 (15-ounce) can black beans, rinsed and drained
6 tablespoons fat-free sour cream
6 tablespoons thinly sliced green onions
6 tablespoons (about 1½ ounces) shredded reduced-fat sharp Cheddar cheese

1. Cook beef in a Dutch oven over medium-high heat until lightly browned; stir to crumble. Drain well; set aside.
2. Add canola oil to pan. Heat pan over medium-high heat. Add chopped onion to pan; sauté 4 minutes or until tender. Add garlic; sauté 30 seconds. Add chili powder, cumin, oregano, and salt; sauté 30 seconds. Stir in corn and tomatoes; bring to a boil. Reduce heat, and simmer 3 minutes, stirring occasionally.
3. Stir in beef, zucchini, water, chipotle chile, and beans; bring to a boil. Cover, reduce heat, and simmer 10 minutes or until zucchini is tender.
4. Spoon 1½ cups chili into each of 6 bowls. Top each serving with 1 tablespoon sour cream, 1 tablespoon green onions, and 1 tablespoon cheese. Yield: 6 servings.

CALORIES 408 (28% from fat); FAT 12.8g (sat 4.4g, mono 4.4g, poly 1.3g); PROTEIN 29g; CARB 45.4g; FIBER 13.2g; CHOL 59mg; IRON 5.4mg; SODIUM 850mg; CALC 180mg

Banana Pumpkin Smoothie

The frozen fruit helps give the smoothie a thick texture; chilling the pumpkin ensures the smoothie stays cold when you blend it. The combination of banana, pumpkin, yogurt, and orange juice gives this breakfast beverage 740 milligrams of potassium per serving.

1 cup low-fat vanilla yogurt
¾ cup canned pumpkin, chilled
½ cup ice cubes
⅓ cup fresh orange juice
1 tablespoon brown sugar
½ teaspoon ground cinnamon
⅛ teaspoon ground nutmeg
Dash of ground cloves
1 ripe banana, sliced and frozen
Dash of ground cinnamon (optional)

1. Combine first 9 ingredients in a blender, and process until smooth. Garnish with dash of cinnamon, if desired. Serve immediately. Yield: 2 servings (serving size: about 1 cup).

CALORIES 218 (9% from fat); FAT 2.2g (sat 1.1g, mono 0.5g, poly 0.1g); PROTEIN 8.4g; CARB 44.5g; FIBER 5.5g; CHOL 6mg; IRON 1.2mg; SODIUM 87mg; CALC 243mg

menu of the month

Outdoor Dining

Invite friends over for a spread that celebrates the flavors of the season.

Menu
serves 4

Pasta with Caramelized Onion Trio, Arugula, and Mozzarella

Baby Artichokes with Creamy Horseradish-Dill Dip

Flatbread with Pancetta and Asparagus

Meyer Lemon and Rosemary Brûlées

Pinot grigio or other crisp white wine

Pasta with Caramelized Onion Trio, Arugula, and Mozzarella

Currants and the caramelized leeks and onions lend sweetness to the pasta, which is contrasted by the peppery arugula. This is best served immediately after tossing.

1 tablespoon olive oil
2 cups coarsely chopped leek
1½ cups coarsely chopped white onion
¼ cup coarsely chopped green onions
8 ounces uncooked linguine
1 cup fat-free, less-sodium chicken broth
¼ cup dried currants
1 tablespoon balsamic vinegar
¼ cup heavy cream
¾ teaspoon salt
2 cups coarsely chopped arugula
½ cup (2 ounces) cubed fresh mozzarella
½ teaspoon chopped fresh thyme

1. Heat oil in a large nonstick skillet over medium heat. Add leek, white onion, and green onions; cook 5 minutes, stirring frequently. Cover, reduce heat to low, and cook 20 minutes or until leek and onions are golden brown, stirring frequently.
2. While onion mixture cooks, prepare pasta according to package directions, omitting salt and fat.
3. Bring broth to a boil in a small saucepan. Add currants and vinegar. Add broth mixture, cream, and salt to onion mixture; cook 2 minutes, stirring frequently. Remove from heat; stir in arugula, mozzarella, and thyme. Add to pasta; toss gently to combine. Yield: 4 servings (serving size: 1¼ cups).

CALORIES 418 (28% from fat); FAT 13.1g (sat 6.2g, mono 4.1g, poly 0.7g); PROTEIN 13g; CARB 63.7g; FIBER 4.7g; CHOL 32mg; IRON 3.6mg; SODIUM 584mg; CALC 170mg

1. *Cut the stem so the artichoke sits on its base without wobbling. Slice off a quarter of the artichoke's top.*

2. *Pull away the outside leaves until you reach the yellow center.*

3. *Cut the artichoke in half lengthwise, and pull or cut out any purple, spiky leaves. You'll see a fuzzy area—that's the choke.*

4. *Using a sharp-edged spoon (such as a grapefruit spoon), scoop out the fuzzy choke until no hair fibers remain, and discard.*

5. *Turn over artichoke, and peel away the tough green exterior at the base with a knife, as if you were peeling an apple. You'll soon reach the yellow flesh.*

6. *Rinse the artichoke in an acid bath of a quarter-cup lemon juice mixed with a cup of water. This helps to stop the browning process.*

Baby Artichokes with Creamy Horseradish-Dill Dip

If there are any pink or purple leaves in the center of the artichoke, scoop them out with a spoon or cut them out with a knife.

    4   cups cold water
    1   tablespoon fresh lemon juice
 2½   pounds baby artichokes (about
        10 artichokes)
    1   lemon, halved
   ¼   cup plain fat-free yogurt
   ¼   cup (2 ounces) ⅓-less-fat cream
        cheese, softened
    1   tablespoon prepared horseradish
 1½   teaspoons chopped fresh dill
 1½   teaspoons fresh lemon juice
   ⅛   teaspoon salt
   ⅛   teaspoon freshly ground black
        pepper
 Dill sprigs (optional)

1. Combine water and 1 tablespoon lemon juice. Working with 1 artichoke at a time, bend back outer green leaves of artichoke, snapping at base, until reaching light green leaves. Trim about 1 inch from top of artichoke. Cut off stem of artichoke to within 1 inch of base; peel stem. Cut artichoke in half vertically. Rub cut surfaces with cut lemon, and place artichoke halves in lemon water. Repeat with remaining artichokes. Steam artichoke halves 12 minutes or until tender.

2. Combine yogurt and next 6 ingredients. Serve artichoke halves with dip; garnish with dill sprigs, if desired. Yield: 4 servings (serving size: about 5 artichoke halves and about 2 tablespoons dip).

CALORIES 101 (32% from fat); FAT 3.6g (sat 2.2g, mono 1g, poly 0.2g); PROTEIN 6.1g; CARB 14.2g; FIBER 6.3g; CHOL 11mg; IRON 1.5mg; SODIUM 261mg; CALC 94mg

Flatbread with Pancetta and Asparagus

DOUGH:

½ cup warm water (100° to 110°)
1 teaspoon dry yeast
1¼ cups all-purpose flour, divided
½ teaspoon sea salt
Cooking spray

TOPPING:

1 teaspoon dried thyme
2 ounces pancetta, finely chopped
1 garlic clove, minced
⅛ teaspoon sea salt
⅛ teaspoon freshly ground black pepper

REMAINING INGREDIENTS:

¼ pound fresh asparagus spears, trimmed
¼ cup (1 ounce) shredded part-skim mozzarella cheese
¼ cup (1 ounce) shaved fresh Parmesan cheese

1. To prepare dough, combine warm water and yeast in a large bowl; let stand 5 minutes. Lightly spoon flour into dry measuring cups; level with a knife. Add 1 cup flour and ½ teaspoon salt to yeast mixture; stir until blended. Turn dough out onto a floured surface. Knead dough until smooth and elastic (about 8 minutes); add enough remaining flour, 1 tablespoon at a time, to prevent dough from sticking to hands (dough will feel sticky).

2. Place dough in a large bowl coated with cooking spray, turning to coat top. Cover and let rise in a warm place (85°), free from drafts, 45 minutes or until doubled in size. (Gently press two fingers into dough. If indentation remains, dough has risen enough.)

3. While dough rises, prepare topping. Heat a small skillet over medium heat. Add thyme, pancetta, and garlic; sauté 5 minutes or until pancetta is crisp. Stir in ⅛ teaspoon salt and pepper.

4. Preheat oven to 475°.

5. Punch dough down; cover and let rest 5 minutes. Roll dough into a 10-inch circle on a floured surface. Place dough on a baking sheet. Spread topping evenly over dough. Arrange asparagus over topping; sprinkle with mozzarella. Bake at 475° for 10 minutes or until crust is golden. Remove from oven. Sprinkle with Parmesan. Yield: 8 servings (serving size: 1 wedge).

CALORIES 132 (31% from fat); FAT 4.6g (sat 2.1g, mono 0.9g, poly 0.2g); PROTEIN 5.8g; CARB 16.2g; FIBER 1.1g; CHOL 9mg; IRON 1.2mg; SODIUM 373mg; CALC 77mg

---

MAKE AHEAD

Meyer Lemon and Rosemary Brûlées

1 cup whole milk
½ cup evaporated fat-free milk
1 tablespoon grated Meyer lemon rind
1 teaspoon chopped fresh rosemary
½ cup sugar
3 large egg yolks
2 large eggs
¼ teaspoon vanilla extract
2 tablespoons sugar

1. Combine first 4 ingredients in a medium saucepan. Heat mixture over medium heat to 180° or until tiny bubbles form around edge (do not boil), stirring occasionally. Remove from heat. Cover and steep 10 minutes.

2. Preheat oven to 325°.

3. Combine ½ cup sugar, egg yolks, and eggs in a medium bowl, stirring with a whisk. Strain milk mixture through a sieve into egg mixture, stirring well with a whisk. Stir in vanilla. Return mixture to pan. Cook over medium-low heat 5 minutes or until mixture coats a spoon.

4. Divide mixture evenly among 4 (6-ounce) ramekins. Place ramekins in a 13 x 9-inch baking pan; add hot water to pan to a depth of 1 inch.

5. Bake at 325° for 30 minutes or until center barely moves when ramekin is touched. Remove ramekins from pan; cool completely on a wire rack. Cover and chill at least 1 hour or overnight.

6. Sift 2 tablespoons sugar evenly over custards. Holding a kitchen blowtorch about 2 inches from top of each custard, heat sugar, moving torch back and forth, until sugar is completely melted and caramelized (for about 1 minute). Serve immediately. Yield: 4 servings (serving size: 1 brûlée).

CALORIES 261 (27% from fat); FAT 7.9g (sat 3.2g, mono 2.9g, poly 1g); PROTEIN 9.5g; CARB 38.6g; FIBER 0.2g; CHOL 267mg; IRON 0.9mg; SODIUM 104mg; CALC 187mg

---

inspired vegetarian

Simple Weeknight Suppers

Speed through dinner prep with these quick-fix recipes.

QUICK & EASY

Quinoa with Leeks and Shiitake Mushrooms

This is tasty with sautéed soy "sausage" links.

2 cups fat-free, less-sodium vegetable broth (such as Swanson Certified Organic)
1 cup water
½ teaspoon salt, divided
1½ cups uncooked quinoa, rinsed
3 tablespoons chopped fresh flat-leaf parsley
1 tablespoon olive oil, divided
¼ teaspoon freshly ground black pepper, divided
3 cups thinly sliced leek (about 2 large)
4 cups thinly sliced shiitake mushroom caps (about 8 ounces)
1½ cups chopped red bell pepper
¼ cup dry white wine
½ cup coarsely chopped walnuts

1. Combine broth, water, and ¼ teaspoon salt in a large saucepan; bring to a boil. Stir in quinoa. Cover, reduce heat, and simmer 15 minutes or until liquid is absorbed. Stir in parsley, 1½ teaspoons oil, and ⅛ teaspoon black pepper. Remove from heat; keep warm.

Continued

2. Heat 1½ teaspoons oil in a medium nonstick skillet over medium-high heat. Add leek; sauté 6 minutes or until wilted. Add mushroom caps, bell pepper, and wine; cook 2 minutes or until vegetables are tender. Stir in ¼ teaspoon salt and ⅛ teaspoon black pepper. Place 1 cup quinoa in each of 4 shallow bowls; top each with 1¼ cups vegetable mixture and 2 tablespoons walnuts. Yield: 4 servings.

CALORIES 495 (29% from fat); FAT 15.7g (sat 1.7g, mono 5.7g, poly 6.2g); PROTEIN 15.8g; CARB 73.8g; FIBER 7.9g; CHOL 0mg; IRON 10.5mg; SODIUM 839mg; CALC 95mg

Greek-Style Potato, Zucchini, and Bean Stew

Add crusty bread and a Greek-style salad of lettuce, tomatoes, red onions, peppers, cured olives, and feta.

- 1½ tablespoons extravirgin olive oil
- 3 cups chopped onion
- 1 cup (¾-inch) cubed peeled baking potato
- ½ cup water
- 3½ cups (½-inch) slices zucchini
- 2½ cups (3-inch) cut green beans (about ½ pound)
- 2 (28-ounce) cans diced tomatoes, undrained
- 1 (15.5-ounce) can Great Northern beans, rinsed and drained
- ¼ cup chopped fresh flat-leaf parsley
- 2 teaspoons chopped fresh dill
- ½ teaspoon dried oregano
- ¼ teaspoon freshly ground black pepper
- ¾ cup (3 ounces) crumbled feta cheese

1. Heat oil in a Dutch oven over medium-high heat. Add onion; sauté 5 minutes or until lightly browned. Add potato and water; bring to a boil. Cover, reduce heat, and cook 5 minutes. Stir in zucchini and next 3 ingredients. Cover and cook 35 minutes or until vegetables are tender. Stir in parsley and next 3 ingredients. Serve with cheese. Yield: 6 servings (serving size: 2 cups stew and 2 tablespoons cheese).

CALORIES 262 (23% from fat); FAT 6.8g (sat 2.6g, mono 3.2g, poly 0.7g); PROTEIN 10g; CARB 45.5g; FIBER 10.8g; CHOL 13mg; IRON 2.8mg; SODIUM 598mg; CALC 187mg

Quick Vegetarian Paella

Despite the length of its ingredient list, this recipe still yields a splendid meal in about 30 minutes. Complete the menu with steamed green beans, and packaged mixed baby greens tossed with bottled orange sections and toasted almond slices.

- 2 tablespoons extravirgin olive oil
- 2 cups chopped onion
- 2 cups (1-inch) chopped green bell pepper
- 1 cup sliced cremini mushrooms
- 2 garlic cloves, minced
- 3 cups uncooked quick-cooking brown rice
- 2 cups fat-free, less-sodium vegetable broth (such as Swanson Certified Organic)
- 1 cup water
- 1 teaspoon saffron threads, crushed, or ground turmeric
- ½ teaspoon dried thyme
- 2 cups chopped tomato
- 1 cup frozen green peas
- ½ cup pimiento-stuffed olives, chopped
- 2 tablespoons chopped fresh flat-leaf parsley
- ¼ teaspoon freshly ground black pepper
- 1 (14-ounce) can artichoke hearts, drained and coarsely chopped
- Chopped fresh flat-leaf parsley (optional)

1. Heat oil in a stockpot over medium-high heat. Add onion, bell pepper, mushrooms, and garlic; sauté 5 minutes. Stir in rice and next 4 ingredients; bring to a boil. Cover, reduce heat, and simmer 10 minutes.
2. Stir in tomato and next 5 ingredients. Cook 3 minutes or until rice is tender and mixture is thoroughly heated. Garnish with additional chopped fresh parsley, if desired. Yield: 5 servings (serving size: about 2 cups).

CALORIES 350 (23% from fat); FAT 8.9g (sat 1g, mono 5.1g, poly 0.9g); PROTEIN 10.8g; CARB 62g; FIBER 7.2g; CHOL 0mg; IRON 3.4mg; SODIUM 686mg; CALC 78mg

Polenta with Spinach, Black Beans, and Goat Cheese

- 1 teaspoon olive oil
- 2 garlic cloves, minced
- ½ cup fat-free, less-sodium vegetable broth (such as Swanson Certified Organic)
- ¼ cup chopped drained oil-packed sun-dried tomato halves
- ½ teaspoon ground cumin
- 1 (15-ounce) can black beans, rinsed and drained
- 1 (6-ounce) package fresh baby spinach
- 4 cups water
- 1 cup uncooked polenta
- 1 tablespoon butter
- ½ teaspoon salt
- ¾ cup (3 ounces) crumbled goat cheese
- Cracked black pepper (optional)

1. Heat oil in a large nonstick skillet over medium-high heat. Add garlic to pan; sauté 1 minute or until golden. Stir in broth, tomatoes, cumin, and beans; bring to a simmer. Cook 2 minutes, stirring occasionally. Remove from heat. Add spinach, tossing to combine.
2. Bring water to a boil in a medium saucepan. Add polenta, butter, and salt; stir well with a whisk. Reduce heat, and simmer 3 minutes or until thick, stirring constantly. Spoon ¾ cup polenta into each of 4 bowls; top each with ¾ cup bean mixture. Sprinkle 3 tablespoons cheese over each serving; garnish with black pepper, if desired. Yield: 4 servings.

CALORIES 356 (30% from fat); FAT 12g (sat 6.5g, mono 3.6g, poly 1.1g); PROTEIN 13.8g; CARB 48.8g; FIBER 9g; CHOL 24mg; IRON 3.9mg; SODIUM 674mg; CALC 135mg

Stir-Fried Tofu and Spring Greens with Peanut Sauce

Bottled Thai peanut sauce is a handy standby. Here we use it to jazz up an otherwise simple combination of tofu and vegetables. Complete the meal with a platter of red and green bell pepper strips, sliced cucumbers, and carrot sticks.

1 (16-ounce) package extrafirm tofu
1 tablespoon canola oil
¼ cup Thai peanut sauce
3½ cups thinly sliced bok choy
1 cup julienne-cut yellow squash
¼ cup sliced green onions
2 cups trimmed watercress
2 tablespoons low-sodium soy sauce
4 cups hot cooked soba (about 10 ounces uncooked buckwheat noodles)
¼ cup chopped dry-roasted peanuts

1. Cut tofu crosswise into ½-inch-thick slices. Press tofu between paper towels until barely moist. Cut slices crosswise into ½-inch cubes.

2. Heat oil in a large nonstick skillet over medium-high heat. Add tofu, and sauté 5 minutes, browning on all sides. Add peanut sauce, and cook 2 minutes, stirring occasionally. Add bok choy, squash, and onions; cook 3 minutes, stirring frequently. Add watercress and soy sauce; cook 1 minute or until watercress is slightly wilted. Remove from heat.

3. Place 1 cup noodles in each of 4 shallow bowls; top each serving with about 1¼ cups vegetable mixture, and sprinkle with 1 tablespoon peanuts. Yield: 4 servings.

CALORIES 444 (29% from fat); FAT 14.4g (sat 2g, mono 5.2g, poly 3g); PROTEIN 20.7g; CARB 59.3g; FIBER 2.8g; CHOL 0mg; IRON 4.4mg; SODIUM 647mg; CALC 116mg

QUICK & EASY
Quick Edamame and Orange Rice

3 cups uncooked quick-cooking brown rice
1 tablespoon canola oil
1½ cups thinly diagonally sliced celery
1 cup sliced green onions
1 cup (2 x ½-inch) julienne-cut red bell pepper
1 cup frozen shelled edamame (green soybeans), thawed
½ cup dry-roasted cashews
¼ cup low-sodium teriyaki sauce
1 teaspoon dark sesame oil
⅛ teaspoon freshly ground black pepper
2 small oranges, peeled and sectioned

1. Cook rice according to package directions, omitting salt and fat. Set aside, and keep warm.

2. Heat canola oil in a large nonstick skillet over medium-high heat. Add celery, onions, and bell pepper; sauté 1 minute. Stir in cooked rice, edamame, and remaining ingredients. Serve immediately. Yield: 4 servings (serving size: 1¾ cups).

CALORIES 476 (29% from fat); FAT 15.6g (sat 2.2g, mono 7.6g, poly 2.2g); PROTEIN 14.7g; CARB 75.9g; FIBER 10.4g; CHOL 0mg; IRON 3.7mg; SODIUM 556mg; CALC 119mg

QUICK & EASY
Hash Browns with Italian-Seasoned Tofu

These just might be the most colorful hash browns you've ever had. Serve with a side salad of mixed greens, tomatoes, and olives. If you'd like, add steamed fresh spinach to each plate.

1½ tablespoons olive oil
1½ cups chopped onion
1 cup chopped carrot
1 garlic clove, minced
1 (20-ounce) package refrigerated diced potatoes with onion (such as Simply Potatoes)
1 cup coarsely chopped red bell pepper
½ teaspoon salt
¼ teaspoon freshly ground black pepper
1 (8-ounce) package water-packed baked garlic and herb Italian-style tofu (such as White Wave), cut into ½-inch cubes
2 tablespoons chopped fresh parsley

1. Heat oil in a large nonstick skillet over medium-high heat. Add onion, carrot, and garlic; sauté 4 minutes. Add potatoes, and sauté 7 minutes or until lightly browned. Stir in bell pepper, salt, black pepper, and tofu; sauté 4 minutes or until thoroughly heated. Remove from heat, and sprinkle with parsley. Yield: 4 servings (serving size: 1½ cups hash browns and 1½ teaspoons parsley).

CALORIES 362 (37% from fat); FAT 10.7g (sat 1.4g, mono 4.1g, poly 1.6g); PROTEIN 9.7g; CARB 34.1g; FIBER 4.7g; CHOL 0mg; IRON 1.2mg; SODIUM 849mg; CALC 219mg

Shop and Stock

The key to getting a simple but satisfying meal on the table on a busy weeknight is twofold. First, shop once or twice a week for fresh, high-quality seasonal fruits and vegetables, and perishable items such as tofu and cheese. Second, stock your pantry and refrigerator with a variety of basic grocery items to avoid unnecessary last-minute trips to the supermarket. Here are some of the items to keep on hand:

• For quick meals, **canned beans** are an indispensable high-protein ingredient in vegetarian soups, stews, chilies, and salads. Stock several varieties, such as black beans, black-eyed peas, cannellini beans, Great Northern beans, chickpeas, and pink, red, and kidney beans.

• **Whole grains,** including bulgur, quinoa, and quick-cooking brown rice, are must-haves on busy weeknights.

• Keep plenty of shapes and varieties of **pasta,** including couscous, angel hair, spaghetti, fusilli, ziti, penne, fettuccine, and linguine, in your pantry. **Asian noodles,** such as udon, soba, rice noodles, and Chinese wheat noodles, also have short cooking times.

• **Nuts and seeds,** such as almonds, cashews, peanuts, walnuts, and sunflower and sesame seeds, are concentrated sources of protein and healthy fats. Nuts add flavor and substance when sprinkled over many dishes, and seeds add crunch to salads.

• Keep a few **prepared condiments and sauces** on hand, such as barbecue sauce (for broiling or stir-frying tofu, tempeh, or seitan), and pasta and pizza sauces. Thai peanut sauce, teriyaki, and stir-fry sauce are also useful.

• **Flavor boosters** for vegetarian dishes include oil-packed sun-dried tomatoes, marinated artichoke hearts, fresh or canned green chiles, low-sodium canned vegetable broth, and preshredded and crumbled cheeses.

Sausage for Supper

Full-flavored sausage makes any supper a hearty meal.

Sausage Menu 1
serves 4

Penne with Sausage, Eggplant, and Feta

Bitter greens with olive vinaigrette*

Lemon sorbet

*Combine 2 tablespoons olive pâté, 2 tablespoons red wine vinegar, 1 tablespoon extravirgin olive oil, 1 teaspoon sugar, 1 teaspoon minced fresh parsley, and 2 teaspoons prepared mustard. Combine 6 cups Italian Blend salad greens and 2 tablespoons pitted, sliced kalamata olives. Toss with vinaigrette.

Game Plan

1. Peel and cube eggplant, mince garlic, and chop parsley for pasta and salad.
2. Boil water for pasta.
3. While sausage mixture cooks:
  - Cook pasta
  - Prepare vinaigrette for salad

QUICK & EASY
Penne with Sausage, Eggplant, and Feta

Meaty breakfast sausage, earthy eggplant, and zesty feta complement each other in this hearty pasta dish. Buy precrumbled feta cheese to save time.

TOTAL TIME: 30 MINUTES

QUICK TIP: Reduce chopping time by substituting two teaspoons bottled minced garlic for four garlic cloves.

4½ cups cubed peeled eggplant (about 1 pound)
½ pound bulk pork breakfast sausage
4 garlic cloves, minced
2 tablespoons tomato paste
1 teaspoon dried oregano
¼ teaspoon freshly ground black pepper
1 (14.5-ounce) can diced tomatoes, undrained
6 cups hot cooked penne (about 10 ounces uncooked tube-shaped pasta)
½ cup (2 ounces) crumbled feta cheese
¼ cup chopped fresh parsley

1. Cook eggplant, sausage, and garlic in a large nonstick skillet over medium-high heat 5 minutes or until sausage is browned and eggplant is tender. Add tomato paste and next 3 ingredients; cook over medium heat 5 minutes, stirring occasionally.
2. Place pasta in a large bowl. Add tomato mixture, cheese, and parsley; toss well. Yield: 4 servings (serving size: 2 cups).

CALORIES 535 (31% from fat); FAT 18.9g (sat 7.6g, mono 7.5g, poly 2.1g); PROTEIN 25.5g; CARB 67.5g; FIBER 4.6g; CHOL 57mg; IRON 4.5mg; SODIUM 884mg; CALC 141mg

Sausage Menu 2
serves 4

Chicken Breasts Stuffed with Italian Sausage and Breadcrumbs

Sautéed zucchini and tomatoes*

Mixed greens with bottled Italian dressing

*Heat a large skillet over medium-high heat. Coat pan with cooking spray. Cut 1 pound zucchini into ¼-inch slices; add zucchini and ½ cup chopped onion to pan. Sauté 5 minutes or until vegetables are tender. Add 1½ cups chopped tomato; cook 5 minutes. Remove from heat; stir in ½ teaspoon dried basil, ¼ teaspoon salt, and ¼ teaspoon pepper.

Game Plan

1. While sausage cooks:
  - Pound chicken
  - Slice zucchini, and chop onion and tomato
2. Stuff chicken breasts with sausage mixture.
3. While chicken cooks:
  - Cook zucchini
  - Toss greens with dressing

QUICK & EASY
Chicken Breasts Stuffed with Italian Sausage and Breadcrumbs

Tangy sourdough bread adds intriguing flavor to the herbed sausage mixture.

TOTAL TIME: 35 MINUTES

QUICK TIP: Rinse and pound chicken when you return home from the supermarket. Wrap flattened chicken breast halves individually in plastic wrap, place in labeled zip-top plastic freezer bags, and freeze. Thaw in the refrigerator overnight.

1 (4-ounce) Italian sausage link
¼ cup finely chopped onion
2 tablespoons finely chopped celery
¼ cup dry white wine
1 (1½-ounce) slice sourdough bread, toasted and crusts removed
1 garlic clove, halved
1 tablespoon minced fresh parsley
½ teaspoon salt, divided
¼ teaspoon freshly ground black pepper
2 (6-ounce) skinless, boneless chicken breast halves
Cooking spray
½ cup fat-free, less-sodium chicken broth

1. Remove casing from sausage; crumble sausage. Heat a large nonstick skillet over medium-high heat. Add sausage, onion, and celery; sauté 5 minutes or until sausage is browned and onion is golden. Add wine to pan; cook 1 minute or until most of liquid evaporates.
2. Rub each side of bread with cut sides of garlic; discard garlic. Coarsely crumble bread; add to sausage mixture. Stir in parsley, ¼ teaspoon salt, and pepper. Let stand 5 minutes or until liquid is absorbed; toss to combine.
3. Place each chicken breast half between 2 sheets of plastic wrap; pound to ¼-inch thickness using a meat mallet or rolling pin. Place half of stuffing on one side of each chicken breast half, leaving a 1-inch border around sides. Fold remaining half of each chicken breast over stuffing, and secure with wooden picks. Sprinkle chicken with ¼ teaspoon salt.

4. Heat a large skillet over medium-high heat. Coat pan with cooking spray. Add stuffed chicken breast halves to pan; cook 3 minutes on each side. Add broth, scraping pan to loosen browned bits. Cover, reduce heat, and simmer 5 minutes or until chicken is done. Remove wooden picks; slice breasts in half. Serve immediately. Yield: 4 servings (serving size: ½ chicken breast).

CALORIES 233 (29% from fat); FAT 7.6g (sat 2.5g, mono 0.5g, poly 0.4g); PROTEIN 21.9g; CARB 11.5g; FIBER 0.9g; CHOL 65mg; IRON 1.6mg; SODIUM 774mg; CALC 47mg

---

Sausage Menu 3
serves 4

Jambalaya with Shrimp and Andouille Sausage

Green beans with rémoulade*

Caramel praline crunch frozen yogurt (such as Edy's/Dreyer's)

*Cook 1 pound trimmed green beans in boiling water 5 minutes; drain. Combine 1 tablespoon light mayonnaise, 1 to 2 tablespoons Creole mustard, 1 tablespoon lemon juice, ¼ teaspoon Worcestershire sauce, ⅛ teaspoon paprika, and ⅛ teaspoon celery salt. Toss with green beans.

Game Plan

1. Chop vegetables and slice sausage.
2. While sausage mixture cooks:
   • Peel shrimp
   • Boil water for green beans
3. While jambalaya simmers and green beans cook:
   • Prepare rémoulade for green beans

QUICK & EASY
Jambalaya with Shrimp and Andouille Sausage

To speed up preparation, pick up peeled and deveined frozen shrimp from the frozen food section. Thaw in the refrigerator or under cold, running water.

TOTAL TIME: 39 MINUTES

1 tablespoon olive oil
1 cup chopped onion
1 cup chopped red bell pepper
1 tablespoon minced garlic
6 ounces andouille sausage, sliced
1 cup uncooked long-grain white rice
1 teaspoon paprika
1 teaspoon freshly ground black pepper
1 teaspoon dried oregano
½ teaspoon onion powder
½ teaspoon dried thyme
¼ teaspoon garlic salt
1 bay leaf
2 cups fat-free, less-sodium chicken broth
¾ cup water
1 tablespoon tomato paste
½ teaspoon hot pepper sauce
1 (14.5-ounce) can no-salt-added diced tomatoes, undrained
½ pound peeled and deveined medium shrimp
2 tablespoons chopped fresh parsley

1. Heat oil in a large Dutch oven over medium-high heat. Add onion, bell pepper, garlic, and sausage; sauté 5 minutes or until vegetables are tender.
2. Add rice and next 7 ingredients; cook 2 minutes. Add broth and next 4 ingredients; bring to a boil. Cover, reduce heat, and simmer 20 minutes. Add shrimp; cook 5 minutes. Let stand 5 minutes. Discard bay leaf. Stir in parsley. Yield: 4 servings (serving size: 1½ cups).

CALORIES 426 (27% from fat); FAT 12.7g (sat 3.9g, mono 2.8g, poly 1g); PROTEIN 25g; CARB 52.7g; FIBER 4.9g; CHOL 117mg; IRON 5.1mg; SODIUM 763mg; CALC 99mg

---

The Road to Key West

Enjoy the best of the Florida Keys with this refreshing concoction.

QUICK & EASY
Mango Mojito

This refreshing drink is an adaptation of the signature cocktail at the Conch Republic Seafood Company in Key West. Store leftover Simple Syrup in the refrigerator up to two weeks; use it to sweeten iced tea or iced coffee.

2 lime wedges
5 fresh mint leaves
¼ cup club soda
3 tablespoons rum
2 tablespoons Simple Syrup
1 tablespoon mango nectar
Crushed ice

1. Squeeze lime wedges into a small glass; add lime wedges and mint to glass. Crush with back of a spoon 30 seconds. Add soda, rum, Simple Syrup, and nectar; stir gently. Serve over ice. Yield: 1 serving (serving size: ½ cup).

(Totals include 2 tablespoons Simple Syrup) CALORIES 205 (0% from fat); FAT 0g; PROTEIN 0.1g; CARB 28.3g; FIBER 0.2g; CHOL 0mg; IRON 0.1mg; SODIUM 14mg; CALC 6mg

QUICK & EASY • MAKE AHEAD
SIMPLE SYRUP:
2 cups sugar
1 cup water

1. Place sugar and water in a small saucepan over medium-high heat until sugar dissolves (about 5 minutes), stirring constantly. Yield: 2 cups (serving size: 2 tablespoons).

CALORIES 97 (0% from fat); FAT 0g; PROTEIN 0g; CARB 25g; FIBER 0g; CHOL 0mg; IRON 0mg; SODIUM 0mg; CALC 1mg

The Real Deal

Homemade ricotta cheese is easy to make, and after tasting the creamy results you'll find it's worth the effort.

Tips for Homemade Ricotta

- Buy a candy thermometer that can clamp onto the lip of the pot, which will allow you to obtain an accurate temperature reading as you heat the milk.
- Before heating the milk mixture, set out everything you need: thermometer; slotted spoon; and moistened cheesecloth, folded in 5 layers, set over a large colander or sieve that has been nestled over a large bowl.
- Resist the temptation to stir the milk mixture after it registers 170° on the thermometer, or the ricotta will have a grainy, thin texture.
- Do not push on the curds while the ricotta is draining over the bowl; let excess whey drip out, then tie the cheesecloth into a bundle and hang it over the faucet for 15 minutes.
- Let the ricotta cool to room temperature before refrigerating.
- Use fresh ricotta within four days.
- If you plan to make several batches of ricotta, always clean the pot between uses, and use a fresh piece of cheesecloth for every batch.

MAKE AHEAD
Homemade Ricotta Cheese

As the milk mixture heats to 170°, stir gently and occasionally; if you stir too vigorously or too frequently (more than every few minutes), the curds may not separate as effectively. If your kitchen sink has a gooseneck faucet, it might be difficult to hang the cheesecloth bag. If so, lay a long wooden spoon across one corner of the sink, and hang the bag on the handle.

1 gallon 2% reduced-fat milk
5 cups low-fat buttermilk
½ teaspoon fine sea salt

1. Line a large colander or sieve with 5 layers of dampened cheesecloth, allowing cheesecloth to extend over outside edges of colander; place colander in a large bowl.
2. Combine milk and buttermilk in a large, heavy stockpot. Attach a candy thermometer to edge of pan so that thermometer extends at least 2 inches into milk mixture. Cook over medium-high heat until candy thermometer registers 170° (about 20 minutes), gently stirring occasionally. As soon as milk mixture reaches 170°, stop stirring (whey and curds will begin separating at this point). Continue to cook, without stirring, until thermometer registers 190°. (Be sure not to stir, or curds that have formed will break apart.) Immediately remove pan from heat. (Bottom of pan may be slightly scorched.)
3. Using a slotted spoon, gently spoon curds into cheesecloth-lined colander; discard whey, or reserve it for another use. Drain over bowl 5 minutes. Gather edges of cheesecloth together; tie securely. Hang cheesecloth bundle from kitchen faucet; drain 15 minutes or until whey stops dripping. Scrape ricotta into a bowl. Sprinkle with salt; toss gently with a fork to combine. Cool to room temperature. Yield: about 3 cups (serving size: ¼ cup).
NOTE: Store in refrigerator up to 4 days.

CALORIES 115 (48% from fat); FAT 6.1g (sat 3.8g, mono 1.8g, poly 0.2g); PROTEIN 11.5g; CARB 3.5g; FIBER 0g; CHOL 23mg; IRON 0mg; SODIUM 191mg; CALC 250mg

Roasted Fennel and Ricotta Gratins with Tarragon

A sprinkling of fresh breadcrumbs gives these easy individual gratins a crispy top. Serve them with steak, roasted chicken, or pork tenderloin.

6¼ cups thinly sliced fennel bulb (about 2 medium bulbs)
Cooking spray
½ teaspoon salt, divided
¾ cup (6 ounces) Homemade Ricotta Cheese (recipe at left)
1 (1½-ounce) slice hearty white bread (such as Pepperidge Farm)
1 teaspoon minced fresh tarragon
¼ teaspoon freshly ground black pepper

1. Preheat oven to 450°.
2. Arrange fennel on a baking sheet coated with cooking spray, and sprinkle evenly with ¼ teaspoon salt. Bake at 450° for 40 minutes or until fennel is crisp-tender, stirring occasionally.
3. Reduce oven temperature to 375°.

4. Combine fennel, ¼ teaspoon salt, and Homemade Ricotta Cheese, tossing well. Divide mixture evenly among 6 (4-ounce) gratin dishes or ramekins coated with cooking spray.

5. Place bread in a food processor; pulse 10 times or until coarse crumbs measure ¾ cup. Combine breadcrumbs, tarragon, and pepper, tossing well. Sprinkle about 2 tablespoons breadcrumb mixture over each gratin dish. Bake at 375° for 20 minutes or until golden. Yield: 6 servings (serving size: 1 gratin).

CALORIES 107 (30% from fat); FAT 3.6g (sat 2g, mono 1g, poly 0.1g); PROTEIN 7.5g; CARB 12g; FIBER 3g; CHOL 11mg; IRON 0.9mg; SODIUM 380mg; CALC 177mg

MAKE AHEAD
Hazelnut-Coated Ricotta Balls with Roasted Grapes

Homemade ricotta is ideal for this memorable dessert. Its firm texture makes it easy to roll into balls (store-bought ricotta tends to be softer and would need to be drained first). You can prepare and chill the ricotta balls up to six hours in advance.

  5 reduced-calorie vanilla
      wafers
  1 tablespoon finely chopped
      hazelnuts, toasted
  2 cups (1 pound) Homemade
      Ricotta Cheese (recipe on
      page 108)
2½ cups seedless red grapes (about
      1 pound)
  2 tablespoons sugar
  ½ cup maple syrup

1. Preheat oven to 450°.

2. Place vanilla wafers in a food processor, and pulse 10 times or until coarse crumbs measure about 2 tablespoons. Combine wafer crumbs and nuts in a shallow dish, stirring to combine.

3. With moist hands, shape Homemade Ricotta Cheese into 24 (1-inch) balls; roll balls in crumb mixture, coating on all sides. Place coated balls on a baking sheet; chill.

4. Place grapes on a jelly-roll pan, and sprinkle with sugar. Bake at 450° for

17 minutes or until grapes begin to burst, stirring occasionally.

5. Place 3 ricotta balls on each of 8 dessert plates, and top each serving with about ¼ cup grapes. Drizzle 1 tablespoon maple syrup over each

serving. Yield: 8 servings.

CALORIES 229 (28% from fat); FAT 7g (sat 3.9g, mono 2.2g, poly 0.4g); PROTEIN 12g; CARB 31.1g; FIBER 0.5g; CHOL 23mg; IRON 0.5mg; SODIUM 202mg; CALC 269mg

How to Make Homemade Ricotta

1. *Immerse tip of the thermometer two inches into liquid to ensure an accurate reading once the curds rise to the top.*

2. *Gently scoop out the curds with a slotted spoon, trying not to agitate them or break them apart.*

3. *Gather the edges of the cheesecloth, and tie into a bag; be careful not to squeeze the bag or push on the curds.*

4. *Hang the cheesecloth bag over the sink to allow the whey to drain out.*

5. *Sprinkle with salt, tossing gently to keep the curds intact.*

Zucchini Boats with Ricotta-Basil Mousse

Use the fragrant cheese stuffing with any mild vegetable, such as bell peppers, mushroom caps, baby eggplant, or tomatoes. Save the scooped-out zucchini pulp for risotto or pasta sauce. You can use a mini chopper to chop the herbs quickly, but do not use it to combine the mousse ingredients because it will liquefy the ricotta.

QUICK TIP: Use a melon baller to make quick work of hollowing out the zucchini halves for the herbed mousse.

    6 small zucchini (about 1½ pounds)
  Cooking spray
    1 cup loosely packed fresh basil
       leaves, finely chopped
    1 cup (8 ounces) Homemade
       Ricotta Cheese (recipe on
       page 108)
    ½ cup loosely packed fresh flat-leaf
       parsley leaves, finely chopped
    ¼ cup (1 ounce) grated fresh
       Parmigiano-Reggiano cheese
    2 tablespoons hot water
    1 tablespoon fresh lemon juice
    ¼ teaspoon salt
    ¼ teaspoon freshly ground black
       pepper
  Parsley sprigs (optional)

1. Preheat oven to 450°.
2. Cut each zucchini in half lengthwise; scoop out pulp, leaving ¼-inch-thick shells. Reserve pulp for another use. Arrange zucchini shells in a single layer in a 13 x 9-inch baking dish coated with cooking spray.
3. Combine basil and next 7 ingredients, stirring well with a whisk. Divide mixture evenly among shells, pressing gently. Bake at 450° for 20 minutes or until zucchini is tender. Garnish with parsley sprigs, if desired. Yield: 12 servings (serving size: 1 stuffed shell).

CALORIES 59 (43% from fat); FAT 2.8g (sat 1.7g, mono 0.8g, poly 0.2g); PROTEIN 5.5g; CARB 3.5g; FIBER 0.8g; CHOL 9mg; IRON 0.5mg; SODIUM 158mg; CALC 129mg

How to Make Zucchini Boats

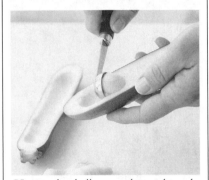

Use a melon baller to make quick work of hollowing out the zucchini halves for the herbed mousse.

Orecchiette and Arugula with Creamy Ricotta Sauce

Fresh ricotta creates an incredibly creamy sauce for this easy pasta dish; try this recipe with any of your other favorite pasta shapes. If arugula isn't available at your market, substitute fresh basil.

    6 quarts water
  2½ teaspoons salt, divided
    1 pound uncooked orecchiette
       ("little ears" pasta)
    1 cup (8 ounces) Homemade
       Ricotta Cheese (recipe on
       page 108)
    ¾ cup (3 ounces) grated fresh
       pecorino Romano cheese,
       divided
    1 tablespoon extravirgin olive oil
    1 teaspoon freshly ground black
       pepper, divided
    3 cups thinly sliced trimmed
       arugula
    2 cups chopped plum tomato
       (about 5 medium)

1. Bring 6 quarts water and 2 teaspoons salt to a boil in a large stockpot. Stir in pasta; cook 12 minutes or until al dente. Drain pasta in a colander over a bowl, reserving ½ cup cooking water.
2. Combine ½ teaspoon salt, Homemade Ricotta Cheese, ¼ cup pecorino, oil, and ½ teaspoon pepper in a large bowl, stirring well. Add hot pasta, ¼ cup reserved cooking water, and arugula; toss well to coat. Add additional cooking water if sauce is too thick. Spoon about 1¼ cups pasta mixture onto each of 8 plates. Top each serving with ¼ cup tomato and 1 tablespoon pecorino. Sprinkle evenly with ½ teaspoon pepper. Serve immediately. Yield: 8 servings.

CALORIES 319 (25% from fat); FAT 8.7g (sat 4.1g, mono 3.1g, poly 0.8g); PROTEIN 16.3g; CARB 43.5g; FIBER 2.5g; CHOL 22mg; IRON 1.1mg; SODIUM 450mg; CALC 265mg

Ricotta Cheesecake with Fresh Berry Topping
(pictured on page 95)

You'll need to make at least 1½ batches of Homemade Ricotta Cheese (recipe on page 108) for this luscious dessert. Although cream cheese-based cheesecakes are served chilled, ricotta-based cheesecakes are often enjoyed warm or at room temperature. If you've made this dessert in advance, cover and refrigerate, then let it stand at room temperature for 30 minutes before serving. While a shiny metal pan makes a delicious cheesecake, a dark metal or nonstick pan consistently gave us a taller, lightly browned cake.

CHEESECAKE:

    4 cups (2 pounds) Homemade
       Ricotta Cheese (recipe on
       page 108)
    1 cup granulated sugar
    2 teaspoons vanilla extract
    1 teaspoon grated lemon
       rind
    ¼ teaspoon salt
    4 large eggs
  Cooking spray
    1 tablespoon powdered sugar

TOPPING:

    2 cups quartered strawberries
    1 pint fresh raspberries
    1 pint fresh blueberries
    2 tablespoons granulated
       sugar
    2 tablespoons fresh lemon
       juice
  Mint sprigs (optional)

1. Preheat oven to 350°.

2. To prepare cheesecake, place first 5 ingredients in a large bowl; beat with a mixer at medium speed 2 minutes or until smooth. Add eggs, 1 at a time, beating well after each addition. Pour batter into a 10-inch springform pan coated with cooking spray. Bake at 350° for 1 hour or until cheesecake center barely moves when pan is touched. Remove cheesecake from oven; run a knife around outside edge of cheesecake. Cool slightly; remove outer ring from pan. Sprinkle cheesecake evenly with powdered sugar.

3. To prepare topping, combine berries, 2 tablespoons granulated sugar, and juice; toss gently to combine. Let stand 5 minutes. Serve berry mixture with cheesecake. Garnish with mint sprigs, if desired. Yield: 12 servings (serving size: 1 cheesecake wedge and about ½ cup berry mixture).

CALORIES 286 (32% from fat); FAT 10.2g (sat 5.6g, mono 3.1g, poly 0.7g); PROTEIN 18g; CARB 31.7g; FIBER 2.5g; CHOL 101mg; IRON 0.6mg; SODIUM 328mg; CALC 353mg

Ricotta Ravioli with Browned Poppy Seed Butter and Asparagus

The contrast between the emerald asparagus and the black poppy seeds is striking atop the ravioli. If you can't find round gyoza skins, cut square won ton wrappers into circles with a 3-inch round cutter. Ricotta salata is a firm aged cheese with a sharp, slightly sweet flavor; substitute Parmesan if your supermarket doesn't carry ricotta salata.

RAVIOLI:

  1 cup (8 ounces) Homemade Ricotta Cheese (recipe on page 108)
  ¼ cup (1 ounce) grated fresh pecorino Romano cheese
  2 tablespoons minced fresh flat-leaf parsley
  ⅛ teaspoon salt
  2 large egg whites
 48 (3-inch) round gyoza skins
  6 quarts water

TOPPING:

 1½ tablespoons butter
  2 cups (2-inch) slices asparagus
  ¼ teaspoon salt
  2 teaspoons poppy seeds
  ⅓ cup (about 1½ ounces) crumbled ricotta salata cheese

1. To prepare ravioli, combine Homemade Ricotta Cheese, pecorino Romano, parsley, ⅛ teaspoon salt, and egg whites; mix with a fork until blended. Working with 1 gyoza skin at a time (cover remaining skins to prevent drying), spoon about 2 teaspoons ricotta mixture into center of skin. Moisten edges of skin with water; place 1 skin over filling, stretching slightly to meet edges of bottom skin. Press edges together with a fork to seal; place on a lightly floured baking sheet (cover with a damp towel to prevent drying). Repeat procedure with remaining skins and ricotta mixture to form 24 ravioli.

2. Bring 6 quarts water to a boil over medium-high heat. Add 4 ravioli; cook 5 minutes, turning ravioli carefully after 2½ minutes. Remove ravioli from water with a slotted spoon; place on a platter. Repeat procedure with remaining ravioli; cover and keep warm. Reserve ½ cup cooking water.

3. To prepare topping, melt butter in a large nonstick skillet over medium heat; cook 3 minutes or until lightly browned, shaking pan occasionally. Add ¼ cup reserved cooking water, asparagus, and ¼ teaspoon salt; cook 3 minutes or until asparagus is crisp-tender and water evaporates. Stir in poppy seeds; cook 30 seconds. Add ¼ cup reserved cooking water; cook over medium-high heat 1 minute or until liquid is reduced by about half. Add ravioli to skillet; toss gently to combine. Sprinkle with ricotta salata; serve immediately. Yield: 6 servings (serving size: 4 ravioli, about ⅓ cup asparagus mixture, and about 1 tablespoon ricotta salata).

CALORIES 356 (30% from fat); FAT 12g (sat 6.6g, mono 2.9g, poly 1.1g); PROTEIN 19.6g; CARB 42.6g; FIBER 2.5g; CHOL 41mg; IRON 3mg; SODIUM 833mg; CALC 288mg

Buying and Storing Ricotta

While supermarket ricotta (usually sold in plastic tubs) will do in a pinch, the richer taste and more compact texture of fresh ricotta sold in specialty food stores will come closer to what you can make at home. Buy it no more than a day or two before using it, and refrigerate immediately because it's highly perishable. If it seems watery, drain by placing it in a cheesecloth-lined sieve set over a bowl for an hour or so in the refrigerator.

What Is Whey?

Aside from the nursery rhyme about Little Miss Muffet, you may not be familiar with whey. It's the light green liquid left behind when butterfat is separated from milk. When heating milk and buttermilk to make ricotta cheese, a thick, creamy layer (curds) forms on top, leaving the whey below. Whey is virtually fat-free and contains some calcium, potassium, B vitamins, zinc, and magnesium. You can discard it or use it in place of water or milk in breads, pancakes, or muffins.

Sweet Ideas

Ricotta's creamy texture and mild flavor make it ideal for easy-to-prepare, healthful desserts and sweet snacks. Here are a few ideas:

• Serve ricotta atop pancakes or French toast, and drizzle with maple syrup for brunch.

• Spread ricotta on toasted slices of baguette or English muffin halves, and dust with cinnamon sugar.

• Whisk honey into ricotta, dollop in dessert goblets, and top with berries.

• Whip ricotta, unsweetened cocoa, and sugar until creamy, spoon into wineglasses, and garnish with toasted pine nuts and crumbled amaretti cookies.

• Combine ricotta, grated orange rind, and honey; spread on store-bought crepes, and roll up. Chill an hour or until firm, and cut into pinwheels.

Sesame-Coated Chicken Stuffed with Ricotta and Spinach

Vary the greens used in the stuffing, depending on your mood and preference. For an earthier flavor, try a combination of arugula and escarole instead of spinach.

CHICKEN:

2 (6-ounce) packages prewashed baby spinach
1 cup (8 ounces) Homemade Ricotta Cheese (recipe on page 108)
½ teaspoon freshly ground black pepper, divided
¼ teaspoon salt, divided
Dash of freshly grated nutmeg
6 (6-ounce) skinless, boneless chicken breast halves
Cooking spray
1 tablespoon extravirgin olive oil
2 tablespoons sesame seeds

SAUCE:

1½ cups chopped tomato
⅔ cup thinly sliced fresh basil
½ cup finely chopped red onion
1 teaspoon extravirgin olive oil
½ teaspoon grated lemon rind
¼ teaspoon ground red pepper
⅛ teaspoon salt

1. Preheat oven to 450°.
2. To prepare chicken, heat a large nonstick skillet over medium heat. Add spinach to pan; cook 5 minutes or until spinach begins to wilt, stirring frequently. Drain spinach in a colander, pressing until barely moist. Place spinach on a cutting board; finely chop. Place spinach in a medium bowl. Add Homemade Ricotta Cheese, ¼ teaspoon black pepper, ⅛ teaspoon salt, and nutmeg; stir well to combine.
3. Place each chicken breast half between 2 sheets of heavy-duty plastic wrap; pound to ¼-inch thickness using a meat mallet or rolling pin. Spread each chicken breast half with ¼ cup ricotta mixture, leaving a ¼-inch border. Starting with a short side, roll up each chicken breast half jelly-roll fashion. Place rolls, seam sides down, in a 13 x 9-inch baking dish coated with cooking

spray. Sprinkle ¼ teaspoon black pepper and ⅛ teaspoon salt evenly over rolls; drizzle rolls evenly with 1 tablespoon oil. Sprinkle rolls with sesame seeds, pressing gently to adhere. Bake at 450° for 20 minutes or until chicken is done.
4. To prepare sauce, combine tomato and remaining 6 ingredients, stirring gently. Serve with chicken. Yield: 6 servings (serving size: 1 chicken roll and about ½ cup sauce).

CALORIES 348 (29% from fat); FAT 11.1g (sat 3.8g, mono 4.6g, poly 1.8g); PROTEIN 49.6g; CARB 12.3g; FIBER 4.1g; CHOL 114mg; IRON 3.6mg; SODIUM 480mg; CALC 245mg

How to Stuff Chicken Breasts

Spread the filling onto a flattened chicken breast half. Starting with a short side, roll up loosely.

sidetracked

Seder Side Dish

Haroset is a delicious, symbolic food eaten during the Passover meal. But it's a speedy condiment that complements meals anytime.

Traditionally, haroset is eaten on matzo during the seder meal. Although haroset is a holiday food, it certainly shouldn't be limited to Passover seders. Its sweet flavors and hearty texture make it a delicious year-round accompaniment with any number of foods, including chicken, turkey, lamb, and brisket. So make up a batch to share during Passover, but don't wait until next year to enjoy it again.

Lemon-Coconut-Almond Haroset

A touch of coconut lends this haroset exotic flavor, and its chunky texture makes it a good accompaniment with roast chicken and carrots. Toast the coconut in a 350° oven for 10 minutes, stirring once; store any extra toasted coconut in a zip-top bag.

4 teaspoons sugar
1 teaspoon grated lemon rind
1 tablespoon fresh lemon juice
3 Gala apples, peeled, cored, and cut into ½-inch pieces
1 Granny Smith apple, peeled, cored, and cut into ½-inch pieces
½ cup coarsely chopped almonds
1½ tablespoons dried coconut chips (such as Melissa's), toasted
Parsley sprigs (optional)

1. Combine first 5 ingredients in a large bowl. Stir in almonds and coconut. Cover and refrigerate 2 hours. Garnish with parsley, if desired. Yield: 4 cups (serving size: 2 tablespoons).

CALORIES 25 (32% from fat); FAT 0.9g (sat 0.1g, mono 0.5g, poly 0.2g); PROTEIN 0.3g; CARB 4.5g; FIBER 1g; CHOL 0mg; IRON 0.1mg; SODIUM 0mg; CALC 4mg

Turkish Haroset

This fruit-filled haroset would be excellent on matzo for a snack during Passover, when leavened bread is forbidden. And it's good spread on toast for breakfast the rest of the year. Try it with Gala apples.

½ cup whole pitted dates
¼ cup raisins
½ cup sweet red wine
½ cup dried apricots
¼ cup dried figs
½ apple, peeled, cored, and cut into 1-inch chunks
⅓ cup orange sections
½ cup chopped walnuts

1. Combine dates, raisins, and wine in a

medium bowl. Cover with plastic wrap, and let stand at room temperature 8 hours or overnight.

2. Place raisin mixture in a food processor. Add apricots and remaining ingredients. Process until almost smooth, scraping sides of bowl occasionally. Cover and chill at least 2 hours. Yield: 1½ cups (serving size: 2 tablespoons).

CALORIES 105 (29% from fat); FAT 3.4g (sat 0.3g, mono 0.5g, poly 2.4g); PROTEIN 1.5g; CARB 17.8g; FIBER 2.3g; CHOL 0mg; IRON 0.7mg; SODIUM 2mg; CALC 23mg

Iranian Haroset

This spiced date-and-almond version hails from Tehran.

⅓ cup hazelnuts
1 cup whole pitted dates
⅓ cup whole blanched almonds
¼ cup raisins
¼ cup golden raisins
2 tablespoons sweet red wine
¼ teaspoon ground ginger
¼ teaspoon ground cardamom
¼ teaspoon ground cinnamon
⅛ teaspoon ground cloves
1 cup shredded peeled
    Granny Smith apple (about
    8 ounces)
⅓ cup sliced banana

1. Preheat oven to 350°.
2. Place hazelnuts on a baking sheet. Bake at 350° for 10 minutes, stirring once. Turn nuts out onto a towel. Roll up towel; rub off skins.
3. Combine hazelnuts, dates, almonds, raisins, and golden raisins in a food processor. Process until ground, scraping sides of bowl occasionally. (Mixture will be thick and crumbly but will hold together when pressed.) Add wine and next 4 ingredients; pulse 4 times or until combined. Add apple and banana; pulse 4 times or until combined. Transfer mixture to a small bowl. Cover and refrigerate 1 hour. Yield: 2 cups (serving size: 2 tablespoons).

CALORIES 84 (29% from fat); FAT 2.7g (sat 0.2g, mono 1.8g, poly 0.5g); PROTEIN 1.3g; CARB 15.5g; FIBER 2.1g; CHOL 0mg; IRON 0.5mg; SODIUM 1mg; CALC 16mg

New England Haroset

Local ingredients have long influenced haroset recipes. In New England, cranberries and maple syrup are natural additions. The Concord grapes used to make sweet kosher wine are a local specialty. Use good-quality maple syrup, because its subtle flavor shines in this unspiced recipe. Use Granny Smith or Gala apples, or a combination of the two. You can grind the walnuts in a food processor.

3 cups finely diced apple (about
    1 pound)
½ cup sweetened dried cranberries,
    minced
¼ cup Concord grape kosher wine
    (such as Manischewitz)
4 teaspoons maple syrup
⅓ cup ground walnuts

1. Combine first 4 ingredients in a large bowl. Stir in walnuts. Refrigerate 2 hours in an airtight container. Yield: 3 cups (serving size: 2 tablespoons).

CALORIES 27 (23% from fat); FAT 0.7g (sat 0.1g, mono 0.1g, poly 0.5g); PROTEIN 0.2g; CARB 4.9g; FIBER 0.6g; CHOL 0mg; IRON 0.1mg; SODIUM 0mg; CALC 2mg

Greek-Style Haroset

Unlike most haroset recipes, this one is cooked. Prepare it a day ahead.

2 cups whole pitted dates
2 cups water
1 Granny Smith apple, peeled,
    cored, and quartered
1 Golden Delicious apple, peeled,
    cored, and quartered
¼ cup sweet red wine
½ cup coarsely chopped walnuts

1. Combine dates, water, and apples in a medium saucepan. Bring to a boil over medium-high heat. Reduce heat, and simmer 25 minutes or until apples are tender, stirring occasionally. Remove from heat; cool at least 15 minutes.
2. Place apple mixture and wine in a food processor; pulse 5 times (mixture will be chunky). Add nuts; pulse 2 times

to combine. Yield: 4 cups (serving size: 2 tablespoons).

CALORIES 36 (20% from fat); FAT 0.8g (sat 0.1g, mono 0.1g, poly 0.6g); PROTEIN 0.4g; CARB 7.3g; FIBER 0.8g; CHOL 0mg; IRON 0.1mg; SODIUM 0mg; CALC 5mg

Classic Apple Haroset

Use the shredding attachment on the food processor to quickly shred the apples. You can also grind or chop them. Don't refrigerate more than two hours before serving.

2 cups shredded peeled Gala apple
    (about 1 pound)
1 cup shredded peeled Granny
    Smith apple (about 8 ounces)
¾ cup coarsely chopped walnuts
3 tablespoons sweet red wine
1½ tablespoons honey
¼ teaspoon ground cinnamon

1. Combine all ingredients; refrigerate 2 hours in an airtight container. Yield: 2¾ cups (serving size: 2 tablespoons).

CALORIES 91 (30% from fat); FAT 3g (sat 0.3g, mono 0.8g, poly 1.7g); PROTEIN 1.6g; CARB 16.2g; FIBER 3.7g; CHOL 0mg; IRON 1mg; SODIUM 18mg; CALC 16mg

Pear-Pecan Haroset

This recipe comes from Arkansas, where pecans are grown locally. Pears add soft, mellow flavor. Try this haroset with fish.

2 cups shredded peeled Golden
    Delicious apple (about 1 pound)
1 cup shredded peeled Bartlett pear
    (about ¾ pound)
2 teaspoons fresh lemon juice
1 teaspoon vanilla extract
1 teaspoon honey
¼ cup coarsely chopped pecans

1. Combine first 5 ingredients in a large bowl. Fold in pecans. Refrigerate 2 hours in an airtight container. Yield: 2½ cups (serving size: 2 tablespoons).

CALORIES 30 (36% from fat); FAT 1.2g (sat 0.1g, mono 0.6g, poly 0.3g); PROTEIN 0.2g; CARB 5.3g; FIBER 1.1g; CHOL 0mg; IRON 0.1mg; SODIUM 0mg; CALC 3mg

Web Cuisine

The Internet provides a worldwide forum for food lovers.

What's really new today is the vast amount of information the Web puts at your fingertips—and at little cost. Crave chocolate mint pudding tonight? Just type "chocolate mint pudding" into the Google search engine, and you'll get 142,000 results. But food Web sites can narrow down those results to something more manageable. Want a brownie that's delicious but not too decadent? Tap into CookingLight.com. Looking for a county-fair prizewinning recipe? Then, go to www.allrecipes.com. Looking for lessons on making stock? Check out eGullet (www.egullet.org). Here are just some of the recipes and lessons (regarding stock) you'll find there.

Seven Steps to Great Stock

1. Prepare the ingredients. Nearly all stocks include carrots, onions, and celery—known as the basic vegetables of *mirepoix*. Halve and peel the onions. Peel the carrots, and trim and rinse the celery; coarsely chop. Although some people skip this step, taking a couple of minutes to prepare the vegetables results in a cleaner-tasting stock and will help infuse it with the flavor of the vegetables.

2. Skim. Cover the ingredients with water, turn on heat to high; simmer. You'll notice a gray scum rising to the surface of the stock. Gently remove and discard this scum with a spoon, ladle, or a dedicated skimmer. If you don't remove the scum, it will eventually reincorporate into the stock, making it cloudy and giving it an off taste.

3. Simmer. After the stock is skimmed, lower the heat, and let the stock simmer for as long as necessary. Find the setting on your stovetop that maintains a simmer: not quite a boil, but with noticeable small bubbles continuously rising to the surface.

4. Strain. Place a colander over a large bowl or pot in a clean sink with the drain shut (if you spill any stock, you can recover it). Start by transferring the stock to a large bowl and straining it in batches until the stockpot is light enough to lift. Pour with the lid affixed slightly off center, which prevents the big chunks of bones and vegetables from splashing into the colander.

5. Defat. Return the strained stock to the stockpot, and put it in the refrigerator. If the stockpot doesn't fit in the refrigerator, divide the stock among a few smaller vessels (quart-sized plastic takeout soup containers work well, as do plain old bowls). As the stock chills, the fat will solidify on top, making it easy to scrape and remove.

6. Reduce. Once it's been defatted, you officially have usable stock. But to save space, reduce all of it right away. Bring the stock to a simmer again, and let it reduce (skim any impurities that rise to the top) as much as you like—you can always dilute its flavor later with a little water.

7. Store. Ice-cube trays are excellent for making frozen cubes of stock. Plastic zip-top bags are also a space-efficient way to store stock. When refrigerated, reduced stock takes on the consistency of gelatin, which makes it easy to handle. Just keep it in a tub, and spoon it out as needed. Reduced stock will keep in the refrigerator for up to a week and in the freezer for up to three months.

Beef Stock

Generally, with stocks made from meat (as opposed to vegetable stocks), the body-enhancing properties of stock come from the natural gelatin in bones. Made from beef or veal bones, brown stock is the basis of many classic European sauces and makes quick, light, deeply flavored pan sauces for meat. It enriches most any dish in which it's used. Roasting the bones lends this stock hearty flavor, while the tomato paste gives it nice color.

3½   pounds meaty beef bones (such as oxtail)
3   cups coarsely chopped celery
1½   cups chopped carrot (about ¾ pound)
2   tablespoons tomato paste
3   onions, peeled and halved (about 1½ pounds)
5   quarts water

1. Preheat oven to 400°.
2. Arrange bones in an even layer in a shallow roasting pan. Bake at 400° for 45 minutes or until browned.
3. Transfer bones to an 8-quart stockpot. Add celery, carrot, tomato paste, and onion to pot; stir well to combine. Pour water over mixture; bring to a simmer. Reduce heat, and simmer 5 hours, skimming surface occasionally.
4. Strain stock through a sieve into a large bowl; discard solids. Cool stock to room temperature. Cover and chill stock 8 to 24 hours. Skim solidified fat from surface; discard. Refrigerate stock in an airtight container for up to 1 week or freeze for up to 3 months. Yield: 10 cups (serving size: 1 cup).

CALORIES 8 (31% from fat); FAT 0.3g (sat 0.1g, mono 0.1g, poly 0g); PROTEIN 0.7g; CARB 0.7g; FIBER 0.1g; CHOL 2mg; IRON 0.1mg; SODIUM 9mg; CALC 4mg

Beef stock is the basis of many classic European sauces.

Slow-Roasted Beef with Creamy Mashed Potatoes

This is one of the most classic and rewarding uses of stock. Beef takes on a new dimension of taste and lusciousness when braised in a beef stock. The braising liquid is then made into a sauce, further enhancing the rich beef flavor.

BEEF:

- 6 cups Beef Stock (recipe on page 114)
- 2 cups water
- 1 pound boneless chuck roast, trimmed and cut across grain into 4 slices
- 1 teaspoon chopped fresh thyme
- ¼ teaspoon salt
- ⅛ teaspoon freshly ground black pepper

POTATOES:

- 1½ pounds baking potatoes, peeled and cut into ½-inch pieces
- ½ cup 2% reduced-fat milk
- 1 tablespoon butter, softened
- ½ teaspoon salt
- ¼ teaspoon freshly ground black pepper

REMAINING INGREDIENT:

- 1 teaspoon chopped fresh thyme

1. Preheat oven to 400°.
2. To prepare beef, combine Beef Stock and water in a saucepan; bring to a simmer. Place beef in a 13 x 9-inch baking dish; pour stock mixture over beef. Bake at 400° for 2 hours or until beef is tender.
3. Remove beef from cooking liquid; cover and keep warm. Strain cooking liquid through a sieve into a bowl. Place a zip-top bag inside a 2-cup glass measure. Pour liquid into bag; let stand 10 minutes (fat will rise to top). Seal bag; carefully snip off 1 corner of bag. Drain liquid into a saucepan, stopping before fat layer reaches opening; discard fat. Bring liquid to a boil; reduce to simmer. Cook 20 minutes or until reduced to 1 cup. Remove from heat, and stir in

1 teaspoon thyme, ¼ teaspoon salt, and ⅛ teaspoon pepper.
4. To prepare potatoes, place potatoes in a saucepan; cover with water. Bring to a boil. Reduce heat, and cook 12 minutes or until very tender. Drain. Return potatoes to pan. Add milk and next 3 ingredients; mash with a potato masher to desired consistency. Cook 2 minutes or until thoroughly heated. Serve with beef. Serve sauce over beef; garnish with 1 teaspoon thyme. Yield: 4 servings (serving size: about 3 ounces beef, ¾ cup potatoes, ¼ cup sauce, and ¼ teaspoon thyme).

CALORIES 341 (24% from fat); FAT 8.9g (sat 3.8g, mono 3.6g, poly 0.4g); PROTEIN 25.2g; CARB 39.6g; FIBER 2.8g; CHOL 73mg; IRON 3.1mg; SODIUM 538mg; CALC 69mg

---

MAKE AHEAD • FREEZABLE
Shellfish Stock

Next time you make lobster, save the shells to prepare this stock. You can also make it with an equivalent quantity of crab shells, or use a combination of crab and lobster shells. For a less expensive option, use shrimp shells. Straining the stock twice makes for a smooth, clean-tasting final product.

- 2½ pounds lobster shells (about 4 small lobsters)
- 2 cups coarsely chopped celery
- 2 cups coarsely chopped fennel bulb
- 1 cup coarsely chopped carrot
- 2 tablespoons no salt-added tomato paste
- 2 onions, peeled and halved (about 1 pound)
- 5 quarts water

1. Preheat oven to 450°.
2. Arrange shells in an even layer in a shallow roasting pan. Bake at 450° for 30 minutes or until toasted.
3. Transfer shells to an 8-quart stockpot. Add celery and next 4 ingredients to pot; stir well. Pour water over vegetable mixture; bring to a boil. Reduce heat, and simmer 4 hours, skimming surface occasionally.
4. Strain stock through a sieve into a

large bowl; discard solids. Strain again through a paper towel-lined sieve. Cool stock to room temperature. Cover and chill stock. Refrigerate stock in an airtight container for up to 2 days, or freeze for up to 3 months. Yield: 10 cups (serving size: 1 cup).

CALORIES 9 (5% from fat); FAT 0.1g (sat 0g, mono 0g, poly 0g); PROTEIN 1.3g; CARB 0.8g; FIBER 0.2g; CHOL 4mg; IRON 0.1mg; SODIUM 35mg; CALC 15mg

---

Lobster "Bouillabaisse"

Traditional bouillabaisse uses a variety of fish and shellfish. Enhanced with stock made from lobster shells, this version focuses on the king of crustaceans: lobster. If you'd rather not wrangle live lobsters, ask your fishmonger to steam the lobsters for you (and save the shells). This "bouillabaisse" is also nice (and less costly) with shrimp.

- 5 cups water, divided
- 2 tablespoons salt
- 4 (1½-pound) whole Maine lobsters
- 2 large baking potatoes, peeled and cut into ¼-inch cubes (about 1⅓ pounds)
- 7 cups Shellfish Stock (recipe at left)
- 1 cup white wine
- 3 tablespoons tomato paste
- ⅛ teaspoon salt
- ⅛ teaspoon freshly ground black pepper
- 2 tablespoons minced fresh tarragon
- Freshly ground black pepper

1. Bring 4 cups water and 2 tablespoons salt to a boil in a 5-gallon stockpot. Place a vegetable steamer or rack in bottom of pot. Add lobsters; steam, covered, 14 minutes or until done. Remove meat from cooked lobster claws; chop meat. Cut each lobster tail in half, lengthwise; chill meat and tails.
2. Place potatoes in a saucepan; cover with water. Bring to a boil; cook 5 minutes or until tender. Drain; set aside.
3. Preheat oven to 300°.

Continued

4. Combine 1 cup water, stock, wine, and tomato paste in a large saucepan; bring to a boil. Cook over medium-high heat 30 minutes or until reduced to 5 cups. Stir in ⅛ teaspoon salt and pepper.
5. While stock reduces, place lobster tails, chopped lobster meat, and potato in a single layer on a baking sheet, keeping separate. Bake at 300° for 20 minutes or until thoroughly heated. Place half a lobster tail in each of 8 shallow soup bowls; place ½ cup potato and ¼ cup chopped lobster in each bowl. Ladle about ⅔ cup stock mixture over each serving; sprinkle each serving with ¾ teaspoon tarragon and black pepper. Yield: 8 servings.

CALORIES 270 (9% from fat); FAT 2.6g (sat 0.4g, mono 0.5g, poly 1g); PROTEIN 36.5g; CARB 21g; FIBER 1.8g; CHOL 119mg; IRON 2.3mg; SODIUM 558mg; CALC 109mg

MAKE AHEAD • FREEZABLE
Chicken Stock

This basic white stock is the foundation of many soups, sauces, and rice and pasta dishes. In addition to the stock, it yields two poached chicken breasts, ideal for salads and sandwiches, such as the Rosemary Chicken Salad Sandwiches (recipe on page 121).

 1   (4-pound) whole chicken
 3   cups coarsely chopped celery
1½ cups chopped carrot
 2   large onions, peeled and halved
     (about 1½ pounds)
3½ quarts water

1. Remove and discard giblets and neck from chicken. Rinse chicken with cold water; place chicken in an 8-quart stockpot. Add celery and remaining ingredients; bring to a simmer. Reduce heat, and simmer 45 minutes; skim surface occasionally, discarding solids.
2. Remove chicken from pot; cool. Remove chicken breast meat from bones; reserve for another use. Return chicken to pot; bring to a boil. Reduce heat, and simmer 2 hours, skimming surface occasionally.
3. Strain stock through a sieve into a large bowl; reserve dark meat for another use, and discard other solids. Cool stock to room temperature. Cover and chill 8 to 24 hours. Skim solidified fat from surface; discard. Refrigerate stock in an airtight container for up to 5 days or freeze for up to 3 months. Yield: 10 cups (serving size: 1 cup).

CALORIES 9 (55% from fat); FAT 0.6g (sat 0.2g, mono 0.2g, poly 0.1g); PROTEIN 0.7g; CARB 0.3g; FIBER 0.1g; CHOL 3mg; IRON 0.1mg; SODIUM 12mg; CALC 9mg

Sautéed Chicken with Chardonnay Sauce

 4   (6-ounce) skinless, boneless
     chicken breast halves
 ¼   teaspoon salt
 ¼   teaspoon freshly ground black
     pepper
 2   tablespoons all-purpose flour
 2   tablespoons butter, divided
1½ cups thinly sliced mushrooms
1½ tablespoons finely chopped
     shallots
 1   cup chardonnay or other dry
     white wine
 2   cups Chicken Stock (recipe at
     left)
 2   tablespoons chopped fresh
     parsley

1. Place each chicken breast half between 2 sheets of heavy-duty plastic wrap; pound to ½-inch thickness using a meat mallet or rolling pin. Sprinkle chicken with salt, pepper, and flour.
2. Heat 1 tablespoon butter in a large nonstick skillet over medium heat. Add chicken; cook 5 minutes on each side or until done. Remove chicken from pan; keep warm. Add mushrooms and shallots to pan; sauté 5 minutes or until tender. Stir in wine, scraping pan to loosen browned bits; add stock. Bring to a boil; cook until reduced to 1 cup (about 10 minutes). Cut 1 tablespoon butter into small pieces. Remove pan from heat. Add butter, stirring until butter melts. Spoon sauce over chicken. Sprinkle with parsley. Yield: 4 servings (serving size: 1 chicken breast half, ¼ cup sauce, and 1½ teaspoons parsley).

CALORIES 288 (26% from fat); FAT 8.2g (sat 3.5g, mono 3g, poly 0.8g); PROTEIN 41.2g; CARB 5.8g; FIBER 0.6g; CHOL 115mg; IRON 1.8mg; SODIUM 309mg; CALC 33mg

Thai-Style Vegetable Curry

 1   tablespoon canola oil
 3   cups chopped onion
 1   tablespoon chopped peeled
     ginger
 4   garlic cloves, minced
 4   cups Vegetable Stock (recipe on
     page 117), divided
 2   tablespoons low-sodium soy
     sauce
 2   to 3 teaspoons red Thai curry
     paste (such as Thai Kitchen)
 ½   teaspoon salt
1½ cups (¼-inch) slices carrot
 2   cups chopped red bell pepper
 2   cups cherry tomatoes
 2   zucchini, halved lengthwise and
     thinly sliced (about 4 cups)
 8   ounces small yellow squash,
     halved lengthwise and thinly
     sliced (about 1½ cups)
 1   (8-ounce) package presliced
     mushrooms
 1   (6-ounce) package fresh baby
     spinach
 4   cups hot cooked rice noodles

1. Heat oil in a Dutch oven over medium-high heat. Add onion, ginger, and garlic; sauté 5 minutes. Add 1 cup Vegetable Stock, soy sauce, curry paste, and salt. Stir in carrot; cook 2 minutes. Add bell pepper and next 4 ingredients; cook 2 minutes, stirring occasionally. Stir in 3 cups stock and spinach; bring to a boil. Reduce heat, and simmer 5 minutes or until carrot is tender, stirring occasionally. Serve over noodles. Yield: 8 servings (serving size: 1½ cups curry and ½ cup noodles).

CALORIES 188 (11% from fat); FAT 2.3g (sat 0.2g, mono 1.1g, poly 0.8g); PROTEIN 4.4g; CARB 40.2g; FIBER 4.4g; CHOL 0mg; IRON 2.3mg; SODIUM 361mg; CALC 77mg

Many think it's hard, but making stock is simple.

Vegetable Stock

You can improvise with your choice of vegetables, but avoid bitter ones, which can compete with the flavors in a finished dish.

    3   cups coarsely chopped cabbage
 2½   cups coarsely chopped fennel
        bulb
    2   cups coarsely chopped celery
    1   cup chopped carrot
    2   tablespoons tomato paste
    2   large onions, peeled and halved
        (about 1½ pounds)
    1   (8-ounce) package mushrooms
  12   black peppercorns
  10   flat-leaf parsley sprigs
    8   thyme sprigs
    6   garlic cloves, peeled
    2   bay leaves
    4   quarts water

1. Combine first 12 ingredients in an 8-quart stockpot. Pour water over vegetable mixture; bring to a boil. Reduce heat, and simmer 45 minutes, skimming surface occasionally.
2. Strain stock through a sieve into a large bowl; discard solids. Cool stock to room temperature. Cover and chill. Refrigerate stock in an airtight container for up to 5 days or freeze for up to 3 months. Yield: 13 cups (serving size: 1 cup).

CALORIES 3 (5% from fat); FAT 0g; PROTEIN 0.1g; CARB 0.6g; FIBER 0.2g; CHOL 0mg; IRON 0.1mg; SODIUM 18mg; CALC 9mg

superfast

. . . And Ready in Just about 20 Minutes

More than a week's worth of quick entrées gets you in and out of the kitchen in a flash.

Steak Salad with Creamy Ranch Dressing

STEAK:

 ½   teaspoon garlic powder
 ½   teaspoon brown sugar
 ½   teaspoon ground red pepper
 ¼   teaspoon salt
 ¼   teaspoon black pepper
  1   (1-pound) boneless sirloin steak, trimmed (about ½ inch thick)
Cooking spray

SALAD:

  4   (1-ounce) slices sourdough bread
  1   garlic clove, halved
  2   cups grape tomatoes
  1   cup halved and sliced cucumber
  1   cup sliced red onion
  1   (16-ounce) bag classic iceberg salad mix (such as Dole's)
 ½   cup fat-free ranch dressing

1. Heat a nonstick grill pan over medium-high heat.
2. Preheat broiler.
3. To prepare steak, combine first 5 ingredients; rub evenly over both sides of steak. Coat grill pan with cooking spray. Cook steak 4 minutes on each side or until desired degree of doneness. Remove from pan; let stand 5 minutes. Cut steak diagonally across grain into thin slices.
4. While steak stands, prepare salad. Place bread slices on a baking sheet. Broil 2 minutes on each side or until lightly browned. Rub cut sides of garlic halves over bread slices. Cut bread into ¾-inch cubes. Combine bread cubes, tomatoes, cucumber, onion, and salad mix in a large bowl. Add dressing, tossing gently to coat. Divide salad evenly among 4 plates; top with steak. Yield: 4 servings (serving size: 3 cups salad and about 3 ounces meat).

CALORIES 334 (20% from fat); FAT 7.5g (sat 2.6g, mono 3.1g, poly 0.6g); PROTEIN 29.2g; CARB 37g; FIBER 4.8g; CHOL 67mg; IRON 3.6mg; SODIUM 733mg; CALC 73mg

Shrimp and Orzo with Cherry Tomatoes and Romano Cheese

Parmesan cheese works in this dish, too, if you don't have pecorino Romano on hand. Serve leftovers as a great cold pasta salad for lunch.

  1   cup uncooked orzo (rice-shaped pasta)
  2   tablespoons olive oil, divided
 ¾   teaspoon salt, divided
 ¼   teaspoon black pepper, divided
  1   pound medium shrimp, peeled and deveined
  1   cup chopped Vidalia or other sweet onion
  1   tablespoon bottled minced garlic
 ¼   teaspoon crushed red pepper
  2   cups cherry tomatoes, halved
 ⅓   cup (about 1½ ounces) grated fresh pecorino Romano cheese
 ⅓   cup chopped fresh basil

1. Cook pasta according to package directions, omitting salt and fat.
2. While pasta cooks, heat 1 tablespoon oil in a large skillet over medium-high heat. Sprinkle ½ teaspoon salt and ⅛ teaspoon black pepper evenly over shrimp. Add shrimp to pan; cook 1½ minutes on each side or until done. Remove from pan.
3. Add 1 tablespoon oil to pan. Add onion, garlic, and red pepper; cook 2 minutes, stirring frequently. Add tomatoes; cook 3 minutes or until tomatoes begin to soften, stirring occasionally. Stir in pasta and shrimp; cook 1 minute or until thoroughly heated. Remove from heat, and stir in ¼ teaspoon salt, ⅛ teaspoon black pepper, cheese, and basil. Yield: 4 servings (serving size: 1¼ cups).

CALORIES 414 (26% from fat); FAT 11.9g (sat 2.9g, mono 6g, poly 1.6g); PROTEIN 33.1g; CARB 43.6g; FIBER 3.1g; CHOL 181mg; IRON 4.9mg; SODIUM 721mg; CALC 178mg

Smoked Paprika Pork Chops with Bell Pepper and Corn Relish

Accompany this dish with refrigerated potato wedges tossed with garlic powder, ground red pepper, and salt, and roasted until crisp.

- 1 tablespoon olive oil
- ½ cup prechopped red onion
- 2 teaspoons bottled minced fresh ginger
- ⅓ cup chopped red bell pepper
- 1 teaspoon ground coriander
- ¼ teaspoon dried thyme
- 1 (15.5-ounce) can no salt-added whole-kernel corn, drained
- 1 teaspoon cider vinegar
- ¾ teaspoon salt, divided
- ¼ teaspoon black pepper, divided
- 1½ teaspoons smoked sweet paprika
- 4 (4-ounce) center-cut boneless pork loin chops, trimmed
- Cooking spray

1. Heat oil in a large nonstick skillet over medium-high heat. Add onion and ginger; sauté 2 minutes or until tender. Add bell pepper and next 3 ingredients; cook 3 minutes or until bell pepper is tender, stirring occasionally. Stir in vinegar, ¼ teaspoon salt, and ⅛ teaspoon black pepper; cook 1 minute, stirring constantly. Spoon relish into a bowl.
2. Combine ½ teaspoon salt, ⅛ teaspoon black pepper, and paprika; sprinkle evenly over pork. Coat pan with cooking spray. Add pork to pan; cook 4 minutes on each side or until done. Serve with relish. Yield: 4 servings (serving size: 1 pork chop and about ⅓ cup relish).

CALORIES 263 (30% from fat); FAT 8.9g (sat 2.5g, mono 4.5g, poly 1.2g); PROTEIN 27.2g; CARB 19.8g; FIBER 1.4g; CHOL 62mg; IRON 1.6mg; SODIUM 508mg; CALC 39mg

Jamaican Chicken with Mango Salsa

Jarred sliced mango can be found in the produce section. You can also use two cups sliced fresh mango. Serve with corn tortilla chips to scoop up any remaining salsa.

- ½ teaspoon Jamaican jerk seasoning (such as Spice Islands)
- ½ teaspoon salt, divided
- 4 (6-ounce) skinless, boneless chicken breast halves
- Cooking spray
- ¼ cup minced fresh cilantro
- ¼ cup finely chopped red onion
- 1 tablespoon chopped fresh mint
- 2 teaspoons fresh lime juice
- 1 teaspoon brown sugar
- ¼ teaspoon black pepper
- ¼ teaspoon crushed red pepper
- 1 (16-ounce) jar sliced peeled mango, drained and chopped (such as Del Monte SunFresh)

1. Heat a large nonstick skillet over medium-high heat. Sprinkle jerk seasoning and ¼ teaspoon salt evenly over chicken. Coat chicken with cooking spray. Add chicken to pan; cook 4 minutes on each side or until done.
2. While chicken cooks, combine ¼ teaspoon salt, cilantro, and remaining 7 ingredients. Serve salsa with chicken. Yield: 4 servings (serving size: 1 chicken breast half and about ½ cup salsa).

CALORIES 244 (9% from fat); FAT 2.4g (sat 0.6g, mono 0.6g, poly 0.5g); PROTEIN 39.8g; CARB 14.7g; FIBER 1.6g; CHOL 99mg; IRON 1.5mg; SODIUM 445mg; CALC 33mg

Sriracha-Glazed Chicken and Onions over Rice

- 1 (3½-ounce) bag boil-in-bag long-grain rice
- 3 tablespoons hoisin sauce
- 1 tablespoon ketchup
- 1¼ teaspoons Sriracha (hot chile sauce, such as Huy Fong)
- 1½ tablespoons canola oil
- 1½ cups presliced onion
- 1 tablespoon bottled minced fresh ginger
- 1 tablespoon bottled minced garlic
- ¾ teaspoon curry powder
- 1 pound skinless, boneless chicken breast, cut into 1-inch-thick slices

1. Prepare rice according to package directions, omitting salt and fat.

2. While rice cooks, combine hoisin, ketchup, and Sriracha in a small bowl.
3. Heat oil in a large nonstick skillet over medium-high heat. Add onion; sauté 3 minutes or until tender. Add ginger and next 3 ingredients; sauté 6 minutes or until chicken is done. Stir in hoisin mixture; cook 1 minute, tossing to coat. Serve over rice. Yield: 4 servings (serving size: ¾ cup chicken mixture and about ½ cup rice).

CALORIES 326 (20% from fat); FAT 7.3g (sat 0.9g, mono 3.6g, poly 2.1g); PROTEIN 29.5g; CARB 34g; FIBER 2.2g; CHOL 66mg; IRON 2mg; SODIUM 338mg; CALC 35mg

Spice-Rubbed Salmon with Cucumber Relish

The bold spice rub works well with rich-flavored salmon and would also be good on pork. Serve with delicate angel hair pasta or mashed potatoes.

- 1 tablespoon brown sugar
- 1 teaspoon garlic powder
- 1 teaspoon dried oregano
- 1 teaspoon ground cumin
- 1 teaspoon chili powder
- 1 teaspoon paprika
- ½ teaspoon salt, divided
- ¼ teaspoon dried thyme
- 4 (6-ounce) salmon fillets, skinned
- Cooking spray
- 2 cups chopped cucumber
- ½ cup chopped red bell pepper
- ¼ cup prechopped onion
- 2 tablespoons chopped fresh mint
- 1 tablespoon capers
- 1 tablespoon cider vinegar

1. Preheat broiler.
2. Combine first 6 ingredients, ¼ teaspoon salt, and thyme; rub evenly over fish. Place fish on a jelly-roll pan coated with cooking spray. Broil 8 minutes or until fish flakes easily when tested with a fork.
3. Combine ¼ teaspoon salt, cucumber, and next 5 ingredients; serve with fish. Yield: 4 servings (serving size: 1 fish fillet and about ½ cup relish).

CALORIES 312 (39% from fat); FAT 13.6g (sat 3.2g, mono 5.7g, poly 3.3g); PROTEIN 37.3g; CARB 8.9g; FIBER 2.3g; CHOL 87mg; IRON 1.7mg; SODIUM 450mg; CALC 53mg

Asian Sandwich
Night Menu
serves 4

Asian-flavored wraps and crunchy won ton chips elevate sandwich night to a new level.

Asian Catfish Wraps

Sweet-spicy won ton chips*

Steamed edamame pods

*Cut 12 won ton wrappers in half diagonally to create 24 triangles; arrange in a single layer on a baking sheet. Brush triangles with 2 teaspoons dark sesame oil. Combine 1 teaspoon sugar, ½ teaspoon wasabi powder, ⅛ teaspoon salt, and ⅛ teaspoon ground red pepper; sprinkle evenly over triangles. Bake at 400° for 5 minutes or until lightly browned and crisp.

QUICK & EASY
Asian Catfish Wraps

Catfish nuggets are fresh catfish pieces that are less expensive than fillets. If they're not available, buy fillets and cut them into bite-sized pieces.

1 teaspoon dark sesame oil, divided
1 pound catfish nuggets
3 cups thinly sliced napa (Chinese) cabbage
1 cup thinly sliced shiitake mushroom caps
¾ cup preshredded carrot
½ cup sliced green onions
1 tablespoon bottled minced fresh ginger
1 tablespoon bottled minced garlic
¼ cup hoisin sauce
1 teaspoon chili garlic sauce (such as Lee Kum Kee)
4 (8-inch) fat-free flour tortillas

1. Heat ½ teaspoon oil in a large non-stick skillet over medium-high heat. Add catfish; cook 3 minutes or until done, stirring frequently. Remove from pan.
2. Add ½ teaspoon oil to pan. Add cabbage and next 5 ingredients; sauté 2 minutes or until carrot is crisp-tender. Stir in catfish nuggets, hoisin, and chili garlic sauce, and cook 1 minute or until thoroughly heated. Remove from heat.

3. Warm tortillas according to package directions. Divide catfish mixture evenly among tortillas; roll up. Yield: 4 servings (serving size: 1 wrap).

CALORIES 344 (27% from fat); FAT 10.4g (sat 2.3g, mono 4.7g, poly 2.6g); PROTEIN 22.8g; CARB 37.8g; FIBER 3.7g; CHOL 54mg; IRON 0.9mg; SODIUM 650mg; CALC 58mg

lighten up

Rise to French Toast

A favorite B&B treat is transformed for home cooks.

Brian Durkee, of St. Charles, Missouri, surprised his wife, Doris, with a weekend getaway at the Main Street Inn, in Ste. Genevieve, Missouri for her 34th birthday. For breakfast, the Durkees enjoyed a fruit preserve-filled French toast baked like an upside-down cake, over caramel and pecans. The dish was so good that Doris asked the innkeepers for the recipe.

Durkee quickly realized the French toast was a far cry from the *Cooking Light* creations she is accustomed to making so she asked us for help.

By making a more traditional caramel syrup with melted sugar, evaporated milk, and one tablespoon of butter, we substantially reduced the amount of butter and sugar. For the syrup alone, the calories per serving dropped from 205 to 74, and the fat fell from 11 grams to one. Instead of using the tricky flipping step, we served the toast straight from the pan.

Although pecans are high in calories and fat, they're rich in the monounsaturated variety (a healthy fat), so we kept three tablespoons of nuts. Since bread is the main ingredient in French toast, we wanted enough of it to fill the pan. We used 16 bread slices but cut them thinner, which saved 46 calories per serving. By combining egg substitute and large eggs in place of the baker's dozen of extralarge, we trimmed more than 100 calories and more than 7 grams of fat per serving. We swapped the original's whole milk for fat-free, saving 112 calories and 16 grams of fat.

BEFORE	AFTER
SERVING SIZE	
1 piece	
CALORIES PER SERVING	
696	332
FAT	
30g	6.7g
PERCENT OF TOTAL CALORIES	
39%	18%

Strawberry-Filled French Toast with Caramel and Pecans

SAUCE:
½ cup granulated sugar
3 tablespoons water
1 tablespoon butter
½ cup evaporated fat-free milk
½ teaspoon vanilla extract
⅛ teaspoon salt

FRENCH TOAST:
Cooking spray
1 (12-ounce) loaf French bread, cut into 16 (¼-inch-thick) slices
½ cup strawberry preserves
2 cups fat-free milk
¾ cup egg substitute
1 tablespoon vanilla extract
¼ teaspoon ground cinnamon
⅛ teaspoon ground nutmeg
⅛ teaspoon salt
2 large eggs, lightly beaten
3 tablespoons chopped pecans
2 tablespoons powdered sugar

1. To prepare sauce, combine granulated sugar and water in a medium, heavy saucepan. Cook over medium-low heat 3 minutes or until sugar dissolves. Cover and cook over medium heat 1 minute. Uncover and cook 5 minutes or until light golden (do not stir).
2. Remove from heat, and let stand 1 minute. Add butter; stir until melted. Add evaporated milk, stirring constantly. Place pan over medium heat; cook 3 minutes or until mixture melts and is smooth, stirring constantly. Remove from heat; stir in vanilla and salt.

Continued

3. Preheat oven to 350°.

4. To prepare French toast, pour sauce into a 13 x 9-inch baking dish coated with cooking spray. Arrange 8 bread slices in dish. Spread preserves evenly over bread; top with remaining bread.

5. Combine 2 cups milk and next 6 ingredients. Pour milk mixture over bread; sprinkle with pecans.

6. Bake, uncovered, at 350° for 35 minutes or until top is golden. Cool 5 minutes. Sprinkle with powdered sugar. Yield: 8 servings (serving size: 1 piece).

CALORIES 332 (18% from fat); FAT 6.7g (sat 1.7g, mono 2.9g, poly 1.5g); PROTEIN 11.9g; CARB 55.2g; FIBER 1.6g; CHOL 58mg; IRON 2mg; SODIUM 453mg; CALC 164mg

enlightened cook

Growing Organically

Earthbound Farm, now one of the largest organic growers in the country, started as a labor of love for founders Drew and Myra Goodman.

While Earthbound Farm is now the largest grower of organic produce in America, the scene isn't that much different than it was 20 years ago. Then, Drew and Myra Goodman, founders of Earthbound Farm, would harvest, wash, and bag armfuls of baby organic lettuce from their backyard in Northern California's Carmel Valley each Sunday to keep in the refrigerator for convenient, healthful salads all week long. That simple practice by a busy, young couple has blossomed into a company that has changed the way America eats. Drew and Myra still pick lettuce—only now, like millions of other Americans, they get a bag of Earthbound Farm salad from the produce shelf.

Grilled Vegetable Lasagna

(pictured on page 94)

Grilling the vegetables deepens their flavors, which makes for a delicious vegetarian entrée. To speed preparation, use no-boil lasagna noodles; the baking time remains the same.

3 eggplants, cut lengthwise into ¼-inch slices (about 3 pounds)
3 zucchini, cut lengthwise into ⅛-inch slices (about 1¼ pounds)
Cooking spray
1 teaspoon salt, divided
¾ teaspoon freshly ground black pepper, divided
2 red bell peppers, quartered and seeded
1 (15-ounce) container fat-free ricotta cheese
1 large egg, lightly beaten
¾ cup grated Asiago cheese, divided
¼ cup minced fresh basil
¼ cup minced fresh parsley
9 lasagna noodles
1 (26-ounce) jar tomato-basil spaghetti sauce (such as Muir Glen)
¾ cup (3 ounces) shredded part-skim mozzarella cheese
¼ cup commercial pesto (such as Alessi)

1. Preheat grill.

2. Coat eggplant and zucchini with cooking spray. Sprinkle with ½ teaspoon salt and ¼ teaspoon black pepper. Grill eggplant and zucchini 1½ minutes on each side or just until tender. Cool; combine in a large bowl.

3. Place bell peppers on grill, skin-side down; grill 3 minutes or until tender. Cut into 1-inch-wide strips. Add bell peppers to eggplant mixture.

4. Combine ricotta cheese, egg, ½ cup Asiago cheese, basil, parsley, ½ teaspoon salt, and ½ teaspoon black pepper.

5. Cook noodles according to package directions, omitting salt and fat.

6. Preheat oven to 375°.

7. Spread ½ cup spaghetti sauce in a 13 x 9-inch baking dish coated with cooking spray. Arrange 3 noodles over tomato sauce. Top with half of eggplant mixture. Spread half of ricotta cheese mixture over eggplant mixture; sprinkle with ¼ cup mozzarella cheese.

8. Arrange 3 noodles and 1 cup of spaghetti sauce over cheese; cover with remaining eggplant mixture. Top with remaining ricotta mixture. Spread pesto over ricotta; sprinkle with ¼ cup mozzarella cheese. Cover with 3 noodles.

9. Spoon 1 cup spaghetti sauce over noodles. Sprinkle with ¼ cup Asiago cheese and ¼ cup mozzarella cheese.

10. Bake at 375° for 1 hour. Let stand 15 minutes before serving. Yield: 10 servings.

CALORIES 318 (29% from fat); FAT 10.4g (sat 4.2g, mono 1.3g, poly 0.4g); PROTEIN 15.2g; CARB 41.9g; FIBER 3.2g; CHOL 40mg; IRON 2.7mg; SODIUM 728mg; CALC 269mg

Roasted Beet Salad with Tarragon Vinaigrette

We call for golden beets, but regular beets work just as well in this flavorful salad. You can also use a mixture of both for a colorful, pretty platter.

3 pounds golden beets
¼ cup olive oil, divided
2 tablespoons minced garlic, divided
1½ teaspoons chopped fresh thyme, divided
1½ teaspoons minced fresh tarragon, divided
1 teaspoon salt, divided
1 teaspoon black pepper, divided
1 cup red wine vinegar
¼ cup sugar
2 tablespoons finely chopped shallots
½ teaspoon chopped fresh oregano
2 cups vertically sliced red onion

1. Preheat oven to 350°.

2. Leave root and 1-inch stem on beets; scrub with a brush. Place beets, 2 tablespoons oil, 1 tablespoon garlic, 1 teaspoon thyme, and 1 teaspoon tarragon in a large bowl; toss gently. Place beet mixture on a jelly-roll pan. Bake at 350° for 1 hour or until beets are tender. Drain and cool slightly. Trim off beet roots; rub off skins. Cut in half. Sprinkle with ½ teaspoon salt and ½ teaspoon pepper.

3. Combine vinegar, sugar, shallots, oregano, 2 tablespoons oil, 1 tablespoon garlic, ½ teaspoon thyme, ½ teaspoon tarragon, ½ teaspoon salt, and ½ teaspoon pepper in a small bowl, stirring with a whisk. Add vinegar mixture and onion to beet mixture; toss gently. Yield: 8 servings (serving size: about ½ cup).

CALORIES 146 (22% from fat); FAT 3.7g (sat 0.5g, mono 2.6g, poly 0.5g); PROTEIN 3.3g; CARB 26.9g; FIBER 5.3g; CHOL 0mg; IRON 1.8mg; SODIUM 428mg; CALC 43mg

---

QUICK & EASY

Black Bean Soup

Top this hearty soup with a dollop of low-fat sour cream and/or chopped green onions.

- 1 tablespoon olive oil
- ½ cup diced celery
- ½ cup minced onion
- ¼ cup diced green bell pepper
- 3 tablespoons chopped carrot
- 1 tablespoon minced garlic
- 1½ teaspoons ground cumin
- 1 teaspoon dried oregano
- 1 teaspoon chili powder
- ¼ teaspoon freshly ground black pepper
- 2 cups vegetable broth
- 1 cup water
- 3 (15-ounce) cans black beans, rinsed and drained
- Sliced green onions (optional)

1. Heat oil in a large saucepan over medium heat. Add celery, minced onion, bell pepper, and carrot. Cook 10 minutes or until tender, stirring occasionally. Add garlic and next 4 ingredients; sauté 3 minutes. Add broth, water, and beans; bring to a boil. Reduce heat, and simmer 15 minutes. Cool slightly.

2. Place half of soup in a blender, and process until smooth. Pour into a bowl. Repeat procedure with remaining soup. Garnish with sliced green onions, if desired. Yield: 6 servings (serving size: about 1 cup).

CALORIES 221 (17% from fat); FAT 4.1g (sat 0.3g, mono 1.7g, poly 1.9g); PROTEIN 12g; CARB 32g; FIBER 12.4g; CHOL 0mg; IRON 4.8mg; SODIUM 643mg; CALC 84mg

---

Wedding Gift

A simple sandwich created for a friend's wedding becomes a Pennsylvania reader's signature creation.

When we tasted Brandy Long's Rosemary Chicken Salad Sandwiches in the Cooking Light Test Kitchens, we gave the recipe a high rating. Long, who lives in Saltillo, Pennsylvania, created the recipe when she was asked by a friend's mother to make chicken salad sandwiches for her daughter's wedding. She held onto the recipe and has been making her Rosemary Chicken Salad Sandwiches for special holidays, baby showers, and church events ever since. Sometimes she skips the bread and serves the fragrant salad with crackers.

QUICK & EASY

Rosemary Chicken Salad Sandwiches

- 3 cups chopped roasted skinless, boneless chicken breasts (about ¾ pound)
- ⅓ cup chopped green onions
- ¼ cup chopped smoked almonds
- ¼ cup plain fat-free yogurt
- ¼ cup light mayonnaise
- 1 teaspoon chopped fresh rosemary
- 1 teaspoon Dijon mustard
- ⅛ teaspoon salt
- ⅛ teaspoon freshly ground black pepper
- 10 slices whole-grain bread

1. Combine first 9 ingredients, stirring well. Spread about ⅔ cup chicken mixture over each of 5 bread slices, and top with remaining bread slices. Cut sandwiches diagonally in half. Yield: 5 servings (serving size: 1 sandwich).

CALORIES 360 (29% from fat); FAT 11.6g (sat 2.1g, mono 3.5g, poly 1.8g); PROTEIN 33.6g; CARB 29.9g; FIBER 4.4g; CHOL 76mg; IRON 2.9mg; SODIUM 529mg; CALC 104mg

---

Rice and Beans with Avocado

—Kathy McCullough, Los Angeles, California

- 2 cups water
- 1 cup long-grain brown rice
- 1 (15-ounce) can black beans, rinsed and drained
- 2 cups halved cherry tomatoes
- ⅔ cup diced peeled avocado (about 1 medium)
- ⅓ cup chopped green onions
- ⅓ cup (1½ ounces) shredded Cheddar cheese
- 1 tablespoon chopped ripe olives
- ¼ teaspoon salt
- ¼ teaspoon freshly ground black pepper

1. Combine water and rice in a medium saucepan; bring to a boil. Cover, reduce heat, and simmer 35 minutes. Stir in beans; cook 10 minutes or until rice is done. Place rice mixture in a large bowl. Add tomatoes and remaining ingredients, tossing gently to combine. Yield: 6 servings (serving size: 1 cup).

CALORIES 215 (25% from fat); FAT 6g (sat 2g, mono 2.8g, poly 0.8g); PROTEIN 7.3g; CARB 35.7g; FIBER 6.3g; CHOL 7mg; IRON 1.8mg; SODIUM 349mg; CALC 81mg

---

QUICK & EASY

Apricot-Glazed Pork Chops

—Lori R. Jobe, Frisco, Texas

- ¼ teaspoon salt
- ⅛ teaspoon black pepper
- 4 (4-ounce) boneless center-cut loin pork chops (about ½ inch thick)
- 1 teaspoon olive oil
- ⅓ cup apricot preserves
- ⅓ cup riesling or other slightly sweet white wine
- ½ teaspoon bottled ground fresh ginger (such as Spice World)

1. Sprinkle salt and pepper evenly over pork. Heat oil in a large nonstick skillet over medium-high heat; add pork. Cook 2 minutes on each side or until browned. Remove pork from pan, and keep warm.

Continued

2. Combine preserves, wine, and ginger in a small bowl, stirring with a whisk. Add preserves mixture to pan; simmer 4 minutes or until mixture thickens. Return pork to pan; cook 1 minute, turning to coat. Yield: 4 servings (serving size: 1 pork chop).

CALORIES 246 (28% from fat); FAT 7.7g (sat 2.6g, mono 3.8g, poly 0.6g); PROTEIN 23.5g; CARB 17.4g; FIBER 0.1g; CHOL 67mg; IRON 1.1mg; SODIUM 208mg; CALC 25mg

---

QUICK & EASY
Roasted Sesame Asparagus

—Lynn Brandt, Franklin, Pennsylvania

1½ pounds asparagus spears
Cooking spray
1½ teaspoons dark sesame oil
1 tablespoon balsamic vinegar
1½ teaspoons sesame seeds, toasted
½ teaspoon crushed red pepper
⅛ teaspoon salt
⅛ teaspoon black pepper
1 tablespoon shaved fresh Parmesan cheese

1. Preheat oven to 450°.
2. Snap off tough ends of asparagus. Arrange asparagus in a single layer on a jelly-roll pan coated with cooking spray; brush with oil. Bake at 450° for 10 minutes or until crisp-tender. Remove from oven. Add vinegar, sesame seeds, and red pepper; toss gently. Place asparagus on a platter; sprinkle with salt and black pepper. Top with cheese. Yield: 6 servings.

CALORIES 50 (31% from fat); FAT 1.7g (sat 0.4g, mono 0.7g, poly 0.6g); PROTEIN 2.9g; CARB 5.6g; FIBER 2.6g; CHOL 1mg; IRON 0.5mg; SODIUM 63mg; CALC 36mg

---

QUICK & EASY
Spinach Salad with Poppy Seed Dressing

—Marie Alana Gardner, North Tonawanda, New York

DRESSING:
⅓ cup plain fat-free yogurt
¼ cup light mayonnaise
2 teaspoons white vinegar
2 teaspoons sugar
1 teaspoon poppy seeds

SALAD:
4 cups torn spinach
2 cups cubed Granny Smith apple
1 cup bite-size pieces navel orange
¼ cup chopped red onion

1. To prepare dressing, combine first 5 ingredients in a small bowl; stir with a whisk.
2. To prepare salad, combine spinach, apple, orange, and onion in a large bowl; add dressing. Toss gently to combine. Yield: 6 servings (serving size: about 1 cup).

CALORIES 105 (32% from fat); FAT 3.7g (sat 0.5g, mono 0g, poly 0.2g); PROTEIN 2.3g; CARB 18.2g; FIBER 2.5g; CHOL 4mg; IRON 1.3mg; SODIUM 118mg; CALC 78mg

---

Garlic Breadsticks

—Faith B. Kerr, Ivoryton, Connecticut

1 tablespoon dry yeast
1 tablespoon honey
1½ cups warm water (100° to 110°)
1 teaspoon salt
1 large egg, lightly beaten
2¾ cups all-purpose flour
2 cups whole wheat flour
Cooking spray
½ teaspoon kosher salt
½ teaspoon garlic powder
½ teaspoon dried basil
½ teaspoon dried oregano

1. Preheat oven to 425°.
2. Dissolve yeast and honey in water in a large bowl; let stand 5 minutes. Add salt and egg, stirring with a whisk. Lightly spoon flours into dry measuring cups; level with a knife. Add flours to yeast mixture, stirring until a stiff dough forms. Turn dough out onto a lightly floured surface; knead until smooth and elastic (about 10 minutes). Shape dough into a log; divide log into 24 equal portions. Working with one portion at a time (cover remaining dough to prevent drying), gently roll each portion into a 6-inch rope. Place ropes on baking sheets coated with cooking spray.
3. Combine salt, garlic powder, basil, and oregano in a small bowl. Spray ropes lightly with cooking spray; sprinkle with garlic mixture. Bake at 425° for 15 minutes

or until golden. Yield: 24 servings (serving size: 1 breadstick).

CALORIES 87 (4% from fat); FAT 0.4g (sat 0.1g, mono 0.1g, poly 0.1g); PROTEIN 3.2g; CARB 18.8g; FIBER 1.7g; CHOL 9mg; IRON 1.2mg; SODIUM 141mg; CALC 6mg

---

season's best

Spring Peas with Pancetta

Baby peas have become a symbol of spring. Also known as petit pois, *they are English peas harvested before maturity so they are sweet and tender.*

QUICK & EASY
Spring Peas with Pancetta

Avoid the temptation to substitute regular bacon for the pancetta, because its smoky quality will overwhelm the delicate flavor of the peas. Get fresh baby peas from your local farmers markets or grocery store.

3 slices pancetta, chopped (about 1 ounce)
¾ cup finely chopped white onion
1 garlic clove, minced
3 cups shelled green peas or frozen petite green peas
1 cup fat-free, less-sodium chicken broth
2 teaspoons sugar
¼ teaspoon salt
¼ cup chopped fresh flat-leaf parsley

1. Heat a large nonstick skillet over medium-high heat. Add pancetta; sauté 5 minutes or until crispy. Remove pancetta from pan, reserving drippings in pan. Add onion and garlic to pan; sauté 2 minutes or until tender. Add peas, broth, sugar, and salt to pan. Simmer 5 minutes or until peas are tender, stirring occasionally. Stir in pancetta and parsley. Yield: 6 servings (serving size: ½ cup).

CALORIES 153 (23% from fat); FAT 3.9g (sat 1.6g, mono 0.1g, poly 0.2g); PROTEIN 8.4g; CARB 21.6g; FIBER 6.4g; CHOL 8mg; IRON 2mg; SODIUM 425mg; CALC 44mg

Happy Birthday

Homemade treats add a touch of love to someone's special day. Here are eight sweet ways to celebrate.

Grand Marnier Meringue Torte

Prepare the meringues up to three days ahead, and store at room temperature in an airtight container. Top with filling and fruit shortly before serving.

MERINGUES:
- 2 teaspoons clear vanilla extract
- ½ teaspoon cream of tartar
- ⅛ teaspoon salt
- 6 large egg whites
- ¾ cup superfine sugar

FILLING:
- 3 cups frozen extracreamy whipped topping, thawed
- 2 tablespoons Grand Marnier (orange-flavored liqueur)
- 1½ teaspoons finely grated orange rind
- 2 tablespoons grated semisweet chocolate, divided
- ½ cup halved strawberries
- ½ cup blueberries
- ½ cup blackberries
- ½ cup raspberries
- Mint sprigs (optional)
- Orange rind strips (optional)

1. Preheat oven to 200°.
2. To prepare meringues, cover a baking sheet with parchment paper. Draw 3 (8-inch) circles on paper. Turn paper over, and secure with masking tape.
3. Place first 4 ingredients in a large bowl, and beat with a mixer at high speed until foamy. Gradually add sugar, 1 tablespoon at a time, beating until stiff peaks form. Divide egg mixture among 3 drawn circles on baking sheet. Spread mixture onto circles using back of a spoon. Bake at 200° for 2 hours or until dry. Turn oven off; cool meringues in closed oven at least 1 hour. Carefully remove meringues from paper.
4. To prepare filling, combine whipped topping, liqueur, and grated rind. Place 1 meringue on a serving platter; top with 1 cup whipped topping mixture and 2 teaspoons chocolate. Repeat layers twice with remaining meringues, whipped topping mixture, and chocolate. Combine berries; arrange over torte. Garnish with mint and rind strips, if desired. Yield: 8 servings (serving size: 1 piece).

CALORIES 206 (31% from fat); FAT 7g (sat 6.5g, mono 0.3g, poly 0.1g); PROTEIN 3.2g; CARB 32.4g; FIBER 1.1g; CHOL 0mg; IRON 0.3mg; SODIUM 95mg; CALC 7mg

Cracking and Separating Eggs

You'll need: Two bowls—one for the whites and one for the yolks. Choose fresh eggs, and make sure they appear clean and the shells are intact.
• Lightly tap the middle of the egg—the widest portion—against the rim of the bowl. You'll hear a slight pop when the egg has cracked. At that point, one more tap will do the trick. The egg should crack evenly with a slightly larger hole at the point of impact. Use this hole to separate the shell.
• Hold a cupped hand up over one bowl. With the other, gently separate the shell along the crack, letting the yolk and whites drop into your waiting hand. Keeping the solid yolk in your hand, allow the whites to fall through your fingers into the bowl below. Place the yolk in the second bowl, and throw away the shell.
• Check to make sure your whites are clean, removing any errant bits of shell.

Carrot Sheet Cake with Cream Cheese Frosting

CAKE:
- Cooking spray
- 9 tablespoons butter, softened
- ⅔ cup packed brown sugar
- ½ cup granulated sugar
- 2 large eggs
- 2 large egg whites
- 2 teaspoons vanilla extract
- 2 cups all-purpose flour
- 2 teaspoons baking soda
- 1 teaspoon ground cinnamon
- ¼ teaspoon salt
- ¾ cup low-fat buttermilk
- 2 cups finely shredded carrot

FROSTING:
- ½ cup (4 ounces) block-style fat-free cream cheese
- ¼ cup butter, softened
- 2 teaspoons vanilla extract
- ⅛ teaspoon salt
- 2¾ cups powdered sugar, divided
- 1 tablespoon orange sugar sprinkles

1. Preheat oven to 350°.
2. To prepare cake, coat a 13 x 9-inch baking pan with cooking spray; line bottom of pan with wax paper. Coat wax paper with cooking spray; set aside.
3. Place 9 tablespoons butter, brown sugar, and granulated sugar in a large bowl; beat with a mixer at medium speed 5 minutes or until well blended. Add eggs and egg whites, 1 at a time, beating well after each addition until pale and fluffy. Beat in 2 teaspoons vanilla.
4. Lightly spoon flour into dry measuring cups; level with a knife. Combine flour, baking soda, cinnamon, and ¼ teaspoon salt, stirring with a whisk. Add flour mixture and buttermilk alternately to sugar mixture, beginning and ending with flour mixture; mix after each addition. Stir in carrot. Spoon batter into prepared pan. Sharply tap pan once on counter to remove air bubbles. Bake at 350° for 30 minutes or until a wooden pick inserted in center comes out clean.
Continued

Cool in pan 10 minutes on a wire rack; remove from pan. Carefully peel off wax paper; cool completely on wire rack.

5. To prepare frosting, place cream cheese and next 3 ingredients in a large bowl; beat with a mixer at medium speed until smooth. Gradually add 2 cups powdered sugar, beating at low speed until smooth (do not overbeat). Stir in ¾ cup powdered sugar. Cover and chill 30 minutes. Spread frosting over top of cake. Garnish with sprinkles. Store cake loosely covered in refrigerator. Yield: 16 servings (serving size: 1 piece).

CALORIES 309 (30% from fat); FAT 10.3g (sat 5g, mono 4.1g, poly 0.5g); PROTEIN 4.5g; CARB 50.2g; FIBER 0.9g; CHOL 52mg; IRON 1.1mg; SODIUM 358mg; CALC 49mg

and buttermilk alternately to sugar mixture, beginning and ending with flour mixture; mix after each addition. Beat in extracts. Pour batter into prepared pan. Sharply tap pan once on counter to remove air bubbles. Bake at 350° for 20 minutes or until a wooden pick inserted in center comes out clean. Cool in pan 10 minutes on a wire rack; remove from pan. Carefully peel off wax paper; cool completely on wire rack. Place cake on a large platter or cutting board; refrigerate until cold (about 2 hours).

5. Spread ice cream evenly over top of cake; cover with plastic wrap. Freeze until firm (6 hours to overnight).

6. Uncover cake. Cut cake with a 2-inch

round cutter into 24 cake rounds. Discard scraps. Working quickly, place one cake round, ice cream side up, in a paper muffin cup liner; top with another cake round, ice cream side down. Repeat procedure with remaining cake rounds to form 12 filled ice-cream cakes.

7. Combine whipped topping and cherry juice, if desired. Top each cake with 2 tablespoons whipped topping; arrange 1 cherry on each cake. Freeze until ready to serve. Let cakes stand at room temperature 5 minutes before serving. Yield: 12 servings (serving size: 1 cake).

CALORIES 274 (24% from fat); FAT 7.2g (sat 3.4g, mono 2.5g, poly 0.4g); PROTEIN 4.6g; CARB 47g; FIBER 1g; CHOL 49mg; IRON 1mg; SODIUM 246mg; CALC 82mg

MAKE AHEAD • FREEZABLE
Mini Ice-Cream Cakes

Cooking spray
1 cup sugar
⅓ cup butter, softened
2 large eggs
1⅔ cups all-purpose flour
1 teaspoon baking powder
¼ teaspoon baking soda
¼ teaspoon salt
1 cup low-fat buttermilk
1 teaspoon vanilla extract
¼ teaspoon almond extract
3 cups low-fat strawberry ice cream, softened
1½ cups fat-free frozen whipped topping, thawed
1 tablespoon red maraschino cherry juice (optional)
12 red maraschino cherries with stems, drained

1. Preheat oven to 350°.

2. Coat a 15 x 10-inch jelly-roll pan with cooking spray; line bottom of pan with wax paper. Coat wax paper with cooking spray; set aside.

3. Place sugar and butter in a large bowl; beat with a mixer at medium speed 5 minutes or until well blended. Add eggs, 1 at a time, beating well after each addition.

4. Lightly spoon flour into dry measuring cups; level with a knife. Combine flour, baking powder, baking soda, and salt, stirring well with a whisk. Add flour mixture

A Baker's Dozen of Decorating Ideas

Test Kitchens staffer Jan Moon offers her tips.

1. Use funky candles, such as tall, slender birthday candles or even a mix of styles—and lots of them.

2. Stencils create lovely designs. Lightly place one over the frosted cake; dust with powdered sugar, unsweetened cocoa, or bright decorator sugars.

3. Fresh flowers are a great way to make any cake special. You can find edible flowers alongside the herbs at the grocery. Or you can grow them yourself—just make sure they are food safe (look online at www. foodsubs.com) and have not been sprayed with pesticides. The flowers I most often use are violets, pansies, nasturtiums, and sweetheart roses.

4. Edible clay, available at craft and specialty stores, is a new way to add pizzazz to any cake. You can mold it into shapes, or roll it out, cut out shapes with cookie cutters, and apply directly to the cake.

5. Ribbons provide an easy way to decorate. I love to put a bow on top. You can also trim the bottom edge with a wide ribbon.

6. Candy is an easy adornment. My favorites are Necco Wafers, Skittles, Wonka Nerd Ropes, colorful suckers, and gummy candies. You can also flatten gumdrops with a rolling pin and cut out shapes.

7. Colored sprinkles, dragées, edible confetti, and edible glitter found in the baking section of your grocery or craft store make for quick decorations.

8. Fresh fruit is always a good embellishment. Lemon, lime, or orange rind strips are also good cake toppers.

9. Mix small party favors or trinkets—party horns, party hats, and streamers—with colored sprinkles for an amusing cake for a child.

10. Toasted nuts, almond brickle, and grated or shaved chocolate are great options for a tailored cake.

11. Tie long, thin ribbons around tiny favors or fortunes. Place the prizes into the opening of a Bundt cake, with the ribbons draping out over the cake. Let each guest pull a ribbon to reveal a surprise.

12. Prepare simple glazes from a combination of milk, powdered sugar, vanilla or almond extract, and food coloring. Make one color—or lots of colors—to drizzle on the cake for a dramatic effect.

13. Bake your favorite cake in one of the new fun-shaped cake pans, such as the Fleur-de-Lis, Sunflower, or Rose Cake Pans from Williams-Sonoma ($29.95; 877-812-6235, www.williams-sonoma.com). Let the cake cool, then dust the cake with powdered sugar.

Yellow Sheet Cake with Chocolate Frosting

(pictured on page 145)

Here's a moist, buttery dessert that can make any occasion a celebration. It was a favorite with our staffers, receiving top scores for its taste. Fresh edible flowers, such as mums, make an easy, pretty decoration; most people remove the flowers before eating the cake. If you're offering the cake at an informal gathering, serve it right from the pan.

CAKE:
Cooking spray
- 1 tablespoon all-purpose flour
- ½ cup butter, melted
- 1 (8-ounce) carton fat-free sour cream
- 1½ cups granulated sugar
- 2 teaspoons vanilla extract
- ½ cup egg substitute
- 2 cups all-purpose flour
- 1 teaspoon baking soda
- ½ teaspoon salt
- ¾ cup low-fat buttermilk

FROSTING:
- ½ cup (4 ounces) block-style fat-free cream cheese, softened
- ¼ cup butter, softened
- 1 teaspoon vanilla extract
- ⅓ cup unsweetened cocoa
- 1 to 2 tablespoons evaporated fat-free milk
- ⅛ teaspoon salt
- 3 cups powdered sugar, divided

1. Preheat oven to 350°.

2. To prepare cake, coat bottom of a 13 x 9-inch baking pan with cooking spray (do not coat sides of pan); line bottom of pan with wax paper. Coat wax paper with cooking spray; dust with 1 tablespoon flour. Set aside.

3. Combine ½ cup butter and sour cream in a large bowl, stirring with a whisk until well blended. Add granulated sugar and 2 teaspoons vanilla. Beat with a mixer at medium speed 3 minutes or until well blended. Add egg substitute; beat 2 minutes or until well blended.

4. Lightly spoon 2 cups flour into dry measuring cups; level with a knife. Combine 2 cups flour, baking soda, and ½ teaspoon salt, stirring well with a whisk. Add flour mixture and buttermilk alternately to sugar mixture, beginning and ending with flour mixture; mix after each addition. Pour batter into prepared pan. Sharply tap pan once on counter to remove air bubbles. Bake at 350° for 30 minutes or until a wooden pick inserted in center comes out clean. Cool in pan 10 minutes on a wire rack; remove from pan. Carefully peel off wax paper; cool completely on wire rack.

5. To prepare frosting, place cream cheese, ¼ cup butter, and 1 teaspoon vanilla in a large bowl; beat with a mixer at high speed until fluffy. Add cocoa, milk, and ⅛ teaspoon salt; beat at low speed until well blended. Gradually add 1½ cups powdered sugar; beat at low speed until creamy. Gradually add 1½ cups powdered sugar. Place cake on a serving platter. Spread frosting over top and sides of cake. Store cake loosely covered in refrigerator. Yield: 18 servings (serving size: 1 piece).

CALORIES 291 (25% from fat); FAT 8.1g (sat 4.1g, mono 3.3g, poly 0.4g); PROTEIN 4.3g; CARB 51.6g; FIBER 0.9g; CHOL 22mg; IRON 1mg; SODIUM 285mg; CALC 54mg

White Birthday Cake with Italian Meringue Icing

This gorgeous white cake is great for any birthday. The fluffy meringue icing glides easily over the layers and acts as a canvas for any decoration you choose.

CAKE:
Cooking spray
- 2 cups sugar
- ¾ cup unsalted butter, softened
- 3 large eggs
- 1 teaspoon clear vanilla extract
- ½ teaspoon almond extract
- 3 cups cake flour
- ½ teaspoon baking powder
- ½ teaspoon baking soda
- ½ teaspoon salt
- ¾ cup low-fat buttermilk

ICING:
- ¼ teaspoon cream of tartar
- 3 large egg whites
- 1 cup sugar
- ¼ cup water
- ¼ teaspoon salt
- 1 teaspoon vanilla extract
- ½ teaspoon almond extract

1. Preheat oven to 350°.

2. To prepare cake, coat 2 (9-inch) round cake pans with cooking spray; line bottoms of pans with wax paper. Coat wax paper with cooking spray; set aside.

3. Place 2 cups sugar and butter in a large bowl; beat with a mixer at medium speed 5 minutes or until well blended. Add eggs, 1 at a time, beating well after each addition. Beat in 1 teaspoon clear vanilla extract and ½ teaspoon almond extract.

4. Lightly spoon flour into dry measuring cups; level with a knife. Combine flour, baking powder, baking soda, and ½ teaspoon salt, stirring with a whisk. Add flour mixture and buttermilk alternately to sugar mixture, beginning and ending with flour mixture, and mix after each addition. Pour batter into prepared pans. Sharply tap pans once on counter to remove air bubbles. Bake at 350° for 30 minutes or until a wooden pick inserted in center comes out clean. Cool cake in pans 10 minutes on a wire rack; remove cake from pans. Carefully peel off wax paper, and cool completely on wire rack.

5. To prepare icing, place cream of tartar and egg whites in a large bowl; beat with a mixer at high speed until soft peaks form using clean, dry beaters.

6. Combine 1 cup sugar, ¼ cup water, and ¼ teaspoon salt in a small saucepan. Cook over medium heat until sugar dissolves, stirring frequently, and bring to a boil. Cook, without stirring, 2 minutes or until a candy thermometer registers 238°. Pour hot sugar syrup in a thin stream over egg whites, beating at high speed until stiff peaks form. Stir in 1 teaspoon vanilla extract and ½ teaspoon almond extract. Place 1 cake layer on a plate; spread with 2 cups icing. Top with second cake layer. Spread remaining
Continued

icing over top and sides of cake. Yield: 16 servings (serving size: 1 slice).

CALORIES 310 (28% from fat); FAT 9.7g (sat 5.8g, mono 2.6g, poly 0.5g); PROTEIN 3.8g; CARB 52.4g; FIBER 0.3g; CHOL 63mg; IRON 1.5mg; SODIUM 202mg; CALC 33mg

Red Velvet Cake with Buttercream Frosting

This classic cake is hard to resist. The striking color combination makes it ideal for Christmas and Valentine's Day, as well as for birthdays. A thick, cooked mixture of flour and milk extends the frosting while keeping the fat at a reasonable amount.

CAKE:
  Cooking spray
1¼ cups granulated sugar
 ⅓ cup vegetable shortening
 ½ cup egg substitute
 1 tablespoon unsweetened cocoa
 1 (1-ounce) bottle red food coloring
 2 cups cake flour
 ½ teaspoon salt
 1 cup low-fat buttermilk
 1 teaspoon vanilla extract
 1 tablespoon white vinegar
 1 teaspoon baking soda

FROSTING:
 ¾ cup fat-free milk
 ¾ cup all-purpose flour
 ½ cup butter, softened
 2 teaspoons vanilla extract
 ⅛ teaspoon salt
2½ cups powdered sugar

1. Preheat oven to 350°.
2. To prepare cake, coat 2 (8-inch) round cake pans with cooking spray; line bottoms of pans with wax paper. Coat wax paper with cooking spray; set pans aside.
3. Place granulated sugar and shortening in a large bowl; beat with a mixer at medium speed 5 minutes or until well blended. Add egg substitute; beat well. Combine cocoa and food coloring in a small bowl, stirring with a whisk; add to sugar mixture, stirring well to combine.
4. Lightly spoon cake flour into dry measuring cups, and level with a knife. Combine cake flour and ½ teaspoon

salt, stirring with a whisk. Add flour mixture and buttermilk alternately to sugar mixture, beginning and ending with flour mixture; mix after each addition. Stir in 1 teaspoon vanilla. Combine vinegar and baking soda; add to batter, stirring well. Pour batter into prepared pans. Sharply tap pans once on counter to remove air bubbles. Bake at 350° for 25 minutes or until a wooden pick inserted in center comes out clean. Cool in pans 10 minutes on a wire rack; remove from pans. Carefully peel off wax paper; cool completely on wire rack.
5. To prepare frosting, combine milk and all-purpose flour in a small, heavy saucepan over medium heat. Cook 3 minutes or until mixture forms a very thick paste, stirring constantly with a whisk. Spoon into a bowl; cover surface with plastic wrap. Refrigerate 45 minutes or until chilled. Place butter in a medium bowl, and beat with a mixer at medium speed until creamy. Add 2 teaspoons vanilla, ⅛ teaspoon salt, and chilled flour mixture; beat until smooth. Gradually add powdered sugar, beating just until blended (do not overbeat).
6. Place 1 cake layer on a plate; spread with ⅓ cup frosting. Top with second cake layer. Spread remaining frosting over top and sides of cake. Store cake loosely covered in refrigerator. Yield: 16 servings (serving size: 1 slice).

CALORIES 324 (28% from fat); FAT 10.1g (sat 4g, mono 3.8g, poly 1.3g); PROTEIN 3.8g; CARB 54.6g; FIBER 0.6g; CHOL 16mg; IRON 1.8mg; SODIUM 249mg; CALC 37mg

---

Waxing Poetic

When baking a cake, the last thing you want is for it to stick to the pan. To ensure an easy release, coat the pan with cooking spray, line the bottom of the pan with wax paper, and coat the paper with cooking spray. For a good fit, trace the bottom of the pan onto wax paper, and cut out the shape just inside the traced line. Once you've turned the cake out onto a wire rack, carefully peel off the wax paper; if the paper cools onto the cake, it might stick.

German Chocolate Cupcakes with Caramel Icing

These chocolate cupcakes tend to sink slightly in the middle as they cool, but the icing hides the dip. The icing will harden quickly as it cools, so you'll need to work quickly when spreading it over the cupcakes; if it becomes too thick, whisk in an additional tablespoon of evaporated milk. Sprinkling the top of the iced cupcakes with toasted pecans and coconut gives a bigger flavor impact than if they were stirred into the icing.

CUPCAKES:
 6 tablespoons butter
 4 ounces sweet baking chocolate, chopped
1¼ cups granulated sugar
 ¼ cup water
 2 teaspoons vanilla extract
 ½ cup egg substitute
 2 cups all-purpose flour
 ½ teaspoon baking powder
 ½ teaspoon baking soda
 ¼ teaspoon salt

ICING:
 ¼ cup butter
 ½ cup packed dark brown sugar
 ½ cup evaporated low-fat milk
 2 teaspoons vanilla extract
 2 cups powdered sugar
 2 tablespoons chopped pecans, toasted
 2 tablespoons flaked sweetened coconut, toasted

1. Preheat oven to 350°.
2. To prepare cupcakes, place 6 tablespoons butter and chocolate in a large microwave-safe bowl; microwave at HIGH 1 minute, stirring after 30 seconds. Stir until chocolate melts. Stir in granulated sugar, water, and 2 teaspoons vanilla. Add egg substitute, stirring with a whisk.
3. Lightly spoon flour into dry measuring cups; level with a knife. Combine flour, baking powder, baking soda, and

salt, stirring with a whisk. Add flour mixture to chocolate mixture, stirring with a whisk until smooth. Place 18 paper muffin cup liners in muffin cups; spoon batter evenly into lined muffin cups. Bake at 350° for 18 minutes or until a wooden pick inserted in center of a cupcake comes out clean. Cool on a wire rack.

4. To prepare icing, melt ¼ cup butter in a medium saucepan over medium heat. Add brown sugar; cook 3 minutes, stirring constantly with a whisk. Add milk, and cook 3 minutes, stirring constantly. Remove from heat; stir in 2 teaspoons vanilla. Gradually add powdered sugar, stirring with a whisk until smooth. Working quickly, spread each cupcake with about 1½ tablespoons frosting; sprinkle cupcakes evenly with pecans and coconut. Yield: 18 servings (serving size: 1 cupcake).

CALORIES 282 (29% from fat); FAT 9g (sat 4.4g, mono 3g, poly 0.5g); PROTEIN 3g; CARB 48.7g; FIBER 0.5g; CHOL 17mg; IRON 1.1mg; SODIUM 149mg; CALC 32mg

---

MAKE AHEAD
Ganache-Topped Chocolate-Raspberry Sheet Cake

The raspberry and dark chocolate flavors give this cake a stylish flair, making it suitable for special occasions. We made it a sheet cake, but you can bake the batter in two 8-inch cake pans for a more sophisticated look; reduce the baking time to 25 minutes or until a wooden pick inserted in the center comes out clean.

CAKE:
Cooking spray
½ cup boiling water
½ cup unsweetened cocoa
1⅓ cups sugar
10 tablespoons butter, softened
1 (8-ounce) carton egg substitute
2 cups cake flour
1 teaspoon baking soda
¼ teaspoon salt
1 (8-ounce) carton fat-free sour cream
2 teaspoons vanilla extract
½ cup seedless raspberry jam

GANACHE:
½ cup sugar
⅓ cup evaporated fat-free milk
¼ cup unsweetened cocoa
½ teaspoon vanilla extract
⅛ teaspoon salt
3 ounces semisweet chocolate, chopped

REMAINING INGREDIENTS:
Fresh raspberries (optional)

1. Preheat oven to 350°.
2. To prepare cake, coat a 13 x 9-inch baking pan with cooking spray; line bottom of pan with wax paper. Coat wax paper with cooking spray; set aside.
3. Pour boiling water over ½ cup cocoa in a small bowl; stir to dissolve cocoa. Cool mixture.
4. Place 1⅓ cups sugar and butter in a large bowl; beat with a mixer at medium speed 5 minutes or until well blended. Add cocoa mixture and egg substitute; beat well.
5. Lightly spoon flour into dry measuring cups; level with a knife. Combine flour, baking soda, and ¼ teaspoon salt, stirring with a whisk. Add flour mixture and sour cream alternately to sugar mixture, beginning and ending with flour mixture; mix after each addition. Beat in vanilla. Pour batter into prepared pan. Sharply tap pan once on counter to remove air bubbles. Bake at 350° for 30 minutes or until a wooden pick inserted in center comes out clean. Cool in pan 10 minutes on a wire rack; remove from pan. Carefully peel off wax paper; cool completely on wire rack. Spread jam over top of cake.
6. To prepare ganache, combine ½ cup sugar, milk, and ¼ cup cocoa in a medium saucepan over medium heat; bring to a boil, stirring frequently. Cook 1 minute, stirring constantly. Remove from heat; add ½ teaspoon vanilla, ⅛ teaspoon salt, and chopped chocolate, stirring until smooth. Spread ganache evenly over top of cake, allowing ganache to run down sides. Let cake stand 20 minutes or until set. Garnish with raspberries and mint leaves, if desired. Yield: 16 servings (serving size: 1 piece).

CALORIES 296 (30% from fat); FAT 9.9g (sat 5.1g, mono 3.9g, poly 0.4g); PROTEIN 4.9g; CARB 50.6g; FIBER 1.8g; CHOL 20mg; IRON 2.4mg; SODIUM 241mg; CALC 51mg

---

Manicotti Made Easy

This spinach and cheese-stuffed pasta became a family favorite.

A few years ago, Catherine Salzman, of Montville, New Jersey, emptied her recipe file and started over. Her husband, David, was diagnosed with diabetes, and to improve their diet Salzman added more vegetable-rich recipes as well as low-fat, lower-calorie choices. Easy Meatless Manicotti was one delicious result of her culinary makeovers. Serve this satisfying dish with a colorful green salad drizzled with tangy vinaigrette and slices of crusty Italian bread.

MAKE AHEAD • FREEZABLE
Easy Meatless Manicotti

2 cups (8 ounces) shredded part-skim mozzarella cheese, divided
1 (16-ounce) carton fat-free cottage cheese
1 (10-ounce) package frozen chopped spinach, thawed, drained, and squeezed dry
¼ cup (1 ounce) grated fresh Parmesan cheese
1½ teaspoons dried oregano
¼ teaspoon salt
¼ teaspoon black pepper
1 (8-ounce) package manicotti (14 shells)
1 (26-ounce) jar fat-free tomato-basil pasta sauce
Cooking spray
1 cup water

1. Preheat oven to 375°.
2. Combine 1½ cups mozzarella, cottage cheese, and next 5 ingredients in a medium bowl. Spoon about 3 tablespoons cheese mixture into each uncooked manicotti. Pour half of pasta sauce into a 13 x 9-inch baking dish coated with cooking spray. Arrange
Continued

stuffed shells in a single layer over sauce, and top with remaining sauce. Pour 1 cup water into dish. Sprinkle ½ cup mozzarella evenly over sauce. Cover tightly with foil. Bake at 375° for 1 hour or until shells are tender. Let stand 10 minutes before serving. Yield: 7 servings (serving size: 2 manicotti).

CALORIES 328 (25% from fat); FAT 9g (sat 4.8g, mono 2.2g, poly 0.5g); PROTEIN 23.8g; CARB 38.3g; FIBER 3.9g; CHOL 23mg; IRON 3mg; SODIUM 891mg; CALC 451mg

MAKE AHEAD
Toasted Coconut Muffins

"I like to toast the coconut so the topping is crunchy."

—Lorraine Fina Stevenski,
Clearwater, Florida

MUFFINS:
1½ cups all-purpose flour
¼ cup granulated sugar
¼ cup light brown sugar
1½ teaspoons baking powder
¼ to ½ teaspoon ground allspice
¼ teaspoon salt
½ cup 1% low-fat milk
3 tablespoons part-skim ricotta
   cheese
3 tablespoons cream of coconut
1 tablespoon canola oil
2 teaspoons vanilla extract
1½ teaspoons grated lemon rind
1 large egg, lightly beaten
1 large egg white, lightly beaten
¼ cup flaked sweetened coconut,
   toasted
Cooking spray

TOPPING:
¼ cup flaked sweetened coconut,
   toasted
3 tablespoons all-purpose flour
3 tablespoons granulated sugar
1 tablespoon canola oil

1. Preheat oven to 350°.
2. To prepare muffins, lightly spoon 1½ cups flour into dry measuring cups; level with a knife. Combine 1½ cups flour and next 5 ingredients in a large bowl, stirring with a whisk. Make a well in center of mixture. Combine milk and

next 7 ingredients; stir well with a whisk. Add milk mixture to flour mixture, stirring just until moist. Fold in ¼ cup coconut. Place 12 muffin cup liners in muffin cups; coat liners with cooking spray. Divide batter evenly among muffin cups.
3. To prepare topping, combine ¼ cup coconut, 3 tablespoons flour, 3 tablespoons granulated sugar, and 1 tablespoon oil in a small bowl; stir with a fork until crumbly. Sprinkle topping evenly over batter. Bake at 350° for 23 minutes or until a wooden pick inserted in center of a muffin comes out clean. Cool in pan on a wire rack 15 minutes. Yield: 12 servings (serving size: 1 muffin).

CALORIES 178 (28% from fat); FAT 5.5g (sat 2.5g, mono 1.7g, poly 0.9g); PROTEIN 3.7g; CARB 28.5g; FIBER 0.8g; CHOL 19mg; IRON 1.2mg; SODIUM 145mg; CALC 76mg

Red Pepper Soup

"I have seen several recipes for red pepper soup. My version is spiced up a bit and has added vegetables."

—Cecil M. Roper, Fort Worth, Texas

2 red bell peppers
2 teaspoons olive oil
1½ cups chopped onion
¼ cup finely chopped shallots
2 garlic cloves, minced
½ cup chopped celery
½ cup sliced carrot
1 tablespoon tomato paste
1 teaspoon Old Bay seasoning
½ teaspoon salt
¼ teaspoon freshly ground black
   pepper
¼ teaspoon hot sauce
1 (14-ounce) can fat-free,
   less-sodium chicken broth
1 (14-ounce) can less-sodium beef
   broth
2 tablespoons reduced-fat sour cream
2 tablespoons chopped fresh chives

1. Preheat broiler.
2. Cut bell peppers in half lengthwise; discard seeds and membranes. Place pepper halves, skin sides up, on a foil-lined baking sheet, and flatten peppers

with hand. Broil 15 minutes or until skin looks blackened. Place in a zip-top plastic bag, and seal. Let stand 10 minutes. Peel and coarsely chop.
3. Heat 2 teaspoons oil in a large saucepan over medium-high heat. Add onion, shallots, and garlic; cook 3 minutes, stirring occasionally. Add celery and carrot; cook 2 minutes. Add bell peppers, tomato paste, and next 6 ingredients, and bring to a boil. Cover, reduce heat, and simmer 15 minutes. Remove pan from heat; let stand 5 minutes. Place half of bell pepper mixture in a blender; process until smooth. Pour into a large bowl. Repeat procedure with remaining bell pepper mixture.
4. Ladle soup into individual bowls; top with sour cream and chives. Yield: 6 servings (serving size: about ¾ cup soup, 1 teaspoon sour cream, and 1 teaspoon chives).

CALORIES 70 (31% from fat); FAT 2.4g (sat 0.7g, mono 1.2g, poly 0.3g); PROTEIN 2.7g; CARB 10.4g; FIBER 1.5g; CHOL 3mg; IRON 0.7mg; SODIUM 569mg; CALC 37mg

Curry-Carrot Dip with Toasted Pita Chips

"I always look for ways to transform vegetables into dips and appetizers. If you can't find cardamom seeds, use an extra ½ teaspoon ground cumin."

—Juliana Goodwin, Springfield, Missouri

3 cups (¼-inch-thick) slices carrot
   (about 2 pounds)
1 (14-ounce) can fat-free,
   less-sodium chicken broth
3 cardamom seeds or dash ground
   cardamom
4 (6-inch) whole wheat pitas, each
   cut into 6 wedges
Cooking spray
2 tablespoons olive oil
2 cups chopped onion (about
   1 large onion)
2 garlic cloves, minced
1 tablespoon curry powder
1 teaspoon ground cumin
¼ cup minced fresh cilantro
1 teaspoon garlic salt
⅛ teaspoon black pepper

1. Place carrot in a saucepan. Cover with water to 1 inch above carrot. Add broth and cardamom; bring to a boil. Reduce heat, and simmer 40 minutes or until carrot is tender. Drain carrot in a colander over a bowl, reserving 1½ cups cooking liquid. Discard cardamom seeds. Combine reserved liquid and carrot; refrigerate overnight.

2. Preheat oven to 350°.

3. Coat pita wedges with cooking spray; place in a single layer on a baking sheet. Bake at 350° for 15 minutes or until crisp.

4. Remove carrot with a slotted spoon. Place carrot and ¾ cup reserved cooking liquid in a blender, and process until smooth. Discard remaining liquid.

5. Heat oil in a nonstick skillet over medium-high heat. Add onion and garlic; sauté 3 minutes. Stir in curry powder and cumin; sauté 1 minute. Add carrot mixture; cook 2 minutes or until thoroughly heated. Stir in cilantro, garlic salt, and pepper. Serve immediately with pita chips. Yield: 12 servings (serving size: about ⅓ cup dip and 2 pita chips).

CALORIES 153 (20% from fat); FAT 3.4g (sat 0.5g, mono 1.8g, poly 0.7g); PROTEIN 4.7g; CARB 28.2g; FIBER 5.3g; CHOL 0mg; IRON 1.5mg; SODIUM 370mg; CALC 41mg

---

Pasta Night Menu
serves 8

Leftovers of the pasta taste great either cold or warmed. Coffee ice cream is a nice finale because it offers a contrast to the tangy pasta and salad.

Greek Chicken with Angel Hair Pasta

Cucumber, tomato, and carrot salad*

Low-fat coffee ice cream with amaretti

*Cut 1 English cucumber in half lengthwise; cut into thin slices. Combine cucumber, 2 cups halved grape tomatoes, and 1 cup thinly diagonally sliced carrot. Combine 2 tablespoons chopped fresh parsley, 3 tablespoons red wine vinegar, 2 teaspoons extravirgin olive oil, ½ teaspoon salt, and ¼ teaspoon pepper, stirring with a whisk. Drizzle vinaigrette over salad; toss well to coat.

Greek Chicken with Angel Hair Pasta

"I came up with this dish from a basic recipe that called for chicken, spices, and tomatoes, and then I added some of my own favorites to it."
—Heather Lanzone, Spokane, Washington

1	pound uncooked angel hair pasta
1	tablespoon olive oil
4	(6-ounce) skinless, boneless chicken breast halves, each cut in half
2	cups chopped red onion
1	cup chopped yellow bell pepper
6	tablespoons fresh lemon juice
1	teaspoon dried basil
½	teaspoon dried oregano
2	(14.5-ounce) cans diced tomatoes with basil, garlic, and oregano
¾	cup (3 ounces) feta cheese, crumbled

1. Cook pasta according to package directions, omitting salt and fat.

2. Heat oil in a large nonstick skillet over medium-high heat. Add chicken to pan; sauté 3 minutes on each side. Add onion and next 5 ingredients to pan; stir well. Cover, reduce heat, and simmer 25 minutes or until chicken is done. Remove from heat; sprinkle with cheese. Serve with pasta. Yield: 8 servings (serving size: ½ chicken breast, about ½ cup tomato mixture, and about 1 cup pasta).

CALORIES 400 (16% from fat); FAT 7.3g (sat 2.7g, mono 2.7g, poly 1.5g); PROTEIN 30g; CARB 54.3g; FIBER 3.1g; CHOL 60mg; IRON 3.9mg; SODIUM 694mg; CALC 148mg

---

lunch box chronicles

Spring Roast

One succulent leg of lamb yields many dining options.

Roast a boneless leg of lamb and enjoy a delectable roast any night of the week. We've provided more than a week's worth of portable dishes, from classic salads to several creative sandwiches—all which begin with Simple Roasted Leg of Lamb.

Simple Roasted Leg of Lamb

This large roast is great as a Sunday dinner centerpiece, and the mild seasonings encourage leftovers to blend into a variety of dishes. For a nice accompaniment, toss halved fingerling potatoes with olive oil and sea salt. Place them on the broiler pan with the lamb during the last half-hour of cooking.

1	cup thinly sliced onion
2	tablespoons grated lemon rind
⅓	cup fresh lemon juice
3	tablespoons water
2	tablespoons chopped fresh parsley
1	tablespoon chopped fresh rosemary
1	tablespoon chopped fresh thyme
½	teaspoon salt
¼	teaspoon freshly ground black pepper
2	garlic cloves, crushed
1	(5-pound) boneless leg of lamb, trimmed
Cooking spray	

1. Place first 10 ingredients in a food processor; pulse until finely chopped. Place onion mixture and lamb in a large zip-top plastic bag. Seal bag; rub onion mixture into lamb. Marinate in refrigerator 4 hours to overnight, turning occasionally.

2. Preheat oven to 450°.

3. Remove lamb from bag; discard marinade. Place lamb on a broiler pan coated with cooking spray. Bake at 450° for 15 minutes. Reduce oven temperature to 350° (do not remove lamb from oven). Bake at 350° for 1 hour and 20 minutes or until a thermometer inserted in thickest portion of lamb registers 145° (medium-rare). Place lamb on a cutting board. Cover loosely with foil; let stand 15 minutes. Yield: 17 servings (serving size: about 3 ounces).

CALORIES 190 (47% from fat); FAT 9.9g (sat 4g, mono 4.2g, poly 0.7g); PROTEIN 23.2g; CARB 0.4g; FIBER 0.1g; CHOL 78mg; IRON 1.8mg; SODIUM 74mg; CALC 9mg

Lamb, Roasted Tomato, and Artichoke Sandwiches with Olive Spread

Roasting the tomatoes makes them sweet and meaty; it also draws out much of the liquid so that you can assemble the sandwiches the night before without worrying about the focaccia becoming soggy.

      4 plum tomatoes, halved lengthwise
         (about ½ pound)
      2 teaspoons olive oil
   1 ½ teaspoons fresh thyme leaves,
         divided
      ¼ teaspoon freshly ground black
         pepper
      ¼ cup low-fat mayonnaise
      2 tablespoons chopped ripe olives
      1 tablespoon grated lemon rind
      2 tablespoons fresh lemon juice
      4 (2-ounce) pieces focaccia (Italian
         flatbread), cut in half horizontally
   1 ¼ cups sliced Simple Roasted Leg of
         Lamb (about 6 ounces) (recipe on
         page 129)
      ½ cup thinly sliced red onion
      1 (14-ounce) can artichoke hearts,
         drained and thinly sliced

1. Preheat oven to 350°.
2. Arrange tomato halves, cut sides up, on a baking sheet. Drizzle with oil; sprinkle with 1 teaspoon thyme and black pepper. Bake at 350° for 45 minutes or until very tender. Cool slightly.
3. Combine ½ teaspoon thyme, mayonnaise, olives, rind, and juice.
4. Spread cut sides of bread evenly with mayonnaise mixture. Divide tomato halves, Simple Roasted Leg of Lamb, onion, and artichokes evenly among 4 bread pieces. Top with remaining bread pieces. Wrap sandwiches in foil or parchment paper; chill. Yield: 4 servings (serving size: 1 sandwich).

CALORIES 368 (25% from fat); FAT 10.3g (sat 2.6g, mono 4.2g, poly 0.9g); PROTEIN 20.9g; CARB 49.9g; FIBER 5.9g; CHOL 39mg; IRON 3.1mg; SODIUM 831mg; CALC 24mg

Tabbouleh with Roast Lamb

The addition of lamb makes this fiber-rich bulgur salad filling and satisfying.

      1 cup uncooked bulgur
      1 cup boiling water
      2 cups chopped fresh parsley
      2 cups chopped seeded tomato
         (about 1 ½ pounds)
   1 ½ cups shredded Simple Roasted
         Leg of Lamb (about 6 ounces)
         (recipe on page 129)
      ½ cup thinly sliced green onions
      ⅓ cup fresh lemon juice (about 1 large)
      1 tablespoon extravirgin olive oil
      ½ teaspoon salt
      ¼ teaspoon freshly ground black
         pepper

1. Combine bulgur and boiling water in a large bowl. Cover and let stand 30 minutes or until liquid is absorbed.
2. Stir in parsley and remaining ingredients. Cover and chill. Yield: 4 servings (serving size: 1½ cups).

CALORIES 282 (29% from fat); FAT 9.2g (sat 2.6g, mono 4.8g, poly 1g); PROTEIN 17.7g; CARB 35g; FIBER 9.1g; CHOL 39mg; IRON 3.9mg; SODIUM 362mg; CALC 69mg

Cavatappi Salad with Roast Lamb

You can use any other short pasta for this salad, such as penne, rigatoni, or farfalle.

      2 red bell peppers
      8 ounces uncooked cavatappi
      3 tablespoons sherry vinegar
   1 ½ tablespoons extravirgin olive oil
      3 cups (1-inch) slices asparagus
         (about 1 pound)
   1 ½ cups shredded Simple Roasted
         Leg of Lamb (about 6 ounces)
         (recipe on page 129)
      1 cup thinly sliced celery
      ½ cup (2 ounces) grated fresh
         Parmesan cheese
      3 tablespoons chopped fresh basil
      ½ teaspoon salt
      ¼ teaspoon freshly ground black pepper

1. Preheat broiler.
2. Cut bell peppers in half lengthwise; discard seeds and membranes. Place pepper halves, skin sides up, on a foil-lined baking sheet; flatten with hand. Broil 10 minutes or until blackened. Place in a zip-top plastic bag; seal. Let stand 10 minutes. Peel and chop.
3. Cook pasta in boiling water 8 minutes or until al dente. Drain and rinse with cold water; drain. Place pasta in a large bowl. Drizzle with vinegar and oil; toss well to coat.
4. Steam asparagus 3 minutes or until crisp-tender. Rinse with cold water; drain. Add asparagus, peppers, Simple Roasted Leg of Lamb, and remaining ingredients to pasta; toss well. Cover and chill. Yield: 6 servings (serving size: 1⅓ cups).

CALORIES 305 (29% from fat); FAT 9.9g (sat 3.5g, mono 4.7g, poly 1g); PROTEIN 18.2g; CARB 35.5g; FIBER 3.7g; CHOL 32mg; IRON 2.8mg; SODIUM 392mg; CALC 152mg

Greek Lamb and Potato Salad

Refrigerated potato wedges are a great time-saver because they don't need to be cooked before going into the salad.

      ¼ cup fresh lemon juice
      1 tablespoon honey
      1 teaspoon dried oregano
      ½ teaspoon salt
      ¼ teaspoon freshly ground black
         pepper
      ⅛ teaspoon ground coriander
      1 (20-ounce) package refrigerated
         new potato wedges (such as
         Simply Potatoes)
   2 ¼ cups chopped Simple Roasted Leg
         of Lamb (about 9 ounces) (recipe
         on page 129)
      2 cups cherry tomatoes, halved
      2 cups chopped seeded cucumber
      1 cup chopped red onion
      ¾ cup thinly sliced celery
      ½ cup (2 ounces) crumbled feta
         cheese

1. Combine first 6 ingredients, stirring with a whisk. Place potatoes in a large bowl. Drizzle with half of dressing; toss to coat. Cover and chill 10 minutes, stirring occasionally.

2. Add Simple Roasted Leg of Lamb and remaining 5 ingredients to potato mixture. Drizzle with remaining dressing, and toss gently to coat. Cover and chill. Yield: 4 servings (serving size: 1¾ cups).

CALORIES 331 (30% from fat); FAT 10.9g (sat 5.2g, mono 3.9g, poly 0.8g); PROTEIN 24.6g; CARB 34g; FIBER 6g; CHOL 71mg; IRON 2.3mg; SODIUM 685mg; CALC 114mg

---

Roast Lamb Pitas with Spicy Sesame Yogurt Sauce

Here's a nice change from typical Greek gyro sandwiches. It's best to pack the yogurt sauce in a separate container so the sandwich won't become soggy before lunchtime; either drizzle the sauce into the pita halves just before eating, or serve it on the side for dunking.

½ cup plain fat-free yogurt
1 tablespoon tahini (sesame-seed paste)
½ teaspoon chile garlic sauce (such as Lee Kum Kee)
¼ teaspoon freshly ground black pepper
⅛ teaspoon salt
2 (6-inch) pitas, cut in half
1¼ cups shredded Simple Roasted Leg of Lamb (about 5 ounces) (recipe on page 129)
1 cup thinly sliced red onion
1 cup thinly sliced cucumber
2 plum tomatoes, seeded and thinly sliced

1. Combine first 5 ingredients, stirring with a whisk.

2. Fill each pita half with about ⅓ cup Simple Roasted Leg of Lamb, ¼ cup onion, and ¼ cup cucumber. Divide tomato slices evenly among pita halves. Wrap sandwiches in foil or parchment paper; chill. Serve with sauce. Yield: 2 servings (serving size: 2 stuffed pita halves and ¼ cup sauce).

CALORIES 434 (28% from fat); FAT 13.7g (sat 4.2g, mono 5.3g, poly 2.8g); PROTEIN 30.8g; CARB 47.7g; FIBER 3.3g; CHOL 70mg; IRON 4mg; SODIUM 596mg; CALC 166mg

---

Lamb Sandwiches with Green Pea Spread and Herbed Mayo

You can use fresh peas in place of the frozen peas called for in the Green Pea Spread. For a quick dinner, stir leftover Green Pea Spread into cooked pasta, and top with Parmesan.

¼ cup fat-free mayonnaise
2 tablespoons chopped fresh basil
2 tablespoons chopped fresh chives
1 (8-ounce) French bread baguette, cut in half horizontally
¼ cup Green Pea Spread
2 cups sliced Simple Roasted Leg of Lamb (about 9 ounces) (recipe on page 129)
½ cup thinly sliced radishes

1. Combine mayonnaise, basil, and chives, stirring with a whisk; spread mayonnaise mixture over top half of baguette. Spread Green Pea Spread over bottom half of baguette, and top with Simple Roasted Leg of Lamb, radishes, and top half of baguette. Cut crosswise into 4 pieces. Wrap sandwiches in foil or parchment paper; chill. Yield: 4 servings (serving size: 1 sandwich).

(Totals include Green Pea Spread) CALORIES 319 (24% from fat); FAT 8.4g (sat 3.1g, mono 3.5g, poly 0.6g); PROTEIN 23.1g; CARB 38.5g; FIBER 1.9g; CHOL 60mg; IRON 3.4mg; SODIUM 578mg; CALC 18mg

GREEN PEA SPREAD:
1 tablespoon olive oil
1 cup finely chopped onion
7 tablespoons water, divided
1 (10-ounce) package frozen green peas, thawed
2 tablespoons fresh lemon juice
¼ teaspoon salt
¼ teaspoon freshly ground black pepper

1. Heat oil in a medium nonstick skillet over medium heat. Add onion; cook 3 minutes or until tender, stirring occasionally. Add ¼ cup water and peas; cook 5 minutes or until peas are tender.

Spoon into a blender or food processor; add 3 tablespoons water, lemon juice, salt, and pepper. Process until smooth. Cover and chill. Yield: 2 cups (serving size: ¼ cup).

CALORIES 52 (31% from fat); FAT 1.8g (sat 0.3g, mono 1.3g, poly 0.2g); PROTEIN 2.1g; CARB 7.3g; FIBER 1.8g; CHOL 0mg; IRON 0.6mg; SODIUM 114mg; CALC 13mg

---

Roast Lamb and White Bean Salad

Two kinds of beans add visual appeal; you can also use two cans of one type of bean.

2 cups trimmed arugula
1½ cups cubed Simple Roasted Leg of Lamb (about 6 ounces) (recipe on page 129)
1 cup chopped yellow bell pepper
½ cup chopped fresh flat-leaf parsley
½ cup (2 ounces) cubed fresh mozzarella cheese
¼ cup thinly sliced shallots
1 (15.5-ounce) can Great Northern beans, rinsed and drained
1 (15-ounce) can cannellini beans or other white beans, rinsed and drained
3 tablespoons white wine vinegar
2 teaspoons extravirgin olive oil
¼ teaspoon freshly ground black pepper
⅛ teaspoon salt

1. Combine first 8 ingredients in a large bowl; toss well. Combine vinegar and remaining 3 ingredients; drizzle over salad. Toss gently to coat. Cover and chill. Yield: 4 servings (serving size: 1½ cups).

CALORIES 352 (29% from fat); FAT 11.3g (sat 4.4g, mono 3.8g, poly 1.1g); PROTEIN 25.3g; CARB 35.3g; FIBER 11.3g; CHOL 50mg; IRON 4.7mg; SODIUM 515mg; CALC 186mg

Lamb and Couscous Salad

Israeli couscous is about the size of small peas, much larger than the more familiar Moroccan couscous.

2½ cups water
1 cup uncooked Israeli couscous
1½ cups chopped Simple Roasted Leg of Lamb (about 6 ounces) (recipe on page 129)
½ cup chopped fresh flat-leaf parsley
3 tablespoons grated orange rind
½ cup fresh orange juice (about 1 orange)
⅓ cup thinly sliced green onions
3 tablespoons coarsely chopped pistachios, toasted
1 tablespoon extravirgin olive oil
½ teaspoon salt
½ teaspoon ground cumin
¼ teaspoon freshly ground black pepper

1. Bring water to a boil in a medium saucepan; gradually stir in couscous. Cover, reduce heat, and simmer 8 minutes or until al dente. Drain and rinse with cold water; drain. Place couscous in a medium bowl. Stir in Simple Roasted Leg of Lamb and remaining ingredients. Cover and chill. Yield: 4 servings (serving size: 1 cup).

CALORIES 347 (30% from fat); FAT 11.6g (sat 2.9g, mono 6.1g, poly 1.7g); PROTEIN 19g; CARB 41g; FIBER 4.1g; CHOL 39mg; IRON 2.3mg; SODIUM 368mg; CALC 45mg

Curried Noodle Salad with Roast Lamb

Udon noodles can be found in Asian markets and many large supermarkets; spaghetti is a good substitute. The flavor intensifies as the salad chills—it's actually better the next day.

⅓ cup rice vinegar
2 tablespoons fresh lime juice
1 tablespoon dark sesame oil
1 tablespoon honey
2 teaspoons grated peeled fresh ginger
1 teaspoon curry powder
1 teaspoon chile garlic sauce (such as Lee Kum Kee)
¾ teaspoon salt
¼ teaspoon freshly ground black pepper
1 garlic clove, minced
8 ounces uncooked udon noodles (thick, round Japanese wheat noodles) or spaghetti
1½ cups shredded Simple Roasted Leg of Lamb (about 6 ounces) (recipe on page 129)
1 cup (3-inch) julienne-cut seeded plum tomato
1 cup chopped peeled mango
½ cup shredded carrot
½ cup thinly sliced green onions
½ cup (2-inch) julienne-cut seeded peeled cucumber
⅓ cup thinly sliced fresh basil

1. Combine first 10 ingredients.
2. Cook noodles in boiling water 10 minutes or until tender. Drain and rinse with cold water; drain. Place noodles in a large bowl; stir in Simple Roasted Leg of Lamb and remaining 6 ingredients. Drizzle with dressing, and toss to coat. Cover and chill. Yield: 6 servings (serving size: 1⅓ cups).

CALORIES 268 (23% from fat); FAT 6.9g (sat 1.7g, mono 2.4g, poly 1.3g); PROTEIN 14g; CARB 38g; FIBER 3.9g; CHOL 26mg; IRON 2.2mg; SODIUM 398mg; CALC 34mg

Barley-Mushroom Salad with Lamb and Goat Cheese

Pearl barley has the outer husk of bran removed, and has been steamed and polished, like a pearl. Toasting the barley in a dry saucepan adds a nutty flavor.

1 cup uncooked pearl barley
3 cups water
1 tablespoon extravirgin olive oil
2 cups thinly sliced cremini mushrooms (about 6 ounces)
2 cups thinly sliced shiitake mushroom caps (about 6 ounces)
½ cup diced celery
¼ cup thinly sliced shallots
2 tablespoons chopped fresh parsley
1½ teaspoons chopped fresh rosemary
2¼ cups shredded Simple Roasted Leg of Lamb (about 9 ounces) (recipe on page 129)
⅓ cup (about 1½ ounces) crumbled goat cheese
2 tablespoons balsamic vinegar
¾ teaspoon salt
¼ teaspoon freshly ground black pepper

1. Cook barley in a large saucepan over medium heat 5 minutes or until golden, stirring occasionally. Add water; bring to a boil. Cover, reduce heat, and simmer 50 minutes or until barley is tender and liquid is absorbed. Place barley in a large bowl; cool slightly.
2. While barley cooks, heat oil in a large nonstick skillet over medium heat. Add mushrooms, celery, and shallots; cook 5 minutes or until mushrooms are tender and liquid evaporates, stirring frequently. Remove from heat; stir in parsley and rosemary. Cool slightly. Stir mushroom mixture, Simple Roasted Leg of Lamb, and remaining ingredients into barley. Cover and chill. Yield: 6 servings (serving size: 1 cup).

CALORIES 279 (30% from fat); FAT 9.2g (sat 3.4g, mono 4.2g, poly 0.8g); PROTEIN 17.9g; CARB 31.3g; FIBER 6g; CHOL 42mg; IRON 2.7mg; SODIUM 380mg; CALC 41mg

Mint for the Cook

Bursting with fragrance and color, this fresh herb adds dimension to sweet and savory dishes.

MAKE AHEAD
Mint Limeade

The fresh, cool flavor of mint is a welcome addition to this warm-weather drink. Try serving it as a refreshing cooler with spicy Asian food.

 6 cups water, divided
1¾ cups sugar
 ⅓ cup coarsely chopped fresh mint
 1 cup fresh lime juice (about 12 limes)
10 mint sprigs (optional)
10 lime slices (optional)

1. Combine 2 cups water, sugar, and chopped mint in a small saucepan; bring to a boil. Cook until sugar dissolves, stirring frequently. Remove from heat; let stand 10 minutes. Strain through a sieve into a bowl; discard solids.
2. Combine 4 cups water, sugar syrup, and lime juice in a large pitcher, stirring well. Serve over ice; garnish with mint sprigs and lime slices, if desired. Yield: 8 cups (serving size: about ¾ cup).

CALORIES 142 (0% from fat); FAT 0g; PROTEIN 0.1g; CARB 37.2g; FIBER 0.1g; CHOL 0mg; IRON 0mg; SODIUM 0mg; CALC 3mg

> Mint is versatile enough to add fresh, cool flavor to both savory dishes and desserts.

Cornmeal-Crusted Scallops with Mint Chimichurri
(pictured on page 146)

Chimichurri is a thick herb sauce commonly made with parsley and oregano, and served with grilled meat in Argentina. Mint gives this version a more delicate taste, making it perfect for seafood. Serve over a bed of rice to soak up the flavorful sauce.

1½ cups loosely packed fresh mint leaves
 ¾ cup sliced green onions
 2 tablespoons water
1½ tablespoons fresh lime juice
 1 tablespoon honey
 1 teaspoon minced seeded serrano chile
 ½ teaspoon salt
 ½ teaspoon freshly ground black pepper
 1 garlic clove
 3 tablespoons yellow cornmeal
1½ pounds sea scallops
 1 tablespoon olive oil
Green onion strips (optional)

1. Place first 9 ingredients in a food processor; process until finely chopped. Set aside.
2. Place cornmeal in a shallow dish. Dredge scallops in cornmeal. Heat oil in a large nonstick skillet over medium-high heat. Add scallops; cook 3 minutes on each side or until done. Serve with chimichurri, and garnish with onion strips, if desired. Yield: 4 servings (serving size: about 4 ounces sea scallops and 2 tablespoons chimichurri).

CALORIES 237 (19% from fat); FAT 4.9g (sat 0.6g, mono 2.6g, poly 0.9g); PROTEIN 29.6g; CARB 17.3g; FIBER 2.1g; CHOL 56mg; IRON 1.4mg; SODIUM 576mg; CALC 68mg

QUICK & EASY
Southeast Asian Cabbage and Shrimp Salad

Fresh mint adds a cooling effect to this peppery salad. For a spicier dish, keep the seeds in the jalapeño peppers. Use steamed, boiled, or grilled shrimp.

DRESSING:
 ½ cup fresh lime juice (about 6 limes)
 ⅓ cup chopped fresh cilantro
 ¼ cup water
 3 tablespoons brown sugar
 2 tablespoons minced seeded jalapeño pepper
 2 tablespoons thinly sliced fresh mint
1½ tablespoons fish sauce
 1 garlic clove, minced

SALAD:
 6 cups thinly sliced Napa cabbage
1½ cups shredded carrot
1½ cups loosely packed fresh mint leaves
 1 cup vertically sliced red onion
1½ pounds medium shrimp, cooked and peeled
 1 English cucumber, halved lengthwise and sliced (about 1½ cups)
 6 tablespoons chopped unsalted, dry-roasted peanuts
Mint sprigs (optional)

1. To prepare dressing, combine first 8 ingredients, stirring with a whisk until sugar dissolves.
2. To prepare salad, combine cabbage and next 5 ingredients in a large bowl. Drizzle dressing over salad, and toss well to coat. Sprinkle with peanuts; garnish with mint sprigs, if desired. Serve immediately. Yield: 6 servings (serving size: 2 cups salad and 1 tablespoon peanuts).

CALORIES 252 (24% from fat); FAT 6.7g (sat 1g, mono 2.6g, poly 2.3g); PROTEIN 27.5g; CARB 21.6g; FIBER 3.8g; CHOL 172mg; IRON 3.7mg; SODIUM 553mg; CALC 170mg

Roasted Potato Salad with Mint Vinaigrette

Initially covering the potato mixture as it cooks with a small amount of broth steams the vegetables so they'll cook through without burning. Once the pan is uncovered, the broth quickly evaporates, and the vegetables brown and caramelize.

- 3 cups (2-inch) cut green beans
- 3 cups (1-inch-square) cut red bell pepper (about 2 large peppers)
- ½ cup chopped fresh mint
- ½ cup fat-free, less-sodium chicken broth
- 4 garlic cloves, sliced
- 2 pounds small red potatoes, quartered
- 2 Vidalia or other sweet onions, trimmed and quartered
- Cooking spray
- ½ cup chopped fresh mint
- ⅓ cup white wine vinegar
- 2 tablespoons olive oil
- 1 teaspoon salt
- ½ to 1 teaspoon coarsely ground black pepper

1. Preheat oven to 400°.
2. Combine first 7 ingredients; toss well. Arrange vegetable mixture in a single layer on a jelly-roll pan coated with cooking spray; cover with foil. Bake at 400° for 20 minutes. Uncover and stir; bake, uncovered, an additional 40 minutes or until lightly browned, stirring after 20 minutes. Let stand 5 minutes. Place vegetable mixture in a large bowl.
3. Combine ½ cup mint, vinegar, oil, salt, and black pepper, stirring well with a whisk. Drizzle vinaigrette over vegetable mixture, and toss well to coat. Serve at room temperature or chilled. Yield: 9 servings (serving size: 1 cup).

CALORIES 139 (22% from fat); FAT 3.4g (sat 0.5g, mono 2.2g, poly 0.5g); PROTEIN 3.7g; CARB 25.2g; FIBER 3.7g; CHOL 0mg; IRON 1.7mg; SODIUM 296mg; CALC 44mg

Choosing and Storing Mint

If you're buying mint at the market, look for bright green, crisp leaves with no signs of wilting. Place the stems in a glass containing a couple inches of water, and cover leaves loosely with plastic wrap or a zip-top plastic bag (do not seal the bag). Refrigerate up to one week, changing the water every other day.

Fresh mint can also be frozen for later use. Simply rinse the leaves, pat dry, and freeze in a zip-top plastic bag (the leaves will darken once they're frozen, but that doesn't affect the flavor). Later, pull out what you need, and return the rest to the freezer. You may prefer to freeze whole or chopped mint leaves in ice-cube trays with water, which preserves the green color. After they freeze, remove cubes from the trays, and store in zip-top plastic bags. Add these minty ice cubes to drinks; or thaw, drain, and use in recipes calling for mint.

Chicken Salad with Mint and Feta

This simple chicken salad is zesty with the flavors of mint, feta cheese, and lemon juice. It's great as is and also good served in a pita or on a bed of greens.

- 3 cups chopped skinless, boneless rotisserie chicken breast
- ½ cup chopped yellow bell pepper
- ½ cup chopped red bell pepper
- ½ cup cubed peeled English cucumber
- ½ cup (2 ounces) crumbled feta cheese
- ¼ cup chopped fresh mint
- 2 tablespoons fresh lemon juice
- 1½ tablespoons chopped fresh oregano
- 1½ teaspoons extravirgin olive oil
- ¼ teaspoon salt
- ¼ teaspoon freshly ground black pepper
- Mint sprigs (optional)

1. Combine all ingredients except mint sprigs in a large bowl; toss gently to combine. Garnish with mint sprigs, if desired. Yield: 6 servings (serving size: about ¾ cup).

CALORIES 233 (28% from fat); FAT 7.3g (sat 2.7g, mono 2.7g, poly 1.1g); PROTEIN 36.9g; CARB 2.9g; FIBER 0.2g; CHOL 105mg; IRON 1.5mg; SODIUM 289mg; CALC 75mg

Fudgy Mint Fallen Soufflé

Fresh mint leaves steep in hot water to create a mint "tea" that pairs with chocolate in this rich dessert. Because this soufflé is meant to be served fallen, there's no mad rush to get it to the table. As it deflates, the rich dessert becomes more dense and fudgy. For a special treat, serve vanilla ice cream on the side.

- ½ cup boiling water
- ½ cup fresh mint leaves
- ⅔ cup unsweetened cocoa
- 2 tablespoons butter
- 3 tablespoons all-purpose flour
- 1 cup fat-free milk
- ½ cup granulated sugar
- ⅛ teaspoon salt
- 4 large egg whites
- 2 tablespoons granulated sugar
- Cooking spray
- 1 tablespoon powdered sugar
- Mint sprigs (optional)

1. Combine boiling water and mint leaves in a small bowl; cover and steep 20 minutes.
2. Preheat oven to 375°.
3. Strain mint mixture through a fine sieve into a large bowl; discard mint leaves. Add cocoa to water; stir well with a whisk.
4. Melt butter in a small saucepan over medium heat. Add flour, stirring with a whisk. Cook 1 minute, stirring constantly. Stir in milk, ½ cup granulated sugar, and salt; cook over medium heat 3 minutes or until thick, stirring constantly. Remove from heat; stir into cocoa mixture. Cool slightly.

5. Place egg whites in a large bowl; beat with a mixer at high speed until foamy. Add 2 tablespoons granulated sugar, 1 tablespoon at a time, beating until stiff peaks form. Gently stir one-fourth of egg white mixture into cocoa mixture; gently fold in remaining egg white mixture. Spoon into a 2-quart soufflé dish coated with cooking spray. Bake at 375° for 30 minutes or until puffy and set. Let stand 5 minutes (soufflé will fall during standing). Sprinkle with powdered sugar; garnish with mint sprigs, if desired. Serve warm or at room temperature. Yield: 6 servings (serving size: about ⅔ cup).

CALORIES 181 (26% from fat); FAT 5.2g (sat 2.7g, mono 2g, poly 0.2g); PROTEIN 6.1g; CARB 32.4g; FIBER 3.3g; CHOL 11mg; IRON 1.7mg; SODIUM 133mg; CALC 53mg

Grilled Tuna over Lemon-Mint Barley Salad

The flavors of the vinaigrette are mirrored in the marinade, so there's a double dose of the refreshing combination of the lemon and mint.

¾ cup finely chopped fresh mint, divided
1 teaspoon grated lemon rind
3 tablespoons plus 1 teaspoon fresh lemon juice, divided
¾ teaspoon salt, divided
½ teaspoon crushed red pepper
3 garlic cloves, minced
4 (6-ounce) Yellowfin tuna steaks
2¼ cups water
1 cup uncooked pearl barley
2 cups chopped tomato
¾ cup chopped green onions
2 tablespoons capers
2 tablespoons chopped pitted kalamata olives
1 tablespoon extravirgin olive oil
Cooking spray

1. Combine ½ cup mint, lemon rind, 4 teaspoons lemon juice, ¼ teaspoon salt, pepper, and garlic in a shallow dish; add tuna, turning to coat. Cover and refrigerate 30 minutes.

2. Combine ¼ teaspoon salt and water in a medium saucepan; bring to a boil. Stir in barley; cover, reduce heat, and simmer 30 minutes or until liquid is absorbed. Remove from heat; cover and let stand 5 minutes. Spoon barley into a large bowl; cool slightly. Add remaining ¼ cup mint, tomato, green onions, capers, and olives; stir well to combine. Combine remaining ¼ teaspoon salt, remaining 2 tablespoons lemon juice, and oil, stirring well with a whisk. Drizzle over barley mixture; toss gently to coat. Set aside.

3. Prepare grill or broiler.

4. Place tuna steaks on a grill rack or broiler pan coated with cooking spray; cook 2 minutes on each side until tuna steaks are medium-rare or until desired degree of doneness. Spoon about 1½ cups barley mixture onto each of 4 plates; top each serving with 1 tuna steak. Yield: 4 servings.

CALORIES 415 (15% from fat); FAT 6.9g (sat 1.2g, mono 3.3g, poly 1.6g); PROTEIN 47.2g; CARB 41.9g; FIBER 10.4g; CHOL 77mg; IRON 4mg; SODIUM 685mg; CALC 88mg

Beef, Mint, and Pepperoncini Burgers with Lemon-Feta Sauce

This large, heaping burger might best be eaten with a knife and fork. The heat, tang, and crunch of pepperoncini peppers are welcome additions to the herb-filled burger. Look for jars of the peppers in the grocery store's pickle aisle. The creamy sauce tames the heat of the pepper.

RELISH:

1½ cups quartered cherry tomatoes
1 tablespoon finely chopped fresh mint
1 tablespoon fresh lemon juice

SAUCE:

½ cup (2 ounces) crumbled reduced-fat feta cheese
¼ cup plain fat-free yogurt
2 tablespoons fresh lemon juice
1 tablespoon honey
1 garlic clove

BURGERS:

½ cup chopped fresh mint
½ cup finely chopped seeded pickled pepperoncini peppers
¼ teaspoon salt
¼ teaspoon ground cinnamon
¼ teaspoon black pepper
1 large egg white, lightly beaten
1 pound ground round
Cooking spray
5 (2-ounce) Kaiser rolls or hamburger buns

1. To prepare relish, combine tomatoes, 1 tablespoon mint, and 1 tablespoon juice; cover and chill.

2. To prepare sauce, place feta cheese and next 4 ingredients in a food processor, and process 2 minutes or until smooth, scraping sides. Cover and chill.

3. Prepare grill or broiler.

4. To prepare burgers, combine ½ cup mint and next 6 ingredients. Divide mixture into 5 equal portions, shaping each into a ½-inch-thick patty. Place patties on a grill rack or broiler pan coated with cooking spray; cook 5 minutes on each side or until done. Place 1 patty on bottom half of each bun; top with ¼ cup relish. Drizzle each serving with about 2 tablespoons sauce; top with top halves of buns. Serve immediately. Yield: 5 servings (serving size: 1 burger).

CALORIES 378 (28% from fat); FAT 11.9g (sat 4.4g, mono 4g, poly 1.3g); PROTEIN 27.9g; CARB 39.8g; FIBER 2.4g; CHOL 62mg; IRON 4.2mg; SODIUM 647mg; CALC 122mg

WINE NOTE: The sauce of lemon, feta cheese, and yogurt on this tasty burger adds a salty, tangy flavor that can make many red wines taste flat and dull. So opt for a fresh, clean, dry white wine instead (whoever said white wines don't go with red meat?). Try a snappy pinot grigio, served well chilled. The 2003 Zenato Pinot Grigio from Veneto, Italy, is an affordable choice at about $10.

Chilled Pea Soup with Mint Pesto

You can substitute fresh peas for frozen.

 1 teaspoon butter
 ½ cup sliced green onions
 1½ tablespoons all-purpose flour
 1½ cups 1% low-fat milk
 1 (14-ounce) can fat-free,
    less-sodium chicken broth
 1 (1-pound) package frozen green
    peas, unthawed
 6 tablespoons Mint Pesto
 ¼ teaspoon salt
 ¼ teaspoon freshly ground black
    pepper
 Mint sprigs (optional)

1. Melt butter in a large saucepan over medium heat. Add onions; cook 2 minutes, stirring frequently. Sprinkle flour over onions, and cook 1 minute, stirring constantly. Stir in milk and broth. Bring to a boil over medium heat, stirring constantly; cook 3 minutes or until slightly thick. Add peas; cook 5 minutes.

2. Place half of pea mixture in a blender. Remove center piece of blender lid (to allow steam to escape); secure lid on blender. Place a clean dishtowel over opening in lid (to prevent spills). Process until smooth. Strain puréed pea mixture through a sieve into a large bowl, pressing mixture with a spatula. Discard solids. Repeat procedure with remaining pea mixture. Stir in Mint Pesto, salt, and pepper; cover and chill. Garnish with mint sprigs, if desired. Yield: 6 servings (serving size: about ⅔ cup).

(Totals include Mint Pesto) CALORIES 149 (30% from fat); FAT 5g (sat 1.8g, mono 2g, poly 0.9g); PROTEIN 9.1g; CARB 17.6g; FIBER 4.6g; CHOL 7mg; IRON 2mg; SODIUM 452mg; CALC 175mg

MINT PESTO:

 2 tablespoons pine nuts
 2 small garlic cloves
 4 cups loosely packed fresh mint
    leaves (about 2 ounces)
 ½ cup (2 ounces) grated fresh
    Parmesan cheese
 ¼ teaspoon salt
 ¼ teaspoon freshly ground black
    pepper
 ¼ cup water
 1 tablespoon extravirgin olive oil

1. With food processor on, drop pine nuts and garlic through food chute; process until minced. Add mint, cheese, salt, and pepper; process until finely minced. With processor on, slowly add water and oil through food chute, and process until well blended. Yield: ¾ cup (serving size: 1 tablespoon).

CALORIES 45 (68% from fat); FAT 3.4g (sat 1g, mono 1.5g, poly 0.7g); PROTEIN 2.2g; CARB 1.8g; FIBER 0.8g; CHOL 3mg; IRON 0.6mg; SODIUM 128mg; CALC 78mg

---

Mint in Your Garden

Members of the genus *Mentha* are hardy perennials that come back year after year. They thrive in sun or partial shade, do well in average soil, and many withstand droughts and heat. Mint plants require little maintenance— but they will take over the garden if allowed. They have a running root system, which is no problem if you have an area devoted entirely to the herb. If space is limited, grow mint in containers or pots to keep it in bounds. To encourage bushy growth, occasionally pinch off the growing tip just above the first set of leaves. This will result in new shoots, yielding more leaves to harvest. Space plants about 12 to 18 inches apart. For easy-to-follow instructions for planting your own mint garden, visit www.backyardgardener.com or www.ehow.com/how_320_grow-mint.html.

Backyard Barbecue Menu

serves 8

Invite the neighbors over for an evening to celebrate warmer weather.

Grilled Corn with Mint Butter

Soy and lime-glazed
pork tenderloin*

Chilled steamed broccoli with
bottled vinaigrette

Grilled garlic bread

*Prepare grill. Place 2 (1-pound) trimmed pork tenderloins on a grill rack coated with cooking spray. Grill 20 minutes or until a thermometer registers 155° or until desired degree of doneness. Combine 3 tablespoons low-sodium soy sauce, 2 tablespoons honey, 1 teaspoon grated lime rind, ¾ teaspoon salt, and ½ teaspoon crushed red pepper. Brush glaze over pork; grill 1 minute. Remove from heat; let stand 5 minutes. Cut across grain into thin slices.

Grilled Corn with Mint Butter

 2 tablespoons butter, melted
 1 tablespoon finely chopped fresh
    mint
 2 teaspoons fresh lemon juice
 ½ teaspoon finely chopped fresh
    cilantro
 ½ teaspoon coarsely ground black
    pepper
 ¼ teaspoon salt
 8 ears shucked corn
 Cooking spray

1. Prepare grill.
2. Combine first 6 ingredients; stir well.
3. Place corn on grill rack coated with cooking spray; grill 10 minutes or until done, turning frequently. Place corn on a platter. Brush with butter mixture. Yield: 8 servings (serving size: 1 ear).

CALORIES 149 (27% from fat); FAT 4.5g (sat 2.1g, mono 1.2g, poly 0.9g); PROTEIN 4.7g; CARB 27.4g; FIBER 3.9g; CHOL 8mg; IRON 0.8mg; SODIUM 115mg; CALC 5mg

Easy Asian Dinners from The Minimalist

These meatless dishes created by Mark Bittman for the home cook appeal to everyone.

Asian Vegetarian Menu
serves 4

Hot and Sour Soup

Tofu with Red Peppers and Black Bean Paste

Ginger Fried Rice

Snow Peas with Ginger

Mango sorbet

Jasmine tea or Chinese beer

QUICK & EASY
Hot and Sour Soup

5   dried shiitake mushrooms (about ¼ ounce)
5   dried wood ear mushrooms (about ¼ ounce)
1   (32-ounce) carton fat-free, less-sodium vegetable broth (such as Swanson Certified Organic)
2¼ cups water, divided
1   tablespoon minced peeled fresh ginger
1   teaspoon minced garlic
¼   cup rice vinegar
1   tablespoon low-sodium soy sauce
½   to 1 teaspoon freshly ground black pepper
½   pound reduced-fat firm or extrafirm tofu, drained and cut into ¼-inch cubes
2½ tablespoons cornstarch
4   large egg whites, lightly beaten
½   cup chopped green onions
¼   cup minced fresh cilantro
1   teaspoon dark sesame oil
Chili oil (optional)

1. Place mushrooms in a medium bowl; cover with boiling water. Cover and let stand 10 minutes or until tender; drain. Thinly slice mushrooms; set aside.
2. Combine broth, 2 cups water, ginger, and garlic in a large saucepan over medium-high heat; bring to a boil. Add mushrooms. Reduce heat, and simmer 5 minutes. Add vinegar, soy sauce, pepper, and tofu; bring to a boil. Reduce heat, and simmer 5 minutes.
3. Combine ¼ cup water and cornstarch, stirring with a whisk. Stir cornstarch mixture into broth mixture; bring to a boil. Reduce heat; simmer 3 minutes or until soup thickens slightly, stirring frequently. Slowly pour egg whites into broth mixture in a steady stream, stirring constantly but gently with a wooden spoon. Remove from heat; stir in onions, cilantro, and sesame oil. Drizzle with chili oil, if desired. Yield: 4 servings (serving size: 1¾ cups).

CALORIES 158 (21% from fat); FAT 3.8g (sat 0.2g, mono 0g, poly 0g); PROTEIN 11.1g; CARB 20.3g; FIBER 6.5g; CHOL 0mg; IRON 1.5mg; SODIUM 770mg; CALC 44mg

---

QUICK & EASY
Tofu with Red Peppers and Black Bean Paste

Black bean paste is a salty sauce made from mashed fermented black beans, garlic, and other spices. It's typically used in Chinese, Korean, and Vietnamese cooking.

1   (12.3-ounce) package reduced-fat firm tofu, drained
2   teaspoons grapeseed or canola oil
1   tablespoon minced garlic
1   tablespoon minced peeled fresh ginger
4   dried hot red chiles
2   cups thinly sliced red bell pepper
2   tablespoons sherry
⅓   cup coarsely chopped green onions
1   tablespoon low-sodium soy sauce
1   tablespoon black bean paste
1   teaspoon dark sesame oil

1. Cut each block of tofu in half lengthwise. Place tofu slices on several layers of paper towels; cover with additional paper towels. Let stand 30 minutes, pressing down occasionally. Cut tofu into ½-inch cubes.
2. Heat grapeseed oil in a large nonstick skillet over medium-high heat. Add garlic, ginger, and chiles; stir-fry 30 seconds. Add bell pepper, and cook 3 minutes or until tender, stirring frequently. Stir in tofu and sherry; cook 3 minutes or until thoroughly heated, stirring frequently. Stir in onions; cook 30 seconds. Remove from heat; add soy sauce, bean paste, and sesame oil, stirring gently to combine. Yield: 4 servings (serving size: about 1 cup).

CALORIES 187 (41% from fat); FAT 9g (sat 0.5g, mono 0.9g, poly 2.4g); PROTEIN 13.2g; CARB 14.3g; FIBER 2.9g; CHOL 0mg; IRON 3.1mg; SODIUM 146mg; CALC 77mg

---

QUICK & EASY
Ginger Fried Rice

Grapeseed oil has a light quality that won't compete with the vivid flavor of the other ingredients. It also has a high smoke point, making it a good choice for stir-frying. Chilling the rice a day ahead helps prevent the grains from sticking together. To chill, spread onto a jelly-roll pan, cover, and refrigerate eight hours or overnight.

1   tablespoon grapeseed or canola oil
3   tablespoons chopped peeled fresh ginger
2   tablespoons minced garlic
2   cups thinly vertically sliced onion
¼   teaspoon salt
4   cups cooked short-grain rice, chilled
2   large eggs, lightly beaten
¼   cup chopped green onions
2   tablespoons low-sodium soy sauce
2   teaspoons dark sesame oil
Cilantro sprigs (optional)

1. Heat grapeseed oil in a large nonstick skillet over medium heat; add ginger and garlic. Cook 10 minutes or until browned and crisp, stirring constantly. Remove from pan; set aside.

Continued

2. Add sliced onion to pan; reduce heat to medium-low. Cover and cook 10 minutes or until soft; stir occasionally. Sprinkle salt over onion; increase heat to medium-high. Add rice; cook 4 minutes or until heated, stirring frequently.

3. Make a well in center of rice; add eggs, stirring to scramble. Gradually incorporate eggs into rice; stir in ginger mixture, green onions, soy sauce, and sesame oil. Garnish with cilantro, if desired. Yield: 4 servings (serving size: 1 cup).

CALORIES 372 (22% from fat); FAT 8.9g (sat 1.7g, mono 2g, poly 2.6g); PROTEIN 8.9g; CARB 62.7g; FIBER 1.9g; CHOL 106mg; IRON 3.4mg; SODIUM 447mg; CALC 41mg

QUICK & EASY
Snow Peas with Ginger
(pictured on page 147)

This simple yet delightful side dish comes together in minutes and adds a colorful note to the menu.

1½ teaspoons dark sesame oil
  3 cups snow peas, trimmed (about 8 ounces)
  1 teaspoon minced peeled fresh ginger
  2 tablespoons low-sodium soy sauce
  ⅛ teaspoon freshly ground black pepper

1. Heat oil in a large nonstick skillet over medium-high heat. Add peas and ginger; sauté 3 minutes. Remove from heat; stir in soy sauce and black pepper. Yield: 4 servings (serving size: about ½ cup).

CALORIES 40 (41% from fat); FAT 1.9g (sat 0.3g, mono 0g, poly 0.1g); PROTEIN 1.8g; CARB 4.4g; FIBER 1.3g; CHOL 0mg; IRON 1.2mg; SODIUM 269mg; CALC 22mg

Cook's Tour

Three renowned culinary figures share their recipes from the cities (Paris, Mexico City, New Orleans) that changed their lives—and their palates.

Greek-Style Leeks
Leeks à la Grecque

Braised in a piquant blend of red wine vinegar, olive oil, and herbs, and then chilled, these leeks are a fine make-ahead Parisian side dish.

—David Rosengarten

  4 leeks (about 2 pounds)
  1 cup water
  3 tablespoons red wine vinegar
  1 teaspoon olive oil
  ½ teaspoon salt
  3 fresh marjoram sprigs
  3 fresh oregano sprigs
  1 (3-inch) cinnamon stick
  1 cup chopped seeded tomato
  2 tablespoons chopped pitted kalamata olives
  ¼ cup (1 ounce) feta cheese, crumbled
  1 teaspoon finely chopped fresh marjoram
  1 teaspoon finely chopped fresh oregano

1. Preheat oven to 400°.
2. Remove roots, outer leaves, and tops from leeks, leaving 1½ to 2 inches of dark leaves. Cut leeks in half lengthwise to within 1 inch of bulb end, and rinse with cold water. Arrange leeks in a single layer in bottom of a 9-inch pie plate.
3. Combine water and next 6 ingredients in a small saucepan; bring to a boil. Reduce heat; simmer 10 minutes. Pour mixture over leeks. Cover with foil; bake at 400° for 30 minutes or until leeks are tender. Using a slotted spoon, remove leeks; reserve liquid. Cool leeks to room temperature. Cover and chill 2 hours.
4. Place cooking liquid in a small saucepan; bring to a boil. Remove from heat; strain mixture through a sieve into a bowl, reserving ¼ cup cooking liquid. Discard solids.
5. Place 2 leek halves on each of 4 small plates; top each serving with ¼ cup tomato and 1½ teaspoons olives. Drizzle 1 tablespoon reserved liquid over each serving, and divide cheese evenly among plates. Sprinkle evenly with chopped marjoram and chopped oregano. Yield: 4 servings.

CALORIES 114 (28% from fat); FAT 3.6g (sat 1.3g, mono 1.5g, poly 0.5g); PROTEIN 3.2g; CARB 19g; FIBER 2.7g; CHOL 6mg; IRON 3mg; SODIUM 439mg; CALC 116mg

Bistro-Style Chicken with Wild Mushrooms and Madeira

This Parisian entrée pairs juicy chicken thighs with earthy mushrooms. Look in the produce aisle for packages of "gourmet blend" mushrooms, or use any combination of cremini, shiitake, oyster, and button mushrooms.

—David Rosengarten

  8 skinless, boneless chicken thighs (about 1½ pounds)
  ½ teaspoon salt, divided
  ½ teaspoon pepper, divided
  ⅛ teaspoon grated whole nutmeg
Cooking spray
  2 pounds red potatoes, halved
  ½ cup 1% low-fat milk
  2 tablespoons butter, divided
  8 ounces sliced mushrooms, such as cremini, shiitake, oyster, and button
  1 cup fat-free, less-sodium chicken broth
  ½ cup Madeira wine or dry sherry
  ¼ cup chopped fresh parsley

1. Preheat oven to 350°.

2. Sprinkle chicken evenly with ¼ teaspoon salt, ¼ teaspoon pepper, and nutmeg. Place chicken in a shallow roasting pan coated with cooking spray; cover with foil. Bake chicken at 350° for 30 minutes. Turn chicken over; bake, uncovered, an additional 30 minutes or until chicken is done. Remove chicken to a serving platter, reserving 1 tablespoon pan drippings. Keep chicken warm.

3. Place potatoes in a medium saucepan; cover with water. Bring to a boil; cook 15 minutes or until very tender. Drain. Return potatoes to pan; add milk, 1 tablespoon butter, ¼ teaspoon salt, and ¼ teaspoon pepper; mash with a potato masher to desired consistency.

4. Heat reserved pan drippings in a large skillet over medium heat. Add mushrooms to pan; cook 3 minutes or until moisture evaporates, stirring constantly. Stir in broth and wine, scraping pan to loosen browned bits; cook 5 minutes, stirring frequently. Remove from heat; stir in 1 tablespoon butter. Drizzle gravy over chicken; sprinkle with parsley. Serve with potatoes. Yield: 4 servings (serving size: 2 chicken thighs, ¼ cup gravy, 1 tablespoon parsley, and about 1 cup potatoes).

CALORIES 526 (29% from fat); FAT 16.7g (sat 5.9g, mono 6g, poly 2.7g); PROTEIN 41.4g; CARB 44.1g; FIBER 5g; CHOL 160mg; IRON 4.2mg; SODIUM 615mg; CALC 93mg

Mussels with Fine Herbs
Moules-Marinière aux Fines Herbes

Parisians love seafood, and mussels in an herb-infused wine broth are a local favorite.
—David Rostengarten

    1 tablespoon butter, divided
    ¼ cup finely chopped shallots
    1 cup dry white wine
    1 cup water
    2 pounds small mussels, scrubbed
       and debearded
    1 bay leaf
    ¼ cup minced fresh flat-leaf
       parsley
    ¾ teaspoon minced fresh tarragon
    4 (½-ounce) slices French bread,
       toasted

1. Melt 1½ teaspoons butter in a Dutch oven over medium-low heat. Add shallots to pan, and cook 4 minutes or until shallots are tender, stirring frequently. Increase heat to medium-high. Stir in wine, water, mussels, and bay leaf; bring to a boil. Cover, reduce heat, and simmer 3 minutes or until shells open. Remove from heat; discard any unopened shells. Divide mussels evenly among 4 serving bowls. Add 1½ teaspoons butter to wine mixture in pan, stirring until melted. Discard bay leaf. Ladle ½ cup wine mixture over each serving. Sprinkle evenly with parsley and tarragon; serve with French bread. Yield: 4 servings (serving size: about 20 mussels and 1 bread slice).

CALORIES 306 (24% from fat); FAT 8g (sat 2.4g, mono 2.3g, poly 1.5g); PROTEIN 28.7g; CARB 19.2g; FIBER 0.4g; CHOL 71mg; IRON 10mg; SODIUM 767mg; CALC 75mg

Chorizo-Stuffed Poblano Chiles with Sweet-Sour Escabeche

Spicy, tangy, a little sweet, and a tad sour, this dish from Rick Bayless is based on a traditional central Mexican version. You can prepare the different components—roast the chiles and make the potato-chorizo stuffing—a day ahead and refrigerate. Then let everything come to room temperature, and stuff the chiles.

    6   large poblano chiles
    Cooking spray
    ⅓   cup finely chopped
        carrot
    ¾   cup water
    ½   cup cider vinegar
    2   tablespoons brown sugar
    ¼   teaspoon ground allspice
    2   garlic cloves, sliced
    2   bay leaves
    1½ cups sliced onion
    ½   teaspoon salt
    3   cups cubed peeled Yukon gold or
        red potato
    8   ounces chorizo sausage
    Chopped fresh cilantro
        (optional)

1. Preheat broiler.

2. Place chiles on a foil-lined baking sheet. Broil 14 minutes or until blackened, turning twice. Place in a zip-top plastic bag; seal. Let stand 10 minutes; peel.

3. Heat a small saucepan over medium heat. Coat pan with cooking spray. Add carrot to pan; cover and cook 5 minutes or until carrot is crisp-tender, stirring occasionally. Add water and next 5 ingredients to pan; stir well. Bring mixture to a simmer; cook 1 minute or until sugar dissolves, stirring frequently. Discard bay leaves. Combine onion and salt in a large bowl; pour vinegar mixture over onion mixture. Cool completely.

4. Place potato in a saucepan; cover with water. Bring to a boil. Reduce heat. Simmer 10 minutes or until tender; drain.

5. Heat a large nonstick skillet over medium heat. Remove casings from sausage. Cook sausage 10 minutes or until browned, stirring to crumble. Remove sausage from pan, reserving 1 teaspoon drippings in pan. Drain sausage on paper towels. Add potato to pan; cook 15 minutes, browning on all sides. Stir in sausage; cook until mixture is thoroughly heated.

6. Cut a lengthwise slit in each chile; discard stems, seeds, and membranes. Place about ½ cup sausage mixture in each chile (chiles will be full). Place onion mixture on each of 6 plates; top each serving with one stuffed chile. Garnish with cilantro, if desired. Yield: 6 servings (serving size: 1 stuffed chile and about ⅓ cup onion mixture).

CALORIES 270 (32% from fat); FAT 9.6g (sat 3.1g, mono 4.2g, poly 1.4g); PROTEIN 13.5g; CARB 34.1g; FIBER 5.4g; CHOL 27mg; IRON 3.5mg; SODIUM 684mg; CALC 30mg

Tortilla Soup with Dried Chile, Fresh Cheese, and Avocado

Epazote is a pungent wild herb frequently used in Mexican cooking and sold in Latin markets. If you can't find it, substitute two teaspoons chopped fresh cilantro.

—Rick Bayless

  6 (6-inch) corn tortillas
     Cooking spray
1¾ cups vertically sliced onion
  4 garlic cloves, peeled
  2 cups chopped tomato
  2 stemmed dried seeded pasilla (or 1 dried ancho) chiles
  6 cups fat-free, less-sodium chicken broth
  1 teaspoon dried crumbled epazote leaves
 ¾ cup (3 ounces) queso fresco
 ⅓ cup cubed peeled avocado
  1 large lime, cut into 6 wedges

1. Preheat oven to 400°.
2. Cut tortillas into ¼-inch-wide strips. Place strips on a baking sheet. Bake at 400° for 8 minutes or until golden. Set strips aside.
3. Heat a large saucepan over medium-high heat. Coat pan with cooking spray. Add onion and garlic; sauté 7 minutes or until golden. Place onion mixture and tomato in a blender or food processor; process until smooth.
4. Recoat pan with cooking spray. Add chiles, and sauté 60 seconds or until fragrant. Remove chiles; cool completely. Remove and discard stems; chop chiles.
5. Place pan over medium-high heat. Add tomato mixture, and cook 15 minutes or until very thick (consistency will resemble tomato paste), stirring frequently. Add broth and epazote; bring to a boil. Partially cover, reduce heat to medium-low, and cook 30 minutes. Strain mixture through a fine-mesh sieve into a bowl. Discard solids.
6. Ladle soup into bowls. Divide cheese, tortilla strips, and avocado evenly among bowls. Sprinkle each serving with chopped chile. Serve with lime wedges. Yield: 6 servings (serving size: about ¾ cup soup, 2 tablespoons cheese, about 1 tablespoon avocado, ⅓ cup tortilla strips, about 1 teaspoon chile, and 1 lime wedge).

CALORIES 154 (28% from fat); FAT 4.9g (sat 1.2g, mono 2g, poly 0.7g); PROTEIN 7.4g; CARB 22.5g; FIBER 4.2g; CHOL 5mg; IRON 0.9mg; SODIUM 485mg; CALC 72mg

Crescent City Gumbo

Creole gumbos all share one ingredient: okra, which came to America with African slaves (the stew's name stems from *ochingombo*, a Bantu word for okra). This version is inspired by Jessica B. Harris's favorite gumbos served at New Orleans restaurants.

     Cooking spray
  3 tablespoons canola oil, divided
 ½ pound skinless, boneless chicken thighs, cut into bite-size pieces
  1 pound low-fat smoked sausage (such as Healthy Choice) or turkey kielbasa, cut into ½-inch-thick rounds
  2 cups chopped onion
  1 cup chopped green bell pepper
 ½ cup chopped celery
  1 tablespoon minced fresh garlic
  1 teaspoon chopped fresh thyme
 ½ teaspoon ground red pepper
 ⅓ cup all-purpose flour
  5 cups fat-free, less-sodium chicken broth
  1 (14.5-ounce) can no salt-added diced tomatoes, undrained
  3 cups (1-inch) slices fresh okra
  2 bay leaves
 ¼ cup chopped fresh flat-leaf parsley
  1 pound medium shrimp, peeled and deveined
2⅔ cups hot cooked long-grain rice

1. Heat a large Dutch oven over medium-high heat. Coat pan with cooking spray. Add 1 teaspoon oil, chicken, and sausage; sauté 3 minutes or until browned. Remove from pan (reserve drippings in pan). Add onion, bell pepper, and celery to pan; sauté 4 minutes. Add garlic, thyme, and red pepper; sauté 4 minutes or until onion is tender and garlic is fragrant. Remove from pan.

2. Add 8 teaspoons oil to pan. Add flour, stirring constantly with a whisk. Cook 10 minutes or until roux is light brown, stirring constantly with a whisk. Gradually add broth, stirring constantly with a whisk. Add chicken and sausage, onion mixture, tomatoes, okra, and bay leaves; bring to a boil. Cover, reduce heat, and simmer 45 minutes, stirring occasionally.
3. Stir in parsley and shrimp; cook 5 minutes or until shrimp are done. Discard bay leaves. Serve over rice. Yield: 8 servings (serving size: 1¼ cups gumbo and ⅓ cup rice).

CALORIES 353 (24% from fat); FAT 9.4g (sat 1.5g, mono 3.8g, poly 2.3g); PROTEIN 29.4g; CARB 36.3g; FIBER 4g; CHOL 130mg; IRON 4.3mg; SODIUM 863mg; CALC 124mg

QUICK & EASY
New Orleans Okra

Onion, celery, and green bell pepper are used so often in Louisiana that locals call them "the trinity." Here, they're combined with another local staple: okra.

—Jessica B. Harris

  1 tablespoon olive oil
  2 cups chopped onion
 ½ cup minced celery
 ½ cup minced green bell pepper
  1 tablespoon tomato paste
  2 (14.5-ounce) cans diced tomatoes, undrained
 ½ teaspoon ground red pepper
1½ pounds small okra pods, trimmed and cut into ½-inch slices
 ¼ teaspoon salt

1. Heat oil in a Dutch oven over medium-high heat. Add onion, and sauté 5 minutes. Add celery, bell pepper, and tomato paste; cook 2 minutes. Stir in diced tomatoes and red pepper; cook 10 minutes or until sauce thickens. Add okra. Cover, reduce heat, and simmer 20 minutes or until okra is tender. Stir in salt. Yield: 8 servings (serving size: ¾ cup).

CALORIES 101 (16% from fat); FAT 1.9g (sat 0.3g, mono 1.3g, poly 0.2g); PROTEIN 4g; CARB 20.3g; FIBER 5.2g; CHOL 0mg; IRON 1.2mg; SODIUM 499mg; CALC 149mg

Creole Tomato Salad

(pictured on page 147)

Tomatoes are an important ingredient in the Creole cooking of New Orleans. This composed salad is easy to put together yet yields abundant, fresh flavor.

—Jessica B. Harris

SALAD:

- 3 ripe tomatoes, cut into ¼-inch-thick slices (about 2 pounds)
- 1 Vidalia or other sweet onion, thinly sliced and separated into rings
- ¼ teaspoon salt
- 1 tablespoon thinly sliced fresh mint
- 2 teaspoons chopped fresh chives

VINAIGRETTE:

- 4 teaspoons olive oil
- 4 teaspoons red wine vinegar
- 1 teaspoon Dijon mustard
- ½ teaspoon minced fresh garlic

1. To prepare salad, alternate tomato and onion slices on a platter. Sprinkle with salt. Top with mint and chives.
2. To prepare vinaigrette, combine oil, vinegar, mustard, and garlic in a jar. Cover tightly; shake vigorously. Drizzle vinaigrette over salad, and serve at room temperature. Yield: 4 servings.

CALORIES 73 (55% from fat); FAT 4.8g (sat 0.7g, mono 3.4g, poly 0.6g); PROTEIN 1.4g; CARB 7.5g; FIBER 1.5g; CHOL 0mg; IRON 0.6mg; SODIUM 185mg; CALC 13mg

dinner tonight

Fresh From the Sea

Fresh seafood nets a quartet of cool, refreshing salads.

When the weather gets warmer there are two things you'll want to eat more of—seafood and salads. So go ahead and combine the two—you get a fabulous, healthy, fresh-tasting meal that's sure to please any night of the week.

Seafood Menu 1

serves 4

Caribbean Grilled Scallop Salad

Grilled baguette*

Coconut sorbet

*Preheat grill. Cut 1 (8-ounce) French baguette into ½-inch-thick slices. Brush both sides of bread evenly with 2 tablespoons olive oil. Grill both sides of bread 1 minute or until golden.

Game Plan

1. While grill heats:
- Peel, core, and slice pineapple
- Slice baguette; brush with oil
- Season scallops

2. While scallops and pineapple cook:
- Place salad greens and avocado in bowl
- Prepare dressing

Caribbean Grilled Scallop Salad

Boston lettuce is pale green with a mild taste and tender texture. To prep it perfectly, rinse gently, pat dry, and refrigerate in moistened paper towels until ready to assemble salad.

TOTAL TIME: 16 MINUTES

QUICK TIP: Speed up preparation by purchasing peeled and cored pineapple and prewashed salad greens in the produce section.

- 12 large sea scallops (about 1½ pounds)
- 2 teaspoons fish rub, divided (such as Emeril's)
- Cooking spray
- 5 (½-inch) slices fresh pineapple
- 4 cups gourmet salad greens or mixed salad greens
- 4 cups torn Boston lettuce (about 2 small heads)
- ⅓ cup diced peeled avocado
- 2 tablespoons mango chutney
- 2 tablespoons fresh lime juice
- 2 teaspoons olive oil

---

1. Prepare grill.
2. Pat scallops dry with a paper towel. Sprinkle 1½ teaspoons fish rub evenly over scallops. Coat scallops with cooking spray. Place scallops on grill rack; grill 3 minutes on each side or until done. Remove scallops. Add pineapple to grill rack; grill 2 minutes on each side. Remove pineapple from grill; chop pineapple.
3. Combine pineapple, salad greens, lettuce, and avocado in a large bowl.
4. Chop large pieces of mango chutney. Combine ½ teaspoon fish rub, chutney, lime juice, and oil. Add to salad, and toss well. Place 1½ cups salad in each of 4 bowls. Arrange 3 scallops over each salad. Yield: 4 servings.

CALORIES 264 (20% from fat); FAT 5.8g (sat 0.8g, mono 3g, poly 1.1g); PROTEIN 30.8g; CARB 22.8g; FIBER 3.4g; CHOL 56mg; IRON 2.3mg; SODIUM 559mg; CALC 101mg

Shellfish and Bacon Spinach Salad

Gently rinse mussels under cold running water, and discard any opened mussels before you cook them. After cooking, be sure to discard any unopened shells.

TOTAL TIME: 30 MINUTES

QUICK TIP: For a milder taste, soak onion slices in ice water for 30 minutes. Drain, and pat dry. This process works great with bold red onions.

- 2 thick slices applewood-smoked bacon, diced (such as Neuske's)
- 2 garlic cloves, minced
- ¼ cup riesling or other dry white wine
- ⅛ teaspoon crushed red pepper
- 3 pounds mussels, scrubbed and debearded
- ⅓ cup thinly sliced red onion, separated into rings
- 2 (6-ounce) packages prewashed baby spinach

1. Cook bacon in a Dutch oven over medium heat until crisp. Remove bacon from pan, reserving 1 tablespoon drippings in pan. Crumble bacon; set aside.

Continued

2. Add garlic to drippings in pan; cook over medium heat 1 minute. Add wine and crushed red pepper. Add mussels; cover and cook 6 minutes or until shells open. Remove from heat; discard any unopened shells. Place mussels in a bowl. Add onion and spinach to wine mixture in pan; cook 1 minute or until spinach wilts. Divide spinach mixture among 4 plates; sprinkle evenly with bacon. Arrange mussels over spinach mixture; drizzle evenly with any remaining wine mixture. Yield: 4 servings (serving size: about 2 dozen mussels, 2 cups spinach mixture, and 1 tablespoon bacon).

CALORIES 165 (25% from fat); FAT 4.6g (sat 1.5g, mono 0.6g, poly 0.7g); PROTEIN 16.7g; CARB 14.9g; FIBER 4.2g; CHOL 37mg; IRON 7.3mg; SODIUM 586mg; CALC 96mg

Seafood Menu 2
serves 4

Shellfish and Bacon Spinach Salad (recipe on page 141)

Herb and Parmesan breadsticks*

Oatmeal-raisin cookies

*Unroll 1 (11-ounce) can refrigerated breadstick dough; separate into 12 pieces. Combine 3 tablespoons grated Parmesan cheese and 2 teaspoons herbes de Provence on a plate. Coat each piece of dough lightly with cheese mixture. Twist each piece several times, forming a spiral; place on an ungreased baking sheet, pressing down lightly on both ends. Bake at 375° for 13 minutes or until lightly browned. Serve warm.

Game Plan

1. While breadsticks bake:
   - Cook bacon
   - Scrub and debeard mussels
   - Mince garlic
2. While mussels cook:
   - Slice onion

Seafood Menu 3
serves 4

Shrimp and Crab Salad Rolls

Quick corn and potato chowder*

Strawberry sorbet

*Combine 2 cups refrigerated hash brown potatoes with onions and peppers (such as Simply Potatoes), 1½ cups 1% low-fat milk, 1 (14¾-ounce) can cream-style corn, ¾ teaspoon salt, and ¼ teaspoon black pepper in a saucepan. Bring to a boil, stirring occasionally. Reduce heat, and simmer 8 minutes or until thickened, stirring occasionally. Ladle chowder into bowls; top each serving with 1½ teaspoons chopped fresh chives.

Game Plan

1. While chowder cooks:
   - Combine mayonnaise mixture
   - Chop shrimp
2. While buns toast:
   - Combine mayonnaise mixture with shrimp and crabmeat
   - Wash lettuce leaves, and pat dry

QUICK & EASY
Shrimp and Crab Salad Rolls

We loved the kick of the horseradish. For milder flavor, use 1 teaspoon horseradish. If you can't find crabmeat, double the amount of coarsely chopped cooked shrimp.

TOTAL TIME: 40 MINUTES

QUICK TIP: Get a head start by using frozen, thawed, cooked, peeled shrimp, available near the meat department or in the frozen foods aisle of the supermarket.

   3   tablespoons chopped green onions
   3   tablespoons light mayonnaise
   1   tablespoon prepared horseradish
   2   teaspoons Dijon mustard
   ¼   teaspoon hot sauce
   8   ounces coarsely chopped cooked shrimp (about 1½ cups chopped)
   8   ounces lump crabmeat, drained and shell pieces removed
   4   small whole wheat hoagie rolls, split and toasted
   4   small Boston lettuce leaves

1. Combine first 5 ingredients in a large bowl, and stir well. Add shrimp and crabmeat, stirring to combine. Line each hoagie roll with 1 lettuce leaf. Place ⅔ cup shrimp mixture in each bun. Yield: 4 servings.

CALORIES 331 (24% from fat); FAT 8.7g (sat 1.3g, mono 1g, poly 1.9g); PROTEIN 29.7g; CARB 35.6g; FIBER 5.4g; CHOL 172mg; IRON 4.2mg; SODIUM 777mg; CALC 153mg

QUICK & EASY
Grilled Tuna Niçoise Salad

Niçoise olives are smaller than the more familiar green or ripe black olives. If you can't find niçoise, choose kalamata olives (they're available with and without pits).

TOTAL TIME: 20 MINUTES

QUICK TIP: If you buy frozen tuna steaks, thaw them in the refrigerator 1 day ahead. Keep hard-cooked eggs on hand to make this salad any evening

   ¾   pound small red potatoes
   ½   pound green beans, trimmed
   ⅓   cup reduced-fat Italian dressing
   2   teaspoons chopped fresh or ½ teaspoon dried tarragon
   4   (6-ounce) tuna steaks (about ¾ inch thick)
      Cooking spray
   8   cups mixed salad greens
   1   hard-cooked large egg, chopped
  16   niçoise olives
   2   tablespoons capers

1. Prepare grill.
2. Scrub potatoes. Place wet potatoes in an 8-inch square baking dish; cover with wax paper. Microwave at HIGH 3 minutes. Add beans to dish; cover. Microwave at HIGH 3 minutes or until vegetables are tender; drain. Rinse with cold water.
3. While vegetables cook, combine dressing and tarragon. Set aside ¼ cup dressing mixture; brush remaining dressing mixture over fish. Place fish on grill rack coated with cooking spray; grill 3 minutes on each side or until medium-rare (140° to 145°) or desired degree of doneness. (Do not overcook or fish will be tough.)

4. Arrange greens on 4 serving plates. Drain potatoes and green beans; thinly slice potatoes. Arrange potatoes, green beans, egg, and olives over greens. Top each salad with a steak; sprinkle with capers. Drizzle evenly with reserved dressing. Yield: 4 servings (serving size: 1 steak, 2 cups salad greens, 4 olives, and 1½ teaspoons capers).

CALORIES 437 (22% from fat); FAT 10.6g (sat 1.9g, mono 4g, poly 3.5g); PROTEIN 57.3g; CARB 26.1g; FIBER 6.2g; CHOL 152mg; IRON 4.2mg; SODIUM 706mg; CALC 146mg

---

Seafood Menu 4
serves 4

**Grilled Tuna Niçoise
Salad (recipe on page 142)**

Crusty whole wheat rolls

Blueberry-yogurt
sundaes*

*Combine 2 tablespoons blueberry spread (such as Polaner All-Fruit) and 1 tablespoon warm water, stirring until blended. Stir in 2 cups fresh or frozen, thawed, blueberries. Scoop ½ cup vanilla low-fat frozen yogurt into each of 4 serving bowls; top with blueberry sauce. Garnish with mint leaves, if desired.

Game Plan

1. While grill heats:
  • Microwave potatoes and green beans
  • Combine dressing and tarragon
2. While tuna cooks:
  • Slice potatoes
  • Divide vegetables, egg, and olives onto four plates
  • Prepare topping for sundaes

Memorial Day Celebration

This all-American menu is a good way to remember the day with friends.

Memorial Day Menu
serves 4

**Honey-Chipotle
Barbecue Chicken Sandwiches**

**Marinated Tomatoes
with Lemon and Summer Savory**

**Green Bean and New Potato
Salad**

Frozen Iced Tea

Lemonade or beer

Honey-Chipotle Barbecue Chicken Sandwiches

(pictured on page 146)

½ cup water
1 teaspoon ground cumin
4 garlic cloves, thinly sliced
1 pound skinless, boneless chicken breast
1 (7-ounce) can chipotle chiles in adobo sauce
1 tablespoon canola oil
1 tablespoon minced garlic
1 teaspoon ground cumin
½ cup canned tomato purée
¼ cup cider vinegar
3 tablespoons honey
1 tablespoon Worcestershire sauce
¼ teaspoon salt
4 (1½-ounce) sandwich rolls
2 ounces Monterey Jack cheese, thinly sliced
4 (⅛-inch-thick) slices red onion

1. Combine first 4 ingredients in a large saucepan. Cover and bring to a boil over medium-high heat. Reduce heat to medium-low; cook 10 minutes or until chicken is done. Drain and place chicken on a cutting board. Cut chicken across grain into thin slices; keep warm.

2. Remove 2 tablespoons adobo sauce from can; set aside. Remove 2 chipotle chiles from can; finely chop, and set aside. Reserve remaining chiles and adobo sauce for another use.

3. Heat oil in a large nonstick skillet over medium-high heat. Add minced garlic; sauté 3 minutes or until just beginning to brown. Add 1 teaspoon cumin; sauté 1 minute. Stir in tomato purée; cook 4 minutes or until mixture thickens to a pastelike consistency, stirring constantly. Stir in reserved 2 tablespoons adobo sauce, 2 chopped chipotle chiles, vinegar, honey, Worcestershire, and salt. Add chicken to sauce; simmer 3 minutes or until thoroughly heated.

4. Preheat broiler.

5. Split rolls; arrange in a single layer, cut sides up, on a baking sheet. Broil 1 minute or until lightly toasted. Remove top halves of rolls from baking sheet. Divide chicken mixture evenly among bottom halves of rolls, and top chicken mixture evenly with cheese. Broil chicken-topped rolls 2 minutes or until cheese melts. Remove from oven; top with onion and top roll halves. Serve immediately. Yield: 4 sandwiches (serving size: 1 sandwich).

CALORIES 424 (25% from fat); FAT 11.8g (sat 3.9g, mono 4.7g, poly 1.9g); PROTEIN 34.5g; CARB 45.1g; FIBER 2.6g; CHOL 78mg; IRON 3.6mg; SODIUM 765mg; CALC 211mg

---

MAKE AHEAD
Marinated Tomatoes with Lemon and Summer Savory

Summer savory is slightly bitter and has an aroma similar to that of thyme.

3 tomatoes, each cut into 6 wedges (about 1 pound)
¼ cup fresh lemon juice
1 teaspoon sugar
1 teaspoon extravirgin olive oil
½ teaspoon chopped fresh or ¼ teaspoon dried summer savory
¼ teaspoon salt
⅛ teaspoon ground red pepper
1 garlic clove, minced

Continued

1. Place tomato in a medium bowl.

2. Combine lemon juice and remaining 6 ingredients, stirring with a whisk. Pour dressing over tomatoes; toss gently to coat. Let stand 1 hour, stirring occasionally. Serve with a slotted spoon. Yield: 4 servings (serving size: ½ cup).

CALORIES 40 (32% from fat); FAT 1.4g (sat 0.2g, mono 0.9g, poly 0.3g); PROTEIN 1.1g; CARB 7.1g; FIBER 1.5g; CHOL 0mg; IRON 0.4mg; SODIUM 153mg; CALC 16mg

MAKE AHEAD

Green Bean and New Potato Salad

(pictured on page 146)

Cook the potatoes and green beans in the same pot of simmering water. The beans take less time, so add them to the pot after the cooked potatoes are scooped out.

1½ pounds small red potatoes
  2 cups (1-inch) cut green beans (about ¾ pound)
  ⅔ cup low-fat mayonnaise
  2 tablespoons whole-grain Dijon mustard
  2 tablespoons rice vinegar
  1 tablespoon fresh lime juice
  1 teaspoon honey
  ⅛ teaspoon freshly ground black pepper
Dash of salt
  1 garlic clove, minced
  ½ cup finely chopped red onion
  ¼ cup chopped fresh basil

1. Place potatoes in a large saucepan; cover with water. Bring to a boil. Reduce heat; simmer 20 minutes or until tender. Remove potatoes with a slotted spoon; place on a cutting board. Cool to room temperature. Add beans to simmering cooking water; cook 3 minutes or until crisp-tender. Drain; cool slightly. Cut potatoes into quarters.

2. Combine mayonnaise and next 7 ingredients in a large bowl, stirring with a whisk. Add potatoes, beans, onion, and basil; toss gently to combine. Yield: 4 servings (serving size: about 1¼ cups).

CALORIES 232 (14% from fat); FAT 3.6g (sat 0.6g, mono 1g, poly 1.7g); PROTEIN 4.7g; CARB 46.1g; FIBER 5.4g; CHOL 0mg; IRON 1.9mg; SODIUM 610mg; CALC 65mg

MAKE AHEAD • FREEZABLE

Frozen Iced Tea

This refreshing, simple dessert is a delicious twist on a summer standby, and it's great to have on hand for hot afternoons. For a frozen mint iced tea, add several fresh mint sprigs with the lemon juice and sugar mixture; discard mint before freezing.

  3 family-size tea bags
  6 cups boiling water
  1 cup sugar
  ½ cup water
  2 tablespoons light-colored corn syrup
  6 tablespoons fresh lemon juice
Lemon slices (optional)
Mint sprigs (optional)

1. Place tea bags in a large bowl. Pour boiling water over tea bags; steep 10 minutes. Remove and discard tea bags.

2. Combine sugar, ½ cup water, and light-colored syrup in a saucepan; bring to a boil over medium-high heat. Remove from heat; let stand 5 minutes. Add sugar mixture and lemon juice to tea; stir to combine. Cool to room temperature. Pour cooled tea mixture into a 13 x 9-inch baking dish; cover and freeze at least 6 hours or until firm. Remove tea mixture from freezer; scrape entire mixture with a fork until fluffy. Spoon into a container; cover and freeze up to 1 month. Garnish with lemon slices and mint sprigs, if desired. Yield: 8 servings (serving size: 1 cup).

CALORIES 115 (0% from fat); FAT 0g; PROTEIN 0g; CARB 30.1g; FIBER 0.1g; CHOL 0mg; IRON 0mg; SODIUM 10mg; CALC 5mg

lighten up

Cookies with Merit

With help from Cooking Light, *Girl Scouts earn their "Let's Get Cooking" badges.*

MAKE AHEAD

Chocolate Malted Cookies

  1 cup packed brown sugar
  6 tablespoons malted milk powder (such as Carnation)
  5 tablespoons butter, softened
  3 tablespoons chocolate syrup
  1 tablespoon vanilla extract
  1 large egg
  2 cups all-purpose flour
  1 teaspoon baking soda
  ½ teaspoon salt
  ½ cup milk chocolate chips
  ⅓ cup semisweet chocolate minichips

1. Preheat oven to 350°.

2. Combine first 6 ingredients in a large bowl; beat with a mixer at medium speed 2 minutes or until light and fluffy. Lightly spoon flour into dry measuring cups; level with a knife. Combine flour, baking soda, and salt in a medium bowl; stir with a whisk. Gradually add flour mixture to sugar mixture, beating at low speed until well blended. Stir in chocolate chips and minichips.

3. Drop dough by heaping teaspoonfuls 2 inches apart onto baking sheets. Bake at 350° for 10 minutes. Cool on pans 2 minutes or until firm. Remove cookies from pans; cool on wire racks. Yield: 2½ dozen cookies (serving size: 1 cookie).

CALORIES 125 (28% from fat); FAT 3.9g (sat 2g, mono 1.5g, poly 0.2g); PROTEIN 1.9g; CARB 20.8g; FIBER 0.5g; CHOL 14mg; IRON 0.7mg; SODIUM 124mg; CALC 28mg

BEFORE	AFTER
SERVING SIZE	
1 cookie	
CALORIES PER SERVING	
227	125
FAT	
11.8g	3.9g
PERCENT OF TOTAL CALORIES	
47%	28%

Yellow Sheet Cake with Chocolate Frosting,
page 125

Honey-Chipotle Barbecue Chicken Sandwiches, page 143, with Green Bean and New Potato Salad, page 144

Cornmeal-Crusted Scallops with Mint Chimichurri, page 133

Snow Peas with Ginger, page 138

Creole Tomato Salad, page 141

Bistro Bouillabaisse, facing page

Beachside Celebration

A Gulf Coast setting inspired Chef Sean Murphy to create a romantic dinner for two.

Even if you don't have a sandy beach nearby, the aroma and flavors of this island-inspired menu—redolent of seafood and citrus—will transport you to a sunny, breezy place. So plan now to prepare this extraordinary meal and celebrate with someone special.

Romantic Island Dinner Menu
serves 2

Crab Cocktail with Parmesan Chips

Bistro Bouillabaisse or **"Floribbean" Grouper with Red Pepper-Papaya Jam**

Baby Spinach Salad with Warm Citrus-Bacon Vinaigrette

Baguette with Homemade Aïoli

Berry-Filled Cinnamon Crepes

MAKE AHEAD

Crab Cocktail with Parmesan Chips

Once cooled, rounds of melted Parmesan cheese crisp like potato chips. You can prepare the crab mixture and salsa a couple of hours before serving; refrigerate until you're ready to assemble the cocktails.

CRAB MIXTURE:

- 1 tablespoon minced shallots
- 2 teaspoons red wine vinegar
- 1 teaspoon sugar
- 1 teaspoon chopped fresh basil
- 1 teaspoon chopped fresh tarragon
- 1 teaspoon fresh lemon juice
- 1 teaspoon Dijon mustard
- ½ teaspoon Worcestershire sauce
- ½ teaspoon olive oil
- ¼ teaspoon hot pepper sauce
- ⅛ teaspoon salt
- ⅛ teaspoon freshly ground black pepper
- 1 garlic clove, minced
- 4 ounces lump crabmeat, shell pieces removed

SALSA:

- 2 tablespoons finely chopped fresh pineapple
- 2 tablespoons finely chopped peeled mango
- 1 tablespoon finely chopped red bell pepper
- 1 teaspoon minced fresh chives

CHIPS:

- 2 tablespoons grated fresh Parmesan cheese

1. To prepare crab mixture, combine first 13 ingredients in a medium bowl, stirring well with a whisk. Add crabmeat; toss gently to coat. Cover and chill.
2. To prepare salsa, combine pineapple, mango, bell pepper, and chives; cover and chill.
3. Preheat oven to 350°.
4. To prepare chips, spread 1 tablespoon cheese into each of 2 (3-inch) circles on a baking sheet, leaving at least 2 inches between circles. Bake at 350° for 8 minutes or until cheese begins to brown. Remove pan from oven; carefully lift chips from pan with a spatula, and place on a wire rack. Cool completely.
5. Spoon ½ cup crab mixture into each of 2 martini glasses or small bowls; top each serving with 2 tablespoons salsa and 1 chip. Serve immediately. Yield: 2 servings.

CALORIES 128 (30% from fat); FAT 4.3g (sat 1.5g, mono 1.6g, poly 0.6g); PROTEIN 14.6g; CARB 7.9g; FIBER 0.6g; CHOL 62mg; IRON 1mg; SODIUM 501mg; CALC 159mg

Bistro Bouillabaisse
(pictured on page 148)

- 1 tablespoon olive oil
- ½ cup vertically sliced onion
- ¼ cup julienne-cut leek
- ¼ cup thinly sliced celery
- 1 garlic clove, minced
- ¾ cup diced plum tomato
- ½ teaspoon fennel seeds
- ¼ teaspoon dried thyme
- ⅛ teaspoon dried tarragon
- Dash of crushed saffron threads
- ½ cup dry white wine
- 1 tablespoon Pernod or sambuca (licorice-flavored liqueur)
- 1 cup bottled clam juice
- ½ cup tomato juice
- ⅛ teaspoon freshly ground black pepper
- 8 littleneck clams
- 4 ounces grouper or other firm white fish fillet, cut into 1-inch pieces
- 6 medium mussels, scrubbed and debearded
- 6 large shrimp, peeled and deveined
- 1 (5-ounce) lobster tail, split in half lengthwise
- 2 tablespoons chopped fresh flat-leaf parsley

1. Heat oil in a large saucepan over medium heat. Add onion and next 3 ingredients; cook 5 minutes, stirring frequently. Add tomato and next 4 ingredients; cook 1 minute. Stir in wine and liqueur; bring to a boil. Reduce heat, and simmer 5 minutes. Add juices and pepper; bring to a simmer. Cook 10 minutes. Add clams and grouper; cook over medium heat 3 minutes or until clams begin to open. Add mussels, shrimp, and lobster; cook 4 minutes or until mussels open. Discard any unopened clams or mussels. Garnish with parsley. Yield: 2 servings (serving size: 2 cups).

CALORIES 399 (27% from fat); FAT 11.9g (sat 2.2g, mono 6g, poly 1.8g); PROTEIN 50.2g; CARB 18.1g; FIBER 2.4g; CHOL 203mg; IRON 9.8mg; SODIUM 977mg; CALC 171mg

WINE NOTE: A still rosé would be fine, but why not heighten the pleasure (and romance) and serve a California sparkling rosé? Gloria Ferrer's nonvintage Brut Rosé is smashing at $35.

STAFF FAVORITE
"Floribbean" Grouper with Red Pepper-Papaya Jam

Flavors and ingredients from Florida and the Caribbean converge in this impressive entrée. The delicate spicy sweetness of the jam balances the fish's crisp coating of coconut and cashews.

JAM:

1 cup chopped red bell pepper
¾ cup diced peeled papaya
½ teaspoon chopped jalapeño pepper
¼ cup water
3 tablespoons red wine vinegar
2 tablespoons sugar
Dash of salt
½ teaspoon fresh lime juice

GROUPER:

¼ cup panko (Japanese breadcrumbs)
2 tablespoons flaked sweetened coconut
1½ tablespoons chopped dry-roasted cashews
2 tablespoons all-purpose flour
2 large egg whites, lightly beaten
2 (6-ounce) grouper fillets
⅛ teaspoon salt
⅛ teaspoon freshly ground black pepper
2 teaspoons butter
Lime wedges (optional)

1. To prepare jam, combine first 3 ingredients in a food processor; process until smooth.

2. Combine water, vinegar, sugar, and dash of salt in a small saucepan over medium-high heat. Cook until sugar dissolves, stirring frequently. Reduce heat to medium. Add puréed pepper mixture; cook 7 minutes or until thickened and reduced to ½ cup, stirring frequently. Remove from heat; stir in lime juice. Cool.

3. Preheat oven to 350°.

4. To prepare grouper, place panko, coconut, and cashews in food processor; pulse 4 times or until cashews are finely chopped. Place panko mixture in a shallow dish. Place flour in another shallow dish; place egg whites in another shallow dish. Sprinkle fillets with ⅛ teaspoon salt and black pepper. Dredge 1 fillet in flour. Dip fillet into egg whites; dredge in panko mixture, gently pressing coating onto fillet to adhere. Repeat procedure with remaining fillet, flour, egg whites, and panko mixture.

5. Melt butter in a large nonstick ovenproof skillet over medium-high heat. Add fillets; cook 2 minutes or until lightly browned on bottom. Turn fillets over; wrap handle of pan with foil. Place pan in oven; bake at 350° for 8 minutes or until fish flakes easily when tested with a fork. Serve immediately with jam and lime wedges, if desired. Yield: 2 servings (serving size: 1 fillet and ¼ cup jam).

CALORIES 411 (23% from fat); FAT 10.6g (sat 4.3g, mono 3.8g, poly 1.4g); PROTEIN 40.5g; CARB 38.5g; FIBER 1.8g; CHOL 73mg; IRON 3mg; SODIUM 466mg; CALC 75mg

Baby Spinach Salad with Warm Citrus-Bacon Vinaigrette

VINAIGRETTE:

2 bacon slices
⅓ cup fresh orange juice
2 tablespoons brandy
1½ tablespoons red wine vinegar
1 teaspoon honey
⅛ teaspoon salt
⅛ teaspoon freshly ground black pepper

SALAD:

1 tablespoon water
¼ teaspoon fresh lemon juice
½ Granny Smith apple, thinly sliced
4 cups bagged prewashed baby spinach
½ cup thinly vertically sliced red onion
¼ cup chopped peeled mango
1 tablespoon chopped walnuts, toasted
12 fresh raspberries
Cracked black pepper (optional)

1. To prepare vinaigrette, cook bacon in a medium nonstick skillet over medium heat until crisp. Remove bacon from pan; crumble. Discard drippings. Add orange juice, brandy, vinegar, and honey to pan; cook over medium-low heat 5 minutes or until reduced to about 2 tablespoons. Stir in bacon, salt, and ⅛ teaspoon pepper.

2. To prepare salad, combine water and lemon juice in a medium bowl. Add apple; toss to coat. Remove apple from bowl with a slotted spoon; place in a large bowl. Add spinach, onion, and mango. Drizzle with vinaigrette, and toss gently to coat. Arrange about 2¼ cups salad on each of 2 plates; top each serving with 1½ teaspoons walnuts and 6 raspberries. Sprinkle with cracked black pepper, if desired. Serve immediately. Yield: 2 servings.

CALORIES 170 (30% from fat); FAT 5.6g (sat 1.2g, mono 1.6g, poly 2.2g); PROTEIN 5.6g; CARB 22.2g; FIBER 3.9g; CHOL 7mg; IRON 2.3mg; SODIUM 345mg; CALC 83mg

MAKE AHEAD
Baguette with Homemade Aïoli

This garlic-flavored mayonnaise contains an uncooked egg yolk, so it's important to use a pasteurized egg, which comes in a carton alongside other eggs in the supermarket. This recipe makes enough aïoli for leftovers, which will keep for three to four days in the refrigerator.

1 tablespoon Dijon mustard
1½ teaspoons fresh lemon
   juice
½ teaspoon minced fresh garlic
⅛ teaspoon salt
⅛ teaspoon freshly ground black
   pepper
1 large pasteurized egg yolk
¼ cup olive oil
1 pound French bread baguette,
   thinly sliced

1. Combine first 6 ingredients in a food processor, and process until well blended. With food processor on, slowly pour oil through food chute; process until smooth. Serve aïoli with baguette. Yield: 16 servings (serving size: about 1 teaspoon aïoli and 1 ounce bread).

CALORIES 112 (37% from fat); FAT 4.6g (sat 0.7g, mono 3g, poly 0.6g); PROTEIN 2.7g; CARB 14.9g; FIBER 0.9g; CHOL 13mg; IRON 0.8mg; SODIUM 215mg; CALC 24mg

Any of your favorite fresh fruits will look and taste great in the elegant berry-filled crepes.

Berry-Filled Cinnamon Crepes

Use any fresh fruit to stuff these lightly spiced crepes—a combination of pineapple, mango, and strawberries, for example. As the fruit filling cooks, be sure to stir gently so the delicate berries don't break apart. Start the crepe batter first, as the batter needs to chill for one hour; this relaxes the gluten in the flour so the crepes will be tender. Stack leftover cooked and cooled crepes between wax paper or paper towels to prevent sticking, place in a large zip-top plastic bag, and refrigerate up to five days, or freeze up to one month.

FILLING:
¼ cup fresh raspberries
¼ cup fresh blueberries
¼ cup fresh blackberries
¼ cup quartered small strawberries
1 tablespoon granulated
   sugar
1 banana, cut into ½-inch
   slices
2 Cinnamon Crepes
Powdered sugar (optional)

1. Combine first 6 ingredients in a saucepan over medium-low heat. Cook 4 minutes or until thoroughly heated, stirring occasionally.
2. Place 1 Cinnamon Crepe on each of 2 plates; spoon about ½ cup fruit mixture in center of each crepe. Fold bottom edge of crepe (closest to you) over fruit; fold in both sides of crepe over fruit. Arrange, seam sides up, on plates. Sprinkle with powdered sugar, if desired. Yield: 2 servings (serving size: 1 filled crepe).

(Totals include Cinnamon Crepes) CALORIES 232 (16% from fat); FAT 4.2g (sat 2.1g, mono 1.3g, poly 0.4g); PROTEIN 5g; CARB 44.9g; FIBER 4.2g; CHOL 65mg; IRON 1.4mg; SODIUM 51mg; CALC 61mg

MAKE AHEAD • FREEZABLE
CINNAMON CREPES:
¾ cup all-purpose flour
¾ cup half-and-half
¼ cup whole milk
¼ cup granulated sugar
½ teaspoon ground cinnamon
¼ teaspoon vanilla extract
Dash of salt
2 large eggs
Cooking spray

1. Lightly spoon flour into a dry measuring cup; level with a knife. Place flour and next 7 ingredients in a food processor, and process until smooth. Pour batter into a bowl; cover and chill at least 1 hour or up to 12 hours.
2. Heat an 8-inch crepe pan or medium nonstick skillet over medium-high heat. Coat pan with cooking spray; remove pan from heat. Pour a scant ¼ cup batter into pan; quickly tilt pan in all directions so batter covers pan with a thin film. Cook 1 minute or until surface of crepe begins to look dry.

3. Carefully lift edge of crepe with a spatula to test for doneness. Turn crepe over when it can be shaken loose from pan and underside is lightly browned; cook crepe 20 seconds on other side.
4. Place crepe on a towel, and cool. Repeat procedure until all of batter is used. Stack crepes between single layers of wax paper or paper towels to prevent them from sticking. Yield: 8 crepes (serving size: 1 crepe).

CALORIES 121 (29% from fat); FAT 3.9g (sat 2.1g, mono 1.3g, poly 0.2g); PROTEIN 3.8g; CARB 16.5g; FIBER 0.4g; CHOL 65mg; IRON 0.8mg; SODIUM 51mg; CALC 48mg

superfast

. . . And Ready in Just About 20 Minutes

More than a week's worth of quick entrées gets you in and out of the kitchen in a flash.

QUICK & EASY
Gingered Scallops

For tender, moist scallops, keep a close eye on their cooking time. Serve with steamed green beans.

1 (3½-ounce) bag boil-in-bag
   long-grain rice
2 tablespoons canola oil
1½ pounds large sea scallops
¼ teaspoon salt
⅛ teaspoon black pepper
2 tablespoons finely chopped green
   onions
2 tablespoons fresh lemon juice
1 tablespoon bottled minced ginger
1 tablespoon honey
2 teaspoons low-sodium soy sauce

1. Prepare rice according to package microwave directions; set aside.
2. While rice cooks, heat oil in a large skillet over high heat. Pat scallops dry

Continued

with a paper towel; sprinkle with salt and pepper. Place scallops in pan; cook 2 minutes on each side or until lightly browned. Remove scallops from pan.

3. Add onions and remaining 4 ingredients to pan. Add scallops; toss well. Serve with rice. Yield: 4 servings (serving size: about 5 scallops and ½ cup rice).

CALORIES 326 (24% from fat); FAT 8.5g (sat 0.7g, mono 4.2g, poly 2.6g); PROTEIN 30.4g; CARB 30.1g; FIBER 0.7g; CHOL 56mg; IRON 1.5mg; SODIUM 510mg; CALC 58mg

Jamaican Chicken Thighs

Reasonably priced chicken thighs make a Caribbean-accented meal when seasoned with classic island spices and sautéed. Serve alongside peaches tossed with lime juice or fresh pineapple with cilantro.

- 2 teaspoons garlic powder
- 1 teaspoon onion powder
- ½ teaspoon ground ginger
- ½ teaspoon dried thyme
- ½ teaspoon ground allspice
- ¼ teaspoon salt
- ¼ teaspoon ground nutmeg
- ¼ teaspoon ground red pepper
- ⅛ teaspoon freshly ground black pepper
- 8 skinless, boneless chicken thighs
- Cooking spray

1. Combine first 9 ingredients in a small bowl. Rub spice mixture evenly over chicken. Heat a large nonstick skillet over medium-high heat. Coat pan with cooking spray. Add chicken, and cook 5 minutes on each side or until done. Yield: 4 servings (serving size: 2 thighs).

CALORIES 175 (29% from fat); FAT 5.5g (sat 1.4g, mono 1.7g, poly 1.4g); PROTEIN 27.5g; CARB 2.2g; FIBER 0.6g; CHOL 115mg; IRON 1.7mg; SODIUM 265mg; CALC 22mg

Chicken Strips with Blue Cheese Dressing

Pair this fiery entrée with cool, crunchy carrot and celery sticks.

CHICKEN:

- ½ cup low-fat buttermilk
- ½ teaspoon hot sauce
- ½ cup all-purpose flour
- ½ teaspoon paprika
- ½ teaspoon ground red pepper
- ½ teaspoon freshly ground black pepper
- ¼ teaspoon salt
- 1 pound chicken breast tenders
- 1 tablespoon canola oil

DRESSING:

- ½ cup fat-free mayonnaise
- ¼ cup (1 ounce) crumbled blue cheese
- 1 tablespoon red wine vinegar
- 1 teaspoon bottled minced garlic
- ¼ teaspoon salt
- ¼ teaspoon freshly ground black pepper

1. To prepare chicken, combine buttermilk and hot sauce in a shallow dish. Combine flour and next 4 ingredients in a shallow dish. Dip chicken in buttermilk mixture, and dredge chicken in flour mixture.

2. Heat oil in a large nonstick skillet over medium-high heat. Add chicken; cook 4 minutes on each side or until done. Remove from pan. Set aside, and keep warm.

3. While chicken cooks, prepare dressing. Combine mayonnaise and remaining 5 ingredients in a small bowl. Serve with chicken strips. Yield: 4 servings (serving size: about 3 chicken tenders and 2 tablespoons dressing).

CALORIES 281 (28% from fat); FAT 8.7g (sat 2.6g, mono 3.2g, poly 1.5g); PROTEIN 30.8g; CARB 18.4g; FIBER 1.3g; CHOL 77mg; IRON 1.9mg; SODIUM 771mg; CALC 101mg

Mediterranean Tuna Sandwiches

- 4 teaspoons olive oil
- 4 teaspoons red wine vinegar
- 8 slices whole-grain bread
- 2 (6-ounce) cans low-sodium tuna in water, drained and flaked
- ⅓ cup roughly chopped drained oil-packed sun-dried tomato halves
- ¼ cup sliced ripe olives
- ¼ cup finely chopped red onion
- 3 tablespoons low-fat mayonnaise
- 2 teaspoons capers
- ¼ teaspoon freshly ground black pepper
- 4 romaine lettuce leaves

1. Combine oil and vinegar in a small bowl; brush oil mixture evenly over 1 side of each bread slice.

2. Combine tuna and next 6 ingredients. Place 1 lettuce leaf on each of 4 bread slices. Top lettuce evenly with tuna mixture, and cover with remaining bread slices. Serve immediately. Yield: 4 servings (serving size: 1 sandwich).

CALORIES 293 (31% from fat); FAT 10g (sat 1.5g, mono 5.7g, poly 1.4g); PROTEIN 21.2g; CARB 31.3g; FIBER 4.6g; CHOL 18mg; IRON 3.5mg; SODIUM 530mg; CALC 73mg

Sweet Orange Salmon

Eight ingredients combine in a spice rub that would also be good on pork tenderloin medallions. Serve with orange wedges.

- 2 tablespoons brown sugar
- 1 teaspoon chili powder
- ½ teaspoon grated orange rind
- ½ teaspoon ground cumin
- ½ teaspoon paprika
- ¼ teaspoon salt
- ¼ teaspoon ground coriander
- ⅛ teaspoon black pepper
- 4 (6-ounce) salmon fillets
- Cooking spray

1. Preheat broiler.

2. Combine first 8 ingredients in a small bowl. Rub spice mixture over both sides of salmon fillets. Place salmon on a broiler pan coated with cooking spray. Broil 8 minutes or until salmon flakes easily when tested with a fork. Yield: 4 servings (serving size: 1 fillet).

CALORIES 303 (39% from fat); FAT 13.3g (sat 3.1g, mono 5.7g, poly 3.2g); PROTEIN 36.2g; CARB 7.5g; FIBER 0.5g; CHOL 87mg; IRON 1mg; SODIUM 235mg; CALC 33mg

QUICK & EASY
Orecchiette with Cannellini Beans and Spinach

Orecchiette, an ear-shaped pasta, holds all the delicious ingredients in its curves. Small pasta shells may be substituted.

    1   (12-ounce) package orecchiette pasta ("little ears" pasta)
    2   teaspoons olive oil
    ¾   cup prechopped onion
    ½   cup preshredded carrot
    2   teaspoons bottled minced garlic
    1   cup fat-free, less-sodium chicken broth
    2   tablespoons preshredded fresh Parmesan cheese
    2   teaspoons dried basil
    1   (28-ounce) can plum tomatoes, undrained and chopped
    1   (16-ounce) can cannellini beans, rinsed and drained
    1   (6-ounce) package fresh baby spinach
    ¼   cup seasoned breadcrumbs
    2   tablespoons preshredded fresh Parmesan cheese

1. Cook pasta according to package directions, omitting salt and fat; drain.
2. Heat oil in a large skillet over medium heat. Stir in onion, carrot, and garlic; sauté 3 minutes. Stir in broth and next 4 ingredients; simmer 5 minutes. Stir in spinach, and cook 1 minute or until spinach is wilted. Stir in pasta; cook until thoroughly heated. Place pasta mixture on each of 6 plates. Sprinkle with breadcrumbs and cheese. Yield: 6 servings (serving size: about 1½ cups pasta, 1 teaspoon cheese, and 2 teaspoons breadcrumbs).

CALORIES 393 (9% from fat); FAT 4g (sat 1g, mono 1.6g, poly 0.7g); PROTEIN 17.9g; CARB 70.1g; FIBER 8g; CHOL 2mg; IRON 6.6mg; SODIUM 495mg; CALC 183mg

QUICK & EASY
Spicy Filet Mignon with Grilled Sweet Onion

If you can't find sweet onions such as Vidalia, white or yellow onions will work fine, too. Serve with a tossed green salad.

        Cooking spray
    2   cups vertically sliced Vidalia or other sweet onion
    ⅛   teaspoon salt
    ⅛   teaspoon black pepper
    1   teaspoon garlic powder
    ½   teaspoon ground cumin
    ½   teaspoon dried oregano
    ¼   teaspoon salt
    ¼   teaspoon ground red pepper
    ¼   teaspoon black pepper
    4   (4-ounce) beef tenderloin steaks

1. Heat a grill pan over medium-high heat. Coat pan with cooking spray. Add onion; sprinkle with ⅛ teaspoon salt and ⅛ teaspoon black pepper. Cook 8 minutes or until browned, stirring occasionally. Remove from pan; keep warm.
2. Combine garlic powder and next 5 ingredients in a small bowl. Sprinkle garlic mixture over both sides of beef. Add beef to pan. Grill 5 minutes on each side or until desired degree of doneness. Serve with onion mixture. Yield: 4 servings (serving size: 1 filet and ¼ cup onion mixture).

CALORIES 313 (63% from fat); FAT 22g (sat 8.7g, mono 9.2g, poly 0.9g); PROTEIN 21g; CARB 6.7g; FIBER 1.1g; CHOL 74mg; IRON 3mg; SODIUM 269mg; CALC 27mg

QUICK & EASY
Italian Chicken Salad

Leftover or rotisserie chicken from the deli speeds this fresh dish to the table.

DRESSING:
    1   tablespoon olive oil
    1   tablespoon fresh lemon juice
    1   tablespoon red wine vinegar
    ½   teaspoon bottled minced garlic
    ½   teaspoon sugar
    ¼   teaspoon freshly ground black pepper
    ⅛   teaspoon salt

SALAD:
    3   cups cubed cooked chicken breast
    1   cup finely chopped red bell pepper
    2   tablespoons finely chopped fresh parsley
    1   teaspoon dried oregano
    ½   teaspoon dried basil
    10 pitted ripe olives, halved
    1   (14-ounce) can quartered artichoke hearts, drained

1. To prepare dressing, combine first 7 ingredients in a medium bowl, stirring with a whisk.
2. To prepare salad, combine chicken and remaining 6 ingredients in a large bowl. Pour dressing over salad, and toss gently to combine. Yield: 4 servings (serving size: 1¼ cups).

CALORIES 262 (32% from fat); FAT 9.4g (sat 1.5g, mono 3.8g, poly 1.2g); PROTEIN 34.6g; CARB 8.3g; FIBER 1.1g; CHOL 89mg; IRON 2.5mg; SODIUM 395mg; CALC 31mg

QUICK & EASY
Spiced Grilled Chicken Breasts with Corn-Pepper Relish

Substitute an equal amount of chopped fresh cilantro for the minced parsley in the relish, if desired.

    1   teaspoon chili powder
    ½   teaspoon salt
    ½   teaspoon ground cumin
    ¼   teaspoon paprika
    ⅛   teaspoon ground red pepper
    ⅛   teaspoon black pepper
    4   (6-ounce) skinless, boneless chicken breast halves
    1   tablespoon canola oil
    2   cups frozen whole-kernel corn, thawed
    1   cup diced red bell pepper
    3   tablespoons prechopped onion
    2   tablespoons minced fresh parsley
    2   tablespoons fresh lime juice
        Dash of black pepper

1. Combine first 6 ingredients in a small bowl. Rub spice mixture over both sides of chicken breasts.

Continued

2. Heat oil in a grill pan over medium-high heat. Add chicken; cook 5 minutes on each side or until done.

3. While chicken cooks, combine corn and remaining 5 ingredients in a bowl. Serve with chicken. Yield: 4 servings (serving size: 1 chicken breast and ½ cup relish).

CALORIES 333 (24% from fat); FAT 9g (sat 1.7g, mono 3.9g, poly 2.5g); PROTEIN 42.7g; CARB 21.5g; FIBER 3.3g; CHOL 108mg; IRON 2.2mg; SODIUM 397mg; CALC 35mg

QUICK & EASY
Scallop and Tomato Sauté

Serve this quick sauté over angel hair pasta with a green salad and crusty bread.

    2   teaspoons olive oil
 1 ½   pounds large sea scallops
    2   teaspoons bottled minced garlic
    1   (28-ounce) can whole tomatoes, undrained
  ⅓   cup dry white wine
  ⅓   cup chopped fresh parsley
    1   tablespoon balsamic vinegar
    2   teaspoons fresh lemon juice
    1   teaspoon capers
  ½   teaspoon crushed red pepper
  ¼   teaspoon salt
  ¼   teaspoon freshly ground black pepper
    2   tablespoons preshredded fresh Parmesan cheese

1. Heat oil in a large nonstick skillet over medium-high heat. Add scallops to pan, and cook 2 minutes on each side. Remove scallops from pan; keep warm.
2. Add garlic to pan; cook 1 minute or until lightly browned. Drain and discard ½ cup liquid from tomatoes. Add tomatoes and remaining liquid to pan, crushing tomatoes slightly with a spoon; cook 2 minutes. Add wine and next 7 ingredients; bring to a boil. Reduce heat, and simmer 4 minutes.
3. Add scallops to pan; cook 1 minute or until thoroughly heated. Sprinkle with cheese. Yield: 4 servings (serving size: about 5 scallops, about ½ cup sauce, and 1 ½ teaspoons cheese).

CALORIES 237 (17% from fat); FAT 4.6g (sat 0.9g, mono 2g, poly 0.8g); PROTEIN 31.4g; CARB 14.3g; FIBER 2.1g; CHOL 58mg; IRON 3mg; SODIUM 742mg; CALC 147mg

QUICK & EASY
Mango and Shrimp Salad

Look for bottled mango in the refrigerated food section of the produce department. Roasted bottled bell pepper is usually in the condiment aisle near the olives.

    2   cups water
    5   tablespoons lemon juice, divided
  ¼   teaspoon salt
  ¼   teaspoon crushed red pepper flakes
    1   bay leaf
    1   pound peeled and deveined shrimp
    1   to 2 tablespoons chili sauce
    1   tablespoon sesame oil
    1   cup halved grape tomatoes
    1   cup bottled chopped mango
  ½   cup sliced bottled red bell pepper
    8   Bibb lettuce leaves

1. Combine water, 1 tablespoon juice, salt, red pepper flakes, and bay leaf in a large saucepan; bring to a boil. Add shrimp. Cover, reduce heat, and simmer 3 minutes or until shrimp are done. Drain shrimp, and discard bay leaf. Set shrimp aside.
2. Combine ¼ cup juice, chili sauce, and oil in a large bowl; stir with a whisk. Gently stir in shrimp, tomatoes, mango, and bell pepper. Line 4 plates with lettuce leaves. Place salad on lettuce. Yield: 4 servings (serving size: 1 cup salad and 2 lettuce leaves).

CALORIES 168 (25% from fat); FAT 4.6g (sat 0.8g, mono 1.6g, poly 1.9g); PROTEIN 18.7g; CARB 13.6g; FIBER 1.6g; CHOL 166mg; IRON 3.1mg; SODIUM 472mg; CALC 46mg

technique

Asian Steaming

Use this ancient cooking method to quickly prepare delicious appetizers, entrées, and even desserts.

Asian cuisine's emphasis on fresh ingredients and natural flavors is the key to its success with steamed dishes. No other cooking method can acheive what can be done with steam.

Steamer Setup

There are many types of steamers on the market, including steamer inserts for standard cookware and electric countertop steamers. Even if you don't own a steamer, you can concoct a makeshift option that will do the trick. We tested several of the recipes using the following method, which works especially well for foods that are steamed with sauce.

1. You will need a small metal vegetable steamer, a pie plate, and a wok with a lid.
2. Open the steamer, and place it upside down in the bottom of the wok. (If you have a nonstick wok, place the steamer on a small, heatproof plate or folded cloth napkin to keep the metal from scratching the bottom.)

3. Fill the wok with 4 cups of water, and bring to a boil.
4. Wearing oven mitts, carefully place a pie plate containing food over the steamer.
5. Cover and steam the food.
6. Wearing oven mitts, carefully remove the pie plate from the wok; be sure to keep your hands covered to help prevent burns.

Eight-Treasure Rice Pudding

The name of this Chinese dessert comes from the tradition of decorating it with eight kinds of fruit, nuts, or candy. Glutinous rice, also called sweet rice, has rounded grains and a moist, sticky texture when cooked; look for it in large supermarkets or Asian groceries. You can make almond butter at home: Process ½ cup slivered or whole almonds in a food processor for 2½ to 3 minutes or until the mixture begins to come away from the sides of the bowl.

- ½ cup chopped peeled mango
- ¼ cup seedless green grapes, halved
- ¼ cup raisins
- ¼ cup dried tart cherries
- ¼ cup chopped dried pineapple
- Cooking spray
- ¼ teaspoon salt
- 3 cups hot cooked glutinous rice
- ¼ cup almond butter
- ¼ cup maple syrup
- 4 cups water
- 1 tablespoon chopped almonds

1. Combine first 5 ingredients; arrange half of fruit mixture in an 8-inch glass bowl coated with cooking spray. Sprinkle salt over rice, and toss to combine. Spread half of rice over fruit mixture, pressing firmly with a spatula to pack. Spread almond butter over rice; drizzle with half of syrup. Top with remaining fruit mixture. Spread remaining rice over fruit mixture, pressing firmly with a spatula to pack. Drizzle with remaining syrup.

2. Open a small metal vegetable steamer; place steamer upside down in a large, deep wok. Add water; bring to a simmer. Wearing oven mitts, carefully place bowl on top of inverted steamer. Cover and cook 5 minutes or until thoroughly heated. Wearing oven mitts, carefully remove bowl from wok. Place a plate upside down on top of bowl; invert pudding onto plate. Sprinkle with almonds. Yield: 6 servings (serving size: 1 wedge).

CALORIES 276 (24% from fat); FAT 7.3g (sat 0.7g, mono 4.5g, poly 1.6g); PROTEIN 4.5g; CARB 51.2g; FIBER 1.8g; CHOL 0mg; IRON 1.9mg; SODIUM 103mg; CALC 58mg

Stuffed Shiitake Mushrooms

This traditional dish from central China is sometimes made by stuffing cucumbers instead of mushroom caps. If you don't find ground chicken at the store, you can grind raw, boneless, skinless chicken in a food processor. Replace the shrimp and chicken with tofu for a great vegetarian version. Although we cooked the mushrooms on a pie plate in a wok, a bamboo steamer would also work well.

- ¼ cup chopped green onions
- 3 tablespoons dry-roasted peanuts
- 1½ tablespoons low-sodium soy sauce
- 1 tablespoon grated peeled fresh ginger
- 1 tablespoon mirin (sweet rice wine)
- 2 teaspoons cornstarch
- 1 teaspoon dark sesame oil
- ½ teaspoon curry powder
- 2 garlic cloves, minced
- 6 ounces large shrimp, peeled, deveined, and chopped
- 4 ounces ground chicken
- 16 shiitake mushroom caps
- 4 cups water
- 1⅓ cups thinly sliced English cucumber
- 1⅓ cups thinly sliced carrot

1. Combine first 11 ingredients in a food processor; process until mixture forms a paste. Spoon about 1½ tablespoons mixture into each mushroom cap. Arrange mushrooms in a 10-inch pie plate.

2. Open a small metal vegetable steamer; place steamer upside down in a large, deep wok. Add water; bring to a simmer. Wearing oven mitts, carefully place pie plate on top of inverted steamer. Cover and cook 6 minutes or until filling is done. Wearing oven mitts, carefully remove pie plate from wok.

3. Arrange ⅓ cup cucumber and ⅓ cup carrot around edge of each of 4 plates; arrange 4 stuffed mushrooms in center of each plate. Yield: 4 servings.

CALORIES 262 (23% from fat); FAT 6.6g (sat 0.8g, mono 2.3g, poly 2g); PROTEIN 16.6g; CARB 36.9g; FIBER 5.7g; CHOL 65mg; IRON 2.6mg; SODIUM 427mg; CALC 76mg

Coconut-Curry Shrimp over Rice

Shrimp needs just a short marinating time to absorb the flavors of the aromatic sauce, making this tasty entrée quick enough for a busy weeknight. Steaming cooks the shrimp gently, so there's less chance of overcooking. Regular coconut milk offers the best flavor for this dish; the taste of light coconut milk is too subtle.

- ¼ cup coconut milk
- 3 tablespoons finely chopped red bell pepper
- 1½ tablespoons fish sauce
- 1 tablespoon minced fresh cilantro
- 1 tablespoon fresh lemon juice
- 1 teaspoon sugar
- 1 teaspoon curry powder
- 1½ pounds large shrimp, peeled and deveined
- 4 cups water
- 3 cups hot cooked basmati rice
- 4 lemon wedges
- Cilantro sprigs (optional)

1. Combine first 7 ingredients in a large zip-top plastic bag. Add shrimp; seal and marinate in refrigerator 30 minutes, turning bag occasionally. Place shrimp mixture in a 10-inch pie plate.

2. Open a small metal vegetable steamer; place steamer upside down in a large, deep wok. Add water; bring to a simmer. Wearing oven mitts, carefully place pie plate on top of inverted steamer. Cover and cook 4 minutes or until shrimp are done. Wearing oven mitts, carefully remove pie plate from wok. Serve shrimp mixture over rice; serve with lemon wedges. Garnish with cilantro sprigs, if desired. Yield: 4 servings (serving size: 1 cup shrimp mixture, ¾ cup rice, and 1 lemon wedge).

CALORIES 375 (15% from fat); FAT 6.4g (sat 3.3g, mono 0.7g, poly 1.3g); PROTEIN 38.6g; CARB 38.3g; FIBER 1g; CHOL 259mg; IRON 6.3mg; SODIUM 777mg; CALC 111mg

QUICK & EASY

Steamed Egg Custard with Prosciutto and Green Onions

Think of this quick-cooking dish as an Asian-style frittata. Substitute ham for prosciutto, if desired. Steamed or sautéed bok choy makes a good accompaniment.

    2 tablespoons minced shiitake
       mushroom caps
    1 tablespoon chopped fresh cilantro
    1 tablespoon rice vinegar
    1 tablespoon low-sodium soy sauce
    1 teaspoon grated peeled fresh ginger
    4 large eggs, lightly beaten
    Cooking spray
    4 cups water
    ¼ cup finely chopped prosciutto
       (about ½ ounce)
    ¼ cup minced green onions
    1 teaspoon dark sesame oil
    3 cups hot cooked basmati rice

1. Combine first 6 ingredients, stirring with a whisk; pour into a 10-inch pie plate coated with cooking spray.
2. Open a small metal vegetable steamer; place steamer upside down in a large, deep wok. Add water; bring to a simmer. Wearing oven mitts, carefully place pie plate on top of inverted steamer. Cover and cook 3 minutes. Carefully remove wok lid; sprinkle custard with prosciutto and onions. Cover and cook 3 minutes or until a knife inserted in center comes out clean. Wearing oven mitts, carefully remove pie plate from wok. Drizzle custard with oil; cut into 4 wedges. Serve over rice. Yield: 4 servings (serving size: 1 custard wedge and ¾ cup rice).

CALORIES 219 (28% from fat); FAT 6.8g (sat 2g, mono 2.5g, poly 1.2g); PROTEIN 10g; CARB 28g; FIBER 1.1g; CHOL 216mg; IRON 1.7mg; SODIUM 270mg; CALC 36mg

Steamed Fish with Spicy Ginger Sauce

Mild-flavored fish works best in this easy recipe.

SAUCE:

    ¼ cup fresh orange juice
    2 tablespoons mirin (sweet rice
       wine)
    2 tablespoons low-sodium soy sauce
    1 tablespoon dark sesame oil
    1 tablespoon grated peeled fresh
       ginger
    ½ to 1 teaspoon crushed red pepper

FISH:

    4 (6-ounce) halibut or trout fillets
    ½ cup chopped green onions
    1 tablespoon grated peeled fresh
       ginger
    ¼ teaspoon salt
    ¼ teaspoon freshly ground black
       pepper
    1 cup thinly sliced leek (about 1 large)
    ½ cup (1-inch) julienne-cut carrot
    ½ cup (1-inch) julienne-cut red bell
       pepper
    4 cups water
    4 cilantro sprigs (optional)

1. To prepare sauce, combine first 6 ingredients, stirring with a whisk.
2. To prepare fish, lightly score each fish fillet by making 3 (¼-inch-deep) crosswise cuts with a sharp knife. Combine onions and 1 tablespoon ginger, tossing well. Rub about 2 tablespoons onion mixture evenly into slits of each fillet. Sprinkle fillets with salt and black pepper. Combine leek, carrot, and bell pepper; arrange half of leek mixture in a 10-inch pie plate. Pour half of sauce over leek mixture; arrange fillets in a single layer over leek mixture. Top fillets with remaining leek mixture, and drizzle with remaining sauce.
3. Open a small metal vegetable steamer; place steamer upside down in a large, deep wok. Add water; bring to a simmer. Wearing oven mitts, carefully place pie plate on top of inverted steamer. Cover and cook 12 minutes or until fish flakes easily when tested with a fork. Wearing oven mitts, carefully remove pie plate from wok. Garnish with cilantro sprigs, if desired. Yield: 4 servings (serving size: 1 fillet, about 3 tablespoons leek mixture, and about 3 tablespoons sauce).

CALORIES 279 (25% from fat); FAT 7.6g (sat 1.1g, mono 2.7g, poly 2.7g); PROTEIN 36.7g; CARB 12.2g; FIBER 2g; CHOL 54mg; IRON 2.3mg; SODIUM 537mg; CALC 104mg

WINE NOTE: The fish demands a wine that is light, delicate, dry, and fruity: riesling. It's also a boon that riesling is high in acidity—always a great counterpoint to the oils in fish (that's why we squeeze lemon on fish). Of all rieslings, German wines are the most delicate and fruity. There are many great German rieslings available in wineshops; be sure to buy one labeled "Kabinett" or "Spätlese." A kabinett riesling is the lightest; spätlese is more full-bodied. Selbach-Oster, Dr. F. Weins-Prüm, and Dr. Loosen are all terrific producers. Prices start at $13.

Shrimp Dumplings with Sweet-and-Sour Dipping Sauce

If you have a standard bamboo steamer, you'll need to cook the dumplings in two batches; with a two-tiered bamboo steamer, though, you can steam all of them at once. If you don't have a bamboo steamer, you can use a wok, vegetable steamer, and pie plate. If the dumplings are touching in the basket, they may stick together once cooked.

SAUCE:

2 tablespoons minced red bell pepper
2 tablespoons fish sauce
2 tablespoons rice vinegar
2 teaspoons sugar
2 teaspoons grated peeled fresh ginger

DUMPLINGS:

2 teaspoons canola oil
1 cup finely chopped leek (about 1 large)
1 tablespoon grated peeled fresh ginger
1 tablespoon mirin (sweet rice wine)
¼ teaspoon salt
¼ teaspoon freshly ground black pepper
¾ pound large shrimp, peeled, deveined, and chopped
30 wonton wrappers
30 (¼-inch-thick) slices carrot (about 3 large carrots)

1. To prepare sauce, combine first 5 ingredients.

2. To prepare dumplings, heat oil in a medium nonstick skillet over medium-high heat. Add leek and 1 tablespoon ginger; sauté 3 minutes. Remove from heat. Combine leek mixture, mirin, salt, black pepper, and shrimp, stirring well.

3. Working with 1 wonton wrapper at a time (cover remaining wrappers with a damp towel to prevent drying), spoon about 1 tablespoon shrimp mixture into center of each wrapper. Moisten edges of wrapper with water; bring 2 opposite corners to center, pinching points to seal. Bring remaining 2 corners to center, pinching points to seal. Pinch 4 edges together to seal.

4. Add water to a wok or large skillet to a depth of 1 inch; bring to a boil. Line a bamboo steamer with 15 carrot slices; arrange 15 dumplings on top of carrot slices. Cover with steamer lid. Place steamer in pan; steam dumplings 12 minutes. Remove dumplings from steamer; cover and keep warm. Repeat procedure with remaining carrot slices and dumplings. Serve with sauce. Yield: 10 servings (serving size: 3 dumplings, 3 carrot slices, and about 2 teaspoons sauce).

CALORIES 133 (14% from fat); FAT 2g (sat 0.3g, mono 0.7g, poly 0.7g); PROTEIN 9.7g; CARB 18.1g; FIBER 0.9g; CHOL 54mg; IRON 1.9mg; SODIUM 533mg; CALC 39mg

well equipped

Immerse Yourself

Hand blenders are a helpful tool in the kitchen.

The immersion blender (also called a hand blender) has become popular in our Test Kitchens. We often reach for it to create smoothies, emulsify sauces, and purée soups.

Easy Puebla-Style Chicken Mole

This quick version of the Mexican classic comes together in minutes. Serve it with black beans and yellow rice, or as a filling for enchiladas.

1 teaspoon olive oil
1 cup thinly sliced onion
1 teaspoon ground cumin
1 teaspoon ground coriander
½ teaspoon ground cinnamon
2 stemmed dried seeded ancho chiles, torn into 2-inch pieces (about ¼ cup)
2 garlic cloves, thinly sliced
3 cups fat-free, less-sodium chicken broth
1⅓ cups coarsely chopped tomato (about 1 medium)
¼ cup golden raisins
3 tablespoons sliced almonds, toasted
3 (2 x ½-inch) orange rind strips
¾ pound skinless, boneless chicken breast halves
¾ pound skinless, boneless chicken thighs
½ ounce unsweetened chocolate
¼ teaspoon salt
¼ teaspoon black pepper

1. Heat oil in a Dutch oven over medium-high heat. Add onion; cook 5 minutes or until almost tender. Combine cumin, coriander, and cinnamon in a small bowl; sprinkle over onion in pan. Cook 1 minute. Add chiles and garlic to pan; cook 2 minutes or until chiles soften. Add broth and next 4 ingredients to pan; bring to a boil. Add chicken to pan; cover, reduce heat, and simmer 10 minutes or until chicken is done. Remove chicken from pan; shred with 2 forks. Set aside.

2. Add chocolate to chile mixture; let stand until chocolate melts. Using an immersion blender in pan, purée chocolate mixture until smooth. Cook over medium heat 20 minutes or until reduced to 3½ cups. Add shredded chicken to sauce; stir in salt and pepper. Yield: 6 servings (serving size: about 1 cup chicken mixture).

CALORIES 211 (29% from fat); FAT 6.8g (sat 1.8g; mono 2.8g; poly 1.3g); PROTEIN 27.2g; CARB 10.5g; FIBER 2.5g; CHOL 80mg; IRON 2.1mg; SODIUM 380mg; CALC 50mg

MAKE AHEAD

Zucchini and Fennel Soup with Roasted Red Pepper Purée

This light soup can be made up to three days ahead and stored in an airtight container in the refrigerator. For a vegetarian soup, use vegetable broth instead of chicken broth. If you're short on time, use bottled roasted red peppers.

6 red bell peppers
1½ teaspoons extravirgin olive oil
⅛ teaspoon salt
⅛ teaspoon black pepper
Cooking spray
2 cups thinly sliced onion
3 cups thinly sliced fennel bulb (about 1 bulb)
1 teaspoon fennel seeds
4½ cups (¼-inch) slices zucchini (about 1½ pounds)
4 garlic cloves
3 cups fat-free, less-sodium chicken broth
¼ teaspoon salt
¼ teaspoon black pepper

1. Preheat broiler.

2. Cut bell peppers in half lengthwise; discard seeds and membranes. Place

Continued

pepper halves, skin sides up, on a foil-lined baking sheet; flatten with hand. Broil 20 minutes or until blackened. Place in a zip-top plastic bag; seal. Let stand 20 minutes. Peel and cut into strips. Place peppers in beaker of an immersion blender; add oil. Purée until smooth. Transfer purée to a bowl. Stir in 1/8 teaspoon salt and 1/8 teaspoon black pepper.

3. Heat a large, heavy saucepan over medium-low heat. Coat pan with cooking spray. Add onion to pan; cover and cook 5 minutes or until tender, stirring occasionally. Add sliced fennel and fennel seeds to pan; cover and cook over medium-low heat 8 minutes or until sliced fennel is tender. Increase heat to medium-high. Add zucchini and garlic to pan, and cook 3 minutes, stirring constantly. Add broth; bring to a boil. Cover, reduce heat, and simmer 20 minutes or until vegetables are tender.

4. Place vegetable mixture, 1/4 teaspoon salt, and 1/4 teaspoon black pepper in beaker of an immersion blender; purée until smooth. Pour 1 cup soup into each of 6 bowls; top each serving with 1/3 cup pepper purée. Yield: 6 servings.

CALORIES 91 (17% from fat); FAT 1.9g (sat 0.3g; mono 1g; poly 0.4g); PROTEIN 4.4g; CARB 17.1g; FIBER 5.7g; CHOL 0mg; IRON 1.6mg; SODIUM 369mg; CALC 63mg

---

Tips to Blend In

• To prevent splattering, be sure the blade is fully immersed in the liquid.

• Use the correct size pot or pan for each recipe to ensure the liquid will cover the blade. Generally, it's easier to use a high-sided pot or beaker than a shallow sauté pan or bowl.

• If the blender suctions to the bottom of the pot, simply tilt the pot slightly to one side with one hand while blending with the other.

• To quickly rinse the immersion blender between uses, fill its beaker with water, submerge the blades, and start the blender. This is helpful when you need to use the blender more than once for one recipe.

Veal Chops with Red Grape Sauce

The sauce provides a pleasant sweet-savory foil to the tender chops. Serve with sautéed spinach.

 1 teaspoon olive oil
 1½ pounds veal loin chops (about 2 chops)
 ½ teaspoon salt
 ¼ teaspoon black pepper
 ½ cup sliced shallots
 4 garlic cloves, sliced
 1 cup seedless red grapes
 ½ cup pinot grigio or other dry white wine
 2 teaspoons fresh marjoram leaves, divided
 1 (14-ounce) can less-sodium beef broth

1. Heat oil in a medium nonstick skillet over medium-high heat. Sprinkle veal with salt and pepper; add to pan. Cook 8 minutes; turn veal. Cook 7 minutes or until medium-rare or desired degree of doneness. Transfer veal to a platter. Cover with foil; set aside.

2. Add shallots to pan; sauté 2 minutes or until golden. Add garlic; sauté 1 minute. Add grapes; cook 4 minutes or until grape skins blister. Stir in wine and 1 teaspoon marjoram; reduce heat, and simmer 2 minutes. Add broth to pan; bring to a boil. Cook 10 minutes or until mixture is reduced to 1¼ cups. Transfer grape mixture to beaker of an immersion blender; purée until smooth. Stir in 1 teaspoon marjoram.

3. Remove veal from bones; cut into thin slices. Serve with sauce. Yield: 4 servings (serving size: 4 ounces veal and about 1/4 cup grape sauce).

CALORIES 223 (22% from fat); FAT 5.5g (sat 1.5g; mono 2.3g; poly 0.7g); PROTEIN 25.1g; CARB 13.1g; FIBER 0.6g; CHOL 87mg; IRON 1.7mg; SODIUM 431mg; CALC 44mg

---

Red Lentil Stew with Yogurt Sauce

This recipe uses an immersion blender to blend the yogurt sauce and again to roughly purée the lentils.

 1 cup plain yogurt
 ¼ cup packed fresh cilantro leaves
 2 teaspoons canola oil
 3 cups coarsely chopped onion (about 1 large)
 2 cups coarsely chopped red bell pepper
 6 garlic cloves, coarsely chopped
 1 tablespoon curry powder
 5¼ cups organic vegetable broth (such as Swanson Certified Organic)
 1 (14.5-ounce) can whole tomatoes, undrained
 1 pound dried small red lentils
 1 tablespoon finely grated peeled fresh ginger
 ⅛ teaspoon ground red pepper

1. Combine yogurt and cilantro in beaker of an immersion blender; blend until cilantro is finely chopped. Cover and chill.

2. Heat oil in a large saucepan over medium heat. Add onion, bell pepper, and garlic; sauté 8 minutes or until tender. Add curry; cook 1 minute, stirring constantly. Add broth and tomatoes; bring to a boil. Stir in lentils. Cover, reduce heat, and simmer 30 minutes or until lentils are very soft. Stir in ginger.

3. Using an immersion blender in pan, coarsely purée lentil mixture. Stir in red pepper. Serve lentil mixture with yogurt sauce. Yield: 8 servings (serving size: 1 cup lentil mixture and 2 tablespoons yogurt sauce).

CALORIES 265 (10% from fat); FAT 3.1g (sat 0.9g; mono 0.6g; poly 0.8g); PROTEIN 17.5g; CARB 45.1g; FIBER 9.9g; CHOL 4mg; IRON 4.4mg; SODIUM 757mg; CALC 119mg

---

In our Test Kitchens, we often use a hand blender to purée sauce right in the pan.

Moroccan-Style Braised Beef with Carrots and Couscous

Dried apricots and North African spices render a hearty stew. Use an immersion blender to thicken the braising mixture gravy—no need for a roux.

BEEF:

- 2 teaspoons olive oil
- 1 pound lean beef stew meat, cut into 1-inch cubes
- ¼ teaspoon salt
- ¼ teaspoon black pepper
- 3 cups thinly sliced onion
- 4 garlic cloves, chopped
- 2 teaspoons ground cumin
- 2 teaspoons ground turmeric
- 2 teaspoons paprika
- 1 teaspoon ground ginger
- 2 (14-ounce) cans less-sodium beef broth
- ¼ cup packed dried apricots
- ⅛ teaspoon salt
- ⅛ teaspoon black pepper
- 2 cups diagonally sliced peeled carrot (about 4 carrots)
- 2 tablespoons water (optional)
- ¼ cup chopped fresh flat-leaf parsley

COUSCOUS:

- 2 teaspoons olive oil
- 1 garlic clove, crushed
- ½ teaspoon salt
- ¼ teaspoon ground turmeric
- ⅓ cup less-sodium beef broth
- ⅓ cup water
- ⅔ cup uncooked couscous
- ¼ cup chopped green onions

REMAINING INGREDIENT:

- ¼ cup chopped fresh flat-leaf parsley, divided

1. To prepare beef, heat 2 teaspoons oil in a large saucepan over medium-high heat. Sprinkle beef with ¼ teaspoon salt and ¼ teaspoon pepper. Add beef to pan, and cook 4 minutes or until beef is browned on all sides, turning occasionally. Transfer beef to a bowl; cover and keep warm.
2. Add 3 cups onion to pan; cook 10 minutes or until tender, stirring frequently. Add 4 garlic cloves and next 4

ingredients; cook 1 minute, stirring constantly. Add 2 cans broth; bring to a boil. Add apricots; reduce heat, and simmer 5 minutes. Cover and cook over medium-low heat 30 minutes. Using an immersion blender in pan, purée onion mixture. Stir in ⅛ teaspoon salt and ⅛ teaspoon pepper.
3. Add beef to onion mixture; cook over medium-low heat 1 hour or until beef is tender. Add carrot to pan; cover and cook 15 minutes or until carrot is tender, adding 2 tablespoons water, if desired, to loosen sauce. Stir in ¼ cup chopped parsley.
4. While beef cooks, prepare couscous. Heat 2 teaspoons oil in a small saucepan over medium heat. Add crushed garlic, ½ teaspoon salt, and ¼ teaspoon turmeric. Stir in ⅓ cup broth and ⅓ cup water; bring to a boil. Gradually stir in couscous. Remove from heat. Cover and let stand 5 minutes; fluff with a fork. Stir in green onions.
5. Spoon couscous onto 4 plates. Top each serving with beef stew, and sprinkle each with 1 tablespoon parsley. Yield: 4 servings (serving size: 1 cup stew and ½ cup couscous).

CALORIES 439 (30% from fat); FAT 14.6g (sat 4.1g; mono 7.4g; poly 1.3g); PROTEIN 32g; CARB 43.7g; FIBER 6g; CHOL 71mg; IRON 5.7mg; SODIUM 681mg; CALC 91mg

---

QUICK & EASY • MAKE AHEAD

Strawberry Sauce with Caramelized Sugar and Pink Peppercorns

Serve this sauce over frozen vanilla yogurt, pound cake, or sliced fresh strawberries. This recipe can be prepared up to four days in advance and refrigerated in an airtight container.

- ⅔ cup sugar
- ¼ cup water
- 1 pound hulled strawberries, quartered
- ½ teaspoon crushed pink peppercorns

1. Combine sugar and water in a large saucepan; bring to a boil. Cook until sugar dissolves; do not stir. Brush down any crystals that form on edges of pan with a wet pastry brush. Cook 2 minutes

or until sugar caramelizes and turns pale amber, swirling pan occasionally. Remove pan from heat; cool 3 minutes. Add strawberries; cover and let stand 10 minutes or until strawberries are tender. Cook over low heat until caramel is liquefied. Stir in peppercorns. Using an immersion blender in pan, purée sauce until smooth. (Sauce will thicken as it cools.) Yield: 1¼ cups (serving size: about 1½ tablespoons).

CALORIES 83 (2% from fat); FAT 0.2g (sat 0g; mono 0g; poly 0.1g); PROTEIN 0.4g; CARB 21.1g; FIBER 1.2g; CHOL 0mg; IRON 0.3mg; SODIUM 1mg; CALC 10mg

---

season's best

Adobo Chips with Warm Goat Cheese and Cilantro Salsa

Add a note of authenticity to your Cinco de Mayo celebration with this appetizer.

The salsa derives smoky heat from chipotle chiles, and adobo sauce adds a piquant, vinegary touch to the chips. The warm blend of goat cheese and cream cheese provides a smooth counterpart to the crunch and the chiles.

Adobo Chips with Warm Goat Cheese and Cilantro Salsa

SALSA:

- 1 (7-ounce) can chipotle chiles in adobo sauce
- 2 cups chopped fresh cilantro (about 1 bunch)
- 1 cup finely chopped tomatillos (about 4 medium)
- ¼ cup minced red onion
- ¼ cup fresh lime juice

Continued

CHIPS:

2½ teaspoons fresh lime juice
1 teaspoon canola oil
½ teaspoon paprika
¼ teaspoon cumin
8 (6-inch) white corn tortillas

CHEESE:

½ cup (4 ounces) block-style fat-free cream cheese, softened
¼ cup (2 ounces) goat cheese

1. To prepare salsa, remove 2 chipotle chiles from can; finely chop to measure 2 teaspoons. Remove 1 teaspoon adobo sauce from can, and set aside (reserve remaining chipotle chiles and adobo sauce for another use). Combine chiles, cilantro, tomatillos, onion, and ¼ cup lime juice in a medium bowl; cover and chill 1 hour.

2. Preheat oven to 375°.

3. To prepare chips, combine reserved 1 teaspoon adobo sauce, 2½ teaspoons lime juice, oil, paprika, and cumin in a small bowl, stirring with a whisk. Brush 1 tortilla with about ¼ teaspoon juice mixture, spreading to edge. Top with another tortilla; repeat procedure with juice mixture. Repeat procedure 6 more times (you will have 1 stack of 8 tortillas). Using a sharp knife, cut tortilla stack into 6 wedges. Place wedges in a single layer on baking sheets. Bake at 375° for 15 minutes; turn wedges. Bake an additional 10 minutes.

4. Reduce oven temperature to 350°.

5. To prepare cheese, combine cream cheese and goat cheese in a small bowl; stir until blended. Spread cheese mixture into a shallow 6-ounce ramekin or baking dish; cover with foil. Bake at 350° for 10 minutes or just until warm. Yield: 8 servings (serving size: 6 chips, 1½ tablespoons cheese mixture, and about ¼ cup salsa).

CALORIES 95 (29% from fat); FAT 3.3g (sat 1.2g, mono 0.9g, poly 0.6g); PROTEIN 4.9g; CARB 13.4g; FIBER 1.8g; CHOL 4.4mg; IRON 0.5mg; SODIUM 131mg; CALC 60mg

The Good Daughter

At her San Francisco restaurant, Mijita, Chef Traci Des Jardins honors the authentic Mexican cuisine of her childhood.

San Francisco Chef Traci Des Jardins, who grew up eating authentic Mexican fare, wants to introduce people to a different way of appreciating this popular cuisine.

"Usually in Mexico, if you see a burrito, it has one ingredient," Des Jardins says. "You don't see the burritos with 50,000 ingredients like meat and beans and rice and avocado and sour cream and all that stuff that has become the norm for Americans."

"I love Mexican food," she says. "I want people to know it's not about those giant burritos, and it can be clean, fresh, and flavorful." Here are some great recipes that reiterate that truth.

MAKE AHEAD • FREEZABLE
Chile Verde

This vibrant chile is even better the next day after the flavors marry. Make it ahead and store in the refrigerator up to two days.

1 tablespoon canola oil
2 (1-pound) pork tenderloins, trimmed and cut into 1-inch cubes
1½ teaspoons salt
¼ teaspoon freshly ground pepper
¼ cup all-purpose flour
4 cups chopped onion
2 pounds small tomatillos, husks and stems removed and tomatillos quartered
1 pound Anaheim or poblano chiles (about 4 medium), cut into 1-inch pieces
6 garlic cloves, chopped
3 cups water
1 cup chopped fresh cilantro
1 teaspoon ground cumin
½ teaspoon dried oregano

1. Heat oil in a stockpot over medium-high heat. Sprinkle pork evenly with salt and pepper. Place flour in a large zip-top plastic bag. Add pork to bag; seal. Shake to coat. Add pork to pan, and sauté 5 minutes, browning on all sides. Remove pork from the pan.

2. Add onion, tomatillos, chiles, and garlic to pan; sauté 8 minutes or until tender. Add pork, water, and remaining ingredients to pan; bring to a simmer. Cook 2 hours or until pork is tender, stirring occasionally. Yield: 8 servings (serving size: about 1⅓ cups).

CALORIES 267 (26% from fat); FAT 7g (sat 1.6g, mono 3g, poly 1.5g); PROTEIN 26.4g; CARB 18.9g; FIBER 3.7g; CHOL 74mg; IRON 2.7mg; SODIUM 511mg; CALC 45mg

Grandma Salazar's Albóndigas Soup

Traci Des Jardins has fond memories of her grandmother's recipe for this soup and has reinterpreted it for her menu at Mijita. Chilling the meatballs for 20 minutes helps them hold their shape when cooked. *Albóndigas* (ahl-BON-dee-gas) is Spanish for meatballs.

1 cup boiling water
½ cup short-grain rice
Cooking spray
2 cups chopped onion, divided
1 (1-ounce) slice white bread
½ cup minced fresh cilantro, divided
1½ teaspoons dried oregano
1 teaspoon ground cumin
¼ teaspoon salt
½ pound lean ground pork
½ pound ground sirloin
2 large egg whites
1 cup chopped carrot
1 garlic clove, minced
1 cup chopped seeded peeled tomato (about 8 ounces)
4 cups (1 [32-ounce] carton) fat-free, less-sodium chicken broth
2 tablespoons chopped fresh mint
2 cups chopped zucchini
½ teaspoon salt
¼ teaspoon freshly ground black pepper

1. Pour water over rice, and let stand 20 minutes. Drain.

2. Heat a nonstick skillet over medium heat. Coat pan with cooking spray. Add ½ cup onion to pan; cook 5 minutes or until tender, stirring occasionally.

3. Place bread in a food processor; pulse 10 times or until coarse crumbs measure 1¼ cups. Combine rice, cooked onion, breadcrumbs, ¼ cup cilantro, oregano, and next 5 ingredients, stirring well. Shape mixture into 29 (1-inch) meatballs. Chill 20 minutes.

4. Heat a Dutch oven over medium-high heat. Coat pan with cooking spray. Add 10 meatballs, and cook 6 minutes, browning on all sides. Remove meatballs from pan; drain well on paper towels. Wipe drippings from pan with a paper towel. Repeat procedure with cooking spray and remaining meatballs. Return pan to heat. Coat with cooking spray. Add 1½ cups onion, carrot, and garlic to pan; sauté 5 minutes or until vegetables are tender. Stir in tomato and broth; bring mixture to a boil. Add meatballs and mint to pan. Reduce heat, and simmer 35 minutes. Add zucchini, ½ teaspoon salt, and pepper to pan. Cook 10 minutes. Garnish with ¼ cup cilantro. Yield: 8 servings (serving size: about 1 cup soup and 1½ teaspoons cilantro).

CALORIES 181 (21% from fat); FAT 4.4g (sat 1.6g, mono 0.6g, poly 0.3g); PROTEIN 15.5g; CARB 20.4g; FIBER 2.9g; CHOL 36mg; IRON 1.9mg; SODIUM 500mg; CALC 43mg

QUICK & EASY
Strawberry Agua Fresca

Spanish for "fresh water," *agua fresca* is a refreshing, fruit-infused drink that's served throughout Mexico. Depending on the ripeness of the berries, adjust the amount of sugar for desired sweetness.

    4   cups water
    ⅓   cup sugar
    6   cups hulled strawberries
    ¼   cup fresh lime juice (about 2
        limes)

1. Combine water and sugar, stirring until sugar dissolves. Place strawberries in a blender, and process until smooth.

Combine sugar mixture, strawberry purée, and juice; stir well. Yield: 8 cups (serving size: 1⅓ cups).

CALORIES 71 (4% from fat); FAT 0.4g (sat 0g, mono 0.1g, poly 0.2g); PROTEIN 0.8g; CARB 17.8g; FIBER 2.3g; CHOL 0mg; IRON 0.5mg; SODIUM 4mg; CALC 21mg

QUICK & EASY
Cabbage Salad

This simple salad is like a Mexican coleslaw. The jalapeño adds a nice touch of heat; use less if you're sensitive to the pepper.

    16 cups thinly sliced cabbage
    4   cups thinly sliced onion
    1   cup chopped fresh cilantro
    3   tablespoons fresh lime juice
    1   tablespoon canola oil
    ½   teaspoon salt
    1   jalapeño pepper, seeded and
        finely chopped

1. Combine all ingredients; toss well. Yield: 8 cups (serving size: 1 cup).

CALORIES 86 (19% from fat); FAT 2.1g (sat 0.2g, mono 1.1g, poly 0.7g); PROTEIN 3.3g; CARB 16.2g; FIBER 4.6g; CHOL 0g; IRON 1.3mg; SODIUM 184mg; CALC 101mg

QUICK & EASY
Guacamole

This dip is a favorite at Mijita. Lime juice, onion, cilantro, and cumin lend the creamy avocado lots of flavor.

    1   cup finely chopped onion
    ¼   cup minced fresh cilantro
    2   tablespoons fresh lime juice
    ½   teaspoon salt
    ¼   teaspoon ground cumin
    ¼   teaspoon freshly ground black pepper
    2   ripe peeled avocados, seeded and
        coarsely mashed
    12 ounces unsalted baked tortilla chips

1. Combine first 7 ingredients, stirring well. Serve with chips. Yield: 16 servings (serving size: 2 tablespoons guacamole and about 10 chips).

CALORIES 122 (27% from fat); FAT 3.9g (sat 0.6g, mono 0g, poly 0g); PROTEIN 3g; CARB 21.1g; FIBER 3.6g; CHOL 0mg; IRON 0mg; SODIUM 74mg; CALC 3mg

---

great starts

Begin the Day with Flaxseed

Stir nutty-flavored ground flax into breads and cereals for great-tasting, healthful breakfasts.

MAKE AHEAD
Banana-Cinnamon Waffles

Crown these lightly spiced waffles with cinnamon sugar, sliced bananas, and/or a drizzle of maple syrup. Buckwheat flour adds a somewhat tangy, robust nuttiness.

    1   cup all-purpose flour
    ½   cup whole wheat flour
    ¼   cup buckwheat flour
    ¼   cup ground flaxseed
    2   tablespoons sugar
    1½   teaspoons baking powder
    ½   teaspoon ground cinnamon
    ¼   teaspoon salt
    1½   cups fat-free milk
    3   tablespoons butter, melted
    2   large eggs, lightly beaten
    1   large ripe banana, mashed
    Cooking spray

1. Lightly spoon flours into dry measuring cups; level with a knife. Combine flours, flaxseed, and next 4 ingredients in a medium bowl, stirring with a whisk.

2. Combine milk, butter, and eggs, stirring with a whisk; add milk mixture to flour mixture, stirring until blended. Fold in mashed banana.

3. Preheat a waffle iron. Coat iron with cooking spray. Spoon about ¼ cup batter for each 4-inch waffle onto hot waffle iron, spreading batter to edges. Cook 3 to 4 minutes or until steaming stops; repeat procedure with remaining batter. Yield: 8 servings (serving size: 2 waffles).

CALORIES 215 (31% from fat); FAT 7.4g (sat 3.3g, mono 1.9g, poly 1.4g); PROTEIN 7.3g; CARB 31.1g; FIBER 3.4g; CHOL 65mg; IRON 1.9mg; SODIUM 205mg; CALC 133mg

Grinding Flaxseed

To reap the benefits of flaxseed, you'll need to grind it; left whole, the seeds pass through the body undigested. Although you can find ground flaxseed, it will keep longer if left whole and ground just before using.

You can easily grind flaxseed in a spice or coffee grinder. Grind the flaxseed until it reaches an almost flourlike consistency. One quarter-cup of whole flaxseeds yields about six tablespoons ground flaxseed.

Finding and Storing Flaxseed

When shopping, you'll find whole flaxseeds and ground flaxseed—labeled either "ground flaxseed" or "flaxseed meal." Choose flaxseed meal that is pure and not combined with flour. You'll find flaxseed products in health-food stores or in the baking aisles or organic/natural-foods aisles of supermarkets. You can also order flaxseed products online at www.bobsredmill.com.

Because flaxseed is high in fat, store it (whether whole or ground) in the refrigerator or freezer to prevent spoilage. Whole seeds will keep for up to one year, while ground flaxseed will keep for three to four months. As with cooking oils, smell the seeds or meal before using in a recipe—if it smells a bit like oil paint, it has spoiled.

Zucchini-Pecan Flaxseed Bread

Ground flaxseed is a novel addition to this dense and sweet breakfast bread. You can freeze individual slices on a baking sheet, then transfer to a zip-top plastic bag to keep in the freezer up to two months. On hurried mornings, grab a slice, and defrost by microwaving at HIGH for 30 seconds to one minute.

1½ cups all-purpose flour
1 cup whole wheat flour
¾ cup granulated sugar
½ cup ground flaxseed
¼ cup packed brown sugar
1 tablespoon baking powder
1 teaspoon ground cinnamon
¾ teaspoon salt
¼ teaspoon baking soda
¼ teaspoon ground nutmeg
2 cups shredded zucchini (about 2 medium zucchini)
1 cup vanilla low-fat yogurt
½ cup egg substitute
3 tablespoons canola oil
1 teaspoon vanilla extract
¼ cup chopped pecans, toasted
Cooking spray
3 tablespoons chopped pecans, toasted

1. Preheat oven to 350°.
2. Lightly spoon flours into dry measuring cups; level with a knife. Combine flours, granulated sugar, and next 7 ingredients in a large bowl, stirring well with a whisk.
3. Spread zucchini onto several layers of heavy-duty paper towels; cover with additional paper towels. Press down firmly to remove excess liquid.
4. Combine yogurt, egg substitute, oil, and vanilla in a medium bowl, stirring well with a whisk. Stir in zucchini.
5. Add zucchini mixture and ¼ cup pecans to flour mixture, stirring until well combined. Pour batter into a 9 x 5-inch loaf pan coated with cooking spray. Sprinkle batter with 3 tablespoons pecans. Bake at 350° for 1 hour or until a wooden pick inserted in center comes out clean. Cool in pan 10 minutes on a wire rack. Remove bread from pan; place on wire rack. Yield: 1 loaf, 18 servings (serving size: 1 slice).

CALORIES 181 (30% from fat); FAT 6.1g (sat 0.6g, mono 2.9g, poly 2.2g); PROTEIN 4.5g; CARB 28.5g; FIBER 2.6g; CHOL 1mg; IRON 1.4mg; SODIUM 223mg; CALC 90mg

Power Granola Parfaits

Vary the dried fruit in the granola according to what you have on hand—try chopped dried apricots, raisins, dried currants, dried blueberries, or even chopped dried mango.

1 cup halved strawberries
1 cup blueberries
1 cup raspberries
3 cups plain low-fat yogurt
3 cups Power Granola (recipe below)
2 tablespoons maple syrup

1. Place first 3 ingredients in a medium bowl; toss gently to combine. Spoon ½ cup berry mixture into each of 6 (8-ounce) parfait glasses; top each serving with ½ cup yogurt and ½ cup Power Granola. Drizzle each serving with 1 teaspoon maple syrup. Yield: 6 servings (serving size: 1 parfait).

(Totals include Power Granola) CALORIES 324 (25% from fat); FAT 9g (sat 1.9g, mono 2.8g, poly 3.5g); PROTEIN 11.1g; CARB 53.7g; FIBER 6.1g; CHOL 7mg; IRON 2mg; SODIUM 92mg; CALC 277mg

MAKE AHEAD
POWER GRANOLA:
2 cups regular oats
⅓ cup ground flaxseed
¼ cup chopped walnuts
¼ cup chopped slivered almonds
2 teaspoons ground cinnamon
⅓ cup orange juice
⅓ cup honey
¼ cup packed brown sugar
2 teaspoons canola oil
1 teaspoon vanilla extract
Cooking spray
⅓ cup dried cranberries

1. Preheat oven to 300°.
2. Combine first 5 ingredients in a bowl.
3. Combine orange juice, honey, and sugar in a small saucepan. Cook over medium heat just until sugar dissolves,

stirring frequently. Remove from heat; stir in oil and vanilla.

4. Pour honey mixture over oat mixture, stirring to coat. Spread mixture in a thin layer on a jelly-roll pan coated with cooking spray. Bake at 300° for 10 minutes; stir well. Bake an additional 10 to 15 minutes or until golden brown. Spoon granola into a bowl; stir in cranberries. Cool completely. Yield: about 4¾ cups (serving size: about ½ cup).

NOTE: Store completely cooled granola in an airtight container at room temperature up to 2 weeks.

CALORIES 196 (31% from fat); FAT 6.8g (sat 0.7g, mono 2.2g, poly 3.3g); PROTEIN 4.1g; CARB 32.5g; FIBER 3.6g; CHOL 0mg; IRON 1.5mg; SODIUM 5mg; CALC 38mg

---

QUICK & EASY

Oatmeal with Apples, Hazelnuts, and Flaxseed

If your market sells hazelnuts with the skins removed, you can skip Steps 1 and 2, and just finely chop the nuts.

- ¼ cup hazelnuts
- 3 cups fat-free milk
- 1½ cups regular oats
- 1½ cups diced Granny Smith apple (about 1 medium)
- ⅓ cup ground flaxseed
- ½ teaspoon ground cinnamon
- ¼ teaspoon salt
- ½ teaspoon vanilla extract
- 3 tablespoons brown sugar
- 3 tablespoons slivered almonds

1. Preheat oven to 350°.
2. Place hazelnuts on a baking sheet. Bake at 350° for 15 minutes, stirring once. Turn nuts out onto a towel. Roll up towel; rub off skins. Finely chop nuts, and set aside.
3. Combine milk and next 5 ingredients in a medium saucepan. Bring to a boil over medium heat. Stir in vanilla. Cover, reduce heat, and simmer 5 minutes or until thick. Sprinkle with hazelnuts, brown sugar, and almonds. Yield: 6 servings (serving size: ⅔ cup).

CALORIES 258 (29% from fat); FAT 8.4g (sat 0.9g, mono 4.1g, poly 2.9g); PROTEIN 9.8g; CARB 36.3g; FIBER 6g; CHOL 2mg; IRON 1.9mg; SODIUM 156mg; CALC 203mg

---

Apple Muffins with Walnut Streusel

MUFFINS:

- 1¼ cups all-purpose flour
- ½ cup whole wheat flour
- ¾ cup ground flaxseed
- ¾ cup packed brown sugar
- 1 teaspoon baking powder
- 1 teaspoon baking soda
- ¼ teaspoon salt
- ½ cup 1% low-fat milk
- ½ cup orange juice
- 1 tablespoon butter, melted
- 1 teaspoon vanilla extract
- 2 large eggs, lightly beaten
- 2 cups finely chopped Granny Smith apple (about 1 large)
- ½ cup golden raisins
- Cooking spray

STREUSEL:

- ¼ cup finely chopped walnuts
- 2 tablespoons brown sugar
- 1 tablespoon chilled butter, cut into small pieces

1. Preheat oven to 350°.
2. To prepare muffins, lightly spoon flours into dry measuring cups; level with a knife. Combine flours, flaxseed, and next 4 ingredients in a medium bowl, stirring with a whisk. Make a well in center of mixture.
3. Combine milk and next 4 ingredients, stirring with a whisk; add to flour mixture, stirring just until moist. Fold in apple and raisins. Spoon batter into 18 muffin cups coated with cooking spray.
4. To prepare streusel, combine walnuts, 2 tablespoons brown sugar, and chilled butter in a small bowl, stirring with a fork until crumbly. Sprinkle streusel evenly over batter. Bake at 350° for 20 minutes or until muffins spring back when touched lightly in center. Remove from pans immediately; place on a wire rack. Serve warm or at room temperature. Yield: 1½ dozen (serving size: 1 muffin).

CALORIES 167 (27% from fat); FAT 5g (sat 1.3g, mono 1.1g, poly 2.2g); PROTEIN 3.8g; CARB 27.9g; FIBER 2.6g; CHOL 27mg; IRON 1.4mg; SODIUM 148mg; CALC 54mg

---

Almond-Crusted French Toast

Top with maple syrup, fresh berries, or bananas sautéed with a bit of butter and cinnamon.

- ⅓ cup ground flaxseed
- ¼ cup sliced almonds
- 1 cup vanilla soy milk (such as Silk)
- ½ cup egg substitute
- 1 tablespoon maple syrup
- ½ teaspoon ground cinnamon
- ½ teaspoon vanilla extract
- 2 large egg whites, lightly beaten
- 6 (1.5-ounce) slices whole wheat or whole-grain bread (such as Earth Grains)
- Cooking spray
- 1 teaspoon butter, divided
- 1½ teaspoons sifted powdered sugar

1. Combine flaxseed and almonds in a shallow dish. Combine milk and next 5 ingredients in a medium bowl, stirring well with a whisk; pour milk mixture into another shallow dish.
2. Working with 1 bread slice at a time, place bread slice into milk mixture, turning to coat both sides. Let bread stand in milk mixture 2 to 3 minutes. Remove bread slice from milk mixture; dredge 1 side of bread in flaxseed mixture, pressing gently to adhere. Repeat procedure with remaining bread slices, milk mixture, and flaxseed mixture.
3. Heat a large nonstick skillet over medium heat. Coat pan with cooking spray. Melt ½ teaspoon butter in pan; swirl to coat bottom of pan. Add 3 coated bread slices, coated sides down; cook 2 minutes on each side or until lightly browned. Repeat procedure with cooking spray, remaining butter, and remaining coated bread slices. Sprinkle powdered sugar evenly over toast. Yield: 6 servings (serving size: 1 piece).

CALORIES 216 (30% from fat); FAT 7.3g (sat 1.1g, mono 2.7g, poly 2.7g); PROTEIN 10.7g; CARB 28g; FIBER 5.2g; CHOL 2mg; IRON 2.6mg; SODIUM 286mg; CALC 126mg

In the Family Kitchen

As with many great cooks, the first inspiration and teacher for Chuck Williams, founder of Williams-Sonoma, was his grandmother.

Chuck Williams benefited from his grandmother's encouragement—and picked up her style of cooking. "There were never any recipes in her kitchen," Williams recalls. "She just knew how things were made. She didn't have recipes for pies and cakes or stews. She knew the basics and built from them." Williams credits his grandmother with teaching him fundamentals that still serve him well.

What follows is a collection of recipes from Williams that reflect the influence of his grandmother. They use simple ingredients, chosen wisely and economically, to make standout recipes that are doable for the everyday cook. And most of the recipes serve almost as a template—once you've made the Country Lima Beans or Roasted Chicken with Onions, Potatoes, and Gravy several times, you've mastered the technique and don't necessarily need to follow the recipe exactly when you want to make the dish again. That's the kind of cooking Williams learned in his grandma's kitchen.

MAKE AHEAD • FREEZABLE
Navy Bean Soup

Williams's grandmother would make a pot of beans most Mondays. Here, ham hocks create a rich stock, and their smoky flavor permeates the entire dish.

2¼ cups dried navy beans (about 1 pound)
6 cups warm water
1 small yellow onion, peeled
3 whole cloves
⅔ cup chopped celery
3 thyme sprigs
3 parsley sprigs
3 smoked ham hocks (about 1⅓ pounds)
1 bay leaf
3 cups chopped kale
2 cups (½-inch) cubed peeled Yukon gold potato
1½ cups chopped Vidalia or other sweet onion
⅔ cup thinly sliced carrot
1 teaspoon salt
¾ teaspoon freshly ground black pepper
2 tablespoons chopped fresh parsley

1. Sort and wash beans; place in a large Dutch oven. Cover with water to 2 inches above beans; bring to a boil. Cook 2 minutes; remove from heat. Cover and let stand 1 hour. Drain beans; rinse and drain.

2. Return beans to pan; cover with 6 cups warm water. Stud whole onion with cloves; place in pan. Add celery and next 4 ingredients; bring to a boil. Cover, reduce heat, and simmer 45 minutes.

3. Discard onion, thyme, parsley sprigs, and bay leaf. Remove ham hocks from pan; cool slightly. Remove meat from bones; finely chop to yield ⅓ cup meat. Discard bones, skin, and fat. Add meat, kale, and next 5 ingredients to pan; stir well. Cover and simmer 30 minutes or until beans and vegetables are tender. Stir in chopped parsley. Yield: 6 servings (serving size: about 1⅔ cups).

CALORIES 396 (13% from fat); FAT 5.5g (sat 1.8g, mono 1.8g, poly 1.1g); PROTEIN 22.7g; CARB 67g; FIBER 21.7g; CHOL 12mg; IRON 6.2mg; SODIUM 455mg; CALC 194mg

MAKE AHEAD • FREEZABLE
Simple White Bread

This recipe is adapted from one prepared by Williams's mother. Three rises give this basic sandwich-style bread a delicate crumb and a soft texture. An egg wash creates a glossy top crust on the baked bread, but be gentle when brushing the egg on the dough so as not to deflate the loaf.

1 teaspoon sugar
1 package dry yeast (about 2¼ teaspoons)
1¼ cups warm water (100° to 110°), divided
3 cups all-purpose flour
1¼ teaspoons salt
Cooking spray
1 large egg, lightly beaten

1. Dissolve sugar and yeast in ¼ cup warm water in a large bowl; let stand 5 minutes.

2. Lightly spoon flour into dry measuring cups, and level with a knife. Add 1 cup warm water, flour, and salt to yeast mixture; stir until a soft dough forms. Turn out onto a floured surface. Knead dough until smooth and elastic (about 5 minutes).

3. Place dough in a large bowl coated with cooking spray, turning to coat top. Cover and let rise in a warm place (85°), free from drafts, 45 minutes or until doubled in size. (Gently press two fingers into dough. If indentation remains, dough has risen enough.)

4. Uncover dough, and punch dough down. Cover and let rise 30 minutes. Uncover dough; punch dough down. Cover and let rest 10 minutes. Roll into a 14 x 7-inch rectangle on a floured surface. Roll up tightly, starting with a short edge, pressing firmly to eliminate air pockets; pinch seam and ends to seal. Place roll, seam side down, in an 8 x 4-inch loaf pan coated with cooking spray. Cover and let rise 30 minutes or until doubled in size.

5. Preheat oven to 425°.

6. Uncover dough; gently brush with egg. Bake at 425° for 12 minutes. Reduce oven temperature to 350° (do not remove bread from oven); bake an additional 15 minutes or until loaf sounds hollow when tapped. Remove from pan; cool on a wire rack. Yield: 12 servings (serving size: 1 slice).

CALORIES 123 (6% from fat); FAT 0.8g (sat 0.2g, mono 0.2g, poly 0.2g); PROTEIN 4g; CARB 24.5g; FIBER 1g; CHOL 18mg; IRON 1.6mg; SODIUM 253mg; CALC 7mg

Country Lima Beans

Humble ingredients were the cornerstone of Grandmother Shaw's cooking, and these modest components create a flavorful, satisfying dish. Oven cooking works well and makes preparation a snap. Serve as a side with roast beef, pork, or chicken; or you can even enjoy this as a main dish with a side salad.

    2 cups dried lima beans (about
       1 pound)
    1 teaspoon salt
    ½ teaspoon freshly ground black
       pepper
    3 bacon slices, chopped
    1 cup chopped onion
    1 cup finely chopped carrot
    2 cups water
    2 tablespoons butter,
       softened

1. Sort and wash beans; place in a large Dutch oven. Cover with water to 2 inches above beans; cover and let stand 8 hours or overnight. Drain beans. Return beans to pan; stir in salt and pepper.
2. Preheat oven to 300°.
3. Cook bacon in a large nonstick skillet over medium heat until crisp. Remove bacon from pan with a slotted spoon; set bacon aside. Add onion and carrot to drippings in pan; sauté 5 minutes or until golden. Add onion mixture, bacon, 2 cups water, and butter to bean mixture in Dutch oven; stir well. Cover and bake at 300° for 2½ hours or until beans are tender, stirring every hour. Yield: 8 cups (serving size: 1 cup).

CALORIES 248 (26% from fat); FAT 7.2g (sat 2.8g, mono 2.9g, poly 0.8g); PROTEIN 11.8g; CARB 35.4g; FIBER 11.2g; CHOL 13mg; IRON 3.3mg; SODIUM 404mg; CALC 53mg

Roasted Chicken with Onions, Potatoes, and Gravy

Thanks to his childhood influence, Williams champions the excellence of simple cooking. This dish received our highest rating. All you need to make this a complete meal is a green vegetable and dinner rolls.

    1 (4-pound) roasting chicken
    1 teaspoon salt, divided
    ¾ teaspoon freshly ground black
       pepper, divided
    4 oregano sprigs
    1 lemon, quartered
    1 celery stalk, cut into 2-inch pieces
  Cooking spray
    2 tablespoons butter, melted
    2 pounds yellow onions, peeled and
       each cut into 8 wedges
    2 pounds small red potatoes,
       quartered
    ¼ cup all-purpose flour
    1 (14-ounce) can fat-free,
       less-sodium chicken broth, divided
  Lemon wedges (optional)
  Fresh oregano sprigs (optional)

1. Preheat oven to 425°.
2. Remove and discard giblets and neck from chicken. Rinse chicken with cold water; pat dry. Trim excess fat. Starting at neck cavity, loosen skin from breast and drumsticks by inserting fingers, gently pushing between skin and meat. Combine ½ teaspoon salt and ½ teaspoon pepper; rub under loosened skin and over breast and drumsticks. Place oregano, quartered lemon, and celery into body cavity. Lift wing tips up and over back; tuck under chicken. Tie legs together with string. Place chicken, breast side up, on the rack of a broiler pan coated with cooking spray.
3. Combine ½ teaspoon salt, ¼ teaspoon pepper, butter, onions, and potatoes in a large bowl; toss well to coat. Arrange onion mixture around chicken on rack. Place rack in pan. Bake at 425° for 20 minutes. Reduce oven temperature to 325° (do not remove pan from oven); bake an additional 1 hour and 15 minutes or until onions and potatoes are

tender and a thermometer inserted into meaty part of chicken thigh registers 180°. Set chicken, onions, and potatoes aside; cover and keep warm.
4. Place a zip-top plastic bag inside a 2-cup glass measure. Pour pan drippings into bag; let stand 10 minutes (fat will rise to top). Seal bag; carefully snip off 1 bottom corner of bag. Drain drippings into a small saucepan, stopping before fat layer reaches opening; discard fat. Combine flour and ½ cup broth in a small bowl, stirring with a whisk. Add flour mixture and remaining broth to saucepan. Bring to a boil over medium-high heat. Reduce heat to medium; cook 5 minutes or until gravy thickens, stirring frequently with a whisk. Serve gravy with chicken and onion mixture. Garnish with lemon wedges and oregano sprigs, if desired. Yield: 6 servings (serving size: about 4 ounces chicken, 1⅓ cups onion mixture, and ⅓ cup gravy).

CALORIES 430 (24% from fat); FAT 11.6g (sat 4g, mono 4.3g, poly 2g); PROTEIN 36.9g; CARB 43.7g; FIBER 5.2g; CHOL 113mg; IRON 3.4mg; SODIUM 654mg; CALC 71mg

---

Indispensable Tools

"The right equipment enhances your enjoyment of cooking," says Chuck Williams, who has spent the last five decades hunting for the best cooking tools to sell in his stores. Here are a few of his essentials:

- one or two sharp paring knives
- a strong whisk
- good-quality wooden spoons
- a few good heavy pots and saucepans
- a sturdy, nonslip chopping board
- tongs
- a silicone spatula

Double-Crusted Apple Pie

Williams especially enjoyed making pies with his grandmother. She would give him pastry scraps that he rolled out and heaped with apples or peaches.

PASTRY:

2½ cups all-purpose flour
½ teaspoon salt
½ cup vegetable shortening
½ cup ice water
Cooking spray

FILLING:

10 cups thinly sliced peeled Granny Smith apple (about 3 pounds)
¾ cup granulated sugar
1½ tablespoons all-purpose flour
1 teaspoon ground cinnamon
½ teaspoon salt
¼ teaspoon ground nutmeg
1 tablespoon chilled butter, cut into small pieces

TOPPING:

1 tablespoon fat-free milk
1 teaspoon turbinado sugar

1. To prepare pastry, lightly spoon 2½ cups flour into dry measuring cups; level with a knife. Combine 2½ cups flour and ½ teaspoon salt in a large bowl, stirring well with a whisk; cut in shortening with a pastry blender or two knives until mixture resembles coarse meal. Gradually add ice water; toss with a fork until flour mixture is moist. Divide dough into 2 equal portions. Gently press each portion into a 4-inch circle on heavy-duty plastic wrap; cover and chill 30 minutes.
2. Preheat oven to 425°.
3. Slightly overlap 2 sheets of plastic wrap on a slightly damp surface. Unwrap and place 1 portion of chilled dough on plastic wrap. Cover dough with 2 additional sheets of overlapping plastic. Roll dough, still covered, into a 12-inch circle. Place dough in freezer 5 minutes or until plastic wrap can be easily removed. Remove top sheets of plastic wrap; fit dough, plastic wrap side

up, into a 9-inch deep-dish pie plate coated with cooking spray. Remove remaining plastic wrap.
4. To prepare filling, combine apple and next 5 ingredients; toss gently to coat. Spoon apple mixture into prepared pie plate; top with butter.
5. Slightly overlap 2 sheets of plastic wrap on a slightly damp surface. Unwrap and place remaining portion of chilled dough on plastic wrap. Cover dough with 2 additional sheets of overlapping plastic wrap. Roll dough, still covered, into an 11-inch circle. Place dough in freezer 5 minutes or until plastic wrap can be easily removed. Remove top sheets of plastic wrap; fit dough, plastic wrap side up, over apple mixture. Remove remaining plastic wrap. Press edges of dough together. Fold edges under, and flute. Cut several slits in top of dough to allow steam to escape.
6. To prepare topping, brush top of dough with milk; sprinkle turbinado sugar evenly over dough. Place pie plate on a foil-lined baking sheet; bake at 425° for 10 minutes. Reduce oven temperature to 350° (do not remove pie from oven); bake an additional 40 minutes or until browned. Cool on a wire rack. Yield: 10 servings (serving size: 1 wedge).

CALORIES 333 (30% from fat); FAT 11.2g (sat 3.1g, mono 3.7g, poly 2.6g); PROTEIN 3.7g; CARB 55.2g; FIBER 2.5g; CHOL 3mg; IRON 1.7mg; SODIUM 245mg; CALC 15mg

Citrus-Scented Angel Food Cake

Grandmother Shaw baked on Fridays and Saturdays, making simple sweets like this.

1 cup sifted all-purpose flour
1½ cups sugar, divided
1 tablespoon grated lime rind
12 large egg whites
1 teaspoon cream of tartar
¼ teaspoon salt
½ teaspoon lemon extract
1 tablespoon fresh lime juice

1. Preheat oven to 325°.
2. Lightly spoon sifted flour into a dry measuring cup; level with a knife. Sift flour again into a small bowl; add ¾ cup sugar and rind, stirring well with a whisk.
3. Place egg whites in a large bowl; beat with a mixer at high speed until foamy. Add cream of tartar and salt; beat until soft peaks form. Gradually add ¾ cup sugar, 1 tablespoon at a time, beating until stiff peaks form. Beat in lemon extract and lime juice. Sift ¼ cup flour mixture over egg white mixture; gently fold in. Repeat procedure with remaining flour mixture, ¼ cup at a time.
4. Spoon batter into an ungreased 10-inch tube pan, spreading evenly. Break air pockets by cutting through batter with a knife. Bake at 325° for 55 minutes or until cake springs back when lightly touched. Remove cake from oven. Invert pan; cool completely. Loosen cake from sides of pan using a narrow metal spatula. Invert cake onto a plate. Yield: 8 servings (serving size: 1 slice).

CALORIES 227 (1% from fat); FAT 0.2g (sat 0g, mono 0g, poly 0.1g); PROTEIN 7g; CARB 49.3g; FIBER 0.4g; CHOL 0mg; IRON 0.7mg; SODIUM 157mg; CALC 7mg

Brown Sugar-Walnut Divinity

Brown sugar gives these candies a rich, caramel-like flavor. It's moister than granulated sugar, so the candies have a fluffy, creamy, melt-in-your-mouth texture.

1½ cups packed brown sugar
½ cup water
1 teaspoon cider vinegar
⅛ teaspoon salt
1 large egg white
¾ teaspoon vanilla extract
½ cup coarsely chopped walnuts, toasted

1. Combine first 3 ingredients in a heavy saucepan over medium heat; bring to a boil, stirring just until sugar dissolves. Cover, reduce heat, and cook 3 minutes. Uncover; cook, without stirring, 10 minutes or until a candy thermometer registers 244°.
2. Place salt and egg white in a large

bowl; beat with a mixer at high speed until foamy. Gradually pour hot sugar syrup into egg white mixture, beating at medium speed, then at high speed until stiff peaks form. Beat in vanilla; stir in nuts. Working quickly, drop mixture by teaspoonfuls on wax paper. Cool completely. Store in an airtight container. Yield: 30 candies (serving size: 1 piece).

CALORIES 55 (21% from fat); FAT 1.3g (sat 0.1g, mono 0.2g, poly 0.9g); PROTEIN 0.4g; CARB 11g; FIBER 0.1g; CHOL 0mg; IRON 0.3mg; SODIUM 16mg; CALC 11mg

happy endings

Mad for Mangoes

The sweet taste of the tropics brightens a sunny assortment of desserts.

MAKE AHEAD
Mango Pie

Crystallized ginger lends a sweet, peppery bite.

CRUST:
2½ cups all-purpose flour
 ½ teaspoon salt
  5 tablespoons chilled butter, cut into small pieces
  3 tablespoons vegetable shortening, chilled
 10 tablespoons ice water
Cooking spray

FILLING:
 ⅔ cup packed brown sugar
  3 tablespoons cornstarch
4½ cups (½-inch-thick) mango wedges (about 4 medium)
  1 tablespoon chilled butter, cut into small pieces

TOPPING:
1½ teaspoons fat-free milk
  2 tablespoons chopped crystallized ginger
  1 tablespoon granulated sugar

1. To prepare crust, lightly spoon flour into dry measuring cups; level with a knife. Combine flour and salt, stirring well with a whisk. Cut in 5 tablespoons butter and shortening with a pastry blender or 2 knives until mixture resembles coarse meal. Add water, stirring just until moist. Divide dough into two equal portions. Gently press each portion into a 4-inch circle on a sheet of plastic wrap; cover. Chill 30 minutes.
2. Preheat oven to 425°.
3. Unwrap 1 dough portion, and place on a lightly floured surface. Roll dough into a 12-inch circle. Fit dough into a 10-inch deep-dish pie plate coated with cooking spray.
4. To prepare filling, combine brown sugar and cornstarch in a large bowl, stirring well with a whisk. Add mango; toss to coat. Add mango mixture to prepared pie plate; sprinkle evenly with 1 tablespoon butter.
5. Unwrap remaining dough portion; place on a lightly floured surface. Roll dough into a 12-inch circle. Fit dough over mango mixture. Press edges of dough together. Fold edges under; flute. Cut several slits in top of dough to allow steam to escape.
6. To prepare topping, brush top of dough with milk. Combine ginger and granulated sugar; sprinkle evenly over dough. Place pie plate on a foil-lined baking sheet; bake at 425° for 20 minutes. Reduce oven temperature to 375°; bake an additional 30 minutes or until pie is golden brown. Cool completely on a wire rack. Yield: 12 servings (serving size: 1 wedge).

CALORIES 274 (30% from fat); FAT 9.1g (sat 4.4g, mono 2.6g, poly 1.1g); PROTEIN 3.1g; CARB 46.1g; FIBER 1.8g; CHOL 15mg; IRON 1.6mg; SODIUM 146mg; CALC 25mg

Tropical Fruit Compote

If you can't find turbinado sugar, use ½ cup unpacked light brown sugar. The red pepper enlivens the fruits' sweetness.

  1 cup water
 ½ cup turbinado sugar
 ⅛ teaspoon crushed red pepper
  4 (⅛-inch) slices peeled fresh ginger
  3 star anise
  1 (2-inch) cinnamon stick
 ½ cup riesling or other slightly sweet white wine
 ½ teaspoon grated orange rind
  3 cups cubed peeled ripe mango (about 1 large)
  3 cups cubed peeled papaya (about 1 small)
  1 cup sliced carambola (star fruit)

1. Bring water and sugar to a boil in a medium saucepan; cook 3 minutes or until sugar dissolves. Add pepper, ginger, anise, and cinnamon. Reduce heat; cook until reduced to ½ cup (about 20 minutes). Remove from heat; stir in wine and rind. Cool completely. Strain mixture through a small sieve into a bowl; discard solids.
2. Combine wine mixture and fruit in a bowl, and toss gently. Chill 30 minutes. Yield: 6 servings (serving size: 1 cup).

CALORIES 166 (2% from fat); FAT 0.4g (sat 0.1g, mono 0.1g, poly 0.1g); PROTEIN 1g; CARB 39.4g; FIBER 3.4g; CHOL 0mg; IRON 0.6mg; SODIUM 12mg; CALC 42mg

---

Buying and Storing Mangoes

• Like peaches, ripe mangoes emit a fragrant aroma and give slightly when gently pressed at the stem.

• Their skin should be smooth. A few black spots are acceptable and won't affect the fruit's flavor.

• Skin color isn't always an indicator of ripeness. Ripe mangoes range in color from green to gold to deep red.

• If purchased when hard, mangoes ripen at room temperature in four to seven days. To speed the process, ripen them in a brown paper bag.

• Ripe, unpeeled mangoes will keep three to four days in the the refrigerator.

How to Prepare Mangoes

1. *Cut an unpeeled mango lengthwise as close to the seed as possible. Place a piece, cut side down, on a cutting board, and peel off the skin with your fingers (ripe mangoes can be peeled by hand), securing with your other hand. Slice or cube the flesh as needed.*

2. *To dice, cut an unpeeled mango lengthwise as close to the seed as possible. With the flesh side up, score the flesh in cube or diamond shapes, being careful not to cut through the skin.*

3. *Turn the skin inside out by pressing gently, and peel off the cut pieces. (You can also use a paring knife to trim mango away from the skin.)*

Caramelized Mangoes

⅓ cup sugar
¼ cup water
1 tablespoon unsalted chilled butter, cut into small pieces
5 cups (½-inch-thick) mango wedges (about 4 large)
Lime wedges (optional)

1. Combine sugar and water in a large, heavy skillet over medium-high heat; cook until sugar dissolves. Cook without stirring 3 minutes or until golden. Stir in butter. Reduce heat to medium. Add mango to pan, tossing gently. Cook 10 minutes or until mango is lightly browned, stirring frequently. Serve with lime wedges, if desired. Yield: 4 cups (serving size: about 1¼ cups).

CALORIES 149 (13% from fat); FAT 2.3g (sat 1.3g, mono 0.6g, poly 0.1g); PROTEIN 0.7g; CARB 34.5g; FIBER 2.5g; CHOL 5mg; IRON 0.2mg; SODIUM 16mg; CALC 14mg

Mango Macadamia Crisp

The fruit's tangy-sweet taste and velvety texture contrasts nicely with the crunchy nut topping. Bottled refrigerated mango may be substituted for fresh.

FILLING:
¼ cup granulated sugar
2 teaspoons cornstarch
4 cups chopped peeled ripe mango (about 4 pounds)
3 tablespoons fresh lime juice
2 teaspoons butter, melted
Cooking spray

TOPPING:
⅓ cup all-purpose flour
3 tablespoons granulated sugar
1½ teaspoons brown sugar
½ teaspoon ground ginger
3 tablespoons butter
3 tablespoons chopped macadamia nuts

1. Preheat oven to 400°.
2. To prepare filling, combine ¼ cup granulated sugar and cornstarch, stirring well with a whisk. Add mango, juice, and melted butter; toss gently to combine. Place mango mixture in an 8-inch square baking dish coated with cooking spray.
3. To prepare topping, lightly spoon flour into a dry measuring cup; level with a knife. Combine flour, 3 tablespoons granulated sugar, brown sugar, and ginger, stirring well. Cut in 3 tablespoons butter with a pastry blender or 2 knives until mixture resembles coarse meal. Stir in nuts. Sprinkle flour mixture evenly over mango mixture. Bake at 400° for 40 minutes or until browned. Yield: 8 servings (serving size: about ½ cup).

CALORIES 238 (31% from fat); FAT 8.1g (sat 3.1g, mono 4.2g, poly 0.3g); PROTEIN 1.7g; CARB 43.7g; FIBER 3.3g; CHOL 14mg; IRON 0.6mg; SODIUM 49mg; CALC 21mg

Mango Mascarpone Ice Cream

1 cup mango nectar
⅓ cup sugar
5 cups cubed peeled ripe mango (about 4½ pounds)
⅔ cup (5 ounces) mascarpone cheese
⅓ cup fat-free sour cream
1 tablespoon fresh lemon juice
Dash of salt

1. Combine nectar and sugar in a small saucepan. Cook over medium heat 5 minutes or until sugar dissolves, stirring constantly. Cool.
2. Place mango in a blender, and process until smooth. Press puréed mango through a fine sieve into a bowl; discard solids. Combine mango purée, cheese, and sour cream in a blender; process until smooth. Pour into a bowl; stir in nectar mixture, juice, and salt. Cover; chill completely.
3. Pour mixture into freezer can of an ice-cream freezer; freeze according to manufacturer's instructions. Spoon ice cream into a chilled, freezer-safe container; cover and freeze 2 hours or until almost firm. Yield: 10 servings (serving size: ½ cup).

CALORIES 169 (32% from fat); FAT 5.9g (sat 3.1g, mono 0.1g, poly 0.1g); PROTEIN 1.8g; CARB 30.3g; FIBER 2.3g; CHOL 16mg; IRON 0.3mg; SODIUM 15mg; CALC 36mg

cooking class

Tour de Cuisine

Kitchen-centered vacations are a great way to visit a beautiful destination, immerse yourself in a country's culture, and sharpen your cooking skills.

A culinary vacation is one of the best and most enjoyable ways to understand other cultures, and the fastest route to experiencing the finest cuisine of a destination. Whether you spend your entire vacation in a country villa kitchen or simply pass a morning in the company of a local chef, your palate will be richer for the experience. But if your travel plans don't include a culinary vacation in the near future, we've shared recipes from culinary guide Joanne Weir's trips to Provence in the south of France. For more information about this and Weir's other programs, visit www.joanneweir.com.

Chicken with 40 Cloves of Garlic

Weir shares this classic dish with tour participants to teach them about French comfort food at its simple and satisfying best. One of the basic tenets of French cuisine is making full use of ingredients—hence, whole chickens in this recipe. In a pinch, you can substitute 6 pounds of chicken pieces. The garlic softens in flavor as it roasts and is easy to spread over the baguette slices. Serve with steamed asparagus.

    2   (3-pound) whole chickens
    1   tablespoon butter
    1   tablespoon extravirgin olive oil
    ½   teaspoon salt
    ¼   teaspoon freshly ground black
        pepper
    40 garlic cloves, peeled
    1¼ cups fat-free, less-sodium chicken
        broth
    1   cup dry white wine
    24 (¼-inch-thick) slices diagonally
        cut French bread baguette
    Chopped fresh flat-leaf parsley
        (optional)

1. Remove and discard giblets and neck from chickens. Rinse chickens with cold water; pat dry. Trim excess fat; remove skin. Cut each chicken into 8 pieces. Combine butter and oil in a 12-inch nonstick skillet over medium-high heat. Sprinkle salt and pepper evenly over chicken. Add half of chicken pieces to pan; cook 2 minutes on each side or until golden. Remove chicken from pan; keep warm. Repeat procedure with remaining chicken.
2. Reduce heat to medium. Add garlic to pan; cook 1 minute or until garlic begins to brown, stirring frequently. Arrange chicken on top of garlic. Add broth and wine; cover and cook 25 minutes or until chicken is done.
3. Remove chicken from pan; keep warm. Increase heat to medium-high; cook 10 minutes or until liquid is reduced to about 1 cup. Serve sauce and garlic with chicken and bread. Garnish with parsley, if desired. Yield: 8 servings (serving size: about 4 ounces chicken, 2 tablespoons sauce, 5 garlic cloves, and 3 bread slices).

CALORIES 343 (36% from fat); FAT 13.7g (sat 3.6g, mono 4.9g, poly 3.4g); PROTEIN 29.6g; CARB 24.2g; FIBER 2g; CHOL 111mg; IRON 2.3mg; SODIUM 468mg; CALC 58mg

---

Provençal Pantry

One of the best things about the cuisine of Provence is its use of simple but fresh ingredients to produce extraordinary dishes. Following are some of the staples of the south-of-France pantry.

Anchovies. These tiny fish, typically sold boned, cured, and packed in oil, lend a subtle, salty flavor to a variety of dishes. They're easily mashed into a paste, and a little goes a long way.

Beans and legumes. Fresh, dried, and even canned beans and legumes are a staple; chickpeas are a particular favorite.

Capers. These are unopened flower buds on a bush native to the Mediterranean, and the world's finest are grown in Provence. Dried and bottled in brine, they add salty, briny zip to a dish.

Garlic. France, and particularly Provence, is a major producer of garlic. Its pungency finds its way into many Provençal dishes.

Herbs. Local cooks reach for fresh and dried flat-leaf parsley, basil, oregano, rosemary, thyme, and lavender—all of which grow abundantly in the region. Keep herbes de Provence—a blend of dried lavender, marjoram, rosemary, sage, savory, thyme, and basil—on hand to add a dash of Mediterranean flavor to any dish.

Olives. Beloved throughout the Mediterranean, the small niçoise and the green picholine are local varieties.

Olive oil. This golden ingredient appears in all manner of dishes, including cakes.

Wine. Provence produces red, white, and rosé wines, to be enjoyed with meals and often added to recipes.

Grilled Lamb Chops with Lavender Salt

Garlic is sautéed in oil and discarded, leaving behind the essence of garlic flavor without overpowering the delicate lavender.

  1 tablespoon kosher salt
  2 teaspoons dried lavender
     flowers
  1 tablespoon olive oil
  3 garlic cloves, halved
  ½ teaspoon freshly ground black
     pepper
  8 (4-ounce) lamb loin chops,
     trimmed

1. Place salt and lavender in a spice or coffee grinder; process until ground.
2. Heat oil in a large nonstick skillet over medium-high heat. Add garlic; cook 2 minutes or until golden. Remove garlic from pan; discard. Sprinkle 1 teaspoon salt mixture and pepper over chops. Add chops to pan; cook 3 minutes on each side or until desired degree of doneness. Serve with additional lavender salt, if desired. Yield: 4 servings (serving size: 2 chops).

CALORIES 239 (48% from fat); FAT 28.9g (sat 3.8g, mono 6.8g, poly 0.9g); PROTEIN 28.7g; CARB 0.4g; FIBER 0.1g; CHOL 90mg; IRON 1.9mg; SODIUM 551mg; CALC 20mg

Vegetable Soup with Pistou

SOUP:
  ½ cup dried navy beans
  6 cups water
1¾ cups chopped leek
  1 cup chopped onion
  1 cup finely chopped carrot (about
     2 medium)
  1 cup chopped seeded peeled tomato
  ¾ cup peeled diced potato
1½ teaspoons salt
  ¼ teaspoon black pepper
Dash of ground thyme
  8 parsley sprigs
  1 bay leaf
 10 cups water
1½ cups diced zucchini (about 2)
  ¾ cup uncooked elbow macaroni
  ¼ pound green beans, trimmed and
     cut in half crosswise

PISTOU:
  1 cup fresh basil leaves
  ⅓ cup grated Parmesan cheese
  4 garlic cloves, peeled
  2 tablespoons extravirgin olive oil

REMAINING INGREDIENT:
Thyme sprigs (optional)

1. To prepare soup, sort and wash beans; place in a large Dutch oven. Cover with water to 2 inches above beans; cover and let stand 8 hours. Drain; return beans to pan. Add 6 cups water; bring to a boil. Reduce heat, and simmer 45 minutes or until tender. Drain; return beans to pan.
2. Add leek and next 9 ingredients to pan, stirring to combine. Add 10 cups water; bring to a boil. Reduce heat; simmer 30 minutes or until potato is tender.
3. Stir in zucchini, macaroni, and green beans; cook 15 minutes or until macaroni is tender. Discard bay leaf.
4. To prepare pistou, place basil, cheese, and garlic in a food processor; process until a stiff paste forms. With processor on, slowly pour oil through food chute; process until well blended. Serve with soup. Garnish with thyme sprigs, if desired. Yield: 6 servings (serving size: 2 cups soup and 2 teaspoons pistou).

CALORIES 243 (24% from fat); FAT 6.6g (sat 1.5g, mono 3.8g, poly 0.9g); PROTEIN 9.9g; CARB 37.6g; FIBER 8.3g; CHOL 4mg; IRON 2.9mg; SODIUM 679mg; CALC 135mg

How to Rinse Leeks

Washing leeks can be a hassle. Chop them first, then rinse in a strainer.

MAKE AHEAD
Warm Olives with Wild Herbs

In this appetizer, the olives stand in the oil mixture and become more flavorful. Save the herb-infused oil for a dipping sauce with crusty French bread.

  ¾ cup niçoise olives
  ¾ cup picholine olives
  ¼ cup extravirgin olive
     oil
  ¼ teaspoon grated lemon
     rind
  ⅛ teaspoon crushed red
     pepper
  2 fresh thyme sprigs
  2 fresh savory sprigs
  1 fresh rosemary sprig

1. Combine all ingredients in a small saucepan over medium-low heat. Cook 5 minutes or until warm. Place olive mixture in a medium bowl; let stand at room temperature at least 6 hours. Drain olives in a colander over a bowl; discard stems. Reserve oil for another use, if desired. Yield: 10 servings (serving size: about 2 tablespoons).

CALORIES 49 (88% from fat); FAT 4.8g (sat 0.5g, mono 3.5g, poly 0.6g); PROTEIN 0.2g; CARB 1.9g; FIBER 0.5g; CHOL 0mg; IRON 0.8mg; SODIUM 182mg; CALC 25mg

QUICK & EASY • MAKE AHEAD

Croutons with Orange and Fennel Tapenade

Olive trees grow throughout Provence, and olive oil is the predominant cooking medium. Add capers and garlic, and you have the makings of the region's signature dish: tapenade. Weir's version incorporates flavorful orange and fennel seed.

½ cup pitted niçoise olives
1 teaspoon grated orange rind
1½ tablespoons orange juice
1 tablespoon capers
1 tablespoon extravirgin olive oil
1 teaspoon fennel seeds
1 teaspoon water
2 garlic cloves, peeled
¼ teaspoon freshly ground black pepper
22 (¼-inch-thick) slices diagonally cut French bread baguette, toasted
1 orange, cut into sections and halved (optional)

1. Place first 8 ingredients in a food processor; process until smooth. Add pepper. Spoon 1 teaspoon tapenade over each baguette slice. Arrange on a serving platter; garnish with orange sections, if desired. Yield: 22 servings (serving size: 1 crouton).

CALORIES 51 (28% from fat); FAT 1.6g (sat 0.2g, mono 1g, poly 0.2g); PROTEIN 1.3g; CARB 7.9g; FIBER 0.6g; CHOL 0mg; IRON 0.4mg; SODIUM 125mg; CALC 15mg

Summer Salad of Seared Tuna, Lima Beans, and Tomatoes

Weir's students make this dish with the various types of fresh beans they find at the local market. If you can't find fresh limas, try flageolets, cranberry beans, or any combination of shell beans.

4 cups water
1½ cups shelled lima beans
¼ cup red wine vinegar
2 tablespoons extravirgin olive oil
4 cups water
¾ pound green beans, trimmed
¾ pound yellow wax beans, trimmed
2 cups cherry tomatoes, halved
6 tablespoons chopped fresh basil
¾ teaspoon salt, divided
½ teaspoon freshly ground black pepper, divided
6 (6-ounce) tuna steaks (about 1 inch thick)
Cooking spray

1. Preheat grill.
2. Bring 4 cups water to a boil in a medium saucepan over medium-high heat. Add lima beans; cook 20 minutes or until tender. Drain. Add vinegar and oil, tossing well.
3. Bring 4 cups water to a boil in a medium saucepan over medium-high heat. Add green beans and wax beans; cook 7 minutes or until crisp-tender. Drain and combine lima beans, green beans, wax beans, tomatoes, and basil in a large bowl. Sprinkle with ½ teaspoon salt and ¼ teaspoon pepper; set aside.
4. Coat both sides of tuna with cooking spray; sprinkle with ¼ teaspoon salt and ¼ teaspoon pepper. Place tuna on a grill rack coated with cooking spray; cook 2 minutes on each side or until desired degree of doneness. Cut each steak crosswise into ¼-inch slices; arrange over bean mixture. Yield: 6 servings (serving size: 1 tuna steak and 1½ cups bean mixture).

CALORIES 334 (18% from fat); FAT 6.6g (sat 1.1g, mono 3.6g, poly 1.1g); PROTEIN 46g; CARB 22g; FIBER 9.1g; CHOL 77mg; IRON 3.5mg; SODIUM 362mg; CALC 105mg

WINE NOTE: The perfect wine for a summer salad needs to be refreshing and crisp, while at the same time capable of standing up to the "meatiness" of the grilled tuna and the acidity inherent in tomatoes. A good choice comes from France: Sancerre. Try the Pascal Jolivet Sancerre 2003 (Loire Valley, France, $25), which is snappy, fresh, and full of citrus flavors.

How to Slice Grilled Tuna Steaks

Cut each steak crosswise into ¼-inch slices.

QUICK & EASY • MAKE AHEAD

Chickpea Salad with Provençal Herbs and Olives

The easiest way to pit a niçoise olive is to smack it with the side of a chef's knife.

¼ cup red wine vinegar
1 tablespoon extravirgin olive oil
¼ teaspoon salt
¼ teaspoon black pepper
4 garlic cloves, minced
2 (15½-ounce) cans chickpeas (garbanzo beans), drained
¾ cup diced red onion
¼ cup pitted niçoise olives
1 tablespoon chopped fresh flat-leaf parsley
1 teaspoon chopped fresh oregano
1 teaspoon chopped fresh rosemary
1 teaspoon chopped fresh thyme

Continued

1. Combine first 5 ingredients in a small bowl. Combine chickpeas and remaining 6 ingredients in a large bowl. Pour vinegar mixture over salad, tossing gently. Yield: 6 servings (serving size: ⅔ cup).

CALORIES 163 (24% from fat); FAT 4.4g (sat 0.6g, mono 2.8g, poly 0.8g); PROTEIN 5.3g; CARB 26.3g; FIBER 4.7g; CHOL 0mg; IRON 1.6mg; SODIUM 449mg; CALC 43mg

MAKE AHEAD
Orange Cake with Fresh Berries

Because of its geographic location on the Mediterranean, Provence has been influenced by other Mediterranean countries. Oranges and olive oil are highly valued. Orange-flower water adds an intense perfume but can be omitted. It can be found in Middle Eastern food stores.

    1   cup sifted cake flour
    ½   cup sugar
    1   teaspoon baking powder
    ¼   teaspoon salt
    1   tablespoon grated orange rind
    ¼   cup fresh orange juice
    1   tablespoon olive oil
    1   teaspoon vanilla extract
    ¼ to ½ teaspoon orange-flower water
    2   large egg yolks
    6   large egg whites
    ¼   teaspoon cream of tartar
    1   tablespoon powdered sugar
    1   cup blueberries
    1   cup raspberries

1. Preheat oven to 350°.
2. Combine flour, sugar, baking powder, and salt in a large bowl; stir well. Add rind and next 5 ingredients; beat with a mixer at medium speed until smooth. Place egg whites and cream of tartar in a bowl. Using clean, dry beaters, beat until stiff peaks form. Gently stir one-fourth of egg whites into batter; fold in remaining egg whites. Pour mixture into a 10-inch tube pan with removable bottom. Bake at 350° for 25 minutes or until cake springs back when lightly touched. Cool in pan 5 minutes on a wire rack. Remove from pan; cool completely. Dust with powdered sugar. Serve with berries. Yield: 8 servings (serving size: 1 cake

slice, 2 tablespoons raspberries, and 2 tablespoons blueberries).

CALORIES 176 (25% from fat); FAT 4.8g (sat 0.9g, mono 3g, poly 0.7g); PROTEIN 4.8g; CARB 28.7g; FIBER 1.7g; CHOL 51mg; IRON 1.3mg; SODIUM 178mg; CALC 50mg

MAKE AHEAD
Olive and Caramelized Onion Tart

Savory tarts are an integral part of French cuisine. Each region has its own variation, and this rustic version has a pizzalike crust. You can prepare the topping while the dough rises.

DOUGH:

    1   package dry yeast (about 2¼ teaspoons)
    ¾   cup warm water (100° to 110°), divided
    2¼ cups all-purpose flour, divided
    2   tablespoons 1% low-fat milk
    1   tablespoon olive oil
    ½   teaspoon salt
    ½   teaspoon finely chopped fresh thyme
    ½   teaspoon finely chopped fresh rosemary
        Cooking spray
    1   tablespoon cornmeal

TOPPING:

    1   tablespoon olive oil
    9   cups vertically sliced yellow onion (about 2½ pounds)
    1   teaspoon chopped fresh thyme
    ½   teaspoon chopped fresh rosemary
    3   garlic cloves, chopped
    1   cup chopped seeded peeled tomato
    ½   cup chopped pitted kalamata olives
    2   canned anchovy fillets, patted dry and mashed
    ½   cup (2 ounces) crumbled goat cheese
    ⅛   teaspoon freshly ground black pepper

1. To prepare dough, dissolve yeast in ¼ cup warm water in a large bowl; let stand 5 minutes. Add ½ cup warm water. Lightly spoon flour into dry measuring cups; level with a knife. Add 2 cups flour

and next 5 ingredients to yeast mixture, stirring until well blended.
2. Turn dough out onto a floured surface. Knead until smooth and elastic (about 8 minutes); add enough of remaining flour, 1 tablespoon at a time, to prevent dough from sticking to hands (dough will feel tacky).
3. Place dough in a large bowl coated with cooking spray, turning to coat top. Cover and let rise in a warm place (85°), free from drafts, 40 minutes or until doubled in size. (Gently press two fingers into dough. If indentation remains, dough has risen enough.)
4. Punch dough down; cover and let rest 5 minutes. Shape dough into a 15 x 13-inch rectangle on a baking sheet coated with cooking spray and sprinkled with cornmeal. Crimp edges of dough with fingers to form a rim.
5. Preheat oven to 400°.
6. To prepare topping, heat 1 tablespoon oil in a large nonstick skillet over medium-high heat. Add onion and next 3 ingredients. Cover and cook 15 minutes or until golden brown, stirring occasionally. Uncover; reduce heat, and cook 15 minutes or until onion is soft, stirring occasionally. Stir in tomato; cook 15 minutes or until mixture is almost dry. Stir in olives and anchovies.
7. Spread onion mixture over dough, leaving a ½-inch border. Bake at 400° for 35 minutes or until crust is crisp. Sprinkle with cheese and pepper. Serve warm or at room temperature. Yield: 9 servings (serving size: 1 piece).

CALORIES 244 (27% from fat); FAT 7.2g (sat 1.6g, mono 3.9g, poly 1.1g); PROTEIN 6.6g; CARB 39.2g; FIBER 3g; CHOL 4mg; IRON 2.2mg; SODIUM 273mg; CALC 51mg

Cooking tours expose you to the life, soul, and cuisine of destinations.

MAKE AHEAD
Lavender and Toasted Almond Ice Cream with Warm Figs

Look for dried lavender flowers in natural foods or specialty grocery stores.

 5 tablespoons sugar
 1 to 2 tablespoons dried lavender flowers
 4 cups 2% reduced-fat milk
 ½ cup honey
 3 egg yolks
 ¼ cup almonds, toasted and chopped
 Cooking spray
 2 tablespoons honey
 12 ripe figs, halved
 2 tablespoons ruby port

1. Place sugar and lavender in a spice or coffee grinder, and process until ground. Discard any large pieces.
2. Combine milk, ½ cup honey, and egg yolks in a heavy saucepan over medium heat. Cook until mixture is slightly thick and coats the back of a spoon (about 8 minutes), stirring constantly (do not boil). Remove from heat; add lavender powder, stirring until blended. Strain mixture through a sieve into a bowl; discard solids. Chill 2 hours.
3. Pour mixture into freezer can of an ice-cream freezer; freeze according to manufacturer's instructions.
4. Spoon ice cream into a freezer-safe container; stir in almonds. Cover and freeze 1 hour or until firm.
5. Preheat oven to 350°.
6. Coat a 13 x 9-inch baking dish with cooking spray. Drizzle 2 tablespoons honey in bottom of dish. Place figs, cut-sides down, in prepared dish. Bake at 350° for 20 minutes or until figs are tender. Turn figs; add port to dish, and baste figs with honey mixture. Bake an additional 5 minutes. Spoon ice cream into bowls, and serve with figs and sauce. Yield: 4 servings (serving size: about ½ cup ice cream and 6 fig halves).

CALORIES 238 (22% from fat); FAT 5.7g (sat 2.2g, mono 2.4g, poly 0.8g); PROTEIN 6.3g; CARB 42.5g; FIBER 2.6g; CHOL 86mg; IRON 0.7mg; SODIUM 66mg; CALC 191mg

My Big Greek Salad

Memories from a childhood in Greece moved this Washington, D.C., reader to create a zesty and colorful rice salad.

MAKE AHEAD
Greek-Style Picnic Salad

For authentic Greek flavor, substitute two teaspoons chopped fresh oregano for dried.
 —Katherine Andrews, Washington, D.C.

 2 cups uncooked white rice
 1 cup boiling water
 ¾ cup sun-dried tomatoes, packed without oil
 1½ tablespoons olive oil, divided
 8 cups bagged prewashed spinach (about 8 ounces)
 2 garlic cloves, minced
 2 cups (8 ounces) reduced-fat feta cheese, crumbled
 ¼ cup chopped pitted kalamata olives
 1 teaspoon dried oregano
 ½ teaspoon salt
 ½ teaspoon freshly ground black pepper
 1 (15½-ounce) can chickpeas (garbanzo beans), rinsed and drained
 3 tablespoons pine nuts, toasted
 10 lemon wedges (optional)

1. Cook rice according to package directions, omitting salt and fat. Cool to room temperature; set aside.
2. Combine boiling water and sun-dried tomatoes in a bowl; let stand 30 minutes or until soft. Drain and cut into 1-inch pieces.
3. Heat 1½ teaspoons oil in a large skillet over medium-high heat. Add spinach and garlic; sauté 3 minutes or until spinach wilts. Combine rice, tomatoes, spinach mixture, cheese, and next 5 ingredients. Drizzle with 1 tablespoon oil; toss gently to coat. Sprinkle with nuts; serve with lemon wedges, if desired. Yield: 10 servings (serving size: 1 cup).

CALORIES 288 (30% from fat); FAT 9.5g (sat 2.6g, mono 3.6g, poly 1.7g); PROTEIN 10.3g; CARB 41.8g; FIBER 4g; CHOL 8mg; IRON 3.4mg; SODIUM 713mg; CALC 110mg

Marinated Grilled Chicken Legs

"This recipe was an experiment, and it turned out to be one of our favorites."
 —Marie Meyer, Greensboro, North Carolina

 1 cup fresh orange juice
 2 tablespoons fresh lemon juice
 4 teaspoons low-sodium soy sauce
 1 tablespoon dry sherry
 1½ teaspoons bottled minced garlic
 1½ teaspoons balsamic vinegar
 1½ teaspoons basil oil
 1 teaspoon onion powder
 1 teaspoon dark sesame oil
 ½ teaspoon salt
 ¼ teaspoon hot pepper sauce
 8 chicken drumsticks (about 2¼ pounds), skinned
 Cooking spray
 Green onion strips (optional)

1. Combine first 11 ingredients in a large zip-top plastic bag. Add chicken to bag; seal. Marinate in refrigerator 2 hours, turning bag occasionally.
2. Prepare grill.
3. Remove chicken from bag, reserving marinade. Place marinade in a small saucepan; cook over medium heat 3 minutes. Place chicken on grill rack coated with cooking spray; grill 30 minutes or until done, turning and basting occasionally with marinade. Garnish with green onion strips, if desired. Yield: 4 servings (serving size: 2 drumsticks).

CALORIES 215 (31% from fat); FAT 7.5g (sat 1.8g, mono 2.8g, poly 1.8g); PROTEIN 30g; CARB 4.4g; FIBER 0.1g; CHOL 97mg; IRON 1.5mg; SODIUM 339mg; CALC 18mg

Salsa Verde

"When a coworker brought me tomatillos from her garden, I came up with this recipe. It's great with tortilla chips."

—Holly Clebnik, Newington, Connecticut

 8 tomatillos (about 12 ounces)
 ¼ cup chopped green onions
 ¼ cup chopped fresh cilantro
 ½ teaspoon salt
 1 jalapeño pepper, seeded and quartered
 1 (4.5-ounce) can chopped green chiles, undrained

1. Discard husks and stems from tomatillos. Combine tomatillos and remaining ingredients in a food processor; pulse until coarsely chopped. Yield: 2 cups (serving size: ¼ cup).

CALORIES 16 (21% from fat); FAT 0.4g (sat 0.1g, mono 0.1g, poly 0.2g); PROTEIN 0.5g; CARB 3.2g; FIBER 1g; CHOL 0mg; IRON 0.3mg; SODIUM 334mg; CALC 4mg

Orange Chicken Salad with Feta

"This salad combines many of my favorite flavors in a new way. Orange juice concentrate in the dressing gives the salad a fresh taste."

—Jenna Bayley-Burke, Hillsboro, Oregon

 1 pound skinless, boneless chicken breast
    Cooking spray
 8 cups torn leaf lettuce
 1 cup orange bell pepper strips
 1 cup grape or cherry tomatoes, halved
 ½ cup matchstick-cut carrots
 ½ cup (2 ounces) feta cheese, crumbled
 ¼ cup chopped green onions
 3 tablespoons thawed orange juice concentrate, undiluted
 1 tablespoon white vinegar
 1 tablespoon olive oil
 ⅛ teaspoon salt
 ⅛ teaspoon black pepper
 1 (11-ounce) can mandarin oranges in light syrup, drained
 2 tablespoons sliced almonds, toasted

1. Prepare grill.
2. Place chicken on a grill rack coated with cooking spray; grill 6 minutes on each side or until done. Cut into ½-inch-thick slices. Set aside.
3. Combine lettuce and next 5 ingredients in a large bowl. Combine orange juice concentrate, vinegar, oil, salt, and black pepper; stir with a whisk. Pour juice mixture over lettuce mixture, tossing to coat. Place lettuce mixture on each of 4 plates; top with chicken, oranges, and almonds. Yield: 4 servings (serving size: about 2 cups salad, 3 ounces chicken, about 10 mandarin orange segments, and 1½ teaspoons almonds).

CALORIES 299 (28% from fat); FAT 9.3g (sat 3g, mono 4.4g, poly 1.2g); PROTEIN 25.1g; CARB 31.2g; FIBER 4.8g; CHOL 62mg; IRON 1.5mg; SODIUM 351mg; CALC 161mg

Roasted Tricolored Peppers with Crostini

"I was having friends over and wanted to make a crostini appetizer with fresh tomatoes. Then I saw the supermarket's colorful bell peppers—they were beautiful, and I knew if I roasted them they would make a perfect substitute."

—Susan Stewart, Plainview, New York

 1 large red bell pepper
 1 large yellow bell pepper
 1 large orange bell pepper
 ½ cup chopped red onion
 ¼ cup thinly sliced fresh basil
 2 tablespoons chopped fresh cilantro
 2 tablespoons white wine vinegar
 1 tablespoon extravirgin olive oil
 1½ teaspoons sugar
 ¼ teaspoon freshly ground black pepper
 20 (¼-inch-thick) slices diagonally cut French bread baguette

1. Preheat broiler.
2. Cut bell peppers in half lengthwise; discard seeds and membranes. Place pepper halves, skin sides up, on a foil-lined baking sheet; flatten with hand. Broil 15 minutes or until blackened. Place in a zip-top plastic bag; seal. Let stand 15 minutes. Peel and finely chop.
3. Combine bell pepper, onion, basil, and cilantro in a medium bowl. Combine vinegar, oil, sugar, and black pepper in a small bowl, stirring with a whisk. Pour vinegar mixture over bell pepper mixture, tossing to coat. Cover and chill 2 hours. Serve with bread slices. Yield: 10 servings (serving size: ¼ cup bell pepper mixture and 2 bread slices).

CALORIES 215 (14% from fat); FAT 3.4g (sat 0.6g, mono 1.8g, poly 0.7g); PROTEIN 6.2g; CARB 40g; FIBER 2.4g; CHOL 0mg; IRON 1.9mg; SODIUM 387mg; CALC 57mg

Tilapia in Mustard Cream Sauce

"Orange roughy or chicken can be used instead of tilapia, and tomatoes or spinach can be substituted for mushrooms."

—Alix McLearen, Wesley Chapel, Florida

 4 (6-ounce) tilapia fillets
 ½ teaspoon chopped fresh thyme
 ½ teaspoon freshly ground black pepper
 ¼ teaspoon salt
    Cooking spray
 ¾ cup fat-free, less-sodium chicken broth
 1 ounce portobello mushrooms, thinly sliced
 2 tablespoons whipping cream
 2 tablespoons Dijon mustard

1. Sprinkle fish with thyme, pepper, and salt. Heat a large nonstick skillet over medium-high heat. Coat pan with cooking spray. Add fish; cook 1 minute on each side. Add broth, and bring to a boil. Cover, reduce heat, and simmer 5 minutes. Add mushrooms; cook, uncovered, 1 minute or until mushrooms are tender. Remove fish from pan; keep warm.
2. Add cream and mustard to pan; stir with a whisk until well combined. Cook 1 minute or until thoroughly heated. Serve sauce over fish. Yield: 4 servings (serving size: 1 fillet and ¼ cup sauce).

CALORIES 184 (22% from fat); FAT 4.6g (sat 2.1g, mono 1g, poly 0.4g); PROTEIN 32.7g; CARB 1.2g; FIBER 0.6g; CHOL 134mg; IRON 2.2mg; SODIUM 536mg; CALC 40mg

Easy Mushroom Orzo

"I cook lots of pasta. One night I had mushrooms that needed to be used and leftover orzo, so I put them together."

—Christine Zerby, Marengo, Ohio

    1   teaspoon olive oil
    2   garlic cloves, minced
    2   tablespoons dry white wine
    2   tablespoons water
    1   tablespoon low-sodium soy sauce
    1   tablespoon finely chopped fresh
        parsley
    ½   teaspoon dried thyme
    ¼   teaspoon dried oregano
    ¼   teaspoon salt
    ¼   teaspoon freshly ground black
        pepper
    1   (8-ounce) package mushrooms,
        halved
    2   cups hot cooked orzo (about 1
        cup uncooked rice-shaped pasta)

1. Heat oil in a large saucepan over medium-high heat. Add garlic; sauté 1 minute. Add wine and next 8 ingredients; cook 10 minutes or until mushrooms are tender, stirring occasionally. Combine mushroom mixture and orzo in a medium bowl, and toss well to combine. Yield: 4 servings (serving size: ⅔ cup).

CALORIES 229 (7% from fat); FAT 1.9g (sat 0.4g, mono 0.8g, poly 0.1g); PROTEIN 9.6g; CARB 43g; FIBER 2.6g; CHOL 0mg; IRON 2.3mg; SODIUM 283mg; CALC 19mg

Pork Tenderloin Diane

"About three years ago, I made this recipe for my mom on Mother's Day. Roasted new potatoes with rosemary and feta make a nice side dish."

—Amy Luce, Mansfield, Texas

    1   (1-pound) pork tenderloin,
        trimmed and cut into 1-inch-thick
        slices
    ¾   teaspoon lemon pepper
    2   teaspoons butter
    2   tablespoons fresh lemon juice
    1   tablespoon Worcestershire sauce
    1   teaspoon Dijon mustard

1. Sprinkle pork with lemon pepper. Melt butter in a large nonstick skillet over medium heat. Add pork slices to pan; cook 3 minutes on each side or until browned. Remove from pan; keep warm. **2.** Add juice, Worcestershire, and mustard to pan; cook 1 minute, stirring frequently. Return pork to pan; cook 1 minute or until thoroughly heated, turning to coat. Yield: 4 servings (serving size: 3 ounces).

CALORIES 160 (33% from fat); FAT 5.9g (sat 2.3g, mono 2.6g, poly 0.5g); PROTEIN 23.9g; CARB 1.7g; FIBER 0.1g; CHOL 79mg; IRON 1.7mg; SODIUM 230mg; CALC 14mg

inspired vegetarian

Hip Dips and Spreads

Bean dips are growing in popularity at restaurant tables. Make some at home, and taste just how versatile they are.

Bold flavor inspires the versatility of the following recipes, which can be the springboard for vegetarian meals.

Curried Tomato Spread

This spread is equally good served warm or cold. Accompany with whole wheat crackers, toasted baguette slices, or raw vegetables, such as cauliflower. Also try it as a condiment in an Indian or Middle Eastern menu.

    ½   cup water
    2   garlic cloves, chopped
    ½   cup crushed fire-roasted tomatoes
        (such as Muir Glen)
    ½   teaspoon ground cumin
    ¼   teaspoon salt
    ¼   teaspoon curry powder
    ⅛   teaspoon ground turmeric
    ⅛   teaspoon crushed red
        pepper
    1   (16-ounce) can cannellini beans
        or other white beans, rinsed and
        drained

1. Place water and garlic in a small saucepan; bring to a boil. Cook about 3 minutes or until reduced to 2 tablespoons. Add tomatoes and next 5 ingredients; cook 2 minutes over medium-low heat. Stir in beans; cook 2 minutes. **2.** Place bean mixture in a food processor, and process until smooth. Yield: 1¼ cups (serving size: 1 tablespoon).

CALORIES 18 (6% from fat); FAT 0.1g (sat 0g, mono 0g, poly 0.1g); PROTEIN 0.9g; CARB 3.3g; FIBER 0.9g; CHOL 0mg; IRON 0.4mg; SODIUM 77mg; CALC 9mg

Cannellini Pesto

A staple of Italian cooking, cannellini beans are an ideal partner for the garlicky basil pesto. Bring out a platter of crisp, fresh green beans and celery sticks for dipping. The spread makes a delicious substitute for tomato sauce in pizza, too.

    2   (16-ounce) cans cannellini beans
        or other white beans, rinsed and
        drained
    1   cup basil leaves
    2   tablespoons grated fresh Parmesan
        cheese
    2   tablespoons water
    1   teaspoon olive oil
    ¼   teaspoon salt
    1   garlic clove, crushed
    1   tablespoon pine nuts, toasted
    Basil sprig (optional)

1. Place first 7 ingredients in a food processor; process until smooth. Add nuts; pulse 5 times or until nuts are chopped. Place mixture in a bowl. Garnish with basil sprig, if desired. Yield: 1½ cups (serving size: 1 tablespoon).

CALORIES 24 (23% from fat); FAT 0.6g (sat 0.1g, mono 0.2g, poly 0.2g); PROTEIN 1.1g; CARB 3.3g; FIBER 1g; CHOL 0.3mg; IRON 0.4mg; SODIUM 78mg; CALC 15mg

Provençal Olive Spread

Serve with round, crisp lavash crackers, thin breadsticks, or baguette slices. The spread is also a terrific condiment on vegetarian burgers and pasta.

  2 (15.5-ounce) cans Great Northern beans or other white beans, rinsed and drained
  4 teaspoons capers
  4 teaspoons red wine vinegar
  1 teaspoon fennel seeds
  ½ teaspoon dried oregano
  ¼ teaspoon salt
  16 kalamata olives, pitted

1. Place all ingredients in a food processor; process until smooth. Place bean mixture in a bowl. Yield: 2 cups (serving size: 1 tablespoon).

CALORIES 21 (26% from fat); FAT 0.6g (sat 0.1g, mono 0.4g, poly 0.1g); PROTEIN 1g; CARB 2.7g; FIBER 1g; CHOL 0mg; IRON 0.2mg; SODIUM 116mg; CALC 7mg

Red-Red Bean Spread

Roasted red peppers give this spread smoky sweetness. You can substitute 1½ cups bottled roasted red bell peppers. Serve with toasted bagel chips or raw vegetables. You can also top crostini with this spread and a slice of fresh mozzarella.

  2 red bell peppers
  1 (15-ounce) can kidney beans, rinsed and drained
  2 tablespoons tomato paste
  ½ teaspoon salt
  ½ teaspoon grated lemon rind
  ¼ teaspoon freshly ground black pepper
  Dash of ground red pepper

1. Preheat broiler.
2. Cut bell peppers in half lengthwise; discard seeds and membranes. Place pepper halves, skin sides up, on a foil-lined baking sheet; flatten with hand. Broil 10 minutes or until blackened. Place in a zip-top plastic bag; seal. Let stand 5 minutes. Peel and chop. Place bell peppers, beans, and remaining ingredients in a food processor, and process until smooth. Yield: 1½ cups (serving size: 1 tablespoon).

CALORIES 14 (6% from fat); FAT 0.1g (sat 0g, mono 0g, poly 0.1g); PROTEIN 0.8g; CARB 2.5g; FIBER 0.6g; CHOL 0mg; IRON 0.2mg; SODIUM 71mg; CALC 7mg

Rosemary-Chickpea Dip

Fresh rosemary and lemon brighten mild, nutty chickpeas. Dip with pita wedges or endive leaves. For a quick lunch, try this in pita bread with sliced cucumbers and tomatoes. Or thin with a little vegetable broth to make an easy soup.

  2 teaspoons olive oil
  1 cup chopped green onions
  2 (15½-ounce) cans chickpeas (garbanzo beans), rinsed and drained
  ¼ cup fat-free, less-sodium vegetable broth (such as Swanson's Certified Organic)
  2 tablespoons fresh lemon juice
  1½ teaspoons chopped fresh rosemary
  ½ teaspoon salt

1. Heat oil in a large nonstick skillet over medium-high heat. Add onions; sauté 3 minutes or until tender. Add beans; sauté 1 minute. Place bean mixture, broth, and remaining ingredients in a food processor; process until smooth. Place bean mixture in a bowl. Yield: 1½ cups (serving size: 1 tablespoon).

CALORIES 27 (30% from fat); FAT 0.9g (sat 0.1g, mono 0.5g, poly 0.3g); PROTEIN 1g; CARB 4.1g; FIBER 1.1g; CHOL 0mg; IRON 0.4mg; SODIUM 107mg; CALC 11mg

Tex-Mex Pinto Bean Spread

Fiber-rich, low-fat pinto beans are the base of this tasty dip, made zesty with lime, cilantro, and jalapeño. Serve with baked tortilla chips. You can also perk up quesadillas or vegetarian tacos with this spread.

  1 (15-ounce) can pinto beans, rinsed and drained
  ½ cup chopped onion
  2 tablespoons chopped fresh cilantro
  2 teaspoons fresh lime juice
  ½ teaspoon kosher salt
  ½ jalapeño pepper, seeded
  ½ cup chopped plum tomato
  1 tablespoon pumpkinseeds, toasted

1. Place first 6 ingredients in a food processor, and process until smooth. Place bean mixture in a bowl. Stir in tomato, and sprinkle with pumpkinseeds. Yield: 1¼ cups (serving size: 1 tablespoon).

CALORIES 15 (12% from fat); FAT 0.2g (sat 0g, mono 0g, poly 0.1g); PROTEIN 0.7g; CARB 2.7g; FIBER 0.7g; CHOL 0mg; IRON 0.2mg; SODIUM 85mg; CALC 7mg

Caramelized Black Bean "Butter"

Caramelized onions lend the black beans an intriguing sweetness and complexity, which is highlighted by balsamic vinegar and cocoa. Spread on a sandwich of sliced ciabatta with grilled vegetables and arugula. It's also great with baked tortilla chips.

  1 tablespoon olive oil
  4 cups chopped onion
  2 (15-ounce) cans black beans, rinsed and drained
  1 tablespoon balsamic vinegar
  2 teaspoons unsweetened cocoa
  ½ teaspoon salt
  ½ teaspoon paprika
  1 tablespoon chopped fresh parsley

1. Heat oil in a large nonstick skillet over medium-high heat. Add onion; sauté 10 minutes or until golden. Place onion, beans, and next 4 ingredients in a food processor; process until smooth. Place bean mixture in a bowl. Sprinkle with parsley. Yield: 3 cups (serving size: 1 tablespoon).

CALORIES 17 (2% from fat); FAT 0.4g (sat 0.1g, mono 0.2g, poly 0g); PROTEIN 0.7g; CARB 3.1g; FIBER 0.8g; CHOL 0mg; IRON 0.2mg; SODIUM 48mg; CALC 7mg

Weighing In

Kitchen scales provide an accurate, convenient, and fast way to measure ingredients.

When precision is key, a scale is the best tool for measuring ingredients. Consider these examples:

• Some recipes, such as herb pesto, call for leafy ingredients that don't fit well into measuring cups. You may end up with a dry pesto if the leaves are tightly, not loosely, packed in the cup.

• Measuring cubed bread can be difficult because large cubes can be unwieldy in a cup measure.

• Measuring cheese can be tricky if it's cubed or grated. It's much easier to weigh the amount of cheese you need before shredding or cubing than to try and pack it into measuring cups.

• When measuring flour, cooks should always spoon it into the measuring cup—but many of us scoop the measuring cup into the flour. This causes the amount of flour to vary greatly and makes a big difference when baking delicate cakes or pastries.

• Scales are good for measuring dried pasta or other bulky items that don't fit well into measuring cups.

• When dividing dough into several equal pieces for dinner rolls, pizzas, and the like, it's much easier to use a scale than to judge each by eye.

You can also employ a kitchen scale to determine serving sizes. Not many people know what a four-ounce portion of uncooked meat looks like. But once you've weighed a few portions, you quickly learn how much meat that actually is.

To become accustomed to using a scale, you may want to start with an inexpensive spring-type model, available in kitchenware stores for as little as $10. Then, as you begin weighing more food items, upgrade to a more precise digital scale.

Cheesy Baked Cavatappi with Onions and Peppers

Determining an accurate cup measure of a wavy pasta, such as cavatappi, can be tricky; weighing the pasta is simpler. And it's much easier to weigh the amount of cheese you need and shred it all at once.

  1 teaspoon olive oil
1½ cups chopped onion
2½ cups chopped red bell pepper (about 2 large peppers)
 12 ounces uncooked cavatappi (about 4 cups)
2½ cups 1% low-fat milk
  1 ounce all-purpose flour (about ¼ cup)
1½ teaspoons butter
  4 ounces sharp white Cheddar cheese, shredded (1 cup)
  4 ounces Gruyère cheese, shredded (1 cup)
  ¾ teaspoon salt
  ¼ teaspoon freshly ground black pepper
Dash of ground nutmeg
Dash of ground red pepper
Cooking spray
  2 tablespoons dry breadcrumbs
Chopped fresh parsley (optional)

1. Preheat oven to 350°.
2. Heat oil in a large saucepan over medium-high heat. Add onion; sauté 3 minutes or until crisp-tender. Add bell pepper; sauté 3 minutes. Set mixture aside.
3. Cook pasta according to package directions, omitting salt and fat. Drain.
4. Combine milk and flour in a medium bowl, stirring with a whisk. Melt butter in saucepan over medium-high heat; add milk mixture, stirring with a whisk. Cook 3 minutes or until slightly thick, stirring constantly. Remove from heat; gradually add cheeses, stirring with a whisk until cheeses melt. Stir in salt, black pepper, nutmeg, and ground red pepper. Add onion mixture and pasta, stirring well to combine. Spoon mixture into a 13 x 9-inch baking dish coated with cooking spray. Sprinkle breadcrumbs evenly over pasta mixture. Bake at 350° for 35 minutes or until bubbly. Garnish with parsley, if desired. Yield: 8 servings (serving size: about 1½ cups).

CALORIES 361 (30% from fat); FAT 12.2g (sat 6.3g, mono 3.8g, poly 1.1g); PROTEIN 17.1g; CARB 46.1g; FIBER 1.7g; CHOL 36mg; IRON 2.3mg; SODIUM 421mg; CALC 360mg

Purchasing Tips

The maximum weight a scale can hold varies from model to model. The smaller the maximum capacity, the more accurate a scale will be. Most home cooks will be content with one that has a maximum capacity of two to four pounds. If you need to weigh the occasional large cut of meat or giant batch of pizza dough, consider a second scale with higher maximum capacity. When shopping, look for these features:

• Select a scale with a platform or bowl that's large enough to hold the types of ingredients you normally use, or one with a flat platform that will accommodate a plate upon which you can place ingredients.

• Make sure the scale has an easy-to-read display—one that you don't need to bend down to view.

• Choose a model with a detachable platform or bowl for easy cleaning, or look for a scale designed without nooks and crannies in which food can become lodged.

• Look for a scale with an easy taring feature. Taring refers to setting the scale to zero after placing a bowl or plate on it so you weigh only the contents of the container, without the weight of the container. For many digital models, all you need to do is press a button to tare the scale. For spring scales, you'll need to turn a dial; just make sure the dial is easy to access.

• For the best of both worlds, select a scale that weighs in both metric (grams) and U.S. measurements (ounces).

• If counter space is a concern, look for a scale with a low profile; many digital scales are slim enough to fit into a drawer.

Kitchen Scale Types

There are three basic styles of scales you'll find for use in the kitchen—balance, spring, and electronic or digital. **Balance scales,** however accurate, are difficult to use and hard to find, so we've focused on the other two types. **Spring scales** are the least expensive, but also the least accurate because they usually measure food in one-ounce increments. They are controlled by a spring that yields to pressure when weight is applied. Spring scales are widely available and come in two basic styles. Flat spring scales have the spring needle contained within the base, and the scale can be tared or zeroed out by turning the base. The second type is more upright and has a bowl or dish that rests on the spring for measuring, and usually has a large round dial on the front that shows the weight. Spring scales range in price from $10 to $100, but most models are less than $40. **Electronic or digital scales** are the most accurate. Most can be switched between metric and U.S. measurements (in ounces and pounds). The most accurate of these show measurements in one-gram increments, while others use five-gram or larger increments. Electronic scales range from $30 to $300, but an adequate model sells for $50 to $70.

Country Potatoes au Gratin

This filling dish works well as an entrée with a side salad completing the meal. If you prefer to have it as a side dish, it will make 12 servings.

2   teaspoons butter
1   onion (about 5½ ounces), thinly sliced
3   garlic cloves, minced
4   cups 2% reduced-fat milk
1   teaspoon salt
¼   teaspoon freshly ground black pepper
3   ounces all-purpose flour (about ⅔ cup)
6   ounces shredded sharp Cheddar cheese (1½ cups), divided
6   ounces diced ham (about 1¼ cups)
3   pounds peeled baking potatoes, cut into ⅛-inch-thick slices
Cooking spray

1. Preheat oven to 350°.
2. Melt butter in a Dutch oven over medium-high heat. Add onion and garlic; sauté 5 minutes or until onion is tender. Combine milk, salt, pepper, and flour, stirring with a whisk. Add milk mixture to pan. Bring to a simmer; cook until slightly thick (about 2 minutes), stirring frequently. Add 4 ounces cheese and ham, stirring until cheese melts. Stir in potatoes.
3. Place potato mixture in a 13 x 9-inch baking dish coated with cooking spray. Sprinkle with 2 ounces cheese. Cover with foil coated with cooking spray. Bake at 350° for 45 minutes. Uncover and bake an additional 30 minutes or until lightly browned and potatoes are tender. Let stand 15 minutes before serving. Yield: 8 servings.

CALORIES 376 (22% from fat); FAT 12g (sat 7.6g, mono 2.8g, poly 0.5g); PROTEIN 16.7g; CARB 50.3g; FIBER 3.8g; CHOL 46mg; IRON 1.3mg; SODIUM 727mg; CALC 321mg

Chocolate-Cinnamon Bread Pudding

Measuring the bread by weight is important in this recipe—12 ounces of cubed bread can vary from seven to 10 cups. If you use too little bread, the dessert will be loose and wet; too much bread, and it will be dry. But just the right amount yields a decadently creamy, rich dessert.

5½   ounces sugar (about ⅔ cup)
3   large eggs, lightly beaten
2½   cups 2% reduced-fat milk
3   ounces semisweet chocolate, finely chopped (about ¾ cup)
2¼   ounces unsweetened cocoa (about ½ cup)
2   teaspoons vanilla extract
½   teaspoon ground cinnamon
Dash of ground nutmeg
12   ounces (1-inch) cubed French bread (about 10 cups)
Cooking spray
1   ounce sugar (about 2 tablespoons)

1. Preheat oven to 350°.
2. Combine 5½ ounces sugar and eggs in a large bowl, stirring with a whisk. Heat milk over medium-high heat in a small, heavy saucepan to 180° or until tiny bubbles form around edge (do not boil). Remove from heat; add chocolate and cocoa, stirring with a whisk until chocolate melts and cocoa dissolves. Gradually add hot milk mixture to sugar mixture, stirring constantly with a whisk. Stir in vanilla, cinnamon, and nutmeg. Add bread, tossing to coat; let stand 30 minutes, tossing occasionally.
3. Spoon bread mixture into an 8-inch square baking dish coated with cooking spray; sprinkle 1 ounce of sugar evenly over bread mixture. Bake at 350° for 40 minutes or until set. Serve warm. Yield: 8 servings.

CALORIES 327 (23% from fat); FAT 8.4g (sat 4.1g, mono 1.9g, poly 0.6g); PROTEIN 10.5g; CARB 55.6g; FIBER 3.7g; CHOL 85mg; IRON 2.3mg; SODIUM 325mg; CALC 144mg

Citrus Chiffon Cake

Weighing the flour and sugar guarantees a billowy cake that's light and airy (and worthy of *Cooking Light* Test Kitchens' highest rating for taste).

1½ teaspoons baking powder
½ teaspoon salt
8 ounces granulated sugar (about 1 cup), divided
6 ounces sifted cake flour (about 1¾ cups)
1 tablespoon grated orange rind
½ cup fresh orange juice (about 1 orange)
5 tablespoons canola oil
1 tablespoon grated lemon rind
1½ teaspoons vanilla extract
3 large egg yolks, lightly beaten
8 large egg whites
¾ teaspoon cream of tartar
2 teaspoons powdered sugar

1. Preheat oven to 325°.
2. Combine baking powder, salt, 7 ounces sugar, and flour in a large bowl, stirring with a whisk until mixture is well combined.
3. Combine orange rind and next 5 ingredients in a medium bowl, stirring with a whisk. Add rind mixture to flour mixture, stirring until smooth.
4. Place egg whites in a large bowl; beat with a mixer at high speed until foamy. Add cream of tartar; beat until soft peaks form. Gradually add 1 ounce sugar, beating until stiff peaks form. Gently stir one-fourth of egg white mixture into flour mixture; gently fold in remaining egg white mixture.
5. Spoon batter into an ungreased 10-inch tube pan, spreading evenly. Break air pockets by cutting through batter with a knife. Bake at 325° for 45 minutes or until cake springs back when lightly touched. Invert pan; cool completely. Loosen cake from sides of pan using a narrow metal spatula. Invert cake onto plate. Sift powdered sugar over top of cake. Yield: 16 servings (serving size: 1 slice).

CALORIES 158 (30% from fat); FAT 5.3g (sat 0.6g, mono 3g, poly 1.5g); PROTEIN 3.3g; CARB 24.2g; FIBER 0.3g; CHOL 38mg; IRON 1mg; SODIUM 149mg; CALC 34mg

Cornmeal, Fennel, and Golden Raisin Dinner Rolls

A scale can also serve as a quick tool to achieve an even division of dough. Just pinch off enough dough to equal the correct weight for each roll. After rolling the dough pieces into balls, freeze the portions you don't want to cook in a single layer on a baking sheet, then transfer to a zip-top plastic bag to keep in the freezer for up to two months. Thaw dough balls at room temperature and allow to rise to double their size before baking as directed in the recipe.

¼ teaspoon sugar
1 package dry yeast (about 2¼ teaspoons)
1¼ cups warm water (100° to 110°)
1 cup golden raisins
1 teaspoon salt
1 teaspoon fennel seeds, crushed
6¼ ounces all-purpose flour (about 1⅓ cups)
5⅓ ounces bread flour (about 1 cup plus 3 tablespoons)
2⅔ ounces cornmeal (about 9 tablespoons)
Cooking spray
1 large egg, lightly beaten

1. Dissolve sugar and yeast in warm water in a large bowl; let stand 5 minutes. Add raisins and next 5 ingredients, stirring until a stiff dough forms. Turn dough out onto a floured surface. Knead until smooth and elastic (about 10 minutes; dough will feel sticky).
2. Place dough in a large bowl coated with cooking spray, turning to coat top. Cover and let rise in a warm place (85°), free from drafts, 1 hour or until doubled in size. (Gently press two fingers into dough. If indentation remains, dough has risen enough.) Punch dough down; cover and let rise 1 hour or until doubled in size.
3. Punch dough down. Divide dough into 16 (1½-ounce) portions. Working with one dough portion at a time (cover remaining dough portions to prevent drying), roll each portion into a ball. Place dough balls on a large baking sheet coated with cooking spray. Cover and let rise 30 minutes or until dough balls are doubled in size.
4. Preheat oven to 450°.
5. Uncover dough. Gently brush egg evenly over dough. Bake at 450° for 10 minutes or until rolls are browned on bottom and sound hollow when tapped. Remove from pan; cool on wire racks. Yield: 16 servings (serving size: 1 roll).

CALORIES 126 (5% from fat); FAT 0.7g (sat 0.2g, mono 0.2g, poly 0.2g); PROTEIN 3.6g; CARB 26.5g; FIBER 1.4g; CHOL 13mg; IRON 1.4mg; SODIUM 154mg; CALC 12mg

Cilantro Pesto Primavera with Seared Tuna

Using too much of an herb in a lower-fat pesto will result in a dry paste because there's not enough oil in the sauce to keep it loose. Weighing the herbs ensures accuracy. You can make the pesto up to two days ahead; it doesn't lose its bright green color as basil pesto is prone to do. Use leftover pesto as a sandwich spread or a thick sauce to dollop over fish or chicken.

8 ounces uncooked penne rigate (about 2 cups)
1 tablespoon butter
1 small zucchini, halved lengthwise and sliced (about ¾ cup)
1 small yellow squash, halved lengthwise and sliced (about ½ cup)
½ cup sugar snap peas, trimmed
½ cup halved grape tomatoes
½ cup Cilantro Pesto
¼ teaspoon salt
¼ teaspoon freshly ground black pepper
6 (6-ounce) Yellowfin tuna fillets
Cooking spray

1. Cook pasta according to package directions, omitting salt and fat. Drain; place in a large bowl.
2. Melt butter in a large nonstick skillet over medium-high heat. Add zucchini, squash, and peas; sauté 2 minutes or until crisp-tender. Stir in tomatoes; sauté 30 seconds. Add vegetable mixture and Cilantro Pesto to pasta, tossing gently to coat.

Continued

3. Sprinkle salt and black pepper evenly over tuna. Return skillet to medium-high heat. Coat pan with cooking spray. Add tuna to pan; cook 2 minutes on each side or until desired degree of doneness. Cut tuna across grain into ½-inch-thick slices. Spoon about 1 cup pasta mixture onto each of 6 plates; top each serving with 1 sliced tuna steak. Yield: 6 servings.

(Totals include Cilantro Pesto) CALORIES 404 (20% from fat); FAT 8.8g (sat 2.9g, mono 3.8g, poly 1.2g); PROTEIN 46.2g; CARB 32.2g; FIBER 2.1g; CHOL 83mg; IRON 3.2mg; SODIUM 478mg; CALC 126mg

MAKE AHEAD

CILANTRO PESTO:

- ½ cup chopped green onions
- 2 tablespoons fresh lime juice
- 1 tablespoon grated peeled fresh ginger
- ¾ teaspoon salt
- ½ teaspoon freshly ground black pepper
- Dash of ground red pepper
- 2 garlic cloves, minced
- 2 ounces grated fresh Parmesan cheese (½ cup)
- 1 ounce fresh cilantro leaves (about 2 cups loosely packed)
- 2 tablespoons extravirgin olive oil

1. Place first 9 ingredients in a food processor, and process until finely minced. With processor on, slowly pour oil through food chute, and process until well blended. Yield: ¾ cup (serving size: 1 tablespoon).

CALORIES 43 (73% from fat); FAT 3.5g (sat 1.1g, mono 2g, poly 0.3g); PROTEIN 1.8g; CARB 1.1g; FIBER 0.3g; CHOL 3mg; IRON 0.1mg; SODIUM 226mg; CALC 59mg

BEFORE	AFTER
SERVING SIZE	
1 wedge	
CALORIES PER SERVING	
370	325
FAT	
22.6g	10.7g
PERCENT OF TOTAL CALORIES	
55%	30%

Scandinavian Souvenir

A favorite Swedish shrimp pie translates into a lighter version that is every bit as good as the original.

On a European vacation, J.G. Humphries of McDonough, Georgia, and her husband, David, stopped to visit friends in the small Swedish town of Säffle. Upon their arrival, they were treated to a casual meal featuring a hearty quichelike pie filled with shrimp and Havarti cheese. After one bite, J.G. knew she couldn't leave without the recipe. Although J.G. obtained the recipe, and often served the pie for Sunday night suppers, she knew it was too high in fat. She asked us to lighten it.

The original filling had more than 122 calories and eight grams of fat per serving, derived mostly from whole eggs, whole milk, and Havarti cheese. We lowered both numbers by using egg substitute, evaporated fat-free milk, and fat-free cream cheese. These changes, along with a slight decrease in the amount of cheese used, lowered the calories per slice by 45. We were also able to trim the fat by more than 50 percent, from 22.6 grams to slightly more than 10 grams.

Shrimp Pie

Much like a cheesecake crust, the crumbly mixture is simply pressed into a deep-dish pie plate—no kneading or rolling required.

PASTRY:

- 1¼ cups all-purpose flour
- ¼ cup semolina or pasta flour
- 2 teaspoons sugar
- ¼ teaspoon salt
- 2 tablespoons butter, chilled and cut into small pieces
- 1 tablespoon vegetable shortening
- ¼ cup ice water
- ½ teaspoon cider vinegar
- Cooking spray

FILLING:

- 12 ounces uncooked large shrimp, peeled, deveined, and chopped
- ¼ cup (2 ounces) fat-free cream cheese, softened
- ½ cup egg substitute, divided
- 2 teaspoons all-purpose flour
- 1 cup evaporated fat-free milk
- ½ cup (2 ounces) shredded Havarti or fontina cheese
- 1½ tablespoons chopped fresh dill
- ⅛ teaspoon salt

1. Preheat oven to 375°.

2. To prepare pastry, lightly spoon 1¼ cups all-purpose flour and semolina flour into dry measuring cups; level with a knife. Combine flours, sugar, and ¼ teaspoon salt in a medium bowl; cut in butter and shortening with a pastry blender or 2 knives until mixture resembles coarse meal.

3. Combine ice water and vinegar in a small bowl. Add water mixture to flour mixture; toss with a fork until well combined (mixture will be crumbly and will not form a ball). Press mixture into bottom and up sides of a 9-inch deep-dish pie plate coated with cooking spray. Bake at 375° for 5 minutes. Remove from oven; cool on a wire rack.

4. To prepare filling, heat a large non-stick skillet over medium-high heat. Coat pan with cooking spray. Add shrimp; cook 1 minute or until shrimp turn pink. Remove from heat.

5. Combine cream cheese and ¼ cup egg substitute in a medium bowl; beat with a mixer at medium speed until well blended. Add 2 teaspoons flour; beat 1 minute. Beat in ¼ cup egg substitute and milk. Stir in shrimp, Havarti cheese, dill, and ⅛ teaspoon salt. Pour shrimp mixture into prepared crust. Bake at 375° for 40 minutes or until set. Remove from oven; let stand 10 minutes before serving. Yield: 6 servings (serving size: 1 wedge).

CALORIES 325 (30% from fat); FAT 10.7g (sat 4.7g, mono 3.4g, poly 1.5g); PROTEIN 24.4g; CARB 32.6g; FIBER 0.9g; CHOL 108mg; IRON 3.5mg; SODIUM 450mg; CALC 249mg

Sparkling Fruit Gelées, page 205

Grilled Vidalia Onion and Steak Sandwiches, page 197

Pike Place Market Salad, page 208

Sesame-Chile Chicken with Gingered Watermelon
Salsa, page 198

Mango Rice Salad with Grilled Shrimp,
page 192

Summer Cookbook

Your A to Z guide to the season's best produce, flavors, tips, and techniques

Apricots

Petite **apricots** are at their peak in June and July. Choose plump, fairly firm fruit that yields to slight pressure. Apricots are delicate and should be eaten within two to three days of purchase; store in a plastic bag in the refrigerator. Their oval pit is easily removed once the fruit is halved.

MAKE AHEAD
Corn Bread with Curried Apricot Chutney

The contrast of smoky bacon, sweet fruit, and spicy jalapeño yields a complex-flavored chutney. Because apricot skins are tender, there's no need to peel the fruit. Serve the chutney and bread warm. You can make them both a day in advance and reheat before serving—wrap the bread in foil, and heat at 300° for about 10 minutes. Microwave the chutney at HIGH about one minute.

CORN BREAD:
- 1 cup all-purpose flour
- 1 cup yellow cornmeal
- 1 tablespoon baking powder
- ¾ teaspoon salt
- 1 cup low-fat buttermilk
- 3 tablespoons butter, melted
- 2 tablespoons honey
- 3 large eggs, lightly beaten
- Cooking spray

CHUTNEY:
- 2 bacon slices, cut into 2-inch pieces
- 1 cup diced Vidalia or other sweet onion
- ¼ teaspoon curry powder
- 1 cup chopped apricots (about 4 medium)
- 1 tablespoon finely chopped seeded jalapeño pepper
- 1 tablespoon honey
- ¼ teaspoon salt

1. Preheat oven to 400°.
2. To prepare corn bread, lightly spoon flour into a dry measuring cup; level with a knife. Combine flour, cornmeal, baking powder, and ¾ teaspoon salt in a large bowl, stirring with a whisk; make a well in center of mixture. Combine buttermilk, butter, 2 tablespoons honey, and eggs, stirring with a whisk; add to flour mixture, stirring just until moist. Spoon batter into a 13 x 9-inch baking pan coated with cooking spray. Bake at 400° for 15 minutes or until a wooden pick inserted in center comes out clean. Cool in pan 10 minutes on a wire rack; remove from pan. Cool completely on wire rack. Cut into 24 (2¼-inch) squares.
3. To prepare chutney, cook bacon in a medium saucepan over medium-high heat until crisp. Remove bacon from pan, reserving 1 teaspoon drippings in pan. Crumble bacon, and set aside. Add onion and curry powder to drippings in pan; sauté 5 minutes. Add apricots and remaining 3 ingredients; cook 3 minutes or until thoroughly heated. Remove from heat; stir in crumbled bacon. Serve chutney with corn bread. Yield: 12 servings (serving size: 2 corn bread squares and 2 tablespoons chutney).

CALORIES 177 (26% from fat); FAT 5.2g (sat 2.2g, mono 1.9g, poly 0.4g); PROTEIN 5g; CARB 27.3g; FIBER 0.8g; CHOL 63mg; IRON 1.3mg; SODIUM 404mg; CALC 106mg

Barbecue & Blueberries

MAKE AHEAD
Peach Barbecue Sauce

- 1 tablespoon olive oil
- 1½ cups chopped onion
- 3 cups chopped peeled peaches (about 4 large)
- 1 teaspoon freshly ground black pepper
- ½ teaspoon salt
- 6 garlic cloves, minced
- 2 cups beer
- 1 cup ketchup
- 1 cup prepared mustard
- ¼ cup packed brown sugar
- 3 tablespoons cider vinegar
- 2 tablespoons Worcestershire sauce
- 2 teaspoons ground cumin
- 2 teaspoons hot pepper sauce
- 1½ teaspoons ground coriander
- ¼ teaspoon ground cinnamon

1. Heat oil in a large saucepan over medium heat. Add onion; cook 5 minutes or until tender, stirring occasionally. Add peaches, pepper, salt, and garlic; cook 1 minute, stirring frequently. Stir in beer and remaining ingredients, and bring to a boil. Reduce heat, and simmer, uncovered, 30 minutes. Place half of mixture in a blender. Remove center piece of blender lid (to allow steam to escape); secure lid on blender. Place a clean dish towel over opening in blender lid (to prevent spills). Process until smooth. Pour puréed mixture into a medium bowl. Repeat procedure with remaining mixture. Yield: 5 cups (serving size: ¼ cup).
NOTE: Refrigerate sauce up to 10 days.

CALORIES 59 (20% from fat); FAT 1.3g (sat 0.1g, mono 0.8g, poly 0.2g); PROTEIN 1.2g; CARB 12g; FIBER 0.9g; CHOL 0mg; IRON 0.7mg; SODIUM 350mg; CALC 27mg

Blueberry-Lemon Coffee Cake

Blueberries and lemon are a natural match, and they come together nicely in this fruit-filled snack cake. Almond paste, a sweet mixture of ground almonds and sugar, contributes a mildly nutty flavor and moist texture. Almond paste is found in the baking section of the grocery store. (Don't substitute marzipan, which is sweeter and has a smoother texture.) If it's hard, soften it by microwaving at HIGH 10 to 15 seconds.

CAKE:

1½ cups all-purpose flour
2 teaspoons baking powder
¼ teaspoon baking soda
½ teaspoon salt
½ cup sugar
⅓ cup almond paste
2 tablespoons chilled butter, cut into small pieces
1 large egg
1 tablespoon lemon juice
¾ cup fat-free milk
1½ cups blueberries
2 teaspoons grated lemon rind
Cooking spray

TOPPING:

¼ cup sugar
3 tablespoons sliced almonds, chopped
1½ tablespoons butter, melted
½ teaspoon ground cinnamon

1. Preheat oven to 350°.
2. To prepare cake, lightly spoon flour into dry measuring cups, and level with a knife. Combine flour, baking powder, baking soda, and salt in a small bowl, stirring with a whisk.
3. Place ½ cup sugar, almond paste, and 2 tablespoons butter in a large bowl; beat with a mixer at medium speed until well blended. Add egg and lemon juice, beating well. Add flour mixture and milk alternately to sugar mixture, beginning and ending with flour mixture. Fold in blueberries and rind. Spoon batter into a 9-inch square baking pan coated with cooking spray.
4. To prepare topping, combine ¼ cup sugar and remaining 3 ingredients in a small bowl, tossing with a fork until moist. Sprinkle topping evenly over batter. Bake at 350° for 35 minutes or until a wooden pick inserted in center comes out clean. Cool in pan on a wire rack. Yield: 12 servings (serving size: 1 piece).

CALORIES 196 (30% from fat); FAT 6.5g (sat 2.1g, mono 3.2g, poly 0.8g); PROTEIN 3.8g; CARB 31.6g; FIBER 1.4g; CHOL 27mg; IRON 1.2mg; SODIUM 243mg; CALC 82mg

Corn

Fresh Corn and Scallop Johnnycakes with Green Onion Sauce

Similar to pancakes, johnnycakes are made with cornmeal for a bit of crunch. This appetizer version pairs sweet bay scallops with crisp summer corn. Place cooked johnnycakes on a baking sheet in a 225° oven to keep them warm while the remaining batter cooks on the stovetop. Garnish with sliced chives, if desired.

SAUCE:

½ cup thinly sliced green onions
¼ cup loosely packed fresh parsley leaves
2 tablespoons fresh lemon juice
2 tablespoons light mayonnaise
1 tablespoon reduced-fat sour cream
1 tablespoon ketchup
1 tablespoon Dijon mustard
⅛ teaspoon ground red pepper

CAKES:

1 cup yellow cornmeal
2 tablespoons all-purpose flour
1 tablespoon sugar
1 teaspoon baking powder
½ teaspoon baking soda
½ teaspoon salt
¼ teaspoon ground red pepper
1¼ cups low-fat buttermilk
1 tablespoon chopped fresh chives
1 large egg, lightly beaten
1 cup fresh corn kernels (about 2 ears)
¾ pound bay scallops, coarsely chopped
Cooking spray

1. To prepare sauce, place first 8 ingredients in a food processor; process until smooth. Cover and chill until ready to serve.
2. To prepare cakes, combine cornmeal and next 6 ingredients in a large bowl; add buttermilk, chives, and egg, stirring with a whisk until blended. Fold in corn and scallops.
3. Heat a nonstick griddle or large nonstick skillet over medium-high heat. Coat pan with cooking spray. Spoon batter by heaping tablespoons onto hot pan. Turn johnnycakes over when edges begin to brown (about 2 minutes). Cook 2 minutes or until lightly browned. Remove johnnycakes from pan; cover and keep warm. Repeat procedure with cooking spray and remaining batter. Serve warm with sauce. Yield: 8 servings (serving size: 3 johnnycakes and 1 tablespoon sauce).

CALORIES 189 (15% from fat); FAT 3.2g (sat 0.8g, mono 1.3g, poly 0.4g); PROTEIN 11.7g; CARB 27.8g; FIBER 1.5g; CHOL 44mg; IRON 1.2mg; SODIUM 509mg; CALC 101mg

Dill

Dill and Beet-Cured Salmon with Cucumber Salad

Dill and salmon are a classic pair. The salt draws moisture from the fish as a way to preserve it. It takes three days to cure, but the results are well worth the wait.

SALMON:

⅔ cup chopped fresh dill
⅓ cup kosher salt
¼ cup sugar
2 teaspoons coarsely ground black pepper
1 teaspoon crushed coriander seeds
1 (3-pound) salmon fillet, cut in half horizontally
1½ cups shredded peeled beets (about 2 medium)

SALAD:

SALAD:

    2   cucumbers, peeled, halved
        lengthwise, seeded, and thinly
        sliced
    1   tablespoon kosher salt
    ¼   cup rice vinegar
    2   tablespoons chopped fresh dill
    2   teaspoons sugar
    ½   teaspoon crushed coriander
        seeds
    ¼   teaspoon freshly ground black
        pepper
        Dill sprigs (optional)

1. To prepare salmon, combine first 5 ingredients in a small bowl. Sprinkle one-third of dill mixture in bottom of a 13 x 9-inch baking dish. Arrange 1 salmon half, skin-side down, on dill mixture. Combine one-third of dill mixture and beets in a small bowl; spread over salmon. Top with remaining salmon half, skin-side up. Spread remaining dill mixture evenly over salmon. Cover loosely with plastic wrap. Place a cast-iron skillet or other heavy object on top of salmon to weigh it down, and refrigerate 24 hours.

2. Remove skillet, and set aside. Uncover salmon, and carefully turn salmon stack over. Cover loosely with plastic wrap. Place skillet on top of salmon, and refrigerate 24 hours. Repeat procedure one more time.

3. To prepare salad, place cucumbers in a colander; sprinkle with 1 tablespoon salt. Toss well. Drain in sink 1 hour. Place cucumbers on several layers of paper towels, and cover with additional paper towels. Let stand 5 minutes, pressing down occasionally. Combine cucumbers, vinegar, and next 4 ingredients. Cover and chill 1 hour or up to 4 hours, stirring occasionally; drain well.

4. Scrape off and discard beet and salt mixtures from salmon. Discard liquid. Cut salmon into ⅛-inch-thick slices; discard skin. Serve with salad. Garnish with dill sprigs, if desired. Yield: 12 servings (serving size: about 2 ounces salmon and about ¼ cup salad).

CALORIES 172 (36% from fat); FAT 6.8g (sat 1.4g, mono 2.4g, poly 2.3g); PROTEIN 24.6g; CARB 1.6g; FIBER 0.1g; CHOL 51mg; IRON 0.7mg; SODIUM 523mg; CALC 43mg

How to Salt-Cure Salmon

Chicken and Rice Avgolemono with Dill

    1   (2¼-pound) whole rotisserie chicken
    9   cups water
    2   cups chopped carrot
    2   cups chopped onion
    ¾   cup chopped celery
    1   teaspoon salt
    1   thyme sprig
    1   tablespoon olive oil
    1   cup sliced green onions
    3   garlic cloves, minced
    ¾   cup uncooked long-grain
        white rice
    ½   cup fresh lemon juice (about
        3 lemons)
    2   large eggs, lightly beaten
    ½   cup chopped fresh dill

1. Remove and discard skin from chicken. Remove meat from bones, reserving bones. Chop meat; cover and chill until ready to use.

2. Combine chicken bones, 9 cups water, and next 5 ingredients in a large Dutch oven; bring to a boil. Reduce heat, and simmer 1 hour. Strain stock through a sieve into a large bowl; discard solids.

3. Heat oil in pan over medium-high heat. Add green onions and garlic; sauté 1 minute. Add strained stock, and bring to a boil. Stir in rice; reduce heat, and simmer, uncovered, 15 minutes or until rice is tender. Stir in chopped chicken.

4. Combine lemon juice and eggs in a medium bowl, stirring well with a whisk. Gradually add 1 cup hot soup to egg mixture; stir constantly with a whisk. Gradually add egg mixture to pan; stir constantly. Cook over medium heat until slightly thick (about 2 minutes); stir constantly. Remove from heat; stir in dill. Yield: 6 servings (serving size: about 1½ cups).

CALORIES 243 (24% from fat); FAT 6.4g (sat 1.5g, mono 3.1g, poly 1.1g); PROTEIN 21.7g; CARB 23g; FIBER 1.2g; CHOL 127mg; IRON 2.3mg; SODIUM 495mg; CALC 34mg

Eggplant

MAKE AHEAD

Seafood Stuffed Eggplant

    3   eggplants, each cut in half
        lengthwise (about 3 pounds)
        Cooking spray
    1   tablespoon olive oil
    ½   cup chopped 33%-less-sodium ham
    ½   cup chopped onion
    ¼   cup chopped red bell pepper
    3   garlic cloves, minced
    ½   cup beer
    ½   pound medium shrimp, peeled,
        deveined, and coarsely chopped
    2½ ounces day-old French bread or
        other firm white bread
    6   tablespoons (1½-ounces) grated
        fresh Parmesan cheese, divided
    ¼   cup finely chopped green
        onions
    1   tablespoon chopped fresh basil
    1½ teaspoons chopped fresh tarragon
    1   teaspoon grated lemon rind
    ¼   teaspoon salt
    ⅛   teaspoon freshly ground black
        pepper

Continued

1. Preheat oven to 425°.
2. Score cut side of each eggplant half in a crisscross pattern; lightly coat cut sides of eggplant halves with cooking spray. Place eggplant halves, cut sides down, on a baking sheet. Bake at 425° for 10 minutes. Turn eggplant halves over; bake an additional 10 minutes or until tender. Remove from oven, and cool 10 minutes. Remove pulp from eggplant, leaving ¼-inch-thick shells. Place shells on baking sheet coated with cooking spray. Chop pulp; set aside.
3. Reduce oven temperature to 350°.
4. Heat oil in a large nonstick skillet over medium-high heat. Add ham, ½ cup onion, bell pepper, and garlic; sauté 5 minutes. Add eggplant pulp and beer; cook 10 minutes or until most of liquid evaporates, stirring occasionally. Stir in shrimp; cook 1 minute. Remove from heat.
5. Place bread in a food processor; process until coarse crumbs form. Add breadcrumbs, 3 tablespoons cheese, green onions, and next 5 ingredients to eggplant mixture; stir gently to combine. Mound about ½ cup shrimp mixture into each eggplant shell. Sprinkle each with 1½ teaspoons cheese. Bake at 350° for 15 minutes or until thoroughly heated and shrimp are done. Yield: 6 servings (serving size: 1 stuffed eggplant half).

CALORIES 203 (27% from fat); FAT 6.2g (sat 2g, mono 2.8g, poly 0.9g); PROTEIN 15.5g; CARB 23.3g; FIBER 0.8g; CHOL 68mg; IRON 2mg; SODIUM 444mg; CALC 142mg

Fava Beans & Figs

Also called broad beans, **favas** come in large, fuzzy pods. Once shelled, the beans must be removed from their tough outer skins. Blanch shelled beans, immerse in cold water, and drain; pinch the beans to slide them out of their skins. As a general rule, one pound of fava bean pods yields about one cup of shelled beans.

MAKE AHEAD
Spelt Salad with Fava Beans

Spelt is a nutty-tasting grain that's similar in taste and texture to wheat berries. Look for it in health-food stores and the natural-foods aisle of large supermarkets. Once the fava beans are shelled, their tough outer skins need to be peeled; blanching and then rinsing the beans in cool water makes the skins easier to remove.

    1   cup uncooked spelt or wheat
        berries
    4   cups water
    2   cups shelled unpeeled fava beans
        (about 2 pounds whole pods)
    ½   cup chopped drained oil-packed
        sun-dried tomato halves
    ½   cup diced celery
    ⅓   cup dried currants
    3   tablespoons balsamic vinegar
    1   tablespoon extravirgin olive oil
    ½   teaspoon salt
    ½   teaspoon freshly ground black
        pepper
    2   garlic cloves, crushed
    ¼   cup chopped fresh parsley

1. Place spelt in a large saucepan; cover with water to 2 inches above spelt. Bring to a boil. Cover, reduce heat, and simmer 1½ hours or until spelt is tender. Drain.
2. Bring 4 cups water to a boil in a medium saucepan. Add fava beans; cook 2 minutes. Drain and rinse with cold water; drain. Remove and discard tough outer skins from beans.
3. Combine spelt, fava beans, tomatoes, celery, and currants in a large bowl. Combine vinegar and next 4 ingredients, stirring with a whisk. Drizzle over spelt mixture; toss well to coat. Sprinkle with chopped parsley. Yield: 6 servings (serving size: 1 cup).

CALORIES 190 (22% from fat); FAT 4.6g (sat 0.5g, mono 2.5g, poly 0.5g); PROTEIN 6.2g; CARB 35.4g; FIBER 2.9g; CHOL 0mg; IRON 2.8mg; SODIUM 252mg; CALC 40mg

Fig and Pork Brochettes

Small figs hold together better on the grill than larger ones. It's necessary to cook the figs and pork separately because the delicate fruit cooks more quickly. If using wooden skewers, soak them in water for 30 minutes before threading the pork.

    ½   cup low-sodium soy sauce
    2   tablespoons brown sugar
    2   tablespoons balsamic vinegar
    2   tablespoons peanut oil
    2   tablespoons hoisin sauce
    1   tablespoon minced peeled fresh
        ginger
    1½ pounds pork tenderloin, trimmed
        and cut into 24 (1-inch) cubes
    24 small dark-skinned fresh figs,
        trimmed (such as Black Mission,
        Celeste, or Brown Turkey)
    Cooking spray

1. Combine first 6 ingredients, stirring with a whisk. Reserve ¼ cup soy sauce mixture; cover and chill.
2. Combine pork and remaining soy sauce mixture in a large zip-top plastic bag; seal and marinate in refrigerator 2 hours or up to overnight, turning bag occasionally.
3. Prepare grill.
4. Remove pork from bag, reserving marinade. Pour marinade into a small saucepan, and bring to a boil. Cook 2 minutes. Thread 4 pork pieces onto each of 6 (12-inch) skewers. Thread 4 figs lengthwise onto each of another 6 (12-inch) skewers. Place pork brochettes on grill rack coated with cooking spray; grill 10 minutes or until tender, turning and basting frequently with cooked marinade. Add fig brochettes to grill during last 5 minutes of cooking time, turning once.
5. Place ¼ cup reserved soy mixture in a small microwave-safe bowl; microwave at HIGH 2 minutes or until thoroughly heated. Serve with brochettes. Yield: 6 servings (serving size: 1 pork brochette, 1 fig brochette, and 2 teaspoons sauce).

CALORIES 326 (19% from fat); FAT 6.9g (sat 1.8g, mono 2.9g, poly 1.4g); PROTEIN 26g; CARB 43.1g; FIBER 6.7g; CHOL 74mg; IRON 2.4mg; SODIUM 457mg; CALC 80mg

Grapes & Gooseberries

Grilled Chicken with Fresh Grape Glaze

The finished glaze will have the consistency of bottled barbecue sauce. Natural sugars in the grapes caramelize on the chicken. The sweet glaze is also delightful on pork tenderloin medallions.

GLAZE:

- 3 cups seedless red grapes
- 2 teaspoons olive oil
- 1 cup chopped onion
- 2 garlic cloves, minced
- 2 tablespoons balsamic vinegar
- 2 teaspoons low-sodium soy sauce
- 1 teaspoon brown sugar
- 1 teaspoon chopped fresh rosemary

CHICKEN:

- 1 tablespoon olive oil
- 6 chicken drumsticks (about 1½ pounds), skinned
- 6 chicken thighs (about 1½ pounds), skinned
- 2 teaspoons chopped fresh rosemary
- 1 teaspoon freshly ground black pepper
- ¾ teaspoon salt
- Cooking spray
- Fresh rosemary leaves (optional)

1. To prepare glaze, place grapes in a blender; process until smooth. Heat 2 teaspoons oil in a saucepan over medium heat. Add onion; cover and cook 10 minutes. Add garlic; cover and cook 3 minutes, stirring occasionally. Stir in puréed grapes, vinegar, soy sauce, sugar, and 1 teaspoon rosemary; bring to a boil. Reduce heat, and simmer 10 minutes or until slightly thick. Cool slightly. Place grape mixture in blender; process until smooth. Set aside.

2. Prepare grill.

3. To prepare chicken, brush 1 tablespoon oil over chicken, and sprinkle with 2 teaspoons rosemary, pepper, and salt. Place chicken on grill rack coated with cooking spray; cover and grill 25 minutes or until done, turning and basting frequently with grape glaze. Garnish with rosemary leaves, if desired. Yield: 6 servings (serving size: 1 thigh and 1 drumstick).

CALORIES 262 (30% from fat); FAT 8.7g (sat 1.8g, mono 4.2g, poly 1.6g); PROTEIN 26.8g; CARB 19.5g; FIBER 1.2g; CHOL 103mg; IRON 2mg; SODIUM 470mg; CALC 37mg

---

MAKE AHEAD

Gooseberry Fool

Tart, grape-sized gooseberries are popular for making jams and jellies since their juice thickens nicely because of its high pectin content. This perennial dessert favorite combines tangy and sweet flavors. It's cool, refreshing, and creamy.

- 4 cups vanilla low-fat yogurt
- 3 cups green or pink gooseberries, halved
- ½ cup sugar
- ¼ cup whipping cream

1. Place a colander in a 2-quart glass measure or medium bowl. Line colander with 4 layers of cheesecloth, allowing cheesecloth to extend over outside edges. Spoon yogurt into colander. Cover loosely with plastic wrap; refrigerate 12 hours or overnight. Spoon yogurt cheese into a bowl; discard liquid. Cover and refrigerate.

2. Combine gooseberries and sugar in a medium nonstick skillet. Cook over medium heat 5 minutes or until mixture begins to thicken, stirring frequently. Gently mash gooseberries with a fork; simmer 2 minutes. Spoon into a small bowl; cover and chill.

3. Place whipping cream in a large bowl; beat with a mixer at high speed until stiff peaks form. Fold in yogurt and gooseberry mixture. Serve chilled. Yield: 4 servings (serving size: about 1 cup).

CALORIES 284 (20% from fat); FAT 6.4g (sat 3.6g, mono 1.7g, poly 0.6g); PROTEIN 10.1g; CARB 48.6g; FIBER 4.8g; CHOL 24mg; IRON 0.5mg; SODIUM 93mg; CALC 264mg

---

Haricots Verts

QUICK & EASY

Haricots Verts and Grape Tomato Salad with Crème Fraîche Dressing

Haricots verts are tender, young French green beans. If not labeled as such in your market, look for slim, petite green beans. Crème fraîche adds a nutty flavor and rich texture to the dressing; look for it near the gourmet cheeses in your supermarket. Substitute whole sour cream, if you prefer.

- 1 pound haricots verts, trimmed
- ¼ cup finely chopped fresh basil
- 2 tablespoons minced shallots
- 2 tablespoons fresh lemon juice
- 2 tablespoons crème fraîche
- 1 tablespoon honey
- ½ teaspoon salt
- 1 pint grape or cherry tomatoes, halved
- 1 tablespoon pine nuts, toasted

1. Cook haricots verts in boiling water 2 minutes or until crisp-tender. Drain and rinse with cold water; drain.

2. Combine basil and next 5 ingredients in a large bowl, stirring with a whisk. Add haricots verts and tomatoes; toss gently to coat. Place mixture on each of 6 plates; sprinkle with nuts. Yield: 6 servings (serving size: about ¾ cup salad and ½ teaspoon nuts).

CALORIES 74 (34% from fat); FAT 2.8g (sat 1.1g, mono 0.8g, poly 0.6g); PROTEIN 1.7g; CARB 11.4g; FIBER 3.5g; CHOL 7mg; IRON 0.7mg; SODIUM 203mg; CALC 47mg

Iced Tea

MAKE AHEAD
Lemon Verbena Iced Tea

Lemon verbena infuses the lightly sweetened iced tea with sunny citrus flavor. You can also use the fragrant syrup to enliven cocktails or moisten pound cake. Blanching the herb leaves brightens their color so the syrup will stay green. Avoid using a strongly flavored tea, such as Earl Grey; it will overpower the taste of the syrup.

½ cup sugar
½ cup water
1 cup lemon verbena leaves
4 cups ice
6 cups brewed tea, chilled
Mint leaves (optional)
Lemon wedges (optional)

1. Combine sugar and water in a small saucepan; bring to a boil. Cook 1 minute or until sugar dissolves. Cool sugar syrup completely.
2. Cook lemon verbena leaves in boiling water 1 minute. Drain and plunge into ice water; drain.
3. Place sugar syrup and verbena leaves in a blender; process until smooth. Cover and chill overnight. Strain sugar syrup through a fine sieve into a bowl. Place ⅔ cup ice into each of 6 tall glasses; add 1 cup brewed tea and 2 tablespoons sugar syrup to each serving, stirring to combine. Garnish with mint leaves and lemon wedges, if desired. Yield: 6 servings.

CALORIES 67 (0% from fat); FAT 0g; PROTEIN 0g; CARB 17.4g; FIBER 0g; CHOL 0mg; IRON 0mg; SODIUM 7mg; CALC 0mg

Jalapeños

The sweetness of fresh cherries softens the fire from **jalapeño** peppers. The season for fresh cherries is late May to early August. Sweet cherries are heart-shaped; the most common varieties are deep-red Bing and gold-and-pink Royal Ann. (Sour cherries are usually sold frozen and canned.) Refrigerate fresh cherries in a plastic bag up to three days, and wash just before using.

MAKE AHEAD
Jalapeño-Spiked Cherry Preserves

Be sure to use the seeds from the jalapeño peppers to infuse the preserves with some heat. Serve as a condiment with toast, as a sandwich spread with smoked turkey, as a sauce for grilled or blackened chicken or pork chops, or as an appetizer topping with cream cheese and crackers.

2 cups sugar
1½ cups water
⅔ cup cider vinegar
1½ teaspoons ground ginger
½ teaspoon ground cinnamon
Dash of salt
Dash of ground cloves
Dash of ground nutmeg
4 jalapeño peppers, sliced
2 pounds sweet cherries, pitted and coarsely chopped
1 large Granny Smith apple, cored and chopped

1. Combine all ingredients in a large, heavy saucepan; bring to a boil. Reduce heat, and simmer until slightly thick and reduced to 4 cups (about 50 minutes), skimming foam from surface of mixture occasionally. Cool; pour into an airtight container. (Mixture will thicken as it

cools.) Cover and chill. Yield: 4 cups (serving size: 2 tablespoons).
NOTE: Refrigerate preserves in an airtight container up to three weeks.

CALORIES 71 (4% from fat); FAT 0.3g (sat 0.1g, mono 0.1g, poly 0.1g); PROTEIN 0.4g; CARB 18g; FIBER 0.7g; CHOL 0mg; IRON 0.2mg; SODIUM 6mg; CALC 5mg

Kiwi & Kebabs

QUICK & EASY
Kiwi Colada

Here's a fun twist on the classic summertime umbrella drink. Kiwifruit and melon liqueur give the cocktail a green hue and slightly tangy flavor. Although we used green kiwi, you can substitute the golden variety for a sweeter taste and golden color.

5 peeled kiwifruit, divided
3 cups ice
¼ cup light rum
¼ cup Midori (melon-flavored liqueur)
3 tablespoons Cream of Coconut (such as Coco Lopez)
1 (8-ounce) can crushed pineapple in juice, undrained

1. Cut 4 kiwifruit into quarters, and place in a blender. Set remaining kiwifruit aside. Add ice and remaining 4 ingredients to blender; process until smooth. Strain mixture through a sieve into a pitcher; discard seeds. Pour into each of 6 glasses. Cut remaining kiwifruit into 6 slices; garnish each glass with 1 kiwifruit slice. Yield: 6 servings (serving size: about ¾ cup).

CALORIES 143 (10% from fat); FAT 1.6g (sat 1g, mono 0g, poly 0.2g); PROTEIN 0.6g; CARB 23.1g; FIBER 2.5g; CHOL 0mg; IRON 0.4mg; SODIUM 11mg; CALC 17mg

Beef, Okra, and Potato Kebabs

Kebabs are a favorite way to grill meat and vegetables. This recipe features an unusual, delicious grilled okra. Grilling infuses the pods with smoky flavor and allows them to maintain their firm texture.

    8 fingerling potatoes, each cut in
       half lengthwise
    2 tablespoons chopped fresh parsley
 1½ tablespoons prepared horseradish
 1½ tablespoons whole-grain Dijon
       mustard
    1 tablespoon Worcestershire sauce
    2 teaspoons olive oil
 1½ teaspoons sugar
   ¼ teaspoon freshly ground black
       pepper
   ½ teaspoon salt, divided
    1 cup (1-inch-square) cut red bell
       pepper
  16 small okra pods
    8 shallots, peeled and halved
    1 pound boneless sirloin steak,
       trimmed and cut into 1-inch cubes
    1 yellow squash, halved lengthwise
       and cut into ½-inch slices (about
       2 cups)
Cooking spray

1. Place potatoes in a saucepan; cover with water. Bring to a boil. Reduce heat, and simmer 15 minutes or until tender; drain. Cool.
2. Combine parsley and next 6 ingredients in a large bowl, stirring well; stir in ¼ teaspoon salt. Add potatoes, bell pepper, and next 4 ingredients; toss well to coat. Cover and chill 1 hour.
3. Prepare grill.
4. Thread vegetables and beef alternately onto 8 (10-inch) skewers. Sprinkle kebabs evenly with ¼ teaspoon salt. Place kebabs on grill rack coated with cooking spray; grill 10 minutes or until desired degree of doneness, turning occasionally. Yield: 4 servings (serving size: 2 kebabs).

CALORIES 338 (30% from fat); FAT 11.3g (sat 3.7g, mono 5.3g, poly 0.7g); PROTEIN 30.6g; CARB 30.4g; FIBER 3.9g; CHOL 76mg; IRON 4.8mg; SODIUM 564mg; CALC 76mg

---

Lima Beans & Lime

MAKE AHEAD
Leek and Lima Bean Soup with Bacon

Fresh limas are at their peak from June to September. Thawed frozen beans substitute well for fresh. Here, the beans are puréed in a creamy soup garnished with bacon, sour cream, and onions.

    3 bacon slices
    2 cups chopped leek (about 2
       leeks)
    4 cups fresh baby lima beans
    4 cups fat-free, less-sodium chicken
       broth
    1 cup water
    2 tablespoons fresh lemon juice
   ½ teaspoon salt
   ¼ teaspoon freshly ground black
       pepper
   ½ cup thinly sliced green onions
   ½ cup reduced-fat sour cream

1. Cook bacon in a large saucepan over medium heat until crisp. Remove bacon from pan, reserving 1 tablespoon drippings in pan. Crumble bacon; set aside. Add leek to drippings in pan; cook 7 minutes or until tender, stirring frequently. Stir in beans, broth, and water; bring to a boil. Reduce heat, and simmer 10 minutes or until beans are tender.
2. Place half of bean mixture in a blender. Remove center piece of blender lid (to allow steam to escape); secure lid on blender. Place a clean dishtowel over opening in blender lid (to prevent spills), and process until smooth. Pour puréed bean mixture into a large bowl. Repeat procedure with remaining bean mixture. Stir in lemon juice, salt, and pepper. Ladle about 1 cup soup into each of 8 bowls; top each serving with 1 tablespoon onions, 1 tablespoon sour cream, and about 1 teaspoon bacon. Yield: 8 servings.

CALORIES 170 (26% from fat); FAT 5g (sat 2.4g, mono 1.8g, poly 0.5g); PROTEIN 8.9g; CARB 22.6g; FIBER 6.1g; CHOL 10mg; IRON 2.3mg; SODIUM 440mg; CALC 55mg

---

MAKE AHEAD
Streusel-Topped Key Lime Squares

If you can't find key limes, you can use regular Persian limes, but the squares won't be quite as tart.

   ¼ cup butter, softened
   ¼ cup granulated sugar
    1 teaspoon grated lime rind
   ⅛ teaspoon salt
   ⅛ teaspoon lemon extract
    1 cup all-purpose flour
Cooking spray
   ⅔ cup granulated sugar
    3 tablespoons all-purpose flour
   ¾ teaspoon baking powder
   ⅛ teaspoon salt
   ½ cup fresh key lime juice
    3 large eggs, lightly beaten
    1 tablespoon powdered sugar

1. Preheat oven to 350°.
2. Place first 5 ingredients in a medium bowl; beat with a mixer at medium speed

Continued

until creamy (about 2 minutes). Lightly spoon 1 cup flour into a dry measuring cup; level with a knife. Gradually add 1 cup flour to butter mixture, beating at low speed until mixture resembles coarse meal. Reserve ⅔ cup mixture for topping. Gently press remaining mixture (about 1⅓ cups) into bottom of an 8-inch square baking pan coated with cooking spray. Bake at 350° for 12 minutes or until just beginning to brown.

3. Combine ⅔ cup sugar, 3 tablespoons flour, baking powder, and ⅛ teaspoon salt in a medium bowl, stirring with a whisk. Add lime juice and eggs, stirring with a whisk until smooth. Pour mixture over crust. Bake at 350° for 12 minutes. Remove pan from oven (do not turn oven off); sprinkle reserved ⅔ cup flour mixture evenly over egg mixture. Bake an additional 8 to 10 minutes or until set. Remove from oven; cool in pan on a wire rack. Sprinkle evenly with powdered sugar. Cut into squares. Yield: 16 servings (serving size: 1 square).

CALORIES 121 (29% from fat); FAT 3.9g (sat 1.7g, mono 1.5g, poly 0.3g); PROTEIN 2.2g; CARB 19.9g; FIBER 0.3g; CHOL 47mg; IRON 0.6mg; SODIUM 93mg; CALC 21mg

Mangoes

The distinctive taste of fresh **mangoes** complements all kinds of sweet and savory dishes. The key to cutting a mango is to work around its large, flat seed. One way to do this is to remove the skin with a paring knife or vegetable peeler; cut a thin slice off the bottom, more rounded end so the mango stands flat on a cutting surface. Make a cut down the length of the mango about one-half inch from its center (you might feel the knife graze the seed); repeat on the other side. Trim off any remaining flesh.

Mango Rice Salad with Grilled Shrimp

(pictured on cover and page 184)

Customize the recipe to suit your preferences—try chicken in place of shrimp, or omit the shrimp and serve the salad cold or at room temperature as a side dish. For added flavor, use basmati or jasmine rice.

    4 teaspoons curry powder
    1 tablespoon minced fresh garlic
    1 tablespoon minced peeled fresh
       ginger
    1 tablespoon low-sodium soy sauce
    ⅛ teaspoon ground red pepper
    ⅛ teaspoon ground cumin
 1½ pounds medium shrimp, peeled
       and deveined (about 36 shrimp)
    2 cups water
    ⅔ cup light coconut milk
 1¼ cups uncooked long-grain rice
    2 cups diced peeled mango (about
       2 mangoes)
 1½ cups diced red bell pepper
    ¾ cup shredded carrot
    ½ cup sliced green onions
    2 tablespoons fresh lime juice
    1 tablespoon chopped fresh cilantro
    1 tablespoon chopped fresh parsley
    ½ teaspoon salt
 Cooking spray
 Cilantro sprigs (optional)

1. Combine first 6 ingredients in a medium bowl. Add shrimp; toss to coat. Cover and chill 1 hour.
2. Bring water and coconut milk to a boil in a medium saucepan; add rice. Cover, reduce heat, and simmer 15 minutes or until liquid is absorbed. Add mango and next 7 ingredients; toss gently to combine.
3. Prepare grill or grill pan to medium-high heat.
4. Thread 3 shrimp onto each of 12 (6-inch) skewers. Place skewers on grill rack or grill pan coated with cooking spray; grill 3 minutes on each side or until shrimp are done. Serve skewers over salad. Garnish with cilantro sprigs, if desired. Yield: 6 servings (serving size: 2 skewers and about 1 cup salad).

CALORIES 342 (11% from fat); FAT 4.1g (sat 1.8g, mono 0.5g, poly 1g); PROTEIN 27.4g; CARB 48.9g; FIBER 2.9g; CHOL 172mg; IRON 5.3mg; SODIUM 478mg; CALC 95mg

How to Cut a Mango

Nectarines

Floral and herbal notes of lavender add a sophisticated touch to sweet-tart **nectarines**. Although there are many varieties of this highly fragrant herb, English lavender is most commonly used in cooking. Look for dried lavender buds in health-food stores or gourmet markets; you'll most likely find fresh edible lavender in garden centers or nurseries.

MAKE AHEAD

Nectarines Poached in Lavender-Honey Syrup

A sweet end to a dinner party, this unique dessert tastes great any way you prefer to serve it—warm, at room temperature, or chilled. Take care not to overcook the nectarines—they should be tender but not too soft.

    4 cups water
    ¾ cup sugar
    ¾ cup honey
    2 teaspoons dried lavender buds
    6 nectarines, halved and pitted
       (about 1½ pounds)
    6 cups vanilla low-fat frozen yogurt
 Lavender sprigs (optional)

1. Bring first 3 ingredients to a boil in a Dutch oven, stirring to dissolve sugar. Stir in lavender buds. Add nectarines. Reduce heat, and simmer 8 minutes or until nectarines are just tender (do not overcook). Remove nectarines from pan with a slotted spoon, reserving liquid in pan.

2. Bring liquid to a boil, and cook until reduced to 3 cups (about 10 minutes). Cool slightly. Serve syrup with nectarines and yogurt. Garnish with fresh lavender, if desired. Yield: 12 servings (serving size: 1 nectarine half, ½ cup yogurt, and ¼ cup syrup).

CALORIES 243 (6% from fat); FAT 1.5g (sat 0.8g, mono 0.4g, poly 0g); PROTEIN 4.9g; CARB 54.9g; FIBER 0.9g; CHOL 5mg; IRON 0.3mg; SODIUM 60mg; CALC 155mg

Okra

Available fresh year-round in the South, and elsewhere from May to October, **okra** has a mild flavor similar to that of green beans and, once cooked, a characteristic viscous texture. Select smaller, more tender okra pods (less than four inches long) that are firm, brightly colored, and free of blemishes. Refrigerate up to three days in a plastic bag.

MAKE AHEAD
Spicy Pickled Okra

2½ cups white vinegar
2 cups water
3 tablespoons sugar
2 tablespoons kosher salt
1 teaspoon white peppercorns
1 teaspoon coriander seeds
1 teaspoon fennel seeds
1 teaspoon cumin seeds
4 dill sprigs
2 green or red jalapeño peppers, halved lengthwise
1½ pounds small okra pods

1. Combine first 8 ingredients in a large saucepan; bring to a boil. Cook 1 minute or until sugar and salt dissolve, stirring frequently. Remove from heat; stir in dill

sprigs, jalapeños, and okra. Cool completely; pour mixture into an airtight container. Cover and chill. Yield: about 5 cups (serving size: ¼ cup).

NOTE: Refrigerate okra in an airtight container up to two weeks.

CALORIES 28 (0% from fat); FAT 0g; PROTEIN 0.7g; CARB 6.8g; FIBER 1.1g; CHOL 0mg; IRON 0.3mg; SODIUM 103mg; CALC 29mg

Passion Fruit, Peaches & Plums

Look for **passion fruit** from March to September in supermarkets or Latin food markets. It has deep purple skin and sweet-tart yellow flesh containing many black seeds. When ripe, passion fruit will have wrinkled, dimpled skin. Refrigerate ripe passion fruit up to five days; store unripe passion fruit at room temperature until it becomes shriveled. Although the seeds are edible, they're often discarded. To extract the seeds, cut the fruit in half with a heavy knife. Scoop out the pulp, and press through a sieve into a bowl; reserve the seeds, if you'd like.

How to Extract Seeds

Try New Things Menu
serves 4

Passion fruit pulp has a sweet-sour flavor that creates a tasty glaze for shrimp kebabs.

Spicy Passion Fruit-Glazed Shrimp

Jasmine rice pilaf with pistachios*

Sautéed yellow squash and red bell peppers

*Heat 1 tablespoon olive oil in a medium saucepan over medium-high heat. Add ⅓ cup chopped shallots and 2 minced garlic cloves; sauté 2 minutes. Add 1 cup jasmine rice; sauté 1 minute. Stir in 2 cups fat-free, less-sodium chicken broth and ½ teaspoon salt; bring to a boil. Cover, reduce heat, and simmer 20 minutes or until rice is done. Stir in ¼ cup chopped toasted pistachios and 2 tablespoons chopped cilantro.

Spicy Passion Fruit-Glazed Shrimp

Passion fruit gives the glaze a sweet-and-sour taste. It's not necessary to strain the pulp initially; the seeds will be strained when preparing the glaze. When straining the glaze, press with the back of a spoon to extract as much passion fruit pulp as possible. Serve these kebabs over a bed of basmati or jasmine rice.

½ cup water
½ cup sugar
½ cup passion fruit pulp (about 4 passion fruit)
2 tablespoons fresh lime juice
1 teaspoon low-sodium soy sauce
½ teaspoon crushed red pepper
¼ teaspoon salt
32 large shrimp, peeled and deveined (about 1½ pounds)
Cooking spray
8 lime wedges

1. Bring water and sugar to a boil in a small saucepan, stirring until sugar dissolves. Add passion fruit pulp, stirring well, and cook 1 minute. Remove from heat; cool 15 minutes.

2. Strain passion fruit mixture through a sieve into a large bowl; discard seeds.
Continued

Add lime juice, soy sauce, red pepper, and salt, stirring well. Set ½ cup fruit mixture aside. Add shrimp to remaining passion fruit mixture, and toss well to coat. Cover and refrigerate 15 minutes.

3. Prepare grill.

4. Thread 4 shrimp on each of 8 (10-inch) skewers. Place skewers on grill rack coated with cooking spray. Grill 2 minutes on each side or until done, basting with reserved ½ cup passion fruit mixture. Serve with lime wedges. Yield: 4 servings (serving size: 2 skewers and 2 lime wedges).

CALORIES 277 (10% from fat); FAT 3.1g (sat 0.6g, mono 0.5g, poly 1.2g); PROTEIN 35.2g; CARB 26.2g; FIBER 0.7g; CHOL 259mg; IRON 4.5mg; SODIUM 403mg; CALC 92mg

MAKE AHEAD
Peach-Vidalia Jam

This jam makes a delicious sandwich or snack when spread on whole-grain bread and topped with sharp Cheddar cheese. It's also a tasty accompaniment to grilled chicken or ham steaks, and is even good dolloped onto a bowl of field peas. The recipe makes a lot of jam, so it's ideal for gift giving. Blanching the peaches makes them easy to peel—the skins slip right off.

    3 pounds ripe peaches
    4 cups sugar
    1 cup basil sprigs
    ¾ cup water
    ¼ cup fresh lemon juice
    ¼ teaspoon salt
    ⅛ teaspoon ground red pepper
    3 pounds Vidalia or other sweet
       onion, vertically sliced (about
       10 cups)

1. Place peaches in a large stockpot of boiling water; cook 1 minute. Drain and plunge peaches into ice water; drain. Peel peaches; coarsely chop.

2. Combine chopped peaches, sugar, and remaining ingredients in a large, heavy stockpot; bring to a boil, stirring occasionally. Reduce heat, and simmer until slightly thick and reduced to 6 cups (about 45 minutes), skimming foam from surface of mixture occasionally. Cool; discard basil. Pour into an airtight

container. (Mixture will thicken as it cools.) Cover and chill. Yield: 6 cups (serving size: 2 tablespoons).

NOTE: Refrigerate jam in an airtight container up to three weeks.

CALORIES 85 (1% from fat); FAT 0.1g (sat 0g, mono 0g, poly 0.1g); PROTEIN 0.5g; CARB 21.6g; FIBER 0.3g; CHOL 0mg; IRON 0.1mg; SODIUM 13mg; CALC 7mg

---

Plums come in an assortment of colors, from golden-hued to purplish-black to bright green. Generally, larger plums are juicier and best for eating out of hand, while smaller, firmer plums work well in recipes. Refrigerate ripe plums in a plastic bag for three to five days. To ripen hard plums, store in a paper bag at room temperature for a day or two.

Plum Galette

Choose tart plums for a less-sweet galette, or very ripe plums for a sugary result. The jam is a tasty glaze for the galette; serve leftovers spread on toast for breakfast.

    1 cup all-purpose flour
    3½ tablespoons chilled butter, cut
       into small pieces
    ¼ teaspoon salt
    3 tablespoons ice water
    1 tablespoon cornmeal
    4 plums, each cut into 8 wedges
    1 tablespoon cornstarch
    ¼ cup Plum Jam
    1 tablespoon Plum Jam
    1 tablespoon sugar

1. Lightly spoon flour into a dry measuring cup; level with a knife. Combine flour, butter, and salt in a food processor; process until mixture resembles coarse meal. With processor on, slowly add ice water through food chute, processing just until combined (do not form a ball). Press mixture gently into a 4-inch circle on plastic wrap. Cover and chill 30 minutes.

2. Preheat oven to 425°.

3. Line a baking sheet with parchment paper; sprinkle paper with cornmeal. Unwrap dough; roll dough into a 9-inch circle on a lightly floured surface. Place dough on baking sheet. Combine plums

and cornstarch in a large bowl, tossing to coat. Add ¼ cup Plum Jam; toss well to coat. Arrange plum mixture on top of dough, leaving a 1½-inch border. Fold edges of dough over plum mixture. Bake at 425° for 20 minutes.

4. Remove galette from oven (do not turn oven off). Brush crust with 1 tablespoon Plum Jam; sprinkle galette with sugar. Bake at 425° for 20 minutes or until crust is golden brown. Cool in pan 10 minutes on a wire rack before serving. Yield: 6 servings (serving size: 1 wedge).

(Totals include Plum Jam) CALORIES 208 (32% from fat); FAT 7.3g (sat 3.4g, mono 2.8g, poly 0.3g); PROTEIN 2.8g; CARB 33.8g; FIBER 1.6g; CHOL 18mg; IRON 1mg; SODIUM 146mg; CALC 5mg

MAKE AHEAD
PLUM JAM:

    4½ cups chopped ripe red plums
       (about 8 medium)
    1 cup sugar
    1 cup water

1. Combine plums, sugar, and water in a large saucepan; bring to a boil. Cover, reduce heat, and simmer 10 minutes. Uncover and simmer 50 minutes or until mixture begins to thicken, skimming foam from surface of mixture occasionally. Cool; pour into an airtight container. (Mixture will thicken as it cools.) Cover and chill. Yield: 2 cups (serving size: 2 tablespoons).

NOTE: Refrigerate jam in an airtight container up to three weeks.

CALORIES 68 (4% from fat); FAT 0.3g (sat 0g, mono 0.1g, poly 0.1g); PROTEIN 0.3g; CARB 17.2g; FIBER 0.5g; CHOL 0mg; IRON 0mg; SODIUM 0mg; CALC 0mg

Fresh summer plums serve double duty in this free-form tart—as both the glaze and the filling.

Quesadilla

Peach and Brie Quesadillas with Lime-Honey Dipping Sauce

This intriguing appetizer is savory-sweet. Ripe—but firm—peaches work best; if they're too soft, they'll make the tortillas soggy. Placing the fillings on one side of the tortilla and folding the other half over (like a taco) makes the quesadillas easier to handle. Whole wheat tortillas would also be great, offering a sweet, nutty taste. The lime-honey dipping sauce balances the richness of the buttery filling.

SAUCE:
2 tablespoons honey
½ teaspoon grated lime rind
2 teaspoons fresh lime juice

QUESADILLAS:
1 cup thinly sliced peeled firm ripe peaches (about 2 large)
1 tablespoon chopped fresh chives
1 teaspoon brown sugar
3 ounces Brie cheese, thinly sliced
4 (8-inch) fat-free flour tortillas
Cooking spray
Chive strips (optional)

1. To prepare sauce, combine first 3 ingredients, stirring with a whisk; set aside.
2. To prepare quesadillas, combine peaches, 1 tablespoon chives, and sugar, tossing gently to coat. Arrange one-fourth of cheese and one-fourth of peach mixture over half of each tortilla; fold tortillas in half. Heat a large nonstick skillet over medium-high heat. Coat pan with cooking spray. Place 2 quesadillas in pan; cook 2 minutes on each side or until tortillas are lightly browned and crisp. Remove from pan; keep warm. Repeat procedure with remaining quesadillas. Cut each quesadilla into 3 wedges; serve with sauce. Garnish with chive strips, if desired. Yield: 6 servings

(serving size: 2 quesadilla wedges and about 1 teaspoon sauce).

CALORIES 157 (23% from fat); FAT 4g (sat 2.5g, mono 1.2g, poly 0.1g); PROTEIN 5.3g; CARB 25.5g; FIBER 0.7g; CHOL 14mg; IRON 0.9mg; SODIUM 316mg; CALC 30mg

Raspberries

Fresh Raspberry Sauce

The vibrant color and fruity flavor of this easy no-cook sauce are the essence of summer. Try it over ice cream, pound cake, or angel food cake. The optional framboise adds sublime flavor; you can also use a raspberry-flavored liqueur, such as Chambord.

4 cups fresh raspberries, divided
¼ cup sugar
1 tablespoon framboise (raspberry brandy; optional)
½ teaspoon fresh lemon juice

1. Combine 2 cups raspberries and sugar in a food processor; process until puréed. Press mixture through a fine sieve over a medium bowl; discard solids. Stir in 2 cups raspberries, framboise, if desired, and lemon juice. Cover and chill. Yield: 2 cups (serving size: ¼ cup).

CALORIES 61 (6% from fat); FAT 0.4g (sat 0g, mono 0g, poly 0.2g); PROTEIN 0.7g; CARB 13.6g; FIBER 1g; CHOL 0mg; IRON 0.4mg; SODIUM 1mg; CALC 15mg

Lemon and liqueur bring out the best in ripe summer berries— especially in the raspberry sauce.

Spinach, Squash Blooms & Strawberries

Summer Steak House Dinner Menu
serves 6

In this twist on the traditional restaurant meal, grilled steak is paired with a light, tender spinach soufflé and updated potato salad that's good eaten warm or at room temperature.

Spinach and Parmesan Fallen Soufflé

Potato-artichoke salad*

Grilled beef tenderloin steaks

*Place 1½ pounds fingerling potatoes (halved lengthwise) in a large saucepan; cover with water. Bring to a boil; reduce heat, and simmer 15 minutes or until tender. Drain. Drain 1 (6-ounce) jar marinated artichoke hearts in a colander over a large bowl. Add 2 tablespoons chopped fresh parsley, ½ teaspoon salt, and ¼ teaspoon black pepper to bowl, stirring with a whisk. Add potatoes, artichoke hearts, and ⅓ cup thinly vertically sliced red onion; toss to combine.

Spinach and Parmesan Fallen Soufflé

Cooking spray
2 tablespoons dry breadcrumbs
2 garlic cloves, minced
10 ounces fresh spinach
1 cup 1% low-fat milk
1 tablespoon cornstarch
⅓ cup (about 1½ ounces) grated fresh Parmigiano-Reggiano cheese
¼ teaspoon salt
⅛ teaspoon freshly ground black pepper
⅛ teaspoon grated whole nutmeg
3 large egg whites
1 large egg

1. Preheat oven to 375°.
2. Lightly coat an 11 x 7-inch baking dish with cooking spray, and dust with breadcrumbs. Set aside.

Continued

3. Heat a large nonstick skillet over medium heat. Coat pan with cooking spray. Add garlic; cook 20 seconds, stirring constantly. Add spinach; cook 3 minutes or until spinach wilts, stirring occasionally. Remove from heat; cool slightly. Place spinach mixture on several layers of heavy-duty paper towels, and squeeze until barely moist. Place spinach mixture in a blender. Add milk and cornstarch; process until smooth. Add cheese, salt, pepper, and nutmeg; pulse until well blended. Pour into a large bowl.

4. Place egg whites and egg in a large bowl; beat with a mixer at high speed 5 minutes or until tripled in volume. Gently fold one-fourth of egg mixture into spinach mixture; gently fold in remaining egg mixture (mixture will seem slightly thin). Spoon mixture into prepared baking dish; smooth top with a spatula.

5. Bake at 375° for 35 minutes or until set in center. Cool 5 minutes on a wire rack before serving. Yield: 6 servings.

CALORIES 92 (34% from fat); FAT 3.5g (sat 1.8g, mono 1g, poly 0.3g); PROTEIN 8.5g; CARB 7.3g; FIBER 1.2g; CHOL 42mg; IRON 1.7mg; SODIUM 326mg; CALC 193mg

How to Seal Squash Blossoms

Stuffed Squash Blossom Bruschetta

You'll find squash blossoms, which have a subtle squash flavor, from late spring to early fall at gourmet grocery stores, farmers' markets, or Latin food markets. They perish quickly and should be kept in the refrigerator for no longer than one day.

16 (½-ounce) slices diagonally cut
    French bread baguette
Cooking spray
 2 garlic cloves, halved
 1 cup part-skim ricotta cheese
 ½ cup (2 ounces) grated fresh
    Parmesan cheese
1½ tablespoons minced shallots
    (about 1 small)
 1 tablespoon chopped fresh dill
 ¼ teaspoon salt
 ¼ teaspoon freshly ground black
    pepper
16 large squash blossoms (about 3
    cups)

1. Prepare grill or grill pan.

2. Place bread on grill rack or grill pan coated with cooking spray; grill 2 minutes on each side or until lightly browned. Remove from grill. Rub cut sides of garlic over one side of each bread slice. Set aside.

3. Preheat oven to 350°.

4. Spoon ricotta onto several layers of heavy-duty paper towels; spread to ½-inch thickness. Cover with additional paper towels; let stand 15 minutes. Scrape into a bowl using a rubber spatula. Stir in Parmesan and next 4 ingredients. Gently spoon about 1 tablespoon ricotta mixture into each blossom. Gently press edges of blossoms to seal in cheese mixture.

5. Place stuffed blossoms in a 13 x 9-inch baking dish coated with cooking spray. Bake at 350° for 15 minutes or until thoroughly heated. Top each bread slice with 1 squash blossom; serve immediately. Yield: 8 servings (serving size: 2 bruschetta).

CALORIES 148 (26% from fat); FAT 4.3g (sat 2.7g, mono 1.3g, poly 0.1g); PROTEIN 8.7g; CARB 19.5g; FIBER 0.6g; CHOL 14mg; IRON 1.2mg; SODIUM 411mg; CALC 172mg

Strawberry-Black Pepper Sorbet

To crush the peppercorns, use a mortar and pestle, the side of a chef's knife, or the bottom of a heavy pan or skillet.

 1 cup sugar
 1 cup water
 2 tablespoons coarsely crushed
    black peppercorns
 6 cups sliced strawberries (about
    2 pounds)
 2 tablespoons fresh lemon juice

1. Combine sugar and water in a small saucepan; bring to a boil, stirring occasionally until sugar dissolves. Remove from heat. Stir in peppercorns; let stand 20 minutes.

2. Strain sugar syrup through a fine sieve into a bowl; discard solids. Place half of sugar syrup, half of strawberries, and lemon juice in a blender, and process until smooth. Pour puréed mixture into a bowl. Repeat procedure with remaining sugar syrup and strawberries.

3. Pour mixture into freezer can of an ice-cream freezer; freeze according to manufacturer's instructions. Spoon sorbet into a freezer-safe container; cover and freeze 4 hours or until firm. Yield: 12 servings (serving size: ½ cup).

CALORIES 93 (3% from fat); FAT 0.3g (sat 0g, mono 0.1g, poly 0.2g); PROTEIN 0.6g; CARB 23.4g; FIBER 2.2g; CHOL 0mg; IRON 0.6mg; SODIUM 2mg; CALC 17mg

Heirloom Tomatoes

Heirloom tomatoes have become more popular and easy to find in summer months. They range in color from yellow to purple, and in form from grape-sized to sausage-shaped to heavy, fat globes. In general, yellow and orange tomatoes are lower in acidity and thus taste sweeter than red or green varieties, which are more tart. Purple varieties have a deep, complex flavor similar to that of red wine.

Stacked Heirloom Tomato Salad with Ricotta Salata Cream

Use a variety of heirloom tomato colors for the prettiest presentation. Unlike ricotta cheese, ricotta salata is firm enough to crumble or grate. Substitute feta cheese for ricotta salata, if you prefer.

- 6 (1-ounce) slices country peasant loaf bread
- Cooking spray
- 1 garlic clove, halved
- ½ cup (2 ounces) crumbled ricotta salata cheese
- ½ cup (4 ounces) reduced-fat silken tofu
- 2 tablespoons water
- 2 tablespoons fresh lemon juice
- 1 garlic clove, minced
- 6 tomatoes, cut into ⅓-inch-thick slices (about 3¼ pounds)
- ¼ cup thinly sliced fresh basil
- 1 teaspoon coarsely ground black pepper

1. Prepare grill or grill pan.
2. Place bread on grill rack or grill pan coated with cooking spray; grill 2 minutes on each side or until lightly browned. Remove from grill. Rub cut sides of halved garlic clove over one side of each bread slice. Set aside.
3. Place cheese, tofu, water, lemon juice, and minced garlic in a blender; process until smooth.
4. Place 1 bread slice on each of 6 plates; divide tomato slices evenly among servings. Spoon cheese mixture on each serving, dividing evenly; sprinkle evenly with basil and pepper. Yield: 6 servings.

CALORIES 168 (26% from fat); FAT 4.9g (sat 2.3g, mono 1.8g, poly 0.6g); PROTEIN 7.6g; CARB 26.7g; FIBER 3.7g; CHOL 10mg; IRON 2mg; SODIUM 339mg; CALC 49mg

Upside-Down Cake

MAKE AHEAD
Cherry-Almond Upside-Down Cake

Cherries and almonds have a natural affinity; in fact, cherry pits have a bitter almond flavor. The ease of this special dessert belies its gorgeous appearance. If you're pitting the cherries, be sure to work over a bowl and save any accumulated juice, which should be added to the recipe with the cherries.

- 1¼ cups sugar, divided
- ¼ cup dry red wine
- 2 pounds dark sweet cherries, pitted
- 1 teaspoon fresh lemon juice
- Cooking spray
- ¾ cup whole blanched almonds, toasted
- 2 large eggs
- 2 large egg whites
- 1 cup all-purpose flour
- ½ teaspoon salt

1. Preheat oven to 375°.
2. Combine ¼ cup sugar and wine in a large saucepan over low heat; stir until sugar dissolves. Increase heat to medium-high; bring to a boil. Stir in cherries. Reduce heat to low, and cook 5 minutes or until cherries just begin to soften, stirring frequently. Remove cherries from pan with a slotted spoon, reserving liquid in pan. Place cherries in a bowl; stir in lemon juice. Arrange cherries in an even layer in bottom of a 9-inch square baking pan coated with cooking spray.
3. Cook wine mixture over medium-high heat 3 minutes or until reduced to ¼ cup. Drizzle over cherries.
4. Place almonds and 2 tablespoons sugar in a food processor; process until finely ground (do not process to a paste).
5. Place eggs and egg whites in a large bowl. Beat with a mixer at high speed until foamy; slowly add ¾ cup plus 2 tablespoons sugar. Beat until thick and lemon-colored (about 2 minutes).

6. Lightly spoon flour into a dry measuring cup; level with a knife. Combine flour and salt. Gradually sift flour mixture over egg mixture; fold in. Fold in ground almond mixture. Carefully spoon batter over cherries. Bake at 375° for 30 minutes or until golden brown. Cool in pan 15 minutes on a wire rack. Place a plate upside down on top of cake; invert onto plate. Yield: 9 servings (serving size: 1 piece).

CALORIES 322 (23% from fat); FAT 8.3g (sat 1.1g, mono 4.6g, poly 2g); PROTEIN 7.5g; CARB 57.8g; FIBER 3.9g; CHOL 47mg; IRON 1.7mg; SODIUM 163mg; CALC 51mg

Vidalia Onions

Grilled Vidalia Onion and Steak Sandwiches
(pictured on page 182)

Cola in the marinade tenderizes the meat.

STEAK:
- ¾ cup cola
- 2 tablespoons red wine vinegar
- 1 teaspoon coarsely ground black pepper
- ½ teaspoon salt
- ½ teaspoon ground chipotle chile pepper
- 4 garlic cloves, crushed
- 1 bay leaf, crushed
- 1 (1½-pound) flank steak, trimmed

DRESSING:
- ¾ cup minced arugula
- ½ cup low-fat mayonnaise

REMAINING INGREDIENTS:
- Cooking spray
- 6 (½-inch-thick) slices Vidalia onion
- 6 (2-ounce) Kaiser rolls
- 12 (¼-inch-thick) slices tomato

1. To prepare steak, combine first 7 ingredients in a large zip-top plastic bag. Add steak; seal and marinate in refrigerator 2 hours, turning bag occasionally.

Continued

Remove steak from bag, reserving marinade. Pour marinade into a microwave-safe bowl; microwave at HIGH 2 minutes or until mixture comes to a boil. Set aside.

2. Prepare grill.

3. To prepare dressing, combine arugula and mayonnaise; set aside.

4. Place steak on a grill rack coated with cooking spray; grill 8 minutes on each side or until steak is medium-rare or desired degree of doneness. Remove steak from grill; cover and let stand 5 minutes. Place onion slices on grill rack; grill 4 minutes on each side, basting occasionally with reserved marinade. Place rolls on grill rack, cut sides down; grill 2 minutes or until lightly browned.

5. Cut steak diagonally across grain into thin slices. Spread 2 tablespoons dressing on bottom half of each roll. Divide steak, tomato, and onion evenly among bottom halves of rolls. Top with top halves of rolls. Yield: 6 servings (serving size: 1 sandwich).

CALORIES 417 (24% from fat); FAT 11g (sat 3.3g, mono 3.8g, poly 2.2g); PROTEIN 30.5g; CARB 49.1g; FIBER 3.2g; CHOL 38mg; IRON 3.9mg; SODIUM 747mg; CALC 104mg

WINE NOTE: A great steak sandwich like this one deserves a rich, fleshy red wine—one that will stand up to the savoriness of the grilled onions and the sweet meatiness of the steak. Since this is a sandwich, the wine shouldn't break the bank. A top choice: a California merlot. The Chateau Souverain Merlot 2001 (Alexander Valley, California, $18) is smooth, with hints of blackberries, plum, sage, and mushrooms.

Vidalia onions only grow in a small corner of Georgia, but they're famous around the country for their subtle sweetness. Vidalias are juicy, mild, and very sweet due to the area's unique combination of soils and climate. Sweet onions from other states share with Vidalias the high sugar and water content that is their delicious signature. But to onion connoisseurs, the pale yellow bulbs are the cream of the crop.

Watermelon

Sesame-Chile Chicken with Gingered Watermelon Salsa

(pictured on page 183)

For ease of preparation, purchase a container of cut-up watermelon from the produce section of your supermarket; then all you have to do is cut the chunks into small pieces. While the liquid from the salsa is tasty, you might want to use a slotted spoon to serve the salsa. Serve over a bed of jasmine or basmati rice.

CHICKEN:

- 2 tablespoons low-sodium soy sauce
- 1 to 2 tablespoons chili sauce with garlic
- 1 tablespoon dark sesame oil
- 4 (6-ounce) skinless, boneless chicken breast halves

SALSA:

- 2 cups diced seeded watermelon
- ¼ cup diced yellow bell pepper
- 2 tablespoons thinly sliced green onions
- 1 tablespoon chopped fresh cilantro
- 2 teaspoons mirin (sweet rice wine)
- 1 teaspoon fresh lime juice
- 1 teaspoon grated peeled fresh ginger
- ⅛ teaspoon salt
- 1 jalapeño pepper, seeded and minced

REMAINING INGREDIENTS:

¼ teaspoon salt
Cooking spray
Cilantro sprigs (optional)
Lime wedges (optional)

1. To prepare chicken, combine first 3 ingredients in a large zip-top plastic bag. Add chicken; seal and marinate in refrigerator 1 hour, turning occasionally.

2. Prepare grill.

3. To prepare salsa, combine watermelon and next 8 ingredients; cover and chill until ready to serve.

4. Remove chicken from marinade; discard marinade. Sprinkle chicken evenly with ¼ teaspoon salt. Place chicken on a grill rack coated with cooking spray. Grill 6 minutes on each side or until done. Remove chicken from grill; let stand 5 minutes. Cut chicken diagonally across grain into thin slices; serve with salsa. Garnish with cilantro sprigs and serve with lime wedges, if desired. Yield: 4 servings (serving size: 1 chicken breast half and about ½ cup salsa).

CALORIES 247 (17% from fat); FAT 4.6g (sat 0.9g, mono 1.5g, poly 1.5g); PROTEIN 40.2g; CARB 8.7g; FIBER 0.7g; CHOL 99mg; IRON 1.8mg; SODIUM 722mg; CALC 27mg

---

Xtra-Easy Appetizer

QUICK & EASY • MAKE AHEAD

Nectarine, Prosciutto, and Arugula Bundles

Your guests will be amazed to find out how tasty these simple snacks are. Peaches or plums also work well in place of the nectarines. You can assemble the bundles up to one hour in advance. Just cover them with plastic wrap, and refrigerate until ready to serve.

- 4 cups lightly packed trimmed arugula
- 1 teaspoon extravirgin olive oil
- ⅛ teaspoon freshly ground black pepper
- 12 (½-ounce) slices prosciutto, each cut in half lengthwise
- 3 nectarines, each cut into 8 wedges (about ¾ pound)

1. Combine first 3 ingredients in a large bowl; toss gently to combine. Arrange 3 or 4 arugula leaves at 1 end of 1 prosciutto strip. Place 1 nectarine wedge on top of arugula; roll up. Place bundle, seam side down, on a serving plate. Repeat procedure with remaining arugula, prosciutto, and nectarines. Yield: 8 servings (serving size: 3 bundles).

CALORIES 79 (40% from fat); FAT 3.5g (sat 1g, mono 1.6g, poly 0.3g); PROTEIN 6.3g; CARB 6.4g; FIBER 0.9g; CHOL 19mg; IRON 0.6mg; SODIUM 412mg; CALC 16mg

Yellow Squash

QUICK & EASY

Yellow Squash Ribbons with Red Onion and Parmesan

This supereasy side can also be made with zucchini or a colorful combination of zucchini and yellow squash.

  4 yellow squash (about 1½ pounds)
  1 teaspoon olive oil
  1 cup thinly vertically sliced red onion
  1 garlic clove, minced
  ¼ teaspoon salt
  ¼ to ½ teaspoon crushed red pepper
  ¼ teaspoon freshly ground black pepper
  ¼ cup (1 ounce) shaved fresh Parmesan cheese

1. Using a vegetable peeler, shave squash into ribbons to measure 5 cups. Discard seeds and core of squash.
2. Heat oil in a large nonstick skillet over medium heat. Add squash, onion, and garlic; cook 4 minutes or until onion is tender, gently stirring occasionally. Remove from heat. Add salt, red pepper, and black pepper, and toss gently to combine. Sprinkle with cheese. Yield: 4 servings (serving size: about ¾ cup).

CALORIES 84 (36% from fat); FAT 3.4g (sat 1.4g, mono 1.4g, poly 0.3g); PROTEIN 4.5g; CARB 10.4g; FIBER 3.8g; CHOL 5mg; IRON 1mg; SODIUM 266mg; CALC 128mg

Zucchini

Eight-Ball Zucchini Parmesan

Eight-ball zucchini is a round, softball-sized variety of summer squash. You can find it at farmers' markets, or purchase it from specialty produce purveyors such as Frieda's (www.friedas.com). This recipe is equally delicious when made with the more commonly found long, slender zucchini squash.

  1 (1-ounce) slice French bread, torn into small pieces
  6 eight-ball zucchini (about 1½ pounds)
  ½ cup packed spinach leaves
  8 basil leaves
  2 garlic cloves, minced
  1 small onion, peeled and quartered (about 5 ounces)
  ¾ teaspoon olive oil
  1 cup chopped plum tomato
  ½ teaspoon salt
  ¼ cup (1 ounce) grated fresh Parmesan cheese
Flat-leaf parsley sprigs (optional)

1. Preheat oven to 350°.
2. Place bread in a food processor; pulse 10 times or until coarse crumbs measure 1 cup. Set aside.
3. Cut each zucchini in half lengthwise; scoop out pulp, leaving ¼-inch-thick shells. Set pulp aside. Steam zucchini shells, covered, 6 minutes or until tender. Drain, cut sides down, on several layers of heavy-duty paper towels.
4. Place zucchini pulp in food processor; process until finely chopped. Spoon into a bowl. Place spinach, basil, garlic, and onion in food processor; process until finely chopped.
5. Heat oil in a large nonstick skillet over medium heat. Add spinach mixture; cook 3 minutes, stirring occasionally. Add zucchini pulp, tomato, and salt; cook 8 minutes, stirring occasionally. Remove from heat; stir in breadcrumbs.

6. Fill each zucchini shell with about 2½ tablespoons spinach mixture. Sprinkle evenly with cheese. Bake at 350° for 20 minutes or until cheese melts. Garnish with parsley, if desired. Yield: 6 servings (serving size: 2 zucchini halves).

CALORIES 67 (30% from fat); FAT 2.2g (sat 0.9g, mono 0.9g, poly 0.3g); PROTEIN 4g; CARB 9g; FIBER 2g; CHOL 3mg; IRON 0.8mg; SODIUM 316mg; CALC 87mg

season's best

Grilled Peaches and Pork

Meat is a natural on the summertime grill, and here we use pork paillards (boneless chops pounded thin for speedy cooking).

While the grill is hot, we add halved peaches (plums would be a good substitute) drizzled with balsamic vinegar. Grilling caramelizes the fruit's sugar, deepens its flavor, and softens its texture to make it a delicious sidekick for the pork. A bed of arugula adds a peppery counterpoint. Enjoy this dish on the deck or patio with a glass of chilled riesling, and you have the ingredients for a fine solstice supper.

Grilled Peaches and Pork

  4 (4-ounce) boneless center-cut pork loin chops
  ¼ cup balsamic vinegar, divided
  2 tablespoons fresh lime juice
  3 teaspoons chopped fresh thyme
  ½ teaspoon salt
  ½ teaspoon freshly ground black pepper
  4 large peaches, peeled, halved, and pitted (about 12 ounces)
Cooking spray
  6 cups trimmed arugula
  1 teaspoon turbinado or granulated sugar

1. Place each piece of pork between 2 sheets of heavy-duty plastic wrap, and
Continued

flatten each piece to ¼-inch thickness using a meat mallet or rolling pin.

2. Combine 2 tablespoons vinegar, juice, thyme, salt, and pepper in a small bowl. Reserve 1 tablespoon juice mixture. Pour remaining juice mixture in a large zip-top plastic bag. Add pork; seal and marinate in refrigerator 1 hour, turning occasionally.

3. Preheat grill.

4. Place peaches, cut sides up, on a plate; drizzle with 2 tablespoons vinegar.

5. Place pork on grill rack coated with cooking spray; grill 3 minutes on each side or until done. Set aside.

6. Place peaches, cut sides down, on grill rack; grill 4 minutes or until soft and slightly browned. Turn and cook 2 minutes or until thoroughly heated. Cut each peach half into 4 slices. Cut pork into 1-inch strips.

7. Drizzle arugula with reserved 1 tablespoon juice mixture, tossing to coat. Place arugula on each of 4 plates. Top with pork strips and peach slices; sprinkle with sugar. Yield: 4 servings (serving size: 3 ounces pork, 8 peach slices, 1½ cups arugula, and ¼ teaspoon sugar).

CALORIES 216 (29% from fat); FAT 7g (sat 2.4g, mono 3g, poly 0.6g); PROTEIN 25.5g; CARB 12.7g; FIBER 0.6g; CHOL 65mg; IRON 1.5mg; SODIUM 234mg; CALC 84mg

sound bites

Creative Culture

Take a cue from Indian cooks, and use yogurt in savory recipes.

Yogurt has remained a key ingredient in Indian kitchens for 5,000 years and is used by everyday cooks as a meat tenderizer, a souring agent, and a base for curries.

Although you can prepare any of the recipes that follow with purchased yogurt, it's simple to make (see "Making Yogurt," at right). You don't need any special utensils, preservatives (the homemade stuff will keep for one week in the refrigerator), or stabilizers, such as gelatin.

Making Yogurt

We use 1% low-fat milk, but fat-free milk will also work in the recipe below. Whole milk produces particularly thick, creamy yogurt that's excellent in cooked dishes. Make sure the starter you use comes from a yogurt that specifies "contains live and active cultures" on the label. Some commercial brands are pasteurized and don't contain live cultures, which are necessary to ferment the milk. An unheated gas oven with the pilot light on offers a warm environment for the cultures to grow; if you have an electric oven, just leave the oven light on. And before you start cooking with homemade yogurt, refrigerate two tablespoons of it in a small container with a tight-fitting lid so you'll have starter for your next homemade batch.

Homemade Yogurt

4 cups 1% low-fat milk
2 tablespoons plain low-fat yogurt

1. Place milk in a large saucepan; heat milk over medium-high heat until bubbles appear. Remove from heat. Cool until it registers 110° to 112° on a thermometer. Transfer milk to a large glass container. Stir yogurt into milk. Cover container tightly with plastic wrap. Place container in an unheated oven with pilot light or oven light left on 8 hours or overnight. Remove wrap, and gently shake container to see if yogurt is very thick. If not, let it sit for a few hours longer. If it is thick, place container in refrigerator to chill. Yield: 4 cups (serving size: ½ cup).

CALORIES 53 (23% from fat); FAT 1.4g (sat 0.8g, mono 0.4g, poly 0.1g); PROTEIN 4.2g; CARB 6.1g; FIBER 0g; CHOL 5mg; IRON 0.1mg; SODIUM 64mg; CALC 157mg

Eggplant with Spinach-Yogurt Sauce
Hariyali Kadhi

A coffee grinder is useful in this recipe for pulverizing coriander seeds and grinding dried chickpeas into flour. (If you'd prefer to buy chickpea flour, it's available in Indian markets.) The sauce can be prepared and refrigerated in a covered container a day ahead; reheat it over low heat while the eggplant cooks.

SAUCE:

1 teaspoon canola oil
1 cup chopped red onion
1 cup chopped tomato
1 teaspoon grated peeled fresh ginger
2 garlic cloves, minced
1 (10-ounce) package frozen chopped spinach, thawed, drained, and squeezed dry
1 cup water
¼ cup chickpea (garbanzo bean) flour
¼ cup water
2 cups plain whole milk yogurt, divided
¾ teaspoon salt

EGGPLANT:

1 (¾-pound) eggplant, cut crosswise into 16 slices
1 teaspoon canola oil
½ teaspoon ground coriander
½ teaspoon ground turmeric
¼ teaspoon ground red pepper

REMAINING INGREDIENTS:

2 teaspoons canola oil
¼ teaspoon ground red pepper
2 garlic cloves, thinly sliced
2 cups hot cooked basmati rice

1. To prepare sauce, heat 1 teaspoon oil in a large nonstick skillet over medium-high heat. Add onion; sauté 5 minutes. Add tomato, ginger, and minced garlic; sauté 5 minutes or until tender. Add spinach, and sauté 3 minutes. Add 1 cup water; cook 5 minutes or until liquid evaporates. Remove from heat; cool.

Spoon spinach mixture into a food processor; process until smooth. Lightly spoon flour into a dry measuring cup; level with a knife. Place flour in a small bowl; whisk in ¼ cup water, ¼ cup yogurt, and salt. Place spinach mixture in a medium saucepan; stir in flour mixture and 1¾ cups yogurt. Cook over medium heat 15 minutes or until mixture begins to thicken, stirring frequently. Cover and remove from heat.

2. Preheat broiler.

3. To prepare eggplant, place eggplant slices in a single layer on a baking sheet. Combine 1 teaspoon oil, coriander, turmeric, and ¼ teaspoon pepper. Using the back of a spoon, spread a small amount of mixture over 1 side of each eggplant slice. Broil 10 minutes or until lightly browned.

4. Heat 2 teaspoons oil in a small skillet over medium heat. Add ¼ teaspoon pepper and sliced garlic; sauté 1 minute or just until garlic is lightly browned. Remove from heat. Pour warm spinach sauce in a shallow serving dish; top with eggplant. Drizzle with garlic mixture. Serve with rice. Yield: 4 servings (serving size: about 4 eggplant slices, ¾ cup sauce, and ½ cup rice).

CALORIES 314 (29% from fat); FAT 10.2g (sat 3.3g, mono 4g, poly 1.9g); PROTEIN 12.1g; CARB 46.7g; FIBER 4.1g; CHOL 16mg; IRON 3.5mg; SODIUM 561mg; CALC 299mg

Cooking with Yogurt

Whether you cook with homemade or commercial yogurt, follow these simple guidelines:

• In cooked dishes, use whole milk yogurt; its fat content keeps the yogurt from curdling during the cooking process. To further guard against curdling, add the yogurt a few tablespoons at a time, and cook over medium-low heat.

• Choose fat-free, low-fat, or whole milk yogurt for uncooked marinades, dips, and drinks.

• Unless otherwise specified, yogurt-based foods are best served immediately.

• Avoid freezing dishes made with yogurt, as freezing can change their texture.

Tandoori-Style Cauliflower
Tandoori Gobhi

CAULIFLOWER:

- 3 cups water
- 1 tablespoon fresh lemon juice
- 1 teaspoon salt
- 6 cups cauliflower florets

SPICE MIX:

- 2 cardamom pods
- 2 whole cloves
- 1 (1-inch) cinnamon stick
- 1 bay leaf

SAUCE:

- 1½ teaspoons canola oil
- 1½ cups chopped white onion
- 1 tablespoon finely ground blanched almonds (about ½ ounce)
- 1½ teaspoons grated peeled fresh ginger
- ½ teaspoon ground turmeric
- ½ teaspoon salt
- ¼ teaspoon ground red pepper
- 3 garlic cloves, minced
- ⅓ cup water
- 6 tablespoons plain whole milk yogurt

REMAINING INGREDIENT:

- ¼ cup chopped fresh cilantro

1. To prepare cauliflower, bring first 3 ingredients to a boil in a large saucepan. Add cauliflower florets; cover, reduce heat, and simmer 5 minutes or just until tender (do not overcook). Drain.

2. To prepare spice mix, combine cardamom, cloves, cinnamon, and bay leaf in a medium nonstick skillet; cook over medium heat 2 minutes or until toasted and fragrant. Place mixture in a coffee or spice grinder; process until ground.

3. To prepare sauce, heat oil in pan over medium heat. Add onion; sauté 8 minutes or until lightly browned. Stir in cardamom mixture, almonds, and next 5 ingredients; cook 2 minutes. Remove from heat; cool slightly.

4. Preheat oven to 350°.

5. Place onion mixture and ⅓ cup water in a blender; process until almost smooth, scraping sides occasionally. Place mixture in pan; gradually stir in yogurt. Cook over low heat 5 minutes, stirring frequently.

6. Place cauliflower in a shallow 2-quart baking dish; pour onion mixture over cauliflower, tossing to coat. Bake at 350° for 20 minutes or until thoroughly heated and just beginning to brown. Sprinkle with cilantro. Yield: 6 servings (serving size: 1 cup).

CALORIES 84 (33% from fat); FAT 3.1g (sat 0.5g, mono 0.9g, poly 0.5g); PROTEIN 3.6g; CARB 12.8g; FIBER 4.4g; CHOL 2mg; IRON 1.3mg; SODIUM 277mg; CALC 70mg

QUICK & EASY • MAKE AHEAD
Saffron-Marinated Chicken Skewers
Kesari Malai Tikka

You can purchase almond meal in specialty stores, or grind the little you need for this recipe in a coffee grinder.

- 2 tablespoons 2% reduced-fat milk
- ½ teaspoon saffron threads, crushed
- ½ cup Yogurt Cheese (recipe on page 202)
- 2 tablespoons almond meal
- 1 tablespoon grated peeled fresh ginger
- 1 teaspoon salt
- 1 teaspoon fresh lemon juice
- ½ teaspoon freshly ground black pepper
- 2 pounds skinless, boneless chicken breast, cut into 1½-inch pieces
- Cooking spray

1. Combine milk and saffron in a small microwave-safe bowl, and microwave at HIGH 20 seconds. Let stand 5 minutes.

2. Combine milk mixture, Yogurt Cheese, and next 5 ingredients in a large zip-top plastic bag. Add chicken, tossing to coat; seal. Marinate in refrigerator 2½ hours, turning occasionally.

3. Prepare grill.

4. Remove chicken from bag, and discard marinade. Thread chicken evenly onto 20 (6-inch) skewers. Place skewers on grill rack coated with cooking spray; grill 15 minutes or until done, turning once. Yield: 10 servings (serving size: 2 skewers).

CALORIES 111 (14% from fat); FAT 1.7g (sat 0.4g, mono 0.3g, poly 0.3g); PROTEIN 21.6g; CARB 0.9g; FIBER 0.2g; CHOL 53mg; IRON 0.7mg; SODIUM 220mg; CALC 24mg

Yogurt Cheese

This cheese is simple to prepare and is good in marinades and dips. If you need a small amount of yogurt cheese and don't have a lot of time, use the quick-drain method: Spread about twice as much yogurt as you need cheese in a ½-inch thickness on several layers of heavy-duty paper towels; cover with additional paper towels, and let stand five minutes. Quick-drained yogurt cheese isn't as thick as this version, but it will do in a pinch.

1 quart plain low-fat yogurt

1. Line a colander with 4 layers of cheesecloth, allowing cheesecloth to extend over outside edges of colander, and place colander in a medium bowl. Spoon yogurt into cheesecloth-lined colander. Refrigerate overnight. Discard liquid. Yield: 2 cups.

(Totals for entire recipe) CALORIES 309 (22% from fat); FAT 7.6g (sat 4.9g, mono 2.1g, poly 0.2g); PROTEIN 25.7g; CARB 34.5g; FIBER 0g; CHOL 29mg; IRON 0.4mg; SODIUM 343mg; CALC 897mg

MAKE AHEAD
Walnut-Yogurt Dip
Akhrot Ka Raita

This sweet-savory dip is delicious with pita wedges and fresh strawberries or cut-up pineapple for breakfast, dessert, or a snack. You can prepare it up to one day ahead and refrigerate.

1 cup Yogurt Cheese (recipe above)
⅓ cup coarsely chopped walnuts
2 tablespoons brown sugar
¼ teaspoon salt
¼ teaspoon cumin seeds
⅛ teaspoon crushed red pepper
12 seedless green grapes, thinly sliced

1. Combine first 4 ingredients in a medium bowl. Sprinkle with cumin and pepper; garnish with grape slices. Cover and chill 20 minutes. Yield: 1 cup (serving size: 2 tablespoons).

CALORIES 67 (46% from fat); FAT 3.5g (sat 0.5g, mono 0.8g, poly 2g); PROTEIN 2.9g; CARB 6.8g; FIBER 0.3g; CHOL 2mg; IRON 0.3mg; SODIUM 97mg; CALC 63mg

QUICK & EASY
Curd Rice
Dahiwale Chawal

Ghee is butter that has been slowly melted so the milk solids sink to the bottom and are discarded. You can purchase it at Middle Eastern and Indian grocery stores. To make ghee at home, simmer 4 tablespoons butter over medium heat until milk solids stop crackling and turn amber (about five minutes), stirring occasionally. Turn off heat, and let the residue settle to the bottom of the pan. Pour the clear butter fat into a small bowl, and use as directed in the recipe.

2 cups uncooked basmati rice
4 cups water
1 tablespoon canola oil
1 teaspoon salt
1 cup plain low-fat yogurt
1 cup chopped peeled ripe mango
½ cup low-fat buttermilk
2 tablespoons minced fresh cilantro
2 tablespoons ghee (clarified butter)
1 teaspoon black mustard seeds
¼ cup unsalted cashews, chopped
1 tablespoon slivered peeled fresh ginger
15 curry leaves, crushed
2 dried hot red chiles

1. Rinse rice in 2 changes of cold water; drain. Bring rice and 4 cups water to a boil in a large saucepan. Add oil and salt. Cover, reduce heat, and simmer 15 minutes or until liquid is absorbed. Fluff with a fork. Spoon rice into a large bowl; cool to room temperature. Add yogurt, mango, buttermilk, and cilantro; stir gently.
2. Heat ghee in a small skillet over medium heat. Add mustard seeds; cook 3 minutes or until seeds begin to pop. Add cashews and remaining 3 ingredients; cook 2 minutes or until fragrant. Pour over rice mixture. Discard chiles, if desired. Serve immediately. Yield: 14 servings (serving size: ½ cup).

CALORIES 164 (30% from fat); FAT 5.5g (sat 1.9g, mono 2.3g, poly 1g); PROTEIN 4g; CARB 26.8g; FIBER 1.8g; CHOL 6mg; IRON 0.6mg; SODIUM 195mg; CALC 57mg

Spiced Salmon Kebabs
Tandoori Rawas

Ajowan, sometimes called *ajwain* or *carom*, is a spice related to caraway and cumin, and you can find it in most Indian markets.

¾ teaspoon cumin seeds
¾ teaspoon coriander seeds
½ teaspoon ajowan (carom seeds)
3 cardamom pods
2 whole cloves
1 bay leaf
1 (1-inch) cinnamon stick
3 tablespoons plain low-fat yogurt
1 tablespoon grated peeled fresh ginger
1 tablespoon fresh lemon juice
1 teaspoon salt
¼ teaspoon crushed red pepper
3 garlic cloves, minced
1 (2¼-pound) salmon fillet, cut into 1-inch cubes
Cooking spray

1. Combine first 7 ingredients in a small skillet over medium heat; cook 2 minutes or until fragrant, stirring constantly. Cool. Place mixture in a spice or coffee grinder, and process until finely ground.
2. Combine spice mixture, yogurt, and next 5 ingredients in a large zip-top plastic bag. Add fish, tossing to coat; seal and marinate in refrigerator 2 hours, turning occasionally. Remove fish from bag; discard marinade.
3. Preheat broiler.
4. Thread fish evenly onto 6 (12-inch) skewers. Place skewers on a broiler pan coated with cooking spray; broil 7 minutes on each side or until done. Yield: 6 servings (serving size: 1 skewer).

CALORIES 245 (41% from fat); FAT 11.1g (sat 2.6g, mono 4.9g, poly 2.6g); PROTEIN 32.6g; CARB 1.9g; FIBER 0.6g; CHOL 84mg; IRON 1.1mg; SODIUM 269mg; CALC 38mg

QUICK & EASY
Pineapple Raita

You can prepare this up to one day ahead; garnish with mint and peppercorns just before serving. Serve with grilled chicken and pita bread.

2 cups plain low-fat yogurt
1 tablespoon sugar
Dash of salt
1½ cups diced pineapple
½ teaspoon dried mint flakes
¼ teaspoon crushed pink peppercorns

1. Place yogurt, sugar, and dash of salt in a bowl; stir with a whisk until smooth. Stir in pineapple. Transfer yogurt mixture to a serving dish, and chill. Before serving, sprinkle with mint flakes and peppercorns. Yield: 3½ cups (serving size: 2 tablespoons).

CALORIES 17 (15% from fat); FAT 0.3g (sat 0.2g, mono 0.1g, poly 0g); PROTEIN 1g; CARB 2.7g; FIBER 0.1g; CHOL 1mg; IRON 0.1mg; SODIUM 18mg; CALC 33mg

Bengali Fish Curry
Doi Maach

Thick, meaty fish like mahimahi works best in this dish. Serve with steamed basmati rice or Curd Rice (recipe on page 202).

SPICE MIX:
2 teaspoons coriander seeds
1 teaspoon cumin seeds
2 dried hot red chiles
2 whole cloves
2 green cardamom pods
1 (1-inch) cinnamon stick

FISH:
2¼ pounds mahimahi, cut into 1½-inch pieces
¾ teaspoon ground turmeric
½ teaspoon salt
2 tablespoons canola oil, divided

SAUCE:
¾ cup finely chopped red onion
1 teaspoon grated peeled fresh ginger
1 garlic clove, minced
1 bay leaf
¼ cup water
1 teaspoon salt
½ teaspoon sugar
1 cup plain whole milk yogurt

1. To prepare spice mix, combine first 6 ingredients in a spice or coffee grinder; process until finely ground.

2. To prepare fish, combine mahimahi, turmeric, and ½ teaspoon salt in a large bowl; toss well. Heat 1 tablespoon oil in a large nonstick skillet over medium-high heat. Add half of fish; cook 5 minutes or until fish is lightly browned and flakes easily when tested with a fork (do not overcook). Remove from pan. Repeat procedure with remaining fish and 1 tablespoon oil.

3. To prepare sauce, add onion to pan; sauté 5 minutes or until tender. Add ginger, garlic, and bay leaf; sauté 2 minutes. Add spice mix; cook 2 minutes. Stir in water, 1 teaspoon salt, and sugar. Remove from heat; gradually stir in yogurt. Cook over low heat 5 minutes, stirring constantly. Return fish and accumulated juices to pan. Cook over low heat 5 minutes or just until heated. Discard bay leaf. Yield: 6 servings (serving size: 1 cup).

CALORIES 235 (29% from fat); FAT 7.6g (sat 1.7g, mono 2.7g, poly 2.5g); PROTEIN 33.6g; CARB 7.6g; FIBER 1.6g; CHOL 129mg; IRON 3.1mg; SODIUM 762mg; CALC 106mg

QUICK & EASY
Indian Cabbage Salad
Hara Salaad

Tamarind paste and palm sugar can be found in Asian markets. Substitute brown sugar for palm sugar, if desired.

½ cup whole pitted dates, chopped
1 (16-ounce) package cabbage-and-carrot coleslaw
2 tablespoons hot water
1½ teaspoons tamarind paste
1 cup plain low-fat yogurt
1 tablespoon packed palm sugar
¼ teaspoon salt

1. Combine chopped dates and coleslaw in a large bowl.

2. Combine hot water and tamarind paste in a small bowl; stir well with a whisk. Stir in yogurt, sugar, and salt. Pour over cabbage mixture; toss well. Chill 30 minutes. Yield: 8 servings (serving size: 1 cup).

CALORIES 71 (7% from fat); FAT 0.6g (sat 0.3g, mono 0.1g, poly 0.1g); PROTEIN 2.7g; CARB 15.3g; FIBER 0.8g; CHOL 2mg; IRON 0.5mg; SODIUM 105mg; CALC 90mg

Alfresco Brunch

Gather friends for an elegant midmorning meal in honor of a bride-to-be, a graduate, or simply the arrival of summer.

Alfresco Brunch Menu
serves 8

Lemon-Buttermilk Scones with Quick Blackberry Jam

Mixed Greens Salad with Honey-Orange Dressing

Fresh Mozzarella, Sun-Dried Tomato, and Prosciutto Strata

Grits Casserole with Pesto Butter

Banana-Chocolate Brunch Cake

Sparkling Fruit Gelées

Sparkling wine and coffee

MAKE AHEAD
Lemon-Buttermilk Scones with Quick Blackberry Jam

Cake flour gives these scones a light, moist texture. You can make and chill the jam up to two weeks ahead. The scones can be baked a day in advance; store and serve the scones at room temperature.

3 cups cake flour
2 tablespoons sugar
2 teaspoons baking powder
½ teaspoon salt
¼ cup chilled butter, cut into small pieces
¾ cup low-fat buttermilk
1½ teaspoons grated lemon rind
1 tablespoon fresh lemon juice
1 teaspoon cake flour
1 large egg white, lightly beaten
1 teaspoon sugar
10 tablespoons Quick Blackberry Jam
Continued

1. Preheat oven to 350°.

2. Lightly spoon 3 cups flour into dry measuring cups; level with a knife. Place 3 cups flour, 2 tablespoons sugar, baking powder, and salt in a food processor; pulse 2 or 3 times or until combined. Add butter; pulse 10 times or until mixture resembles coarse meal. Add buttermilk, rind, and lemon juice; pulse until just combined. Scrape dough onto a lightly floured surface with a rubber spatula; sprinkle with 1 teaspoon flour (dough will be soft).

3. With floured hands, pat dough into a 4-inch circle; place on a baking sheet lined with parchment paper. Pat dough into an 8-inch circle. Cut dough into 10 wedges, cutting into but not through dough. Brush egg white over dough; sprinkle with 1 teaspoon sugar. Bake at 350° for 25 minutes or until golden. Cool on a wire rack. Serve with Quick Blackberry Jam. Yield: 10 servings (serving size: 1 scone and 1 tablespoon jam).

(Totals include Quick Blackberry Jam) CALORIES 237 (20% from fat); FAT 5.2g (sat 2.4g, mono 2g, poly 0.4g); PROTEIN 4.7g; CARB 41.7g; FIBER 0.8g; CHOL 13mg; IRON 3.3mg; SODIUM 274mg; CALC 89mg

QUICK & EASY • MAKE AHEAD
QUICK BLACKBERRY JAM:

2   cups blackberries
½   cup crème de cassis (black currant-flavored liqueur)
3   tablespoons fresh lemon juice
2   tablespoons sugar
¼   cup water
1   tablespoon cornstarch

1. Combine first 4 ingredients in a medium saucepan over medium heat. Cook 8 minutes or until berries begin to soften; stir frequently.

2. Combine water and cornstarch in a small bowl, stirring with a whisk; stir into berry mixture. Bring to a boil, and cook 1 minute or until thick, stirring constantly. Cool; pour into an airtight container. Cover and chill. Yield: 1 cup (serving size: 1 tablespoon).

NOTE: Refrigerate jam in an airtight container up to two weeks.

CALORIES 25 (4% from fat); FAT 0.1g (sat 0g, mono 0g, poly 0.1g); PROTEIN 0.3g; CARB 5.2g; FIBER 0g; CHOL 0mg; IRON 0.1mg; SODIUM 0mg; CALC 5mg

QUICK & EASY
Mixed Greens Salad with Honey-Orange Dressing

This easy, all-purpose salad goes with almost any early summer dinner.

3   tablespoons fresh orange juice
1   tablespoon honey
2   teaspoons minced shallots
2   teaspoons white wine vinegar
½   teaspoon Dijon mustard
¼   teaspoon salt
¼   teaspoon freshly ground black pepper
4   cups chopped romaine lettuce
4   cups torn radicchio
3   cups bagged baby spinach leaves

1. Combine first 7 ingredients in a large bowl, stirring with a whisk. Add lettuce, radicchio, and spinach; toss gently to coat. Yield: 8 servings (serving size: about 1 cup).

CALORIES 24 (8% from fat); FAT 0.2g (sat 0g, mono 0g, poly 0.1g); PROTEIN 1.1g; CARB 5.3g; FIBER 1.1g; CHOL 0mg; IRON 0.8mg; SODIUM 97mg; CALC 26mg

MAKE AHEAD
Fresh Mozzarella, Sun-Dried Tomato, and Prosciutto Strata

Assemble the ingredients, chill overnight, and bake in the morning. If you don't have enough time to refrigerate the bread mixture overnight, you can chill it for as little as three hours.

1   pound rosemary focaccia, cut into ¾-inch cubes (about 15 cups)
3¼ cups fat-free milk
¼   cup (2 ounces) crème fraîche or sour cream
1   (8-ounce) carton egg substitute
¼   cup oil-packed sun-dried tomatoes, drained and chopped
1   garlic clove, minced
Cooking spray
4   ounces prosciutto, chopped
4   ounces fresh mozzarella cheese, cut into ¼-inch-wide strips
½   cup (2 ounces) grated fresh Parmesan cheese

1. Preheat oven to 350°.

2. Arrange bread cubes in a single layer on a large baking sheet. Bake at 350° for 10 minutes or until toasted, stirring once.

3. Combine milk, crème fraîche, and egg substitute in a large bowl, stirring with a whisk until smooth. Add tomatoes and garlic, stirring with a whisk. Add bread; stir gently to combine. Let stand 5 minutes.

4. Pour half of bread mixture into a 13 x 9-inch baking dish coated with cooking spray. Arrange prosciutto and mozzarella evenly over bread mixture. Top with remaining bread mixture. Cover and chill 8 hours or overnight.

5. Preheat oven to 350°.

6. Uncover dish. Bake at 350° for 20 minutes. Sprinkle evenly with Parmesan. Bake an additional 20 minutes. Remove from oven; let stand 5 minutes. Serve warm. Yield: 8 servings.

CALORIES 325 (30% from fat); FAT 11g (sat 5.4g, mono 4.3g, poly 0.7g); PROTEIN 20.3g; CARB 36.9g; FIBER 1.2g; CHOL 36mg; IRON 3.2mg; SODIUM 738mg; CALC 263mg

STAFF FAVORITE
Grits Casserole with Pesto Butter

The classic Italian basil sauce freshens a down-home favorite. Beaten egg whites give the grits a light, airy texture; the casserole will rise as it bakes but then fall shortly after coming out of the oven. Use caution as the grits cook on the stovetop; they tend to spatter, so stir them with a long-handled wooden spoon.

PESTO BUTTER:

½   cup loosely packed fresh basil leaves
¼   cup loosely packed fresh parsley leaves
2   tablespoons grated fresh Parmesan cheese
2   tablespoons fat-free, less-sodium chicken broth
1   large garlic clove, minced
2   tablespoons butter, softened

CASEROLE:

4 cups 1% low-fat milk
1 cup fat-free, less-sodium chicken broth
½ teaspoon salt
1¼ cups uncooked quick-cooking grits
½ cup (2 ounces) grated fresh Parmesan cheese
½ teaspoon freshly ground black pepper
4 large egg whites
Dash of cream of tartar
Cooking spray

1. To prepare pesto butter, place first 5 ingredients in a food processor; process until finely chopped. Scrape down sides; add butter. Process until well combined. Cover and chill.
2. Preheat oven to 375°.
3. To prepare casserole, combine milk, 1 cup broth, and salt in a large saucepan; bring to a boil. Gradually add grits, stirring constantly. Reduce heat to medium-low; simmer 5 minutes or until thick, stirring occasionally with a wooden spoon. Remove from heat; add ½ cup cheese and pepper, stirring until cheese melts. Cool slightly.
4. Place egg whites in a large bowl; beat with a mixer at high speed until foamy. Add cream of tartar; beat until stiff peaks form. Gently stir one-fourth of egg white mixture into grits mixture; gently fold in remaining egg white mixture. Spoon into a 2-quart soufflé dish coated with cooking spray. Bake at 375° for 40 minutes or until casserole has risen and begins to brown. Serve warm with pesto butter. Yield: 8 servings (serving size: about ¾ cup casserole and about 2 teaspoons pesto butter).

CALORIES 219 (28% from fat); FAT 6.8g (sat 3.7g, mono 2.3g, poly 0.4g); PROTEIN 11.8g; CARB 27.5g; FIBER 0.8g; CHOL 18mg; IRON 1.4mg; SODIUM 458mg; CALC 272mg

Banana-Chocolate Brunch Cake

Mashed banana in the batter keeps the cake moist, like banana bread. Bake the cake up to two days ahead; cool completely, wrap in plastic wrap, and store in the refrigerator. For best results, glaze the cake the morning of the brunch.

2 cups all-purpose flour
¾ cup packed brown sugar
1½ teaspoons baking powder
½ teaspoon baking soda
½ teaspoon salt
¼ teaspoon ground cinnamon
2 cups mashed banana (about 3 large)
¼ cup fat-free milk
1 large egg, lightly beaten
4 ounces bittersweet chocolate, chopped and divided
Cooking spray
8 teaspoons hot water

1. Preheat oven to 350°.
2. Lightly spoon flour into dry measuring cups; level with a knife. Combine flour and next 5 ingredients in a large bowl, stirring with a whisk.
3. Combine banana, milk, and egg, stirring until well blended. Add banana mixture to flour mixture, stirring just until moist. Gently fold in half of chocolate. Spoon batter into a 9-inch round cake pan coated with cooking spray. Bake at 350° for 35 minutes or until a wooden pick inserted in center comes out clean. Cool in pan 5 minutes on a wire rack; remove from pan. Cool completely.
4. Combine remaining chocolate and hot water in a small microwave-safe bowl; microwave at HIGH 30 seconds or until almost melted. Stir until smooth. Drizzle glaze over cooled cake. Yield: 10 servings (serving size: 1 slice).

CALORIES 260 (20% from fat); FAT 5.8g (sat 2.7g, mono 2.1g, poly 0.4g); PROTEIN 4.7g; CARB 51.7g; FIBER 2.7g; CHOL 21mg; IRON 2.1mg; SODIUM 271mg; CALC 69mg

Sparkling Fruit Gelées
(pictured on page 181)

These stylish individual cups can be prepared and refrigerated up to two days before the gathering. Substitute your favorite fresh fruits in any combination.

3½ teaspoons unflavored gelatin
2⅔ cups sparkling wine, divided
⅔ cup sugar
4 teaspoons fresh lemon juice
2 cups sliced strawberries
1⅓ cups fresh blueberries
⅔ cup sliced banana
⅔ cup fresh raspberries

1. Sprinkle gelatin over ⅔ cup wine in a small saucepan, and let stand 5 minutes. Place saucepan over low heat; cook 5 minutes or until gelatin dissolves, stirring constantly.
2. Combine ⅔ cup wine and sugar in a medium saucepan over medium heat; cook 5 minutes or until sugar dissolves, stirring frequently. Remove from heat; stir in 1⅓ cups wine. Add gelatin mixture and lemon juice, stirring well.
3. Divide mixture evenly among 8 (6-ounce) Champagne flutes or wineglasses. Combine strawberries and remaining 3 ingredients. Stir about ½ cup fruit mixture into each glass; cover and chill 6 hours or overnight. Yield: 8 servings (serving size: 1 gelée).

CALORIES 166 (2% from fat); FAT 0.3g (sat 0g, mono 0g, poly 0.2g); PROTEIN 1.7g; CARB 28.3g; FIBER 2.4g; CHOL 0mg; IRON 0.6mg; SODIUM 7mg; CALC 19mg

Pasta Salads

Pasta salads toss together to satisfy even the heartiest appetites.

Pasta Salad Menu 1
serves 4

Chicken and Farfalle Salad with Walnut Pesto

Strawberries in balsamic vinegar with angel food cake*

White wine

*Combine 4 cups hulled, halved strawberries and 2 teaspoons sugar; let stand 30 minutes. Drizzle with 2 tablespoons balsamic vinegar; toss gently to coat. Let stand 15 minutes; serve over slices of purchased angel food cake.

Game Plan

1. While strawberries and sugar stand:
- Bring water for farfalle to a boil
2. While pasta cooks:
- Prepare pesto
3. Toss pasta salad. Drizzle strawberries with vinegar; toss.

QUICK & EASY
Chicken and Farfalle Salad with Walnut Pesto

To make sure the walnut pesto ingredients are evenly minced, stop the food processor halfway through processing, and scrape down the sides.

TOTAL TIME: 26 MINUTES

SMART INGREDIENT: Keep kalamata olives on hand to add zesty saltiness to salads, sandwiches, and spreads.

SALAD:
- 2 cups uncooked farfalle (bow tie pasta; about 6 ounces)
- 2 cups cubed cooked skinless, boneless chicken breast
- 1 cup quartered cherry tomatoes
- 2 tablespoons chopped pitted kalamata olives

WALNUT PESTO:
- 1 cup basil leaves
- ½ cup fresh parsley leaves
- 3 tablespoons coarsely chopped walnuts, toasted
- 1½ tablespoons extravirgin olive oil
- 1 tablespoon white wine vinegar
- ½ teaspoon salt
- 1 garlic clove

REMAINING INGREDIENT:
- 4 curly leaf lettuce leaves

1. To prepare salad, cook pasta according to package directions, omitting salt and fat. Drain; rinse with cold water. Combine pasta, chicken, tomatoes, and olives in a large bowl.
2. To prepare walnut pesto, combine basil and next 6 ingredients in a food processor; pulse 6 times or until finely minced. Add pesto to pasta mixture, tossing gently to coat. Place 1 lettuce leaf on each of 4 plates; top with salad mixture. Yield: 4 servings (serving size: 1½ cups salad and 1 lettuce leaf).

CALORIES 374 (30% from fat); FAT 12.5g (sat 2g, mono 5.5g, poly 3.9g); PROTEIN 29.4g; CARB 36.3g; FIBER 3g; CHOL 60mg; IRON 3.6mg; SODIUM 393mg; CALC 62mg

Pasta Salad Menu 2
serves 4

Soba and Slaw Salad with Peanut Dressing

Melon and lime compote*

Fortune cookies

*Peel and cut 1 honeydew melon into 1-inch pieces. Drizzle with ½ cup fresh lime juice, tossing gently to coat. Sprinkle with 1 tablespoon grated lime rind.

Game Plan

1. While water for soba noodles comes to a boil:
- Prepare compote
- Shred cabbage and grate carrot
2. While noodles cook:
- Prepare soy sauce mixture
- Chop shrimp and slice green onions
3. Assemble salad.

QUICK & EASY
Soba and Slaw Salad with Peanut Dressing

Look for soba noodles, rice vinegar, chile paste, and soy sauce in the specialty-foods aisle of your supermarket or in Asian markets. Use packaged slaw mix in place of the red cabbage and carrot if you're in a hurry. Try this recipe with coarsely chopped rotisserie chicken instead of shrimp.

TOTAL TIME: 40 MINUTES

QUICK TIP: Use the shredding attachment of a food processor to make quick work of preparing cabbage and carrots.

- 6 ounces uncooked soba (buckwheat) noodles, broken in half
- 6 cups shredded red cabbage
- 2 cups grated carrot
- ¾ cup thinly sliced green onions, divided
- ½ pound coarsely chopped cooked shrimp
- 3 tablespoons low-sodium soy sauce
- 3 tablespoons rice vinegar
- 2½ tablespoons creamy peanut butter
- 1 tablespoon canola oil
- 2 teaspoons Thai chile paste with garlic
- 2 tablespoons chopped dry-roasted peanuts

1. Cook noodles according to package directions, omitting salt and fat. Drain; rinse with cold water.
2. Combine noodles, shredded cabbage, carrot, ½ cup green onions, and shrimp in a large bowl.
3. Combine soy sauce and next 4 ingredients in a small bowl; stir with a whisk until blended. Add soy sauce mixture to noodle mixture, tossing gently to coat. Sprinkle with ¼ cup green onions and peanuts. Yield: 4 servings (serving size: 2½ cups salad, 1 tablespoon onions, and 1½ teaspoons peanuts).

CALORIES 393 (30% from fat); FAT 12.9g (sat 1.8g, mono 5.8g, poly 3.5g); PROTEIN 24.6g; CARB 47.7g; FIBER 4.7g; CHOL 111mg; IRON 5.5mg; SODIUM 753mg; CALC 127mg

Pasta Salad Menu 3

serves 4

Rotini, Summer Squash, and Prosciutto Salad with Rosemary Dressing

Tomato bruschetta*

Fresh blueberries with low-fat vanilla yogurt

*Combine 1 cup cherry tomatoes, 1 teaspoon olive oil, 4 fresh basil leaves, and a pinch of salt and pepper in a food processor; process until coarsely chopped. Coat 8 (½-ounce) French bread baguette slices with cooking spray. Broil 2 minutes or until lightly browned. Spoon 2 tablespoons cherry tomato mixture onto each baguette slice.

Game Plan

1. While water for rotini comes to a boil:
- Chop yellow squash, zucchini, prosciutto, and red onion
- Cook prosciutto

2. While pasta cooks:
- Prepare bruschetta
- Combine ingredients for balsamic vinegar mixture

3. Assemble salad.

Rotini, Summer Squash, and Prosciutto Salad with Rosemary Dressing

Using white balsamic vinegar maintains the salad dressing's pure golden color.

TOTAL TIME: 45 MINUTES

QUICK TIP: Add yellow squash and zucchini to pasta during the last minute of cooking.

- 3 cups uncooked rotini (corkscrew pasta; about 8 ounces)
- 1½ cups coarsely chopped yellow squash
- 1½ cups coarsely chopped zucchini
- 4 ounces thinly sliced prosciutto, chopped
- 3 tablespoons chopped red onion
- 2 ounces fresh mozzarella cheese, chopped
- ¼ teaspoon salt
- ¼ teaspoon freshly ground black pepper

- 2 tablespoons white balsamic vinegar
- 1 tablespoon extravirgin olive oil
- 1½ teaspoons Dijon mustard
- ½ teaspoon finely chopped fresh rosemary

1. Cook pasta according to package directions, omitting salt and fat. Add squash and zucchini during last minute of cooking. Drain pasta mixture; rinse with cold water.

2. Heat a large nonstick skillet over medium-high heat until hot. Add prosciutto; cook 5 minutes or until crisp, stirring frequently.

3. Combine pasta mixture, prosciutto, onion, and cheese in a large bowl; sprinkle with salt and pepper. Combine vinegar, oil, mustard, and rosemary in a small bowl, stirring with a whisk. Add vinegar mixture to pasta mixture, tossing gently to coat. Yield: 4 servings (serving size: 2¼ cups).

CALORIES 359 (28% from fat); FAT 11.1g (sat 4g, mono 2.8g, poly 0.4g); PROTEIN 18.7g; CARB 46.3g; FIBER 2.4g; CHOL 36mg; IRON 2.5mg; SODIUM 771mg; CALC 103mg

Pasta Salad Menu 4

serves 4

Mediterranean Orzo Salad with Feta Vinaigrette

Pita wedges

Mint iced tea*

*Combine 1 quart cold water, ¾ cup fresh mint leaves, and 5 regular-sized tea bags in a saucepan; bring to a simmer. Remove from heat; cover and steep 3 minutes. Strain mixture, discarding mint and tea bags. Add 3 tablespoons sugar, stirring to dissolve. Serve over ice.

Game Plan

1. While water for orzo and water for tea comes to a boil:
- Chop spinach, sun-dried tomatoes, red onion, and kalamata olives

2. While pasta cooks:
- Steep tea bags and mint in water
- Chop marinated artichokes

3. Combine salad.

Mediterranean Orzo Salad with Feta Vinaigrette

This salad is chock-full of zesty ingredients. If pitted kalamata olives aren't available, press each olive with the flat side of a wide chef's knife to loosen the pits for easy removal.

TOTAL TIME: 45 MINUTES

QUICK TIP: The marinade from the artichokes does double duty—it saturates the artichokes and becomes a quick vinaigrette for the salad.

- 1 cup uncooked orzo (rice-shaped pasta; about 8 ounces)
- 2 cups bagged prewashed baby spinach, chopped
- ½ cup chopped drained oil-packed sun-dried tomato halves
- 3 tablespoons chopped red onion
- 3 tablespoons chopped pitted kalamata olives
- ½ teaspoon freshly ground black pepper
- ¼ teaspoon salt
- 1 (6-ounce) jar marinated artichoke hearts, undrained
- ¾ cup (3 ounces) feta cheese, crumbled and divided

1. Cook orzo according to package directions, omitting salt and fat. Drain; rinse with cold water. Combine cooked orzo, spinach, and next 5 ingredients in a large bowl.

2. Drain artichokes, reserving marinade. Coarsely chop artichokes, and add artichokes, reserved marinade, and ½ cup feta cheese to orzo mixture, tossing gently to coat. Sprinkle each serving with feta cheese. Yield: 4 servings (serving size: 1¼ cups salad and about 1 tablespoon cheese).

CALORIES 338 (29% from fat); FAT 11g (sat 3.8g, mono 2.7g, poly 0.5g); PROTEIN 11.9g; CARB 52g; FIBER 5.1g; CHOL 19mg; IRON 3mg; SODIUM 620mg; CALC 138mg

Northwest Exposure

For anyone who loves to eat, Seattle is one of the most dynamic and satisfying places to be in the country.

The combination of Northwest tradition, international influence, and pure individuality put Seattle dining in a satisfyingly modern and delicious context. Here are some recipes from the northwest pantry.

Pike Place Market Salad

(pictured on page 182)

The salad calls for herb salad mix, which can be found prebagged in the supermarket, or use any combination of lettuces and herbs. Any fresh cherry or berry (blackberries, blueberries, etc.) will do nicely. The dressing and caramelized walnuts can be made a day ahead (store the nuts in an airtight container and the dressing in the refrigerator).

WALNUTS:
- 1 tablespoon sugar
- 3 tablespoons coarsely chopped walnuts
- Cooking spray

DRESSING:
- ½ cup apple cider
- 3 tablespoons water
- ¼ teaspoon cornstarch
- 1 tablespoon finely chopped shallots
- 1 tablespoon champagne vinegar
- ⅛ teaspoon salt
- ⅛ teaspoon freshly ground black pepper

REMAINING INGREDIENTS:
- 8 cups herb salad mix
- 2 cups berries and/or pitted sweet cherries
- ¼ cup (1 ounce) blue cheese, crumbled

1. To prepare nuts, place sugar in a small skillet over medium heat; cook 90 seconds or until sugar dissolves, stirring as needed so sugar dissolves evenly and doesn't burn. Reduce heat; stir in walnuts. Cook over low heat 30 seconds or until golden. Spread mixture onto foil coated with cooking spray. Cool completely; break into small pieces.

2. To prepare dressing, place cider in a small saucepan over medium-high heat; bring to a boil. Cook until reduced to 2 tablespoons (about 5 minutes). Combine water and cornstarch in a small bowl; add to pan. Bring cider mixture to a boil, stirring constantly; cook 30 seconds. Remove from heat. Stir in shallots, vinegar, salt, and pepper; cool.

3. To prepare salad, place salad mix in a large bowl. Drizzle with dressing; toss gently to coat. Place salad on each of 4 plates; top with berries, cheese, and walnuts. Serve immediately. Yield: 4 servings (serving size: 2 cups salad, ½ cup berries, 1 tablespoon cheese, and 2¼ teaspoons walnuts).

CALORIES 165 (37% from fat); FAT 6.7g (sat 1.8g, mono 0.7g, poly 3g); PROTEIN 5.2g; CARB 24.6g; FIBER 4.5g; CHOL 6mg; IRON 1.9mg; SODIUM 199mg; CALC 116mg

WINE NOTE: This market salad is a kaleidoscope of bold flavors and compelling textures, from the berries to the caramelized walnuts to the crumbled blue cheese. It needs a powerhouse of a wine to match it all: Walla Walla Village Gewürztraminer 2003 (Walla Walla, Washington; $16). It's sassy with bright tropical fruit flavors (a great counterpoint to the saltiness of the cheese), a citrusy edge, and loads of spice.

Thai Iced Coffee

A popular combination of coffee, sweetened milk, and spice, this Thai coffee celebrates Seattle's ethnic diversity while giving a nod to the city's daily celebration of java. This recipe makes one serving; multiply it to serve as many as you like. It's sweet enough to be a light dessert.

- ¼ cup hot espresso or very strong brewed coffee
- 5 teaspoons fat-free sweetened condensed milk
- 2 tablespoons hot water
- Dash of cardamom

1. Combine all ingredients; stir well. Cool completely; chill in refrigerator. Serve over ice. Yield: 1 serving (serving size: about ½ cup).

CALORIES 96 (2% from fat); FAT 0.2g (sat 0.1g, mono 0g, poly 0.1g); PROTEIN 2.9g; CARB 20.6g; FIBER 0g; CHOL 2mg; IRON 0.1mg; SODIUM 43mg; CALC 93mg

Ponzu Grilled Salmon with Golden Beet Couscous

This dish highlights the wild salmon so abundant in Seattle, and the many cultural influences (chief among them Asian) that coalesce in Pacific Northwest cuisine. Wild Alaskan salmon is in season in June, and you can find it in supermarkets and fish markets across the country. Its rich flavor is worth paying a bit more. The ponzu sauce may be made up to a day ahead and refrigerated. Golden beets add sweetness and beautiful color, but don't stain like red beets. Israeli couscous has lovely pearl-like grains that are much larger than regular couscous. Use regular couscous if you can't find Israeli.

COUSCOUS:
- 1 teaspoon extravirgin olive oil
- 2 tablespoons thinly sliced peeled shallot (about 1 large)
- 8 ounces small golden beets, peeled, quartered, and thinly sliced (about 1½ cups)
- 1 cup uncooked Israeli couscous
- 2 cups water
- ¼ teaspoon salt
- 1 cup raw spinach leaves, trimmed

SAUCE:
- ½ cup fresh orange juice
- 3 tablespoons low-sodium soy sauce
- 2 tablespoons brown sugar
- 2 tablespoons sake (rice wine)
- 1 tablespoon fresh lime juice
- ½ teaspoon cornstarch
- ⅛ teaspoon crushed red pepper

REMAINING INGREDIENTS:
  4 (6-ounce) salmon fillets with skin
     (about 1 inch thick)
  Cooking spray
  Lime wedges (optional)

1. Prepare grill.
2. To prepare couscous, heat oil in a large nonstick skillet over medium-high heat. Add shallots and beets; sauté 5 minutes or until shallots are tender and just beginning to brown. Stir in couscous; cook 1 minute, stirring frequently. Add water and salt; cover and simmer 8 minutes or until couscous is tender. Remove from heat; stir in spinach. Toss gently until combined and spinach wilts. Keep warm.
3. To prepare sauce, combine orange juice and next 6 ingredients in a small saucepan, stirring well with a whisk; bring to a boil over medium-high heat. Cook 1 minute.
4. To prepare fish, brush cut sides of fillets with ¼ cup sauce; place, skin sides up, on grill rack coated with cooking spray. Grill salmon 2 minutes. Turn salmon fillets; brush with remaining sauce. Grill 3 minutes or until fish flakes easily when tested with a fork or desired degree of doneness. Serve with couscous mixture and lime wedges, if desired. Yield: 4 servings (serving size: 1 fillet and ¾ cup couscous).

CALORIES 500 (22% from fat); FAT 12.4g (sat 1.9g, mono 4.5g, poly 4.6g); PROTEIN 41.4g; CARB 51.6g; FIBER 4.1g; CHOL 94mg; IRON 3mg; SODIUM 828mg; CALC 60mg

Lemon Drop Liqueur

Locals often unwind at Ray's Boathouse with a bracing summer cocktail like this one. Fresh lemon juice and lemon rind add bright tang and a beautiful hue to this liqueur. Begin a batch three weeks before you plan to serve it. Pour over ice with two parts sparkling water for a cool, delicious lemon spritzer. To serve straight up, coat the rim of a chilled martini glass in lemon juice, then dip the rim in sugar. Garnish with a slice of lemon.

  2 cups sugar
  1 cup water
  5 lemon rinds, cut into strips
  3 cups vodka
  ¼ cup lemon juice

1. Combine sugar and water in a medium saucepan; cook over medium heat 5 minutes or until sugar dissolves, stirring constantly. Remove from heat; stir in rind. Cool completely. Stir in vodka and lemon juice.
2. Sterilize 2 wide-mouthed, 1-quart jars according to manufacturer's directions. Divide vodka mixture between jars. Cover each jar with metal lid; screw on band. Store in a cool, dark place for 3 weeks, shaking jar every other day.
3. Line a fine-mesh sieve with a double layer of cheesecloth; strain mixture through cheesecloth into a bowl. Discard solids. Pour liqueur into jars, a clean decanter, or freezer-safe container; store in refrigerator or freezer. Yield: 4¾ cups (serving size: ¼ cup).
NOTE: Mixture will keep in freezer up to one year.

CALORIES 170 (0% from fat); FAT 0g; PROTEIN 0g; CARB 21.4g; FIBER 0.1g; CHOL 0mg; IRON 0mg; SODIUM 1mg; CALC 1mg

Fish Tacos with Two Salsas

Fish tacos like these are sold at numerous vendors along the shore of Elliott Bay. You can prepare one or the other salsa, or make both of them and serve the extra with baked tortilla chips.

TOMATO SALSA:
  1 cup chopped seeded tomato
     (about 2 medium)
  ½ cup chopped seeded yellow
     or orange tomato (about 1
     medium)
  ¼ cup finely chopped red
     onion
  1 tablespoon chopped parsley
  1 tablespoon fresh lime juice
  ½ teaspoon minced habanero
     pepper
  ½ teaspoon extravirgin olive oil
  ¼ teaspoon salt

MANGO SALSA:
  1 cup chopped peeled
     mango
  ½ cup chopped seeded peeled
     cucumber
  ¼ cup chopped green onions
  ¼ cup chopped fresh cilantro
  2 tablespoons minced jalapeño
     pepper
  1 tablespoon fresh lime
     juice
  1 teaspoon extravirgin olive
     oil
  ⅛ teaspoon salt

FISH:
  2 tablespoons lime juice
  2 teaspoons olive oil
  ¼ teaspoon ground cumin seed
  2 garlic cloves, minced
  4 (6-ounce) halibut fillets
  ¼ teaspoon salt
  Cooking spray

REMAINING INGREDIENTS:
  4 (10-inch) flour tortillas
  1 cup shredded red cabbage
  ¼ cup reduced-fat sour
     cream
  Lime wedges (optional)

1. To prepare tomato salsa, combine first 8 ingredients in a small bowl; cover and chill at least 1 hour.
2. To prepare mango salsa, combine mango and next 7 ingredients in a small bowl. Cover and chill at least 1 hour.
3. Prepare grill.
4. To prepare fish, combine 2 tablespoons lime juice, 2 teaspoons olive oil, cumin, and garlic in a large zip-top plastic bag. Add fish to bag; seal. Marinate 15 minutes, turning once. Remove fish from bag; discard marinade. Sprinkle both sides of fish evenly with ¼ teaspoon salt. Place fish on grill rack coated with cooking spray; grill 4 minutes on each side or until fish flakes easily when tested with a fork or desired degree of doneness. Flake fish into large chunks.
5. To prepare tacos, place tortillas on grill rack coated with cooking spray; grill 10 seconds on each side. Arrange ¼ of fish and ¼ cup cabbage over one half
Continued

of each tortilla; top each with salsa and 1 tablespoon sour cream. Fold tortillas in half. Serve with lime wedges, if desired. Yield: 4 servings (serving size: 1 taco and about ¼ cup salsa).

CALORIES 541 (25% from fat); FAT 15.3g (sat 3.6g, mono 7.1g, poly 2.5g); PROTEIN 43.9g; CARB 55.9g; FIBER 4.6g; CHOL 62mg; IRON 4.5mg; SODIUM 835mg; CALC 162mg

MAKE AHEAD
Hazelnut Bread

The soaking water for the nuts is used again to proof the yeast, which infuses the entire loaf with nutty flavor.

  ¾ cup chopped hazelnuts
1½ cups boiling water
  2 tablespoons packed brown sugar
  1 package dry yeast (about
       2¼ teaspoons)
  3 cups bread flour, divided
1¼ teaspoons salt
     Cooking spray
  1 teaspoon cornmeal

1. Preheat oven to 350°.
2. Spread hazelnuts in an even layer on a baking sheet. Bake at 350° for 10 minutes or until light brown. Remove from heat; transfer to a small bowl. Pour boiling water over hazelnuts; cover and let stand 20 minutes. Strain hazelnut mixture through a sieve into a bowl, reserving liquid and nuts. Spread nuts in an even layer on a double thickness of paper towels; pat lightly with additional paper towels to dry. Set aside. Place reserved liquid in a small saucepan; heat until warm (100° to 104°). Transfer liquid to a large bowl. Add sugar and yeast, stirring well with a whisk; let stand 5 minutes.
3. Lightly spoon flour into dry measuring cups; level with a knife. Add 2¾ cups flour and salt to yeast mixture; stir until a soft dough forms. Turn dough out onto a floured surface. Knead until smooth and elastic (about 8 minutes); add enough of remaining flour, 1 tablespoon at a time, to prevent dough from sticking to hands (dough will feel tacky). Cover dough; let rest 10 minutes. Uncover; knead in reserved hazelnuts.
4. Place dough in a large bowl coated with cooking spray, turning to coat top. Cover and let rise in a warm place (85°), free from drafts, 1 hour or until doubled in size. (Press two fingers into dough. If indentation remains, dough has risen enough.) Punch dough down; cover and let rest 5 minutes. Shape dough into a 9-inch oval; place on a baking sheet sprinkled with cornmeal. Lightly spray dough with cooking spray; cover. Let rise in a warm place (85°), free from drafts, 30 minutes or until doubled in size.
5. Preheat oven to 375°.
6. Uncover and bake at 375° for 30 minutes or until browned on bottom and loaf sounds hollow when tapped. Cool on wire rack. Yield: 16 servings (serving size: 1 slice).

CALORIES 135 (25% from fat); FAT 3.7g (sat 0.3g, mono 2.5g, poly 0.6g); PROTEIN 4.1g; CARB 21.5g; FIBER 1.3g; CHOL 0mg; IRON 0.6mg; SODIUM 186mg; CALC 12mg

Honey Crème Brûlée with Raspberries

  2 cups 2% reduced-fat milk
  ¾ cup nonfat dry milk
  2 tablespoons sugar
  2 tablespoons honey
  5 large egg yolks
     Dash of salt
  3 tablespoons sugar
24 fresh raspberries

1. Preheat oven to 300°.
2. Combine first 4 ingredients in a large saucepan. Heat mixture over medium heat to 180° or until tiny bubbles form around edge (do not boil), stirring occasionally. Remove from heat.
3. Combine egg yolks and salt in a medium bowl; stir well with a whisk. Gradually add hot milk mixture to egg mixture, stirring constantly with a whisk. Divide milk mixture evenly among 4 shallow (6-ounce) baking dishes. Place dishes in a 13 x 9-inch baking pan; add hot water to pan to a depth of 1 inch. Bake at 300° for 1 hour or until center barely moves when dish is touched. Remove dishes from pan; cool completely on a wire rack. Cover and chill at least 4 hours or overnight.
4. Sift 3 tablespoons sugar evenly over custards. Holding a kitchen blow torch about 2 inches from top of each custard, heat sugar, moving torch back and forth, until sugar is completely melted and caramelized (about 1 minute). Top evenly with raspberries. Serve immediately. Yield: 4 servings (serving size: 1 crème brûlée and 6 raspberries).

CALORIES 275 (26% from fat); FAT 7.9g (sat 3.4g, mono 3.1g, poly 1g); PROTEIN 12.6g; CARB 39.2g; FIBER 0.8g; CHOL 265mg; IRON 0.8mg; SODIUM 185mg; CALC 364mg

superfast

...And Ready in Just About 20 Minutes

More than a week's worth of quick entrées gets you in and out of the kitchen in a flash.

QUICK & EASY
Wasabi Seafood Salad

Start cooking the clams for a minute before adding the shrimp so both will be done at the same time.

  1 cup water
  1 pound littleneck clams, cleaned
       (about 16 clams)
  ½ pound peeled and deveined large
       shrimp
  ¼ cup low-fat mayonnaise
  3 tablespoons fresh lime juice
  1 teaspoon wasabi paste
  8 cups bagged salad greens
  ¼ cup chopped fresh cilantro

1. Bring 1 cup water to a boil in a large saucepan. Add clams; cover and cook 1 minute. Add shrimp; cover and cook 3 minutes or until shrimp are done and clam shells open. Drain; discard any unopened clam shells.
2. Combine mayonnaise, lime juice, and wasabi, stirring with a whisk. Place

2 cups greens on each of 4 salad plates; divide clams and shrimp evenly over greens. Drizzle each serving with about 1 tablespoon wasabi mixture; sprinkle each serving with 1 tablespoon cilantro. Yield: 4 servings.

CALORIES 220 (30% from fat); FAT 7.4g (sat 1.1g, mono 1.7g, poly 3.4g); PROTEIN 28g; CARB 9.9g; FIBER 2.5g; CHOL 130mg; IRON 18.7mg; SODIUM 322mg; CALC 146mg

QUICK & EASY
Whole Trout with Tarragon Aïoli

We call for broiling the fish; you also can cook it on the grill. Aïoli is a garlic-flavored mayonnaise. This version is enhanced with mustard and fragrant tarragon.

4 (8-ounce) dressed trout, heads and tails removed
Cooking spray
½ teaspoon salt
¼ teaspoon black pepper
10 tarragon sprigs, divided
12 thin slices lemon
¼ cup low-fat mayonnaise
1½ tablespoons Dijon mustard
¼ teaspoon bottled minced garlic
Tarragon sprigs (optional)

1. Preheat broiler.
2. Open trout, skin sides down, on a foil-lined baking sheet coated with cooking spray. Sprinkle salt and pepper evenly over fish. Arrange 2 tarragon sprigs and 3 lemon slices on 1 side of each fish. Fold fish over tarragon and lemon. Broil fish 6 minutes on each side or until fish flakes easily when tested with a fork.
3. While fish cooks, chop 2 tarragon sprigs to equal 1 teaspoon. Combine chopped tarragon, mayonnaise, mustard, and garlic, stirring with a whisk. Serve fish with aïoli. Garnish with tarragon sprigs, if desired. Yield: 4 servings (serving size: 1 fish and about 1 tablespoon aïoli).

CALORIES 281 (40% from fat); FAT 12.4g (sat 3g, mono 3.4g, poly 3.7g); PROTEIN 35.7g; CARB 5.9g; FIBER 5.9g; CHOL 96mg; IRON 0.5mg; SODIUM 626mg; CALC 128mg

QUICK & EASY
Chopped Vegetable and Chicken Salad

This high-fiber salad makes a great lunch.

¼ cup sherry vinegar
4 teaspoons olive oil
2 teaspoons lemon juice
1 teaspoon sugar
½ teaspoon bottled minced garlic
¼ teaspoon pepper
2½ cups arugula leaves
2 cups chopped cooked chicken breast
1 cup chopped English cucumber
1 cup prechopped green bell pepper
1 cup prechopped tomato
¼ cup finely chopped fresh parsley
1 (15½-ounce) can chickpeas (garbanzo beans), rinsed and drained
2 tablespoons crumbled feta cheese

1. Combine first 6 ingredients in a large bowl, stirring with a whisk. Add arugula and next 6 ingredients; toss well. Sprinkle with cheese. Yield: 4 servings (serving size: 1¾ cups).

CALORIES 282 (31% from fat); FAT 9.6g (sat 2.1g, mono 4.7g, poly 1.1g); PROTEIN 27.8g; CARB 20.5g; FIBER 5.1g; CHOL 64mg; IRON 2.5mg; SODIUM 373mg; CALC 98mg

QUICK & EASY
Spicy-Sweet Pork Tenderloin

Spooning the soy sauce mixture over the top of each piece of pork lets it soak into the meat like a quick marinade. Serve with mashed potatoes and steamed baby carrots.

1 tablespoon low-sodium soy sauce
1 teaspoon bottled minced fresh ginger
1 teaspoon bottled minced garlic
1 teaspoon canola oil
1 (1-pound) pork tenderloin, trimmed and cut crosswise into 12 (¾-inch-thick) slices
⅓ cup bottled salsa
1 tablespoon seedless raspberry preserves
2 tablespoons chopped fresh cilantro

1. Combine first 3 ingredients in a bowl.
2. Heat oil in a large nonstick skillet over medium-high heat. Flatten each pork piece to ½-inch thickness using your fingertips. Add pork to pan; spoon soy sauce mixture evenly over pork slices. Cook 3 minutes or until browned. Turn pork over; cook 3 minutes or until done. Remove from pan.
3. Add salsa and preserves to pan; increase heat to medium-high. Cook 30 seconds or until slightly thick, stirring constantly. Serve pork with salsa mixture, and sprinkle with cilantro. Yield: 4 servings (serving size: 3 pork slices, about 1 tablespoon salsa mixture, and 1½ teaspoons cilantro).

CALORIES 169 (28% from fat); FAT 5.1g (sat 1.4g, mono 2.4g, poly 0.8g); PROTEIN 24.4g; CARB 5.3g; FIBER 0.4g; CHOL 74mg; IRON 1.7mg; SODIUM 285mg; CALC 15mg

QUICK & EASY
Apricot Lamb Chops

Serve with couscous and green beans.

½ cup apricot preserves
2 teaspoons Dijon mustard
1 teaspoon bottled minced garlic
1 teaspoon low-sodium soy sauce
½ teaspoon Worcestershire sauce
¼ teaspoon salt
⅛ teaspoon ground cinnamon
⅛ teaspoon black pepper
8 (4-ounce) lamb loin chops, trimmed
Cooking spray

1. Combine first 5 ingredients in a small bowl; set aside. Combine salt, cinnamon, and pepper, and sprinkle over both sides of lamb. Heat a large nonstick skillet over medium-high heat. Coat pan with cooking spray. Add lamb to pan; cook 5 minutes on each side or until desired degree of doneness. Remove pan from heat; add apricot mixture, turning lamb to coat. Place chops on each of 4 plates; spoon apricot mixture over chops. Yield: 4 servings (serving size: 2 lamb chops and about 2 tablespoons apricot mixture).

CALORIES 287 (27% from fat); FAT 8.6g (sat 3g, mono 3.8g, poly 0.6g); PROTEIN 26.1g; CARB 26.7g; FIBER 0.3g; CHOL 81mg; IRON 2.1mg; SODIUM 350mg; CALC 32mg

Skillet Pork with Sweet Balsamic Peaches

  1   teaspoon chili powder
 ¼   teaspoon salt
 ¼   teaspoon black pepper
  4   (4-ounce) boneless center-cut loin
      pork chops (about ½ inch thick)
Cooking spray
 ⅛   teaspoon salt
  1   cup finely chopped onion
1¼   cups finely chopped peaches
      (about 3)
  2   tablespoons dark brown sugar
  2   teaspoons balsamic vinegar
  1   teaspoon bottled ground fresh
      ginger (such as Spice World)
 ⅛   teaspoon crushed red pepper

1. Combine first 3 ingredients; sprinkle evenly over both sides of chops. Heat a large nonstick skillet over medium heat. Coat pan with cooking spray. Add pork to pan; cook 3 minutes on each side or until done.
2. Place chops on a serving platter; sprinkle with ⅛ teaspoon salt. Keep warm.
3. Add onion to pan; cook 4 minutes or until tender. Stir in peaches and remaining 4 ingredients. Cook 3 minutes or until slightly thick, stirring constantly. Serve peach mixture with chops. Yield: 4 servings (serving size: 1 pork chop and about ⅓ cup peach mixture).

CALORIES 215 (23% from fat); FAT 5g (sat 1.7g, mono 2.2g, poly 0.6g); PROTEIN 24.9g; CARB 17.4g; FIBER 2.1g; CHOL 71mg; IRON 1.4mg; SODIUM 289mg; CALC 35mg

Tomato Soup with Chicken and Gorgonzola Cheese

  1   teaspoon olive oil
  1   teaspoon bottled minced garlic
  1   cup sliced celery (about 2 stalks)
  1   teaspoon crushed red pepper
 ¾   pound shredded cooked chicken
      breast
  1   (28-ounce) can diced tomatoes,
      undrained
  1   (14-ounce) can fat-free,
      less-sodium chicken broth
 ½   cup (2 ounces) crumbled
      Gorgonzola cheese

1. Heat oil in a large nonstick skillet over medium-high heat. Add garlic; sauté 1 minute. Add celery, pepper, and chicken; cook 6 minutes or until thoroughly heated. Add tomatoes and broth; bring to a simmer. Cook 8 minutes. Sprinkle with cheese. Yield: 4 servings (serving size: 1½ cups soup and 2 tablespoons cheese).

CALORIES 254 (30% from fat); FAT 8.4g (sat 4.1g, mono 2g, poly 0.9g); PROTEIN 32.3g; CARB 11.8g; FIBER 4.2g; CHOL 85mg; IRON 1.8mg; SODIUM 699mg; CALC 140mg

Fresh Tortellini with Mushrooms and Pancetta

  1   (9-ounce) package fresh cheese
      tortellini (such as DiGiorno)
  3   ounces pancetta, diced
  1   cup chopped onion
  1   teaspoon bottled minced garlic
  1   (8-ounce) package presliced
      cremini mushrooms
  2   cups bagged baby spinach
  1   cup organic vegetable broth (such
      as Swanson Certified Organic)
 ½   cup sun-dried tomato bits
 ¼   teaspoon black pepper
 ¼   cup (1 ounce) preshredded
      Parmesan cheese

1. Cook pasta according to package directions, omitting salt and fat; drain and keep warm.
2. Heat a large nonstick skillet over medium-high heat; add pancetta. Cook 5 minutes or until almost crisp, stirring occasionally; drain. Add onion, garlic, and mushrooms; cook 4 minutes or until onion is tender, stirring frequently. Add spinach, broth, tomato, and pepper. Cook 2 minutes or until spinach wilts, stirring constantly. Toss with pasta. Place pasta mixture in each of 4 bowls. Sprinkle with cheese. Yield: 4 servings (serving size: about 1½ cups pasta mixture and 1 tablespoon cheese).

CALORIES 333 (31% from fat); FAT 11.4g (sat 5.6g, mono 2g, poly 0.5g); PROTEIN 16.4g; CARB 42.7g; FIBER 3.6g; CHOL 42mg; IRON 2.4mg; SODIUM 880mg; CALC 223mg

Thai Shrimp and Tofu with Asparagus

 ⅓   cup oyster sauce
  1   tablespoon fish sauce
  2   teaspoons sugar
  1   teaspoon Thai red curry paste
  1   tablespoon canola oil, divided
  1   (14-ounce) package reduced-fat
      firm tofu, drained and cut into
      ½-inch cubes
 ½   pound frozen peeled and
      deveined medium shrimp, thawed
  2   cups thinly sliced shiitake
      mushrooms (about 4 ounces)
  1   cup chopped onion
  1   tablespoon bottled minced fresh
      ginger
  1   tablespoon bottled minced garlic
  1   pound asparagus, trimmed and cut
      into ½-inch pieces (about 5 cups)

1. Combine first 4 ingredients in a bowl.
2. Heat 1 teaspoon oil in a large nonstick skillet over medium-high heat; add tofu. Cook 3 minutes or until lightly browned; set aside. Heat 1 teaspoon oil in pan; add shrimp. Cook 2 minutes on each side or just until opaque; set aside. Heat 1 teaspoon oil in pan; add mushrooms, onion, ginger, and garlic. Cook 2 minutes or until mushrooms are tender, stirring frequently. Add asparagus; cook 4 minutes or until crisp-tender. Add sauce mixture, tofu, and shrimp to pan; cook 1 minute or until heated. Yield: 3 servings (serving size: 2 cups).

CALORIES 358 (31% from fat); FAT 12.2g (sat 0.7g, mono 3g, poly 2.1g); PROTEIN 36.8g; CARB 27.9g; FIBER 4.2g; CHOL 115mg; IRON 9.5mg; SODIUM 822mg; CALC 173mg

By the Book

When it comes to learning the basics of cuisine, cookbooks still set the standard.

Despite the increasing number of ways that we can learn to cook—television, the Internet, and cooking classes, to name a few—cookbooks remain a stable point of reference. They're an ideal way for the beginner to learn basic techniques or for the home cook to discover a new cuisine.

Cookbook author James Peterson is an example of the best of contemporary food writers. Peterson's goal is to teach readers to master basic techniques with detailed written descriptions and clear step-by-step photographs. Cookbooks like his are a handy tool you can pull from the bookshelf any time you need a little guidance—or just inspiration for tonight's supper.

QUICK & EASY
Shrimp Cocktail with Tropical Fruit Salsa

Peterson's version of the traditional shrimp cocktail with tomato sauce and lemon has charm and character. The papaya-mango salsa is spiced with chiles, cilantro, and plenty of lime juice to balance the sweetness of the fruit.

24 jumbo shrimp (about 1½ pounds)
1 poblano chile, halved and seeded
1 jalapeño pepper, halved and seeded
1 cup finely chopped peeled mango
1 cup finely chopped peeled papaya
⅓ cup finely chopped red onion
¼ cup chopped fresh cilantro
¼ cup fresh lime juice
½ teaspoon salt
Cooking spray

1. Peel and devein shrimp; set aside.
2. Preheat broiler.
3. Place poblano chile and jalapeño pepper halves, skin sides up, on a foil-lined broiler pan; flatten with hand. Broil 10 minutes or until blackened. Place in a zip-top plastic bag; seal. Let stand 10 minutes. Peel and finely chop, and place in a bowl. Add mango and next 5 ingredients.

4. Heat a large nonstick skillet over medium-high heat. Coat pan with cooking spray. Add shrimp; sauté 2½ minutes on each side or until done. Place ½ cup salsa in center of each of 6 small serving plates; arrange 4 shrimp over each serving. Yield: 6 servings.

CALORIES 140 (10% from fat); FAT 2g (sat 0.4g, mono 0.3g, poly 0.8g); PROTEIN 23.4g; CARB 6.1g; FIBER 0.7g; CHOL 172mg; IRON 2.8mg; SODIUM 366mg; CALC 69mg

STAFF FAVORITE • QUICK & EASY
Sautéed Scallops with Parsley and Garlic

The secret to perfectly browned scallops is patience. Peterson recommends cooking in batches. Heat the oil until it ripples in the pan. Add the scallops, a few at a time, and wait for them to sizzle before adding more. If you add too many at once, the pan will lose heat and its ability to brown them all.

16 large sea scallops (about 1½ pounds)
¼ teaspoon salt
¼ teaspoon freshly ground black pepper
1½ tablespoons olive oil
2 tablespoons butter
¼ cup chopped fresh flat-leaf parsley
2 garlic cloves, minced

1. Sprinkle scallops with salt and pepper. Heat oil in a large nonstick skillet over medium-high heat. Add 8 scallops; sauté 2½ minutes on each side or until browned. Set aside, and keep warm. Repeat procedure with remaining 8 scallops. Wipe pan clean with a paper towel.
2. Add butter to pan; reduce heat, and cook until butter melts. Stir in parsley and garlic, and cook 15 seconds. Return scallops to pan; toss to coat. Yield: 4 servings (serving size: 4 scallops).

CALORIES 241 (43% from fat); FAT 11.5g (sat 3.6g, mono 5.7g, poly 1.1g); PROTEIN 28.7g; CARB 4.3g; FIBER 0.2g; CHOL 71mg; IRON 0.8mg; SODIUM 464mg; CALC 48mg

Papaya and Avocado Crab Salad

This refreshing summer salad is also good with other seafood, such as shrimp.

1 poblano chile, halved and seeded
1 jalapeño pepper, halved
1 cup diced peeled papaya
1 cup diced peeled avocado
⅔ cup finely chopped red onion
¼ cup fresh lime juice (about 2 limes)
2 tablespoons minced fresh cilantro
½ teaspoon salt
1 pound lump crabmeat, shell pieces removed
1 garlic clove, minced
6 (6-inch) pitas, split

1. Preheat broiler.
2. Place chile and pepper halves, skin sides up, on a foil-lined broiler pan; flatten with hand. Broil 10 minutes or until blackened. Place in a zip-top plastic bag; seal. Let stand 10 minutes. Peel and finely chop; place in a large bowl.
3. Add papaya and next 7 ingredients; toss gently to combine. Serve with pitas. Yield: 6 servings (serving size: 1 cup salad and 1 pita).

CALORIES 294 (17% from fat); FAT 5.4g (sat 0.8g, mono 2.6g, poly 1.1g); PROTEIN 19.5g; CARB 41.2g; FIBER 3.3g; CHOL 45mg; IRON 2.2mg; SODIUM 746mg; CALC 101mg

Selecting Shellfish

The most important step in buying good fresh seafood is finding a reliable fishmonger. A well-kept fish store should smell like the sea. These are some of James Peterson's quick guidelines for common shellfish varieties:

• Where you live usually dictates the variety of **clams** you can find. Fortunately, most varieties are interchangeable. Ask the fishmonger for the best substitute. Hard-shell clams may gape slightly. Give them a squeeze; they should close back up. If you have a bad clam in your bunch, it will open and usually fall apart while you're handling it.

• With the exception of lobster tails, **lobsters** should always be bought live. Try to buy from a vendor that keeps them in tanks and preferably one that has a thriving business.

• Unless you live near the Gulf, you'll probably have to buy your **shrimp** frozen. Fortunately, shrimp freeze well and lose little of their original flavor and texture. If you buy frozen shrimp, thaw as needed and use quickly.

• Much of the crabmeat comes from **Atlantic blue crabs**. The best grade is called lump, jumbo, or backfin; the second-best grade consists of smaller pieces of body meat and is called flake.

• Perfectly healthy **mussels** will sometimes gape slightly, but if you tap two together, they should close quickly. Also, sniff them; they should smell like a clean beach. Store in a bowl in the refrigerator, covered with a wet towel to keep them moist.

• **Sea scallops** are almost always shucked at sea. Scallops labeled "wet" have been soaked and are less expensive than "dry" scallops. Look for scallops that are cream colored or slightly pink and not dull looking. Avoid ones that are pure white, brownish, or dull looking. Ask to smell the scallops; they shouldn't have a strong odor.

Corn Bread Oyster Stuffing

If you use fresh oysters in the shell, buy about three dozen. We opted for the preshucked variety for convenience.

- 1 (6-ounce) package yellow corn bread mix (such as Martha White)
- ⅔ cup fat-free milk
- 2 large egg whites, lightly beaten
- 2 links (about 6 ounces) andouille sausage, chopped (such as Gerhard's)
- Cooking spray
- 1½ cups chopped onion
- 2 (3½-ounce) packages shiitake mushrooms, stems removed and caps quartered
- 1 (10-ounce) package frozen chopped spinach, thawed, drained, and squeezed dry
- 1 (1-pound) container standard oysters, undrained
- 4 cups cubed day-old French bread
- ½ cup half-and-half
- ⅓ cup egg substitute
- ¼ cup fat-free milk
- 2 teaspoons chopped fresh sage
- 1 teaspoon chopped fresh rosemary
- 2 tablespoons chopped fresh parsley
- ½ teaspoon salt

1. Preheat oven to 400°.
2. Prepare corn bread mix according to package directions, using ⅔ cup fat-free milk and 2 egg whites; cool completely. Crumble to measure 3 cups; reserve remaining corn bread for another use.
3. Reduce oven temperature to 375°.
4. Place sausage in a food processor, and pulse until finely chopped. Heat a large nonstick skillet over medium-high heat. Coat pan with cooking spray. Add onion and mushroom caps to pan; sauté 5 minutes or until tender. Stir in sausage and spinach; sauté 2 minutes.
5. Drain oysters, reserving ⅓ cup oyster liquor. Combine oysters, reserved oyster liquor, corn bread crumbs, spinach mixture, French bread, and remaining ingredients in a large bowl; toss well. Place mixture in a 13 x 9-inch baking dish coated with cooking spray. Bake at 375°

for 35 minutes or until lightly browned. Yield: 10 servings (serving size: about 1 cup).

CALORIES 230 (31% from fat); FAT 8.1g (sat 2.8g, mono 3.1g, poly 1.2g); PROTEIN 12.3g; CARB 26.5g; FIBER 2.9g; CHOL 44mg; IRON 5.9mg; SODIUM 675mg; CALC 141mg

QUICK & EASY
Spaghetti with Clams

Clams are steamed, and the steaming liquid is simmered with tomatoes, garlic, parsley, and olive oil. Unlike mussels, clams that do not open are usually fine and need only a thin knife to pry open the shells.

- 6 quarts water
- 1 pound uncooked spaghetti
- ½ teaspoon salt
- 1 cup water
- 48 littleneck clams (about 3 pounds)
- 2½ cups chopped seeded peeled tomato (about 1½ pounds)
- 3 garlic cloves, minced
- ⅓ cup minced fresh flat-leaf parsley
- ¼ cup extravirgin olive oil
- Flat-leaf parsley sprigs

1. Bring 6 quarts water to a boil in a large stockpot. Stir in pasta; partially cover, and return to a boil, stirring frequently. Cook 6 minutes or until pasta is al dente, stirring occasionally. Drain; place in a large bowl. Sprinkle with salt, tossing well; keep warm.
2. While pasta cooks, bring 1 cup water to a boil in a large Dutch oven. Add clams; cover and cook 6 minutes or until shells open. Remove clams from pan with a slotted spoon; reserve 2 cups cooking liquid in pan. Add tomato and garlic; reduce heat, and simmer 5 minutes. Stir in minced parsley and oil; cook 15 seconds. Serve tomato mixture and clams over spaghetti. Garnish with parsley sprigs. Yield: 8 servings (serving size: 1 cup pasta, 6 clams, and ½ cup tomato mixture).

CALORIES 329 (24% from fat); FAT 8.7g (sat 1.2g, mono 5.6g, poly 1.2g); PROTEIN 14.8g; CARB 47.1g; FIBER 2.1g; CHOL 18mg; IRON 10.2mg; SODIUM 189mg; CALC 44mg

Steamed Mussels with Curry and Mint

1½ teaspoons curry powder
  1 cup dry white wine
  ½ cup finely chopped shallots
  4 pounds mussels
  ⅓ cup chopped fresh mint
  2 tablespoons whipping cream
  ½ teaspoon freshly ground black pepper
  12 (½-inch-thick) slices French bread baguette (about 4 ounces)

1. Cook curry in a small saucepan over medium heat 2 minutes or until toasted; stir constantly. Remove from pan; set aside.
2. Bring wine and shallots to a boil in a large Dutch oven; cover and cook 5 minutes. Add mussels; cover and cook 5 minutes or until shells open. Remove mussels from pan with a slotted spoon, reserving cooking liquid; discard any unopened shells. Keep warm.
3. Add curry, mint, cream, and pepper to cooking liquid in pan. Place pan over medium-high heat; bring to a simmer. Remove from heat. Place mussels in each of 4 large shallow bowls; spoon curry mixture over mussels. Serve with bread. Yield: 4 servings (serving size: 1 pound mussels, ½ cup curry mixture, and 3 bread slices).

CALORIES 313 (22% from fat); FAT 7.5g (sat 2.6g, mono 2g, poly 1.3g); PROTEIN 23.3g; CARB 28.1g; FIBER 1.3g; CHOL 55mg; IRON 8.8mg; SODIUM 640mg; CALC 139mg

How to Extract Meat from Lobster Claws

1. *Snap the claws away from the body of the lobster. Gently move the pincher side to side until you feel it snap; gently pull it away.*

2. *Place the claw on a cutting board with the thorny bottom facing up. Hack straight down into the shell with the dull edge of a heavy-duty chef's knife or cleaver. As soon as you make contact with the shell, pull up the knife to avoid going through the claw.*

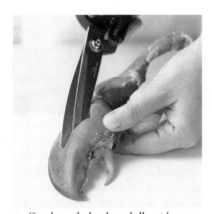

3. *Cut through the claw shells with kitchen shears to expose meat.*

4. *Once you've cut through the shell, break pieces apart, and remove the claw meat.*

Steamed Lobster with Parsley Emulsion

  4 cups water
  1 tablespoon salt
  2 (1½-pound) Maine lobsters
  ½ cup dry white wine
  ¼ cup finely chopped shallots
  2 tablespoons whipping cream
  1 cup chopped fresh flat-leaf parsley
  ¼ teaspoon freshly ground black pepper

1. Bring 4 cups water and salt to a boil in a 5-gallon stockpot. Place a vegetable steamer or rack in bottom of pan. Add lobsters; cover and cook 14 minutes or until done. Remove lobsters from pan; reserve ½ cup cooking liquid.
2. Working with 1 lobster, twist tail from body. Cut tail lengthwise on top with scissors to split open; remove meat from tail. Remove dark green tomalley from head; set aside.
3. Break claws from body. Pull pincers apart; remove lower pincer. Hack into shell, cutting through, but not all the way through, claw. Break pieces apart; remove meat from claws. Repeat procedure with other lobster.
4. Combine ½ cup reserved cooking liquid, wine, and shallots in a small saucepan; bring to a boil. Cover, reduce heat, and simmer 5 minutes. Add cream and tomalley, if desired. Bring to a simmer; remove from heat. Place cream mixture, parsley, and pepper in a blender; process until smooth. Strain mixture through a sieve into a bowl, and discard solids. Serve with lobster. Yield: 2 servings (serving size: 1 tail, 2 claws, and about ⅓ cup sauce).
NOTE: Pregnant women and people with compromised immune systems should not eat the tomalley because of its toxicity.

CALORIES 304 (21% from fat); FAT 7g (sat 3.7g, mono 2g, poly 0.4g); PROTEIN 38.6g; CARB 11.7g; FIBER 2.1g; CHOL 147mg; IRON 4.7mg; SODIUM 709mg; CALC 208mg

Smokin'

If you yearn for full, robust flavor, but not the fat that often comes with it, try smoking food over smoldering wood.

Smoking is an easy cooking method that adds terrific depth and complexity in taste without added fat or salt. Meats are the foods one typically thinks of as being smoked, but vegetables can be smoked, as well, and turned into soup or sauce (or enjoyed on their own).

Smoked Onion and Garlic Soup

(pictured on page 234)

Mellow smoked onions and garlic give body and depth to this delightfully fragrant twist on a classic. Fresh thyme sprigs are an aromatic garnish. Heavy-duty foil creates a disposable "tray" for the onions and garlic, exposing them to lots of smoke. For added sturdiness, keep the foil tray on a baking sheet when transporting the onion mixture to and from the grill.

    2 cups wood chips
    Cooking spray
    6 cups thinly vertically sliced
       yellow onion
   15 garlic cloves, peeled
    2 teaspoons tomato paste
  1½ teaspoons chopped fresh or
       ½ teaspoon dried thyme
    ½ teaspoon freshly ground black
       pepper
    ¼ cup dry sherry
    3 (14-ounce) cans less-sodium beef
       broth
   12 (½-ounce) slices French bread
       baguette, toasted
    ¾ cup (3 ounces) shredded Gruyère
       cheese

1. Soak wood chips in water 30 minutes; drain.
2. Prepare grill for indirect grilling, heating one side to low and leaving one side with no heat. Maintain temperature at 200° to 225°.

3. Place wood chips on hot coals. Place a disposable aluminum foil pan on unheated side of grill. Pour 2 cups water into pan. Place grill rack on grill. Fold a 24 x 12-inch sheet of heavy-duty foil in half crosswise to form a 12-inch square. Fold edges of foil up to form a rim. Coat foil with cooking spray. Place foil tray on a baking sheet; arrange onion and garlic on foil tray. Carefully place foil tray on grill rack over foil pan on unheated side. Close lid; cook 1 hour and 15 minutes. Carefully remove foil tray from grill; place on baking sheet.
4. Heat a large Dutch oven over medium-high heat. Add onion mixture, tomato paste, thyme, and pepper; cook 1 minute, stirring constantly. Add sherry and broth; bring to a boil. Cover, reduce heat, and simmer 1 hour.
5. Preheat broiler.
6. Ladle about 1 cup soup into each of 6 ovenproof soup bowls. Top each serving with 2 toast slices and 2 tablespoons cheese. Broil 3 minutes or until cheese melts. Serve immediately. Yield: 6 servings.

CALORIES 189 (22% from fat); FAT 4.7g (sat 2.7g, mono 1.4g, poly 0.3g); PROTEIN 9.6g; CARB 27.5g; FIBER 1.9g; CHOL 16mg; IRON 1.3mg; SODIUM 601mg; CALC 175mg

WINE NOTE: Do as the French would, and drink bubbly. The sprightly texture and crisp freshness of a good sparkling wine will partner with the soup famously. A good value is the Gloria Ferrer Sonoma Brut from California, about $18.

STAFF FAVORITE • MAKE AHEAD
Smoky Tomato Salsa

Smoked tomatoes and jalapeño pepper make a world of difference in this salsa and blend beautifully with the garlic and lime. Garnish with a cilantro sprig, if desired.

    2 cups wood chips
    Cooking spray
    5 large plum tomatoes (about
       2 pounds)
    1 jalapeño pepper
    1 tablespoon fresh lime juice
    ½ teaspoon dried marjoram or
       oregano
    2 garlic cloves, minced
    1 cup diced red onion
    3 tablespoons chopped fresh
       cilantro
    ½ teaspoon salt

1. Soak wood chips in water 30 minutes; drain well.
2. Prepare grill for indirect grilling, heating one side to low and leaving one side with no heat. Maintain grill temperature at 200° to 225°.
3. Place wood chips on hot coals. Place a disposable aluminum foil pan on unheated side of grill. Pour 2 cups water into pan. Coat grill rack with cooking spray, and place on grill. Place tomatoes and pepper on grill rack over foil pan on unheated side. Close lid; cook 50 minutes. Remove tomatoes and pepper from grill; discard stem from pepper.
4. Place tomatoes, pepper, lime juice, marjoram, and garlic in a food processor; process 1 minute or until smooth. Pour mixture into a medium bowl; stir in onion, cilantro, and salt. Cover and chill at least 45 minutes before serving. Yield: 2 cups (serving size: ¼ cup).

CALORIES 16 (11% from fat); FAT 0.2g (sat 0g, mono 0g, poly 0.1g); PROTEIN 0.6g; CARB 3.7g; FIBER 0.7g; CHOL 0mg; IRON 0mg; SODIUM 152mg; CALC 8mg

Chips off the Old Block

Serious barbecue cooks talk about preferred woods, such as alder for fish and hickory for pork. But there's not a big flavor difference unless you're smoking for hours. Still, you might want to try various wood chips, or a combination of them, for subtle nuances in taste. Whatever wood you choose, be sure to soak it in water first so it will smoke and not flame. Look for wood chips or chunks at outdoor-supply stores, supermarkets, and specialty stores.

Alder has a delicate, slightly sweet flavor and is traditionally used to smoke salmon. It's a good choice for other fish, as well.

Apple and **cherry** give off smoke with a sweet, fruity flavor that pairs well with poultry and pork.

Hickory is popular in the South and offers the deep, strong flavor many people associate with barbecue. Use it with pork, beef, or poultry; it's too strong for fish.

Maple produces sweet, mild smoke that's great for salmon, chicken, and pork.

Mesquite burns hot and is better suited to grilling than smoking.

Oak is another popular wood for smoking, with an assertive flavor that's suited to most any meat.

Pecan is favored among chefs, offering a mellowed richness with notes of hickory.

How to Smoke Foods on a Charcoal Grill

To smoke food on a covered charcoal grill, cook over indirect heat with a small amount of charcoal and wood chips.

1. Soak wood chips for 30 minutes; drain.

2. Using a charcoal chimney, fire up about two dozen briquettes or a dozen handfuls of lump charcoal. Pour the coals into a single layer on just one side of the lower grate, or pile them into a charcoal basket placed on one side of the grill. The charcoal is ready when coated with thick gray ash. You should be able to hold your hand about five inches above the coals for about five seconds.

3. Place a disposable aluminum foil pan filled with water on the other side of the lower grate, and toss a handful of soaked wood chips on the charcoal. Place the upper grate, or grill rack, on the grill. Arrange the food on the grill rack above the pan on the unheated side of the grill.

4. If the grill lid has a built-in thermometer, place the lid on the grill so that the thermometer is directly over the food. If there's no thermometer, place the lid's vent directly over the food and insert a candy thermometer in the opening so the probe is in the air near the food; close the vent to secure the thermometer.

5. Maintain a temperature of 200° to 225°. Close the grill's bottom vents as needed to lower the heat, and open them to raise it.

6. If you'll be smoking longer than an hour, you will need to add more preheated charcoal (about one-third of the original amount of briquettes) (see Step 2) and another generous handful of wood chips. Refuel when the temperature starts to sink toward 200°, and add more presoaked wood chips when you no longer see smoke coming from the grill.

If smoking one large piece of food, rotate it midway through the cook time for even cooking. Avoid lifting the lid except to add more charcoal, rotate the food, or check for doneness.

Smoky Peppered Pork Tenderloins

Since most cuts of pork and beef taste best with a crusty surface, we take the extra step of searing the tenderloins on all sides before smoking them. The dense meat takes longer to cook than you might expect, but offers a rewarding entrée.

- 2 tablespoons mixed peppercorns
- 2 teaspoons dried onion flakes
- 1 teaspoon mustard seeds
- ¾ teaspoon salt
- 2 (12-ounce) pork tenderloins, trimmed
- 4 cups wood chips
- Cooking spray

1. Place first 4 ingredients in a spice or coffee grinder; process until coarsely ground. Rub over all sides of tenderloins. Wrap tenderloins in plastic wrap; refrigerate 1½ hours or overnight.
2. Soak wood chips in water 30 minutes; drain.
3. Prepare grill for indirect grilling, heating one side to low and leaving one side with no heat. Maintain temperature at 200° to 225°.
4. Heat a large, heavy skillet over high heat. Unwrap tenderloins. Coat pan with cooking spray. Add tenderloins to pan; cook 1½ minutes on each side or until browned. Remove from pan.
5. Place half of wood chips on hot coals. Place a disposable aluminum foil pan on unheated side of grill. Pour 2 cups water into pan. Coat grill rack with cooking spray; place on grill. Place tenderloins on grill rack over foil pan on unheated side. Close lid; cook 1 hour. Place remaining wood chips on hot coals. Close lid; cook 1 hour or until a thermometer inserted into thickest portion of 1 tenderloin registers 155° or until desired degree of doneness. Remove from grill; cover and let stand 10 minutes. Cut crosswise into thin slices. Yield: 6 servings (serving size: 3 ounces).

CALORIES 167 (30% from fat); FAT 5.6g (sat 1.9g, mono 2.3g, poly 0.5g); PROTEIN 26.2g; CARB 1.2g; FIBER 0.4g; CHOL 80mg; IRON 1.4mg; SODIUM 351mg; CALC 12mg

---

Scandinavian Tastes Menu
serves 4

Smoked salmon and dill are a classic Nordic pairing. You can easily double the recipes if you're cooking for more.

Smoked Salmon with Mustard and Dill

Creamy cucumber salad*

Roasted potato wedges

*Combine 3 cups (2-inch) julienne-cut English cucumber, ⅓ cup plain low-fat yogurt, 1 tablespoon prepared horseradish, 2 teaspoons fresh lemon juice, and ½ teaspoon salt, tossing well to coat.

Smoked Salmon with Mustard and Dill

- 2 cups wood chips
- 1 tablespoon minced fresh dill
- 1 tablespoon fresh lemon juice
- 3 tablespoons sweet-hot mustard (such as Inglehoffer)
- ½ teaspoon salt
- 1 (1½-pound) salmon fillet
- Cooking spray

1. Soak wood chips in water 30 minutes; drain.
2. Combine dill, juice, mustard, and salt, stirring well. Place salmon, skin side down, in a shallow baking dish; brush mustard mixture over salmon. Cover and refrigerate 20 minutes.
3. Prepare grill for indirect grilling, heating one side to low and leaving one side with no heat. Maintain temperature at 200° to 225°.
4. Place wood chips on hot coals. Place a disposable aluminum foil pan on unheated side of grill. Pour 2 cups water into pan. Coat grill rack with cooking spray; place on grill. Place salmon, skin side down, on grill rack over foil pan on unheated side. Close lid; cook 35 minutes or until fish flakes easily when tested with a fork or until desired degree of doneness. Yield: 4 servings (serving size: about 4½ ounces).

CALORIES 262 (40% from fat); FAT 11.6g (sat 2.5g, mono 4.6g, poly 2.5g); PROTEIN 31g; CARB 4.8g; FIBER 0g; CHOL 80mg; IRON 0.5mg; SODIUM 429mg; CALC 16mg

---

Smoked Trout Salad with Apples and Pecans

Substitute any other white fish, or even salmon. You can use other fruit in place of the apples, if you prefer; pears or berries would work nicely.

- 2 cups wood chips
- 3 tablespoons fresh lemon juice
- 1 teaspoon prepared horseradish
- 4 (6-ounce) rainbow trout fillets
- Cooking spray
- ½ teaspoon salt, divided
- ½ teaspoon freshly ground black pepper, divided
- 2 tablespoons white wine vinegar
- 1 tablespoon walnut oil or olive oil
- ¼ teaspoon chili powder
- 8 cups mixed salad greens
- 2 cups thinly sliced Golden Delicious apple (about 1 large apple)
- 2 cups thinly sliced Braeburn apple (about 1 large apple)
- 1 cup thinly sliced red onion
- 2 tablespoons chopped pecans, toasted

1. Soak wood chips in water 30 minutes, and drain well.
2. Combine lemon juice, horseradish, and fillets in a large zip-top plastic bag. Seal and marinate in refrigerator 20 minutes, turning bag occasionally.
3. Prepare grill for indirect grilling, heating one side to low and leaving one side with no heat. Maintain temperature at 200° to 225°.
4. Place wood chips on hot coals. Place a disposable aluminum foil pan on unheated side of grill. Pour 2 cups water into pan. Coat grill rack with cooking spray; place on grill. Remove fillets from bag; discard marinade. Sprinkle fillets with ¼ teaspoon salt and ¼ teaspoon pepper. Place fillets on grill rack over foil pan on unheated side. Close lid; cook 30 minutes or until fish flakes easily when tested with a fork or until desired degree of doneness.
5. Combine ¼ teaspoon salt, ¼ teaspoon pepper, vinegar, oil, and chili powder, stirring with a whisk. Combine greens, apples, and onion in a large bowl; drizzle with vinaigrette. Toss gently to

coat. Remove skin from fillets; discard skin. Break fillets into pieces; serve over salad. Sprinkle with nuts. Yield: 4 servings (serving size: 3 cups salad, 1 fillet, and 1½ teaspoons nuts).

CALORIES 324 (38% from fat); FAT 13.5g (sat 2.6g, mono 4.3g, poly 5.5g); PROTEIN 29.4g; CARB 23.3g; FIBER 6g; CHOL 75mg; IRON 2.2mg; SODIUM 376mg; CALC 165mg

Spicy Smoked Shrimp with Orange and Lime

The smoky taste from the grill complements the dry rub. Shrimp are fully cooked when opaque and slightly firm.

  2 cups wood chips
  ½ teaspoon salt
  ½ teaspoon ground red pepper
  ¼ teaspoon freshly ground black pepper
  ⅛ teaspoon garlic powder
  ⅛ teaspoon ground coriander
1½ pounds large shrimp, peeled and deveined
Cooking spray
Orange wedges
Lime wedges

1. Soak wood chips in water 30 minutes; drain.
2. Combine salt, red pepper, black pepper, garlic powder, and coriander in a small bowl. Rub mixture over shrimp. Cover and chill 20 minutes.
3. Prepare grill for indirect grilling, heating one side to low and leaving one side with no heat. Maintain temperature at 200° to 225°.
4. Place wood chips on hot coals. Place a disposable aluminum foil pan on unheated side of grill. Pour 2 cups water into pan. Coat grill rack with cooking spray; place on grill.
5. Place shrimp on grill rack over foil pan on unheated side. Close lid; cook 30 minutes or until shrimp are done. Serve with orange and lime wedges. Yield: 6 servings (serving size: about 5 shrimp).

CALORIES 123 (15% from fat); FAT 2g (sat 0.4g, mono 0.3g, poly 0.8g); PROTEIN 23.1g; CARB 1.7g; FIBER 0.1g; CHOL 172mg; IRON 2.8mg; SODIUM 365mg; CALC 60mg

How to Smoke Foods on a Gas Grill

On some gas grills, it's impossible to hold the heat down to the desirable smoking range of 200° to 225°. In that case, smoke on the lowest heat level you can maintain, and reduce the cooking time called for in the recipes. You won't get as much smokiness, but you'll still get a good sense of the scent.

1. Soak wood chips for 30 minutes; drain. Many newer gas grills include a smoker box nestled near one of the burners. Added to the box, soaked wood chips will smolder from the heat of the nearest burner. If your gas grill doesn't have a built-in box, make a foil pouch to hold the wood. Place the wood on a piece of heavy-duty foil, and fold up and close loosely. Pierce the foil about a half-dozen times with a fork to allow smoke to escape.

2. Turn on the burner at the end of the grill nearest the smoker box. If you're using a foil pouch, turn on the burner at one end of the grill, and arrange the pouch very near that burner. If your grill is longer than 36 inches, you may need to turn on two burners to get the proper heat.

3. Place a disposable aluminum foil pan filled with water on the unheated side of the grill. Place the grill rack on the grill. Arrange food on the grill rack directly above the pan on the unheated side of the grill.

4. If your gas grill has no thermometer in its lid, place an oven thermometer on the cooking grate near the food. Adjust the grill knobs as needed to maintain the desired temperature.

5. If you see no more smoke escaping from the grill, add more soaked wood chips to the smoker box or carefully toss on another foil pouch. If you're smoking one large piece of food, rotate it when you have the grill open, but avoid raising the lid more than necessary.

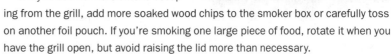

Smoked Strip Steaks

Strip steaks offer a lot of surface area relative to their total size, which allows them to absorb a maximum amount of smoke. Serve thin slices of the steak over rice pilaf.

2 cups wood chips
2 teaspoons freshly ground black pepper
1 teaspoon garlic powder
½ teaspoon salt
¼ teaspoon dry mustard
2 (12-ounce) New York strip or sirloin strip steaks, trimmed
2 teaspoons Worcestershire sauce
Cooking spray

1. Soak wood chips in water 30 minutes; drain.
2. Combine pepper, garlic powder, salt, and mustard, and rub evenly over both sides of steaks. Place coated steaks in a large zip-top plastic bag; add Worcestershire sauce. Seal and shake to coat. Marinate in refrigerator 30 minutes.
3. Prepare grill for indirect grilling, heating one side to low and leaving one side with no heat. Maintain temperature at 200° to 225°.
4. Heat a large, heavy skillet over high heat. Remove steaks from bag, and discard marinade. Coat pan with cooking spray. Add steaks to pan; cook 1½ minutes on each side or until browned. Remove from pan.
5. Place wood chips on hot coals. Place a disposable aluminum foil pan on unheated side of grill. Pour 2 cups water into pan. Coat grill rack with cooking spray, and place on grill. Place steaks on grill rack over foil pan on unheated side. Close lid; cook 1 hour and 15 minutes or until a thermometer inserted into steak registers 145° (medium-rare) or until desired degree of doneness. Remove steaks from grill; cover and let stand 5 minutes. Cut steaks across grain into thin slices. Yield: 6 servings (serving size: about 3 ounces).

CALORIES 186 (43% from fat); FAT 8.8g (sat 3.4g, mono 3.6g, poly 0.3g); PROTEIN 24.1g; CARB 1.2g; FIBER 0.2g; CHOL 65mg; IRON 2.4mg; SODIUM 273mg; CALC 13mg

Grilled Freshness

A bruschetta appetizer inspires a grilled chicken dish with Italian flair.

The bruschetta at a North Carolina restaurant was the inspiration for Ruth Powers's grilled chicken recipe. Ruth, from Goodrich, Michigan, using basil and tomatoes from her garden, recreated the restaurant's bruschetta topping. "I remember that the tomato topping tasted sweet, so I used orange juice concentrate instead," she says.

Grilled Chicken with Italian Salsa

SALSA:
2¼ cups chopped tomatoes (about 2 medium)
½ cup chopped fresh basil
1 tablespoon thawed orange juice concentrate
½ teaspoon salt
½ teaspoon minced fresh garlic
½ teaspoon balsamic vinegar
¼ teaspoon freshly ground black pepper

CHICKEN:
2 tablespoons fresh lemon juice
2 tablespoons balsamic vinegar
1 tablespoon olive oil
1 tablespoon Dijon mustard
1 tablespoon chopped fresh oregano
1 teaspoon chopped fresh rosemary
1 teaspoon chopped fresh parsley
½ teaspoon garlic powder
½ teaspoon chopped fresh thyme
½ teaspoon freshly ground black pepper
¼ teaspoon salt
4 (6-ounce) skinless, boneless chicken breast halves
Cooking spray

1. To prepare salsa, combine first 7 ingredients in a medium bowl. Cover and chill 1 hour.
2. To prepare chicken, combine lemon juice and next 10 ingredients in a large zip-top plastic bag. Add chicken; seal. Marinate in refrigerator 1 hour, turning occasionally.
3. Preheat grill.
4. Remove chicken from bag; discard marinade. Place chicken on grill rack coated with cooking spray; grill 6 minutes on each side or until chicken is done. Serve with salsa. Yield: 4 servings (serving size: 1 chicken breast half and ½ cup salsa).

CALORIES 293 (29% from fat); FAT 9.5g (sat 1.8g, mono 4.5g, poly 1.9g); PROTEIN 41.7g; CARB 10.1g; FIBER 1.6g; CHOL 108mg; IRON 2.2mg; SODIUM 633mg; CALC 46mg

Cheese and Olive-Stuffed Tomatoes

"This is a wonderful side dish for steak or warm tuna salad, and it's great heated in the microwave for a quick lunch."
—Tamara Dial Gray, Cape Coral, Florida

4 ripe tomatoes (about 2¼ pounds)
½ cup (2 ounces) feta cheese, crumbled
¼ cup chopped pitted kalamata olives
2 tablespoons chopped fresh flat-leaf parsley
2 tablespoons chopped fresh basil

1. Preheat broiler.
2. Cut tops off tomatoes; discard. Carefully scoop out tomato pulp, leaving shells intact; finely chop pulp. Combine pulp, cheese, and remaining 3 ingredients. Place tomato shells in an 8-inch square baking dish. Divide pulp mixture evenly among tomato shells. Broil 2 minutes or until tomatoes just begin to blister and topping is browned. Yield: 4 servings (serving size: 1 tomato).

CALORIES 79 (55% from fat); FAT 4.9g (sat 2.3g, mono 1.8g, poly 0.4g); PROTEIN 3.2g; CARB 7g; FIBER 1.5g; CHOL 13mg; IRON 0.8mg; SODIUM 257mg; CALC 83mg

The sweet salad tames the heat from the casserole. Since you'll have to open a bag of chips for the casserole topping, go ahead and serve the rest on the side with salsa.

Spicy Chicken with Poblano Peppers and Cheese

Tossed salad with fruit*

Chips and salsa

*Combine 4 cups torn romaine lettuce, 1 cup fresh orange sections, 1 cup sliced kiwifruit, and 1/3 cup very thinly vertically sliced red onion. Combine 2 tablespoons fresh lime juice, 1 tablespoon honey, 2 teaspoons extravirgin olive oil, 2 teaspoons Dijon mustard, 1/4 teaspoon salt, and 1/8 teaspoon black pepper, stirring with a whisk. Drizzle dressing over salad; toss gently to coat. Sprinkle with 2 tablespoons toasted slivered almonds.

Spicy Chicken with Poblano Peppers and Cheese

"This family favorite changes a bit every time I make it."

—Jean Hardin, DeSoto, Texas

    4   poblano chiles, halved and seeded
    2   cups chopped cooked chicken
        breast
    1   cup (4 ounces) reduced-fat
        shredded Cheddar cheese
    1   cup fresh corn kernels (about
        2 ears)
    1/2 cup chopped onion
    1/2 cup chopped zucchini
    1/2 cup chopped red bell pepper
    2   tablespoons finely chopped fresh
        cilantro
    1/2 teaspoon kosher salt
    1/2 teaspoon ground cumin
    1/2 teaspoon paprika
    1/2 teaspoon freshly ground black
        pepper
    1/2 teaspoon bottled minced garlic
    1/4 cup bottled salsa
        Cooking spray
    3/4 cup crushed baked tortilla chips,
        divided

1. Preheat broiler.
2. Place chile halves, skin sides up, on a foil-lined baking sheet, and flatten with hand. Broil 8 minutes or until blackened. Place peppers in a zip-top plastic bag; seal. Let stand 15 minutes. Peel and discard skins.
3. Reduce oven temperature to 375°.
4. Combine chicken and next 11 ingredients in a large bowl; stir in salsa, stirring until well combined.
5. Place peppers, cut sides up, in an 11 x 7-inch baking dish coated with cooking spray; top evenly with 1/4 cup chips. Spoon chicken mixture evenly over chips; sprinkle with 1/2 cup chips. Lightly coat chips with cooking spray. Bake at 375° for 20 minutes or until cheese melts and casserole is thoroughly heated. Yield: 4 servings (serving size: 2 chile halves).

CALORIES 331 (30% from fat); FAT 11.1g (sat 4.9g, mono 1.5g, poly 1.5g); PROTEIN 32.4g; CARB 25.2g; FIBER 4.2g; CHOL 80mg; IRON 2mg; SODIUM 688mg; CALC 256mg

Chicken Marsala

"I wanted a chicken recipe with less salt and fat and came up with this tasty dish."

—Stephanie Troia, Tampa, Florida

    4   (6-ounce) skinless, boneless
        chicken breast halves
    1/4 teaspoon salt
    1/4 teaspoon freshly ground black
        pepper
    2   tablespoons all-purpose flour
    1   tablespoon olive oil
    1   cup presliced mushrooms
    1/2 cup Marsala wine
    1/2 cup fat-free, less-sodium chicken
        broth
    2   tablespoons fresh lemon
        juice
    1   tablespoon chopped fresh
        parsley

1. Place chicken between 2 sheets of heavy-duty plastic wrap; pound each piece to 1/2-inch thickness using a meat mallet or rolling pin. Sprinkle both sides of chicken evenly with salt and pepper. Place flour in a shallow dish. Dredge chicken in flour, turning to coat; shake off excess flour.
2. Heat oil in a large skillet over medium-high heat. Add chicken; cook 3 minutes on each side or until browned. Remove chicken from pan; keep warm. Add mushrooms, wine, broth, and juice to pan; reduce heat, and simmer 10 minutes or until mixture is reduced to 2/3 cup. Return chicken to pan, turning to coat well. Cover and cook 5 minutes or until chicken is done. Sprinkle with parsley. Yield: 4 servings (serving size: 1 chicken breast and about 2 1/2 tablespoons sauce).

CALORIES 241 (21% from fat); FAT 5.6g (sat 1g, mono 3g, poly 0.9g); PROTEIN 40.7g; CARB 4.9g; FIBER 0.5g; CHOL 99mg; IRON 1.8mg; SODIUM 308mg; CALC 26mg

MAKE AHEAD
Cucumber, Mango, and Black Bean Salad

"This combo is fast and bursting with great flavor."

—Robin Ohlgren-Evans, Moscow, Idaho

    1   cup chopped seeded cucumber
    1/2 cup chopped mango
    1/2 cup canned black beans, rinsed
        and drained
    2   tablespoons minced seeded
        jalapeño pepper
    2   tablespoons fresh lime juice
    1   tablespoon fresh orange juice
    1   tablespoon chopped fresh
        cilantro
    1/2 teaspoon salt

1. Combine all ingredients in a bowl, stirring gently. Let stand 15 minutes before serving. Yield: 4 servings (serving size: 1/2 cup).

CALORIES 39 (3% from fat); FAT 0.1g (sat 0g, mono 0g, poly 0g); PROTEIN 1.6g; CARB 9.7g; FIBER 2.1g; CHOL 0mg; IRON 0.6mg; SODIUM 422mg; CALC 18mg

MAKE AHEAD
Pasta Salad

"I made this so my three-year-old would eat more veggies."

—Tricia Taylor, Louisville, Kentucky

    3   cups (8 ounces) uncooked
        vegetable rotini (corkscrew pasta)
 1½   cups (¼-inch-thick) slices
        zucchini
 1¼   cups yellow bell pepper strips
    1   cup drained canned quartered
        artichoke hearts
   ½   cup (2 ounces) cubed part-skim
        mozzarella cheese
   ½   cup grape or cherry tomatoes,
        halved
   ¼   cup reduced-fat Greek or Italian
        dressing
   ¼   cup sliced ripe olives
  34   slices turkey pepperoni, cut into
        strips (about 2 ounces)

1. Cook pasta according to package directions, omitting salt and fat; drain. Place pasta and remaining ingredients in a large bowl; toss well to combine. Yield: 6 servings (serving size: 1½ cups).

CALORIES 248 (32% from fat); FAT 8.9g (sat 2.7g, mono 1.9g, poly 0.7g); PROTEIN 14.3g; CARB 29.2g; FIBER 2g; CHOL 31mg; IRON 2.5mg; SODIUM 725mg; CALC 121mg

Veggie Tostadas

"My husband loves this dinner's Mexican flavors."

—Barbara Mehlman, Los Angeles, California

    2   (10-inch) 98%-fat-free flour
        tortillas
    1   (16-ounce) can fat-free refried beans
    2   tablespoons enchilada sauce
    2   cups gourmet salad greens
    1   cup diced plum tomato
   ¼   cup chopped green onions
    2   tablespoons sliced ripe olives
    1   peeled avocado, cut into 12
        wedges
    1   tablespoon finely chopped bottled
        jalapeño pepper
   ¼   cup (1 ounce) crumbled reduced-
        fat feta cheese

1. Preheat broiler.
2. Place a tortilla on a baking sheet, and broil 1 minute on each side or until lightly browned. Repeat procedure with remaining tortilla.
3. Combine beans and enchilada sauce in a small saucepan; cook over medium heat until hot. Spread half of bean mixture over each tortilla; top evenly with remaining ingredients. Yield: 4 servings (serving size: ½ tostada).

CALORIES 318 (27% from fat); FAT 9.8g (sat 1.9g, mono 5.2g, poly 1.1g); PROTEIN 14.3g; CARB 46g; FIBER 11.9g; CHOL 3mg; IRON 4.7mg; SODIUM 924mg; CALC 140mg

MAKE AHEAD
Three-Pepper Slaw

"I tossed some cabbage and bell peppers with a lone jalapeño, and we really liked the combination. I love the crunchy texture, and, fortunately, the ingredients are available year-round."

—Mickey Strang,
McKinleyville, California

   ½   cup thinly sliced red bell pepper
        strips
   ½   cup thinly sliced green bell
        pepper strips
   ⅓   cup chopped green onions
   ¼   cup finely chopped seeded
        jalapeño pepper
    1   (10-ounce) package angel
        hair coleslaw (about 6
        cups)
   ¼   cup white wine vinegar
    2   tablespoons fresh lime
        juice
    2   teaspoons canola oil
    1   teaspoon sugar
   ½   teaspoon salt
   ¼   teaspoon white pepper

1. Place first 5 ingredients in a large bowl, tossing to combine.
2. Combine vinegar and remaining 5 ingredients in a small bowl, stirring with a whisk. Pour vinegar mixture over cabbage mixture, tossing to coat. Yield: 8 servings (serving size: about ¾ cup).

CALORIES 29 (39% from fat); FAT 1.3g (sat 0.1g, mono 0.7g, poly 0.4g); PROTEIN 0.8g; CARB 4.5g; FIBER 0.2g; CHOL 0mg; IRON 0.3mg; SODIUM 153mg; CALC 21mg

inspired vegetarian

Of All the Crust

Two menus offer savory vegetable pies and make-ahead side dishes for alfresco dining.

Menu 1
serves 6

Summer Squash Chowder

**Spinach and Gruyère Tart
in a Three-Pepper Crust**

**Tossed Greens and Beets
with Pistachio Dressing**

**Strawberries with
Crunchy Almond Topping**

QUICK & EASY • MAKE AHEAD
Summer Squash Chowder

To purée the soup even faster, use an immersion blender. You can prepare the squash purée a day in advance; cover and refrigerate. To serve, combine the purée, milk, salt, and pepper in a Dutch oven; heat as directed.

 5½   cups diced yellow squash (about
        1½ pounds)
    1   cup fresh corn kernels (about 2 ears)
    1   cup chopped yellow or red bell
        pepper
   ½   cup chopped Vidalia or other
        sweet onion
    1   (14-ounce) can organic vegetable
        broth (such as Swanson Certified
        Organic)
 1¾   cups whole milk
   ¾   teaspoon salt
   ⅛   teaspoon white pepper

1. Combine first 5 ingredients in a Dutch oven, and bring to a boil. Cover; reduce heat, and simmer 20 minutes. Cool mixture.
2. Place half of squash mixture in a blender; process until smooth. Pour puréed squash mixture into a large bowl. Repeat procedure with remaining squash mixture. Return mixture to pan. Stir in milk, salt, and white pepper. Cook over

low heat until thoroughly heated, stirring occasionally. Yield: 6 servings (serving size: 1 cup).

CALORIES 96 (26% from fat); FAT 2.8g (sat 1.3g, mono 0.6g, poly 0.3g); PROTEIN 4.7g; CARB 15.1g; FIBER 1.6g; CHOL 6.9mg; IRON 0.7mg; SODIUM 497mg; CALC 93mg

Spinach and Gruyère Tart in a Three-Pepper Crust

To speed up preparation, prepare potatoes and spinach mixture either while the dough chills or while the crust bakes.

CRUST:
  1 cup all-purpose flour
  ½ teaspoon salt
  ¼ teaspoon white pepper
  ¼ teaspoon freshly ground black pepper
  ¼ teaspoon ground red pepper
  3 tablespoons chilled butter, cut into small pieces
  4½ tablespoons ice water
     Cooking spray

FILLING:
  4 small Yukon gold potatoes (about 1 pound)
  ½ cup chopped onion
  ¼ cup water
  1 (10-ounce) package fresh spinach
  ½ teaspoon salt, divided
  ½ cup (2 ounces) shredded Gruyère cheese, divided
  1 (8-ounce) carton egg substitute

1. To prepare crust, lightly spoon flour into a dry measuring cup; level with a knife. Place flour, ½ teaspoon salt, and peppers in a food processor; pulse 2 times. Add chilled butter; pulse 4 times or until mixture resembles coarse meal. Place mixture in a bowl. Sprinkle surface with ice water, 1 tablespoon at a time; toss until moist and crumbly (do not form a ball). Place mixture on a lightly floured surface, and knead lightly 2 or 3 times. Press mixture into a 4-inch circle on plastic wrap; cover. Chill 30 minutes.
2. Preheat oven to 450°.
3. Slightly overlap 2 sheets of plastic wrap on a slightly damp surface. Unwrap and place chilled dough on plastic wrap. Cover dough with 2 additional sheets of overlapping plastic wrap. Roll dough, still covered, into a 10-inch circle. Place dough in freezer 5 minutes or until plastic wrap can be easily removed.
4. Remove top sheets of plastic wrap; fit dough, plastic wrap side up, into a 9-inch round removable-bottom tart pan coated with cooking spray. Remove remaining plastic wrap. Press dough against bottom and sides of pan. Line bottom of dough with a piece of parchment paper; arrange pie weights or dried beans on paper. Bake at 450° for 20 minutes or until edge is lightly browned. Carefully remove pie weights and paper; cool on a wire rack. Reduce oven to 400°.
5. To prepare filling, bring a large saucepan of water to a boil. Add potatoes; cook 20 minutes or until tender. Cool; cut into ¼-inch-thick slices. Heat a large nonstick skillet over medium-high heat. Coat pan with cooking spray. Add onion; sauté 5 minutes or until tender. Stir in ¼ cup water. Add spinach; cover and cook 3 minutes or until spinach wilts, stirring occasionally. Remove from heat; cool.
6. Spoon half of spinach mixture into cooled crust. Arrange half of potato slices over spinach. Sprinkle with ¼ teaspoon salt and ¼ cup cheese. Repeat procedure with remaining spinach, potato, and salt. Pour egg substitute over mixture. Sprinkle with ¼ cup cheese. Bake at 400° for 25 minutes or until mixture is set and cheese is golden brown. Cool 15 minutes on a wire rack. Yield: 6 servings (serving size: 1 wedge).

CALORIES 260 (32% from fat); FAT 9.2g (sat 4.7g, mono 3.3g, poly 0.6g); PROTEIN 11.9g; CARB 33.4g; FIBER 2.8g; CHOL 25mg; IRON 3.6mg; SODIUM 585mg; CALC 173mg

Round out your meal with a side of tossed greens or green beans and of course, dessert.

Tossed Greens and Beets with Pistachio Dressing

  ¼ cup fresh lime juice
  3 tablespoons water
  2 tablespoons pistachios
  2 tablespoons honey
  1 tablespoon canola oil
  ½ teaspoon crushed red pepper
     Dash of salt
  8 cups torn curly leaf lettuce
  ½ cup vertically sliced red onion
  1 (15-ounce) can sliced beets, drained and chilled

1. Place first 7 ingredients in a blender; process until finely chopped. Spoon into a small bowl; chill.
2. Combine lettuce, onion, and pistachio mixture in a large bowl; toss. Place salad on each of 6 plates, and top with beets. Yield: 6 servings (serving size: 1 cup salad and about 5 beet slices).

CALORIES 94 (37% from fat); FAT 3.9g (sat 0.4g, mono 2.1g, poly 1.2g); PROTEIN 2.2g; CARB 14.8g; FIBER 3g; CHOL 0mg; IRON 1.9mg; SODIUM 143mg; CALC 39mg

Strawberries with Crunchy Almond Topping

This easy but stylish dessert is best made early in the day to let the strawberries macerate in the sweetened almond liqueur.

  6 cups sliced strawberries
  ½ cup sugar
  2 tablespoons amaretto (almond-flavored liqueur)
  6 amaretti cookies, crushed
  6 tablespoons reduced-fat sour cream

1. Combine first 3 ingredients in a bowl. Cover and chill 4 to 8 hours. Spoon into individual dessert dishes. Sprinkle with crushed cookies; top with sour cream. Yield: 6 servings (serving size: ½ cup strawberries, 1 crushed cookie, and 1 tablespoon sour cream).

CALORIES 207 (11% from fat); FAT 2.6g (sat 0.4g, mono 0.3g, poly 0.3g); PROTEIN 2.8g; CARB 44g; FIBER 4.8g; CHOL 2mg; IRON 0.7mg; SODIUM 29mg; CALC 32mg

Menu 2

serves 6

**Summer Squash Chowder
(recipe on page 222)**

**Roasted Fresh Corn, Poblano,
and Cheddar Pizza**

**Green Beans with Lemon and
Garlic**

**Fresh Orange Sorbet with
Bittersweet Chocolate**

Roasted Fresh Corn,
Poblano, and Cheddar Pizza

(pictured on page 233)

      2 poblano chiles
Cooking spray
      2 cups fresh corn kernels (about
         4 ears)
    ½ cup chopped green onions
      1 garlic clove, minced
    ½ cup 1% low-fat milk
      2 large egg whites
      1 large egg
    ½ teaspoon salt
    ¼ teaspoon freshly ground black
         pepper
      1 cup (4 ounces) shredded sharp
         Cheddar cheese
      1 (13.8-ounce) can refrigerated
         pizza crust dough
      2 tablespoons fat-free sour cream
      2 tablespoons chopped fresh cilantro

1. Preheat broiler.
2. Place chiles on a foil-lined baking sheet; broil 10 minutes or until blackened and charred, turning occasionally. Place in a heavy-duty zip-top plastic bag; seal. Let stand 10 minutes. Peel and discard skins, seeds, and stems. Chop peppers.
3. Reduce oven temperature to 425°.
4. Heat a large nonstick skillet over medium-high heat. Coat pan with cooking spray. Add corn, onions, and garlic; sauté 2 minutes or until lightly browned. Stir in milk; cook over medium heat 2 minutes or until liquid almost evaporates. Cool slightly. Place egg whites, egg, salt, and black pepper in a bowl; stir with a whisk. Stir in poblano peppers, corn mixture, and cheese.
5. Line a baking sheet with parchment paper. Unroll dough onto parchment paper; pat dough to form a 13 x 8-inch rectangle. Spread corn mixture over dough, leaving a 1-inch border. Fold border of dough over corn mixture. Bake at 425° for 12 minutes or until set. Serve with sour cream; sprinkle with cilantro. Yield: 6 servings (serving size: 1 pizza piece, 1 teaspoon sour cream, and 1 teaspoon cilantro).

CALORIES 331 (28% from fat); FAT 10.3g (sat 4.4g, mono 2.2g, poly 0.3g); PROTEIN 15.8g; CARB 44.5g; FIBER 1.6g; CHOL 57mg; IRON 2.5mg; SODIUM 808mg; CALC 186mg

QUICK & EASY
Green Beans with Lemon
and Garlic

      2 cups water
    1½ pounds green beans, trimmed
    1½ tablespoons olive oil
    1½ tablespoons butter
      1 garlic clove, minced
      2 tablespoons fresh lemon juice
    ¼ teaspoon salt
    ¼ teaspoon freshly ground black
         pepper
      2 tablespoons chopped fresh parsley

1. Bring water to a boil in a large skillet. Add beans; cover, reduce heat, and simmer 8 minutes or until tender. Drain beans; pat dry.
2. Heat oil and butter in pan over medium heat. Add garlic, and sauté 30 seconds. Add beans, juice, salt, and pepper; cook 2 minutes or until thoroughly heated. Sprinkle with parsley. Yield: 6 servings.

CALORIES 49 (40% from fat); FAT 2.2g (sat 0.6g, mono 1.2g, poly 0.2g); PROTEIN 1.7g; CARB 7.2g; FIBER 1.1g; CHOL 2.5mg; IRON 1.1mg; SODIUM 111mg; CALC 37mg

Fresh Orange Sorbet with
Bittersweet Chocolate

    1½ cups fresh orange juice (about
         5 oranges)
    ½ cup sugar
      4 oranges, sectioned and
         chopped
      1 cup water
      1 ounce bittersweet chocolate,
         coarsely grated

1. Combine juice and sugar in a large bowl, stirring until sugar dissolves. Add oranges and water.
2. Pour orange mixture into freezer can of an ice-cream freezer; freeze according to manufacturer's instructions. Spoon sorbet into a freezer-safe container; cover and freeze 1 hour or until firm. Garnish with bittersweet chocolate. Yield: 6 servings (serving size: about 1 cup sorbet).

CALORIES 150 (14% from fat); FAT 2.3g (sat 1g, mono 0g, poly 0.1g); PROTEIN 1.4g; CARB 34.1g; FIBER 2g; CHOL 0mg; IRON 0.3mg; SODIUM 2mg; CALC 37mg

menu of the month

Fourth of July
Cookout

Celebrate the holiday with this colorful backyard barbecue.

Fourth of July
Cookout Menu

serves 8

**Grilled Flatbreads with
Tomatoes and Basil**

**Orzo, Corn, and Roasted Bell
Pepper Salad**

Spicy Lamb Kebabs

**Polenta Cake with Late-
Summer Berries**

Beer or iced tea

Grilled Flatbreads with
Tomatoes and Basil

BREAD:
    2¼ cups bread flour, divided
    ¾ cup plus 2 tablespoons warm
         water (100° to 110°), divided
      1 package dry yeast (about
         2¼ teaspoons)
      1 tablespoon extravirgin
         olive oil
    ¾ teaspoon salt
      1 tablespoon bread flour
Cooking spray

TOPPING:

- 2 tablespoons balsamic vinegar
- 1 tablespoon extravirgin olive oil
- ½ teaspoon salt
- ½ teaspoon freshly ground black pepper
- 2 garlic cloves, minced
- 4 cups (¼-inch-thick) slices plum tomatoes
- 1 cup finely chopped fresh basil

1. To prepare bread, lightly spoon 2¼ cups flour into dry measuring cups; level with a knife. Combine ¼ cup flour, ¼ cup water, and yeast in a large bowl, stirring with a whisk; let stand 30 minutes. Stir in 2 cups flour, ½ cup water, 1 tablespoon oil, and ¾ teaspoon salt. Turn dough out onto a lightly floured surface; sprinkle with 1 tablespoon flour (dough will feel slightly tacky). Knead until smooth and elastic (about 8 minutes).

2. Place dough in a large bowl coated with cooking spray, turning to coat top. Cover and let rise in a warm place (85°), free from drafts, 1 hour or until doubled in size. (Gently press two fingers into dough. If indentation remains, dough has risen enough.)

3. Prepare grill.

4. Divide dough into 8 equal portions. Working with one dough portion at a time (cover remaining dough to prevent drying), roll each portion into a 6-inch circle on a lightly floured surface. Place dough circles on a lightly floured baking sheet. Place dough circles on a grill rack coated with cooking spray, and grill 2 minutes on each side or until golden and crisp.

5. To prepare topping, combine vinegar and next 4 ingredients in a medium bowl, stirring with a whisk. Add tomatoes, and toss gently to coat. Spoon ½ cup tomato mixture onto each flatbread; sprinkle each flatbread with 2 tablespoons basil. Serve immediately. Yield: 8 servings (serving size: 1 flatbread).

CALORIES 172 (20% from fat); FAT 3.8g (sat 0.5g, mono 2.6g, poly 0.4g); PROTEIN 5.9g; CARB 31.1g; FIBER 2.3g; CHOL 0mg; IRON 2.5mg; SODIUM 376mg; CALC 17mg

MAKE AHEAD

Orzo, Corn, and Roasted Bell Pepper Salad

Grilling the vegetables lends this pasta salad a pleasant, smoky flavor. You can prepare and chill it up to a day ahead. To save time, drain and chop a 7-ounce jar of roasted red bell peppers. Slide a skewer or wooden pick through the red onion slices to hold them together as they cook. If you're sensitive to spicy food, seed the jalapeño.

- 2 red bell peppers
- 1 cup uncooked orzo (rice-shaped pasta)
- 3 tablespoons extravirgin olive oil, divided
- 3 ears shucked corn
- 1 red onion, peeled and cut into ½-inch-thick slices
- Cooking spray
- ¼ cup thinly sliced green onions
- ¼ cup chopped fresh flat-leaf parsley
- 3 tablespoons white wine vinegar
- 1 teaspoon salt
- ½ teaspoon freshly ground black pepper
- 1 jalapeño pepper, minced
- 1 garlic clove, minced

1. Preheat broiler.

2. Cut bell peppers in half lengthwise; discard seeds and membranes. Place pepper halves, skin sides up, on a foil-lined baking sheet; flatten with hand. Broil 15 minutes or until blackened. Place in a zip-top plastic bag; seal. Let stand 15 minutes. Peel and chop.

3. Prepare grill.

4. Cook orzo according to package directions, omitting salt and fat. Drain. Place orzo in a large bowl; drizzle with 1 tablespoon oil. Cool slightly.

5. Place corn and red onion on grill rack coated with cooking spray; grill 5 minutes or until lightly browned, turning occasionally. Cut kernels from ears of corn; chop red onion. Add bell pepper, corn, red onion, 2 tablespoons oil, green onions, and remaining ingredients to orzo. Toss gently to combine. Yield: 8 servings (serving size: about ⅔ cup).

CALORIES 180 (30% from fat); FAT 5.9g (sat 0.9g, mono 3.9g, poly 0.7g); PROTEIN 5g; CARB 28.6g; FIBER 2.8g; CHOL 0mg; IRON 1.3mg; SODIUM 302mg; CALC 15mg

Spicy Lamb Kebabs

The yogurt-based marinade would also work well with cubed beef sirloin steak.

- 1 cup plain fat-free yogurt
- 1 tablespoon grated lemon rind
- 2 tablespoons fresh lemon juice
- 1½ tablespoons grated peeled fresh ginger
- 2 teaspoons paprika
- 1½ teaspoons salt
- 1 teaspoon ground coriander
- 1 teaspoon ground cumin
- ½ teaspoon freshly ground black pepper
- ¼ teaspoon ground red pepper
- 2 garlic cloves, minced
- 2½ pounds boneless leg of lamb, trimmed and cubed
- Cooking spray
- 2 tablespoons chopped fresh mint
- 8 lemon wedges

1. Combine first 11 ingredients in a large zip-top plastic bag. Add lamb to bag; seal and marinate in refrigerator 3 hours, turning bag occasionally.

2. Prepare grill.

3. Remove lamb from bag, and discard marinade. Thread lamb onto 8 (10-inch) skewers. Place kebabs on grill rack coated with cooking spray; grill 8 minutes or until desired degree of doneness, turning occasionally. Place kebabs on a platter; sprinkle with mint. Serve with lemon wedges. Yield: 8 servings (serving size: 1 kebab and 1 lemon wedge).

CALORIES 163 (29% from fat); FAT 5.2g (sat 1.8g, mono 2.1g, poly 0.5g); PROTEIN 24.8g; CARB 3.5g; FIBER 0.4g; CHOL 73mg; IRON 2.2mg; SODIUM 528mg; CALC 52mg

Polenta Cake with Late-Summer Berries

Grilling the cake slices is optional but makes for a lovely presentation.

CAKE:

Cooking spray
1½ cups all-purpose flour
⅓ cup finely ground dry polenta
1 teaspoon baking powder
⅛ teaspoon salt
½ teaspoon vanilla extract
2 large eggs, lightly beaten
1 cup sugar
6 tablespoons butter, softened
2 large egg whites

BERRY TOPPING:

2 tablespoons water
1 tablespoon sugar
1 (10-ounce) package frozen unsweetened raspberries, thawed
2 cups halved strawberries
1 cup blueberries
1 cup fresh raspberries
1 cup blackberries

1. Preheat oven to 350°.
2. To prepare cake, coat an 8 x 4-inch loaf pan with cooking spray; set aside.
3. Lightly spoon flour into dry measuring cups; level with a knife. Combine flour, polenta, baking powder, and salt in a medium bowl, stirring with a whisk; set aside.
4. Combine vanilla and 2 eggs in a small bowl, stirring well with a whisk. Combine 1 cup sugar and butter in a medium bowl; beat with a mixer at medium speed until mixture is light and fluffy (about 5 minutes). Gradually add vanilla mixture and egg whites to sugar mixture, beating well (about 2 minutes). Gradually add flour mixture, and stir just until moist.
5. Pour batter into prepared pan. Bake at 350° for 1 hour or until a wooden pick inserted in center comes out clean. Cool cake in pan 10 minutes on a wire rack; remove cake from pan. Cool completely on wire rack. Cut cake into 9 equal slices.

6. To prepare berry topping, place water, 1 tablespoon sugar, and thawed raspberries in a food processor or blender; process until smooth. Strain mixture through a sieve into a bowl, pressing with back of a spoon; discard solids. Combine raspberry sauce, strawberries, blueberries, fresh raspberries, and blackberries in a large bowl; toss gently to combine.
7. Prepare grill.
8. Place cake slices on grill rack coated with cooking spray; grill 1 minute on each side or until golden brown and grill marks form. Serve grilled cake slices with berry topping. Yield: 9 servings (serving size: 1 cake slice and about ½ cup berry topping).

CALORIES 312 (27% from fat); FAT 9.3g (sat 5.1g, mono 2.7g, poly 0.7g); PROTEIN 5.4g; CARB 53.5g; FIBER 5.6g; CHOL 68mg; IRON 1.6mg; SODIUM 219mg; CALC 75mg

dinner tonight

Saté

Bright, full flavors are served on skewers in saté, the Indonesian way with grilled meat.

Saté Menu 1

serves 4

Chicken Saté with Ponzu Sauce

Asian slaw*

Raspberry sorbet

*Combine 2 tablespoons rice vinegar, 2 tablespoons low-sodium soy sauce, 2 teaspoons light brown sugar, and 1 teaspoon sesame oil in a large bowl, stirring with a whisk. Add 1 (16-ounce) package cabbage-and-carrot coleslaw, ¼ cup minced fresh cilantro, ¼ cup chopped green onions, and 2 tablespoons chopped dry-roasted peanuts; toss to coat.

Game Plan

1. While grill preheats:
  • Slice chicken; combine with sake mixture
  • Prepare slaw and chill
2. Thread chicken on skewers, and grill

Chicken Saté with Ponzu Sauce

To prevent wooden skewers from burning while grilling, soak for 30 minutes in hot water beforehand.

TOTAL TIME: 30 MINUTES

SMART INGREDIENT: Sesame oil provides a distinctive nutty flavor. Since its shelf life is shorter than that of canola or vegetable oil, purchase it in small bottles and store in the refrigerator. It will become cloudy and partially solid when chilled, but clear and fluid as it returns to room temperature.

4 (6-ounce) skinless, boneless chicken breast halves
¼ cup packed light brown sugar
¼ cup sake (rice wine)
¼ cup rice vinegar
¼ cup fresh lime juice
2 teaspoons low-sodium soy sauce
1 teaspoon dark sesame oil
¼ teaspoon crushed red pepper
1 garlic clove, minced
Cooking spray

1. Prepare grill.
2. Cut each chicken breast half lengthwise into 4 strips. Combine sugar and next 7 ingredients in a small bowl; stir until sugar dissolves. Combine chicken and half of sake mixture in a large bowl. Let stand 10 minutes. Reserve remaining sake mixture.
3. Drain chicken, discarding marinade. Thread 1 chicken strip onto each of 16 (8-inch) skewers. Place chicken on grill rack coated with cooking spray; grill 2 minutes on each side or until done. Serve with remaining sake mixture. Yield: 4 servings (serving size: 4 skewers and about 1½ tablespoons sake mixture).

CALORIES 267 (12% from fat); FAT 3.5g (sat 0.7g, mono 0.5g, poly 0.5g); PROTEIN 39.6g; CARB 13.3g; FIBER 0.1g; CHOL 99mg; IRON 1.6mg; SODIUM 216mg; CALC 30mg

WINE NOTE: This dish calls for a wine that's bold yet refreshing. Dry rosé does this admirably. Try a chilled bottle of Chateau Potelle's Riviera Rosé from Paso Robles, California. The 2002 is about $15.

Saté Menu 2

serves 4

Salmon Saté with Dill Mustard Glaze

Asparagus with tarragon vinaigrette*

Angel hair pasta

*Combine 1 pound trimmed fresh asparagus and 1 tablespoon water in a shallow microwave-safe dish; cover with plastic wrap. Microwave at HIGH 3 minutes or until asparagus is crisp-tender; drain. Rinse with cold water. Drain well; cool. Combine 2 tablespoons tarragon vinegar, 1½ teaspoons Dijon mustard, 1 teaspoon olive oil, ⅛ teaspoon freshly ground black pepper, 1 minced garlic clove, and a dash of salt in a small bowl, stirring with a whisk. Drizzle over asparagus; toss to combine. Sprinkle with 2 tablespoons Parmesan cheese.

Game Plan

1. While grill preheats:
- Microwave asparagus
- Prepare vinaigrette for asparagus

2. While water comes to a boil and pasta cooks:
- Prepare glaze for salmon
- Thread salmon on skewers

3. Grill salmon

QUICK & EASY
Salmon Saté with Dill Mustard Glaze

To prevent fish from falling off skewers, resist turning them more than once while they cook.

TOTAL TIME: 30 MINUTES

2 tablespoons chopped fresh dill
2 tablespoons whole-grain Dijon mustard
1 teaspoon grated lemon rind
2 tablespoons fresh lemon juice
¼ teaspoon salt
¼ teaspoon ground red pepper
2 garlic cloves, minced
1 (1-pound) salmon fillet, skinned and cut crosswise into 16 pieces
Cooking spray
Dill sprigs (optional)

1. Prepare grill.

2. Combine first 7 ingredients in a bowl; stir with a whisk. Add salmon pieces; toss gently to coat. Thread 4 salmon pieces onto each of 4 (8-inch) skewers. Place salmon on grill rack coated with cooking spray, and grill 3 minutes on each side or until fish flakes easily when tested with a fork or until desired degree of doneness. Garnish with dill sprigs, if desired. Yield: 4 servings (serving size: 1 skewer).

CALORIES 223 (49% from fat); FAT 12.1g (sat 3.5g, mono 5g, poly 3.2g); PROTEIN 23.2g; CARB 3g; FIBER 1.1g; CHOL 57mg; IRON 0.5mg; SODIUM 321mg; CALC 43mg

Saté Menu 3

serves 4

Shrimp Saté with Pineapple Salsa

Lemony broccoli*

White wine

*Cook 1 (12-ounce) package broccoli florets in boiling water 3 minutes or until crisp-tender; drain. Place broccoli in a large bowl. Add 2 teaspoons fresh lemon juice, 2 teaspoons butter, ¼ teaspoon salt, and ¼ teaspoon pepper. Toss gently to coat.

Game Plan

1. While grill preheats:
- Bring water to a boil for broccoli
- Squeeze juice for broccoli
- Prepare salsa
- Season shrimp

2. While broccoli cooks:
- Thread shrimp on skewers

3. Grill shrimp

QUICK & EASY
Shrimp Saté with Pineapple Salsa

TOTAL TIME: 45 MINUTES

SALSA:

¾ cup finely chopped pineapple
¼ cup finely chopped red onion
1 tablespoon minced seeded jalapeño pepper
1 tablespoon chopped fresh cilantro
1 tablespoon cider vinegar
1 teaspoon honey

SATÉ:

2 tablespoons chopped fresh mint
2 tablespoons fresh lime juice
¼ teaspoon salt
¼ teaspoon chili powder
24 large shrimp, peeled and deveined (about 1½ pounds)
Cooking spray
4 cilantro sprigs (optional)

1. Prepare grill.

2. To prepare salsa, combine first 6 ingredients in a medium bowl.

3. To prepare saté, combine mint, juice, salt, and chili powder in a large bowl; add shrimp, tossing gently to coat. Thread 3 shrimp onto each of 8 (6-inch) skewers. Place shrimp on grill rack coated with cooking spray; grill 1½ minutes on each side or until shrimp turn pink. Serve with salsa. Garnish with cilantro sprigs, if desired. Yield: 4 servings (serving size: 2 skewers and ¼ cup salsa).

CALORIES 208 (13% from fat); FAT 3g (sat 0.6g, mono 0.4g, poly 1.2g); PROTEIN 34.9g; CARB 8.7g; FIBER 0.7g; CHOL 259mg; IRON 4.3mg; SODIUM 403mg; CALC 98mg

Saté Menu 4

serves 4

Chicken Saté with Peanut Sauce (recipe on page 228)

Spicy cucumber salad*

Rice noodles

*Combine ½ cup rice vinegar, 1 tablespoon sugar, 1 tablespoon minced seeded jalapeño pepper, and 1 teaspoon grated lime rind in a large bowl. Add 3 cups thinly sliced English cucumber and ½ cup thinly sliced red onion; toss to coat.

Game Plan

1. While grill preheats and water for noodles comes to a boil:
- Marinate chicken
- Prepare peanut sauce

2. While noodles cook:
- Slice cucumber and red onion for salad
- Toss salad

3. Thread chicken on skewers, and grill

Continued

Chicken Saté with Peanut Sauce

Serve the zesty peanut sauce in condiment bowls on individual serving plates.

TOTAL TIME: 40 MINUTES

QUICK TIP: You can broil instead of grill. In fact, traditional Indonesian saté skewers are often broiled. Place on a broiler pan coated with cooking spray; broil eight to 10 minutes, turning once.

SATÉ:

  1   pound skinless, boneless chicken breast, cut into 8 strips
  1   tablespoon light brown sugar
2½   tablespoons low-sodium soy sauce
  2   teaspoons bottled ground fresh ginger (such as Spice World)
  1   teaspoon grated lime rind
  ¼   teaspoon crushed red pepper
  2   garlic cloves, minced

SAUCE:

  1   tablespoon light brown sugar
1½   tablespoons low-sodium soy sauce
  1   tablespoon fresh lime juice
  2   tablespoons natural-style, reduced-fat creamy peanut butter (such as Smucker's)
  ¼   teaspoon crushed red pepper
  1   garlic clove, minced

REMAINING INGREDIENT:

  Cooking spray

1. Prepare grill.
2. To prepare saté, combine chicken and next 6 ingredients in a medium bowl. Let stand 10 minutes.
3. To prepare sauce, combine 1 tablespoon brown sugar and next 5 ingredients in a medium bowl, stirring until sugar dissolves.
4. Thread chicken strips onto each of 8 (8-inch) skewers. Place chicken on grill rack coated with cooking spray; grill 5 minutes on each side or until chicken is done. Serve chicken with sauce. Yield: 4 servings (serving size: 2 skewers and 1 tablespoon sauce).

CALORIES 205 (20% from fat); FAT 4.5g (sat 1g, mono 0.4g, poly 0.4g); PROTEIN 29.3g; CARB 11.2g; FIBER 0.8g; CHOL 66mg; IRON 1.5mg; SODIUM 672mg; CALC 26mg

Your Lucky Number

Seven beat-the-heat recipes that use seven or fewer ingredients

When you make your ingredients count, there's no need to go higher than seven. These recipes will get you in and out of the kitchen with little effort. Each contains only seven ingredients (not counting salt, pepper, or water).

Menu 1
serves 6

Steak Diane

Roasted potato wedges

Steamed asparagus spears

Steak Diane
(pictured on page 235)

For an easy side of roasted potatoes, start with precut potato wedges from the refrigerated section of the grocery store.

  ½   teaspoon salt, divided
  ¼   teaspoon black pepper
  6   (4-ounce) beef tenderloin steaks, trimmed (about 1 inch thick)
  1   teaspoon butter
  ½   cup finely chopped shallots
  ⅓   cup water
  2   tablespoons Worcestershire sauce
1½   tablespoons fresh lemon juice
1½   tablespoons dry sherry
  2   tablespoons chopped fresh parsley

1. Heat a large, heavy skillet over medium-high heat. Sprinkle ¼ teaspoon salt and pepper evenly over steaks. Add steaks to pan; cook 4 minutes on each side or until desired degree of doneness. Remove from pan; cover and keep warm.
2. Melt butter in pan over medium heat. Add shallots, and cook 2 minutes or until tender, stirring occasionally. Add water and next 3 ingredients, stirring with a whisk. Reduce heat, and simmer 1 minute. Stir in ¼ teaspoon salt. Spoon sauce over steaks, and sprinkle with parsley. Yield: 6 servings (serving size: 1 steak and 1½ tablespoons sauce).

CALORIES 197 (40% from fat); FAT 8.7g (sat 3.3g, mono 3.3g, poly 0.3g); PROTEIN 24.2g; CARB 3.8g; FIBER 0.1g; CHOL 73mg; IRON 3.5mg; SODIUM 312mg; CALC 18mg

Double-Duty Ingredients

Lots of everyday ingredients pack a one-two punch. That is, they give you two or more different tastes in one compact package.

Bacon imparts smoky flavor, meaty richness, and saltiness.

Balsamic vinegar lends a tangy note and a little sweetness, particularly when reduced to a syrup.

Canned **green chiles** give dishes pungency and a hit of heat.

Capers offer a sharp grassiness and a briny-salty quality.

Fresh **citrus** brightens. Lemon or lime rind, in particular, provides a floral aroma and flavor with a touch of bitterness. Citrus juice enhances all flavors by adding acidity and a touch of sweetness.

Hoisin sauce imparts sweetness, a hint of spice, and salt.

Olives contribute a slightly bitter edge and meaty texture to recipes. They also provide saltiness.

Soy sauce imparts complexity to dishes by adding a savory, salty, meaty, and decidedly Asian flavor.

Menu 2

serves 6

**Balsamic-Glazed Chicken and
Bell Pepper Sandwiches**

Baked taro chips

Orange wedges

Place a cast-iron or heavy skillet on top of sandwiches; let stand 5 minutes. Cut each sandwich into 6 wedges. Yield: 6 servings (serving size: 2 wedges).

CALORIES 433 (24% from fat); FAT 11.4g (sat 4.2g, mono 5.4g, poly 1g); PROTEIN 34g; CARB 49g; FIBER 1.9g; CHOL 68mg; IRON 3.6mg; SODIUM 709mg; CALC 170mg

Menu 4

serves 6

**Seviche-Style Shrimp and
Avocado Tacos**

Yellow rice

Mango slices

QUICK & EASY

Balsamic-Glazed Chicken and Bell Pepper Sandwiches

Balsamic vinegar cooks down to a glaze that clings to the sandwich fillings. Pressing the sandwich after assembling it conducts the heat from the chicken and cooked vegetables to melt the cheese.

    4   teaspoons olive oil, divided
    ½   teaspoon salt, divided
 1¼   pounds chicken breast tenders
    ½   cup balsamic vinegar, divided
    2   cups red bell pepper strips (about
        2 medium)
    2   cups vertically sliced onion (about
        1 large)
    2   (8-ounce) loaves focaccia bread,
        cut in half horizontally
    4   ounces provolone cheese, thinly
        sliced
    ⅛   teaspoon black pepper

1. Heat 2 teaspoons oil in a large non-stick skillet over medium-high heat. Sprinkle ¼ teaspoon salt over chicken. Add chicken to pan; cook 1 minute on each side or until lightly browned. Add ¼ cup vinegar; cook 2 minutes or until chicken is done and vinegar is syrupy. Remove chicken mixture from pan; cover and keep warm. Wipe pan clean with a paper towel.
2. Return pan to medium-high heat; add 2 teaspoons oil. Add bell pepper and onion; sauté 7 minutes or until tender. Stir in ¼ teaspoon salt and ¼ cup vinegar; cook 1 minute or until vinegar is syrupy.
3. Arrange chicken mixture evenly over bottom halves of bread, and top with bell pepper mixture. Arrange cheese over pepper mixture; sprinkle with black pepper. Top with top halves of bread.

Menu 3

serves 8

**Spaghetti with Peppery
No-Cook Tomato Sauce**

Sautéed broccolini

Garlic breadsticks

QUICK & EASY

Spaghetti with Peppery No-Cook Tomato Sauce

Strong ingredients—like pungent cheese, sharp olives, fruity olive oil, and briny capers—give this pasta sauce plenty of flavor so there's no cooking necessary. Quickly peel tomatoes by plunging them into the boiling pasta water (before adding the pasta) for 20 seconds; remove with a slotted spoon, and quickly rinse under cold water. The skins will slip right off.

    1   pound uncooked spaghetti
    2   cups chopped seeded peeled
        tomato (about 5 medium tomatoes)
    1   cup (4 ounces) crumbled ricotta
        salata or feta cheese
    ⅓   cup chopped pitted kalamata
        olives
    ¼   cup capers
 1½   tablespoons extravirgin olive oil
    ¾   teaspoon salt
    ½   teaspoon black pepper
    4   garlic cloves, minced

1. Cook pasta according to package directions, omitting salt and fat. Drain.
2. Combine tomato and remaining 7 ingredients in a large bowl. Add pasta, and toss well to combine. Serve immediately. Yield: 8 servings (serving size: about 1⅓ cups).

CALORIES 330 (29% from fat); FAT 10.7g (sat 3.9g, mono 3.9g, poly 1g); PROTEIN 11g; CARB 48.2g; FIBER 2.8g; CHOL 15mg; IRON 1.3mg; SODIUM 685mg; CALC 48mg

QUICK & EASY

Seviche-Style Shrimp and Avocado Tacos

Look for cooked, peeled shrimp at the seafood counter. Marinate shrimp in a non-reactive bowl, such as one that is glass or ceramic; an aluminum or copper bowl will react with the citrus juice to give the shrimp a metallic taste.

    3   limes
    1   cup chopped seeded tomato
    1   cup diced peeled avocado (about
        1 avocado)
    ½   cup chopped fresh cilantro
    ¾   teaspoon salt
    ¼   teaspoon black pepper
    3   garlic cloves, minced
    1   pound cooked peeled medium
        shrimp
  12   (6-inch) corn tortillas

1. Finely grate rind from limes to measure 1 tablespoon; juice limes to measure ¼ cup. Place rind and juice in a large bowl. Add tomato and next 6 ingredients; toss well. Cover and chill 15 minutes, stirring occasionally.
2. Heat tortillas according to package directions. Spoon about ½ cup shrimp mixture down center of each tortilla; fold in half. Serve immediately. Yield: 6 servings (serving size: 2 tacos).

CALORIES 261 (27% from fat); FAT 7.8g (sat 1.3g, mono 3.8g, poly 1.8g); PROTEIN 19.5g; CARB 30.3g; FIBER 5g; CHOL 115mg; IRON 3.1mg; SODIUM 498mg; CALC 114mg

Menu 5

serves 6

**Summer Corn and
White Bean Soup**

Tossed salad

Corn bread sticks

Menu 6

serves 6

Five-Spice Pork Lo Mein

Sautéed snow peas
and carrot coins

Jasmine tea

Menu 7

serves 6

**Roast Chicken Pitas with
Cumin-Lemon Dressing**

Tomato, red onion, and feta
cheese salad

Red grapes

QUICK & EASY
Summer Corn and White Bean Soup

This quick, fiber-packed soup is a terrific way to use fresh corn. Add a slight kick with a sprinkle of Monterey Jack cheese with jalapeño peppers just before serving.

- 1 tablespoon canola oil
- 1 cup sliced green onions
- ¾ cup chopped cooked ham (about 4 ounces)
- 3 cups fresh corn kernels (about 5 ears)
- ½ teaspoon salt
- 2 (15-ounce) cans navy beans, rinsed and drained
- 2 (14-ounce) cans fat-free, less-sodium chicken broth
- 2 (4.5-ounce) cans chopped green chiles, undrained

1. Heat oil in a Dutch oven over medium heat. Add onions and ham, and cook 3 minutes, stirring frequently. Stir in corn and remaining ingredients. Bring to a boil; reduce heat, and simmer 5 minutes or until thoroughly heated. Yield: 6 servings (serving size: about 1½ cups).

CALORIES 278 (17% from fat); FAT 5.3g (sat 1g, mono 2.5g, poly 1.4g); PROTEIN 17g; CARB 42.8g; FIBER 10.1g; CHOL 16mg; IRON 4.2mg; SODIUM 593mg; CALC 150mg

These recipes, with few ingredients, get you out of the kitchen quickly.

QUICK & EASY
Five-Spice Pork Lo Mein

Chinese five-spice powder is a common spice blend that can be found in most supermarkets. Its five assertive components are cinnamon, cloves, fennel seed, star anise, and Szechuan peppercorns. Cutting the cooked noodles makes them easier to combine with the other ingredients and serve.

- 8 ounces uncooked Chinese-style noodles
- 1 tablespoon grated peeled fresh ginger
- 2 teaspoons five-spice powder
- 1 (¾-pound) pork tenderloin, trimmed and cut into thin strips
- ½ teaspoon salt, divided
- 2 tablespoons toasted peanut oil
- ¼ cup water
- ¼ cup hoisin sauce
- ½ cup chopped green onions

1. Cook noodles according to package directions, omitting salt and fat; drain. Place in a large bowl. Snip noodles several times with kitchen scissors.
2. Combine ginger, five-spice powder, and pork in a medium bowl; add ¼ teaspoon salt, tossing to coat. Heat oil in a large nonstick skillet over medium-high heat. Add pork mixture; sauté 2 minutes or until browned. Stir in ¼ teaspoon salt, water, and hoisin sauce; cook 2 minutes or until pork is done. Add pork mixture and green onions to noodles; toss well to combine. Yield: 6 servings (serving size: 1⅓ cups).

CALORIES 273 (29% from fat); FAT 8.9g (sat 1.9g, mono 3.6g, poly 2g); PROTEIN 16.3g; CARB 34.8g; FIBER 5.7g; CHOL 38mg; IRON 2.8mg; SODIUM 399mg; CALC 31mg

QUICK & EASY
Roast Chicken Pitas with Cumin-Lemon Dressing

This recipe is best made when the rotisserie chicken is still warm. If your pitas are a bit stale and don't roll up well, cut them into half circles, and stuff the pita pockets with the chicken mixture.

- 3 cups shredded skinless, boneless rotisserie chicken (about 1 [2-pound] chicken)
- 1 cup cubed seeded peeled cucumber (about 1 cucumber)
- ⅓ cup fresh lemon juice (about 2 lemons)
- ¾ teaspoon salt
- 2 tablespoons extravirgin olive oil
- 2 teaspoons cumin seeds
- 4 garlic cloves, sliced
- 6 (6-inch) pitas

1. Preheat oven to 375°.
2. Combine first 4 ingredients in a large bowl, tossing to coat.
3. Heat oil in a small skillet over medium heat. Add cumin and garlic; cook 1 minute or until toasted, stirring frequently. Pour cumin mixture over chicken mixture; toss well.
4. Wrap pitas in foil; bake at 375° for 10 minutes or until heated. Spoon ⅔ cup chicken mixture on each pita; roll up. Yield: 6 servings (serving size: 1 pita roll).

CALORIES 333 (27% from fat); FAT 10.1g (sat 2g, mono 5.2g, poly 1.9g); PROTEIN 23.4g; CARB 36g; FIBER 1.6g; CHOL 53mg; IRON 3mg; SODIUM 671mg; CALC 74mg

Snap into Summer

Discover the varied shapes, sizes, colors, and textures of the season's best beans.

QUICK & EASY
Haricots Verts with Browned Garlic

Slender haricots verts need little embellishment. Here they're tossed with a good dose of browned garlic. Once it's cooked, garlic's flavor mellows considerably. If you can't find the tiny French green beans, substitute regular green beans and increase the cook time in boiling water to five minutes to ensure they're done.

     2 quarts water
  2½ teaspoons salt, divided
  1½ pounds haricots verts
     4 teaspoons butter
   ⅓ cup thinly sliced garlic (about
         1 head)
     2 tablespoons finely chopped
         shallots
     1 teaspoon chopped fresh rosemary
   ½ teaspoon freshly ground black
         pepper

1. Bring 2 quarts water and 2 teaspoons salt to a boil in a large saucepan. Add beans; cook 2 to 3 minutes or until crisp-tender. Drain.

2. Melt butter in pan over medium heat. Add garlic and shallots; cook 4 minutes or until lightly browned, stirring occasionally. Add ½ teaspoon salt, beans, rosemary, and pepper; cook 4 minutes or until thoroughly heated, stirring occasionally. Yield: 8 servings (serving size: about 1 cup).

CALORIES 54 (33% from fat); FAT 2g (sat 1g, mono 0.8g, poly 0.1g); PROTEIN 2g; CARB 8.5g; FIBER 3.1g; CHOL 5mg; IRON 1.1mg; SODIUM 226mg; CALC 45mg

Wax Bean, Roasted Pepper, and Tomato Salad with Goat Cheese

A tart vinaigrette dresses this fresh combination of mild-tasting wax beans, sweet roasted red bell pepper, and juicy cherry tomatoes. Pungent goat cheese adds an extra dimension of flavor. To save time, you can use bottled roasted red bell peppers; just rinse them well to remove as much of the briny flavor as possible.

     1 red bell pepper
     2 quarts water
  2½ teaspoons salt, divided
     1 pound wax beans, trimmed and
         cut in half crosswise
     2 cups cherry tomatoes, halved
   ½ cup sliced green onions
   ¼ cup chopped fresh parsley
     2 tablespoons cider vinegar
     2 tablespoons fresh lemon juice
     1 tablespoon Dijon mustard
  1½ teaspoons sugar
     1 teaspoon extravirgin olive oil
   ½ cup (2 ounces) crumbled goat
         cheese

1. Preheat broiler.

2. Cut pepper in half lengthwise, and discard seeds and membranes. Place pepper halves, skin sides up, on a foil-lined baking sheet; flatten with hand. Broil pepper halves 10 minutes or until blackened. Place in a zip-top plastic bag, and seal. Let stand 15 minutes. Peel and cut into strips.

3. Bring 2 quarts water and 2 teaspoons salt to a boil in a large saucepan. Add beans; cook 4 minutes or until beans are crisp-tender. Drain; place in a large bowl. Add pepper strips, tomatoes, onions, and parsley; toss to combine.

4. Combine ½ teaspoon salt, vinegar, and next 4 ingredients, stirring with a whisk. Drizzle over salad; toss gently. Sprinkle with cheese. Yield: 8 servings (serving size: about 1 cup).

CALORIES 63 (36% from fat); FAT 2.5g (sat 1.2g, mono 0.9g, poly 0.3g); PROTEIN 3g; CARB 8.9g; FIBER 2.7g; CHOL 3mg; IRON 1.2mg; SODIUM 289mg; CALC 40mg

QUICK & EASY
Rattlesnake Beans with Olive Tapenade

     2 quarts water
  2½ teaspoons salt, divided
  1½ pounds rattlesnake beans or pole
         beans, trimmed and cut into
         1-inch pieces
   ¼ cup kalamata olives, pitted
  1½ teaspoons grated lemon rind
  1½ teaspoons fresh lemon juice
  1½ teaspoons extravirgin olive oil
     1 teaspoon chopped fresh rosemary
     1 garlic clove, chopped
     1 shallot, peeled and quartered

1. Bring 2 quarts water and 2 teaspoons salt to a boil in a large saucepan. Add beans; cook 25 minutes or until beans are tender. Drain.

2. Place olives and remaining 6 ingredients in a food processor; add ½ teaspoon salt. Process until finely chopped, scraping sides of bowl occasionally. Combine beans and olive mixture in a large bowl; toss well. Yield: 6 servings (serving size: about ¾ cup).

CALORIES 66 (35% from fat); FAT 2.6g (sat 0.3g, mono 1.9g, poly 0.3g); PROTEIN 2.4g; CARB 10.1g; FIBER 4g; CHOL 0mg; IRON 1.3mg; SODIUM 365mg; CALC 49mg

Selecting and Storing Beans

Look closely at the beans in the market. If the sides of the pods are bulging from the seeds, the beans will be tough because they were picked too late. Make sure the skin is taut. Old beans have leathery, discolored skin, and they may be limp. Next, pick up a bean, and break it in half. If you hear the signature snap, the bean is fresh.

Once you get them home, cook snap beans as soon as possible. To preserve, wrap in a damp paper towel, place in a plastic bag, and refrigerate up to one week. If you can't cook them within a week, trim the stem ends, blanch the beans, cool, and freeze until you're ready to use in a recipe.

Snap Bean Glossary

Green beans: They're called green beans, but these slender beans with tiny seeds tucked in the pods can also be yellow or purple. (When cooked, the purple beans turn green.) These beans should be cooked briefly in boiling salted water to seal in the bright green color.

Haricots verts (ah-ree-koh VEHR): Also referred to as French filet beans, these tiny beans are picked young and prized for their intense, slightly sweet flavor and crisp texture. They should be no longer than about three inches and only a bit larger in diameter than a matchstick. Even though these beans are commonly called haricots verts (*vert* is French for "green"), you'll also find yellow and purple varieties. These beans are similar to green beans, but they cook more quickly.

Pole beans: These beans are longer and broader than regular green beans. Pole beans can be flat or round. Always check pole beans for strings by snapping off the ends and peeling back before cooking. Pole beans taste much like green beans, but they're tougher than other snap beans and thus need to cook longer.

Rattlesnake beans: An heirloom variety of pole bean, this bean gets its name from its mottled skin. Cook them as you would other varieties of pole beans. Once cooked, these beans turn green and lose their dappled appearance.

Wax beans: Wax beans are a hybrid first grown as a hothouse plant in England. Their waxy texture earned them the name, and in addition to classic yellow, there are purple and light green varieties. These beans aren't as flavorful as green beans. They can be treated much like green beans for cooking purposes.

Basic Pot of Pole Beans

Serve this basic side dish with anything you'd normally have with green beans.

- 3 bacon slices
- 1 cup chopped onion
- ¼ teaspoon salt
- ¼ teaspoon freshly ground black pepper
- 3 (14-ounce) cans fat-free, less-sodium chicken broth
- 1½ pounds pole beans, trimmed and cut in half crosswise

1. Cook bacon in a large Dutch oven over medium heat until crisp. Remove bacon from pan, reserving 1 teaspoon drippings in pan. Crumble bacon; set aside. Add onion to drippings in pan; cook 3 minutes, stirring frequently. Add bacon, salt, and remaining ingredients; bring to a boil. Reduce heat, and simmer, uncovered, 25 minutes or until beans are tender. Yield: 8 servings (serving size: about 1 cup).

CALORIES 63 (26% from fat); FAT 1.8g (sat 0.6g, mono 0.5g, poly 0.2g); PROTEIN 4.1g; CARB 8.8g; FIBER 3.8g; CHOL 3mg; IRON 1.3mg; SODIUM 370mg; CALC 45mg

Spicy Pickled Beans

Keep these crunchy, sweet-sour-spicy beans on hand for snacking, set them out on a relish tray at a cocktail party, or use in place of celery for Bloody Marys.

- 2 quarts water
- 1 tablespoon salt
- ½ pound green beans, trimmed
- ½ pound wax beans, trimmed
- 1¼ cups red wine vinegar
- ½ cup sugar
- ½ cup sherry vinegar or cider vinegar
- ½ cup vodka
- 2 tablespoons mustard seeds
- 1 tablespoon black peppercorns
- 2 teaspoons fennel seeds
- 1 to 2 teaspoons crushed red pepper
- 4 garlic cloves
- 4 fresh dill sprigs
- 2 bay leaves

1. Bring 2 quarts water and salt to a boil in a large saucepan. Add beans; cook 4 minutes or until crisp-tender. Drain; place in a large bowl.

2. Combine red wine vinegar and next 10 ingredients in a medium saucepan. Bring to a boil; cook 1 minute or until sugar dissolves. Pour over beans; cover and marinate in refrigerator at least 24 hours. Discard dill and bay leaves. Drain, if desired. Yield: 16 servings (serving size: 1 ounce beans).

NOTE: Refrigerate beans in an airtight container up to two weeks.

CALORIES 21 (13% from fat); FAT 0.3g (sat 0g, mono 0.1g, poly 0.1g); PROTEIN 0.8g; CARB 3.8g; FIBER 1.3g; CHOL 0mg; IRON 0.5mg; SODIUM 47mg; CALC 18mg

Fettuccine with Clams, Haricots Verts, and Parsley

- 3 tablespoons butter
- 1 cup coarsely chopped peeled tomato
- ¼ cup finely chopped shallots
- ½ teaspoon salt
- 3 garlic cloves, minced
- 1 cup dry white wine
- 1 (8-ounce) bottle clam juice
- 42 littleneck clams in shells (about 2 pounds), scrubbed
- 8 ounces haricots verts, trimmed and cut in half crosswise
- 1 cup chopped fresh flat-leaf parsley
- 7 cups hot cooked fettuccine (about 1 pound uncooked pasta)

1. Melt butter in a Dutch oven over medium-high heat. Add tomato, shallots, salt, and garlic; sauté 3 minutes. Stir in wine and clam juice. Add clams; bring to a boil. Cover, reduce heat, and simmer 5 minutes or until shells begin to open. Stir in beans; cover and cook 2 minutes or until beans are crisp-tender. Remove from heat; stir in parsley. Serve immediately over pasta. Yield: 6 servings (serving size: about 1 cup clam mixture and about 1 cup pasta).

CALORIES 390 (17% from fat); FAT 7.4g (sat 3.3g, mono 2.4g, poly 0.4g); PROTEIN 17.9g; CARB 64.2g; FIBER 4.4g; CHOL 31mg; IRON 10.3mg; SODIUM 361mg; CALC 80mg

Roasted Fresh Corn, Poblano, and Cheddar Pizza, page 224

Smoked Onion
and Garlic Soup,
page 216

Grilled Fig and Arugula Salad with
Gorgonzola Toasts, page 241

Steak Diane, page 228

Orange Yogurt Cake,
page 239

Spanish Nights

Serve this mix-and-match menu inspired by Old Madrid for a relaxing dinner at dusk.

Spanish Nights Menu
serves 6

Asparagus Salad with Piquillo Peppers and Capers
or
Shrimp-Filled Piquillo Peppers in Sherry Vinaigrette
or
Moorish-Style Salad with Cumin and Smoked Paprika
or
Steamed Mussels with Lemon, Onion, and Wine

Chicken with White Wine, Grape Juice, and Cilantro
or
Dried Plum-Stuffed Pork Loin in Sweet Sherry Sauce

Baked Rice

Orange Yogurt Cake
or
Spiced Peaches in Crisp Phyllo Pastry

Spanish wine
Rioja or albariño

QUICK & EASY
Moorish-Style Salad with Cumin and Smoked Paprika
Ensalada Morisca

DRESSING:

1½ tablespoons minced fresh parsley
1 teaspoon chopped canned anchovy fillets
½ teaspoon cumin seeds
¼ teaspoon Spanish smoked sweet paprika
3 garlic cloves, minced
3 tablespoons white wine vinegar
1 tablespoon extravirgin olive oil

SALAD:

6 cups torn escarole
2 cups halved cherry tomatoes
½ cup vertically sliced red onion

1. To prepare dressing, combine first 5 ingredients in a mortar or small bowl; grind with a pestle until mixture forms a smooth paste. Add vinegar and oil; stir with a whisk.

2. To prepare salad, combine escarole, tomatoes, and onion in a large bowl. Add dressing; toss well. Yield: 6 servings (serving size: 1⅓ cups).

CALORIES 65 (44% from fat); FAT 3.4g (sat 0.6g, mono 2.1g, poly 0.5g); PROTEIN 3.5g; CARB 6.1g; FIBER 2.3g; CHOL 6mg; IRON 1.2mg; SODIUM 292mg; CALC 54mg

MAKE AHEAD
Shrimp-Filled Piquillo Peppers in Sherry Vinaigrette
Pimientos del Piquillo con Tartar de Langostinos

4 teaspoons sherry vinegar
½ teaspoon Dijon mustard
1 tablespoon extravirgin olive oil
1⅛ teaspoons salt, divided
¼ teaspoon sugar
⅛ teaspoon freshly ground black pepper
6 cups water
½ pound medium shrimp, peeled and deveined
2 tablespoons finely chopped fresh parsley
2 teaspoons finely chopped Vidalia or other sweet onion
10 small roasted piquillo peppers
2 cups sliced Belgian endive (about 2 small heads)
2 cups trimmed watercress
¼ cup vertically sliced onion

1. Combine vinegar and mustard in a small bowl, stirring with a whisk. Add oil, ⅛ teaspoon salt, sugar, and black pepper, stirring with a whisk until blended.

2. Combine water and 1 teaspoon salt in a large Dutch oven; bring to a boil. Add shrimp; cook 3 minutes or until done. Drain and rinse with cold water; finely chop. Combine shrimp, parsley, and chopped onion in a medium bowl; stir in 4 teaspoons vinegar mixture. Gently fill each piquillo pepper with about 1½ tablespoons shrimp mixture.

3. Place endive, watercress, and sliced onion on a large platter, tossing to combine. Top with stuffed peppers, and drizzle with remaining vinegar mixture. Yield: 10 servings (serving size: 1 stuffed pepper and about ⅓ cup greens).

CALORIES 43 (37% from fat); FAT 1.8g (sat 0.3g, mono 1.1g, poly 0.2g); PROTEIN 4.1g; CARB 2.3g; FIBER 1.1g; CHOL 34mg; IRON 0.8mg; SODIUM 144mg; CALC 30mg

Asparagus Salad with Piquillo Peppers and Capers
Ensalada de Espárragos con Alcaparras

2 tablespoons chopped fresh parsley, divided
1 tablespoon chopped shallots
½ teaspoon kosher salt
1 garlic clove, minced
2 tablespoons chopped roasted piquillo peppers
2 tablespoons chopped seeded peeled plum tomato
1 tablespoon white wine vinegar
1 tablespoon extravirgin olive oil
¼ teaspoon Dijon mustard
⅛ teaspoon freshly ground black pepper
1 pound asparagus spears, steamed and cooled
1 hard-cooked large egg
1½ teaspoons capers

1. Place 1 tablespoon parsley, shallots, salt, and garlic in a mortar or small bowl; grind with a pestle until mixture forms a smooth paste. Stir in piquillo peppers and tomato. Add vinegar, oil, mustard, and black pepper; stir well. Place asparagus in a shallow dish, and drizzle with pepper mixture. Gently toss, using a serving fork and spoon. Place asparagus on a serving platter.

2. Cut egg in half lengthwise; remove
Continued

and reserve yolk for another use. Chop egg white. Sprinkle egg white, capers, and 1 tablespoon parsley evenly over asparagus. Yield: 6 servings.

CALORIES 51 (42% from fat); FAT 2.4g (sat 0.3g, mono 1.8g, poly 0.2g); PROTEIN 2.4g; CARB 4.7g; FIBER 1.9g; CHOL 0mg; IRON 0.5mg; SODIUM 212mg; CALC 23mg

---

The Spanish Pantry

These ingredients lend dishes quintessential Spanish flavor. You'll find most at large supermarkets and specialty stores. Or order them from La Tienda (888-472-1022, www.tienda.com).

Quince paste is a sweet confection made from quince, a fruit that tastes like a mix of apple and pear. For a quick tapa, top triangles of manchego cheese with thin slices of quince paste.

Prized for its earthy flavor and rich aroma, **Spanish smoked paprika** brings a host of dishes to life, from grilled meats and fish to salads and stews. It may be sweet, bittersweet, or hot.

Cream sherry is a very sweet sherry used in Spanish cooking; it's also appropriate as a dessert wine.

Small, thin-fleshed, slightly piquant **roasted piquillo peppers** are sold in jars. They hold their shape, making them ideal for stuffing; they're also nice lightly sautéed with garlic and olive oil.

Made from the stigmas of the purple saffron crocus, the spice **saffron** is used in small amounts for the flavor and the golden hue it imparts to food. Buy from a reputable source to ensure authenticity and high quality.

Manchego cheese, Spain's unique sheep's milk cheese from the plains of La Mancha, has become popular in the United States; you can find it at supermarkets. Manchego is available semicured and mild (labeled *curado)* or well-cured and slightly sharp (labeled *viejo)*.

Cured, air-dried **Serrano ham** can be eaten thinly sliced (like prosciutto) and is commonly used in Spanish cooking as a flavor accent.

Dried Plum-Stuffed Pork Loin in Sweet Sherry Sauce
Lomo Relleno

Our method of butterflying the pork tenderloins allows the flavors of the sweet dried plum and piquant piquillo peppers to permeate the meat as it cooks. Serve leftover pork over polenta with a tossed green salad for an easy dinner another night.

- 2 (1-pound) pork tenderloins, trimmed
- 2 tablespoons minced fresh parsley, divided
- ¾ teaspoon kosher salt, divided
- ¼ teaspoon freshly ground black pepper
- 1 garlic clove, minced
- 12 bite-size pitted dried plums
- ¼ cup sliced roasted piquillo peppers
- 1 tablespoon all-purpose flour
- 1 tablespoon olive oil
- 1½ cups vertically sliced Vidalia or other sweet onion
- 4 black peppercorns
- 2 garlic cloves, unpeeled
- 1 bay leaf
- ⅓ cup fat-free, less-sodium chicken broth
- ⅓ cup cream sherry
- ½ teaspoon ground cumin

1. Preheat oven to 400°.
2. Cut 1 pork tenderloin in half lengthwise, cutting to, but not through, other side; open halves, laying pork flat. Cut each half lengthwise, cutting to, but not through, other side; open halves, laying pork flat. Repeat procedure with remaining tenderloin. Sprinkle inside of tenderloins with 1 tablespoon parsley, ½ teaspoon salt, black pepper, and minced garlic. Top each tenderloin with 6 dried plums and 2 tablespoons piquillo peppers. Roll up each pork tenderloin, jelly-roll fashion, starting at long side. Secure pork at 2-inch intervals with twine; dust with flour.
3. Heat oil in a large ovenproof nonstick skillet over medium-high heat. Add pork; cook 6 minutes on each side or until browned. Add 1 tablespoon parsley, onion, peppercorns, unpeeled garlic,

and bay leaf; sauté 2 minutes. Stir in broth, sherry, and cumin. Wrap handle of pan with foil, and transfer pan to oven. Cover and bake at 400° for 25 minutes or until a thermometer registers 160° (slightly pink). Transfer pork to a platter; let stand 5 minutes. Cut pork into ¾-inch-thick slices, and sprinkle with ¼ teaspoon salt. Remove whole garlic cloves; squeeze to extract pulp. Stir into pan juices (discard garlic skins and bay leaf). Serve pan juices with pork. Yield: 8 servings (serving size: 3 ounces pork [3 slices] and about 2 tablespoons pan juices).

CALORIES 204 (29% from fat); FAT 6.6g (sat 1.7g, mono 3.6g, poly 0.7g); PROTEIN 24.7g; CARB 11g; FIBER 2g; CHOL 74mg; IRON 1.9mg; SODIUM 279mg; CALC 25mg

---

Chicken with White Wine, Grape Juice, and Cilantro
Pollo a la Uva Blanco con Cilantro

This dish combines the flavors of the Spanish vineyards in Andalucía (white wine and white grape juice) with the tastes of the region's Moorish palate (pungent cilantro).

- 6 (6-ounce) skinless, boneless chicken breast halves
- ¾ teaspoon kosher salt
- ⅛ teaspoon freshly ground black pepper
- 3 tablespoons olive oil
- 1 cup vertically sliced onion
- 2 garlic cloves, minced
- ¾ cup dry white wine
- 6 tablespoons finely chopped fresh cilantro, divided
- ⅓ cup unsweetened white grape juice
- ½ teaspoon ground coriander
- ¼ teaspoon ground cumin
- ¼ teaspoon crushed red pepper
- 1½ cups seedless green grapes, halved

1. Sprinkle chicken with salt and black pepper. Heat oil in a 12-inch nonstick skillet over medium-high heat. Add chicken; cook 2 minutes on each side or until lightly browned. Add onion and garlic; sauté 2 minutes or until onion is tender. Stir in wine, 3 tablespoons cilantro, and next 4 ingredients; bring to a boil. Cover, reduce heat, and simmer 30 minutes or until chicken is done.

2. Transfer chicken to a serving platter, and keep warm. Increase heat to medium-high; cook until sauce is reduced to 1 cup (about 5 minutes). Stir in grapes. Spoon sauce over chicken; sprinkle with remaining cilantro. Yield: 6 servings (serving size: 1 chicken breast, about ¼ cup sauce, and 1½ teaspoons cilantro).

CALORIES 297 (27% from fat); FAT 9.1g (sat 1.5g, mono 5.5g, poly 1.2g); PROTEIN 40.1g; CARB 12.4g; FIBER 1g; CHOL 99mg; IRON 1.8mg; SODIUM 352mg; CALC 38mg

---

QUICK & EASY
Steamed Mussels with Lemon, Onion, and Wine
Mijillones al Limón

After adding the mussels, don't remove the lid until the minimum amount of cooking time has elapsed.

    2 teaspoons olive oil
  2¼ cups vertically sliced onion
       (1 medium)
    2 tablespoons finely chopped shallots
  1½ teaspoons chopped fresh thyme
    1 garlic clove, minced
    1 bay leaf
   ¼ cup dry white wine
  1¾ pounds small mussels, scrubbed
       and debearded
   ¼ cup fresh lemon juice
   ⅛ teaspoon salt
   ⅛ teaspoon freshly ground black
       pepper
    2 tablespoons finely chopped fresh
       parsley

1. Heat oil in a large nonstick skillet over medium heat. Add onion, shallots, thyme, garlic, and bay leaf; sauté 2 minutes. Reduce heat to low; cover and cook 10 minutes. Add wine; uncover and cook over medium-high heat 2 minutes or until liquid almost evaporates. Add mussels, juice, salt, and pepper. Cover and cook 3 minutes or until mussels open; discard any unopened shells and bay leaf. Serve with pan juices; sprinkle with parsley. Yield: 6 servings (serving size:

about 8 mussels, about 1 tablespoon pan juices, and 1 teaspoon parsley).

CALORIES 152 (27% from fat); FAT 4.5g (sat 0.8g, mono 1.8g, poly 1g); PROTEIN 16.4g; CARB 11.1g; FIBER 0.8g; CHOL 37mg; IRON 5.5mg; SODIUM 431mg; CALC 50mg

---

QUICK & EASY
Baked Rice
Arroz al Horno

Traditional in Valencia, baked rice is delicious with pork or chicken.

  1½ tablespoons olive oil
   ⅓ cup finely chopped shiitake
       mushroom caps
    2 tablespoons minced onion
  1¼ cups uncooked Arborio or other
       short-grain rice
  2½ cups fat-free, less-sodium chicken
       broth
   ¼ teaspoon salt
   ⅛ teaspoon crushed saffron threads
    2 tablespoons minced fresh parsley
  1½ teaspoons minced fresh thyme

1. Preheat oven to 400°.
2. Heat oil in a 2-quart ovenproof saucepan. Add mushrooms and onion; cook 5 minutes. Add rice, broth, salt, and saffron; bring to a boil. Wrap handle of pan with foil; cover and transfer pan to oven. Bake at 400° for 15 minutes. Remove from oven; let stand, covered, 10 minutes. Add parsley and thyme. Yield: 6 servings (serving size: ⅔ cup).

CALORIES 107 (29% from fat); FAT 3.5g (sat 0.5g, mono 2.5g, poly 0.4g); PROTEIN 2.5g; CARB 16g; FIBER 0.8g; CHOL 0mg; IRON 0.5mg; SODIUM 261mg; CALC 11mg

---

MAKE AHEAD • FREEZABLE
Orange Yogurt Cake
Bizcocho de Naranja
(pictured on page 236)

Seville and Valencia are famous for oranges. This moist cake offers a triple punch of orange flavor: juice, marmalade, and liqueur. Wrap cooled, unglazed cake in plastic wrap to freeze. Allow to thaw overnight in refrigerator. Bring to room temperature, glaze, and serve. Garnish with fresh raspberries or strawberries, mint, and grated orange rind, if desired.

    1 cup fresh orange juice
   ⅛ teaspoon crushed saffron
       threads
    2 cups all-purpose flour
  1½ teaspoons baking powder
   ¼ teaspoon salt
    1 cup sugar
    1 large egg
    1 large egg white
   ¼ cup plain low-fat yogurt
    6 tablespoons olive oil
       Cooking spray
    3 tablespoons sweet orange
       marmalade
    1 tablespoon Grand Marnier or
       other orange-flavored liqueur

1. Preheat oven to 350°.
2. Place juice in a small saucepan; bring to a simmer over medium-high heat. Remove from heat; stir in saffron. Let stand 10 minutes.
3. Lightly spoon flour into dry measuring cups, and level with a knife. Combine flour, baking powder, and salt, stirring well with a whisk. Set aside.
4. Place sugar, egg, and egg white in a large bowl, and beat with a mixer at medium speed 5 minutes or until thickened. Add yogurt, beating well. Gradually add oil and juice mixture, beating until well blended. Add half of flour mixture to sugar mixture; beat just until blended. Repeat procedure with remaining flour mixture.
5. Spoon batter into a 9-inch round cake pan coated with cooking spray. Bake at 350° for 40 minutes or until a wooden pick inserted in center comes out clean. Cool 5 minutes in pan on a wire rack; remove from pan. Cool completely on wire rack.
6. Place cake on a serving platter. Combine marmalade and liqueur in a small saucepan; bring to a simmer over medium heat, stirring constantly. Remove from heat; strain through a fine sieve directly onto surface of cake. Discard solids. Spread marmalade mixture evenly over top of cake, allowing excess to drizzle down sides of cake. Yield: 12 servings (serving size: 1 slice).

CALORIES 240 (29% from fat); FAT 7.9g (sat 1.1g, mono 5.3g, poly 1g); PROTEIN 3.4g; CARB 39.3g; FIBER 0.6g; CHOL 18mg; IRON 1.2mg; SODIUM 135mg; CALC 32mg

Spiced Peaches in Crisp Phyllo Pastry
Bric de Melocotón Perfumado

The filling for this strudel-like dessert is similar to homemade peach preserves. Pay close attention during the last 15 minutes of cooking the peaches to prevent burning. Prepare this dessert a day or two ahead, and store in an airtight container.

½ cup unsweetened white grape juice, divided
⅓ cup granulated sugar
½ cup riesling or other sweet white wine
½ teaspoon grated lemon rind
2 teaspoons fresh lemon juice
⅛ teaspoon ground nutmeg
3 whole cloves
1 (3-inch) cinnamon stick
4 cups coarsely chopped peeled peaches (about 1½ pounds)
12 (14 x 9-inch) sheets frozen phyllo dough, thawed (such as Athens)
Cooking spray
1 teaspoon powdered sugar

1. Combine 3 tablespoons grape juice and granulated sugar in a medium saucepan. Cook over high heat 4 minutes or until golden, stirring constantly. Remove from heat. Stir in 5 tablespoons grape juice, wine, and next 5 ingredients; bring to a boil. Reduce heat, and simmer 10 minutes. Remove and discard cloves and cinnamon stick. Stir in peaches; bring to a boil. Reduce heat to medium; cook 25 minutes or until very thick, stirring frequently. Cool 1 hour.
2. Preheat oven to 375°.
3. Place 1 phyllo sheet on work surface (cover remaining dough to prevent drying); lightly coat with cooking spray. Place another phyllo sheet on top of first; lightly coat with cooking spray. Repeat procedure with remaining phyllo and cooking spray, ending with cooking spray.
4. Spoon peach mixture along 1 long edge of phyllo, leaving a 2-inch border. Fold over short edges of phyllo to cover 2 inches of peach mixture on each end. Starting at long edge with 2-inch border,

roll up jelly-roll fashion. (Do not roll tightly, or pastry may split.) Place pastry, seam side down, on a baking sheet coated with cooking spray. Divide pastry into 6 equal portions by scoring 5 diagonal slits on top using a sharp knife. Lightly coat pastry with cooking spray.
5. Bake at 375° for 25 minutes or until golden brown. Cool 10 minutes on baking sheet on a wire rack. Sprinkle with powdered sugar. Cut along scored slits into equal portions using a serrated knife. Yield: 6 servings (serving size: 1 slice).

CALORIES 217 (36% from fat); FAT 8.7g (sat 0.4g, mono 3.1g, poly 2.6g); PROTEIN 2.8g; CARB 37.5g; FIBER 0.5g; CHOL 0mg; IRON 1.1mg; SODIUM 111mg; CALC 14mg

lighten up

Zucchini Bread Winner

A lighter, healthier version gets high praise from an Oregon office manager.

After almost a decade of making Zucchini Bread, Peggy Schliebe's baking days came to a halt. Her favorite community church cookbook recipe was suddenly banished from her diet. "I was diagnosed with type 1 diabetes," Schliebe says, "and my Zucchini Bread recipe is loaded with sugar and oil." Soon after, she asked us to give her recipe a makeover.

BEFORE	AFTER
SERVING SIZE	
1 slice	
CALORIES PER SERVING	
213	150
FAT	
10.1g	4.3g
PERCENT OF TOTAL CALORIES	
43%	26%

Zucchini Bread

This quick bread recipe makes two loaves. Enjoy a loaf now, and store the other in the freezer up to one month. Toasted slices are delicious for breakfast.

3 cups all-purpose flour
1 teaspoon baking powder
1 teaspoon ground cinnamon
½ teaspoon salt
¼ teaspoon baking soda
½ cup egg substitute
⅓ cup canola oil
2 teaspoons vanilla extract
1 teaspoon grated lemon rind
1 large egg, lightly beaten
1½ cups sugar
3 cups shredded zucchini (12 ounces)
¼ cup coarsely chopped walnuts, toasted
Cooking spray

1. Preheat oven to 350°.
2. Lightly spoon flour into dry measuring cups; level with a knife. Combine flour and next 4 ingredients in a large bowl.
3. Combine egg substitute and next 4 ingredients in a large bowl; stir in sugar. Add zucchini; stir until well combined. Add flour mixture; stir just until combined. Stir in walnuts.
4. Divide batter evenly between 2 (8 x 4-inch) loaf pans coated with cooking spray. Bake at 350° for 1 hour or until a wooden pick inserted in center comes out clean. Cool 10 minutes in pans on a wire rack; remove from pans. Cool completely on wire rack. Yield: 2 loaves, 12 servings per loaf (serving size: 1 slice).

CALORIES 150 (26% from fat); FAT 4.3g (sat 0.4g, mono 2g, poly 1.6g); PROTEIN 2.7g; CARB 25.3g; FIBER 0.6g; CHOL 9mg; IRON 1mg; SODIUM 96mg; CALC 21mg

Thomas Jefferson's Garden

A passionate gardener and food lover, Jefferson was an advocate of healthful eating, and his tastes helped shape those of a new nation.

The next time you're at the local farmers' market perusing the rows of heirloom lettuces or debating whether to buy purple or white eggplant, say a word of thanks to America's third president. We believe Thomas Jefferson would have enjoyed the following recipes. We think you will, too.

Grilled Fig and Arugula Salad with Gorgonzola Toasts

(pictured on page 234)

Marseilles fig bushes from France had a place of pride in Monticello's orchards.

⅓ cup (about 1½ ounces) crumbled Gorgonzola cheese
1 tablespoon butter, softened
8 (1-ounce) slices peasant bread
12 fresh figs, halved
Cooking spray
2 tablespoons balsamic vinegar
1 tablespoon extravirgin olive oil
½ teaspoon salt
¼ teaspoon freshly ground black pepper
3 cups baby spinach
3 cups arugula
8 Boston lettuce leaves
2 tablespoons chopped green onions

1. Preheat grill.
2. Combine cheese and butter in a small bowl; stir until well blended.
3. Grill bread 5 minutes on each side or until golden; cool. Spread 1 teaspoon cheese mixture on each slice; set aside.
4. Thread 4 fig halves lengthwise onto each of 6 (8-inch) skewers; coat figs with cooking spray. Place fig kebabs on grill rack, and grill 4 minutes on each side. Cool slightly; remove figs from skewers.

5. Combine vinegar, oil, salt, and pepper in a small bowl. Place spinach and arugula in a large bowl; add dressing, tossing gently to coat. Place on each of 8 serving plates. Top with figs and lettuce leaves; sprinkle evenly with onions. Serve with toasts. Yield: 8 servings (serving size: 1 cup salad, 1 lettuce leaf, 3 fig halves, and 1 toast).

CALORIES 180 (30% from fat); FAT 6.2g (sat 2.3g, mono 2g, poly 0.4g); PROTEIN 4.5g; CARB 30.2g; FIBER 4.1g; CHOL 8mg; IRON 1.1mg; SODIUM 378mg; CALC 103mg

Peach Melba with Blackberry Sauce

This includes two of Jefferson's favorites: peaches, which he grew, and ice cream, which he discovered in France. The ice house at Monticello was kept cool with winter ice harvested from the Rivanna River, so he enjoyed ice cream year-round.

1½ cups water
1 cup sugar
1 (1-inch) piece vanilla bean, split lengthwise
6 peeled peaches, halved and pitted
2 cups blackberries
½ teaspoon lemon juice
3 cups vanilla reduced-fat ice cream (such as Healthy Choice)

1. Combine water and sugar in a large saucepan over medium heat. Scrape seeds from vanilla bean; add seeds and bean to pan. Bring mixture to a simmer, stirring constantly; cook 10 minutes. Add peaches to sugar mixture; simmer 5 minutes or just until tender. Remove peaches with a slotted spoon, and place in a bowl.
2. Bring sugar mixture to a boil over medium-high heat; cook until reduced to 1 cup (about 5 minutes). Remove and discard vanilla bean. Add blackberries; cook 10 minutes, stirring occasionally. Remove from heat; cool 5 minutes. Place berry mixture in a blender or food processor; process until smooth. Strain mixture through a fine sieve over a bowl; discard solids. Stir in juice.
3. Place ice cream in each of 6 bowls; top with peaches and blackberry sauce. Yield: 6 servings (serving size: ½ cup ice cream, 2 peach halves, and about 2½ tablespoons sauce).

CALORIES 288 (8% from fat); FAT 2.5g (sat 1g, mono 1.1g, poly 0.2g); PROTEIN 4.6g; CARB 65g; FIBER 1g; CHOL 5mg; IRON 1mg; SODIUM 52mg; CALC 121mg

QUICK & EASY
Fruit Medley with Mint and Lime

Jefferson's stone fruit trees produced heavily. Serve this as a salad or light dessert.

1 cup seedless green grapes, halved
1 cup seedless red grapes, halved
3 plums, cut into ½-inch-thick wedges
2 peaches, peeled and cut into ½-inch-thick wedges
2 nectarines, cut into ½-inch-thick wedges
2 limes
1 cup water
¼ cup sugar
6 mint sprigs
2 tablespoons chopped fresh mint
1 teaspoon grated lime rind
1 tablespoon fresh lime juice
Mint sprigs (optional)

Continued

1. Combine first 5 ingredients in a large bowl; cover and chill.

2. Carefully remove 6 (2-inch) strips of rind from limes using a vegetable peeler, making sure to avoid white pithy part of rind. Combine lime strips, water, sugar, and 6 mint sprigs in a small saucepan; bring to a boil. Cook until reduced to ½ cup (about 5 minutes). Discard lime strips and mint sprigs; cool. Stir in chopped mint, grated rind, and juice. Pour over fruit, tossing gently to coat. Garnish with additional mint sprigs, if desired. Yield: 6 servings (serving size: 1 cup).

CALORIES 122 (4% from fat); FAT 0.5g (sat 0.1g, mono 0.2g, poly 0.2g); PROTEIN 1.5g; CARB 30.6g; FIBER 1.9g; CHOL 0mg; IRON 0.7mg; SODIUM 2mg; CALC 17mg

Baked Couscous with Summer Squash and Herbs

This side dish—good for a summer brunch or buffet—highlights the squash and kitchen herbs grown at Monticello.

 1 (14-ounce) can fat-free, less-sodium chicken broth, divided
 ¾ cup uncooked couscous
 Cooking spray
 2 cups sliced yellow squash (about 2 small)
 ½ cup sliced green onions
 2 tablespoons chopped fresh basil
 1 tablespoon chopped fresh oregano
 1 garlic clove, minced
 ¼ cup (1 ounce) shredded fontina cheese
 ¼ cup (1 ounce) grated Parmigiano-Reggiano cheese
 ¼ cup egg substitute
 ¼ teaspoon salt
 ¼ teaspoon freshly ground black pepper

1. Preheat oven to 400°.

2. Bring 1 cup chicken broth to a boil in a medium saucepan; gradually stir in couscous. Remove from heat; cover and let stand 5 minutes. Fluff couscous with a fork.

3. Heat a large nonstick skillet over medium-high heat. Coat pan with cooking spray. Add squash and next 4

ingredients; sauté 3 minutes or until squash is tender. Set aside.

4. Combine fontina and Parmigiano-Reggiano; set aside. Combine couscous, squash mixture, and half of cheese mixture in a large bowl; stir in remaining chicken broth, egg substitute, salt, and pepper. Spoon mixture into an 8 x 8-inch baking dish lightly coated with cooking spray. Top with remaining cheese mixture. Bake at 400° for 35 minutes or until golden. Serve warm. Yield: 6 servings (serving size: about 1½ cups).

CALORIES 161 (31% from fat); FAT 5.6g (sat 1.9g, mono 1.6g, poly 1.3g); PROTEIN 8.1g; CARB 19.9g; FIBER 2.2g; CHOL 9mg; IRON 0.8mg; SODIUM 351mg; CALC 112mg

Antipasto Salad

Jefferson acquired globe artichokes to grow at Monticello from Bernard McMahon, a noted Philadelphia nurseryman and the author of *The American Gardener's Calendar*. In addition, Jefferson was particularly fond of parsley, which is used to garnish this salad. Placing the artichokes in lemon water as they're cut minimizes discoloration. Cooking the cauliflower, squash, and carrots briefly retains the crispness of the vegetables.

 6 cups water
 ¼ cup fresh lemon juice, divided
 4 artichokes (each about 12 ounces)
 1 (7-ounce) bag whole baby carrots with tops
 3 cups small cauliflower florets
 1 (8-ounce) bag baby pattypan squash, halved
 3 tablespoons red wine vinegar
 2 tablespoons extravirgin olive oil
 1 teaspoon chopped fresh thyme
 ½ teaspoon sugar
 ½ teaspoon salt
 ½ teaspoon freshly ground black pepper
 2 garlic cloves, minced
 ½ cup vertically sliced red onion
 ⅓ cup pitted kalamata olives, halved
 ⅓ cup fresh flat-leaf parsley leaves

1. Combine water and 2 tablespoons juice in a large bowl. Cut off stem from each artichoke to within 1 inch of base;

peel stem. Remove bottom leaves and tough outer leaves, leaving tender heart and bottom. Cut lengthwise into quarters. Remove fuzzy thistle from bottom with a spoon; place in lemon water. Drain artichokes. Cook artichokes in boiling water 6 minutes or until tender. Remove from pan with a slotted spoon; plunge into a large bowl of ice water. Add carrots to pan; cook 1 minute. Add cauliflower and squash to pan; cook 1 minute or until crisp-tender. Drain and plunge into ice water with artichokes. Drain artichoke mixture well.

2. Combine 2 tablespoons juice, vinegar, and next 6 ingredients in a large bowl; stir with a whisk. Add artichoke mixture, onion, and olives; toss gently to coat. Cover and chill. Sprinkle with parsley just before serving. Yield: 8 servings (serving size: 1¼ cups).

CALORIES 117 (44% from fat); FAT 5.8g (sat 0.8g, mono 4g, poly 0.8g); PROTEIN 3.9g; CARB 15.3g; FIBER 5.7g; CHOL 0mg; IRON 1.7mg; SODIUM 360mg; CALC 62mg

Green Salad Scented with Sesame Oil

Jefferson especially enjoyed salads made with the fresh herbs and lettuces grown at Monticello. When he failed at cultivating olives, he turned to sesame plants and pressed the seeds for oil to dress his salads. Mâche is a "gourmet" green with a tangy, nut-like flavor. You can substitute arugula, spinach, or watercress.

 8 cups salad greens
 4 cups mâche
 2 cups thinly sliced Belgian endive (about 2 heads)
 1 cup orange sections
 1 cup thinly sliced radishes
 ¼ cup thinly sliced green onions
 2 tablespoons white wine vinegar
 2 tablespoons fresh orange juice
 1 tablespoon light-colored sesame oil
 ¼ teaspoon salt
 ⅛ teaspoon black pepper

1. Combine first 6 ingredients in a large bowl. Combine vinegar, juice, oil, salt, and pepper in a small bowl; stir with a whisk. Pour over salad, tossing gently to coat. Serve immediately. Yield: 6 servings (serving size: 2 cups).

CALORIES 65 (35% from fat); FAT 2.5g (sat 0.4g, mono 1g, poly 1.1g); PROTEIN 2.2g; CARB 10.1g; FIBER 3.9g; CHOL 0mg; IRON 1.4mg; SODIUM 138mg; CALC 61mg

QUICK & EASY
Cold Summer Pasta with Vegetables

Jefferson imported squash from Italy and peppers from Mexico. In Jefferson's time, tomatoes were considered an exotic new fruit—one for which he had a fondness. He discovered pasta during his diplomatic tenure in France. Noodles were fashionable there at the time, and he sketched plans for a pasta machine during a foray to Northern Italy.

- ¾ pound uncooked cavatappi
- 1 cup (1-inch) diagonally cut asparagus
- ½ cup shelled green peas
- ¼ cup olive oil, divided
- 1 cup red cherry tomatoes, halved
- 1 cup yellow cherry tomatoes, halved
- ½ cup chopped red bell pepper
- ½ cup chopped yellow bell pepper
- ½ cup chopped orange bell pepper
- ½ cup chopped yellow squash
- 1 tablespoon chopped fresh chives
- 6 tablespoons fresh lemon juice
- 1½ teaspoons salt
- ½ teaspoon freshly ground black pepper
- 3 garlic cloves, minced

1. Cook pasta according to package directions; omit salt and fat. Add asparagus and peas during last minute of cooking. Drain; rinse with cold running water. Drain well; place in a large bowl. Add 1 tablespoon oil; toss to coat. Stir in red cherry tomatoes and next 6 ingredients.
2. Combine 3 tablespoons oil, juice, salt, black pepper, and garlic in a small bowl; stir with a whisk. Pour dressing over pasta mixture, and toss well. Serve chilled or at room temperature. Yield: 6 servings (serving size: about 2 cups).

CALORIES 335 (28% from fat); FAT 10.6g (sat 1.5g, mono 6.9g, poly 1.6g); PROTEIN 13.5g; CARB 47.8g; FIBER 3g; CHOL 0mg; IRON 3.6mg; SODIUM 593mg; CALC 43mg

Creamed Collard Greens with Ham

Collards are among the hundreds of different vegetables grown at Monticello. Serve with Cornmeal Buttermilk Biscuits (recipe below).

- 1 (1-pound) bag prewashed, chopped collard greens
- 1½ cups chopped onion
- ¼ teaspoon crushed red pepper
- 2 ounces 33%-less-sodium smoked ham, chopped (½ cup)
- ¾ cup 1% low-fat milk
- ¼ cup all-purpose flour
- ½ teaspoon salt
- ¼ teaspoon freshly ground black pepper

1. Place first 4 ingredients in a large stockpot; cover with water to 1 inch above greens. Bring to a boil over medium-high heat. Uncover, reduce heat, and simmer 1½ hours. Drain greens in a colander over a bowl; reserve 2 cups liquid.
2. Combine milk and flour in pan, stirring with a whisk until blended. Stir in reserved cooking liquid, salt, and black pepper; bring to a boil over medium-high heat. Reduce heat, and simmer 3 minutes or until mixture thickens, stirring constantly. Add greens; simmer 10 minutes, stirring occasionally. Yield: 6 servings (serving size: about ¾ cup).

CALORIES 83 (15% from fat); FAT 1.4g (sat 0.5g, mono 0.4g, poly 0.3g); PROTEIN 5.3g; CARB 13.6g; FIBER 3.4g; CHOL 7mg; IRON 0.6mg; SODIUM 325mg; CALC 156mg

MAKE AHEAD
Cornmeal Buttermilk Biscuits

Serve with Creamed Collard Greens with Ham (recipe above).

- 1 cup all-purpose flour
- ½ cup cornmeal
- 1½ tablespoons sugar
- 2 teaspoons baking powder
- ½ teaspoon salt
- 3 tablespoons chilled butter, cut into small pieces
- ½ cup low-fat buttermilk

1. Preheat oven to 450°.
2. Lightly spoon flour into a dry measuring cup; level with a knife. Combine flour, cornmeal, sugar, baking powder, and salt in a medium bowl; cut in butter with a pastry blender or 2 knives until mixture resembles coarse meal. Add buttermilk; stir just until moist.
3. Turn dough out onto a lightly floured surface. Pat dough into an 8 x 4-inch rectangle. Cut dough by making 1 lengthwise cut and 3 crosswise cuts to form 8 biscuits. Place biscuits, 1 inch apart, on an ungreased baking sheet.
4. Bake at 450° for 12 minutes or until golden. Serve biscuits warm or at room temperature. Yield: 8 servings (serving size: 1 biscuit).

CALORIES 136 (30% from fat); FAT 4.5g (sat 2.3g, mono 1.8g, poly 0.2g); PROTEIN 2.8g; CARB 20.9g; FIBER 1g; CHOL 12mg; IRON 1.2mg; SODIUM 316mg; CALC 87mg

MAKE AHEAD
Grape-Black Cumin Flatbread

Jefferson cultivated table grapes at Monticello, as well as black cumin seeds (seeds from a plant known in Jefferson's time as Nutmeg Plant). Black cumin seeds have a stronger, more peppery flavor than the more common amber variety and are a delicious foil for the sweet grapes. Omit them if you wish, and substitute poppy seeds, caraway seeds, or dried onion flakes. Sesame seeds are another option—and another crop Jefferson cultivated.

- 1 package dry yeast (about 2¼ teaspoons)
- 1¼ cups warm water (100° to 110°)
- 3¼ cups all-purpose flour, divided
- 2 tablespoons sugar
- ½ cup plus 1 teaspoon stone-ground cornmeal, divided
- 2 tablespoons olive oil, divided
- ¾ teaspoon black cumin seeds, divided
- 1 teaspoon salt
- Cooking spray
- 1 cup red grape halves, divided
- ¼ teaspoon kosher salt

Continued

1. Dissolve yeast in warm water in a large bowl; let stand 5 minutes. Lightly spoon flour into dry measuring cups; level with a knife. Add 2 cups flour and sugar to yeast mixture; stir until well combined. Cover and let stand at room temperature 1 hour to form a sponge (mixture will rise and bubble slightly).

2. Add 1 cup flour, ½ cup cornmeal, 1 tablespoon olive oil, ¼ teaspoon black cumin seeds, and 1 teaspoon salt to sponge; stir until a soft dough forms. Turn dough out onto a floured surface. Knead until smooth and elastic (about 8 minutes); add enough of remaining flour, 1 tablespoon at a time, to prevent dough from sticking to hands.

3. Place dough in a large bowl coated with cooking spray, turning to coat top. Cover and let rise in a warm place (85°), free from drafts, 1 hour or until doubled in size. (Gently press two fingers into dough. If indentation remains, dough has risen enough.) Punch dough down; cover and let rest 5 minutes. Turn dough out onto a lightly floured surface; gently knead in ⅔ cup grape halves. Cover dough with plastic wrap, and let rest 10 minutes.

4. Transfer dough onto a baking sheet sprinkled with remaining 1 teaspoon cornmeal. Pat dough into a 14 x 10-inch rectangle; brush with remaining 1 tablespoon olive oil. Cover and let rise 30 minutes or until doubled in size. (Gently press two fingers into dough. If indentation remains, dough has risen enough.)

5. Preheat oven to 475°.

6. Uncover dough, and sprinkle with remaining ½ teaspoon cumin seeds and kosher salt. Sprinkle remaining ⅓ cup grape halves over dough; gently press into dough.

7. Bake at 475° for 15 minutes or until lightly browned. Loosen bread from pan with a thin spatula. Serve warm or at room temperature. Yield: 12 servings (serving size: 1 piece).

CALORIES 184 (14% from fat); FAT 2.9g (sat 0.4g, mono 1.8g, poly 0.5g); PROTEIN 4.3g; CARB 35.2g; FIBER 1.6g; CHOL 0mg; IRON 2mg; SODIUM 240mg; CALC 9mg

. . . And Ready in Just About 20 Minutes

More than a week's worth of quick entrées gets you in and out of the kitchen in a flash.

QUICK & EASY
Seared Mediterranean Tuna Steaks

Coriander has a lemon-sage flavor that complements the tuna and the fresh tomato sauce. Serve with a side of refrigerated potato wedges, roasted according to package instructions.

    4   (6-ounce) Yellowfin tuna steaks
        (about ¾ inch thick)
    ½   teaspoon salt, divided
    ½   teaspoon ground coriander
    ⅛   teaspoon black pepper
        Cooking spray
   1½   cups chopped seeded tomato
    ¼   cup chopped green onions
    3   tablespoons chopped fresh parsley
    1   tablespoon capers, drained
    1   tablespoon extravirgin olive oil
    1   tablespoon lemon juice
    ½   teaspoon bottled minced garlic
   12   chopped pitted kalamata olives

1. Heat a large nonstick skillet over medium-high heat. Sprinkle fish with ¼ teaspoon salt, coriander, and pepper. Coat pan with cooking spray. Add fish to pan; cook 4 minutes on each side or until desired degree of doneness.

2. While fish cooks, combine ¼ teaspoon salt, tomato, and next 7 ingredients. Serve tomato mixture over fish. Yield: 4 servings (serving size: 1 tuna steak and ⅔ cup tomato mixture).

CALORIES 268 (28% from fat); FAT 8.4g (sat 1.3g, mono 5.3g, poly 1.2g); PROTEIN 40.9g; CARB 5.8g; FIBER 1.4g; CHOL 77mg; IRON 2mg; SODIUM 610mg; CALC 48mg

Southeast Asian Supper Menu

serves 4

Quick-cooked vegetables offer a crunchy counterpoint to the creamy entrée. Bold ingredients boost the flavor while keeping prep time to a minimum.

Pork Strips with Peanut Sauce and Rice Noodles

Sugar snap pea and carrot sauté*

Coconut sorbet

*Heat a large nonstick skillet over medium-high heat. Coat pan with cooking spray. Add 2 cups sugar snap peas and 1 cup diagonally cut carrot; sauté 3 minutes or until crisp-tender. Remove from heat; stir in 1 tablespoon low-sodium soy sauce, 1 teaspoon rice vinegar, and 1 teaspoon dark sesame oil.

QUICK & EASY
Pork Strips with Peanut Sauce and Rice Noodles

Rice noodles soak up liquid quickly, so if you're not serving immediately, reserve about ¼ cup cooked sauce, and add to remaining pork mixture just before serving, tossing gently.

    ½   cup boiling water
    ¼   cup reduced-fat peanut butter
    2   tablespoons rice vinegar
    2   tablespoons low-sodium soy sauce
    2   teaspoons fresh lime juice
    1   teaspoon bottled minced garlic
    1   teaspoon bottled ground fresh
        ginger (such as Spice World)
    1   teaspoon sesame oil
    1   teaspoon chile paste with garlic
        (such as Sambal oelek)
    1   teaspoon honey
    ½   teaspoon cornstarch
        Cooking spray
    4   (4-ounce) boneless loin pork
        chops, trimmed and cut into
        ½-inch strips
    1   red bell pepper, seeded and thinly
        sliced (about 2 cups)
    1   (6-ounce) package rice noodles
    ½   cup thinly sliced green onions
        Lime wedges (optional)

1. Combine first 11 ingredients in a bowl, stirring with a whisk; set aside.

2. Heat a large nonstick skillet over medium-high heat. Coat pan with cooking spray. Add pork and pepper; cook 6 minutes or until pork is done. Add peanut butter mixture to pan, stirring well to coat pork; bring to a boil. Reduce heat, and simmer 1 minute.

3. Cook rice noodles according to package directions, omitting salt and fat; drain. Add noodles to pork mixture, tossing gently. Sprinkle with onions. Serve with lime wedges, if desired. Yield: 4 servings (serving size: 2 cups pork mixture and 2 tablespoons onions).

CALORIES 461 (31% from fat); FAT 15.8g (sat 4g, mono 4.1g, poly 1.7g); PROTEIN 29.6g; CARB 49.9g; FIBER 2.3g; CHOL 73mg; IRON 2mg; SODIUM 563mg; CALC 28mg

Cajun Salmon Cakes with Lemon-Garlic Aïoli

Boneless, canned, or foil-packed cooked salmon makes this an easy entrée. Serve with steamed broccoli and oven-baked fries.

AÏOLI:
- 2 tablespoons fat-free mayonnaise
- 2 teaspoons fresh lemon juice
- ¼ teaspoon bottled minced garlic

CAKES:
- 3 (6-ounce) cans skinless, boneless pink salmon in water, drained
- ¼ cup sliced green onions
- ¼ cup fat-free mayonnaise
- 2 tablespoons dry breadcrumbs
- 2 teaspoons Dijon mustard
- 1 teaspoon Cajun seasoning blend
- ½ cup dry breadcrumbs
- 1 tablespoon canola oil

1. To prepare aïoli, combine first 3 ingredients in a small bowl; set aside.

2. To prepare cakes, combine salmon and next 5 ingredients in a medium bowl. Divide salmon mixture into 8 equal portions, shaping each portion into a ½-inch-thick patty. Dredge patties in ½ cup breadcrumbs.

3. Heat oil in a large nonstick skillet over medium-high heat. Place patties in pan; cook 3 minutes on each side or until lightly browned and heated through. Serve aïoli over salmon. Yield: 4 servings (serving size: 2 patties and about 1½ teaspoons aïoli).

CALORIES 254 (32% from fat); FAT 9.1g (sat 0.6g, mono 2.6g, poly 1.3g); PROTEIN 29g; CARB 16.3g; FIBER 1.1g; CHOL 78mg; IRON 1.9mg; SODIUM 924mg; CALC 46mg

Open-Faced Steak, Pear, and Gorgonzola Sandwiches

Sharp Gorgonzola cheese, sweet pears, and savory seared flank steak make a scrumptious combination. For added convenience in making this open-faced sandwich, purchase presliced onions and prewashed bagged salad greens.

- Cooking spray
- 1 pound flank steak, trimmed
- ½ teaspoon salt
- ½ teaspoon freshly ground black pepper
- 1 cup thinly sliced red onion, separated into rings (about ½ onion)
- 2 small Bartlett pears
- 3 tablespoons bottled lemon juice, divided
- 2 tablespoons white wine vinegar
- 1 tablespoon water
- 1 teaspoon olive oil
- 1 teaspoon bottled minced garlic
- 6 cups prewashed gourmet salad greens
- ¼ cup (1 ounce) crumbled Gorgonzola cheese
- 6 (2.8-ounce) Mediterranean-style white flatbread (such as Toufayan)

1. Heat a large cast-iron skillet over medium-high heat. Coat pan with cooking spray. Sprinkle both sides of steak with salt and pepper. Add steak to pan; cook 6 minutes. Turn steak; add onion to pan. Lightly coat onion with cooking spray. Cook steak 6 minutes or until desired degree of doneness, stirring onion frequently. Transfer steak to a cutting board. Cook onion 2 minutes or until tender and lightly browned. Remove pan from heat.

2. Core pears; cut into thin slices. Place pears in a large bowl. Drizzle pears with 2 tablespoons lemon juice; toss well to coat. Combine 1 tablespoon lemon juice, vinegar, water, oil, and garlic in a small bowl; stir well with a whisk. Add salad greens and cheese to pear mixture. Drizzle with oil mixture; toss to coat.

3. Cut steak diagonally into thin slices. Top each flatbread with about 7 slices (about 2 ounces) steak, about 1 tablespoon onions, and about 1⅓ cups salad mixture. Yield: 6 servings (serving size: 1 sandwich).

CALORIES 397 (21% from fat); FAT 9.4g (sat 3.3g, mono 3.7g, poly 1g); PROTEIN 26.7g; CARB 54.2g; FIBER 11.4g; CHOL 31mg; IRON 4.6mg; SODIUM 435mg; CALC 145mg

Apricot Pork Chops

Peach preserves or orange marmalade can be used instead of apricot preserves. Serve these tangy chops with a dressed baked potato and sugar snap peas.

- Cooking spray
- 4 (4-ounce) boneless loin pork chops
- ¼ cup chopped onion
- ¼ cup apricot preserves
- 1 tablespoon low-sodium soy sauce
- 2 teaspoons bottled minced garlic
- ¼ teaspoon salt
- ¼ cup sliced green onions

1. Heat a large nonstick skillet over medium-high heat. Coat pan with cooking spray. Add pork to pan; cook 6 minutes on each side or until done. Remove from pan; keep warm.

2. Add chopped onion to pan; sauté 4 minutes or until lightly browned. Stir in preserves, soy sauce, garlic, and salt; cook 3 minutes or until thickened. Add pork to pan, turning to coat. Sprinkle evenly with green onions. Yield: 4 servings (serving size: 1 pork chop and 1 tablespoon sauce).

CALORIES 231 (32% from fat); FAT 8.3g (sat 2.5g, mono 3.6g, poly 1.2g); PROTEIN 23.9g; CARB 15.2g; FIBER 0.5g; CHOL 73mg; IRON 1.2mg; SODIUM 345mg; CALC 24mg

Pesto Tortellini and Zucchini Salad

Serve this fragrant, colorful salad with warm whole wheat rolls and precut fresh cantaloupe or honeydew melon. Look for fresh tortellini in the refrigerated section of your supermarket. You can substitute yellow squash for zucchini.

    2 (9-ounce) packages fresh
        three-cheese tortellini
  Cooking spray
    2 teaspoons bottled minced garlic
    4 cups zucchini, halved and thinly
        sliced (about 2 zucchini)
    2 cups chopped plum tomato (about
        4 tomatoes)
    3 tablespoons prepared pesto
   ½ teaspoon salt
   ¼ teaspoon freshly ground black
        pepper
    2 tablespoons shredded Parmesan
        cheese

1. Cook pasta according to package directions, omitting salt and fat; drain, reserving ¼ cup cooking liquid.
2. While pasta cooks, heat a large non-stick skillet over medium-high heat. Coat pan with cooking spray. Add garlic and zucchini, and sauté 5 minutes or until zucchini is tender. Combine pasta, zucchini mixture, and tomato in a large bowl, tossing gently.
3. Combine reserved ¼ cup cooking liquid, pesto, salt, and pepper in a small bowl. Drizzle over pasta, tossing gently to coat. Sprinkle with cheese. Yield: 6 servings (serving size: about 2 cups pasta mixture and 1 teaspoon cheese).

CALORIES 336 (30% from fat); FAT 11.2g (sat 4.4g, mono 4.4g, poly 1g); PROTEIN 14.9g; CARB 45.9g; FIBER 3.3g; CHOL 39mg; IRON 2.1mg; SODIUM 586mg; CALC 220mg

Spinach and Cheese-Stuffed Portobello Caps

Serve these Italian-style mushroom caps with crusty bread and salad tossed with a zesty vinaigrette. To serve four, simply double the recipe. Squeeze excess liquid from spinach before adding to filling.

    4 large portobello caps
  Cooking spray
   ¼ teaspoon salt, divided
    1 cup fat-free ricotta cheese
   ¼ teaspoon garlic powder
   ¼ teaspoon ground black pepper
   ½ (10-ounce) package frozen
        chopped spinach, thawed and
        drained thoroughly
   ⅓ cup chopped bottled roasted red
        bell peppers
   ¾ cup tomato sauce
   ½ cup (2 ounces) shredded part-
        skim mozzarella cheese
   ½ teaspoon dried oregano

1. Preheat oven to 400°.
2. Remove brown gills from undersides of mushrooms using a spoon; discard gills. Place mushrooms, stem sides up, on a baking sheet coated with cooking spray. Sprinkle with ⅛ teaspoon salt. Bake at 400° for 5 minutes.
3. While mushrooms bake, combine ricotta, garlic powder, black pepper, and ⅛ teaspoon salt in a medium bowl, stirring well. Gently stir in spinach and bell pepper. Divide mixture evenly among mushroom caps. Top evenly with tomato sauce and mozzarella cheese. Sprinkle evenly with oregano. Bake at 400° for 8 minutes. Increase oven temperature to broil. Broil 1½ minutes or until cheese is melted. Yield: 2 servings (serving size: 2 mushroom caps).

CALORIES 305 (22% from fat); FAT 6.9g (sat 4.1g, mono 0g, poly 0.1g); PROTEIN 22.9g; CARB 31.6g; FIBER 6.2g; CHOL 42mg; IRON 2.8mg; SODIUM 949mg; CALC 466mg

Smoked Mozzarella, Spinach, and Pepper Omelet Sandwiches

Serve with fresh fruit salad drizzled with berry or vanilla yogurt.

    2 tablespoons fat-free milk
   ¼ teaspoon salt
   ¼ teaspoon freshly ground black
        pepper
    6 large egg whites
    3 large eggs
  Dash of hot pepper sauce
  Cooking spray
    1 cup finely diced red bell pepper
   ¾ cup chopped onion
    4 sourdough English muffins, split
   ½ cup (2 ounces) shredded smoked
        mozzarella cheese
  1½ cups bagged baby spinach leaves

1. Preheat broiler.
2. Combine first 6 ingredients in a large bowl, stirring with a whisk; set aside.
3. Heat a large nonstick skillet over medium-high heat. Coat pan with cooking spray. Add bell pepper and onion; sauté 4 minutes or until tender. Reduce heat to medium. Pour egg mixture into pan; let egg mixture set slightly. Tilt pan; carefully lift edges of omelet with a spatula to allow uncooked portion to flow underneath cooked portion. Cook 3 minutes. Wrap handle of pan with foil; place pan under broiler. Broil 1 minute or until set and lightly browned.
4. Arrange muffin halves in a single layer on a baking sheet. Sprinkle muffin halves evenly with cheese, and broil 1 minute or until cheese begins to brown.
5. Divide omelet into 4 portions; place 1 portion on bottom half of each muffin. Top evenly with spinach leaves; top with remaining muffin halves. Yield: 4 servings (serving size: 1 sandwich).

CALORIES 295 (28% from fat); FAT 9g (sat 3.6g, mono 1.6g, poly 1.1g); PROTEIN 19g; CARB 33.8g; FIBER 2.4g; CHOL 168mg; IRON 2.7mg; SODIUM 686mg; CALC 173mg

Spicy Shrimp in Coconut Sauce

Serve this dish with fresh mango and pineapple cubes. Add more or less crushed red pepper to make it as spicy as you like.

- ½   cup light coconut milk
- 1   tablespoon fresh lime juice
- 1   teaspoon bottled minced ginger
- 1   teaspoon low-sodium soy sauce
- 1   teaspoon honey
- ½   teaspoon cornstarch
- ½   teaspoon chile paste with garlic (such as Sambal oelek)
- ½   teaspoon bottled minced garlic
- ¼   teaspoon salt
- 2   teaspoons canola oil
- 1½ pounds large shrimp, peeled and deveined
- 2   tablespoons chopped green onions (about 1 onion)
- ½   teaspoon crushed red pepper
- 2   cups hot cooked jasmine rice

1. Combine first 9 ingredients in a medium bowl; set aside.
2. Heat oil in a large nonstick skillet over medium-high heat. Add shrimp, and sauté 2 minutes. Add green onions and red pepper; cook 1 minute. Add coconut milk mixture to pan; bring to a boil. Reduce heat, and simmer 1 minute or until shrimp turn pink. Serve immediately with rice. Yield: 4 servings (serving size: about 1 cup shrimp mixture and ½ cup rice).

CALORIES 310 (20% from fat); FAT 7g (sat 2.2g, mono 1.9g, poly 1.9g); PROTEIN 36.8g; CARB 23.2g; FIBER 0.7g; CHOL 259mg; IRON 4.8mg; SODIUM 513mg; CALC 97mg

Crisp Lemon-Pepper Catfish

This recipe is versatile—just change the spice mixture to create a different flavor. Use Cajun seasoning, Greek seasoning, or your favorite spice blend instead of lemon pepper. Serve with herbed rice and steamed asparagus.

- Cooking spray
- 4   (6-ounce) catfish fillets
- 2   teaspoons fresh lemon juice
- ½   cup panko (Japanese) breadcrumbs
- 2   tablespoons all-purpose flour
- 2   teaspoons lemon pepper seasoning
- ¼   teaspoon salt

1. Preheat broiler.
2. Cover a baking sheet with foil; coat with cooking spray. Set aside.
3. Coat both sides of fish with cooking spray; drizzle with lemon juice. Combine breadcrumbs, flour, seasoning, and salt in a shallow dish. Dredge fish in breadcrumb mixture.
4. Place fish on prepared baking sheet; broil 10 minutes or until fish flakes easily when tested with a fork or until desired degree of doneness. Yield: 4 servings (serving size: 1 fillet).

CALORIES 303 (43% from fat); FAT 14.4g (sat 3g, mono 6.5g, poly 3.1g); PROTEIN 28.2g; CARB 13.5g; FIBER 0.5g; CHOL 80mg; IRON 1.1mg; SODIUM 508mg; CALC 20mg

California Crab Wraps

Canned lump crabmeat is a budget-friendly way to enjoy this meal any night of the week.

- 1½ cups diced plum tomato (about 3 tomatoes)
- ½   cup chopped red onion
- ½   cup diced avocado (about ½ avocado)
- 1   tablespoon fresh lime juice
- ½   teaspoon ground cumin
- ¼   teaspoon salt
- ⅛   teaspoon black pepper
- 1¼ cups canned lump crabmeat (such as Chicken of the Sea)
- ½   cup (4 ounces) ⅓-less-fat cream cheese
- ¼   cup chopped fresh cilantro
- 4   (10-inch) whole wheat flour tortillas
- 4   romaine lettuce leaves, trimmed

1. Combine first 7 ingredients in a small bowl; set aside.
2. Combine crabmeat, cream cheese, and cilantro in a small bowl; spread evenly down centers of tortillas. Place 1 lettuce leaf over crabmeat mixture. Spoon tomato mixture evenly over lettuce, and roll up. Yield: 4 servings (serving size: 1 wrap).

CALORIES 312 (29% from fat); FAT 11.7g (sat 0.9g, mono 2.7g, poly 1.1g); PROTEIN 18.5g; CARB 44.8g; FIBER 6g; CHOL 58mg; IRON 2.5mg; SODIUM 602mg; CALC 100mg

Black Bean, Corn, and Shrimp Salad

Serve this salad with toasted pita wedges.

- 1   tablespoon chili powder
- ½   teaspoon garlic salt
- ½   teaspoon ground cumin
- 1½ pounds medium shrimp, peeled and deveined
- Cooking spray
- 2   tablespoons fresh lime juice, divided
- 1½ cups frozen whole-kernel corn, thawed
- ¾   cup bottled salsa
- ¼   cup chopped fresh cilantro
- 1   (15-ounce) can black beans, rinsed and drained

1. Heat a large nonstick skillet over medium-high heat.
2. Combine first 3 ingredients in a large bowl. Add shrimp; toss to coat.
3. Coat pan with cooking spray. Add shrimp; sauté 3 minutes or until done. Add 1 tablespoon lime juice. Remove shrimp from pan. Add corn to pan; sauté 1 minute. Stir in salsa, cilantro, and beans; cook 30 seconds or until thoroughly heated. Stir in 1 tablespoon lime juice. Serve shrimp over bean mixture. Yield: 4 servings (serving size: ⅓ cup shrimp and about ⅔ cup bean mixture).

CALORIES 354 (12% from fat); FAT 4.8g (sat 0.7g, mono 0.7g, poly 2.4g); PROTEIN 43.3g; CARB 34.9g; FIBER 9.1g; CHOL 259mg; IRON 7.6mg; SODIUM 827mg; CALC 148mg

Grill Once, Eat Twice

Prepare a flank steak entrée to enjoy for dinner—and have the makings for lunch the next day.

QUICK & EASY • MAKE AHEAD
Basic Grilled Flank Steak

An easy marinade gives this steak a robust flavor—yet the seasonings are subtle enough that leftovers work in a variety of applications. Embellish with a cilantro sprig garnish.

- 1 (2-pound) flank steak, trimmed
- 2 teaspoons Worcestershire sauce
- ½ teaspoon sea salt
- ½ teaspoon freshly ground black pepper
- Cooking spray

1. Place steak in an 11 x 7-inch baking dish. Sprinkle both sides with Worcestershire sauce, salt, and pepper; rub mixture into steak. Cover and refrigerate at least 20 minutes.
2. Prepare grill.
3. Place steak on grill rack coated with cooking spray; grill 8 minutes on each side or until desired degree of doneness. Place on a cutting board; cover loosely with foil. Let stand 10 minutes. Cut steak diagonally across grain into thin slices. Yield: 8 servings (serving size: 3 ounces).

CALORIES 158 (38% from fat); FAT 6.7g (sat 2.8g, mono 2.7g, poly 0.3g); PROTEIN 22.6g; CARB 0.4g; FIBER 0g; CHOL 45mg; IRON 1.6mg; SODIUM 203mg; CALC 14mg

MAKE AHEAD
Southwestern Steak, Corn, and Black Bean Wraps

You can use fresh corn in place of frozen; if it's fresh enough, it doesn't need to be cooked. To keep the wraps from getting soggy in the refrigerator, dole out the corn mixture with a slotted spoon. Try this with flavored tortillas to suit your taste.

- 1 cup frozen whole-kernel corn, thawed
- ½ cup chopped fresh cilantro
- 2 tablespoons minced red onion
- 2 tablespoons fresh lime juice
- 1 tablespoon extravirgin olive oil
- ½ teaspoon ground cumin
- ⅛ teaspoon salt
- ⅛ teaspoon freshly ground black pepper
- 1 (15-ounce) can black beans, rinsed and drained
- 2¼ cups chopped Basic Grilled Flank Steak (about 9 ounces) (recipe at left)
- 6 (8-inch) fat-free flour tortillas
- ¾ cup (3 ounces) shredded Monterey Jack cheese with jalapeño peppers

1. Combine first 9 ingredients; stir well.
2. Arrange about ⅓ cup Basic Grilled Flank Steak down center of each tortilla. Top each tortilla with about ⅓ cup corn mixture and 2 tablespoons cheese; roll up. Wrap sandwiches in aluminum foil or wax paper, and chill. Yield: 6 servings (serving size: 1 wrap).

CALORIES 327 (29% from fat); FAT 10.4g (sat 4.7g, mono 4.3g, poly 0.7g); PROTEIN 21g; CARB 39.8g; FIBER 4.6g; CHOL 37mg; IRON 3mg; SODIUM 796mg; CALC 131mg

MAKE AHEAD
Steak Salad Wraps with Horseradish Sauce

Look for the flatbreads near the deli counter in your supermarket; they're larger than pitas and thicker than tortillas, so they hold up well in this saucy wrap.

- ½ cup plain low-fat yogurt
- 1 tablespoon prepared horseradish
- 3 cups thinly sliced Basic Grilled Flank Steak (about 12 ounces) (recipe at left)
- 4 (2.8-ounce) whole wheat flatbreads (such as Flatout)
- 1 cup chopped romaine lettuce
- 1 cup halved cherry tomatoes
- 1 cup diced cucumber

1. Combine yogurt and horseradish, stirring with a whisk.
2. Arrange ¾ cup Basic Grilled Flank Steak on each flatbread. Top each flatbread with ¼ cup lettuce, ¼ cup tomatoes, and ¼ cup cucumber. Spoon 2 tablespoons yogurt mixture over each serving; roll up. Wrap in aluminum foil or wax paper; chill. Yield: 4 servings (serving size: 1 wrap).

CALORIES 414 (25% from fat); FAT 11.5g (sat 3.1g, mono 4.5g, poly 1.9g); PROTEIN 34.9g; CARB 41.9g; FIBER 5.1g; CHOL 46mg; IRON 3.8mg; SODIUM 722mg; CALC 104mg

MAKE AHEAD
Steak, Sun-Dried Tomato, and Mozzarella Couscous Salad

Gently heating the garlic in olive oil infuses the oil with flavor and cooks the garlic enough to keep the dressing mellow.

- 2 teaspoons extravirgin olive oil
- 2 garlic cloves, minced
- 2½ cups water
- 1 cup uncooked couscous
- ½ cup chopped sun-dried tomatoes, packed without oil (about 1 ounce)
- 1½ cups chopped Basic Grilled Flank Steak (about 6 ounces) (recipe at left)
- ½ cup (2 ounces) cubed part-skim mozzarella cheese
- ½ cup chopped drained bottled roasted red bell peppers
- ¼ cup chopped fresh basil
- 2 tablespoons red wine vinegar
- ¼ teaspoon salt
- ¼ teaspoon freshly ground black pepper

1. Combine oil and garlic in a small non-stick skillet; cook over medium-low heat 2 minutes or just until fragrant. Remove from heat; set aside.

2. Bring 2½ cups water to a boil in a medium saucepan. Add couscous and tomatoes; reduce heat to medium, and cook 5 minutes or until water is absorbed. Remove from heat; fluff with a fork. Spoon couscous mixture into a large bowl. Add Basic Grilled Flank Steak, cheese, roasted peppers, and basil; toss well to combine.

3. Combine garlic mixture, vinegar, salt, and black pepper, stirring with a whisk. Drizzle dressing over couscous mixture; toss gently to coat. Cover and chill. Yield: 4 servings (serving size: about 1 cup).

CALORIES 332 (25% from fat); FAT 9.1g (sat 3.6g, mono 3.9g, poly 0.7g); PROTEIN 21.9g; CARB 39.8g; FIBER 3.3g; CHOL 30mg; IRON 2.3mg; SODIUM 548mg; CALC 139mg

MAKE AHEAD

Mixed Bean Salad with Flank Steak

A colorful trio of beans enlivens this fiber- and iron-rich main-dish salad. Look for pink beans on the Latin foods aisle of your supermarket; if you can't find them, substitute light kidney beans.

2   cups (1-inch) cut green beans (about ½ pound)
1½ cups chopped Basic Grilled Flank Steak (about 6 ounces) (recipe on page 248)
1½ tablespoons minced shallots (about 1 small)
1   (15-ounce) can pink beans, rinsed and drained
1   (15-ounce) can black soybeans, rinsed and drained
3   tablespoons red wine vinegar
1   tablespoon extravirgin olive oil
¼   teaspoon salt
¼   teaspoon dried oregano
¼   teaspoon freshly ground black pepper

1. Steam green beans 5 minutes or until crisp-tender; drain. Place green beans in a large bowl. Add Basic Grilled Flank Steak, shallots, pink beans, and soybeans; toss to combine.

2. Combine vinegar and next 4 ingredients, stirring with a whisk. Drizzle over bean mixture; toss gently to coat. Cover and chill. Yield: 4 servings (serving size: 1½ cups).

CALORIES 355 (30% from fat); FAT 11.8g (sat 2.6g, mono 5.2g, poly 3.3g); PROTEIN 28.6g; CARB 35.9g; FIBER 8.5g; CHOL 22mg; IRON 7.1mg; SODIUM 548mg; CALC 141mg

MAKE AHEAD

Beef, Orange, and Gorgonzola Sandwiches

Grilled flank steak with oranges and blue cheese combine in a sandwich that will make you the envy of coworkers when you open your lunch box. For the best results, use crusty rolls because they stay pleasantly crisp.

2   tablespoons cider vinegar
1½ teaspoons extravirgin olive oil
½   teaspoon grated orange rind
⅛   teaspoon salt
⅛   teaspoon freshly ground black pepper
1   cup fresh orange sections (about 2 oranges)
4   (2-ounce) Italian or French rolls
2   cups thinly sliced Basic Grilled Flank Steak (about 8 ounces) (recipe on page 248)
1   cup bagged prewashed baby spinach
¼   cup (1 ounce) crumbled Gorgonzola or other blue cheese

1. Combine first 5 ingredients, stirring with a whisk.

2. Pat orange sections dry with a paper towel. Cut each roll in half horizontally. Layer bottom of each roll with ½ cup Basic Grilled Flank Steak, ¼ cup spinach, 1 tablespoon cheese, and ¼ cup orange sections. Drizzle each serving with about 2 teaspoons vinaigrette; top with top halves of rolls. Wrap in aluminum foil or wax paper; chill. Yield: 4 servings (serving size: 1 sandwich).

CALORIES 318 (29% from fat); FAT 10.2g (sat 4.6g, mono 3.7g, poly 0.5g); PROTEIN 21.6g; CARB 34.7g; FIBER 2.4g; CHOL 36mg; IRON 3.5mg; SODIUM 533mg; CALC 148mg

MAKE AHEAD

Soba-Edamame Salad with Flank Steak

You can substitute whole wheat spaghetti for soba, if desired.

2   quarts water
12   ounces uncooked soba (buckwheat noodles)
2   cups frozen shelled edamame (green soybeans), thawed
2   cups thinly sliced Basic Grilled Flank Steak (about 8 ounces) (recipe on page 248)
1   cup (2-inch) julienne-cut red bell pepper
1   cup shredded carrot
1   cup (1-inch) slices green onions
¼   cup rice vinegar
2   tablespoons canola oil
1   tablespoon low-sodium soy sauce
2   teaspoons grated peeled fresh ginger
1   teaspoon chili garlic sauce (such as Lee Kum Kee)
¼   teaspoon salt

1. Bring 2 quarts water to a boil in a large saucepan. Add soba; cook 4 minutes. Add edamame; cook 2 minutes or until soba is done. Drain and rinse with cold water; drain. Place soba mixture in a large bowl. Add Basic Grilled Flank Steak, bell pepper, carrot, and onions; toss well to combine.

2. Combine vinegar and next 5 ingredients, stirring with a whisk. Drizzle over soba mixture; toss gently to coat. Cover and chill. Yield: 6 servings (serving size: 1⅓ cups).

CALORIES 389 (25% from fat); FAT 10.8g (sat 1.6g, mono 4.2g, poly 2.4g); PROTEIN 22.8g; CARB 48.3g; FIBER 5.4g; CHOL 20mg; IRON 4.5mg; SODIUM 417mg; CALC 60mg

Peppery Beef and Two-Potato Salad

Double the potato mixture, and use half to accompany the Basic Grilled Flank Steak (recipe on page 248). Refrigerate leftovers to use in this salad. If you prefer less of a bite, reduce the amount of red and black pepper by half.

- 4 cups (1-inch) cubed sweet potatoes (about 1 pound)
- 3 cups (1-inch) cubed small red potatoes (about 1 pound)
- 2 tablespoons olive oil, divided
- ½ teaspoon salt, divided
- Cooking spray
- 2 cups chopped Basic Grilled Flank Steak (about 8 ounces) (recipe on page 248)
- 1 cup thinly sliced green onions
- 3 tablespoons fresh lemon juice
- ¼ teaspoon ground red pepper
- ¼ teaspoon freshly ground black pepper

1. Preheat oven to 450°.
2. Combine potatoes, 1 tablespoon oil, and ¼ teaspoon salt on a baking sheet coated with cooking spray; toss well to coat. Bake at 450° for 30 minutes or until tender. Place potatoes in a large bowl. Add Basic Grilled Flank Steak and onions; toss to combine.
3. Combine 1 tablespoon oil, ¼ teaspoon salt, juice, and peppers, stirring with a whisk. Drizzle over potato mixture; toss gently to coat. Cover and chill. Yield: 4 servings (serving size: 2 cups).

CALORIES 346 (30% from fat); FAT 11.5g (sat 2.8g, mono 6.8g, poly 0.9g); PROTEIN 19g; CARB 41.1g; FIBER 6.5g; CHOL 30mg; IRON 2.7mg; SODIUM 458mg; CALC 56mg

Lentil and Orzo Salad with Flank Steak and Feta

While small green lentils are prettiest, you can also use brown lentils in this filling Greek-inspired salad.

- 1 cup dried petite green lentils
- 1¼ cups uncooked orzo (about 8 ounces rice-shaped pasta)
- 1½ cups chopped Basic Grilled Flank Steak (about 6 ounces) (recipe on page 248)
- ¾ cup (3 ounces) crumbled feta cheese
- ½ cup chopped fresh basil
- ¼ cup chopped pitted kalamata olives
- 1 tablespoon chopped fresh oregano
- ¼ cup white balsamic vinegar
- 2 tablespoons extravirgin olive oil
- ½ teaspoon salt
- ¼ teaspoon freshly ground black pepper
- 2 garlic cloves, minced

1. Place lentils in a medium saucepan, and cover with water to 2 inches above lentils. Bring to a boil. Cover, reduce heat, and simmer 20 minutes or until tender. Drain and rinse with cold water; drain. Place lentils in a large bowl.
2. Cook pasta according to package directions, omitting salt and fat. Drain and rinse with cold water; drain. Add pasta, Basic Grilled Flank Steak, cheese, basil, olives, and oregano to lentils; toss well to combine.
3. Combine vinegar and next 4 ingredients, stirring with a whisk. Drizzle over pasta mixture; toss gently to coat. Cover and chill. Yield: 6 servings (serving size: about 1⅓ cups).

CALORIES 391 (27% from fat); FAT 11.6g (sat 4g, mono 5.8g, poly 0.8g); PROTEIN 22.3g; CARB 49.5g; FIBER 6.1g; CHOL 27mg; IRON 3.9mg; SODIUM 515mg; CALC 124mg

season's best

Stone Fruit Salad with Toasted Almonds

This salad is inspired by the abundance of summer's plums, peaches, nectarines, apricots, and cherries.

Stone Fruit Salad with Toasted Almonds

- 1 cup riesling or other sweet white wine
- 1 tablespoon white wine vinegar
- 1 tablespoon almond oil
- ¼ teaspoon salt
- ⅛ teaspoon black pepper
- 8 cups mixed salad greens
- 3 plums, sliced
- 2 peaches, peeled and sliced
- 2 nectarines, peeled and sliced
- 2 apricots, peeled and sliced
- ¾ cup pitted fresh cherries, halved
- ¼ cup (2 ounces) crumbled goat cheese
- 2 tablespoons sliced almonds, toasted

1. Heat wine in a medium saucepan over medium-high heat until reduced to 2 tablespoons (about 10 minutes). Remove from heat, and stir in vinegar, oil, salt, and pepper.
2. To serve salad, toss salad greens and fruit with dressing. Sprinkle with cheese and almonds. Serve immediately. Yield: 6 servings (serving size: 1¼ cups salad, 2 teaspoons cheese, and 1 teaspoon almonds).

CALORIES 146 (39% from fat); FAT 6.8g (sat 2.3g, mono 2.9g, poly 0.8g); PROTEIN 4.2g; CARB 19.6g; FIBER 3g; CHOL 7mg; IRON 0.8mg; SODIUM 152mg; CALC 51mg

Cool and Creamy

These frosty, easy-to-assemble ice cream and yogurt pies are welcome summertime desserts.

Malt Shop Ice Cream Pie

Think of this no-cook pie as a deconstructed hot fudge sundae in an ice-cream cone—crushed cones form the crust cradling the malt-flavored ice cream and toppings.

- 2 tablespoons honey
- 2 tablespoons butter, melted
- 12 sugar cones, crushed (about 2 cups)
- 2 cups strawberry low-fat ice cream, softened
- 1/4 cup malted milk powder, divided
- 1/2 cup strawberry topping
- 2 cups vanilla low-fat ice cream, softened
- 1/2 cup fat-free hot fudge topping
- 1 1/4 cups canned whipped light cream (such as Reddi-wip)

1. Combine first 3 ingredients, stirring well. Firmly press mixture into bottom and up sides of a 9-inch pie plate. Freeze 30 minutes or until firm.
2. Place strawberry ice cream and 2 tablespoons milk powder in a medium bowl; beat with a mixer at medium speed until smooth. Spoon mixture evenly into crust; spread with strawberry topping. Freeze 30 minutes or until firm.
3. Place vanilla ice cream and 2 tablespoons milk powder in a medium bowl; beat with a mixer at medium speed until smooth. Spread mixture evenly over strawberry topping. Cover and freeze 4 hours or until firm. Top with hot fudge and whipped cream just before serving. Yield: 10 servings (serving size: 1 pie wedge, about 2 1/2 teaspoons hot fudge, and 2 tablespoons whipped cream).

CALORIES 316 (22% from fat); FAT 7.8g (sat 3.8g, mono 2.4g, poly 0.2g); PROTEIN 4.5g; CARB 57.7g; FIBER 2.1g; CHOL 15mg; IRON 1.7mg; SODIUM 155mg; CALC 128mg

Peppermint-Marshmallow Ice Cream Pie

Spreading melted ice cream into the pie plate "glues" the crust into place. Crushed chocolate wafers create the crust, while whole cookies define the edges of the pie.

- 4 cups vanilla low-fat ice cream, softened and divided
- 20 chocolate wafer cookies (such as Nabisco's Famous Chocolate Wafers), coarsely crushed and divided
- 1 1/4 cups miniature marshmallows, divided
- 15 hard peppermint candies, crushed
- 8 chocolate wafer cookies
- 5 hard peppermint candies, crushed

1. Place 2 tablespoons ice cream in a small microwave-safe bowl. Microwave at HIGH 20 seconds or until ice cream melts. Spread melted ice cream in bottom of a 9-inch pie plate. Arrange half of crushed cookies in bottom of pie plate.
2. Place remaining ice cream, 1 cup marshmallows, and 15 crushed candies in a large bowl; beat with a mixer at medium speed until well combined. Spoon half of mixture evenly into crust, and sprinkle evenly with remaining crushed cookies. Spread remaining ice cream mixture over crushed cookies. Arrange whole cookies around outside edge of pie; sprinkle top of pie with 1/4 cup marshmallows and 5 crushed candies. Cover and freeze 4 hours or until firm. Yield: 8 servings (serving size: 1 wedge).

CALORIES 281 (18% from fat); FAT 5.5g (sat 2.8g, mono 1.6g, poly 0.5g); PROTEIN 5.1g; CARB 53g; FIBER 0.9g; CHOL 20mg; IRON 0.8mg; SODIUM 221mg; CALC 77mg

Cherries Jubilee Ice Cream Pie

(pictured on page 269)

All the flavors of the classic summertime dessert combine in this easy-to-prepare pie. Since the cherries are cooked, frozen ones work just fine—and they save you the trouble of pitting fresh ones.

- 1/3 cup water
- 1/4 cup sugar
- 2 tablespoons brandy
- 1 tablespoon cornstarch
- 1 (12-ounce) package frozen pitted dark sweet cherries
- 2 tablespoons butter, melted
- 2 tablespoons honey
- 1 1/2 cups graham cracker crumbs (about 9 cookie sheets)
- 4 cups vanilla low-fat ice cream, softened

1. Preheat oven to 375°.
2. Combine first 5 ingredients in a medium saucepan. Bring to a boil; cook 2 minutes or until thick, stirring constantly. Cool completely.
3. Combine butter and honey in a medium bowl. Add cracker crumbs, stirring to blend. Press into bottom and up sides of a 9-inch pie plate. Bake at 375° for 8 minutes. Cool completely.
4. Place 1/2 cup cherry mixture in a food processor; process until smooth. Place remaining cherry mixture in an airtight container; cover and chill.
5. Place ice cream in a large bowl, and beat with a mixer at medium speed until smooth. Add puréed cherry mixture, and gently fold in to achieve a swirl pattern. Spoon mixture into cooled crust. Cover and freeze 4 hours or until firm. Top with reserved cherry sauce just before serving. Yield: 8 servings (serving size: 1 pie wedge and 3 tablespoons sauce).

CALORIES 277 (23% from fat); FAT 7g (sat 3.4g, mono 2.4g, poly 0.8g); PROTEIN 5g; CARB 47.3g; FIBER 1.6g; CHOL 24mg; IRON 0.7mg; SODIUM 165mg; CALC 88mg

MAKE AHEAD • FREEZABLE

Chocolate-Banana Frozen Pie with Peanut Butter Crust

This pie's no-bake crust is a sweet and simple concoction of graham cracker crumbs, honey, and peanut butter. Cooking softens the mashed banana so that once frozen, the filling stays velvety smooth.

1¼ cups graham cracker crumbs (about 8 cookie sheets)
½ cup honey, divided
⅓ cup creamy peanut butter
3 cups mashed ripe banana (about 4 bananas)
2 cups chocolate low-fat frozen yogurt, softened
8 teaspoons chocolate syrup

1. Combine cracker crumbs, ¼ cup honey, and peanut butter, stirring well. Press mixture into bottom and up sides of a 9-inch pie plate.
2. Combine ¼ cup honey and banana in a large nonstick skillet. Cook over medium heat 6 minutes or until mixture thickens, stirring frequently. Cool completely.
3. Place yogurt in a medium bowl; beat with a mixer at medium speed until smooth. Fold banana mixture into yogurt. Spoon mixture into crust. Cover and freeze 4 hours or until firm. Drizzle with chocolate syrup just before serving. Yield: 8 servings (serving size: 1 pie wedge and 1 teaspoon syrup).

CALORIES 312 (23% from fat); FAT 8.1g (sat 2g, mono 3.5g, poly 2.1g); PROTEIN 7g; CARB 58.2g; FIBER 3.5g; CHOL 2mg; IRON 1.5mg; SODIUM 169mg; CALC 87mg

MAKE AHEAD • FREEZABLE

Turtle Ice Cream Pie

A thin layer of chocolate brownie batter forms the crust for this rich-tasting pie that is great for grown-ups, yet sassy enough for a kid's birthday party.

CRUST:

½ cup all-purpose flour
¼ cup unsweetened cocoa
⅛ teaspoon salt
⅓ cup sugar
2½ tablespoons fat-free milk
½ teaspoon vanilla extract
1 large egg, lightly beaten
2 tablespoons butter
2 tablespoons mini semisweet chocolate chips
Cooking spray

FILLING:

4 cups vanilla low-fat ice cream, softened
⅓ cup fat-free caramel sundae syrup
¼ cup chopped pecans, toasted
3 tablespoons fat-free caramel sundae syrup

1. Preheat oven to 350°.
2. Lightly spoon flour into a dry measuring cup; level with a knife. Combine flour, cocoa, and salt in a medium bowl, stirring with a whisk; set aside. Combine sugar, milk, vanilla, and egg in a medium bowl, stirring with a whisk; set aside.
3. Place butter and chocolate chips in a small microwave-safe bowl. Microwave at HIGH 1 minute or until butter and chocolate melt, stirring every 20 seconds. Add chocolate mixture to sugar mixture, stirring with a whisk. Fold in flour mixture. Spread batter into a 9-inch deep-dish pie plate coated with cooking spray. Bake at 350° for 15 minutes or until a wooden pick inserted in center comes out clean. Cool completely on a wire rack.
4. To prepare filling, place ice cream in a large bowl; beat with a mixer at medium speed until smooth. Spoon half of ice cream over cooled crust, and place remaining ice cream in refrigerator. Drizzle pie with ⅓ cup caramel. Freeze pie 30 minutes or until firm. Spread remaining ice cream over caramel. Sprinkle evenly with pecans; drizzle with 3 tablespoons caramel. Cover and freeze 4 hours or until firm. Yield: 8 servings (serving size: 1 wedge).

CALORIES 308 (29% from fat); FAT 10g (sat 4.3g, mono 3.9g, poly 1.2g); PROTEIN 6.3g; CARB 50.5g; FIBER 1.8g; CHOL 51mg; IRON 1.3mg; SODIUM 181mg; CALC 104mg

STAFF FAVORITE • MAKE AHEAD
FREEZABLE

Lemon Meringue Baked Alaska

The layer of meringue insulates the ice cream mixture, keeping it from melting under the broiler.

32 vanilla wafers
2 cups vanilla low-fat ice cream, softened
2 cups lemon sorbet, softened
4 large egg whites
1 cup sugar
¼ cup water
1 tablespoon grated lemon rind

1. Line bottom and sides of a 9-inch deep-dish pie plate with wafers; set aside.
2. Place ice cream and sorbet in a large bowl; beat with a mixer at medium speed until smooth. Spoon into prepared pie plate; place in freezer.
3. Place egg whites in a large bowl; beat with a mixer at high speed until foamy using clean, dry beaters. Combine sugar and water in a small saucepan; bring to a boil. Cook, without stirring, until a candy thermometer registers 238°. Pour

hot sugar syrup in a thin stream over egg whites, beating at medium speed. Increase speed to high; beat until stiff peaks form. Fold in rind. Spread over ice cream. Cover loosely, and freeze 4 hours or until firm.

4. Preheat broiler.

5. Broil frozen pie 1 minute or until meringue is lightly browned. Serve immediately. Yield: 8 servings (serving size: 1 wedge).

CALORIES 290 (12% from fat); FAT 3.8g (sat 1.4g, mono 1g, poly 0.1g); PROTEIN 4.1g; CARB 61.6g; FIBER 0.9g; CHOL 11mg; IRON 0.6mg; SODIUM 105mg; CALC 51mg

reader recipes

Can't Eat Just One

An Illinois reader transforms her fried zucchini into baked chips.

When Linda Oldenburg was growing up, one of her favorite foods was her mother's fried zucchini. Using squash from the garden, her mother sliced the zucchini into rounds and panfried it in butter. "I loved it," says Oldenburg, who lives in Rockford, Illinois.

Until a few years ago, when Oldenburg and her husband, David, went out for dinner, they started with an order of fried zucchini. But then the couple became more concerned about their diet. Linda decided the zucchini was a good place to start making changes and set out to create a trimmed-down zucchini chip.

Besides incorporating healthful ingredients into the recipe, Oldenburg also changed her cooking method to keep the fat content low. She used a seasoned baking stone to bake the zucchini. (Since many kitchens don't have this item, we baked the zucchini slices on a rack and achieved similar results. Baking the zucchini slices on a wire rack exposes all sides to the oven's heat, resulting in a crisp chip.)

QUICK & EASY
Zucchini Oven Chips

¼ cup dry breadcrumbs
¼ cup (1 ounce) grated fresh Parmesan cheese
¼ teaspoon seasoned salt
¼ teaspoon garlic powder
⅛ teaspoon freshly ground black pepper
2 tablespoons fat-free milk
2½ cups (¼-inch-thick) slices zucchini (about 2 small)
Cooking spray

1. Preheat oven to 425°.
2. Combine first 5 ingredients in a medium bowl, stirring with a whisk. Place milk in a shallow bowl. Dip zucchini slices in milk, and dredge in breadcrumb mixture. Place coated slices on an oven-proof wire rack coated with cooking spray; place rack on a baking sheet. Bake at 425° for 30 minutes or until browned and crisp. Serve immediately. Yield: 4 servings (serving size: about ¾ cup).

CALORIES 61 (28% from fat); FAT 1.9g (sat 1g, mono 0.5g, poly 0.2g); PROTEIN 3.8g; CARB 7.6g; FIBER 1g; CHOL 5mg; IRON 0.6mg; SODIUM 231mg; CALC 87mg

QUICK & EASY • MAKE AHEAD
Bean and Corn Salsa

"I came up with this recipe when my crop of tomatoes was more plentiful than I expected. It's delicious, healthful, and perfect for chips, baked potatoes, and grilled chicken."

—Sherri Matheson, Wadsworth, Ohio

3 cups chopped seeded tomato (about 3 medium)
¾ cup chopped Vidalia or other sweet onion
½ cup chopped tomatillos (about 2 medium)
¼ cup canned black beans, rinsed and drained
¼ cup fresh corn kernels
2 tablespoons finely chopped fresh parsley
2 tablespoons fresh lime juice
½ teaspoon salt
½ teaspoon freshly ground black pepper
½ teaspoon hot sauce

1. Combine all ingredients in a large bowl; cover and chill at least 2 hours. Yield: 4 cups (serving size: ¼ cup).

CALORIES 15 (12% from fat); FAT 0.2g (sat 0g, mono 0g, poly 0.1g); PROTEIN 0.6g; CARB 3.3g; FIBER 0.8g; CHOL 0mg; IRON 0.2mg; SODIUM 83mg; CALC 7mg

Get Grilling Menu
serves 6

Don't save your pesto for pasta only—it makes a great rub for poultry or meat. Dress the pasta salad with your favorite commercial vinaigrette.

Pesto turkey tenderloins*

Pasta salad with cherry tomatoes and kalamata olives

Grilled asparagus spears

*Spread ¾ cup Classic Basil Pesto (recipe below) evenly over 2 (¾-pound) turkey tenderloins. Place tenderloins on a grill rack coated with cooking spray. Grill 7 minutes on each side or until done. Let stand 5 minutes; cut across grain into thin slices.

QUICK & EASY • MAKE AHEAD
FREEZABLE
Classic Basil Pesto

"Commercial pestos have so much oil. Using a couple of recipes as a guide, I fiddled around until I came up with one that had the right consistency."

—Kris McDowell, Eagan, Minnesota

2 cups loosely packed basil leaves
⅓ cup (about 1½ ounces) grated fresh Parmesan cheese
¼ cup fat-free, less-sodium chicken broth
1 tablespoon coarsely chopped walnuts
1 tablespoon extravirgin olive oil
½ teaspoon salt
¼ teaspoon freshly ground black pepper
1 garlic clove, minced

1. Place all ingredients in a food processor; process until smooth. Yield: ¾ cup (serving size: 2 tablespoons).

CALORIES 54 (75% from fat); FAT 4.5g (sat 1.2g, mono 2.3g, poly 0.9g); PROTEIN 2.4g; CARB 1.2g; FIBER 0.7g; CHOL 4mg; IRON 0.6mg; SODIUM 279mg; CALC 74mg

Couscous and Summer Vegetable Sauté

"This easy recipe is a good way to use extra corn on the cob or zucchini."

—Mary Kate Long, Ninde, Virginia

¾ cup uncooked couscous
1½ teaspoons olive oil
1½ cups shredded zucchini (about 1 medium)
¼ cup chopped onion
1½ cups fresh corn kernels
½ teaspoon salt
⅛ teaspoon black pepper

1. Cook couscous according to package directions, omitting salt and fat. Keep couscous warm.
2. Heat oil in a large nonstick skillet over medium-high heat. Add zucchini and onion; sauté 3 minutes or until tender. Stir in couscous and corn; cook 1 minute or until thoroughly heated. Stir in salt and pepper. Yield: 6 servings (serving size: ⅔ cup).

CALORIES 133 (12% from fat); FAT 1.8g (sat 0.3g, mono 1g, poly 0.4g); PROTEIN 4.5g; CARB 25.9g; FIBER 2.6g; CHOL 0mg; IRON 0.6mg; SODIUM 205mg; CALC 13mg

Flounder Baked in Parchment Paper

"Opening the parchment package at the table is dramatic and lots of fun."

—Carolyn Gedutis, Chelsea, Massachusetts

4 (6-ounce) flounder fillets
½ teaspoon salt
¼ teaspoon black pepper
1 (2-inch) piece peeled fresh ginger, thinly sliced
1 large lemon, thinly sliced
½ cup thinly sliced cherry tomatoes
½ cup thinly sliced green onions
Cooking spray

1. Preheat oven to 425°.
2. Cut a 36-inch-long piece of parchment paper. Fold in half crosswise; open. Place fillets, slightly overlapping, in center of right half of paper. Sprinkle with salt and pepper. Top with ginger, lemon, tomatoes, and onions.
3. Fold paper; seal edges with narrow folds. Slide packet onto a baking sheet; lightly coat packet with cooking spray. Bake at 425° for 15 minutes or until browned. Place on a platter; cut open. Yield: 4 servings (serving size: 1 fillet, about 2 tablespoons tomatoes, and about 2 tablespoons green onions).

CALORIES 171 (12% from fat); FAT 2.2g (sat 0.5g, mono 0.4g, poly 0.6g); PROTEIN 32.9g; CARB 3.7g; FIBER 1.2g; CHOL 82mg; IRON 1.2mg; SODIUM 439mg; CALC 56mg

Summer Day Soup

"With a whole-grain bread, this soup makes a quick, comforting lunch."

—Natasha Leigh Yates, Red Wing, Minnesota

4 cups vegetable juice, chilled
2 cups chopped tomato
1½ cups chopped sweet onion
1½ cups chopped seeded peeled cucumber
1 cup chopped bell pepper
¼ cup finely chopped fresh parsley
2 tablespoons fresh lime juice
2 tablespoons fresh lemon juice
2 tablespoons tarragon vinegar
1 tablespoon extravirgin olive oil
1 teaspoon dried basil
1 teaspoon honey
½ teaspoon dried tarragon
¼ teaspoon ground cumin
¼ teaspoon dried oregano
2 garlic cloves, minced

1. Combine all ingredients in a large bowl. Place 4 cups vegetable mixture in a blender or food processor, and process until smooth. Return puréed vegetable mixture to bowl, stirring to combine. Cover and chill. Yield: 8 servings (serving size: 1 cup).

CALORIES 69 (27% from fat); FAT 2.1g (sat 0.3g, mono 1.3g, poly 0.3g); PROTEIN 1.8g; CARB 12.7g; FIBER 2.3g; CHOL 0mg; IRON 1.1mg; SODIUM 334mg; CALC 34mg

Banana Corn Muffins

—Tara Bennett, Arlington, Virginia

½ cup mashed ripe banana (about 1 medium)
½ cup 2% reduced-fat milk
1 (8½-ounce) package corn muffin mix (such as Jiffy)
Cooking spray

1. Preheat oven to 350°.
2. Combine banana, milk, and mix in a medium bowl; stir just until moist. Spoon batter evenly into 6 muffin cups coated with cooking spray (batter will be slightly thin). Bake at 350° for 22 minutes or until a wooden pick inserted in center comes out clean. Cool in pan 10 minutes. Yield: 6 servings (serving size: 1 muffin).

CALORIES 199 (24% from fat); FAT 5.4g (sat 1.5g, mono 2.8g, poly 0.7g); PROTEIN 3.7g; CARB 34.2g; FIBER 3.2g; CHOL 2mg; IRON 1.1mg; SODIUM 457mg; CALC 49mg

Sesame Cucumber Salad

"This salad is great with rice and grilled teriyaki chicken or a peanut noodle dish."

—Greta Snyder, Chehalis, Washington

1¾ cups (2-inch) julienne-cut English cucumber (about 1 large)
¼ teaspoon kosher salt
1 cup red bell pepper strips
2 tablespoons rice vinegar
2 teaspoons grated peeled fresh ginger
2 teaspoons dark sesame oil
¼ teaspoon crushed red pepper
¼ teaspoon black pepper

1. Place cucumber in a colander; sprinkle with salt. Toss well. Drain 20 minutes. Combine cucumber and bell pepper in a medium bowl.
2. Combine vinegar, ginger, and oil, stirring with a whisk. Pour over cucumber mixture; toss gently to coat. Stir in crushed red pepper and black pepper. Yield: 5 servings (serving size: ½ cup).

CALORIES 30 (60% from fat); FAT 2g (sat 0.3g, mono 0.7g, poly 0.8g); PROTEIN 0.6g; CARB 2.9g; FIBER 0.5g; CHOL 0mg; IRON 0.3mg; SODIUM 96mg; CALC 10mg

Mix and Match

Choose from soups, salads, and sandwiches to customize light summer meals.

QUICK & EASY

Creamy Truffle-Scented White Bean Soup

1 tablespoon olive oil
1 cup chopped onion
1 tablespoon bottled minced roasted garlic
¼ teaspoon freshly ground black pepper
1½ teaspoons chopped fresh rosemary
2 cups organic vegetable broth (such as Swanson Certified Organic)
2 (19-ounce) cans cannellini beans or other white beans, rinsed and drained
2 tablespoons fresh lemon juice
1 teaspoon truffle oil

1. Heat olive oil in a large saucepan over medium-high heat. Add onion; sauté 2 minutes. Stir in garlic and pepper; sauté 2 minutes or until onion is tender. Add rosemary; sauté 30 seconds. Stir in broth and beans. Bring to a boil; cover, reduce heat, and simmer 15 minutes. Remove from heat; stir in lemon juice. Let stand 5 minutes. Pour half of mixture into a blender; process until smooth. Pour puréed bean mixture into a large bowl. Repeat procedure with remaining bean mixture. Spoon 1 cup soup into each of 4 bowls, and drizzle each serving with ¼ teaspoon truffle oil. Yield: 4 servings.

CALORIES 222 (21% from fat); FAT 5.3g (sat 0.6g, mono 3.3g, poly 1.2g); PROTEIN 8.2g; CARB 34.5g; FIBER 8.3g; CHOL 0mg; IRON 3mg; SODIUM 563mg; CALC 76mg

Fried Green Tomato Salad with Warm Corn Salsa

The sweet salsa of corn, Vidalia onion, and red bell pepper vibrantly complements the tart green tomatoes.

TOMATOES:

12 (¼-inch-thick) slices green tomato (about 2 tomatoes)
¼ teaspoon salt
⅛ teaspoon freshly ground black pepper
⅓ cup yellow cornmeal
4 teaspoons olive oil, divided
Cooking spray

SALSA:

1 cup finely chopped Vidalia or other sweet onion
½ cup finely chopped red bell pepper
1 cup fresh corn kernels
1 garlic clove, minced
2 teaspoons balsamic vinegar
¼ teaspoon salt
⅛ teaspoon freshly ground black pepper
2 teaspoons minced fresh parsley

1. To prepare tomatoes, sprinkle tomato slices evenly with ¼ teaspoon salt and ⅛ teaspoon black pepper. Dredge tomato slices in cornmeal.
2. Heat 2 teaspoons oil in a large nonstick skillet over medium-high heat. Add 6 tomato slices to pan, and cook 2 minutes or until lightly browned. Coat tops of tomato slices with cooking spray; turn slices over. Cook 2 minutes or until lightly browned. Remove from pan. Repeat procedure with 2 teaspoons olive oil, remaining tomato slices, and cooking spray.
3. To prepare salsa, return pan to medium-high heat. Coat pan with cooking spray. Add onion and bell pepper; sauté 3 minutes. Add corn and garlic; sauté 1 minute. Stir in vinegar, ¼ teaspoon salt, and ⅛ teaspoon black pepper. Remove from heat; stir in parsley. Serve warm salsa over tomato slices. Yield: 4 servings (serving size: 3 tomato slices and about ⅓ cup salsa).

CALORIES 161 (29% from fat); FAT 5.2g (sat 0.7g, mono 3.5g, poly 0.8g); PROTEIN 3.5g; CARB 27g; FIBER 2.7g; CHOL 0mg; IRON 1.1mg; SODIUM 311mg; CALC 22mg

STAFF FAVORITE • QUICK & EASY

Southwestern Falafel with Avocado Spread

Inspired by the traditional Middle Eastern sandwich of chickpea patties in pita bread, this Southwestern-accented version features cumin-flavored pinto bean patties and a spread that is much like guacamole.

PATTIES:

1 (15-ounce) can pinto beans, rinsed and drained
½ cup (2 ounces) shredded Monterey Jack cheese
¼ cup finely crushed baked tortilla chips (about ¾ ounce)
2 tablespoons finely chopped green onions
1 tablespoon finely chopped cilantro
⅛ teaspoon ground cumin
1 large egg white, lightly beaten
1½ teaspoons canola oil

SPREAD:

¼ cup mashed peeled avocado
2 tablespoons finely chopped plum tomato
2 tablespoons fat-free sour cream
1 tablespoon finely chopped red onion
1 teaspoon fresh lime juice
⅛ teaspoon salt

REMAINING INGREDIENT:

2 (6-inch) pitas, each cut in half crosswise

1. To prepare patties, place pinto beans in a medium bowl; partially mash with a fork. Add cheese and next 5 ingredients; stir until well combined. Divide into 4 equal portions, shaping each into a ¼-inch-thick oval patty.

Continued

2. Heat oil in a large nonstick skillet over medium-high heat. Add patties; cook 3 minutes on each side or until browned and thoroughly heated.

3. To prepare spread, while patties cook, combine avocado and next 5 ingredients. Place 1 patty in each pita half. Spread about 2 tablespoons avocado spread over patty in each pita half. Yield: 4 servings (serving size: 1 stuffed pita half).

CALORIES 281 (30% from fat); FAT 9.5g (sat 3.4g, mono 3.9g, poly 1.5g); PROTEIN 12.2g; CARB 37.4g; FIBER 5.9g; CHOL 13mg; IRON 2.4mg; SODIUM 625mg; CALC 188mg

---

QUICK & EASY • MAKE AHEAD
Chickpea and Hearts of Palm Salad

This salad holds up well and would make a good take-to-work lunch. For a bruschetta topping, omit the chickpeas and finely chop the remaining elements.

  1 cup drained canned chickpeas (garbanzo beans)
  ½ cup chopped plum tomato
  ⅓ cup (about 1½ ounces) diced provolone cheese
  ¼ cup finely chopped red onion
  1 (14-ounce) can hearts of palm, drained and cut crosswise into ½-inch slices
  2 tablespoons red wine vinegar
  1 tablespoon minced fresh parsley
  1 teaspoon olive oil

1. Combine first 5 ingredients in a medium bowl.

2. Combine vinegar, parsley, and oil, stirring with a whisk. Drizzle over salad; toss well to combine. Yield: 4 servings (serving size: about ¾ cup).

CALORIES 149 (31% from fat); FAT 5.2g (sat 2.2g, mono 1.9g, poly 0.7g); PROTEIN 8g; CARB 19.4g; FIBER 5g; CHOL 7mg; IRON 3.5mg; SODIUM 479mg; CALC 151mg

---

Get-Together with Friends Menu
serves 4

Summer Squash and Pasta Soup

Green Salad with Apples and Maple-Walnut Dressing

Feta-Basil Sandwiches

WINE NOTE: The summer squash soup, green salad with apples, and the feta and basil in the sandwiches all cry out for a clean, fresh white with enough snap to stand up to the feta. Sancerre from the Loire Valley of France is a good choice. Made from sauvignon blanc grapes, it's about as tangy and pristine as white wine gets. Many of the small Sancerre producers export to the United States. Try Domaine Vacheron. The 2004 is $28.50.

QUICK & EASY
Summer Squash and Pasta Soup

  2 teaspoons butter
  ¾ cup chopped onion
  1 garlic clove, minced
  1½ cups small yellow squash, halved lengthwise and thinly sliced
  ¼ cup dry white wine
  2 cups organic vegetable broth (such as Swanson Certified Organic)
  1 cup water
  ⅔ cup uncooked ditalini (very short tube-shaped macaroni)
  1 tablespoon fresh lemon juice
  ½ teaspoon chopped fresh thyme
  ¼ teaspoon salt
  ¼ teaspoon freshly ground black pepper

1. Melt butter in a large saucepan over medium-high heat. Add onion and garlic; sauté 3 minutes or until tender. Add squash; sauté 2 minutes. Add wine; cook 1 minute or until liquid almost evaporates. Add broth and water; bring to a boil. Add pasta; cook 10 minutes or until pasta is done. Stir in juice, thyme, salt, and pepper. Yield: 4 servings (serving size: about 1 cup).

CALORIES 124 (17% from fat); FAT 2.3g (sat 1.1g, mono 0.8g, poly 0.1g); PROTEIN 3.8g; CARB 22.7g; FIBER 1.6g; CHOL 5mg; IRON 1mg; SODIUM 450mg; CALC 21mg

---

QUICK & EASY
Green Salad with Apples and Maple-Walnut Dressing

This salad contains sweet, spicy, nutty, and salty notes. Walnut oil adds the depth; you can substitute extravirgin olive oil—albeit with milder results.

  6 cups gourmet salad greens
  1 cup (2-inch) julienne-cut Braeburn or Honeycrisp apple
  2 tablespoons cider vinegar
  2 tablespoons maple syrup
  2 teaspoons whole-grain Dijon mustard
  1½ teaspoons walnut oil
  ⅛ teaspoon salt
  ⅛ teaspoon ground red pepper

1. Combine salad greens and apple in a large bowl.

2. Combine vinegar and remaining 5 ingredients, stirring with a whisk. Drizzle over salad; toss gently to coat. Yield: 4 servings (serving size: about 1¼ cups).

CALORIES 73 (27% from fat); FAT 2.2g (sat 0.2g, mono 0.5g, poly 1.3g); PROTEIN 1.6g; CARB 13.7g; FIBER 2.5g; CHOL 0mg; IRON 1.4mg; SODIUM 159mg; CALC 58mg

---

QUICK & EASY
Feta-Basil Sandwiches

  1 cup (4 ounces) crumbled feta cheese
  ¼ cup chopped fresh basil
  ¼ cup fat-free mayonnaise
  ¼ teaspoon freshly ground black pepper
  8 (1½-ounce) slices firm white bread (such as Pepperidge Farm Hearty White), toasted
  8 (¼-inch-thick) slices tomato

1. Combine first 4 ingredients, tossing with a fork until well combined. Spread about 2½ tablespoons cheese mixture onto each of 4 bread slices; top each sandwich with 2 tomato slices and 1 bread slice. Yield: 4 servings (serving size: 1 sandwich).

CALORIES 313 (28% from fat); FAT 9.6g (sat 4.3g, mono 2.7g, poly 0.9g); PROTEIN 14.4g; CARB 44.8g; FIBER 0.9g; CHOL 27mg; IRON 1.9mg; SODIUM 954mg; CALC 227mg

---

QUICK & EASY
Asian Cucumber Soup

Gazpacho inspired this chilled soup.

1 (1-ounce) slice day-old white bread or other firm white bread, torn into pieces
1 cup chopped yellow bell pepper
½ cup chopped green onions
3 tablespoons chopped fresh cilantro
1½ teaspoons minced peeled fresh ginger
2 pounds cucumber, peeled, halved lengthwise, seeded, and chopped
1 small garlic clove, minced
1⅔ cups organic vegetable broth (such as Swanson Certified Organic), divided
3 tablespoons rice vinegar
1 teaspoon sugar
½ to 1 teaspoon Sriracha (hot chile sauce, such as Huy Fong)
¼ teaspoon salt
2 teaspoons roasted peanut oil

1. Place bread in a blender. Pulse 10 times or until coarse crumbs form. Place breadcrumbs in a large bowl.
2. Combine bell pepper and next 5 ingredients. Place half of bell pepper mixture and 1 cup broth in blender, and process until smooth. Add puréed bell pepper mixture to breadcrumbs; stir well. Repeat procedure with remaining bell pepper mixture and ⅔ cup broth. Stir in vinegar, sugar, Sriracha, and salt. Cover and chill. Spoon 1¼ cups soup into each of 4 bowls; drizzle each serving with ½ teaspoon oil. Yield: 4 servings.

CALORIES 88 (30% from fat); FAT 2.9g (sat 0.4g, mono 1.1g, poly 0.8g); PROTEIN 2.4g; CARB 13.9g; FIBER 1.9g; CHOL 0mg; IRON 1mg; SODIUM 488mg; CALC 44mg

QUICK & EASY
Monterey Jack and Jalapeño Sandwiches

Monterey Jack cheese and pickled peppers combine for a new twist on pimiento cheese sandwiches. While this version is mild, you can increase the amount of jalapeño or use Monterey Jack cheese with jalapeño peppers for spicier sandwiches.

8 (1½-ounce) slices sourdough bread
1 garlic clove, halved
1 cup (4 ounces) shredded Monterey Jack cheese
¼ cup fat-free mayonnaise
1 tablespoon minced green onions
1 tablespoon finely chopped pickled jalapeño peppers

1. Heat a large grill pan over medium-high heat. Add 4 bread slices; cook 2 minutes on each side or until lightly browned. Remove from pan. Repeat procedure with remaining bread slices. Rub 1 side of each bread slice with cut sides of garlic clove; discard garlic.
2. Combine cheese and remaining 3 ingredients, stirring well. Spread about 3 tablespoons cheese mixture over garlic side of each of 4 bread slices; top each sandwich with 1 bread slice, garlic side down. Yield: 4 servings (serving size: 1 sandwich).

CALORIES 352 (30% from fat); FAT 11.6g (sat 6g, mono 3.5g, poly 0.9g); PROTEIN 14.6g; CARB 46.8g; FIBER 3g; CHOL 27mg; IRON 2.4mg; SODIUM 817mg; CALC 279mg

sidetracked

Summer Gratins

These versatile accompaniments crown fresh vegetables with a crunchy, golden crust.

Because these savory sides almost make a meal on their own (some are substantial enough to serve as a light entrée on a warm evening), the main dishes you choose to accompany them can be simple, such as grilled or roasted meats or fish seasoned with nothing more than salt and pepper.

Individual Spinach-Asiago Gratins

Cooking spray
1 teaspoon butter
½ cup finely chopped Walla Walla or other sweet onion
2 garlic cloves, minced
1 (10-ounce) bag fresh spinach, coarsely chopped
1½ tablespoons all-purpose flour
1 cup 1% low-fat milk
¼ teaspoon salt
¼ teaspoon freshly ground black pepper
Dash of ground nutmeg
¼ cup (1 ounce) grated fresh Asiago cheese
1 (1-ounce) slice white bread, torn into pieces
1 tablespoon chopped fresh parsley

1. Preheat broiler.
2. Heat a large nonstick skillet over medium-high heat. Coat pan with cooking spray. Add butter; swirl pan until butter melts. Add onion and garlic; sauté 3 minutes or until tender. Add half of spinach; cook 2 minutes or until spinach begins to wilt, stirring frequently. Add remaining spinach; cook 2 minutes or until spinach wilts, stirring frequently. Remove pan from heat.
3. Place flour in a small bowl; gradually add milk, stirring with a whisk. Stir flour mixture into spinach mixture; add salt, pepper, and nutmeg. Cook over medium-high heat 3 minutes or until thick and bubbly, stirring constantly. Remove from heat. Add cheese, stirring until cheese melts. Divide mixture evenly among 4 (4-ounce) ramekins or custard cups coated with cooking spray. Place ramekins on a baking sheet.
4. Place bread in a food processor; process until coarse crumbs measure ½ cup. Add parsley; pulse 3 times or until combined. Sprinkle about 2 tablespoons breadcrumb mixture over each serving. Broil 1 minute or until browned. Yield: 4 servings (serving size: 1 gratin).

CALORIES 118 (31% from fat); FAT 4.1g (sat 2.3g, mono 1.2g, poly 0.4g); PROTEIN 7.2g; CARB 14.2g; FIBER 2.2g; CHOL 11mg; IRON 2.5mg; SODIUM 309mg; CALC 234mg

Double-Squash Basmati Gratin

Basmati rice and feta cheese distinguish this updated squash-rice casserole from its classic counterpart. Serve with roasted chicken or grilled chicken breasts.

    4   cups zucchini, halved lengthwise
        and thinly sliced (about 1¼
        pounds)
    4   cups yellow squash, halved
        lengthwise and thinly sliced
        (about 1¼ pounds)
    2   cups thinly sliced leek (about
        2 large)
    ¼   cup fat-free, less-sodium chicken
        broth
    1   teaspoon salt, divided
    1   teaspoon freshly ground black
        pepper, divided
    3   garlic cloves, minced
    1   cup fat-free sour cream
    ⅔   cup 1% low-fat milk
    2   large egg whites, lightly beaten
    3   cups cooked basmati rice
    1   cup (4 ounces) crumbled feta
        cheese
    ½   cup (2 ounces) grated fresh
        Parmesan cheese
    ¼   cup chopped fresh parsley
    2   teaspoons chopped fresh oregano
  Cooking spray
   25   onion or garlic melba snack
        crackers
    2   tablespoons butter, melted

1. Preheat oven to 375°.
2. Combine zucchini, squash, leek, broth, ½ teaspoon salt, ½ teaspoon pepper, and garlic in a Dutch oven. Cover and cook over medium-high heat 20 minutes or until squash is very tender, stirring occasionally. Uncover and remove from heat; cool slightly.
3. Combine ½ teaspoon salt, ½ teaspoon pepper, sour cream, milk, and egg whites in a large bowl, stirring with a whisk. Add squash mixture, rice, cheeses, parsley, and oregano; stir well. Pour into a 13 x 9-inch baking dish coated with cooking spray.
4. Place crackers in a food processor; process until coarsely ground. Drizzle

with butter; pulse 3 times or until moist. Sprinkle cracker crumb mixture evenly over rice mixture. Bake at 375° for 25 minutes or until browned on top and bubbly around edges. Let stand 10 minutes before serving. Yield: 9 servings (serving size: about 1 cup).

CALORIES 251 (29% from fat); FAT 8.1g (sat 4.7g, mono 2.3g, poly 0.5g); PROTEIN 11g; CARB 34.1g; FIBER 2.4g; CHOL 25mg; IRON 2.1mg; SODIUM 656mg; CALC 246mg

Succotash-Cheddar Casserole with Crunchy Bacon Topping

The popular summertime combination of corn, lima beans, and bell pepper is tossed with a creamy cheese sauce and baked under a crisp cracker crumb topping. Place the crackers in a zip-top plastic bag, and crush with a rolling pin or bottle. Serve with grilled or roasted chicken.

    2   cups frozen baby lima beans
    3   bacon slices
    ⅔   cup finely chopped onion
    ½   cup finely chopped red bell
        pepper
    ½   teaspoon salt, divided
    2   garlic cloves, minced
    2   cups fresh corn kernels (about
        3 ears)
   2½   tablespoons all-purpose flour
   1⅓   cups 1% low-fat milk, divided
    ¼   teaspoon freshly ground black
        pepper
    ¾   cup (3 ounces) shredded
        reduced-fat extrasharp Cheddar
        cheese
  Cooking spray
   15   reduced-fat round buttery
        crackers (such as Ritz), coarsely
        crushed

1. Preheat oven to 375°.
2. Cook lima beans in boiling water 5 minutes or until crisp-tender; drain.
3. Cook bacon in a large nonstick skillet over medium heat until crisp. Remove bacon from pan, reserving 2 teaspoons drippings in pan. Crumble bacon, and set aside. Add onion, bell pepper, ¼ teaspoon salt, and garlic to drippings in pan;

cook 4 minutes or until tender, stirring frequently. Stir in lima beans and corn.
4. Place flour in a small bowl; gradually add ⅓ cup milk, stirring with a whisk to form a slurry. Add slurry, ¼ teaspoon salt, 1 cup milk, and black pepper to corn mixture; cook over medium heat 2½ minutes or until thick and bubbly. Remove from heat. Add cheese; stir until cheese melts. Spoon into an 8-inch square baking dish coated with cooking spray. Sprinkle with cracker crumbs and bacon. Bake at 375° for 20 minutes or until lightly browned on top and bubbly around edges. Yield: 6 servings (serving size: about ¾ cup).

CALORIES 258 (29% from fat); FAT 8.2g (sat 3.5g, mono 2.5g, poly 1g); PROTEIN 12.9g; CARB 34.4g; FIBER 5g; CHOL 17mg; IRON 2.1mg; SODIUM 514mg; CALC 201mg

Individual Corn Custards with Bacon-Potato Crust

Crushed potato chips top this side dish. Serve with grilled pork chops or with barbecued chicken.

    3   bacon slices
    3   cups fresh corn kernels (about
        5 ears), divided
    ¼   cup finely chopped onion
    1   jalapeño pepper, seeded and
        minced
    1   garlic clove, minced
   1¼   cups fat-free milk, divided
    2   teaspoons all-purpose flour
    ½   teaspoon salt
    ¼   teaspoon freshly ground black
        pepper
    2   large eggs, lightly beaten
  Cooking spray
    ⅓   cup crushed baked potato chips
        (about 1 ounce)

1. Preheat oven to 375°.
2. Cook bacon in a large nonstick skillet over medium heat until crisp. Remove bacon from pan, reserving 1 teaspoon drippings in pan. Crumble bacon; set aside. Add 2 cups corn, onion, jalapeño, and garlic to pan; sauté 2 minutes or until lightly browned. Remove from heat; cool slightly.

3. Place 1 cup corn and ¼ cup milk in a blender or food processor; process until smooth. Pour puréed corn mixture into a medium bowl. Add sautéed corn mixture, 1 cup milk, flour, salt, black pepper, and eggs, stirring with a whisk until well combined. Divide mixture evenly among 6 (6-ounce) ramekins or custard cups coated with cooking spray.

4. Place ramekins in a 13 x 9-inch baking pan; add hot water to pan to a depth of 1 inch. Bake at 375° for 30 minutes or until a knife inserted in center of each custard comes out clean. Remove pan from oven.

5. Preheat broiler.

6. Combine bacon and potato chips; sprinkle about 1½ tablespoons bacon mixture over each custard. Broil 1 minute or until browned. Yield: 6 servings (serving size: 1 custard).

CALORIES 158 (28% from fat); FAT 4.9g (sat 1.4g, mono 1.5g, poly 0.8g); PROTEIN 8g; CARB 22.9g; FIBER 2.6g; CHOL 76mg; IRON 1.2mg; SODIUM 354mg; CALC 67mg

---

MAKE AHEAD
Eggplant-Noodle Gratin

A touch of balsamic vinegar gives this gratin a slight sweetness reminiscent of caponata. Serve with pork chops or pork tenderloin.

- 1 tablespoon olive oil
- 4 cups coarsely chopped peeled eggplant
- 1 cup chopped yellow onion
- 1 cup chopped red bell pepper
- 2 cups chopped tomato
- 3 garlic cloves, minced
- 3 cups hot cooked medium egg noodles (about 2⅔ cups uncooked pasta)
- ¼ cup chopped fresh basil
- 1 tablespoon balsamic vinegar
- 1 teaspoon chopped fresh oregano
- ¾ teaspoon salt
- ¼ teaspoon freshly ground black pepper
- Cooking spray
- ⅔ cup (about 2½ ounces) shredded provolone cheese

1. Preheat oven to 350°.

2. Heat oil in a large nonstick skillet over medium-high heat. Add eggplant, onion, and bell pepper; sauté 5 minutes or until eggplant is tender. Add tomato and garlic; sauté 1 minute. Remove from heat; stir in noodles and next 5 ingredients. Spoon into an 11 x 7-inch baking dish coated with cooking spray; sprinkle evenly with cheese. Bake at 350° for 25 minutes or until thoroughly heated and cheese melts. Yield: 6 servings (serving size: about 1 cup).

CALORIES 222 (29% from fat); FAT 7.2g (sat 2.7g, mono 3.1g, poly 1g); PROTEIN 8.5g; CARB 32.3g; FIBER 3.8g; CHOL 37mg; IRON 2mg; SODIUM 401mg; CALC 119mg

---

Cheesy Polenta-Green Tomato Gratin

This unique side tastes somewhat like a tamale. Serve with grilled chicken or fish.

POLENTA:
- 1¾ cups 1% low-fat milk
- ¾ cup water
- ½ teaspoon salt
- ¾ cup yellow cornmeal
- Cooking spray

TOMATOES:
- 1½ teaspoons olive oil
- 2½ cups chopped firm green tomato (about 2 large)
- ½ cup chopped green onions
- ¼ teaspoon salt
- ¼ teaspoon ground cumin
- 1 jalapeño pepper, seeded and finely chopped
- 1 garlic clove, minced
- 2 tablespoons chopped fresh cilantro
- ¾ cup (3 ounces) crumbled queso fresco
- ½ cup (2 ounces) shredded Monterey Jack cheese
- Cilantro sprigs (optional)

1. Preheat oven to 425°.

2. To prepare polenta, combine first 3 ingredients in a medium saucepan; bring to a boil. Gradually add cornmeal, stirring constantly. Reduce heat, and simmer 5 minutes or until thick, stirring frequently. Spread mixture into an 8-inch square baking dish coated with cooking spray.

3. To prepare tomatoes, heat oil in a large nonstick skillet over medium-high heat. Add tomato and next 5 ingredients; sauté 6 minutes or until tomato is tender. Remove from heat; stir in chopped cilantro. Spoon tomato mixture over polenta; sprinkle with cheeses. Bake at 425° for 20 minutes or until lightly browned. Garnish with cilantro sprigs, if desired. Yield: 6 servings.

CALORIES 191 (29% from fat); FAT 6.1g (sat 3.2g, mono 2.3g, poly 0.3g); PROTEIN 8.7g; CARB 25g; FIBER 1.7g; CHOL 16mg; IRON 1.1mg; SODIUM 412mg; CALC 211mg

---

Great Gratin Toppings

Toppings provide the true pleasure factor in any gratin. Explore these options.
Baked potato or tortilla chips Crushed chips create a crunchy topping that complements most gratin ingredients.
Cheese Either on its own or used along with bread or cracker crumbs, cheese is the classic topping for gratins. Some of the best varieties include Gruyère, which takes on a silky texture when melted, and blue cheese, which browns nicely. Grated hard cheeses like Parmigiano-Reggiano, pecorino Romano, and Asiago add sharp, nutty tones.
Cornflake crumbs The flakes can be seasoned as desired, but by themselves, the crumbs lend a slightly sweet note.
Panko These coarse Japanese breadcrumbs are lighter and airier than their Western counterparts, and stay crisper after baking. Panko is also known for its superior browning qualities.
Sourdough breadcrumbs An alternative to standard white breadcrumbs, sourdough adds a welcome tang to mild summer vegetables.

Two-Tomato Gratin

With all the flavors of bruschetta, this dish goes well with grilled fish or steak.

1 garlic clove
3 ounces French bread, torn into pieces
2 teaspoons butter, melted
1 teaspoon olive oil
⅓ cup finely chopped shallots
1 pint grape tomatoes
1 pint yellow pear tomatoes
½ teaspoon salt
¼ teaspoon freshly ground black pepper
3 tablespoons chopped fresh parsley
Cooking spray

1. Preheat oven to 425°.
2. With food processor on, drop garlic through food chute; process until finely chopped. Add bread; pulse until coarse crumbs measure 1¾ cups. Drizzle breadcrumbs with butter; pulse to combine.
3. Heat oil in a medium ovenproof skillet over medium-high heat. Add shallots; sauté 3 minutes or until tender. Add tomatoes, salt, and pepper; sauté 1½ minutes or just until heated. Stir in parsley. Sprinkle evenly with breadcrumb mixture. Lightly coat with cooking spray. Bake at 425° for 7 minutes or until golden brown. Let stand 5 minutes before serving. Yield: 6 servings (serving size: about ⅔ cup).

CALORIES 86 (29% from fat); FAT 2.8g (sat 0.9g, mono 1.3g, poly 0.4g); PROTEIN 2.4g; CARB 13.8g; FIBER 1.7g; CHOL 3mg; IRON 1.1mg; SODIUM 303mg; CALC 23mg

2 for 1

Zesty concoctions perform dinnertime double duty as dressings for salads and marinades for entrées.

The following recipes provide versatile, fresh-tasting dressings and vinaigrettes and multiple dishes that can help you with dinner on even your busiest weeknights.

Couscous Salad Cups
(pictured on page 270)

This pasta salad is satisfying with grilled lamb chops, chicken, or shrimp. For a picnic, try serving it in halved bell peppers. You can use whole wheat couscous for added fiber. To quickly turn this into a vegetarian main dish, add a can of drained chickpeas and some crumbled feta cheese.

2 cups organic vegetable broth (such as Swanson Certified Organic)
1 cup uncooked couscous
1 cup shredded carrot
½ cup chopped green onions
½ cup diced English cucumber
½ cup diced plum tomato
½ cup Pomegranate-Orange Dressing (recipe on page 261)
¼ cup chopped fresh parsley
¼ cup chopped fresh mint
¼ teaspoon salt
¼ teaspoon freshly ground black pepper
8 Boston lettuce leaves

1. Bring broth to a boil in a medium saucepan; gradually stir in couscous. Remove from heat; cover and let stand 5 minutes. Fluff with a fork; cool.
2. Combine cooled couscous, carrot, and next 8 ingredients in a large bowl; toss well. Spoon about ⅔ cup couscous mixture into each lettuce leaf. Yield: 8 servings (serving size: 1 filled lettuce leaf).

CALORIES 139 (17% from fat); FAT 2.7g (sat 0.4g, mono 1.8g, poly 0.3g); PROTEIN 3.5g; CARB 24.8g; FIBER 2.3g; CHOL 0mg; IRON 1mg; SODIUM 331mg; CALC 30mg

Mediterranean Grilled Chicken Kebabs

These kebabs would be handsomely garnished with fresh pomegranate seeds. If you have any leftover dressing, serve it as a dipping sauce.

1 cup Pomegranate-Orange Dressing (recipe on page 261), divided
2 pounds skinless, boneless chicken thighs, trimmed and cut into bite-size pieces
2 large oranges
¼ teaspoon salt
¼ teaspoon freshly ground black pepper
Cooking spray
¼ cup chopped fresh mint

1. Combine ½ cup Pomegranate-Orange Dressing and chicken in a large zip-top plastic bag. Seal and marinate in refrigerator 30 minutes, turning bag occasionally.
2. Prepare grill.
3. Cut each orange into 8 wedges; cut each wedge crosswise into 3 pieces.
4. Remove chicken from marinade; discard marinade. Thread chicken and orange pieces alternately onto 16 (10-inch) skewers. Sprinkle evenly with salt and pepper. Place kebabs on a grill rack coated with cooking spray; grill 5 minutes on each side or until chicken is done, basting occasionally with ½ cup Pomegranate-Orange Dressing. Place kebabs on a platter; sprinkle with mint. Yield: 8 servings (serving size: 2 kebabs).

CALORIES 205 (35% from fat); FAT 8g (sat 1.6g, mono 4.1g, poly 1.4g); PROTEIN 22.7g; CARB 9g; FIBER 0.7g; CHOL 94mg; IRON 1.6mg; SODIUM 320mg; CALC 35mg

Pomegranate-Orange Dressing

Look for pomegranate molasses in Middle Eastern markets and health-foods stores.

1 cup fresh orange juice
2½ tablespoons balsamic vinegar
2 tablespoons fresh lemon juice
2 tablespoons pomegranate molasses
2 teaspoons grated orange rind
2 teaspoons minced fresh rosemary
1 teaspoon salt
1 teaspoon brown sugar
½ teaspoon ground cumin
½ teaspoon ground black pepper
¼ teaspoon ground red pepper
4 garlic cloves, minced
¼ cup extravirgin olive oil

1. Combine all ingredients except oil, stirring with a whisk. Gradually add oil, stirring constantly with a whisk until well combined. Yield: about 1½ cups (serving size: 1 tablespoon).

NOTE: Refrigerate dressing in an airtight container up to five days; stir well before using.

CALORIES 39 (55% from fat); FAT 2.4g (sat 0.3g, mono 1.8g, poly 0.2g); PROTEIN 0.1g; CARB 4.1g; FIBER 0.1g; CHOL 0mg; IRON 0.3mg; SODIUM 99mg; CALC 9mg

Jícama and Orange Salad

Serve this crunchy salad alongside grilled chicken or fish. To speed preparation, look for jars of fresh orange sections and precut vegetables in the refrigerated section of your supermarket's produce department.

6 cups (3 x ¼-inch) strips peeled jícama (about 1 pound)
6 cups lightly packed baby spinach (about 3 ounces)
1 cup orange sections (about 2 oranges)
1 cup red bell pepper strips
½ cup thinly sliced red onion
⅔ cup Ginger-Sesame Vinaigrette (recipe at right)
2 tablespoons sesame seeds, toasted

1. Combine first 5 ingredients in a large bowl. Drizzle with Ginger-Sesame Vinaigrette, and toss well to coat. Sprinkle with sesame seeds. Yield: 8 servings (serving size: 1¼ cups).

CALORIES 103 (29% from fat); FAT 3.3g (sat 0.4g, mono 1.4g, poly 1.3g); PROTEIN 2.7g; CARB 17.2g; FIBER 6.5g; CHOL 0mg; IRON 1.5mg; SODIUM 287mg; CALC 49mg

Ginger-Sesame Grilled Tofu Steaks

All you need to complete this meal is a side of steamed snow peas, sugar snap peas, or asparagus. Draining the tofu on paper towels helps it absorb more marinade.

1 pound reduced-fat extrafirm water-packed tofu, drained and cut crosswise into 8 slices
⅔ cup Ginger-Sesame Vinaigrette (recipe at right)
1 tablespoon finely chopped fresh cilantro
1 tablespoon low-sodium soy sauce
8 lime slices
Cooking spray
2 cups hot cooked short-grain white rice

1. Place tofu slices on several layers of paper towels; cover with additional paper towels. Let stand 20 minutes, pressing down occasionally. Combine Ginger-Sesame Vinaigrette, cilantro, and soy sauce in a 13 x 9-inch baking dish. Remove ¼ cup cilantro mixture; set aside. Add tofu to dish in a single layer, turning to coat. Cover and marinate in refrigerator 30 minutes, turning occasionally.
2. Prepare grill.
3. Add lime slices to marinade; turning to coat. Remove tofu and lime slices from marinade, reserving marinade. Place tofu and lime slices on grill rack coated with cooking spray; grill 2 minutes on each side or until browned and thoroughly heated, basting occasionally with reserved marinade. Spoon ½ cup rice onto each of 4 plates. Top each serving with 2 tofu slices and 2 lime slices; drizzle each serving with 1 tablespoon reserved cilantro mixture. Yield: 4 servings.

CALORIES 307 (27% from fat); FAT 9.3g (sat 0.4g, mono 3.2g, poly 4.4g); PROTEIN 16.3g; CARB 40.6g; FIBER 4.8g; CHOL 0mg; IRON 3.4mg; SODIUM 669mg; CALC 57mg

Ginger-Sesame Vinaigrette

Try tossing this vinaigrette with salad greens or rice noodles, or use it as a dipping sauce for pot stickers or spring rolls. Many supermarkets stock miso with the refrigerated foods; if yours doesn't, you'll need to visit an Asian market.

½ cup rice wine vinegar
¼ cup water
¼ cup yellow miso (soybean paste)
¼ cup chopped green onions
2 tablespoons sugar
2 tablespoons minced peeled fresh ginger
2 tablespoons low-sodium soy sauce
4 teaspoons canola oil
2 teaspoons dark sesame oil

1. Combine first 3 ingredients in a medium bowl, stirring with a whisk until smooth. Stir in green onions and remaining ingredients. Yield: about 1⅓ cups (serving size: 1 tablespoon).

NOTE: Refrigerate vinaigrette in an airtight container up to five days; stir well before using.

CALORIES 23 (59% from fat); FAT 1.5g (sat 0.1g, mono 0.7g, poly 0.6g); PROTEIN 0.5g; CARB 2.1g; FIBER 0.1g; CHOL 0mg; IRON 0mg; SODIUM 192mg; CALC 0mg

From an easy make-ahead Asian vinaigrette base, you get two distinctly different dishes that come together quickly.

Honeyed Lemon-Dijon Vinaigrette

This bright, zesty vinaigrette is great on any tossed salad. It's also a good marinade for fish, seafood, or chicken, and it makes a tasty sauce for roast veal.

¼ cup chopped fresh dill
¼ cup white wine vinegar
2 tablespoons chopped red onion
2 tablespoons capers
1 tablespoon grated lemon rind
2 tablespoons fresh lemon juice
4 teaspoons honey
2 teaspoons Dijon mustard
1 teaspoon salt
¾ teaspoon freshly ground black pepper
½ teaspoon hot pepper sauce
2 garlic cloves, minced
⅓ cup boiling water
¼ cup extravirgin olive oil

1. Place first 12 ingredients in a blender; process until mixture is smooth. Add water and oil; process until well combined. Yield: about 1½ cups (serving size: 1 tablespoon).

NOTE: Refrigerate vinaigrette in an airtight container up to five days, and stir well before using.

CALORIES 27 (80% from fat); FAT 2.4g (sat 0.3g, mono 1.8g, poly 0.2g); PROTEIN 0.1g; CARB 1.6g; FIBER 0.1g; CHOL 0mg; IRON 0.1mg; SODIUM 133mg; CALC 2mg

> When you use this tasty citrus vinaigrette as a foundation of a recipe, you don't need to add many other seasonings.

How to Butterfly Shrimp

First peel the shrimp, leaving tails intact. Using a paring knife, cut deeply down the back of each shrimp, cutting to, but not through, the underside.

Spicy Grilled Jumbo Shrimp

This easy entrée is great for casual backyard get-togethers. With the vinaigrette already made, the shrimp take less than 30 minutes to prepare.

2¼ pounds unpeeled jumbo shrimp
¾ cup Honeyed Lemon-Dijon Vinaigrette (recipe at left), divided
½ teaspoon crushed red pepper
¼ teaspoon salt
¼ teaspoon coarsely ground black pepper
Cooking spray
Lemon wedges

1. Peel shrimp, leaving tails intact. Starting at tail end, butterfly each shrimp, cutting to, but not through, underside of shrimp.
2. Combine shrimp, 6 tablespoons Honeyed Lemon-Dijon Vinaigrette, and red pepper in a large zip-top plastic bag. Seal and marinate in refrigerator 15 minutes, turning bag occasionally.
3. Prepare grill.
4. Remove shrimp from marinade; discard marinade. Sprinkle shrimp evenly with salt and black pepper. Place shrimp, cut sides down, on grill rack coated with cooking spray; grill 2 minutes on each side or until done, basting frequently with 6 tablespoons Honeyed Lemon-Dijon

Vinaigrette. Serve shrimp with lemon wedges. Yield: 6 servings (serving size: about 4½ ounces).

CALORIES 223 (27% from fat); FAT 6.6g (sat 1.1g, mono 3.2g, poly 1.5g); PROTEIN 34.7g; CARB 4.1g; FIBER 0.3g; CHOL 259mg; IRON 4.2mg; SODIUM 549mg; CALC 93mg

Grilled New Potato Salad

Smoky flavors from the grill enrich this potato salad. Serve at room temperature to enjoy the most flavor and best texture it has to offer. You can combine all the ingredients except the arugula up to one hour ahead; just before serving, stir in the delicate greens.

2 pounds small red potatoes, halved
½ cup Honeyed Lemon-Dijon Vinaigrette (recipe at left), divided
Cooking spray
3 cups loosely packed baby arugula
¼ cup thinly vertically sliced red onion
¼ teaspoon salt
¼ teaspoon freshly ground black pepper

1. Prepare grill.
2. Place potatoes in a medium saucepan; cover with water. Bring to a boil. Reduce heat; simmer 10 minutes or until potatoes are almost tender. Drain and rinse with cold water; drain well. Place potatoes in a bowl. Drizzle with 2 tablespoons Honeyed Lemon-Dijon Vinaigrette; toss gently to coat.
3. Place potatoes, cut sides down, on grill rack coated with cooking spray; grill 3 minutes on each side or until potatoes are very tender.
4. Combine potatoes, arugula, and remaining 3 ingredients in a large bowl. Drizzle with 6 tablespoons Honeyed Lemon-Dijon Vinaigrette, and toss gently to coat. Yield: 8 servings (serving size: ¾ cup).

CALORIES 125 (17% from fat); FAT 2.4g (sat 0.3g, mono 1.8g, poly 0.3g); PROTEIN 3.1g; CARB 22.4g; FIBER 1.8g; CHOL 0mg; IRON 1.4mg; SODIUM 222mg; CALC 15mg

Maple-Balsamic Dressing

The sweet, tangy dressing is ideal for peppery greens, such as arugula, or bitter greens like radicchio or endive. It also complements rich meats, such as pork or dark-meat chicken.

½ cup tomato juice
⅓ cup balsamic vinegar
¼ cup maple syrup
1 tablespoon minced fresh rosemary
2 teaspoons Dijon mustard
½ teaspoon salt
½ teaspoon freshly ground black pepper
2 garlic cloves, minced
2½ tablespoons extravirgin olive oil

1. Combine all ingredients except oil, stirring well. Gradually add oil, stirring constantly with a whisk until well combined. Yield: about 1 cup (serving size: 1 tablespoon).
NOTE: Refrigerate dressing in an airtight container up to five days; stir well before using.

CALORIES 39 (53% from fat); FAT 2.3g (sat 0.3g, mono 1.7g, poly 0.2g); PROTEIN 0.2g; CARB 4.7g; FIBER 0.1g; CHOL 0mg; IRON 0.2mg; SODIUM 118mg; CALC 8mg

Arugula, Roasted Tomato, and Goat Cheese Salad

Use your favorite salad greens for this tasty first course. We liked the spiciness of arugula, but any other greens will work.

1 cup grape or cherry tomatoes, halved
¼ cup Maple-Balsamic Dressing (recipe above), divided
Cooking spray
8 cups loosely packed baby arugula, watercress, or spinach (about 4 ounces)
¼ cup thinly vertically sliced red onion
2 tablespoons crumbled goat cheese
¼ teaspoon freshly ground black pepper

1. Preheat oven to 350°.
2. Combine tomatoes and 2 tablespoons Maple-Balsamic Dressing; toss well to coat. Arrange tomatoes, cut sides up, on a jelly-roll pan coated with cooking spray. Bake at 350° for 30 minutes or until tomatoes soften. Cool completely.
3. Combine tomatoes, arugula, and onion in a large bowl. Drizzle with 2 tablespoons Maple-Balsamic Dressing; toss gently to coat. Sprinkle with cheese and pepper. Yield: 6 servings (serving size: about 1⅓ cups salad and 1 teaspoon cheese).

CALORIES 47 (44% from fat); FAT 2.3g (sat 0.6g, mono 1.3g, poly 0.3g); PROTEIN 1.5g; CARB 6g; FIBER 0.9g; CHOL 1mg; IRON 0.7mg; SODIUM 97mg; CALC 54mg

Maple-Balsamic Pork Tenderloins

Butterflying the pork increases the surface area to absorb the marinade, and the thinner meat cooks more quickly on the grill.

2 (¾-pound) pork tenderloins, trimmed
½ cup Maple-Balsamic Dressing (recipe at left), divided
½ teaspoon salt
½ teaspoon freshly ground black pepper
Cooking spray

1. Cut tenderloins lengthwise, cutting to, but not through, other side. Open halves, laying tenderloins flat. Place tenderloins in a large zip-top plastic bag. Add ¼ cup Maple-Balsamic Dressing; seal and shake to coat. Marinate in refrigerator 20 minutes or up to 8 hours, turning bag occasionally.
2. Prepare grill.
3. Place ¼ cup Maple-Balsamic Dressing in a small saucepan, and bring to a boil. Reduce heat, and simmer 2 minutes or until syrupy.
4. Remove tenderloins from marinade; discard marinade. Sprinkle tenderloins evenly with salt and pepper. Place on a grill rack coated with cooking spray; grill 8 minutes on each side or until a thermometer registers 155° or until

desired degree of doneness. Remove pork from grill; cover and let stand 5 minutes. Cut pork across grain into thin slices, and drizzle with reduced Maple-Balsamic Dressing. Yield: 6 servings (serving size: 3 ounces).

CALORIES 176 (32% from fat); FAT 6.2g (sat 1.7g, mono 3.5g, poly 0.6g); PROTEIN 24g; CARB 4.8g; FIBER 0.1g; CHOL 74mg; IRON 1.6mg; SODIUM 372mg; CALC 14mg

Apple-Kiwi Dressing

Kiwifruit contains enzymes that act as a tenderizer, making it ideal for meat marinades.

2 tablespoons cider vinegar
2 tablespoons apple juice
1 tablespoon olive oil
1 tablespoon water
½ teaspoon sugar
½ teaspoon salt
¼ teaspoon freshly ground black pepper
¼ teaspoon hot pepper sauce
3 kiwifruit, peeled and cut into chunks (about ½ pound)
1 small garlic clove

1. Place all ingredients in a blender, and process until smooth. Yield: 1 cup (serving size: 1 tablespoon).
NOTE: Refrigerate dressing in an airtight container up to five days; stir well before using.

CALORIES 18 (45% from fat); FAT 0.9g (sat 0.1g, mono 0.6g, poly 0.1g); PROTEIN 0.2g; CARB 2.7g; FIBER 0.5g; CHOL 0mg; IRON 0.1mg; SODIUM 77mg; CALC 4mg

Poached Chicken and Asparagus Salad

Here's a cool, light salad that's great for hot, humid days. If you anticipate having leftovers, toss together only what will be eaten at dinner to keep all the components at their peak.

    6   cups water
    2   tablespoons fresh lemon juice
    ½   teaspoon salt
    ½   teaspoon cracked black pepper
    1   bay leaf
    1   small onion, halved
    ½   pound skinless, boneless chicken
        breast
    2½ cups (1-inch) slices asparagus
    1   cup yellow bell pepper strips
    ¼   cup Apple-Kiwi Dressing (recipe
        on page 263)
    1   teaspoon finely chopped fresh
        tarragon

1. Combine first 6 ingredients in a large saucepan; bring to a boil. Cook 5 minutes. Add chicken. Cover, reduce heat, and simmer 15 minutes or until chicken is tender. Remove chicken from pan with a slotted spoon. Place chicken on a cutting surface; cover loosely with foil. Let stand 10 minutes; cut chicken into bite-size pieces.
2. Return poaching liquid to a boil. Add asparagus; cook 2 minutes or until crisp-tender. Drain and rinse with cold water; drain well. Discard bay leaf and onion. Combine chicken, asparagus, bell pepper, Apple-Kiwi Dressing, and tarragon; toss well. Yield: 2 servings (serving size: 2 cups).

CALORIES 216 (15% from fat); FAT 3.6g (sat 0.7g, mono 1.6g, poly 0.8g); PROTEIN 31g; CARB 16.8g; FIBER 1.7g; CHOL 66mg; IRON 4.9mg; SODIUM 303mg; CALC 72mg

Grilled Peppercorn Sirloin

This steak is best marinated for just a few hours. Mixed black, green, and pink peppercorns offer slightly less heat than all black peppercorns, though you can use them instead.

    ½   cup Apple-Kiwi Dressing (recipe
        on page 263)
    1   (¾-pound) boneless sirloin steak
        (about 1½ inches thick),
        trimmed
    2   teaspoons coarsely ground mixed
        peppercorns
    ¼   teaspoon salt
        Cooking spray

1. Combine Apple-Kiwi Dressing and steak in a large zip-top plastic bag. Seal and marinate in refrigerator 4 hours, turning bag occasionally.
2. Prepare grill.
3. Remove steak from marinade; discard marinade. Combine peppercorns and salt; sprinkle over both sides of steak. Place on grill rack coated with cooking spray; grill 4 minutes on each side or until desired degree of doneness. Remove from grill; cover and let stand 10 minutes. Cut across grain into thin slices. Yield: 3 servings (serving size: 3 ounces).

CALORIES 203 (40% from fat); FAT 9.1g (sat 3.2g, mono 4.1g, poly 0.5g); PROTEIN 24.5g; CARB 4.3g; FIBER 1g; CHOL 59mg; IRON 1.8mg; SODIUM 348mg; CALC 25mg

WINE NOTE: Steak says cabernet sauvignon. But with this dish, cabernet is good for another reason, too—the peppercorns, which have a definitive flavor that's bold enough to need a structured red as a contrast. Cabernets are usually pricey, but here's a terrific quaffer that's a steal: Raymond Vineyards "Amberhill" Cabernet Sauvignon. The 2002 is $13.

Herbed Lemon-Buttermilk Dressing

This all-purpose dressing is similar to ranch dressing. It's great as a marinade on chicken, dressing on salad, and dip with cut-up vegetables.

    ¾   cup fat-free buttermilk
    ⅓   cup low-fat mayonnaise
    1   tablespoon grated lemon
        rind
    1   tablespoon finely chopped
        onion
    2   teaspoons fresh lemon juice
    2   teaspoons Dijon mustard
    1   teaspoon finely chopped fresh
        chives
    1   teaspoon finely chopped fresh
        basil
    1   teaspoon finely chopped fresh
        thyme
    ½   teaspoon coarsely ground black
        pepper
    ¼   teaspoon salt
    1   garlic clove, minced

1. Combine all ingredients, stirring with a whisk until well blended. Yield: 1¼ cups (serving size: 1 tablespoon).
NOTE: Refrigerate dressing in an airtight container up to five days; stir well before using.

CALORIES 12 (23% from fat); FAT 0.3g (sat 0g, mono 0.1g, poly 0.2g); PROTEIN 0.4g; CARB 1.9g; FIBER 0.1g; CHOL 0mg; IRON 0mg; SODIUM 89mg; CALC 13mg

Iceberg Wedge with Pancetta

Pancetta, unsmoked Italian bacon, updates this classic, but you can also use regular bacon in its place.

        Cooking spray
    1   ounce pancetta, diced (about
        3 tablespoons)
    1   head iceberg lettuce
    ½   cup Herbed Lemon-Buttermilk
        Dressing (recipe at left)
    1   cup chopped tomato
    ½   cup diced English cucumber

1. Heat a nonstick skillet over medium-high heat. Coat pan with cooking spray. Add pancetta to pan; cook 3 minutes or until crisp. Drain on paper towels.
2. Cut lettuce head in half; cut each half into 2 wedges. Place 1 wedge on each of 4 salad plates. Drizzle each wedge with 2 tablespoons Herbed Lemon-Buttermilk Dressing; top each with ¼ cup tomato and 2 tablespoons cucumber. Sprinkle evenly with pancetta. Serve immediately. Yield: 4 servings.

CALORIES 64 (27% from fat); FAT 1.9g (sat 0.4g, mono 0.7g, poly 0.7g); PROTEIN 3.7g; CARB 9.9g; FIBER 0.8g; CHOL 3mg; IRON 0.9mg; SODIUM 251mg; CALC 71mg

Grilled Herb-Coated Chicken Breasts

¾ cup Herbed Lemon-Buttermilk Dressing (recipe on page 264)
4 (6-ounce) skinless, boneless chicken breast halves
½ teaspoon salt
½ teaspoon freshly ground black pepper
2 tablespoons finely chopped fresh parsley
2 tablespoons finely chopped fresh chives
1 teaspoon canola oil
1 teaspoon honey
Cooking spray

1. Combine Herbed Lemon-Buttermilk Dressing and chicken in a large zip-top plastic bag. Seal and marinate in refrigerator 1 hour or up to 8 hours, turning bag occasionally.
2. Prepare grill.
3. Remove chicken from marinade, and discard marinade. Sprinkle chicken evenly with salt and pepper. Combine parsley, chives, oil, and honey, stirring well. Spoon herb mixture evenly over tops of chicken breast halves. Place chicken, herb side down, on grill rack coated with cooking spray; grill 8 minutes each side or until done. Yield: 4 servings (serving size: 1 chicken breast half).

CALORIES 222 (15% from fat); FAT 3.8g (sat 0.7g, mono 1.4g, poly 1.2g); PROTEIN 40g; CARB 4.6g; FIBER 0.3g; CHOL 99mg; IRON 1.5mg; SODIUM 540mg; CALC 44mg

menu of the month

Riverside Repast

Chill out by the water with a picnic.

Menu
serves 4

Papaya-Carrot Slaw

Antipasto Chicken Sandwich

Chewy Chocolate-Coconut Macaroons

Ginger Limeade

QUICK & EASY • MAKE AHEAD
Papaya-Carrot Slaw

Prepare and refrigerate the slaw up to 1 day in advance.

1 cup shredded peeled green papaya
½ cup shredded carrot
½ cup red bell pepper strips
1 teaspoon grated lime rind
2 tablespoons fresh lime juice
1 tablespoon grated peeled fresh ginger
¼ teaspoon salt
¼ teaspoon pepper

1. Combine all ingredients in a medium bowl. Stir well; cover and refrigerate. Yield: 4 servings (serving size: ½ cup).

CALORIES 29 (4% from fat); FAT 0.1g (sat 0g, mono 0g, poly 0.1g); PROTEIN 0.6g; CARB 7.2g; FIBER 1.4g; CHOL 0mg; IRON 0.2mg; SODIUM 158mg; CALC 17mg

QUICK & EASY • MAKE AHEAD
Antipasto Chicken Sandwich
(pictured on page 271)

To speed preparation, purchase roasted chicken breasts and shred the meat. Prepare this sandwich the morning of your picnic, and wrap it tightly in foil.

1 (10-ounce) loaf round focaccia, cut in half horizontally
2 tablespoons olive paste
2 cups shredded roasted skinless, boneless chicken breast
½ cup coarsely chopped drained marinated artichoke hearts
½ cup chopped drained oil-packed sun-dried tomato halves
½ cup coarsely chopped bottled roasted red bell peppers
2 ounces thinly sliced prosciutto
½ cup (2 ounces) shredded fontina cheese

1. Spread bottom half of focaccia with olive paste. Arrange chicken on top of paste. Arrange artichokes, tomatoes, peppers, and prosciutto over chicken. Sprinkle with cheese. Top with top half of focaccia; press gently.

---

2. Heat a large nonstick skillet over medium heat. Add sandwich to pan. Place a cast-iron or heavy skillet on top of sandwich; press gently to flatten. Cook 2 minutes on each side or until bread is lightly toasted (leave cast-iron skillet on sandwich while cooking). Cut into 4 wedges. Yield: 4 servings (serving size: 1 wedge).

CALORIES 447 (29% from fat); FAT 14.5g (sat 5g, mono 4.2g, poly 2.1g); PROTEIN 36.8g; CARB 42.1g; FIBER 3.8g; CHOL 89mg; IRON 3.6mg; SODIUM 986mg; CALC 156mg

MAKE AHEAD • FREEZABLE
Chewy Chocolate-Coconut Macaroons

Prepare these cookies a couple of days before your picnic, and store them in an airtight container. To freeze leftovers, layer cookies between sheets of waxed paper in an airtight container. Thaw about 30 minutes before serving.

2 ounces unsweetened chocolate, chopped
½ cup sifted cake flour
2 tablespoons unsweetened cocoa
⅛ teaspoon salt
2½ cups lightly packed flaked sweetened coconut
1 teaspoon vanilla extract
1 (14-ounce) can fat-free sweetened condensed milk

1. Preheat oven to 250°.
2. Line a large baking sheet with parchment paper, and secure with masking tape.
3. Place chocolate in a small microwave-safe bowl. Microwave at HIGH 1 minute or until almost melted. Remove from microwave; stir until completely melted.
4. Combine flour, cocoa, and salt in a large bowl. Add coconut, and toss well. Stir in melted chocolate, vanilla, and condensed milk (mixture will be stiff). Drop by level tablespoons 2 inches apart onto prepared baking sheet. Bake at 250° for 45 minutes or until edges of cookies are firm and centers of cookies are soft, rotating baking sheet once during baking time. Remove from oven, and cool 10 minutes on pan on a wire rack.
Continued

Remove cookies from parchment paper, and cool completely on rack. Store in an airtight container. Yield: 3 dozen cookies (serving size: 1 cookie).

CALORIES 84 (38% from fat); FAT 3.7g (sat 3.3g, mono 0.3g, poly 0g); PROTEIN 1.9g; CARB 11.7g; FIBER 0.9g; CHOL 1mg; IRON 0.2mg; SODIUM 45mg; CALC 33mg

---

MAKE AHEAD
Ginger Limeade

This sweet-tart beverage is refreshing on a hot day. Feel free to adjust the sugar to suit your taste. Tote the limeade in a thermos so it stays cold.

    6 cups cold water, divided
    ½ cup sugar
    3 tablespoons chopped peeled fresh
       ginger
    3 tablespoons grated lime rind
   10 mint leaves
   1¼ cups fresh lime juice (about 6
       limes)
    4 lime wedges (optional)

1. Place ¼ cup water, sugar, ginger, rind, and mint leaves in a blender, and process until well blended. Cover; chill 2 hours.
2. Add 5¾ cups water and juice; stir to combine. Garnish with lime wedges, if desired. Yield: 4 servings (serving size: 2 cups).

CALORIES 124 (1% from fat); FAT 0.1g (sat 0g, mono 0g, poly 0g); PROTEIN 0.6g; CARB 33.5g; FIBER 0.9g; CHOL 0mg; IRON 0.1mg; SODIUM 9mg; CALC 21mg

---

Chicken Tonight—and Tomorrow

A bird on the grill takes flight in sandwiches and salads to go.

MAKE AHEAD
Grilled Lemon-Herb Chicken

If your grill is large enough, cook two chickens at the same time to feed a larger group or just to have more leftovers for quick lunches. Refrigerate leftover chicken up to three days. Butterflying the chicken is easier to do with strong kitchen shears than with a knife.

    1 (5-pound) roasting chicken
    3 tablespoons fresh lemon juice
    2 tablespoons chopped fresh
       parsley
    1 tablespoon chopped fresh
       thyme
    1 teaspoon salt
    ½ teaspoon freshly ground black
       pepper
       Cooking spray

1. Remove and discard giblets and neck from chicken. Rinse chicken with cold water, and pat dry. Trim excess fat. Place chicken, breast side down, on a cutting surface. Cut chicken in half lengthwise along backbone (do not cut through breastbone). Turn chicken over. Starting at neck cavity, loosen skin from breast and drumsticks by inserting fingers, gently pushing between skin and meat.
2. Combine juice and next 4 ingredients; rub mixture under loosened skin and over breast and drumsticks. Gently press skin to secure. Place chicken in a large zip-top plastic bag. Seal and marinate in refrigerator 30 minutes.
3. Prepare grill.
4. Place chicken, skin side up, on grill rack coated with cooking spray. Grill 55

---

minutes or until a thermometer inserted into meaty part of thigh registers 180°. Remove chicken from grill; cover and let stand 10 minutes. Remove and discard skin. Yield: 5 servings (serving size: about 4 ounces meat).

CALORIES 203 (27% from fat); FAT 6.2g (sat 1.7g, mono 2.2g, poly 1.4g); PROTEIN 33.5g; CARB 1.1g; FIBER 0.2g; CHOL 100mg; IRON 1.5mg; SODIUM 565mg; CALC 21mg

---

MAKE AHEAD
Curried Chicken Salad with Apples and Raisins

Enjoy this fruit-studded chicken salad with whole-grain crackers, or spread it on whole wheat bread for a sandwich.

    ¼ cup low-fat mayonnaise
    2 teaspoons water
    1 teaspoon curry powder
    1 cup chopped skinless, boneless
       Grilled Lemon-Herb Chicken
       (about 4 ounces) (recipe at left)
    ¾ cup chopped Braeburn apple
       (about 1 small)
    ⅓ cup diced celery
    3 tablespoons raisins
    ⅛ teaspoon salt

1. Combine first 3 ingredients in a medium bowl, stirring with a whisk until well blended. Add Grilled Lemon-Herb Chicken and remaining ingredients; stir well. Cover and chill. Yield: 2 servings (servings size: about 1 cup).

CALORIES 222 (22% from fat); FAT 5.4g (sat 0.9g, mono 1.7g, poly 2g); PROTEIN 17.5g; CARB 26.9g; FIBER 2.5g; CHOL 50mg; IRON 1.5mg; SODIUM 731mg; CALC 30mg

---

MAKE AHEAD
Guacamole Chicken Wraps

    2 tablespoons fresh lime juice
    ¼ teaspoon salt
    1 ripe peeled avocado
    ½ cup chopped seeded plum
       tomato
    4 green leaf lettuce leaves
    4 (8-inch) fat-free flour tortillas
    2 cups shredded skinless, boneless
       Grilled Lemon-Herb Chicken
       (about 8 ounces) (recipe at left)

1. Place first 3 ingredients in a medium bowl; mash with a fork until smooth. Stir in tomato.

2. Place 1 lettuce leaf on each tortilla; spread about ¼ cup avocado mixture on each lettuce leaf. Top each serving with ½ cup Grilled Lemon-Herb Chicken. Roll up. Wrap in foil or parchment paper; chill. Yield: 4 servings (serving size: 1 wrap).

CALORIES 300 (33% from fat); FAT 10.9g (sat 2.1g, mono 6g, poly 1.7g); PROTEIN 21.1g; CARB 30.2g; FIBER 4.1g; CHOL 50mg; IRON 2.5mg; SODIUM 777mg; CALC 22mg

MAKE AHEAD

Grilled Chicken and Zucchini Sandwich

Although you can use both light and dark meat on this sandwich, it's best with breast meat. To kick-start lunch preparation, cook the zucchini on the grill while you're cooking the chicken; you can even assemble the sandwich the night before.

    2 tablespoons low-fat mayonnaise
    1 teaspoon fresh lemon juice
    ¼ teaspoon bottled minced
       garlic
    ⅛ teaspoon freshly ground black
       pepper
    1½ teaspoons extravirgin olive oil
    2 small zucchini, thinly sliced
       lengthwise (about 12 ounces)
    1 (8-ounce) package plain focaccia,
       cut in half horizontally
    2 ounces thinly sliced sharp
       provolone cheese
    2 cups thinly sliced skinless,
       boneless Grilled Lemon-Herb
       Chicken (about 8 ounces) (recipe
       on page 266)
    ¼ cup sliced bottled roasted red bell
       peppers

1. Combine first 4 ingredients; set aside.

2. Preheat grill or grill pan over medium-high heat.

3. Brush oil evenly over both sides of zucchini slices. Place half of zucchini on grill rack or grill pan; grill 2 minutes on each side or until lightly browned. Remove from grill or grill pan. Repeat procedure with remaining zucchini.

4. Layer bottom half of focaccia with cheese, zucchini, mayonnaise mixture, Grilled Lemon-Herb Chicken, bell peppers, and top half of focaccia. Cut into 4 wedges. Wrap in foil or parchment paper; chill. Yield: 4 servings (serving size: 1 wedge).

CALORIES 351 (30% from fat); FAT 11.6g (sat 3.9g, mono 4.7g, poly 1.4g); PROTEIN 26.5g; CARB 36.7g; FIBER 2.2g; CHOL 64mg; IRON 3.1mg; SODIUM 785mg; CALC 132mg

MAKE AHEAD

Grilled Eggplant Pitas with Chicken and Goat Cheese

Grilling one thinly sliced eggplant alongside your chicken will give you a side dish for dinner and the basis for this lunch later in the week.

    4 (¼-inch-thick) slices eggplant
       Cooking spray
    2 (6-inch) pitas, cut in half
    1⅓ cups thinly sliced skinless,
       boneless Grilled Lemon-Herb
       Chicken (about 5 ounces) (recipe
       on page 266)
    ½ cup (2 ounces) crumbled goat
       cheese
    ½ cup thinly sliced plum tomato
       (about 2 tomatoes)
    ¼ cup thinly sliced fresh basil
       leaves

1. Preheat grill or grill pan over medium-high heat.

2. Lightly coat both sides of eggplant slices with cooking spray. Place eggplant on grill rack or grill pan; grill 2 minutes on each side or until eggplant is lightly browned.

3. Fill each pita half with 1 eggplant slice, ⅓ cup Grilled Lemon-Herb Chicken, 2 tablespoons goat cheese, 2 tablespoons tomato, and 1 tablespoon basil. Wrap in foil or parchment paper; chill. Yield: 4 servings (serving size: 1 stuffed pita half).

CALORIES 415 (24% from fat); FAT 11.2g (sat 5.4g, mono 3g, poly 1.2g); PROTEIN 34.4g; CARB 43.6g; FIBER 4.9g; CHOL 80mg; IRON 3.8mg; SODIUM 807mg; CALC 125mg

MAKE AHEAD

Summer Vegetable Tabbouleh with Chicken

With fresh tastes and crunchy textures, this cold salad is great for a hot afternoon. It holds well once prepared and will keep in the refrigerator up to three days. Serve with toasted pita chips.

    1 cup uncooked bulgur
    1 cup boiling water
    1½ cups chopped skinless, boneless
       Grilled Lemon-Herb Chicken
       (about 6 ounces) (recipe on page
       266)
    1 cup chopped fresh parsley
    1 cup chopped cucumber
    1 cup chopped red onion
    1 cup chopped plum tomato (about
       4 tomatoes)
    ¼ cup chopped fresh mint
    ¼ cup fresh lemon juice (about
       2 lemons)
    2 tablespoons extravirgin olive oil
    ½ teaspoon salt
    ⅛ teaspoon freshly ground black
       pepper
    1 garlic clove, minced

1. Combine bulgur and boiling water in a large bowl; let stand 30 minutes. Add Grilled Lemon-Herb Chicken and next 5 ingredients, and toss gently to combine.

2. Combine lemon juice and remaining 4 ingredients, stirring well with a whisk. Drizzle juice mixture over salad; toss gently to coat. Yield: 4 servings (serving size: 1½ cups).

CALORIES 296 (30% from fat); FAT 9.9g (sat 1.7g, mono 6g, poly 1.5g); PROTEIN 18.5g; CARB 36.3g; FIBER 8.5g; CHOL 38mg; IRON 2.8mg; SODIUM 526mg; CALC 66mg

Southwestern Chicken Pasta Salad

Fresh summer corn is sweet, tender, and juicy—cooked or raw. If your corn is a bit past its prime, boil it for two minutes.

- ½ pound uncooked penne rigate
- 2 cups shredded skinless, boneless Grilled Lemon-Herb Chicken (about 8 ounces) (recipe on page 266)
- 1 cup fresh corn kernels
- ¾ cup (3 ounces) shredded sharp Cheddar cheese
- ½ cup sliced green onions
- ½ cup diced red bell pepper
- ½ cup chopped plum tomato (about 2 tomatoes)
- ¼ cup fresh orange juice
- 2 tablespoons fresh lime juice
- 1 tablespoon extravirgin olive oil
- 1 tablespoon chopped canned chipotle chiles in adobo sauce
- ½ teaspoon salt

1. Cook pasta according to package directions, omitting salt and fat. Drain and place in a large bowl. Add Grilled Lemon-Herb Chicken and next 5 ingredients; toss well to combine.

2. Combine orange juice and remaining 4 ingredients, stirring with a whisk. Drizzle over pasta mixture; toss gently to coat. Cover and chill. Yield: 6 servings (serving size: 1⅓ cups).

CALORIES 322 (28% from fat); FAT 9.9g (sat 3.6g, mono 3.8g, poly 1g); PROTEIN 21g; CARB 38.2g; FIBER 2.5g; CHOL 48mg; IRON 2.1mg; SODIUM 523mg; CALC 121mg

Spinach Salad with Chicken, Melon, and Mango

Thanks to an ample amount of spinach, this is a big, satisfying salad. Though the spinach is less prone to wilting than lettuce, it's best to store the dressing and salad separately and toss together shortly before eating.

DRESSING:
- ½ cup plain low-fat yogurt
- ¼ cup minced fresh mint
- 1 tablespoon honey
- 2 teaspoons fresh orange juice
- 2 teaspoons fresh lemon juice
- ¼ teaspoon salt

SALAD:
- 3 cups thinly sliced skinless, boneless Grilled Lemon-Herb Chicken (about 12 ounces) (recipe on page 266)
- 2 cups cubed honeydew melon
- 1½ cups cubed peeled ripe mango (about 1 mango)
- 1 (6-ounce) package fresh baby spinach

1. To prepare dressing, combine first 6 ingredients, stirring well with a whisk; cover and chill.

2. To prepare salad, combine Grilled Lemon-Herb Chicken, melon, mango, and spinach in a large bowl; cover and chill. Just before serving, drizzle yogurt mixture over salad, and toss gently to coat. Yield: 4 servings (serving size: about 3 cups salad and about 3 tablespoons dressing).

CALORIES 277 (18% from fat); FAT 5.4g (sat 1.7g, mono 1.9g, poly 1.2g); PROTEIN 28.5g; CARB 30.7g; FIBER 4.1g; CHOL 77mg; IRON 2.9mg; SODIUM 676mg; CALC 114mg

season's best

Pasta with Five Fresh Herbs

This recipe works because it has one predominant herb (basil) layered with other fresh herbs in smaller amounts to deepen the taste without becoming a flavor battle.

Pasta with Five Fresh Herbs

- 1 pound uncooked penne rigate
- 4 teaspoons extravirgin olive oil, divided
- ¼ cup chopped fresh basil
- ½ teaspoon chopped fresh oregano
- ½ teaspoon salt
- ½ teaspoon freshly ground black pepper
- 2 pints fresh cherry tomatoes
- 1 garlic clove, minced
- 1 tablespoon chopped fresh chives
- ½ teaspoon chopped fresh thyme
- ½ cup fat-free, less-sodium chicken broth
- 2 tablespoons chopped fresh parsley
- ½ cup (about 3 ounces) goat cheese, crumbled

1. Cook pasta according to package directions, omitting salt and fat; drain. Place in a large bowl. Add 2 teaspoons oil, basil, and next 3 ingredients to hot pasta, and toss well.

2. Heat 2 teaspoons oil in a large nonstick skillet over medium-high heat. Add tomatoes and garlic; sauté 2 minutes. Add chives and thyme; sauté 1 minute or until tomatoes are slightly charred and skins are just beginning to burst. Add broth; bring to a boil. Cook over high heat 1 minute. Add tomato mixture and parsley to pasta; toss gently to combine. Sprinkle with cheese; serve immediately. Yield: 6 servings (serving size: about 1½ cups pasta and about 1½ teaspoons cheese).

CALORIES 379 (21% from fat); FAT 8.8g (sat 3.7g, mono 3.4g, poly 0.5g); PROTEIN 14.6g; CARB 61.9g; FIBER 3.8g; CHOL 11mg; IRON 3.3mg; SODIUM 313mg; CALC 69mg

Cherries Jubilee Ice Cream Pie,
page 251

Couscous Salad Cups, page 260

Antipasto Chicken Sandwich,
page 265

Grilled Vegetables with Feta,
facing page

Baked Salmon with Dill, Grilled Asparagus with Balsamic Vinegar, page 275
Mashed Potatoes with Chives, page 276

Campus Cuisine

Elective courses, clubs, and other programs teach novice cooks their way around a kitchen.

Savvy college administrators from Harvard, Yale, University of Colorado at Boulder, and beyond, along with committed chefs and teachers, are helping adventuresome students learn the skills they need in the kitchen. The recipes we share here are simple for novice cooks to prepare yet creative enough to appeal to seasoned cooks who just want to get a satisfying dinner on the table tonight.

Grilled Vegetables with Feta

(facing page)

Yale students hone their knife skills chopping and slicing vegetables for this recipe. Served with basmati rice, it's a satisfying meatless entrée.

VINAIGRETTE:
- ¼ cup balsamic vinegar
- 2 tablespoons Dijon mustard
- 2 tablespoons olive oil
- 1 teaspoon freshly ground black pepper
- ½ teaspoon salt
- 3 garlic cloves, minced

VEGETABLES:
- 2 zucchini, halved lengthwise (about 1 pound)
- 1 red bell pepper, quartered
- 1 yellow bell pepper, quartered
- 4 (½-inch-thick) slices Vidalia or other sweet onion
- 4 (4-inch) portobello caps
- Cooking spray

REMAINING INGREDIENTS:
- 4 cups hot cooked basmati rice
- ½ cup (2 ounces) feta cheese, crumbled

1. Prepare grill.
2. To prepare vinaigrette, combine first 6 ingredients in a small bowl; stir well with a whisk.

3. To prepare vegetables, combine ¼ cup vinaigrette, zucchini, and bell peppers in a large bowl. Brush remaining vinaigrette over both sides of onion slices and mushroom caps. Place vegetables on grill rack coated with cooking spray; grill 2½ minutes on each side or until vegetables are tender and browned. Place vegetables on a cutting board; cut each vegetable piece in half. Serve over rice; sprinkle with cheese. Yield: 8 servings (serving size: ½ cup rice, about 2 cups vegetables, and 1 tablespoon cheese).

CALORIES 348 (36% from fat); FAT 13.9g (sat 5.4g, mono 6.4g, poly 1.3g); PROTEIN 12.3g; CARB 47.6g; FIBER 3.8g; CHOL 25mg; IRON 3.4mg; SODIUM 634mg; CALC 208mg

Easy Schnitzel

Maureen Clancy, the author of this story, developed an easier and lighter version of Wiener schnitzel after her two college-aged sons discovered the dish on a trip abroad. Serve with a tossed salad of mixed greens, cherry tomatoes, sliced cucumber, and onion. See page 274 for technique images on how to prepare the chicken for Easy Schnitzel.

- 4 (6-ounce) skinless, boneless chicken breast halves
- ¼ teaspoon salt
- ¼ teaspoon freshly ground black pepper
- 2 tablespoons all-purpose flour
- 2 tablespoons Dijon mustard
- 1 large egg, lightly beaten
- ½ cup dry breadcrumbs
- 1½ tablespoons grated fresh Parmesan cheese
- 2 teaspoons finely chopped fresh parsley
- 2 teaspoons chopped fresh chives
- 1 garlic clove, minced
- 1 tablespoon olive oil
- 4 lemon wedges (optional)

1. Preheat oven to 350°.
2. Place each chicken breast half between 2 sheets of heavy-duty plastic
Continued

How to Quarter a Pepper

To quarter a pepper: Use a knife to slice pepper in half; pull away stem. Slice halves.

wrap; pound to ½-inch thickness using a meat mallet or rolling pin. Sprinkle chicken with salt and pepper.

3. Place flour in a shallow bowl. Combine mustard and egg in a shallow dish. Combine breadcrumbs, cheese, parsley, chives, and garlic in a shallow dish. Dredge 1 chicken breast half in flour, turning to coat; shake off excess flour. Dip in egg mixture; dredge in breadcrumb mixture. Repeat procedure with remaining chicken, flour, egg mixture, and breadcrumb mixture.

4. Heat oil in a large ovenproof nonstick skillet over medium-high heat. Add chicken; sauté 2½ minutes or until browned. Remove from heat. Turn chicken over; place pan in oven. Bake at 350° for 10 minutes or until chicken is done. Serve with lemon wedges, if desired. Yield: 4 servings (serving size: 1 chicken breast half).

CALORIES 328 (22% from fat); FAT 8.1g (sat 1.9g, mono 3.8g, poly 1.3g); PROTEIN 45.3g; CARB 16.7g; FIBER 0.7g; CHOL 153mg; IRON 2.6mg; SODIUM 636mg; CALC 85m

Brennan's Bananas Foster

Chef John Turenne at Yale notes that this recipe, a hit in every class, was created at New Orleans's Brennan's Restaurant in the 1950s. Look for firm, ripe bananas. Because it contains alcohol, this recipe is not appropriate for underage students.

- 4 bananas
- ¼ cup butter
- 1 cup packed brown sugar
- ¼ cup crème de banane (banana liqueur)
- ½ teaspoon ground cinnamon
- ¼ cup dark rum
- 2 cups vanilla low-fat ice cream

1. Peel bananas; cut each banana in half lengthwise. Cut each half into 2 pieces.
2. Melt butter in a large nonstick skillet over medium heat. Stir in sugar, liqueur, and cinnamon. Bring to a simmer, and cook 2 minutes. Add bananas; cook 4 minutes or until tender. Remove from heat. Add rum to pan, and ignite rum with a long match. Stir bananas gently until flame dies down. Serve over ice cream. Yield: 8 servings (serving size: ¼ cup ice cream, 2 banana pieces, and 2 tablespoons sauce).

CALORIES 290 (21% from fat); FAT 6.9g (sat 3.4g, mono 2.4g, poly 0.3g); PROTEIN 2.2g; CARB 51.4g; FIBER 2.1g; CHOL 18mg; IRON 0.7mg; SODIUM 74mg; CALC 79mg

Rosemary Grilled Lamb Chops

Students at Harvard also discover that just a few ingredients, such as garlic and chopped fresh rosemary, lend a heady fragrant aroma to a humble lamb chop. An instant-read thermometer is crucial for determining when to remove the lamb from the grill (from 140° for rare to 170° for well done), since doneness is a matter of personal preference.

- 1 tablespoon chopped fresh rosemary
- 1 teaspoon olive oil
- ½ teaspoon kosher salt, divided
- 1 garlic clove, minced
- 4 (4-ounce) lamb loin chops, trimmed
- ⅛ teaspoon freshly ground black pepper
- Cooking spray

1. Combine rosemary, oil, ¼ teaspoon salt, and garlic; rub mixture evenly over both sides of lamb. Cover and marinate in refrigerator at least 2 hours or overnight.
2. Prepare grill.
3. Remove lamb from bag. Sprinkle both sides of lamb with ¼ teaspoon salt and pepper. Place lamb on a grill rack coated with cooking spray; grill 3 minutes on each side or until desired degree of doneness (145° for medium-rare). Yield: 4 servings (serving size: 1 chop).

CALORIES 232 (59% from fat); FAT 15.2g (sat 5.9g, mono 7.2g, poly 0.9g); PROTEIN 22g; CARB 0.5g; FIBER 0.2g; CHOL 72mg; IRON 2.1mg; SODIUM 290mg; CALC 17mg

How to Prepare Easy Schnitzel

1. *Pound chicken breasts to ½-inch thickness using a meat mallet or rolling pin.*

2. *Dredge chicken breast half in flour.*

3. *Dip chicken breast half in egg mixture.*

4. *Dredge chicken breast half in breadcrumb mixture.*

For a casual get-together, this easy meal accommodates a crowd. Plain couscous soaks up all the tasty sauce from the pork.

Pork Tenderloin with Onions and Dried Cranberries

Parmesan spinach*

Couscous

*Heat 2 teaspoons olive oil in a large non-stick skillet over medium-high heat. Add 3 minced garlic cloves; sauté 2 minutes. Add 2 (10-ounce) packages thawed frozen chopped spinach; cook 5 minutes or until thoroughly heated. Stir in ½ cup shredded fresh Parmesan cheese, ½ teaspoon salt, and ¼ teaspoon freshly ground black pepper.

Pork Tenderloin with Onions and Dried Cranberries

"I used this recipe to teach my college-aged sons about the ease of cooking with pork tenderloins because they are so versatile," Maureen Clancy says. "Now they prepare the dish on their own, experimenting with different beers and dried fruits." As with any dish that incorporates alcohol, this is intended for students who are of legal drinking age.

    2 (1-pound) pork tenderloins,
       trimmed
    1 teaspoon salt, divided
    ¼ teaspoon freshly ground black
       pepper
    1 tablespoon olive oil
    3 cups (¼-inch-thick) slices onion
       (about 3 medium)
    1 cup light beer
    1 cup fat-free, less-sodium chicken
       broth
    ½ cup dried cranberries

1. Sprinkle pork with ¾ teaspoon salt and pepper. Heat oil in a large nonstick skillet over medium-high heat. Add pork; cook 6 minutes, browning on all sides. Remove pork from pan. Add onion to pan; reduce heat, and cook 8 minutes

or until browned. Remove onion from pan; sprinkle with ¼ teaspoon salt, and set aside. Add beer to pan; cook 1 minute over high heat or until reduced to ½ cup.

2. Return pork and onion to pan; add broth, and bring to a boil. Cover, reduce heat, and simmer 30 minutes. Stir in cranberries; cover and cook 30 minutes or until pork is tender. Remove from heat. Place pork on a cutting board; cover and let stand 5 minutes. Cut each tenderloin into 12 slices. Serve with onion mixture. Yield: 8 servings (serving size: 3 pork slices and ¼ cup onion mixture).

CALORIES 178 (27% from fat); FAT 5.4g (sat 1.5g, mono 2.9g, poly 0.6g); PROTEIN 22.5g; CARB 9.4g; FIBER 0.8g; CHOL 68mg; IRON 1.5mg; SODIUM 394mg; CALC 14mg

Back-to-School Basics

Beginner cooks may be more inspired to spend time in the kitchen if they have good-quality, basic tools. Many students start out with Mom's hand-me-downs, but well-priced, high-quality starter sets of cookware are available at department and discount stores. Here's a checklist of tools to ensure students' success in the kitchen:

- eight-inch chef's knife
- garlic press
- kitchen timer with large readout and three distinctive alarms
- vegetable peeler
- colanders (plastic and stainless steel)
- two cutting boards (designate separate boards for meat and vegetables)
- instant-read thermometer
- silicone pot holders
- heat-resistant spatulas, wire whisks, and wooden spoons
- measuring cups and spoons
- pepper grinder

Grilled Asparagus with Balsamic Vinegar

(pictured on page 272)

One cooking class at Harvard teaches students how to prepare and cook fresh vegetables. In this recipe, students learn how to cook asparagus.

    1 pound thin asparagus spears
    1 teaspoon olive oil
    ¼ teaspoon kosher salt
    ⅛ teaspoon freshly ground black
       pepper
       Cooking spray
    1 tablespoon balsamic vinegar

1. Prepare grill.
2. Snap off tough ends of asparagus; place asparagus in a bowl or shallow dish. Drizzle with oil; sprinkle with salt and pepper, tossing well to coat. Place asparagus on a grill rack coated with cooking spray; grill 2 minutes on each side or until crisp-tender. Place asparagus in a bowl; drizzle with vinegar. Serve immediately. Yield: 4 servings.

CALORIES 25 (43% from fat); FAT 1.2g (sat 0.2g, mono 0.8g, poly 0.2g); PROTEIN 1.3g; CARB 3g; FIBER 0g; CHOL 0mg; IRON 1.3mg; SODIUM 120mg; CALC 16mg

Baked Salmon with Dill

(pictured on page 272)

Chef Martin Breslin's approach is to build a student's confidence in the kitchen with simple recipes using basic ingredients. The delicate combination of fresh dill and lemon lend just enough flavor to add interest to plain baked fish.

    4   (6-ounce) salmon fillets (about 1
        inch thick)
        Cooking spray
    1½ tablespoons finely chopped fresh
        dill
    ½   teaspoon kosher salt
    ⅛   teaspoon freshly ground black
        pepper
    4   lemon wedges

Continued

1. Preheat oven to 350°.

2. Place fish on a baking sheet lightly coated with cooking spray; lightly coat fish with cooking spray. Sprinkle fish with dill, salt, and pepper. Bake at 350° for 10 minutes or until fish flakes easily when tested with a fork or until desired degree of doneness. Serve with lemon wedges. Yield: 4 servings (serving size: 1 fillet and 1 lemon wedge).

CALORIES 263 (54% from fat); FAT 15.8g (sat 3.2g, mono 5.7g, poly 5.7g); PROTEIN 28.2g; CARB 0.1g; FIBER 0g; CHOL 80mg; IRON 0.5mg; SODIUM 313mg; CALC 20mg

---

QUICK & EASY

Mashed Potatoes with Chives

(pictured on page 272)

In class, Breslin points out the differences among potato varieties. Yukon gold potatoes lend a buttery color and flavor, and they're great for mashing.

    2 pounds Yukon gold potatoes,
       peeled
    ½ cup whole milk
    3 tablespoons butter
    ½ teaspoon kosher salt
    ½ teaspoon freshly ground black
       pepper
    2 tablespoons chopped fresh chives

1. Place potatoes in a large saucepan; cover with water. Bring to a boil over medium-high heat. Reduce heat, and simmer 15 minutes or until tender; drain.
2. Combine milk and butter in a small saucepan, and cook over medium-high heat until butter melts. Remove milk mixture from heat.
3. Return potatoes to pan; mash with a potato masher to desired consistency. Add milk mixture, salt, and pepper, stirring until well combined. Stir in chives. Yield: 6 servings (serving size: ¾ cup).

CALORIES 187 (30% from fat); FAT 6.3g (sat 3.2g, mono 2.5g, poly 0.2g); PROTEIN 4.3g; CARB 27.7g; FIBER 1.8g; CHOL 17mg; IRON 1.3mg; SODIUM 215mg; CALC 24mg

---

dinner tonight

Weeknight Pizza

A world of flavor tops these quick weeknight pizzas.

Weeknight Pizza Menu 1
serves 4

Pizza Olympia

Mixed olives and pepperoncini

Yogurt with honey and walnuts*

*Place ¼ cup chopped walnuts in a small skillet; toast over medium heat 3 minutes or until fragrant and lightly browned. Spoon ½ cup plain low-fat yogurt into each of 4 small serving bowls. Drizzle 2 tablespoons honey over each serving. Sprinkle each with 1 tablespoon walnuts.

Game Plan

1. While oven preheats:
   • Prepare tomato paste mixture for pizza
2. Assemble pizza
3. While pizza bakes:
   • Combine olives and pepperoncini
   • Prepare yogurt; chill

QUICK & EASY

Pizza Olympia

The feta cheese will not melt, so use the crust's golden color as an indicator of doneness.

TOTAL TIME: 25 MINUTES

    1 (10-ounce) focaccia, cut in half
       horizontally
    1 tablespoon minced fresh garlic
    2 tablespoons tomato paste
    2 teaspoons dried oregano
    1 (7-ounce) bottle roasted red bell
       peppers, drained and chopped
    ½ cup chopped red onion
    1 tablespoon drained capers
    1 cup (4 ounces) crumbled feta
       cheese

---

1. Preheat oven to 450°.
2. Place focaccia halves, cut sides up, on a baking sheet. Combine garlic, tomato paste, and oregano in a small bowl; spread evenly over focaccia halves. Top each half evenly with roasted peppers, onion, and capers; sprinkle with feta cheese. Bake at 450° for 12 minutes or until focaccia is golden. Cut each pizza in half. Yield: 4 servings (serving size: ½ pizza).

CALORIES 301 (25% from fat); FAT 8.4g (sat 4.5g, mono 2.7g, poly 0.5g); PROTEIN 11.4g; CARB 45.6g; FIBER 2.6g; CHOL 25mg; IRON 3.2mg; SODIUM 648mg; CALC 160mg

---

Weeknight Pizza Menu 2
serves 4

Turkish Turkey Pizza

Minted cucumber and cherry tomato salad*

Iced grapes

*Combine 1 tablespoon extravirgin olive oil, 2 teaspoons red wine vinegar, ¼ teaspoon salt, and ¼ teaspoon freshly ground black pepper in a small bowl, stirring with a whisk. Combine 2 cups thinly sliced English cucumber and 2 cups halved cherry tomatoes in a serving bowl. Drizzle dressing over cucumber and tomato, tossing to coat. Sprinkle with ¼ cup chopped fresh mint.

Game Plan

1. While oven preheats:
   • Cook topping for pizza
   • Combine salad ingredients (except mint)
2. While pizza bakes:
   • Sprinkle mint over salad
   • Freeze grapes

Turkish Turkey Pizza

Pomegranate molasses may be sold as concentrated pomegranate juice. Look for it in Middle Eastern markets, gourmet shops, and some large supermarkets. Its unique flavor makes it well worth seeking out, and a bottle lasts indefinitely in the refrigerator. If you can't find it, combine 2 tablespoons fresh lemon juice and 2 teaspoons honey, stirring until blended.

TOTAL TIME: 36 MINUTES

    1   tablespoon olive oil
    ¾   cup chopped red onion
    ½   cup chopped red bell pepper
    ½   pound lean ground turkey
    1   cup diced canned tomatoes, drained
    ¼   cup chopped fresh flat-leaf parsley, divided
    1   tablespoon tomato paste
    1½ teaspoons pomegranate molasses
    ¼   teaspoon ground cumin
    ⅛   teaspoon ground allspice
    4   (4-inch) pitas
    ¼   cup plain low-fat yogurt
    ½   teaspoon salt
    ½   teaspoon freshly ground black pepper
    ½   teaspoon ground red pepper

1. Preheat oven to 450°.
2. Heat oil in a large nonstick skillet over medium-high heat. Add onion and bell pepper; cook 2 minutes or until tender. Add turkey; cook 3 minutes. Add tomato, 2 tablespoons parsley, tomato paste, and next 3 ingredients to pan; reduce heat to medium. Cook 5 minutes or until liquid almost evaporates.
3. Place pitas on a baking sheet. Combine yogurt, salt, black pepper, and red pepper in a small bowl; spread evenly over pitas. Divide turkey mixture evenly among pitas; sprinkle evenly with 2 tablespoons parsley. Bake at 450° for 5 minutes; serve immediately. Yield: 4 servings (serving size: 1 pizza).

CALORIES 248 (30% from fat); FAT 8.3g (sat 1.7g, mono 2.8g, poly 0.5g); PROTEIN 15.7g; CARB 27.4g; FIBER 2.5g; CHOL 49mg; IRON 2.7mg; SODIUM 667mg; CALC 109mg

---

Weeknight Pizza Menu 3
serves 4

Garden Tomato and Basil Pesto Pizza

Baby arugula salad with balsamic vinaigrette*

Melon slices

*Combine 2 tablespoons extravirgin olive oil, 2 teaspoons balsamic vinegar, 1 teaspoon sugar, ½ teaspoon Dijon mustard, ¼ teaspoon salt, and ¼ teaspoon freshly ground black pepper in a small bowl, stirring with a whisk. Combine ¼ cup thinly sliced red onion, ¼ cup toasted sliced almonds, and 1 (5-ounce) package prewashed baby arugula in a serving bowl. Pour vinaigrette over arugula mixture; toss to coat.

Game Plan

1. While oven preheats:
 • Slice tomatoes and cheese for pizza
 • Prepare vinaigrette for salad
2. While pizza bakes:
 • Combine salad and vinaigrette

Garden Tomato and Basil Pesto Pizza

Fresh mozzarella is easier to slice when it's very firm. Place mozzarella in the freezer just until firm, and thinly slice. Any brand of prebaked pizza crust will work for this recipe.

TOTAL TIME: 15 MINUTES

    1   (12-ounce) prebaked pizza crust (such as Mama Mary's)
Cooking spray
    2   tablespoons commercial pesto
    1   cup (4 ounces) thinly sliced fresh mozzarella cheese
    2   cups chopped tomato (about 2 large)
    ¼   teaspoon crushed red pepper
    ¼   cup thinly sliced fresh basil

1. Preheat oven to 450°.
2. Spray crust with cooking spray.
3. Place crust on a baking sheet; bake at 450° for 10 minutes. Spread pesto evenly over crust, leaving a ½-inch border. Top with cheese slices and tomato; sprinkle with pepper. Bake at 450° for 5 minutes or until cheese melts and crust is golden. Sprinkle with basil. Yield: 4 servings (serving size: ¼ pizza).

CALORIES 377 (32% from fat); FAT 13.5g (sat 4.9g, mono 0.1g, poly 0.2g); PROTEIN 14.8g; CARB 48.1g; FIBER 3.1g; CHOL 24mg; IRON 3.2mg; SODIUM 687mg; CALC 209mg

---

technique

Preserving the Bounty

Extend the season with simple jams, chutneys, and relishes—no special equipment is needed.

Raspberry-Almond Jam

This bright, fruity jam, a tasty topping for toast, is also good stirred into oatmeal or layered with ice cream for a quick parfait.

    5   cups fresh raspberries
    2   cups sugar
    ½   cup amaretto (almond-flavored liqueur)
    2   tablespoons fresh lime juice
    ¼   teaspoon salt
    ¼   teaspoon almond extract

1. Combine first 4 ingredients in a large saucepan; bring to a boil. Reduce heat, and simmer, uncovered, 40 minutes or until thick, stirring frequently. Remove from heat; stir in salt and extract. Cool; pour into airtight containers. Yield: 3½ cups (serving size: 2 tablespoons).
NOTE: Refrigerate Raspberry-Almond Jam in airtight containers up to six weeks.

CALORIES 74 (2% from fat); FAT 0.2g (sat 0g, mono 0g, poly 0.1g); PROTEIN 0.3g; CARB 17.9g; FIBER 1.4g; CHOL 0mg; IRON 0.2mg; SODIUM 21mg; CALC 6mg

Red Tomato Chutney

This sweet-tart chutney pairs summery tomatoes with fall-flavored cranberries, making it an all-purpose condiment for late-summer and fall barbecues. Spoon it over burgers and grilled chicken. In cooler weather, toss a little chutney with roasted vegetables, such as parsnips, turnips, or sweet potatoes. Or mix it with low-fat mayonnaise to make a dip for raw vegetables.

    3   cups finely chopped peeled
        tomato (about 4 large)
    1   cup finely chopped red bell pepper
    1   cup finely chopped red onion
    ½   cup dried cranberries
    ½   cup cider vinegar
    ¼   cup granulated sugar
    ¼   cup packed brown sugar
    2   tablespoons minced peeled fresh
        ginger
    ½   teaspoon salt
    ½   teaspoon mustard seeds
    ¼   teaspoon ground cinnamon
    ¼   teaspoon ground cumin
    ¼   teaspoon ground allspice
    ⅛   teaspoon ground red pepper

1. Combine all ingredients in a large saucepan; bring to a boil. Reduce heat, and simmer, uncovered, 45 minutes or until thick, stirring frequently. Cool; pour into airtight containers. Yield: 3½ cups (serving size: 2 tablespoons).

NOTE: Refrigerate Red Tomato Chutney in airtight containers up to two months.

CALORIES 30 (3% from fat); FAT 0.1g (sat 0g, mono 0g, poly 0.1g); PROTEIN 0.3g; CARB 7.5g; FIBER 0.5g; CHOL 0mg; IRON 0.2mg; SODIUM 44mg; CALC 6mg

---

Preserve the Best

To prepare preserves, jam, or chutney, use the best fruit you can find. Whether you're at the supermarket, the local farmers' market, or out in the berry patch, there's one rule for picking the best produce: Smell it. If it lacks fragrance, it probably lacks taste.

Fig and Ginger Jam

Spoon this condiment onto English muffins, dab it on crackers and top with a sliver of Brie cheese, or slather it on toast points and top with smoked salmon or salmon caviar.

    4   cups coarsely chopped dark-
        skinned fresh figs (such as Black
        Mission, Celeste, or Brown
        Turkey; about 15 large figs)
    2¼ cups sugar
    ⅓   cup water
    ¼   cup fresh lemon juice
    3   tablespoons chopped crystallized
        ginger
    ¼   teaspoon salt

1. Combine all ingredients in a large saucepan; bring to a boil. Reduce heat, and simmer, uncovered, 30 minutes or until thick, stirring frequently. Cool; pour into airtight containers. Yield: 3 cups (serving size: 2 tablespoons).

NOTE: Refrigerate Fig and Ginger Jam in airtight containers up to six weeks.

CALORIES 107 (1% from fat); FAT 0.1g (sat 0g, mono 0g, poly 0.1g); PROTEIN 0.3g; CARB 27.7g; FIBER 1.2g; CHOL 0mg; IRON 0.2mg; SODIUM 25mg; CALC 16mg

---

Blueberry-Chipotle Chutney

Consider using this chutney as a barbecue sauce, basting it onto meat on the grill. Or spread it on a tortilla, top with sliced grilled chicken and goat cheese, and roll up.

    4   cups fresh blueberries
    1   cup finely chopped Granny Smith
        apple
    ½   cup white wine vinegar
    ⅓   cup sugar
    ⅓   cup honey
    3   tablespoons grated orange rind
    2   tablespoons chopped canned
        chipotle chiles in adobo sauce
        (about 2 chiles)
    1   tablespoon mustard seeds
    ½   teaspoon salt
    ½   teaspoon ground ginger

1. Combine all ingredients in a large saucepan; bring to a boil. Reduce heat, and simmer, uncovered, 25 minutes or until thick, stirring frequently. Cool; pour into airtight containers. Yield: 4 cups (serving size: 2 tablespoons).

NOTE: Refrigerate Blueberry-Chipotle Chutney in airtight containers up to two months.

CALORIES 34 (5% from fat); FAT 0.2g (sat 0g, mono 0.1g, poly 0.1g); PROTEIN 0.3g; CARB 8.5g; FIBER 0.7g; CHOL 0mg; IRON 0.2mg; SODIUM 48mg; CALC 4mg

---

Watermelon Rind Relish

For this recipe, you'll need the rind of a 5-pound melon. Use the white inner rind, not the outer green part, which might have been waxed. Shred the rind with the large holes of a box grater, or cut it into chunks and shred it in a food processor. Serve the relish with ham or fish, or stir a little into steamed carrots.

    3   quarts water
    6   cups shredded watermelon
        rind
    1   cup sugar
    1   cup cider vinegar
    1½ tablespoons dry mustard
    2   teaspoons ground turmeric
    1½ teaspoons ground ginger
    ½   teaspoon salt
    ½   teaspoon celery seeds

1. Bring 3 quarts water to a boil in a large saucepan. Add rind; cook 3 minutes. Drain well.

2. Combine sugar and remaining 6 ingredients in pan; bring mixture to a boil. Reduce heat, and simmer 2 minutes. Stir in watermelon rind; simmer, uncovered, 30 minutes or until most of liquid evaporates, stirring frequently. Cool; pour into airtight containers. Yield: 3½ cups (serving size: 2 tablespoons).

NOTE: Refrigerate Watermelon Rind Relish in airtight containers up to two months.

CALORIES 42 (6% from fat); FAT 0.3g (sat 0g, mono 0.1g, poly 0.1g); PROTEIN 0.4g; CARB 10.4g; FIBER 0.2g; CHOL 0mg; IRON 0.3mg; SODIUM 43mg; CALC 5mg

Green Tomato Chutney

This sweet, tangy chutney is a fine topping for burgers, fish tacos, rice and beans, or grilled chicken.

    2   cups chopped green tomato
        (about 3 medium)
    1   cup chopped Granny Smith apple
    ½   cup sugar
    ½   cup chopped green bell pepper
    ½   cup chopped onion
    ¼   cup cider vinegar
    2   teaspoons grated lemon rind
    2   tablespoons fresh lemon juice
    1   tablespoon minced peeled fresh
        ginger
    ½   teaspoon salt
    ½   teaspoon ground coriander
    ¼   teaspoon ground cinnamon
    ¼   teaspoon ground allspice
    ¼   teaspoon ground red pepper
    2   garlic cloves, minced
    1   jalapeño pepper, seeded and chopped

1. Combine all ingredients in a large saucepan; bring to a boil. Reduce heat, and simmer, uncovered, 45 minutes or until thick, stirring frequently. Cool; pour into airtight containers. Yield: 4 cups (serving size: 2 tablespoons).

NOTE: Refrigerate Green Tomato Chutney in airtight containers up to two months.

CALORIES 20 (5% from fat); FAT 0.1g (sat 0g, mono 0g, poly 0g); PROTEIN 0.2g; CARB 5g; FIBER 0.3g; CHOL 0mg; IRON 0.1mg; SODIUM 39mg; CALC 4mg

Spiced Pepper Relish

This tastes like traditional sweet pickle relish, but with a peppery spike. Use it on sandwiches or salads, or enjoy it spooned onto field peas or other beans.

   3½   cups shredded onion (about 2 large)
    3   cups shredded red bell pepper
        (about 4 medium)
    2   cups sugar
    1   cup white wine vinegar
    ½   cup water
    1   teaspoon salt
    1   teaspoon crushed red pepper

1. Combine all ingredients in a large saucepan; bring to a boil. Reduce heat, and simmer, uncovered, 35 minutes or until thick, stirring frequently. Cool; pour into airtight containers. Yield: 5 cups (serving size: 2 tablespoons).

NOTE: Refrigerate Spiced Pepper Relish in airtight containers up to one month.

CALORIES 48 (2% from fat); FAT 0.1g (sat 0g, mono 0g, poly 0g); PROTEIN 0.3g; CARB 12.1g; FIBER 0.2g; CHOL 0mg; IRON 0.1mg; SODIUM 60mg; CALC 4mg

Blackberry-Rhubarb Chutney

This spiced chutney is great as a condiment to roasts and sautés, but don't stop there. For an aromatic side dish, stir a couple of tablespoons into any cooked whole grain, such as brown rice, spelt, or barley. Or use a little to spice up homemade chicken salad. For the best taste, use fresh blackberries; fresh rhubarb can be hard to find, so use frozen.

    4   cups fresh blackberries
    2   cups thinly sliced frozen rhubarb,
        thawed
    2   cups thinly sliced celery
    1   cup chopped red onion
    1   cup granulated sugar
    1   cup packed dark brown sugar
    ¾   cup dry red wine
    ¼   cup red wine vinegar
    1   teaspoon ground ginger
    ½   teaspoon ground cinnamon
    ¼   teaspoon ground cloves
    ¼   teaspoon salt
    2   garlic cloves, minced

1. Combine all ingredients in a large saucepan, and bring to a boil. Reduce heat, and simmer, uncovered, 1 hour or until thick, stirring frequently. Cool and pour into airtight containers. Yield: 4½ cups (serving size: 2 tablespoons).

NOTE: Refrigerate Blackberry-Rhubarb Chutney in airtight containers up to two months.

CALORIES 60 (2% from fat); FAT 0.1g (sat 0g, mono 0g, poly 0.1g); PROTEIN 0.4g; CARB 14.2g; FIBER 0.3g; CHOL 0mg; IRON 0.3mg; SODIUM 25mg; CALC 21mg

Lemon-Zucchini Relish

This unusual relish is reminiscent of Middle Eastern condiments, particularly those made with preserved lemon. While it will go well with roasted chicken or any grilled entrée, you can also use it as a spread on sandwiches.

    6   cups shredded zucchini (about
        6 medium)
    1   teaspoon salt
    1   large lemon
   1½   cups chopped yellow onion
   1½   cups golden raisins
    1   cup white wine
    ¾   cup fresh lemon juice (about
        4 lemons)
    ¾   cup honey
    ¼   cup sugar

1. Place zucchini in a colander; sprinkle with salt. Toss well. Drain 30 minutes, tossing occasionally. Place zucchini on paper towels; squeeze until barely moist.
2. Carefully remove rind from lemon using a vegetable peeler, making sure to avoid white pithy part of the rind. Place rind in a small saucepan; cover with water. Bring to a boil; cover, reduce heat, and simmer 15 minutes or until rind is tender. Drain; cool. Finely chop rind.
3. Combine zucchini, rind, onion, and remaining ingredients in a large saucepan; bring to a boil. Reduce heat, and simmer, uncovered, 35 minutes or until thick, stirring frequently. Cool; pour into airtight containers. Yield: 4 cups (serving size: 2 tablespoons).

NOTE: Refrigerate Lemon-Zucchini Relish in airtight containers up to 1 month.

CALORIES 60 (2% from fat); FAT 0.1g (sat 0g, mono 0g, poly 0.1g); PROTEIN 0.7g; CARB 15.7g; FIBER 0.7g; CHOL 0mg; IRON 0.3mg; SODIUM 54mg; CALC 11mg

Spicy Cucumber Relish

It used to be a tradition among many German farm families in the Midwest to always have a bowl of these vinegary cucumbers in the refrigerator. They're the easiest relish of all, as they require no cooking, and they're a refreshing salad alongside any meal.

     4 cups water
     1 cup thinly sliced shallots
     1 cup white wine vinegar
     ⅓ cup sugar
     ¼ cup chopped fresh dill
  1½ teaspoons salt
     1 teaspoon crushed red pepper
     6 cups thinly sliced peeled cucumber
         (about 3 large)

1. Combine water, shallots, vinegar, sugar, dill, salt, and pepper in a large glass bowl, stirring until sugar dissolves. Stir in cucumber. Cover and refrigerate at least 24 hours. Serve with a slotted spoon. Yield: 5 cups (serving size: ¼ cup).
NOTE: Refrigerate Spicy Cucumber Relish in airtight containers up to one week.

CALORIES 19 (5% from fat); FAT 0.1g (sat 0g, mono 0g, poly 0g); PROTEIN 0.4g; CARB 4.4g; FIBER 0.4g; CHOL 0mg; IRON 0.2mg; SODIUM 120mg; CALC 9mg

---

Contain Yourself

Although refrigerator preserving is more straightforward than traditional canning, you must store jams, chutneys, and relishes in nonreactive, airtight containers. The best containers to use are glass canning jars, found in large supermarkets and some hardware stores. You can also forgo the glass jars and use stainless steel bowls or plastic containers with tight-fitting lids. Avoid reactive metals, such as aluminum, copper, and cast iron—when they come in contact with acidic ingredients, they often give the food an unpleasant metallic flavor. Store containers in the refrigerator for two weeks to two months, depending on the recipe.

Alfresco Italian

Like most Italian cooking, grilling emphasizes simplicity and flavor.

Italian-style grilling is a delicious way to lend new flair to a familiar way of cooking. Simply choose the freshest seasonal produce available, a great cut of meat or a fresh piece of fish, and a handful of fresh herbs. Invite friends over for a party, and enjoy a platter of bruschetta, roll out dough for a fire-kissed pizza, and throw a few rosemary sprigs into the fire to help perfume the afternoon air.

Salmon Trout with Garlic and Grilled Fennel

If you can't find salmon trout, buy regular trout instead. Fennel imparts an aniselike flavor and aroma.

     2 (8-ounce) skin-on salmon trout
         fillets
  1½ teaspoons olive oil, divided
     ½ teaspoon salt, divided
     ½ teaspoon freshly ground black
         pepper, divided
     ¼ cup fresh lemon juice, divided
     ½ cup (2 ounces) finely chopped
         prosciutto
     ¼ cup chopped fennel fronds
     ⅛ teaspoon fennel seeds, crushed
     2 garlic cloves, minced
  Cooking spray
     2 fennel bulbs
     4 lemon wedges

1. Prepare grill.
2. Brush fish evenly with 1 teaspoon oil; sprinkle evenly with ¼ teaspoon salt and ⅛ teaspoon pepper. Combine ½ teaspoon oil and 2 tablespoons juice. Set aside.
3. Combine ⅛ teaspoon pepper, prosciutto, fennel fronds, fennel seeds, and garlic, stirring well. Heat a large nonstick skillet over medium-high heat. Coat pan with cooking spray. Sauté prosciutto mixture 3 minutes or until prosciutto is crisp.
4. Cut fennel bulbs in half vertically. Grill 2 minutes on each side or until golden. Cut into ¼-inch-thick slices. Keep warm.

5. Place fish on grill rack coated with cooking spray. Grill 5 minutes on each side or until fish flakes easily when tested with a fork or until desired degree of doneness, basting occasionally with juice mixture. Transfer fish to a serving platter; sprinkle fish evenly with ¼ teaspoon salt and ¼ teaspoon pepper. Top with prosciutto mixture, and drizzle with 2 tablespoons juice. Serve immediately with grilled fennel and lemon wedges. Yield: 4 servings (serving size: ½ fillet).

CALORIES 176 (34% from fat); FAT 6.6g (sat 1.6g, mono 2.1g, poly 0.7g); PROTEIN 19.1g; CARB 11.7g; FIBER 4g; CHOL 73mg; IRON 1.4mg; SODIUM 651mg; CALC 80mg

Eggplant and Tomato-Mint Salsa

Allow grilled eggplant pulp to stand one hour to drain excess liquid. Otherwise the salsa will be watery. Serve salsa with crusty bread, sturdy crackers, or alongside fish or chicken.

     2 eggplants (about 1½ pounds)
  Cooking spray
  1½ cups chopped seeded
         tomato
     ¼ cup chopped fresh mint
     2 teaspoons fresh lemon
         juice
     1 teaspoon extravirgin olive oil
     ½ teaspoon salt
     ½ teaspoon freshly ground black
         pepper
     1 garlic clove, minced

1. Prepare grill.
2. Cut each eggplant in half lengthwise. Lightly score cut sides of eggplant. Place eggplant, cut sides down, on grill rack coated with cooking spray. Grill 20 minutes or until very tender, turning occasionally. Scoop pulp from eggplant halves, and place in a sieve over a bowl. Discard peels. Let pulp stand 1 hour or until cool and thoroughly drained. Discard liquid. Coarsely mash pulp, and place in a small bowl. Stir in tomato and remaining ingredients. Serve at room temperature, stirring just before serving. Yield: 4 servings (serving size: ½ cup).

CALORIES 61 (25% from fat); FAT 1.7g (sat 0.3g, mono 1g, poly 0.3g); PROTEIN 2.1g; CARB 11.9g; FIBER 1g; CHOL 0mg; IRON 0.8mg; SODIUM 305mg; CALC 22mg

Grilled Bread with Tuscan-Style Lamb

Ask your butcher to cut the leg of lamb into thin slices, or scaloppine (the Italian name for very thin slices of veal). Also, try the lamb over couscous or inside a warm pita.

    1 tablespoon chopped fresh
       flat-leaf parsley
    1 tablespoon chopped fresh rosemary
    1 tablespoon chopped fresh thyme
    1 tablespoon chopped fresh sage
    1 tablespoon white wine vinegar
    1 teaspoon extravirgin olive oil
    ¼ teaspoon freshly ground black
       pepper
    2 garlic cloves, minced
    1 (1-pound) boneless leg of lamb,
       trimmed
    ½ teaspoon salt
       Cooking spray
    1 (8-ounce) French bread baguette
    ½ cup thinly sliced bottled roasted
       red bell peppers

1. Combine first 8 ingredients, stirring well; place mixture in a large zip-top plastic bag. Cut lamb crosswise into 8 (¼-inch-thick) slices. Place each slice between 2 sheets of heavy-duty plastic wrap; pound each piece to ⅛-inch thickness using a meat mallet or rolling pin. Add lamb to bag; seal and marinate in

refrigerator 8 hours or overnight, turning bag occasionally. Remove lamb from bag; discard marinade.
2. Prepare grill.
3. Sprinkle lamb evenly with salt. Place lamb on grill rack coated with cooking spray, and grill 1 minute on each side or until desired degree of doneness.
4. Cut baguette in half horizontally. Coat cut sides of bread with cooking spray. Place bread, cut sides down, on grill rack, and grill 2 minutes or until golden. Cut bread into 16 slices. Serve lamb with grilled bread and bell peppers. Yield: 4 servings (serving size: about 2 slices lamb, 4 slices bread, and 2 tablespoons peppers).

CALORIES 207 (29% from fat); FAT 6.6g (sat 1.7g, mono 2.5g, poly 1.7g); PROTEIN 14.2g; CARB 22.3g; FIBER 1.9g; CHOL 37mg; IRON 1.7mg; SODIUM 353mg; CALC 18mg

Polenta with Chunky Tomato Sauce and Pecorino Romano

Polenta may be prepared ahead, covered, and refrigerated overnight.

POLENTA:

    1½ cups uncooked instant cornmeal
     6 cups water
    ½ teaspoon salt
    ½ cup (2 ounces) grated pecorino
       Romano cheese
       Cooking spray

TOMATO SAUCE:

    2½ cups chopped tomato (about
       2 large)
    ¼ cup thinly sliced shallots (about
       1 large or 2 small shallots)
    3 tablespoons thinly sliced fresh
       basil (about 12 leaves)
    1 tablespoon minced fresh
       marjoram or oregano
    1 teaspoon extravirgin olive oil
    ½ teaspoon salt
    ⅛ teaspoon freshly ground black
       pepper

REMAINING INGREDIENT:

    ¼ cup (1 ounce) shaved pecorino
       Romano cheese

1. To prepare polenta, place cornmeal in a large saucepan. Gradually add water and ½ teaspoon salt, stirring constantly with a whisk. Bring to a boil. Reduce heat to medium; cook 15 minutes, stirring frequently. Remove from heat; stir in grated cheese. Spoon polenta into a 13 x 9-inch pan coated with cooking spray, spreading evenly. Press plastic wrap onto surface of polenta; chill 2 hours or until firm.
2. To prepare sauce, combine tomato and next 6 ingredients in a medium bowl; set aside.
3. Prepare grill.
4. Cut polenta into rounds using a 2½-inch cookie cutter; coat both sides of rounds evenly with cooking spray. Grill polenta 5 minutes on each side or until golden brown. Serve with tomato sauce, and sprinkle with shaved cheese. Serve immediately. Yield: 6 servings (serving size: 2 polenta rounds and ½ cup tomato sauce).

CALORIES 251 (24% from fat); FAT 6.7g (sat 2.4g, mono 2.4g, poly 1g); PROTEIN 9g; CARB 40.4g; FIBER 5g; CHOL 14mg; IRON 1.1mg; SODIUM 549mg; CALC 154mg

Grilling Basics

Whether you cook on a charcoal, gas, or electric grill, or a grill pan, you can enjoy great flavor with these tips:

- Regulate the heat: In general, thicker pieces of food require lower heat for a longer time, and smaller pieces call for more intense heat for a shorter period.
- Wipe off excess marinade before placing food on the grill to minimize flare-ups.
- Keep the grill clean to prevent sticking, burning, or off flavors.
- Coat the grill rack with cooking spray before adding the food to prevent food from sticking and to create more prominent grill marks.

Chocolate Pizza with Apricot Preserves and Bananas

The recipe calls for letting the dough rise one hour. You can also let it stand at room temperature overnight with the same great results. Slice the bananas just before adding them to pizza to avoid discoloration. Serve this deliciously gooey dessert with a knife and fork.

    3 cups all-purpose flour, divided
    1 tablespoon sugar
    1 teaspoon dry yeast
    ¼ teaspoon salt
    1 cup warm water (110° to 120°)
    1 tablespoon extravirgin olive oil
Cooking spray
    ¾ cup apricot preserves
    2 ripe bananas, sliced
    ½ cup (4 ounces) semisweet
       chocolate chips

1. Lightly spoon flour into dry measuring cups; level with a knife. Combine 2¾ cups flour, sugar, yeast, and salt in a large bowl, stirring well with a whisk. Make a well in center of mixture. Combine water and oil; add to flour mixture. Stir until a soft dough forms. Turn dough out onto a floured surface. Knead until smooth and elastic, about 10 minutes (dough will feel sticky), using enough remaining flour, 1 tablespoon at a time, to keep hands from sticking.
2. Place dough in a large bowl coated with cooking spray, turning to coat top. Cover and let rise in a warm place (85°), free from drafts, 1 hour or until doubled in size. (Gently press two fingers into dough. If indentation remains, dough has risen enough.)
3. Prepare grill.
4. Punch dough down. Divide dough into 5 equal portions. Shape each portion into a ball; cover and let rest 15 minutes. Working with one portion at a time (cover remaining dough to prevent drying), roll each portion into a 9-inch circle on a floured surface. Combine preserves and banana in a small bowl, stirring gently.
5. Working with 1 portion at a time, place dough circle on grill rack coated with cooking spray, and cook 2 minutes or until lightly browned. Turn dough, and top with about ⅓ cup apricot mixture. Spread mixture over dough, leaving a 1-inch border. Sprinkle about 1½ tablespoons chocolate chips over apricot mixture. Cook 1 minute or until pizza is crisp. Repeat with remaining dough, apricot mixture, and chocolate chips. Cut into 4 wedges. Yield: 10 servings (serving size: 2 wedges).

CALORIES 393 (15% from fat); FAT 6.5g (sat 2.7g, mono 1.7g, poly 0.5g); PROTEIN 6.8g; CARB 78.4g; FIBER 2.7g; CHOL 1mg; IRON 3.1mg; SODIUM 88mg; CALC 20mg

Shrimp Kebabs

Grilling takes this fast shrimp appetizer from simple to super. For an authentic Italian presentation, thread the shrimp on sturdy rosemary sprigs before grilling. If you can't find fresh rosemary sprigs, thread shrimp onto wooden skewers (soak skewers in water for 30 minutes first).

    1 teaspoon chopped fresh thyme
    1 teaspoon chopped fresh oregano
    ½ teaspoon chopped fresh rosemary
    ½ teaspoon grated lemon rind
    ½ teaspoon olive oil
    ¼ teaspoon salt
    ⅛ teaspoon freshly ground black
       pepper
    1 garlic clove, minced
Dash of ground red pepper
   18 large shrimp, peeled and deveined
    6 (6-inch) rosemary sprigs
Cooking spray

1. Prepare grill.
2. Combine first 10 ingredients in a zip-top plastic bag; seal and shake well. Marinate in refrigerator 15 minutes, turning occasionally.
3. Thread 3 shrimp on each rosemary sprig. Place prepared sprigs on grill rack coated with cooking spray; grill 2 minutes on each side or until shrimp are done. Yield: 6 servings (serving size: 1 kebab).

CALORIES 27 (25% from fat); FAT 0.8g (sat 0.1g, mono 0.3g, poly 0.2g); PROTEIN 4.3g; CARB 0.5g; FIBER 0.1g; CHOL 32mg; IRON 0.6mg; SODIUM 128mg; CALC 14mg

Grilled Squid with Lemon Caper Sauce

This colorful salad is a favorite on the Aeolian Islands off the northeastern coast of Sicily. Many of the seafood, vegetable, and pasta dishes on these islands, as in the rest of Sicily, call for locally produced salted capers, which have a more decisive flavor than capers packed in brine. Look for salted capers in Italian markets; rinse thoroughly before using. Serve this salad with grilled bread.

    ⅓ cup pitted Sicilian or other green
       olives
    3 tablespoons salted capers,
       rinsed
    3 tablespoons fresh lemon
       juice
    2 tablespoons white wine
       vinegar
   12 basil leaves
    1 garlic clove, peeled
    2 teaspoons extravirgin olive oil,
       divided
    ¼ cup water
    1 cup red bell pepper strips
    ½ cup thinly sliced red onion
    1 pound cleaned skinless
       squid
    ⅛ teaspoon salt
    ⅛ teaspoon freshly ground black
       pepper
Cooking spray

1. Prepare grill.
2. Combine first 6 ingredients and 1 teaspoon oil in a food processor, and process until smooth. With processor on, slowly add water through food chute; process until smooth. Transfer mixture to a large bowl. Add bell pepper and onion, and set aside.
3. Combine remaining 1 teaspoon oil and squid; toss well. Sprinkle salt and black pepper over squid. Place squid on grill rack coated with cooking spray; grill 3 minutes or until done, turning once. Cut squid into thin strips; add to olive mixture, tossing to coat. Yield: 4 servings (serving size: ¾ cup).

CALORIES 159 (29% from fat); FAT 5.2g (sat 0.9g, mono 2.7g, poly 1g); PROTEIN 18.6g; CARB 9.5g; FIBER 1.6g; CHOL 264mg; IRON 1.6mg; SODIUM 415mg; CALC 62mg

Chicken Skewers with Mint Sauce

These succulent bites of marinated, grilled chicken taste delicious with the refreshing sauce.

CHICKEN:

    2   tablespoons fresh lemon juice
    1   teaspoon olive oil
    ½   teaspoon salt
    ¼   teaspoon crushed red pepper
    ¼   teaspoon crushed black
        peppercorns
    2   garlic cloves, minced
    1   pound skinless, boneless chicken
        breast, cut into 1-inch pieces
    Cooking spray

MINT SAUCE:

    2   (1½-ounce) slices white bread
    ¾   cup packed fresh mint leaves
        (about ¾ ounce)
    1   tablespoon extravirgin olive oil
    2   teaspoons white wine vinegar
    ½   teaspoon salt
    2   garlic cloves, minced
    ½   cup water

1. To prepare chicken, combine first 6 ingredients in a large zip-top plastic bag. Add chicken; seal and marinate in refrigerator 15 minutes, turning bag occasionally. Remove chicken from bag; discard marinade.
2. Prepare grill.
3. Thread chicken pieces onto 6 (8-inch) skewers. Place skewers on grill rack coated with cooking spray; grill 8 minutes or until chicken is done, turning frequently.
4. To prepare mint sauce, place bread slices in a food processor, and pulse until coarsely crumbled. Add mint, olive oil, white wine vinegar, ½ teaspoon salt, and 2 garlic cloves; pulse until combined. With processor on, slowly pour water through food chute, and process until smooth and well blended. Yield: 6 servings (serving size: 1 skewer [about 2½ ounces chicken] and 2 tablespoons sauce).

CALORIES 193 (29% from fat); FAT 6.1g (sat 1.2g, mono 3g, poly 0.9g); PROTEIN 25.4g; CARB 8.4g; FIBER 0.4g; CHOL 64mg; IRON 1.3mg; SODIUM 467mg; CALC 37mg

Fruit Skewers with Vin Santo Glaze

Vin santo is an amber-hued Tuscan dessert wine. You can substitute Marsala, a fortified dessert wine from Sicily.

GLAZE:

    1   cup vin santo
    ¼   cup sugar
    1   (4-inch-long) orange rind strip
    1   (2-inch) cinnamon stick
    1   tablespoon butter

SKEWERS:

    1   cup cubed, peeled peaches (about
        2 medium)
    1   cup cubed ripe plums (about 4)
    ¾   cup seedless green grapes
    ¾   cup pitted sweet cherries
    Cooking spray

CHEESE:

    1   cup part-skim ricotta cheese
    2   tablespoons orange blossom
        honey
    1   teaspoon grated orange rind

1. Prepare grill.
2. To prepare glaze, combine first 4 ingredients in a medium saucepan; bring to a boil. Cook 15 minutes or until reduced to ⅓ cup. Remove and discard rind and cinnamon. Add butter, stirring with a whisk. Remove from heat, and keep warm.
3. To prepare skewers, thread peaches, plums, grapes, and cherries alternately onto each of 8 (8-inch) skewers; brush with 2 tablespoons glaze, reserving remaining glaze. Place skewers on grill rack coated with cooking spray; grill 4 minutes on each side or until lightly browned.
4. To prepare cheese, combine ricotta, honey, and rind, stirring well. Spoon about ¾ tablespoon remaining glaze on each of 4 dessert plates; top with 2 skewers. Spoon about ¼ cup cheese mixture on each plate. Yield: 4 servings.

CALORIES 323 (23% from fat); FAT 8.4g (sat 4.6g, mono 2.8g, poly 0.4g); PROTEIN 8.6g; CARB 49.1g; FIBER 2.8g; CHOL 27mg; IRON 0.7mg; SODIUM 101mg; CALC 185mg

Marinades and Pastes— What's the Difference?

Marinades season and tenderize food. They're liquid and often include an acid, such as lemon juice, vinegar, buttermilk, or wine. Acids tenderize meat, poultry, and seafood by weakening muscle tissue and increasing its ability to retain moisture. Because of the acidity, place marinating meats in glass or plastic containers—never in aluminum or copper (acids react with the metal, discoloring both the food and the pan). Meats, such as beef, pork, and lamb, call for longer marinating times because their flesh is more dense. Poultry, which is more tender, requires shorter marinating times. Fish's delicate texture calls for the shortest marinating time; 30 minutes is plenty. (Longer marinating turns fish mealy or mushy.) Marinades infuse flavor slowly and are ideal for larger cuts, such as flank steak and leg of lamb (as is the case with Grilled Bread with Tuscan-Style Lamb [recipe on page 281]), but they also add great flavor to vegetables.

Pastes (often composed of herbs, garlic, and oil) put aromatics directly on the surface of the food, imparting flavor with every bite. Pastes also form a protective layer to keep meat, poultry, and fish tender and juicy on the inside while cooking. Use pastes on steaks, pork tenderloin, chicken breasts, and fish fillets, such as Salmon Trout with Garlic and Grilled Fennel (recipe on page 280).

Dinner Party Pasta

A Michigan couple's recipe for entertaining gets a dramatic makeover that puts it back on the menu.

At a dinner party with some college friends a few years ago, Heidi Van Til of Traverse City, Michigan, was served a bowl of fettuccine with shrimp and bacon. The pasta dish was so delicious that she asked the hostess for the recipe.

Her friend's famed fettuccine became one of Heidi's favorites to serve at dinner parties, but she and husband Ethan harbored reservations about preparing such a high-calorie entrée. "The recipe has sentimental value, and I want to keep using it, but it's so decadent," Heidi wrote, asking us to lighten it.

We began by substituting two percent reduced-fat milk for heavy cream. We whisked a little flour into the milk to achieve a thickened texture similar to cream. Next, we adjusted the bacon and Parmesan cheese.

We added a garlic clove for its assertive taste and fragrance, and a little salt and pepper to balance the sauce's flavor. Lowering the fat overaccentuated the parsley, so we used less to balance its fresh, earthy quality. Finally, we increased the peas by half a cup, adding fiber, vibrant color, and a lightly sweet snap to each bite.

Heidi prepared the lightened fettuccine for a Saturday night dinner with her husband. She says it was easy to make, and both she and Ethan were pleased with the new version.

Creamy Fettuccine with Shrimp and Bacon

Cook the fettuccine al dente so the strands remain intact and maintain a slightly firm texture.

- 1 pound uncooked fettuccine
- 2 bacon slices (uncooked)
- 1 pound large shrimp, peeled and deveined
- 1 garlic clove, minced
- 1½ cups frozen green peas, thawed
- 1 cup shredded carrot
- 2 cups 2% reduced-fat milk
- 2 tablespoons all-purpose flour
- ½ teaspoon salt
- ½ teaspoon freshly ground black pepper
- 1 cup (4 ounces) grated Parmesan cheese
- ½ cup chopped fresh flat-leaf parsley, divided

1. Cook pasta according to package directions, omitting salt and fat. Drain well; keep warm.

2. Cook bacon in a large nonstick skillet over medium-high heat 6 minutes or until crisp. Remove bacon from pan, reserving 1 tablespoon drippings in pan. Crumble bacon; set aside.

3. Add shrimp and garlic to pan; sauté over medium-high heat 2 minutes. Add peas and carrot; cook 2 minutes or just until shrimp are done. Transfer shrimp mixture to a large bowl; keep warm.

4. Combine milk, flour, salt, and pepper, stirring with a whisk. Add milk mixture to pan; cook over medium heat 3 minutes or until thickened and bubbly, stirring constantly with a whisk. Remove pan from heat; add cheese, stirring until blended. Add milk mixture to shrimp mixture; stir until combined. Add pasta and ¼ cup parsley, tossing gently to coat. Transfer pasta mixture to a platter, or place on each of 8 plates; sprinkle evenly with ¼ cup parsley and crumbled bacon. Serve immediately. Yield: 8 servings (serving size: about 1¼ cups pasta and 1½ teaspoons parsley).

CALORIES 382 (18% from fat); FAT 7.7g (sat 3.7g, mono 1.2g, poly 0.5g); PROTEIN 25g; CARB 52.9g; FIBER 3.6g; CHOL 101mg; IRON 4.1mg; SODIUM 505mg; CALC 218mg

WINE NOTE: While Heidi's pairing choice of sauvignon blanc is fine, this pasta dish is beautifully enhanced by chardonnay—a wine with its own creaminess. A delicious, food-friendly find is Santa Rita Chardonnay "120" from the Maipo Valley of Chile. The 2004 is just $8.

BEFORE	AFTER
SERVING SIZE	
1¼ cups	
CALORIES PER SERVING	
723	382
FAT	
40.8g	7.7g
PERCENT OF TOTAL CALORIES	
51%	18%

. . . And Ready in Just About 20 Minutes

More than a week's worth of quick entrées gets you in and out of the kitchen in a flash.

QUICK & EASY
Pan-Seared Pork Chops with Dried Fruit

Serve this dish with couscous or brown rice. Add a green salad or steamed vegetables to balance the sweetness of the pork chops.

- Cooking spray
- 4 (6-ounce) bone-in center-cut pork chops (about ½ inch thick)
- ¼ teaspoon salt
- ¼ teaspoon freshly ground black pepper
- ⅓ cup sliced shallots
- 1 cup fat-free, less-sodium chicken broth
- 1 (7-ounce) package dried mixed fruit bits (such as SunMaid)

1. Heat a large nonstick skillet over medium-high heat. Coat pan with cooking spray. Sprinkle both sides of pork with salt and pepper. Add pork to pan; cook 3 minutes on each side or until lightly browned. Remove from pan, and set aside.

2. Add shallots to pan; cook 1 minute, stirring constantly. Add broth and fruit; cover and simmer 1 minute. Return pork to pan, and cook 1 minute or until thoroughly heated. Yield: 4 servings (serving size: 1 pork chop and ⅓ cup sauce).

CALORIES 380 (30% from fat); FAT 12.6g (sat 4.5g, mono 5.5g, poly 0.9g); PROTEIN 28.5g; CARB 38.7g; FIBER 4.7g; CHOL 76mg; IRON 1.8mg; SODIUM 299mg; CALC 56mg

QUICK & EASY
Speedy Chicken and Cheese Enchiladas

Rotisserie chicken and prechopped vegetables make this a quick casserole.

Cooking spray
1 cup chopped white onion
1 cup chopped bell pepper
1 (10-ounce) can enchilada sauce (such as Old El Paso)
2 cups chopped skinless, boneless rotisserie chicken breast (about 8 ounces)
1 cup (4 ounces) preshredded, reduced-fat Mexican blend cheese, divided
½ teaspoon ground cumin
8 (6-inch) corn tortillas
¼ cup fat-free sour cream
¼ cup chopped fresh cilantro

1. Preheat broiler.
2. Heat a large nonstick skillet over medium-high heat. Coat pan with cooking spray. Add onion and pepper; sauté 2 minutes or until crisp-tender. Add enchilada sauce; bring to a boil. Cover, reduce heat, and simmer 5 minutes.
3. Combine chicken, ¾ cup cheese, and cumin, tossing well.
4. Wrap tortillas in paper towels; microwave at HIGH 30 seconds or until warm. Spoon ¼ cup chicken mixture in center of each tortilla; roll up. Place tortillas, seam sides down, in an 11 x 7-inch baking dish coated with cooking spray. Pour sauce mixture over enchiladas; broil 3 minutes or until thoroughly heated. Sprinkle ¼ cup cheese evenly over enchiladas, and broil 1 minute or until cheese melts. Serve with sour cream and cilantro. Yield: 4 servings (serving size: 2 enchiladas, 1 tablespoon sour cream, and 1 tablespoon cilantro).

CALORIES 364 (27% from fat); FAT 10.9g (sat 4.9g, mono 2.9g, poly 1.4g); PROTEIN 29.7g; CARB 37.2g; FIBER 4.1g; CHOL 70mg; IRON 1.7mg; SODIUM 701mg; CALC 339mg

QUICK & EASY
Chipotle Chicken Tortilla Soup

If you like spicy food, you'll love this. Purchase corn muffins from your supermarket bakery to round out the meal.

1 tablespoon canola oil
1½ teaspoons bottled minced garlic
¾ pound chicken breast tenders, cut into bite-size pieces
1 teaspoon chipotle chile powder
1 teaspoon ground cumin
1 cup water
¼ teaspoon salt
1 (14-ounce) can fat-free, less-sodium chicken broth
1 (14.5-ounce) can stewed tomatoes, undrained
1 cup crushed baked tortilla chips
¼ cup chopped fresh cilantro
1 lime, cut into 4 wedges

1. Heat oil in a large saucepan over medium-high heat. Add garlic and chicken; sauté 2 minutes. Add chile powder and cumin; stir well. Add water, salt, broth, and tomatoes; bring to a boil. Cover, reduce heat, and simmer 5 minutes. Top with tortilla chips and cilantro, and serve with lime wedges. Yield: 4 servings (serving size: 1¼ cups soup, ¼ cup chips, 1 tablespoon cilantro, and 1 lime wedge).

CALORIES 228 (21% from fat); FAT 5.4g (sat 0.6g, mono 2.5g, poly 1.7g); PROTEIN 22.9g; CARB 21.8g; FIBER 3.5g; CHOL 49mg; IRON 1.7mg; SODIUM 873mg; CALC 62mg

Asian in an Instant Menu
serves 4

From start to finish, this entire meal takes about 30 minutes to prepare.

Seared Sea Scallops on Asian Slaw

Noodle and vegetable toss*

Jasmine tea

*Cook 8 ounces vermicelli according to package directions, omitting salt and fat. Drain; place in a large bowl. Combine 2 tablespoons fresh orange juice, 1 tablespoon low-sodium soy sauce, 1 tablespoon dark sesame oil, and 1 teaspoon bottled ground fresh ginger, stirring with a whisk. Drizzle over pasta; toss to coat. Stir in ½ cup red bell pepper strips and ½ cup green bell pepper strips.

QUICK & EASY
Seared Sea Scallops on Asian Slaw

Look for pretoasted sesame seeds in Asian markets. Serve this with quick-cooking rice tossed with edamame.

4 cups thinly sliced napa (Chinese) cabbage (about 1 small head)
½ cup thinly sliced radishes (about 6 small)
2 tablespoons rice vinegar
2 tablespoons low-sodium soy sauce
2 teaspoons dark sesame oil, divided
⅛ teaspoon crushed red pepper
16 large sea scallops (about 1½ pounds)
¼ teaspoon salt
¼ teaspoon freshly ground black pepper
2 teaspoons sesame seeds, toasted

1. Combine cabbage and radishes in a large bowl; set aside.
2. Combine rice vinegar, soy sauce, 1 teaspoon oil, and red pepper, stirring well with a whisk.
3. Heat 1 teaspoon oil in a large nonstick skillet over medium-high heat. Sprinkle scallops with salt and black

Continued

pepper. Add scallops to pan; cook 3 minutes on each side or until done. Arrange 1 cup cabbage mixture on each of 4 plates; top each serving with 4 scallops. Drizzle each serving with 1 tablespoon vinegar mixture; sprinkle each serving with ½ teaspoon sesame seeds. Serve immediately. Yield: 4 servings.

CALORIES 135 (25% from fat); FAT 3.8g (sat 0.5g, mono 1.2g, poly 1.3g); PROTEIN 16.4g; CARB 7g; FIBER 1.3g; CHOL 37mg; IRON 0.6mg; SODIUM 597mg; CALC 78mg

QUICK & EASY
Spicy Orange Beef

A side of sliced cucumbers dressed with rice vinegar and a pinch of sugar would offer a good balance for this fiery entrée.

1 (3½-ounce) bag boil-in-bag brown rice
½ teaspoon salt
1 teaspoon bottled minced garlic
½ teaspoon crushed red pepper
1 pound boneless sirloin steak, cut into ¼-inch strips
½ teaspoon grated orange rind
¼ cup fresh orange juice
2 tablespoons low-sodium soy sauce
1 tablespoon cornstarch
1 teaspoon dark sesame oil
¾ cup (1-inch) slices green onions

1. Cook rice according to package directions, omitting salt and fat. Combine rice and salt, tossing well.
2. Combine garlic, pepper, and beef, tossing well.
3. Combine rind, juice, soy sauce, and cornstarch, stirring with a whisk.
4. Heat oil in a large nonstick skillet over medium-high heat. Add beef mixture and onions; sauté 2 minutes. Add juice mixture; cook 2 minutes or until sauce thickens, stirring frequently. Serve beef mixture over rice. Yield: 4 servings (serving size: ½ cup beef mixture and about ⅓ cup rice).

CALORIES 274 (22% from fat); FAT 6.8g (sat 1.9g, mono 2.4g, poly 0.7g); PROTEIN 26.5g; CARB 24.9g; FIBER 2.1g; CHOL 69mg; IRON 3.7mg; SODIUM 627mg; CALC 25mg

QUICK & EASY
Pork Tenderloin with Exotic Mushrooms

Enjoy this pork version of creamy Stroganoff; it has a short prep time. Serve with steamed broccoli.

8 ounces uncooked wide egg noodles
1 pound pork tenderloin, trimmed
Cooking spray
1 teaspoon olive oil
1 teaspoon salt
½ teaspoon dried thyme
½ teaspoon freshly ground black pepper
1 (8-ounce) package presliced exotic mushroom blend (such as shiitake, cremini, and oyster)
½ cup water
2 tablespoons Worcestershire sauce
1 tablespoon all-purpose flour
1 (8-ounce) carton reduced-fat sour cream
2 tablespoons chopped fresh parsley

1. Cook pasta according to package directions, omitting salt and fat. Drain; keep warm.
2. Cut pork crosswise into 4 pieces; cut each piece in half lengthwise. Slice each half into thin strips.
3. Heat a large nonstick skillet over medium-high heat. Coat pan with cooking spray. Add oil. Add pork, salt, thyme, pepper, and mushrooms to pan; sauté 4 minutes or until pork is desired degree of doneness and mushrooms are tender. Remove from heat.
4. Combine water, Worcestershire sauce, and flour in a medium bowl, stirring with a whisk until smooth. Stir in sour cream. Add sour cream mixture to pan, stirring to combine. Return pan to medium-high heat. Bring to a boil; cook 1 minute or until sauce thickens, stirring constantly. Serve pork mixture over noodles; sprinkle with parsley. Serve immediately. Yield: 4 servings (serving size: 1 cup pork mixture, 1¼ cups noodles, and 1½ teaspoons parsley).

CALORIES 479 (29% from fat); FAT 15.5g (sat 7g, mono 5.7g, poly 1.1g); PROTEIN 34.8g; CARB 50.2g; FIBER 2.7g; CHOL 98mg; IRON 4.4mg; SODIUM 760mg; CALC 97mg

QUICK & EASY
Shrimp Pad Thai

This Thai noodle specialty is a speedy one-dish meal. For a twist, substitute rice noodles or sweet potato noodles from the Asian market for the spaghetti.

8 ounces uncooked spaghetti
¼ cup low-sodium teriyaki sauce
3 tablespoons creamy peanut butter
2 tablespoons hot water
¼ teaspoon Sriracha (hot chile sauce, such as Huy Fong)
2 teaspoons dark sesame oil
1 teaspoon bottled minced garlic
1 pound peeled and deveined large shrimp
4 cups snow peas
⅓ cup chopped fresh cilantro
⅓ cup chopped dry-roasted peanuts
5 lime wedges

1. Cook pasta according to package directions, omitting salt and fat; drain and set aside.
2. Combine teriyaki sauce, peanut butter, hot water, and Sriracha, stirring with a whisk.
3. Heat oil in a large nonstick skillet over medium-high heat. Add garlic, and sauté 1 minute. Add shrimp; sauté 2 minutes or until shrimp are almost done. Add teriyaki sauce mixture, and cook 2 minutes or until sauce thickens. Add pasta and snow peas; cook 2 minutes or until thoroughly heated, stirring well. Sprinkle with cilantro and peanuts. Serve with lime wedges. Yield: 5 servings (serving size: about 1½ cups Pad Thai, about 1 tablespoon cilantro, about 1 tablespoon peanuts, and 1 lime wedge).

CALORIES 431 (29% from fat); FAT 13.9g (sat 2.3g, mono 5.8g, poly 4.5g); PROTEIN 31.3g; CARB 45.8g; FIBER 3.9g; CHOL 138mg; IRON 5.5mg; SODIUM 522mg; CALC 90mg

Get Together

Whether you're hosting a few friends for an evening or a group for the weekend, we have no-fuss menus and terrific recipes for memorable gatherings, large and small.

Stay for the Weekend

Welcome guests with meals featuring the season's best fare and no-cook options to keep you free from the kitchen.

Friday Night Welcome Menu
serves 8

Fresh Ginger Beer

Turkey Burgers with Goat Cheese

Grilled Pepper Relish

Cabbage and Celery Root Slaw

Oranges and Raspberries with Lavender Honey and Yogurt

QUICK & EASY
Fresh Ginger Beer

If you like ginger ale, you'll love this tangy beverage. Add your favorite rum to create a memorable cocktail. If you can't find superfine sugar, place granulated sugar in a blender, and process until fine. You can find bottled ground fresh ginger in the produce section of the supermarket.

2   cups cold water
1   cup fresh lime juice
4   teaspoons bottled ground fresh ginger (such as Spice World)
¾   cup superfine sugar
3   cups sparkling water
Lime slices (optional)

1. Place water, juice, and ginger in a blender; process until blended.
2. Line a strainer with cheesecloth. Strain mixture into a pitcher; discard solids. Add sugar to pitcher; stir until dissolved.
3. Add sparkling water just before serving. Serve over ice. Garnish with lime slices, if desired. Yield: 8 servings (serving size: 1 cup).

CALORIES 81 (0% from fat); FAT 0g; PROTEIN 0.1g; CARB 21.5g; FIBER 0.1g; CHOL 0mg; IRON 0mg; SODIUM 3mg; CALC 21mg

Turkey Burgers with Goat Cheese

Top these burgers with Grilled Pepper Relish (recipe on page 288), sliced onion, and Dijon mustard.

3   pounds lean ground turkey
3   tablespoons chopped fresh parsley
1   tablespoon chopped fresh rosemary
¼   teaspoon kosher salt
¼   teaspoon freshly ground black pepper
Cooking spray
8   (1½-ounce) hamburger buns
4   ounces goat cheese, cut into 8 slices

1. Prepare grill.
2. Combine first 5 ingredients in a large bowl. Divide turkey mixture into 8 equal portions, shaping each into a ½-inch-thick patty. Place patties on grill rack coated with cooking spray; cook 5 minutes on each side or until done. Place buns, cut sides down, on grill rack; cook 1 minute or until lightly browned. Top each patty with 1 slice goat cheese. Serve on buns. Yield: 8 servings (serving size: 1 burger).

CALORIES 336 (19% from fat); FAT 7.1g (sat 2.5g, mono 1.1g, poly 1g); PROTEIN 48.2g; CARB 22.2g; FIBER 1.2g; CHOL 74mg; IRON 3.5mg; SODIUM 466mg; CALC 60mg

---

Travel Plans

If your group is meeting at a lake house or cabin, make a list of the items you'll need in order to avoid repeated trips to the mini-market. Call your lodging's caretaker to learn which household and kitchen items are on site. Many rentals are equipped with cutting boards, blenders, and so on.

• You'll need a grill for several of these recipes, so if one isn't available, take a charcoal grill. Don't forget to pick up a sack of charcoal, matches, foil, and grilling utensils.

• You'll need a blender and strainer for the Fresh Ginger Beer (recipe at left), plus a baking dish for the Corn Pudding (recipe on page 290). And don't forget the cooking spray for easy cleanup. Grab a couple bags of ice, too.

• If you can't stir without your favorite spoon, or if a dish just won't taste right without a dash from your black pepper grinder, by all means bring them along. For many cooks, a favorite chef's knife, mini-whisk, or good balsamic vinegar are a must.

• Pack plastic disposable containers with lids to store leftovers or to take picnic food.

• Bamboo torches illuminate the night, and citronella candles discourage the season's last mosquitoes. Music lovers: Grab your portable stereo.

Here's a game plan for a couple of kicked-back days. With Friday and Saturday night's menus planned, follow our breakfast, lunch, and snack suggestions to keep the gang nourished and satisfied all weekend long without having to spend time cooking at every meal.

Plan a Satisfying Breakfast

Start the day with a meal outdoors, and offer tempting breakfast items guests can serve themselves. Bowls of crunchy, nutty muesli with ice-cold milk or tangy yogurt drizzled with honey need no preparation.

For a savory, equally simple breakfast, cut thick slices of rustic whole-grain bread to serve with olive oil, sea salt, and black pepper. Top bread with part-skim ricotta cheese and juicy tomato slices for a hearty start.

For another self-service option, set the table with a toaster, a loaf of whole wheat bread, smoked salmon, butter, cream cheese, and lemon wedges. These simple ingredients look impressive, taste divine, and require nothing more than opening a few packages. (No matter what you serve for breakfast, don't forget the fresh fruit—buy it precut at the supermarket—and offer pots of coffee and tea.)

Picnic Pointers

At lunchtime, enjoy the scenery outdoors with a flavor-packed picnic. Choose no-prep ingredients, such as fresh figs, wafer-thin prosciutto slices, a wedge of pecorino Romano cheese, assorted olives, bottled roasted red bell peppers, grissini (breadsticks) purchased from the supermarket, and a selection of grapes. Pack foods separately in resealable plastic containers to avoid bruising delicate items. Fill a thermos with iced tea or apple cider to round out your lunch.

And Don't Forget Snacks

Guests will want some nibbles between meals, too, especially if you've planned an active weekend. Apples, pears, flatbreads, nuts, and cheeses laid out on a wooden board invite self-service anytime. Other options include popcorn, peanut butter-filled celery sticks, or hard-cooked eggs drizzled with balsamic vinegar and sprinkled with sea salt and black pepper.

MAKE AHEAD
Grilled Pepper Relish

4 bell peppers (assorted colors, such as red, yellow, and orange)
¼ cup chopped fresh basil
2 tablespoons chopped pitted kalamata olives
1 tablespoon balsamic vinegar
1½ teaspoons olive oil
1 teaspoon chopped fresh thyme
¼ teaspoon salt
¼ teaspoon black pepper

1. Prepare grill.
2. Place bell peppers on grill rack. Grill, uncovered, over medium-high heat 5 to 7 minutes until peppers blister, turning frequently. Place peppers in a zip-top plastic bag; seal. Let stand 15 minutes. Peel peppers; remove and discard seeds. Cut peppers into ½-inch pieces.
3. Combine bell peppers and remaining ingredients in a medium bowl; toss well. Yield: 8 servings (serving size: ¼ cup).
NOTE: To roast peppers in the oven instead of grilling them, cut bell peppers in half lengthwise; discard seeds and membranes. Place pepper halves, skin sides up, on a foil-lined baking sheet; flatten with hand. Broil 15 minutes or until blackened. Place in a zip-top plastic bag; seal. Let stand 15 minutes. Proceed with recipe as directed.

CALORIES 33 (47% from fat); FAT 1.7g (sat 0.2g, mono 1.2g, poly 0.3g); PROTEIN 0.7g; CARB 4.3g; FIBER 0.4g; CHOL 0mg; IRON 0.4mg; SODIUM 118mg; CALC 10mg

---

Cabbage and Celery Root Slaw

⅓ cup cider vinegar
1½ tablespoons Dijon mustard
1 tablespoon canola oil
1 tablespoon honey
½ teaspoon celery seeds
¼ teaspoon black pepper
⅛ teaspoon kosher salt
2 (10-ounce) bags angel hair coleslaw (about 10 cups)
2 cups diced Granny Smith apple
1 cup shredded peeled celeriac (celery root)

1. Combine first 7 ingredients in a large bowl; stir with a whisk. Add coleslaw, apple, and celeriac; toss well. Yield: 8 servings (serving size: 1 cup).

CALORIES 58 (25% from fat); FAT 2.3g (sat 0.2g, mono 1.4g, poly 0.6g); PROTEIN 1.9g; CARB 13.7g; FIBER 1.2g; CHOL 0mg; IRON 0.9mg; SODIUM 145mg; CALC 58mg

---

MAKE AHEAD
Oranges and Raspberries with Lavender Honey and Yogurt

Prepare the lavender honey and fruit mixture ahead, and serve it over vanilla frozen yogurt with an extra drizzle of lavender honey. Look for dried lavender blossoms in specialty markets or health-food stores. You can also purchase lavender honey in some specialty markets and skip infusing the honey.

1 cup honey
1 tablespoon dried lavender blossoms
4 cups orange sections (about 6 large oranges)
2 cups fresh raspberries
1 tablespoon grated orange rind
4 cups low-fat vanilla frozen yogurt
Fresh lavender blossoms (optional)

1. Combine honey and dried lavender blossoms in a small saucepan. Cook over low heat 20 minutes. Remove from heat; cool. Strain mixture through a sieve into a small bowl; discard solids.

2. Combine orange sections, raspberries, rind, and ½ cup lavender honey in a large bowl; toss to coat. Cover and chill 1 hour.

3. Spoon fruit mixture over frozen yogurt. Drizzle with remaining lavender honey. Garnish with fresh lavender, if desired. Yield: 8 servings (serving size: ¾ cup fruit mixture, ½ cup yogurt, and 1 tablespoon honey).

CALORIES 287 (5% from fat); FAT 1.6g (sat 0.9g, mono 0.4g, poly 0.2g); PROTEIN 5.7g; CARB 67.5g; FIBER 4g; CHOL 5mg; IRON 0.6mg; SODIUM 62mg; CALC 200mg

---

Saturday Evening Supper Menu

serves 8

Striped Bass with Fennel over Sautéed Spinach

Mixed Bean-Cherry Tomato Salad with Basil Vinaigrette

Corn Pudding

Plum Upside-Down Cake

WINE NOTE: Even though the delicious corn pudding in this menu is stellar with chardonnay, the menu as a whole works better with a good, crisp sauvignon blanc. That's because herbal-tasting sauvignon blanc is one of the best white wine choices for a menu with lots of green and herbal notes—in this case, fennel, spinach, green beans, and basil. Fine sauvignon blancs are available from all over the world at good prices. A good one from California is Chateau Souverain Sauvignon Blanc 2004 (Alexander Valley, California), about $14.

Striped Bass with Fennel over Sautéed Spinach

This peppery fish dish is a good source of lean protein, iron, and fiber.

RELISH:

    4 cups diced fennel bulb (about 1
       pound)
    2 cups diced red onion
    2 teaspoons olive oil
    ½ teaspoon salt
    ½ teaspoon freshly ground black
       pepper
       Cooking spray
    2 teaspoons sugar
    2 teaspoons capers, drained
    1 tablespoon balsamic
       vinegar

BASS:

    8 (6-ounce) striped bass fillets
       without skin
    2 teaspoons olive oil
    ½ teaspoon salt
    ½ teaspoon freshly ground black
       pepper

SPINACH:

    2 teaspoons olive oil
    6 garlic cloves, thinly sliced
    2 pounds fresh spinach, trimmed
    ½ teaspoon salt
    ¼ teaspoon freshly ground black
       pepper

1. Preheat oven to 450°.
2. To prepare relish, combine first 5 ingredients, tossing well to coat. Arrange fennel mixture in a single layer on a jelly-roll pan coated with cooking spray. Bake at 450° for 30 minutes or until lightly browned, stirring once. Place fennel mixture in a bowl; stir in sugar, capers, and vinegar.
3. Preheat grill.
4. To prepare fish, place fillets on grill rack coated with cooking spray. Brush fillets evenly with 2 teaspoons oil; sprinkle evenly with ½ teaspoon salt and ½ teaspoon pepper. Grill fish 4 minutes on each side or until fish flakes easily when tested with a fork or until desired degree of doneness. Remove from grill; keep warm.

---

5. To prepare spinach, heat 2 teaspoons oil in a Dutch oven over medium-high heat. Add garlic; cook 2 minutes or until golden, stirring frequently. Add half of spinach, and cook 1 minute, stirring constantly. Add remaining spinach; cook 2 minutes or until wilted, stirring frequently. Sprinkle with ½ teaspoon salt and ¼ teaspoon pepper.

6. Place ½ cup spinach mixture on each of 8 plates; top each with 1 fillet and about ¼ cup relish. Yield: 8 servings.

CALORIES 287 (24% from fat); FAT 7.8g (sat 1.4g, mono 3.9g, poly 1.7g); PROTEIN 34.7g; CARB 21.5g; FIBER 7.4g; CHOL 140mg; IRON 5.6mg; SODIUM 779mg; CALC 142mg

---

MAKE AHEAD

Mixed Bean-Cherry Tomato Salad with Basil Vinaigrette

A bright assemblage of flavors, textures, and colors, this salad can be made early in the day and refrigerated until ready to serve.

    1 pound fresh green beans, trimmed
    1 pound fresh wax beans, trimmed
    ¼ cup balsamic vinegar
    2 tablespoons extravirgin olive oil
    ½ teaspoon kosher salt
    ½ teaspoon freshly ground black
       pepper
    3 cups cherry tomatoes, halved
       (2 pints)
    1 cup loosely packed basil leaves,
       coarsely chopped
    ½ cup finely chopped red onion
       Basil sprigs (optional)

1. Cook green and wax beans in boiling water 5 minutes. Drain and plunge beans into ice water; drain.
2. Combine vinegar, oil, salt, and pepper in a large bowl. Add beans, tomatoes, basil leaves, and onion; toss gently. Cover and chill. Garnish with basil sprigs, if desired. Yield: 8 servings (serving size: ¾ cup bean mixture).

CALORIES 86 (38% from fat); FAT 3.6g (sat 0.5g, mono 2.5g, poly 0.4g); PROTEIN 2.1g; CARB 11.2g; FIBER 4.4g; CHOL 0mg; IRON 1mg; SODIUM 132mg; CALC 57mg

Corn Pudding

If you use frozen corn, thaw it before adding it to the recipe. If you can't find fresh chives, chop the green part of green onions.

- 3 cups corn kernels (about 6 ears)
- ¼ cup chopped fresh chives
- 1 tablespoon chopped fresh thyme
- ¾ teaspoon salt
- ¼ teaspoon freshly ground black pepper
- 1½ cups 1% low-fat milk
- ½ cup egg substitute
- 2 tablespoons ⅓-less-fat cream cheese
- 1 large egg, lightly beaten
- Cooking spray

1. Preheat oven to 350°.
2. Combine first 5 ingredients in a medium bowl. Combine milk, egg substitute, cream cheese, and egg in a medium bowl. Add milk mixture to corn mixture, and stir well. Pour corn mixture into an 11 x 7-inch baking dish coated with cooking spray. Bake at 350° for 55 minutes or until pudding is golden brown. Yield: 8 servings (serving size: 1 square).

CALORIES 113 (32% from fat); FAT 4.1g (sat 1.3g, mono 1.1g, poly 1.4g); PROTEIN 6.5g; CARB 14.4g; FIBER 1.7g; CHOL 31mg; IRON 0.8mg; SODIUM 308mg; CALC 80mg

> Serve
> # Plum Upside-Down Cake
> with a scoop of vanilla yogurt or a dollop of fat-free whipped topping.

MAKE AHEAD
Plum Upside-Down Cake

- 2 teaspoons butter
- 6 large red plums, pitted and quartered (about 1 pound)
- 1¼ cups sugar, divided
- ¼ teaspoon ground cardamom
- Dash of salt
- Cooking spray
- 1½ cups all-purpose flour (about 6¾ ounces)
- 1½ teaspoons baking powder
- ¼ teaspoon salt
- ¼ cup butter, softened
- 2 large eggs
- ¾ cup fat-free buttermilk
- 1 tablespoon amaretto (almond-flavored liqueur)

1. Melt 2 teaspoons butter in a large nonstick skillet over medium heat. Add plums, and cook 3 minutes. Add ½ cup sugar, cardamom, and dash of salt. Cook 10 minutes or until plums are tender, stirring frequently. Remove plums from pan using a slotted spoon. Bring cooking liquid to a boil. Cook 5 minutes or until liquid is very thick (consistency of jam).
2. While cooking liquid reduces, arrange plums in bottom of a 9-inch round cake pan coated with cooking spray. Pour reduced cooking liquid over plums. Cool.
3. Preheat oven to 350°.
4. Lightly spoon flour into dry measuring cups; level with a knife. Combine flour, baking powder, and ¼ teaspoon salt, stirring well with a whisk. Beat ¼ cup butter and ¾ cup sugar with a mixer at medium speed until fluffy. Add eggs, one at a time, beating well after each addition. Add flour mixture and buttermilk alternately to sugar mixture, beginning and ending with flour mixture. Beat in amaretto.
5. Pour batter over plums, spreading batter evenly. Bake at 350° for 50 minutes or until a wooden pick inserted in center comes out clean. Cool 10 minutes. Run a knife around outside edge. Place a plate upside down on top of cake. Invert cake onto plate; cool. Yield: 8 servings (serving size: 1 wedge).

CALORIES 326 (23% from fat); FAT 8.4g (sat 3.8g, mono 3.4g, poly 0.6g); PROTEIN 5.3g; CARB 58.1g; FIBER 1.4g; CHOL 71mg; IRON 1.5mg; SODIUM 270mg; CALC 93mg

Supper Club Beach Party

Use supper club gatherings to strengthen community ties. Our tips and mostly make-ahead menu will help it happen.

End-of-Summer Beach Party Menu
serves 10

Mix and match to suit your group's tastes. Have all the recipes on hand for people to pick and choose from, or make just one recipe for each course.

Appetizers
Tomato and Parmesan Focaccia with Caramelized Onions

Smoky Shrimp and Avocado Seviche

Entrées
California Burgers

Cumin-Crusted Pork Soft Tacos

Tex-Mex Pasta Salad (kids' option)

Sides
End-of-Summer Tomato Salad

Roasted Asparagus with Orange Vinaigrette

Tuscan White Beans

Desserts
Strawberry-Topped Pavlovas with Honey-Balsamic Sauce

Lemon-Blueberry Bundt Cake

Tomato and Parmesan Focaccia with Caramelized Onions

Serve this tasty appetizer bread warm or at room temperature. While you can make it a day in advance, it's best the day it's baked.

DOUGH:

- 1 cup warm water (100° to 110°)
- 2 tablespoons olive oil
- 1 teaspoon sugar
- 1 package dry yeast (about 2¼ teaspoons)
- 2¾ cups all-purpose flour (about 12⅓ ounces), divided
- ¼ cup yellow cornmeal
- 1 teaspoon salt
- Cooking spray

TOPPING:

- 1 tablespoon olive oil
- 4 cups thinly sliced yellow onion
- 1 teaspoon dried basil
- ½ teaspoon salt
- ¼ teaspoon freshly ground black pepper
- 12 (⅛-inch-thick) slices tomato
- ⅓ cup (about 1½ ounces) grated fresh Parmesan cheese
- ¼ cup thinly sliced fresh basil

1. To prepare dough, combine first 4 ingredients in a large bowl, stirring to dissolve yeast; let stand 5 minutes. Lightly spoon flour into dry measuring cups; level with a knife. Add 2½ cups flour, cornmeal, and 1 teaspoon salt to yeast mixture; stir well. Turn dough out onto a floured surface. Knead until smooth and elastic (about 10 minutes); add enough remaining flour, 1 tablespoon at a time, to prevent dough from sticking to hands.

2. Place dough in a large bowl coated with cooking spray, turning to coat top. Cover and let rise in a warm place (85°), free from drafts, 1½ hours or until doubled in size. (Gently press two fingers into dough. If indentation remains, dough has risen enough.)

3. To prepare topping, heat 1 tablespoon oil in a large nonstick skillet over medium-high heat. Add onion, dried

basil, ½ teaspoon salt, and pepper; cook 20 minutes or until onion is golden, stirring occasionally. Cool.

4. Arrange tomato slices between several layers of paper towels. Let stand 10 minutes, pressing down occasionally.

5. Uncover dough. Punch dough down; cover and let rest 5 minutes. Pat dough into an even layer in a 15 x 10-inch jelly-roll pan coated with cooking spray. Cover and let rise 30 minutes.

6. Preheat oven to 425°.

7. Uncover dough. Arrange onion mixture over dough, leaving a ½-inch border. Top with tomato slices; sprinkle with cheese. Bake at 425° for 23 minutes or until browned. Sprinkle with fresh basil. Cool at least 10 minutes before serving. Yield: 16 servings (serving size: 1 piece).

CALORIES 138 (23% from fat); FAT 3.5g (sat 0.8g, mono 2.1g, poly 0.4g); PROTEIN 3.9g; CARB 22.5g; FIBER 1.4g; CHOL 2mg; IRON 1.3mg; SODIUM 266mg; CALC 45mg

Smoky Shrimp and Avocado Seviche

Most seviche recipes call for marinating raw seafood in citrus juice, but this recipe starts with cooked shrimp. An ice bath quickly cools down the boiled shrimp to prevent overcooking. You can make this appetizer earlier in the day, but don't marinate it for more than four hours, as the citrus juice will start to affect the texture of the shrimp.

- 1½ pounds medium shrimp, peeled and deveined
- 1 cup diced peeled avocado
- ⅓ cup finely chopped red bell pepper
- ⅓ cup finely chopped peeled jícama
- ⅓ cup fresh lime juice
- ¼ cup finely chopped onion
- ¼ cup fresh orange juice
- 3 tablespoons chopped fresh cilantro
- 1 tablespoon finely chopped canned chipotle chile in adobo sauce
- ½ teaspoon sugar
- ½ teaspoon salt
- 4 ounces baked tortilla chips

1. Cook shrimp in boiling water 2 minutes. Drain and plunge shrimp into ice water. Let stand 3 minutes; drain.

2. Combine shrimp, avocado, and remaining ingredients except chips in a large bowl, stirring well. Cover and chill up to 4 hours. Serve with chips. Yield: 10 servings (serving size: ½ cup seviche and about 8 chips).

CALORIES 152 (23% from fat); FAT 3.9g (sat 0.6g, mono 1.7g, poly 1g); PROTEIN 15.1g; CARB 14.2g; FIBER 2g; CHOL 103mg; IRON 2.1mg; SODIUM 317mg; CALC 56mg

California Burgers

Alfalfa sprouts and avocados crown these juicy burgers. A combination of regular ground turkey and ground turkey breast offers superior texture.

SAUCE:

- ½ cup ketchup
- 1 tablespoon Dijon mustard
- 1 tablespoon fat-free mayonnaise

PATTIES:

- ½ cup finely chopped shallots
- ¼ cup dry breadcrumbs
- 1 teaspoon salt
- 1 teaspoon Worcestershire sauce
- ¼ teaspoon freshly ground black pepper
- 3 garlic cloves, minced
- 1¼ pounds ground turkey
- 1¼ pounds ground turkey breast
- Cooking spray

REMAINING INGREDIENTS:

- 10 (2-ounce) hamburger buns
- 10 red leaf lettuce leaves
- 20 bread-and-butter pickles
- 10 (¼-inch-thick) slices red onion, separated into rings
- 2 peeled avocados, each cut into 10 slices
- 3 cups alfalfa sprouts

1. Prepare grill.

2. To prepare sauce, combine first 3 ingredients; set aside.

3. To prepare patties, combine shallots and next 7 ingredients, mixing well.

Continued

Divide mixture into 10 equal portions, shaping each into a ½-inch-thick patty. Place patties on grill rack coated with cooking spray; grill 4 minutes on each side or until done.

4. Spread 1 tablespoon sauce on top half of each bun. Layer bottom half of each bun with 1 lettuce leaf, 1 patty, 2 pickles, 1 onion slice, 2 avocado slices, and about ⅓ cup sprouts. Cover with top halves of buns. Yield: 10 servings (serving size: 1 burger).

CALORIES 384 (29% from fat); FAT 12.4g (sat 2.6g, mono 5.1g, poly 2.8g); PROTEIN 31.4g; CARB 37.5g; FIBER 3.9g; CHOL 68mg; IRON 4mg; SODIUM 828mg; CALC 94mg

Cumin-Crusted Pork Soft Tacos

(pictured on page 305)

To keep the tortillas from splitting, lightly coat them with cooking spray before heating. They can also be heated in a grill pan. Garnish with sliced green onions, if desired.

PORK:
- 2 teaspoons ground cumin
- 1 teaspoon cumin seeds, crushed
- 1 teaspoon paprika
- ½ teaspoon salt
- ¼ teaspoon black pepper
- 2 (1-pound) pork tenderloins, trimmed
- 1 tablespoon olive oil

SALSA:
- 2 cups frozen whole-kernel corn, thawed
- 1 cup quartered grape tomatoes
- 1 cup cubed peeled avocado
- ½ cup diced red onion
- ⅓ cup chopped fresh cilantro
- 2 tablespoons fresh lime juice
- ½ teaspoon salt
- 2 (15-ounce) cans black beans, rinsed and drained

REMAINING INGREDIENTS:
- 2 cups reduced-fat sour cream
- 1 tablespoon canned chipotle chile in adobo sauce, chopped
- 30 (6-inch) corn tortillas

1. Preheat oven to 425°.

2. To prepare pork, combine first 5 ingredients. Rub cumin mixture over pork. Heat oil in a large cast-iron skillet over medium-high heat. Add pork; cook 4 minutes or until browned on all sides. Bake at 425° for 12 minutes or until a thermometer registers 155°. Remove pork from oven; let stand 5 minutes. Cut pork across grain into ¼-inch slices.

3. To prepare salsa, combine corn and next 7 ingredients.

4. Place sour cream and chipotle in a blender; process until smooth.

5. Wrap tortillas, 3 at a time, in a damp paper towel. Microwave at HIGH 20 seconds. Spoon about 1 ounce pork onto each tortilla. Top each tortilla with about 2 tablespoons salsa and about 2 teaspoons sour cream mixture. Fold in half. Yield: 15 servings (serving size: 2 tacos).

CALORIES 345 (29% from fat); FAT 11.1g (sat 4g, mono 4.1g, poly 1.4g); PROTEIN 24.6g; CARB 40g; FIBER 5.8g; CHOL 68mg; IRON 2.6mg; SODIUM 427mg; CALC 157mg

MAKE AHEAD
Tex-Mex Pasta Salad

- 1 pound uncooked radiatore pasta (short coiled pasta)
- 2 teaspoons olive oil
- 3 garlic cloves, minced
- 1½ pounds ground turkey
- ⅔ cup water
- 1 (1.25-ounce) package 40%-less-sodium taco seasoning (such as Old El Paso)
- 2 cups (8 ounces) preshredded reduced-fat Mexican blend cheese
- 2 cups chopped seeded tomato
- 1 cup chopped bell pepper
- ½ cup chopped fresh cilantro
- ½ cup chopped green onions
- ½ cup sliced ripe olives
- 1 (15.5-ounce) can black beans, rinsed and drained
- 2 tablespoons fresh lime juice
- ½ teaspoon salt
- ¼ teaspoon ground cumin
- 1 (8-ounce) container reduced-fat sour cream
  Salsa (optional)

1. Cook pasta according to package directions, omitting salt and fat. Drain and rinse with cold water. Drain; set aside.

2. Heat oil in a large nonstick skillet over medium-high heat. Add garlic; sauté 1 minute. Add turkey; cook until browned, stirring to crumble. Stir in water and taco seasoning; bring to a boil. Reduce heat, and simmer 4 minutes or until liquid almost evaporates and turkey is done, stirring frequently. Remove from heat; cool slightly.

3. Combine pasta, turkey mixture, cheese, and next 6 ingredients in a large bowl.

4. Combine lime juice, salt, cumin, and sour cream, stirring until well blended. Pour over pasta mixture; toss gently to coat. Serve with salsa, if desired. Yield: 12 servings (serving size: about 1⅓ cups).

CALORIES 344 (30% from fat); FAT 11.4g (sat 5.3g, mono 4.1g, poly 1.4g); PROTEIN 23.4g; CARB 38.5g; FIBER 3.6g; CHOL 51mg; IRON 2.9mg; SODIUM 632mg; CALC 193mg

MAKE AHEAD
End-of-Summer Tomato Salad

The assortment of tomato colors and sizes creates a gorgeous, yet simple, salad. Juicy summer tomatoes don't need much embellishment to shine. Here, they're lightly dressed with a simple vinaigrette that doesn't mask their sweet flavor.

- 1 cup cherry tomatoes, halved
- 1 cup grape tomatoes
- 1 cup yellow pear tomatoes
- 2 tablespoons chopped fresh chives
- 2 tablespoons chopped fresh basil
- 2 tablespoons chopped fresh mint
- 1 teaspoon minced fresh tarragon
- 1 tablespoon capers
- ¾ pound tomatoes, cut into ¼-inch-thick wedges
- ¾ pound yellow tomatoes, cut into ¼-inch-thick wedges
- 1½ teaspoons extravirgin olive oil
- 1½ teaspoons champagne vinegar
- ¼ teaspoon salt
- ¼ teaspoon freshly ground black pepper

1. Combine first 10 ingredients in a large bowl. Combine oil, vinegar, salt, and pepper, stirring with a whisk. Drizzle oil mixture over tomato mixture; toss gently to coat. Yield: 10 servings (serving size: about ¾ cup).

CALORIES 26 (35% from fat); FAT 1g (sat 0.1g, mono 0.6g, poly 0.2g); PROTEIN 1.1g; CARB 4.2g; FIBER 1.1g; CHOL 0mg; IRON 0.5mg; SODIUM 99mg; CALC 13mg

QUICK & EASY • MAKE AHEAD

Roasted Asparagus with Orange Vinaigrette

Elegant and simple, this side dish has the added benefit of being equally tasty warm or at room temperature.

    1 tablespoon grated orange rind
    3 tablespoons fresh orange
       juice
    2 tablespoons finely chopped
       shallots
    1 teaspoon sugar
    1 teaspoon salt, divided
   ¼   teaspoon freshly ground black
       pepper, divided
    3 pounds asparagus spears,
       trimmed
   Cooking spray
    2 tablespoons extravirgin olive oil

1. Preheat oven to 450°.
2. Combine first 4 ingredients; stir in ½ teaspoon salt and ⅛ teaspoon pepper. Set aside.
3. Arrange asparagus in a single layer on a jelly-roll pan coated with cooking spray. Drizzle with oil, and sprinkle with ½ teaspoon salt and ⅛ teaspoon pepper. Toss well to coat. Bake at 450° for 10 minutes, stirring well after 5 minutes. Remove from oven (do not turn oven off). Drizzle with juice mixture; toss to coat. Bake at 450° for 5 minutes or until crisp-tender. Yield: 10 servings (serving size: about 4 ounces).

CALORIES 44 (57% from fat); FAT 2.8g (sat 0.4g, mono 2g, poly 0.3g); PROTEIN 1.7g; CARB 4.2g; FIBER 0.1g; CHOL 0mg; IRON 1.6mg; SODIUM 237mg; CALC 20mg

QUICK & EASY • MAKE AHEAD

Tuscan White Beans

You can combine the ingredients and refrigerate up to two days, but bring to room temperature for full flavor.

   ½   cup chopped onion
   ½   cup chopped celery
   ½   cup chopped carrot
   ⅓   cup chopped fresh parsley
    1 tablespoon grated lemon
       rind
   ⅓   cup fresh lemon juice
    2 tablespoons chopped fresh
       sage
    2 tablespoons extravirgin olive oil
   ½   teaspoon salt
   ¼   teaspoon crushed red pepper
    3 (15.5-ounce) cans cannellini beans
       or other white beans, rinsed and
       drained
    2 garlic cloves, minced

1. Combine all ingredients in a large bowl. Let stand at room temperature at least 30 minutes before serving. Yield: 10 servings (serving size: about ⅔ cup).

CALORIES 114 (25% from fat); FAT 3.2g (sat 0.4g, mono 2g, poly 0.7g); PROTEIN 4.3g; CARB 17g; FIBER 4.4g; CHOL 0mg; IRON 1.6mg; SODIUM 341mg; CALC 45mg

MAKE AHEAD

Strawberry-Topped Pavlovas with Honey-Balsamic Sauce

(pictured on page 306)

The components of this dessert can be prepared in stages and assembled shortly before serving. Store meringues in an airtight container at room temperature up to one week; refrigerate strawberries and sauce up to two days. Garnish with mint.

STRAWBERRIES:
    3 quarts strawberries, quartered
   ⅓   cup sugar

MERINGUES:
   ¼   teaspoon cream of tartar
    4 large egg whites
   ¾   cup sugar
    1 teaspoon vanilla extract

SAUCE:
   ¾   cup balsamic vinegar
    1 (2-inch) cinnamon stick
    3 tablespoons honey

1. Preheat oven to 250°.
2. To prepare strawberries, combine strawberries and ⅓ cup sugar; cover and chill.
3. To prepare meringues, cover 2 baking sheets with parchment paper. Draw 5 (4-inch) circles on each piece of paper. Turn paper over; secure with masking tape. Place cream of tartar and egg whites in a large bowl; beat with a mixer at high speed until foamy. Gradually add ¾ cup sugar, 1 tablespoon at a time, beating until stiff peaks form (do not underbeat). Beat in vanilla. Divide egg white mixture evenly among 10 drawn circles on baking sheets. Shape meringues into nests with 1-inch sides using back of a spoon.
4. Bake at 250° for 1 hour, rotating baking sheets after 30 minutes. Turn oven off, and cool meringues in closed oven 30 minutes. Carefully remove meringues from paper. Cool completely.
5. To prepare sauce, combine vinegar and cinnamon stick in a small saucepan over medium-high heat. Bring to a boil; cook until syrupy and reduced to about ⅓ cup (about 5 to 6 minutes). Remove from heat. Discard cinnamon stick; stir in honey.
6. Place 1 meringue nest on each of 10 dessert plates; top each serving with about ¾ cup strawberry mixture. Drizzle with about 2 teaspoons sauce. Yield: 10 servings.

CALORIES 182 (3% from fat); FAT 0.6g (sat 0g, mono 0.1g, poly 0.3g); PROTEIN 2.8g; CARB 43.9g; FIBER 3.7g; CHOL 0mg; IRON 1mg; SODIUM 29mg; CALC 36mg

Lemon-Blueberry Bundt Cake

Both kids and adults will love this golden cake bursting with blueberries and drizzled with tangy lemon glaze.

CAKE:

Cooking spray
2 tablespoons granulated sugar
3 cups all-purpose flour (about 13½ ounces)
1½ teaspoons baking powder
½ teaspoon baking soda
¼ teaspoon salt
1¾ cups granulated sugar
¼ cup butter, softened
1 tablespoon grated lemon rind
4 large eggs
½ teaspoon vanilla extract
1 (16-ounce) container reduced-fat sour cream
2 cups fresh blueberries

GLAZE:

1 cup powdered sugar
3 tablespoons fresh lemon juice

1. Preheat oven to 350°.
2. To prepare cake, coat a 12-cup Bundt pan with cooking spray; dust with 2 tablespoons granulated sugar. Set aside.
3. Lightly spoon flour into dry measuring cups; level with a knife. Combine flour, baking powder, baking soda, and salt, stirring with a whisk.
4. Place 1¾ cups granulated sugar, butter, and rind in a large bowl; beat with a mixer at medium speed until well blended (about 2 minutes). Add eggs, 1 at a time, beating well after each addition (about 4 minutes total). Beat in vanilla and sour cream. Add flour mixture; beat at medium speed just until combined. Gently fold in blueberries. Spoon batter into prepared pan. Bake at 350° for 1 hour or until a wooden pick inserted in center comes out clean. Cool in pan 15 minutes on a wire rack; remove from pan. Cool completely on wire rack.

5. To prepare glaze, combine powdered sugar and lemon juice, stirring well with a whisk. Drizzle over cooled cake. Yield: 16 servings (serving size: 1 slice).

CALORIES 299 (23% from fat); FAT 7.8g (sat 4g, mono 2.7g, poly 0.5g); PROTEIN 5g; CARB 53.2g; FIBER 1.1g; CHOL 71mg; IRON 1.5mg; SODIUM 172mg; CALC 68mg

Tapas Today

A small-plates buffet lets you prepare dishes ahead of time, so you can entertain with ease and continental charm.

Who would have thought that a small plate set atop a glass of wine would turn into an international phenomenon? Tapas, the plural of tapa—meaning "cover"—is a custom that began nearly 200 years ago in Spain. At the time, smart bar owners realized that if they put savory food on the little plates, their patrons would drink more.

The popularity of tapas spread much farther than Spain. You can find small plates served all around the Mediterranean. In France, they're called hors d'oeuvres; in Italy, antipasti. In Greece, Turkey, Syria, Lebanon, Israel, and Egypt, they use the word meze; and in Morocco, mukabalatt. Even Venice has its own custom of cicheti, the local equivalent of tapas and meze.

What started as a simple cover has developed into a dizzying array of flavorful, healthful, and colorful dishes. The variety can be staggering, which makes tapas ideal for entertaining at home. And don't think that everything has to come straight from the oven or frying pan at the last moment. Some dishes can be made in advance and reheated before serving. Even better, tapas are often served at room temperature, to be consumed at leisure. So relax, join your guests, and enjoy the Mediterranean charm of tapas.

Baked Omelet with Zucchini, Leeks, Feta, and Herbs

This classic Greek dish can be prepared several hours in advance, refrigerated, and brought to room temperature before serving. A spoonful of the Smoky Tomato Relish (recipe on page 297) makes a suitable condiment.

¾ cup water
¼ cup uncooked long-grain rice
Cooking spray
2¼ cups thinly sliced leek (about 3 medium)
4 cups shredded zucchini (about 2 medium)
½ cup egg substitute
1½ tablespoons chopped fresh mint
1 tablespoon chopped fresh dill
½ teaspoon salt
¼ teaspoon freshly ground black pepper
4 large eggs, lightly beaten
½ cup (2 ounces) crumbled feta cheese

1. Bring water to a boil in a medium saucepan; add rice. Cover, reduce heat, and simmer 20 minutes or until liquid is absorbed. Place rice in a large bowl.
2. Preheat oven to 325°.
3. Heat a large nonstick skillet over medium-low heat. Coat pan with cooking spray. Add leek; cover and cook 12 minutes or until tender, stirring occasionally. Remove from pan; add leek to rice. Coat pan with cooking spray; increase heat to medium. Add zucchini; cook 6 minutes or until tender, stirring occasionally. Remove from pan; add zucchini to rice. Add egg substitute and next 5 ingredients to rice mixture; stir until blended.
4. Pour egg mixture into an 8-inch square baking dish coated with cooking spray. Sprinkle with cheese. Bake at 325° for 35 minutes or until golden brown and set. Yield: 16 servings (serving size: 1 piece).

CALORIES 60 (35% from fat); FAT 2.3g (sat 0.9g, mono 0.6g, poly 0.4g); PROTEIN 3.9g; CARB 6.4g; FIBER 0.8g; CHOL 54mg; IRON 1mg; SODIUM 154mg; CALC 42mg

Warm Spiced Lentils

Serve this dish with pita bread wedges. Make sure not to overcook the lentils, or they will split and their texture will suffer. Substitute red or yellow lentils, if you prefer.

    1   cup petite green lentils
    1   small onion, peeled
    4   whole cloves
    2   bay leaves
    1   (2-inch) lemon rind strip
    1   tablespoon extravirgin olive oil
    ¾   cup chopped red onion
    1   cup chopped seeded tomato
    ¾   teaspoon ground ginger
    ¾   teaspoon ground cumin
    ½   teaspoon ground turmeric
    ½   teaspoon Hungarian sweet
        paprika
    ⅛   teaspoon ground red pepper
    3   garlic cloves, minced
    ¼   cup chopped fresh cilantro
    3   tablespoons chopped fresh
        flat-leaf parsley
  1 ½   tablespoons fresh lemon juice
    ½   teaspoon salt
    ⅛   teaspoon freshly ground black
        pepper
    8   lemon wedges

1. Place lentils in a large saucepan, and cover with water to 2 inches above lentils. Stud whole onion with cloves. Add studded onion, bay leaves, and rind to pan; bring to a boil. Cover, reduce heat, and simmer 20 minutes or until lentils are just tender. Drain well. Discard onion, bay leaves, and rind.
2. Heat oil in a large nonstick skillet over medium heat. Add chopped red onion; cook 5 minutes or until tender, stirring occasionally. Stir in tomato and next 6 ingredients; cook 2 minutes. Stir in lentils, cilantro, and parsley; cook 2 minutes. Stir in juice, salt, and black pepper. Serve warm with lemon wedges. Yield: 8 servings (serving size: about ⅓ cup lentil mixture and 1 lemon wedge).

CALORIES 112 (17% from fat); FAT 2.1g (sat 0.3g, mono 1.3g, poly 0.3g); PROTEIN 7.4g; CARB 17.2g; FIBER 8.2g; CHOL 0mg; IRON 2.6mg; SODIUM 152mg; CALC 25mg

The full flavors and authentic ingredients of tapas account for their popularity.

Grilled Bread with Serrano Ham, Manchego, and Olives

This simple dish shines when you use the ripest tomatoes you can find.

        Dash of salt
    2   garlic cloves
    3   tablespoons extravirgin olive oil
    8   (½-inch-thick) slices Italian or
        French bread
    6   tomatoes, halved
    ¼   teaspoon salt
    ⅛   teaspoon freshly ground black
        pepper
    ½   cup (about 2 ounces) very thin
        slices serrano ham or prosciutto
    ½   cup (2 ounces) shaved Manchego
        cheese
    ½   cup chopped pitted green olives

1. Prepare grill.
2. Mash dash of salt and garlic with a mortar and pestle or the back of a spoon to make a fine paste. Combine garlic mixture and oil in a small bowl.
3. Place bread on grill rack; grill 1 minute on each side or until golden brown.
4. Rub both sides of bread slices with cut sides of tomatoes, squeezing slightly to leave pulp, seeds, and juice on bread. Discard peels. Spread garlic mixture over bread slices; sprinkle with ¼ teaspoon salt and pepper. Cut each slice diagonally in half. Arrange ham and cheese evenly over bread pieces, and sprinkle evenly with olives. Serve immediately. Yield: 8 servings (serving size: 2 pieces).

CALORIES 192 (42% from fat); FAT 8.9g (sat 2.1g, mono 3.7g, poly 0.6g); PROTEIN 7.7g; CARB 23.6g; FIBER 3.5g; CHOL 11mg; IRON 1.2mg; SODIUM 620mg; CALC 95mg

---

Sip Suitably

Tapas foods feature robust, assertive flavors, so select beverages to complement them. But be adventurous—a tapas party gives people a chance to sample drinks they might not find at another kind of gathering.

• Sherry is among the most traditional beverages to accompany tapas.

• In general, full-bodied wines harmonize with tapas dishes. Consider Spanish wines, including those from the Rioja, Catalonia, and Ribera del Duero regions, as well as Italian wines, such as Barolo or Bolgheri.

• Spanish beers, such as Estrella Damm, may be hard to come by. Most light-bodied, crisp lagers and pilsners will do.

• To make the party even more special, pour glasses of cava, a Spanish sparkling wine, or Italian prosecco.

• Branch out and serve other beverages, such as Greek ouzo, Italian grappa, or French Pernod.

• Include sparkling water, such as Perrier or San Pellegrino. Follow the European custom and serve water chilled, but hold the ice.

Garlic Flatbreads with Smoked Mozzarella and Tomato Vinaigrette

(pictured on page 307)

Smoked mozzarella infuses this dish with distinctive flavor, though you can substitute regular mozzarella, if you prefer. Serve warm, or prepare in advance and serve at room temperature (store flatbreads and topping separately).

FLATBREADS:

¼ cup whole wheat flour (about 1 ounce)
1 cup warm water (100° to 110°), divided
1 package dry yeast (about 2¼ teaspoons)
2¼ cups all-purpose flour, divided (about 10 ounces)
½ teaspoon salt
Cooking spray
1 teaspoon cornmeal
4 garlic cloves, thinly sliced

TOPPING:

3 tablespoons balsamic vinegar
2 tablespoons extravirgin olive oil
¼ teaspoon salt
⅛ teaspoon freshly ground black pepper
1 garlic clove, minced
¾ cup halved red cherry tomatoes (about 4 ounces)
¾ cup halved yellow cherry tomatoes (about 4 ounces)
1 cup (4 ounces) shredded smoked mozzarella cheese
½ cup thinly sliced fresh basil

1. To prepare flatbreads, lightly spoon whole wheat flour into a dry measuring cup; level with a knife. Combine whole wheat flour, ¼ cup water, and yeast in a bowl; let stand 10 minutes.
2. Lightly spoon all-purpose flour into dry measuring cups, and level with a knife. Combine 2 cups all-purpose flour, ½ teaspoon salt, and ¾ cup water in a large bowl. Add yeast mixture, and stir until a dough forms. Turn dough out onto a lightly floured surface. Knead until smooth and elastic (about 10 minutes); add enough of remaining ¼ cup all-purpose flour, 1 tablespoon at a time, to prevent dough from sticking to hands (dough will feel sticky). Place dough in a large bowl coated with cooking spray, turning to coat top. Cover and let rise in a warm place (85°), free from drafts, 1 hour or until doubled in size. (Gently press two fingers into dough. If indentation remains, dough has risen enough.)
3. Preheat oven to 450°.
4. Punch dough down; cover and let rest 5 minutes. Divide dough in half. Roll each half into a 9-inch circle on a lightly floured surface; place on baking sheets sprinkled with cornmeal. Lightly coat dough with cooking spray. Sprinkle dough evenly with sliced garlic; press garlic into dough using fingertips. Bake at 450° for 10 minutes or until crisp and garlic begins to brown. Remove flatbreads from oven; cool on wire racks.
5. To prepare topping, combine vinegar and next 4 ingredients in a medium bowl. Add tomatoes; toss gently.
6. Preheat broiler.
7. Sprinkle each flatbread with ½ cup cheese; broil flatbreads 1 minute or until cheese melts. Remove from oven; top each flatbread with half of tomato mixture. Sprinkle each flatbread with ¼ cup basil. Cut each flatbread into 6 equal wedges. Yield: 12 servings (serving size: 1 wedge).

CALORIES 139 (27% from fat); FAT 4.1g (sat 1.3g, mono 2.1g, poly 0.4g); PROTEIN 5.3g; CARB 20.2g; FIBER 1.3g; CHOL 5mg; IRON 1.4mg; SODIUM 194mg; CALC 73mg

---

When More Is More

Variety accounts for much of the fun of a tapas party. Because portions are small, guests can enjoy a wide selection of dishes. Ideally, your spread will include meats, fish, cheeses, vegetables, salads, and bread-based dishes like pizza, flatbread, or crostini. While many of these dishes will be served at room temperature—both for convenience and optimum flavor—try to include some hot and chilled dishes, as well, which will help stimulate your guests' palates.

Stewed Mussels with Feta

Serve with crusty baguette slices so you can sop up the tasty broth.

Cooking spray
¾ cup minced yellow onion
4 cups chopped seeded peeled tomato (about 4 large)
1 cup dry white wine
1 teaspoon red wine vinegar
¼ teaspoon dried oregano
¼ teaspoon crushed red pepper
64 small mussels, scrubbed and debearded (about 2 pounds)
1 cup (4 ounces) crumbled feta cheese
¼ teaspoon salt
⅛ teaspoon freshly ground black pepper
1 tablespoon chopped fresh flat-leaf parsley

1. Heat a large nonstick skillet over medium heat. Coat pan with cooking spray. Add onion; cook 4 minutes or until tender, stirring occasionally. Increase heat to medium-high. Stir in tomato and next 4 ingredients; bring to a boil. Reduce heat; simmer 30 minutes or until thick. Add mussels; cover and cook 5 minutes or until shells open. Remove from heat; discard any unopened shells. Stir in cheese, salt, and pepper. Sprinkle with parsley. Yield: 8 servings (serving size: 8 mussels and about ½ cup tomato mixture).

CALORIES 177 (29% from fat); FAT 5.8g (sat 2.6g, mono 1.3g, poly 0.9g); PROTEIN 16.5g; CARB 10.1g; FIBER 1.2g; CHOL 44mg; IRON 5mg; SODIUM 562mg; CALC 114mg

---

Classic Tzatziki

A traditional Greek dip and gyro condiment, tzatziki also makes a tasty topping for sandwiches and even hamburgers.

1 cup grated seeded peeled cucumber
⅛ teaspoon salt
1 cup plain fat-free yogurt
1 tablespoon chopped fresh mint
2 teaspoons chopped fresh dill
2 teaspoons fresh lemon juice
¼ teaspoon salt
2 garlic cloves, minced

1. Place cucumber on several layers of paper towels; sprinkle with ⅛ teaspoon salt. Let stand 30 minutes.

2. Combine cucumber, yogurt, and remaining ingredients, stirring until well blended. Refrigerate at least 1 hour before serving. Yield: 14 servings (serving size: 2 tablespoons).

CALORIES 9 (0% from fat); FAT 0g; PROTEIN 0.8g; CARB 1.8g; FIBER 0.1g; CHOL 0mg; IRON 0mg; SODIUM 72mg; CALC 24mg

MAKE AHEAD
Smoky Tomato Relish

Serve this rustic relish with pita wedges, or grilled shrimp or chicken. You can prepare it up to one day ahead and refrigerate.

    1 green bell pepper
    2 tomatoes (about 1 pound)
    ½ cup chopped onion
    1 tablespoon extravirgin olive oil
    2 teaspoons red wine vinegar
 1 ½ teaspoons chopped fresh thyme
    1 teaspoon chopped fresh mint
    ½ teaspoon salt
    ¼ teaspoon freshly ground black
       pepper
    ¼ teaspoon ground red pepper
    2 garlic cloves, minced
       Flat-leaf parsley leaves (optional)
    6 (6-inch) pitas, each cut into 4
       wedges

1. Heat a large cast-iron skillet over medium-high heat. Cut bell pepper in half lengthwise; discard seeds and membranes. Flatten one bell pepper half with hand; add to pan, skin side down. Reserve remaining bell pepper half for another use. Add tomatoes to pan. Cook 10 minutes or until blackened, turning frequently. Remove from heat; cool pepper and tomatoes to room temperature.

2. Chop tomatoes, and place in a medium bowl. Chop bell pepper; add to tomato. Stir in onion and next 8 ingredients. Garnish with parsley, if desired. Serve chilled or at room temperature with pita wedges. Yield: 8 servings (serving size: ¼ cup relish and 3 pita wedges).

CALORIES 156 (14% from fat); FAT 2.4g (sat 0.3g, mono 1.3g, poly 0.5g); PROTEIN 4.8g; CARB 29.1g; FIBER 2.1g; CHOL 0mg; IRON 1.5mg; SODIUM 390mg; CALC 51mg

MAKE AHEAD
Grape Leaves Stuffed with Rice, Currants, and Herbs

Make this dish the night before a gathering, refrigerate overnight, and serve at room temperature.

   24 large grape leaves
       Cooking spray
    1 cup finely chopped onion
    ½ cup uncooked long-grain rice
    ½ cup chopped green onions
    2 tablespoons pine nuts
    1 cup water
    2 tablespoons dried currants
    2 tablespoons chopped fresh
       flat-leaf parsley
 1 ½ tablespoons chopped fresh mint
 1 ½ tablespoons chopped fresh dill
    ½ teaspoon salt
    ¼ teaspoon freshly ground black
       pepper
    ⅛ teaspoon ground cinnamon
    ½ cup plain fat-free yogurt
    8 lemon wedges

1. Rinse grape leaves with cold water; drain well. Pat dry with paper towels. Remove stems; discard. Set leaves aside.

2. Heat a large nonstick skillet over medium heat. Coat pan with cooking spray. Add 1 cup onion; cook 7 minutes or until tender, stirring occasionally. Add rice, green onions, and nuts; cook 4 minutes, stirring frequently. Stir in water and next 7 ingredients; bring to a boil. Cover, reduce heat, and simmer 15 minutes or until rice is tender. Cool slightly.

3. Spoon 1 rounded tablespoon rice mixture onto center of 1 grape leaf. Fold one side of leaf over filling. Fold opposite side over filling. Beginning at one short side, roll up leaf tightly, jelly-roll fashion. Repeat procedure with remaining grape leaves and filling. Steam grape leaves, covered, 10 minutes or until thoroughly heated. Cool to room temperature. Serve with yogurt and lemon wedges. Yield: 8 servings (serving size: 3 stuffed grape leaves, 1 tablespoon yogurt, and 1 lemon wedge).

CALORIES 88 (12% from fat); FAT 1.8g (sat 0.2g, mono 0.4g, poly 0.9g); PROTEIN 2.7g; CARB 16.5g; FIBER 1g; CHOL 0mg; IRON 1.3mg; SODIUM 500mg; CALC 72mg

How to Stuff Grape Leaves

1. *Spoon 1 rounded tablespoon rice mixture onto center of 1 grape leaf.*

2. *Fold one side of leaf over filling.*

3. *Fold opposite side over filling.*

4. *Beginning at one short side, roll up leaf tightly, jelly-roll fashion.*

Roasted Peppers, Anchovies, and Basil à la Merenda

A welcome addition to a tapas spread, this salad also makes a delicious side for beef, chicken, or fish, and can be made ahead.

    3 yellow bell peppers
    3 red bell peppers
    1 tablespoon anchovy paste
    1 teaspoon extravirgin olive oil
    1 teaspoon red wine vinegar
    ½ teaspoon chopped fresh oregano
    ¼ teaspoon freshly ground black pepper
    1 garlic clove, minced
    ¼ cup chopped fresh basil
    ¼ cup niçoise olives, pitted

1. Preheat broiler.
2. Cut bell peppers in half lengthwise; discard seeds and membranes. Place pepper halves, skin sides up, on a foil-lined baking sheet; flatten with hand. Broil 15 minutes or until blackened. Place in a zip-top plastic bag; seal. Let stand 15 minutes. Peel and cut into 1-inch strips.
3. Combine bell peppers, anchovy paste, and next 5 ingredients in a medium bowl, stirring until well blended; let stand 30 minutes. Sprinkle with basil and olives. Yield: 6 servings (serving size: about ⅓ cup).

CALORIES 51 (32% from fat); FAT 1.8g (sat 0.3g, mono 1g, poly 0.3g); PROTEIN 1.7g; CARB 8.6g; FIBER 0.3g; CHOL 1mg; IRON 2mg; SODIUM 346mg; CALC 29mg

Toasted Pita with Mint, Cucumber, and Tomato Salad

Put late-summer tomatoes to good use in this bright and herby salad.

    ¼ cup fresh lemon juice
    2 tablespoons extravirgin olive oil
    ½ teaspoon salt
    ¼ teaspoon freshly ground black pepper
    2 garlic cloves, minced
    3¾ cups chopped tomato (about 3 medium)
    1½ cups chopped peeled English cucumber (about 1)
    ⅓ cup thinly sliced green onions
    ⅓ cup chopped fresh flat-leaf parsley
    ¼ cup chopped fresh mint
    1 tablespoon chopped fresh cilantro
    3 (6-inch) pitas, each cut into 8 wedges

1. Preheat oven to 425°.
2. Combine first 5 ingredients in a large bowl, stirring with a whisk. Add tomato and next 5 ingredients; toss well.
3. Arrange pita wedges in a single layer on a baking sheet. Bake at 425° for 6 minutes or until golden. Serve with salad. Yield: 8 servings (serving size: about ⅔ cup salad and 3 pita wedges).

CALORIES 116 (30% from fat); FAT 3.9g (sat 0.5g, mono 2.6g, poly 0.6g); PROTEIN 3.2g; CARB 18g; FIBER 2g; CHOL 0mg; IRON 1.2mg; SODIUM 274mg; CALC 43mg

New Chapter for a Creamy Casserole

The story of a New Jersey family's favorite dish now has a happy ending.

After her mother died, Betsy Bacon and her sisters inherited her mother's recipe for Chicken and Broccoli Casserole. Betsy prepared the dish for her two children and husband. But as they became more health conscious, the family shifted toward a lower-fat diet. She missed the flavor and the fond memories of her mother's chicken casserole. That's when she asked *Cooking Light* to lighten it.

Chicken and Broccoli Casserole

For crisper broccoli, remove it from the boiling water after three minutes. Serve with a simple green salad.

    3 quarts water
    1 (12-ounce) package broccoli florets
    4 (6-ounce) skinless, boneless chicken breast halves
    1 (12-ounce) can evaporated fat-free milk
    ¼ cup all-purpose flour (about 1 ounce)
    ¼ teaspoon salt
    ¼ teaspoon freshly ground black pepper
       Dash of nutmeg
    1 cup (4 ounces) grated fresh Parmesan cheese, divided
    1 cup fat-free mayonnaise
    ½ cup fat-free sour cream
    ¼ cup dry sherry
    1 teaspoon Worcestershire sauce
    1 (10.75-ounce) can condensed 30%-reduced-sodium 98%-fat-free cream of mushroom soup, undiluted
       Cooking spray

Keep It Simple

Your tapas offerings may include refined dishes, but they can also feature something as simple as a plate of olives. Here are suggestions:

• Cured olives—niçoise, picholine, lucques (France), kalamata (Greece), and manzanilla (Spain), to name a few—are tasty party snacks.

• Include a selection of cheeses. As with any cheese board, present a wide variety that ranges from soft to hard textures and from mild to strong flavors (for instance, goat cheese, Manchego, Parmgiano-Reggiano, and gorgonzola). Ask a cheese merchant for advice; he should steer you from cheeses that might be popular but aren't at peak quality, and encourage you to sample new varieties.

• Provide an assortment of cured hams and sausages, such as sopressata, prosciutto, and serrano ham.

• Offer a crudités medley to enjoy with tapas-style dips, such as Classic Tzatziki (recipe on page 296).

1. Preheat oven to 400°.

2. Bring water to a boil in a large Dutch oven over medium-high heat. Add broccoli, and cook 5 minutes or until crisp-tender. Transfer broccoli to a large bowl with a slotted spoon. Add chicken to boiling water; reduce heat, and simmer 15 minutes or until done. Transfer chicken to a cutting board; cool slightly. Cut chicken into bite-sized pieces, and add chicken to bowl with broccoli.

3. Combine evaporated milk, flour, salt, pepper, and nutmeg in a saucepan, stirring with a whisk until smooth. Bring to a boil over medium-high heat; cook 1 minute, stirring constantly. Remove from heat. Add ½ cup cheese, mayonnaise, and next 4 ingredients, stirring well. Add mayonnaise mixture to broccoli mixture; stir gently to combine.

4. Spoon mixture into a 13 x 9-inch baking dish coated with cooking spray. Sprinkle with ½ cup cheese. Bake at 400° for 50 minutes or until mixture bubbles at edges and cheese begins to brown. Remove from oven; cool on a wire rack 5 minutes. Yield: 8 servings (serving size: about 1 cup).

CALORIES 276 (25% from fat); FAT 7.8g (sat 3.5g, mono 1.8g, poly 1.1g); PROTEIN 31.1g; CARB 18.9g; FIBER 2.1g; CHOL 66mg; IRON 1.6mg; SODIUM 696mg; CALC 365mg

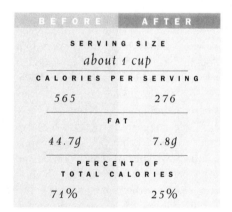

BEFORE	AFTER
SERVING SIZE	
about 1 cup	
CALORIES PER SERVING	
565	276
FAT	
44.7g	7.8g
PERCENT OF TOTAL CALORIES	
71%	25%

Grand Grilling

Enjoy the smoky sweetness that develops when vegetables are cooked on the grill.

Since vegetables cook quickly on the grill, you should use medium-hot heat to sear in flavor. The hand test is a reliable measure of the grill's readiness. Place your hand about two inches above the grate; if you can keep it there for only two to three seconds, then the grill is sufficiently heated. Once you place the food on the grate, don't move it until it has had time to sear. Watch your vegetables carefully as they cook; you want them to get nice grill marks and be browned, but not blackened.

Other than a timer, the only major grill tools you need are long-handled, strong spatulas and tongs for turning food. You might also want a vegetable grill rack, which makes it possible to cook bite-sized vegetables. It's simply a metal sheet perforated with small holes that allow flames and smoke to permeate the food.

Tandoori Tofu and Vegetable Kebabs
(pictured on page 306)

Prebaking makes the tofu appealingly chewy, allows it to absorb the marinade more effectively, and reduces sticking and crumbling on the grill. Golden raisins in the rice pilaf are a sweet balance to the intense spices in the tandoori marinade.

  1 (16-ounce) package water-packed firm tofu, drained and cut into 16 cubes
Cooking spray
  1 cup finely chopped onion
  ¾ cup plain low-fat yogurt
  2 teaspoons grated peeled fresh ginger
  2 teaspoons canola oil
  2 teaspoons ground coriander
1½ teaspoons ground cumin
  ½ teaspoon ground turmeric

  ¼ teaspoon freshly ground black pepper
  1 garlic clove, minced
16 large mushrooms (about 10 ounces)
  2 small red onions, each cut into 8 wedges
2⅔ cups water
1⅓ cups uncooked basmati rice
  ⅔ cup golden raisins
  1 teaspoon salt, divided

1. Preheat oven to 375°.

2. Arrange tofu in a single layer on a foil-lined baking sheet coated with cooking spray. Bake at 375° for 25 minutes or until tofu releases 3 or more tablespoons liquid.

3. Prepare grill.

4. Combine chopped onion and next 8 ingredients in a large bowl. Add tofu, mushrooms, and onion wedges; toss gently to coat. Let stand at room temperature 30 minutes.

5. While tofu and vegetables marinate, prepare rice. Bring water to a boil in a medium saucepan; stir in rice. Cover, reduce heat, and simmer 15 minutes or until liquid is absorbed. Stir in raisins and ¼ teaspoon salt. Let stand 5 minutes; fluff with a fork.

6. Remove tofu and vegetables from bowl; discard marinade. Thread tofu cubes, mushrooms, and onion wedges alternately onto 8 (6-inch) skewers. Lightly coat kebabs with cooking spray; sprinkle with ¾ teaspoon salt. Place kebabs on grill rack coated with cooking spray; grill 4 minutes on each side or until lightly browned. Serve with rice. Yield: 4 servings (serving size: 2 kebabs and 1 cup rice).

CALORIES 421 (21% from fat); FAT 9.6g (sat 1.7g, mono 1.9g, poly 5g); PROTEIN 20.2g; CARB 72.9g; FIBER 5.4g; CHOL 2mg; IRON 4.9mg; SODIUM 625mg; CALC 190mg

Pasta and Grilled Vegetables with Goat Cheese

This vibrant vegetable entrée is light and delicious. To ensure even grilling, cut the vegetables into large, similar-sized pieces. After they're cooked, they're chopped into bite-sized pieces. You can substitute yellow squash for zucchini.

  1 large zucchini, quartered
     lengthwise (about 8 ounces)
  1 red bell pepper, cut into
     4 wedges
  1 leek, trimmed and halved
  1 (14-ounce) can artichoke hearts,
     drained
  1 head radicchio, quartered
  ½ teaspoon salt, divided
  ¼ teaspoon freshly ground black
     pepper
  2 garlic cloves, minced
Cooking spray
  4 cups hot cooked rotini (about 4
     cups uncooked corkscrew pasta)
  1 cup grape or cherry tomatoes
  ¾ cup (3 ounces) crumbled goat
     cheese
  2 tablespoons chopped fresh basil

1. Prepare grill.
2. Arrange first 5 ingredients in a single layer in a jelly-roll pan; sprinkle evenly with ¼ teaspoon salt, black pepper, and garlic. Lightly coat vegetables with cooking spray. Place vegetables on grill rack; grill 3 minutes on each side or until browned and tender. Remove vegetables to a cutting board; chop into bite-sized pieces.
3. Place pasta in a large bowl; sprinkle with ¼ teaspoon salt, tossing well. Stir in grilled vegetables and tomatoes; sprinkle each serving with cheese and basil. Yield: 4 servings (serving size: 2½ cups pasta, 3 tablespoons cheese, and 1½ teaspoons basil).

CALORIES 327 (16% from fat); FAT 5.8g (sat 3.5g, mono 1g, poly 0.3g); PROTEIN 14g; CARB 56.3g; FIBER 3.4g; CHOL 19mg; IRON 3.8mg; SODIUM 682mg; CALC 149mg

Grilled Onion Raita

A chunkier version of a typically smooth *raita* (RI-tah), this Indian condiment is easy to prepare if you're firing up the grill for other foods. Serve with any of the main dishes featured here or as a cooling complement to a fiery curry. Store in an airtight container in the refrigerator up to two days.

 1½ teaspoons extravirgin olive oil
  1 onion, cut into ½-inch-thick slices
  ¾ cup finely chopped English
     cucumber
  ¾ cup plain fat-free yogurt
  1 tablespoon minced fresh cilantro
  ¾ teaspoon cumin seeds
  ¼ teaspoon salt
  ¼ teaspoon freshly ground black
     pepper

1. Prepare grill.
2. Brush oil over onion. Place onion on grill rack; grill 4 minutes on each side or until browned and tender. Remove onion to a cutting board, and cool completely; chop.
3. Combine onion, cucumber, and remaining ingredients in a medium bowl; stir well. Yield: 2 cups (serving size: ¼ cup).

CALORIES 24 (26% from fat); FAT 0.7g (sat 0.1g, mono 0.5g, poly 0.1g); PROTEIN 1.3g; CARB 3.8g; FIBER 0.4g; CHOL 0mg; IRON 0.5mg; SODIUM 87mg; CALC 39mg

Grilled Veggie Pizzas

Homemade pizza on the grill tastes like wood-fired restaurant pizza. Personalize the recipe by using your favorite vegetable or cheese combinations. Mushrooms, asparagus, yellow squash, or eggplant would also work well for the vegetable toppings.

DOUGH:

  1 package dry yeast (about
     2¼ teaspoons)
 1½ cups warm water (100° to 110°)
  2 tablespoons extravirgin olive oil
  4 cups all-purpose flour, divided
     (about 18 ounces)
  ½ teaspoon salt
Cooking spray

TOPPINGS:

  2 large zucchini, cut lengthwise
     into ¼-inch strips (about 1
     pound)
  2 red bell peppers, cut into ¼-inch
     rings
  1 large onion, halved and cut into
     ½-inch slices (about 1 cup)
  1 tablespoon extravirgin
     olive oil
  ¼ teaspoon freshly ground black
     pepper
  2 garlic cloves, minced
  6 tablespoons (about 1½
     ounces) shredded part-skim
     mozzarella
  6 tablespoons (about 1½ ounces)
     shredded Gruyère cheese

1. To prepare dough, dissolve yeast in warm water in a large bowl. Stir in 2 tablespoons oil, and let stand 5 minutes. Lightly spoon flour into dry measuring cups; level with a knife. Add 3½ cups flour and salt to yeast mixture; stir until a dough forms. Turn dough out onto a lightly floured surface. Knead until smooth and elastic (about 10 minutes); add enough remaining flour, 1 tablespoon at a time, to prevent dough from sticking to hands.
2. Place dough in a large bowl coated with cooking spray, turning to coat top. Cover and let rise in a warm place (85°), free from drafts, 1 hour or until doubled in size. (Gently press two fingers into dough. If indentation remains, dough has risen enough.) Punch dough down; cover and let rest 5 minutes.
3. Prepare grill.
4. While dough rises, prepare topping. Place zucchini, bell pepper, and onion in a large bowl; stir in 1 tablespoon oil and black pepper, tossing well. Place on grill rack coated with cooking spray; grill 5 minutes on each side or until tender. Remove from grill; stir in garlic.
5. Divide dough into 6 equal portions, pressing each portion into a 7-inch round. Coat both sides of dough rounds with cooking spray. Place 3 dough rounds on grill rack. Grill 4 minutes or until puffed and golden. Remove from grill. Turn rounds over; top each round with 1 tablespoon mozzarella, about

one-sixth of vegetables, and 1 tablespoon Gruyère. Place topped rounds on grill. Cover and cook 1½ minutes or until bottoms are browned. Repeat procedure with remaining dough rounds, vegetables, and cheeses. Yield: 6 servings (serving size: 1 pizza).

CALORIES 458 (28% from fat); FAT 14.5g (sat 5.4g, mono 7.3g, poly 1.1g); PROTEIN 17.8g; CARB 63g; FIBER 3.1g; CHOL 23mg; IRON 4.6mg; SODIUM 326mg; CALC 266mg

QUICK & EASY
Grilled Eggplant and Tomato Sandwiches with Roquefort Dressing

When grilled to perfection, eggplant peel is slightly crusty—a nice contrast to its tender, moist flesh. Roasted eggplant makes a hearty sandwich when combined with a coarse-textured bread, such as an Italian ciabatta or sourdough.

    ¼ cup plain fat-free yogurt
    3 tablespoons (about ¾ ounce) crumbled Roquefort or other blue cheese
    2 tablespoons minced fresh parsley
    1 tablespoon light mayonnaise
    1 garlic clove, minced
    2 Japanese eggplants (about 1 pound)
      Cooking spray
    8 (1-ounce) slices ciabatta or sourdough bread
    8 (¼-inch-thick) slices tomato (about 2 tomatoes)
    ¼ teaspoon salt
    ¼ teaspoon freshly ground black pepper
    2 cups trimmed arugula

1. Prepare grill.
2. Combine first 5 ingredients in a small bowl, stirring well.
3. Trim ends from eggplants. Cut each eggplant lengthwise into 3 slices; lightly coat eggplant with cooking spray. Place eggplant on grill rack coated with cooking spray; grill 3 minutes on each side or until browned and tender. Remove from grill; cut slices crosswise in half. Place bread slices on grill rack; grill 3 minutes on each side or until lightly toasted.

4. Spread yogurt mixture evenly over 4 toast slices. Top each with 3 eggplant pieces and 2 tomato slices; sprinkle evenly with salt and pepper. Top each with ½ cup arugula. Cover with remaining toast slices. Yield: 4 servings (serving size: 1 sandwich).

CALORIES 261 (29% from fat); FAT 8.4g (sat 1.8g, mono 3.2g, poly 1.3g); PROTEIN 9g; CARB 42.6g; FIBER 2g; CHOL 7mg; IRON 2.7mg; SODIUM 700mg; CALC 95mg

QUICK & EASY • MAKE AHEAD
Corn and Pepper Relish

Roasting corn without the husks gives the relish a smoky flavor. If you leave the husks on, the corn flavor is more pronounced. Serve with a veggie burger or grilled vegetable wrap.

    4 ears shucked corn
      Cooking spray
    ¼ cup cider vinegar
    2 tablespoons sugar
    2 tablespoons fresh lime juice
    2 teaspoons mustard seeds
    1 teaspoon minced peeled fresh ginger
    ½ teaspoon salt
    ½ teaspoon curry powder
    ¼ teaspoon crushed red pepper
    ¼ teaspoon freshly ground black pepper
    ¾ cup chopped orange or red bell pepper (about 1 large)
    ¾ cup chopped red onion

1. Prepare grill.
2. Place corn on grill rack coated with cooking spray, and grill 12 minutes or until corn is lightly browned, turning frequently. Cool and cut kernels from ears of corn.
3. Combine vinegar and next 8 ingredients in a large bowl, stirring until sugar dissolves. Add corn kernels, bell pepper, and onion; toss well. Store in an airtight container in refrigerator. Yield: 8 servings (serving size: ½ cup).

CALORIES 80 (11% from fat); FAT 1g (sat 0.1g, mono 0.4g, poly 0.4g); PROTEIN 2.5g; CARB 18g; FIBER 2.4g; CHOL 0mg; IRON 0.6mg; SODIUM 156mg; CALC 12mg

Grilled Vegetables and Chickpeas with Couscous

Served over couscous, this vegetable-bean combination makes a one-dish meal with rich flavors of the Middle East. Add the Grilled Onion Raita (recipe on page 300) as a side dish, or serve with hot pepper sauce.

    1 large zucchini (about 8 ounces)
    1 large yellow squash (about 6 ounces)
    1 small green bell pepper, quartered
    1 small red bell pepper, quartered
    1 small onion, cut into ¼-inch-thick slices (about ½ cup)
      Cooking spray
    1 cup water
    ¾ cup uncooked couscous
    ½ teaspoon hot pepper sauce
    ¼ teaspoon salt
    ¼ teaspoon freshly ground black pepper
    ¼ teaspoon ground cumin
      Dash of ground cinnamon
    ¾ cup cherry tomatoes, halved
    3 tablespoons fresh lemon juice
    2 tablespoons chopped fresh cilantro
    1 tablespoon extravirgin olive oil
    1 (15½-ounce) can chickpeas (garbanzo beans), drained
    ¼ cup (1 ounce) crumbled feta cheese

1. Prepare grill.
2. Cut zucchini and squash lengthwise into ¼-inch-thick slices. Place zucchini, squash, bell peppers, and onion on a grill rack coated with cooking spray; grill 3 minutes on each side or until well browned. Remove vegetables to a cutting board; cool. Chop vegetables into bite-sized pieces; place in a large bowl.
3. Bring water to a boil in a medium saucepan. Stir in couscous and next 5 ingredients. Cover, remove from heat, and let stand 5 minutes. Fluff with a fork.
4. Add couscous, tomatoes, and next 4 ingredients to vegetable mixture; toss well. Sprinkle each serving with cheese. Yield: 4 servings (serving size: 1¾ cups couscous mixture and 1 tablespoon cheese).

CALORIES 325 (22% from fat); FAT 7.8g (sat 2.2g, mono 3.6g, poly 1.4g); PROTEIN 13.2g; CARB 53g; FIBER 8.6g; CHOL 8mg; IRON 3mg; SODIUM 270mg; CALC 113mg

Garden Minestrone

A bowl of this soup will satisfy your craving for comfort food that comes with the approach of cool fall evenings.

MAKE AHEAD • FREEZABLE

Garden Minestrone

2 teaspoons olive oil
1 cup chopped onion
2 teaspoons chopped fresh oregano
4 garlic cloves, minced
3 cups chopped yellow squash
3 cups chopped zucchini
1 cup chopped carrot
1 cup fresh corn kernels (about 2 ears)
4 cups chopped tomato, divided
3 (14-ounce) cans fat-free, less-sodium chicken broth, divided
½ cup uncooked ditalini pasta (very short tube-shaped macaroni)
1 (15.5-ounce) can Great Northern beans, rinsed and drained
1 (6-ounce) package fresh baby spinach
1 teaspoon salt
½ teaspoon freshly ground black pepper
1 cup (4 ounces) grated Asiago cheese
Coarsely ground black pepper (optional)

1. Heat oil in a Dutch oven over medium-high heat. Add onion to pan; sauté 3 minutes or until softened. Add oregano and garlic; sauté 1 minute. Stir in squash, zucchini, carrot, and corn; sauté 5 minutes or until vegetables are tender. Remove from heat.
2. Place 3 cups tomato and 1 can broth in a blender; process until smooth. Add tomato mixture to pan; return pan to heat. Stir in 1 cup tomato and 2 cans broth; bring mixture to a boil. Reduce heat, and simmer 20 minutes.

3. Add pasta and beans to pan; cook 10 minutes or until pasta is tender, stirring occasionally. Remove from heat. Stir in spinach, salt, and ½ teaspoon pepper. Ladle soup into individual bowls; top with cheese. Garnish with coarsely ground black pepper, if desired. Yield: 8 servings (serving size: 1½ cups soup and 2 tablespoons cheese).

CALORIES 217 (25% from fat); FAT 6.1g (sat 2.7g, mono 2g, poly 0.6g); PROTEIN 12.6g; CARB 30.5g; FIBER 7.9g; CHOL 12mg; IRON 2.7mg; SODIUM 812mg; CALC 206mg

. . . And Ready in Just About 20 Minutes

More than a week's worth of quick entrées gets you in and out of the kitchen in a flash.

QUICK & EASY

Mussels in Tomato-Wine Broth

Serve with chilled white wine and Italian bread. To save prep time, use kitchen scissors to cut the tomatoes in the can.

2 teaspoons olive oil
2 teaspoons bottled minced garlic
¼ cup dry white wine
1 teaspoon fresh lemon juice
¼ teaspoon crushed red pepper
1 (14.5-ounce) can no-salt-added stewed tomatoes, undrained and chopped
1 (8-ounce) bottle clam juice
2 pounds small mussels, scrubbed and debearded
2 tablespoons chopped fresh flat-leaf parsley

1. Heat olive oil in a Dutch oven over medium-high heat. Add garlic; sauté 1 minute. Add wine and next 4 ingredients; bring to a boil. Add mussels. Cover,

reduce heat, and simmer 5 minutes or until shells open. Remove from heat, and discard any unopened shells. Stir in parsley. Yield: 2 servings (serving size: about 15 mussels and 1 cup tomato mixture).

CALORIES 295 (27% from fat); FAT 8.9g (sat 1.4g, mono 4.3g, poly 1.7g); PROTEIN 25.4g; CARB 21.4g; FIBER 3.6g; CHOL 57mg; IRON 10.8mg; SODIUM 823mg; CALC 145mg

Meal in Minutes Menu
serves 4

Pleasantly bitter broccoli rabe complements the sweet fruit sauce; blanching lessens its bite.

Chicken in Cherry Marsala Sauce

Broccoli rabe with garlic*

Buttered egg noodles

*Cook 8 cups coarsely chopped broccoli rabe in boiling water 2 minutes; drain. Melt 2 teaspoons butter in a large nonstick skillet over medium heat. Add 3 thinly sliced garlic cloves; cook 1 minute, stirring frequently. Add blanched broccoli rabe, ½ teaspoon salt, and ¼ teaspoon freshly ground black pepper; toss to combine. Serve with lemon wedges.

QUICK & EASY

Chicken in Cherry Marsala Sauce

If you can't find dried cherries, use regular dried cranberries.

⅓ cup dried cherries
⅓ cup Marsala
2 teaspoons olive oil
4 (6-ounce) skinless, boneless chicken breast halves
½ teaspoon salt, divided
½ teaspoon black pepper, divided
1 teaspoon butter
¼ cup finely chopped shallots
1 tablespoon chopped fresh thyme
½ cup fat-free, less-sodium chicken broth

1. Combine cherries and Marsala in a small microwave-safe bowl. Microwave at HIGH 45 seconds, and set aside.

2. Heat oil in a large nonstick skillet over medium-high heat. Add chicken; cook 4 minutes on each side or until done. Remove chicken from pan; sprinkle with ¼ teaspoon salt and ¼ teaspoon pepper. Cover and keep warm.

3. Add butter to pan, and cook until butter melts. Add shallots and thyme; sauté 1 minute or until tender. Stir in broth, scraping pan to loosen browned bits. Add cherry mixture, ¼ teaspoon salt, and ¼ teaspoon pepper; bring to a boil. Reduce heat to medium, and simmer 2 minutes or until sauce is slightly thick. Serve chicken with sauce. Yield: 4 servings (serving size: 1 breast half and about ¼ cup sauce).

CALORIES 297 (16% from fat); FAT 5.4g (sat 1.4g, mono 2.6g, poly 0.8g); PROTEIN 40.5g; CARB 13.7g; FIBER 1.1g; CHOL 101mg; IRON 2.1mg; SODIUM 464mg; CALC 33mg

QUICK & EASY
Seared Scallop Salad

To keep splatters down, buy dry-packed scallops, if available. Serve with sourdough bread and purchased fresh fruit salad.

 2 teaspoons bottled ground fresh ginger (such as Spice World)
 2 teaspoons olive oil
 1 teaspoon bottled minced garlic
 ¼ teaspoon salt
 ¼ teaspoon black pepper
 1½ pounds large sea scallops
 Cooking spray
 4 cups packaged gourmet salad greens
 2 cups halved cherry tomatoes (about 1 pound)
 1 cup preshredded carrot
 1 cup sliced cucumber
 ¼ cup chopped red onion
 ¼ cup light red wine vinaigrette

1. Combine first 6 ingredients in a large bowl; toss gently to coat. Heat a large nonstick skillet over medium-high heat. Coat pan with cooking spray. Add scallop mixture to pan; cook 3 minutes on each side or until done. Combine greens and remaining 5 ingredients in a large bowl, and toss well. Place salad on each

of 4 plates; top with scallops. Yield: 4 servings (serving size: 1¾ cups salad and about 3 scallops).

CALORIES 235 (16% from fat); FAT 4.1g (sat 0.5g, mono 1.8g, poly 0.9g); PROTEIN 30.7g; CARB 18g; FIBER 3.3g; CHOL 56mg; IRON 1.8mg; SODIUM 680mg; CALC 92mg

QUICK & EASY
Skillet Pork and Warm Pineapple Salsa

Pineapple is a sweet foil for the fiery jalapeño. Either fresh or canned pineapple chunks work well in this recipe. If you like a spicier kick, remember that smaller jalapeño peppers are typically hotter than the larger ones. To complete the meal, serve with rice and steamed snow peas.

 2 teaspoons olive oil, divided
 4 (4-ounce) boneless loin pork chops
 1 teaspoon salt-free Jamaican jerk seasoning (such as Spice Islands)
 ½ teaspoon salt
 ⅛ teaspoon ground red pepper
 1⅓ cups pineapple chunks
 ½ cup coarsely chopped onion
 1 tablespoon fresh lime juice
 1 small jalapeño pepper, seeded and chopped

1. Heat 1 teaspoon oil in a large non-stick skillet over medium-high heat. Sprinkle both sides of pork with jerk seasoning, salt, and red pepper. Add pork to pan; cook 4 minutes on each side or until done. Remove pork from pan; cover and keep warm.

2. Add 1 teaspoon oil to pan. Add pineapple, reserving 2 tablespoons juice. Add onion; cook 2 minutes or until lightly browned, stirring frequently. Stir in lime juice, jalapeño, and reserved pineapple juice. Serve warm salsa over pork. Yield: 4 servings (serving size: 1 chop and ½ cup salsa).

CALORIES 235 (29% from fat); FAT 7.5g (sat 2g, mono 3.9g, poly 0.7g); PROTEIN 24.5g; CARB 17.2g; FIBER 1g; CHOL 70mg; IRON 1.3mg; SODIUM 490mg; CALC 32mg

QUICK & EASY
Poblano, Mango, and Black Bean Quesadillas

The sweetness of the mango balances the snappiness of the chile. Top quesadillas with fat-free sour cream and salsa, and serve with spinach and carrot salad.

 1 teaspoon olive oil
 1½ cups sliced onion
 ½ teaspoon dried oregano
 ¼ teaspoon salt
 ⅛ teaspoon black pepper
 1 poblano chile, seeded and chopped
 1 (15-ounce) can black beans, rinsed and drained
 1 cup jarred sliced peeled mango (such as Del Monte SunFresh)
 ⅓ cup cubed peeled avocado
 4 (8-inch) fat-free flour tortillas
 Cooking spray
 ½ cup (2 ounces) shredded reduced-fat sharp Cheddar cheese

1. Preheat broiler.

2. Heat oil in a large nonstick skillet over medium-high heat. Add onion and next 4 ingredients; sauté 5 minutes or until onion is tender. Add beans; cook 1 minute or until thoroughly heated. Remove from heat; stir in mango and avocado.

3. Place flour tortillas on a baking sheet coated with cooking spray. Arrange about ¾ cup bean mixture on half of each tortilla, leaving ½-inch borders. Sprinkle cheese evenly over bean mixture, and fold tortillas in half. Lightly coat tortillas with cooking spray. Broil 3 minutes or until cheese melts. Yield: 4 servings (serving size: 1 quesadilla).

CALORIES 334 (25% from fat); FAT 9.3g (sat 2.9g, mono 3.5g, poly 0.9g); PROTEIN 13.2g; CARB 54.5g; FIBER 7.2g; CHOL 10mg; IRON 3mg; SODIUM 753mg; CALC 253mg

Lemon Chicken Pita Burgers with Spiced Yogurt Sauce

You can also serve the chicken patties with couscous tossed with golden raisins.

  ½ cup chopped green onions
  ⅓ cup Italian-seasoned breadcrumbs
  1 tablespoon Moroccan or Greek seasoning blend
  ½ teaspoon coarsely ground black pepper
  2 large egg whites, lightly beaten
  1 pound ground chicken
  2 teaspoons grated lemon rind, divided
  1 tablespoon olive oil
  ½ cup plain low-fat yogurt
  1½ teaspoons chopped fresh oregano
  4 (6-inch) pitas, cut in half
  2 cups shredded lettuce
  ½ cup diced tomato

1. Combine first 6 ingredients; add 1 teaspoon rind, stirring well. Divide mixture into 8 equal portions, shaping each into a ¼-inch-thick oval patty.
2. Heat oil in a large nonstick skillet over medium-high heat. Add patties; cook 2 minutes on each side or until browned. Cover, reduce heat to medium, and cook 4 minutes.
3. Combine 1 teaspoon rind, yogurt, and oregano, stirring well. Fill each pita half with 1 patty, 1 tablespoon yogurt mixture, ¼ cup lettuce, and 1 tablespoon tomato. Yield: 4 servings (serving size: 2 stuffed pita halves).

CALORIES 426 (30% from fat); FAT 14g (sat 3.4g, mono 6.3g, poly 2.7g); PROTEIN 28.9g; CARB 46.4g; FIBER 3.3g; CHOL 77mg; IRON 2.1mg; SODIUM 776mg; CALC 137mg

Chicken Yakitori on Watercress

Yakitori means "grilled fowl" in Japanese and is traditionally served on skewers, but this skillet version is just as tasty and even easier. The sweet-salty chicken and sauce make a lovely main-dish salad when served on watercress with a side of sticky rice.

  2 tablespoons low-sodium soy sauce
  2 tablespoons rice wine vinegar
  2 tablespoons mirin
  1½ tablespoons dark sesame oil
  2 teaspoons sugar
  ¼ teaspoon crushed red pepper
  1 pound chicken breast tenders
  Cooking spray
  ½ cup sliced green onions
  4 cups trimmed watercress (about 1 bunch)
  ¼ cup sliced radishes

1. Combine first 6 ingredients in a large bowl. Reserve half of soy sauce mixture.
2. Add chicken to marinade in bowl, turning to coat. Let stand 5 minutes.
3. While chicken marinates, heat a large nonstick skillet over medium-high heat. Coat pan with cooking spray. Drain chicken; discard marinade. Add chicken to pan; cook 4 minutes on each side or until done.
4. Remove pan from heat; add reserved soy sauce mixture and onions. Toss mixture to coat.
5. Place watercress on each of 4 plates. Place chicken mixture on each serving; top with radishes and sauce. Yield: 4 servings (serving size: 4 ounces chicken, 1 cup watercress, about 2 tablespoons sauce, and 1 tablespoon radishes).

CALORIES 174 (21% from fat); FAT 4g (sat 0.8g, mono 1.4g, poly 1.4g); PROTEIN 27.2g; CARB 4.7g; FIBER 0.8g; CHOL 66mg; IRON 1mg; SODIUM 225mg; CALC 56mg

Chipotle Turkey and Corn Soup

Stacking the turkey cutlets and then thinly slicing them will save you some time during preparation. You can freeze leftover chipotle chiles in the adobo sauce (package chiles individually with a little sauce in small plastic freezer bags) and use in salsas, with pork, or for Mexican-inspired scrambled eggs.

  1 tablespoon canola oil
  1 pound turkey cutlets, cut into thin strips
  2 teaspoons adobo sauce
  1 to 2 teaspoons chopped canned chipotle chiles in adobo sauce
  2 (14-ounce) cans fat-free, less-sodium chicken broth
  1 (14¾-ounce) can cream-style corn
  ¼ cup chopped fresh cilantro, divided
  ¼ teaspoon salt
  ½ cup crushed lime-flavored tortilla chips (about 1½ ounces)
  4 lime wedges

1. Heat oil in a large saucepan over medium-high heat. Add turkey; cook 3 minutes or until browned, stirring occasionally. Stir in adobo sauce, chiles, broth, and corn; bring to a boil. Reduce heat to medium-low; simmer 5 minutes. Stir in 3 tablespoons cilantro and salt. Ladle soup into each of 4 bowls; sprinkle with cilantro and crushed chips. Serve with lime wedges. Yield: 4 servings (serving size: 1½ cups soup, ¾ teaspoon cilantro, 2 tablespoons chips, and 1 lime wedge).

CALORIES 263 (19% from fat); FAT 5.5g (sat 0.7g, mono 2.8g, poly 1.6g); PROTEIN 32g; CARB 22.1g; FIBER 2.8g; CHOL 45mg; IRON 2.3mg; SODIUM 943mg; CALC 25mg

Cumin-Crusted Pork Soft Tacos,
page 292

Strawberry-Topped Pavlovas with Honey-Balsamic Sauce, page 293

Tandoori Tofu and Vegetable Kebabs, page 299

Garlic Flatbreads with Smoked Mozzarella and
Tomato Vinaigrette, page 296

Hand-Hacked Pot Stickers and
Tangy Ginger Dipping Sauce,
page 310

Culinary Walking Tours

Discover a unique way for intrepid travelers and food lovers to learn about cuisine and culture.

Culinary walking tours are a delightful way to steep in the native culture of a place, something more travelers are seeking today. "Consumers want to do more 'sight-doing' rather than 'sightseeing,' " says Bob Whitley, president of the United States Tour Operators Association (USTOA). "They want to get into the life, experience the culture and people and place, not just ride by." Whitley suggests tapping local convention and visitors bureaus to find walking tours, along with browsing the Internet—including USTOA's own Web site (www.ustoa.com); a hotel concierge can also help guests find tours. Tours can last a couple of hours, a whole day, or longer, and you don't have to venture far to find one. Most large cities offer some kind of walking tour that focuses on food, and participants are as likely to be local residents as out-of-towners. Here are some sample recipes you might find on a walking tour in San Francisco's Chinatown.

Sesame-Onion Pancakes

Not pancakes as Westerners know them, these sesame-infused savory flatbreads pair well with spicy dips or saucy dishes.

    2   cups all-purpose flour (about
        9 ounces)
    3   tablespoons sesame seeds
    ¼   teaspoon salt
    ¼   teaspoon baking powder
    1   tablespoon canola oil
    ½   cup minced green onions
    ¾   cup water
    Cooking spray

1. Lightly spoon flour into dry measuring cups, and level with a knife. Place flour, sesame seeds, salt, and baking powder in a food processor; pulse just until combined. Add oil, and pulse until combined. Add onions; pulse until combined. Add water; pulse until mixture begins to hold together (do not allow dough to form a ball).
2. Place dough on a lightly floured surface. Divide into 12 equal portions, shaping each portion into a ball. Working with 1 portion at a time (cover remaining portions to prevent drying), roll each portion into a 5-inch circle between 2 sheets of heavy-duty plastic wrap. Stack pancakes between layers of wax paper or paper towels to prevent sticking.
3. Heat a large nonstick skillet over medium-high heat. Coat pan with cooking spray. Place 1 pancake in pan, and cook 20 seconds or until lightly browned. Turn and cook 20 seconds or until lightly browned. Remove from pan, and keep warm. Repeat procedure with cooking spray and remaining pancakes. Cut each pancake into 6 wedges. Serve warm. Yield: 12 servings (serving size: 6 wedges).

CALORIES 104 (22% from fat); FAT 2.5g (sat 0.3g, mono 1.1g, poly 0.9g); PROTEIN 2.7g; CARB 17.5g; FIBER 1g; CHOL 0mg; IRON 1.4mg; SODIUM 61mg; CALC 31mg

Rice Congee Soup
Jook

Creamy, slightly salty, and thick like porridge, *jook* is a popular Chinese breakfast. Make a pot of congee, and set out bowls of condiments (chopped onions, parsley, ginger, and soy sauce) so diners can season to taste.

    9   cups water
    1   cup uncooked long-grain rice
    2   teaspoons salt
    1   fresh turkey wing (about
        1 pound)
    1   (½-inch) piece peeled fresh
        ginger (about ¼ ounce)
    Chopped green onions (optional)
    Minced fresh parsley (optional)
    Julienne-cut peeled fresh ginger
        (optional)
    Low-sodium soy sauce (optional)

1. Combine first 5 ingredients in a large Dutch oven, and bring to a boil over medium-high heat. Cover, reduce heat, and cook 1½ hours or until soup has a creamy consistency, stirring occasionally. Remove from heat; keep warm.
2. Discard ginger piece. Remove turkey from soup; place on a cutting board or work surface. Cool 10 minutes. Remove skin from turkey; discard. Remove meat from bones; discard bones. Chop meat into bite-size pieces, and stir meat into soup. Ladle soup into each of 6 bowls; garnish with green onions, parsley, julienne-cut ginger, and soy sauce, if desired. Yield: 6 servings (serving size: about 1 cup).

CALORIES 207 (23% from fat); FAT 5.3g (sat 1.5g, mono 2g, poly 1.3g); PROTEIN 13.5g; CARB 24.7g; FIBER 0.4g; CHOL 33mg; IRON 1.9mg; SODIUM 809mg; CALC 26mg

Many culinary walking tours are led by locals eager to share their favorite foods.

Chinese-Style Roast Pork
Char Sil

In San Francisco's Chinatown, *char sil* is often displayed hanging in a market window or layered in pans in Chinese delicatessens or restaurants. This versatile pork works well in stir-fries, lo meins, or dumplings. Wrap leftovers tightly in foil or heavy-duty plastic wrap, and place in a plastic bag. Freeze up to three months. Serve with snow peas.

½ cup hoisin sauce
½ cup ketchup
¼ cup packed brown sugar
¼ cup dry sherry
¼ cup low-sodium soy sauce
2 tablespoons honey
2 teaspoons minced green onions
1 teaspoon dark sesame oil
4 garlic cloves, minced
2 pounds boneless Boston butt pork roast, trimmed and cut into 2-inch cubes

1. Combine first 9 ingredients in a large zip-top plastic bag. Add pork; seal and marinate in refrigerator 24 hours, turning bag occasionally. Remove pork from bag, reserving marinade.
2. Preheat oven to 350°.
3. Place pork on the rack of a broiler pan lined with foil. Bake at 350° for 30 minutes. Turn pork over, and baste with reserved marinade. Discard remaining marinade. Bake an additional 20 minutes or until a thermometer registers 160° (slightly pink).
4. Preheat broiler. Broil pork 5 minutes or until browned. Yield: 8 servings (serving size: 3 ounces).

CALORIES 193 (41% from fat); FAT 8.9g (sat 3g, mono 4g, poly 1.1g); PROTEIN 21.2g; CARB 5.8g; FIBER 0.2g; CHOL 73mg; IRON 1.5mg; SODIUM 249mg; CALC 28mg

Tangy Ginger Dipping Sauce
(pictured on page 308)

This chunky, flavorful sauce lends pork, chicken, or even tofu a lively flavor and color. Try it with the Hand-Hacked Pot Stickers (recipe at right).

½ cup chopped peeled tomato
⅓ cup chopped green onions
¼ cup fresh lime juice
¼ cup rice vinegar
1½ tablespoons sugar
2 teaspoons chopped peeled fresh ginger
2 garlic cloves, chopped
1 jalapeño pepper, seeded and chopped

1. Combine all ingredients in a small bowl; stir well with a whisk until sugar dissolves. Yield: 1 cup (serving size: 1 tablespoon).

CALORIES 11 (0% from fat); FAT 0g; PROTEIN 0.1g; CARB 2.7g; FIBER 0.2g; CHOL 0mg; IRON 0.1mg; SODIUM 1mg; CALC 2mg

Rainbow Fried Rice

For variety, substitute chicken or shrimp for the pork.

1 tablespoon canola oil
2 large eggs, lightly beaten
¾ cup minced yellow onion
1 cup chopped Chinese-Style Roast Pork (recipe at left)
4 cups cooked long-grain rice, chilled
3 tablespoons low-sodium soy sauce
2 cups shredded iceberg lettuce
½ cup frozen green peas, thawed
¼ teaspoon salt
⅛ teaspoon white pepper
½ cup minced green onions
1 teaspoon dark sesame oil

1. Heat canola oil in a large nonstick skillet over medium-high heat. Add eggs; stir-fry 1 minute or until done. Remove from pan.
2. Add yellow onion to pan; sauté 2 minutes or until translucent. Stir in Chinese-Style Roast Pork; stir-fry 2 minutes over medium-high heat. Add rice and soy sauce; stir-fry 2 minutes. Return eggs to pan; cook 1 minute. Stir in lettuce, peas, salt, and pepper; stir-fry 1 minute. Sprinkle with green onions, and drizzle with sesame oil. Yield: 6 servings (serving size: 1 cup).

CALORIES 219 (28% from fat); FAT 6.7g (sat 1.4g, mono 3.1g, poly 1.5g); PROTEIN 9.7g; CARB 29g; FIBER 1.7g; CHOL 85mg; IRON 1.7mg; SODIUM 455mg; CALC 33mg

Hand-Hacked Pot Stickers
(pictured on page 308)

1 cup chopped napa (Chinese) cabbage
1 cup chopped spinach
¼ cup minced green onions
1 tablespoon low-sodium soy sauce
1 teaspoon minced peeled fresh ginger
½ teaspoon dark sesame oil
Dash of white pepper
3 garlic cloves, minced
⅓ pound lean ground pork
¼ pound peeled and deveined shrimp, chopped
24 round wonton wrappers or gyoza skins
1 tablespoon canola oil, divided
2 cups fat-free, less-sodium chicken broth, divided
Green onion strips (optional)

1. Combine first 10 ingredients in a bowl. Working with 1 wonton wrapper at a time (cover remaining wrappers with a damp towel to prevent drying), spoon about 1 heaping teaspoon filling into center of each wrapper. Moisten edges of wrapper with water. Fold in half, pinching edges together to seal. Holding sealed edges of pot sticker between thumb and first two fingers of each hand, form 3 or 4 pleats along seal. Place dumplings, seam sides up, on a platter.
2. Heat 1½ teaspoons canola oil in a large nonstick skillet.
3. Arrange 12 pot stickers, seam sides up, in pan, and cook 30 seconds or until browned. Add 1 cup chicken broth to pan; cover and cook 5 minutes. Uncover and cook about 1 minute or until liquid evaporates. Remove pot stickers from pan; cover and keep warm. Repeat procedure with 1½ teaspoons canola oil, 12 pot stickers, and 1 cup broth. Garnish with green onion strips, if desired. Serve immediately. Yield: 8 servings (serving size: 3 pot stickers).

CALORIES 150 (27% from fat); FAT 4.5g (sat 1g, mono 1.3g, poly 0.9g); PROTEIN 11.1g; CARB 15.7g; FIBER 1g; CHOL 45mg; IRON 1.7mg; SODIUM 346mg; CALC 43mg.

Sandwich to the Rescue

Using ingredients on hand, a Cooking Light *reader from New York City creates a delectable chicken sandwich.*

Kara Hamelly's Chicken Focaccia Sandwiches were a spur-of-the-moment creation she first assembled a couple of years ago with her friend Russ Medbery.

Chicken Focaccia Sandwiches

2 (6-ounce) skinless, boneless chicken breast halves
Cooking spray
1 teaspoon dried Italian seasoning
½ teaspoon garlic powder
½ teaspoon freshly ground black pepper
¼ teaspoon salt, divided
1 tablespoon olive oil
½ cup water
1½ cups (¼-inch-thick) slices red onion
2½ cups red bell pepper strips (about 2 medium)
⅓ cup chopped green onions
10 ounces focaccia bread, cut in half horizontally
½ cup (2 ounces) shredded sharp Cheddar cheese

1. Cut each chicken breast half in half horizontally, and lightly coat chicken with cooking spray. Sprinkle Italian seasoning, garlic powder, black pepper, and ⅛ teaspoon salt over chicken. Heat oil in a large nonstick skillet over medium-high heat. Add chicken; cook 2 minutes on each side or until browned. Reduce heat to medium; add water. Cook 10 minutes or until chicken is done. Remove chicken from pan; keep warm.
2. Return pan to medium-high heat. Add red onion; sauté 2 minutes. Add bell pepper, green onions, and ⅛ teaspoon salt; sauté 2 minutes or until tender.
3. Preheat broiler.

4. Place bottom half of focaccia on a baking sheet; top with chicken. Arrange onion mixture evenly over chicken; sprinkle with cheese. Broil 2 minutes or until cheese melts. Top with remaining bread; cut into 4 equal portions. Yield: 4 servings (serving size: 1 sandwich).

CALORIES 421 (28% from fat); FAT 13.2g (sat 4.6g, mono 5.4g, poly 2.2g); PROTEIN 29.8g; CARB 46.4g; FIBER 2.4g; CHOL 64mg; IRON 3mg; SODIUM 586mg; CALC 143mg

---

QUICK & EASY
Broccoli with Pan-Roasted Peppers

"I always had difficulty coming up with exciting vegetable side dishes. This one is so colorful, it livens up the plate and incorporates so many different flavors."
—Courtney Shepler, Baton Rouge, Louisiana

4 cups broccoli florets (about 1½ pounds)
1 tablespoon olive oil
1¾ cups (1-inch) red bell pepper strips (2 medium)
1¾ cups (1-inch) yellow bell pepper strips (2 medium)
¼ cup red wine vinegar
1 teaspoon sugar
¾ teaspoon salt
¼ teaspoon freshly ground black pepper

1. Cook broccoli in boiling water 4 minutes or until crisp-tender; drain. Rinse with cold water; drain.
2. Heat oil in a large nonstick skillet over medium-high heat. Add bell peppers and vinegar. Cover, reduce heat to medium, and cook 15 minutes or until peppers are tender, stirring frequently. Uncover; sprinkle with sugar. Increase heat to medium-high; cook 2 minutes or until liquid evaporates and bell peppers begin to brown, stirring constantly. Add broccoli; cook 2 minutes or until thoroughly heated, tossing to combine. Remove from heat; stir in salt and black pepper. Yield: 6 servings (serving size: 1 cup).

CALORIES 65 (39% from fat); FAT 2.8g (sat 0.4g, mono 1.7g, poly 0.5g); PROTEIN 2.5g; CARB 9.9g; FIBER 1.4g; CHOL 0mg; IRON 1mg; SODIUM 311mg; CALC 31mg

---

Sizzling Chicken Fajitas

"This is one of my favorite dishes to serve to company for a casual meal."
—Ann Bahm, Sammamish, Washington

½ cup low-sodium soy sauce
⅓ cup water
⅓ cup white vinegar
¼ teaspoon garlic powder
¼ teaspoon black pepper
1½ pounds skinless, boneless chicken breast
Cooking spray
1 tablespoon canola oil
1 cup green bell pepper strips (about 1 medium)
1 cup red bell pepper strips (about 1 medium)
1 cup vertically sliced red onion
1 teaspoon seasoned salt
6 (8-inch) fat-free flour tortillas
¾ cup bottled salsa
¾ cup fat-free sour cream

1. Combine first 5 ingredients; reserve ¼ cup soy sauce mixture. Combine remaining mixture and chicken in a large zip-top plastic bag. Seal and marinate in refrigerator 3 hours, turning occasionally.
2. Prepare grill.
3. Remove chicken from marinade; discard marinade. Place chicken on grill rack coated with cooking spray; cover and grill 10 minutes on each side or until done.
4. Heat oil in a large nonstick skillet over medium-high heat. Add bell peppers and onion; sprinkle with seasoned salt. Sauté 4 minutes or until tender. Add reserved soy sauce mixture, and cook 2 minutes. Cut chicken into thin slices; add to vegetable mixture.
5. Place a 10-inch cast-iron skillet, upside down, over high heat for 1½ minutes. Turn pan over, and add chicken mixture. Warm tortillas according to package directions. Serve chicken mixture immediately with warm tortillas, salsa, and sour cream. Yield: 6 servings (serving size: 1 cup chicken mixture, 2 tablespoons salsa, 2 tablespoons sour cream, and 1 tortilla).

CALORIES 340 (10% from fat); FAT 3.9g (sat 0.6g, mono 1.7g, poly 1.1g); PROTEIN 32.4g; CARB 41.5g; FIBER 2.2g; CHOL 71mg; IRON 2.4mg; SODIUM 997mg; CALC 66mg

This is a satisfying meal that's easy to prepare for a simple weeknight supper. Look for lemon curd near the jams and jellies in your grocery store.

Potato-Leek Chowder

Rainbow salad*

Angel food cake with lemon curd

*Combine 6 cups mixed salad greens, 1 cup thinly sliced mushrooms, ½ cup thinly sliced cucumber, ½ cup red bell pepper strips, and ⅓ cup thinly vertically sliced red onion in a large bowl. Drizzle with ⅓ cup reduced-fat balsamic vinaigrette; toss gently to coat. Sprinkle with 2 tablespoons toasted pine nuts.

heat, and simmer 25 minutes or until potato is tender. Cool 10 minutes; stir in milk. Place one-third of potato mixture in a blender; process until smooth. Pour puréed potato mixture into a large bowl. Repeat procedure twice with remaining potato mixture.

3. Return puréed potato mixture to pan; stir in leek, pepper, salt, and corn. Cook over medium-high heat 5 minutes or until thoroughly heated, stirring frequently. Sprinkle with crumbled bacon just before serving. Yield: 6 servings (serving size: 1⅔ cups chowder and about 2 tablespoons bacon).

CALORIES 227 (31% from fat); FAT 7.7g (sat 1.5g, mono 2.6g, poly 1g); PROTEIN 9.1g; CARB 39g; FIBER 5.4g; CHOL 4mg; IRON 2.3mg; SODIUM 629mg; CALC 90mg

If your local markets don't carry flatbreads, you can use pita bread. Sweet mango chutney helps balance the spice in the Indian-flavored vegetables.

Cumin Potatoes

Curried carrot and cauliflower*

Grilled lamb loin chops

Flatbreads and mango chutney

*Heat 1 tablespoon canola oil in a large nonstick skillet over medium-high heat. Add 2 cups cauliflower florets and 1 cup thinly sliced carrot; sauté 5 minutes or until crisp-tender. Stir in 2 tablespoons fresh lemon juice, ½ teaspoon curry powder, ½ teaspoon salt, and ¼ teaspoon black pepper; toss well to combine.

MAKE AHEAD • FREEZABLE
Potato-Leek Chowder

"After a week of especially cold weather, I craved some thick and hearty soup but was short on time. Adding cauliflower is a great way to lightly thicken the soup. For extra zip, add a little shredded sharp Cheddar cheese before serving."

—Julie Blum, Mollusk, Virginia

1 tablespoon olive oil
3 cups finely chopped leek (about 4 leeks)
5 cups fat-free, less-sodium chicken broth
3 cups (2-inch) cubed peeled Yukon gold or red potato
3 cups (2-inch) chopped cauliflower florets
1 cup fat-free milk
¼ teaspoon freshly ground black pepper
⅛ teaspoon salt
1 (14¾-ounce) can cream-style corn
3 bacon slices, cooked and crumbled (drained)

1. Heat oil in a large Dutch oven over medium heat. Add leek; cook 15 minutes or until tender, stirring frequently (do not brown). Set aside.
2. Combine broth, potato, and cauliflower in pan; bring to a boil. Reduce

---

QUICK & EASY • MAKE AHEAD
Black Bean Salsa

Refrigerate the salsa overnight to reduce some of the jalapeño's heat, if desired. "This is one of my favorite recipes that I make for potlucks at work and get-togethers with friends."

—Krista Oldiges, Huntsville, Ohio

3 cups chopped tomato (about 2 medium)
1 cup chopped red bell pepper (about 1 medium)
1 cup chopped green bell pepper (about 1 medium)
½ cup chopped red onion
⅓ cup chopped fresh cilantro
⅓ cup fresh lime juice (about 2 limes)
1 tablespoon olive oil
1 teaspoon salt
½ teaspoon ground cumin
½ teaspoon chili powder
1 jalapeño pepper, finely chopped
1 (15-ounce) can black beans, rinsed and drained
1 (11-ounce) can extrasweet whole kernel corn, drained

1. Combine all ingredients in a large bowl, stirring well. Yield: 6 cups (serving size: ⅓ cup).

CALORIES 38 (24% from fat); FAT 1g (sat 0.1g, mono 0.6g, poly 0.2g); PROTEIN 1.5g; CARB 7.4g; FIBER 1.6g; CHOL 0mg; IRON 0.5mg; SODIUM 186mg; CALC 13mg

---

QUICK & EASY
Cumin Potatoes

"Cumin potatoes are common in India; this is a different accompaniment for steak."

—Veenu Chopra, New Delhi, India

4 cups cubed peeled baking potato (about 1¼ pounds)
1 tablespoon canola oil
1 teaspoon cumin seeds
½ cup finely chopped red onion
½ teaspoon salt
½ teaspoon ground coriander
½ teaspoon paprika
2 tablespoons minced fresh cilantro

1. Cook potato in boiling water 10 minutes or until tender; drain. Rinse with cold water; drain.
2. Heat oil in a large nonstick skillet over medium-high heat. Add cumin seeds to pan, and sauté 30 seconds. Add onion, salt, coriander, and paprika; sauté 3 minutes, stirring constantly. Add potato; sauté 2 minutes or until thoroughly heated. Remove from heat, and sprinkle with cilantro. Yield: 4 servings (serving size: about 1 cup).

CALORIES 175 (20% from fat); FAT 3.9g (sat 0.3g, mono 2.1g, poly 1.1g); PROTEIN 3.1g; CARB 33.1g; FIBER 2.7g; CHOL 0mg; IRON 0.9mg; SODIUM 300mg; CALC 19mg

Delicious Duck

Duck is a delicious alternative to chicken and requires minimal preparation.

Duck Menu 1

serves 4

Apricot Grilled Duck Breasts

Sautéed green beans with pecans*

Israeli couscous

*Cook 1 (12-ounce) package prewashed cut green beans in boiling water 1½ minutes or until crisp-tender. Drain and plunge green beans into ice water; drain. Melt 2 teaspoons butter in a large nonstick skillet over medium-high heat. Add ¼ cup chopped shallots; sauté 5 minutes or until lightly browned. Add green beans, ¼ cup chopped pecans, ¼ teaspoon salt, and ¼ teaspoon freshly ground black pepper. Cook 1 minute or until thoroughly heated.

Game Plan

1. While duck marinates:
   • Preheat grill
   • Chop shallots and pecans for green beans
2. While duck cooks:
   • Prepare couscous
   • Sauté green beans

QUICK & EASY

Apricot Grilled Duck Breasts

Serve this savory-sweet entrée over couscous, brown or white rice, or even pasta.

TOTAL TIME: 36 MINUTES

½ cup apricot preserves
2½ tablespoons sherry vinegar
¼ teaspoon salt
¼ teaspoon ground cumin
⅛ teaspoon ground red pepper
4 (6-ounce) boneless duck breast halves (1½ pounds), skinned
Cooking spray

1. Combine first 5 ingredients in a bowl, stirring with a whisk. Add duck; cover and marinate in refrigerator 20 minutes.
2. Prepare grill.
3. Remove duck from marinade, reserving marinade. Bring marinade to a boil in a small saucepan over medium-high heat; boil 1 minute. Remove from heat.
4. Place duck on grill rack coated with cooking spray. Grill 6 minutes on each side or until a thermometer inserted into thickest portion registers 170°, basting occasionally with reserved marinade. Yield: 4 servings (serving size: 1 duck breast half).

CALORIES 299 (11% from fat); FAT 3.7g (sat 0.8g, mono 1.3g, poly 0.5g); PROTEIN 39.4g; CARB 26.8g; FIBER 0.2g; CHOL 203mg; IRON 6.7mg; SODIUM 311mg; CALC 23mg

Duck Menu 2

serves 6

Duck Stew

Goat cheese crostini*

Spinach salad with low-fat bottled vinaigrette

*Combine 1 tablespoon chopped bottled roasted red bell peppers, 1 tablespoon chopped fresh parsley, 1½ teaspoons chopped fresh rosemary, and 1 (3-ounce) package goat cheese in a small bowl, stirring until blended. Cut 1 (8-ounce) baguette into 8 slices; lightly toast bread slices. Spread goat cheese mixture evenly over bread slices.

Game Plan

1. While duck and sausage cook:
   • Rinse and drain beans
   • Chop celery, carrot, and onion
2. While stew cooks:
   • Prepare crostini; slice and toast bread
   • Assemble spinach salad

QUICK & EASY

Duck Stew

For a thicker consistency, coarsely mash one can of beans with a fork or potato masher before adding to Dutch oven. Enjoy leftover stew for lunch the next day.

TOTAL TIME: 44 MINUTES

QUICK TIP: Buy prechopped celery, onions, and carrot for the stew, and prewashed fresh spinach for the salad if you're making the entire menu.

2 teaspoons canola oil
1 pound boneless duck breast halves, skinned and cut into 1-inch pieces
½ pound smoked turkey sausage, sliced
1 cup chopped celery
1 cup chopped carrot
1 cup chopped onion
1½ teaspoons bottled minced garlic
1 cup fat-free, less-sodium chicken broth
2 (15.8-ounce) cans Great Northern beans, rinsed and drained
1 (14½-ounce) can diced tomatoes, undrained

1. Heat oil in a Dutch oven over medium-high heat. Add duck and sausage; cook 7 minutes or until browned. Remove duck and sausage from pan. Add celery and next 3 ingredients to pan; sauté 7 minutes. Return duck mixture to pan. Add broth, beans, and tomatoes; bring to a boil. Reduce heat, and simmer 10 minutes. Yield: 6 servings (serving size: about 1⅓ cups).

CALORIES 296 (24% from fat); FAT 7.8g (sat 2.3g, mono 2.7g, poly 1.5g); PROTEIN 27.5g; CARB 30g; FIBER 8.6g; CHOL 71mg; IRON 8.9mg; SODIUM 712mg; CALC 107mg

Duck Menu 3

serves 4

Duck with Dried Cherries and Rosemary

Roasted thyme potatoes*

Low-fat coffee ice cream with fat-free hot fudge topping

*Cut 1½ pounds red potatoes (about 6 medium) into 4 wedges each. Combine potatoes, 1 tablespoon fresh or 1 teaspoon dried thyme, 2 tablespoons chopped fresh parsley, 1 tablespoon olive oil, ¼ teaspoon salt, ¼ teaspoon freshly ground black pepper, ¼ teaspoon paprika, and 2 minced garlic cloves in a large bowl, tossing well to coat. Arrange wedges in a single layer in a shallow roasting pan. Bake at 400° for 30 minutes or until potatoes are golden and tender, stirring occasionally.

Game Plan

1. While oven preheats:
   - Cut potatoes
   - Chop herbs and mince garlic for potatoes
   - Prepare topping for duck
2. While potatoes bake:
   - Cook duck

QUICK & EASY

Duck with Dried Cherries and Rosemary

We used pinot noir for the red wine in the sauce. Substitute beef broth for an alcohol-free version. Use sweetened dried cranberries instead of cherries, if desired.

TOTAL TIME: 25 MINUTES

½	cup dried sweet cherries
½	cup dry red wine
2	tablespoons raspberry vinegar
1	tablespoon chopped fresh rosemary
2	teaspoons grated peeled fresh ginger
⅛	teaspoon sugar
2	teaspoons olive oil
4	(6-ounce) boneless duck breast halves, skinned
¼	teaspoon salt
¼	teaspoon freshly ground black pepper

Rosemary sprigs (optional)

1. Combine first 6 ingredients, and set aside.
2. Heat oil in a large nonstick skillet over medium-high heat. Sprinkle both sides of duck with salt and pepper. Add duck to pan, and cook 3 minutes on each side or until a thermometer inserted into thickest portion registers 170°. Place duck on a cutting board; cover with foil.
3. Add cherry mixture to pan; cook over medium-low heat 5 minutes. Remove from heat. Cut duck into thin slices; spoon cherry mixture over duck. Garnish with rosemary sprigs, if desired. Yield: 4 servings (serving size: 1 duck breast half and 2 tablespoons sauce).

CALORIES 279 (27% from fat); FAT 8.3g (sat 2.2g, mono 3.4g, poly 1.1g); PROTEIN 28.7g; CARB 16.8g; FIBER 2.2g; CHOL 109mg; IRON 7mg; SODIUM 230mg; CALC 29mg

Duck Menu 4

serves 4

Curried Duck Sandwiches

Quick creamy tomato soup*

Sliced fresh fruit

*Combine ¼ cup buttermilk, ¼ teaspoon freshly ground black pepper, 2 (14½-ounce) cans undrained petite diced tomatoes, and 2 (10¾-ounce) cans undiluted fat-free, less-sodium condensed tomato soup in a large saucepan. Cook over medium heat 8 minutes or until thoroughly heated, stirring frequently. Sprinkle with sliced fresh basil, if desired.

Game Plan

1. While duck cooks:
   - Combine soup ingredients
2. While soup cooks:
   - Prepare duck mixture
   - Halve pitas

QUICK & EASY

Curried Duck Sandwiches

If you don't have white wine on hand, use two tablespoons chicken broth, white cranberry juice, or apple juice instead. The filling can also be served with crackers or fruit salad.

TOTAL TIME: 40 MINUTES

QUICK TIP: You can substitute two cups cooked chicken, turkey, or shrimp for duck.

	Cooking spray
¾	pound boneless duck breast halves, skinned (about 2 breast halves)
½	cup chopped celery
¼	cup golden raisins
3	tablespoons low-fat mayonnaise
2	tablespoons mango chutney
2	tablespoons dry white wine
2	tablespoons chopped dry-roasted cashews
1	tablespoon curry powder
1	tablespoon chopped green onions
4	(6-inch) pitas, cut in half
8	small lettuce leaves

1. Heat a small nonstick skillet over medium-high heat. Coat pan with cooking spray. Add duck; cook 4 minutes on each side or until a thermometer inserted into thickest portion registers 170°. Cool slightly; coarsely chop duck.
2. Combine duck, celery, and next 7 ingredients in a large bowl. Line each pita half with 1 lettuce leaf; spoon duck mixture evenly into pita halves. Yield: 4 servings (serving size: 2 pita halves).

CALORIES 382 (14% from fat); FAT 5.8g (sat 1g, mono 2g, poly 1g); PROTEIN 28.4g; CARB 52.4g; FIBER 2.5g; CHOL 111mg; IRON 6.2mg; SODIUM 651mg; CALC 83mg

Baker's Secrets

Cooking Light baking expert Kathryn Conrad shares her techniques for achieving bakery-quality results at home.

In addition to the satisfaction of mastering home-baking, these recipes allow you to control the fat and sodium that go into them, as well as the portion sizes. Another reason to try some of these top-rated recipes: They smell and taste so luscious, which makes them a pleasure for pros and amateurs alike.

Caramel-Pecan Sticky Buns

CARAMEL:

⅓ cup packed dark brown muscovado sugar or dark brown sugar
3 tablespoons butter
4 teaspoons light corn syrup
Cooking spray
2 tablespoons chopped pecans

DOUGH:

1 package dry yeast (about 2¼ teaspoons)
1⅔ cups warm water (100° to 110°)
1½ teaspoons salt
5¼ cups all-purpose flour, divided (about 23½ ounces)
⅓ cup granulated sugar
1 teaspoon ground cinnamon
2 tablespoons butter, softened

1. To prepare caramel, combine first 3 ingredients in a saucepan over medium heat; stir frequently until butter melts. Continue cooking until mixture thickens and becomes smooth (about 1 minute), stirring constantly. Remove from heat; pour into center of a 9-inch square baking pan; quickly spread caramel onto pan bottom using a spatula coated with cooking spray. Sprinkle with pecans; cool to room temperature. Lightly coat sides of pan with cooking spray.

2. To prepare dough, dissolve yeast in warm water in a large bowl; let stand 5 minutes. Stir in salt.

3. Lightly spoon flour into dry measuring cups; level with a knife. Add 5 cups flour to yeast mixture; stir until a soft dough forms. Turn dough out onto a floured surface. Knead until smooth and elastic (about 8 minutes); add enough of remaining flour, 1 tablespoon at a time, to keep dough from sticking to hands.

4. Place dough in a large bowl coated with cooking spray, turning to coat top. Cover and let rise in a warm place (85°), free from drafts, 1 hour or until doubled in size. (Gently press two fingers into dough. If indentation remains, dough has risen enough.) Punch dough down; cover and let rest 5 minutes.

5. Combine granulated sugar and cinnamon in a small bowl; set aside.

6. Roll dough into a 16 x 12-inch rectangle on a lightly floured surface; spread softened butter over dough. Sprinkle with cinnamon mixture, leaving a ½-inch border. Roll up rectangle tightly, starting with long edge, pressing firmly to eliminate air pockets; pinch seam to seal (do not seal ends). Cut into 16 (1-inch) slices. Place slices, cut sides up, in prepared pan (rolls will be crowded). Cover and let rise 30 minutes or until doubled in size.

7. Preheat oven to 375°.

8. Uncover and bake at 375° for 20 minutes or until light golden brown. Cool in pan 5 minutes on a wire rack. Place a serving platter upside down on top of pan; invert rolls onto platter. Serve warm. Yield: 16 servings (serving size: 1 roll).

CALORIES 232 (21% from fat); FAT 5.3g (sat 1.9g, mono 2.1g, poly 0.7g); PROTEIN 4.5g; CARB 41.7g; FIBER 1.4g; CHOL 9mg; IRON 2.1mg; SODIUM 249mg; CALC 14mg

How to Make Sticky Buns

Place slices, cut sides up, in prepared pan (rolls will be crowded). Cover and let rise 30 minutes or until doubled in size.

Three Common Mistakes

Baking is a skill that improves with practice. It takes experience to know how dough should feel as it's kneaded or to determine if it has risen enough. "The hardest thing for most new bakers to learn is that there are no absolutes," says *Cooking Light* Test Kitchens staffer Kathryn Conrad. "The results are influenced by the conditions—everything from humidity in the air to the warmth of your hands when you handle the dough." Novice bread bakers make three common—and easily rectified—errors.

1. Adding too much flour when kneading and shaping the dough. In an effort to keep dough from sticking to their hands, many bakers add too much flour while kneading, which will make the bread tough and dense.

2. Not kneading long enough. Kneading time varies from one recipe to the next. Knead dough until it reaches the desired texture (usually "smooth and elastic"), using the suggested time as a guideline.

3. Not proofing long enough. Use the recommended time as a guideline. But remember, the texture of the dough is the true indicator of whether it's risen enough.

Special Bread Secrets

Caramel-Pecan Sticky Buns

Professional bakers' secret: Create a treat with tons of butter and nuts.

Conrad's trick: Trim the butter and use muscovado dark brown sugar. Chopping the pecans distributes their flavor while allowing you to use fewer nuts.

Tip for the home baker: "Although dark brown muscovado sugar adds an extrarich caramel flavor," Conrad says, "these buns are fantastic with regular dark brown sugar, as well."

Baguette

Professional bakers' secret: A technique called autolyse produces the characteristic airy interior and crunchy crust.

Conrad's trick: "*Autolyse* is a French term for allowing the mixture of flour, yeast, and water to rest for 15 minutes."

Tip for the home baker: Resist the urge to add too much flour when kneading and shaping the dough.

Bagels

Professional bakers' secret: Bagels need a poaching step to achieve a chewy texture. Professionals use a malt syrup bath.

Conrad's trick: Malt syrup is hard for home bakers to find, so our recipe substitutes brown beer and brown sugar. "If you've ever had a homogeneous ring of bread called a 'bagel,' it probably hasn't been through the poaching step."

Tip for the home baker: Once you've made the recipe a few times, experiment with different beers and even cola to achieve slight variations.

Potato-Dill Bread

Professional bakers' secret: Add butter, and lots of it, plus whole milk.

Conrad's trick: Use Yukon gold potatoes, fat-free milk, and ⅓-less-fat cream cheese for buttery flavor and color.

Tip for the home baker: "Avoid the temptation to substitute a different type of potato for the Yukons," Conrad says. Other types of potatoes won't yield the same rich-tasting results.

Whole Wheat Sunflower Oat Bread

Professional bakers' secret: The sponge method, which allows the yeast-flour-liquid mixture time to ferment before adding more flour. This gives an otherwise very dense bread lighter texture.

Conrad's trick: Knead vigorously for about 10 minutes to enhance the texture.

Tip for the home baker: Toast the groats for a subtle nutty flavor.

Soft Pretzels

Professional bakers' secret: Dip pretzels in a lye bath to produce a chewy exterior and caramel color.

Conrad's trick: Obviously we don't want you to use lye at home—that's hazardous. But Conrad found that dunking pretzels in a mixture of simmering water and baking soda yields similar toothsome results. "I tried skipping this step before baking the pretzels and ended up with pretzel-shaped bread."

Tip for the home baker: Be sure to cover the pretzels while they rise. For a lower-sodium option, top the pretzels with two teaspoons of sesame seeds instead of kosher salt.

Cinnamon-Raisin Bread

Professional bakers' secret: Use lots of butter and plump raisins.

Conrad's trick: Trim the amount of butter, and use it judiciously. "One tablespoon goes into the dough, and another is melted and brushed on the loaf pan. This brings the butter flavor to the forefront." In addition, the raisins are soaked in hot water so they become plump and soft.

Tip for the home baker: After nestling the dough into the loaf pan, remove any raisins that are visible on the surface to prevent burning as the loaf is baked.

Baguette

1 package dry yeast (about 2¼ teaspoons)
1¼ cups warm water (100° to 110°)
3 cups bread flour, divided (about 14¼ ounces)
1 teaspoon salt
Cooking spray
1 teaspoon cornmeal

1. Dissolve yeast in warm water in a large bowl; let stand 5 minutes. Lightly spoon flour into dry measuring cups; level with a knife. Add 2¾ cups flour to yeast mixture; stir until a soft dough forms. Cover and let stand 15 minutes. Turn dough out onto a lightly floured surface; sprinkle evenly with salt. Knead until salt is incorporated and dough is smooth and elastic (about 6 minutes); add enough of remaining flour, 1 tablespoon at a time, to prevent dough from sticking to hands (dough will feel slightly sticky).

2. Place dough in large bowl coated with cooking spray, turning to coat top. Cover and let rise in a warm place (85°), free from drafts, 40 minutes or until doubled in size. (Gently press two fingers into dough. If indentation remains, dough has risen enough.) Punch dough down; cover and let rest 5 minutes. Divide in half. Working with 1 portion at a time (cover remaining dough to prevent drying), roll each portion on a floured surface into a 12-inch rope, slightly tapered at ends. Place ropes on a large baking sheet sprinkled with cornmeal. Lightly coat dough with cooking spray, and cover; let rise 20 minutes or until doubled in size.

3. Preheat oven to 450°.

4. Uncover dough. Cut 3 (¼-inch-deep) diagonal slits across top of each loaf. Bake at 450° for 20 minutes or until loaves are browned on bottom and sound hollow when tapped. Yield: 2 loaves, 12 servings per loaf (serving size: 1 slice).

CALORIES 53 (3% from fat); FAT 0.2g (sat 0g, mono 0.1g, poly 0.1g); PROTEIN 2.1g; CARB 11.2g; FIBER 0.5g; CHOL 0mg; IRON 0.8mg; SODIUM 97mg; CALC 1mg

Bagels

1 (12-ounce) can brown beer (such as Newcastle Brown Ale), divided
1 cup water
1 package dry yeast (about 2¼ teaspoons)
1 large egg white, lightly beaten
4½ cups bread flour, divided (about 21½ ounces)
1½ teaspoons salt
 Cooking spray
4 cups water
1 teaspoon brown sugar
1 teaspoon stone-ground yellow cornmeal
1 teaspoon water
1 large egg yolk
1 teaspoon sesame seeds
1 teaspoon poppy seeds

1. Heat ½ cup beer and 1 cup water over low heat in a small, heavy saucepan to between 100° and 110°. Combine beer mixture and yeast in a large bowl, stirring until yeast dissolves. Let stand 5 minutes. Stir in egg white.

2. Lightly spoon flour into dry measuring cups; level with a knife. Add 4¼ cups flour and salt to beer mixture; stir until a soft dough forms. Turn dough out onto a floured surface. Knead until smooth and elastic (about 8 minutes); add enough of remaining flour, 1 tablespoon at a time, to prevent dough from sticking to hands (dough will feel sticky).

3. Place dough in a large bowl coated with cooking spray, turning to coat top. Cover and let rise in a warm place (85°), free from drafts, 1 hour and 15 minutes or until doubled in size. (Gently press two fingers into dough. If indentation remains, dough has risen enough.) Punch dough down; cover and let rest 5 minutes.

4. Turn dough out onto a lightly floured surface. Divide dough into 10 equal portions. Working with 1 portion at a time (cover remaining dough to prevent drying), shape each portion into a ball. Make a hole in center of each ball using your index finger. Using fingers of both hands, gently pull dough away from center to make a 1½-inch hole. Place bagels on a baking sheet coated with cooking spray.

5. Lightly coat bagels with cooking spray; cover with plastic wrap. Let rise 10 minutes (bagels will rise only slightly).

6. Preheat oven to 400°.

7. Combine remaining beer, 4 cups water, and sugar in a Dutch oven. Bring to a boil; reduce heat, and simmer. Gently lower 1 bagel into simmering beer mixture. Cook 30 seconds. Turn bagel with a slotted spoon; cook 30 seconds. Transfer bagel to a wire rack lightly coated with cooking spray. Repeat procedure with remaining bagels.

8. Place bagels on a baking sheet sprinkled with cornmeal. Combine 1 teaspoon water and egg yolk in a small bowl; stir with a fork until blended. Brush bagels with yolk mixture; sprinkle with sesame and poppy seeds.

9. Bake at 400° for 17 minutes or until golden. Transfer bagels to a wire rack to cool. Yield: 10 servings (serving size: 1 bagel).

CALORIES 211 (14% from fat); FAT 3.2g (sat 0.2g, mono 1.1g, poly 1g); PROTEIN 8.3g; CARB 40.8g; FIBER 1.6g; CHOL 20mg; IRON 2.8mg; SODIUM 357mg; CALC 11mg

How to Make Bagels

Using fingers of both hands, gently pull dough away from center to make a 1½-inch hole.

Potato-Dill Bread

1 teaspoon olive oil
2 cups chopped onion
2 packages dry yeast (about 4½ teaspoons)
2 cups warm fat-free milk (100° to 110°)
1 cup mashed cooked peeled Yukon gold potatoes
2 teaspoons salt
1 (8-ounce) block ⅓-less-fat cream cheese, softened
1 tablespoon chopped fresh dill
7 cups all-purpose flour, divided (about 32 ounces)
 Cooking spray
1 teaspoon water
1 large egg, lightly beaten

1. Heat oil in a large nonstick skillet over medium-high heat. Add onion, and sauté 5 minutes. Remove from heat; cool.

2. Dissolve yeast in warm milk in a small bowl; let stand 5 minutes.

3. Combine onion, potato, salt, and cheese in a large bowl. Add milk mixture and dill; stir until well combined.

4. Lightly spoon flour into dry measuring cups; level with a knife. Add 6 cups flour to onion mixture; stir until a soft dough forms. Turn dough out onto a floured surface. Knead until smooth and elastic (about 8 minutes); add enough of remaining flour, 1 tablespoon at a time, to keep dough from sticking to hands.

5. Place dough in a large bowl coated with cooking spray, turning to coat top. Cover and let rise in a warm place (85°), free from drafts, 40 minutes or until doubled in size. (Gently press two fingers into dough. If indentation remains, dough has risen enough.) Punch dough down; cover and let rest 5 minutes.

6. Divide dough into 2 portions. Roll each portion into a 14 x 7-inch rectangle on a lightly floured surface. Roll up rectangles tightly, starting with short edges, pressing firmly to eliminate air pockets; pinch seams and ends to seal. Place each roll, seam side down, in a 9 x 5-inch loaf pan coated with cooking spray. Coat dough with cooking spray. Cover and let
Continued

rise in a warm place (85°), free from drafts, 20 minutes or until doubled in size.

7. Preheat oven to 350°.

8. Uncover dough. Combine water and egg, stirring with a whisk. Gently brush loaves with egg mixture. Bake at 350° for 40 minutes or until browned on bottom and sound hollow when tapped. Yield: 2 loaves, 32 servings (serving size: 1 slice).

CALORIES 126 (20% from fat); FAT 2.8g (sat 1.2g, mono 0.9g, poly 0.4g); PROTEIN 4.2g; CARB 21g; FIBER 0.9g; CHOL 12mg; IRON 1.3mg; SODIUM 185mg; CALC 31mg

MAKE AHEAD • FREEZABLE
Whole Wheat Sunflower Oat Bread

  1 cup oat groats
  1 package dry yeast (about
     2¼ teaspoons)
2½ cups warm water (100° to 110°)
  2 tablespoons honey
  2 teaspoons salt, divided
5¾ cups stone-ground whole wheat
     flour, divided (about 26 ounces)
  ½ cup sunflower seed
     kernels
     Cooking spray
  1 teaspoon water
  1 large egg white
  2 tablespoons sunflower seed
     kernels

1. Preheat oven to 375°.

2. Spread groats on a baking sheet in an even layer. Bake at 375° for 10 minutes. Remove from heat; cool completely.

3. Dissolve yeast in warm water in a large bowl; let stand 5 minutes. Stir in honey and ¼ teaspoon salt.

4. Lightly spoon flour into dry measuring cups; level with a knife. Add 3 cups flour to yeast mixture; stir well. Stir in groats. Cover and let stand at room temperature 1 hour to form a sponge (mixture will rise and bubble slightly).

5. Stir 1¾ teaspoons salt and ½ cup sunflower seeds into sponge. Add 2½ cups flour; stir until a soft dough forms. Turn dough out onto a floured surface. Knead until elastic (about 10 minutes); add enough remaining flour, 1 tablespoon at a time, to prevent dough from sticking to hands.

6. Place dough in a large bowl coated with cooking spray, turning to coat top. Cover and let rise in a warm place (85°), free from drafts, 1 hour or until doubled in size. (Press two fingers into dough. If indentation remains, dough has risen enough.) Punch down; cover and let rest 5 minutes.

7. Divide dough into 2 equal portions. Roll each portion into a 14 x 7-inch rectangle on a lightly floured surface. Roll up each rectangle tightly, starting with short edges, pressing firmly to eliminate air pockets; pinch seams and ends to seal. Place each roll, seam side down, in an 8½ x 4½-inch loaf pan coated with cooking spray. Lightly coat dough with cooking spray. Cover and let rise in a warm place (85°), free from drafts, 30 minutes or until doubled in size.

8. Preheat oven to 400°.

9. Combine 1 teaspoon water and egg white, stirring with a whisk. Uncover loaves, and gently brush with egg white mixture. Sprinkle with 2 tablespoons sunflower seeds. Bake at 400° for 40 minutes or until loaves are browned on bottom and sound hollow when tapped. Cool on a wire rack. Yield: 2 loaves, 32 servings (serving size: 1 slice).

CALORIES 136 (17% from fat); FAT 2.5g (sat 0.1g, mono 0.4g, poly 1.1g); PROTEIN 4.9g; CARB 23.3g; FIBER 3.2g; CHOL 0mg; IRON 1.1mg; SODIUM 148mg; CALC 20mg

Soft Pretzels

  1 package dry yeast (about 2¼
     teaspoons)
1½ teaspoons sugar
  1 cup warm water (100° to 110°)
3¼ cups all-purpose flour, divided
     (about 14½ ounces)
  1 teaspoon salt
     Cooking spray
  6 cups water
  2 tablespoons baking soda
  1 teaspoon cornmeal
  1 teaspoon water
  1 large egg
  2 teaspoons kosher salt

1. Dissolve yeast and sugar in warm water in a large bowl; let stand 5 minutes.

2. Lightly spoon flour into dry measuring cups; level with a knife. Add 3 cups flour and 1 teaspoon salt to yeast mixture; stir until a soft dough forms. Turn dough out onto a lightly floured surface; knead until smooth and elastic (about 8 minutes). Add enough remaining flour, 1 tablespoon at a time, to prevent dough from sticking to hands (dough will feel slightly sticky).

3. Place dough in a large bowl coated with cooking spray, turning to coat top. Cover and let rise in a warm place (85°), free from drafts, 40 minutes or until doubled in size. (Gently press two fingers into dough. If indentation remains, dough has risen enough.) Punch dough down; cover and let rest 5 minutes.

4. Preheat oven to 425°.

5. Divide dough into 12 equal portions. Working with 1 portion at a time (cover remaining dough to prevent drying), roll each portion into an 18-inch-long rope with tapered ends. Cross one end of rope over the other to form a circle, leaving about 4 inches at each end of rope. Twist rope at base of circle. Fold ends over circle and into a traditional pretzel shape, pinching gently to seal. Place pretzels on a baking sheet lightly coated with cooking spray. Cover and let rise 10 minutes (pretzels will rise only slightly).

6. Combine 6 cups water and baking soda in a nonaluminum Dutch oven. Bring to a boil; reduce heat, and simmer. Gently lower 1 pretzel into simmering water mixture; cook 15 seconds. Turn pretzel with a slotted spatula; cook 15 seconds. Transfer pretzel to a wire rack coated with cooking spray. Repeat procedure with remaining pretzels.

7. Place pretzels on a baking sheet sprinkled with cornmeal. Combine 1 teaspoon water and egg in a small bowl, stirring with a fork until smooth. Brush a thin layer of egg mixture over pretzels; sprinkle with kosher salt. Bake at 425° for 12 minutes or until pretzels are deep golden brown. Transfer pretzels to a wire rack to cool. Yield: 12 servings (serving size: 1 pretzel).

CALORIES 141 (12% from fat); FAT 1.9g (sat 0.2g, mono 0.6g, poly 0.6g); PROTEIN 4.3g; CARB 26.8g; FIBER 1.1g; CHOL 18mg; IRON 1.8mg; SODIUM 541mg; CALC 8mg

How to Make Soft Pretzels

1. *Cross one end of rope over the other to form a circle, leaving about 4 inches at each end of rope. Twist the rope at the base of the circle.*

2. *Fold the ends over the circle and into a traditional pretzel shape, pinching gently to seal.*

3. *Gently lower 1 pretzel into simmering water mixture; cook 15 seconds. Turn pretzel with a slotted spatula; cook an additional 15 seconds.*

Cinnamon-Raisin Bread

¾ cup raisins
¾ cup fat-free milk
⅓ cup packed brown sugar
1 package dry yeast (about 2¼ teaspoons)
4¼ cups all-purpose flour, divided (about 19 ounces)
1 teaspoon salt
1¼ teaspoons ground cinnamon, divided
½ cup egg substitute
2 tablespoons butter, melted, cooled, and divided
Cooking spray
¼ cup granulated sugar
1 large egg white, lightly beaten

1. Place raisins in a small bowl, and cover with very hot tap water. Let stand 10 minutes; drain well.

2. Heat milk over low heat in a small, heavy saucepan to between 100° and 110°; remove from heat. Combine warm milk, brown sugar, and yeast in a large bowl, stirring until yeast dissolves. Let stand 5 minutes.

3. Lightly spoon flour into dry measuring cups; level with a knife. Combine 4 cups flour, salt, and ¼ teaspoon cinnamon.

4. Add egg substitute and 1 tablespoon butter to milk mixture; stir well with a whisk. Add to flour mixture; stir until a soft dough forms. Turn dough out onto a lightly floured surface. Knead until smooth and elastic (about 8 minutes); add enough of remaining flour, 1 tablespoon at a time, to prevent dough from sticking to hands. Lightly coat dough with cooking spray; cover and let stand 10 minutes. Knead in raisins.

5. Place dough in a large bowl coated with cooking spray, turning to coat top. Cover and let rise in a warm place (85°), free from drafts, 1 hour or until doubled in size. (Gently press two fingers into dough. If indentation remains, dough has risen enough.) Punch dough down; cover and let rest 5 minutes.

6. Brush a 9 x 5-inch loaf pan with 1 tablespoon butter.

7. Roll dough into a 14 x 7-inch rectangle on a lightly floured surface; lightly coat surface of dough with cooking spray. Combine granulated sugar and 1 teaspoon cinnamon in a small bowl. Sprinkle sugar mixture evenly over dough; lightly recoat with cooking spray. Cover dough with plastic wrap; press to help sugar mixture adhere. Remove and discard plastic wrap. Roll up rectangle tightly, starting with a short edge, pressing firmly to eliminate air pockets; pinch seam and ends to seal. Place roll, seam side down, into prepared pan. Cover and let rise 40 minutes or until doubled in size.

8. Preheat oven to 350°.

9. Uncover loaf; carefully remove exposed raisins, and gently brush dough with egg white. Bake at 350° for 50 minutes or until loaf is browned on bottom and sounds hollow when tapped. Remove from pan; cool on wire rack. Yield: 1 loaf, 18 servings (serving size: 1 slice).

CALORIES 172 (8% from fat); FAT 1.6g (sat 0.7g, mono 0.6g, poly 0.2g); PROTEIN 4.6g; CARB 34.9g; FIBER 1.4g; CHOL 4mg; IRON 1.8mg; SODIUM 165mg; CALC 27mg

How to Make Cinnamon-Raisin Bread

Sprinkle sugar mixture evenly over dough; lightly recoat with cooking spray. Cover dough with plastic wrap; press to help sugar mixture adhere. Remove and discard plastic wrap.

A Better Brunch Tradition

A new rendition of her family's sausage casserole is welcomed by a Washington reader.

Some of Elizabeth Walker's best childhood memories revolve around the holidays with her parents and four older brothers in their suburban Seattle home. "With such a large family, traditions were big—including this casserole," she recalls. Walker wanted to continue preparing her late mother's recipe and hoped a lower-calorie version might taste just as good as the original.

We substituted one pound of turkey breakfast sausage for the high-fat pork sausage, saving 127 calories and 13.2 grams of fat per serving. Although we used less turkey sausage than pork sausage, it yielded about the same amount of cooked meat because the turkey rendered less fat than the pork. We kept the regular sharp Cheddar cheese but trimmed the amount to ⅔ cup from ¾ cup without losing a bit of its tangy richness. Switching from whole eggs to egg substitute cut another 2.5 grams of fat per serving. We also lost 2.6 grams of fat per serving by substituting 30 percent reduced-sodium, 98 percent fat-free cream of mushroom soup for regular cream of mushroom soup.

By changing to reduced-sodium soup and omitting one teaspoon of salt called for in the original recipe, we shaved 400 milligrams of sodium per serving.

BEFORE	AFTER
SERVING SIZE	
1 piece	
CALORIES PER SERVING	
482	321
FAT	
31.6g	10.8g
PERCENT OF TOTAL CALORIES	
59%	30%

Breakfast Sausage Casserole

This satisfying recipe is perfect to make for weekend guests. Assemble and refrigerate the casserole the night before, and just pop it in the oven the next morning. Look for turkey sausage near other breakfast-style sausage in the frozen foods section.

Cooking spray
1   (16-ounce) package frozen turkey sausage, thawed (such as Louis Rich)
8   (1½-ounce) slices sourdough bread, cut into ½-inch cubes (about 8 cups)
⅔   cup (about 2½ ounces) shredded sharp Cheddar cheese
3   cups 1% low-fat milk, divided
1   cup egg substitute
1   tablespoon Dijon mustard
1   (10.75-ounce) can condensed 30% reduced-sodium, 98%-fat-free cream of mushroom soup, undiluted

1. Heat a large nonstick skillet over medium-high heat. Coat pan with cooking spray. Add sausage; cook 5 minutes or until browned, stirring to crumble.
2. Arrange bread in a 13 x 9-inch baking dish coated with cooking spray. Top evenly with sausage and Cheddar cheese. Combine 2½ cups milk, egg substitute, and mustard, stirring with a whisk. Pour over bread mixture. Cover and refrigerate 8 hours or overnight.
3. Preheat oven to 350°.
4. Uncover casserole. Combine ½ cup milk and soup, stirring with a whisk. Pour over bread mixture. Bake at 350° for 1 hour and 5 minutes or until set and lightly browned. Let stand 15 minutes before serving. Yield: 8 servings.

CALORIES 321 (30% from fat); FAT 10.8g (sat 5.3g, mono 2.5g, poly 1.1g); PROTEIN 22g; CARB 32.2g; FIBER 1.6g; CHOL 58mg; IRON 2.8mg; SODIUM 968mg; CALC 238mg

Candied Apples

Cinnamon candied apples are a traditional Halloween treat.

When we prepared these Candied Apples in our Test Kitchens, we were won over by their simple charm. We liked the way the cinnamon candy coating complemented the sweetness and cool crunch of the fruit.

Candied Apples

Apples sold in bulk in bags, which tend to be smaller than those sold individually, are the ideal size for these treats. You'll find white dowels at hobby and craft stores, or use wooden craft sticks. Store Candied Apples in an airtight container up to three days.

Cooking spray
8   (4-ounce) Red Delicious apples, stemmed
1   cup sugar
⅓   cup light-colored corn syrup
⅓   cup water
⅓   cup cinnamon decorator candies (such as Red Hots)

1. Line a large baking sheet with foil, and coat with cooking spray. Insert 1 (6-inch) white dowel into stem end of each apple.
2. Combine sugar, corn syrup, water, and candies in a small, heavy saucepan over medium heat. Cook until sugar dissolves, stirring occasionally. Cook, without stirring, until a candy thermometer registers 300° (about 8 minutes). Remove from heat.
3. Working with 1 apple at a time, holding apple by its dowel, dip in syrup, tilting pan. Turn apple quickly to coat evenly with syrup; let excess syrup drip back into pan. Place apple, dowel side up, on prepared baking sheet to harden (about 5 minutes). Yield: 8 servings (serving size: 1 apple).

CALORIES 237 (0% from fat); FAT 0.2g (sat 0g, mono 0g, poly 0.1g); PROTEIN 0.3g; CARB 61.4g; FIBER 2.7g; CHOL 0mg; IRON 0.2mg; SODIUM 20mg; CALC 8mg

The Aromatic Kitchen

Chef Floyd Cardoz tells how to get the most from spices to boost flavor—without extra calories.

As executive chef at Tabla Restaurant and Bread Bar in New York City, Chef Floyd Cardoz uses an abundance of spices to prepare his creative Indian-inflected American cuisine. "When you cook with spices, you don't need fat to enhance flavor and add excitement." Spices, such as those frequently used in Indian cuisine—cardamom, coriander, turmeric, mustard seed, and cumin, to name just a few—add intrigue, zest, and depth to food without increasing calories. Try Cardoz's recipes, or use them as a springboard for inventing your own distinctive spice blends. Either way, you're in for a flavorful adventure.

Halibut with Cumin-Pepper Curry

(pictured on page 343)

Cooking the spice paste briefly before adding liquid deepens the flavor of the sauce. Serve this dish over basmati rice.

- 1 tablespoon chopped peeled fresh ginger
- 1 tablespoon water
- 1 teaspoon ground coriander
- 1 teaspoon ground cumin
- ¼ teaspoon ground turmeric
- ¼ teaspoon crushed red pepper
- 4 garlic cloves, minced
- ½ teaspoon freshly ground black pepper, divided
- 2 teaspoons canola oil
- ¼ cup finely chopped onion
- 1 (14-ounce) can fat-free, less-sodium chicken broth
- ¾ cup light coconut milk
- 3 tablespoons fresh lemon juice
- 4 (6-ounce) halibut fillets
- ½ teaspoon salt
- 4 teaspoons chopped fresh parsley (optional)

1. Combine first 7 ingredients in a small bowl. Add ¼ teaspoon black pepper, stirring until well blended.
2. Heat oil in a large nonstick skillet over medium heat. Add onion; cook 3 minutes, stirring occasionally. Add ginger mixture; cook 1 minute, stirring frequently. Add broth; bring to a boil. Reduce heat, and simmer 5 minutes. Add coconut milk and juice; simmer 2 minutes.
3. Sprinkle fish with ¼ teaspoon black pepper and salt. Add fish to pan; cook 8 minutes or until fish flakes easily when tested with a fork or until desired degree of doneness. Garnish with parsley, if desired. Yield: 4 servings (serving size: 1 fillet and ¼ cup sauce).

CALORIES 260 (30% from fat); FAT 8.8g (sat 2.9g, mono 2.7g, poly 2g); PROTEIN 37.8g; CARB 5.9g; FIBER 0.8g; CHOL 54mg; IRON 2mg; SODIUM 597mg; CALC 96mg

Marinated Flank Steak with Horseradish Raita

This tender, marinated beef is crusted with a dry spice rub and served with spicy-sweet yogurt sauce. The cooling raita also has a little bite of its own.

RAITA:
- 1½ teaspoons finely grated fresh horseradish root
- ½ teaspoon finely grated peeled fresh ginger
- ¼ teaspoon salt
- ¼ teaspoon sugar
- 1 (8-ounce) carton fat-free yogurt

STEAK:
- 1 tablespoon mustard seeds
- 2 teaspoons Szechuan peppercorns
- 1½ teaspoons whole allspice
- 1½ teaspoons coriander seeds
- 1 teaspoon cumin seeds
- ½ teaspoon kosher salt
- 1 (1-pound) flank steak, trimmed
- Cooking spray
- Parsley sprigs (optional)

1. To prepare raita, combine first 5 ingredients in a small bowl. Cover mixture, and chill.
2. To prepare steak, combine mustard seeds and next 4 ingredients in a spice or coffee grinder; pulse until coarsely ground. Stir kosher salt into spice mixture. Rub spice mixture over both sides of steak; cover and chill 4 hours.
3. Heat a large nonstick skillet over medium-high heat. Coat pan with cooking spray. Add steak; cook 3 minutes on each side or until desired degree of doneness. Place steak on a platter or cutting board; let stand 5 minutes. Cut steak diagonally across grain into thin slices. Serve with raita. Garnish with parsley, if desired. Yield: 4 servings (serving size: 3 ounces steak and ¼ cup raita).

CALORIES 216 (33% from fat); FAT 7.8g (sat 2.9g, mono 3.2g, poly 0.4g); PROTEIN 27.1g; CARB 7.7g; FIBER 1.6g; CHOL 46mg; IRON 3.2mg; SODIUM 475mg; CALC 165mg

Safety Tip

If you use whole cinnamon, cloves, cardamom, mace, chiles, or bay leaf, be sure to remove them before serving. They have an unpleasant texture and can be a choking hazard. You can fish them out of a cooked dish before serving—as Cardoz prefers—or wrap them in a cheesecloth pouch to make a bouquet garni that can be discarded after cooking. Seeds, such as cumin, mustard, coriander, fennel, and nigella, can be eaten whole.

Chef Floyd Cardoz's Spice Tips

At the restaurant and at home, Cardoz considers the best ways to select, store, and cook with spices. Here are his tips for getting the most out of them.

Buy fresh: Begin with the freshest possible product. Buy from a vendor with frequent turnover, such as an online spice store (like www.vannsspices.com or www.penzeys.com), or a local Indian or Asian market. Cardoz suggests purchasing whole spices whenever possible. They stay fresh longer, and you can use them whole, or grind them coarse or fine, depending on a recipe.

Purchase small quantities: After a year, ground spices tend to lose flavor. Old spices don't spoil, but they won't add much to your cooking, either. The best way to test if spices are still effective is to smell them. Spices should be vibrant when you use them, giving you a strong, powerful rush of very aromatic scent.

Enhance the flavor: You'll treat spices differently depending on the dish you're cooking. For instance, you can cook whole spices in oil, toast them, or grind them. Cardoz uses a technique he's dubbed "blooming" because when the spices release their fragrances, "it's like a flower opening." Heat the oil until hot, but not smoking. Then add whole spices and cook until the oil shimmers with the spices' aromatic essences. You can then start cooking the rest of the dish's ingredients in the same pan, imparting powerful spice flavors to the food. Apply this technique to risottos, sautés, and vegetable dishes.

For a smoky, earthy flavor, Cardoz toasts whole spices in a heavy-bottomed cast-iron skillet over medium-low heat, then cools and grinds them to add to a dish as a final flourish. Burned spices are bitter, so pay close attention while toasting spices, and don't toast already ground spices—they tend to burn. Cardoz suggests adding toasted spices to dishes like soups and stews just before serving.

To grind spices, try using a coffee grinder (ideally, one reserved for spices). To clean the grinder, wipe with a slice of bread, which will absorb the spice oil. You can also grind spices with a mortar and pestle. If you don't have these or a grinder,

a rolling pin will do the job—just put whole spices in a zip-top plastic bag, fold it over, and roll. The goal is to rupture the plant cells and release the aromatic oils.

Choose the method: Cardoz adds whole spices to soups, stews, and braises. In his recipe for Poached Chicken with Salsa Verde and Bok Choy (recipe on page 323), the poaching liquid takes on the citrus notes of crushed coriander seeds and the sweet licorice flavor of fennel seeds. Whole spices can also flavor a simple side dish of rice: Sauté uncooked rice in oil with cinnamon, cloves, bay leaf, cumin, fennel, or mustard seeds before boiling. (Remove the whole cloves, cinnamon, and bay leaf before serving.)

Spice **pastes** combine finely ground spices with vinegar, wine, broth, or water. Halibut with Cumin-Pepper Curry (recipe on page 321) uses a mixture of ground turmeric, ground coriander, ground cumin, black pepper, and water to make a traditional curry paste that results in a thick sauce. While it's best to grind only the amount needed for a recipe, any leftover spice blend can be mixed with vinegar because, in addition to binding the spices, it also acts as a preservative. Apply the spice-vinegar paste to chicken or lamb before grilling, among other uses.

Spice **rubs,** on the other hand, are typically dry, ground coarsely, mixed with salt, and rubbed directly onto meat. Rubs work well when grilling, barbecuing, broiling, or pan-searing (see Marinated Flank Steak with Horseradish Raita on page 321).

Start with what you know: One of the best ways to get acquainted with spices is to use them in familiar dishes. For example, Cardoz adds sizzle to scrambled eggs by seasoning sautéed onions with turmeric, ginger, ground red pepper, and chopped tomato before adding beaten eggs to the pan. He also likes to spark up a midweek dinner by marinating chicken in soy sauce, chiles, cinnamon, black pepper, cloves, ginger, fresh lime juice, coriander, and garlic for four to six hours. Pot-roasting the chicken requires little attention and results in a tender, full-flavored main course with a zesty sauce.

Goan-Style Steamed Mussels with Calamari

Goa is a state on the west coast of India known for its seafood dishes. Curry leaves resemble small, narrow bay leaves and are available in Indian and gourmet markets. "Blooming" the mustard seeds in oil intensifies their aroma and flavor. Serve this entrée with Indian flatbread, called *naan*. When purchasing a serrano chile here's a tip: Look for a deep green color and smooth skin, which indicates the chile is fresh.

1 1/2 tablespoons canola oil
1 tablespoon mustard seeds
2 1/2 cups thinly sliced onion (about 2 medium)
1 tablespoon crumbled dried curry leaves (about 2 leaves)
2 tablespoons fresh lemon juice
2 teaspoons chopped peeled fresh ginger
1/2 teaspoon salt, divided
1/2 teaspoon freshly ground black pepper, divided
3 garlic cloves, minced
1 serrano chile, seeded and thinly sliced
2 cups cleaned skinless squid (about 1 pound), thinly sliced
32 mussels (about 1 1/4 pounds), scrubbed and debearded
3 tablespoons chopped fresh cilantro

1. Heat oil in a large Dutch oven over medium heat. Add mustard seeds; cook 2 minutes or until seeds begin to pop. Add onion and curry leaves; cook 8 minutes or until onion is lightly browned, stirring occasionally. Stir in juice, ginger, 1/4 teaspoon salt, 1/4 teaspoon pepper, garlic, and chile.

2. Sprinkle squid with 1/4 teaspoon salt and 1/4 teaspoon pepper. Add squid and mussels to pan; cover and cook 3 minutes or until mussels open and squid begins to curl around edges. Discard any unopened shells. Remove from heat, and sprinkle evenly with cilantro. Yield: 4 servings (serving size: 1 1/2 cups).

CALORIES 331 (30% from fat); FAT 10.9g (sat 1.5g, mono 4g, poly 3.2g); PROTEIN 38.4g; CARB 18.8g; FIBER 1.8g; CHOL 309mg; IRON 7.6mg; SODIUM 806mg; CALC 111mg

Black Pepper Shrimp with Coriander-Coconut Chutney

We used a finger hot chile, which is hotter than jalapeño and similar to cayenne, but you can substitute a serrano or an Anaheim chile. For the freshest flavor, grind whole cumin and coriander seeds.

SHRIMP:
- 2 teaspoons canola oil
- 1½ teaspoons ground coriander
- ¼ teaspoon freshly ground black pepper
- 12 jumbo shrimp, peeled and deveined (about 1½ pounds)
- ¼ teaspoon salt
- Cooking spray
- 2 tablespoons fresh lime juice

CHUTNEY:
- 1 cup chopped onion
- ⅓ cup chopped fresh cilantro
- 3 tablespoons flaked sweetened coconut
- 2 tablespoons fresh lime juice
- 1 tablespoon mango chutney
- 1 teaspoon sugar
- 1 teaspoon ground cumin
- 1 teaspoon minced fresh green chile
- ¼ teaspoon salt
- 2 garlic cloves
- Cilantro sprigs (optional)

1. To prepare shrimp, combine first 3 ingredients in a large zip-top plastic bag. Add shrimp to bag; seal. Marinate in refrigerator 2 hours; turn bag occasionally.
2. Prepare grill.
3. Remove shrimp from bag. Sprinkle shrimp with ¼ teaspoon salt. Place shrimp on grill rack coated with cooking spray; grill 3 minutes on each side or until shrimp are done. Drizzle 2 tablespoons juice over shrimp; keep warm.
4. To prepare chutney, place onion and next 9 ingredients in a food processor; process until smooth. Serve with shrimp. Garnish with cilantro sprigs, if desired. Yield: 4 servings (serving size: 3 shrimp and about ¼ cup chutney).

CALORIES 252 (25% from fat); FAT 6.9g (sat 1.9g, mono 1.9g, poly 1.9g); PROTEIN 35.4g; CARB 11g; FIBER 1.4g; CHOL 259mg; IRON 4.7mg; SODIUM 614mg; CALC 109mg

Shaved Fennel with Maple Gastrique

Serve with roasted salmon or pork.

- 1 tablespoon canola oil
- 1 teaspoon fennel seeds
- 1 teaspoon sliced peeled fresh ginger
- 2 star anise
- 2 garlic cloves, minced
- 1 fennel bulb, thinly sliced
- ¼ cup cider vinegar
- ¼ cup maple syrup
- ¼ teaspoon sea salt
- ⅛ teaspoon ground red pepper

1. Heat oil in a large nonstick skillet over medium heat. Add fennel seeds, ginger, star anise, and garlic to pan; cook 2 minutes, stirring occasionally. Add sliced fennel to pan; cook 5 minutes or until lightly browned, stirring occasionally. Add vinegar, scraping pan to loosen browned bits. Stir in syrup, salt, and pepper; bring to a simmer. Cook 15 minutes or until fennel is tender. Discard anise. Yield: 8 servings (serving size: ¼ cup).

CALORIES 55 (31% from fat); FAT 1.9g (sat 0.1g, mono 1.1g, poly 0.6g); PROTEIN 0.5g; CARB 9.9g; FIBER 1.1g; CHOL 0mg; IRON 0.5mg; SODIUM 89mg; CALC 28mg

Golden Smashed Potatoes

Serve these potatoes with Marinated Flank Steak with Horseradish Raita (recipe on page 321).

- 2½ pounds Yukon gold potatoes, quartered
- 1 tablespoon olive oil
- 1 teaspoon mustard seeds
- 1 cup fat-free milk
- 2 tablespoons maple syrup
- ½ teaspoon ground turmeric
- 1 teaspoon salt
- ½ teaspoon freshly ground black pepper

1. Place potatoes in a large saucepan; cover with water. Bring to a boil; reduce heat, and simmer 15 minutes or until tender. Drain; return potatoes to pan.

2. While potatoes cook, heat oil in a small saucepan over medium heat. Add mustard seeds; cook 2 minutes or until seeds begin to pop. Add milk, syrup, and turmeric; simmer until reduced to ½ cup (about 10 minutes). Add milk mixture, salt, and pepper to potatoes, and mash with potato masher or fork to desired consistency. Serve immediately. Yield: 6 servings (serving size: about 1 cup).

CALORIES 212 (10% from fat); FAT 2.4g (sat 0.3g, mono 1.8g, poly 0.3g); PROTEIN 6.1g; CARB 40.4g; FIBER 2.4g; CHOL 0.8mg; IRON 1.8mg; SODIUM 421mg; CALC 59mg

Poached Chicken with Salsa Verde and Bok Choy

CHICKEN:
- 4 cups water
- 1½ cups chopped leek (about 1 large)
- 1 cup chopped onion
- 1 cup chopped carrot
- ¾ cup chopped celery
- 1 tablespoon grated peeled fresh ginger
- 1 teaspoon crushed coriander seeds
- 1 teaspoon fennel seeds
- 1 teaspoon ground turmeric
- 5 garlic cloves, minced
- 2 serrano chiles
- 1 bay leaf
- 4 (14-ounce) cans fat-free, less-sodium chicken broth
- ½ teaspoon salt
- ¼ teaspoon freshly ground black pepper
- 6 (6-ounce) skinless, boneless chicken breast halves

SALSA VERDE:
- ½ cup minced fresh cilantro
- ¼ cup fresh lime juice
- 2 tablespoons minced fresh basil
- 2 tablespoons minced fresh flat-leaf parsley
- 1 tablespoon minced fresh tarragon
- 1 tablespoon olive oil
- 2 teaspoons finely chopped serrano chile
- ¼ teaspoon freshly ground black pepper
- ⅛ teaspoon salt
- 3 garlic cloves, minced

Continued

VEGETABLES:

- 2 teaspoons olive oil
- 2 tablespoons finely chopped shallots
- 1 tablespoon grated peeled fresh ginger
- ½ teaspoon ground cumin
- ½ teaspoon freshly ground black pepper
- ¼ teaspoon salt
- 3 garlic cloves, minced
- 2 cups sliced peeled kohlrabi
- 12 radishes, sliced
- ½ cup fat-free, less-sodium chicken broth
- 3 cups halved baby bok choy

1. To prepare chicken, combine first 13 ingredients in a large Dutch oven; bring to a boil. Reduce heat, and simmer 15 minutes. Sprinkle ½ teaspoon salt and ¼ teaspoon black pepper over chicken; add chicken to pan. Bring to a boil; reduce heat, and simmer 5 minutes. Remove pan from heat. Cover and let stand 30 minutes. Remove chicken from pan with a slotted spoon; cut into ¼-inch-thick slices. Reserve poaching liquid for another use.

2. To prepare salsa verde, combine cilantro and next 9 ingredients, stirring until well blended.

3. To prepare vegetables, heat 2 teaspoons oil in a large nonstick skillet over medium-high heat. Add shallots and next 5 ingredients to pan; sauté 1 minute. Add kohlrabi and radishes; sauté 2 minutes. Stir in ½ cup broth; bring to a simmer. Cook 8 minutes or until vegetables are almost tender. Add bok choy; cook 2 minutes or until vegetables are tender. Serve with chicken and salsa. Yield: 6 servings (serving size: 1 chicken breast half, about 2 tablespoons salsa, and ½ cup vegetables).

CALORIES 314 (20% from fat); FAT 6.9g (sat 1.2g, mono 3.4g, poly 1.3g); PROTEIN 47.9g; CARB 17.5g; FIBER 6.6g; CHOL 99mg; IRON 5.3mg; SODIUM 832mg; CALC 499mg

Spice Primer

We often associate the word "spicy" with heat, but spices boast a broad spectrum of flavors and aromas. They can be earthy, smoky, musky, astringent, or even citrusy. Grown primarily in South Asia, Central America, and the Mediterranean, spices are derived from rootstocks (ginger), bark (cinnamon), berries (juniper), fruits (chiles), seeds (coriander), leaves (bay leaf), buds (cloves), and flowers (saffron), or other dry, hardened, aromatic parts of plants. Ann Wilder, president of Vann's Spices, provides some additional information on just a few of Floyd Cardoz's favorite spices.

SPICE	NATIVE TO	FLAVOR	WITH
Coriander seed	Morocco, India	Citrusy, sweet; balances bitterness and sourness	Fish, curries, chili, braises, stews and soups, baked goods; often paired with cumin
Green cardamom	India	Sweet, delicate, aromatic	Desserts, chai tea, Arabian coffee
Star anise	China	Sweet licorice	Duck, pork roast, chocolate cake, brownies; major component of Chinese five-spice powder
Fennel seed	India	Savory licorice	Fish, Italian sausage, meat curries
Fenugreek	India	Musky, peppery	Indian curry blends
Nigella seed	Middle East	Nutty, smoky	Flatbreads
Mustard seed	Canada, India, Middle East, Thailand, China	Spicy, strong bite	Grilled vegetables, seafood, potato salad
Cloves	Southeast Asia	Strong, pungent	Ham, meats, mulled apple cider, desserts
Mace	Indonesia	Subtler version of nutmeg	Oyster stew, lobster, and other seafood; desserts
Cumin	North Africa, Middle East, China	Earthy, peppery, toasty, bittersweet	Stews, chili, beef, lamb, pork, chicken, chutneys, and curries
Allspice	Jamaica, Central and South America	Pungent, peppery combination of clove, cinnamon, and nutmeg flavors	Cakes, jams, fruit pies, sausages, soups, stews, and curries
Turmeric	India	Pungent, bitter, musky	Curries, bean and lentil dishes, rice, chicken, chutneys, relishes

dinner tonight

Latin-Inspired Dishes

Zesty or mild, these Latin-inspired dishes shake up a weeknight.

Latin-Inspired Menu 1
serves 4

Coconut Crab and Shrimp Salad

Spicy pita wedges*

Pineapple sorbet

*Cut 4 (6-inch) pita breads into wedges; arrange wedges in a single layer on a baking sheet. Lightly coat wedges with cooking spray. Combine 2 teaspoons sesame seeds, ½ teaspoon ground cumin, ¼ teaspoon salt, ¼ teaspoon garlic powder, and ¼ teaspoon ground red pepper. Sprinkle evenly over wedges. Bake at 450° for 5 minutes or until lightly browned.

Game Plan

1. While pita wedges bake:
   • Toast coconut
   • Chop cilantro and jalapeño
   • Chop onion and dice avocado
2. While shrimp cooks:
   • Tear lettuce
3. Assemble salad
4. Scoop sorbet; freeze until time to serve

QUICK & EASY
Coconut Crab and Shrimp Salad

This fresh, colorful seafood salad also makes a terrific appetizer. For a spicier dish, add the jalapeño pepper seeds or use two peppers.

TOTAL TIME: 45 MINUTES

QUICK TIP: To avoid using two pans, toast the coconut over medium-high heat until golden before cooking the shrimp.

Cooking spray
½ pound medium shrimp, peeled and deveined
½ teaspoon salt, divided
1 cup fresh (about 2 ears) or frozen corn kernels, thawed
⅓ cup finely chopped onion
⅓ cup chopped fresh cilantro
⅓ cup diced peeled avocado
½ pound lump crabmeat, drained and shell pieces removed
1 jalapeño pepper, seeded and chopped
3 tablespoons fresh lemon juice
2 teaspoons extravirgin olive oil
6 cups torn Boston lettuce (about 3 small heads)
¼ cup flaked sweetened coconut, toasted

1. Heat a medium nonstick skillet over medium-high heat. Coat pan with cooking spray. Add shrimp and ¼ teaspoon salt; cook 4 minutes or until shrimp are done, turning once. Remove from pan. Coarsely chop shrimp.
2. Combine corn and next 5 ingredients in a medium bowl. Gently stir in shrimp. Combine juice, oil, and ¼ teaspoon salt, stirring with a whisk. Drizzle juice mixture over shrimp mixture; toss gently to coat. Place lettuce on each of 4 plates; top with shrimp mixture. Sprinkle with coconut. Yield: 4 servings (serving size: 1½ cups lettuce, about 1 cup shrimp mixture, and 1 tablespoon coconut).

CALORIES 223 (34% from fat); FAT 8.5g (sat 2.2g, mono 3.6g, poly 1.3g); PROTEIN 24g; CARB 16g; FIBER 3g; CHOL 124mg; IRON 3mg; SODIUM 613mg; CALC 94mg

Latin-Inspired Menu 2
serves 4

Tacos al Carbón

Spicy cabbage salad*

Salsa and baked tortilla chips

*Combine 6 cups thinly sliced cabbage, ½ cup thinly sliced green onions, 2 tablespoons fresh lime juice, 1 tablespoon extravirgin olive oil, 1 teaspoon salt, and 1 seeded and minced jalapeño pepper; toss well.

Game Plan

1. While peppers and onion cook:
   • Trim and slice beef
2. While beef cooks:
   • Squeeze lime and mince garlic
   • Prepare salad
   • Heat tortillas

QUICK & EASY
Tacos al Carbón

Substitute chicken breast or thighs, lamb, or shrimp for the steak. Serve with lime wedges.

TOTAL TIME: 30 MINUTES

Cooking spray
1½ cups thinly sliced red bell pepper (about 1 medium)
1½ cups thinly sliced onion (about 1 medium)
1 (1-pound) flank steak, trimmed and thinly sliced
1 tablespoon chili powder
1 tablespoon fresh lime juice
2½ teaspoons olive oil
¾ teaspoon salt
8 garlic cloves, minced
8 (6-inch) corn tortillas
3 tablespoons chopped fresh cilantro
6 tablespoons fat-free sour cream

1. Heat a grill pan over medium-high heat. Coat pan with cooking spray. Add bell pepper to pan, and cook 4 minutes.
Continued

Add onion to pan, and sauté 10 minutes or until vegetables are tender. Place pepper mixture in a large bowl; cover and keep warm.

2. Add beef to pan; cook 7 minutes or until desired degree of doneness. Add to pepper mixture. Add chili powder, juice, oil, salt, and garlic to bowl; toss to coat.

3. Heat tortillas according to package directions. Spoon steak mixture evenly over tortillas. Top each taco with about 1 teaspoon cilantro and 2¼ teaspoons sour cream. Yield: 4 servings (serving size: 2 tacos).

CALORIES 371 (32% from fat); FAT 13.1g (sat 3.8g, mono 5.7g, poly 1.7g); PROTEIN 29g; CARB 36g; FIBER 4g; CHOL 49mg; IRON 2.9mg; SODIUM 608mg; CALC 164mg

---

Latin-Inspired Menu 3
serves 4

Margarita-Braised Chicken Thighs

Green rice*

Pineapple sherbet

*Bring 2 cups fat-free, less-sodium chicken broth to a boil in a medium saucepan; stir in 1 cup long-grain white rice. Cover and cook 20 minutes or until liquid is absorbed and rice is tender. Stir in 2 tablespoons butter and ½ teaspoon salt. Combine ¾ cup chopped fresh cilantro, ¾ cup sliced green onions, and 2 tablespoons fresh lime juice. Add to rice; stir well.

Game Plan

1. While chicken browns:
- Slice onion and mince garlic
- Combine fruit, juice, and tequila

2. While chicken bakes:
- Chop cilantro and onion for rice
- Squeeze lime juice for rice

Margarita-Braised Chicken Thighs

This juicy, fruity chicken dish received rave reviews in our Test Kitchens.

TOTAL TIME: 43 MINUTES

QUICK TIP: Purchase boneless, skinless chicken thighs, presliced onion, and bottled minced garlic to slash prep time.

- ½ cup flour (about 2¼ ounces)
- 1 tablespoon paprika
- 2 teaspoons garlic powder
- 8 skinless, boneless chicken thighs (about 1½ pounds)
- ½ teaspoon salt
- 1 tablespoon olive oil
- Cooking spray
- 1 cup thinly sliced onion (about 1 medium)
- 5 garlic cloves, minced
- ½ cup dried tropical fruit
- ½ cup orange juice
- ¼ cup tequila
- 1 lime, thinly sliced

1. Preheat oven to 400°.

2. Combine first 3 ingredients in a small baking dish. Sprinkle chicken with salt; dredge chicken in flour mixture.

3. Heat oil in a large nonstick skillet over medium-high heat. Add chicken to pan; cook 4 minutes on each side or until lightly browned. Transfer chicken to an 11 x 7-inch baking dish coated with cooking spray. Add onion to pan; cook 3 minutes. Add garlic, and sauté 1 minute.

4. Combine fruit, juice, and tequila in a microwave-safe dish, and microwave at HIGH 2 minutes. Pour fruit mixture into pan; bring to a boil, scraping pan to loosen browned bits. Cook 1 minute. Pour onion mixture over chicken; top with lime slices. Bake at 400° for 20 minutes or until chicken is done. Yield: 4 servings (serving size: 2 thighs and about ⅓ cup fruit mixture).

CALORIES 350 (25% from fat); FAT 9.9g (sat 2.2g, mono 4.3g, poly 2.1g); PROTEIN 25.1g; CARB 37.9g; FIBER 2.7g; CHOL 94mg; IRON 2.7mg; SODIUM 416mg; CALC 55mg

---

Firehouse Gourmets

Chicago-area firefighters visit Chef John des Rosiers's kitchen to heat up their culinary repertoires.

Lunch service is winding down at Bank Lane Bistro in suburban Chicago when Chef John des Rosiers greets two uniformed firemen who have come, not to inspect the potential hazards of the kitchen's wood-burning oven and flaming gas range, but to pick up kitchen knives and a few tips.

Beginning in 2004, des Rosiers hatched a plot to teach firefighters cooking that they could practice in the station house. "I wanted to give something back to the community. These guys are true heroes, and the least they deserve is some tasty, healthy food." Here are some samples of the recipes des Rosiers teaches his students to make.

Provençal Herb-Marinated Roast Chicken

Chef John des Rosiers prefers to marinate his chickens for two days. We found that even a four-hour soak yields satisfying results.

- 2 (3-pound) roasting chickens
- ¼ cup chopped fresh rosemary
- ¼ cup chopped fresh thyme
- ¼ cup chopped fresh basil
- 1½ tablespoons extravirgin olive oil
- 1¼ teaspoons salt
- 1 teaspoon freshly ground black pepper
- 4 garlic cloves, minced
- Cooking spray

1. Remove and discard giblets and necks from chickens. Rinse chickens with cold water; pat dry. Trim excess fat. Place chickens on a cutting surface. Split chickens in half lengthwise. Starting at neck cavity, loosen skin from breasts and drumsticks by inserting fingers, gently pushing between skin and meat.

2. Combine rosemary and next 6 ingredients. Rub mixture under loosened skin and over breasts and drumsticks. Place chicken halves in large zip-top plastic bags; seal and marinate in refrigerator 4 hours or up to 2 days.

3. Preheat oven to 500°.

4. Remove chicken halves from bags. Place chicken halves, skin sides up, on a broiler pan coated with cooking spray. Bake at 500° for 30 minutes or until a thermometer inserted into meaty part of thigh registers 175°. Remove chicken halves from pan; cover and let stand 15 minutes. Discard skin. Yield: 8 servings (serving size: about 4½ ounces meat).

CALORIES 221 (30% from fat); FAT 7.3g (sat 1.5g, mono 3.3g, poly 1.4g); PROTEIN 35.5g; CARB 1.2g; FIBER 0.5g; CHOL 113mg; IRON 2.2mg; SODIUM 500mg; CALC 31mg

QUICK & EASY
Olive Oil-Whipped Potatoes

Chef John des Rosiers cuts potatoes into thin, uniform pieces so they'll cook quickly and evenly. We've called for a potato masher, but for the fluffiest, most finely textured potatoes, use a ricer.

    4   pounds large baking potatoes, peeled
    ⅔   cup warm half-and-half
    ¼   cup extravirgin olive oil
    1½ teaspoons salt
    ½   teaspoon freshly ground black
        pepper

1. Cut each potato lengthwise into quarters; cut each quarter crosswise into ¼-inch-thick pieces. Place potatoes in a Dutch oven; cover with warm water. Bring to a boil; reduce heat, and simmer 5 minutes or until just tender.

2. Drain potatoes; let stand 5 minutes. Return potatoes to pan. Add half-and-half and remaining ingredients; mash with a potato masher until desired consistency. Yield: 10 servings (serving size: about ¾ cup).

CALORIES 225 (29% from fat); FAT 7.2g (sat 1.8g, mono 4.5g, poly 0.6g); PROTEIN 3.7g; CARB 36.9g; FIBER 3.3g; CHOL 8mg; IRON 0.6mg; SODIUM 371mg; CALC 36mg

Herb-Coated Pork Tenderloin with Creamy Polenta

A quartet of fresh herbs permeates pork tenderloin with heady aroma. The longer you marinate the pork, the stronger the herb flavor will be.

PORK:

    1   tablespoon chopped fresh rosemary
    1   tablespoon chopped fresh thyme
    1   tablespoon chopped fresh
        marjoram
    1   tablespoon chopped fresh
        oregano
    1   tablespoon extravirgin olive oil
    ½   teaspoon salt
    ¼   teaspoon freshly ground black
        pepper
    4   garlic cloves, minced
    2   (1-pound) pork tenderloins,
        trimmed
        Cooking spray

POLENTA:

    ½   cup finely chopped onion
    2   garlic cloves, minced
    ½   cup dry white wine
    5   cups water, divided
    1   cup dry polenta
    1   tablespoon butter
    1   teaspoon salt
    ¼   teaspoon freshly ground black
        pepper

1. To prepare pork, combine first 9 ingredients in a large zip-top plastic bag; seal and marinate in refrigerator overnight or up to 2 days.

2. Preheat oven to 400°.

3. Remove pork from bag. Place pork on a broiler pan coated with cooking spray. Bake at 400° for 30 minutes or until a thermometer registers 155°. Remove from oven; cover and let stand 10 minutes before slicing.

4. To prepare polenta, heat a medium saucepan over medium-high heat. Coat pan with cooking spray. Add onion and 2 garlic cloves; sauté 2 minutes. Add wine; cook 5 minutes or until liquid almost evaporates. Add 2½ cups water; reduce heat, and simmer 5 minutes. Gradually add polenta, stirring constantly with a

whisk. Cook over medium heat 15 minutes or until thick and creamy, stirring frequently and gradually adding 2½ cups water. Stir in butter, 1 teaspoon salt, and ¼ teaspoon pepper. Serve with pork. Yield: 8 servings (serving size: about 3 ounces pork and about ¾ cup polenta).

CALORIES 221 (29% from fat); FAT 7.1g (sat 2.3g, mono 3.6g, poly 0.7g); PROTEIN 25.3g; CARB 13g; FIBER 1.6g; CHOL 77mg; IRON 2mg; SODIUM 511mg; CALC 23mg

Butternut Squash Soup with Toasted Walnuts

This soup's delicious taste and creamy texture belie its simple preparation. Roasting the squash creates browned edges for a richer flavor.

    8   cups (1-inch) cubed peeled
        butternut squash (about
        2¼ pounds)
    1½ teaspoons olive oil
    ¾   teaspoon salt, divided
    ½   teaspoon freshly ground black
        pepper, divided
        Cooking spray
    4   cups warm 2% reduced-fat milk,
        divided
    1   (14-ounce) can fat-free,
        less-sodium chicken broth, divided
    ¼   cup chopped walnuts, toasted

1. Preheat oven to 400°.

2. Combine squash, oil, ¼ teaspoon salt, and ¼ teaspoon pepper on a foil-lined baking sheet coated with cooking spray. Bake at 400° for 45 minutes or until tender. Place half of squash, half of milk, and half of broth in a blender; process until smooth. Pour puréed mixture into a large saucepan. Repeat procedure with remaining squash, milk, and broth. Cook over medium heat 5 minutes or until thoroughly heated (do not bring to a boil). Stir in ½ teaspoon salt and ¼ teaspoon pepper. Ladle 1 cup soup into each of 8 bowls; sprinkle each serving with 1½ teaspoons nuts. Yield: 8 servings.

CALORIES 204 (26% from fat); FAT 5.9g (sat 1.9g, mono 1.7g, poly 2.1g); PROTEIN 7.5g; CARB 34.7g; FIBER 5.3g; CHOL 9mg; IRON 2mg; SODIUM 370mg; CALC 271mg

Grilled Duck with Warm Mushroom Salad and Truffle Vinaigrette

Be sure not to overcook the duck, or it will be tough; it's safe to cook duck until 160°, when it's still a little pink (medium).

2 tablespoons chopped fresh rosemary
2 tablespoons chopped fresh parsley
1 tablespoon olive oil
4 (6-ounce) boneless duck breast halves, skinned
3 garlic cloves, minced
½ teaspoon salt, divided
¼ teaspoon freshly ground black pepper, divided
Cooking spray
3 cups thinly sliced shiitake mushroom caps (about 5 ounces)
2 cups thinly sliced cremini mushroom caps (about 5 ounces)
¾ cup (¼-inch) diagonally cut asparagus
1½ tablespoons Champagne vinegar
1½ teaspoons truffle oil

1. Combine first 5 ingredients in a large zip-top plastic bag; seal and marinate in refrigerator overnight or up to 2 days.
2. Prepare grill.
3. Remove duck from bag; sprinkle evenly with ¼ teaspoon salt and ⅛ teaspoon pepper. Place duck on a grill rack coated with cooking spray, and grill 4 minutes on each side or until desired degree of doneness. Remove duck from grill; cover and let stand 10 minutes. Cut duck across grain into thin slices.
4. While duck stands, heat a large nonstick skillet over medium-high heat. Coat pan with cooking spray. Add mushrooms, ⅛ teaspoon salt, and ⅛ teaspoon pepper; sauté 10 minutes or until tender. Add asparagus; sauté 2 minutes. Combine ⅛ teaspoon salt, vinegar, and truffle oil, stirring with a whisk. Arrange about ½ cup mushroom mixture in center of each of 4 plates. Top each serving with 1 sliced duck breast half. Drizzle about 1½ teaspoons vinaigrette over each serving. Yield: 4 servings.

CALORIES 250 (30% from fat); FAT 8.4g (sat 1.5g, mono 4.9g, poly 1g); PROTEIN 37.7g; CARB 5.3g; FIBER 0.9g; CHOL 182mg; IRON 7.2mg; SODIUM 434mg; CALC 35mg

Finding The Sweet Spot

In the honey business, location is everything, so consider the (flower) source when pairing varietal honey with food.

With more than 300 varieties of floral-source honey in the United States, there's not one all-purpose varietal (see "Homegrown Honey," page 331). Some are best drizzled on warm buttered biscuits, while others are the perfect addition to blended smoothies or the hearty emulsifier for salad dressings. "Cooking with varietal honey impacts the taste and flavor of the food more than run-of-the-mill clover honey," Helene Marshall—who runs the San Francisco Bay Area-based Marshall's Farm Honey with her beekeeper husband—explains. She adds a little star thistle honey to her iced tea, which she says enhances the flavor of the tea instead of overpowering it with sweetness. And really, that is the bottom line: While these honeys might taste sweet, they're not simply sweeteners. With that being said, there's nothing quite like enjoying a spoonful of cotton or orange blossom honey to sweeten your afternoon.

Sweetly Spiced Supper Menu
serves 4

Honey and ginger bookend this delicious meal—they both flavor the entrée and enhance the dessert. You can substitute basil or parsley for the cilantro in the side dish, if you prefer.

Honey-Ginger Glazed Salmon with Arugula Salad

Cilantro orzo pilaf*

Vanilla yogurt with honey and gingersnap cookies

*Cook 1½ cups orzo according to package directions, omitting salt and fat. Drain; place in a medium bowl. Add 1 tablespoon finely chopped cilantro, 1 tablespoon extravirgin olive oil, 1 teaspoon grated lemon rind, and ¼ teaspoon salt. Toss well to coat.

Honey-Ginger Glazed Salmon with Arugula Salad

If sage honey isn't available, substitute alfalfa or another light-colored, mild honey. For bolder flavor, try a dark honey, such as gallberry.

⅔ cup sage honey
¼ cup fresh lemon juice, divided
2 tablespoons warm water (100° to 110°)
1½ teaspoons grated peeled fresh ginger
1 garlic clove, minced
4 (6-ounce) skinless salmon fillets (1 inch thick)
½ teaspoon salt, divided
1 tablespoon olive oil
¼ teaspoon freshly ground black pepper
4 cups trimmed arugula

1. Preheat oven to 350°.
2. Combine honey, 2 tablespoons juice, water, ginger, and garlic in a small bowl,

stirring with a whisk until blended. Pour honey mixture into a 13 x 9-inch baking pan; arrange fish in pan, skinned side up. Let stand 20 minutes. Turn fish over; sprinkle with ¼ teaspoon salt. Bake at 350° for 7 minutes. Remove from oven.

3. Preheat broiler.

4. Brush fish with honey mixture; broil 7 minutes or until fish is browned and flakes easily when tested with a fork or until desired degree of doneness.

5. Combine 2 tablespoons juice, ¼ teaspoon salt, oil, and pepper in a medium bowl; stir with a whisk until blended. Add arugula; toss gently to coat. Serve salad with fish. Yield: 4 servings (serving size: 1 fillet and about ½ cup salad).

CALORIES 396 (38% from fat); FAT 16.6g (sat 3.6g, mono 8.2g, poly 3.6g); PROTEIN 36.9g; CARB 25g; FIBER 0.5g; CHOL 87mg; IRON 1.1mg; SODIUM 378mg; CALC 56mg

WINE NOTE: Honey intensifies the rich meatiness of salmon in this dish, which requires a clean, crisp wine. Try Havens Albariño 2004 from Napa Valley, California ($24). (Albariño is a Spanish white grape.)

Combing the Web

Find more varietal honeys through Internet vendors.

Branches
(www.katzandco.com/zindex3.html)
Beautifully packaged black button sage, wildflower, and citrus honeys

City Bees (www.citybees.com)
Neighborhood honey from the San Francisco Bay area

Glorybee Honey (www.glorybee.com)
Red raspberry and blackberry honey from Eugene, Oregon

McClendon's Select
(www.mcclendonsselect.com)
Citrus-blossom honey from Arizona

The Savannah Bee Company
(www.savannahbee.com/story.htm)
Georgia tupelo and orange blossom honey

Volcano Island Honey
(www.volcanoislandhoney.com)
Pure white kiawe honey from Hawaii

Orange Blossom Honey Butter

This simple recipe earned our Test Kitchens' highest rating for its balance of sweet honey, tangy citrus, and creamy butter. Store, covered, in the refrigerator up to a week. For best results, bring to room temperature and beat with a mixer again before serving. Serve with biscuits or English muffins.

½ cup orange blossom honey
¼ cup butter, softened
¼ teaspoon grated orange rind
¼ teaspoon grated lemon rind

1. Combine all ingredients in a medium bowl; beat with a mixer at medium speed until blended (about 2 minutes). Serve butter at room temperature. Yield: 16 servings (serving size: about 2¼ teaspoons).

CALORIES 57 (44% from fat); FAT 2.8g (sat 1.8g, mono 0.7g, poly 0.1g); PROTEIN 0.1g; CARB 8.7g; FIBER 0g; CHOL 8mg; IRON 0.1mg; SODIUM 1mg; CALC 2mg

---

Spicy Flank Steak

If you can't find almond blossom honey, substitute a dark, rich honey, such as avocado.

SAUCE:
1 cup boiling water
1 stemmed dried seeded pasilla chile
1 stemmed dried seeded Anaheim chile
½ teaspoon olive oil
2 garlic cloves, minced
1 cup less-sodium beef broth
⅓ cup almond blossom honey
2 tablespoons fresh lime juice
½ teaspoon salt
½ teaspoon ground cumin

STEAK:
½ teaspoon salt
¼ teaspoon freshly ground black pepper
⅛ teaspoon Spanish smoked paprika
1 pound flank steak, trimmed
Cooking spray

---

1. To prepare sauce, combine first 3 ingredients in a small bowl; cover and let stand 10 minutes.

2. Heat oil in a large nonstick skillet over medium-high heat. Add garlic; sauté 2 minutes or just until garlic begins to brown. Add chile mixture, broth, and next 4 ingredients; bring to a boil. Reduce heat; cook until reduced to about ½ cup (about 15 minutes), stirring frequently. Place mixture in a blender or food processor; process until smooth. Keep warm.

3. To prepare steak, heat a grill pan over high heat. Combine ½ teaspoon salt, pepper, and paprika; rub salt mixture evenly over both sides of steak. Lightly coat steak with cooking spray. Add steak to pan; cook 4 minutes on each side or until desired degree of doneness. Place steak on a platter; let stand 5 minutes. Cut steak diagonally across grain into thin slices; drizzle with sauce. Yield: 4 servings (serving size: 3 ounces steak and 2 tablespoons sauce).

CALORIES 259 (26% from fat); FAT 7.4g (sat 2.9g, mono 3.1g, poly 0.4g); PROTEIN 23.4g; CARB 25.1g; FIBER 0.3g; CHOL 45mg; IRON 1.8mg; SODIUM 740mg; CALC 22mg

---

Honey-Roasted Root Vegetables

Honey amplifies the natural sugars of the caramelized vegetables in this dish. If you can't find tupelo honey, substitute another medium-color, floral variety, such as dandelion, loosestrife, or orange blossom.

2 cups coarsely chopped peeled sweet potato (about 1 large)
1½ cups coarsely chopped peeled turnip (about 2 medium)
1½ cups coarsely chopped parsnip (about 2 medium)
1½ cups coarsely chopped carrot (about 2 medium)
¼ cup tupelo honey
2 tablespoons olive oil
½ teaspoon salt
3 shallots, halved
Cooking spray

Continued

1. Preheat oven to 450°.

2. Combine all ingredients except cooking spray in a large bowl; toss to coat. Place vegetable mixture on a jelly-roll pan coated with cooking spray. Bake at 450° for 35 minutes or until vegetables are tender and begin to brown, stirring every 15 minutes. Yield: 8 servings (serving size: ½ cup).

CALORIES 118 (27% from fat); FAT 3.5g (sat 0.5g, mono 2.5g, poly 0.4g); PROTEIN 1.3g; CARB 21.7g; FIBER 2.3g; CHOL 0mg; IRON 0.5mg; SODIUM 171mg; CALC 33mg

MAKE AHEAD

Baklava with Wildflower Honey

(pictured on page 342)

Wildflower honey adds a delicate floral scent to this classic dessert, but almond honey would also work well in this recipe. If you can't find unsalted pistachios, use salted and omit the added ⅛ teaspoon salt.

SYRUP:
1½ cups wildflower honey
½ cup water
1 tablespoon fresh lemon juice
3 whole cloves
1 (3-inch) cinnamon stick

FILLING:
⅔ cup unsalted pistachios, coarsely chopped
½ cup blanched unsalted almonds, coarsely chopped
⅓ cup walnuts, coarsely chopped
¼ cup sugar
¾ teaspoon ground cinnamon
¼ teaspoon ground cardamom
⅛ teaspoon salt

REMAINING INGREDIENTS:
Cooking spray
24 (14 x 9-inch) sheets frozen phyllo dough, thawed
1 tablespoon water

1. To prepare syrup, combine first 5 ingredients in a medium saucepan over low heat; stir until honey is completely dissolved (about 2 minutes). Increase heat to medium; cook, without stirring, until a candy thermometer registers 230° (about 10 minutes). Remove from heat; keep warm. Remove solids with a slotted spoon; discard.

2. Preheat oven to 350°.

3. To prepare filling, combine pistachios and next 6 ingredients; set aside.

4. Lightly coat a 13 x 9-inch baking dish with cooking spray. Working with 1 phyllo sheet at a time (cover remaining dough to prevent drying), place phyllo sheet lengthwise in bottom of prepared pan, allowing end of sheet to extend over edges of dish; lightly coat with cooking spray. Repeat procedure with 5 phyllo sheets and cooking spray for a total of 6 layers. Sprinkle phyllo evenly with one-third of nut mixture (about ⅔ cup). Repeat procedure with phyllo, cooking spray, and nut mixture 2 more times. Top last layer of nut mixture with remaining 6 sheets phyllo, each one lightly coated with cooking spray. Lightly coat top phyllo sheet with cooking spray; press baklava gently into pan. Sprinkle baklava surface with 1 tablespoon water.

5. Make 3 lengthwise cuts and 7 crosswise cuts to form 32 equal portions using a sharp knife. Bake at 350° for 30 minutes or until phyllo is golden brown. Remove from oven. Drizzle honey mixture evenly over baklava. Cool in pan on a wire rack. Store covered at room temperature. Yield: 32 servings (serving size: 1 piece).

CALORIES 117 (27% from fat); FAT 3.5g (sat 0.3g, mono 1g, poly 0.9g); PROTEIN 1.9g; CARB 20.7g; FIBER 0.9g; CHOL 0mg; IRON 0.6mg; SODIUM 53mg; CALC 12mg

---

Keep It Flowing

To minimize sticking, lightly coat the inside of a measuring cup or spoon with cooking spray before measuring honey. This step also ensures a more accurate measure and less waste.

How to Make Baklava

1. *Before baking, make 3 even lengthwise cuts and 7 even crosswise cuts in baklava to form 32 portions using a sharp knife.*

2. *Bake at 350° for 30 minutes or until the phyllo is golden brown.*

3. *Remove from oven. Drizzle honey mixture evenly over baklava.*

Homegrown Honey

You can find locally produced artisanal honey in supermarkets, specialty stores, and at farmers' markets. Experiment with different varieties from your area. The color and flavor of a particular honey depend on its nectar source. The Colorado-based National Honey Board provides this information on some of the more common American honey varietals and their characteristics.

HONEY	COLOR	FLAVOR	SUGGESTED USES
Alfalfa	Light	Mild, with beeswax aroma	Mix into dough for tarts, cookies, and other pastries.
Avocado	Dark	Rich, buttery, caramelized	Drizzle on top of butternut squash soup; glaze roasted vegetables, fish, or chicken.
Blueberry	Light to medium amber	Fruity, with lemony scent	Top scones; add to cake batters.
Buckwheat	Dark	Pungent, malty, molasses-like	Add to barbecue sauces.
Eucalyptus	Often dark, though color varies widely	Mildly sweet, slight menthol flavor and aroma	Brush on roasted pork or lamb.
Fireweed	Light	Delicate, with hints of tea	Pour onto pancakes, waffles, or French toast.
Orange blossom	Light to medium	Mild, delicate, with hints of citrus	Stir into cold fruit smoothies.
Sage	Light	Cloverlike, with floral aftertaste	Drizzle on bread and crackers.
Tupelo	Light golden amber with a greenish tint	Complex floral, herbal, and fruity flavor and aftertaste	Spread on biscuits; blend into butter or mustard sauces.
Wildflower	Dark, though color can vary	Pungent, floral	Blend into dressings and marinades.

Honey Barbecued Chicken Breasts

Buckwheat honey's malty pungency makes it ideal for barbecue sauces.

- 1 cup low-sodium bottled chili sauce
- ½ cup ketchup
- ½ cup buckwheat honey
- ⅓ cup Worcestershire sauce
- 1 tablespoon cider vinegar
- 1 tablespoon Dijon mustard
- 1 tablespoon Sriracha (hot chile sauce, such as Huy Fong)
- 1 teaspoon paprika
- ¼ teaspoon salt
- 2 garlic cloves, minced
- 6 (6-ounce) skinless, boneless chicken breast halves
- Cooking spray
- 6 lemon wedges

1. Combine first 10 ingredients in a small saucepan. Bring mixture to a boil over medium-high heat; reduce heat, and simmer 30 minutes, stirring occasionally. Remove from heat, and cool. Reserve ⅓ cup honey mixture. Combine chicken and remaining mixture in a large zip-top plastic bag; seal and marinate in refrigerator 1 hour, turning bag occasionally.

2. Prepare grill.

3. Remove chicken from bag; discard marinade. Place chicken on grill rack coated with cooking spray; grill 5 minutes on each side or until chicken is done, basting occasionally with reserved honey mixture. Serve with lemon wedges. Yield: 6 servings (serving size: 1 breast half and 1 lemon wedge).

CALORIES 273 (8% from fat); FAT 2.4g (sat 0.6g, mono 0.6g, poly 0.6g); PROTEIN 40.2g; CARB 23g; FIBER 0.4g; CHOL 99mg; IRON 2mg; SODIUM 412mg; CALC 37mg

Honey-Hoisin Pork Tenderloin

Look for hoisin sauce in the Asian section of your market. Clover honey would work for this dish if you can't find sage honey. Serve with a green salad and mashed potatoes.

- 2 tablespoons sliced green onions
- 2 tablespoons hoisin sauce
- 2 tablespoons low-sodium soy sauce
- 2 tablespoons sage honey
- 1 tablespoon hot water
- 2 garlic cloves, minced
- 1 (1-pound) pork tenderloin, trimmed
- ¼ teaspoon salt
- Cooking spray
- ½ teaspoon sesame seeds

Continued

1. Combine first 6 ingredients in a small bowl. Pour ¼ cup honey mixture into a large zip-top plastic bag; reserve remaining honey mixture. Add pork to bag; seal and marinate in refrigerator 30 minutes, turning bag occasionally.

2. Preheat oven to 400°.

3. Remove pork from bag; discard marinade. Sprinkle pork with salt. Heat a large ovenproof skillet over medium-high heat. Coat pan with cooking spray. Add pork; cook 2 minutes, browning on all sides. Brush 1 tablespoon reserved honey mixture over pork; sprinkle with sesame seeds. Place skillet in oven. Bake at 400° for 20 minutes or until a thermometer registers 160° (slightly pink) or until desired degree of doneness.

4. Place pork on a platter; let stand 5 minutes. Cut pork across grain into thin slices. Drizzle with 3 tablespoons reserved honey mixture. Yield: 4 servings (serving size: 3 ounces pork

CALORIES 195 (20% from fat); FAT 4.3g (sat 1.4g, mono 1.9g, poly 0.6g); PROTEIN 24.7g; CARB 13.6g; FIBER 0.5g; CHOL 74mg; IRON 1.7mg; SODIUM 633mg; CALC 12mg

inspired vegetarian

Autumn Harvest

Vegetables come into their own this time of year in these sides and entrées.

QUICK & EASY
Pan Catalan

This flavorful Spanish side dish is worth adding to your repertoire. Use good-quality bread and olive oil. Squeeze the tomatoes as you rub them over the bread to transfer some of the seeds and juice.

- 1 garlic clove, halved
- 4 (2-ounce) slices country white bread, toasted
- 2 plum tomatoes, halved
- ¼ teaspoon kosher salt
- 1 tablespoon extravirgin olive oil

1. Rub cut sides of garlic over one side of each bread slice. Discard garlic. Rub 1 side of each bread slice with cut sides of tomato halves; reserve tomatoes for another use. Sprinkle bread evenly with salt. Drizzle with oil. Yield: 4 servings (serving size: 1 slice).

CALORIES 197 (21% from fat); FAT 4.5g (sat 0.5g, mono 2.7g, poly 0.8g); PROTEIN 6.3g; CARB 34.5g; FIBER 2.4g; CHOL 0mg; IRON 1.7mg; SODIUM 491mg; CALC 3mg

QUICK & EASY
Golden Potato-Leek Soup with Cheddar Toasts
(pictured on page 341)

Yukon gold potatoes are the key ingredient to give the soup rich, buttery flavor.

CHEDDAR TOASTS:

- 8 (¼-inch-thick) slices diagonally cut sourdough French bread baguette

  Cooking spray
- ½ cup (2 ounces) shredded sharp Cheddar cheese
- ⅛ teaspoon ground red pepper

SOUP:

- 1 tablespoon butter
- 3 cups thinly sliced leek (about 3 medium)
- 6 cups cubed peeled Yukon gold potato (about 2¼ pounds)
- 2 cups water
- ½ teaspoon salt
- 2 (14-ounce) cans organic vegetable broth (such as Swanson Certified Organic)
- 2 thyme sprigs

REMAINING INGREDIENTS:

- ⅓ cup whipping cream
- ¼ teaspoon freshly ground black pepper

  Thyme sprigs (optional)

1. Preheat oven to 375°.

2. To prepare Cheddar toasts, place baguette slices in a single layer on a baking sheet. Bake at 375° for 7 minutes or until toasted. Turn slices over; coat with cooking spray, and sprinkle 1 tablespoon cheese over each slice. Bake 5 minutes or

until cheese melts. Sprinkle evenly with red pepper.

3. To prepare soup, melt butter in a Dutch oven over medium heat. Add leek; cook 10 minutes or until tender, stirring occasionally (do not brown).

4. Add potatoes and next 4 ingredients. Bring to a boil; reduce heat, and simmer, uncovered, 20 minutes or until potatoes are very tender.

5. Remove pan from heat; discard thyme sprigs. Partially mash potatoes with a potato masher; stir in cream. Sprinkle with black pepper. Serve with Cheddar toasts. Garnish with thyme sprigs, if desired. Yield: 8 servings (serving size: about 1 cup soup and 1 toast).

CALORIES 299 (25% from fat); FAT 8.6g (sat 4.7g, mono 2.7g, poly 0.6g); PROTEIN 7.5g; CARB 48.4g; FIBER 3.9g; CHOL 25mg; IRON 2mg; SODIUM 660mg; CALC 113mg

QUICK & EASY
Pasta with Winter Squash and Pine Nuts

The texture of the squash breaks down as it cooks to create a smooth, hearty sauce for the pasta in this one-dish meal. The slightly sweet squash contrasts with the sharp Parmesan cheese. Use the grating attachment of a food processor to shred the squash.

- 2 tablespoons butter
- 2 tablespoons pine nuts, toasted
- 1 tablespoon chopped fresh sage
- 1 teaspoon olive oil
- 1 garlic clove, minced
- 2½ cups water, divided
- 1 pound butternut squash, peeled, seeded, and shredded
- 1 teaspoon sugar
- ¾ teaspoon salt
- ½ teaspoon black pepper
- 12 ounces uncooked penne (tube-shaped pasta)
- 1 cup (4 ounces) finely shredded Parmesan cheese, divided

1. Melt butter in a large nonstick skillet over medium-high heat until lightly browned. Add pine nuts and sage; remove from heat. Remove from pan, and set aside.

2. Heat oil in pan over medium-high heat. Add garlic to pan, and sauté 30 seconds. Reduce heat to medium. Add 1 cup water and squash to pan. Cook 12 minutes or until water is absorbed, stirring occasionally. Add 1½ cups water, ½ cup at a time, stirring occasionally until each portion of water is absorbed before adding next (about 15 minutes). Stir in sugar, salt, and pepper.

3. Cook pasta according to package directions, omitting salt and fat. Drain, reserving ½ cup pasta water. Combine pasta and squash mixture in a large bowl. Add reserved ½ cup pasta water, butter mixture, and ¾ cup cheese; toss well. Sprinkle with ¼ cup cheese. Serve immediately. Yield: 6 servings (serving size: 1 cup pasta mixture and 2 teaspoons cheese).

CALORIES 351 (28% from fat); FAT 11g (sat 4.7g, mono 3.8g, poly 1.3g); PROTEIN 13.8g; CARB 50.8g; FIBER 3.8g; CHOL 20mg; IRON 2.5mg; SODIUM 554mg; CALC 209mg

QUICK & EASY • MAKE AHEAD
Beets with Walnut-Garlic Sauce
Pkhali

Made throughout the Balkans, Russia, and Turkey, this side dish can be eaten alone or spread on pita bread. Make it a few hours ahead, and let it sit at room temperature to allow the flavors to mellow and meld. Use precooked beets (available in the refrigerated section of the produce department), or roast them. To roast beets, trim stems to one inch, wash, and place on a foil-lined baking sheet; bake at 425° for 45 minutes or until tender. Trim off ¼ inch of beet roots, and rub off skins.

  1 cup chopped onion (about
      1 small)
  ¼ cup walnuts, toasted
  2 tablespoons red wine
      vinegar
  ¾ teaspoon salt
  ½ teaspoon ground red pepper
  ½ teaspoon ground coriander
  1 garlic clove, peeled
  4 cups finely chopped, precooked
      beets (such as Melissa's)

1. Place first 7 ingredients in a food processor; process until smooth.

2. Combine walnut mixture and beets in a large bowl. Yield: 6 servings (serving size: ⅔ cup).

CALORIES 93 (29% from fat); FAT 3g (sat 0.3g, mono 0.4g, poly 2.1g); PROTEIN 2.9g; CARB 15.5g; FIBER 3.1g; CHOL 0mg; IRON 1.2mg; SODIUM 379mg; CALC 31mg

QUICK & EASY
Kale with Garlic and Peppers
(pictured on page 342)

Although you can find kale in supermarkets year-round, this member of the cabbage family is at its peak flavor in cool-weather months. Kale also brings a good dose of protein and iron to this side dish, and the jalapeño pepper adds a pleasant kick. You can substitute collard greens for kale, if you prefer.

  2 teaspoons olive oil
  2 cups sliced red bell pepper (about
      2 medium)
  1 tablespoon chopped seeded
      jalapeño pepper (about 1 small)
  ¼ teaspoon salt
  ¼ teaspoon freshly ground black
      pepper
  14 cups chopped kale, stems
      removed (about 1 pound)
  ½ cup organic vegetable broth (such
      as Swanson Certified Organic)
  1 garlic clove, minced
Lemon wedges (optional)

1. Heat olive oil in a Dutch oven over medium-high heat. Add bell pepper, jalapeño, salt, and black pepper; sauté 3 minutes or until tender. Add kale and broth; cover. Reduce heat to medium-low; cook 10 minutes or until tender, stirring once. Stir in garlic; increase heat to medium. Cook, uncovered, 2 minutes or until liquid evaporates. Serve with lemon wedges, if desired. Yield: 4 servings (serving size: 1 cup).

CALORIES 157 (24% from fat); FAT 4.1g (sat 0.6g, mono 1.8g, poly 1.1g); PROTEIN 8.4g; CARB 28.2g; FIBER 4.9g; CHOL 0mg; IRON 4.3mg; SODIUM 321mg; CALC 323mg

How to Prepare Kale

1. *Pull apart the bunch and examining each leaf. Remove and discard any yellowed or limp portions.*

2. *Wash greens in cool water, agitating with your hands. Replace water two or three times, until there are no traces of dirt or grit.*

3. *Lay flat to dry on a dishtowel, or use a salad spinner.*

4. *To remove the hard center vein, fold the leaf in half and tear or cut away.*

Fennel and Orange Salad

This salad is welcome on a fall or winter evening. Save the juice from the oranges as you chop them, and add it to the salad. Use crimson-fleshed blood oranges if you can find them in your market.

    4   cups thinly sliced fennel bulb
        (about 1 small bulb)
    3   cups coarsely chopped navel
        orange sections (about 4 medium)
    2   tablespoons coarsely chopped
        pitted kalamata olives (about 7)
    1   tablespoon extravirgin olive oil
    ½   teaspoon chopped fresh thyme
    ¼   teaspoon salt
    ¼   teaspoon freshly ground black
        pepper
        Thyme sprigs (optional)

1. Combine all ingredients except thyme sprigs, and toss gently. Garnish with thyme sprigs, if desired. Yield: 6 servings (serving size: 1 cup).

CALORIES 92 (37% from fat); FAT 3.8g (sat 0.5g, mono 2.7g, poly 0.4g); PROTEIN 1.3g; CARB 14.9g; FIBER 3.7g; CHOL 0mg; IRON 0.4mg; SODIUM 190mg; CALC 65mg

Spicy Carrot Salad
Houria

Toasting the cumin seeds intensifies their flavor. To toast the seeds, place them in a small, heavy skillet over medium heat and cook, stirring constantly, one to three minutes or until they smell toasty.

    4   (¼-inch) diagonally cut carrots
        (about 1½ pounds)
    1   teaspoon cumin seeds, toasted
    1   teaspoon Hungarian sweet
        paprika
    ¼   cup chopped fresh cilantro
    2   teaspoons extravirgin olive oil
    ½   teaspoon freshly ground black
        pepper
    ¼   teaspoon salt
    ¼   teaspoon ground red pepper
    1   garlic clove, minced
    ¼   cup (1 ounce) crumbled
        reduced-fat feta cheese

1. Place carrots, cumin, and paprika in a large saucepan. Cover with water to just above carrots; bring to a boil. Cook 5 minutes or until carrots are just tender; drain. Combine carrots, cilantro, and next 5 ingredients in a large bowl; sprinkle with cheese. Yield: 4 servings (serving size: 1 cup).

CALORIES 112 (32% from fat); FAT 4g (sat 1g, mono 1.9g, poly 0.5g); PROTEIN 3.4g; CARB 17.6g; FIBER 5.6g; CHOL 3mg; IRON 1mg; SODIUM 364mg; CALC 85mg

Fettuccine with Wild Mushrooms and Parmesan

The rich mushroom flavor makes this an ideal pasta dish for autumn.

    12 ounces uncooked fettuccine
    2   tablespoons butter
    ¼   cup finely chopped shallots
        (about 1 medium)
    8   ounces sliced cremini mushrooms
        (about 2½ cups)
    4   ounces sliced oyster mushroom
        caps (about 2 cups)
    4   ounces thinly sliced shiitake
        mushroom caps (about 2 cups)
    4   garlic cloves, minced
    ¼   cup dry sherry
    1   cup organic vegetable broth (such
        as Swanson Certified Organic)
    2   tablespoons crème fraîche or sour
        cream
    1½ tablespoons chopped fresh
        parsley
    2   teaspoons chopped fresh thyme
    ½   teaspoon salt
    ¼   teaspoon freshly ground black
        pepper
    2   ounces shaved fresh Parmesan
        cheese (about ½ cup)

1. Cook pasta according to package directions, omitting salt and fat. Drain and set aside.
2. Melt butter in a large nonstick skillet over medium-high heat. Add shallots, mushrooms, and garlic; sauté 6 minutes or until moisture evaporates. Add sherry; cook 2 minutes or until liquid almost evaporates. Add broth; reduce heat, and simmer 5 minutes. Stir in crème fraîche

and next 4 ingredients. Add pasta, tossing to coat. Spoon about 1⅓ cups pasta mixture into each of 6 shallow bowls; top evenly with cheese. Yield: 6 servings.

CALORIES 328 (25% from fat); FAT 9g (sat 4.8g, mono 2.8g, poly 0.3g); PROTEIN 13.8g; CARB 48.8g; FIBER 2.8g; CHOL 23mg; IRON 2.8mg; SODIUM 485mg; CALC 146mg

Green Beans Tossed with Walnut-Miso Sauce

Squeezing the grated ginger and using the juice in the sauce for the beans creates mild ginger flavor. The nutty, salty sauce is a nice complement to the beans.

    4   cups green beans, trimmed (about
        10 ounces)
    2   tablespoons grated peeled fresh
        ginger
    3   tablespoons coarsely chopped
        walnuts, toasted
    2   tablespoons water
    1½ tablespoons yellow miso (soybean
        paste)
    ½   teaspoon low-sodium soy
        sauce

1. Place beans in a large saucepan of boiling water; cook 5 minutes. Drain and plunge beans into ice water; drain.
2. Place ginger on several layers of damp cheesecloth. Gather edges of cheesecloth; squeeze cheesecloth bag over a small bowl. Set ½ teaspoon ginger juice aside; reserve remaining juice for another use. Discard ginger. Place ½ teaspoon ginger juice, walnuts, water, miso, and soy sauce in a food processor; process until nuts are minced. Combine walnut mixture and beans in a large bowl. Yield: 4 servings (serving size: 1 cup).

CALORIES 63 (49% from fat); FAT 3.4g (sat 0.3g, mono 0.5g, poly 2.4g); PROTEIN 2.3g; CARB 6.2g; FIBER 3g; CHOL 0mg; IRON 0.5mg; SODIUM 300mg; CALC 39mg

Pasta Perfected

A Boise, Idaho, reader gives a back-of-the-box recipe a new identity.

Gerry Mitchell's Shrimp, Broccoli, and Sun-Dried Tomatoes with Pasta was inspired by a recipe on the back of a box of farfalle, but by the time it reached the table, the dish had a new identity. Mitchell left out the soft canned mushrooms the original recipe called for and added crunchy broccoli and zesty sun-dried tomatoes, one of her favorite combinations. Instead of cream, she used reduced-fat cream cheese and chicken broth, and replaced the olive oil with cooking spray to sauté the garlic and shrimp. After only one try, the pasta was perfect. "It's light and tasty, and the tomatoes give it a sweet flavor that we enjoy," Mitchell says.

Shrimp, Broccoli, and Sun-Dried Tomatoes with Pasta

½   cup sun-dried tomatoes, packed without oil
½   cup boiling water
3   cups uncooked farfalle (bow tie pasta)
1½ cups chopped broccoli
Cooking spray
1   garlic clove, minced
1   pound large shrimp, peeled and deveined
½   cup fat-free, less-sodium chicken broth
½   cup (4 ounces) ⅓-less-fat cream cheese
½   teaspoon dried basil
¼   cup (1 ounce) grated fresh Parmesan cheese
2   teaspoons fresh lemon juice

1. Place tomatoes and boiling water in a bowl. Cover and let stand 30 minutes or until tender; drain and chop.
2. While tomatoes steep, cook pasta according to package directions, omitting salt and fat. Drain.
3. Steam broccoli, covered, 4 minutes or until crisp-tender. Set aside.
4. Heat a large nonstick skillet over medium-high heat. Coat pan with cooking spray. Add garlic to pan; sauté 30 seconds. Add shrimp; cook 4 minutes. Add broth and cream cheese, stirring to combine; bring to a boil. Reduce heat, and simmer 2 minutes. Add tomatoes, broccoli, and basil; stir well. Cook 2 minutes or until thoroughly heated, stirring frequently. Remove from heat. Stir in pasta, Parmesan cheese, and juice. Serve immediately. Yield: 4 servings (serving size: 2 cups).

CALORIES 493 (22% from fat); FAT 12g (sat 5.7g, mono 2.8g, poly 1.2g); PROTEIN 39.8g; CARB 58.7g; FIBER 5.6g; CHOL 198mg; IRON 7.5mg; SODIUM 862mg; CALC 210mg

Black Beans and Rice with Cheese

"This is a variation on a black bean dish my husband liked in Guatemala. I have come up with several different variations, but this one is both easy and delicious."
—Joann Hoye, Raleigh, North Carolina

1   tablespoon olive oil
½   cup chopped onion
½   cup chopped red bell pepper
3   garlic cloves, minced
½   cup water
1   teaspoon chili powder
½   teaspoon salt
½   teaspoon ground cumin
½   teaspoon dried oregano
¼   teaspoon ground coriander
¼   teaspoon ground red pepper
1   (15-ounce) can black beans, rinsed and drained
1   cup hot cooked long-grain rice
¼   cup (1 ounce) reduced-fat shredded Cheddar cheese

1. Heat oil in a medium saucepan over medium heat. Add onion and bell pepper; cook 5 minutes or until tender, stirring occasionally. Add garlic; cook 1 minute. Add water and next 7 ingredients; bring to a boil. Cover, reduce heat, and simmer 10 minutes or until thoroughly heated. Place ¼ cup rice on each of 4 plates; top each with ½ cup bean mixture. Sprinkle each serving with 1 tablespoon cheese. Yield: 4 servings.

CALORIES 158 (30% from fat); FAT 5.3g (sat 1.5g, mono 2.6g, poly 0.5g); PROTEIN 6.1g; CARB 24.6g; FIBER 4.1g; CHOL 5mg; IRON 1.9mg; SODIUM 664mg; CALC 93mg

QUICK & EASY
Wasabi Mashed Potatoes

"I used to think mashed potatoes could only be good if they were smothered in butter, but one day I improvised this recipe. These potatoes are great paired with hearty red-sauced meat or Asian-inspired fish entrées, like sesame grilled tuna or honey-orange salmon."
—John Tyler Connoley, Silver City, New Mexico

4   cups cubed peeled baking potato (about 1¾ pounds)
¾   cup plain low-fat yogurt
¾   teaspoon wasabi powder (dried Japanese horseradish)
½   teaspoon salt

1. Place potatoes in a saucepan; cover with water. Bring to a boil; cook 10 minutes or until very tender. Drain.
2. Combine potatoes and remaining ingredients in a medium bowl, and beat with a mixer at medium speed until well blended. Serve immediately. Yield: 6 servings (serving size: ⅔ cup).

CALORIES 113 (5% from fat); FAT 0.6g (sat 0.3g, mono 0.1g, poly 0.1g); PROTEIN 3.4g; CARB 23.3g; FIBER 1.9g; CHOL 2mg; IRON 0.4mg; SODIUM 233mg; CALC 65mg

Spinach Custard Pie

"I received this treasure from a seasoned cook in Tennessee. I've added my own touches, such as using fat-free sour cream and cutting down on the butter."

—Susan Beckes,
Wake Forest, North Carolina

2 (10-ounce) packages frozen chopped spinach
Cooking spray
¼ cup chopped onion
¼ cup chopped red bell pepper
2 large eggs, lightly beaten
2 large egg whites, lightly beaten
2 tablespoons all-purpose flour
2 tablespoons grated fresh Parmesan cheese
2 teaspoons butter, melted
¼ teaspoon salt
⅛ teaspoon black pepper
1 (8-ounce) carton fat-free sour cream
¼ teaspoon paprika

1. Preheat oven to 350°.
2. Cook spinach according to package directions; drain well. Place spinach in a large bowl.
3. Heat a large nonstick skillet over medium-high heat. Coat pan with cooking spray. Add onion and bell pepper; sauté 2 minutes or until tender.
4. Add onion mixture, eggs, and egg whites to spinach. Stir in flour and next 5 ingredients. Spoon mixture into a 9-inch pie plate coated with cooking spray. Sprinkle evenly with paprika. Bake at 350° for 30 minutes or until set. Let stand 5 minutes before serving. Yield: 6 servings (serving size: 1 wedge).

CALORIES 115 (31% from fat); FAT 3.9g (sat 1.5g, mono 1.3g, poly 0.5g); PROTEIN 8.5g; CARB 13.1g; FIBER 2.9g; CHOL 78mg; IRON 1.9mg; SODIUM 301mg; CALC 193mg

QUICK & EASY • MAKE AHEAD
Tomato, Caper, and Artichoke Sauce

"This recipe is a version of a dish I had at a restaurant. It's quick to make and can be served as a pasta sauce or over fish or chicken. I love it over chicken ravioli."

—Alison Hughes, Union City, California

Cooking spray
¼ cup chopped onion
1 garlic clove, minced
1¾ cups presliced mushrooms
1 tablespoon capers
1 (14-ounce) can artichoke hearts, rinsed, drained, and chopped
½ cup tomato sauce
¼ cup sliced ripe olives
¼ cup dry white wine
1 (14.5-ounce) can diced tomatoes, undrained

1. Heat a large nonstick skillet over medium heat. Coat pan with cooking spray. Add onion and garlic; cook 2 minutes or until tender, stirring occasionally. Add mushrooms; cook 3 minutes, stirring frequently. Stir in capers and artichokes; cook 30 seconds. Add tomato sauce, olives, wine, and tomatoes; bring to a boil. Reduce heat, and simmer 20 minutes, stirring occasionally. Yield: 3 cups (serving size: ¾ cup).

CALORIES 104 (27% from fat); FAT 3.1g (sat 0.6g, mono 1.7g, poly 0.1g); PROTEIN 4.1g; CARB 16.9g; FIBER 4.7g; CHOL 0mg; IRON 0.6mg; SODIUM 767mg; CALC 22mg

QUICK & EASY • MAKE AHEAD
Apple, Pear, and Cranberry Compote

"I developed this recipe in the fall, when apples and pears were coming in. I like to serve this compote instead of regular cranberry sauce with turkey or ham."

—Meg Wilson, Anderson, South Carolina

3 cups coarsely chopped peeled Fuji apple (about 2 medium)
2¼ cups coarsely chopped peeled Bartlett pear (about 2 medium)
¾ cup apple cider
½ cup fresh cranberries
2 tablespoons brown sugar
¾ teaspoon ground cinnamon
⅛ teaspoon salt
⅛ teaspoon ground nutmeg
2 teaspoons fresh lemon juice

1. Combine first 8 ingredients in a medium saucepan over medium heat. Bring to a boil. Cover, reduce heat, and simmer 15 minutes or until fruit is tender. Remove

from heat, and stir in lemon juice. Yield: 12 servings (serving size: ⅓ cup).

CALORIES 42 (2% from fat); FAT 0.1g; PROTEIN 0.2g; CARB 11g; FIBER 1.4g; CHOL 0mg; IRON 0.2mg; SODIUM 27mg; CALC 7mg

Veni, Vidi, Vegetarian Menu
serves 6

This meal works well for casual entertaining because all the elements are easy to put together.

Polenta Lasagna

Salad with lemon, garlic, and Parmesan vinaigrette*

Breadsticks

*Combine 2 tablespoons fresh lemon juice, 1 tablespoon extravirgin olive oil, ¼ teaspoon salt, ¼ teaspoon sugar, ⅛ teaspoon freshly ground black pepper, and 3 minced garlic cloves, stirring with a whisk. Drizzle over 6 cups baby spinach; toss gently to coat. Sprinkle each serving with 1 tablespoon grated fresh Parmesan cheese; top each serving with 2 tablespoons croutons.

MAKE AHEAD
Polenta Lasagna

"Sun-dried tomato and garlic polenta is also good in this because the flavors complement the vegetables. The lasagna is delicious with or without the sausage, or you could substitute lean ground beef."

—Angela McKinlay, Everett, Washington

1 (26-ounce) jar marinara sauce, divided
1 teaspoon olive oil
1 cup finely chopped onion
½ cup chopped red bell pepper
1 cup meatless fat-free sausage, crumbled (such as Lightlife Gimme Lean)
1 cup chopped mushrooms
½ cup chopped zucchini
2 garlic cloves, minced
1 (16-ounce) tube of polenta, cut into 18 slices
½ cup (2 ounces) preshredded part-skim mozzarella cheese

1. Preheat oven to 350°.
2. Spoon ½ cup marinara sauce into an 8-inch square baking dish to cover bottom, and set aside.
3. Heat oil in a large nonstick skillet over medium-high heat. Add onion and bell pepper; sauté 4 minutes or until tender. Stir in sausage; cook 2 minutes. Add mushrooms, zucchini, and garlic; sauté 2 minutes or until mushrooms are tender, stirring frequently. Add remaining marinara sauce; reduce heat, and simmer 10 minutes.
4. Arrange 9 polenta slices over marinara in baking dish, and top evenly with half of vegetable mixture. Sprinkle ¼ cup cheese over vegetable mixture; arrange remaining polenta over cheese. Top polenta with remaining vegetable mixture, and sprinkle with ¼ cup cheese.
5. Cover and bake at 350° for 30 minutes. Uncover and bake an additional 15 minutes or until bubbly. Let stand 5 minutes before serving. Yield: 6 servings (serving size: 1 piece).

CALORIES 221 (20% from fat); FAT 4.9g (sat 1.4g, mono 2.1g, poly 1.1g); PROTEIN 12.3g; CARB 30.9g; FIBER 4.6g; CHOL 5mg; IRON 2.8mg; SODIUM 880mg; CALC 125mg

QUICK & EASY
Couscous with Caramelized Onion and Goat Cheese

"We love couscous because it is so quick and easy to prepare. For a twist, sometimes I will add sun-dried tomatoes, roasted red pepper, or lemon zest to this."

—Judy Hasselkus, Indianapolis, Indiana

  1 tablespoon olive oil
  2 cups thinly vertically sliced red onion
  1 cup uncooked couscous
  1 teaspoon garlic pepper (such as Lawry's)
  ¼ cup (1 ounce) crumbled goat cheese
  1 cup fat-free, less-sodium chicken broth

1. Heat oil in a medium nonstick skillet over medium-high heat. Add onion, and sauté 7 minutes or until browned.
2. Combine couscous and garlic pepper in a medium bowl; top with onion and cheese. Place broth in a microwave-safe measuring cup; microwave at HIGH 2½ minutes or until hot. Slowly pour over couscous mixture. Cover; let stand 5 minutes. Fluff with a fork, tossing until well combined. Yield: 5 servings (serving size: about ¾ cup).

CALORIES 132 (30% from fat); FAT 4.4g (sat 1.2g, mono 2.3g, poly 0.3g); PROTEIN 4.9g; CARB 19.7g; FIBER 3.2g; CHOL 3mg; IRON 1mg; SODIUM 155mg; CALC 22mg

MAKE AHEAD
Maple Raisin Bran Muffins

"My favorite cookies are oatmeal-raisin, and this muffin comes closer to their taste than any I have found."

—Lorraine Stevenski, Clearwater, Florida

BATTER:
  ⅔ cup all-purpose flour (about 3 ounces)
  ½ cup whole wheat flour (about 2 ounces)
  ½ cup oat bran
  ½ cup raisins
  ⅓ cup packed dark brown sugar
  ¼ cup granulated sugar
  1 teaspoon ground cinnamon
  ¼ teaspoon salt
  ½ cup reduced-fat sour cream
  ½ cup 2% reduced-fat milk
  ¼ cup butter, melted and cooled
  2 tablespoons maple syrup
  1 teaspoon vanilla extract
  1 large egg, lightly beaten
Cooking spray

TOPPING:
  ½ cup packed dark brown sugar
  ¼ cup quick-cooking oats
  2 tablespoons all-purpose flour
  1 tablespoon canola oil
  1 tablespoon maple syrup
  1 teaspoon ground cinnamon

1. Preheat oven to 375°.
2. To prepare batter, lightly spoon flours into dry measuring cups; level with a knife. Place flours in a large bowl. Stir in oat bran and next 5 ingredients; make a well in center of dry ingredients. Combine sour cream and next 5 ingredients; stir well with a whisk. Add to dry ingredients; stir just until moist. Spoon mixture evenly into 12 muffin cups coated with cooking spray.
3. To prepare topping, combine ½ cup dark brown sugar and remaining 5 ingredients in a small bowl; toss with a fork until moist. Sprinkle topping evenly over batter. Bake at 375° for 15 minutes or until a wooden pick inserted in center comes out clean. Cool 10 minutes in pan on a wire rack. Yield: 1 dozen (serving size: 1 muffin).

CALORIES 249 (29% from fat); FAT 7.8g (sat 3.8g, mono 1.9g, poly 1.2g); PROTEIN 4.6g; CARB 43.1g; FIBER 2.1g; CHOL 52mg; IRON 1.6mg; SODIUM 274mg; CALC 65mg

in season

The Seductive Quince

Try this romantically fragrant fruit that's equally at home in sweet and savory preparations.

MAKE AHEAD
Poached Quinces

Serve with whole-grain toast at breakfast or as a topping for ice cream at dessert. Or use the poached fruit as an ingredient in other sweet and savory recipes.

  4 cups water
  1 cup sugar
  1 teaspoon black peppercorns
  1 cinnamon stick
  1 (1-inch) julienne-cut lemon rind
  4 quinces, cored, peeled, and quartered (about 1¾ pounds)

1. Bring first 5 ingredients to a boil in a Dutch oven, and cook 2 minutes. Add

Continued

quinces; reduce heat, and simmer 45 minutes or until tender, stirring occasionally. Remove from heat, and cool to room temperature. Remove quinces from liquid with a slotted spoon. Strain liquid through a sieve into a bowl; discard solids. Pour liquid over quinces. Yield: 16 servings (serving size: 1 quince quarter and about 1 tablespoon liquid).

NOTE: Refrigerate in an airtight container up to two weeks.

CALORIES 66 (0% from fat); FAT 0g; PROTEIN 0.1g; CARB 17.1g; FIBER 0.6g; CHOL 0mg; IRON 0.2mg; SODIUM 1mg; CALC 3mg

---

MAKE AHEAD

Moroccan Lamb Stew with Quince Sambal

Many North African dishes include somewhat astringent fruits, such as quince, to act as a foil for rich meats like lamb. Serve leftover sambal over grilled chicken.

STEW:

 1 tablespoon all-purpose flour
 1 pound boneless leg of lamb, trimmed and cut into bite-sized pieces
 2 teaspoons canola oil
 1½ cups finely chopped onion
 ½ cup finely chopped carrot
 2 tablespoons tomato paste
 1 tablespoon grated peeled fresh ginger
 1 teaspoon dried oregano
 1 teaspoon ground cinnamon
 ½ teaspoon ground coriander
 ¼ teaspoon salt
 ¼ teaspoon ground cardamom
 ¼ teaspoon freshly ground black pepper
 2 garlic cloves, minced
 ½ cup water
 1 teaspoon grated lime rind
 1 teaspoon grated orange rind
 2 (14-ounce) cans fat-free, less-sodium chicken broth
 1 (15½-ounce) can chickpeas (garbanzo beans), rinsed and drained

SAMBAL:

 ⅔ cup finely chopped Poached Quinces (recipe on page 337; about 2 quince quarters)
 1 tablespoon chopped fresh mint
 1 teaspoon Sambal oelek (ground fresh chile paste) or chile paste with garlic
 ½ teaspoon grated peeled fresh ginger
 ⅛ teaspoon ground cinnamon
 1 garlic clove, minced

1. To prepare stew, combine flour and lamb in a medium bowl; toss well to coat. Heat oil in a large saucepan over medium-high heat. Add lamb mixture; cook 5 minutes, browning on all sides. Add onion and next 10 ingredients; sauté 5 minutes. Stir in water, lime rind, orange rind, and broth; bring to a boil. Cover, reduce heat, and simmer 45 minutes. Uncover and cook 55 minutes or until lamb is tender. Stir in chickpeas; cook 2 minutes or until thoroughly heated.

2. To prepare sambal, combine Poached Quinces and remaining 5 ingredients, tossing well. Serve over stew. Yield: 4 servings (serving size: about 1 cup stew and about ¼ cup sambal).

CALORIES 342 (27% from fat); FAT 10.1g (sat 2.3g, mono 4.3g, poly 2.2g); PROTEIN 27.5g; CARB 35.9g; FIBER 7.2g; CHOL 65mg; IRON 4.2mg; SODIUM 747mg; CALC 88mg

---

How to Core Quince

Quinces are very hard and require some elbow grease to prepare. Coring them with a traditional apple corer is very difficult, so try this method instead. Stand the fruit upright, and use a sharp, heavy knife to cut the four "sides" of the fruit away from the core. Peel each quarter of fruit with a vegetable peeler.

MAKE AHEAD

Free-Form Quince and Apple Pie

For this pie, choose a sweet cooking apple that will remain firm.

DOUGH:

 2¼ cups all-purpose flour (about 10 ounces)
 3 tablespoons granulated sugar
 ½ teaspoon salt
 ½ cup chilled butter, cut into small pieces and divided
 ¼ cup plus 1 teaspoon ice water
 ½ teaspoon white vinegar

FILLING:

 4½ cups thinly sliced Poached Quinces (recipe on page 337; about 16 quince quarters)
 2 tablespoons cognac or brandy
 1 teaspoon vanilla extract
 2 Braeburn or Fuji apples, peeled, cored, and thinly sliced
 1 tablespoon all-purpose flour

REMAINING INGREDIENTS:

 Cooking spray
 2 teaspoons turbinado sugar or granulated sugar

1. Preheat oven to 400°.

2. To prepare dough, lightly spoon 2¼ cups flour into dry measuring cups; level with a knife. Place 2¼ cups flour, granulated sugar, and salt in a food processor; pulse to combine. Add all but 1 teaspoon butter; pulse 10 times or until mixture resembles coarse meal. Combine ice water and vinegar. With processor on, slowly add ice water mixture through food chute, processing just until combined (do not form a ball). Press mixture gently into a 6-inch circle on plastic wrap. Cover and chill 30 minutes.

3. To prepare filling, combine Poached Quinces, cognac, vanilla, and apples in a large bowl. Sprinkle with 1 tablespoon flour; toss well to combine.

4. Remove dough from refrigerator. Slightly overlap 2 sheets of plastic wrap on a slightly damp surface. Unwrap and place chilled dough on plastic wrap. Cover dough with 2 additional sheets of overlapping plastic wrap. Roll dough, still covered, into a 14-inch circle. Remove top sheets of plastic wrap; place dough, plastic wrap side up, on a baking sheet lined with parchment paper.

5. Remove plastic wrap. Spoon filling into center of dough, leaving a 2-inch border. Fold edges of dough toward center, pressing gently to seal (dough will only partially cover filling). Lightly coat dough with cooking spray. Sprinkle turbinado sugar over dough; dot filling evenly with 1 teaspoon butter. Bake at 400° for 30 minutes or until crust is golden brown. Yield: 10 servings (serving size: 1 wedge).

CALORIES 324 (26% from fat); FAT 9.5g (sat 4.6g, mono 3.8g, poly 0.5g); PROTEIN 3.3g; CARB 57.2g; FIBER 2.2g; CHOL 24mg; IRON 1.7mg; SODIUM 186mg; CALC 15mg

---

MAKE AHEAD

Rustic Quince and Sour Cherry Crumble

Tart cherries balance the sweet, slightly spiced quince in this homey dessert.

FILLING:

4   cups chopped Poached Quinces (recipe on page 337; about 16 quince quarters)
½ cup packed brown sugar
2   teaspoons cornstarch
1   (14.5-ounce) can pitted tart cherries in water, drained
Cooking spray

TOPPING:

¾ cup all-purpose flour (about 3⅓ ounces)
¼ cup regular oats
2   tablespoons brown sugar
⅛ teaspoon salt
¼ cup chilled butter, cut into small pieces

1. Preheat oven to 375°.
2. To prepare filling, combine first 4 ingredients in a large bowl, tossing well. Spoon into an 8-inch square baking dish coated with cooking spray.
3. To prepare topping, lightly spoon flour into dry measuring cups; level with a knife. Place flour, oats, 2 tablespoons

sugar, and salt in a food processor; pulse until just combined. Add butter; process until mixture resembles coarse meal. Squeeze handfuls of topping to form large pieces; crumble evenly over filling. Bake at 375° for 40 minutes or until filling is bubbly and topping begins to brown. Yield: 8 servings (serving size: about 1 cup).

CALORIES 279 (17% from fat); FAT 5.4g (sat 2.6g, mono 2.2g, poly 0.3g); PROTEIN 1.9g; CARB 58.1g; FIBER 1.9g; CHOL 13mg; IRON 1.7mg; SODIUM 79mg; CALC 27mg

---

STAFF FAVORITE

Five-Spice Duck Breasts with Caramelized Quince

Duck breasts are marinated in the liquid reserved from Poached Quinces (recipe on page 337), and once cooked, they're brushed with more of the lightly spiced liquid. This creates incredibly moist and flavorful meat. Serve with a simple salad of spinach and radicchio.

Poached Quinces (recipe on page 337)
2   teaspoons minced peeled fresh ginger
1   teaspoon five-spice powder
2   garlic cloves, minced
2   (12-ounce) packages boneless whole duck breasts, thawed and cut in half
½ teaspoon salt
½ teaspoon freshly ground black pepper
1   tablespoon thinly sliced green onions

1. Reserve 4 quince quarters and ¾ cup poaching liquid from Poached Quinces. Reserve remaining quince quarters and liquid for another use. Cut 4 quince quarters into cubes; set aside.
2. Combine ½ cup reserved poaching liquid, ginger, five-spice powder, and garlic in a large zip-top plastic bag. Add duck to bag; seal and toss to coat. Marinate in refrigerator at least 24 hours or up to 2 days, turning bag occasionally.
3. Preheat oven to 400°.
4. Remove duck from marinade; discard marinade. Sprinkle duck evenly with salt

and pepper. Heat a large ovenproof skillet over medium-high heat. Place duck, skin side down, in pan; cook 1½ minutes or until skin is golden brown. Turn meat over; cook 1 minute. Place pan in oven. Bake at 400° for 15 minutes or until a thermometer registers 160° (medium) or until desired degree of doneness. Remove duck from pan, reserving 2 teaspoons drippings in pan. Place duck, skin side down, on a cutting board or work surface. Brush meaty side of duck with ¼ cup poaching liquid.

5. Heat reserved drippings in pan over medium-high heat. Add cubed quince quarters; sauté 5 minutes or until golden brown. Remove from heat; stir in green onions.

6. Remove skin from duck; discard. Cut duck diagonally across grain into thin slices. Divide duck slices evenly among 4 plates; top each serving with ¼ cup quince mixture. Serve immediately. Yield: 4 servings.

CALORIES 307 (13% from fat); FAT 4.4g (sat 1.2g, mono 1.8g, poly 0.6g); PROTEIN 23.8g; CARB 43.6g; FIBER 0.8g; CHOL 124mg; IRON 4.5mg; SODIUM 386mg; CALC 21mg

WINE NOTE: These duck breasts have it all—sweetness from the Poached Quinces, richness from the duck, and spiciness from the five-spice powder. Is there one wine that can act as a perfect counterpoint? Yes: pinot noir. A top pinot will have the acidity to balance the richness of the duck while possessing grace notes of ripe fruit and spiciness to mirror the quince and five-spice powder. A terrific choice: Alderbrook Pinot Noir 2002 from California's Russian River Valley ($24).

The Quintessential Quince

•North American cooks can find round or pear-shaped quinces in stores between October and December. The round variety is the most common, but both kinds will work well in our recipes.

•To ripen quinces, keep them at room temperature on the counter or in a paper bag; store ripened fruit in the crisper section of the refrigerator or in a cold cellar up to eight weeks.

Marmelo-Glazed Pork Tenderloin

Marmelo is the Portuguese word for quince; the term marmalade is derived from this word. Here is a great way to enjoy our Quince-Lemon Marmalade—besides just savoring it on toast.

- ½ cup Quince-Lemon Marmalade (recipe at right)
- 1 tablespoon Dijon mustard
- 2 teaspoons chopped fresh rosemary
- 2 garlic cloves, minced
- 2 (¾-pound) pork tenderloins, trimmed
- ¾ teaspoon salt
- ¾ teaspoon freshly ground black pepper

1. Preheat oven to 400°.
2. Combine first 4 ingredients, stirring until well blended. Sprinkle pork evenly with salt and pepper. Place pork on a baking sheet lined with foil. Brush half of marmalade mixture evenly over pork. Bake at 400° for 20 minutes. Brush remaining marmalade mixture over pork; bake an additional 5 minutes or until a thermometer registers 155° or until desired degree of doneness. Let stand 5 minutes before serving. Yield: 6 servings (serving size: about 3 ounces).

CALORIES 190 (25% from fat); FAT 5.2g (sat 1.8g, mono 2.1g, poly 0.5g); PROTEIN 23g; CARB 12g; FIBER 0.3g; CHOL 65mg; IRON 1.5mg; SODIUM 404mg; CALC 15mg

MAKE AHEAD
Quince Butter

Try this silky-smooth fruit spread on crusty bread, then top it with thin shavings of Manchego cheese.

- 4 cups water
- 1 cup sugar
- 1½ pounds quince, cored, peeled, and quartered
- 2 teaspoons fresh lemon juice

1. Bring water and sugar to a boil; cook 2 minutes. Add quince, and cook over medium-low heat 45 minutes or until very tender. Remove from heat. Remove quince from pan with a slotted spoon, reserving liquid. Place quince in a food processor; process until smooth.
2. Cook reserved cooking liquid over medium-high heat, without stirring, until candy thermometer registers 234°. Remove from heat; stir in puréed quince and juice. Cool; pour into an airtight container. Yield: 1⅓ cups (serving size: 2 tablespoons).
NOTE: Refrigerate butter in an airtight container up to two months.

CALORIES 92 (0% from fat); FAT 0g; PROTEIN 0.2g; CARB 24g; FIBER 0.7g; CHOL 0mg; IRON 0.3mg; SODIUM 2mg; CALC 4mg

MAKE AHEAD
Polenta with Port-Poached Quince and Blue Cheese

This elegant appetizer will impress your guests, and it's easy to make. Prepare the quince topping and brown the polenta slices up to two days ahead. Just before serving, warm the assembled hors d'oeuvres under the broiler.

- 1 cup apple juice
- 1 cup tawny port
- ¼ cup sugar
- 1 rosemary sprig
- 1 cup chopped cored peeled quince (about 1 medium quince)
- Cooking spray
- 1 (16-ounce) tube of polenta, cut into 14 (½-inch) slices
- ½ teaspoon coarsely ground black pepper
- ⅓ cup (about 1½ ounces) crumbled blue cheese

1. Bring first 4 ingredients to a boil in a medium saucepan over medium-high heat. Add quince; reduce heat to medium-low (mixture will just barely simmer), and cook 45 minutes or until quince is tender. Remove from heat, and cool to room temperature. Strain quince mixture through a sieve into a bowl, reserving quince and liquid; discard rosemary. Return liquid to pan; bring to a boil over medium-high heat. Cook 10 minutes or until reduced to about ¼ cup; keep warm.

2. Preheat broiler.
3. Heat a large nonstick skillet over medium-high heat. Coat pan with cooking spray. Arrange polenta slices in pan in a single layer; sprinkle with pepper. Cook 8 minutes or until lightly browned; turn and cook 8 minutes or until lightly browned. Place polenta rounds on a baking sheet. Top each round with 1 tablespoon quince and about 1 teaspoon cheese. Broil 2 minutes or until cheese melts. Place rounds on a platter; drizzle evenly with reduced poaching liquid. Serve warm. Yield: 7 servings (serving size: 2 topped polenta rounds).

CALORIES 146 (11% from fat); FAT 1.8g (sat 1.1g, mono 0.5g, poly 0.1g); PROTEIN 2.6g; CARB 25g; FIBER 1.5g; CHOL 5mg; IRON 0.7mg; SODIUM 201mg; CALC 38mg

MAKE AHEAD
Quince-Lemon Marmalade

The very first marmalades were made with quinces, perhaps because they contain a high amount of pectin. A hint of vanilla mellows the tangy flavors of this version. With its gorgeous color and delicious taste, this marmalade would make a great gift.

- 4 cups chopped cored peeled quince (about 1½ pounds)
- ½ lemon, seeded and coarsely chopped
- 2 cups sugar
- 2 cups water
- 1 (1-inch) piece vanilla bean, split lengthwise

1. Place quince and lemon in a food processor; pulse 10 times or until finely chopped. Place quince mixture, sugar, water, and vanilla in a large, heavy saucepan. Bring to a boil; reduce heat, and simmer 55 minutes or until reduced to about 3½ cups. Cool; pour into an airtight container. Yield: 3½ cups (serving size: 2 tablespoons).
NOTE: Refrigerate marmalade in an airtight container up to two months.

CALORIES 64 (0% from fat); FAT 0g; PROTEIN 0.1g; CARB 16.6g; FIBER 0.3g; CHOL 0mg; IRON 0.1mg; SODIUM 1mg; CALC 2mg

Golden Potato-Leek Soup with
Cheddar Toasts, page 332

Baklava with Wildflower Honey,
page 330

Kale with Garlic and Peppers,
page 333

Halibut with Cumin-Pepper Curry,
page 321

Roasted Potato Salad and
Grilled Pork Tenderloin Sandwich,
facing page

We Break for a Tailgate

This all-American spread will garner cheers from fellow fans and fuel game-day spirits.

MAKE AHEAD

Grilled Pork Tenderloin Sandwiches

(pictured on facing page)

Prepare pork and assemble sandwiches at home. Wrapped in foil, they'll stay warm while you travel. Or slice and refrigerate roasted tenderloin, and serve the sandwiches cold. Take along the dressing, and allow people to dress their sandwiches themselves.

- ¼ cup hot jalapeño jelly
- 1 teaspoon water
- 1 tablespoon paprika
- 1½ teaspoons salt
- 1 teaspoon granulated sugar
- 1 teaspoon brown sugar
- 1 teaspoon chili powder
- 1 teaspoon ground cumin
- ½ teaspoon freshly ground black pepper
- 2 (1-pound) pork tenderloins, trimmed
- Cooking spray
- ¼ cup light ranch dressing
- ¼ cup sweet hickory smoke tomato-based barbecue sauce (such as Bull's-Eye)
- 8 (1½-ounce) hamburger buns or Kaiser rolls

1. Prepare grill.

2. Combine jelly and water; set aside.

3. Combine paprika and next 6 ingredients; rub evenly over pork. Place pork on grill rack coated with cooking spray; cover and grill 15 minutes, turning pork occasionally. Brush pork with jelly mixture. Grill 5 minutes or until thermometer registers 155° (slightly pink).

4. Place pork on a cutting surface. Cover loosely with foil; let stand 10 minutes. Cut pork into thin slices. Combine ranch dressing and barbecue sauce. Serve pork and ranch mixture with buns. Yield: 8 servings (serving size: 1 bun, 3 ounces pork, and 1 tablespoon sauce).

CALORIES 329 (22% from fat); FAT 8g (sat 2g, mono 2.1g, poly 1.6g); PROTEIN 27.8g; CARB 34.6g; FIBER 1.8g; CHOL 76mg; IRON 3.1mg; SODIUM 920mg; CALC 73mg

MAKE AHEAD

Roasted Potato Salad

(pictured on facing page)

Store the vinaigrette separately and toss with the potato mixture right before serving. Don't have a jar for the dressing? Whisk the ingredients in a small bowl, then transfer to a sturdy zip-top plastic bag to take to the game.

POTATOES:

- 2 teaspoons olive oil
- ¼ teaspoon salt
- 4 pounds small red potatoes, quartered
- Cooking spray
- ½ cup chopped green onions
- ¼ cup chopped fresh parsley
- 4 bacon slices, cooked and crumbled

VINAIGRETTE:

- 2½ tablespoons balsamic vinegar
- 1 tablespoon Dijon mustard
- 2 teaspoons olive oil
- ½ teaspoon black pepper
- ¼ teaspoon salt

1. Preheat oven to 450°.

2. To prepare potatoes, combine first 3 ingredients. Arrange evenly on a jelly-roll pan coated with cooking spray. Bake at 450° for 30 minutes or until tender. Cool. Combine potatoes, onions, parsley, and bacon.

3. To prepare vinaigrette, combine vinegar and remaining 4 ingredients in a jar. Cover tightly; shake vigorously. Add vinaigrette to potato mixture; toss well. Serve immediately. Yield: 8 servings (serving size: 1 cup).

CALORIES 210 (18% from fat); FAT 4.3g (sat 0.9g, mono 2.5g, poly 0.5g); PROTEIN 5.5g; CARB 37.7g; FIBER 4.2g; CHOL 3mg; IRON 2mg; SODIUM 260mg; CALC 30mg

MAKE AHEAD

Braised Cranberry-Barbecue Beef Sandwiches

- 1 cup less-sodium beef broth
- ¼ cup instant minced onion
- 2 tablespoons coarsely ground black pepper
- 1 (4-pound) boneless chuck roast, trimmed
- 1 cup sweet hickory smoke barbecue sauce (such as Bull's-Eye)
- 1 cup whole-berry cranberry sauce
- 16 (1½-ounce) hamburger buns

1. Combine first 3 ingredients in a Dutch oven. Add beef; bring to a boil. Cover, reduce heat, and simmer 3 hours or until very tender, turning beef occasionally. Remove beef from pan. Reserve 2 cups cooking liquid; discard remaining cooking liquid. Shred beef with 2 forks. Return shredded beef to pan. Add reserved cooking liquid, barbecue sauce, and cranberry sauce; stir well. Cook over medium-low heat 10 minutes or until thoroughly heated. Serve beef mixture on buns. Yield: 16 servings (serving size: 1 bun and about ⅓ cup beef mixture).

CALORIES 295 (21% from fat); FAT 7g (sat 2.4g, mono 2.3g, poly 1.6g); PROTEIN 24.7g; CARB 33.6g; FIBER 1.7g; CHOL 56mg; IRON 3.4mg; SODIUM 517mg; CALC 67mg

A Taste of the Middle East Menu

serves 7

While the tabbouleh chills, prepare and assemble the kebabs.

Tabbouleh Salad

Beef and veggie kebabs*

Pita bread

*Combine 1 teaspoon salt, ½ teaspoon ground cumin, ½ teaspoon ground coriander, ¼ teaspoon ground red pepper, and ¼ teaspoon freshly ground black pepper. Sprinkle over 1½ pounds beef tenderloin, cut into bite-sized pieces; toss well to coat. Combine 1 cup (1-inch) pieces red bell pepper, 1 cup (1-inch) pieces red onion, 1 cup (1-inch) pieces zucchini, 1 tablespoon olive oil, and 2 teaspoons fresh lemon juice. Thread beef and vegetables alternately onto 14 (10-inch) skewers. Broil 10 minutes or until done, turning after 5 minutes.

MAKE AHEAD

Tabbouleh Salad

1½ cups uncooked bulgur
1½ cups boiling water
1½ cups diced English cucumber
 1 cup chopped fresh parsley
 1 cup diced tomato
 ¼ cup chopped green onions
 ¼ cup fresh lemon juice
 1 tablespoon extravirgin olive oil
 ½ teaspoon salt
 ½ teaspoon black pepper
 4 garlic cloves, minced

1. Combine bulgur and boiling water in a large bowl. Cover and let stand 30 minutes. Drain; return bulgur to bowl.
2. Add cucumber and remaining ingredients to bulgur; toss well. Cover and chill at least 1 hour. Yield: 8 servings (serving size: about 1 cup).

CALORIES 120 (17% from fat); FAT 2.2g (sat 0.3g, mono 1.3g, poly 0.4g); PROTEIN 3.9g; CARB 23.3g; FIBER 5.7g; CHOL 0mg; IRON 1.3mg; SODIUM 159mg; CALC 29mg

MAKE AHEAD • FREEZABLE

Molasses Cookies

This classic spice cookie is about as quick to shape as it is to eat.

 1 cup packed brown sugar
 ½ cup vegetable shortening
 ½ cup molasses
 1 large egg
2¼ cups all-purpose flour (about 10 ounces)
 2 teaspoons baking soda
 1 teaspoon ground cinnamon
 ½ teaspoon ground cloves
 ½ teaspoon ground ginger
 ¼ teaspoon salt
 ½ cup water
 ¼ cup granulated sugar
 Cooking spray

1. Combine brown sugar and shortening in a large bowl; beat with a mixer at medium speed until light and fluffy. Add molasses and egg; beat well. Lightly spoon flour into dry measuring cups; level with a knife. Combine flour and next 5 ingredients, stirring with a whisk. Add flour mixture to sugar mixture; beat at low speed just until blended. Cover and freeze 1 hour.
2. Preheat oven to 375°.
3. Place water in a small bowl. Place granulated sugar in another small bowl. Lightly coat hands with cooking spray. Shape dough into 1-inch balls. Dip one side of each ball in water; dip wet side in sugar. Place balls, sugar side up, 1 inch apart, on baking sheets coated with cooking spray. Bake at 375° for 8 minutes. Remove from pans; cool on wire racks. Yield: 4 dozen (serving size: 1 cookie).

CALORIES 66 (27% from fat); FAT 2g (sat 0.5g, mono 0.7g, poly 0.5g); PROTEIN 0.7g; CARB 11.8g; FIBER 0.2g; CHOL 4mg; IRON 0.5mg; SODIUM 67mg; CALC 12mg

superfast

. . . And Ready in Just About 20 Minutes

More than a week's worth of quick entrées gets you in and out of the kitchen in a flash.

QUICK & EASY

One-Dish Poached Halibut and Vegetables

To complete this meal, you can add your favorite bread and a crisp white wine.

 2 cups thinly sliced fennel bulb (about 6 ounces)
 2 cups organic vegetable broth (such as Swanson Certified Organic)
 1 (20-ounce) package refrigerated red potato wedges (such as Simply Potatoes)
 8 ounces baby carrots
 4 (6-ounce) halibut fillets
 ½ teaspoon paprika
 ⅛ teaspoon salt
 ⅛ teaspoon freshly ground black pepper
 ½ teaspoon chopped fresh thyme
 4 lemon wedges

1. Combine first 4 ingredients in a large nonstick skillet; bring to a boil. Cover, reduce heat, and simmer 4 minutes.
2. Sprinkle one side of fish with paprika, salt, and pepper. Add fish, seasoning side up, and thyme to pan; bring to a boil. Cover, reduce heat, and simmer 6 minutes or until fish flakes easily when tested with a fork or until desired degree of doneness. Serve with lemon wedges. Yield: 4 servings (serving size: 1 fillet, about 1½ cups vegetable mixture, and 1 lemon wedge).

CALORIES 314 (12% from fat); FAT 4.1g (sat 0.6g, mono 1.3g, poly 1.3g); PROTEIN 39.7g; CARB 26.6g; FIBER 5.6g; CHOL 54mg; IRON 3.3mg; SODIUM 659mg; CALC 115mg

QUICK & EASY
Pasta Fagioli Soup

This Italian soup derives its name—*fagioli*—and its high fiber content from kidney beans. Serve with crusty Italian bread and a Caesar salad for a quick weeknight supper.

- 12 ounces Santa Fe chicken sausage, halved lengthwise and sliced (such as Amy's)
- 3 cups fat-free, less-sodium chicken broth
- ½ cup uncooked small seashell pasta
- 2 cups coarsely chopped zucchini (about 2 small zucchini)
- 1 (14.5-ounce) can stewed tomatoes, undrained
- 1 teaspoon dried basil
- 1 teaspoon dried oregano
- 1 (15-ounce) can kidney beans, rinsed and drained
- ⅓ cup (about 1½ ounces) shredded Asiago cheese

1. Heat a large saucepan over high heat. Add sausage; cook 2 minutes, stirring constantly. Add broth and pasta; bring to a boil. Cover, reduce heat, and simmer 4 minutes. Add zucchini and tomatoes; bring to a boil. Cover, reduce heat, and simmer 2 minutes. Stir in basil, oregano, and beans; cover and simmer 3 minutes or until pasta and zucchini are tender. Sprinkle with cheese. Yield: 5 servings (serving size: about 1⅓ cups soup and about 1 tablespoon Asiago cheese).

CALORIES 319 (26% from fat); FAT 9.2g (sat 3.3g, mono 3.8g, poly 0.8g); PROTEIN 21.9g; CARB 39.7g; FIBER 9.6g; CHOL 56mg; IRON 4.4mg; SODIUM 858mg; CALC 56mg

QUICK & EASY
Quick Pork Picadillo Sandwiches

This version of a Cuban favorite uses pumpkin pie spice and chili powder to make short work of the usual long list of spices that go into picadillo. You can serve picadillo with rice instead of hamburger buns. A side of sweet potato chips rounds out the meal.

- 1½ cups chopped onion (about 1 medium)
- 1 teaspoon bottled minced garlic
- 1 pound lean ground pork
- ½ cup golden raisins
- 2 tablespoons red wine vinegar
- 1 tablespoon chili powder
- 1 teaspoon pumpkin pie spice
- ½ teaspoon salt
- 1 (28-ounce) can diced tomatoes, drained
- ¼ cup sliced pimiento-stuffed green olives
- 8 (1½-ounce) whole wheat hamburger buns

1. Cook onion, garlic, and pork in a large nonstick skillet over medium-high heat 5 minutes or until browned, stirring to crumble. Drain and return mixture to pan. Stir in raisins and next 5 ingredients. Reduce heat, and cook 5 minutes, stirring occasionally. Stir in olives. Spread about ⅔ cup picadillo mixture on bottom half of each bun; cover with top half of bun. Yield: 8 servings (serving size: 1 sandwich).

CALORIES 289 (29% from fat); FAT 9.2g (sat 2.5g, mono 4.2g, poly 1.9g); PROTEIN 15.8g; CARB 37.7g; FIBER 3.3g; CHOL 43mg; IRON 1.6mg; SODIUM 754mg; CALC 64mg

QUICK & EASY
Andouille Rice and White Beans

Serve with salad greens tossed with your favorite vinaigrette.

- 1 cup fat-free, less-sodium chicken broth
- 1½ teaspoons dried thyme
- ⅛ teaspoon ground red pepper
- 1 (16-ounce) package frozen pepper stir-fry mix, thawed
- 1 (14.5-ounce) can diced tomatoes with basil, garlic, and oregano, undrained
- 1 (3½-ounce) bag boil-in-bag long-grain rice
- 6 ounces andouille sausage, diced
- ½ cup finely chopped green onions
- ½ (15-ounce) can Great Northern beans, rinsed and drained (about ¾ cup)

1. Combine first 5 ingredients in a Dutch oven; bring to a boil. Open bag of rice; add rice to pepper mixture. Cover, reduce heat, and simmer 10 minutes or until rice is tender.
2. While rice mixture cooks, heat a medium nonstick skillet over medium-high heat. Add sausage; sauté 6 minutes or until browned.
3. Add sausage, onions, and beans to rice mixture; cook until thoroughly heated. Yield: 5 servings (serving size: 1 cup).

CALORIES 269 (22% from fat); FAT 6.6g (sat 2.5g, mono 2.8g, poly 0.8g); PROTEIN 12.8g; CARB 34.7g; FIBER 3.5g; CHOL 24mg; IRON 3.9mg; SODIUM 798mg; CALC 91mg

Go with a Quick Grain

Cooking regular long-grain rice can take more than 20 minutes. We tested the three most commonly available types of quick-cooking rice.

Boil-in-bag rice: The results from the brands we tried were comparable, regardless of whether the rice was cooked in the microwave or on the stovetop. The microwave method is faster since you don't have to wait for water to boil on the stove.

Instant rice: This rice takes half as much time to prepare as boil-in-bag rice; however, our instant rice tended to be mushy.

Precooked rice in a pouch: Since the rice is already cooked, all you need to do is open the pouch and microwave 60 to 90 seconds. Precooked rice contains oil to coat and separate the grains. Some of our staff liked the taste of the oil, while others thought it had an off flavor. Since some precooked rice products can contain as much as 500 milligrams of sodium per cup, be sure to check the labels.

Chicken Drumsticks with Apricot Glaze

Speed preparation by reducing the glaze while the chicken broils.

> 8   (4-ounce) chicken drumsticks, skinned
> ¼   teaspoon salt
> ⅛   teaspoon black pepper
> Cooking spray
> ½   cup apricot spread (such as Polaner All Fruit)
> 2   tablespoons cider vinegar
> 1   tablespoon dark brown sugar
> 1   tablespoon low-sodium soy sauce
> 1   teaspoon bottled ground fresh ginger (such as Spice World)
> ¼   teaspoon crushed red pepper

1. Preheat broiler.
2. Line bottom of a broiler pan with foil. Sprinkle chicken with salt and black pepper. Place chicken on rack of a broiler pan coated with cooking spray; place rack in pan. Broil chicken 12 minutes, turning once.
3. While chicken cooks, combine apricot spread and remaining 5 ingredients in a small saucepan; bring to a boil over medium heat. Cook 5 minutes or until reduced to ½ cup, stirring frequently. Brush ¼ cup apricot mixture evenly over chicken; broil 2 minutes. Brush remaining apricot mixture over chicken; broil 2 minutes or until done. Yield: 4 servings (serving size: 2 drumsticks).

CALORIES 232 (15% from fat); FAT 3.9g (sat 1g, mono 1.2g, poly 0.9g); PROTEIN 23.6g; CARB 24.3g; FIBER 0.1g; CHOL 87mg; IRON 1.4mg; SODIUM 382mg; CALC 17mg

Peppered Pork and Pears

Ground mixed peppercorns give a slightly sweet, barely hot flavor to the pork and pears. If you don't have pear brandy, substitute regular brandy or additional chicken broth. Serve with egg noodles.

> 1   teaspoon olive oil
> 4   (4-ounce) boneless center-cut loin pork chops (about ½ inch thick)
> 2   teaspoons coarsely ground mixed peppercorns or black pepper
> ½   teaspoon salt, divided
> 1   teaspoon butter
> 1   cup thinly sliced leek (about 1 large)
> 2   firm Bartlett pears, cored and cut lengthwise into ½-inch-thick slices
> ⅓   cup fat-free, less-sodium chicken broth
> ¼   cup white wine
> 2   tablespoons pear brandy
> 1   tablespoon chopped fresh sage
> Sage leaves (optional)

1. Heat oil in a large nonstick skillet over medium-high heat. Sprinkle pork with pepper and ¼ teaspoon salt. Add pork to pan; cook 4 minutes on each side or until browned. Remove pork from pan; cover and keep warm.
2. Add butter and leek to pan; sauté 2 minutes or until leek is tender. Add pears. Reduce heat to medium; cook about 2 minutes, stirring gently. Add broth, wine, brandy, chopped sage, and ¼ teaspoon salt; bring to a boil. Cook until sauce is slightly thickened (about 2 minutes). Spoon sauce over pork. Garnish with sage leaves, if desired. Yield: 4 servings (serving size: 1 pork chop and 1 cup pear mixture).

CALORIES 259 (26% from fat); FAT 7.5g (sat 2.4g, mono 3.5g, poly 0.6g); PROTEIN 24.8g; CARB 16.8g; FIBER 3.3g; CHOL 73mg; IRON 1.7mg; SODIUM 384mg; CALC 43mg

Lemony Shrimp with Broiled Veggies

When the vegetables are cooked, fold foil into a pouch to keep them warm until dinnertime.

> Cooking spray
> 1½   cups green bell pepper strips
> 1   cup grape or small cherry tomatoes
> 1   yellow squash, halved lengthwise and cut into 1-inch pieces (about 1 cup)
> 1   small yellow onion, cut into 8 wedges
> 6   cups water
> ¾   teaspoon ground turmeric
> 1   (3½-ounce) bag boil-in-bag long-grain rice
> 1½   pounds peeled and deveined medium shrimp
> ¼   cup chopped fresh parsley
> ½   teaspoon salt
> 2   tablespoons butter
> 2   teaspoons grated lemon rind
> 2   tablespoons fresh lemon juice
> 1½   teaspoons Old Bay seasoning
> 4   lemon wedges

1. Preheat broiler.
2. Line baking sheet or broiler pan with foil, and coat foil with cooking spray. Arrange pepper, tomatoes, squash, and onion in a single layer in pan; coat with cooking spray. Broil 14 minutes or until browned, stirring after 10 minutes.
3. While vegetables broil, bring water and turmeric to a boil in a large saucepan. Add rice; cover, reduce heat, and simmer 6 minutes. Add shrimp to pan; cover and cook 5 minutes or until shrimp are done. Drain. Remove rice from cooking bag. Set shrimp aside.
4. Remove vegetables from broiler, and sprinkle with parsley and salt.
5. Return shrimp to pan. Add butter and next 3 ingredients; toss gently until butter melts. Spoon vegetables and shrimp mixture over rice; serve with lemon wedges. Yield: 4 servings (serving size: ⅔ cup shrimp mixture, ½ cup vegetables, ⅓ cup rice, and 1 lemon wedge).

CALORIES 377 (21% from fat); FAT 9g (sat 3.5g, mono 2.8g, poly 1.5g); PROTEIN 38.3g; CARB 35.3g; FIBER 2.9g; CHOL 274mg; IRON 5.7mg; SODIUM 851mg; CALC 136mg

Broiled Lamb with Cilantro-Papaya Salsa

2 teaspoons garam masala
½ teaspoon salt, divided
¼ teaspoon black pepper
12 (3-ounce) lamb loin chops, trimmed
1 cup diced peeled papaya (about 1 medium)
½ cup prechopped red onion
¼ cup chopped fresh cilantro
1 tablespoon fresh lemon juice
1 teaspoon chopped jalapeño pepper

1. Preheat broiler.
2. Combine garam masala, ¼ teaspoon salt, and black pepper. Rub both sides of lamb chops with garam masala mixture. Arrange lamb in a single layer on a broiler pan; broil 4 minutes on each side or until desired degree of doneness. Remove from heat; sprinkle lamb with ¼ teaspoon salt.
3. While lamb cooks, combine papaya and remaining 4 ingredients; stir well. Serve with lamb. Yield: 6 servings (serving size: 2 lamb chops and ¼ cup salsa).

CALORIES 160 (32% from fat); FAT 5.6g (sat 2g, mono 2.2g, poly 0.5g); PROTEIN 19.7g; CARB 7.2g; FIBER 1.5g; CHOL 61mg; IRON 1.9mg; SODIUM 261mg; CALC 34mg

Greek Chicken with Capers and Orzo

1 cup uncooked orzo (rice-shaped pasta)
Cooking spray
12 ounces chicken breast tenders
2 tablespoons capers
2 tablespoons fresh lemon juice
2 tablespoons extravirgin olive oil
1 tablespoon salt-free dried Greek seasoning blend
1 teaspoon bottled minced garlic
½ teaspoon salt
1 large red bell pepper, cut into thin strips
½ cup finely chopped green onions

1. Cook orzo according to package directions, omitting salt and fat. Drain.

2. While orzo cooks, heat a 12-inch nonstick skillet over medium high heat. Coat pan with cooking spray. Add chicken; cook 3 minutes on each side or until done. Remove chicken from pan; cover and keep warm.
3. Combine capers and next 5 ingredients; set aside.
4. Recoat pan with cooking spray. Add bell pepper, and sauté 2 minutes. Add onions; sauté 1 minute or until peppers begin to brown. Return chicken to pan. Stir in caper mixture, tossing gently to coat chicken. Spoon chicken mixture over orzo. Serve immediately. Yield: 4 servings (serving size: ¾ cup chicken mixture and about ½ cup orzo).

CALORIES 337 (24% from fat); FAT 9g (sat 1.5g, mono 5.7g, poly 1g); PROTEIN 26.3g; CARB 37.2g; FIBER 2.4g; CHOL 49mg; IRON 2.7mg; SODIUM 514mg; CALC 41mg

simple suppers
Spirited Sauces

Beer, wine, and liquor rouse the taste of meaty dinners.

Guinness-Braised Chuck Steaks with Horseradish Mashed Potatoes

STEAK:
1½ pounds boneless chuck steak, trimmed
½ teaspoon freshly ground black pepper
¼ teaspoon salt
2 teaspoons olive oil
1½ cups finely chopped onion
½ cup chopped carrot
½ cup fat-free, less-sodium chicken broth, divided
1 teaspoon dark brown sugar
1 teaspoon chopped fresh rosemary
1 (8-ounce) package presliced mushrooms
1 garlic clove, minced
2 bay leaves
1 (12-ounce) bottle Guinness Stout

POTATOES:
2 pounds peeled baking potatoes, quartered
2 tablespoons butter
½ cup fat-free milk
¼ cup finely chopped green onions
¼ cup reduced-fat sour cream
2 tablespoons prepared horseradish
½ teaspoon salt
½ teaspoon freshly ground black pepper

1. To prepare steak, sprinkle steak with ½ teaspoon pepper and ¼ teaspoon salt. Heat oil in a Dutch oven over medium-high heat. Add steak; cook 5 minutes on each side or until browned. Remove steak from pan; set aside. Add 1½ cups onion, carrot, 2 tablespoons broth, and sugar. Cover, reduce heat to medium, and cook 10 minutes. Stir in rosemary, mushrooms, and garlic. Cover and cook 2 minutes. Add bay leaves, stout, 6 tablespoons broth, and steak; bring to a boil. Cover, reduce heat, and simmer 1½ hours or until steak is tender.
2. To prepare potatoes, place potatoes in a large saucepan; cover with water. Bring to a boil; simmer 20 minutes or until potatoes are tender; drain. Return potatoes to pan. Add butter; beat with a mixer at medium speed just until smooth. Stir in milk and remaining 5 ingredients. Keep warm.
3. Remove steak from pan; keep warm. Discard bay leaves. Increase heat to medium-high; cook 5 minutes or until slightly thickened. Spoon stout mixture over steak. Serve with potatoes. Yield: 6 servings (serving size: 3 ounces beef, ¾ cup potatoes, and ⅓ cup sauce).

CALORIES 428 (27% from fat); FAT 13.1g (sat 5g, mono 6g, poly 0.9g); PROTEIN 35.2g; CARB 42.3g; FIBER 4.6g; CHOL 86mg; IRON 4.3mg; SODIUM 872mg; CALC 82mg

Veal Scallops in Irish Whiskey Sauce

For a more affordable alternative, use pork loin chops cut into ¼-inch-thick slices instead of veal. To slice pork easily, place it in the freezer 15 minutes before slicing.

    1 teaspoon Hungarian sweet
       paprika
    ½ teaspoon salt
    ½ teaspoon freshly ground black
       pepper
    ¼ teaspoon ground sage
    ¼ teaspoon ground ginger
    1 pound (¼-inch-thick) veal
       scaloppine
    2 teaspoons olive oil, divided
    2 teaspoons butter, divided
    2 tablespoons freshly chopped
       shallots
    1 (8-ounce) package presliced
       mushrooms
    ¼ cup Irish whiskey
    ½ cup fat-free, less-sodium chicken
       broth
    2 tablespoons sherry
    2 tablespoons chopped fresh parsley
       (optional)

1. Combine first 5 ingredients in a small bowl; sprinkle evenly over veal.
2. Heat 1 teaspoon oil and 1 teaspoon butter in a large nonstick skillet over medium-high heat. Add half of veal to skillet. Cook 1 minute on each side or until lightly browned. Remove from pan; set aside, and keep warm. Repeat procedure with remaining olive oil, butter, and veal.
3. Reduce heat to medium. Add shallots and mushrooms to pan, and cook 1 minute. Add whiskey, scraping pan to loosen browned bits. Add broth and sherry; simmer 3 minutes or just until sauce begins to thicken. Return veal to pan. Cover and simmer 1 minute or until thoroughly heated. Place veal on a serving platter, and top with sauce. Sprinkle with parsley, if desired. Serve immediately. Yield: 4 servings (serving size: 2 veal slices and ¼ cup sauce).

CALORIES 208 (43% from fat); FAT 10g (sat 3.4g, mono 4.5g, poly 0.9g); PROTEIN 23.5g; CARB 3.4g; FIBER 1.1g; CHOL 90mg; IRON 1.4mg; SODIUM 433mg; CALC 26mg

Pork Loin with Brandy and Dried Cherries

Serve with rice, and garnish with flat-leaf parsley.

    ½ cup dried tart cherries
    ½ cup brandy
    2 pounds boneless pork loin, trimmed
    1 teaspoon dry mustard
    1 teaspoon freshly ground black
       pepper
    ½ teaspoon salt
       Cooking spray
    1 cup finely chopped onion
    3 garlic cloves, minced
    1 cup fat-free, less-sodium chicken
       broth
    1 tablespoon red currant jelly
    1 teaspoon chopped fresh thyme
    1 bay leaf

1. Combine cherries and brandy in a small bowl. Let stand 1 hour.
2. Preheat oven to 325°.
3. Sprinkle pork evenly with mustard, pepper, and salt.
4. Heat a Dutch oven over medium-high heat. Coat pan with cooking spray. Add pork; cook 8 minutes, turning pork every 2 minutes or until browned. Remove pork from pan. Reduce heat to medium; add onion and garlic. Cover and cook 5 minutes. Add cherry mixture, broth, jelly, thyme, and bay leaf; bring to a boil. Return pork to pan. Cover and bake at 325° for 2 hours or until tender. Remove pork from pan; let stand 10 minutes. Discard bay leaf. Bring broth mixture to a boil; cook until reduced to 1½ cups (about 3 minutes). Yield: 6 servings (serving size: 3 ounces pork and ½ cup sauce).

CALORIES 307 (31% from fat); FAT 10.6g (sat 3.6g, mono 4.7g, poly 1g); PROTEIN 31.4g; CARB 16.4g; FIBER 2.1g; CHOL 83mg; IRON 1.8mg; SODIUM 315mg; CALC 47mg

WINE NOTE: The best match depends on the flavors used to cook the pork. In this case, the dried cherries, brandy, and jelly add sweetness. As a result, a thick, soft, jammy, fruity red like Australian shiraz would be a terrific partner. Try Grant Burge "Barossa Vines" Shiraz from Australia's Barossa Valley. The 2001 is about $11.

Lager and Lemon-Grilled Chicken

Beer brings out the fresh citrusy flavor of lemon. Double this easy recipe to enjoy zesty chicken strips over mixed salad greens, in warm corn tortillas with salsa, or as the basis of a cool chicken salad.

    1   cup lager beer (such as Budweiser)
    ¼   cup fresh lemon juice
    3   tablespoons low-sodium soy sauce
    1½   tablespoons olive oil
    2   teaspoons honey
    2   teaspoons chopped fresh oregano
    1   teaspoon chopped fresh thyme
    1   teaspoon freshly ground black
         pepper
    ¼   teaspoon Worcestershire sauce
    3   garlic cloves, minced
    4   (6-ounce) skinless, boneless
         chicken breast halves
         Cooking spray

1. Combine first 10 ingredients in a large zip-top plastic bag. Add chicken; seal and marinate in refrigerator 3 hours, turning bag occasionally. Remove chicken from bag; discard marinade.
2. Prepare grill.
3. Place chicken on grill rack coated with cooking spray; grill 5 minutes on each side or until done. Yield: 4 servings (serving size: 1 chicken breast half).

CALORIES 304 (24% from fat); FAT 8.1g (sat 1.8g, mono 3.1g, poly 1.8g); PROTEIN 53g; CARB 2.1g; FIBER 0.1g; CHOL 145mg; IRON 1.9mg; SODIUM 195mg; CALC 30mg

---

What Happens to the Alcohol?

Depending on how it's cooked, at least some of the alcohol evaporates. In general, the longer alcohol comes into contact with heat, the more of it is lost during cooking. For example, a dish that is quickly flambéed, such as the New Orleans dessert bananas Foster (cooked in rum), retains 75 percent of the alcohol. In a dish that is baked or simmered for two hours or longer, 90 to 95 percent of the alcohol cooks off, while still imparting flavor to the food.

Grilled Flank Steak with Bourbon Barbecue Sauce

Allowing the meat to rest for 10 minutes lets the juices redistribute throughout the steak for richer flavor.

1½ pounds flank steak, trimmed
1 tablespoon chopped fresh rosemary
½ teaspoon freshly ground black pepper
¼ teaspoon kosher salt
Cooking spray
1 teaspoon olive oil
2 tablespoons finely chopped shallots
2 tablespoons tomato paste
½ cup less-sodium beef broth
2 teaspoons brown sugar
1 tablespoon bourbon
2 teaspoons balsamic vinegar
⅛ teaspoon salt

1. Prepare grill.
2. Sprinkle steak with rosemary, pepper, and kosher salt. Place steak on grill rack coated with cooking spray; grill 7 minutes on each side or until desired degree of doneness. Remove from grill; let stand 10 minutes. Cover and keep warm.
3. While steak rests, heat oil in a small saucepan over medium-high heat. Add shallots; sauté 1 minute. Add tomato paste; cook 1 minute. Stir in broth and sugar. Bring to a boil; cook 3 minutes or until thickened. Remove from heat; stir in bourbon, vinegar, and ⅛ teaspoon salt. Cut steak diagonally across grain into thin slices. Serve with sauce. Yield: 4 servings (serving size: 3 ounces beef and 3 tablespoons sauce).

CALORIES 310 (35% from fat); FAT 12g (sat 4.6g, mono 5g, poly 0.6g); PROTEIN 36.3g; CARB 9.7g; FIBER 0.6g; CHOL 70mg; IRON 2.9mg; SODIUM 372mg; CALC 33mg

Spirited Pairings

Depending on which type of alcohol you choose and how it's used, beer, spirits, or wine add subtle, robust, sweet, or earthy flavor to meats, poultry, and seafood. In addition to the recipes, we offer these combinations.

Spirit	Best with . . .	Cooking Tip
Lager (light, bubbly)	Fish, chicken, shrimp, lobster, bratwurst	Simmer bratwurst (or other sausages) in lager. Substitute lager for some of the chicken broth in chicken and rice dishes.
Stout (strong, dark)	Chicken, pork, beef	Add stout to pork roast (such as Boston butt) marinades before slow roasting until tender.
Brandy	Pork, beef, ham, chicken, duck	Add brandy to applesauce; cook until thickened, and serve over roasted duck or chicken.
Bourbon	Beef, lamb, buffalo, venison	Combine beef tips, bourbon, Dijon mustard, and brown sugar; bake or cook in a slow cooker.
Scotch	Pork, lobster, shrimp, scallops	Deglaze pan with scotch after sautéing scallops; finish the sauce with a touch of butter.
Irish whiskey	Veal, chicken, pork	Deglaze pan with whiskey and broth after sautéing pork chops.
Port	Pork, duck, ham, turkey	Combine port, balsamic vinegar, and apricot preserves; cook until thickened, and drizzle sauce over pork tenderloin or ham.
White wine	Chicken, fish, seafood, veal, pork	Add wine to browned chicken with capers, lemon juice, and fresh parsley.
Sherry	Pork, chicken liver, chicken	Add a splash of sherry to chicken and dumplings.

Dining Among the Leaves

Celebrate the fine flavors and scenery of the season with our two outdoor menus.

You can prepare most of the dishes well in advance and enjoy them at room temperature—meaning you can savor them at your leisure. However, our Lunch Under the Trees Menu works best for a backyard experience, where the food doesn't have to travel far from home. If you're planning a hike, quick road trip, or picnic, pack up our easily totable Autumn Picnic Menu, and enjoy it in a scenic spot along the trail.

Lunch Under the Trees Menu
serves 4

Because the pasta salad can't be made too far in advance, this menu is best for a backyard meal.

Antipasto Plate

Creamy Tomato-Balsamic Soup

Pumpkin-Walnut Focaccia with Gruyère

Cavatappi Pasta Salad with Walnut-Sage Pesto

Apple Crumb Croustades

WINE NOTE: With all the savory flavors in this alfresco menu, especially the walnut-sage pesto, this meal needs a wine that isn't shy and has bright herbal flavors of its own. Sauvignon blanc—especially one of the outrageously flavorful examples from New Zealand—hits the mark perfectly. A top choice: Lawson's Dry Hills Sauvignon Blanc 2004 from Marlborough ($13).

MAKE AHEAD
Antipasto Plate

A creamy red bell pepper dip and sweet-savory caponata spread pair with thinly sliced prosciutto from the deli and purchased crackers for an easy antipasto plate. Add fresh fruit and use an assortment of crackers, if you prefer. Both the dip and the spread can be made and refrigerated up to a day in advance; serve them chilled or at room temperature.

DIP:

- 2 tablespoons golden raisins
- 2 tablespoons balsamic vinegar
- 3 tablespoons part-skim ricotta cheese
- 2 tablespoons chopped fresh parsley
- 2 tablespoons chopped fresh basil
- 2 tablespoons ⅓-less-fat cream cheese
- ¾ teaspoon honey
- ⅛ teaspoon salt
- 1 (5½-ounce) bottle roasted red peppers, rinsed and drained

SPREAD:

- 4 plum tomatoes, quartered and seeded
- 2 garlic cloves
- 1 eggplant (about 1 pound), cubed
- ½ onion, peeled and cut into 4 wedges
- 1 teaspoon olive oil
- ⅛ teaspoon salt
- 2 tablespoons chopped fresh basil
- 2 tablespoons balsamic vinegar
- ¼ teaspoon anchovy paste

REMAINING INGREDIENTS:

- 16 water crackers
- 2 ounces very thin slices prosciutto

1. To prepare dip, combine raisins and 2 tablespoons vinegar in a microwave-safe bowl. Microwave at HIGH 45 seconds. Let stand 10 minutes; drain. Place raisins, ricotta, and next 6 ingredients in a food processor; pulse until well combined.

2. Preheat oven to 450°.

3. To prepare spread, combine tomatoes, garlic, eggplant, and onion on a foil-lined jelly-roll pan; toss gently to combine. Drizzle with oil; sprinkle with ⅛ teaspoon salt. Toss to coat. Arrange vegetables in a single layer on pan. Bake at 450° for 20 minutes or until vegetables are lightly blistered and eggplant is tender, stirring after 10 minutes. Cool slightly. Place vegetable mixture, 2 tablespoons basil, 2 tablespoons vinegar, and anchovy paste in food processor; pulse until combined. Serve dip and spread with crackers and prosciutto slices. Yield: 4 servings (serving size: 3 tablespoons dip, 3 tablespoons spread, 4 crackers, and ½ ounce prosciutto).

CALORIES 226 (30% from fat); FAT 7.5g (sat 2.5g, mono 2.9g, poly 0.6g); PROTEIN 10.2g; CARB 33.1g; FIBER 1.4g; CHOL 22mg; IRON 1.8mg; SODIUM 687mg; CALC 72mg

MAKE AHEAD
Creamy Tomato-Balsamic Soup

Cooking the vegetables at the high temperature of 500° caramelizes their natural sugars and deepens their flavor; the liquid poured over them ensures they won't burn. Prepare the soup up to two days ahead; reheat over medium heat before serving.

- 1 cup less-sodium beef broth, divided
- 1 tablespoon brown sugar
- 3 tablespoons balsamic vinegar
- 1 tablespoon low-sodium soy sauce
- 1 cup coarsely chopped onion
- 5 garlic cloves
- 2 (28-ounce) cans whole tomatoes, drained
- Cooking spray
- ¾ cup half-and-half
- Cracked black pepper (optional)

1. Preheat oven to 500°.
2. Combine ½ cup broth, sugar, vinegar, and soy sauce in a small bowl. Place onion, garlic, and tomatoes in a 13 x 9-inch baking pan coated with cooking spray. Pour broth mixture over tomato mixture. Bake at 500° for 50 minutes or until vegetables are lightly browned.
3. Place tomato mixture in a blender. Add ½ cup broth and half-and-half, and process until smooth. Strain mixture through a sieve into a bowl; discard solids. Garnish with cracked black pepper, if desired. Yield: 4 servings (serving size: about ½ cup).

CALORIES 120 (35% from fat); FAT 4.7g (sat 3g, mono 1.5g, poly 0.1g); PROTEIN 3.8g; CARB 14.9g; FIBER 1.7g; CHOL 23mg; IRON 1.7mg; SODIUM 452mg; CALC 120mg

MAKE AHEAD • FREEZABLE
Pumpkin-Walnut Focaccia with Gruyère

The recipe makes two generous free-form loaves—one to enjoy now, and one to freeze for later or give as a gift. If you're making the bread for the Chicken and Ham Sandwich with Artichoke-Tomato Spread (recipe on page 354), pat the dough into a 9-inch circle so the sandwiches will be easier to eat.

- ¾ cup warm water (100° to 110°)
- ⅓ cup packed brown sugar
- 1 package dry yeast (about 2¼ teaspoons)
- 3½ cups bread flour, divided (about 15¾ ounces)
- 3 tablespoons butter, melted
- 1 cup canned pumpkin
- 1 teaspoon salt
- ¼ teaspoon ground nutmeg
- ¾ cup (3 ounces) grated Gruyère cheese, divided
- Cooking spray
- 1 teaspoon cornmeal
- ⅓ cup coarsely chopped walnuts

1. Combine water, sugar, and yeast in a large bowl; let stand 5 minutes. Lightly spoon flour into dry measuring cups; level with a knife. Add 1 cup flour and butter to yeast mixture; stir just until combined. Cover and let rise in a warm place (85°), free from drafts, 30 minutes.
2. Add pumpkin, salt, and nutmeg to flour mixture; stir until well combined. Add 2¼ cups flour and 6 tablespoons cheese; stir until a soft dough forms. Turn dough out onto a floured surface. Knead until smooth and elastic (about 8 minutes); add enough of remaining flour, 1 tablespoon at a time, to prevent dough from sticking to hands (dough will feel tacky).
3. Place dough in a large bowl coated with cooking spray, turning to coat top. Cover and let rise in a warm place (85°), free from drafts, 1 hour or until doubled in size. (Press two fingers into dough. If indentation remains, dough has risen enough.) Punch dough down; cover and let rest 5 minutes. Divide dough in half; shape each half into an 8-inch circle. Place dough circles on a baking sheet sprinkled with cornmeal. Sprinkle 6 tablespoons cheese and nuts evenly over dough circles; press lightly to adhere. Lightly coat dough circles with cooking spray; cover and let rise 20 minutes (dough will not double in size).
4. Preheat oven to 400°.
5. Uncover dough; bake at 400° for 30 minutes or until loaves are browned on bottom and cheese melts (shield loaves with foil to prevent overbrowning, if necessary). Cool on a wire rack. Yield: 2 loaves, 8 servings each (serving size: 1 wedge).

CALORIES 169 (30% from fat); FAT 5.6g (sat 2.3g, mono 1.7g, poly 1.4g); PROTEIN 5.8g; CARB 25.6g; FIBER 1.4g; CHOL 11mg; IRON 1.7mg; SODIUM 219mg; CALC 65mg

> You can prepare most of these dishes well in advance and enjoy them at room temperature.

Cavatappi Pasta Salad with Walnut-Sage Pesto

The flavorful pesto clings to the corkscrew-shaped pasta. Any small pasta, such as farfalle, penne, or seashell, would also work well. The pesto sauce darkens upon standing, so try to serve the salad shortly after tossing the ingredients.

- 2½ cups (½-inch) cubed peeled butternut squash
- Cooking spray
- ¾ teaspoon salt, divided
- ½ cup fresh flat-leaf parsley leaves
- 2½ tablespoons chopped walnuts
- 2 tablespoons fresh sage leaves
- 2 tablespoons fresh lemon juice
- 2 tablespoons extravirgin olive oil
- 1 garlic clove
- ⅓ cup fat-free, less-sodium chicken broth
- 3 cups cooked cavatappi pasta (about 6 ounces uncooked)
- 4 cups torn arugula
- ¼ cup thinly sliced shallots
- ½ teaspoon freshly ground black pepper

1. Preheat oven to 450°.
2. Arrange squash in a single layer on a jelly-roll pan coated with cooking spray. Lightly coat squash with cooking spray; sprinkle evenly with ¼ teaspoon salt. Bake at 450° for 20 minutes or until squash is tender, stirring after 10 minutes. Cool squash slightly.
3. Place ¼ teaspoon salt, parsley, and next 5 ingredients in a food processor; process until finely chopped, scraping sides. With processor on, slowly pour broth through food chute, processing until well blended.
4. Combine ¼ teaspoon salt, squash, pesto, and pasta in a large bowl, and toss well to coat. Add arugula, shallots, and pepper; toss to combine. Serve immediately. Yield: 4 servings (serving size: 2 cups).

CALORIES 325 (30% from fat); FAT 10.9g (sat 1.4g, mono 5.5g, poly 3.3g); PROTEIN 8.5g; CARB 51.8g; FIBER 5.5g; CHOL 0mg; IRON 2.8mg; SODIUM 493mg; CALC 140mg

Apple Crumb Croustades

This is a romantic dessert because two people share each free-form tart. You can cut them in half and serve on two plates, or just dig into one with two forks.

CRUST:

- 1 cup all-purpose flour (about 4½ ounces)
- ⅛ teaspoon salt
- 3 tablespoons chilled butter, cut into small pieces
- 3½ tablespoons ice water

FILLING:

- 2 cups chopped peeled Granny Smith apple (about 2 medium)
- 1½ tablespoons fresh lemon juice
- ¼ cup packed brown sugar
- 1 tablespoon all-purpose flour
- ⅛ teaspoon salt
- ⅛ teaspoon ground cinnamon
- 1 tablespoon water
- 1 large egg white, lightly beaten

TOPPING:

- 2 tablespoons all-purpose flour
- 1 tablespoon brown sugar
- ⅛ teaspoon salt
- ⅛ teaspoon ground cinnamon
- 1½ teaspoons chilled butter, cut into small pieces

1. To prepare crust, lightly spoon 1 cup flour into a dry measuring cup; level with a knife. Combine 1 cup flour and ⅛ teaspoon salt in a medium bowl; cut in 3 tablespoons butter with a pastry blender or 2 knives until mixture resembles coarse meal. Add ice water; stir just until moist. Turn dough out onto a heavily floured surface; knead lightly 5 times. Divide dough into 2 equal portions. Place each dough portion between 2 sheets of plastic wrap; roll each dough portion, still covered, into an 8-inch circle. Chill 10 minutes. Uncover dough; place dough circles on a baking sheet lined with parchment paper.
2. Preheat oven to 350°.
3. To prepare filling, combine apple and juice; toss to coat. Add ¼ cup sugar and next 3 ingredients; toss to combine.

Place half of apple mixture in center of each dough circle, leaving 2-inch borders; fold edges of dough toward center, pressing gently to seal (dough will only partially cover apple mixture). Combine 1 tablespoon water and egg white; brush mixture gently over outside of crust.
4. To prepare topping, combine 2 tablespoons flour and next 3 ingredients; cut in 1½ teaspoons butter with a pastry blender or 2 knives until mixture resembles coarse meal. Sprinkle mixture evenly over apple mixture in center of each croustade. Bake at 350° for 45 minutes or until golden. Yield: 4 servings (serving size: ½ croustade).

CALORIES 320 (29% from fat); FAT 10.4g (sat 5.1g, mono 4.1g, poly 0.5g); PROTEIN 5g; CARB 52.7g; FIBER 1.8g; CHOL 26mg; IRON 2.2mg; SODIUM 313mg; CALC 29mg

Autumn Picnic Menu
serves 4

Take the soup in a thermos to ensure it stays warm. Bring extra fig bars—you'll be sorry if you don't.

Creamy Tomato-Balsamic Soup

Marinated Chickpeas

Chicken and Ham Sandwich with Artichoke-Tomato Spread

Fig and Cream Cheese Bars

Marinated Chickpeas

This zesty side dish holds up well for two or three days. Try tossing leftovers with penne or rigatoni for a main-dish pasta salad.

- ¼ cup chopped fresh flat-leaf parsley
- ¼ cup kalamata olives, pitted and coarsely chopped
- ¼ cup pickled banana peppers, coarsely chopped
- ¼ cup (1 ounce) crumbled feta cheese
- 2 teaspoons chopped fresh chives
- 1 teaspoon chopped fresh rosemary
- 2 (15-ounce) cans chickpeas, rinsed and drained
- 3 tablespoons fresh lemon juice
- 1 tablespoon extravirgin olive oil
- 2 garlic cloves, minced

1. Combine first 7 ingredients in a medium bowl. Combine juice, oil, and garlic, stirring with a whisk. Drizzle over bean mixture; toss to coat. Chill at least 1 hour. Yield: 6 servings (serving size: ½ cup).

CALORIES 162 (30% from fat); FAT 5.4g (sat 1.2g, mono 2.9g, poly 0.9g); PROTEIN 5.6g; CARB 23.7g; FIBER 4.4g; CHOL 4mg; IRON 1.6mg; SODIUM 305mg; CALC 63mg

Chicken and Ham Sandwich with Artichoke-Tomato Spread

This recipe yields more sandwiches than you'll need, but you'll be glad for the leftovers. Wrap the two extra sandwich wedges in plastic wrap, and refrigerate up to one day. Remember to pat the focaccia dough out into a larger, thinner circle so the bread won't be too thick.

- ¼ cup chopped drained oil-packed sun-dried tomato halves
- 1 garlic clove
- ½ (14-ounce) can quartered artichoke hearts, drained
- 1 loaf Pumpkin-Walnut Focaccia with Gruyère (recipe on page 353), cut in half horizontally
- 4 ounces chopped roasted skinless, boneless rotisserie chicken breast
- 4 ounces thinly sliced 33%-less-sodium ham (about ⅛ inch thick)
- 2 cups trimmed arugula

1. Place first 3 ingredients in a food processor; process until smooth. Spread mixture on bottom half of Pumpkin-Walnut Focaccia with Gruyère; top with chicken, ham, and arugula. Place top half of bread on sandwich. Cut sandwich into 6 wedges. Yield: 6 servings (serving size: 1 wedge).

CALORIES 315 (29% from fat); FAT 10.3g (sat 3.8g, mono 3.6g, poly 2.3g); PROTEIN 19.3g; CARB 38.5g; FIBER 3.2g; CHOL 42mg; IRON 3.1mg; SODIUM 649mg; CALC 115mg

Fig and Cream Cheese Bars

With the honeyed flavor of dried figs, a sweet cream cheese layer, and a buttery, crumbly crust, these bars garnered our Test Kitchens' highest rating. Store leftovers in an airtight container in the refrigerator up to five days.

1⅓ cups all-purpose flour (about 6 ounces)
 ¾ cup packed brown sugar
 ½ teaspoon salt
  6 tablespoons chilled butter, cut into small pieces
Cooking spray
  2 cups dried figs, stems removed
  1 cup water
 ½ cup granulated sugar, divided
  3 tablespoons fresh lemon juice
 ¾ cup (6 ounces) ⅓-less-fat cream cheese, softened
  1 teaspoon vanilla extract
  1 large egg
  2 teaspoons powdered sugar

1. Preheat oven to 350°.
2. Lightly spoon flour into dry measuring cups; level with a knife. Combine flour, brown sugar, and salt, stirring well with a whisk. Cut in butter with a pastry blender or 2 knives until mixture resembles coarse meal. Press mixture firmly into a 13 x 9-inch baking dish coated with cooking spray.
3. Combine figs, water, and ¼ cup granulated sugar in a medium saucepan; bring to a boil over medium-high heat. Cook 5 minutes or until figs are tender and sugar dissolves. Cool slightly. Place fig mixture and juice in a blender; process until smooth. Gently spread fig mixture over prepared crust.
4. Place ¼ cup granulated sugar, cheese, vanilla, and egg in a medium bowl; beat with a mixer at medium speed until smooth. Pour over fig mixture; spread to edges. Bake at 350° for 30 minutes or until set and lightly browned. Cool in pan on a wire rack; sprinkle with powdered sugar. Yield: 30 servings (serving size: 1 bar).

CALORIES 125 (28% from fat); FAT 3.9g (sat 2.1g, mono 1.4g, poly 0.2g); PROTEIN 1.8g; CARB 21.7g; FIBER 1.5g; CHOL 17mg; IRON 0.7mg; SODIUM 84mg; CALC 33mg

sidetracked

Cool-Weather Salads

Starring full-flavored fresh produce, these crisp-tasting sides are a great match for hearty entrées.

Fennel, Parsley, and Radicchio Salad with Pine Nuts and Raisins

Pale fennel, dark green parsley, and magenta radicchio glisten with the citrusy vinaigrette. Serve with Butternut Squash Soup with Toasted Walnuts (recipe on page 327).

 ⅓ cup golden raisins
  4 cups thinly sliced fennel bulb (about 1 large bulb)
  4 cups torn radicchio (about 1 medium head)
1½ cups loosely packed fresh flat-leaf parsley leaves
 ¼ cup fresh orange juice
1½ tablespoons red wine vinegar
  2 teaspoons extravirgin olive oil
 ½ teaspoon salt
 ¼ teaspoon freshly ground black pepper
  2 tablespoons pine nuts, toasted

1. Place raisins in a small saucepan, and cover with water. Bring to a boil; remove from heat. Cover and let stand 10 minutes. Drain well.
2. Place fennel, radicchio, and parsley in a large bowl, and toss gently to combine. Combine orange juice and next 4 ingredients, stirring well with a whisk. Stir in raisins. Drizzle orange juice mixture over fennel mixture, and toss gently to coat. Arrange 1⅓ cups salad on each of 6 plates; sprinkle each serving with 1 teaspoon nuts. Yield: 6 servings.

CALORIES 91 (38% from fat); FAT 3.8g (sat 0.4g, mono 1.7g, poly 1.2g); PROTEIN 2.3g; CARB 14.3g; FIBER 3g; CHOL 0mg; IRON 1.9mg; SODIUM 243mg; CALC 61mg

Spinach and Goat Cheese Salad with Frizzled Prosciutto

  2 thin slices prosciutto, cut into ½-inch strips (about ¼ cup)
2½ tablespoons balsamic vinegar
  1 teaspoon extravirgin olive oil
 ¼ teaspoon salt
 ¼ teaspoon freshly ground black pepper
  1 (10-ounce) package fresh spinach (about 10 cups)
 ½ cup (2 ounces) crumbled goat cheese

1. Preheat oven to 400°.
2. Arrange prosciutto in a single layer on a baking sheet. Bake at 400° for 6 minutes or until crisp. Cool completely.
3. Combine vinegar, oil, salt, and pepper, stirring with a whisk. Combine prosciutto and spinach in a large bowl. Drizzle vinegar mixture over spinach mixture; toss gently to combine. Sprinkle with goat cheese. Serve immediately. Yield: 8 servings (serving size: about 1¼ cups salad and about 1 tablespoon cheese).

CALORIES 42 (54% from fat); FAT 2.5g (sat 1.2g, mono 0.9g, poly 0.2g); PROTEIN 3.2g; CARB 2.1g; FIBER 0.8g; CHOL 5mg; IRON 1.2mg; SODIUM 182mg; CALC 47mg

Roasted Squash Salad with Bacon and Pumpkinseeds

  4 cups (½-inch) cubed peeled butternut squash (about 1 pound)
Cooking spray
 ½ teaspoon salt, divided
 ½ teaspoon freshly ground black pepper, divided
  2 tablespoons sherry vinegar
  1 teaspoon Dijon mustard
  1 bacon slice
  1 shallot, minced
 10 cups gourmet salad greens (about 10 ounces)
  3 tablespoons unsalted pumpkinseed kernels, toasted

1. Preheat oven to 400°.

Continued

2. Arrange squash in a single layer on a jelly-roll pan coated with cooking spray. Coat squash with cooking spray; sprinkle evenly with ¼ teaspoon salt and ¼ teaspoon pepper. Bake at 400° for 30 minutes or until squash is tender and lightly browned, stirring after 15 minutes. Remove from heat; keep warm.

3. Combine ¼ teaspoon salt, ¼ teaspoon pepper, vinegar, and mustard.

4. Cook bacon in a small nonstick skillet over medium-high heat until crisp. Remove bacon from pan, reserving 1 teaspoon drippings in pan. Crumble bacon; set aside. Add shallot to drippings in pan; sauté 1 minute. Add shallot and bacon to vinegar mixture, stirring with a whisk.

5. Place salad greens in a large bowl. Drizzle vinegar mixture over greens; toss gently to coat. Arrange about 1⅓ cups salad on each of 6 plates. Top each serving with ⅔ cup squash and 1½ teaspoons pumpkinseed kernels. Yield: 6 servings.

CALORIES 130 (25% from fat); FAT 3.6g (sat 0.9g, mono 0.9g, poly 1.2g); PROTEIN 4.8g; CARB 23.8g; FIBER 5.5g; CHOL 2mg; IRON 3.2mg; SODIUM 275mg; CALC 134mg

Roasted Potato Salad with Peppers and Parmesan

2 pounds small red potatoes, quartered
1 tablespoon extravirgin olive oil, divided
½ teaspoon salt, divided
¼ teaspoon freshly ground black pepper
1 cup finely chopped bottled roasted red bell peppers
½ cup thinly sliced green onions
¼ cup chopped fresh cilantro
2 tablespoons minced seeded jalapeño pepper (about 1 pepper)
2 teaspoons chopped fresh oregano
2 garlic cloves, minced
½ teaspoon ground cumin
⅛ teaspoon freshly ground black pepper
¾ cup (3 ounces) shaved Parmigiano-Reggiano cheese

1. Preheat oven to 375°.

2. Place potatoes in a 13 x 9-inch baking dish. Drizzle with 1 teaspoon oil; sprinkle with ¼ teaspoon salt and ¼ teaspoon black pepper. Toss well to coat. Cover and bake at 375° for 30 minutes. Uncover and bake an additional 30 minutes or until tender, stirring occasionally. Remove from oven; place potatoes in a large bowl. Add bell peppers and next 5 ingredients; toss well.

3. Combine 2 teaspoons oil, ¼ teaspoon salt, cumin, and ⅛ teaspoon black pepper, stirring with a whisk. Drizzle dressing over potato mixture, and toss gently to coat. Sprinkle with cheese. Yield: 6 servings (serving size: about ⅔ cup salad and 2 tablespoons cheese).

CALORIES 202 (29% from fat); FAT 6.4g (sat 2.7g, mono 2.8g, poly 0.5g); PROTEIN 8.5g; CARB 27.6g; FIBER 3.3g; CHOL 10mg; IRON 1.6mg; SODIUM 552mg; CALC 194mg

Autumn Apple, Pear, and Cheddar Salad with Pecans

1 cup apple juice
2 tablespoons cider vinegar
1 teaspoon extravirgin olive oil
½ teaspoon salt
¼ teaspoon freshly ground black pepper
10 cups gourmet salad greens (about 10 ounces)
1 cup seedless red grapes, halved
1 McIntosh apple, cored and cut into 18 wedges
1 Bartlett pear, cored and cut into 18 wedges
¼ cup (1 ounce) finely shredded sharp Cheddar cheese
3 tablespoons chopped pecans, toasted

1. Place apple juice in a small saucepan, and bring to a boil over medium-high heat. Cook until reduced to about 3 tablespoons (about 10 minutes). Combine reduced apple juice, vinegar, oil, salt, and pepper, stirring with a whisk.

2. Combine greens, grapes, apple, and pear in a large bowl. Drizzle with apple juice mixture; toss gently to coat. Sprinkle with cheese and nuts. Yield: 6

servings (serving size: about 1⅔ cups salad, 2 teaspoons cheese, and 1½ teaspoons nuts).

CALORIES 134 (36% from fat); FAT 5.4g (sat 1.2g, mono 2.6g, poly 1.1g); PROTEIN 3.4g; CARB 21.1g; FIBER 4.1g; CHOL 5mg; IRON 1.5mg; SODIUM 255mg; CALC 93mg

Arugula Salad with Port-Cooked Pears and Roquefort Cheese

2 Bartlett pears, peeled, cored and quartered
Cooking spray
½ cup port or other sweet red wine
1 teaspoon sugar
1 tablespoon white wine vinegar
1 teaspoon walnut oil
¼ teaspoon salt
¼ teaspoon freshly ground black pepper
8 cups trimmed arugula (about 8 ounces)
2 cups (½-inch) slices Belgian endive (about ½ pound)
¼ cup (1 ounce) crumbled Roquefort or other blue cheese
2 tablespoons chopped walnuts, toasted

1. Preheat oven to 400°.

2. Arrange pears in a 13 x 9-inch baking dish coated with cooking spray; drizzle with port. Sprinkle evenly with sugar. Cover and bake at 400° for 10 minutes. Uncover and bake an additional 15 minutes or until pears are almost tender. Cool completely; reserve 1 tablespoon liquid from dish. Thinly slice pears; set aside. Combine reserved 1 tablespoon liquid, vinegar, oil, salt, and pepper, stirring with a whisk.

3. Combine sliced pears, arugula, and endive in a large bowl. Drizzle vinegar mixture over arugula mixture; toss gently to coat. Arrange about 1⅓ cups salad on each of 8 plates. Sprinkle each serving with 1½ teaspoons cheese and ¾ teaspoon nuts. Yield: 8 servings.

CALORIES 88 (31% from fat); FAT 3g (sat 0.9g, mono 0.6g, poly 1.4g); PROTEIN 2g; CARB 11g; FIBER 2.5g; CHOL 3mg; IRON 0.6mg; SODIUM 131mg; CALC 62mg

Chef's Table

Dining in the restaurant kitchen of a well-known chef provides a great meal—and a unique way to learn.

What goes on behind most restaurants' kitchen doors remains a happily unsolved mystery for most diners, unless they have to wait a long time for their food or their steak is overdone.

But sitting at the chef's table—a special table often tucked into a corner of the kitchen—means that diners are in for more than just a good meal. They're in the middle of the action where they can hear meat sizzling on the grill, see waiters rushing back and forth with hot plates, and hear the chef shouting instructions to the cooks.

At Cantina in San Diego, visitors to Chef Isabel Cruz's kitchen table are in for more than culinary entertainment. Whether it's a birthday celebration or a girls'-night-out dinner, Cruz's kitchen-table dinners usually turn into classes on her style of healthy Latin- and Asian-influenced cuisine. Here are some examples of what Cruz "teaches" in her kitchen.

Grilled Tuna with Chipotle Ponzu and Avocado Salsa

This recipe is a great example of how bold Asian and Latin flavors work well together. Orange and lime juice substitute for rice vinegar, the acidic ingredient typically used in a Japanese ponzu dipping sauce. It gets a kick from the hot, smoky chipotle chiles. You can also try the ponzu with chicken.

PONZU:
- ½ cup orange juice
- ½ cup lime juice
- ¼ cup grated onion
- ¼ cup low-sodium soy sauce
- 1 tablespoon chopped peeled fresh ginger
- 1½ chipotle chiles in adobo sauce

SALSA:
- ¾ cup diced English cucumber
- ½ cup diced plum tomato
- ½ cup diced peeled avocado
- ¼ cup chopped fresh cilantro

REMAINING INGREDIENTS:
- 4 (6-ounce) tuna steaks
- ¼ teaspoon salt
- Cooking spray
- 2 cups hot cooked medium-grain rice

1. To prepare ponzu, place first 6 ingredients in a blender, and process until smooth.

2. To prepare salsa, combine cucumber, tomato, avocado, and cilantro in a small bowl.

3. Sprinkle fish with salt. Heat a large nonstick grill pan over medium-high heat. Coat pan with cooking spray. Add fish; cook 3 minutes on each side or until desired degree of doneness. Cut each tuna steak diagonally across grain into thin slices. Arrange sliced tuna over rice; top with salsa, and drizzle with ponzu. Yield: 4 servings (serving size: 1 tuna steak, ½ cup rice, ½ cup salsa, and about ⅓ cup ponzu).

CALORIES 447 (26% from fat); FAT 12.6g (sat 2.8g, mono 5.2g, poly 3.1g); PROTEIN 44g; CARB 37.8g; FIBER 2.5g; CHOL 64mg; IRON 3.9mg; SODIUM 606mg; CALC 34mg

Vegetable and Tofu Lettuce Wraps with Miso Sambal

In this appetizer, the fresh flavors of the vegetables come alive with the spicy, gingery sambal. This popular Indonesian condiment takes on many variations of the basic combination of chiles, brown sugar, and salt. Prepare a double batch, and serve the extra with fish. The creamy texture of the avocado and tofu slices are a pleasant contrast to the crisp vegetables.

MISO SAMBAL:
- 2 tablespoons chile paste with garlic (such as Sambal oelek)
- 2 tablespoons chopped peeled fresh ginger
- 2 tablespoons white miso (soybean paste)
- 2 tablespoons rice wine vinegar
- 1½ tablespoons sugar
- 1½ teaspoons dark sesame oil

WRAPS:
- 1 cup matchstick-cut English cucumber
- ½ cup cilantro sprigs
- 2 tablespoons chopped dry-roasted peanuts
- 1 (12.3-ounce) package reduced-fat firm tofu, drained and cut into ½-inch-thick strips
- ½ avocado, peeled and thinly sliced
- 12 large Boston lettuce leaves

1. To prepare miso sambal, place first 6 ingredients in a blender, and process until smooth.

2. To prepare wraps, divide cucumber, cilantro, peanuts, tofu, and avocado evenly among lettuce leaves. Drizzle each with about 1½ teaspoons sambal; roll up. Yield: 6 servings (serving size: 2 wraps).

CALORIES 106 (51% from fat); FAT 6g (sat 0.9g, mono 2.9g, poly 1.5g); PROTEIN 5.5g; CARB 8.5g; FIBER 1.5g; CHOL 0mg; IRON 1.1mg; SODIUM 261mg; CALC 27mg

Vietnamese Grilled Steak with Portobellos and Mint-Cilantro Mojo

A hint of nutmeg in the sauce reflects the French influence in Vietnamese cooking. Combining mint with cilantro adds a refreshing element to the mojo, a Caribbean condiment consisting of garlic, citrus juice, and oil. It would also be good with grilled or roasted lamb. Steamed green beans make a colorful side on the plate.

SAUCE:
- ¼ cup chopped green onions
- ¼ cup low-sodium soy sauce
- 1½ tablespoons chopped peeled fresh ginger
- 1 tablespoon brown sugar
- 1 tablespoon dark sesame oil
- 1 tablespoon honey
- ⅛ teaspoon ground nutmeg
- 1 garlic clove

MOJO:
- ½ cup cilantro leaves
- ½ cup mint leaves
- 3 tablespoons water
- 1 tablespoon olive oil
- 1 tablespoon fresh lemon juice
- 1 garlic clove

REMAINING INGREDIENTS:
- 2 portobello mushroom caps (about 4 ounces)
- 1 pound green beans, trimmed
- Cooking spray
- 1 (1-pound) boneless beef shoulder steak

1. To prepare sauce, place first 8 ingredients in a food processor; process until smooth. Place in a small bowl.
2. To prepare mojo, place cilantro and next 5 ingredients in a food processor; process until smooth. Place in a small bowl.
3. Remove brown gills from undersides of mushrooms using a spoon; discard gills. Cut each mushroom into 6 slices; set aside.
4. Steam green beans 3 minutes or until tender; keep warm.
5. Heat a nonstick grill pan over medium-high heat. Coat pan with cooking spray. Add steak; cook 2 minutes on each side or until browned. Remove from pan; cut steak diagonally across grain into thin slices. Toss mushrooms with half of soy mixture; add to pan. Stir-fry 1 minute; remove from pan. Return steak to pan; cook 2 minutes or until desired degree of doneness. Drizzle steak with remaining soy mixture. Arrange steak, mushrooms, and green beans on serving plates. Serve with mojo. Yield: 4 servings (serving size: 3 ounces steak, 3 mushroom slices, 1 cup green beans, and about 1 tablespoon mojo).

CALORIES 364 (41% from fat); FAT 16.6g (sat 4.9g, mono 7.6g, poly 2.2g); PROTEIN 35.6g; CARB 18.9g; FIBER 4.5g; CHOL 62mg; IRON 4.2mg; SODIUM 608mg; CALC 84mg

Asian Marinated Salmon

This basic marinade is also tasty with chicken, tofu, or beef.

- ½ cup mirin (sweet rice wine)
- ⅓ cup white miso (soybean paste)
- 2 tablespoons dark sesame oil
- 2 tablespoons honey
- 4 (6-ounce) salmon fillets (about 1 inch thick)
- Cooking spray

1. Combine first 4 ingredients in a large zip-top plastic bag. Add fish; seal and marinate in refrigerator 2 hours, turning bag occasionally.
2. Prepare grill.
3. Remove fish from bag; discard marinade. Place fish on grill rack coated with cooking spray; grill 3½ minutes on each side or until fish flakes easily when tested with a fork or until desired degree of doneness. Yield: 4 servings (serving size: 1 fillet).

CALORIES 285 (40% from fat); FAT 12.8g (sat 2.8g, mono 5.4g, poly 3.5g); PROTEIN 32.1g; CARB 6.9g; FIBER 0.5g; CHOL 80mg; IRON 0.8mg; SODIUM 380mg; CALC 22mg

QUICK & EASY • MAKE AHEAD
Guava Sauce

Try this sauce as a salad dressing or as a marinade for pork, chicken, or fish. Guava paste is about an inch-thick block wrapped in cellophane in a 16-ounce package. It's sold in Latin markets and large supermarkets. Store any unused product in the refrigerator because it's easier to cut when chilled.

- ⅔ cup water
- ¼ cup minced shallots
- 3 ounces (about ⅓ cup) commercial guava paste, cut into cubes
- ¼ cup rice vinegar
- 1 teaspoon dark sesame oil

1. Combine first 3 ingredients in a small saucepan. Place over medium heat; cook 5 minutes or until guava paste dissolves, stirring frequently. Remove from heat. Add vinegar and oil, stirring with a whisk until blended. Store in an airtight container in refrigerator up to 1 week. Yield: about ¾ cup (serving size: 1 tablespoon).

CALORIES 19 (19% from fat); FAT 0.4g (sat 0.1g, mono 0.2g, poly 0.2g); PROTEIN 0.1g; CARB 4g; FIBER 0g; CHOL 0mg; IRON 0mg; SODIUM 1mg; CALC 1mg

Chicken with Mango Salsa, Edamame, and Coconut Rice

The sauce and salsa are versatile and go well with shrimp, pork, or salmon.

SAUCE:
    2 tablespoons low-sodium soy sauce
    ¾ teaspoon grated lime rind
    4 teaspoons fresh lime juice
    1 tablespoon chopped green onions
    1 tablespoon chopped fresh cilantro
    2 teaspoons chopped peeled fresh ginger
  1½ teaspoons brown sugar
  1½ teaspoons dark sesame oil
  1½ teaspoons honey
    1 garlic clove, minced

SALSA:
    1 cup cubed peeled ripe mango
    ¼ cup diced red onion
    ¼ cup chopped fresh mint
  1½ tablespoons finely chopped seeded jalapeño pepper

COCONUT RICE:
    1 cup uncooked basmati rice
    ¼ cup sweetened coconut, toasted
    ¼ teaspoon salt
    1 (13.5-ounce) can light coconut milk

REMAINING INGREDIENTS:
    1 cup frozen shelled edamame (green soybeans)
       Cooking spray
    4 (6-ounce) skinless, boneless chicken breast halves

1. To prepare sauce, place first 10 ingredients in a blender; process until well combined. Set aside.

2. To prepare salsa, combine mango, red onion, mint, and jalapeño in a medium bowl, tossing to combine.

3. To prepare coconut rice, combine rice, coconut, salt, and coconut milk in a medium saucepan; bring to a boil over medium-high heat, stirring once. Cover, reduce heat, and simmer 15 minutes or until liquid is absorbed. Remove from heat; cover and let stand 10 minutes. Fluff with a fork; keep warm.

4. Cook edamame according to package directions, omitting salt and fat. Keep warm.

5. Heat a large nonstick skillet over medium-high heat. Coat pan with cooking spray. Add chicken; cook 3 minutes on each side or until browned. Remove from heat, and cut chicken into ¼-inch slices. Combine chicken and sauce in pan; cook 3 minutes or until done. Serve over rice; top with edamame and salsa. Yield: 4 servings (serving size: 1 chicken breast half, ½ cup rice, ¼ cup edamame, and ⅓ cup salsa).

CALORIES 562 (19% from fat); FAT 11.6g (sat 6.5g, mono 1.4g, poly 1.4g); PROTEIN 50.2g; CARB 64.1g; FIBER 2.9g; CHOL 99mg; IRON 5.7mg; SODIUM 603mg; CALC 105mg

Potato, Chicken, and Coconut Soup

Fish sauce, lemongrass, and chile paste lend this Latin dish Asian flair.

    5 cups water
    2 cups chopped peeled baking potato
    1 cup chopped onion
    1 cup chopped celery
    1 cup chopped carrot
    2 tablespoons minced peeled fresh ginger
    ½ teaspoon salt
    2 (5-inch) stalks lemongrass, cut in half lengthwise
    3 garlic cloves, minced
    2 cups shredded cooked chicken breast (about 2 breasts)
    3 tablespoons chopped fresh cilantro
    4 teaspoons fish sauce
    1 tablespoon fresh lime juice
    ½ teaspoon chile paste with garlic (such as Sambal oelek)
    1 (13.5-ounce) can light coconut milk

1. Combine first 9 ingredients in a large saucepan; bring to a boil. Reduce heat; simmer 25 minutes or until vegetables are tender. Discard lemongrass. Cool slightly. Pour 2 cups potato mixture into a blender; process until smooth. Pour into a bowl. Repeat procedure with 2 cups potato mixture. Return puréed mixture to pan. Stir in chicken and remaining ingredients; cook over medium heat 5 minutes or until thoroughly heated. Yield: 6 servings (serving size: 1⅓ cups).

CALORIES 191 (23% from fat); FAT 4.9g (sat 3.3g, mono 0.6g, poly 0.4g); PROTEIN 17.3g; CARB 20.5g; FIBER 1.9g; CHOL 40mg; IRON 1.2mg; SODIUM 581mg; CALC 31mg

MAKE AHEAD
Espresso Cream Cake with Chile-Chocolate Sauce

Mocha beverages are popular at Isabel Cruz's restaurants. The addition of a chile pepper to one of her chocolate-coffee concoctions was the inspiration for this chocolate sauce. It has just a little heat and could also be served over vanilla ice cream. She added the espresso cream "to give you something creamy to drag a bite of your cake through." Strong brewed coffee can substitute for the brewed espresso, if you don't have an espresso machine. Instant coffee will work in a pinch for the finely ground espresso.

CAKE:
  1⅓ cups sifted cake flour (about 5⅓ ounces)
  1¼ cups sugar, divided
    6 large eggs, separated
    3 tablespoons brewed espresso, cooled
  1½ teaspoons finely ground espresso
    ½ teaspoon vanilla extract
    ¼ teaspoon salt
    ¾ teaspoon cream of tartar

ESPRESSO CREAM:
    ½ cup firm silken tofu (about ½ [12.3-ounce] package)
    6 tablespoons fat-free sweetened condensed milk
    ¼ cup brewed espresso, cooled

Continued

CHOCOLATE SAUCE:

¼ cup (2 ounces) bittersweet chocolate
2 tablespoons fat-free milk
¼ teaspoon ancho chile powder

1. Preheat oven to 350°.
2. To prepare cake, sift together flour and 3 tablespoons sugar; set aside.
3. Combine 1 cup sugar and egg yolks in a large bowl; beat with a mixer at high speed 5 minutes or until thick and pale. Combine 3 tablespoons brewed espresso, ground espresso, vanilla, and salt in a small bowl; add to egg yolk mixture, beating at low speed until blended. Sift flour mixture evenly over egg yolk mixture; stir just until moist.
4. Beat egg whites with a mixer at high speed until foamy using clean, dry beaters. Add cream of tartar; beat until soft peaks form. Slowly add 1 tablespoon sugar, beating until stiff peaks form. Gently stir one-fourth of egg white mixture into batter; gently fold remaining egg white mixture into batter.
5. Pour batter into a 9-inch springform pan. Bake at 350° for 40 minutes or until cake springs back when touched lightly in center. Cool in pan 1 hour; run a knife around outside edge; remove sides of pan. Cool completely on a wire rack.
6. To prepare espresso cream, place tofu, condensed milk, and ¼ cup brewed espresso in a blender; process until smooth. Chill.
7. To prepare chocolate sauce, combine chocolate and fat-free milk in a 1-cup glass measure; microwave at HIGH 1 minute or until chocolate is almost melted. Add chile powder, stirring until smooth. Spoon espresso cream onto dessert plates, spreading evenly. Drizzle chocolate sauce in center of espresso cream; top with cake slices. Yield: 12 servings (serving size: 1 cake slice, about 1½ tablespoons espresso cream, and about 2½ teaspoons chocolate sauce).

CALORIES 220 (19% from fat); FAT 4.7g (sat 1.6g, mono 1.1g, poly 0.4g); PROTEIN 6.6g; CARB 38.4g; FIBER 0.5g; CHOL 108mg; IRON 1.4mg; SODIUM 95mg; CALC 52mg

Three Family Favorites

Cooking Light shows three readers how to lighten dishes just in time for the holidays.

Pumpkin Pie Cake

Evangeline "Vange" Millard of Dunedin, Florida, has been baking Pumpkin Pie Cake since the mid-1980s, after she and her husband threw a party where a friend brought the cake. These days, "I bake the cake either for Thanksgiving or Christmas and for my daughter's birthday," Vange says. But Vange was interested in a lightened version.

We started by cutting back on the oil and the eggs. By using ¼ cup oil and two eggs, plus ½ cup egg substitute for some of the whole eggs, we eliminated almost 11 grams of fat per serving in the cake layers. For the frosting, we used butter instead of margarine because it tastes better, but only used 2 tablespoons combined with one eight-ounce package of ⅓-less-fat cream cheese to create the smooth frosting. This reduced the fat in the frosting by almost 6 grams per serving without sacrificing creaminess. Canned pumpkin adds moisture and body to the cake, so the lighter version tastes just as rich and decadent as the original. Sugar makes cake layers tender in addition to adding sweetness, so we kept 1 cup of granulated sugar and added ½ cup of brown sugar, producing a deeper color. For deeper flavor, we substituted pumpkin-pie spice for cinnamon.

Pumpkin Pie Cake

(pictured on page 377)

If you like pumpkin pie, you'll love this cake's subtle spice flavors and velvety cream cheese frosting. Pumpkin-pie spice is a combination of warm spices: cinnamon, ginger, nutmeg, allspice, cloves, and mace. Use it to enliven applesauce, vanilla ice cream, or tea.

CAKE:

Cooking spray
2 tablespoons all-purpose flour
1 cup granulated sugar
½ cup packed brown sugar
¼ cup canola oil
½ cup egg substitute
2 large eggs
1 (15-ounce) can unsweetened pumpkin
2 cups all-purpose flour (about 9 ounces)
2 teaspoons pumpkin-pie spice
1 teaspoon baking powder
1 teaspoon baking soda
½ teaspoon salt

FROSTING:

2 tablespoons butter, softened
1 (8-ounce) block ⅓-less-fat cream cheese
3 cups powdered sugar
2 teaspoons fresh orange juice
¼ cup chopped pecans, toasted
Orange slices (optional)

1. Preheat oven to 350°.
2. To prepare cake, coat 2 (8-inch) round cake pans with cooking spray. Dust pans evenly with 2 tablespoons flour.
3. Combine granulated sugar, brown sugar, and oil in a large bowl; beat with a mixer at medium speed 2 minutes or until well blended. Add egg substitute and eggs; beat until well blended. Add pumpkin, beating until blended.
4. Lightly spoon 2 cups flour into dry measuring cups; level with a knife. Combine 2 cups flour and next 4 ingredients in a medium bowl. Gradually add flour mixture to pumpkin mixture, beating just until blended. Spoon batter into prepared pans. Bake at 350° for 30

minutes or until a wooden pick inserted in center comes out clean. Cool in pans 10 minutes on a wire rack. Remove cake from pans; cool completely on wire rack.

5. To prepare frosting, beat butter and cream cheese at medium speed until creamy. Gradually add powdered sugar, beating until blended (do not overbeat). Add juice, stirring until blended.

6. Place 1 cake layer on a serving plate. Spread 1 cup frosting over layer, and top with remaining cake layer. Spread remaining frosting over top of cake. Sprinkle with pecans, and garnish with orange slices, if desired. Yield: 16 servings (serving size: 1 slice).

CALORIES 318 (30% from fat); FAT 10.6g (sat 3.5g, mono 3.8g, poly 1.8g); PROTEIN 5.2g; CARB 51.8g; FIBER 1.4g; CHOL 40mg; IRON 1.6mg; SODIUM 284mg; CALC 42mg

BEFORE	AFTER
SERVING SIZE	
1 slice	
CALORIES PER SERVING	
541	318
FAT	
28.9g	10.6g
PERCENT OF TOTAL CALORIES	
48%	30%

Rachel's Special Occasion Lasagna

When Sarah Jones of Greensboro, North Carolina, learned to make her sister Rachel's lasagna, she served the dish for her own special occasions. But the calories and fat made her feel guilty.

To reduce calories and fat, and preserve flavor, we kept the assortment of cheeses but substituted reduced-fat and fat-free versions. This trimmed 86 calories and 8 grams of fat. Eliminating the butter shaved 102 calories and 12 grams of fat per portion, and allowed other flavorful ingredients to stand out. We decided a smaller portion size would also be reasonable.

Rachel's Special Occasion Lasagna

Serve with a salad and breadsticks to round out the meal.

1 (8-ounce) package uncooked lasagna noodles (about 9 noodles)
1⅓ cups (6 ounces) fat-free cottage cheese
¾ cup (6 ounces) ⅓-less-fat cream cheese, softened
⅔ cup (6 ounces) part-skim ricotta cheese
¼ cup (1 ounce) grated fresh Parmesan cheese
2 tablespoons minced fresh chives
1 teaspoon Dijon mustard
½ teaspoon salt
½ teaspoon dry mustard
½ teaspoon freshly ground black pepper
4 garlic cloves, minced
2 large egg whites, lightly beaten
1 large egg, lightly beaten
1 (26-ounce) jar fat-free pasta sauce, divided
Cooking spray
¼ cup (1 ounce) shredded part-skim mozzarella cheese

1. Preheat oven to 350°.
2. Cook noodles according to package directions, omitting salt and fat.
3. Combine cottage cheese, cream cheese, and ricotta cheese in a large bowl; stir to blend well. Stir in Parmesan and next 8 ingredients.
4. Spread ½ cup pasta sauce in bottom of a 13 x 9-inch baking dish coated with cooking spray. Arrange 3 noodles over pasta sauce; top with half of cheese mixture and one third of remaining pasta sauce. Repeat layers once, and end with noodles. Spread remaining pasta sauce over noodles.
5. Bake at 350° for 20 minutes. Sprinkle with mozzarella; bake an additional 20 minutes or until cheese is melted. Remove from oven; let stand 10 minutes before serving. Yield: 8 servings.

CALORIES 284 (28% from fat); FAT 8.8g (sat 5.2g, mono 2.5g, poly 0.4g); PROTEIN 15.7g; CARB 34.2g; FIBER 3.3g; CHOL 53mg; IRON 0.9mg; SODIUM 657mg; CALC 179mg

BEFORE	AFTER
SERVING SIZE	
1 portion	
CALORIES PER SERVING	
588	284
FAT	
30.3g	8.8g
PERCENT OF TOTAL CALORIES	
46%	28%

Potluck Potato Casserole

When her interest in nutrition led to second thoughts about this "all-time favorite" dish (recipe on page 362), Lenna Watson of Grand Junction, Colorado, asked for help. "This casserole was so heavy, and I wanted it to be healthier for me."

With a stick of butter, a half-pound of Cheddar cheese, and 2 cups of sour cream, the Potluck Potato Casserole tipped the scales with fat and calories.

We focused on the sour cream, cheese, and butter, which contributed about 270 calories and 25 grams of fat per serving. Substituting fat-free sour cream for regular cut calories and fat, and provided moisture. We used reduced-fat sharp Cheddar because reduced-fat cheeses provide good flavor and melt easier than fat-free versions. Since we reduced the overall amount of cheese, we liked the flavor punch offered by the sharp cheese. We left 5 teaspoons of butter for flavor. These changes trimmed 176 calories and 19 grams of fat per portion, and reduced cholesterol and saturated fat more than 75 percent. To keep the dish moist, we used light cream of chicken soup for regular and added chicken broth. Salt and ground red pepper helped to perk up the flavor.

Potluck Potato Casserole

The crunchy topping on this side-dish casserole gives way to a cheesy interior, resulting in a comfort food winner. Sprinkle the cornflakes over the casserole just before baking.

1½   cups fat-free sour cream
1¼   cups (5 ounces) finely shredded reduced-fat sharp Cheddar cheese
½   cup fat-free, less-sodium chicken broth
2   tablespoons minced fresh onion
5   teaspoons butter, melted
½   teaspoon freshly ground black pepper
¼   teaspoon salt
⅛   teaspoon ground red pepper
1   (30-ounce) package frozen hash browns, thawed (such as Ore-Ida)
1   (10.75-ounce) can reduced-fat cream of chicken soup (such as Campbell's Healthy Request)
Cooking spray
1   cup coarsely crushed cornflakes
2   tablespoons chopped fresh parsley

1. Preheat oven to 350°.
2. Combine first 10 ingredients in a large bowl; spread evenly into a 13 x 9-inch baking dish coated with cooking spray. Sprinkle cornflakes over potato mixture.
3. Bake at 350° for 1 hour or until bubbly. Sprinkle casserole with parsley. Yield: 10 servings.

CALORIES 194 (30% from fat); FAT 6.4g (sat 3.7g, mono 1.8g, poly 0.4g); PROTEIN 7.9g; CARB 27.1g; FIBER 1.5g; CHOL 21mg; IRON 1.5mg; SODIUM 283mg; CALC 166mg

BEFORE	AFTER
SERVING SIZE	
1 portion	
CALORIES PER SERVING	
380	194
FAT	
26.9g	6.4g
PERCENT OF TOTAL CALORIES	
64%	30%

dinner tonight

Turkey Leftovers

Turn leftover turkey into a soothing soup, colorful salad, or hearty sandwich.

Turkey Leftovers Menu 1
serves 4

Shredded Five-Spice Turkey with Herb and Noodle Salad

Edamame*

Green tea sorbet

*Bring 2 quarts water and 1 teaspoon salt to a boil in a large saucepan. Add 1 (1-pound) package frozen edamame in pods; cook 3 minutes. Drain. Place edamame in a bowl; sprinkle with kosher or other coarse-grain salt.

Game Plan

1. While water boils for edamame:
• Prepare vegetables and herbs for turkey mixture and salad
• Prepare dressing
• Boil water for noodles
2. While noodles cook:
• Assemble turkey mixture

Shredded Five-Spice Turkey with Herb and Noodle Salad

TOTAL TIME: 30 MINUTES

QUICK TIP: If you don't have leftover turkey, shredded rotisserie chicken makes a great substitute.

TURKEY:
1   tablespoon dark sesame oil
1   cup thinly sliced shiitake mushrooms (about 2 ounces)
¾   cup chopped onion
2   cups shredded cooked skinless dark-meat turkey (about 8 ounces)
½   cup fat-free, less-sodium chicken broth
1   tablespoon rice wine vinegar
1   tablespoon low-sodium soy sauce
½   teaspoon five-spice powder
¼   teaspoon kosher salt

DRESSING:
2   tablespoons rice wine vinegar
1   tablespoon low-sodium soy sauce
1   tablespoon oyster sauce
1   tablespoon fresh lime juice
1   teaspoon hot chili sauce with garlic
1   teaspoon dark sesame oil
3   garlic cloves, minced

SALAD:
4   ounces uncooked rice vermicelli
4   cups torn butter lettuce
2   cups thinly sliced red bell pepper
1   cup chopped green onions
½   cup chopped fresh basil
½   cup chopped fresh cilantro
½   cup chopped fresh mint
Mint sprigs (optional)

1. To prepare turkey, heat 1 tablespoon oil in a large nonstick skillet over medium-high heat. Add mushrooms and ¾ cup onion to pan; sauté 5 minutes or until lightly browned. Add turkey and next 5 ingredients to pan; cook 5 minutes or until liquid evaporates.
2. To prepare dressing, combine 2 tablespoons vinegar and next 6 ingredients in a small bowl, stirring with a whisk.

3. To prepare salad, cook pasta according to package directions, omitting salt and fat; drain. Combine lettuce and next 5 ingredients. Place about 2 cups lettuce mixture into each of 4 bowls. Top each with 1 cup noodles and 1½ cups turkey mixture; drizzle each with 1½ table-spoons dressing. Garnish with mint sprigs, if desired. Yield: 4 servings.

CALORIES 315 (26% from fat); FAT 9.2g (sat 2.1g, mono 2.9g, poly 3.3g); PROTEIN 21.2g; CARB 35.3g; FIBER 3.2g; CHOL 48mg; IRON 3.9mg; SODIUM 570mg; CALC 75mg

Turkey Leftovers Menu 2

serves 4

Turkey-Sausage Paella

Orange, avocado, and olive salad*

Low-fat dulce de leche ice cream (such as Häagen-Dazs)

*Place ½ cup watercress on each of 4 plates. Top each with ¼ avocado, sliced; 4 sections of an orange; and 2 sliced pimiento-stuffed olives. Combine 1 table-spoon olive oil, 1 tablespoon red wine vinegar, 1 teaspoon minced shallots, 1 tea-spoon honey, ⅛ teaspoon salt, and ⅛ tea-spoon pepper, stirring with a whisk. Drizzle evenly over salads.

Game Plan

1. While broth and saffron stand:
  • Cook chorizo
  • Shred turkey
  • Chop onion, pepper, and parsley
  • Mince garlic
2. While paella simmers:
  • Prepare dressing, and assemble salad

Turkey-Sausage Paella

Use smoked Spanish paprika for this recipe, as regular paprika will not impart the same rich, smoky flavor.

TOTAL TIME: 42 MINUTES

FLAVOR TIP: Look for saffron and smoked Spanish paprika in the spice aisle of mar-kets, or order online at www.penzeys.com or www.tienda.com.

2¾ cups fat-free, less-sodium chicken broth
¼ teaspoon saffron threads
Cooking spray
2 ounces Spanish chorizo sausage
½ cup chopped onion
½ cup chopped red bell pepper
3 garlic cloves, minced
¾ cup uncooked Arborio rice
¼ cup dry white wine
½ teaspoon smoked Spanish paprika
1 (14.5-ounce) can petite diced tomatoes, drained
2 cups shredded cooked turkey breast (about 8 ounces)
½ cup frozen peas, thawed
2 tablespoons chopped fresh parsley

1. Combine broth and saffron in a small saucepan over low heat; bring to a sim-mer. Remove from heat.
2. Heat a large nonstick skillet over medium-high heat. Coat pan with cooking spray. Add chorizo to pan; cook 5 minutes or until browned, stirring to crumble. Remove chorizo from pan with a slotted spoon; drain on paper towels. Add onion and pepper to pan; cook 5 minutes or until lightly browned. Add garlic; cook 2 min-utes. Add rice; cook 3 minutes, stirring constantly. Add wine and paprika; cook 1 minute or until liquid evaporates, scraping pan to loosen browned bits. Stir in broth mixture and tomatoes; bring to a boil. Cover, reduce heat, and simmer 20 min-utes or until rice is tender and liquid is absorbed, stirring occasionally. Gently stir in chorizo, turkey, peas, and parsley; cook 2 minutes or until thoroughly heated. Yield: 4 servings (serving size: 1½ cups).

CALORIES 297 (30% from fat); FAT 9.8g (sat 3.3g, mono 4g, poly 1.6g); PROTEIN 25.5g; CARB 26.2g; FIBER 3.1g; CHOL 54mg; IRON 2.6mg; SODIUM 746mg; CALC 61mg

Turkey Leftovers Menu 3

serves 4

Turkey Noodle Soup

Grilled cheese toasts*

Mixed green salad with bottled vinaigrette

*Lightly toast 8 (½-inch-thick) slices baguette. Rub each slice with cut half of garlic clove; top each with 1 teaspoon grated Cheddar cheese. Broil 1 minute or until cheese melts.

Game Plan

1. Slice and chop vegetables for soup.
2. While vegetables cook:
  • Measure remaining soup ingredients
3. While soup cooks:
  • Assemble cheese toasts
  • Prepare salad

Turkey Noodle Soup

Enjoy this soup year-round with shredded chicken instead of turkey.

TOTAL TIME: 35 MINUTES

QUICK TIP: Purchase prechopped onion, bottled minced garlic, and presliced celery and carrot in the supermarket produce section.

Cooking spray
1 cup (¼-inch-thick) slices carrot
¾ cup chopped onion
4 garlic cloves, minced
1 cup (¼-inch-thick) slices celery
¼ teaspoon salt
¼ teaspoon freshly ground black pepper
6 cups fat-free, less-sodium chicken broth
2 cups (3 ounces) uncooked egg noodles
1 tablespoon low-sodium soy sauce
1 bay leaf
2 cups shredded cooked turkey (about 8 ounces)
Coarsely ground black pepper (optional)
Continued

1. Heat a large saucepan over medium-high heat. Coat pan with cooking spray. Add carrot, onion, and garlic; sauté 5 minutes or until onion is lightly browned. Add celery, salt, and ¼ teaspoon pepper; sauté 3 minutes. Add broth and next 3 ingredients; bring to a boil. Reduce heat, and simmer 5 minutes. Add turkey; cook 3 minutes. Discard bay leaf. Sprinkle with coarsely ground black pepper, if desired. Yield: 4 servings (serving size: 2 cups).

CALORIES 280 (23% from fat); FAT 7.2g (sat 2.6g, mono 1.1g, poly 1.4g); PROTEIN 29.1g; CARB 24.3g; FIBER 2.3g; CHOL 80mg; IRON 2.6mg; SODIUM 544mg; CALC 79mg

---

Turkey Leftovers Menu 4

serves 4

Hot Turkey Sandwiches

Cranberry-shallot chutney*

Sour cream and onion-flavored baked potato chips

*Combine ¼ cup cranberry sauce, 1 tablespoon minced shallots, 1 tablespoon cider vinegar, and 1 teaspoon Dijon mustard in a small bowl.

Game Plan

1. While bacon for sandwiches cooks:
- Slice bread
- Rinse arugula

2. While sandwiches bake:
- Prepare chutney

QUICK & EASY
Hot Turkey Sandwiches

Serve these quick-to-make sandwiches for lunch on the Friday after Thanksgiving or any time you have turkey leftovers and crave a hearty sandwich. Cranberry-shallot chutney adds a sweet, tangy flavor. Bottled gravy will work fine in this recipe.

TOTAL TIME: 38 MINUTES

FLAVOR TIP: Experiment with different cheeses in this sandwich. Swiss, sharp Cheddar, or Monterey Jack cheese would all be delicious substitutes.

---

8   (1-ounce) slices French bread
2   tablespoons light mayonnaise
¼   cup turkey gravy
4   reduced-sodium bacon slices, cooked and cut in half
12 ounces sliced cooked turkey breast
2   slices provolone cheese, halved
1   cup arugula
1   tablespoon cranberry-shallot chutney

1. Preheat oven to 400°.
2. Place bread on a baking sheet. Spread mayonnaise evenly over 4 slices. Spread turkey gravy evenly over remaining 4 slices. Top mayonnaise-spread slices evenly with bacon, turkey, and cheese. Bake at 400° for 10 minutes or until cheese melts. Top cheese evenly with arugula. Drizzle with cranberry-shallot chutney. Top with gravy-spread bread slices. Press sandwiches together. Yield: 4 servings (serving size: 1 sandwich).

CALORIES 402 (25% from fat); FAT 11g (sat 4.5g, mono 3.5g, poly 1.2g); PROTEIN 38.2g; CARB 35.1g; FIBER 2.1g; CHOL 89mg; IRON 3.3mg; SODIUM 787mg; CALC 174mg

---

inspired vegetarian

Bountiful Harvest Menu

The season's produce is showcased in this celebratory feast.

Meatless Thanksgiving Menu

serves 8

Roasted Pepper and Zucchini Crostini

Beet and Fennel Soup

Butternut-Cheese Pie

Green Beans with Roasted Tomatoes and Cumin

Parmesan-Buttermilk Biscuits

Caramel, Orange, and Date Sundaes with Pistachio Brittle
or
Baked Pears with Cranberry-Ginger Filling and Cider Sauce

Holiday Countdown

Up to one week ahead:
- Prepare pistachio brittle; store in an airtight container.
- Bake biscuits; freeze in a zip-top plastic bag.

Up to two days ahead:
- Prepare roasted pepper and zucchini relish; cover and refrigerate.
- Toast baguette slices; store at room temperature in a zip-top plastic bag.
- Prepare soup; cover and chill.
- Cook green beans, and prepare tomato dressing; cover and refrigerate in separate containers.
- Prepare filling for pears; chill.

Thanksgiving morning:
- Prepare filling for butternut pie.
- Prepare orange and date sauce for sundaes.
- Core pears, and rub with lemons; cover and refrigerate.
- Scoop ice cream for sundaes onto a baking sheet; freeze.

A few hours before dinner:
- Fill and bake pears.

One hour before dinner:
- Finish crostini.
- Finish butternut pie.

At the last minute:
- Reheat green beans and tomatoes.
- Reheat biscuits.
- Reheat soup.
- Finish sundaes.
- Prepare sauce for baked pears.

QUICK & EASY • MAKE AHEAD
Roasted Pepper and Zucchini Crostini

4   red bell peppers
2   small zucchini, sliced
Cooking spray
2   tablespoons coarsely chopped fresh basil
1   tablespoon extravirgin olive oil
½   teaspoon white balsamic vinegar
¼   teaspoon salt
¼   teaspoon ground cumin
¼   teaspoon crushed red pepper
24 (¼-inch-thick) slices diagonally cut French bread baguette

1. Preheat broiler.

2. Cut bell peppers in half lengthwise; discard seeds and membranes. Place pepper halves, skin sides up, on a foil-lined baking sheet; flatten with hand. Broil 12 minutes or until blackened and charred. Place in a zip-top plastic bag, and seal. Let stand 15 minutes. Peel and discard skins.

3. Place zucchini on a foil-lined baking sheet, and coat with cooking spray. Broil 5 minutes or until tender and lightly browned. Cool.

4. Dice roasted peppers and zucchini; combine peppers, zucchini, basil, and next 5 ingredients, tossing to coat. Let stand 30 minutes. Spoon 2 tablespoons relish over each bread slice. Yield: 8 servings (serving size: 3 crostini).

CALORIES 102 (24% from fat); FAT 2.7g (sat 0.4g, mono 1.6g, poly 0.4g); PROTEIN 3.1g; CARB 17.1g; FIBER 1.2g; CHOL 0mg; IRON 1mg; SODIUM 220mg; CALC 29mg

Beet and Fennel Soup

Baking the beets concentrates their flavor; the onion is roasted whole. Fennel fronds are the wispy dill-like tops of the bulb.

    4   beets (about 1 pound)
    ¼   cup water
    1   large onion (about 1 pound)
    4   cups organic vegetable broth (such as Swanson Certified Organic)
 1¾   cups chopped fennel bulb (about 1 large)
    1   cup chopped peeled Granny Smith apple
    2   teaspoons white wine vinegar
    2   teaspoons lemon juice
    ½   teaspoon salt
    ½   teaspoon freshly ground black pepper
    8   teaspoons reduced-fat sour cream
        Chopped fennel fronds

1. Preheat oven to 375°.

2. Leave root and 1 inch of stem on beets; scrub with a brush. Place beets on a large sheet of aluminum foil; sprinkle beets with water. Wrap beets in foil; arrange packet of beets and onion on a baking sheet. Bake at 375° for 1 hour or until tender. Cool.

3. Combine broth, fennel, and apple in a medium saucepan. Bring to a boil; reduce heat, and simmer 15 minutes or until fennel is tender. Cool.

4. Trim off beet roots; rub off skins, and coarsely chop. Peel and quarter onion. Add beets and onion to broth mixture, stirring to combine. Place half of beet mixture in a blender; process until smooth. Pour puréed beet mixture into a large bowl. Repeat procedure with remaining beet mixture. Stir in vinegar, juice, salt, and pepper. Return beet mixture to pan.

5. Place beet mixture over medium heat, and cook 2 minutes or until thoroughly heated. Ladle soup into bowls, and top with sour cream. Sprinkle evenly with fennel fronds. Yield: 8 servings (serving size: ¾ cup soup and 1 teaspoon sour cream).

CALORIES 74 (11% from fat); FAT 0.9g (sat 0.4g, mono 0.2g, poly 0.1g); PROTEIN 2.2g; CARB 15.3g; FIBER 3.3g; CHOL 2mg; IRON 0.8mg; SODIUM 496mg; CALC 42mg

Butternut-Cheese Pie

Let the salted squash and bulgur stand about a half-hour before proceeding to soften the bulgur.

    4   cups coarsely shredded butternut squash (about 1 pound)
    ¼   cup uncooked bulgur
    ½   teaspoon salt
    1   teaspoon olive oil
    1   cup chopped onion
    ¾   cup (3 ounces) crumbled feta cheese
    ½   cup (2 ounces) grated fresh Parmesan cheese
    ½   cup chopped fresh mint
    ½   teaspoon freshly ground black pepper
    8   sheets frozen phyllo dough, thawed and divided
        Cooking spray

1. Combine first 3 ingredients in a large bowl; cover and chill 30 minutes.

2. Preheat oven to 350°.

3. Heat oil in a medium skillet over medium-high heat. Add onion; sauté 3 minutes. Add onion, feta cheese, and next 3 ingredients to squash mixture, stirring to combine.

4. Working with 1 phyllo sheet at a time (cover remaining dough to prevent drying), place 1 sheet in a 10-inch deep-dish pie plate coated with cooking spray. Gently press sheet into pie plate, allowing ends to extend over edges; lightly coat with cooking spray. Place another phyllo sheet across first sheet to form a crisscross design; lightly coat phyllo with cooking spray. Repeat procedure with 2 phyllo sheets and cooking spray.

5. Spoon squash mixture over phyllo. Place another phyllo sheet over squash, repeating crisscross design with remaining phyllo and cooking spray. Fold in edges of phyllo to fit dish and form a rim. Bake at 350° for 40 minutes or until golden brown. Yield: 8 servings (serving size: 1 wedge).

CALORIES 190 (20% from fat); FAT 4.3g (sat 2g, mono 1.5g, poly 0.4g); PROTEIN 5.5g; CARB 35.2g; FIBER 5.1g; CHOL 9mg; IRON 2mg; SODIUM 366mg; CALC 131mg

Green Beans with Roasted Tomatoes and Cumin

An easy way to peel tomatoes is to place them in a pot of boiling water for 30 seconds. Remove them with a slotted spoon, then plunge the tomatoes into a bowl of ice water to stop the cooking process. The skins will slide off easily.

    2   cups sliced red onion
    1   garlic clove, sliced
        Cooking spray
    4   large tomatoes, peeled and halved (about 2 pounds)
    1   teaspoon chopped fresh thyme
    1   teaspoon cumin seeds, lightly crushed
    ½   teaspoon salt
    ¼   teaspoon freshly ground black pepper
    ⅛   teaspoon crushed red pepper
    ¼   teaspoon balsamic vinegar
 1½   pounds green beans, trimmed
    1   tablespoon olive oil

Continued

1. Preheat oven to 375°.
2. Place onion and garlic on a baking sheet coated with cooking spray. Place tomato halves, cut sides up, over onion. Combine thyme and next 4 ingredients; sprinkle over tomatoes. Lightly coat vegetables with cooking spray. Bake at 375° for 40 minutes or until onion is browned and tomatoes are tender. Cool. Place mixture in a food processor; pulse 6 times or until mixture is slightly chunky. Stir in vinegar.
3. Cook beans in boiling water in a medium saucepan 7 minutes or just until tender. Drain. Return to pan, and toss with oil. Add tomato mixture, and cook 2 minutes or until thoroughly heated. Yield: 8 servings (serving size: ¾ cup).

CALORIES 64 (30% from fat); FAT 2.1g (sat 0.3g, mono 1.3g, poly 0.4g); PROTEIN 2.6g; CARB 10.9g; FIBER 4.3g; CHOL 0mg; IRON 1.4mg; SODIUM 159mg; CALC 47mg

MAKE AHEAD • FREEZABLE
Parmesan-Buttermilk Biscuits

You will need to roll the dough out twice to be able to make eight round biscuits. To keep the dough from becoming too tough, handle it as little as possible.

    1⅓ cups all-purpose flour (about
        6 ounces)
    1½ tablespoons sugar
     2 teaspoons baking powder
     ½ teaspoon salt
     ¼ teaspoon freshly ground black pepper
    Pinch of ground red pepper
     2 tablespoons chilled butter, cut
        into small pieces
     ⅓ cup plus 1 tablespoon low-fat
        buttermilk, divided
     3 tablespoons grated fresh Parmesan
        cheese
    Cooking spray

1. Preheat oven to 400°.
2. Lightly spoon flour into dry measuring cups; level with a knife. Combine flour and next 5 ingredients in a bowl; cut in butter with a pastry blender or 2 knives until mixture resembles coarse meal. Add ⅓ cup buttermilk and Parmesan cheese, and stir just until moist.

3. Turn dough out onto a heavily floured surface; knead lightly 5 times. Roll dough to a ½-inch thickness; cut with a 2½-inch biscuit cutter. Place on a baking sheet coated with cooking spray. Brush with 1 tablespoon buttermilk. Bake at 400° for 15 minutes or until golden. Yield: 8 servings (serving size: 1 biscuit).

CALORIES 144 (32% from fat); FAT 5.1g (sat 2.6g, mono 2g, poly 0.3g); PROTEIN 3.4g; CARB 21.1g; FIBER 0.7g; CHOL 13mg; IRON 1.3mg; SODIUM 330mg; CALC 104mg

MAKE AHEAD
Caramel, Orange, and Date Sundaes with Pistachio Brittle

The brittle also makes a tasty holiday food gift. If you use the same saucepan to prepare the caramel (Step 3) and the sauce (Step 5), make sure the pan is scrupulously clean.

     6 large navel oranges
     ⅓ cup chopped pistachios
    Cooking spray
     ½ cup plus 2 tablespoons sugar,
        divided
    1⅓ cups plus 2 tablespoons water,
        divided
    10 whole pitted dates, chopped
     ½ cup dried cranberries
     4 cups vanilla low-fat ice cream

1. Peel and section oranges over a bowl; squeeze membranes to extract juice. Discard membranes. Reserve ¼ cup juice for sauce; refrigerate remaining juice for another use. Place orange sections in a medium bowl. Cover and chill in separate containers.
2. Sprinkle pistachios into an 8-inch circle on a baking sheet coated with cooking spray.
3. Place ½ cup sugar and ⅓ cup water in a small, heavy saucepan over medium-high heat; cook until sugar dissolves, stirring frequently (about 2 minutes). Cook until golden, without stirring (about 5 minutes).
4. Pour caramel over pistachios; cool completely. Break brittle into about 8 large pieces; place in an airtight container. Add 1 cup water to pan; bring to a boil. Cook until any remaining caramel in pan

dissolves; discard. Wipe pan clean with paper towels.
5. Place 2 tablespoons sugar and 2 tablespoons water in pan over medium-high heat; cook until sugar dissolves, stirring frequently (about 1 minute). Cook until golden, without stirring (about 3 minutes). Remove from heat; carefully add ¼ cup reserved orange juice, stirring until sugar dissolves. Return pan to heat, and cook just until caramel dissolves, stirring frequently.
6. Combine orange juice mixture, orange sections, dates, and cranberries. Serve over ice cream; top with brittle. Yield: 8 servings (serving size: ½ cup ice cream, ½ cup sauce, and 1 brittle piece).

CALORIES 310 (14% from fat); FAT 4.7g (sat 1.3g, mono 1.3g, poly 0.8g); PROTEIN 4.3g; CARB 64.7g; FIBER 5.2g; CHOL 5mg; IRON 0.5mg; SODIUM 51mg; CALC 150mg

Baked Pears with Cranberry-Ginger Filling and Cider Sauce

Use a miniature food processor to chop the filling. Rubbing the peeled pears with cut lemon prevents discoloration. Use a corer to remove the center of the pears and to create even-sized cavities that hold the same amount of filling. Be careful when you tent with foil not to knock off the pear caps.

     8 firm, ripe Bartlett pears
     1 lemon, halved
     1 cup fresh cranberries
     ½ cup packed brown sugar
     1 tablespoon chopped crystallized
        ginger
     1 teaspoon grated orange rind
     1 cup apple cider
     1 tablespoon butter, melted
     1 tablespoon brown sugar
     ½ teaspoon ground ginger

1. Preheat oven to 400°.
2. Peel pears, leaving stems intact. Slice 1 inch from top of each pear to form a cap. Slice about ¼ inch from base of each pear so it will sit flat. Core each pear. Rub outside of pears with cut sides of lemon halves. Discard lemon.

3. Place cranberries and next 3 ingredients in a food processor; pulse until finely chopped. Place pears in a 13 x 9-inch baking dish. Fill each pear cavity with 3 teaspoons cranberry mixture, 1 teaspoon at a time. Top each pear with its cap. Pour cider over pears.

4. Drizzle butter evenly over pears. Combine 1 tablespoon sugar and ground ginger; sprinkle evenly over pears. Carefully cover with foil. Bake at 400° for 1 hour or until tender, basting every 20 minutes.

5. Using a spatula, carefully remove pears from baking dish; place on individual dessert plates. Pour liquid from baking dish into a medium saucepan. Cook over medium-high heat until reduced to ½ cup (about 12 minutes). Drizzle 1 tablespoon sauce over each pear. Yield: 8 servings.

CALORIES 206 (14% from fat); FAT 3.1g (sat 1.8g, mono 0.8g, poly 0.2g); PROTEIN 0.7g; CARB 47.3g; FIBER 5.7g; CHOL 8mg; IRON 0.6mg; SODIUM 31mg; CALC 31mg

enlightened cook

Another Turkey Day Tradition

A Michigan family's annual Thanksgiving morning jaunt is a treasured neighborhood ritual, and so is the breakfast that follows.

For nearly 15 years, the LaReau family, along with almost 30 of their neighbors in Kalamazoo, Michigan, gather on Thanksgiving morning for an invigorating run. The Turkey Trot, as the event has come to be called, kicks off every year at 9 a.m. It's not competitive—just a fun four-mile jaunt that's a way to get some exercise while catching up with friends. Anything goes, but the most important thing is to show up with a smile.

In that spirit, the run is followed by a healthy breakfast—alfresco style. The food celebrates the hearty flavors of a Midwestern autumn: hot spiced apple cider, Cranberry-Orange Muffins (recipe at right), warm Baked Apples (recipe at right), and thick slices of Spiced Pumpkin Bread (recipe at right).

Cranberry-Orange Muffins

Bake these a day ahead, and store cooled muffins in an airtight container. Freeze any leftover muffins in heavy-duty zip-top plastic bags.

2 cups all-purpose flour (about 9 ounces)
1 cup sugar, divided
1½ teaspoons baking powder
1 teaspoon salt
½ teaspoon baking soda
2 teaspoons grated orange rind
¾ cup orange juice (about 1 large orange)
¼ cup canola oil
1 large egg, lightly beaten
2 cups coarsely chopped fresh cranberries (about 8 ounces)
⅓ cup chopped walnuts, toasted
Cooking spray

1. Preheat oven to 400°.
2. Lightly spoon flour into dry measuring cups; level with a knife. Set aside 1 tablespoon sugar. Combine flour, remaining sugar, baking powder, salt, and baking soda in a large bowl; make a well in center of mixture.
3. Combine rind, juice, oil, and egg in a small bowl, stirring well with a whisk. Add to flour mixture, stirring just until moist. Fold in cranberries and walnuts. Spoon batter into 16 muffin cups coated with cooking spray. Sprinkle evenly with 1 tablespoon sugar. Bake at 400° for 15 minutes or until muffins spring back when touched lightly in center. Run a knife or spatula around outer edge of each muffin cup. Carefully remove each muffin; place on a wire rack. Yield: 16 servings (serving size: 1 muffin).

CALORIES 169 (30% from fat); FAT 5.6g (sat 0.5g, mono 2.5g, poly 2.4g); PROTEIN 2.5g; CARB 27.9g; FIBER 1.3g; CHOL 2mg; IRON 1mg; SODIUM 236mg; CALC 35mg

Baked Apples

Chop the nuts and apples the night before, and combine with the rest of the ingredients in the morning. Serve these juicy baked apples over slices of Spiced Pumpkin Bread (recipe below), warm bowls of oatmeal, or pancakes. Ida Red and McIntosh apples also work well.

2 cups dried cranberries
1¼ cups coarsely chopped walnuts
1 cup packed brown sugar
1 cup water
2 teaspoons ground cinnamon
6 Gala Apples, cored and chopped (about 3 pounds)

1. Combine all ingredients in a large microwave-safe dish. Microwave at HIGH 20 minutes or until apples are soft, stirring occasionally. Yield: 6 cups (serving size: ¼ cup).

CALORIES 126 (29% from fat); FAT 4.1g (sat 0.4g, mono 0.6g, poly 3g); PROTEIN 1g; CARB 23.7g; FIBER 2.3g; CHOL 0mg; IRON 0.5mg; SODIUM 4mg; CALC 16mg

Spiced Pumpkin Bread

This recipe makes two generous loaves. Freeze one, or give it as a gift. The bread is also delicious toasted and topped with Baked Apples (recipe above).

3 cups all-purpose flour (about 13½ ounces)
2 cups sugar
2 teaspoons baking soda
1 teaspoon baking powder
1 teaspoon ground cinnamon
½ teaspoon salt
¼ teaspoon ground cloves
¼ teaspoon ground nutmeg
⅔ cup canola oil
3 eggs, lightly beaten
1 (15-ounce) can pumpkin
½ cup dried currants or raisins
Cooking spray

1. Preheat oven to 350°.

Continued

2. Lightly spoon flour into dry measuring cups; level with a knife. Combine flour and next 7 ingredients in a large bowl; make a well in center of mixture. Combine oil, eggs, and pumpkin in a medium bowl; stir with a whisk until smooth. Add to flour mixture, stirring just until moist. Fold in currants.

3. Spoon batter into 2 (9 x 5-inch) loaf pans coated with cooking spray. Bake at 350° for 1 hour or until a wooden pick inserted in center comes out clean. Cool loaves in pans 10 minutes on a wire rack; remove from pans. Cool loaves completely. Yield: 2 loaves, 16 servings per loaf (serving size: 1 slice).

CALORIES 150 (31% from fat); FAT 5.2g (sat 0.5g, mono 3g, poly 1.5g); PROTEIN 2g; CARB 24.4g; FIBER 0.9g; CHOL 20mg; IRON 0.9mg; SODIUM 170mg; CALC 18mg

entertaining

Enticing Dips and Spreads

Bring variety to the menu with these savory snacks that require minimal preparation.

Chunky Cherry Tomatoes with Basil

This holiday-hued mixture shouldn't stand for much longer than an hour before serving or the salt will draw all the juices from the tomatoes. Serve with slices of toasted country bread.

  3   cups quartered cherry
       tomatoes
  1   cup loosely packed, thinly sliced
       fresh basil
  1   tablespoon extravirgin olive
       oil
  1   tablespoon red wine vinegar
  1   tablespoon balsamic vinegar
  ½   teaspoon salt
  ¼   teaspoon freshly ground black
       pepper
  1   large garlic clove, minced

1. Combine all ingredients in a medium bowl; let stand 1 hour. Yield: 12 servings (serving size: ¼ cup).

CALORIES 20 (59% from fat); FAT 1.3g (sat 0.2g, mono 0.9g, poly 0.2g); PROTEIN 0.4g; CARB 2.3g; FIBER 0.6g; CHOL 0mg; IRON 0.3mg; SODIUM 101mg; CALC 9mg

Artichoke and Fennel Caponata

The ingredients in this sweet-and-sour Sicilian side dish are roughly chopped to create a chunky spread. Caponata is typically made with eggplant, but this version features artichoke hearts. Spoon over toasted baguette slices.

  1   tablespoon olive oil
  1   cup chopped onion
  1   cup chopped celery
  1   cup chopped fennel bulb
  2   garlic cloves, thinly
       sliced
  ½   cup golden raisins
  ⅓   cup white wine vinegar
  3   tablespoons sugar
  2   tablespoons capers
  1½ teaspoons grated lemon
       rind
  ¼   teaspoon salt
  ¼   teaspoon freshly ground black
       pepper
  1   (15-ounce) can tomato sauce
  1   (9-ounce) package frozen
       artichoke hearts, thawed and
       chopped
  2   tablespoons chopped fresh
       flat-leaf parsley

1. Heat oil in a large nonstick skillet over medium-high heat. Add onion, celery, fennel, and garlic; sauté 5 minutes or until tender. Stir in raisins and next 8 ingredients. Bring to a simmer; cook over medium-low heat 5 minutes or until liquid almost evaporates. Sprinkle with parsley. Serve chilled or at room temperature. Yield: 14 servings (serving size: ¼ cup).

CALORIES 62 (17% from fat); FAT 1.2g (sat 0.2g, mono 0.7g, poly 0.2g); PROTEIN 1.4g; CARB 13g; FIBER 2.2g; CHOL 0mg; IRON 0.7mg; SODIUM 257mg; CALC 22mg

Persian Spinach and Yogurt Dip
Borani Esfanaj

Variations of this dish are popular throughout the Mediterranean region. We like the thick, creamy texture of organic yogurt, though you can use any kind of plain, fat-free yogurt. Letting the dip stand before refrigerating it allows flavors to meld. To minimize prep time, you can use frozen spinach, chopped and squeezed dry, and omit the first step. Serve with crudités, pita, or crispy flatbread.

  2   quarts water
  1   (10-ounce) package fresh spinach,
       chopped
  2   teaspoons butter
  ⅓   cup finely chopped sweet
       onion
  1   garlic clove, minced
  ½   teaspoon salt
  1   cup plain fat-free organic yogurt
       (such as Stonyfield Farm)
  ¼   teaspoon freshly ground black
       pepper
  ⅛   teaspoon ground cinnamon

1. Bring 2 quarts water to a boil in a Dutch oven. Add spinach, and cook 1 minute. Drain well. Place spinach on several layers of paper towels; squeeze until barely moist.

2. Melt butter in a medium nonstick skillet over medium heat. Add onion and garlic; cook 6 minutes or until onion is tender, stirring occasionally. Remove from heat; stir in spinach and salt. Cool to room temperature.

3. Combine spinach mixture, yogurt, pepper, and cinnamon in a medium bowl. Let stand 30 minutes. Refrigerate until chilled. Yield: 13 servings (serving size: about 2 tablespoons).

CALORIES 20 (32% from fat); FAT 0.7g (sat 0.3g, mono 0.3g, poly 0g); PROTEIN 1.5g; CARB 2.8g; FIBER 0.3g; CHOL 2mg; IRON 0.6mg; SODIUM 121mg; CALC 47mg

QUICK & EASY • MAKE AHEAD
Green Pea Hummus

Sumac grows in abundance throughout the Mediterranean, and its dried, ground berries are a fruity and astringent spice widely used in Middle Eastern cooking. If you can't find sumac, substitute ¼ teaspoon grated lemon rind. You may need to add up to a tablespoon of water if the mixture is too thick to process smoothly. Serve with pita wedges.

    2   cups frozen green peas
    ½   cup chopped fresh flat-leaf parsley
    3   tablespoons tahini (sesame-seed paste)
    2   tablespoons fresh lemon juice
    ¾   teaspoon ground cumin
    ½   teaspoon salt
    1   garlic clove, chopped
    1   teaspoon extravirgin olive oil
    ¼   teaspoon ground sumac

1. Cook peas in boiling water 3 minutes; drain and rinse with cold water. Drain. Place peas and next 6 ingredients in a food processor, and process until smooth. Spoon pea mixture into a small serving bowl; chill. Drizzle with oil, and sprinkle with sumac just before serving. Yield: 6 servings (serving size: about 3 tablespoons).

CALORIES 93 (48% from fat); FAT 5g (sat 0.7g, mono 2.1g, poly 1.9g); PROTEIN 4.1g; CARB 9.3g; FIBER 2.7g; CHOL 0mg; IRON 1.5mg; SODIUM 254mg; CALC 32mg

MAKE AHEAD
Spicy Spanish Eggplant Dip

Choose medium-sized eggplants with taut skin and uniform coloration that feel firm and heavy for their size. Large eggplants, particularly older ones, may be seedy or bitter. Serve with crispy flatbread.

    2   eggplants (about 1 pound each)
    ¼   cup tomato paste
    2   tablespoons red wine vinegar
    1   tablespoon balsamic vinegar
    1   teaspoon Hungarian sweet paprika
    ½   teaspoon salt
    ¼   teaspoon ground red pepper
    2   tablespoons extravirgin olive oil
    1   cup finely chopped onion
    2   garlic cloves, minced
    ½   cup chopped bottled roasted red bell peppers
    4   canned anchovy fillets, chopped (about ⅓ ounce)
    2   tablespoons finely chopped fresh flat-leaf parsley

1. Preheat oven to 450°.
2. Pierce eggplants several times with a fork; place on a foil-lined baking sheet. Bake at 450° for 45 minutes or until blackened, turning frequently. Cool slightly; peel. Drain eggplant pulp in a colander 5 minutes; chop.
3. Combine tomato paste and next 5 ingredients in a small bowl, stirring until smooth.
4. Heat oil in a large nonstick skillet over medium-low heat. Add onion and garlic; cook 6 minutes or until tender, stirring occasionally. Stir in eggplant, tomato paste mixture, bell peppers, and anchovies; cook 10 minutes. Remove from heat; stir in parsley. Spoon mixture into a medium bowl. Cover and chill. Yield: 12 servings (serving size: ¼ cup).

CALORIES 52 (43% from fat); FAT 2.5g (sat 0.4g, mono 1.7g, poly 0.3g); PROTEIN 1.4g; CARB 7.3g; FIBER 1g; CHOL 1mg; IRON 0.5mg; SODIUM 157mg; CALC 15mg

Most dips can be made ahead, which benefits their flavor.

QUICK & EASY • MAKE AHEAD
Mixed Olive Tapenade

This piquant specialty of Provence, France, features classic ingredients from the region—olives, capers, and anchovies. Serve at room temperature with baguette slices and lemon wedges or crackers. For a fast entrée option, stir the tapenade into hot cooked pasta.

    1   cup kalamata olives, pitted (about 4 ounces)
    1   cup green olives, pitted (about 4 ounces)
    1   tablespoon chopped fresh flat-leaf parsley
    1   tablespoon capers, rinsed and drained
    2   teaspoons chopped fresh thyme
    1   teaspoon grated lemon rind
    ¼   teaspoon freshly ground black pepper
    10 oil-cured olives, pitted (about 1 ounce)
    3   canned anchovy fillets (about ¼ ounce)
    1   garlic clove, chopped

1. Place all ingredients in a food processor; pulse 10 times or until olives are finely chopped. Yield: 16 servings (serving size: about 2 tablespoons).

CALORIES 39 (83% from fat); FAT 3.6g (sat 0.4g, mono 2.3g, poly 0.5g); PROTEIN 0.3g; CARB 2g; FIBER 0.4g; CHOL 0mg; IRON 0.1mg; SODIUM 310mg; CALC 5mg

Pomegranate Power

Pomegranates have been celebrated since the time of Aphrodite for their beauty, sublime taste, and superior health benefits.

Smoky Baked Beans with Pomegranate Molasses

Look for pomegranate molasses in Middle Eastern markets and other specialty groceries. You can also spread it on bread, drizzle it over pound cake, or use it as a glaze for meats and fish.

    1   tablespoon canola oil
    ½   cup finely chopped
         onion
    2   garlic cloves, minced
    ⅓   cup ketchup
    ¼   cup pomegranate juice
    3   tablespoons pomegranate
         molasses
    2   tablespoons brown sugar
    ¾   teaspoon kosher salt
    ½   teaspoon chili powder
    ¼   teaspoon smoked Spanish
         paprika
    ¼   teaspoon ground cumin
    ⅛   teaspoon ground red
         pepper
    1   (14.5-ounce) can diced tomatoes,
         drained
    1   (15-ounce) can black beans,
         rinsed and drained
    1   (15-ounce) can kidney beans,
         rinsed and drained
         Cooking spray

1. Preheat oven to 325°.
2. Heat oil in a medium skillet over medium heat. Add onion; sauté 6 minutes or until tender. Add garlic, and sauté 1 minute.
3. Add ketchup and next 9 ingredients to pan; stir to combine. Add beans, stirring until well combined. Pour into an 11 x 7-inch baking dish lightly coated with cooking spray. Bake at 325° for 30 minutes. Let stand 10 minutes. Yield: 8 servings (serving size: ½ cup).

CALORIES 181 (11% from fat); FAT 2.3g (sat 0.1g, mono 1.1g, poly 0.8g); PROTEIN 4.7g; CARB 35.5g; FIBER 5.5g; CHOL 0mg; IRON 1.9mg; SODIUM 442mg; CALC 48mg

Warm Roasted Apples with Pomegranate-Caramel Sauce

Pomegranate juice adds a twist to the fall flavors featured in this decadent dessert. Covering the saucepan briefly as the caramel sauce boils helps dissolve any granulated sugar crystals clinging to the side of the pan.

APPLES:
         Cooking spray
    ¼   cup packed brown sugar
    3   tablespoons fresh lemon juice
    ¾   teaspoon ground cinnamon
    ¼   teaspoon ground nutmeg
    ⅛   teaspoon salt
    6   large Rome apples, peeled, cored,
         and sliced (about 2½ pounds)
    1   tablespoon chilled butter, cut into
         small pieces

SAUCE:
    ¾   cup granulated sugar
    ¼   cup water
    3   tablespoons lemon juice
    1   teaspoon light corn syrup
    2   tablespoons butter
    ½   cup pomegranate juice

REMAINING INGREDIENT:
    2   cups low-fat vanilla ice cream

1. Preheat oven to 400°.
2. To prepare apples, line a jelly-roll pan with foil. Coat with cooking spray.
3. Combine brown sugar and next 5 ingredients in a large bowl; toss to coat. Place apples in a single layer on prepared pan; top with 1 tablespoon butter pieces. Bake at 400° for 15 minutes. Turn slices over; bake an additional 20 minutes or until lightly browned, stirring occasionally.
4. To prepare sauce, combine granulated sugar, water, 3 tablespoons lemon juice, and syrup in a small, heavy saucepan over medium-low heat; cook 5 minutes or until sugar dissolves. Cover, increase heat to medium, and boil 30 seconds. Uncover and boil 3 minutes or until golden (do not stir). Remove from heat; let stand 1 minute. Carefully add 2 tablespoons butter, stirring until butter melts. Gradually add pomegranate juice, stirring constantly until mixture is smooth. Return to heat; cook over medium-low heat 8 minutes or until thickened. Cool.
5. To serve, spoon ¼ cup ice cream into each of 8 small bowls. Top each serving with about ¾ cup roasted apples and 1 tablespoon sauce. Yield: 8 servings.

CALORIES 295 (17% from fat); FAT 5.6g (sat 3g, mono 2g, poly 0.2g); PROTEIN 1.8g; CARB 63g; FIBER 4g; CHOL 20mg; IRON 0.7mg; SODIUM 95mg; CALC 49mg

QUICK & EASY
Bibb and Radicchio Salad with Persimmons and Pomegranates

Serve this salad alongside broiled salmon.

    1   pomegranate
    1   tablespoon balsamic
         vinegar
    1   tablespoon red wine vinegar
    2   teaspoons extravirgin olive oil
    ½   teaspoon salt
    ⅛   teaspoon freshly ground black
         pepper
    4   cups torn Bibb lettuce (about
         2 small heads)
    4   cups torn radicchio (about
         1 small head)
    1   ripe Fuyu persimmon, halved
         lengthwise and thinly sliced

1. Cut pomegranate in half. Remove seeds from one pomegranate half, being careful not to burst individual juice sacs; set seeds aside. Squeeze 2 tablespoons juice from other pomegranate half using a citrus reamer or juicer. Combine pomegranate juice, vinegars, oil, salt, and pepper, stirring with a whisk.
2. Combine lettuce, radicchio, persimmon, and pomegranate seeds in a large bowl. Drizzle juice mixture over lettuce mixture; toss gently to coat. Serve

immediately. Yield: 6 servings (serving size: 1⅓ cups).

CALORIES 68 (24% from fat); FAT 1.8g (sat 0.2g, mono 1.1g, poly 0.2g); PROTEIN 1.2g; CARB 13.5g; FIBER 1.7g; CHOL 0mg; IRON 0.8mg; SODIUM 206mg; CALC 22mg

Chocolate Soufflés with Pomegranate Sauce

Pomegranate makes a refreshing substitute for the more common raspberry sauce in this light, fluffy dessert. Serve immediately.

SOUFFLÉS:
  Cooking spray
  ½ teaspoon sugar
  1 cup 2% reduced-fat milk
  ½ cup sugar
  ½ cup unsweetened cocoa
  2 tablespoons all-purpose flour
  ⅛ teaspoon salt
  2 tablespoons semisweet chocolate chips
  ½ teaspoon vanilla extract
  ¼ teaspoon ground allspice
  2 large egg yolks, lightly beaten
  4 large egg whites
  2 tablespoons sugar

POMEGRANATE SAUCE:
  1 cup pomegranate juice
  ¼ cup water
  2 teaspoons sugar
  1 tablespoon cold water
  1 teaspoon cornstarch
  2 tablespoons Chambord (raspberry-flavored liqueur)

1. Preheat oven to 350°.
2. To prepare soufflés, coat 6 (8-ounce) ramekins with cooking spray; sprinkle with ½ teaspoon sugar.
3. Combine milk and next 4 ingredients in a medium saucepan. Bring to a boil, stirring constantly until slightly thickened (about 1 minute); remove from heat. Add chocolate chips, vanilla, and allspice, stirring constantly; cool slightly.
4. Place egg yolks in a large bowl. Gradually add chocolate mixture to egg yolks, stirring constantly with a whisk.
5. Place egg whites in a large bowl; beat with a mixer at high speed until soft peaks form. Gradually add 2 tablespoons sugar, 1 tablespoon at a time, beating until stiff peaks form. Gently stir one-fourth of egg white mixture into chocolate mixture; gently fold in remaining egg white mixture. Spoon into prepared ramekins.
6. Place ramekins in a 13 x 9-inch baking pan; add hot water to pan to a depth of 1 inch. Bake at 350° for 20 minutes or until puffy and set.
7. To prepare sauce, place juice, ¼ cup water, and 2 teaspoons sugar in a small saucepan; bring to a boil. Reduce heat, and simmer 8 minutes. Combine 1 tablespoon water and cornstarch in a small bowl, stirring with a whisk to create a slurry. Add slurry and liqueur to juice mixture. Cook 2 minutes or until mixture is slightly syrupy. Remove from heat. Drizzle over chocolate soufflés. Yield: 6 servings (serving size: 1 soufflé and about 1 tablespoon sauce).

CALORIES 300 (13% from fat); FAT 4.4g (sat 2.2g, mono 1.6g, poly 0.3g); PROTEIN 6.5g; CARB 62.8g; FIBER 2.7g; CHOL 71mg; IRON 1.9mg; SODIUM 111mg; CALC 70mg

How to Seed a Pomegranate

While pomegranates are known for their tendency to stain anything they touch, a bowl of water is the only tool you will need to keep you and your kitchen stain-free. This method keeps the pomegranate and its stain-causing seeds safely underwater. Still, we recommend that you wear an apron while you follow these steps for seeding a pomegranate:

1. Place the pomegranate in a bowl of water large enough to fit both the fruit and your hands without spilling over.

2. Under the water, use a medium-sized knife to carefully slice off the crown and opposite end of the pomegranate so the seeds are just visible (don't slice too deeply), then score the pomegranate lengthwise into 1½-inch-wide wedges.

3. With your thumbs, carefully pry the pomegranate apart beneath the water and turn each section inside out. Begin to separate the seeds from the inner white membrane, taking care not to burst the individual juice sacs. The membrane will float to the top while the seeds sink to the bottom.

4. With a large slotted spoon, skim off the floating membrane. Sort through the seeds beneath the water, discarding any stray pieces of membrane (it's unpleasantly bitter).

5. Drain the pomegranate seeds in a fine mesh strainer. Use immediately, or refrigerate up to one week.

Mexican Salad with Pomegranate-Lime Dressing

For this dish, cut a small pomegranate in half, and remove the seeds from one half. Squeeze juice from the other half.

 2 tablespoons fresh lime juice
 2 tablespoons fresh pomegranate
    juice
 1 teaspoon sugar
 ¾ teaspoon salt
 ¼ teaspoon ground cumin
 1 small garlic clove, minced
 1 teaspoon olive oil
 2 cups arugula leaves
 1½ cups (3-inch) julienne-cut peeled
    jícama
 ½ cup vertically sliced red onion
 ½ cup diced peeled avocado
 2 tablespoons chopped fresh
    cilantro
 ¼ cup fresh pomegranate seeds
 4 teaspoons pine nuts, toasted

1. Combine first 6 ingredients in a large bowl. Add oil, and stir with a whisk. Add arugula and next 4 ingredients, and toss gently. Place 1 cup salad on each of 4 salad plates. Top each with 1 tablespoon seeds and 1 teaspoon pine nuts. Serve immediately. Yield: 4 servings.

CALORIES 126 (44% from fat); FAT 6.1g (sat 0.8g, mono 3.1g, poly 1.5g); PROTEIN 1.8g; CARB 18.7g; FIBER 4g; CHOL 0mg; IRON 1mg; SODIUM 444mg; CALC 32mg

When choosing a pomegranate, look for fruit that is round, plump, and blemish-free.

Buttermilk-Banana Pancakes with Pomegranate Syrup

The combination of banana pancakes and pomegranate syrup is a healthy way to start your morning.

PANCAKES:
 1 cup all-purpose flour (about 4½
    ounces)
 1 tablespoon sugar
 ½ teaspoon baking soda
 ½ teaspoon baking powder
 ½ teaspoon ground cinnamon
 ¼ teaspoon salt
 1 (1-ounce) package uncooked
    instant farina (such as Cream of
    Wheat)
 1¼ cups low-fat buttermilk
 1 tablespoon canola oil
 ½ teaspoon vanilla extract
 1 large egg, lightly beaten
 1 cup mashed banana (about
    1 large)

SYRUP:
 ½ cup pomegranate juice
 ½ cup maple syrup
 2 tablespoons pomegranate juice
 2 teaspoons cornstarch

1. To prepare pancakes, lightly spoon flour into a dry measuring cup; level with a knife. Combine flour and next 6 ingredients in a large bowl; stir with a whisk. Combine buttermilk, oil, vanilla, and egg; add to flour mixture, stirring until smooth. Fold in banana.
2. Spoon ¼ cup batter for each pancake onto a hot nonstick griddle. Turn when tops are covered with bubbles and edges look cooked.
3. To prepare syrup, combine ½ cup juice and syrup in a medium saucepan. Bring to a boil over medium-high heat. Combine 2 tablespoons juice and cornstarch in a bowl; add to pan. Cook 1 minute or until thickened; remove from heat. Serve with pancakes. Yield: 6 servings (serving size: 3 pancakes and about 2 tablespoons syrup).

CALORIES 315 (11% from fat); FAT 4g (sat 1g, mono 0.5g, poly 0.3g); PROTEIN 5.7g; CARB 66.6g; FIBER 1.4g; CHOL 37mg; IRON 3.3mg; SODIUM 312mg; CALC 128mg

great starts

Make-Ahead Brunch Casseroles

Ideal for overnight company, these dishes are assembled the night before to pop in the oven the next morning and serve.

Hash Brown Casserole with Bacon, Onions, and Cheese

Though filling enough as a main dish, you can also serve smaller portions of this creamy, cheesy casserole as a tasty side to scrambled eggs. We enjoyed the way the Classic Melts cheese blend melted over the casserole; substitute Cheddar cheese if you can't find this product.

 6 bacon slices
 1 cup chopped onion
 2 garlic cloves, minced
 1 (32-ounce) package frozen
    Southern-style hash brown
    potatoes
 1 cup (4 ounces) preshredded
    Classic Melts Four Cheese blend,
    divided
 ½ cup chopped green onions
 ½ cup fat-free sour cream
 ½ teaspoon salt
 ¼ teaspoon freshly ground black
    pepper
 1 (10.75-ounce) can condensed
    30%-reduced-sodium, 98%-fat-
    free cream of mushroom soup,
    undiluted
 Cooking spray

1. Cook bacon in a large nonstick skillet over medium heat until crisp. Remove bacon from pan, and crumble. Discard drippings in pan. Add 1 cup onion and garlic to pan; cook 5 minutes or until tender, stirring frequently. Stir in potatoes; cover and cook 15 minutes, stirring occasionally.

2. Combine crumbled bacon, ¼ cup cheese, green onions, sour cream, salt, pepper, and soup in a large bowl. Add potato mixture; toss gently to combine. Spoon mixture into an 11 x 7-inch baking dish coated with cooking spray. Sprinkle with ¾ cup cheese. Cover with foil coated with cooking spray. Refrigerate 8 hours or overnight.

3. Preheat oven to 350°.

4. Remove casserole from refrigerator; let stand at room temperature 15 minutes. Bake casserole, covered, at 350° for 30 minutes. Uncover and bake an additional 30 minutes or until bubbly around edges and cheese begins to brown. Yield: 6 servings (servings size: about 1 cup).

CALORIES 293 (31% from fat); FAT 10g (sat 4.8g, mono 3.3g, poly 0.7g); PROTEIN 12.2g; CARB 41.4g; FIBER 4.7g; CHOL 31mg; IRON 0.2mg; SODIUM 720mg; CALC 214mg

MAKE AHEAD

Baked Coconut French Toast with Tropical Fruit Compote

While the fruit compote really complements this dish, you can omit it and pour on maple syrup instead. If you do so, reduce the amount of sugar in the milk mixture by half.

COMPOTE:
1½ cups chopped fresh pineapple
1 cup chopped peeled mango
1 cup chopped peeled papaya
1 cup chopped peeled kiwifruit
3 tablespoons sugar
3 tablespoons fresh lime juice

FRENCH TOAST:
16 (1-inch-thick) slices diagonally cut French bread baguette (about 10 ounces)
Cooking spray
1¼ cups light coconut milk
1¼ cups egg substitute
½ cup sugar
1 tablespoon vanilla extract
½ cup flaked sweetened coconut

1. To prepare compote, combine first 6 ingredients. Cover and chill 8 hours or overnight.

2. To prepare French toast, arrange bread in a single layer in a 13 x 9-inch baking dish coated with cooking spray. Combine coconut milk and next 3 ingredients, stirring with a whisk, and pour evenly over bread. Turn bread over to coat. Cover and refrigerate 8 hours or overnight.

3. Preheat oven to 350°.

4. Remove bread mixture from refrigerator, and uncover. Turn bread slices over, and sprinkle evenly with flaked coconut. Let stand at room temperature 15 minutes. Bake, uncovered, at 350° for 30 minutes or until coconut is golden. Serve warm with fruit compote. Yield: 8 servings (serving size: 2 French toast slices and ½ cup compote).

CALORIES 349 (22% from fat); FAT 8.6g (sat 3.5g, mono 1.5g, poly 2.5g); PROTEIN 8.6g; CARB 60.3g; FIBER 4.1g; CHOL 0mg; IRON 1.8mg; SODIUM 309mg; CALC 44mg

MAKE AHEAD

Ham, Mushroom, and Gruyère Strata

Rich and savory, this strata is packed with traditional omelet fillings: mushrooms, ham, and Swiss cheese. Substitute other favorite omelet ingredients to vary this simple recipe.

1 teaspoon olive oil
1½ cups thinly sliced shallots
6 cups sliced cremini mushrooms (about 14 ounces)
½ cup chopped reduced-fat ham
¼ cup chopped fresh parsley
12 (1-ounce) slices hearty white bread, cut into ½-inch cubes (about 9 cups)
Cooking spray
1 cup (4 ounces) shredded Gruyère or other Swiss cheese
1⅔ cups fat-free milk
1 cup egg substitute
2 teaspoons Dijon mustard
½ teaspoon salt
¼ teaspoon freshly ground black pepper
1 tablespoon chopped fresh chives (optional)

1. Heat oil in a large nonstick skillet over medium-high heat. Add shallots; sauté 3 minutes or until translucent. Add mushrooms, and sauté 7 minutes or until mushrooms release moisture. Cool slightly. Stir in ham and parsley.

2. Arrange half of bread in a 13 x 9-inch baking dish coated with cooking spray. Top bread with half of mushroom mixture and ½ cup shredded cheese. Repeat layers with remaining bread, mushroom mixture, and ½ cup cheese.

3. Combine milk and next 4 ingredients, stirring with a whisk; pour evenly over bread mixture. Cover with foil coated with cooking spray. Refrigerate 8 hours.

4. Preheat oven to 350°.

5. Remove strata from refrigerator, and let stand at room temperature 15 minutes. Bake strata, covered, at 350° for 30 minutes. Uncover and bake an additional 20 minutes or until set and golden brown. Sprinkle with chives, if desired. Yield: 8 servings.

CALORIES 284 (28% from fat); FAT 8.7g (sat 3.5g, mono 2.6g, poly 0.8g); PROTEIN 18.7g; CARB 31.7g; FIBER 2.4g; CHOL 25mg; IRON 3mg; SODIUM 753mg; CALC 271mg

MAKE AHEAD

Chicken Chilaquiles

This easy Mexican casserole is a traditional way to use leftovers. Freshly assembled, the dish will be very full, but the contents settle a bit overnight. Because there's not much liquid, the chips around the edges of the dish remain crunchy.

12 (6-inch) corn tortillas, each cut into 8 wedges
1½ cups salsa verde (such as Herdez)
¾ cup chopped green onions
½ cup fat-free sour cream
Cooking spray
2 cups shredded skinless, boneless rotisserie chicken breast
1 cup (4 ounces) preshredded Mexican blend cheese

1. Preheat oven to 375°.

2. Arrange half of tortilla wedges on a large baking sheet, overlapping some if necessary. Bake at 375° for 10 minutes or

Continued

until crisp. Remove tortilla wedges from pan. Repeat procedure with remaining tortilla wedges.

3. Combine salsa, green onions, and ½ cup sour cream, stirring with a whisk. Place half of tortilla wedges in an 11 x 7-inch baking dish coated with cooking spray. Top evenly with 1 cup chicken, about 1 cup salsa mixture, and ½ cup cheese. Repeat layers with remaining tortilla wedges, 1 cup chicken, 1 cup salsa mixture, and ½ cup cheese (dish will be very full). Cover with foil coated with cooking spray. Refrigerate 8 hours or overnight.

4. Preheat oven to 350°.

5. Remove casserole from refrigerator; let stand at room temperature 15 minutes. Bake casserole, covered, at 350° for 30 minutes. Uncover and bake an additional 20 minutes or until bubbly around edges and cheese begins to brown. Yield: 6 servings.

CALORIES 311 (27% from fat); FAT 9.3g (sat 4.9g, mono 2.2g, poly 1.1g); PROTEIN 22.5g; CARB 33.1g; FIBER 3.2g; CHOL 58mg; IRON 1.2mg; SODIUM 461mg; CALC 263mg

---

MAKE AHEAD
Cheddar Rice Casserole with Tomato Chutney

    2 cups water
    1 cup uncooked basmati rice
 1½ teaspoons butter
   ½ cup chopped green onions
    3 garlic cloves, minced
2¼ cups 1% low-fat milk
   ¾ cup (3 ounces) shredded
        extrasharp Cheddar cheese
    1 tablespoon all-purpose flour
   ¾ teaspoon salt
   ¼ teaspoon freshly ground black
        pepper
    2 large eggs, lightly beaten
   ⅔ cup tomato chutney
        Cooking spray
   ½ cup (2 ounces) grated fresh
        Parmesan cheese

1. Bring water and rice to a boil in a medium saucepan; cover. Reduce heat, and simmer 20 minutes or until liquid is absorbed. Cool slightly.

2. Melt butter in a nonstick skillet over medium-high heat. Add onions and garlic;

---

sauté 2 minutes. Combine rice, onion mixture, milk, and next 5 ingredients, stirring well. Spread chutney in bottom of an 11 x 7-inch baking dish coated with cooking spray. Carefully spoon rice mixture over chutney. Cover with foil coated with cooking spray. Refrigerate 8 hours or overnight.

3. Preheat oven to 350°.

4. Remove casserole from refrigerator; uncover and let stand at room temperature 15 minutes. Sprinkle with Parmesan. Cover and bake at 350° for 30 minutes. Uncover and bake an additional 30 minutes or until set. Let stand 5 minutes before serving. Yield: 6 servings (serving size: about 1 cup).

CALORIES 338 (30% from fat); FAT 11.4g (sat 6.9g, mono 2g, poly 0.5g); PROTEIN 14.3g; CARB 43.6g; FIBER 1.5g; CHOL 98mg; IRON 2.2mg; SODIUM 622mg; CALC 355mg

---

superfast

. . . And Ready in Just About 20 Minutes

More than a week's worth of quick entrées gets you in and out of the kitchen in a flash.

QUICK & EASY
Pasta Margherita

The toppings on this pasta are reminiscent of margherita pizza.

    8 ounces uncooked angel hair pasta
   ½ cup chopped fresh basil
   ¼ cup chopped green onions (about 2)
    1 teaspoon bottled minced garlic
    1 (16-ounce) package cherry
        tomatoes, halved
   ½ cup (2 ounces) preshredded
        Parmesan cheese
    2 teaspoons olive oil
   ½ teaspoon salt
   ½ teaspoon black pepper
   ½ cup (2 ounces) diced fresh
        mozzarella

---

1. Cook pasta according to package directions, omitting salt and fat. Drain. Place in a large bowl.

2. While pasta cooks, place basil, onions, garlic, and tomatoes in a food processor. Pulse 10 times or until coarsely chopped. Add Parmesan to pasta, and stir until cheese melts. Stir in tomato mixture, oil, salt, and pepper, tossing gently to coat pasta. Top with mozzarella. Yield: 4 servings (serving size: 2 cups pasta and 2 tablespoons mozzarella).

CALORIES 343 (25% from fat); FAT 9.5g (sat 4.2g, mono 3.7g, poly 1g); PROTEIN 14.8g; CARB 49.5g; FIBER 3.2g; CHOL 20mg; IRON 3.1mg; SODIUM 480mg; CALC 218mg

---

QUICK & EASY
Cinnamon-Spiced Pork and Plums

Serve the pork with couscous for a one-dish supper.

   ½ teaspoon ground cinnamon
   ¼ teaspoon salt
   ¼ teaspoon ground cloves
   ¼ teaspoon coarsely ground black
        pepper
    4 (4-ounce) boneless center-cut
        loin pork chops (about ½ inch
        thick)
    1 teaspoon olive oil
   ¼ cup finely chopped shallots
    1 teaspoon butter
    1 cup pitted dried plums, halved
        (about 4 ounces)
   ⅓ cup dry white wine
   ⅓ cup fat-free, less-sodium chicken
        broth
    2 tablespoons chopped fresh
        parsley

1. Combine first 4 ingredients in a small bowl; sprinkle evenly over pork. Heat oil in a large nonstick skillet over medium-high heat. Add pork, and cook 2 minutes on each side or until browned. Add shallots and butter; cook 30 seconds or until butter melts, stirring frequently. Add plums, wine, and broth, turning pork to coat. Cover, reduce heat to medium-low, and cook 2 minutes or until pork is done. Sprinkle with parsley. Yield: 4 servings

---

(serving size: 1 pork chop, ¼ cup sauce, and 1½ teaspoons parsley).

CALORIES 334 (33% from fat); FAT 12.3g (sat 4.3g, mono 5.7g, poly 1g); PROTEIN 32g; CARB 20.6g; FIBER 2.7g; CHOL 94mg; IRON 2.1mg; SODIUM 252mg; CALC 43mg

Quick Chicken and Dumplings

In this recipe, flour tortillas stand in for the traditional biscuit dough. To quickly thaw frozen mixed vegetables, place them in a colander and rinse with warm water for about 1 minute.

  1 tablespoon butter
  ½ cup prechopped onion
  2 cups chopped roasted skinless, boneless chicken breasts
  1 (10-ounce) box frozen mixed vegetables, thawed
1½ cups water
  1 tablespoon all-purpose flour
  1 (14-ounce) can fat-free, less-sodium chicken broth
  ¼ teaspoon salt
  ¼ teaspoon black pepper
  1 bay leaf
  8 (6-inch) flour tortillas, cut into ½-inch strips
  1 tablespoon chopped fresh parsley

1. Melt butter in a large saucepan over medium-high heat. Add onion; sauté 5 minutes or until tender. Stir in chicken and vegetables; cook 3 minutes or until thoroughly heated, stirring constantly.
2. While chicken mixture cooks, combine water, flour, and broth. Gradually stir broth mixture into chicken mixture. Stir in salt, pepper, and bay leaf; bring to a boil. Reduce heat, and simmer 3 minutes. Stir in tortilla strips, and cook 2 minutes or until tortilla strips soften. Remove from heat; stir in parsley. Discard bay leaf. Serve immediately. Yield: 4 servings (serving size: about 1½ cups).

CALORIES 366 (23% from fat); FAT 9.3g (sat 3.1g, mono 3.9g, poly 1.4g); PROTEIN 29.8g; CARB 40.3g; FIBER 5.3g; CHOL 67mg; IRON 3.4mg; SODIUM 652mg; CALC 104mg

Nana's Chicken Pastina Soup

You can substitute orzo or alphabets for pastina in this Sicilian-style chicken soup.

  ½ cup water
  2 (14-ounce) cans fat-free, less-sodium chicken broth
2¼ cups prechopped celery, onion, and carrot mix
  ½ teaspoon black pepper
  ⅛ teaspoon salt
  1 pound chicken breast tenders, cut into 1-inch cubes
  ¼ cup (1½ ounces) uncooked pastina (tiny star-shaped pasta)
  3 tablespoons commercial pesto
  2 tablespoons fresh lemon juice
  ¼ cup (1 ounce) preshredded fresh Parmesan cheese

1. Bring water and broth to a boil in a large saucepan. Stir in celery mix, pepper, salt, and chicken; bring to a boil. Add pasta; cook 4 minutes. Stir in pesto and juice, and simmer 1 minute. Sprinkle with cheese. Yield: 4 servings (serving size: 1½ cups soup and 1 tablespoon cheese).

CALORIES 288 (28% from fat); FAT 9.1g (sat 2.5g, mono 5.2g, poly 1g); PROTEIN 33.7g; CARB 16.3g; FIBER 2.7g; CHOL 73mg; IRON 1.9mg; SODIUM 2mg; CALC 156mg

Asian Beef

Serve atop soba noodles or vermicelli.

  ⅓ cup chopped green onions
  3 tablespoons low-sodium soy sauce
  2 tablespoons rice wine vinegar
  2 tablespoons brown sugar
  1 teaspoon toasted sesame oil
  1 teaspoon bottled minced garlic
  1 teaspoon bottled minced ginger (such as Spice World)
  1 pound flank steak, trimmed
Cooking spray

1. Preheat broiler.
2. Combine first 7 ingredients in a small bowl, stirring with a whisk. Place steak

on a broiler rack coated with cooking spray. Pour soy mixture over steak.
3. Broil steak 3 inches from heat 5 minutes on each side or until desired degree of doneness. Let stand 5 minutes; cut across grain into thin slices. Yield: 4 servings (serving size: 3 ounces beef).

CALORIES 190 (33% from fat); FAT 7g (sat 2.4g, mono 2.5g, poly 0.5g); PROTEIN 24.8g; CARB 5.3g; FIBER 0.2g; CHOL 37mg; IRON 2mg; SODIUM 300mg; CALC 31mg

Lemon-Basil Chicken with Basil Aïoli

This dish makes delicious sandwiches, using the chicken as filling and the aïoli as spread.

CHICKEN:
  ½ cup chopped fresh basil
  ⅓ cup chopped green onions
  2 tablespoons fresh lemon juice
  2 tablespoons white wine vinegar
  ½ teaspoon lemon pepper
  ¼ teaspoon freshly ground black pepper
  4 (6-ounce) skinless, boneless chicken breast halves
Cooking spray

BASIL AÏOLI:
  ¼ cup finely chopped fresh basil
  2 tablespoons low-fat mayonnaise
  1 tablespoon fresh lemon juice
1½ teaspoons Dijon mustard
  ¾ teaspoon bottled minced garlic
  ½ teaspoon olive oil

1. To prepare chicken, combine first 6 ingredients in a large bowl. Add chicken, turning to coat.
2. Heat a large nonstick skillet over medium-high heat. Coat pan with cooking spray. Add chicken to pan; cook 8 minutes on each side or until done.
3. While chicken cooks, prepare aïoli. Combine ¼ cup basil and remaining 5 ingredients in a small bowl, stirring with a whisk. Serve with chicken. Yield: 4 servings (serving size: 1 chicken breast half and 1 tablespoon aïoli).

CALORIES 284 (32% from fat); FAT 10.3g (sat 1.7g, mono 1.4g, poly 0.6g); PROTEIN 40.1g; CARB 6.1g; FIBER 1g; CHOL 106mg; IRON 1.9mg; SODIUM 410mg; CALC 51mg

Turkey and Cranberry Port Wine Sauce

Use cranberry sauce left over from your holiday meal to make this easy supper. The recipe calls for shallots, which have a milder, sweeter flavor than onions. A sweet onion will work, as well.

  1 tablespoon canola oil
  4 (4-ounce) turkey breast cutlets
  ½ teaspoon salt, divided
  ½ teaspoon black pepper, divided
  1 tablespoon butter
  ¼ cup chopped shallots
  ⅔ cup whole-berry cranberry sauce
  ¼ cup port wine
  1 tablespoon chopped fresh sage
  1 tablespoon red wine vinegar
Whole sage leaves (optional)

1. Heat oil in a large nonstick skillet over medium-high heat. Sprinkle turkey with ¼ teaspoon salt and ¼ teaspoon pepper. Add turkey to pan; cook 5 minutes on each side or until done. Transfer turkey to a plate.
2. Melt butter in pan. Add shallots; sauté 30 seconds. Reduce heat to medium; stir in cranberry sauce, port, chopped sage, vinegar, ¼ teaspoon salt, and ¼ teaspoon pepper. Cook 2 minutes or until slightly thickened, stirring occasionally.
3. Return turkey to pan. Cook 1 minute or until thoroughly heated. Serve with sauce. Garnish with sage leaves, if desired. Yield: 4 servings (serving size: 1 cutlet and ¼ cup sauce).

CALORIES 276 (23% from fat); FAT 6.9g (sat 1.7g, mono 3.2g, poly 1.1g); PROTEIN 28.4g; CARB 21.5g; FIBER 0.8g; CHOL 53mg; IRON 1.7mg; SODIUM 428mg; CALC 16mg

Seared Salmon on Herbed Mashed Peas

You may need to thin the puréed pea mixture; add one tablespoon of water at a time until you achieve the desired consistency. Serve with sautéed sliced fennel.

  1 teaspoon butter
  1 cup thinly sliced leek
  ¼ cup water
  1 (10-ounce) package frozen green peas, thawed
  1 tablespoon chopped fresh basil
  2 tablespoons fresh lemon juice
  2 teaspoons chopped fresh tarragon
  ½ teaspoon salt, divided
  ½ teaspoon black pepper, divided
  4 (6-ounce) salmon fillets
Cooking spray
Lemon wedges (optional)

1. Heat butter in a medium nonstick skillet over medium heat. Add leek; cook 5 minutes or until tender, stirring occasionally. Add water and peas; cook 5 minutes or until peas are tender.
2. Place pea mixture in a food processor. Add basil, juice, and tarragon; process until smooth, adding more water if necessary. Stir in ¼ teaspoon salt and ¼ teaspoon pepper; keep warm.
3. Sprinkle salmon with ¼ teaspoon salt and ¼ teaspoon pepper. Heat a nonstick skillet over medium-high heat. Coat pan with cooking spray. Add salmon, skin side down, and cook 6 minutes or until golden. Turn and cook 8 minutes or until fish flakes easily when tested with a fork or until desired degree of doneness. Serve salmon over warm mashed peas. Garnish with lemon wedges, if desired. Yield: 4 servings (serving size: 1 salmon fillet and about ½ cup mashed peas).

CALORIES 393 (46% from fat); FAT 19.9g (sat 4.4g, mono 7g, poly 6.9g); PROTEIN 38g; CARB 13.8g; FIBER 3.5g; CHOL 103mg; IRON 2.2mg; SODIUM 482mg; CALC 54mg

season's best

Harvest Sweet Potato Pecan Pie Tarts

Our Harvest Sweet Potato Pecan Pie Tarts boast sweet potato filling with a pecan pie-like topping, all tucked into miniature phyllo pastry shells.

Harvest Sweet Potato Pecan Pie Tarts

Pierce each sweet potato a few times with a fork, place in a pie plate with two tablespoons water, cover loosely with wax paper, and microwave at HIGH five minutes or until tender.

  1 cup mashed cooked sweet potato
  3 tablespoons granulated sugar
  ¼ teaspoon ground cinnamon
  ⅛ teaspoon salt
  ⅓ cup chopped toasted pecans
  ¼ cup firmly packed brown sugar
  1 tablespoon dark corn syrup
  ½ teaspoon vanilla extract
  1 egg white
  2 (2.1-ounce) packages mini phyllo shells (such as Athens)

1. Preheat oven to 350°.
2. Combine first 4 ingredients in a small bowl, stirring well.
3. Combine pecans and next 4 ingredients, stirring well.
4. Spoon about 1 teaspoon sweet potato mixture into each phyllo shell, spreading to edges. Top each tart with about ½ teaspoon pecan mixture. Place filled shells on an ungreased baking sheet. Bake at 350° for 20 minutes. Cool completely on a wire rack. Yield: 15 servings (serving size: 2 tarts).

CALORIES 89 (39% from fat); FAT 3.9g (sat 0.2g, mono 2.2g, poly 0.9g); PROTEIN 0.6g; CARB 13.1g; FIBER 0.5g; CHOL 0mg; IRON 0.6mg; SODIUM 55mg; CALC 9mg

Pumpkin Pie Cake, page 360

Southwestern Chicken Soup, page 407

Sour Cream Muffins with Poppy Seed Streusel, page 395

Roasted Beet, Avocado, and Watercress Salad, page 381

Clockwise from bottom: Parmesan-Sage Roast Turkey with Sage Gravy (page 385); Cranberry, Cherry, and Walnut Chutney (page 395); Sourdough Stuffing with Pears and Sausage (page 391); Flaky Dinner Rolls (page 396); Camembert Mashed Potatoes (page 393); and Oven-Roasted Green Beans (page 392)

The *Cooking Light*® Holiday Cookbook

Your guide to the season's best recipes, menus, tips, and techniques

Getting Started

Kick off the festivities with crowd-pleasing soups, salads, drinks, and snacks.

MAKE AHEAD

Roasted Beet, Avocado, and Watercress Salad

(pictured on page 379)

This dish features holiday colors and a variety of textures, from crisp watercress and crunchy pecans to juicy oranges and buttery avocados. To make the most of the presentation, use a combination of red and yellow beets. You can prepare the beets and dressing in advance, then just assemble the salad before serving.

6 large red or yellow beets (about 4½ pounds)
¼ cup water
1½ teaspoons finely grated orange rind
⅓ cup fresh orange juice
3 tablespoons extravirgin olive oil
2½ tablespoons sherry vinegar
¾ teaspoon sugar
½ teaspoon salt
¼ teaspoon freshly ground black pepper
1 large avocado, peeled
3 bunches watercress (about 9 cups trimmed)
3 cups orange sections (about 3 large navel oranges)
¾ cup vertically sliced red onion
3 tablespoons chopped pecans, toasted

1. Preheat oven to 375°.
2. Remove root and 1 inch stem on beets; scrub with a brush. Cut beets in half; place beets in a 13 x 9-inch baking dish. Add ¼ cup water. Cover with foil, and bake at 375° for 1 hour or until tender. Cool; rub off skins. Cut beets into ½-inch slices.
3. Combine rind and next 6 ingredients in a small bowl. Toss half of juice mixture with beets.
4. Cut avocado in half lengthwise. Cut each half into 12 slices. Place watercress on a platter; top with beets, orange sections, onion, and avocado. Drizzle remaining juice mixture over salad, and top with pecans. Serve immediately. Yield: 12 servings (serving size: ¾ cup watercress, ⅓ cup beets, ¼ cup orange sections, 2 slices avocado, ¾ teaspoon pecans, and 1 tablespoon dressing).

CALORIES 168 (41% from fat); FAT 7.7g (sat 1.1g, mono 5.1g, poly 1.1g); PROTEIN 4g; CARB 24g; FIBER 5.2g; CHOL 0mg; IRON 1.6mg; SODIUM 232mg; CALC 66mg

Spiked Pumpkin Soup

This silky, slightly sweet soup is a fitting starter for various holiday entrées, including roast turkey, ham, or pork tenderloin. Bourbon enhances the natural sweetness of the pumpkin.

Cooking spray
1 cup chopped onion
½ teaspoon minced peeled fresh ginger
½ teaspoon ground cumin
2 garlic cloves, minced
1½ cups apple cider
⅓ cup bourbon
¼ cup maple syrup
1 (29-ounce) can pumpkin
1 (14-ounce) can fat-free, less-sodium chicken broth
2 cups 2% reduced-fat milk
1 teaspoon all-purpose flour
½ teaspoon salt
¼ teaspoon freshly ground black pepper
9 tablespoons reduced-fat sour cream
3 tablespoons chopped fresh parsley (optional)

1. Heat a large Dutch oven over medium-high heat. Coat pan with cooking spray. Add onion, ginger, cumin, and garlic; sauté 5 minutes or until lightly browned. Stir in cider and next 4 ingredients; bring to a boil. Reduce heat, and simmer 10 minutes.
2. Place half of pumpkin mixture in a blender; process until smooth. Pour puréed mixture into a large bowl. Repeat procedure with remaining pumpkin mixture. Return puréed mixture to pan. Stir

Continued

in milk, flour, salt, and pepper; cook until thoroughly heated (do not boil), stirring frequently. Serve with sour cream. Garnish with parsley, if desired. Yield: 9 servings (serving size: about 1 cup soup and 1 tablespoon sour cream).

CALORIES 163 (19% from fat); FAT 3.4g (sat 1.8g, mono 0.3g, poly 0.1g); PROTEIN 5.1g; CARB 24.9g; FIBER 4.2g; CHOL 12mg; IRON 0.8mg; SODIUM 255mg; CALC 119mg

MAKE AHEAD
Smoked Trout with Apple-Horseradish Cream on Potato Pancakes

For convenience, make the pancakes up to a day ahead and reheat them in the oven before serving.

½ cup all-purpose flour (about 2¼ ounces)
4¾ cups shredded peeled baking potato (about 2 pounds)
½ cup grated fresh onion
1 teaspoon salt
½ teaspoon freshly ground black pepper
2 large egg whites, lightly beaten
3 tablespoons olive oil, divided
Cooking spray
¼ cup reduced-fat mayonnaise
3 tablespoons finely chopped Granny Smith apple
2 tablespoons plain fat-free yogurt
4 teaspoons prepared horseradish
4 ounces smoked rainbow trout, bones removed, broken into 48 pieces
3 tablespoons chopped fresh chives

1. Preheat oven to 400°.
2. Lightly spoon flour into a dry measuring cup; level with a knife. Combine flour and next 5 ingredients in a large bowl, stirring until blended. Divide mixture into 48 level tablespoon-sized pancakes, squeezing each to remove excess moisture.
3. Heat 1 tablespoon oil in a nonstick

skillet over medium-high heat. Add 16 pancakes; cook 3 minutes on each side or until browned. Arrange on two baking sheets coated with cooking spray. Repeat procedure twice with remaining oil and pancakes. Bake at 400° for 5 minutes or until thoroughly heated.
4. Combine mayonnaise, apple, yogurt, and horseradish in a small bowl; place ½ teaspoon mayonnaise mixture on each pancake. Top each with a trout piece; sprinkle with chives. Yield: 12 servings (serving size: 4 pancakes).

CALORIES 149 (28% from fat); FAT 4.6g (sat 0.7g, mono 2.7g, poly 0.6g); PROTEIN 5.4g; CARB 22g; FIBER 1.7g; CHOL 8mg; IRON 0.6mg; SODIUM 260mg; CALC 12mg

Apple, Walnut, and Mixed Greens Salad with Zinfandel-Cranberry Vinaigrette

Tossing the cubed apples with lemon juice will help keep them from turning brown. If you prefer sharper onion flavor, use red onions instead of Walla Wallas.

1 cup sweetened dried cranberries (such as Craisins)
¾ cup apple juice
½ cup zinfandel or other fruity dry red wine
½ cup cranberry juice cocktail
3 tablespoons minced shallots
1½ tablespoons fresh lemon juice
½ teaspoon salt
¼ teaspoon freshly ground black pepper
1 tablespoon walnut oil
10 cups gourmet salad greens
3 cups cubed Gala apple (about 2 apples)
1 cup thinly sliced Walla Walla or other sweet onion (about 1 medium onion)
⅓ cup coarsely chopped walnuts, toasted

1. Combine cranberries and apple juice in a medium saucepan; bring to a boil. Remove from heat; let stand 10 minutes.

Drain cranberries; discard apple juice. Set cranberries aside.
2. Bring wine and cranberry juice to a boil in pan, and cook until reduced to ⅓ cup (about 8 minutes). Pour wine mixture into a medium bowl; add shallots, lemon juice, salt, and pepper. Gradually add oil, stirring with a whisk.
3. Combine cranberries, greens, apple, and onion in a large bowl. Drizzle dressing over salad; toss gently to coat. Sprinkle with walnuts. Yield: 10 servings (serving size: about 1⅓ cups salad and about 1½ teaspoons walnuts).

CALORIES 140 (28% from fat); FAT 4.4g (sat 0.4g, mono 0.7g, poly 2.8g); PROTEIN 2.7g; CARB 25.2g; FIBER 4.3g; CHOL 0mg; IRON 1.7mg; SODIUM 146mg; CALC 58mg

MAKE AHEAD
Roasted Cauliflower Soup

Roasting the cauliflower deepens its flavor.

3 pounds cauliflower florets (about 2 large heads)
2 teaspoons olive oil
1½ teaspoons minced fresh thyme
1 teaspoon kosher salt
Cooking spray
4 cups fat-free, less-sodium chicken broth, divided
1¾ cups 2% reduced-fat milk
Dash of finely ground black pepper
Thyme sprigs (optional)

1. Preheat oven to 400°.
2. Combine florets and oil in a large bowl; toss to coat. Add thyme and salt; toss well. Arrange florets on a jelly-roll pan coated with cooking spray. Bake at 400° for 1 hour or until golden brown, stirring after 30 minutes.
3. Place florets, 2 cups broth, and milk in a blender. Process 3 minutes or until smooth. Pour puréed mixture into a large saucepan. Add 2 cups broth and pepper. Cook over medium heat until thoroughly heated. Garnish with fresh thyme sprigs, if desired. Yield: 8 servings (serving size: 1 cup).

CALORIES 88 (26% from fat); FAT 2.5g (sat 0.9g, mono 1.2g, poly 0.3g); PROTEIN 6.4g; CARB 12.1g; FIBER 4.8g; CHOL 4mg; IRON 1.1mg; SODIUM 506mg; CALC 110mg

Winter-Spiced
Red Wine Sangría

You can substitute navel oranges.

1 cup apple juice
⅓ cup Triple Sec (orange-flavored liqueur)
¼ cup sugar
4 whole cloves
3 blood oranges, cut into ¼-inch slices
2 lemons, cut into ¼-inch slices
2 (3-inch) cinnamon sticks
1 Bartlett pear, cut into ½-inch cubes
1 (750-milliliter) bottle fruity red wine

1. Combine all ingredients in a large pitcher; stir until sugar dissolves. Cover and refrigerate at least 4 hours or overnight. Remove cloves and cinnamon sticks before serving. Yield: 10 servings (serving size: ¾ cup).

CALORIES 149 (0% from fat); FAT 0.1g (sat 0g, mono 0g, poly 0g); PROTEIN 0.5g; CARB 22g; FIBER 1.6g; CHOL 0mg; IRON 0.4mg; SODIUM 7mg; CALC 31mg

Baba Ghanoush
with Red Pepper Swirl

Store the dip and purée separately.

3 (1-pound) eggplants
¼ cup fresh lemon juice
3 tablespoons tahini (sesame-seed paste)
2 tablespoons extravirgin olive oil
¾ teaspoon salt
¼ teaspoon freshly ground black pepper
2 garlic cloves, peeled
¼ cup fat-free sour cream
1 (7-ounce) bottle roasted red bell peppers, drained
6 (6-inch) pitas, each cut into 6 wedges

1. Preheat oven to 375°.
2. Pierce eggplants several times with a fork; place on a foil-lined baking sheet. Bake at 375° for 45 minutes or until tender. Cut eggplants in half; scoop out pulp. Discard shells. Drain pulp in a colander 30 minutes. Place pulp in a food processor; pulse 5 times. Add juice and next 5 ingredients, and process until almost smooth. Remove from processor.
3. Place sour cream and bell peppers in food processor, and process until smooth. Swirl bell pepper mixture into eggplant mixture. Serve with pita wedges. Yield: 12 servings (serving size: ½ cup dip and 3 pita wedges).

CALORIES 164 (27% from fat); FAT 5g (sat 0.7g, mono 2.6g, poly 1.3g); PROTEIN 4.9g; CARB 26.8g; FIBER 0.9g; CHOL 0mg; IRON 0.9mg; SODIUM 337mg; CALC 50mg

Vanilla-Scented
Mulled Cider

Loose spices permeate the cider more than those wrapped in cheesecloth.

8 cups apple cider
12 black peppercorns, crushed
8 whole allspice
2 bay leaves
1 (3-inch) piece vanilla bean, split lengthwise and scraped
1 (2 x ½-inch) strip lemon rind

1. Combine all ingredients in a large saucepan; bring to a simmer. Cook 20 minutes, stirring occasionally. Strain cider through a sieve, and discard solids. Yield: 8 servings (serving size: ¾ cup).

CALORIES 140 (0% from fat); FAT 0g; PROTEIN 1g; CARB 35g; FIBER 0g; CHOL 0mg; IRON 0mg; SODIUM 0mg; CALC 0mg

Cranberry Mimosa

This drink starts your gathering in style.

4 cups cranberry juice cocktail
4 cups orange juice
2 (750-milliliter) bottles chilled Champagne or sparkling wine
12 orange slices (optional)

1. Fill 12 (12-ounce) glasses with ice; pour ⅓ cup cranberry juice into each glass. Top each serving with ⅓ cup orange juice and about ½ cup Champagne. Garnish with orange slices, if desired. Yield: 12 servings (serving size: 1 mimosa).

CALORIES 170 (2% from fat); FAT 0.3g (sat 0g, mono 0g, poly 0.1g); PROTEIN 0.7g; CARB 21.7g; FIBER 0.3g; CHOL 0mg; IRON 0.7mg; SODIUM 9mg; CALC 23mg

Pumpkin Hummus

This dish offers a holiday-style twist on the traditional Middle Eastern spread. You can find pumpkinseeds—also called *pepitas*—in groceries and Mexican markets. Prepare up to a day ahead, and refrigerate.

4 (6-inch) pitas, each cut into 8 wedges
Cooking spray
2 tablespoons tahini (sesame-seed paste)
2 tablespoons fresh lemon juice
1 teaspoon ground cumin
1 teaspoon olive oil
¾ teaspoon salt
⅛ teaspoon ground red pepper
1 (15-ounce) can pumpkin
1 garlic clove, chopped
2 tablespoons chopped fresh flat-leaf parsley
1 tablespoon pumpkinseed kernels, toasted (optional)

1. Preheat oven to 425°.
2. Place pita wedges on baking sheets; coat with cooking spray. Bake at 425° for 6 minutes or until toasted.
3. Place tahini and next 7 ingredients in a food processor, and process until smooth. Add parsley; pulse until blended. Spoon hummus into a serving bowl; sprinkle with pumpkinseed kernels, if desired. Serve with pita wedges. Yield: 10 servings (serving size: about 3 tablespoons hummus and about 3 pita wedges).

CALORIES 117 (20% from fat); FAT 2.6g (sat 0.4g, mono 1g, poly 0.9g); PROTEIN 3.7g; CARB 20.4g; FIBER 2.1g; CHOL 0mg; IRON 1.6mg; SODIUM 330mg; CALC 43mg

Winter Plum Soup

This rosy purée of canned plums, wine, and Cointreau is equally good served warm, at room temperature, or chilled. It makes a wonderful first course or a refreshingly light dessert. Prepare up to one day ahead, and chill in the refrigerator, allowing the flavors to meld before serving.

2   (16-ounce) cans plums in light
        syrup, undrained
2   cups dry red wine
1   tablespoon honey
½   teaspoon ground cinnamon
¼   teaspoon ground cloves
¼   cup Cointreau or other
        orange-flavored liqueur
½   teaspoon grated lemon rind
6   tablespoons vanilla low-fat yogurt
6   mint sprigs (optional)

1. Strain plums through a sieve into a bowl, reserving juice. Cut plums in half; discard pits. Combine plums, reserved juice, wine, honey, cinnamon, and cloves in a medium saucepan. Bring to a boil. Cover; reduce heat, and simmer 15 minutes. Place half of soup in a blender; process until smooth. Pour into a bowl. Repeat procedure with remaining soup. Stir in liqueur and rind. Place ¾ cup soup into each of 6 wine goblets. Top each serving with 1 tablespoon yogurt and 1 mint sprig, if desired. Yield: 6 servings.

CALORIES 133 (3% from fat); FAT 0.4g (sat 0.1g, mono 0.2g, poly 0.1g); PROTEIN 1.5g; CARB 32g; FIBER 1.5g; CHOL 1mg; IRON 1.7mg; SODIUM 47mg; CALC 49mg

Creamy Crab Cocktail Salad on Garlic-Rubbed Crostini

This flavorful hors d'oeuvre is sure to please your guests. If you make this dish ahead of time, top the crostini with salad just before serving to keep the bread from becoming soggy. Common condiments provide flavor boosts in this dish.

40   (½-inch-thick) slices diagonally
         cut French bread baguette (about
         10 ounces)
  2   garlic cloves, halved
 ¼   cup finely chopped red onion
 ¼   cup finely chopped celery
 ¼   cup finely chopped red bell
         pepper
  1   pound lump crabmeat, drained
         and shell pieces removed
  5   tablespoons low-fat mayonnaise
  3   tablespoons reduced-fat sour
         cream
  2   tablespoons fresh lemon juice
  1   tablespoon chopped fresh parsley
  2   teaspoons Dijon mustard
  1   teaspoon Worcestershire sauce
 ¼   teaspoon salt
 ¼   teaspoon hot pepper sauce (such
         as Tabasco)

1. Preheat oven to 400°.
2. Place bread slices on a large baking sheet. Bake at 400° for 10 minutes or until crisp. Cool slightly. Lightly rub 1 side of each bread slice with cut sides of garlic. Discard garlic.
3. Combine onion, celery, bell pepper, and crab in a bowl. Combine mayonnaise and remaining 7 ingredients. Spoon over crab mixture, and toss gently. Top each bread slice with 1 tablespoon crab mixture. Yield: 20 servings (serving size: 2 crostini).

CALORIES 74 (18% from fat); FAT 1.5g (sat 0.5g, mono 0.5g, poly 0.5g); PROTEIN 5.8g; CARB 9.4g; FIBER 0.5g; CHOL 15mg; IRON 0.6mg; SODIUM 246mg; CALC 33mg

Roasted Butternut Squash Soup with Apples and Garam Masala

While traditional curry powders often use turmeric as a base, garam masala, a North Indian spice blend, starts with a mix of cardamom, coriander, and black pepper. If you can't find Braeburn apples, Cortland apples will do. Use two percent reduced-fat milk in place of soy milk, if you prefer.

8   cups (1-inch) cubed peeled
        butternut squash (about
        2 medium)
3   tablespoons olive oil, divided
2   tablespoons maple syrup
1   teaspoon kosher salt
1¼ teaspoons garam masala
⅛   teaspoon freshly ground black
        pepper
Cooking spray
¼   cup finely chopped shallots
4   cups chopped peeled Braeburn
        apple (about 1 pound)
¼   cup sweet white wine
3   cups water
1   (14-ounce) can fat-free,
        less-sodium chicken broth
2   tablespoons soy milk

1. Preheat oven to 400°.
2. Combine squash, 2 tablespoons oil, syrup, salt, garam masala, and pepper in a large bowl. Arrange squash in a single layer on a jelly-roll pan coated with cooking spray. Bake at 400° for 45 minutes or until soft.
3. Heat 1 tablespoon oil in a large skillet over medium-high heat. Add shallots; sauté 2 minutes or until tender. Stir in apple; sauté 2 minutes or until tender. Stir in wine; cook 1 minute. Stir in squash, water, and broth. Bring to a simmer; cook 3 minutes. Place half of soup in a blender; process until smooth. Strain mixture through a sieve into a bowl; discard solids. Repeat procedure with remaining soup. Stir in soy milk. Yield: 8 servings (serving size: about 1 cup).

CALORIES 203 (25% from fat); FAT 5.6g (sat 0.8g, mono 3.8g, poly 0.7g); PROTEIN 3.4g; CARB 40g; FIBER 5.9g; CHOL 0mg; IRON 2.1mg; SODIUM 327mg; CALC 130mg

The Main Event

Show-stopping entrées take the spotlight at the holiday table.

Parmesan-Sage Roast Turkey with Sage Gravy

(pictured on page 380)

For a handsome garnish, roast lemon halves and peeled shallots at 425° for 20 minutes; arrange with sage sprigs on the turkey platter.

- 3 cups chopped onion
- 1 cup chopped celery
- 1 cup chopped carrot
- 10 garlic cloves
- Cooking spray
- 1 (13-pound) fresh or frozen turkey, thawed
- ⅓ cup (1½ ounces) grated fresh Parmigiano-Reggiano cheese
- 5 tablespoons chopped fresh sage, divided
- 2 tablespoons butter, softened
- 1 tablespoon minced garlic
- 1 teaspoon salt, divided
- ½ teaspoon freshly ground black pepper, divided
- 1 lemon, halved
- 2½ cups fat-free, less-sodium chicken broth, divided
- ⅓ cup chopped shallots
- 1 cup sherry
- ¼ cup all-purpose flour (about 1 ounce)
- ¼ cup water

1. Preheat oven to 425°.

2. Combine first 4 ingredients in a shallow roasting pan coated with cooking spray. Remove and discard giblets and neck from turkey. Rinse turkey with cold water; pat dry. Trim excess fat. Starting at neck cavity, loosen skin from breast and drumsticks by inserting fingers, gently pushing between skin and meat. Lift wing tips up and over back; tuck under turkey.

3. Combine cheese, ¼ cup sage, butter, minced garlic, ¾ teaspoon salt, and ¼ teaspoon pepper; rub mixture under loosened skin and over breast and drumsticks. Rub turkey skin with cut sides of lemon halves; squeeze juice into turkey cavity. Place lemon halves in turkey cavity; tie legs together with kitchen string.

4. Place turkey, breast side up, on vegetable mixture in pan. Bake at 425° for 30 minutes, and pour 2 cups broth over turkey. Tent turkey breast loosely with foil. Bake an additional 30 minutes.

5. Reduce oven temperature to 325° (do not remove turkey from oven). Bake at 325° for 1½ hours or until a thermometer inserted into meaty part of thigh registers 180°, basting every 30 minutes. Remove turkey from pan. Cover and let stand 30 minutes; discard skin.

6. Place a large zip-top plastic bag inside a 4-cup glass measure. Pour drippings through a sieve into bag; discard solids. Let drippings stand 10 minutes (fat will rise to top). Seal bag; carefully snip off 1 bottom corner of bag. Drain drippings into a medium bowl, stopping before fat layer reaches opening; discard fat. Add enough of remaining chicken broth to drippings to equal 3 cups.

7. Heat a medium saucepan over medium-high heat. Coat pan with cooking spray. Add shallots; sauté 1 minute. Add sherry; bring to a boil. Cook until reduced to ½ cup (about 5 minutes). Stir in 1 tablespoon sage, and cook 30 seconds. Add reserved drippings; bring to a boil.

8. Lightly spoon flour into a dry measuring cup; level with a knife. Combine flour and water, stirring well with a whisk. Stir flour mixture into drippings mixture; bring to a boil. Cook 2 minutes or until thickened, stirring constantly. Stir in ¼ teaspoon salt and ¼ teaspoon pepper. Serve gravy with turkey. Yield: 16 servings (serving size: about 5 ounces turkey meat and about 3 tablespoons gravy).

CALORIES 285 (30% from fat); FAT 9.6g (sat 3.5g, mono 2.5g, poly 2.2g); PROTEIN 40.9g; CARB 3.5g; FIBER 0.3g; CHOL 108mg; IRON 2.7mg; SODIUM 339mg; CALC 64mg

WINE NOTE: One of the best wines for roast turkey (and poultry in general) is pinot noir. In this case, the seasonings—sage, Parmesan, garlic—underscore that choice. Pinot noir's earthy flavors provide a delicious backdrop for the meatiness of the turkey, the herbal quality of the sage, the salty-nuttiness of the cheese, and the pungency of the garlic. As an added boon, pinot noir has a supple, silky texture—just the ticket for a savory bird. Be forewarned: Great pinot noirs are expensive, but this is the time of year to splurge. Try Merry Edwards Estate Pinot Noir 2003 from California's Sonoma Coast ($48).

Smoked Ham Soup with White Beans

If you have the time, soak the beans overnight instead of using the quick-soak method called for; this will result in creamier beans. This high-fiber soup is also great when made with dried cannellini beans. Serve with your favorite corn bread recipe.

- 1 (16-ounce) package dried navy beans
- 1 tablespoon olive oil
- 2 cups chopped yellow onion
- 4 garlic cloves, minced
- 8 cups fat-free, less-sodium chicken broth
- 4 cups water
- 2 tablespoons chopped fresh parsley
- 1 teaspoon chopped fresh thyme
- ¼ teaspoon salt
- ¼ teaspoon freshly ground black pepper
- 2 smoked ham hocks (about 1 pound)
- 2 bay leaves
- 1 (14.5-ounce) can petite diced tomatoes, undrained

1. Sort and wash beans; place in a large Dutch oven. Cover with water to 2 inches above beans; bring to a boil. Cook 2 minutes. Remove from heat; cover and let stand 1 hour. Drain.

2. Heat oil in pan over medium heat. Add onion; cook until tender, stirring occasionally. Add garlic, and cook 1 minute, stirring frequently. Add drained beans, broth, and remaining ingredients;

Continued

bring to a boil. Cover, reduce heat, and simmer 2½ hours or until beans are tender. Discard bay leaves.

3. Remove ham hocks with a slotted spoon, and cool slightly. Remove meat from bones; discard fat, gristle, and bones. Shred meat with 2 forks.

4. Place 1 cup bean mixture in a blender; process until smooth. Return puréed bean mixture to pan; stir until blended. Stir in meat. Yield: 8 servings (serving size: 1¼ cups).

CALORIES 323 (23% from fat); FAT 8.4g (sat 2.6g, mono 4g, poly 1.1g); PROTEIN 22g; CARB 40.7g; FIBER 16.2g; CHOL 27mg; IRON 5.6mg; SODIUM 558mg; CALC 137mg

Penne with Brussels Sprouts and Crisp Bacon

To trim Brussels sprouts, discard the tough outer leaves and trim off about ¼ inch from stems. Don't trim too much from the stems, or the sprouts will fall apart.

    12 ounces uncooked penne
        (tube-shaped pasta)
     3 cups trimmed, halved Brussels
        sprouts (about 1 pound)
     ¼ teaspoon salt
     2 bacon slices
     1 cup 1% low-fat milk
     2 tablespoons all-purpose
        flour
     1 (14-ounce) can fat-free,
        less-sodium chicken broth
     1 tablespoon butter
     ¾ cup (3 ounces) grated Parmigiano-
        Reggiano cheese, divided
     1 tablespoon chopped hazelnuts,
        toasted
     ¼ teaspoon freshly ground black
        pepper

1. Cook pasta according to package directions, omitting salt and fat. Drain well.
2. Steam Brussels sprouts, covered, 7 minutes or until tender. Drain and sprinkle with salt.
3. Cook bacon in a Dutch oven over medium-high heat until crisp. Remove bacon from pan, reserving 1 teaspoon drippings in pan. Crumble bacon; set aside.

4. Add Brussels sprouts to drippings in pan; sauté 5 minutes or until lightly browned. Stir in pasta; cover mixture, and keep warm.
5. Combine milk, flour, and broth, stirring well with a whisk. Melt butter in a medium saucepan over medium heat. Gradually add milk mixture, stirring constantly with a whisk until well blended. Cook 6 minutes or until thickened, stirring constantly. Stir in ¼ cup cheese, stirring until cheese melts. Pour sauce over pasta mixture, tossing to coat. Top with ½ cup cheese, nuts, bacon, and pepper; serve immediately. Yield: 6 servings (serving size: 1½ cups).

CALORIES 384 (28% from fat); FAT 12g (sat 5.3g, mono 4.3g, poly 1.3g); PROTEIN 17.4g; CARB 53.3g; FIBER 4.9g; CHOL 23mg; IRON 3.3mg; SODIUM 476mg; CALC 207mg

Oven-Braised Lentils with Sausage

Comforting and easy to prepare, this hearty dish is good for busy nights, as the lentils cook in the oven and leave you free to tend to other things.

     2 teaspoons olive oil
     2 cups chopped onion
    1¼ cups chopped celery
     ½ cup chopped carrot
     2 garlic cloves, minced
     3 tablespoons tomato paste
     1 cup dry white wine
     3 cups water
     ¼ teaspoon salt
     ¼ teaspoon freshly ground black
        pepper
     3 thyme sprigs
     1 bay leaf
     2 (14-ounce) cans fat-free,
        less-sodium chicken broth
     1 (16-ounce) bag dried lentils
     1 (14-ounce) package turkey
        kielbasa, cut into ½-inch slices

1. Preheat oven to 375°.
2. Heat oil in a large Dutch oven over medium-high heat. Add onion, celery, carrot, and garlic; sauté 5 minutes. Stir in tomato paste, and cook 1 minute, stirring constantly. Add wine, scraping pan

to loosen browned bits; cook 1 minute. Add water and remaining ingredients; bring to a boil. Cover and place in oven. Bake at 375° for 1 hour and 15 minutes or until lentils are tender; discard bay leaf. Yield: 10 servings (serving size: about 1¼ cups).

CALORIES 234 (14% from fat); FAT 3.6g (sat 1.3g, mono 1.6g, poly 0.4g); PROTEIN 20g; CARB 33g; FIBER 15.4g; CHOL 10mg; IRON 5.2mg; SODIUM 450mg; CALC 109mg

MAKE AHEAD
Blackberry-Mustard Glazed Ham

This classic recipe will be well received at all your holiday gatherings; try it with any flavor of fruit preserves you enjoy. Adorn the platter with fresh blackberries, apple slices, oregano, and flat-leaf parsley.

     1 (5-pound) 33%-less-sodium
        smoked, fully-cooked, bone-in
        ham half
        Cooking spray
     ½ cup apple juice
     1 (13-ounce) jar blackberry
        preserves
     1 (7.3-ounce) jar whole-grain Dijon
        mustard

1. Preheat oven to 350°.
2. Trim fat and rind from ham. Score outside of ham in a diamond pattern. Place ham on a broiler pan coated with cooking spray.
3. Combine juice, preserves, and mustard in a medium bowl, stirring well. Set aside half of preserves mixture.
4. Bake ham at 350° for 1½ hours or until a thermometer registers 140°, basting with remaining half of preserves mixture every 20 minutes. Remove ham from oven. Place ham on a platter; cover and let stand 15 minutes before slicing.
5. Place reserved preserves mixture in a large nonstick skillet over medium-low heat. Cook until reduced to 1 cup (about 15 minutes). Serve sauce with ham. Yield: 20 servings (serving size: 3 ounces ham and about 2 teaspoons sauce).

CALORIES 185 (27% from fat); FAT 5.6g (sat 1.6g, mono 2.3g, poly 0.5g); PROTEIN 18.3g; CARB 14.8g; FIBER 1g; CHOL 45mg; IRON 1.5mg; SODIUM 1,011mg; CALC 15mg

Maple-Planked Mahimahi with Charmoula

If it's warm enough to grill outdoors, try serving your family this exotic entrée. *Charmoula* is a traditional Moroccan herb-and-spice mixture similar to pesto. A bed of rice ensures that none of the flavorful sauce goes to waste.

  1 (15 x 6½ x ⅜-inch) maple wood grilling plank
  ½ cup chopped fresh flat-leaf parsley
  ½ cup chopped fresh cilantro
  2 tablespoons fresh lemon juice
  2 tablespoons extravirgin olive oil
  1½ teaspoons ground cumin
  1½ teaspoons paprika
  ¼ teaspoon ground red pepper
  1 garlic clove, minced
  ¾ teaspoon salt, divided
  4 (6-ounce) mahimahi or other firm white fish fillets (about 1 inch thick)
  Cooking spray
  2 cups hot cooked basmati rice

1. Immerse and soak plank in water 1 hour; drain.
2. Prepare grill, heating one side to medium and one side to high heat.
3. Place parsley and next 7 ingredients in a food processor; add ¼ teaspoon salt. Process until herbs are finely chopped.
4. Lightly coat fish with cooking spray; sprinkle with ½ teaspoon salt.
5. Place plank on grill rack over high heat side of grill. Cover and grill 5 minutes or

until lightly charred. Carefully turn plank over; move to medium heat side of grill. Place fish, skin sides down, on charred side of plank. Cover and grill 12 minutes or until fish flakes easily when tested with a fork or until desired degree of doneness. Serve with sauce and rice. Yield: 4 servings (serving size: 1 fillet, 1 tablespoon sauce, and ½ cup rice).

CALORIES 337 (23% from fat); FAT 8.5g (sat 1.3g, mono 5.3g, poly 1g); PROTEIN 34.3g; CARB 28.9g; FIBER 1.1g; CHOL 124mg; IRON 4.3mg; SODIUM 597mg; CALC 50mg

Braised Lamb Shanks with Rosemary Polenta

The flavors in this recipe are reminiscent of the Italian dish osso buco (though we use lamb shanks instead of veal). If you can't find three-quarter-pound lamb shanks, try using one-pound cuts or the closest weight you can find. Ask your butcher for help.

LAMB:
  6 (¾-pound) lamb shanks, trimmed
  ½ teaspoon salt, divided
  ½ teaspoon freshly ground black pepper, divided
  2 cups diced onion
  1 cup diced carrot
  ½ cup diced celery
  2 garlic cloves, minced
  ¾ cup dry red wine
  1 (14.5-ounce) can no-salt-added petite diced tomatoes, undrained
  1 (14-ounce) can less-sodium beef broth
  1 tablespoon chopped fresh rosemary
  1 teaspoon water
  ½ teaspoon cornstarch

POLENTA:
  4 cups fat-free, less-sodium chicken broth
  1 teaspoon chopped fresh rosemary
  ¼ teaspoon freshly ground black pepper
  1 cup finely ground yellow cornmeal
  ¼ cup (1 ounce) grated fresh Parmesan cheese

1. Preheat oven to 300°.
2. To prepare lamb, sprinkle lamb evenly with ¼ teaspoon salt and ¼ teaspoon pepper. Heat a large, wide Dutch oven over medium-high heat. Add lamb, and cook 12 minutes, browning on all sides. Remove lamb from pan.
3. Add onion, carrot, and celery to pan; sauté 8 minutes or until lightly browned. Add garlic, and sauté 1 minute. Add wine; bring to a boil. Cook 2 minutes or until most of liquid evaporates. Return lamb to pan; stir in tomatoes, beef broth, and 1 tablespoon rosemary. Bring to a boil.
4. Cover pan; place in oven. Bake at 300° for 2 hours or until lamb is tender. Remove lamb from pan; set aside, and keep warm. Add ¼ teaspoon salt and ¼ teaspoon pepper to pan; bring to a boil over high heat. Cook until sauce is reduced to about 3½ cups (about 30 minutes), stirring frequently. Combine water and cornstarch in a small bowl, stirring with a whisk. Add cornstarch mixture to pan; cook 30 seconds or until sauce thickens, stirring constantly.
5. To prepare polenta, bring chicken broth, 1 teaspoon rosemary, and ¼ teaspoon pepper to a boil in a large saucepan. Gradually add cornmeal, stirring constantly with a whisk. Reduce heat to medium; cook 4 minutes or until thick, stirring constantly. Remove from heat, and stir in cheese. Serve immediately with lamb and sauce. Yield: 6 servings (serving size: 1 lamb shank, ⅔ cup polenta, and about ½ cup sauce).

CALORIES 447 (20% from fat); FAT 10.1g (sat 3.9g, mono 4.2g, poly 0.7g); PROTEIN 51.1g; CARB 34.4g; FIBER 4g; CHOL 151mg; IRON 4.9mg; SODIUM 815mg; CALC 135mg

Slow-Roasted Salmon with Bok Choy and Coconut Rice

Cooking the salmon at a low temperature ensures moist results. This is ideal for a dinner party—just serve with hot jasmine tea and offer ginger sorbet for dessert.

SALMON:
- 8 (6-ounce) salmon fillets
- ½ teaspoon salt
- ½ teaspoon freshly ground black pepper
- Cooking spray

RICE:
- 2 cups uncooked basmati rice
- 1½ cups light coconut milk
- 1½ cups water
- ¼ teaspoon salt
- 1 cup chopped green onions

BOK CHOY:
- 2 teaspoons canola oil
- 16 cups bok choy, trimmed and cut into 1½-inch pieces (about 4 pounds)
- 1 tablespoon minced peeled fresh ginger
- ½ cup sake (rice wine)
- ¼ teaspoon salt

SAUCE:
- ⅓ cup fresh lime juice
- ¼ cup seasoned rice vinegar
- 2 tablespoons chopped fresh cilantro
- 3 tablespoons brown sugar
- 2 tablespoons Thai fish sauce
- ½ teaspoon red curry paste (such as Thai Kitchen)

1. Preheat oven to 250°.
2. To prepare salmon, sprinkle salmon evenly with ½ teaspoon salt and pepper. Place salmon, skin sides down, on a baking sheet coated with cooking spray. Bake at 250° for 30 minutes until fish flakes easily when tested with a fork or until desired degree of doneness.
3. To prepare rice, rinse with cold water; drain. Combine rice and next 3 ingredients in a medium saucepan. Bring to a boil over high heat; stir once. Cover, reduce heat, and simmer 20 minutes until liquid is absorbed. Let stand 10 minutes; stir in onions.
4. To prepare bok choy, heat oil in a large nonstick skillet over medium-high heat. Add bok choy and ginger; sauté 1 minute. Add sake and ¼ teaspoon salt; cover and cook 2 minutes or until bok choy wilts. Cover and keep warm.
5. To prepare sauce, combine juice and remaining 5 ingredients, stirring well with a whisk. Serve salmon with rice, bok choy, and sauce. Yield: 8 servings (serving size: 1 fillet, about ⅔ cup rice, about ½ cup bok choy, and 1½ tablespoons sauce).

CALORIES 570 (27% from fat); FAT 16.9g (sat 5.4g, mono 6.4g, poly 3.7g); PROTEIN 43.3g; CARB 60.6g; FIBER 1.9g; CHOL 87mg; IRON 4.7mg; SODIUM 965mg; CALC 237mg

Garlic and Herb Standing Rib Roast

A standing rib roast makes a grand statement at the table. You don't need to ask your butcher for a frenched roast (one that has had the meat stripped from the bones); a regular standing rib roast will work just as well.

- 1 (5-pound) standing rib roast, trimmed
- Cooking spray
- 1½ tablespoons chopped fresh thyme
- ½ teaspoon salt
- ¼ teaspoon freshly ground black pepper
- 4 garlic cloves, minced
- Parsley sprigs (optional)
- Roasted garlic heads (optional)

1. Preheat oven to 450°.
2. Place roast on a broiler pan coated with cooking spray. Combine thyme, salt, pepper, and 4 garlic cloves; rub over roast. Bake at 450° for 45 minutes.
3. Reduce heat to 350° (do not remove roast from oven). Bake roast at 350° for 1 hour and 20 minutes or until a thermometer registers 145° (medium-rare) or until desired degree of doneness. Let stand 10 minutes before slicing. Garnish with parsley and roasted garlic, if desired. Yield: 12 servings (serving size: about 3 ounces meat).

CALORIES 226 (53% from fat); FAT 13.3g (sat 5.3g, mono 5.6g, poly 0.4g); PROTEIN 24.4g; CARB 0.4g; FIBER 0.1g; CHOL 72mg; IRON 2.6mg; SODIUM 162mg; CALC 10mg

Pork Tenderloin with Dried Apricot and Onion Marmalade

Serve with hot rice infused with ginger. To infuse the rice, steam white rice with several slices of peeled fresh ginger.

PORK:
- 1 teaspoon salt
- 1 teaspoon ground ginger
- ½ teaspoon ground allspice
- ¼ teaspoon ground red pepper
- 2 (1-pound) pork tenderloins, trimmed
- Cooking spray

MARMALADE:
- 2 tablespoons butter
- 4 cups thinly vertically sliced yellow onion (about 2 large)
- 1 cup dried apricots, diced (about 7 ounces)
- 1 cup water
- 2 cups fat-free, less-sodium chicken broth
- 1 tablespoon grated orange rind
- 1 cup fresh orange juice (about 4 oranges)
- ¼ cup sherry vinegar
- 4 teaspoons sugar
- ½ teaspoon salt
- ¼ teaspoon ground cloves

1. Preheat oven to 350°.
2. To prepare pork, combine first 4 ingredients; rub evenly over pork. Heat a large nonstick skillet over medium-high heat. Coat pan with cooking spray. Add pork; cook 3 minutes on each side or until browned. Remove from pan; wrap pork in foil. Place in a 13 x 9-inch baking dish. Bake at 350° for 25 minutes or until thermometer registers 160°

(slightly pink). Let stand 5 minutes before slicing.

3. To prepare marmalade, heat butter in pan over medium heat. Add onion; cook 8 minutes or until tender, stirring occasionally. Add apricots; cook 2 minutes, stirring occasionally. Stir in water, scraping bottom of pan to loosen browned bits. Stir in broth and remaining 6 ingredients; bring to a boil over medium-high heat. Reduce heat, and simmer 10 minutes or until liquid almost evaporates. Serve marmalade with pork. Yield: 8 servings (serving size: 3 ounces pork and about ¼ cup marmalade).

CALORIES 262 (24% from fat); FAT 7g (sat 2.8g, mono 3g, poly 0.6g); PROTEIN 25.8g; CARB 23.2g; FIBER 2.1g; CHOL 81mg; IRON 2.6mg; SODIUM 619mg; CALC 35mg

---

MAKE AHEAD • FREEZABLE

Pizza with Winter Squash and Bacon

This pizza dough recipe works great for making focaccia and calzones, and can easily be doubled. You can also make it ahead and freeze.

DOUGH:

- 1 teaspoon sugar
- 1 package dry yeast (about 2¼ teaspoons)
- 1 cup warm water (100° to 110°)
- 2¼ cups all-purpose flour, divided (about 10 ounces)
- ¼ teaspoon salt
- Cooking spray
- 1 tablespoon cornmeal

TOPPING:

- 3 cups (½-inch) cubed peeled butternut squash (about 1 pound)
- ½ cup chopped onion
- 1 teaspoon olive oil
- 2 teaspoons chopped fresh sage
- ¼ teaspoon salt
- ¼ teaspoon freshly ground black pepper
- 2 tablespoons fat-free, less-sodium chicken broth
- 1 cup (4 ounces) shredded fontina cheese
- 2 bacon slices, cooked and crumbled

1. To prepare dough, dissolve sugar and yeast in warm water in a large bowl; let stand 5 minutes. Lightly spoon flour into dry measuring cups; level with a knife. Add 1 cup flour and ¼ teaspoon salt to yeast mixture; stir well. Add 1 cup flour, stirring well. Turn dough out onto a floured surface. Knead until smooth and elastic (about 10 minutes); add enough remaining flour, 1 tablespoon at a time, to prevent dough from sticking to hands (dough will feel tacky).

2. Place dough in a large bowl coated with cooking spray, turning to coat top. Cover and let rise in a warm place (85°), free from drafts, 45 minutes or until doubled in size. (Press two fingers into dough. If an indentation remains, dough has risen enough.)

3. Preheat oven to 450°.

4. Punch dough down; cover and let rest 5 minutes. Roll dough into a 14 x 12-inch rectangle on a lightly floured surface. Place dough on a baking sheet coated with cooking spray and sprinkled with cornmeal. Crimp edges of dough with fingers to form a rim. Bake at 450° for 5 minutes.

5. To prepare topping, combine squash, onion, and oil in a large bowl, tossing to coat. Place on a jelly-roll pan coated with cooking spray. Bake at 450° for 25 minutes or until tender, stirring once. Sprinkle with sage, ¼ teaspoon salt, and pepper; toss to combine.

6. Set half of squash mixture aside. Combine remaining half of squash mixture and chicken broth in a medium bowl, and mash with a fork until smooth. Spread mashed squash mixture over pizza crust, leaving a ½-inch border. Top with remaining squash mixture, shredded cheese, and crumbled bacon. Bake at 450° for 15 minutes or until lightly browned. Place pizza on a cutting board, and cut into 8 equal pieces. Yield: 8 servings (serving size: 1 piece).

NOTE: To freeze, let dough rise once, punch down, and shape into a ball. Place in a heavy-duty zip-top plastic bag coated with cooking spray; squeeze out all air, and seal. Store in freezer up to one month. To thaw, place dough in refrigerator 12 hours or overnight. With scissors, cut away plastic bag. Place dough on a floured surface, and shape according to recipe directions.

CALORIES 226 (24% from fat); FAT 6.1g (sat 2.5g, mono 2.1g, poly 0.6g); PROTEIN 8.6g; CARB 35g; FIBER 2.3g; CHOL 15mg; IRON 2.3mg; SODIUM 295mg; CALC 125mg

---

Cherry-Glazed Cornish Hens with Sourdough-Cherry Stuffing

The cherry glaze adds beautiful color to the hens. Serve with a side of steamed broccolini or green beans. For easier clean-up, line the bottom of the broiler pan with foil.

- 2 tablespoons butter
- ⅓ cup finely chopped onion
- ¼ cup finely chopped carrot
- ¼ cup finely chopped celery
- 1½ teaspoons poultry seasoning
- 1 cup fat-free, less-sodium chicken broth
- ½ cup coarsely chopped dried sweet cherries
- 3 cups (½-inch) cubed sourdough bread, toasted
- ½ teaspoon freshly ground black pepper, divided
- ½ teaspoon salt, divided
- ½ cup cherry preserves
- ⅓ cup port or other sweet red wine
- 2 teaspoons finely chopped onion
- 2 teaspoons fresh lemon juice
- ¼ teaspoon dried thyme
- ⅛ teaspoon ground ginger
- 1 garlic clove, minced
- 4 (1¼-pound) Cornish hens
- Cooking spray

1. Preheat oven to 475°.

2. Melt butter in a medium nonstick skillet over medium heat. Add ⅓ cup onion, carrot, celery, and poultry seasoning; cook 7 minutes or until vegetables are tender, stirring occasionally. Add broth and cherries. Bring to a simmer, cook 2 minutes. Combine vegetable mixture, bread cubes, and ¼ teaspoon pepper in a large bowl. Stir well; cool completely.

3. Combine ¼ teaspoon salt, preserves, and next 6 ingredients in a small saucepan over medium heat. Bring to a
Continued

simmer; cook 10 minutes or until slightly thick, stirring occasionally. Set aside.

4. Remove and discard giblets and necks from hens. Rinse hens with cold water; pat dry. Remove skin; trim excess fat. Working with 1 hen at a time, loosely stuff each hen with about ¾ cup bread mixture. Tie ends of legs together with twine. Lift wing tips up and over back; tuck under hen. Place hens, breast sides up, on a broiler pan coated with cooking spray. Sprinkle with ¼ teaspoon pepper and ¼ teaspoon salt.

5. Bake at 475° for 15 minutes; remove from oven. Brush hens with preserves mixture; reduce oven temperature to 400°. Bake an additional 35 minutes or until a thermometer inserted into stuffing registers 165°, basting every 10 minutes with preserves mixture. Remove from oven; let stand 5 minutes. Remove twine before serving. Yield: 4 servings (serving size: 1 stuffed hen).

CALORIES 515 (21% from fat); FAT 12.3g (sat 5.3g, mono 3.5g, poly 2g); PROTEIN 38.3g; CARB 57.7g; FIBER 2.9g; CHOL 170mg; IRON 2.9mg; SODIUM 758mg; CALC 91mg

Lobster Stew

Buy lobsters live, and have them steamed at the grocery store. A two-pound lobster is suitable if two (one-pound) ones aren't available.

     2 (1-pound) lobsters, cooked
     1 pound unpeeled large shrimp
     1 tablespoon butter
    ¼ cup chopped onion
    ¼ cup chopped celery
     1 bay leaf
    ½ cup dry sherry
     6 cups 1% low-fat milk
     2 cups water, divided
  1½ cups cubed peeled baking potato
        (about 8 ounces)
    ¼ cup all-purpose flour (about
        1 ounce)
    ¾ teaspoon salt
    ¼ cup whipping cream
     1 teaspoon dry sherry
     1 tablespoon chopped fresh
        parsley

1. Remove meat from lobster tail and claws, reserving shells. Chop meat; cover and chill. Place lobster shells in a large zip-top plastic bag. Coarsely crush shells using a meat mallet or rolling pin; set shells aside.

2. Peel shrimp, reserving shells. Cover shrimp, and chill.

3. Melt butter in a Dutch oven over medium-high heat. Add onion and celery; sauté 2 minutes. Add reserved lobster shells, shrimp shells, and bay leaf; sauté 5 minutes or until shrimp shells turn orange. Slowly add ½ cup sherry, and cook 1 minute, stirring frequently. Add milk; bring mixture to a simmer. Reduce heat to medium; simmer 10 minutes, stirring occasionally (do not boil). Remove pan from heat. Cool milk mixture to room temperature; cover and chill overnight.

4. Strain milk mixture through a fine sieve into a bowl; discard solids. Set milk mixture aside.

5. Bring 1½ cups water to a boil in a large saucepan over medium-high heat. Add potato; cook 5 minutes or until tender. Lightly spoon flour into a dry measuring cup; level with a knife. Combine flour and ½ cup water, stirring well with a whisk. Add flour mixture to potato mixture; cook 1 minute or until thick, stirring occasionally. Stir in milk mixture; bring to a simmer. Stir in shrimp; cook 3 minutes or until shrimp are done. Remove from heat.

6. Pour one-third of shrimp mixture into a blender, and process until smooth. Pour puréed mixture into a large bowl. Repeat procedure with remaining mixture in two batches. Return puréed mixture to pan. Stir in lobster meat and salt. Cook over medium heat 5 minutes or until thoroughly heated, stirring occasionally. Remove from heat; stir in cream and 1 teaspoon sherry. Ladle 1⅓ cups stew into each of 6 bowls; sprinkle each serving with ½ teaspoon chopped parsley. Yield: 6 servings.

CALORIES 339 (26% from fat); FAT 9.8g (sat 5.2g, mono 2.9g, poly 0.9g); PROTEIN 32.9g; CARB 25.2g; FIBER 0.9g; CHOL 171mg; IRON 2.9mg; SODIUM 700mg; CALC 377mg

On the Side

Whether you're hosting a special occasion or a weeknight supper, these creative accompaniments will complement the menu.

Stuffing vs. Dressing

Is there a difference between stuffing and dressing? Stuffing can be stuffed into the bird or baked alongside it in a separate dish, and the same holds true for dressing.

Whether you refer to the Thanksgiving turkey's best friend as stuffing or dressing depends more on where you live than how the dish is prepared. In the southern and eastern United States, people generally call it "dressing," a term that came about during the 19th century. Elsewhere, it's referred to as "stuffing."

Some believe that stuffing is typically made with bread cubes or crumbs, while dressing is often (but not always) made with corn bread. However, both can be made with rice, wild rice, or potatoes. Whatever you call it, no holiday table is complete without this festive favorite.

MAKE AHEAD

Colby-Jack, Poblano, and Corn Bread Dressing

Toast the corn bread pieces and sauté the vegetable mixture a day ahead; toss them together with the remaining ingredients just before baking.

CORN BREAD:
    ¾ cup all-purpose flour (about
        3⅓ ounces)
  1¼ cups yellow cornmeal
     2 tablespoons sugar
     1 teaspoon baking powder
    ¾ teaspoon salt
    ¼ teaspoon baking soda
  1½ cups low-fat buttermilk
     2 large eggs, lightly beaten
Cooking spray

3 tablespoons sugar
¾ teaspoon salt
½ teaspoon chipotle chile powder
2 large eggs, lightly beaten
1 large egg white, lightly beaten
1 tablespoon butter
2 cups chopped onion
1 cup chopped poblano pepper
1 cup chopped red bell pepper
1 tablespoon minced garlic
1½ teaspoons ground cumin
1 (10-ounce) package frozen
   whole-kernel corn
1½ cups (6 ounces) preshredded
   reduced-fat colby-Jack cheese
¾ cup fat-free, less-sodium chicken
   broth
⅓ cup chopped fresh cilantro

1. Preheat oven to 425°.

2. To prepare corn bread, lightly spoon flour into a dry measuring cup; level with a knife. Combine flour and next 5 ingredients in a medium bowl. Combine buttermilk and 2 eggs; stir well. Add to flour mixture; stir just until moist. Spoon into an 11 x 7-inch baking dish coated with cooking spray. Bake at 425° for 20 minutes or until lightly browned and a wooden pick inserted in center comes out clean. Cool on a wire rack. Cut into ½-inch pieces; arrange on a large baking sheet.

3. Reduce oven temperature to 375°.

4. Bake corn bread pieces at 375° for 20 minutes, stirring occasionally.

5. To prepare stuffing, combine 3 tablespoons sugar and next 4 ingredients; set aside.

6. Melt butter in a large nonstick skillet over medium-high heat. Add onion, poblano, bell pepper, and garlic; sauté 7 minutes or until tender. Add cumin and corn; cook 5 minutes. Combine corn bread pieces, egg mixture, onion mixture, cheese, broth, and cilantro in a large bowl; toss well. Spoon into a 13 x 9-inch baking dish coated with cooking spray; cover with foil. Bake at 375° for 30 minutes. Uncover; bake 5 minutes or until top of dressing is slightly crisp. Yield: 12 servings (serving size: about ⅔ cup).

CALORIES 230 (26% from fat); FAT 6.6g (sat 3.4g, mono 2g, poly 0.6g); PROTEIN 10.4g; CARB 33.4g; FIBER 2.5g; CHOL 84mg; IRON 1.7mg; SODIUM 556mg; CALC 183mg

Sourdough Stuffing with Pears and Sausage

(pictured on page 380)

Sourdough bread gives the stuffing a tangier flavor than French bread, but you can use the latter in a pinch.

8 cups (½-inch) cubed sourdough
   bread (about 12 ounces)
1 pound turkey Italian sausage
Cooking spray
5 cups chopped onion (about
   2 pounds)
2 cups chopped celery
1 cup chopped carrot
1 (8-ounce) package presliced
   mushrooms
2 cups (½-inch) cubed peeled
   Bartlett pear (about 2 medium)
1½ tablespoons chopped fresh basil
2 teaspoons chopped fresh
   tarragon
1 teaspoon salt
1½ cups fat-free, less-sodium chicken
   broth
½ teaspoon freshly ground black
   pepper

1. Preheat oven to 425°.

2. Arrange bread in a single layer on a baking sheet. Bake at 425° for 9 minutes or until golden. Place in a large bowl.

3. Remove casings from sausage. Heat a large nonstick skillet over medium-high heat. Coat pan with cooking spray. Add sausage, and cook 8 minutes or until browned, stirring to crumble. Add sausage to bread cubes, tossing to combine. Set aside.

4. Return pan to medium-high heat. Add onion, celery, and carrot; sauté 10 minutes or until onion begins to brown. Stir in mushrooms; cook 4 minutes. Stir in pear, basil, tarragon, and salt; cook 4 minutes or until pear begins to soften, stirring occasionally. Add pear mixture to bread mixture, tossing gently to combine. Stir in broth and pepper.

5. Place bread mixture in a 13 x 9-inch baking dish coated with cooking spray, and cover with foil. Bake at 425° for 20 minutes. Uncover, and bake an additional 15 minutes or until top is crisp.

Yield: 12 servings (serving size: about ¾ cup).

CALORIES 199 (24% from fat); FAT 5.2g (sat 1.6g, mono 1.5g, poly 1g); PROTEIN 10.7g; CARB 28.6g; FIBER 3.4g; CHOL 23mg; IRON 1.8mg; SODIUM 684mg; CALC 54mg

Sweet Corn Soufflé with Bacon

The sweet-salty flavor of this soufflé makes it well suited to roasted pork. It bakes in a standard 11 x 7-inch baking dish instead of a special soufflé dish.

3 cups fresh corn kernels, divided
   (about 4 ears)
2 bacon slices
½ cup chopped onion
½ cup chopped celery
½ cup chopped red bell pepper
2 tablespoons finely chopped
   seeded jalapeño pepper (about
   1 pepper)
¼ cup white cornmeal
2 tablespoons all-purpose flour
1 cup fat-free, less-sodium chicken
   broth
1 cup 2% reduced-fat milk
½ teaspoon salt
¼ teaspoon freshly ground black
   pepper
½ teaspoon cream of tartar
4 large egg whites
1 tablespoon sugar
⅓ cup chopped fresh cilantro
Cooking spray

1. Preheat oven to 400°.

2. Place 1 cup corn in a blender or food processor; process until puréed. Set aside.

3. Cook bacon in a large saucepan over medium heat until crisp. Remove bacon from pan, reserving drippings in pan. Crumble bacon; set aside. Increase heat to medium-high. Add 2 cups corn, onion, celery, bell pepper, and jalapeño to drippings in pan; sauté 7 minutes. Combine cornmeal and flour; sprinkle over vegetables. Cook 1 minute, stirring frequently. Stir in puréed corn, broth, milk, salt, and black pepper; bring to a

Continued

boil. Reduce heat; simmer 20 minutes or until very thick, stirring frequently. Spoon into a large bowl; cool 15 minutes, stirring occasionally.

4. Place cream of tartar and egg whites in a medium bowl; beat with a mixer at high speed until foamy. Gradually add sugar, beating at high speed until stiff peaks form. Gently stir one-fourth of egg white mixture into corn mixture; gently fold in remaining egg white mixture, bacon, and cilantro. Spoon mixture into an 11 x 7-inch baking dish coated with cooking spray.

5. Place in a 400° oven; immediately reduce oven temperature to 375° (do not remove soufflé from oven). Bake 35 minutes or until puffy and set. Serve immediately. Yield: 10 servings (serving size: about ½ cup).

CALORIES 112 (26% from fat); FAT 3.2g (sat 1.1g, mono 1.2g, poly 0.6g); PROTEIN 5.3g; CARB 17.1g; FIBER 1.9g; CHOL 5mg; IRON 0.7mg; SODIUM 241mg; CALC 40mg

QUICK & EASY
Roasted Cauliflower with Fresh Herbs and Parmesan

Use any fresh herbs you have on hand for this holiday recipe. While parsley, tarragon, and thyme make a nice combination, you can also try sage, chives, and rosemary.

- 12 cups cauliflower florets (about 2 heads)
- 1½ tablespoons olive oil
- 1 tablespoon chopped fresh parsley
- 2 teaspoons chopped fresh thyme
- 2 teaspoons chopped fresh tarragon
- 3 garlic cloves, minced
- ¼ cup (1 ounce) grated fresh Parmesan cheese
- 2 tablespoons fresh lemon juice
- ½ teaspoon salt
- ¼ teaspoon pepper

1. Preheat oven to 450°.

2. Place cauliflower in a large roasting pan or jelly-roll pan. Drizzle with oil; toss well to coat. Bake at 450° for 20 minutes or until tender and browned,

stirring every 5 minutes. Sprinkle with parsley, thyme, tarragon, and garlic. Bake 5 minutes. Combine cauliflower mixture, cheese, and remaining ingredients in a large bowl; toss well to combine. Yield: 8 servings (serving size: about 1 cup).

CALORIES 89 (35% from fat); FAT 3.5g (sat 0.8g, mono 2.1g, poly 0.4g); PROTEIN 5.2g; CARB 12.1g; FIBER 5.4g; CHOL 2mg; IRON 1.1mg; SODIUM 251mg; CALC 83mg

QUICK & EASY
Sautéed Wild Mushrooms with Wilted Spinach

This savory side can become a main dish if you serve it over soft polenta with a sprinkling of Parmesan or feta cheese.

- 1 tablespoon dark sesame oil, divided
- 4½ cups sliced shiitake mushroom caps (about 8 ounces)
- 3 cups sliced oyster mushroom caps (about 8 ounces)
- ⅓ cup sliced shallots
- 2 teaspoons grated peeled fresh ginger
- 3 garlic cloves, minced
- ¼ cup dry sherry
- 7 teaspoons low-sodium soy sauce, divided
- ½ teaspoon sugar
- ⅓ cup chopped green onions
- 2 (10-ounce) packages fresh spinach (about 20 cups)
- 1 teaspoon fresh lemon juice

1. Heat 2 teaspoons oil in a large non-stick skillet over medium-high heat. Add mushrooms, shallots, ginger, and garlic; sauté 3 minutes or until mushrooms are tender. Add sherry, 5 teaspoons soy sauce, and sugar; cook 1 minute or until liquid is almost evaporated. Remove from heat, and stir in onions. Spoon mushroom mixture into a medium bowl; keep warm.

2. Return pan to medium-high heat; add 1 teaspoon oil. Add one-third of spinach, and cook 2 minutes or until spinach wilts, stirring frequently. Repeat procedure with remaining spinach in 2 more batches. Spoon spinach into a

medium bowl; stir in 2 teaspoons soy sauce and lemon juice. Top with mushroom mixture. Yield: 6 servings (serving size: ⅓ cup spinach and ½ cup mushroom mixture).

CALORIES 81 (33% from fat); FAT 3g (sat 0.5g, mono 1g, poly 1.2g); PROTEIN 6.1g; CARB 9.8g; FIBER 3.5g; CHOL 0mg; IRON 3.3mg; SODIUM 289mg; CALC 104mg

QUICK & EASY
Oven-Roasted Green Beans
(pictured on page 380)

This easy side dish adds color to the meal, and you can roast it at the last minute while you finish setting the table.

- 2 pounds green beans, trimmed
- 4 teaspoons extravirgin olive oil
- 1 teaspoon sea salt
- ½ teaspoon freshly ground black pepper

1. Preheat oven to 425°.

2. Place a jelly-roll pan in oven 10 minutes. Place beans in a large bowl. Drizzle with oil; sprinkle with salt and pepper. Toss well to coat. Arrange green bean mixture in a single layer on preheated baking sheet. Bake at 425° for 8 minutes or until crisp-tender. Yield: 12 servings (serving size: about ⅔ cup).

CALORIES 37 (39% from fat); FAT 1.6g (sat 0.2g, mono 1.1g, poly 0.2g); PROTEIN 1.4g; CARB 5.5g; FIBER 2.6g; CHOL 0mg; IRON 0.8mg; SODIUM 196mg; CALC 29mg

Choosing colorful side dishes for your festive holiday feast will make the meal an extra-special treat.

Balsamic-Dressed Roasted Beets

A simple sweet-and-sour dressing complements earthy roasted beets. Its bright flavors make this dish a fitting accompaniment for roasted meats.

    6   beets (about 2½ pounds)
    ½   cup fresh orange juice
    ¼   cup balsamic vinegar
    1   tablespoon sugar
    1   star anise
    ½   teaspoon salt
    ⅛   teaspoon freshly ground black
        pepper

1. Preheat oven to 400°.
2. Leave root and 1 inch of stem on beets; scrub with a brush. Wrap beets in foil. Bake at 400° for 1 hour or until tender. Cool beets to room temperature. Peel and cut each beet into 8 wedges.
3. Combine juice, vinegar, sugar, and star anise in a small saucepan; bring to a boil. Cook until reduced to ⅓ cup (about 10 minutes). Discard star anise. Combine beets, vinegar mixture, salt, and pepper; toss well. Yield: 8 servings (serving size: ½ cup).

CALORIES 79 (3% from fat); FAT 0.3g (sat 0g, mono 0.1g, poly 0.1g); PROTEIN 2.4g; CARB 17.9g; FIBER 4g; CHOL 0mg; IRON 1.2mg; SODIUM 258mg; CALC 27mg

STAFF FAVORITE • QUICK & EASY
Camembert Mashed Potatoes
(pictured on page 380)

The buttery taste and creamy texture of Camembert cheese glorifies these potatoes. Camembert is similar in flavor and texture to Brie, which makes a fine substitute. The rind is easiest to remove if the cheese is well chilled.

    1½ (8-ounce) rounds Camembert cheese
    11 cups cubed peeled Yukon gold
        potato (about 4½ pounds)
    ½   cup 1% low-fat milk
    ¾   teaspoon salt
    ¾   teaspoon freshly ground black
        pepper
    Chopped fresh chives (optional)
    Freshly ground black pepper (optional)

1. Cut cheese into 6 wedges. Carefully remove rind from cheese; discard rind. Chop cheese; let stand at room temperature while potato cooks.
2. Place potato in a large Dutch oven; cover with water. Bring to a boil. Reduce heat; simmer 12 minutes or until tender. Drain in a colander; return potato to pan. Add cheese, milk, salt, and ¾ teaspoon pepper; mash with a potato masher until smooth. Garnish with chives and additional pepper, if desired. Yield: 12 servings (serving size: about ⅔ cup).

CALORIES 198 (20% from fat); FAT 4.4g (sat 2.8g, mono 1.3g, poly 0.1g); PROTEIN 7.9g; CARB 30.7g; FIBER 2g; CHOL 13mg; IRON 1.5mg; SODIUM 310mg; CALC 82mg

MAKE AHEAD
Blue Cheese and Bacon Twice-Baked Potatoes

You can stuff and refrigerate the potato shells up to two days ahead. Add about five minutes to the cook time if starting with cold potatoes. Serve with everything from steak to Thanksgiving dinner.

    5   (12-ounce) baking
        potatoes
    1½ cups low-fat buttermilk
    ½   cup (2 ounces) crumbled blue
        cheese
    ¼   cup finely chopped fresh
        chives
    2   tablespoons butter
    1¼ teaspoons salt
    ¼   teaspoon freshly ground black
        pepper
    4   bacon slices, cooked and
        crumbled

1. Preheat oven to 375°.
2. Bake potatoes at 375° for 1 hour or until tender. Cool 10 minutes or until cool enough to handle. Cut each potato in half lengthwise; scoop out pulp, leaving ¼-inch-thick shells. Place pulp, buttermilk, and remaining 6 ingredients in a large bowl; beat with a mixer at medium speed until well blended. Spoon about ½ cup potato mixture into each of 8 shells (reserve remaining shells for another use). Arrange stuffed shells on a baking sheet. Bake at 375° for 20 minutes

or until thoroughly heated. Yield: 8 servings (serving size: 1 stuffed shell).

CALORIES 264 (25% from fat); FAT 7.4g (sat 3.8g, mono 2.7g, poly 0.4g); PROTEIN 8.5g; CARB 41.7g; FIBER 3.8g; CHOL 20mg; IRON 2.3mg; SODIUM 658mg; CALC 117mg

---

Spud Smarts

Here's how to choose the best potatoes for sides and desserts (see our Praline-Sweet Potato Cheesecake, recipe on page 400).

Russet, or baking, potatoes
Characteristics: High-starch and low-moisture content make these fluffy and dry when cooked.
Best uses: Baked, mashed, fried, or in gratins

Yukon gold potatoes
Characteristics: With moist, butter-yellow flesh, these hold their shape well when cooked.
Best uses: Mashed, sliced in gratins, or cubed in soups, stews, and potato salad

Red potatoes
Characteristics: High-moisture, low-starch, waxy flesh is dense and doesn't fall apart when cooked.
Best uses: Roasted, boiled, and used in soups or potato salad

Sweet potatoes
Characteristics: Not really potatoes (they're a member of the morning glory family), these are sweet, with moist, bright orange flesh.
Best uses: Baked, mashed, or used in soups and stews

Broccoli Purée with Parmesan

Mashed potatoes and broccoli combine with tangy cheese.

    2   cups packaged refrigerated
        mashed potatoes (such as Simply
        Potatoes)
    1   pound broccoli crowns (about
        8 cups)
    ½   cup (2 ounces) grated Parmigiano-
        Reggiano cheese
    ¼   cup 1% low-fat milk
    1   teaspoon extravirgin olive
        oil
    ¾   teaspoon salt
    ¼   teaspoon crushed red
        pepper

1. Heat potatoes according to package directions. Keep warm.
2. Cook broccoli in boiling water 7 minutes or until tender. Drain. Place broccoli, cheese, and remaining 4 ingredients in a food processor; process until smooth, scraping sides of bowl occasionally. Combine potatoes and broccoli mixture in a large bowl, stirring until well blended. Yield: 12 servings (serving size: ⅓ cup).

CALORIES 56 (31% from fat); FAT 1.9g (sat 0.7g, mono 0.6g, poly 0.1g); PROTEIN 3.1g; CARB 7.4g; FIBER 1.6g; CHOL 3mg; IRON 0.5mg; SODIUM 302mg; CALC 67mg

Vegetable purées are a classic French accompaniment to meats. Serve all three purées at dinner, or make just one.

Carrot-Coriander Purée

This lightly sweetened side is a nice alternative to sweet potatoes.

    2   cups packaged refrigerated
        mashed potatoes (such as Simply
        Potatoes)
  2¼   cups chopped carrot
    ¼   cup 1% low-fat milk
    1   tablespoon butter
    2   teaspoons sugar
    ½   teaspoon salt
    ½   teaspoon ground coriander
    ⅛   teaspoon freshly ground black
        pepper

1. Heat potatoes according to package directions. Keep warm.
2. Cook carrot in boiling water 15 minutes or until tender. Drain. Place carrot, milk, and remaining 5 ingredients in a food processor; process until smooth, scraping sides of bowl occasionally. Combine potatoes and carrot mixture in a large bowl, stirring until well blended. Yield: 12 servings (serving size: ⅓ cup).

CALORIES 48 (28% from fat); FAT 1.5g (sat 0.5g, mono 0.4g, poly 0.1g); PROTEIN 0.9g; CARB 8.3g; FIBER 1.3g; CHOL 3mg; IRON 0.2mg; SODIUM 215mg; CALC 20mg

Cauliflower-Garlic Purée

Don't be alarmed by the amount of garlic; cooking it in milk mellows the flavor. Try this purée in place of basic mashed potatoes.

    2   cups packaged refrigerated
        mashed potatoes (such as Simply
        Potatoes)
  5½   cups coarsely chopped cauliflower
        (about 1 small head)
    ½   cup fat-free milk
    6   garlic cloves
    1   bay leaf
    3   tablespoons butter
    1   teaspoon salt

1. Heat potatoes according to package directions. Keep warm.
2. Cook cauliflower in boiling water 7 minutes or until tender. Drain.

3. Place milk, garlic, and bay leaf in a small saucepan; bring to a simmer. Cover and cook over low heat 10 minutes. Discard bay leaf. Place cauliflower, milk mixture, butter, and salt in a food processor; process until smooth, scraping sides of bowl occasionally. Combine mashed potatoes and cauliflower mixture in a large bowl, stirring until well blended. Yield: 12 servings (serving size: ⅓ cup).

CALORIES 72 (41% from fat); FAT 3.3g (sat 1.5g, mono 1.2g, poly 0.2g); PROTEIN 2.3g; CARB 9.5g; FIBER 2.2g; CHOL 8mg; IRON 0.5mg; SODIUM 331mg; CALC 33mg

Smoked Gouda Grits

These grits are great with roasted meats at dinner or with ham and eggs at breakfast.

    1   teaspoon butter
    4   cups chopped onion (about
        2 large)
    2   garlic cloves, minced
    3   cups fat-free, less-sodium chicken
        broth
    2   cups 1% low-fat milk
    ½   teaspoon salt
  1¼   cups uncooked quick-cooking
        grits
    1   cup (4 ounces) shredded smoked
        Gouda cheese
    ½   cup egg substitute
    ¼   teaspoon freshly ground black
        pepper
        Cooking spray

1. Preheat oven to 375°.
2. Melt butter in a large saucepan over medium heat. Add onion and garlic; cook 5 minutes or until golden, stirring occasionally. Stir in broth, milk, and salt; bring to a boil. Gradually add grits, stirring constantly with a whisk; simmer 5 minutes, stirring frequently. Remove pan from heat; stir in cheese, egg substitute, and pepper. Spoon grits mixture into an 11 x 7-inch baking dish coated with cooking spray. Bake at 375° for 40 minutes. Yield: 8 servings (serving size: about 1 cup).

CALORIES 199 (27% from fat); FAT 5.9g (sat 3.3g, mono 1.7g, poly 0.5g); PROTEIN 10.7g; CARB 25.3g; FIBER 1.1g; CHOL 20mg; IRON 1.6mg; SODIUM 469mg; CALC 195mg

Delicious Extras

These breads and sauces are the special touches that make a meal complete.

Sour Cream Muffins with Poppy Seed Streusel

(pictured on page 379)

STREUSEL:

3 tablespoons sugar
2 tablespoons all-purpose flour
1 tablespoon butter, melted
1 teaspoon poppy seeds

MUFFINS:

2 cups all-purpose flour (about 9 ounces)
¾ cup sugar
2 teaspoons baking powder
1 teaspoon baking soda
½ teaspoon salt
¾ cup fat-free buttermilk
¼ cup butter, melted
1 tablespoon grated orange rind
1 teaspoon vanilla extract
1 large egg, lightly beaten
1 (8-ounce) container reduced-fat sour cream
Cooking spray

1. Preheat oven to 375°.
2. To prepare streusel, combine first 4 ingredients in a small bowl; set aside.
3. To prepare muffins, lightly spoon 2 cups flour into dry measuring cups; level with a knife. Combine 2 cups flour and next 4 ingredients in a medium bowl, stirring with a whisk. Make a well in center of mixture. Combine buttermilk and next 5 ingredients in a small bowl; add to flour mixture, stirring just until moist. Spoon batter into 15 muffin cups coated with cooking spray. Sprinkle streusel evenly over batter. Bake at 375° for 18 minutes or until golden brown. Remove muffins from pans immediately; place on a wire rack. Yield: 15 servings (serving size: 1 muffin).

CALORIES 180 (32% from fat); FAT 6.3g (sat 3.2g, mono 2.3g, poly 0.4g); PROTEIN 3.3g; CARB 27.8g; FIBER 0.5g; CHOL 31mg; IRON 1mg; SODIUM 277mg; CALC 77mg

Cranberry, Cherry, and Walnut Chutney

(pictured on page 380)

Aside from making a stellar accompaniment to roast turkey, this chutney is great for gift giving; pack in a ribbon-tied jelly jar. It also goes well with roast chicken, pork tenderloin, or ham.

1 cup sugar
1 cup water
½ cup port or other sweet red wine
¼ teaspoon ground allspice
½ cup dried tart cherries
1 (12-ounce) package fresh cranberries
⅔ cup chopped walnuts, toasted
½ teaspoon grated orange rind
¼ teaspoon almond extract
Orange rind strips (optional)

1. Combine first 4 ingredients in a medium saucepan; bring to a boil. Add cherries, and cook 1 minute. Stir in cranberries; bring to a boil. Reduce heat, and simmer 10 minutes or until cranberries pop. Remove from heat. Stir in walnuts, grated rind, and extract. Garnish with orange rind strips, if desired. Cover and chill. Yield: 16 servings (serving size: ¼ cup).

CALORIES 108 (25% from fat); FAT 3g (sat 0.2g, mono 0.7g, poly 2g); PROTEIN 1.5g; CARB 19.7g; FIBER 1.8g; CHOL 0mg; IRON 0.3mg; SODIUM 2mg; CALC 11mg

How to Shape Challah

Braid ropes; pinch loose ends to seal. Cover and let rise 20 minutes or until almost doubled in size.

Sweet Challah

Allowing the dough to rise three times gives the yeast more time to develop, resulting in a rich, complex flavor. Although this bread is best eaten the day it's made, you can also bake it one day in advance. Cool the bread completely, wrap in plastic wrap, and then wrap in foil; store at room temperature. Leftovers make excellent bread pudding.

1 package dry yeast (about 2¼ teaspoons)
1 cup warm water (100° to 110°)
3 tablespoons honey
Dash of saffron threads, crushed
3 tablespoons butter, melted and cooled
1 teaspoon salt
1 large egg
3 cups bread flour (about 14¼ ounces), divided
Cooking spray
1 teaspoon cornmeal
1 teaspoon water
1 large egg yolk, lightly beaten
¼ teaspoon poppy seeds

1. Dissolve yeast in warm water in a large bowl; stir in honey and saffron. Let stand 5 minutes. Add butter, salt, and egg; stir well with a whisk.
2. Lightly spoon flour into dry measuring cups; level with a knife. Add 2¾ cups flour to yeast mixture, and stir until a soft dough forms. Cover and let stand 15 minutes.
3. Turn dough out onto a lightly floured surface. Knead until smooth and elastic (about 8 minutes); add enough remaining flour, 1 tablespoon at a time, to prevent dough from sticking to hands (dough will be very soft).
4. Place dough in a large bowl coated with cooking spray, turning to coat top. Cover and let rise in a warm place (85°), free from drafts, 40 minutes or until doubled in size. (Press two fingers into dough. If indentation remains, dough has risen enough.)
5. Punch dough down. Shape dough into a ball; return to bowl. Cover and let
Continued

rise 40 minutes or until doubled in size. Punch dough down; cover and let rest 15 minutes.

6. Divide dough into 3 equal portions. Working with 1 portion at a time (cover remaining dough to prevent drying), on a lightly floured surface, roll each portion into a 25-inch rope with one slightly tapered end. Place ropes lengthwise on a large baking sheet sprinkled with cornmeal; pinch untapered ends together to seal. Braid ropes; pinch loose ends to seal. Cover and let rise 20 minutes or until almost doubled in size.

7. Preheat oven to 375°.

8. Combine 1 teaspoon water and egg yolk, stirring with a fork until blended. Uncover loaf, and gently brush with egg yolk mixture. Sprinkle evenly with poppy seeds. Bake at 375° for 30 minutes or until loaf sounds hollow when tapped. Cool on a wire rack. Yield: 1 loaf, 12 servings (serving size: 1 slice).

CALORIES 157 (24% from fat); FAT 4.1g (sat 2.1g, mono 1.2g, poly 0.4g); PROTEIN 5g; CARB 26.9g; FIBER 0.9g; CHOL 42mg; IRON 1.7mg; SODIUM 202mg; CALC 7mg

STAFF FAVORITE • MAKE AHEAD
FREEZABLE
Flaky Dinner Rolls
(pictured on page 380)

These superlative rolls derive their texture and beautiful shape from employing a simple folding technique twice and allowing them to rise just once.

  3 tablespoons sugar
  1 package dry yeast (about 2¼ teaspoons)
  1 cup warm fat-free milk (100° to 110°)
  3 cups all-purpose flour (about 13½ ounces), divided
  ¾ teaspoon salt
  3 tablespoons butter, softened
Cooking spray

1. Dissolve sugar and yeast in milk in a large bowl; let stand 5 minutes. Lightly spoon flour into dry measuring cups; level with a knife. Add 2¾ cups flour and salt to yeast mixture; stir until a dough forms. Turn dough out onto a lightly floured surface. Knead until smooth (about 5 minutes); add enough remaining flour, 1 tablespoon at a time, to prevent dough from sticking to hands (dough will feel slightly sticky). Cover with plastic wrap, and let rest 10 minutes.

2. Roll dough into a 12 x 10-inch rectangle on a lightly floured baking sheet. Gently spread butter over dough. Working with a long side, fold up bottom third of dough. Fold top third of dough over first fold to form a 12 x 3-inch rectangle. Cover with plastic wrap; place in freezer 10 minutes.

3. Remove dough from freezer; remove plastic wrap. Roll dough, still on baking sheet (sprinkle on a little more flour, if needed), into a 12 x 10-inch rectangle. Working with a long side, fold up bottom third of dough. Fold top third of dough over first fold to form a 12 x 3-inch rectangle. Cover with plastic wrap; place in freezer 10 minutes.

4. Remove dough from freezer; remove plastic wrap. Roll dough, still on baking sheet, into a 12 x 8-inch rectangle. Beginning with a long side, roll up dough jelly-roll fashion; pinch seam to seal (do not seal ends of roll). Cut roll into 12 equal slices. Place slices, cut sides up, in muffin cups coated with cooking spray. Lightly coat tops of dough slices with cooking spray. Cover and let rise in a warm place (85°), free from drafts, 45 minutes or until doubled in size.

5. Preheat oven to 375°.

6. Bake dough at 375° for 20 minutes or until golden brown. Remove from pan, and cool 5 minutes on a wire rack. Serve rolls warm. Yield: 12 servings (serving size: 1 roll).

CALORIES 160 (18% from fat); FAT 3.2g (sat 1.5g, mono 1.2g, poly 0.2g); PROTEIN 4.2g; CARB 28.3g; FIBER 1g; CHOL 8mg; IRON 1.7mg; SODIUM 178mg; CALC 25mg

How to Make Flaky Diner Rolls

1. *Working with a long side, fold up bottom third of dough.*

2. *Fold top third of dough over first fold to form a 12 x 3-inch rectangle.*

3. *Cut roll into 12 equal slices*

Flaky Dinner Rolls can be made ahead and frozen for about 1 month.

Clementine-Cranberry Relish

Using the clementine peel lends the relish a pleasant bitterness reminiscent of marmalade. It tastes best at room temperature.

2 clementines, quartered and seeded (about 6 ounces)
1 cup packed brown sugar
½ cup fresh clementine juice (about 7 clementines)
1 tablespoon minced crystallized ginger
¼ teaspoon ground cinnamon
⅛ teaspoon salt
Dash of ground cloves
1 (12-ounce) package fresh cranberries

1. Place clementines in a food processor; process until coarsely chopped.
2. Combine clementines, sugar, and remaining ingredients in a medium saucepan. Bring to a boil; reduce heat, and simmer 10 minutes or until cranberries pop. Remove from heat; cool completely. Serve at room temperature. Yield: 12 servings (serving size: ¼ cup).

CALORIES 97 (1% from fat); FAT 0.1g (sat 0g, mono 0g, poly 0g); PROTEIN 0.2g; CARB 24.5g; FIBER 1.4g; CHOL 0mg; IRON 0.4mg; SODIUM 32mg; CALC 20mg

White Cheddar and Black Pepper Biscuits

The richness of buttermilk and Cheddar cheese mellows the spicy black pepper. Make these for your family, and prepare a second batch to give as a gift.

2 cups all-purpose flour (about 9 ounces)
1 tablespoon baking powder
½ teaspoon salt
½ teaspoon baking soda
½ teaspoon freshly ground black pepper
½ cup (2 ounces) shredded extrasharp white Cheddar cheese
3 tablespoons chilled butter, cut into small pieces
1 cup fat-free buttermilk
Cooking spray

1. Preheat oven to 400°.
2. Lightly spoon flour into dry measuring cups; level with a knife. Place flour and next 4 ingredients in a food processor; pulse 5 times or until well combined. Add cheese and butter; pulse 5 times or until well combined.
3. Place mixture in a large bowl. Add buttermilk; stir just until moist.
4. Turn dough out onto a floured surface. Knead lightly 5 times. Roll dough out to a ½-inch thickness; cut with a 2-inch biscuit cutter into 24 biscuits. Place on a baking sheet coated with cooking spray. Bake at 400° for 15 minutes or until golden. Yield: 12 servings (serving size: 2 biscuits).

CALORIES 129 (33% from fat); FAT 4.7g (sat 2.6g, mono 1.2g, poly 0.2g); PROTEIN 3.9g; CARB 17.4g; FIBER 0.6g; CHOL 13mg; IRON 1.1mg; SODIUM 342mg; CALC 130mg

Mini Corn Muffins with Currants

Ricotta cheese in the batter keeps these muffins moist. Try them in place of bread or rolls at your Thanksgiving meal. Or serve them to complement a savory soup, such as our Smoked Ham Soup with White Beans (recipe on page 385).

½ cup dried currants
½ cup hot water
½ cup all-purpose flour (about 2¼ ounces)
1 cup yellow cornmeal
⅓ cup sugar
2 teaspoons baking powder
¾ teaspoon salt
1 cup part-skim ricotta cheese
2 large eggs, lightly beaten
Cooking spray

1. Preheat oven to 350°.
2. Place currants and hot water in a bowl. Cover and let stand 20 minutes or until soft. Drain currants.
3. Lightly spoon flour into a dry measuring cup; level with a knife. Combine flour and next 4 ingredients in a medium bowl. Combine ricotta and eggs, stirring with a whisk; stir in currants. Add ricotta mixture to flour mixture, stirring just until moist.
4. Spoon batter into 24 miniature muffin cups coated with cooking spray. Bake at 350° for 20 minutes or until a wooden pick inserted in center comes out clean. Remove from pans immediately; place on a wire rack. Serve warm. Yield: 12 servings (serving size: 2 muffins).

CALORIES 148 (15% from fat); FAT 2.5g (sat 1.3g, mono 0.8g, poly 0.2g); PROTEIN 5.1g; CARB 26.1g; FIBER 0.9g; CHOL 42mg; IRON 1.1mg; SODIUM 306mg; CALC 134mg

---

Pair Up for Gifts

Homemade presents are always welcome—especially if they're edible. Try giving one of these delicious combinations.

• Cranberry, Cherry, and Walnut Chutney (recipe on page 395) with White Cheddar and Black Pepper Biscuits (recipe on page 397): Present the chutney in a decorative jar nestled into a towel-lined basket of biscuits. Include a card with reheating instructions for the biscuits.

• Papaya-Golden Raisin Chutney (recipe on page 398) with Sweet Challah (recipe on page 395): Cover the bread in plastic wrap, then secure a pretty kitchen towel around it with a festive ribbon. Attach a small spoon to a jar of the chutney with raffia or ribbon.

• Flaky Dinner Rolls (recipe on page 396) with herb butter: Combine ½ cup softened butter, 1 tablespoon finely chopped parsley, 1 teaspoon chopped fresh thyme, and 1 to 2 minced garlic cloves; beat with a mixer at medium speed until fluffy. Spoon into a ramekin or small crock, and place inside a parchment-lined box or basket filled with rolls. Be sure to attach reheating instructions for the rolls. For more great gift ideas, see Share the Flavor on page 402.

Papaya-Golden Raisin Chutney

The sweet-tart flavor of this chutney goes well with turkey, especially smoked turkey, and roast pork and lamb. If you don't have cheesecloth, wrap the spices in a coffee filter and tie with strings.

- 12 whole cloves
- 10 black peppercorns
- ½ cup water
- ⅓ cup sugar
- ⅓ cup cider vinegar
- 4 cups diced peeled papaya (about 2½ pounds)
- 1 cup golden raisins
- 1 tablespoon minced crystallized ginger
- 1 teaspoon hot pepper sauce
- ½ teaspoon ground coriander

1. Place cloves and peppercorns on a double layer of cheesecloth. Gather edges of cheesecloth together; tie securely to form a bag.
2. Combine water, sugar, and vinegar in a saucepan; bring to a boil. Add cheesecloth bag, papaya, and remaining ingredients; reduce heat, and simmer 35 minutes or until liquid evaporates. Remove from heat; let stand 5 minutes. Discard cheesecloth bag. Spoon chutney into a bowl; cover and chill. Yield: 13 servings (serving size: ¼ cup).

CALORIES 77 (1% from fat); FAT 0.1g (sat 0g, mono 0g, poly 0g); PROTEIN 0.7g; CARB 19.9g; FIBER 1.3g; CHOL 0mg; IRON 0.3mg; SODIUM 5mg; CALC 18mg

Sweet Endings

Save room for dessert, because you won't want to miss a bite of these cakes, pies, and assorted treats.

Cinnamon Streusel-Topped Pumpkin Pie

Using refrigerated pie dough makes this luscious dessert a breeze to prepare. Look for the dough in the dairy section of your supermarket.

FILLING:

- ¾ teaspoon ground cinnamon
- ¼ teaspoon ground allspice
- ¼ teaspoon ground ginger
- ¼ teaspoon ground nutmeg
- ⅛ teaspoon ground cloves
- 2 large eggs, lightly beaten
- 1 (15-ounce) can unsweetened pumpkin
- 1 (14-ounce) can fat-free sweetened condensed milk

CRUST:

- ½ (15-ounce) package refrigerated pie dough (such as Pillsbury)
- Cooking spray

STREUSEL:

- ⅓ cup all-purpose flour (about 1½ ounces)
- ⅓ cup packed dark brown sugar
- ¼ cup regular oats
- ¼ cup chopped pecans
- ¾ teaspoon ground cinnamon
- ⅛ teaspoon ground ginger
- 2 tablespoons chilled butter, cut into small pieces
- 2 to 3 teaspoons water

1. Preheat oven to 375°.
2. To prepare filling, combine first 8 ingredients in a large bowl; stir with a whisk.
3. To prepare crust, roll dough into an 11-inch circle. Fit dough into a 9-inch pie plate coated with cooking spray. Fold edges under; flute.

4. To prepare streusel, lightly spoon flour into a dry measuring cup; level with a knife. Combine flour and next 5 ingredients in a bowl. Cut in butter with a fork or fingertips until crumbly. Sprinkle with water, tossing with a fork just until lightly moistened.
5. Pour pumpkin mixture into crust; sprinkle with streusel. Place pie on a baking sheet. Bake at 375° for 50 minutes or until a knife inserted in center comes out clean. Remove from baking sheet; cool completely on a wire rack. Yield: 12 servings (serving size: 1 wedge).

CALORIES 273 (31% from fat); FAT 9.4g (sat 3.7g, mono 1.9g, poly 0.8g); PROTEIN 5.9g; CARB 41.8g; FIBER 1.7g; CHOL 46mg; IRON 1.1mg; SODIUM 117mg; CALC 118mg

Warm Caramelized Pears with Clove Zabaglione

This dessert calls for very little preparation. It can easily be doubled to serve more diners. Use sweet Marsala for this recipe.

- 1 teaspoon sugar
- ¼ teaspoon ground cloves
- ¼ teaspoon allspice
- ¼ teaspoon ground cinnamon
- ⅛ teaspoon ground nutmeg
- ½ cup Marsala
- 3 tablespoons honey
- 1 tablespoon butter
- 2 pieces lemon rind (1 x 3-inches)
- 4 large Bosc pears, halved and cored (about 2 pounds)
- Cooking spray
- 6 tablespoons Marsala
- ¼ cup sugar
- 2 tablespoons water
- ⅛ teaspoon salt
- 4 large egg yolks
- 1 teaspoon butter
- Lemon zest (optional)
- Ground nutmeg (optional)

1. Preheat an oven to 350°.
2. Combine first 5 ingredients in a small bowl; set aside.
3. Combine ½ cup Marsala, honey, 1 tablespoon butter, rind, and 1 teaspoon spice mixture in a small saucepan. Heat over medium heat until butter is melted.

4. Place pear halves, cut sides up, in a 13 x 9-inch baking dish coated with cooking spray. Pour Marsala mixture over pears. Bake at 350° for 30 minutes or until pears are tender, basting occasionally. Remove from oven; keep warm.

5. Combine 6 tablespoons Marsala, ¼ cup sugar, water, salt, and egg yolks in a medium, heavy saucepan, stirring with a whisk. Cook over low heat, whisking constantly, until mixture is thick (about 5 minutes). Stir in remaining spice mixture and 1 teaspoon butter until blended. Place 1 pear half in each of 8 bowls. Spoon ¼ cup sauce over each pear half. Garnish with lemon zest and nutmeg, if desired. Serve immediately. Yield: 8 servings.

CALORIES 196 (19% from fat); FAT 4.2g (sat 1.8g, mono 1.8g, poly 0.5g); PROTEIN 1.8g; CARB 33.4g; FIBER 3.4g; CHOL 107mg; IRON 0.5mg; SODIUM 58mg; CALC 25mg

---

A Good-to-Know Sauce

Zabaglione (known as *sabayon* to French cooks) is a thin Italian custard made from egg yolks and Marsala wine. It's a frothy, versatile dessert sauce that's worth learning to master. Here, we pair it with warm pears, but you can also drizzle it over other fruit, cake, and ice cream. Try it with Real Old-Fashioned Fruitcake (recipe below) or the Amaretto-Amaretti Pear Crumble (recipe on page 400). Zabaglione is best enjoyed warm.

Real Old-Fashioned Fruitcake

Look for candied citron in gourmet stores, or buy it online from Vine Tree Orchards (www.vinetreeorchards.com). Store leftover citron in a zip-top plastic bag in the freezer. You can substitute candied pineapple for the citron. Make the fruitcake at least a day ahead so the flavors have time to meld. To freeze, wrap cake in layers of plastic wrap, and place in a zip-top plastic freezer bag. Store up to one month.

5 cups hot water
Cooking spray
2 teaspoons all-purpose flour
2 cups raisins
1 cup dried currants
½ cup diced candied citron
2 tablespoons all-purpose flour
¾ cup all-purpose flour (about 3½ ounces)
½ teaspoon grated whole nutmeg
¼ teaspoon salt
¼ teaspoon ground mace
¼ teaspoon ground cinnamon
⅛ teaspoon baking soda
⅛ teaspoon ground cloves
½ cup butter
½ cup sugar
3 tablespoons brandy, divided
2 tablespoons dark molasses
2 large eggs, lightly beaten

1. Preheat oven to 250°.

2. Pour water in a 13 x 9-inch baking pan; place pan on bottom rack in oven.

3. Coat an 8 x 4-inch loaf pan with cooking spray; dust with 2 teaspoons flour.

4. Combine raisins, currants, citron, and 2 tablespoons flour, tossing well to coat; set aside.

5. Lightly spoon ¾ cup flour into a dry measuring cup; level with a knife. Combine ¾ cup flour, nutmeg, and next 5 ingredients, stirring with a whisk.

6. Melt butter in a large saucepan over medium heat. Remove from heat; add sugar, stirring with a whisk. Stir in 1½ tablespoons brandy, molasses, and eggs. Add flour mixture, stirring until smooth. Gradually stir in fruit mixture. Spoon batter into prepared pan; sharply tap pan once on counter to remove air bubbles. Bake at 250° on middle rack for 2 hours. Remove pan of water from oven; bake cake an additional 30 minutes or until a wooden pick inserted in center comes out clean. Brush with 1½ tablespoons brandy. Cool in pan 1 hour on a wire rack. Loosen cake from sides of pan with a knife. Remove cake from pan; cool completely. Wrap cake in plastic wrap; wrap in foil. Chill 24 hours before serving. Yield: 16 servings (serving size: 1 slice).

CALORIES 213 (26% from fat); FAT 6.6g (sat 3.9g, mono 2g, poly 0.4g); PROTEIN 2.4g; CARB 37.2g; FIBER 2.2g; CHOL 42mg; IRON 1.3mg; SODIUM 123mg; CALC 25mg

---

Dark Chocolate Orange Cake

You will need an eight-inch springform pan for this rich and fudgy dessert. Garnish the center of the cake with curls of orange rind for a great finishing touch.

Cooking spray
¾ cup powdered sugar
3 large eggs
3 tablespoons unsweetened cocoa
2 tablespoons cornstarch
2 tablespoons fresh orange juice
1 tablespoon Triple Sec (orange-flavored liqueur)
1 tablespoon hot water
Dash of salt
2 ounces bittersweet chocolate, chopped
Orange rind strips (optional)

1. Preheat oven to 350°.

2. Coat an 8-inch springform pan with cooking spray; line bottom of pan with parchment or wax paper. Wrap outside of pan with aluminum foil.

3. Place ¾ cup sugar and eggs in a bowl; beat with a mixer at high speed 7 minutes.

4. Combine cocoa and cornstarch in a small bowl; set aside. Place juice and next 4 ingredients in a small glass bowl; microwave at HIGH 1 minute or until almost melted, stirring every 20 seconds until smooth. Add cornstarch mixture; whisk until smooth.

5. Gently stir one-fourth of egg mixture into chocolate mixture; gently fold into remaining egg mixture. Scrape batter into prepared pan. Place pan in a 13 x 9-inch baking pan; add hot water to larger pan to a depth of 1 inch. Bake at 350° for 20 minutes or until top is set. Remove cake pan from water; cool 5 minutes on a wire rack. Loosen cake from sides of pan using a narrow metal spatula; cool to room temperature. Cover and chill at least 4 hours or overnight. Garnish with orange rind strips just before serving, if desired. Yield: 6 servings (serving size: 1 slice).

CALORIES 175 (31% from fat); FAT 6.1g (sat 3g, mono 1.3g, poly 0.4g); PROTEIN 4.3g; CARB 26.1g; FIBER 1.7g; CHOL 107mg; IRON 0.8mg; SODIUM 33mg; CALC 17mg

Persimmon Cake

Choose persimmons that are soft but not mushy. If they're firm, let them ripen in a paper bag on the kitchen counter for a couple of days.

1½ pounds ripe persimmons (about 4 medium)
1¾ cups 1% low-fat milk
¾ cup sugar
3 large eggs
1¼ cups all-purpose flour (about 5½ ounces)
¾ teaspoon baking soda
¾ teaspoon baking powder
½ teaspoon ground cinnamon
¼ teaspoon salt
2 tablespoons butter
¾ cup chopped pecans
Cooking spray

1. Preheat oven to 350°.
2. Cut tops off persimmons; scrape pulp away from skin with a spoon. Place persimmon pulp, milk, sugar, and eggs in a food processor or blender, and process until smooth.
3. Lightly spoon flour into dry measuring cups; level with a knife. Combine flour and next 4 ingredients in a large bowl; make a well in center of mixture.
4. Gradually add persimmon mixture to flour mixture, stirring just until blended. (Batter will be thin but will thicken quickly.) Let batter stand 10 minutes to thicken.
5. While batter stands, melt butter in a small skillet over medium-high heat. Add pecans; cook 3 minutes or until pecans are toasted. Pour batter into a 9-inch springform pan coated with cooking spray. Sprinkle pecan mixture over batter. Swirl pecan mixture into batter using a knife or skewer. Bake at 350° for 1½ hours or until cake is set in center and a wooden pick inserted into center comes out clean. Cool 15 minutes; remove cake from pan. Cut into wedges. Yield: 12 servings (serving size: 1 wedge).

CALORIES 270 (31% from fat); FAT 9.2g (sat 2.1g, mono 4.5g, poly 2g); PROTEIN 5.3g; CARB 44.4g; FIBER 2g; CHOL 59mg; IRON 2.5mg; SODIUM 208mg; CALC 91mg

MAKE AHEAD
Eggnog and Dried Fruit Bread Pudding

This recipe calls for eight ounces of country white bread. Buy a rustic loaf that weighs 16 ounces; once you remove the crust you will have eight ounces. Day-old bread works well for bread puddings because it has lost moisture and, thus, absorbs more liquid.

2 tablespoons brandy
1 (7-ounce) package dried fruit bits
2 cups 2% reduced-fat milk
3 tablespoons butter
1 teaspoon vanilla
½ teaspoon freshly grated nutmeg
⅔ cup sugar
3 large eggs, lightly beaten
3 large egg yolks, lightly beaten
8 ounces country white bread, crusts removed and cut into 1-inch pieces
Cooking spray
1 tablespoon powdered sugar

1. Combine brandy and fruit bits in a small saucepan; bring to a boil. Remove from heat; let stand 1 hour.
2. Combine milk, butter, vanilla, and nutmeg in a medium saucepan. Heat to 180° or until tiny bubbles form around edge of pan, stirring frequently (do not boil). Remove from heat. Combine ⅔ cup sugar, eggs, and egg yolks in a large bowl. Pour hot milk mixture into egg mixture in a slow, steady stream, stirring constantly with a whisk. Return milk mixture to saucepan over medium-low heat; cook, stirring constantly, until thickened (about 6 minutes).
3. Preheat oven to 375°.
4. Combine bread and fruit mixture in a large bowl; pour milk mixture over bread mixture. Transfer mixture to an 11 x 7-inch baking dish coated with cooking spray. Place dish in a 13 x 9-inch baking pan; add hot water to pan to a depth of 1 inch. Bake at 375° for 45 minutes or until set. Sprinkle with powdered sugar. Yield: 10 servings (serving size: 1 square).

CALORIES 272 (26% from fat); FAT 8g (sat 3.7g, mono 2.5g, poly 1g); PROTEIN 7.5g; CARB 41.6g; FIBER 1g; CHOL 138mg; IRON 1.4mg; SODIUM 195mg; CALC 106mg

Amaretto-Amaretti Pear Crumble

This dish is very juicy, so we suggest serving it with ice cream.

4 firm Bosc pears, peeled, cored, and cut into ½-inch-thick wedges (about 2 pounds)
1 tablespoon fresh lemon juice
½ cup apricot preserves
¼ cup amaretto (almond-flavored liqueur)
1½ tablespoons chilled butter, cut into small pieces
1 cup amaretti cookie crumbs (about 16 cookies)
1½ cups vanilla low-fat ice cream

1. Preheat oven to 375°.
2. Combine pears and juice in a large bowl; spoon into a 1-quart baking dish.
3. Combine preserves and liqueur in a small bowl; spoon evenly over pears. Sprinkle butter over pear mixture, and top with cookie crumbs. Bake at 375° for 30 minutes or until golden brown. Spoon pear mixture evenly into 6 bowls, and top each serving with ¼ cup ice cream. Yield: 6 servings.

CALORIES 298 (17% from fat); FAT 5.7g (sat 2.3g, mono 1g, poly 0.3g); PROTEIN 3g; CARB 60.2g; FIBER 4.5g; CHOL 10mg; IRON 0.5mg; SODIUM 68mg; CALC 73mg

MAKE AHEAD
Praline-Sweet Potato Cheesecake

It's natural for this cheesecake to have cracks on the top, but they will be covered by the buttery praline mixture.

PRALINE:
Cooking spray
⅓ cup granulated sugar
3 tablespoons water
1 tablespoon light-colored corn syrup
½ teaspoon vanilla extract
¾ cup chopped pecans
2 teaspoons butter
¼ teaspoon salt

CRUST:

- 1¾ cups graham cracker crumbs
- 3 tablespoons granulated sugar
- 1½ tablespoons butter, melted
- 1 tablespoon water

FILLING:

- 2 (15-ounce) cans sweet potatoes in syrup, drained
- 1 cup packed dark brown sugar
- 1 (8-ounce) package ⅓-less-fat cream cheese
- 1 (8-ounce) block fat-free cream cheese
- 1 (8-ounce) container fat-free sour cream
- ¼ cup all-purpose flour (about 1 ounce)
- 1½ teaspoons vanilla extract
- 1 teaspoon ground cinnamon
- ¼ teaspoon ground allspice
- ¼ teaspoon ground ginger
- 2 large eggs
- 2 large egg whites

1. To prepare praline, coat a 10-inch sheet of aluminum foil with cooking spray. Place ⅓ cup granulated sugar and next 3 ingredients in a small, heavy saucepan over medium-high heat; cook until sugar dissolves, stirring as needed to dissolve sugar evenly (about 5 minutes). Continue cooking 5 minutes or until golden. Remove from heat; carefully stir in pecans, 2 teaspoons butter, and salt. Immediately pour onto prepared foil, spreading to a thin layer. Cool completely. Break praline into small pieces. Place in a food processor, and process until coarsely ground.

2. Preheat oven to 350°.

3. To prepare crust, combine cracker crumbs and next 3 ingredients in a bowl. Toss well with a fork. Press crumb mixture into bottom and up sides of a 9-inch springform pan coated with cooking spray. Bake at 350° for 10 minutes. Cool on a wire rack.

4. Reduce oven temperature to 325°.

5. To prepare filling, place sweet potatoes in food processor; process until smooth. Remove from processor. Place brown sugar, cheeses, and sour cream in processor; process until smooth. Add

sweet potatoes, flour, and remaining 6 ingredients, and process until smooth. Add one-half of ground praline mixture; pulse 3 times or until blended. Pour filling into crust. Bake at 325° for 55 minutes. Turn off oven. (Do not remove cheesecake from oven.) Let cheesecake stand in oven 1 hour. Remove from oven; cool on a wire rack. Cover and chill 3 hours or overnight. Sprinkle top with remaining ground praline mixture before serving. Yield: 16 servings (serving size: 1 wedge).

CALORIES 287 (32% from fat); FAT 10.3g (sat 3.8g, mono 4g, poly 1.7g); PROTEIN 7.2g; CARB 42.5g; FIBER 1.9g; CHOL 43mg; IRON 1.3mg; SODIUM 223mg; CALC 86mg

---

MAKE AHEAD
Pecan Pie Coffee Cake

This dessert is at its best with coffee. Make sure you lower the oven temperature to 325° before adding the topping to prevent it from burning.

CAKE:

- ¾ cup granulated sugar
- 3 tablespoons butter, softened
- 2 ounces fat-free cream cheese
- 1 large egg
- 1 large egg white
- 1 teaspoon vanilla extract
- 1¼ cups all-purpose flour (about 5½ ounces)
- ½ teaspoon baking powder
- ¼ teaspoon baking soda
- ¼ teaspoon salt
- ¾ cup nonfat buttermilk
- Cooking spray

TOPPING:

- ⅓ cup light-colored corn syrup
- ¼ cup packed dark brown sugar
- 2 tablespoons butter
- ⅓ cup finely chopped pecans
- 1 large egg, beaten

1. Preheat oven to 350°.

2. To prepare cake, place first 3 ingredients in a large bowl; beat with a mixer at medium speed until well blended (about 5 minutes). Add egg and egg white, 1 at a time, beating well after each addition.

Beat in vanilla. Lightly spoon flour into dry measuring cups; level with a knife. Combine flour, baking powder, baking soda, and salt, stirring well with a whisk. Add flour mixture and buttermilk alternately to sugar mixture, beginning and ending with flour mixture.

3. Pour batter into a 9-inch round cake pan coated with cooking spray. Bake at 350° for 30 minutes or until a wooden pick inserted in center comes out clean. Remove cake from oven. Reduce oven temperature to 325°.

4. To prepare topping, combine syrup, brown sugar, and 2 tablespoons butter in a 4-cup glass measure. Microwave at HIGH 1 minute. Stir with a whisk until butter melts. Stir in pecans and beaten egg with a whisk.

5. Using a wooden skewer, poke holes in top of warm cake. Pour pecan mixture over top of cake. Return cake to oven; bake at 325° for 10 minutes. Cool completely on a wire rack. Yield: 10 servings (serving size: 1 wedge).

CALORIES 275 (32% from fat); FAT 9.8g (sat 3.5g, mono 4.4g, poly 1.3g); PROTEIN 5.2g; CARB 43.1g; FIBER 0.8g; CHOL 58mg; IRON 1.2mg; SODIUM 238mg; CALC 64mg

---

MAKE AHEAD
Pumpkin-Maple Trifle

A trifle is an English dessert composed of layers of sponge cake or ladyfingers doused with sherry, jam, custard, and whipped cream. This distinctly American version contains pumpkin and maple syrup. A trifle bowl is a large, footed vessel made of clear glass (so you can see all of the layers). If you don't have one, use any two-quart bowl or even a soup tureen.

CUSTARD:

- ⅓ cup packed brown sugar
- 3 tablespoons cornstarch
- ¼ teaspoon salt
- 1¾ cups 2% reduced-fat milk, divided
- 1 large egg, lightly beaten
- ⅓ cup canned pumpkin
- 1 teaspoon vanilla extract

Continued

    2 tablespoons fresh lemon
       juice
    4 firm Bosc pears, cored and each
       cut into 16 wedges (about
       2 pounds)
    1 tablespoon butter
    6 tablespoons Frangelico (hazelnut-
       flavored liqueur), divided
    2 tablespoons maple syrup

REMAINING INGREDIENTS:

    6 ounces frozen low-fat pound
       cake, thawed and cut into
       1/4-inch-thick slices (such as
       Sara Lee)
    1 cup frozen reduced-calorie
       whipped topping, thawed
    1/4 teaspoon ground cinnamon

1. To prepare custard, combine first 3 ingredients in a medium saucepan, stirring well with a whisk. Stir in 1 1/2 cups milk; bring to a boil over medium heat, stirring constantly. Cook 1 minute, stirring constantly; remove from heat. Combine 1/4 cup milk and egg in a small bowl. Stir one-fourth of hot milk mixture into egg mixture. Add egg mixture to remaining milk mixture in pan, stirring well. Cook over medium heat 1 minute or until thick, stirring constantly. Remove from heat; stir in pumpkin and vanilla. Pour mixture into a bowl; cover surface with plastic wrap. Chill completely.

2. To prepare pears, combine lemon juice and pears. Melt butter in a large nonstick skillet over medium-high heat. Add pear mixture; cook 4 minutes. Drizzle 3 tablespoons liqueur over pears; cover and simmer 5 minutes or until tender. Remove pears from pan with a slotted spoon, reserving liquid in pan. Add syrup to pan; bring to a boil. Cook 1 minute, stirring frequently. Pour syrup mixture into a small bowl; stir in 3 tablespoons liqueur. Cover and chill.

3. Line bottom of a 2-quart trifle bowl with half of cake slices (cut slices to fit bowl, if necessary); drizzle with half of liqueur mixture. Top with half of pear mixture and any accumulated juices. Spoon half of custard over pears. Repeat procedure with remaining cake, liqueur

mixture, pear mixture, and custard. Spread whipped topping over custard, and sprinkle with cinnamon. Cover and chill 3 hours. Yield: 10 servings.

CALORIES 238 (14% from fat); FAT 3.6g (sat 2.3g, mono 0.8g, poly 0.3g); PROTEIN 3.4g; CARB 44.8g; FIBER 3.3g; CHOL 28mg; IRON 0.9mg; SODIUM 155mg; CALC 80mg

Share the Flavor

Edible gifts are simple to make and always welcome.

Ginger-Pear Preserves

A jar of these preserves is nice for neighbors, friends, and coworkers. Package it with a pretty spreader. Serve on English muffins, crackers, or as a condiment for baked ham.

    6 cups cubed ripe Bosc or Bartlett
       pear (about 1 3/4 pounds)
    3/4 cup chopped seeded lemon (1
       large)
    1/4 cup pear-flavored liqueur
    1 to 2 tablespoons grated peeled
       fresh ginger
    4 cups sugar
    1/2 cup water

1. Combine first 4 ingredients in a large saucepan. Stir in sugar and water; bring to a boil. Reduce heat, and simmer 15 minutes. Remove from heat; cover and let stand 12 hours (do not refrigerate).

2. Bring to a boil, uncovered, over high heat. Reduce heat, and simmer 1 hour and 15 minutes or until thick, stirring occasionally. Place 1 cup preserves into each of 4 sterilized (8-ounce) jars. Cover with lids, and cool upside down on a wire rack. Chill. Yield: 4 cups (serving size: 1 tablespoon).

NOTE: Preserves will keep in the refrigerator up to six weeks.

CALORIES 51 (0% from fat); FAT 0g; PROTEIN 0.1g; CARB 13.1g; FIBER 0.3g; CHOL 0mg; IRON 0mg; SODIUM 1mg; CALC 2mg

Toasted Coconut Marshmallows

These are good as a snack or dropped into a mug of hot chocolate. The mixture for the marshmallows becomes quite thick and requires substantial beating time, so you'll want to use a heavy-duty stand mixer instead of a handheld mixer. Using a stand mixer also makes it safer (and easier) to gradually add the hot gelatin mixture to the beaten egg whites. Use a dough scraper to cut the marshmallows into squares with a quick vertical motion (avoid dragging it as you cut the marshmallows). If the dough scraper sticks to the marshmallows, dust it with powdered sugar.

    Cooking spray
    2 cups flaked sweetened coconut,
       toasted
    2 1/2 envelopes unflavored gelatin (2
       tablespoons plus 1 1/4 teaspoons)
    3/4 cup cold water, divided
    2 cups granulated sugar, divided
    2/3 cup light-colored corn syrup
    1 tablespoon vanilla extract
    1/4 teaspoon salt
    2 large egg whites
    2/3 cup powdered sugar
    3 tablespoons cornstarch

1. Line a 13 x 9-inch baking pan with heavy-duty plastic wrap, allowing plastic wrap to extend 1 inch over sides of pan. Lightly coat plastic wrap with cooking spray. Spread coconut in an even layer in bottom of pan; set aside.

2. Sprinkle gelatin over 1/2 cup cold water in a small bowl; set aside.

3. Combine 1/4 cup water, 1 3/4 cups granulated sugar, and syrup in a large saucepan. Cook, without stirring, over medium-high heat until a candy thermometer registers 260° (about 15 minutes). Remove from heat; gradually stir in softened gelatin (mixture will appear foamy).

4. While sugar mixture cooks, beat vanilla, salt, and egg whites at high speed in a heavy-duty stand mixer with whisk attachment until foamy. Gradually add 1/4 cup granulated sugar, 1 tablespoon at a time, until stiff peaks form.

Gradually pour in gelatin mixture, beating until very thick (about 5 minutes). Gently spread marshmallow mixture over coconut in prepared pan. Coat 1 side of another sheet of plastic wrap with cooking spray. Place plastic wrap, coated side down, over marshmallow mixture. Chill 8 hours or until firm.

5. Sprinkle powdered sugar and cornstarch over a cutting board. Remove top sheet of plastic wrap. Invert marshmallow mixture over powdered sugar mixture. Using a dough scraper, cut mixture into about 1-inch squares. Store between sheets of wax or parchment paper in an airtight container. Yield: 8 dozen (serving size: 3 marshmallows).

CALORIES 107 (12% from fat); FAT 1.5g (sat 1.3g, mono 0.1g, poly 0g); PROTEIN 0.9g; CARB 23.4g; FIBER 0.2g; CHOL 0mg; IRON 0.1mg; SODIUM 43mg; CALC 2mg

How to Make Toasted Coconut Marshmallows

1. *Gradually pour in gelatin mixture, beating until very thick (about 5 minutes.)*

2. *Using a dough scraper, cut mixture into about 1-inch squares.*

MAKE AHEAD
Yogurt Cheese Torte

Drain yogurt of most of its liquid to create a soft spread similar to cream cheese. One cup of yogurt yields approximately ½ cup cheese. Serve with crackers, croutons, or baguette slices. If you're planning to give this torte as a gift, layer the cheese and herb mixture in a small glass container that can double as a serving dish.

  6 cups plain low-fat yogurt
  3 tablespoons extravirgin olive oil
  2 tablespoons sliced garlic
  2 tablespoons chopped fresh basil
  1 tablespoon chopped fresh rosemary
  1 tablespoon chopped fresh thyme
  1 tablespoon chopped fresh sage
  1 tablespoon minced shallots
  1 teaspoon grated lemon rind
  ½ teaspoon sea salt
  ¼ teaspoon crushed red pepper

1. Place a colander in a large bowl. Line colander with 4 layers of cheesecloth, allowing cheesecloth to extend over outside edges.
2. Spoon yogurt into colander. Cover loosely with plastic wrap; refrigerate 12 hours. Spoon yogurt cheese into a medium bowl, and discard liquid. Cover and chill 3 hours.
3. Combine oil and remaining 9 ingredients in a small bowl.
4. Place half of yogurt cheese in a serving bowl; spread with half of herb mixture. Repeat with remaining cheese and herb mixture. Cover and chill torte at least 12 hours and up to 1 week. Serve at room temperature. Yield: 32 servings (serving size: 1 tablespoon yogurt cheese and about 1 teaspoon oil mixture).

CALORIES 42 (43% from fat); FAT 2g (sat 0.7g, mono 1.2g, poly 0.1g); PROTEIN 2.5g; CARB 3.5g; FIBER 0.1g; CHOL 3mg; IRON 0.1mg; SODIUM 68mg; CALC 86mg

MAKE AHEAD
Mini Fruit and Sunflower Loaves

This not-too-sweet bread is good for breakfast or with coffee or tea in the afternoon. Mini loaves are nice for gifts, but you can also bake the batter in a full-sized loaf pan. Just increase the cooking time.

  2 cups all-purpose flour (about 9 ounces)
  1 cup yellow cornmeal
  2 teaspoons baking soda
  ¼ teaspoon salt
  2 cups vanilla fat-free yogurt
  ½ cup canola oil
  ½ cup maple syrup
  ½ cup honey
  1 teaspoon vanilla extract
  1 cup chopped dried mixed fruit
  ½ cup sunflower seed kernels
  1 teaspoon grated orange rind
Cooking spray

1. Preheat oven to 350°.
2. Lightly spoon flour into dry measuring cups, and level with a knife. Combine flour and next 3 ingredients in a large bowl. Combine yogurt, oil, syrup, honey, and vanilla. Add yogurt mixture to flour mixture, stirring just until moist. Fold in fruit, sunflower seeds, and rind.
3. Spoon batter into 4 (6-inch) loaf pans coated with cooking spray. Bake at 350° for 35 minutes or until a wooden pick inserted in center comes out clean. Remove from pans; cool completely on a wire rack. Yield: 4 loaves, 8 servings per loaf (serving size: 1 slice).

CALORIES 151 (30% from fat); FAT 5.1g (sat 0.4g, mono 2.4g, poly 2g); PROTEIN 2.6g; CARB 24.5g; FIBER 1.2g; CHOL 0mg; IRON 0.8mg; SODIUM 111mg; CALC 36mg

MAKE AHEAD

Sesame Bread

This recipe is inspired by Cuban bread, which requires a different baking method than most yeast breads; it undergoes one rise and is placed in an unheated oven (the dough rises a little more as the oven heats up). For best results, give this bread soon after baking. It's wonderful toasted with the Ginger-Pear Preserves (recipe on page 402).

    2   cups warm water (100°
          to 110°)
    1   tablespoon sugar
    2   teaspoons sea salt
    1   package dry yeast (about
          2¼ teaspoons)
    6   cups all-purpose flour, divided
          (about 27 ounces)
        Cooking spray
    ½   cup yellow cornmeal
    ¼   cup sesame seeds

1. Combine first 4 ingredients in a large bowl, stirring with a whisk. Let stand 5 minutes. Lightly spoon flour into dry measuring cups, and level with a knife. Add 5½ cups flour, about 1 cup at a time, to yeast mixture, stirring until a soft dough forms. Turn dough out onto a floured surface. Knead until dough is smooth and elastic (about 8 minutes); add enough remaining flour, 1 tablespoon at a time, to prevent dough from sticking to hands.

2. Place dough in a large bowl coated with cooking spray, turning to coat top. Cover and let rise in a warm place (85°), free from drafts, 1½ hours or until doubled in size. (Press two fingers into dough. If indentation remains, dough has risen enough.)

3. Divide dough into 2 equal portions, shaping each portion into a 12-inch-long loaf. Place loaves on a baking sheet sprinkled with cornmeal. Lightly brush loaves with cold water. Sprinkle evenly with sesame seeds.

4. Place a shallow pan of boiling water on bottom rack of cold oven. Place loaves on middle rack of oven. Set oven temperature to 400°. (Do not preheat oven.) Bake 35 minutes or until loaves

sound hollow when tapped. Cool on a wire rack. Yield: 2 loaves, 12 servings per loaf (serving size: 1 slice).

CALORIES 128 (7% from fat); FAT 1.1g (sat 0.2g, mono 0.3g, poly 0.5g); PROTEIN 3.7g; CARB 25.5g; FIBER 1.1g; CHOL 0mg; IRON 1.7mg; SODIUM 193mg; CALC 20mg

MAKE AHEAD

Maple-Date Bars

Wrap these moist bars individually, or place them in a cookie tin between layers of wax or parchment paper.

    1¾ cups finely chopped pitted dates
          (about 12 ounces)
    ¾   cup water
    ⅓   cup maple syrup
    1   teaspoon grated lemon rind
    ⅔   cup sugar
    ½   cup butter, softened
    1   cup all-purpose flour (about
          4½ ounces)
    1   cup regular oats
    ¼   teaspoon baking soda
    ¼   teaspoon salt
        Cooking spray

1. Combine first 3 ingredients in a heavy saucepan over medium heat. Bring to a boil; cook 12 minutes or until most liquid is absorbed, stirring frequently. (Mixture will look like jam.) Stir in rind; cool completely.

2. Preheat oven to 400°.

3. Beat sugar and butter with a mixer at medium speed until smooth. Lightly spoon flour into a dry measuring cup; level with a knife. Combine flour, oats, baking soda, and salt. Stir flour mixture into sugar mixture (mixture will be crumbly). Press 2 cups flour mixture into bottom of a 13 x 9-inch baking pan coated with cooking spray. Spread date mixture over flour mixture. Sprinkle with remaining flour mixture. Bake at 400° for 20 minutes or until golden brown. Cool completely in pan on a wire rack. Yield: 20 servings (serving size: 1 bar).

CALORIES 162 (28% from fat); FAT 5g (sat 2.3g, mono 2g, poly 0.3g); PROTEIN 1.6g; CARB 29.5g; FIBER 1.8g; CHOL 12mg; IRON 0.7mg; SODIUM 78mg; CALC 14mg

MAKE AHEAD
Italian Anise Cookies

These cookies are similar to biscotti, just cut thinner. Present a half-dozen in a large coffee mug to give with a pound of coffee. Or divide them among small paper gift bags to give with tins of tea or a pretty teacup and saucer.

   3   cups all-purpose flour (about 13½ ounces)
   2   teaspoons baking powder
   1   cup sugar
   2   large eggs
   2   large egg whites
   ¼   cup melted butter
   ½   cup chopped almonds
   1½ teaspoons aniseed
Cooking spray

1. Lightly spoon flour into dry measuring cups; level with a knife. Combine flour and baking powder, stirring well with a whisk. Place sugar, eggs, and egg whites in a large bowl; beat with a mixer at high speed until light and fluffy. Beat in butter. Gradually add flour mixture, almonds, and aniseed, beating until well blended (dough will be sticky).

2. Divide dough in half. Turn each half of dough out onto wax paper; shape each portion into an 8-inch roll. Wrap rolls in wax paper. Chill 1 hour or until firm.

3. Preheat oven to 350°.

4. Unwrap rolls, and place on a baking sheet coated with cooking spray. Bake at 350° for 30 minutes or until lightly browned. Remove rolls from baking sheet; cool 10 minutes on a wire rack. Cut each roll crosswise into 24 (⅜-inch) slices. Place slices on baking sheet. Bake at 350° for 5 minutes. Turn slices over, and bake an additional 5 minutes. Remove from baking sheet, and cool completely on wire rack. Yield: 4 dozen (serving size: 1 cookie).

CALORIES 66 (27% from fat); FAT 2g (sat 0.6g, mono 1g, poly 0.3g); PROTEIN 1.6g; CARB 10.5g; FIBER 0.4g; CHOL 11mg; IRON 0.5mg; SODIUM 33mg; CALC 18mg

QUICK & EASY • MAKE AHEAD
Lemon-Curry Rice

This fragrant gift can be stored in a cool, dry place up to one month. Be sure to include these cooking directions with it: Bring 3 cups water to a boil; add 1½ cups rice mixture. Cook 18 minutes or until rice is tender; stir in ½ teaspoon salt.

   2   tablespoons grated lemon rind
   4   cups uncooked jasmine rice
   1   cup golden raisins
   1   cup shelled pistachios
   1   tablespoon curry powder
   2   teaspoons dried curry leaves
   1   teaspoon white pepper
   ½   teaspoon ground cumin
   ½   teaspoon crushed red pepper

1. Spread rind evenly on a plate; set aside 1 hour or until dry.

2. Combine rind and remaining ingredients in a large zip-top bag, turning bag until mixture is blended. Place 1½ cups rice mixture into each of 4 containers. Seal tightly. Yield: 6 cups uncooked rice mixture (serving size, cooked: 1 cup).

(Totals include ½ teaspoon salt added for cooking) CALORIES 155 (21% from fat); FAT 3.7g (sat 0.5g, mono 1.9g, poly 1.1g); PROTEIN 3.6g; CARB 28g; FIBER 1.7g; CHOL 0mg; IRON 0.8mg; SODIUM 297mg; CALC 18mg

QUICK & EASY • MAKE AHEAD
Seasoned Basmati Rice

Spices are tied in a bouquet garni so they're easy to remove after cooking. And the cheesecloth-wrapped bouquets, bundled in food-safe cellophane, are also good stocking stuffers. Include these directions with each package of rice: Bring 3 cups water to a boil; add bouquet garni and 1½ cups rice mixture, and cook 18 minutes or until rice and lentils are tender. Discard bouquet garni; stir ½ teaspoon salt into rice mixture.

BOUQUET GARNI:

   1   teaspoon cardamom pods, toasted
   16 whole cloves
   8   black peppercorns
   2   (3-inch) cinnamon sticks, halved

REMAINING INGREDIENTS:

   4   cups uncooked basmati rice
   1   cup lentils
   ¼   cup minced crystallized ginger
   2   teaspoons cumin seeds, toasted
   1   teaspoon white pepper

1. To prepare bouquet garni, combine first 4 ingredients in a small bowl. Divide mixture evenly among 4 packages of a double layer of (4-inch-square) cheesecloth. Gather edges of cheesecloth together; tie securely with kitchen twine.

2. Place 1 bouquet garni, 1 cup rice, ¼ cup lentils, 1 tablespoon ginger, ½ teaspoon cumin, and ¼ teaspoon white pepper in each of 4 containers. Seal tightly. Yield: about 6 cups uncooked rice mixture (serving size, cooked: ½ cup).

(Totals include ½ teaspoon salt added for cooking) CALORIES 118 (3% from fat); FAT 0.4g (sat 0.1g, mono 0.1g, poly 0.2g); PROTEIN 3.7g; CARB 25.3g; FIBER 2.1g; CHOL 0mg; IRON 0.8mg; SODIUM 150mg; CALC 9mg

*To make planning meals easier, we composed six all-occasion menus with recipes
from our holiday cookbook.*

Holiday Dinner Menu
serves 8

**Pork Tenderloin with
Dried Apricot and
Onion Marmalade**
(recipe on page 388)

Carrot-Coriander Purée
(recipe on page 394)

Seasoned Basmati Rice
(recipe on page 405)

**White Cheddar and Black
Pepper Biscuits**
(recipe on page 397)

Steamed broccoli

Persimmon Cake
(recipe on page 400)

Open House Menu
serves 8

**Vanilla-Scented
Mulled Cider**
(recipe on page 383)

Pumpkin Hummus
(recipe on page 383)

**Smoked Ham Soup
with White Beans**
(recipe on page 385)

**Mini Corn Muffins with
Currants** (recipe on page 397)

**Eggnog and Dried Fruit
Bread Pudding**
(recipe on page 400)

Thanksgiving Feast Menu
serves 12

**Roasted Beet, Avocado, and
Watercress Salad**
(recipe on page 381)

**Parmesan-Sage Roast Turkey
with Sage Gravy**
(recipe on page 385)

Camembert Mashed Potatoes
(recipe on page 393)

**Sourdough Stuffing with Pears
and Sausage**
(recipe on page 391)

Oven-Roasted Green Beans
(recipe on page 392)

Flaky Dinner Rolls
(recipe on page 396)

**Cranberry, Cherry, and Walnut
Chutney**
(recipe on page 395)

**Cinnamon Streusel-Topped
Pumpkin Pie**
(recipe on page 398)

Dinner Party Menu
serves 6

Roasted Cauliflower Soup
(recipe on page 382)

Green salad

**Braised Lamb Shanks with
Rosemary Polenta**
(recipe on page 387)

Baguette

Dark Chocolate Orange Cake
(recipe on page 399)

Festive Brunch Menu
serves 10

Cranberry Mimosa
(recipe on page 383)

**Blackberry-Mustard
Glazed Ham**
(recipe on page 386)

**Sour Cream Muffins
with Poppy Seed Streusel**
(recipe on page 395)

Mixed fruit salad

Pecan Pie Coffee Cake
(recipe on page 401)

Cocktail Party Menu
serves 12

**Winter-Spiced Red Wine
Sangría**
(recipe on page 383)
(Prepare a double batch.)

Yogurt Cheese Torte
(recipe on page 403)

**Baba Ghanoush with
Red Pepper Swirl**
(recipe on page 383)

**Smoked Trout
with Apple-Horseradish Cream
on Potato Pancakes**
(recipe on page 382)

Assorted cheeses and crackers

Italian Anise Cookies
(recipe on page 405)

Sopa del Día

Leftover chicken inspires a lightened version of Mexican tortilla soup.

With the help of *Cooking Light*, Ann Parker of Kennesaw, Georgia, has become a paragon of good health. She goes to the gym regularly, reworks recipes to make them higher in fiber and lower in fat and calories, and eats what she likes—in moderation. Taking her cue from the magazine's recipes, she knows that there is no such thing as a forbidden ingredient. Parker's Southwestern Chicken Soup is a good example of her newfound culinary know-how.

QUICK & EASY
Southwestern Chicken Soup
(pictured on page 378)

Cooking spray
1 cup chopped onion
3 garlic cloves, minced
6 cups fat-free, less-sodium chicken broth
¼ cup uncooked white rice
1 teaspoon ground cumin
1 (16-ounce) can Great Northern beans, rinsed and drained
3 cups chopped skinless, boneless rotisserie chicken breast
½ cup coarsely chopped fresh cilantro
½ teaspoon black pepper
¼ teaspoon salt
1 cup chopped seeded tomato
¾ cup diced peeled avocado (about 1 medium)
1 tablespoon fresh lime juice
6 lime wedges

1. Heat a large sauté pan over medium-high heat. Coat pan with cooking spray. Add onion and garlic, and sauté 3 minutes. Add broth, rice, cumin, and beans; bring to a boil. Reduce heat; simmer 15 minutes. Stir in chicken, cilantro, pepper, and salt; simmer 5 minutes or until chicken is thoroughly heated.

2. Remove from heat, and stir in tomato, avocado, and juice. Serve with lime wedges. Yield: 6 servings (serving size: 1⅔ cups soup and 1 lime wedge).

CALORIES 274 (25% from fat); FAT 7.7g (sat 1.5g, mono 3.9g, poly 1.3g); PROTEIN 28.4g; CARB 23.1g; FIBER 6g; CHOL 60mg; IRON 2.6mg; SODIUM 516mg; CALC 65mg

QUICK & EASY
Roasted Salmon with Citrus and Herbs

"Everyone in my family loves salmon, even my four-year-old twin boys. There are never any leftovers when I make this dish."

—Karen Ensign, Providence, Utah

1 tablespoon finely chopped fresh parsley
1 tablespoon finely chopped fresh thyme
1 tablespoon minced garlic
2 teaspoons grated lemon rind
2 teaspoons grated lime rind
1 teaspoon sea salt
½ teaspoon freshly ground black pepper
1 (2¼-pound) salmon fillet
Cooking spray

1. Preheat oven to 400°.
2. Combine first 7 ingredients in a small bowl. Place salmon on rack of a broiler pan coated with cooking spray; place rack in pan. Rub parsley mixture over salmon. Bake at 400° for 15 minutes or until fish flakes easily when tested with a fork or until desired degree of doneness. Yield: 6 servings (serving size: 4½ ounces salmon).

CALORIES 282 (42% from fat); FAT 13.3g (sat 3.1g, mono 5.7g, poly 3.2g); PROTEIN 36.3g; CARB 1g; FIBER 0.3g; CHOL 87mg; IRON 0.7mg; SODIUM 464mg; CALC 26mg

MAKE AHEAD
Apple-Cinnamon Granola

"Ever since I realized I didn't have to buy granola in a box, I have experimented with different recipes. This is one of my favorites; the granola is great with yogurt or on top of vanilla ice cream."

—Corrie Francis, Moraga, California

3 cups regular oats
1 cup whole-grain toasted oat cereal (such as Cheerios)
⅓ cup oat bran
⅓ cup finely chopped walnuts
2 teaspoons ground cinnamon
¼ teaspoon ground cardamom
2 tablespoons butter
⅓ cup applesauce
¼ cup honey
2 tablespoons brown sugar
Cooking spray
1 cup chopped dried apple

1. Preheat oven to 250°.
2. Combine first 6 ingredients in a large bowl, stirring well.
3. Melt butter in a medium saucepan over medium heat. Add applesauce, honey, and sugar, and bring to a boil. Cook 1 minute, stirring frequently. Pour applesauce mixture over oat mixture, stirring to coat. Spread mixture in an even layer on a jelly-roll pan coated with cooking spray. Bake at 250° for 1½ hours, stirring every 30 minutes. Cool completely. Stir in chopped apple. Yield: 6 cups (serving size: ½ cup).
NOTE: Store granola in an airtight container up to one week.

CALORIES 196 (27% from fat); FAT 5.8g (sat 1.4g, mono 1.6g, poly 2.2g); PROTEIN 4.4g; CARB 35g; FIBER 4g; CHOL 5mg; IRON 2.2mg; SODIUM 128mg; CALC 28mg

QUICK & EASY
Spicy String Bean Sauté

—Denise Boba, Bloomingdale, Illinois

⅔ pound green beans, trimmed
⅓ pound wax beans, trimmed
1 tablespoon olive oil
4 cups (⅓-inch-thick) vertically sliced Peruvian or other sweet onion (about 1 large)
2 garlic cloves, minced
3 tablespoons fresh lemon juice
1 teaspoon dried oregano
½ teaspoon crushed red pepper
1 tablespoon capers
½ teaspoon kosher salt
¼ teaspoon freshly ground black pepper

Continued

1. Cook beans in boiling water 2 minutes or until crisp-tender; drain. Rinse with cold water; drain.

2. Heat oil in a large nonstick skillet over medium-high heat. Add onion, and sauté 3 minutes or until onion begins to brown. Add garlic; sauté 1 minute. Add beans, juice, oregano, and red pepper; cook 1 minute or until thoroughly heated. Remove from heat. Add capers, salt, and black pepper, tossing to coat. Yield: 6 servings (serving size: 1 cup).

CALORIES 73 (30% from fat); FAT 2.4g (sat 0.3g, mono 1.7g, poly 0.2g); PROTEIN 1.7g; CARB 11.1g; FIBER 3.4g; CHOL 0mg; IRON 0.7mg; SODIUM 209mg; CALC 52mg

---

QUICK & EASY
Pumpkin Muffins

"I combined several recipes and adjusted them to get the flavor we love. Sometimes I add raisins or finely chopped apple or pear."

—Cindy Kahn, Londonderry, New Hampshire

  1 cup all-purpose flour (about 4½ ounces)
  ½ cup whole wheat flour (about 2½ ounces)
  ½ cup granulated sugar
  ½ cup packed brown sugar
  1¼ teaspoons pumpkin-pie spice
  1 teaspoon baking soda
  ¼ teaspoon baking powder
  ¼ teaspoon salt
  1 cup canned pumpkin
  ½ cup fat-free buttermilk
  ½ cup egg substitute
  ¼ cup canola oil
  ¼ cup applesauce
  Cooking spray

1. Preheat oven to 375°.

2. Lightly spoon flours into dry measuring cups; level with a knife. Combine flours, granulated sugar, and next 5 ingredients in a large bowl, stirring with a whisk.

3. Combine pumpkin and next 4 ingredients in a medium bowl, stirring with a whisk. Add pumpkin mixture to flour mixture, stirring just until moist. Spoon batter into 16 muffin cups coated

with cooking spray. Bake at 375° for 20 minutes or until muffins spring back when touched lightly in center. Cool muffins in pans 5 minutes on a wire rack; remove from pans. Cool completely on wire rack. Yield: 16 servings (serving size: 1 muffin).

CALORIES 145 (28% from fat); FAT 4.6g (sat 0.5g, mono 2.3g, poly 1.6g); PROTEIN 2.6g; CARB 24.1g; FIBER 1.2g; CHOL 0mg; IRON 1.1mg; SODIUM 149mg; CALC 33mg

---

QUICK & EASY
Braised Kale with Pinto Beans and Pancetta

"I've been trying to incorporate a variety of vitamin-packed, fiber-rich vegetables and legumes into our diets, and this dish meets both criteria."

—Colette Russo, Barboursville, Virginia

  Cooking spray
  2 cups finely chopped red onion
  ¼ cup chopped pancetta (about 1 ounce)
  3 garlic cloves, minced
  11 cups chopped kale (about 1¼ pounds)
  ½ teaspoon freshly ground black pepper
  ¼ teaspoon salt
  1 (15-ounce) can pinto beans, rinsed and drained
  1 (14-ounce) can less-sodium beef broth

1. Heat a large Dutch oven over medium-high heat. Coat pan with cooking spray. Add onion, pancetta, and garlic; sauté 5 minutes or until pancetta browns. Stir in kale, pepper, and salt. Add beans and broth; bring to a boil. Cover, reduce heat, and simmer 15 minutes or until kale is tender. Uncover and cook 10 minutes or until liquid almost evaporates. Yield: 6 servings (serving size: 1 cup).

CALORIES 109 (19% from fat); FAT 2.3g (sat 0.8g, mono 0.7g, poly 0.5g); PROTEIN 5.8g; CARB 18.1g; FIBER 3.9g; CHOL 3mg; IRON 1.8mg; SODIUM 451mg; CALC 111mg.

---

happy endings

Sweet Soiree

Indulge guests with an extravagant spread of bite-sized luxuries.

Dessert Buffet Menu
serves 12

Popcorn Brittle

Brownie Bourbon Balls

Chocolate Gingersnap Cookies

Chocolate-Speckled Toffee

Key Lime Coconut Snowballs

Bittersweet Chocolate Meringues

Goat Cheese and Chocolate-Stuffed Dates

Assorted beverages

MAKE AHEAD
Popcorn Brittle

While replacing the nuts in brittle with popcorn certainly removes a lot of fat, it also results in a wonderful hybrid—part caramel corn, part brittle. About ¼ cup kernels yields the correct amount of popcorn.

  Cooking spray
  5½ cups popcorn, popped without salt or fat
  1½ cups sugar
  6 tablespoons light-colored corn syrup
  ¼ cup water
  3 tablespoons molasses
  1 tablespoon butter
  ½ teaspoon baking soda
  ½ teaspoon vanilla extract
  ¼ teaspoon salt

1. Line a baking sheet with foil; coat foil with cooking spray. Set aside.

2. Place popcorn in a large zip-top plastic bag; seal. Crush popcorn using a meat mallet or rolling pin; set aside.

3. Combine sugar, syrup, and water in a medium saucepan over medium heat. Cook 1 minute or until sugar dissolves, stirring constantly. Cook, without stirring, until candy thermometer registers 270° (about 8 minutes). Stir in molasses and butter; cook until thermometer registers 290° (about 5 minutes). Stir in baking soda, vanilla, and salt. Stir popcorn into boiling syrup mixture. Working quickly, pour popcorn mixture onto prepared pan; spread to ¼-inch thickness using a wooden spoon coated with cooking spray. Cool completely; break into large pieces. Yield: 12 servings (serving size: about 1½ ounces).

NOTE: Store brittle in an airtight container at room temperature up to four days.

CALORIES 165 (6% from fat); FAT 1.1g (sat 0.5g, mono 0.4g, poly 0.1g); PROTEIN 0.5g; CARB 39.9g; FIBER 0.6g; CHOL 3mg; IRON 0.4mg; SODIUM 123mg; CALC 12mg.

MAKE AHEAD
Brownie Bourbon Balls

In this quick-and-easy rendition, we used packaged brownie mix, a little bourbon, and chopped toasted walnuts.

⅓ cup applesauce
¼ cup egg substitute
1 tablespoon water
1 (16.7-ounce) package double fudge brownie mix (such as Duncan Hines)
Cooking spray
3 tablespoons bourbon
⅓ cup finely chopped walnut pieces, toasted

1. Preheat oven to 350°.
2. Combine first 4 ingredients (including fudge packet from mix), stirring well. Spread into an 8-inch square baking pan coated with cooking spray. Bake at 350° for 30 minutes or until a wooden pick inserted near edge of pan comes out clean. Cool in pan on a wire rack.
3. Crumble brownies; place in a food processor. Add bourbon; process until mixture forms a ball (about 30 seconds).
4. Shape brownie mixture into 24 balls, about 1½ tablespoons each. Place nuts in a shallow bowl. Roll balls in nuts, pressing gently to coat. Yield: 2 dozen (serving size: 1 ball).

NOTE: Store balls in an airtight container at room temperature up to three days.

CALORIES 100 (30% from fat); FAT 3.3g (sat 0.6g, mono 0.9g, poly 1.7g); PROTEIN 1.6g; CARB 16g; FIBER 0.7g; CHOL 1mg; IRON 0.9mg; SODIUM 82mg; CALC 2mg

MAKE AHEAD • FREEZABLE
Chocolate Gingersnap Cookies

A hint of chocolate enhances these crisp, spicy cookies. It's best to bake each tray of cookies separately; while one tray bakes, keep the other tray in the refrigerator to prevent the dough from becoming too soft.

½ cup all-purpose flour (about 2¼ ounces)
2 tablespoons unsweetened cocoa, sifted
1 teaspoon ground ginger
¼ teaspoon baking soda
⅛ teaspoon salt
¼ cup packed brown sugar
2 tablespoons butter, softened
2 tablespoons molasses
1 tablespoon egg substitute
Cooking spray

1. Preheat oven to 350°.
2. Lightly spoon flour into a dry measuring cup; level with a knife. Combine flour and next 4 ingredients, stirring with a whisk. Place sugar and butter in a medium bowl; beat with a mixer at medium speed 2 minutes or until creamy. Add molasses; beat until smooth. Add egg substitute; beat until well combined. Add flour mixture to sugar mixture, stirring until well combined.
3. Shape dough into 24 balls, about 1½ teaspoons each. Place 2 inches apart on 2 baking sheets coated with cooking spray; flatten balls to ½-inch thickness with bottom of a glass. Bake each batch at 350° for 10 minutes. Cool on pan 4 minutes on a wire rack; remove from pan. Cool completely on wire rack. Yield: 2 dozen (serving size: 2 cookies).

NOTE: Store cookies in an airtight container at room temperature up to three days.

CALORIES 66 (29% from fat); FAT 2.1g (sat 1g, mono 0.8g, poly 0.1g); PROTEIN 0.9g; CARB 11.6g; FIBER 0.5g; CHOL 5mg; IRON 0.7mg; SODIUM 70mg; CALC 14mg

Tips for a Successful Dessert Buffet

• Make bites and tidbits; avoid the scenario of trying to balance a plate with a three-layer wedge of cake in one hand and a mug of coffee in the other while making conversation. Bite-sized sweets also mean there's no need for silverware.
• Make desserts that can be served at room temperature. By doing so, you can set up the spread before the party starts, then just relax and enjoy time with your friends.
• Offer a range of textures and tastes: creamy to crunchy, mild to spicy.
• Mix and match your tableware. Don't feel hemmed in by dish sets and serving platters. Use food-safe rose petals, dried fruit, or colorful ribbons to visually tie the tabletop setting together. Or consider putting small, framed snapshots of everyone present among the desserts on the table to help your guests feel special and to inspire lively chitchat. You can even send them home with their pictures as party favors.
• Set napkins around the room where guests can get to them, not just on the buffet.
• To keep traffic moving, set up separate stations for coffee and for other drinks away from the buffet spread.

You can make all these recipes well in advance so that party setup is a breeze.

MAKE AHEAD
Goat Cheese and Chocolate-Stuffed Dates

Use a high-quality chocolate bar (such as Scharffen Berger) and soft Medjool dates for the best flavor. Substitute Neufchâtel cheese in place of goat cheese for more sweetness.

24 whole pitted Medjool dates
¼ cup (2 ounces) goat cheese
1 tablespoon grated unsweetened chocolate
1½ teaspoons powdered sugar

1. Open slit in each date; stuff about ½ teaspoon goat cheese and about ⅛ teaspoon chocolate inside each date. Close date around filling; press gently to seal. Arrange stuffed dates in a single layer on a platter; sift powdered sugar over dates. Yield: 12 servings (serving size: 2 stuffed dates).

NOTE: Refrigerate stuffed dates in an airtight container up to two days.

CALORIES 65 (18% from fat); FAT 1.3g (sat 0.9g, mono 0.3g, poly 0g); PROTEIN 1.3g; CARB 13.4g; FIBER 1.4g; CHOL 2mg; IRON 0.3mg; SODIUM 18mg; CALC 13mg

MAKE AHEAD
Key Lime Coconut Snowballs

Use regular limes if the Key limes aren't available. Unsweetened coconut is often labeled "desiccated" or "pulverized," and is often sold in health-food stores.

⅔ cup graham cracker crumbs (about 4 cookie sheets)
6 tablespoons fat-free sweetened condensed milk
1 teaspoon grated Key lime rind
1½ tablespoons fresh Key lime juice
1 teaspoon vanilla extract
1 cup shredded unsweetened coconut, divided
1¼ cups powdered sugar

1. Combine first 5 ingredients in a medium bowl. Add ⅔ cup coconut, and beat with a mixer at medium speed 1 minute or until no longer grainy. Add sugar, ¼ cup at a time, beating until well combined. Cover and chill 20 minutes.

2. Shape crumb mixture into 24 balls, about 1 teaspoon each. Place ⅓ cup coconut in a shallow bowl; roll balls in coconut. Yield: 12 servings (serving size: 2 balls).

NOTE: Refrigerate balls in an airtight container up to one day.

CALORIES 121 (20% from fat); FAT 2.7g (sat 2.1g, mono 0.3g, poly 0.2g); PROTEIN 1.4g; CARB 23.2g; FIBER 0.8g; CHOL 1mg; IRON 0.4mg; SODIUM 40mg; CALC 30mg

MAKE AHEAD
Bittersweet Chocolate Meringues

⅛ teaspoon salt
⅛ teaspoon cream of tartar
3 large egg whites
½ cup sugar
¼ cup finely chopped bittersweet chocolate

1. Preheat oven to 225°.
2. Line 2 baking sheets with parchment paper; set aside.
3. Place first 3 ingredients in a large bowl, and beat with a mixer at high speed until foamy. Add sugar, 1 tablespoon at a time, beating until stiff peaks form. Beat 1 minute at high speed or until mixture is shiny. Gently fold in chocolate.
4. Spoon mixture into a large zip-top plastic bag. Snip a ¼-inch hole in 1 bottom corner of bag. Pipe 24 (4-inch-long) zigzag shapes onto each prepared pan.
5. Bake at 225° for 30 minutes with 1 pan on bottom rack and 1 pan on second rack from top. Rotate pans; bake an additional 30 minutes or until dry to the touch. Cool on pans 30 minutes on wire racks. Carefully remove meringues from paper; cool completely on wire racks. Yield: 12 servings (serving size: 4 meringues).

NOTE: Store meringues in an airtight container at room temperature up to 2 weeks.

CALORIES 54 (18% from fat); FAT 1.1g (sat 0.6g, mono 0.4g, poly 0g); PROTEIN 1.1g; CARB 10.7g; FIBER 0.2g; CHOL 0mg; IRON 0.1mg; SODIUM 39mg; CALC 2mg

How to Make Meringues

Pipe 24 (4-inch-long) zigzag shapes onto each prepared pan.

How to Make Toffee

1. *Sprinkle ½ teaspoon baking soda over surface of mixture; carefully stir baking soda into mixture. Immediately pour sugar mixture onto prepared pan.*

2. *Working quickly, spread to about ⅛-inch thickness using prepared spatula.*

Chocolate-Speckled Toffee

A candy thermometer is a must for preparing this rich, buttery treat. The syrup mixture bubbles up when you sprinkle it with baking soda, so use a long-handled spoon for stirring. Because the toffee holds well at room temperature, it also makes a good gift.

Cooking spray
1 cup sugar
½ cup light-colored corn syrup
¼ cup butter, cut into small pieces
1 tablespoon water
¼ teaspoon salt
2 teaspoons vanilla extract
½ teaspoon baking soda
1 ounce semisweet chocolate, coarsely chopped

1. Line a baking sheet with foil; lightly coat foil with cooking spray. Lightly coat a metal spatula with cooking spray; set aside.
2. Combine sugar and next 4 ingredients in a medium saucepan. Bring to a boil over medium-high heat, stirring occasionally with a wooden spoon until ingredients are just combined. Cook, without stirring, until candy thermometer registers 300° (about 5 minutes).
3. Remove from heat. Stir in vanilla. Sprinkle baking soda over surface of mixture; carefully stir baking soda into mixture. Immediately pour sugar mixture onto prepared pan. Working quickly, spread to about ⅛-inch thickness using prepared spatula. Let stand 2 minutes. Sprinkle chocolate evenly over toffee, and cool completely. Break into bite-sized pieces. Yield: 12 servings (serving size: about 1 ounce).
NOTE: Store toffee in an airtight container at room temperature up to one week.

CALORIES 152 (27% from fat); FAT 4.5g (sat 2.3g, mono 1.6g, poly 0.1g); PROTEIN 0.2g; CARB 29.1g; FIBER 0.1g; CHOL 10mg; IRON 0mg; SODIUM 145mg; CALC 2mg

culinary postcard

Windy City Cuisine

From steak and potatoes to deep-dish pizza, Chicago is home to many all-American favorites.

Described by poet Carl Sandburg as "Hog Butcher for the World" and "Stacker of Wheat," Chicago has a meat-and-potatoes reputation when it comes to food. The city is also richly influenced by outsiders. Chicago boasts the largest population of Poles outside of Warsaw. And outside Mexico, the Mexican concentration here is second in the United States only to Los Angeles. Clusters of Indians, Vietnamese, Irish, Italians, Koreans, and Filipinos dot the city. You can spend lots of time sampling the diversity or just try one of these recipes at home.

Pan-Seared Steak with Mushrooms

A classic combination, steak and mushrooms are the heart of a meat-and-potatoes, Chicago steak house dinner. Serve with Potatoes Lyonnaise (recipe on page 413) and Creamed Spinach (recipe on page 413), and pair the dish with a hearty red wine.

STEAKS:
4 (4-ounce) beef tenderloin steaks, trimmed (1 inch thick)
¼ teaspoon salt
¼ teaspoon freshly ground black pepper
1 garlic clove, minced
1 tablespoon butter

MUSHROOMS:
½ cup finely chopped shallots
1 pound large button mushrooms, quartered
2 garlic cloves, minced
¼ cup dry white wine
2 tablespoons Worcestershire sauce
¼ teaspoon black pepper
⅛ teaspoon salt
2 tablespoons finely chopped fresh parsley

1. To prepare steaks, sprinkle beef evenly with ¼ teaspoon salt and ¼ teaspoon pepper. Rub 1 minced garlic clove over both sides of steaks. Melt butter in a large nonstick skillet over medium-high heat. Add steaks; cook 3 minutes on each side until browned or until desired degree of doneness. Remove steaks from pan; keep warm.
2. To prepare mushrooms, add shallots and mushrooms to pan; sauté 4 minutes or until lightly browned. Add 2 garlic cloves; sauté 30 seconds. Add wine and next 3 ingredients; cook 3 minutes or until liquid is nearly evaporated. Remove pan from heat, and stir in parsley. Serve mushroom mixture with steaks. Yield: 4 servings (serving size: 1 steak and about ½ cup mushroom mixture).

CALORIES 282 (43% from fat); FAT 13.6g (sat 5.5g, mono 5.5g, poly 0.5g); PROTEIN 26.6g; CARB 10.4g; FIBER 0.4g; CHOL 87mg; IRON 2.9mg; SODIUM 381mg; CALC 47mg

Shrimp De Jonghe

De Jonghe Hotel on Chicago's Monroe Street first served this dish in the 1920s. Bake the shrimp mixture in individual portions using six (six-ounce) ramekins, if you prefer.

- 2 (1-ounce) slices white bread
- 2 tablespoons butter, divided
- 4 garlic cloves, minced and divided
- 1½ tablespoons finely chopped fresh tarragon, divided
- 1½ tablespoons finely chopped green onions, divided
- 1½ pounds large shrimp, peeled and deveined
- ½ cup dry vermouth
- 1 tablespoon Dijon mustard
- ¼ teaspoon salt
- ⅛ teaspoon freshly ground black pepper

1. Preheat oven to 400°.
2. Place bread in a food processor, and pulse 10 times or until coarse crumbs measure 1 cup.
3. Melt 1 tablespoon butter in a large nonstick skillet over medium-high heat. Add half of garlic; sauté 30 seconds. Add breadcrumbs, 1½ teaspoons tarragon, and 1½ teaspoons green onions; cook 2 minutes, stirring constantly. Place breadcrumb mixture in a bowl.
4. Add 1 tablespoon butter to pan; cook 1 minute or until butter begins to brown. Add remaining garlic; sauté 30 seconds, stirring constantly. Add shrimp; sauté 2 minutes. Stir in vermouth and mustard; simmer 1 minute or until shrimp are done. Stir in 1 tablespoon tarragon, 1 tablespoon green onions, salt, and pepper.
5. Arrange shrimp mixture in an 8-inch square baking dish, and sprinkle breadcrumb mixture evenly over shrimp. Bake at 400° for 10 minutes or until breadcrumbs are golden. Yield: 6 servings (serving size: about 5 shrimp and about 2½ tablespoons breadcrumb mixture).

CALORIES 133 (26% from fat); FAT 3.8g (sat 1.7g, mono 1.3g, poly 0.5g); PROTEIN 14.3g; CARB 5.7g; FIBER 0.3g; CHOL 134mg; IRON 2.3mg; SODIUM 301mg; CALC 49mg

Chicago-Style Deep-Dish Pizza

Tomato sauce layered on top of mozzarella cheese and a biscuit-like crust distinguish this fork-and-knife pizza from other styles around the country. You can prepare the dough the night before and let it rise in the refrigerator overnight, if you prefer.

DOUGH:
- 1 teaspoon sugar
- 1 package dry yeast (about 2¼ teaspoons)
- 1 cup warm water (100° to 110°)
- 3 cups all-purpose flour (about 13½ ounces), divided
- ¼ teaspoon salt
- Cooking spray

TOPPING:
- ½ pound turkey Italian sausage (about 2 links)
- 1 cup finely chopped onion
- 1 (8-ounce) package presliced mushrooms
- 1½ teaspoons olive oil, divided
- 3 garlic cloves, minced
- 1 tablespoon tomato paste
- 1 teaspoon dried oregano
- ¼ teaspoon fennel seeds, crushed
- 2 (8-ounce) cans tomato sauce
- 1 tablespoon cornmeal
- 1¼ cups (5 ounces) preshredded part-skim mozzarella cheese
- 2 tablespoons grated fresh Parmesan cheese

1. To prepare dough, dissolve sugar and yeast in warm water in a large bowl; let stand 10 minutes. Lightly spoon flour into dry measuring cups; level with a knife. Add 1 cup flour and salt to yeast mixture, stirring with a whisk until well combined. Add 1¾ cups flour, stirring until a dough forms. Turn dough out onto a lightly floured surface. Knead dough until smooth and elastic (about 8 minutes); add enough of remaining flour, 1 tablespoon at a time, to prevent dough from sticking to hands (dough will feel sticky).
2. Place dough in a large bowl coated with cooking spray, turning to coat top. Cover and let rise in a warm place (85°), free from drafts, 1 hour or until doubled in size. (Press two fingers into dough. If indentation remains, dough has risen enough.) Punch dough down; cover and let stand 5 minutes.
3. Preheat oven to 375°.
4. To prepare topping, heat a large nonstick skillet over medium-high heat. Remove casings from sausage. Coat pan with cooking spray. Add sausage and onion; cook 5 minutes or until sausage is browned, stirring to crumble. Drain; set sausage mixture aside.
5. Return pan to medium-high heat. Add mushrooms; cook 5 minutes or until moisture evaporates, stirring frequently. Remove mushrooms from pan, and set aside.
6. Return pan to medium heat; add 1 teaspoon oil. Add garlic; cook 30 seconds or until lightly browned, stirring constantly. Add tomato paste; cook 1 minute, stirring frequently. Stir in oregano, fennel, and tomato sauce; simmer 5 minutes or until sauce mixture is slightly thickened.
7. Coat a 12-inch cast-iron skillet with ½ teaspoon oil, and sprinkle cornmeal over oil. Place dough in skillet, gently stretching edges to evenly coat bottom and sides of pan. Sprinkle mozzarella evenly over bottom of dough; top evenly with sausage mixture and mushrooms. Top mushrooms with sauce mixture; sprinkle Parmesan over sauce. Bake at 375° for 40 minutes or until crust browns and topping is bubbly. Let pizza stand 10 minutes before serving. Yield: 8 servings (serving size: 1 slice).

CALORIES 323 (22% from fat); FAT 8g (sat 3g, mono 2.8g, poly 1.4g); PROTEIN 16.7g; CARB 46.1g; FIBER 2.9g; CHOL 35mg; IRON 3.6mg; SODIUM 694mg; CALC 156mg

Chicken Vesuvio

If the chicken pieces don't fit in the bottom of your Dutch oven comfortably, brown them in two batches—crowded meat is hard to brown. Buy peeled garlic from the grocery store produce section for easier preparation of this one-dish meal. Versions of this classic Chicago dish are served at many eateries throughout the city, most notably Harry Caray's Restaurant, named for the famous baseball announcer and voice of the Chicago Cubs from 1982 until his death in 1998.

    4   chicken thighs (about
        1¼ pounds), skinned
    4   chicken drumsticks (about
        1 pound), skinned
    ¾   teaspoon salt, divided
    ¼   teaspoon freshly ground black
        pepper
    1   tablespoon olive oil
    12 garlic cloves
    2   large peeled baking potatoes, each
        cut into 8 wedges
    1   cup fat-free, less-sodium chicken
        broth
    ½   cup dry white wine
    3   tablespoons finely chopped fresh
        oregano
    2   garlic cloves, minced
    1   cup frozen green peas

1. Preheat oven to 350°.
2. Sprinkle chicken evenly with ¼ teaspoon salt and pepper. Heat oil over medium-high heat in a large Dutch oven. Add chicken; cook 3 minutes on each side or until browned. Remove chicken from pan.
3. Add whole garlic cloves to pan; sauté 1 minute or until lightly browned. Remove from pan.
4. Add potatoes to pan; sauté 6 minutes or until lightly browned. Return chicken and whole garlic cloves to pan. Add ½ teaspoon salt, broth, white wine, oregano, and minced garlic; bring to a simmer.
5. Cover and bake at 350° for 30 minutes or until chicken is done and potatoes are tender. Add peas; bake an additional 8 minutes or until peas are tender. Yield: 4 servings (serving size: 1 chicken thigh, 1 chicken drumstick, and about 1 cup potato mixture).

CALORIES 448 (19% from fat); FAT 9.5g (sat 2g, mono 4.3g, poly 1.9g); PROTEIN 35.6g; CARB 49.8g; FIBER 5.6g; CHOL 119mg; IRON 3.1mg; SODIUM 712mg; CALC 79mg

---

QUICK & EASY
Creamed Spinach

This lightened version of the popular steak house side dish still delivers full flavor. Serve with Pan-Seared Steak with Mushrooms (recipe on page 411).

    ½   cup fat-free milk
    2   teaspoons all-purpose flour
        Cooking spray
    1   cup thinly sliced leek (about 1 large)
    2   garlic cloves, minced
    1   (10-ounce) package frozen
        chopped spinach, thawed,
        drained, and squeezed dry
    ¼   cup (2 ounces) ⅓-less-fat cream
        cheese
    ¼   teaspoon salt
    ¼   teaspoon freshly ground black
        pepper

1. Combine milk and flour, stirring well with a whisk; set aside.
2. Heat a medium saucepan over medium-high heat. Coat pan with cooking spray. Add leek and garlic; sauté 2 minutes or until tender. Add spinach, and sauté 1 minute. Stir in milk mixture; cook 1½ minutes or until slightly thick, stirring occasionally. Stir in cheese, salt, and pepper, stirring until smooth; cook 1 minute. Yield: 4 servings (serving size: about ½ cup).

CALORIES 86 (39% from fat); FAT 3.7g (sat 2.2g, mono 1g, poly 0.3g); PROTEIN 5.2g; CARB 9.4g; FIBER 2.5g; CHOL 11mg; IRON 1.7mg; SODIUM 276mg; CALC 149mg

---

Potatoes Lyonnaise

Named for Lyons, a city in France renowned for the quality of its food, Lyonnaise-style dishes are prepared or garnished with onions. A signature side dish at Chicago's Morton's steak house, this combination of potatoes and onions is ideal with a juicy steak.

        Cooking spray
    2   small yellow onions, peeled,
        halved lengthwise and cut into
        ¼-inch slices (about 5 cups)
    4   teaspoons olive oil
    1¾ pounds peeled baking potatoes,
        halved lengthwise and cut into
        ¼-inch slices (about 5 cups)
    ½   cup fat-free, less-sodium chicken
        broth
    ½   cup water
    1   tablespoon chopped fresh thyme
    ¾   teaspoon salt
    ¼   teaspoon freshly ground black
        pepper

1. Heat a large nonstick skillet over medium-high heat. Coat pan with cooking spray. Add onions; sauté 5 minutes or until browned, stirring occasionally. Spoon onions into a bowl.
2. Heat oil in pan over medium-high heat. Add potatoes; cook 10 minutes or until browned, stirring occasionally. Reduce heat to low. Stir in onions, broth, and remaining ingredients. Cover and cook 8 minutes or until potatoes are very tender, stirring occasionally. Yield: 6 servings (serving size: about ¾ cup).

CALORIES 159 (18% from fat); FAT 3.2g (sat 0.5g, mono 2.2g, poly 0.4g); PROTEIN 3.1g; CARB 30.1g; FIBER 3.1g; CHOL 0mg; IRON 0.6mg; SODIUM 330mg; CALC 19mg

---

MAKE AHEAD
Melitzanosalata

This eggplant dip is a favorite in Chicago's Greektown section. Prepare up to a day ahead, and refrigerate.

    1   (1¼-pound) eggplant
    2   (1½-ounce) slices white bread
    ¾   cup chopped onion
    ¾   cup chopped plum tomato
    ½   cup fresh parsley leaves
    2   tablespoons fresh lemon juice
    2   tablespoons olive oil
    1   tablespoon red wine vinegar
    ¼   teaspoon salt
    3   garlic cloves, chopped
    2   teaspoons chopped fresh parsley
    4   (6-inch) whole wheat pitas, each
        cut into 8 wedges

Continued

1. Preheat oven to 350°.

2. Pierce eggplant several times with a fork; place on a foil-lined baking sheet. Bake at 350° for 1 hour or until tender; cool slightly. Carefully remove pulp; discard peels.

3. Place bread in a food processor; pulse 10 times or until coarse crumbs measure 2 cups.

4. Place eggplant pulp, breadcrumbs, onion, and next 7 ingredients in a food processor; process until smooth. Spoon eggplant mixture into a serving bowl. Sprinkle evenly with chopped parsley. Serve with pita wedges. Yield: 8 servings (serving size: about ⅓ cup eggplant mixture and 4 pita wedges).

CALORIES 173 (25% from fat); FAT 4.8g (sat 0.7g, mono 2.7g, poly 0.9g); PROTEIN 5.1g; CARB 30g; FIBER 3.2g; CHOL 0mg; IRON 2mg; SODIUM 325mg; CALC 39mg

Cracker Jack Brownie Sundae

Brownies and Cracker Jacks both debuted at the 1893 World's Colombian Exposition in Chicago. Chefs at the city's still-operating Palmer Hotel created the brownie. The "brownie" in this recipe is similar to flourless cake—decadently dense and fudgy.

- ½ cup sugar
- 2 tablespoons butter, softened
- 1 teaspoon vanilla extract
- 1 large egg
- ¼ cup semisweet chocolate chips
- ¼ cup fat-free milk
- ¼ cup all-purpose flour (about 1 ounce)
- ½ cup unsweetened cocoa
- ¼ teaspoon salt
  Cooking spray
- 2¼ cups vanilla reduced-fat ice cream (such as Healthy Choice)
- 1 cup fat-free caramel sundae syrup
- 1 cup Cracker Jacks, coarsely chopped

1. Preheat oven to 375°.

2. Place first 3 ingredients in a large bowl; beat with a mixer at medium speed until well blended (about 2 minutes). Add egg; beat 2 minutes or until pale.

Place chocolate chips in a small microwave-safe bowl, and microwave at HIGH in 20-second intervals until completely melted, stirring after each interval. Add chocolate to sugar mixture; beat until combined. Stir in milk.

3. Lightly spoon flour into a dry measuring cup; level with a knife. Combine flour, cocoa, and salt; add to sugar mixture, stirring just until blended.

4. Scrape batter into an 8-inch square baking dish coated with cooking spray. Bake at 375° for 18 minutes or until completely set. Cool to room temperature in pan on a wire rack. Cut brownies into 9 equal portions.

5. Place one brownie on each of 9 small plates; top each brownie with ¼ cup ice cream and about 1½ tablespoons caramel syrup. Sprinkle Cracker Jacks evenly over sundaes. Serve immediately. Yield: 9 servings (serving size: 1 sundae).

CALORIES 318 (19% from fat); FAT 6.8g (sat 3.6g, mono 1.7g, poly 0.3g); PROTEIN 5.6g; CARB 57.3g; FIBER 2.1g; CHOL 33mg; IRON 1.1mg; SODIUM 215mg; CALC 88mg

MAKE AHEAD
Frango Mint Cheesecake

The Chicago-based department store chain Marshall Field's has sold the addictive mint-infused Frango chocolates since 1918. You can order them online ($4.90 for ⅓ pound; www.fields.com), or substitute 10 dark chocolate mint candies (such as Andes mints). Wrapping the outside of the pan with aluminum foil helps keep the water bath where it belongs. Serve chilled.

- 2 sheets chocolate graham crackers
  Cooking spray
- 1¼ cups sugar
- 3 tablespoons all-purpose flour
- ⅛ teaspoon salt
- 1 cup 1% low-fat cottage cheese
- 1 (8-ounce) block fat-free cream cheese, softened
- 1 (8-ounce) block ⅓-less-fat cream cheese, softened
- 2 teaspoons vanilla extract
- 3 large eggs
- 1 large egg white
- 5 Frango mint candies, chopped and divided

1. Preheat oven to 350°.

2. Place crackers in a food processor; process 30 seconds or until finely ground. Sprinkle crumbs over bottom of a 9-inch springform pan coated with cooking spray. Lightly coat crumbs with cooking spray. Wrap outside of pan with a double layer of foil.

3. Combine sugar, flour, and salt. Place cottage cheese and cream cheeses in a food processor; process 1 minute or until smooth. Add sugar mixture; process 1 minute or until smooth. Add vanilla, eggs, and egg white; process 1 minute or until well blended. Add half of chopped mints; pulse once to combine. Pour batter into prepared pan. Sprinkle remaining chopped mints evenly over batter. Place springform pan in a jelly-roll pan or large roasting pan; add hot water to pan to a depth of 1 inch.

4. Bake at 350° for 50 minutes or until cheesecake center barely moves when pan is touched. Remove cheesecake from oven; cool in pan on a wire rack 5 minutes. Run a knife around outside edge. Cool to room temperature. Cover and chill at least 8 hours. Yield: 12 servings (serving size: 1 slice).

CALORIES 222 (31% from fat); FAT 7.6g (sat 4.2g, mono 1.9g, poly 0.3g); PROTEIN 9.5g; CARB 29.1g; FIBER 0.2g; CHOL 69mg; IRON 0.4mg; SODIUM 229mg; CALC 67mg

december

Christmas Morning Breakfast

A mostly make-ahead spread encourages a leisurely morning of opening gifts from Santa.

Christmas Morning Breakfast Menu 1
serves 6
Bundt Coffee Cake
Bacon, Gruyère, and Ham Strata
Country Sausage Patties
Festive Fruit Punch

MAKE AHEAD
Bundt Coffee Cake
(pictured on page 429)

If you like coffee cakes, you'll love this recipe. It's a moist, light cake with a surprise middle layer of nuts and cinnamon. Prepare it up to one month ahead, and freeze. Defrost at room temperature 24 hours before serving.

Cooking spray
1 tablespoon dry breadcrumbs
1½ cups granulated sugar
¼ cup butter, softened
2 large eggs
1 large egg white
1¼ cups fat-free sour cream
1 teaspoon vanilla extract
2½ cups cake flour (about 10 ounces)
2 teaspoons baking powder
½ teaspoon baking soda
½ teaspoon salt
¼ cup all-purpose flour (about 1 ounce)
¾ cup packed brown sugar
1 teaspoon ground cinnamon
¼ teaspoon salt
1 tablespoon butter, chilled and cut into small pieces
¼ cup chopped pecans
1 teaspoon powdered sugar

1. Preheat oven to 350°.
2. Coat a 12-cup bundt pan with cooking spray; dust with breadcrumbs.
3. Place granulated sugar and ¼ cup butter in a large bowl; beat with a mixer at medium speed until well blended. Add eggs and egg white, 1 at a time, beating well after each addition. Beat in sour cream and vanilla.
4. Lightly spoon cake flour into dry measuring cups; level with a knife. Combine cake flour and next 3 ingredients, stirring with a whisk. Add cake flour mixture to butter mixture, beating at low speed until blended.
5. Lightly spoon all-purpose flour into a dry measuring cup; level with a knife. Combine all-purpose flour, brown sugar, cinnamon, and ¼ teaspoon salt; cut in 1 tablespoon butter with a pastry blender or 2 knives until mixture resembles coarse meal. Stir in pecans.
6. Pour half of batter into prepared pan. Sprinkle with pecan mixture. Pour remaining half of batter over pecan mixture. Bake at 350° for 40 minutes or until a wooden pick inserted in center comes out clean. Cool completely on a wire rack. Invert onto a platter. Sprinkle with powdered sugar. Yield: 14 servings (serving size: 1 slice).

CALORIES 316 (19% from fat); FAT 6.6g (sat 2.4g, mono 2.8g, poly 0.8g); PROTEIN 5.1g; CARB 59.2g; FIBER 0.8g; CHOL 45mg; IRON 2.4mg; SODIUM 309mg; CALC 91mg

MAKE AHEAD
Bacon, Gruyère, and Ham Strata

This make-ahead casserole is blissfully easy to prepare, especially if you purchase diced ham from your supermarket. Gruyère is a type of Swiss cheese. Its sweet nuttiness enhances this dish.

2 cups fat-free milk
1 cup chopped green onions
1 cup egg substitute
1 tablespoon Dijon mustard
¼ teaspoon ground red pepper
12 ounces sourdough French bread, cut into ½-inch cubes (about 10 cups), toasted
¾ cup diced ham
Cooking spray
1 cup (4 ounces) shredded Gruyère cheese
4 bacon slices, cooked and crumbled (drained)

1. Combine milk, green onions, egg substitute, mustard, and pepper in a large bowl, stirring with a whisk. Add bread cubes and ham; stir well to combine. Pour into a 2-quart baking pan coated with cooking spray. Sprinkle with shredded cheese. Cover and chill 8 hours or overnight.
2. Preheat oven to 350°.
3. Uncover dish, and bake at 350° for 20 minutes. Sprinkle with bacon. Bake an additional 15 minutes or until bread mixture is set and cheese is bubbly. Yield: 6 servings.

CALORIES 330 (31% from fat); FAT 11.5g (sat 4.6g, mono 3.5g, poly 1.8g); PROTEIN 23.7g; CARB 34.1g; FIBER 2.2g; CHOL 34mg; IRON 4.2mg; SODIUM 898mg; CALC 348mg

415

Country Sausage Patties

Sausage patties require some fat to stay moist, which is why Boston butt is a good cut of pork for this recipe. The sausage is best when the mixture is made a day ahead and refrigerated, allowing the spices to permeate the meat overnight. You can, however, cook the patties right away. Refrigerate cooked sausage up to three days, or freeze up to two months.

1½ pounds boneless Boston butt pork roast, trimmed and cut into 1-inch cubes
¼ cup cold water
1 teaspoon salt
1 teaspoon dark brown sugar
1 teaspoon minced fresh or
 ¼ teaspoon dried rubbed sage
1 teaspoon minced fresh or
 ¼ teaspoon dried thyme
1 teaspoon crushed red pepper
1 teaspoon freshly ground black pepper
½ teaspoon ground coriander
½ teaspoon hot pepper sauce (such as Tabasco)
¼ teaspoon grated whole nutmeg
Cooking spray

1. Place half of pork in a food processor; pulse until coarsely ground. Place ground pork in a large bowl. Repeat procedure with remaining pork. Add water and next 9 ingredients. Knead mixture until well blended. Cover and refrigerate mixture 8 hours or overnight.
2. Divide mixture into 16 equal portions, shaping each into a ½-inch-thick patty. Heat a large nonstick skillet over medium-high heat. Coat pan with cooking spray. Add half of patties; cook 6 minutes. Turn patties over; cook 5 minutes or until done. Repeat procedure with remaining patties. Yield: 8 servings (serving size: 2 patties).

CALORIES 111 (42% from fat); FAT 5.2g (sat 1.8g, mono 2.3g, poly 0.6g); PROTEIN 14g; CARB 1.1g; FIBER 0.3g; CHOL 47mg; IRON 1mg; SODIUM 349mg; CALC 15mg

Festive Fruit Punch

If you prefer a sweeter beverage, use ginger ale or lemon-lime soda instead of tonic water.

4 cups tonic water
3 cups ice cubes
2 cups pineapple juice, chilled
2 cups orange juice, chilled
2 cups light cranberry juice cocktail, chilled
1 lime, sliced
1 orange, sliced
1 carambola (star fruit), sliced

1. Combine all ingredients in a pitcher. Serve immediately. Yield: 10 servings (serving size: 1 cup).

CALORIES 101 (2% from fat); FAT 0.2g (sat 0g, mono 0g, poly 0.1g); PROTEIN 0.6g; CARB 24.7g; FIBER 0.9g; CHOL 0mg; IRON 0.2mg; SODIUM 8mg; CALC 16mg

Christmas Morning Breakfast Menu 2
serves 6

Individual Potato-Bacon Frittatas

Blueberry-Pecan Scones

Fresh Fruit Salad with Nutmeg-Cinnamon Syrup

Mocha-Spiced Coffee

Individual Potato-Bacon Frittatas

To make breakfast preparation faster and easier, sauté the onion, bell pepper, and garlic the night before.

¾ pound small red potatoes (about 6)
Cooking spray
½ cup chopped onion
½ cup chopped red bell pepper
2 garlic cloves, minced
¾ cup (3 ounces) shredded reduced-fat Swiss cheese
4 bacon slices, cooked and crumbled (drained)
1¾ cups egg substitute
¼ teaspoon salt
¼ teaspoon freshly ground black pepper

1. Place potatoes in a large saucepan, and cover with water. Bring to a boil, and cook 25 minutes or until tender. Drain; cool slightly. Cut potatoes into ½-inch cubes.
2. Preheat oven to 375°.
3. Heat a medium nonstick skillet over medium heat. Coat pan with cooking spray. Add onion, bell pepper, and garlic; sauté 5 minutes or until tender. Remove from heat. Stir in potato, cheese, and bacon.
4. Combine egg substitute, salt, and black pepper. Spoon vegetable mixture evenly into 12 muffin cups or 6-ounce ramekins coated with cooking spray. Pour egg mixture evenly over vegetable mixture. Bake at 375° for 18 minutes or until set. Remove from muffin cups, and cool slightly. Yield: 6 servings (serving size: 2 frittatas).

CALORIES 184 (25% from fat); FAT 5.2g (sat 1.6g, mono 1.6g, poly 1.4g); PROTEIN 16g; CARB 17.8g; FIBER 1.8g; CHOL 10mg; IRON 2.6mg; SODIUM 366mg; CALC 188mg

Blueberry-Pecan Scones

Make these scones a day or two ahead, and store in an airtight container. Resist the temptation to knead the dough; doing so would break apart the tender blueberries. Leftover scones are nice with tea later in the day.

½ cup 2% reduced-fat milk
¼ cup sugar
2 teaspoons grated lemon rind
1 teaspoon vanilla extract
1 large egg
2 cups all-purpose flour (about 9 ounces)
1 tablespoon baking powder
½ teaspoon salt
3 tablespoons chilled butter, cut into small pieces
1 cup fresh or frozen blueberries
¼ cup finely chopped pecans, toasted
Cooking spray
1 large egg white, lightly beaten
2 tablespoons sugar

1. Preheat oven to 375°.

2. Combine first 5 ingredients in a medium bowl, stirring with a whisk. Lightly spoon flour into dry measuring cups; level with a knife. Combine flour, baking powder, and salt in a large bowl, stirring with a whisk. Cut in butter with a pastry blender or 2 knives until mixture resembles coarse meal. Gently fold in blueberries and pecans. Add milk mixture, stirring just until moist (dough will be sticky).

3. Turn dough out onto a floured surface; pat dough into an 8-inch circle. Cut dough into 10 wedges; place dough wedges on a baking sheet coated with cooking spray. Brush egg white over dough wedges; sprinkle evenly with 2 tablespoons sugar. Bake at 375° for 18 minutes or until golden. Serve warm. Yield: 10 servings (serving size: 1 scone).

CALORIES 196 (30% from fat); FAT 6.6g (sat 2.2g, mono 2.9g, poly 1g); PROTEIN 4.4g; CARB 30.2g; FIBER 1.4g; CHOL 31mg; IRON 1.5mg; SODIUM 308mg; CALC 107mg

Fresh Fruit Salad with Nutmeg-Cinnamon Syrup

Substitute your favorite apple for Granny Smith, if desired.

- 2 cups thinly sliced Granny Smith apple (about 1 large apple)
- 2 cups thinly sliced ripe pear (about 1 large pear)
- 1 cup sliced strawberries
- ½ cup orange sections (about 1 orange)
- ½ cup sliced banana (about 1 medium)
- ¼ cup fresh lemon juice
- ¼ cup maple syrup
- ⅛ teaspoon ground nutmeg
- ⅛ teaspoon ground cinnamon

1. Combine first 5 ingredients in a large bowl. Drizzle with juice; toss gently.

2. Combine syrup, nutmeg, and cinnamon in a small saucepan. Cook over low heat 10 minutes, stirring occasionally. Spoon over fruit; toss gently. Serve immediately. Yield: 8 servings (serving size: ½ cup).

CALORIES 76 (2% from fat); FAT 0.2g (sat 0g, mono 0g, poly 0.1g); PROTEIN 0.6g; CARB 19.9g; FIBER 2.3g; CHOL 0mg; IRON 0.4mg; SODIUM 2mg; CALC 19mg

Mocha-Spiced Coffee

Use a high-quality unflavored coffee, such as French roast, for a properly robust cup.

- ½ cup ground coffee
- 1½ teaspoons ground cinnamon
- ½ teaspoon ground nutmeg
- 5 cups water
- 1 cup fat-free milk
- ¼ cup packed brown sugar
- ⅓ cup light chocolate syrup (such as Hershey's Lite Syrup)
- 1 teaspoon vanilla extract
- Whipped cream (optional)

1. Place first 3 ingredients in a coffee filter or filter basket of a coffeemaker. Add 5 cups water to coffeemaker; brew according to manufacturer's instructions.

2. Combine milk, sugar, and syrup in a heavy saucepan. Cook over low heat, stirring constantly, until sugar dissolves. Stir in brewed coffee and vanilla. Serve with whipped cream, if desired. Serve immediately. Yield: 6 servings (serving size: 1 cup).

CALORIES 83 (18% from fat); FAT 1.7g (sat 0.1g, mono 0g, poly 0g); PROTEIN 1.8g; CARB 16.8g; FIBER 0.4g; CHOL 1mg; IRON 0.7mg; SODIUM 39mg; CALC 56mg

menu of the month

Tree Trimming Party

Invite guests over to decorate the tree, and treat them to a lovely dinner.

One tradition that is a favorite among our staff is the trimming of the Christmas tree. The lights, the tinsel, the festive ornaments—old and new—get the season started off right. What's even more special is inviting friends and family over to help.

Have beverages ready when your guests arrive, and enjoy the meal when you finish decorating. Simmer the stew and bake the biscuits while you work on the tree. If children are helping, serve them sparkling nonalcoholic grape juice.

Rossini Bellini

Wild Mushroom and Beef Stew

Asiago-Black Pepper Drop Biscuits

Double-Chocolate Meringue Cookies

Rossini Bellini

(pictured on page 430)

Strawberries take the place of peaches in this version of the classic Italian drink.

- ¼ cup sugar
- 2 tablespoons water
- 3 cups hulled strawberries
- 2 tablespoons fresh lemon juice
- 1 (750-milliliter) bottle prosecco or other sparkling wine, chilled

1. Combine sugar and water in a small saucepan, stirring until sugar dissolves. Bring mixture to a boil over medium-high heat. Remove from heat.

2. Place sugar mixture, strawberries, and lemon juice in a blender; process until smooth. Strain puréed mixture through a sieve into a medium bowl, reserving liquid. Discard solids.

3. Place 3 tablespoons strawberry mixture into each of 8 Champagne flutes. Pour ⅓ cup wine into each flute. Yield: 8 servings (serving size: about ½ cup).

CALORIES 110 (2% from fat); FAT 0.2g (sat 0g, mono 0g, poly 0.1g); PROTEIN 0.6g; CARB 12.3g; FIBER 0.5g; CHOL 0mg; IRON 0.6mg; SODIUM 8mg; CALC 17mg

Wild Mushroom and Beef Stew

Roasted red onions give this stew a rich, almost smoky flavor. Make an extra batch of the tasty onions to use as a pizza or sandwich topping; refrigerate onions up to four days.

    5   cups water
    3   cups fat-free, less-sodium chicken
        broth
    1   cup dried porcini mushrooms
        (about 1 ounce)
    2   tablespoons all-purpose flour
    1   teaspoon salt
    2   garlic cloves, minced
    2   pounds beef stew meat
    1   tablespoon canola oil, divided
Cooking spray
    2   (8-ounce) packages presliced
        button mushrooms
    1   pound cremini mushrooms, sliced
        (about 10 cups)
  ¼   cup tomato paste
    4   cups coarsely chopped red onion
    2   teaspoons chopped fresh or
        ½ teaspoon dried rosemary
  ½   teaspoon freshly ground black
        pepper
    2   tablespoons chopped fresh
        flat-leaf parsley

1. Bring water and broth to a boil in a saucepan. Add porcini; remove from heat, and let stand 15 minutes. Drain in a colander over a bowl, reserving liquid. Chop porcini; set aside.
2. Combine flour, salt, garlic, and beef, tossing well to coat. Heat 1 teaspoon oil in a large Dutch oven over medium-high heat. Add half of beef mixture; sauté 4 minutes or until browned. Remove from pan. Repeat procedure with 1 teaspoon oil and remaining beef mixture. Wipe pan clean with a paper towel; coat with cooking spray. Add button and cremini mushrooms; cover, reduce heat to medium, and cook 10 minutes or until mushrooms release liquid. Stir in reserved porcini liquid, chopped porcini, beef mixture, and tomato paste; bring to a boil. Cover, reduce heat, and simmer 45 minutes.

3. Preheat oven to 450°.
4. Combine 1 teaspoon oil and onion on a foil-lined jelly-roll pan; toss well to coat. Bake at 450° for 25 minutes, stirring twice.
5. Add roasted onion, rosemary, and pepper to stew. Cover and simmer stew 30 minutes or until beef is tender. Sprinkle with parsley. Yield: 8 servings (serving size: 1½ cups).

CALORIES 324 (30% from fat); FAT 10.7g (sat 3.3g, mono 4.8g, poly 1.2g); PROTEIN 32.6g; CARB 25.2g; FIBER 6.1g; CHOL 71mg; IRON 7.4mg; SODIUM 509mg; CALC 51mg

Asiago-Black Pepper Drop Biscuits

These savory biscuits are incredibly easy to make, as there's no need to roll or cut out the dough. If the batter seems too thick, you can add another tablespoon of fat-free buttermilk.

  1¼   cups all-purpose flour (about 5½
        ounces)
    1   teaspoon baking powder
  ½   teaspoon salt
  ¼   teaspoon cracked black
        pepper
  1½   tablespoons chilled butter, cut
        into small pieces
  ½   cup (2 ounces) grated fresh
        Asiago cheese
  ¾   cup fat-free buttermilk
Cooking spray

1. Preheat oven to 450°.
2. Lightly spoon flour into dry measuring cups; level with a knife. Combine flour, baking powder, salt, and pepper in a medium bowl; stir well with a whisk. Cut in butter with a pastry blender or 2 knives until mixture resembles coarse meal. Add cheese; toss well to combine. Add buttermilk; stir just until moist. Drop dough into 8 equal mounds on a baking sheet coated with cooking spray. Bake at 450° for 13 minutes or until edges are lightly browned. Yield: 8 servings (serving size: 1 biscuit).

CALORIES 125 (31% from fat); FAT 4.3g (sat 2.4g, mono 1.4g, poly 0.2g); PROTEIN 4.9g; CARB 16.7g; FIBER 0.6g; CHOL 12mg; IRON 1mg; SODIUM 285mg; CALC 134mg

Double-Chocolate Meringue Cookies

These cookies have a slightly fudgy texture. They're baked, then cooled for 1½ hours in the oven (don't forget to turn it off).

  ½   cup powdered sugar
  ⅓   cup unsweetened cocoa
    5   large egg whites
  ¼   teaspoon cream of tartar
  ⅔   cup granulated sugar
    1   teaspoon vanilla extract
  ¼   cup semisweet chocolate
        minichips
    1   tablespoon powdered sugar

1. Preheat oven to 300°.
2. Cover 2 large baking sheets with parchment paper; secure with masking tape. Sift together ½ cup powdered sugar and cocoa.
3. Place egg whites and cream of tartar in a large bowl; beat with a mixer at high speed until soft peaks form. Gradually add granulated sugar and cocoa mixture, 1 tablespoon at a time, beating until stiff peaks form. Add vanilla; beat until combined. Fold in chocolate chips.
4. Drop dough by rounded tablespoons onto prepared baking sheets to form 36 mounds. Bake at 300° for 30 minutes, rotating racks after 15 minutes. Turn oven off; cool meringues in closed oven 1½ hours or until dry. Sprinkle evenly with 1 tablespoon powdered sugar. Carefully remove cookies from paper. Yield: 36 cookies (serving size: 3 cookies).
NOTE: Store cooled cookies in an airtight container up to two weeks.

CALORIES 135 (30% from fat); FAT 4.5g (sat 2.7g, mono 1.5g, poly 0.3g); PROTEIN 3g; CARB 24.6g; FIBER 2.1g; CHOL 0mg; IRON 0.9mg; SODIUM 27mg; CALC 9mg

Festive Foods Around the Globe

Inspire your meals with some of the world's favorite dishes for the season.

This time of year, Americans tend to focus on Christmas and New Year's Day. It's a chance to slow down, savor the company of loved ones, and close out another year. But many other cultures mark this season in their own special ways, and be it Hanukkah or Pongal, a central part of each celebration is food. We've gathered some of the best of the world's holiday dishes, and we hope they'll inspire you with their wonderful flavors, and soon become a part of your traditions.

MAKE AHEAD • FREEZABLE
Sesame Sweets

Sweet treats made from sesame seeds are common to the Hindu Makar Sankrat/Pongal celebrations. Traditionally, these cookies are made by encasing the dough around the filling and dropping into hot oil to fry. This version, similar in concept to a thumbprint cookie, is baked and just as tasty.

FILLING:
- ¼ cup slivered almonds, toasted
- ¼ cup packed brown sugar
- 2 tablespoons sesame seeds, toasted
- 2½ tablespoons honey
- ¼ teaspoon ground cardamom
- ¼ teaspoon ground ginger
- ⅛ teaspoon ground nutmeg

DOUGH:
- 2 cups sifted cake flour (about 7 ounces)
- 3 tablespoons granulated sugar
- ¼ teaspoon salt
- ¼ cup chilled butter, cut into small pieces
- 4 to 5 tablespoons ice water
- Cooking spray
- 2 tablespoons powdered sugar

1. Preheat oven to 325°.
2. To prepare filling, place first 7 ingredients in a food processor; pulse 6 times or until combined and almonds are finely chopped. Remove almond mixture from food processor; set aside. Wipe processor bowl and blade with a paper towel.
3. To prepare dough, lightly spoon flour into dry measuring cups; level with a knife. Combine flour, granulated sugar, and salt in food processor; pulse 3 times. Add butter; pulse 4 times or just until combined. Add ice water, 1 tablespoon at a time, pulsing just until combined. (Mixture may appear crumbly but will stick together when pressed between fingers.)
4. Shape dough into 24 balls. Place dough 2 inches apart on a baking sheet coated with cooking spray. Press thumb in center of each ball to form an indentation. Fill each indentation with about 1 teaspoon almond mixture. Bake at 325° for 20 minutes or until set. Remove from pan; cool completely on a wire rack. Sprinkle evenly with powdered sugar. Yield: 2 dozen (serving size: 1 cookie).

CALORIES 81 (33% from fat); FAT 3g (sat 1.1g, mono 1.3g, poly 0.4g); PROTEIN 1.1g; CARB 12.9g; FIBER 0.4g; CHOL 5mg; IRON 0.8mg; SODIUM 40mg; CALC 8mg

Two-Potato Latkes

One of the most well-known dishes of the Jewish holiday, Hanukkah, is latkes—potato pancakes cooked in symbolic olive oil. Use a food processor's shredding blade for fast preparation. Serve with applesauce and reduced-fat sour cream.

- 2 tablespoons olive oil
- ¼ cup grated fresh onion
- 1 pound shredded peeled baking potato
- ½ pound shredded peeled sweet potato
- ½ cup all-purpose flour (about 2¼ ounces)
- ⅓ cup finely chopped green onions
- ½ teaspoon salt
- ¼ teaspoon freshly ground black pepper
- 1 garlic clove, minced
- 1 large egg, lightly beaten
- Cooking spray
- Green onion strips (optional)

1. Preheat oven to 425°.
2. Drizzle a jelly-roll pan evenly with oil, tilting pan to coat.
3. Combine grated onion and potatoes in a sieve; squeeze out excess moisture. Lightly spoon flour into a dry measuring cup; level with a knife. Combine potato mixture, flour, and next 5 ingredients in a large bowl. Divide mixture into 8 equal portions, squeezing out excess liquid. Shape each portion into a ¼-inch-thick patty; place on prepared pan. Lightly coat tops of patties with cooking spray. Bake at 425° for 12 minutes. Carefully turn patties over; cook 30 minutes or until lightly browned, turning every 10 minutes. Garnish with green onion strips, if desired. Yield: 4 servings (serving size: 2 latkes).

CALORIES 256 (29% from fat); FAT 8.3g (sat 1.4g, mono 5.5g, poly 1g); PROTEIN 5.7g; CARB 40g; FIBER 4g; CHOL 53mg; IRON 1.7mg; SODIUM 337mg; CALC 38mg

Enhance your holidays with classic dishes from other cultures.

Turkey-Mushroom Bread Pudding

The British holiday Boxing Day is linked to ideas of charity and also to the tradition of boxing up Christmas leftovers. This savory bread pudding is the answer to holiday dinner leftovers, making use of extra turkey and bread.

- 2 teaspoons olive oil
- 4 cups sliced cremini mushrooms
- 2 cups chopped celery
- 1 cup chopped onion
- ½ teaspoon chopped fresh thyme
- 3 garlic cloves, minced
- 2 cups shredded cooked turkey breast (about 8 ounces)
- ¾ teaspoon salt
- ½ teaspoon freshly ground black pepper
- 2 cups 1% low-fat milk
- 1 teaspoon dry mustard
- ¼ teaspoon ground red pepper
- 5 large eggs
- 6 cups French or Italian bread, cut into 1-inch cubes (about 8 ounces)
- Cooking spray
- ½ cup (2 ounces) grated fresh Parmesan cheese

1. Preheat oven to 350°.
2. Heat oil in a large nonstick skillet over medium heat. Add mushrooms, celery, onion, thyme, and garlic; cook 10 minutes or until tender, stirring occasionally. Stir in turkey, salt, and black pepper. Remove mixture from heat; cool slightly.
3. Combine milk, mustard, red pepper, and eggs in a large bowl, stirring with a whisk. Stir in mushroom mixture and bread; toss well. Spoon into an 11 x 7-inch baking dish coated with cooking spray. Sprinkle with cheese. Bake at 350° for 1 hour or until golden brown. Let stand 10 minutes before serving. Yield: 8 servings.

CALORIES 242 (30% from fat); FAT 8.1g (sat 3g, mono 3g, poly 1.1g); PROTEIN 20.7g; CARB 21.3g; FIBER 1.4g; CHOL 163mg; IRON 2.5mg; SODIUM 628mg; CALC 241mg

Garlic Chicken

Ending the Muslim 30 days of fasting, Eid ul-Fitr celebrations include an abundance of dishes like this one—full of heady aromas, sweet spices, and lots of flavor. Marinating and cooking the chicken in tangy yogurt keeps it moist, but the yogurt mixture curdles and should be discarded after cooking. Serve alongside basmati rice pilaf tossed with almonds, raisins, and cumin seeds.

- 1 cup plain low-fat yogurt
- ¼ cup fresh lemon juice
- 2 tablespoons minced garlic (about 6 cloves)
- ½ teaspoon salt, divided
- ½ teaspoon freshly ground black pepper, divided
- ¼ teaspoon ground cardamom
- ¼ teaspoon ground cumin
- ¼ teaspoon ground cinnamon
- ¼ teaspoon ground nutmeg
- 6 (6-ounce) skinless, boneless chicken breast halves
- 1 cup fat-free, less-sodium chicken broth
- 1½ tablespoons olive oil
- 1 tablespoon chopped fresh parsley

1. Combine yogurt, juice, garlic, ¼ teaspoon salt, ¼ teaspoon pepper, cardamom, cumin, cinnamon, and nutmeg in a large zip-top plastic bag. Add chicken; seal and marinate in refrigerator overnight, turning bag occasionally.
2. Remove chicken from bag, reserving marinade; pat chicken dry with paper towels. Combine reserved marinade and chicken broth.
3. Heat oil in a large nonstick skillet over medium-high heat. Sprinkle chicken with remaining ¼ teaspoon salt and remaining ¼ teaspoon pepper. Add half of chicken to pan; cook 1½ minutes on each side or until browned. Repeat procedure with remaining chicken. Return chicken to pan; pour broth mixture over chicken. Bring to a boil. Cover, reduce heat, and simmer 12 minutes or until chicken is done. Place chicken on a serving platter; discard liquid in pan. Sprinkle chicken evenly with parsley. Yield: 6 servings (serving size: 1 chicken breast half).

CALORIES 256 (22% from fat); FAT 6.2g (sat 1.4g, mono 3.2g, poly 0.9g); PROTEIN 42.1g; CARB 5.7g; FIBER 0.5g; CHOL 101mg; IRON 1.6mg; SODIUM 400mg; CALC 104mg

MAKE AHEAD
Five-Spice Sweet Potato Pie

This southern American dessert is a classic for Kwanzaa celebrations. Five-spice powder is a blend of cinnamon, cloves, fennel seed, star anise, and Szechuan peppercorns that can be found in the spice aisle of most supermarkets. If five-spice powder is unavailable, use pumpkin pie spice.

- 2 pounds sweet potatoes (about 5 medium)
- ¾ cup packed brown sugar
- ½ cup 2% reduced-fat milk
- 2 tablespoons butter, softened
- 1 teaspoon vanilla extract
- ½ teaspoon ground cinnamon
- ½ teaspoon five-spice powder or pumpkin pie spice
- ¼ teaspoon salt
- ¼ teaspoon ground nutmeg
- 3 large eggs, lightly beaten
- ½ (15-ounce) package refrigerated pie dough (such as Pillsbury)

1. Preheat oven to 375°.
2. Pierce sweet potatoes several times with a fork. Place sweet potatoes on a baking sheet. Bake at 375° for 1 hour and 15 minutes or until tender. Cool slightly. Peel and discard skins. Place pulp in a medium bowl; mash. Add sugar and next 8 ingredients to pulp. Beat with a mixer at medium speed until well blended.
3. Fit dough into a 9-inch pie plate; fold edges under, and flute. Pour sweet potato mixture into pie shell. Bake at 375° for 55 minutes or until a knife inserted in center comes out clean. Cool completely on a wire rack. Yield: 10 servings (serving size: 1 wedge).

CALORIES 289 (30% from fat); FAT 9.7g (sat 4.2g, mono 3.7g, poly 0.4g); PROTEIN 4.9g; CARB 46.1g; FIBER 3.1g; CHOL 74mg; IRON 1.3mg; SODIUM 220mg; CALC 74mg

Saffron and Carrot Halvah

Halvah is a Middle Eastern specialty.

⅔ cup blanched almonds
3 cups finely grated carrot
1½ cups 1% low-fat milk
⅛ teaspoon saffron threads
½ cup granulated sugar
¼ cup packed brown sugar
¼ cup raisins
½ teaspoon vanilla extract
¼ teaspoon salt
¼ teaspoon ground nutmeg
⅛ teaspoon ground cardamom

1. Place almonds in a food processor; process until finely ground.
2. Combine carrot, milk, and saffron in a small saucepan; bring to a boil, stirring occasionally. Reduce heat to medium-low; cook until most of milk evaporates (about 35 minutes), stirring frequently. Add ground almonds, sugars, and remaining ingredients. Cook on low heat 20 minutes or until mixture pulls away from sides of pan, stirring almost constantly. Yield: 6 servings (serving size: about ⅓ cup).

CALORIES 260 (31% from fat); FAT 9g (sat 1.1g, mono 5.4g, poly 2g); PROTEIN 6.2g; CARB 41.9g; FIBER 3.8g; CHOL 2mg; IRON 1.1mg; SODIUM 177mg; CALC 138mg

Peanut and Squash Soup

Kwanzaa celebrations incorporate foods and dishes native to Africa, such as this soup

1½ teaspoons peanut oil
4 cups (½-inch) cubed peeled butternut squash
1 cup chopped onion
2 tablespoons minced garlic (about 6 cloves)
½ teaspoon salt
½ teaspoon ground cumin
¼ teaspoon ground coriander
4 cups fat-free, less-sodium chicken broth
¾ cup reduced-fat creamy peanut butter
2 tablespoons tomato paste
½ teaspoon crushed red pepper
¼ cup chopped fresh cilantro

1. Heat oil in a large saucepan over medium-high heat. Add squash and next 5 ingredients; sauté 5 minutes or until onion is tender. Add broth, peanut butter, tomato paste, and pepper, stirring well to combine; bring to a boil. Reduce heat; simmer, uncovered, 10 minutes or until squash is tender. Sprinkle with cilantro. Yield: 6 servings (serving size: about 1 cup).

CALORIES 264 (38% from fat); FAT 11.2g (sat 2.4g, mono 5.2g, poly 3.4g); PROTEIN 11.3g; CARB 34.6g; FIBER 6.4g; CHOL 0mg; IRON 2.3mg; SODIUM 621mg; CALC 111mg

season's best

Peppermint Ice Cream Cake

What better way to showcase the bright flavor of one of the season's best treats than an ice cream cake?

This merry confection earned our Test Kitchens' highest rating. It's easy and fun to put together—and you can do much of the work in advance.

Peppermint Ice Cream Cake

Cooking spray
¾ cup unsweetened cocoa
¾ cup boiling water
6 tablespoons butter, melted
1 cup packed dark brown sugar
½ cup granulated sugar
¾ cup egg substitute
1½ cups all-purpose flour (about 6¾ ounces)
½ teaspoon baking powder
½ teaspoon baking soda
½ teaspoon salt
2 teaspoons vanilla extract
3 cups low-fat peppermint ice cream (such as Edy's/Dreyer's Slow-Churned Light), softened
3 cups frozen fat-free whipped topping, thawed
⅛ teaspoon peppermint extract
8 peppermint candies, crushed

1. Preheat oven to 350°.
2. Coat 2 (8-inch) round cake pans with cooking spray. Line bottom of each pan with wax paper.
3. Combine cocoa, water, and butter, stirring with a whisk until mixture is blended. Cool.
4. Combine sugars in a large bowl, stirring well until blended. Add egg substitute; beat with a mixer at medium speed 2 minutes or until light and creamy. Add cocoa mixture; beat 1 minute.
5. Lightly spoon flour into dry measuring cups; level with a knife. Combine flour, baking powder, baking soda, and salt. Gradually add flour mixture to bowl; beat with a mixer at low speed 1 minute or until blended. Stir in vanilla. Pour batter into prepared pans. Bake at 350° for 28 minutes or until a wooden pick inserted in center comes out clean. Cool in pan 10 minutes on a wire rack. Remove cakes from pans. Wrap in plastic wrap; freeze 2 hours or until slightly frozen.
6. Spread ice cream in an 8-inch round cake pan lined with plastic wrap. Cover and freeze 4 hours or until firm.
7. To assemble cake, place one cake layer, bottom side up, on a cake pedestal. Remove peppermint ice cream layer from freezer; remove plastic wrap. Place ice cream layer, bottom side up, on top of cake layer. Top with remaining cake layer.
8. Combine whipped topping and peppermint extract; stir until blended. Spread frosting over top and sides of cake. Sprinkle with crushed peppermints. Freeze until ready to serve. Let cake stand at room temperature 10 minutes before slicing. Yield: 16 servings (serving size: 1 slice).

CALORIES 251 (24% from fat); FAT 6.8g (sat 3.3g, mono 2.1g, poly 0.4g); PROTEIN 4.3g; CARB 44.4g; FIBER 1.7g; CHOL 19mg; IRON 1.6mg; SODIUM 207mg; CALC 63mg

Ring in the New Year

Welcome 2006 in style with a grand appetizer buffet.

Skip the big, blow-out New Year's Eve party this year, opt out of the frenzy, and hail 2006 in a more intimate fashion with a close group of friends and family. You can pay homage to this special night by sending invitations encouraging your guests to dress elegantly, and of course, by toasting the occasion with plenty of Champagne.

Choose a selection of buffet appetizers like the Cherry Chutney Cheese Torte and little Roast Pork Sandwiches. As the party progresses, bring out different hot hors d'oeuvres. This helps to keep the party lively and your guests well fed throughout the evening as they nibble stuffed mushrooms, salmon skewers, and other tidbits. These mostly make-ahead dishes allow you to relax and enjoy the fun, too. Each recipe makes at least 12 servings, so you can mix and match dishes to suit the size of your party. For the perfect celebratory pièce de résistance, serve the Chocolate Fondue at midnight. It's blissful paired with a glass of bubbly.

New Year's Eve Buffet Menu
serves 12

Cherry Chutney Cheese Torte

Salmon Skewers with Romesco Sauce

Curried Chicken Turnovers

Creamy Corn and Chorizo-Stuffed Mushrooms

Roast Pork Sandwiches

Hot Artichoke Dip

Pear Gorgonzola Butter

Sweet-and-Sour Red Onions

Chocolate Fondue

Champagne or other sparkling wine

MAKE AHEAD

Cherry Chutney Cheese Torte

Prepare the chutney up to two days ahead so you can bake the torte the night before the party. Serve leftover chutney with ham, pork, or duck. You can also spread this slightly sweet torte on crackers or gingersnaps.

    2   cups plain low-fat yogurt
    ⅔   cup (about 5 ounces) ⅓-less-fat
        cream cheese, softened
    ¼   cup packed brown sugar
    ¼   cup egg substitute
    1   tablespoon fresh lemon juice
    ¼   teaspoon salt
        Cooking spray
    ½   cup Cherry Chutney
    12 pecan halves
    1   (8-ounce) loaf French bread
        baguette, cut into ¼-inch slices

1. Place colander in a 2-quart glass measure or medium bowl. Line colander with 4 layers of cheesecloth, allowing cheesecloth to extend over outside edges. Spoon yogurt into colander. Cover loosely with plastic wrap; refrigerate 12 hours. Spoon yogurt cheese into a bowl; discard liquid. Cover and refrigerate.

2. Preheat oven to 325°.

3. Place yogurt cheese and cream cheese in a medium bowl; beat with a mixer at medium speed until smooth. Add sugar, egg substitute, juice, and salt; beat until combined. Pour cheese mixture into a 6-inch springform pan coated with cooking spray. Wrap bottom and sides of pan with foil. Place pan in a 13 x 9-inch baking pan; add hot water to pan to a depth of 1 inch. Bake at 325° for 30 minutes or until torte center barely moves when pan is touched. Remove torte from oven; run a knife around outside edge. Cool to room temperature. Cover and chill at least 8 hours. Spoon Cherry Chutney over cooled torte; arrange pecan halves over the top. Serve with bread. Yield: 12 servings (serving size: 1 torte wedge and 5 bread slices).

(Totals include Cherry Chutney) CALORIES 182 (28% from fat); FAT 5.8g (sat 2.1g, mono 1.9g, poly 1.4g); PROTEIN 5.3g; CARB 28g; FIBER 1.8g; CHOL 9mg; IRON 0.7mg; SODIUM 189mg; CALC 62mg

---

MAKE AHEAD

CHERRY CHUTNEY:

    2   cups chopped peeled Granny
        Smith apple (about 1 medium)
    1   cup dried sweet cherries
    ⅔   cup chopped onion
    ½   cup water
    ½   cup red wine
    ⅓   cup sugar
    2   tablespoons white wine
        vinegar
    1   tablespoon grated peeled fresh
        ginger
    1   jalapeño pepper, chopped

1. Combine all ingredients in a small saucepan, and bring to a boil. Cover, reduce heat, and simmer 45 minutes. Uncover; increase heat to medium-high. Cook 15 minutes or until most of liquid evaporates. Cool completely. Yield: 12 servings (serving size: about 2 tablespoons).

CALORIES 78 (0% from fat); FAT 0g; PROTEIN 0.5g; CARB 18.5g; FIBER 1.6g; CHOL 0mg; IRON 0.3mg; SODIUM 3mg; CALC 17mg

How to Make a Torte

Place pan in a 13 x 9-inch baking pan; add hot water to pan to a depth of 1 inch. Bake at 325° for 30 minutes or until torte center barely moves when pan is touched.

Salmon Skewers with Romesco Sauce

Prepare and refrigerate the no-cook sauce the night before the party; assemble and refrigerate the salmon skewers in the morning, and place them in the broiler for five minutes before you're ready to serve them. You can substitute shrimp for the fish.

ROMESCO SAUCE:

1 cup canned fire-roasted diced tomatoes (such as Muir Glen), drained
¼ cup slivered almonds, toasted
2 tablespoons olive oil
1 tablespoon red wine vinegar
2 teaspoons crushed red pepper
1 teaspoon ground cumin
¾ teaspoon salt
3 garlic cloves, chopped
2 (7½-ounce) jars roasted red bell peppers, drained
1 (1-ounce) slice white bread

SALMON:

2 pounds salmon fillets, skinned and cut into 48 cubes
1 teaspoon paprika
1 teaspoon dried oregano
¼ teaspoon salt
Cooking spray

1. Preheat broiler.
2. To prepare romesco sauce, place first 10 ingredients in a food processor; process until smooth.
3. To prepare salmon, sprinkle salmon with paprika, oregano, and ¼ teaspoon salt. Thread 2 salmon pieces onto each of 24 (6-inch) skewers. Arrange on a broiler pan coated with cooking spray. Lightly coat salmon skewers with cooking spray. Broil 5 minutes or until fish flakes easily when tested with a fork or until desired degree of doneness. Serve with sauce. Yield: 12 servings (serving size: 2 skewers and about 2½ tablespoons sauce).

CALORIES 146 (50% from fat); FAT 8.1g (sat 1.5g, mono 4.3g, poly 1.7g); PROTEIN 13.4g; CARB 4.7g; FIBER 1.1g; CHOL 29mg; IRON 0.8mg; SODIUM 354mg; CALC 27mg

Curried Chicken Turnovers

2½ cups chopped onion
1 tablespoon chopped peeled fresh ginger
3 garlic cloves, chopped
1 teaspoon olive oil
1½ teaspoons curry powder
1½ teaspoons ground coriander
¾ cup water
½ cup currants
2 tablespoons sugar
1¼ teaspoons salt
1¾ pounds skinless, boneless chicken breast, chopped
½ cup fat-free sour cream
35 sheets frozen phyllo dough, thawed and divided
Cooking spray
¾ cup shredded coconut, divided

1. Preheat oven to 400°.
2. Place onion, ginger, and garlic in a food processor; process until finely chopped. Heat oil in a large nonstick skillet over medium-high heat. Add onion mixture; sauté 5 minutes or until lightly browned. Add curry and coriander; cook 1 minute, stirring constantly. Add water, currants, sugar, salt, and chicken; bring to a boil. Cover, reduce heat, and simmer 20 minutes. Uncover; cook 20 minutes or until most of liquid evaporates. Remove from heat; cool slightly. Stir in sour cream. Place chicken mixture in food processor; pulse until finely chopped.
3. Place 1 phyllo sheet on a large cutting board or work surface (cover remaining dough to prevent drying); lightly coat with cooking spray. Sprinkle with 1 teaspoon coconut. Repeat layers 4 times. Cut crosswise into 4 strips. Spoon about 2 tablespoons chicken mixture onto one end of each strip. Fold 1 corner of edge over mixture, forming a triangle; continue folding back and forth into a triangle to end of strip. Repeat procedure with remaining phyllo, cooking spray, coconut, and chicken mixture.
4. Place triangles on a large baking sheet coated with cooking spray; coat with cooking spray. Bake at 400° for 18 minutes or until golden brown. Yield: 28 servings (serving size: 1 turnover).

CALORIES 131 (21% from fat); FAT 3.1g (sat 1.6g, mono 1g, poly 0.3g); PROTEIN 8.8g; CARB 16.3g; FIBER 1g; CHOL 17mg; IRON 1.1mg; SODIUM 252mg; CALC 16mg

Creamy Corn and Chorizo-Stuffed Mushrooms

STUFFING:

6 ounces Mexican chorizo sausage
½ cup finely chopped onion
2 garlic cloves, minced
1 (11-ounce) can extrasweet whole-kernel corn, drained
2 ounces ⅓-less-fat cream cheese, softened
¼ cup fat-free sour cream
½ teaspoon salt

REMAINING INGREDIENTS:

2 (1-ounce) slices white bread
24 stuffer mushroom caps (or large mushrooms with stems removed)
Cooking spray

1. Preheat oven to 400°.
2. To prepare stuffing, remove casings from chorizo. Cook chorizo, onion, and garlic in a large nonstick skillet over medium heat 6 minutes or until browned, stirring to crumble. Drain chorizo mixture; pat dry with paper towels. Combine chorizo mixture and corn. Combine cream cheese and sour cream. Stir with a whisk until smooth. Stir cheese mixture and salt into chorizo mixture.
3. Place white bread in a food processor; pulse 10 times or until fine crumbs measure 1 cup.
4. Fill each mushroom cap with about ¾ teaspoon breadcrumbs. Stuff each with 2 teaspoons corn mixture; top with remaining breadcrumbs. Place on a baking sheet coated with cooking spray. Coat each mushroom with cooking spray. Bake at 400° for 20 minutes or until tops are browned. Yield: 12 servings (serving size: 2 mushrooms).

CALORIES 105 (48% from fat); FAT 5.6g (sat 2.3g, mono 2.3g, poly 0.6g); PROTEIN 5.7g; CARB 9.1g; FIBER 1.1g; CHOL 13mg; IRON 0.8mg; SODIUM 325mg; CALC 23mg

Roast Pork Sandwiches

This course has several make-ahead elements. The pork brines overnight, a simple process well worth the effort. The roast makes enough for leftovers. You can prepare the horseradish cream up to a day ahead. The rolls are best baked the morning of the party; you can substitute Parmesan or Gruyère for the nutty-tasting Parrano cheese. Not in the mood to bake? Buy rolls instead.

½ cup Horseradish Cream
12 Parrano Cheese-Thyme Rolls, cut in half horizontally
12 ounces Roast Pork, thinly sliced

1. Spread 1 teaspoon horseradish cream on tops and bottoms of rolls. Place 1 ounce pork on bottom half of each roll; top with top halves of rolls. Yield: 12 servings (serving size: 1 sandwich).

CALORIES 202 (22% from fat); FAT 5g (sat 2.3g, mono 1.7g, poly 0.5g); PROTEIN 13.8g; CARB 24g; FIBER 1.1g; CHOL 51mg; IRON 2mg; SODIUM 379mg; CALC 77mg

ROAST PORK:
3 cups water
¼ cup packed brown sugar
¼ cup kosher salt
1 (12-ounce) bottle beer
6 whole peppercorns, lightly crushed
2 whole allspice, lightly crushed
2 thyme sprigs
1 (2-pound) boneless pork loin roast, trimmed
2 tablespoons brown sugar
½ teaspoon freshly ground black pepper
¼ teaspoon salt
1 tablespoon prepared mustard
Cooking spray

1. Combine water, ¼ cup brown sugar, kosher salt, and beer in a bowl; stir until sugar dissolves. Place beer mixture, peppercorns, allspice, thyme, and pork in a large zip-top plastic bag. Marinate in refrigerator 8 hours or overnight, turning occasionally. Remove pork from bag; discard marinade.
2. Preheat oven to 325°.

3. Combine 2 tablespoons brown sugar, ground pepper, ¼ teaspoon salt, and mustard in a small bowl. Evenly coat all sides of roast with mustard mixture. Heat a large nonstick skillet over medium-high heat. Coat pan with cooking spray. Add pork; cook 2 minutes on all sides or until browned.
4. Place pork on a broiler pan coated with cooking spray. Bake at 325° for 1 hour or until a thermometer registers 160° (slightly pink) or until desired degree of doneness. Place pork on a platter; let stand 10 minutes before slicing. Cut into thin slices; serve warm or cold. Yield: 24 servings (serving size: 1 ounce).

CALORIES 54 (28% from fat); FAT 1.7g (sat 0.6g, mono 0.8g, poly 0.2g); PROTEIN 8.1g; CARB 1.1g; FIBER 0.1g; CHOL 24mg; IRON 0.4mg; SODIUM 192mg; CALC 9mg

HORSERADISH CREAM:
2½ tablespoons prepared horseradish
5 tablespoons reduced-fat sour cream
1 teaspoon prepared mustard

1. Combine all ingredients in a small bowl. Chill. Yield: 12 servings (serving size: 2 teaspoons).

CALORIES 10 (72% from fat); FAT 0.8g (sat 0.5g, mono 0.2g, poly 0g); PROTEIN 0.2g; CARB 0.7g; FIBER 0.1g; CHOL 2mg; IRON 0mg; SODIUM 17mg; CALC 9mg

PARRANO CHEESE-THYME ROLLS:
1 teaspoon sugar
1 package dry yeast (about 2¼ teaspoons)
¾ cup warm water (100° to 110°)
2¾ cups all-purpose flour (about 12⅓ ounces), divided
1 teaspoon chopped fresh thyme
½ teaspoon salt
1 large egg, lightly beaten
¾ cup (3 ounces) freshly grated Parrano cheese
1 teaspoon cornmeal
Cooking spray

1. Dissolve sugar and yeast in warm water in a large bowl; let stand 5 minutes. Lightly spoon flour into dry measuring cups; level with a knife. Add 2½

cups flour, thyme, salt, and egg to yeast mixture; stir until a soft dough forms. Turn dough out onto a floured surface. Knead until smooth and elastic (about 10 minutes); add enough remaining flour, 1 tablespoon at a time, to prevent dough from sticking to hands (dough will feel slightly sticky). Cover dough; let stand 10 minutes. Knead in Parrano cheese until well combined.
2. Divide mixture into 12 equal portions; form each portion into a ball. Place balls onto a baking sheet sprinkled with cornmeal. Lightly coat tops of balls with cooking spray; cover with plastic wrap. Let rise in a warm place (85°), free from drafts, 45 minutes or until doubled in size.
3. Preheat oven to 400°.
4. Bake rolls at 400° for 18 minutes or until browned on tops and bottoms. Remove rolls from baking sheet; cool completely on a wire rack. Yield: 12 servings (serving size: 1 roll).

CALORIES 138 (16% from fat); FAT 2.5g (sat 1.3g, mono 0.7g, poly 0.2g); PROTEIN 5.5g; CARB 22.7g; FIBER 0.9g; CHOL 24mg; IRON 1.5mg; SODIUM 169mg; CALC 59mg

Hot Artichoke Dip

Though initially served hot, this dip will stay delicious as it cools. A combination of canned beans gives the dip body and creamy texture, and minimizes the need for a lot of sour cream and mayonnaise. Serve with fresh vegetables (such as carrots and celery) and crackers.

½ cup reduced-fat sour cream
⅓ cup reduced-fat mayonnaise
1 tablespoon fresh lemon juice
½ teaspoon salt
2 (14-ounce) cans artichoke hearts, rinsed and drained, divided
1 (15.5-ounce) can Great Northern beans, rinsed and drained
1 cup (4 ounces) grated fresh Parmigiano-Reggiano cheese, divided
2 tablespoons chopped fresh parsley, divided
3 garlic cloves, minced
Cooking spray

1. Preheat oven to 400°.
2. Place first 4 ingredients in a food processor; add 1 can artichokes and beans. Process until smooth. Add remaining can artichokes, ¾ cup Parmigiano-Reggiano cheese, 1 tablespoon parsley, and garlic. Pulse 20 times or until artichokes are coarsely chopped.
3. Spoon mixture into an 8-inch square baking dish coated with cooking spray; sprinkle top with remaining ¼ cup Parmigiano-Reggiano cheese and remaining 1 tablespoon parsley. Bake at 400° for 25 minutes or until bubbly. Yield: 12 servings (serving size: ⅓ cup).

CALORIES 98 (37% from fat); FAT 4g (sat 2.2g, mono 0.9g, poly 0.1g); PROTEIN 5.8g; CARB 10.3g; FIBER 2.4g; CHOL 9mg; IRON 0.5mg; SODIUM 488mg; CALC 108mg

QUICK & EASY • MAKE AHEAD • FREEZABLE
Pear Gorgonzola Butter

This butter is a nice staple during the holidays on crackers, baked potatoes, or muffins. Make it a few days before the party, and store in the refrigerator.

½ cup chopped canned pear halves, drained
½ cup (2 ounces) crumbled Gorgonzola cheese
1 tablespoon (1 ounce) ⅓-less-fat cream cheese, softened
1 (8-ounce) loaf French bread baguette, cut into 12 slices and toasted

1. Combine first 3 ingredients in a small bowl; mash with a fork until well blended. Serve with bread. Yield: ¾ cup (serving size: 1 tablespoon butter and 1 bread slice).

CALORIES 78 (22% from fat); FAT 1.9g (sat 1.3g, mono 0.5g, poly 0g); PROTEIN 3g; CARB 13g; FIBER 0.8g; CHOL 6mg; IRON 0.6mg; SODIUM 186mg; CALC 27mg

MAKE AHEAD
Sweet-and-Sour Red Onions

Although these pickled onions are tasty on their own, we also liked them on the Roast Pork Sandwiches (recipe on page 424).

2 cups red wine vinegar
1 cup sugar
¼ teaspoon salt
4 cups thinly vertically sliced red onion (about 2 large)

1. Combine vinegar, sugar, and salt in a small saucepan; cook over medium-high heat until sugar dissolves, stirring frequently. Pour vinegar mixture over onion; let stand 1 hour, stirring occasionally. Chill. Drain before serving. Yield: 12 servings (serving size: about ¼ cup).

CALORIES 17 (0% from fat); FAT 0g; PROTEIN 0.2g; CARB 4.2g; FIBER 0.4g; CHOL 0mg; IRON 0.1mg; SODIUM 6.1mg; CALC 6mg

Chocolate Fondue

In its native Switzerland, chocolate fondue is popular during the holidays. Serve fresh fruit and cut-up angel food cake as dippers.

2 cups fat-free milk
½ cup powdered sugar, sifted
2 tablespoons all-purpose flour
2 tablespoons dark corn syrup
2 teaspoons vanilla extract
5 ounces semisweet chocolate, chopped (about 1 cup)

1. Combine first 5 ingredients in a large saucepan over medium heat. Bring to a simmer; cook 5 minutes, stirring constantly. Reduce heat to medium-low; cook 2 minutes or until mixture is smooth, stirring constantly. Place chocolate in a medium bowl. Pour milk mixture over chocolate; stir until smooth. Transfer chocolate mixture to a fondue pot. Keep warm over a low flame. Yield: 12 servings (serving size: about 2 tablespoons).

CALORIES 103 (31% from fat); FAT 3.6g (sat 2.1g, mono 1.2g, poly 0.1g); PROTEIN 2g; CARB 17.4g; FIBER 0.7g; CHOL 1mg; IRON 0.7mg; SODIUM 25mg; CALC 42mg

in season

Citrus Circumstance

Here are some flavorful strategies to use surplus winter fruit.

Lamb and Orange Tagine

Beef stew meat can stand in for the lamb.

Cooking spray
2½ pounds boneless leg of lamb, trimmed and cut into 1-inch pieces
1½ teaspoons olive oil
2 cups sliced onion
1½ teaspoons ground ginger
1½ teaspoons ground cumin
1½ teaspoons ground coriander
1 teaspoon crushed red pepper
¼ teaspoon ground cardamom
4 garlic cloves, minced
1 (3-inch) cinnamon stick
2 cups fat-free, less-sodium chicken broth
¼ teaspoon salt
1½ cups orange sections (about 3 oranges)
½ cup chopped pitted dates or golden raisins
3 cups hot cooked couscous
¼ cup chopped fresh cilantro
2 tablespoons slivered almonds, toasted

1. Heat a large Dutch oven over medium-high heat. Coat pan with cooking spray. Add half of lamb; cook 5 minutes or until lamb is browned. Remove from pan. Repeat procedure with remaining lamb.
2. Heat oil in pan over medium-high heat. Add onion; sauté 7 minutes or until tender. Add ginger and next 6 ingredients, stirring to combine; sauté 2 minutes. Return lamb to pan; stir in broth and salt. Bring to a boil; cover, reduce heat, and simmer 1½ hours, stirring occasionally. Uncover and simmer 30
Continued

minutes, stirring frequently. Discard cinnamon stick. Add orange sections and dates, stirring gently to combine; cook 5 minutes. Place ½ cup couscous into each of 6 shallow bowls; top with about ¾ cup lamb mixture. Sprinkle each serving with 2 teaspoons cilantro and 1 teaspoon almonds. Yield: 6 servings.

CALORIES 425 (26% from fat); FAT 12.5g (sat 3.5g, mono 5.4g, poly 1.5g); PROTEIN 37.5g; CARB 40.2g; FIBER 4.9g; CHOL 100mg; IRON 3.9mg; SODIUM 358mg; CALC 74mg

QUICK & EASY
Fennel and Orange Salad

Licorice-flavored fennel adds a little crunch to this pretty winter salad. Substitute a crisp green, such as endive, and use feta instead of goat cheese, if you like.

    4   cups thinly sliced fennel bulb
        (about 2 large bulbs)
 1½   cups orange sections (about 3
        oranges)
    2   tablespoons white wine vinegar
    1   teaspoon poppy seeds
    2   teaspoons olive oil
   ¼   teaspoon salt
   ¼   teaspoon ground cumin
   ¼   teaspoon freshly ground black
        pepper
    1   garlic clove, minced
   ¼   cup (1 ounce) crumbled goat
        cheese

1. Combine fennel and orange sections in a large bowl. Combine vinegar and next 6 ingredients, stirring well with a whisk. Drizzle vinegar mixture over fennel mixture; toss gently to coat. Sprinkle with cheese. Serve immediately. Yield: 6 servings (serving size: about ¾ cup).

CALORIES 71 (37% from fat); FAT 2.9g (sat 0.9g, mono 1.4g, poly 0.3g); PROTEIN 2.2g; CARB 10.4g; FIBER 3g; CHOL 2mg; IRON 0.7mg; SODIUM 145mg; CALC 62mg

MAKE AHEAD
Grapefruit Curd

If you don't have a double boiler, place a small saucepan or metal bowl over another saucepan filled with an inch or two of water. This sweet-tart spread will keep refrigerated up to one week.

    2   teaspoons grated grapefruit rind
        (about 2 grapefruit)
   ⅔   cup fresh grapefruit juice
   ½   cup sugar
    2   tablespoons fresh lemon juice
    4   large egg yolks
    2   tablespoons chilled butter, cut
        into small pieces

1. Combine first 5 ingredients in top of a double boiler, stirring well with a whisk. Cook over simmering water until thick (about 10 minutes), stirring constantly. Strain juice mixture through a fine sieve into a bowl; discard solids. Add butter, stirring well with a whisk. Cool completely. Yield: 1 cup (serving size: 1 tablespoon).

CALORIES 56 (43% from fat); FAT 2.7g (sat 1.3g, mono 0.9g, poly 0.2g); PROTEIN 0.8g; CARB 7.4g; FIBER 0.4g; CHOL 57mg; IRON 0.2mg; SODIUM 16mg; CALC 8mg

MAKE AHEAD
Orange and Grapefruit Syrup

Use a large saucepan so the mixture won't boil over. The syrup makes a tasty topping for ice cream or cake, or spoon it over pancakes. Refrigerate up to one week.

    2   cups sugar
    1   cup fresh orange juice
   ¾   cup fresh grapefruit juice (about 2
        grapefruit)
    1   cup orange sections (about 2
        oranges)
    1   cup grapefruit sections (about 1
        grapefruit)

1. Combine first 3 ingredients in a large saucepan, stirring with a whisk; bring to a boil over medium-high heat. Cook, without stirring, until a candy thermometer registers 238° (about 25 minutes).

Remove from heat; let stand 10 minutes. Add orange sections and grapefruit sections, stirring gently. Yield: 3 cups (serving size: ¼ cup).

CALORIES 157 (1% from fat); FAT 0.1g (sat 0g, mono 0.1g, poly 0g); PROTEIN 0.5g; CARB 40g; FIBER 0.7g; CHOL 0mg; IRON 0.1mg; SODIUM 1mg; CALC 12mg

Orange-Maple Marinated Pork Loin

Tangy mustard and soy sauce balance the sweetness of fresh orange juice and maple syrup in this versatile marinade. It's also good with chicken or salmon. Adding water to the pan prevents the juices from burning on the bottom of the roaster.

    2   teaspoons grated orange rind
 1⅓   cups fresh orange juice (about 3
        oranges)
   ⅔   cup maple syrup
    3   tablespoons stone-ground mustard
 2½   tablespoons chopped fresh basil
 2½   tablespoons low-sodium soy sauce
   ¾   teaspoon freshly ground black
        pepper
    4   garlic cloves, minced
 3½   pounds boneless pork loin,
        trimmed
        Cooking spray
   ½   teaspoon salt

1. Combine first 8 ingredients in a bowl, stirring well with a whisk. Combine 2 cups orange mixture and pork in a zip-top plastic bag; seal. (Reserve remaining orange mixture for another use.) Marinate pork in refrigerator 8 hours, turning bag occasionally.
2. Preheat oven to 350°.
3. Remove pork from bag, reserving marinade. Place marinade in a large saucepan; bring to a boil. Reduce heat; cook until reduced to 1 cup, stirring occasionally (about 20 minutes).
4. Place pork on a rack coated with cooking spray; place rack in a shallow roasting pan. Sprinkle pork with salt. Bake at 350° for 1 hour, basting occasionally with reduced marinade. Carefully pour ½ cup water into bottom of pan (do not remove pan from oven).

Bake an additional 45 minutes or until a thermometer registers 160° (slightly pink), basting occasionally with marinade. Discard remaining marinade. Remove pork from oven. Cover with foil; let stand 10 minutes before slicing. Yield: 12 servings (serving size: about 3 ounces).

CALORIES 229 (29% from fat); FAT 7.4g (sat 2.7g, mono 3.2g, poly 0.6g); PROTEIN 22.7g; CARB 16.5g; FIBER 0.7g; CHOL 63mg; IRON 1.3mg; SODIUM 324mg; CALC 44mg

Roasted Sweet Potato and Orange Salad

(pictured on page 431)

Roast the sweet potatoes, section the oranges, and slice the onion ahead. Keep them all refrigerated separately until you're ready to toss the salad.

SALAD:

1 tablespoon chopped fresh rosemary
2 teaspoons olive oil
3 garlic cloves, unpeeled and crushed
1½ pounds peeled sweet potato, cut into ¾-inch pieces
3 cups orange sections (about 6 oranges)
½ cup vertically sliced red onion
3 tablespoons pine nuts, toasted
1 (6-ounce) bag prewashed baby spinach

DRESSING:

3 tablespoons fresh orange juice
2 tablespoons olive oil
1 tablespoon stone-ground mustard
1 tablespoon rice vinegar
1 tablespoon honey
¼ teaspoon salt
¼ teaspoon freshly ground black pepper
1 garlic clove, minced

1. Preheat oven to 400°.
2. To prepare salad, combine first 4 ingredients, tossing well. Place potato mixture on a jelly-roll pan lined with parchment paper. Bake at 400° for 40 minutes, stirring occasionally. Remove from oven; cool. Discard garlic. Combine potato mixture, orange sections, onion, pine nuts, and spinach in a large bowl.
3. To prepare dressing, combine orange juice and remaining 7 ingredients in a small bowl, stirring well with a whisk. Drizzle dressing over salad; toss gently to coat. Yield: 10 servings (serving size 1 cup).

CALORIES 160 (30% from fat); FAT 5.3g (sat 3.2g, mono 1g, poly 0.8g); PROTEIN 2.9g; CARB 27g; FIBER 4.1g; CHOL 0mg; IRON 1.3mg; SODIUM 101mg; CALC 59mg

MAKE AHEAD
Grapefruit, Orange, and Ginger Marmalade

The marmalade is a good holiday gift because it doubles as a glaze for pork or chicken. It will keep refrigerated up to two weeks. Chop the citrus, rind and all. The marmalade thickens as it cooks and will continue to do so as it cools. Stir more often toward the end of the cook time.

¼ to ½ cup chopped crystallized ginger
1 orange, cut into 1-inch pieces
1 red or pink grapefruit, cut into 1-inch pieces
3 cups water
6 cups sugar

1. Place ginger, half of orange, and half of grapefruit in a food processor; pulse 4 times or until finely chopped. Place orange mixture in a Dutch oven. Repeat procedure with remaining orange and grapefruit. Add water to pan; bring mixture to a boil. Cover, reduce heat, and simmer until mixture is reduced to 6 cups (about 50 minutes), stirring occasionally.
2. Add 6 cups sugar; uncover and cook until sugar is dissolved. Increase heat to medium-high; bring mixture to a boil. Cook until mixture is thick and reduced to 5 cups (about 35 minutes), stirring occasionally. Remove from heat; cool. Yield: 5 cups (serving size: 2 tablespoons).

CALORIES 123 (1% from fat); FAT 0.1g (sat 0.1g, mono 0g, poly 0g); PROTEIN 0.1g; CARB 31.6g; FIBER 0.2g; CHOL 0mg; IRON 0.1mg; SODIUM 1mg; CALC 4mg

MAKE AHEAD • FREEZABLE
Citrus Tea Sorbet

Use an unflavored black tea, or substitute your favorite tea. This refreshing sorbet makes a great ending to a spicy meal. If you use loose tea, strain it out and discard before adding the sugar.

2¼ cups boiling water
4 black tea bags or 4 teaspoons loose black tea
2 cups sugar
4 cups grapefruit juice (about 8 grapefruit)
1 tablespoon grated orange rind
1 cup fresh orange juice (about 2 oranges)

1. Pour boiling water over tea bags in a large saucepan; steep 5 minutes. Remove and discard tea bags. Add sugar to pan; cook over medium heat 5 minutes or until sugar dissolves. Cool completely.
2. Combine tea mixture, grapefruit juice, orange rind, and orange juice in freezer can of an ice-cream freezer; freeze according to manufacturer's instructions. Spoon sorbet into a freezer-safe container; cover and freeze 1 hour or until firm. Yield: 8 servings (serving size: about ¾ cup).

CALORIES 252 (1% from fat); FAT 0.2g (sat 0.1g, mono 0.1g, poly 0g); PROTEIN 0.8g; CARB 63.8g; FIBER 0.3g; CHOL 0mg; IRON 0.3mg; SODIUM 2mg; CALC 15mg

---

Sectioning Fresh Citrus

To section an orange or grapefruit, peel the fruit, removing as much of the white pith as possible. Holding the fruit over a bowl to catch the juice, use a sharp knife to cut between the membranes and separate them from the flesh. Discard the membranes and any seeds. (If you need it, squeeze the juice from the membranes before discarding them.)

Orange-Rum Cocktail

Freeze fresh cranberries to float in the drink for a festive garnish. Use any orange-flavored liqueur.

> 6 cups fresh orange juice (about 12 oranges)
> ½ cup Grand Marnier (orange-flavored liqueur)
> ½ cup white rum
> ¾ cup orange sections

1. Combine first 3 ingredients in a pitcher; chill. Add orange sections just before serving. Yield: 7 servings (serving size: 1 cup).

CALORIES 199 (2% from fat); FAT 0.5g (sat 0.1g, mono 0.1g, poly 0.1g); PROTEIN 1.7g; CARB 31.5g; FIBER 0.9g; CHOL 0mg; IRON 0.5mg; SODIUM 3mg; CALC 31mg

lighten up

Sweet Tradition

A century-old steamed pudding now personifies the spirit of Christmas present.

Steamed Pudding with Lemon Sauce is a highlight of Kristi Portugue's family's Christmas Eve dinner. But Kristi, of Lakeville, Minnesota, wanted it to be lighter so her family could enjoy it more often, and she was concerned about the uncooked eggs in the sauce.

We reduced the amount of butter in the pudding to just three tablespoons. When choosing a substitute for whole milk, we can often get away with fat-free milk, but in this case we found that two percent reduced-fat milk made for a better dessert.

We stirred a modest one-third cup of applesauce into the batter, which added a subtle fruit flavor, moisture, and only four calories per serving.

The original lemon sauce had its own challenge. For starters, it was too sweet, so we reduced the sugar by more than a cup. Then we addressed the eggs. We achieved fine results with one whole

yolk. And we cooked the sauce on the stovetop, easing Portugue's apprehension about serving uncooked eggs.

We maintained the silkiness and sheen that butter lends a sauce by reducing it to one tablespoon. Finally, we replaced lemon extract with fresh lemon juice and grated lemon rind for a fresher taste.

Steamed Pudding with Lemon Sauce

Golden raisins or dried cherries may be used instead of raisins. If available, you can use blackstrap molasses, a surprising source of iron, to add rich color and flavor. Coating both the dish and the plastic wrap with cooking spray makes it easier to remove the pudding after it's cooked.

PUDDING:
> Cooking spray
> ⅓ cup applesauce
> 3 tablespoons butter, softened
> 2½ cups all-purpose flour (11¼ ounces)
> ½ teaspoon baking soda
> Dash of salt
> 1¼ cups 2% reduced-fat milk
> ½ cup plus 1 tablespoon molasses
> 1 cup raisins

SAUCE:
> ¾ cup sugar
> ½ cup egg substitute
> ⅓ cup 2% reduced-fat milk
> ¼ cup fresh lemon juice
> 1 tablespoon butter
> 1 large egg yolk
> Dash of salt
> ½ teaspoon grated lemon rind
> ¼ teaspoon vanilla extract

1. Preheat oven to 350°.
2. Lightly coat a 2½-quart oven-safe bowl with cooking spray; line with plastic wrap. Lightly coat surface of wrap with cooking spray. Set aside.
3. Spoon applesauce onto several layers of paper towels; spread to ½-inch thickness. Cover with additional paper towels; let stand 5 minutes. Scrape into a small bowl using a rubber spatula.

4. Beat 3 tablespoons butter with a mixer at medium speed 2 minutes or until fluffy. Lightly spoon flour into dry measuring cups; level with a knife. Combine flour, baking soda, and salt. Add flour mixture, 1¼ cups milk, and molasses to butter, beating until blended. Stir in applesauce and raisins. Spoon mixture into prepared bowl; cover bowl with plastic wrap.

5. Place bowl in a deep roasting pan. Add hot water to pan until water is one-third way up sides of bowl. Tightly cover bowl and pan with aluminum foil. Bake at 350° for 2 hours or until a wooden pick inserted in center comes out clean. Remove bowl from roasting pan. Carefully invert bowl onto a serving plate; remove bowl. Remove and discard plastic wrap.

6. To prepare sauce, combine ¾ cup sugar and next 6 ingredients in a medium saucepan over medium heat, stirring constantly with a whisk until smooth. Cook, stirring frequently, 4 minutes or until thickened. Remove from heat. Stir in rind and vanilla. Let stand at least 5 minutes before serving. Yield: 10 servings (serving size: 1 slice pudding and 2½ tablespoons sauce).

CALORIES 351 (17% from fat); FAT 6.7g (sat 3.1g, mono 2.2g, poly 0.6g); PROTEIN 6.9g; CARB 66.9g; FIBER 1.8g; CHOL 36mg; IRON 5.4mg; SODIUM 180mg; CALC 222mg

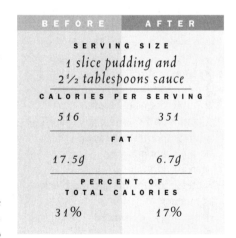

BEFORE	AFTER
SERVING SIZE	
1 slice pudding and 2½ tablespoons sauce	
CALORIES PER SERVING	
516	351
FAT	
17.5g	6.7g
PERCENT OF TOTAL CALORIES	
31%	17%

Bundt Coffee Cake, page 415

Rossini Bellini, page 417

Roasted Sweet Potato and Orange Salad, page 427

Sweet Vermouth Chicken, page 452

(front to back) Chewy Chocolate-Cherry Cookies, page 436, Maple-Walnut Spice Cookies, page 436, Pecan Sandies, page 435 and Pecan-Date Bars, page 437

Cookie Swap

Plan a party, and share a bounty of baked goodies.

As holiday traditions go, a cookie swap is a great way to multitask—offering a chance to get together and exchange tokens with friends during the busy season, as well as a way to shortcut your holiday baking.

All you need to do for a successful cookie swap is prepare a bunch of your favorite cookies, then exchange them and the recipe with other partygoers who've brought their own favorite treats. It's an easy party to throw, especially when you follow our tips and advice. We have a variety of tasty recipes for portable, packable cookies that are ideal for this type of party, plus some ideas for nibbles to serve guests.

MAKE AHEAD
Citrus Tea Punch

A fun change from the more expected mulled wine or cider, this punch is sweet, tangy, and lightly spiced. You can prepare it up to one day in advance.

    6 cups water, divided
  ½ cup sugar
    3 whole cloves
    2 family-sized tea bags
    1 (3-inch) cinnamon stick
    1 cup orange juice
    1 (6-ounce) can thawed lemonade
      concentrate, undiluted
  Ice cubes
  Lemon slices (optional)

1. Combine 4 cups water and sugar in a heavy saucepan; bring to a boil. Cook until sugar dissolves; remove from heat. Add cloves, tea bags, and cinnamon; steep 5 minutes. Strain mixture through a sieve into a pitcher; discard solids. Add remaining 2 cups water, juice, and lemonade concentrate; stir well. Chill. Serve over ice; garnish with lemon slices, if desired. Yield: 12 servings (serving size: about ⅔ cup).

CALORIES 68 (1% from fat); FAT 0.1g (sat 0g, mono 0g, poly 0g); PROTEIN 0.2g; CARB 17.5g; FIBER 0.1g; CHOL 0mg; IRON 0.2mg; SODIUM 4mg; CALC 3mg

MAKE AHEAD
Pomegranate-Avocado Salsa with Spiced Chips

If you can't find clementines, substitute tangerines. Bake the chips up to a day ahead, and store at room temperature in a zip-top plastic bag. You can also prepare the salsa, minus the avocado mixture, a day ahead. Prepare and stir in avocado mixture shortly before serving to keep the avocado green.

CHIPS:

    1 teaspoon paprika
  ¾ teaspoon ground cumin
  ½ teaspoon salt
  ½ teaspoon sugar
  ½ teaspoon garlic powder
  ½ teaspoon onion powder
   12 (6-inch) corn tortillas, each cut
      into 8 wedges
  Cooking spray

SALSA:

  1⅓ cups diced peeled avocado (about
      2 avocados)
    3 tablespoons fresh lime juice
    2 cups clementine sections (about 6
      clementines)
    1 cup pomegranate seeds (about 1
      medium pomegranate)
  ½ cup thinly sliced green onions
  ½ cup minced fresh cilantro
    2 tablespoons honey
  ½ teaspoon salt
    1 jalapeño pepper, seeded and
      minced

1. Preheat oven to 500°.
2. To prepare chips, combine first 6 ingredients. Arrange tortilla wedges in a single layer on 2 baking sheets; coat with cooking spray. Bake at 500° for 5 minutes. Turn wedges over; coat with cooking spray. Sprinkle paprika mixture evenly over wedges. Bake an additional 2 minutes or until lightly browned. Cool completely.
3. To prepare salsa, combine avocado and juice in a medium bowl; toss gently to coat. Add clementine sections and remaining 6 ingredients; toss gently to combine. Serve salsa with chips. Yield: 12 servings (serving size: 8 chips and about ¼ cup salsa).

CALORIES 122 (24% from fat); FAT 3.3g (sat 0.5g, mono 1.8g, poly 0.7g); PROTEIN 2.3g; CARB 22.7g; FIBER 3.3g; CHOL 0mg; IRON 0.7mg; SODIUM 243mg; CALC 63mg

MAKE AHEAD
Bacon and Cheddar Tea Sandwiches

While this recipe calls for country white bread, you can use any sandwich bread. For a nice color contrast, try pumpernickel or rye.

  1½ cups (6 ounces) shredded
      reduced-fat extrasharp Cheddar
      cheese
    5 tablespoons block-style fat-free
      cream cheese, softened
    5 tablespoons thinly sliced green
      onions
  3½ tablespoons fat-free mayonnaise
  1¼ teaspoons hot sauce
    3 bacon slices, cooked and crumbled
   12 (1-ounce) slices country white
      bread, crusts removed

1. Combine first 6 ingredients, stirring well.
2. Spread 3 tablespoons cheese mixture on each of 6 bread slices; top with remaining bread slices. Cut each sandwich in half diagonally; cut each half diagonally again to form 4 wedges. Yield: 12 servings (serving size: 2 wedges).

CALORIES 131 (32% from fat); FAT 4.6g (sat 2.3g, mono 1.1g, poly 0.2g); PROTEIN 7.2g; CARB 15.8g; FIBER 1.7g; CHOL 13mg; IRON 0.6mg; SODIUM 370mg; CALC 127mg

Step-by-Step Guide to Hosting a Cookie Swap

1. Plan early. People are more likely to attend if you give as much advance notice as possible.

2. Track guests' responses. Invite friends, relatives, neighbors, coworkers, or anyone who loves cookies. In this case, more is better—you'll have that many more kinds of cookies to swap. Ask everyone to respond promptly and tell you what type of cookies they'll bring. It's the host's job to keep a running list to avoid duplications. Remind partygoers to bring a few extra empty tins or zip-top bags to take their cookies home in.

3. Determine the number of cookies guests should bring. One suggestion: Ask each guest to bring six dozen cookies from a single recipe—about two or three batches of an average cookie recipe.

Or you can base the number of cookies to bring on the number of guests, and be sure to account for yourself, the host. For example, if you expect 12 guests, ask each person to bring 13 dozen cookies. The advantage to this approach is that everyone will leave with a full dozen of each cookie. Regardless of which strategy appeals to you, consider asking each guest to bring an extra half-dozen, so you can eat a few cookies during the party.

4. Get copies of the recipes. Each guest should go home with a copy of all of the cookie recipes. You can ask guests to bring enough copies of their recipes for all. Or, for a more creative approach, ask each guest to email you a copy of his or her recipe a few days ahead of time. Then you can print the recipes on recipe cards. For a souvenir, bind them into a cookie swap cookbook complete with the year and date.

5. Prepare some savory snacks. You and your guests will be sampling lots of cookies during the party, so it's nice to offer some savory snacks and drinks to balance the sweets.

Cream Cheese Meltaways with Lemon Glaze

Melt-in-your-mouth buttery cookies are covered with a tangy citrus glaze. When shaping these cookies, don't try to form perfectly smooth balls. If the dough is handled too much, the cookies will become heavy and dense.

COOKIES:
- 1¼ cups all-purpose flour (about 5½ ounces)
- ½ cup cornstarch
- ⅛ teaspoon salt
- 1 cup powdered sugar
- ½ cup butter, softened
- ¼ cup (2 ounces) block-style ⅓-less-fat cream cheese, softened
- 1 teaspoon vanilla extract

GLAZE:
- 1¾ cups powdered sugar
- ¼ cup fresh lemon juice

1. Preheat oven to 375°.

2. To prepare cookies, lightly spoon flour into dry measuring cups; level with a knife. Combine flour, cornstarch, and salt in a medium bowl, stirring well with a whisk.

3. Combine 1 cup powdered sugar, butter, cheese, and vanilla in a large bowl; beat with a mixer at medium speed until light and fluffy (about 4 minutes). Add flour mixture; stir until just combined (dough will be dry and crumbly). Shape dough into 36 (1-inch) balls. Place balls 2 inches apart on baking sheets. Bake at 375° for 10 minutes or until bottoms of cookies are lightly browned. Cool 5 minutes on pans on wire racks. Remove from pans; cool completely on wire racks.

4. To prepare glaze, combine 1¾ cups powdered sugar and lemon juice, stirring with a whisk until smooth. Dip tops of cookies in glaze; place on wire racks. Let cookies stand 30 minutes or until glaze is set. Yield: 36 cookies (serving size: 1 cookie).

CALORIES 85 (32% from fat); FAT 3g (sat 1.5g, mono 1.2g, poly 0.1g); PROTEIN 0.6g; CARB 14.3g; FIBER 0.1g; CHOL 8mg; IRON 0.2mg; SODIUM 33mg; CALC 3mg

---

How to Shape Tassies

A special tool called a tart tamper makes shaping the dough easier.

Orange-Walnut Tassies

The cream cheese dough needs to be elastic before it's divided into portions. You can determine if it's ready by pressing one finger onto the surface of the dough. If the dough springs back to take its original shape, the dough is ready to be shaped; if it doesn't, knead a few more times.

CRUST:
- 1 cup all-purpose flour (about 4½ ounces)
- 1 tablespoon granulated sugar
- ⅛ teaspoon salt
- ¼ cup (2 ounces) ⅓-less-fat cream cheese, softened
- 2 tablespoons butter, softened
- 2 tablespoons fat-free milk
- Cooking spray

FILLING:
- ⅓ cup chopped walnuts, toasted
- ½ cup packed brown sugar
- ¼ cup light-colored corn syrup
- ½ teaspoon grated orange rind
- 2 tablespoons fresh orange juice
- ⅛ teaspoon salt
- 1 large egg

1. Preheat oven to 350°.

2. To prepare crust, lightly spoon flour into a dry measuring cup; level with a knife. Combine flour, granulated sugar, and ⅛ teaspoon salt, stirring with a whisk. Combine cream cheese, butter,

---

and milk in a large bowl; beat with a mixer at medium speed until well blended. Add flour mixture; beat at low speed just until blended (mixture will be crumbly).

3. Turn dough out onto a lightly floured surface; knead lightly 3 or 4 times. Divide dough into 24 portions. Place 1 dough portion into each of 24 miniature muffin cups coated with cooking spray. Press dough into bottom and up sides of cups using lightly floured fingers.

4. To prepare filling, spoon about ½ teaspoon walnuts into each muffin cup. Combine brown sugar and remaining 5 ingredients, stirring well with a whisk; spoon about 2 teaspoons filling over walnuts in each muffin cup.

5. Bake at 350° for 20 minutes or until crust is lightly browned and filling is puffy. Cool in pans 10 minutes on a wire rack. Run a knife around outside edge of each tassie; remove from pan. Cool completely on wire racks. Yield: 2 dozen tassies (serving size: 1 tassie).

CALORIES 78 (33% from fat); FAT 2.9g (sat 1g, mono 0.8g, poly 0.9g); PROTEIN 1.4g; CARB 12.2g; FIBER 0.3g; CHOL 13mg; IRON 0.4mg; SODIUM 50mg; CALC 11mg

STAFF FAVORITE • MAKE AHEAD
FREEZABLE
Pecan Sandies
(pictured on page 432)

These buttery, nutty cookies received our Test Kitchens' highest rating. It's important for your butter to be soft when you prepare the crumbly dough, which holds together nicely when you shape it into balls.

  2 cups all-purpose flour (about 9 ounces)
  ¼ cup finely chopped pecans
  ⅛ teaspoon salt
  ¾ cup granulated sugar
  9 tablespoons butter, softened
  2 teaspoons vanilla extract
Cooking spray
  ¼ cup powdered sugar

1. Preheat oven to 350°.
2. Lightly spoon flour into dry measuring cups; level with a knife. Combine flour, pecans, and salt, stirring well with a whisk.

3. Place granulated sugar and butter in a medium bowl; beat with a mixer at medium speed until fluffy (about 2 minutes). Beat in vanilla. Beating at low speed, gradually add flour mixture; beat just until combined (mixture will be crumbly).

4. Shape dough into 34 (1-inch) balls (about 1 tablespoon each). Place dough balls 2 inches apart on baking sheets coated with cooking spray. Bake at 350° for 20 minutes or until lightly browned.

5. While cookies are still hot, sift powdered sugar evenly over tops. Remove from pans; cool completely on wire racks. Yield: 34 cookies (serving size: 1 cookie).

CALORIES 81 (41% from fat); FAT 3.7g (sat 1.6g, mono 1.6g, poly 0.3g); PROTEIN 0.9g; CARB 11.1g; FIBER 0.3g; CHOL 8mg; IRON 0.4mg; SODIUM 30mg; CALC 3mg

MAKE AHEAD • FREEZABLE
Sugared Vanilla Cookies

Use any color of sugar sprinkles—or combination of colors—you like. After freezing the dough, let it thaw for a few minutes before rolling it in sugar. Then slice and bake as directed.

  2½ cups all-purpose flour (about 11¼ ounces)
  ½ teaspoon baking soda
  ¼ teaspoon salt
  1 cup granulated sugar
  10 tablespoons butter, softened
  2 teaspoons vanilla extract
  2 large egg whites
Cooking spray
  ½ cup red sugar sprinkles

1. Lightly spoon flour into dry measuring cups; level with a knife. Combine flour, baking soda, and salt, stirring well with a whisk.
2. Place granulated sugar and butter in a large bowl; beat with a mixer at medium-high speed until light and fluffy (about 1 minute). Add vanilla and egg whites, beating until well blended. Beating at low speed, gradually add flour mixture, beating just until a soft dough forms. Divide dough into 2 equal portions. Place each portion on plastic wrap; shape each portion into an 8-inch log.

Wrap logs in plastic wrap; freeze at least 2 hours or until very firm.
3. Preheat oven to 375°.
4. Working with one dough log at a time, lightly coat log with cooking spray, and roll log in sugar sprinkles, pressing gently to adhere. Cut log into 32 (¼-inch-thick) slices; place 1 inch apart on baking sheets coated with cooking spray. Bake at 375° for 10 minutes or until set. Remove from pans; cool completely on wire racks. Yield: 64 cookies (serving size: 1 cookie).

CALORIES 53 (31% from fat); FAT 1.8g (sat 0.9g, mono 0.7g, poly 0.1g); PROTEIN 0.6g; CARB 8.4g; FIBER 0.1g; CHOL 5mg; IRON 0.2mg; SODIUM 33mg; CALC 1mg

---

Packaging Panache

If you decide on a packaging theme, try some of these ideas for presenting your holiday treats.

• Heap cookies into inexpensive tins lined with parchment paper—retro tins with holiday scenes, galvanized tins, or red and silver tins.

• Stack cookies onto a pretty saucer from a flea market, wrap with cellophane, and tie with a ribbon.

• Pile a wide juice glass high with cookies, and remind guests that they can fill the glass with milk for dunking.

• Use colorful takeout boxes.

• Place cookies in glassine bags, and tie with colorful ribbon.

• Put cookies in a paper bag, fold over the top, punch two holes, string ribbon through the holes, and tie a bow.

• Line a small basket with a holiday napkin, and fill with cookies.

• Stack cookies in a colorful café au lait bowl, and wrap with cellophane.

• Wrap cookies in wax paper, secure with a ribbon, and tie a cookie cutter to the ribbon.

• Package cookies in small wooden boxes lined with colorful tissue paper.

MAKE AHEAD • FREEZABLE
Chewy Chocolate-Cherry Cookies

(pictured on page 432)

 1   cup all-purpose flour (about 4½ ounces)
 ⅓   cup unsweetened cocoa
 ½   teaspoon baking powder
 ¼   teaspoon baking soda
 ¼   teaspoon salt
 1   cup sugar
 ⅓   cup butter, softened
 1   teaspoon vanilla extract
 1   large egg
 ⅔   cup dried tart cherries
 3   tablespoons semisweet chocolate chips
Cooking spray

1. Preheat oven to 350°.
2. Lightly spoon flour into a dry measuring cup; level with a knife. Combine flour, cocoa, baking powder, baking soda, and salt, stirring with a whisk. Place sugar and butter in a large bowl; beat with a mixer at high speed until well blended. Add vanilla and egg; beat well. With mixer on low speed, gradually add flour mixture. Beat just until combined. Fold in cherries and chocolate chips.
3. Drop dough by tablespoonfuls 2 inches apart onto baking sheets coated with cooking spray. Bake at 350° for 12 minutes or just until set. Remove from oven; cool on pans 5 minutes. Remove from pans; cool completely on a wire rack. Yield: 30 cookies (serving size: 1 cookie).

CALORIES 80 (30% from fat); FAT 2.7g (sat 1.3g, mono 1.1g, poly 0.1g); PROTEIN 1.1g; CARB 13.4g; FIBER 0.8g; CHOL 12mg; IRON 0.4mg; SODIUM 56mg; CALC 10mg

MAKE AHEAD •FREEZABLE
Maple-Walnut Spice Cookies

(pictured on page 432)

COOKIES:

 1½   cups all-purpose flour (about 6¾ ounces)
 ½   teaspoon baking soda
 ½   teaspoon ground ginger
 ½   teaspoon ground cinnamon
 ¼   teaspoon salt
 ⅛   teaspoon ground nutmeg
 ⅛   teaspoon ground cloves
 ¾   cup packed dark brown sugar
 ¼   cup butter, softened
 2   tablespoons maple syrup
 1   large egg

FROSTING:

 1   cup powdered sugar
 2   tablespoons maple syrup
 1   tablespoon fat-free milk
 2   teaspoons butter, softened

REMAINING INGREDIENT:

 ½   cup finely chopped walnuts, toasted

1. Preheat oven to 350°.
2. To prepare cookies, lightly spoon flour into dry measuring cups; level with a knife. Combine flour and next 6 ingredients in a medium bowl; stir well with a whisk.
3. Place brown sugar and ¼ cup butter in a large bowl; beat with a mixer at high speed until light and fluffy (about 4 minutes). Add 2 tablespoons syrup and egg; beat until well blended. Beating at low speed, gradually add flour mixture; beat just until combined.
4. Spoon batter evenly into 30 mounds (about 1 tablespoon) 2 inches apart on baking sheets. Bake at 350° for 14 minutes or until lightly browned. Cool on pans 5 minutes. Remove from pans; cool completely on wire racks.
5. To prepare frosting, combine powdered sugar, 2 tablespoons syrup, milk, and 2 teaspoons butter, stirring with a whisk until smooth. Spread frosting evenly over cooled cookies. Working quickly, sprinkle cookies with nuts. Yield: 30 cookies (serving size: 1 cookie).

CALORIES 98 (30% from fat); FAT 3.3g (sat 1.1g, mono 1g, poly 1.1g); PROTEIN 1.2g; CARB 16.3g; FIBER 0.3g; CHOL 12mg; IRON 0.5mg; SODIUM 58mg; CALC 12mg

How to Make Windowpane Cookies

Place 1 cut-out cookie on top of each whole cookie.

MAKE AHEAD • FREEZABLE
Raspberry Linzer Windowpane Cookies

Cut these cookies into shapes—round, rectangular, or even star-shaped. You can reroll the dough scraps, but chill them first.

 2   cups all-purpose flour (about 9 ounces)
 ½   teaspoon baking soda
 ¼   teaspoon salt
 ¼   teaspoon ground cinnamon
 ¾   cup granulated sugar
 ½   cup butter, softened
 ¼   cup egg substitute
 ¼   cup seedless raspberry jam
 2   teaspoons powdered sugar

1. Lightly spoon flour into dry measuring cups; level with a knife. Combine flour, baking soda, salt, and cinnamon, stirring well with a whisk.
2. Place granulated sugar and butter in a large bowl; beat with a mixer at high speed until light and fluffy. Add egg substitute; beat until well blended. Beating at low speed, gradually add flour mixture; beat just until a soft dough forms. Divide dough into 2 equal portions; wrap each dough portion in plastic wrap. Chill at least 1 hour.
3. Preheat oven to 375°.
4. Roll each dough portion into a ⅛-inch thickness on a lightly floured surface; cut with a 2-inch square cookie cutter with

fluted edges to form 32 cookies. Repeat procedure with remaining dough portion. Place cookies 1 inch apart on parchment-lined baking sheets. Cut out centers of 32 cookies with a 1-inch square cookie cutter with fluted edges. Bake cookies at 375° for 10 minutes or until edges are lightly browned. Cool on pans 5 minutes. Remove from pans; cool completely on wire racks.

5. Spread center of each whole cookie with about ½ teaspoon jam. Sprinkle cut-out cookies with powdered sugar. Place 1 cut-out cookie on top of each whole cookie. Yield: 32 cookies (serving size: 1 cookie).

CALORIES 79 (33% from fat); FAT 2.9g (sat 1.4g, mono 1.2g, poly 0.1g); PROTEIN 1g; CARB 12.5g; FIBER 0.2g; CHOL 8mg; IRON 0.4mg; SODIUM 62mg; CALC 3mg

MAKE AHEAD
Pecan-Date Bars

(pictured on page 432)

These bars are actually easier to cut once they have been completely chilled.

CRUST:
1 cup all-purpose flour (about 4½ ounces)
⅓ cup packed brown sugar
¼ teaspoon salt
¼ cup chilled butter, cut into small pieces
Cooking spray

FILLING:
¾ cup dark corn syrup
⅓ cup packed brown sugar
¼ cup egg substitute
2 tablespoons all-purpose flour
1 tablespoon bourbon
1 teaspoon vanilla extract
¼ teaspoon salt
1 large egg
½ cup chopped pitted dates
⅓ cup chopped pecans, toasted
2 tablespoons semisweet chocolate minichips

1. Preheat oven to 400°.
2. To prepare crust, lightly spoon 1 cup flour into a dry measuring cup; level with a knife. Combine 1 cup flour, ⅓ cup sugar, and ¼ teaspoon salt, stirring well with a whisk. Cut in butter with a pastry blender or two knives until mixture resembles coarse meal. Press mixture into bottom of an 11 x 7-inch baking dish coated with cooking spray. Bake at 400° for 12 minutes or until lightly browned. Cool completely.
3. Reduce oven temperature to 350°.
4. To prepare filling, combine corn syrup and next 7 ingredients in a large bowl, stirring well with a whisk. Stir in dates, pecans, and chocolate chips. Pour mixture over prepared crust. Bake at 350° for 35 minutes or until set. Cool in pan on a wire rack. Cover and chill 1 hour or until firm. Yield: 24 servings (serving size: 1 bar).

CALORIES 123 (26% from fat); FAT 3.6g (sat 1.3g, mono 1.6g, poly 0.5g); PROTEIN 1.4g; CARB 22g; FIBER 0.7g; CHOL 14mg; IRON 0.6mg; SODIUM 89mg; CALC 13mg

dinner tonight

Asian Dinners

Serve fresh and easy Asian meals any night of the week.

Asian Dinner Menu 1
serves 4

Kung Pao Chicken

Cool cucumber salad*

Short-grain or sticky rice

*Whisk together 1 tablespoon sugar, 2 tablespoons rice wine vinegar, ½ teaspoon salt, and ¼ teaspoon black pepper in a medium bowl. Add ¼ cup chopped fresh mint; 2 tablespoons chopped fresh basil; 2 seeded, peeled, and sliced cucumbers; 1 medium tomato, cut into wedges; and 2 chopped green onions. Toss to combine.

Game Plan

1. While water boils for rice:
  • Prepare and chill salad
2. While rice cooks:
  • Cut vegetables and slice chicken
3. Cook chicken and vegetables.

QUICK & EASY
Kung Pao Chicken

This traditionally spicy Szechuan dish is nicely balanced by the menu's slightly sweet cucumber salad. If you like fiery flavors, add up to one teaspoon of crushed red pepper. Speed up dinner by using bottled ground fresh ginger and bottled minced garlic.

TOTAL TIME: 30 MINUTES

QUICK TIP: To make it easier to cut chicken into thin strips, freeze 15 minutes before slicing. And look for cut-up broccoli florets in the supermarket produce department.

1 tablespoon canola oil, divided
4 cups broccoli florets
1 tablespoon ground fresh ginger (such as Spice World), divided
2 tablespoons water
½ teaspoon crushed red pepper
1 pound skinless, boneless chicken breast, cut into ¼-inch strips
½ cup fat-free, less-sodium chicken broth
2 tablespoons hoisin sauce
2 tablespoons rice wine vinegar
2 tablespoons low-sodium soy sauce
1 teaspoon cornstarch
4 garlic cloves, minced
2 tablespoons coarsely chopped salted peanuts

1. Heat 1 teaspoon oil in a large non-stick skillet over medium-high heat. Add broccoli and 2 teaspoons ginger to pan; sauté 1 minute. Add water. Cover; cook 2 minutes or until broccoli is crisp-tender. Remove broccoli from pan; keep warm.
2. Heat remaining 2 teaspoons oil in pan; add remaining 1 teaspoon ginger, crushed red pepper, and chicken. Cook 4 minutes or until chicken is lightly browned, stirring frequently.
3. Combine broth and next 5 ingredients in a small bowl; stir with a whisk. Add broth mixture to pan; cook 1 minute or until mixture thickens, stirring constantly. Return broccoli to pan; toss to coat. Sprinkle with peanuts. Yield: 4 servings (serving size: about 1 cup chicken mixture and 1½ teaspoons peanuts).

CALORIES 239 (30% from fat); FAT 7.9g (sat 1.1g, mono 3.7g, poly 2.3g); PROTEIN 30.9g; CARB 11.4g; FIBER 3g; CHOL 66mg; IRON 1.8mg; SODIUM 589mg; CALC 60mg

Asian Dinner Menu 2

serves 4

Five-Spice Salmon with Leeks in Parchment

Sautéed snow peas*

Store-bought almond cookies and jasmine tea

*Heat 2 teaspoons toasted sesame oil in a large nonstick skillet over medium-high heat. Add 2 cups fresh snow peas; sauté 4 minutes or until crisp-tender. Stir in 2 teaspoons rice wine vinegar and 2 teaspoons low-sodium soy sauce.

Game Plan

1. While spices toast:
   - Slice leeks
2. While oven preheats:
   - Grind spices
   - Assemble salmon packets
3. While salmon bakes:
   - Cook snow peas
   - Prepare tea

QUICK & EASY

Five-Spice Salmon with Leeks in Parchment

Cooking this fish in a parchment pouch uses both the radiant heat of the oven and steam inside the packet to produce moist, succulent results. Toasting and grinding the spices takes a little extra time but pays off with vivid flavor.

TOTAL TIME: 45 MINUTES

QUICK TIP: If you can't find some of the whole spices, substitute one tablespoon five-spice powder for the freshly ground spice mixture.

1¼ teaspoons whole fennel seeds
6 whole black peppercorns
2 whole cloves
1 whole star anise
1 (1½-inch) cinnamon stick
4 (6-ounce) skinless salmon fillets
½ teaspoon salt
1 leek, halved lengthwise and thinly sliced (about 1 cup)

1. Preheat oven to 425°.
2. Combine first 5 ingredients in a small

skillet over medium heat; cook 1 minute or until fragrant. Transfer spices to a spice grinder or coffee grinder; grind until fine.
3. Cut 4 (12-inch) squares of parchment paper. Place 1 fillet in center of each square. Sprinkle evenly with salt and spice mixture; top fillets evenly with leeks. Fold paper; seal edges with narrow folds. Place packets on a baking sheet. Bake at 425° for 20 minutes or until puffy and lightly browned. Place on plates; cut open. Serve immediately. Yield: 4 servings (serving size: 1 salmon fillet and ¼ cup leeks).

CALORIES 295 (41% from fat); FAT 13.5g (sat 3.1g, mono 5.8g, poly 3.3g); PROTEIN 36.8g; CARB 5g; FIBER 1.5g; CHOL 87mg; IRON 1.8mg; SODIUM 382mg; CALC 60mg

QUICK & EASY

Steak, Shiitake, and Bok Choy Stir-Fry

Pick up sliced onions, bell peppers, and mushrooms at the supermarket deli salad bar. You can use Asian stir-fry greens (usually a mix of bok choy and mustard greens) from the produce aisle in place of bok choy.

TOTAL TIME: 45 MINUTES

NUTRITION TIP: At 4.5 milligrams per serving, this recipe is an excellent source of heme iron (the most readily absorbed type). Women over 50 and men need 10 milligrams of iron per day; women under 50 need 15 milligrams each day. Pregnant women should consume 30 milligrams daily.

2 tablespoons grated peeled fresh ginger
1 tablespoon minced fresh garlic
3 tablespoons low-sodium soy sauce
4 teaspoons cornstarch, divided
1 teaspoon toasted sesame oil
½ teaspoon crushed red pepper
1 pound flank steak, trimmed and thinly sliced
Cooking spray
2 cups thinly sliced shiitake mushrooms (about ½ pound)
1 cup thinly vertically sliced onion
1 cup red bell pepper strips
4 cups sliced bok choy (about 1 medium head)
1 cup less-sodium beef broth

1. Combine ginger, garlic, soy sauce, 2 teaspoons cornstarch, oil, and crushed red pepper in a large zip-top bag; add steak to bag. Seal and marinate in refrigerator 20 minutes.
2. Heat a large nonstick skillet over medium-high heat. Coat pan with cooking spray; add mushrooms, onion, and bell pepper to pan. Cook 3 minutes or until crisp-tender; transfer to a large bowl. Add bok choy to pan; sauté 2 minutes or until slightly wilted; add to bowl; keep warm.
3. Recoat pan with cooking spray. Add half of steak mixture to pan; cook 3 minutes or until browned, stirring occasionally. Transfer to a large bowl; keep warm. Coat pan with cooking spray. Add remaining steak mixture to pan; cook 3 minutes or until browned, stirring occasionally. Add to bowl; keep warm.
4. Combine broth and remaining 2 teaspoons cornstarch, stirring with a whisk. Add to pan, scraping pan to loosen browned bits. Bring to a boil, and cook 1 minute or until mixture thickens, stirring constantly. Return steak and vegetables to pan; toss gently to coat. Yield: 4 servings (serving size: about 1½ cups).

CALORIES 270 (30% from fat); FAT 9g (sat 3.1g, mono 3.2g, poly 1g); PROTEIN 28.6g; CARB 16.9g; FIBER 3.4g; CHOL 45mg; IRON 4.5mg; SODIUM 706mg; CALC 244mg

Asian Dinner Menu 3

serves 4

Steak, Shiitake, and Bok Choy Stir-Fry

Jasmine rice*

Coconut sorbet with fresh mangoes

*Bring 2 cups water, 1 tablespoon unsalted butter, and ½ teaspoon salt to a boil in a medium saucepan; add 2 cups jasmine rice. Cover, reduce heat, and simmer 20 minutes or until liquid is absorbed. Fluff with a fork. Stir in ⅓ cup sliced green onions.

Game Plan

1. While steak marinates:
   - Slice vegetables for stir-fry
   - Boil water for rice
2. While rice simmers:
   - Cook steak and vegetables

Taking Issue

Millions of readers turn to culinary magazines to find great recipes and learn about food trends and tips. Here's how we do it at *Cooking Light*.

On most weekdays, the editors, chefs, and other staffers at *Cooking Light* meet at noon around the big maple table in the Test Kitchens to taste and discuss a recipe's merits—or lack thereof. It's a democratic process, and recipes are rated from one to three (our highest accolade). We confer about everything from the ingredients (Do all of them contribute to the flavor of the dish, and will any of them be difficult for readers to find?) to the procedure (Should we streamline the number of steps, or alter the method to enhance the final product?). A recipe makes it into the magazine if it's delicious, meets our nutritional criteria, looks appetizing, and, finally, merits the effort and expense it will take a reader to prepare at home.

"Our Test Kitchens are an incredibly creative, collaborative, and busy place," says Editor in Chief Mary Kay Culpepper. "The math tells the story: We publish more than 1,000 recipes a year. Many of those recipes must be tested a few times before they pass. Then they have to be prepared for photography. It means our team prepares nearly 5,000 recipes a year."

Most of our recipes are provided by the dozens of developers we work with, who are scattered all over the world. Some of our recipes are developed by food editors and Test Kitchens professionals, who share some of their favorites here.

QUICK & EASY
Grilled Grouper with Browned Butter-Orange Couscous

"We used a stainless steel pan, which makes it easier to watch the browning process and prevent the butter from burning, but a dark-surface nonstick skillet can be used as well."

—Kathryn Conrad

COUSCOUS:
2 tablespoons butter
¼ cup slivered almonds
1 cup uncooked couscous
1 (14-ounce) can fat-free, less-sodium chicken broth
½ cup coarsely chopped orange sections
¼ cup pomegranate seeds
3 tablespoons chopped fresh parsley
¼ teaspoon salt

GROUPER:
¼ teaspoon salt
½ teaspoon coriander seeds
½ teaspoon black peppercorns
Dash of ground red pepper
4 (6-ounce) grouper fillets
Cooking spray

1. To prepare couscous, melt butter in a large stainless steel skillet over medium-high heat. Add almonds; sauté 2 minutes or until almonds are toasted and butter is lightly browned. Add couscous. Cook 1 minute; stir constantly. Remove from heat.
2. Bring broth to a boil in a medium saucepan over high heat. Gradually add broth to couscous mixture in pan; cover and let stand 5 minutes. Fluff with a fork. Stir in oranges, pomegranate seeds, parsley, and ¼ teaspoon salt.
3. To prepare grouper, place ¼ teaspoon salt, coriander, peppercorns, and red pepper in a spice or coffee grinder; process until finely ground. Rub spice mixture evenly over fish.
4. Heat a grill pan over medium-high heat. Coat pan with cooking spray. Arrange fillets in pan; cook 4 minutes. Turn fillets over; cook 4 minutes or until fish flakes easily when tested with a fork or until desired degree of doneness. Serve with couscous. Yield: 4 servings (serving size: 1 fillet and 1 cup couscous).

CALORIES 453 (24% from fat); FAT 12.1g (sat 3.6g, mono 5.5g, poly 1.8g); PROTEIN 42.2g; CARB 42g; FIBER 3.9g; CHOL 78mg; IRON 2.6mg; SODIUM 704mg; CALC 95mg

WINE NOTE: Oranges in the couscous and ground coriander on the fish are the biggest factors to consider. Try a riesling from Washington State. Like the dish, it is light yet bold; its subtle sweetness balances the intensity of the coriander. Try Chateau Ste. Michelle 2004 Johannisberg Riesling from Washington's Columbia Valley ($10).

Warm Cabbage Salad with Bacon and Blue Cheese

"Bacon drippings add flavor to the sautéed shallots, and the bacon crumbles are the finishing touch on top of the salad. A simple reduction of the cider concentrates the apple essence in the dressing."

—Kathryn Conrad

3 bacon slices
1 tablespoon peeled chopped shallot (about 1 small)
2 cups apple cider
¼ teaspoon salt
¼ teaspoon black pepper
1½ ounces Roquefort or other blue cheese, crumbled (about ⅓ cup)
8 cups shredded cabbage
½ cup diced red bell pepper

1. Cook bacon in a Dutch oven over medium-high heat until crisp. Remove bacon from pan, reserving 1 teaspoon drippings in pan. Crumble bacon; set aside.

Continued

2. Heat drippings over medium-high heat. Add shallot; sauté 1 minute. Remove from heat.

3. Bring cider to a boil in a small saucepan over medium heat; cook until reduced to ¼ cup (about 15 minutes). Remove from heat. Add shallot mixture, salt, and pepper. Place cider mixture and cheese in a blender or small food processor; process until smooth.

4. Combine cabbage and bell pepper in a large bowl; drizzle cider mixture over cabbage mixture, tossing well to coat. Top with crumbled bacon. Serve immediately. Yield: 6 servings (serving size: 1 cup).

CALORIES 118 (28% from fat); FAT 3.7g (sat 1.8g, mono 1.2g, poly 0.3g); PROTEIN 4.6g; CARB 18.4g; FIBER 0.1g; CHOL 10mg; IRON 0.8mg; SODIUM 317mg; CALC 94mg

STAFF FAVORITE
Chicken and Dumplings from Scratch

"I wanted to create a chicken and dumplings recipe that was creamy, rich, and thick without all of the fat of traditional versions. Thickening the base was the challenge. Relying solely on cornstarch produced a gluey consistency and thin flavor, and using all flour created pasty results. So I settled for a little of each to achieve the thickness and texture I wanted. Toasting the flour, a process similar to making a dry roux, added some richness. Then I finished the dish with a splash of cream for flavor."

—Kathryn Conrad

STEW:
- 1 (4-pound) whole chicken
- 3 quarts water
- 3 cups chopped onion
- 1 cup chopped celery
- 1 cup chopped carrot
- 1 teaspoon salt
- ¼ teaspoon freshly ground black pepper
- 10 garlic cloves, peeled
- 4 thyme sprigs
- 2 bay leaves
- ¼ cup all-purpose flour (about 1 ounce)
- 2 teaspoons cornstarch
- 3 tablespoons heavy cream

DUMPLINGS:
- ¾ cup 1% low-fat milk
- 1 large egg
- 1½ cups all-purpose flour (about 6¾ ounces)
- 1 tablespoon baking powder
- 1 tablespoon cornmeal
- ½ teaspoon salt

REMAINING INGREDIENTS:
- 1 tablespoon chopped parsley
- Freshly ground black pepper

1. To prepare stew, remove and discard giblets and neck from chicken. Rinse chicken with cold water; place chicken in an 8-quart stockpot. Add 3 quarts water and next 8 ingredients; bring to a boil. Reduce heat, and simmer 45 minutes; skim surface occasionally, discarding solids. Remove chicken from pot; cool. Strain stock through a sieve into a large bowl; discard solids. Remove chicken meat from bones; tear into 2-inch pieces, and store in refrigerator. Cool stock to room temperature.

2. Pour stock into two zip-top plastic bags. Let stand 15 minutes. Working with one bag at a time, snip off a corner of bag; drain liquid into stockpot, stopping before fat layer reaches opening. Discard fat. Repeat procedure with remaining bag. Bring stock to a boil over medium-high heat; reduce heat, and simmer until reduced to 8 cups (about 15 minutes).

3. Heat a cast-iron skillet over medium-high heat 5 minutes. Lightly spoon ¼ cup flour into a dry measuring cup; level with a knife. Add flour to pan; cook 1 minute or until lightly browned, stirring constantly. Combine browned flour and cornstarch in a large bowl; add ⅔ cup stock to flour mixture, stirring with a whisk until smooth. Add flour mixture to remaining stock in pan; bring to a boil over medium-high heat. Cook 2 minutes or until slightly thickened. Reduce heat; stir in cream. Add chicken; keep warm over low heat.

4. To prepare dumplings, combine milk and egg in a medium bowl. Lightly spoon 1½ cups flour into dry measuring cups; level with a knife. Combine flour, baking powder, cornmeal, and ½ teaspoon salt.

Add flour mixture to milk mixture, stirring with a fork just until dry ingredients are moistened.

5. Drop one-third dumpling batter by 8 heaping teaspoonfuls onto chicken mixture. Cover and cook 3 minutes or until dumplings are done (do not allow chicken mixture to boil). Remove dumplings with a slotted spoon; place in a large serving bowl or on a deep serving platter; keep warm. Repeat procedure with remaining dumpling batter.

6. Remove pan from heat; slowly pour stew over dumplings. Sprinkle with chopped parsley and freshly ground black pepper. Serve immediately. Yield: 6 servings (serving size: 1⅓ cups stew and 4 dumplings).

CALORIES 334 (21% from fat); FAT 7.9g (sat 3.2g, mono 2.4g, poly 1.2g); PROTEIN 31.4g; CARB 32.2g; FIBER 1.2g; CHOL 130mg; IRON 3.3mg; SODIUM 755mg; CALC 211mg

Cranberry-Apple Crisp with Cinnamon-Maple Cream

"The topping is an easy alternative to making a pastry crust. Cooking the fruit on the stovetop ensures that it is tender when the topping is browned. I prefer using dark brown sugar with the assertive spices and brandy in the filling, but the light variety will work as well."

—Jan Moon

MAPLE CREAM:
- 2 cups frozen reduced-calorie whipped topping, thawed
- 1 teaspoon maple syrup
- ⅛ teaspoon ground cinnamon

FILLING:
- ¾ cup dried cranberries
- 3 tablespoons brandy
- Cooking spray
- 6 cups chopped peeled Granny Smith apple (about 2½ pounds)
- 2 tablespoons fresh lemon juice
- ¼ cup granulated sugar
- ¼ cup packed dark brown sugar
- 2 teaspoons all-purpose flour
- 1 teaspoon ground cinnamon
- 1 teaspoon finely grated orange rind
- ¼ teaspoon salt
- ⅛ teaspoon ground nutmeg

TOPPING:

- ⅔ cup all-purpose flour (about 3 ounces)
- ⅓ cup packed dark brown sugar
- ¼ teaspoon salt
- ¼ cup chilled butter, cut into small pieces
- ⅔ cup regular oats
- 2 tablespoons walnuts, toasted and finely chopped

1. Preheat oven to 375°.

2. To prepare maple cream, combine whipped topping, maple syrup, and cinnamon. Cover and chill.

3. To prepare filling, combine cranberries and brandy in a small bowl. Microwave at HIGH 30 seconds; set aside.

4. Heat a large nonstick skillet over medium-high heat. Coat pan with cooking spray. Add apple and juice; sauté 3 minutes. Stir in cranberry mixture, granulated sugar, and next 6 ingredients. Spoon apple mixture into an 11 x 7-inch baking dish or shallow 2-quart baking dish coated with cooking spray.

5. To prepare topping, lightly spoon ⅔ cup flour into a dry measuring cup; level with a knife. Combine flour, ⅓ cup brown sugar, and ¼ teaspoon salt in a bowl; cut in butter with a pastry blender or 2 knives until mixture is crumbly. Add oats and walnuts; toss well. Sprinkle over apple mixture.

6. Bake at 375° for 30 minutes or until bubbly and topping is browned. Serve with maple cream. Yield: 12 servings (serving size: ½ cup crisp and about 2½ tablespoons cream).

CALORIES 265 (23% from fat); FAT 6.7g (sat 3.5g, mono 1.9g, poly 1g); PROTEIN 2.7g; CARB 47.9g; FIBER 3g; CHOL 10mg; IRON 1.1mg; SODIUM 130mg; CALC 25mg

Shrimp Fritters with Spicy Moroccan Dipping Sauce

"The spice mixture in the dipping sauce is similar to a zesty Moroccan spice blend called *ras-el-hanout*. You can use the remaining spice mixture as a rub for pork and lamb. Panko, breadcrumbs used in Japanese cooking, can be found at Asian markets or in your supermarket's ethnic-food aisle. "

—Mary Drennen

FRITTERS:

- Cooking spray
- 1 cup thinly sliced leek (about 1 large)
- 1½ teaspoons minced peeled fresh ginger
- 1 tablespoon chopped fresh cilantro
- 1 tablespoon chopped fresh mint
- 12 large shrimp, peeled and deveined (about ½ pound)
- 24 gyoza skins
- 1 tablespoon water
- 1 large egg
- ½ cup panko (Japanese) breadcrumbs
- 4 teaspoons all-purpose flour
- 2 teaspoons olive oil, divided

DIPPING SAUCE:

- ½ teaspoon olive oil
- 2 tablespoons minced shallots
- 1 teaspoon Moroccan Spice Blend
- ½ cup red wine
- 1 tablespoon rice vinegar
- ¾ cup fat-free, less-sodium chicken broth
- 2 tablespoons low-sodium soy sauce
- ¼ teaspoon cornstarch
- 1 teaspoon water

1. Heat a large nonstick skillet over medium-high heat. Coat pan with cooking spray. Add leek to pan; cook 4 minutes or until slightly tender. Add ginger; sauté 1 minute. Remove leek mixture from pan; set aside. Wipe pan dry with a paper towel. Combine cilantro and mint in a small bowl.

2. Cut each shrimp in half lengthwise. Place 2 shrimp halves, 2 teaspoons leek mixture, and ½ teaspoon cilantro mixture on 1 gyoza skin (cover remaining gyoza skins to prevent drying). Moisten edges of skin with water; top with another gyoza skin. Repeat procedure with remaining shrimp halves, leek mixture, cilantro mixture, and gyoza skins (cover shrimp packets with a damp towel to prevent drying). Combine 1 tablespoon water and egg in a small bowl, stirring with a whisk. Place panko in a small bowl; place flour in another small bowl. Dip each shrimp packet in flour; dip in egg mixture, and dredge in panko. Place packets on a baking sheet.

3. Heat 1 teaspoon oil in a large nonstick skillet coated with cooking spray over medium-high heat. Add 6 packets to pan. Cook 3 minutes on each side or until browned; remove from pan. Repeat procedure with 1 teaspoon oil and remaining packets; wipe pan dry with a paper towel.

4. To prepare dipping sauce, heat ½ teaspoon oil in pan. Add shallots; sauté 3 minutes or until tender. Add 1 teaspoon Moroccan Spice Blend; cook 1 minute. Add red wine and vinegar, scraping bottom of pan to loosen browned bits; bring to a boil. Cook until reduced to ½ cup (about 3 minutes). Add broth and soy sauce; cook until reduced to ½ cup (about 3 minutes). Combine cornstarch and 1 teaspoon water; add cornstarch mixture to pan. Cook 30 seconds or until slightly thickened, stirring constantly. Serve dipping sauce with fritters. Yield: 4 servings (serving size: 3 fritters and 2 tablespoons dipping sauce).

(Totals include Moroccan Spice Blend) CALORIES 354 (17% from fat); FAT 6.7g (sat 1.3g, mono 3g, poly 1.5g); PROTEIN 21.3g; CARB 46.1g; FIBER 2.4g; CHOL 143mg; IRON 5.1mg; SODIUM 821mg; CALC 109mg

QUICK & EASY • MAKE AHEAD

MOROCCAN SPICE BLEND:

- 1½ teaspoons freshly ground black pepper
- 1 teaspoon ground ginger
- 1 teaspoon ground cumin
- 1 teaspoon ground cinnamon
- 1 teaspoon ground coriander
- ¼ teaspoon grated whole nutmeg
- ⅛ teaspoon ground cardamom
- ⅛ teaspoon ground cloves

1. Combine all ingredients in a small bowl. Store spice mixture in an airtight container. Yield: 2 tablespoons (serving size: 1 teaspoon).

CALORIES 7 (26% from fat); FAT 0.2g (sat 0g, mono 0g, poly 0g); PROTEIN 0.2g; CARB 1.3g; FIBER 1g; CHOL 0mg; IRON 0.4mg; SODIUM 1mg; CALC 12mg

Tips from the Test Kitchens

When it comes to making food delicious and light, our Test Kitchens professionals have learned all the tricks. And they share some of them with the recipes in this story.

Use the right technique. Often, flavor comes from how food is cooked as much as from the food itself. Toasting flour to make a dry roux for the Chicken and Dumplings from Scratch (recipe on page 440) lends the finished product deep flavor. Roasting caramelizes and intensifies the flavor of vegetables (butternut squash is a terrific example) without lots of extra fat. Reducing liquid ingredients, such as cider, broth, and sauces, also magnifies flavor.

Try new ingredients. Once-hard-to-find ethnic foods are now readily available in supermarkets and superstores. And many are surprisingly versatile. One of our favorites: panko (Japanese bread-crumbs), which we use to give a crunchy coating to oven-fried chicken or Shrimp Fritters with Spicy Moroccan Dipping Sauce (recipe on page 441).

Flavor with fat intelligently. Anyone who is familiar with *Cooking Light* recipes knows we're fond of bacon and its Italian cousin, pancetta. A little of either goes a long way to infuse a dish with smokiness, as in the Warm Cabbage Salad with Bacon and Blue Cheese (recipe on page 439). In our Test Kitchens, we opt for high-flavor cheeses like blue, Parmesan, feta, and sharp Cheddar. And we know that stirring in a little cream or butter at the end of cooking a soup or sauce also adds body without loading up on fat. We can use these items in our kitchens—and recommend them to our

readers—because whenever possible, we use full-fat ingredients judiciously. In Risotto with Porcini Mushrooms and Mascarpone (recipe on page 443), for example, just ¼ cup of each cheese endows the dish with luscious texture.

Rely on quality. High-caliber products help ensure good results. For example, we use a top-notch name-brand butter in our Test Kitchens. (Organic and European butters are good, too.) It's not because we're food chauvinists. We've found that substituting a generic brand of butter can yield a less-than-spectacular result, says Test Kitchens Director Vanessa Johnson, because these products may have a higher water content than their name-brand counterparts. "For that reason, we never swap real butter for margarine," she says.

Embrace reduced- and nonfat products, too. To keep fat and calories in check, we often turn to lower-fat versions of cream cheese, yogurt, milk, sour cream, and cheese. Egg substitute is another option. Often, the secret to using these products successfully is combining them with small amounts of full-fat ingredients. Chicken and Dumplings from Scratch (recipe on page 440) pairs 1% low-fat milk with a few tablespoons of heavy cream for a richer texture.

Balance the flavors. When flavor seems flat, most people reach for the saltshaker. But because we watch the sodium content of a recipe as closely as the fat, we may add a smidgen of acid (in the form of citrus juice or vinegar), sugar, or heat (from peppers or hot sauce) to balance the overall flavor of a dish.

Our goal is to inspire, teach, and entertain readers whenever we can.

Spicy Collard Greens

"A smoked turkey wing gives this vegetable side dish its robust flavor. The meaty flavor of the turkey bone is drawn out during the long simmering time for the collard greens (similar to the way chicken or beef bones infuse a stock with flavor). The dried Anaheim chile is red in color, distinguishing it from the fresh green Anaheim. Heatwise, both are rather mild."

—Kathryn Conrad

- 1 smoked turkey wing, skinned
- ½ teaspoon olive oil
- 1 dried Anaheim chile, stemmed and chopped (about 3 tablespoons)
- 1 cup chopped onion
- 1 garlic clove, minced
- 1 (16-ounce) package collard greens, chopped
- ½ teaspoon salt
- ½ teaspoon crushed red pepper
- ¼ teaspoon freshly ground black pepper
- 2 teaspoons lemon juice

1. Remove meat from turkey wing; chop and reserve ½ cup. Reserve remaining turkey meat for another use. Separate wing bone at the joint; reserve drumstick portion of wing. Discard remaining bones.

2. Heat oil in a Dutch oven over medium-high heat. Add chile; sauté 30 seconds. Add onion; sauté 2 minutes. Add garlic; sauté 30 seconds. Add reserved drumstick bone, greens, salt, red pepper, and black pepper to pot; cover with water to 1 inch above greens. Bring to a boil over medium-high heat; reduce heat, and simmer, uncovered, 2 hours.

3. Drain greens in a colander over a bowl, reserving cooking liquid. Discard turkey bone. Return cooking liquid to pan; cook over high heat until reduced to ¾ cup (about 40 minutes). Add greens and reserved ½ cup chopped turkey to pan; reduce heat, and cook 3 minutes or until thoroughly heated, stirring frequently. Stir in lemon juice. Serve warm. Yield: 6 servings (serving size: ¾ cup).

CALORIES 54 (17% from fat); FAT 1g (sat 0.5g, mono 0.3g, poly 0.1g); PROTEIN 4.8g; CARB 6g; FIBER 2.1g; CHOL 12mg; IRON 0.4mg; SODIUM 358mg; CALC 75mg

Key Lime Brûlées

"Regular limes can be used for Key limes."
—Ann Taylor Pittman

- ¾ cup 2% reduced-fat milk
- ½ cup sugar
- ½ cup half-and-half
- 3 tablespoons fresh Key lime juice or lime juice
- 3 large egg yolks
- 1 large egg
- 3 tablespoons sugar

1. Preheat oven to 325°.

2. Combine milk, sugar, and half-and-half in a small, heavy saucepan. Heat mixture over medium heat to 180° or until tiny bubbles form around edge (do not boil), stirring occasionally. Remove from heat.

3. Combine lime juice, egg yolks, and egg in a medium bowl; stir well with a whisk. Gradually add hot milk mixture to egg mixture, stirring constantly with a whisk.

4. Divide mixture evenly among 6 (4-ounce) ramekins or custard cups. Place ramekins in a 13 x 9-inch baking pan; add hot water to pan to a depth of 1 inch. Bake at 325° for 30 minutes or until center barely moves when ramekin is touched. Remove ramekins from pan; cool completely on a wire rack. Cover and chill 4 hours or overnight.

5. Carefully sift 1½ teaspoons sugar over each custard. Holding a kitchen blowtorch about 2 inches from top of each custard, heat sugar, moving torch back and forth, until sugar is completely melted and caramelized (about 1 minute). Serve custards immediately. Yield: 6 servings (serving size: 1 custard).

NOTE: If you don't have a kitchen torch, you can make the sugar topping on the stovetop. Place ¼ cup sugar and 1 tablespoon water in a small, heavy saucepan. Cook over medium heat 5 to 8 minutes or until golden. (Resist the urge to stir, since doing so may cause the sugar to crystallize.) Immediately pour the sugar mixture evenly over cold custards, spreading to form a thin layer.

CALORIES 172 (29% from fat); FAT 5.6g (sat 2.8g, mono 2.1g, poly 0.5g); PROTEIN 4.1g; CARB 26.1g; FIBER 0g; CHOL 150mg; IRON 0.4mg; SODIUM 41mg; CALC 80mg

Risotto with Porcini Mushrooms and Mascarpone

"Mascarpone is a buttery-rich cheese that gives risotto its luxurious creamy consistency."
—Kathleen Kanen

- 1½ cups boiling water
- ½ cup dried porcini mushrooms (about ½ ounce)
- 1 (14-ounce) can less-sodium beef broth
- Cooking spray
- 1 cup uncooked Arborio rice or other short-grain rice
- ¾ cup chopped shallots
- 2 garlic cloves, minced
- ½ cup dry white wine
- ¼ cup (2 ounces) grated Parmigiano-Reggiano cheese
- ¼ cup (1 ounce) mascarpone cheese
- 1 tablespoon chopped fresh or 1 teaspoon dried thyme
- ½ teaspoon salt
- ½ teaspoon freshly ground black pepper

1. Combine boiling water and mushrooms; let stand 10 minutes or until soft. Drain in a colander over a bowl. Reserve 1¼ cups soaking liquid; chop mushrooms.

2. Bring soaking liquid and broth to a simmer in a small saucepan (do not boil). Keep broth mixture warm over low heat.

3. Heat a large saucepan over medium-high heat. Coat pan with cooking spray. Add rice, shallots, and garlic; sauté 5 minutes. Add wine; cook until liquid evaporates (about 2 minutes).

4. Add 1 cup broth mixture to rice mixture; cook over medium heat 5 minutes or until the liquid is nearly absorbed, stirring occasionally. Add remaining broth mixture, ½ cup at a time, stirring occasionally until each portion of broth mixture is absorbed before adding next (about 25 minutes total). Add mushrooms, cheeses, thyme, salt, and pepper; stir gently just until cheese melts. Serve warm. Yield: 4 servings (serving size: 1 cup).

CALORIES 198 (28% from fat); FAT 6.1g (sat 3.2g, mono 1g, poly 0.3g); PROTEIN 8.9g; CARB 27g; FIBER 1.2g; CHOL 15mg; IRON 1.9mg; SODIUM 449mg; CALC 113mg

Overnight Caramel French Toast

"This is one of my favorite holiday brunch dishes because it can be prepared the night before and popped in the oven to bake the next morning. I adapted it from a family favorite by reducing the amount of butter and eggs, and switching to low-fat milk; it still tastes decadent and rich."
—Vanessa Johnson

- 1 cup packed light brown sugar
- ½ cup light-colored corn syrup
- ¼ cup butter
- Cooking spray
- 10 (1-ounce) slices French bread (soft bread such as Pepperidge Farm)
- 2½ cups 1% low-fat milk
- 1 tablespoon all-purpose flour
- 1½ teaspoons vanilla extract
- ¼ teaspoon salt
- 2 large eggs
- 2 tablespoons granulated sugar
- 1 teaspoon ground cinnamon

1. Combine first 3 ingredients in a small saucepan. Cook over medium heat 5 minutes or until mixture is bubbly, stirring constantly. Pour mixture into a 13 x 9-inch baking dish coated with cooking spray, spreading evenly.

2. Arrange bread slices in a single layer over syrup in dish.

3. Combine milk and next 4 ingredients in a large bowl, stirring with a whisk. Pour egg mixture over bread. Cover and refrigerate 8 hours or overnight.

4. Preheat oven to 350°.

5. Combine 2 tablespoons granulated sugar and cinnamon. Sprinkle evenly over bread.

6. Bake at 350° for 50 minutes or until golden. Let stand 5 minutes before serving. Yield: 10 servings (serving size: 1 piece).

CALORIES 314 (21% from fat); FAT 7.2g (sat 3.2g, mono 2.8g, poly 0.6g); PROTEIN 6.2g; CARB 57.4g; FIBER 1.1g; CHOL 57mg; IRON 1.6mg; SODIUM 360mg; CALC 128mg

Home for the Holidays

A celebration of a white Christmas in New England, where yuletide rituals and food span generations.

Lobster Bisque

Lobster shells flavor the broth in this dish, while potato adds body. Finished with a splash of brandy, this rich soup is most satisfying as a first course.

- 5 cups water, divided
- 2 cups clam juice
- ¾ cup dry white wine, divided
- 2 (1¼-pound) whole Maine lobsters
- 1½ cups chopped carrot, divided
- 1½ cups chopped celery, divided
- 1½ cups chopped onion, divided
- 1 cup chopped fennel bulb, divided
- 1 cup fat-free, less-sodium chicken broth
- 1 teaspoon dried tarragon
- ½ teaspoon dried thyme
- 5 fresh parsley sprigs
- 2 bay leaves
- 1½ tablespoons butter
- 2 garlic cloves, minced
- 2 tablespoons all-purpose flour
- 1 cup chopped peeled baking potato
- 1 (14.5-ounce) can diced tomatoes, drained
- 1 cup fat-free milk
- ¼ cup whipping cream
- 2 tablespoons brandy
- Chive sprigs (optional)

1. Combine 3 cups water, clam juice, and ½ cup wine in an 8-quart stockpot; bring to a boil. Add lobsters; cover and cook 10 minutes or until bright red. Remove lobsters from pan, reserving liquid in pan. Cool lobsters. Remove meat from tail and claws. Discard any roe or tomalley. Chop meat; chill until ready to use. Place lobster shells in pan. Add remaining 2 cups water, 1 cup carrot, 1 cup celery, 1 cup onion, ½ cup fennel, broth, tarragon, thyme, parsley, and bay leaves; bring to a boil. Reduce heat, and simmer, partially covered, 1½ hours. Strain through a fine sieve into a bowl; discard solids, and reserve broth.

2. Melt butter in pan over medium heat; add remaining ½ cup carrot, remaining ½ cup celery, remaining ½ cup onion, remaining ½ cup fennel, and garlic; sauté 5 minutes. Add remaining ¼ cup wine; cook 3 minutes or until liquid almost evaporates. Sprinkle flour over carrot mixture; cook 1 minute, stirring constantly. Stir in reserved broth and potato; cook 20 minutes or until potato is tender. Add tomatoes; cook 10 minutes. Place one-third of mixture in a blender; process until smooth. Pour puréed mixture into a large bowl. Repeat procedure with remaining mixture. Return puréed mixture to pan. Stir in lobster, milk, cream, and brandy; cook 5 minutes over medium-low heat or until thoroughly heated (do not boil). Garnish with chive sprigs, if desired. Yield: 12 servings (serving size: ⅔ cup).

CALORIES 153 (24% from fat); FAT 4.1g (sat 2g, mono 1.3g, poly 0.3g); PROTEIN 16.3g; CARB 9g; FIBER 1.4g; CHOL 84mg; IRON 0.8mg; SODIUM 407mg; CALC 83mg

Coriander and Black Pepper-Crusted Rib Roast with Roasted Onions

Coriander lends subtle but exotic flavor to this homey favorite. Use a meat thermometer to ensure the roast is cooked to your liking, and remember its internal temperature will rise another five to 10 degrees as it stands. The longer the meat rests, the more juice it will retain.

- 1 (5-pound) rib-eye roast, trimmed
- 1 teaspoon salt
- 1 tablespoon Dijon mustard
- 1 tablespoon honey
- 1 tablespoon ground coriander
- 1½ teaspoons freshly ground black pepper
- 1 teaspoon garlic powder
- Cooking spray
- 6 cups thinly sliced Rio or other sweet onion (about 5 large)
- 1 teaspoon dried rosemary
- 1 teaspoon sugar
- 6 garlic cloves, sliced
- ½ cup less-sodium beef broth
- Parsley sprigs (optional)
- Sage sprigs (optional)
- Rosemary sprigs (optional)
- Small pears (optional)
- Orange wedges (optional)

1. Preheat oven to 450°.

2. Sprinkle roast with salt. Combine mustard and honey in a small bowl; rub over roast to coat.

3. Combine coriander, pepper, and garlic powder in a small bowl. Sprinkle evenly over roast. Place roast in a roasting pan coated with cooking spray.

4. Bake at 450° for 20 minutes. Reduce oven temperature to 300° (do not remove roast from oven), and bake 1½ hours or until a thermometer inserted into center of roast registers 135°. Remove from oven, and tent loosely with foil. Let stand at least 15 minutes before cutting into thin slices.

5. While roast bakes, heat a large non-stick skillet over medium-high heat. Coat pan with cooking spray. Add onion and next 3 ingredients; cook 20 minutes or until onions are golden brown, stirring occasionally. Stir in broth, scraping pan to loosen browned bits. Add onion mixture to roasting pan for last 15 minutes of baking time. Garnish with parsley, sage, rosemary, pears, and orange wedges, if desired. Yield: 12 servings (serving size: 3 ounces beef and about ¼ cup onions).

CALORIES 321 (47% from fat); FAT 16.8g (sat 6.7g, mono 6.7g, poly 0.9g); PROTEIN 34.4g; CARB 9g; FIBER 1.2g; CHOL 83mg; IRON 3.3mg; SODIUM 336mg; CALC 21mg

Cranberry-Studded Whipped Butter

½ cup boiling water
¼ cup finely chopped dried
   cranberries
6 tablespoons (2 ounces) light
   whipped butter, softened
2 tablespoons whipping cream
2 teaspoons powdered sugar

1. Combine water and cranberries; let stand 5 minutes. Drain and cool.
2. Combine cranberries and remaining ingredients in a small bowl; stir until blended. Spoon into a decorative bowl, and refrigerate until ready to serve. Yield: 12 servings (serving size: about 2½ teaspoons).

CALORIES 42 (74% from fat); FAT 3.5g (sat 2.2g, mono 1g, poly 0.1g); PROTEIN 0.2g; CARB 2.6g; FIBER 0.1g; CHOL 98mg; IRON 0.1mg; SODIUM 505mg; CALC 4mg

Roasted Brussels Sprouts with Chestnuts

Chestnuts, in season through February, are perennially associated with the holidays. Bottled chestnuts are a timesaver.

1½ cups thinly sliced onion
¾ cup (½ x 1½-inch) julienne-cut
   red bell pepper
3 tablespoons extravirgin olive oil
1¼ teaspoons salt
½ teaspoon freshly ground black
   pepper
½ teaspoon caraway seeds
3 pounds Brussels sprouts, trimmed
   and halved (about 10 cups)
8 garlic cloves, thinly sliced
Cooking spray
1 (8.5-ounce) bottle chestnuts,
   coarsely chopped

1. Preheat oven to 400°.
2. Combine first 8 ingredients in a large bowl, tossing to coat. Spread onto a large roasting pan coated with cooking spray. Bake at 400° for 25 minutes, stirring occasionally. Add chestnuts; stir well. Bake 8 minutes or until vegetables

are tender. Serve immediately. Yield: 12 servings (serving size: about ⅔ cup).

CALORIES 129 (28% from fat); FAT 4g (sat 0.6g, mono 2.8g, poly 0.5g); PROTEIN 5g; CARB 21.6g; FIBER 4.7g; CHOL 0mg; IRON 1.9mg; SODIUM 272mg; CALC 60mg

Cardamom Pork Roast with Apples and Figs

While the ingredient list is long, this fruited roast is actually simple to make.

ROAST:
3 tablespoons brown sugar
1 teaspoon garlic powder
1 teaspoon ground cumin
1 teaspoon ground cinnamon
½ teaspoon salt
½ teaspoon ground ginger
½ teaspoon freshly ground black
   pepper
¼ teaspoon ground cardamom
¼ teaspoon ground fennel
1 (3-pound) pork loin, trimmed
Cooking spray
2 cups dried figs, halved lengthwise
2 cups dried apples
¼ cup minced crystallized ginger
¾ cup pear nectar
1 (14-ounce) can fat-free,
   less-sodium chicken broth

SAUCE:
½ cup pear nectar
½ cup port
2 tablespoons currant jelly
¼ cup heavy cream

1. Preheat oven to 400°.
2. To prepare roast, combine first 9 ingredients in a small bowl. Rub mixture over surface of roast; place in a shallow roasting pan coated with cooking spray.
3. Place figs, apples, and crystallized ginger around roast. Pour ¾ cup nectar and broth over fruit. Bake at 400° for 1 hour and 10 minutes or until meat thermometer registers 160°, stirring fruit frequently. Remove from oven; place roast on a carving board, and place fruit in a bowl using a slotted spoon.
4. To prepare sauce, pour any pan juices into a saucepan. Add ½ cup pear nectar,

port, and jelly; bring to a boil. Cook 4 minutes or until thick enough to lightly coat back of a spoon. Stir in heavy cream; simmer 2 minutes or until sauce has thickened, stirring occasionally. Yield: 12 servings (serving size: 3 ounces pork, ¼ cup fruit, and about 1½ tablespoons sauce).

CALORIES 363 (18% from fat); FAT 7.3g (sat 3g, mono 2.6g, poly 0.6g); PROTEIN 26g; CARB 46.4g; FIBER 4.9g; CHOL 82mg; IRON 2.8mg; SODIUM 212mg; CALC 61mg

WINE NOTE: Here's a dish that begs for riesling from Alsace, France. In general, the white wines of Alsace are known for their affinity for pork dishes. But in particular, both the acidity and the fruitiness of riesling make it a star pick when flavors go several directions—sweet (figs), spicy (cardamom), herbal (fennel), and exotic (ginger) all at the same time. Try the Hugel et Fils Riesling 2003 from Alsace ($20).

Warm Chocolate Soufflé Cakes with Raspberry Sauce

You can make the sauce a day ahead and keep it refrigerated. Garnish the soufflés with fresh raspberries or mint, if desired.

SAUCE:
⅔ cup granulated sugar
¼ cup fresh orange juice
1 (12-ounce) package frozen
   unsweetened raspberries, thawed

CAKES:
Cooking spray
2 tablespoons granulated sugar
¾ cup fat-free milk
¼ cup half-and-half
2 ounces unsweetened chocolate,
   chopped
¼ cup unsweetened cocoa
1 teaspoon vanilla extract
1¼ cups granulated sugar, divided
¼ cup butter, softened
3 large egg yolks
¼ cup all-purpose flour (about 1 ounce)
¼ teaspoon cream of tartar
5 large egg whites
1 tablespoon powdered sugar

Continued

1. To prepare sauce, place first 3 ingredients in a food processor; process until smooth. Strain through a sieve into a bowl; discard solids. Cover and chill.

2. To prepare cakes, coat 12 (6-ounce) ramekins with cooking spray; sprinkle evenly with 2 tablespoons granulated sugar. Set aside.

3. Combine milk and half-and-half in a small saucepan. Bring to a simmer over medium-high heat (do not boil). Remove from heat; add chocolate, stirring until chocolate melts. Add cocoa and vanilla, stirring with a whisk. Pour into a large bowl; cool completely.

4. Preheat oven to 325°.

5. Place 1 cup granulated sugar and butter in a medium bowl; beat with a mixer at high speed until light and fluffy. Beat in egg yolks. Add cooled chocolate mixture; beat until blended. Lightly spoon flour into a dry measuring cup; level with a knife. Stir into chocolate mixture.

6. Place cream of tartar and egg whites in a large bowl; beat with a mixer at high speed until soft peaks form, using clean dry beaters. Gradually add remaining ¼ cup granulated sugar, 1 tablespoon at a time, beating until stiff peaks form. Gently stir one-fourth of egg white mixture into chocolate mixture; gently fold in remaining egg white mixture. Spoon into prepared ramekins.

7. Place ramekins in 2 (13 x 9-inch) baking pans; add hot water to pans to a depth of 1 inch. Bake at 325° for 33 minutes or until puffy and set. Loosen cakes from sides of ramekins using a narrow metal spatula. Invert cakes onto each of 12 dessert plates. Sprinkle evenly with powdered sugar; serve with raspberry sauce. Yield: 12 servings (serving size: 1 cake and 2 tablespoons sauce).

CALORIES 273 (27% from fat); FAT 8.1g (sat 4.3g, mono 2.3g, poly 0.4g); PROTEIN 4.5g; CARB 48.1g; FIBER 2.5g; CHOL 64mg; IRON 1.2mg; SODIUM 63mg; CALC 54mg

Hot Mulled Ginger-Spiced Cider

This recipe is prepared in an electric slow cooker, freeing up the stovetop. However, it can be heated in a pot on the stove, if you prefer.

    3 whole cloves
    2 (1 x 4-inch) strips orange rind
    2 whole allspice
    1 (3-inch) cinnamon stick
    1 (½-inch) piece peeled fresh ginger
   12 cups apple cider
    ½ cup apple jelly
    ¼ teaspoon ground nutmeg

1. Place first 5 ingredients on a 5-inch-square double layer of cheesecloth. Gather edges of cheesecloth together; tie securely.

2. Place cheesecloth bag, cider, jelly, and nutmeg in an electric slow cooker. Cover and cook at HIGH 4 hours. Remove and discard cheesecloth bag. Yield: 12 servings (serving size: 1 cup).

CALORIES 174 (0% from fat); FAT 0g; PROTEIN 1g; CARB 43.8g; FIBER 0g; CHOL 0mg; IRON 0mg; SODIUM 0mg; CALC 0mg

Eggnog

The combination of whole and evaporated low-fat milk helps achieve a slimmed-down version of the traditional holiday beverage.

    4 cups whole milk
    1 (12-ounce) can evaporated low-fat milk
    ½ cup sugar
    ¼ teaspoon ground cinnamon
    ⅛ teaspoon ground nutmeg
    6 large eggs
    ¼ cup brandy
    1 teaspoon vanilla extract

1. Place milk and evaporated milk in a large saucepan. Bring to a simmer over medium heat.

2. Combine sugar, cinnamon, nutmeg, and eggs in a large bowl. Gradually add hot milk to egg mixture, stirring constantly with a whisk. Return milk mixture to pan; cook over medium-low heat until thick (about 8 minutes), stirring constantly. Pour into a bowl; stir in brandy and vanilla. Press plastic wrap onto surface of eggnog, and chill 8 hours or overnight. Yield: 12 servings (serving size: about ½ cup).

CALORIES 152 (33% from fat); FAT 5.6g (sat 2.7g, mono 1.6g, poly 0.5g); PROTEIN 7.6g; CARB 15g; FIBER 0g; CHOL 118mg; IRON 0.5mg; SODIUM 101mg; CALC 168mg

Raisin-Stout Loaves

These hearty oval-shaped breads are delicious served with the slightly sweet Cranberry-Studded Whipped Butter (recipe on page 445). We used Guinness for the dough, but you can substitute another dark beer, such as Newcastle Brown Ale, if desired.

    ¾ cup golden raisins
    1 cup boiling water
    ½ cup warm water (100° to 110°)
    1 package dry yeast (about 2¼ teaspoons)
    5 tablespoons honey, divided
    1 cup stout or other dark beer, at room temperature
   3¼ cups all-purpose flour, divided (about 14½ ounces)
    1 cup whole-grain rye flour (about 4 ounces)
    2 teaspoons salt
    ½ cup coarsely chopped walnuts
   Cooking spray

1. Combine raisins and 1 cup boiling water in a small bowl; let stand 10 minutes. Drain and reserve raisins.

2. Combine warm water, yeast, and 1 tablespoon honey in a bowl; let stand 5 minutes or until bubbly. Stir in ¼ cup honey and beer.

3. Lightly spoon flours into dry measuring cups; level with a knife. Combine 3 cups all-purpose flour, rye flour, and salt in a large bowl; make a well in center of mixture. Add yeast mixture to flour mixture, stirring until a soft dough forms. Turn dough out onto a lightly floured surface. Knead until smooth and elastic

(about 7 minutes); add enough of remaining all-purpose flour, 1 tablespoon at a time, to prevent dough from sticking to hands (dough will feel sticky). Flatten dough; top with raisins and walnuts. Fold over dough sides to cover; knead until raisins and walnuts are well distributed. Place dough in a large bowl coated with cooking spray, turning to coat top. Cover and let rise in a warm place (85°), free from drafts, 1¼ hours or until doubled in size. (Gently press two fingers into dough. If indentation remains, dough has risen enough.)

4. Punch dough down; turn out onto a floured surface. Knead 1 minute; cover and let rest 5 minutes. Divide dough into 2 equal portions. Roll each portion into an 8-inch-long football shape. Place on a baking sheet lined with parchment paper. Cover and let rise 30 minutes or until doubled in size.

5. Preheat oven to 450°.

6. Uncover dough, and make 3 (¼-inch-deep) diagonal cuts across top of each loaf using a sharp knife. Bake at 450° for 10 minutes. Reduce oven temperature to 350° (do not remove loaves from oven); bake loaves 30 minutes or until browned on bottom and sound hollow when tapped. Cool on a wire rack 30 minutes before slicing. Yield: 2 loaves, 16 slices per loaf (serving size: 1 slice).

CALORIES 95 (13% from fat); FAT 1.4g (sat 0.1g, mono 0.3g, poly 0.8g); PROTEIN 2.7g; CARB 18.2g; FIBER 1.1g; CHOL 0mg; IRON 0.9mg; SODIUM 147mg; CALC 8mg

MAKE AHEAD
Classic Shrimp Cocktail with Red and Green Sauces

For convenience, make this dish ahead, and refrigerate until time to serve.

SHRIMP:
- 4 quarts water
- 1 tablespoon salt
- 2 tablespoons fresh lemon juice
- 1 onion, cut into 8 wedges
- 1 bay leaf
- 48 jumbo shrimp, peeled and deveined (about 2 pounds)

SALSA VERDE:
- 1½ cups packed fresh flat-leaf parsley leaves
- 1 cup packed fresh basil leaves
- 1½ tablespoons sliced almonds
- 3 tablespoons cold water
- 2 tablespoons extravirgin olive oil
- 2 tablespoons red wine vinegar
- 1 tablespoon capers, drained
- 2 teaspoons Dijon mustard
- ¼ teaspoon salt
- ⅛ teaspoon freshly ground black pepper
- 1 garlic clove, peeled

HORSERADISH SAUCE:
- ¾ cup bottled chili sauce (such as Heinz)
- ¼ cup ketchup
- 2 tablespoons prepared horseradish
- 2 tablespoons fresh lemon juice
- 3 drops hot pepper sauce (such as Tabasco; optional)

1. To prepare shrimp, combine first 5 ingredients in a Dutch oven. Bring to a boil and cook, covered, 5 minutes. Add shrimp; cook, uncovered, 3 minutes or until shrimp are done. Drain; discard bay leaf and onion. Rinse shrimp with cold water. Chill 1 hour.

2. To prepare salsa verde, combine flat-leaf parsley and next 10 ingredients in a blender. Process until smooth. Pour into a bowl; cover and chill.

3. To prepare horseradish sauce, combine chili sauce, ketchup, horseradish, and 2 tablespoons juice. Add hot pepper sauce, if desired. Cover and chill. Serve shrimp with sauces. Yield: 12 servings (4 shrimp, 1 tablespoon salsa verde, and about 1 tablespoon horseradish sauce).

CALORIES 136 (27% from fat); FAT 4.1g (sat 0.6g, mono 2.2g, poly 0.8g); PROTEIN 16.1g; CARB 7.9g; FIBER 0.5g; CHOL 115mg; IRON 2.5mg; SODIUM 512mg; CALC 60mg

Twisted Fennel and Coarse Salt Breadsticks

These golden breadsticks are both pretty and delicious. Keep the recipe in mind throughout the season—a batch makes a fine hostess gift.

- 1 tablespoon sugar
- 1 package dry yeast (about 2¼ teaspoons)
- 1 cup plus 2 tablespoons warm fat-free milk (100° to 110°)
- 3 tablespoons extravirgin olive oil
- 2¾ cups all-purpose flour (about 12⅓ ounces), divided
- ½ cup yellow cornmeal
- ¾ teaspoon salt
- Cooking spray
- 1 tablespoon water
- 1 egg white, lightly beaten
- 1 tablespoon fennel seeds
- 1½ teaspoons kosher salt

1. Dissolve sugar and yeast in warm milk in a bowl; let stand 5 minutes. Stir in olive oil.

2. Lightly spoon flour into dry measuring cups; level with a knife. Combine 2½ cups flour, cornmeal, and ¾ teaspoon salt in a large bowl. Add yeast mixture; stir until a soft dough forms. Turn dough out onto a lightly floured surface. Knead until smooth and elastic (about 10 minutes); add enough remaining flour, 1 tablespoon at a time, to prevent dough from sticking to hands (dough will feel sticky). Place dough in a large bowl coated with cooking spray, turning to coat top. Cover and let rise in a warm place (85°), free from drafts, 1 hour or until doubled in size. (Gently press two fingers into dough. If indentation remains, dough has risen enough.)

3. Line 2 baking sheets with parchment paper. Punch dough down; turn out onto a lightly floured surface. Divide dough into 24 equal portions. Working with 1 portion at a time (cover remaining portions to prevent drying), shape each portion into a 9-inch rope. Twist two ropes together; pinch ends to seal. Place on prepared baking sheets. Repeat with remaining dough. Cover dough, and let rise 30 minutes or until doubled in size.

4. Preheat oven to 425°.

5. Combine water and egg white in a small bowl. Combine fennel seeds and kosher salt in another bowl. Brush breadsticks with egg white mixture, and sprinkle evenly with fennel seed mixture. Bake at 425° for 15 minutes or until
Continued

puffed and lightly golden. Cool on a wire rack before serving. Yield: 12 servings (serving size: 1 breadstick).

CALORIES 164 (22% from fat); FAT 4g (sat 0.6g, mono 2.8g, poly 0.5g); PROTEIN 4.6g; CARB 27g; FIBER 1.5g; CHOL 0mg; IRON 1.7mg; SODIUM 399mg; CALC 58mg

Whipped Sweet Potatoes with Hazelnut Topping

Beaten egg whites give this version of sweet potato casserole a light texture beneath the sweet, nutty streusel. This side pairs well with beef, pork, or poultry.

⅓ cup packed brown sugar
1 teaspoon grated orange rind
1 tablespoon fresh orange juice
1 teaspoon salt
1½ teaspoons ground cinnamon
1 teaspoon ground nutmeg
¼ teaspoon ground allspice
3 (29-ounce) cans sweet potatoes, drained and halved
3 large egg whites
Cooking spray
½ cup chopped hazelnuts, toasted
½ cup packed brown sugar
¼ cup all-purpose flour (about 1 ounce)
¼ teaspoon ground cinnamon
3 tablespoons chilled butter, cut into small pieces

1. Preheat oven to 400°.
2. Combine first 8 ingredients in a large bowl; mash well. Beat egg whites with a mixer at high speed until stiff peaks form. Gently fold beaten egg whites into sweet potato mixture. Spoon mixture into a shallow 3-quart baking dish coated with cooking spray.
3. Combine hazelnuts and next 3 ingredients in a bowl. Cut in butter with a fork until mixture is crumbly. Sprinkle over sweet potato mixture. Bake at 400° for 25 minutes or until topping is lightly browned. Yield: 12 servings (serving size: about ⅔ cup).

CALORIES 248 (22% from fat); FAT 6.1g (sat 1.8g, mono 3.4g, poly 0.6g); PROTEIN 3.3g; CARB 46.2g; FIBER 4.1g; CHOL 8mg; IRON 1.8mg; SODIUM 293mg; CALC 44mg

Blue Ribbon Creation

A Greensboro, North Carolina, reader lightens classic Chicken Cordon Bleu.

When Marie Meyer's recipe came in the mail, it caught our attention. We don't often receive French-inspired recipes, since the classic form of the cuisine is typified by dishes rich with butter and cream. But with some culinary tweaking, Meyer was able to create a cordon bleu dish that is délicieuse.

Chicken Cordon Bleu

¼ cup fat-free, less-sodium chicken broth
5 teaspoons butter, melted
1 large garlic clove, minced
½ cup dry breadcrumbs
1 tablespoon grated fresh Parmigiano-Reggiano cheese
1 teaspoon paprika
4 (6-ounce) skinless, boneless chicken breast halves
¼ teaspoon salt
¼ teaspoon dried oregano
¼ teaspoon freshly ground black pepper
4 thin slices prosciutto (about 2 ounces)
¼ cup (1 ounce) shredded part-skim mozzarella cheese
Cooking spray

1. Preheat oven to 350°.
2. Place broth in a small microwave-safe bowl; microwave at HIGH 15 seconds or until warm. Stir in butter and garlic. Combine breadcrumbs, Parmigiano-Reggiano, and paprika in a medium shallow bowl; set aside.
3. Place each chicken breast half between 2 sheets of heavy-duty plastic wrap, and pound each to ¼-inch thickness using a meat mallet or rolling pin. Sprinkle both sides of chicken with salt, oregano, and pepper. Top each breast

half with 1 slice prosciutto and 1 tablespoon mozzarella. Roll up each breast half jelly-roll fashion. Dip each roll in chicken broth mixture; dredge in breadcrumb mixture. Place rolls, seam side down, in an 8-inch square baking dish coated with cooking spray. Pour remaining broth mixture over chicken. Bake at 350° for 28 minutes or until juices run clear and tops are golden. Yield: 4 servings (serving size: 1 rolled chicken breast half).

CALORIES 297 (30% from fat); FAT 9.9g (sat 4.4g, mono 3.6g, poly 1g); PROTEIN 45.5g; CARB 3.8g; FIBER 0.5g; CHOL 125mg; IRON 1.9mg; SODIUM 619mg; CALC 94mg

Orange-Coconut Bread

"This bread is good with a cup of tea and makes an easy on-the-go snack."
—Trisha Kruse, Eagle, Idaho

1 cup sugar
1 tablespoon canola oil
1 large egg
¼ cup 2% reduced-fat milk
1 (8-ounce) carton orange fat-free yogurt
2 cups all-purpose flour (about 9 ounces)
5 tablespoons flaked sweetened coconut, divided
2 teaspoons grated orange rind
1 teaspoon baking soda
½ teaspoon salt
Cooking spray

1. Preheat oven to 350°.
2. Combine first 3 ingredients in a medium bowl; stir with a whisk until smooth. Stir in milk and yogurt. Lightly spoon flour into dry measuring cups; level with a knife. Combine flour, ¼ cup coconut, rind, baking soda, and salt in a large bowl, stirring with a whisk. Make a well in center of flour mixture; add milk mixture to flour mixture, stirring just until moist.
3. Spoon batter into a 9 x 5-inch loaf pan coated with cooking spray. Sprinkle with remaining 1 tablespoon coconut. Bake at 350° for 50 minutes or until a wooden pick inserted in center comes

out clean. Cool in pan 10 minutes. Yield: 12 servings (serving size: 1 slice).

CALORIES 178 (13% from fat); FAT 2.6g (sat 1g, mono 1g, poly 0.5g); PROTEIN 4.1g; CARB 34.8g; FIBER 0.8g; CHOL 18mg; IRON 1.1mg; SODIUM 228mg; CALC 53mg

Flavor Fiesta Menu
serves 6

Mellow sweet potatoes balance the smoky spiciness of the meat loaf and the tangy-sweet salsa. Use extralean ground beef instead of turkey, if you prefer.

Chipotle Meat Loaf
Pineapple-pepper salsa*
Whipped sweet potatoes

*Combine 1 cup chopped pineapple, 1 cup chopped papaya, and 3 tablespoons diced red onion in a medium bowl. Stir in 3 tablespoons chopped cilantro, 2 tablespoons vinegar, ¼ teaspoon salt, and ⅛ teaspoon ground red pepper, tossing to combine.

Chipotle Meat Loaf

"With the addition of chipotles, cumin, and cilantro, this meat loaf has a very fresh, slightly smoky, and moderately spicy flavor."
—Henna Verburg,
Worcester, Massachusetts

MEAT LOAF:
- 1 (7-ounce) can chipotle chiles in adobo sauce
- ½ cup finely chopped onion
- ½ cup coarsely chopped fresh cilantro
- ¼ cup regular oats
- ¼ cup dry breadcrumbs
- ¼ cup tomato sauce
- 2 teaspoons chopped fresh parsley
- 1 teaspoon salt
- ½ teaspoon ground cumin
- ½ teaspoon dried oregano
- ¼ teaspoon dried basil
- ¼ teaspoon freshly ground black pepper
- 2 garlic cloves, minced
- 2 large egg whites
- 1 pound ground turkey
- 1 pound ground turkey breast
- Cooking spray

TOPPING:
- ¼ cup tomato sauce
- 1 tablespoon ketchup
- ½ teaspoon hot sauce

1. Preheat oven to 350°.
2. To prepare meat loaf, remove 1 chipotle chile and 1 teaspoon adobo sauce from can; reserve remaining chiles and sauce for another use. Chop chile. Combine chile, sauce, onion, and next 14 ingredients in a large bowl, stirring well. Place turkey mixture in a 9 x 5-inch loaf pan coated with cooking spray. Bake, uncovered, at 350° for 30 minutes.
3. To prepare topping, combine ¼ cup tomato sauce, ketchup, and hot sauce in a small bowl; brush mixture evenly over meat loaf. Cover and bake an additional 30 minutes or until thermometer registers 160°. Let stand 10 minutes before slicing. Yield: 6 servings (serving size: 1 slice).

CALORIES 239 (24% from fat); FAT 7.1g (sat 1.9g, mono 2.5g, poly 1.9g); PROTEIN 36.3g; CARB 8.4g; FIBER 1.3g; CHOL 94mg; IRON 2.1mg; SODIUM 753mg; CALC 55mg

MAKE AHEAD • FREEZABLE
Black Bean Chili

"Everyone is happy to be included in a black bean chili meal at our house. I serve the chili on top of baked tortilla chips, rice, or corn bread, and dress it up with dollops of sour cream and a sprinkle of coarsely chopped cilantro."
—Robin Johnson, Portland, Oregon

- 1 tablespoon canola oil
- 1¾ cups finely chopped onion (about 1 large)
- 2 garlic cloves, minced
- 2 tablespoons chili powder
- 2 teaspoons ground cumin
- 4 cups canned black beans, rinsed and drained (about 3 [15-ounce] cans)
- 1 cup water
- ¼ cup bottled chipotle sauce
- 1 tablespoon sugar
- 1 (28-ounce) can diced tomatoes, undrained

1. Heat oil in a small Dutch oven over medium heat. Add onion and garlic; sauté 6 minutes or just until onion mixture begins to brown. Add chili powder and cumin; cook 1 minute, stirring constantly. Add beans and remaining ingredients, stirring to combine. Bring to a boil; reduce heat, and simmer 30 minutes or until slightly thick, stirring occasionally. Yield: 6 servings (serving size: about 1 cup).

CALORIES 172 (16% from fat); FAT 3g (sat 0.3g, mono 1.5g, poly 0.9g); PROTEIN 8g; CARB 35.5g; FIBER 11.1g; CHOL 0mg; IRON 3.3mg; SODIUM 878mg; CALC 95mg

MAKE AHEAD
Pumpkin Pie Cheesecake

"After trying many versions, I developed this cheesecake. The cream cheese makes the filling very moist, and the dessert tastes more like a pumpkin pie than a cheesecake. Our family loves it."
—Beth Berenis, Ocoee, Florida

- Cooking spray
- ½ cup graham cracker crumbs (about 4 cookie sheets)
- ¾ cup granulated sugar
- ¼ cup packed brown sugar
- 1 (8-ounce) block fat-free cream cheese
- ½ cup (4 ounces) ⅓-less-fat cream cheese
- 1 cup canned pumpkin
- 2 tablespoons reduced-fat sour cream
- 1 tablespoon all-purpose flour
- ½ teaspoon ground cinnamon
- ½ teaspoon ground ginger
- ¼ teaspoon salt
- ¼ teaspoon ground nutmeg
- ¾ teaspoon vanilla extract
- ⅛ teaspoon ground cloves
- 2 large eggs
- ½ cup frozen reduced-calorie whipped topping, thawed
- Cinnamon (optional)

1. Preheat oven to 325°.
2. Coat an 8-inch springform pan with cooking spray, and sprinkle pan evenly with crumbs.

Continued

3. Combine sugars and cream cheeses in a large bowl; beat with a mixer at medium speed until smooth. Add pumpkin and next 9 ingredients, and beat well.

4. Pour cheese mixture into prepared pan. Bake at 325° for 35 minutes or until center is just set. Turn oven off, and partially open oven door. Cool cheesecake in oven 1 hour.

5. Remove cheesecake from oven; cover. Chill at least 8 hours or overnight. Serve with whipped topping, and sprinkle topping with cinnamon, if desired. Yield: 8 servings (serving size: 1 wedge and 1 tablespoon whipped topping).

CALORIES 235 (25% from fat); FAT 6.4g (sat 3.6g, mono 1.8g, poly 0.5g); PROTEIN 8.1g; CARB 36.4g; FIBER 1.2g; CHOL 67mg; IRON 1.2mg; SODIUM 340mg; CALC 95mg

inspired vegetarian

Beyond Butternut

Cool-weather months yield an abundance of winter squash varieties that make satisfying, savory dishes.

Pumpkin Risotto Cakes

Since the risotto needs to chill overnight, these cakes come together quickly. Add mixed greens topped with roasted red bell pepper wedges and crumbled feta for a light supper.

Brown Rice Risotto with Pumpkin (recipe at right), chilled
1 tablespoon olive oil, divided
Basil sprigs (optional)

1. Divide Brown Rice Risotto with Pumpkin into 18 equal portions, shaping each into a ½-inch-thick patty. Heat 1½ teaspoons oil in a large nonstick skillet over medium-high heat. Add 9 patties; cook 3 minutes on each side or until golden. Repeat procedure with 1½ teaspoons oil and remaining patties.

Garnish with basil, if desired. Yield: 6 appetizer servings (serving size: 3 cakes).

CALORIES 195 (24% from fat); FAT 5.1g (sat 0.9g, mono 3.1g, poly 0.4g); PROTEIN 5.1g; CARB 30.8g; FIBER 3.1g; CHOL 2mg; IRON 1.3mg; SODIUM 242mg; CALC 77mg

Brown Rice Risotto with Pumpkin

Brown Arborio rice tends to be chewier than the regular white Arborio, the short-grain rice most commonly used in risottos. It's perfect for this dish.

4 cups organic vegetable broth (such as Swanson Certified Organic)
3½ cups water
2 tablespoons olive oil
⅓ cup finely chopped shallots
1 (8-ounce) package presliced cremini mushrooms
2 garlic cloves, minced
½ cup dry white wine
1¼ cups uncooked brown Arborio or other short-grain rice
2½ cups (½-inch) cubed peeled fresh pumpkin
¼ cup (1 ounce) grated fresh Parmesan cheese
2 tablespoons chopped fresh or 2 teaspoons dried basil
1 tablespoon chopped fresh or 1 teaspoon dried oregano
¼ teaspoon freshly ground black pepper

1. Bring broth and water to a simmer in a medium saucepan (do not boil). Keep warm over low heat.

2. Heat oil in a large saucepan over medium-high heat. Add shallots; cook 1 minute or until tender, stirring constantly. Add mushrooms and garlic; cook 3 minutes, stirring constantly. Add wine; cook 1 minute or until liquid has evaporated. Add rice; cook 1 minute, stirring constantly. Stir in 1 cup broth mixture; cook 6 minutes or until liquid is nearly absorbed, stirring constantly. Add remaining broth, ½ cup at a time, stirring constantly until each portion is absorbed before adding next (about 55 minutes

total). Stir in pumpkin during last 15 minutes of cooking time. Stir in cheese and remaining ingredients. Yield: 6 servings (serving size: about 1 cup).

CALORIES 262 (15% from fat); FAT 4.3g (sat 0.9g, mono 2.1g, poly 0.3g); PROTEIN 7.6g; CARB 46.3g; FIBER 4.6g; CHOL 2.9mg; IRON 1.9mg; SODIUM 363mg; CALC 116mg

Greek Spaghetti Squash Salad

This recipe makes about 10 cups; it stores well in the refrigerator one to two days, and is even better the second day. Here the squash is cooked in the microwave to save time.

1 (3-pound) spaghetti squash
5 cups chopped plum tomato
1 cup (4 ounces) crumbled reduced-fat feta cheese
1 cup chopped seeded cucumber
1 cup green bell pepper strips
¼ cup vertically sliced red onion
¼ cup chopped pitted kalamata olives
3 tablespoons sherry or red wine vinegar
2 tablespoons chopped fresh or 2 teaspoons dried oregano
¼ teaspoon salt
¼ teaspoon freshly ground black pepper
1 garlic clove, minced

1. Pierce squash with a fork; place on paper towels in microwave. Microwave at HIGH 15 minutes or until tender. Let stand 10 minutes. Cut squash in half lengthwise; discard seeds. Scrape inside of squash with a fork to remove spaghetti-like strands.

2. Combine cooked squash and next 6 ingredients in a large bowl; toss well. Combine vinegar and remaining 4 ingredients, stirring with a whisk. Add to squash mixture, tossing to coat. Cover and chill. Yield: 8 servings (serving size: 1¼ cups).

CALORIES 100 (37% from fat); FAT 4.1g (sat 1.7g, mono 0.1g, poly 0.5g); PROTEIN 4.7g; CARB 13.8g; FIBER 1.5g; CHOL 5mg; IRON 0.7mg; SODIUM 350mg; CALC 85mg

Spaghetti Squash Gratins with Chunky Tomato Sauce

These individual casseroles are like little lasagnas with spaghetti squash replacing the traditional lasagna noodles.

    1   (2-pound) spaghetti squash
    1   teaspoon olive oil
    2   garlic cloves, minced
    1   teaspoon kosher salt, divided
    ½   teaspoon freshly ground black pepper, divided
    ¼   teaspoon crushed red pepper
    2   (28-ounce) cans whole tomatoes, drained and chopped
    3   oregano sprigs
    3   thyme sprigs
    ½   cup (2 ounces) grated fresh Parmesan cheese
    2   teaspoons chopped fresh oregano
    1   teaspoon chopped fresh thyme
    1   (15-ounce) carton fat-free ricotta cheese

1. Preheat oven to 400°.
2. Pierce squash with a fork. Place squash on a baking sheet; bake at 400° for 1 hour or until tender. Cool. Cut squash in half lengthwise; discard seeds. Scrape inside of squash with a fork to remove spaghetti-like strands to measure 4 cups.
3. Heat oil in a large saucepan over medium heat. Add garlic; cook 2 minutes, stirring frequently. Add ½ teaspoon salt, ¼ teaspoon black pepper, red pepper, tomatoes, oregano sprigs, and thyme sprigs; bring to a boil. Reduce heat, and simmer 20 minutes or until thickened, stirring occasionally. Discard oregano and thyme sprigs.
4. Combine remaining ½ teaspoon salt, remaining ¼ teaspoon black pepper, Parmesan, and remaining 3 ingredients. Spoon ½ cup squash into each of 8 (8-ounce) ramekins. Spoon tomato sauce evenly over squash; divide ricotta mixture evenly among ramekins, spreading to cover. Bake at 400° for 50 minutes or until lightly browned. Yield: 8 servings (serving size: 1 gratin).

CALORIES 117 (21% from fat); FAT 2.7g (sat 1.1g, mono 0.9g, poly 0.4g); PROTEIN 7.8g; CARB 15.1g; FIBER 1.1g; CHOL 13mg; IRON 1.5mg; SODIUM 531mg; CALC 200mg

How to Prepare Spaghetti Squash

1. *Pierce shell of squash with a fork, and bake according to directions, or until tender when pierced with a fork.*

2. *Remove from oven, and allow squash to sit until cool to the touch—about 10 minutes—then use a chef's knife to cut in half lengthwise.*

3. *Carefully scoop away seeds and pulp from center of squash with a small spoon or melon baller, and discard.*

4. *Hold squash in a vertical position with one hand, and use a fork to gently scrape out the flesh, working from top to base.*

Southwestern Squash Stew

MAKE AHEAD

Chayote, a gourdlike fruit also known as mirliton, has a mild flavor and texture similar to summer squash and doesn't have to be peeled. Kabocha is a medium-sized, flattened-turban-shaped squash with a rough skin that ranges in color from jade green to tan.

    1   tablespoon olive oil
    1   cup chopped onion
    2½ cups chopped chayote
    1   poblano chile, seeded and chopped
    1   garlic clove, minced
    4   cups (1-inch) cubed peeled kabocha squash
    2   cups organic vegetable broth (such as Swanson Certified Organic)
    2   cups water
    1   teaspoon ground cumin
    1   teaspoon chili powder
    1   (15-ounce) can hominy, drained
    1   (14.5-ounce) can diced tomatoes, undrained
    2   oregano sprigs
    1   teaspoon kosher salt
    ¼   teaspoon freshly ground black pepper
    6   lime wedges

1. Heat oil in a Dutch oven over medium heat. Add onion; cook 4 minutes, stirring frequently. Add chayote, poblano, and garlic; cook 4 minutes, stirring frequently. Add kabocha squash and next 7 ingredients; bring to a boil. Reduce heat, and simmer 1 hour or until vegetables are tender. Discard oregano sprigs. Stir in salt and black pepper. Ladle stew into individual bowls; serve with lime wedges. Yield: 6 servings (serving size: about 1½ cups stew and 1 lime wedge).

CALORIES 131 (25% from fat); FAT 3.7g (sat 0.8g, mono 1.8g, poly 0.5g); PROTEIN 3g; CARB 23.5g; FIBER 4.7g; CHOL 3mg; IRON 1.3mg; SODIUM 704mg; CALC 67mg

Hubbard Squash and Pinto Bean Stew

Hubbard squash are very large with thick, bumpy skin that ranges from medium green to bright orange. Really big hubbards are often sold in pieces. The yellow-orange flesh has a grainy texture and is best in recipes where it's boiled or baked.

    3   cups dried pinto beans
    4   cups water
    3   tablespoons olive oil
    4   cups chopped onion
    4   cups (½-inch) cubed peeled
        hubbard squash or fresh
        pumpkin
    1   cup sliced carrot
    1   tablespoon chipotle chile in
        adobo sauce, chopped
    2   tablespoons chopped fresh or
        2 teaspoons dried sage
    1   tablespoon chopped fresh or
        1 teaspoon dried thyme
    1   (28-ounce) can crushed tomatoes,
        undrained
    ¾   teaspoon salt
    2   tablespoons pumpkinseed kernels,
        toasted

1. Sort and wash beans; place in a large Dutch oven. Cover with water to 2 inches above beans; cover and let stand 8 hours. Drain beans. Combine beans and 4 cups water in pan; bring to a boil. Reduce heat, and simmer 30 minutes. Cover and simmer 30 minutes or until tender.
2. Heat oil in a large nonstick skillet over medium heat. Add onion, squash, carrot, and chile; cook 10 minutes, stirring frequently. Add to bean mixture. Stir in sage, thyme, and tomatoes; bring to a boil. Cover, reduce heat, and simmer 10 minutes or until squash is tender. Stir in salt. Ladle stew into individual bowls; sprinkle with pumpkinseed kernels. Yield: 6 servings (serving size: 1½ cups stew and 1 teaspoon kernels).

CALORIES 171 (27% from fat); FAT 5.1g (sat 0.8g, mono 2.4g, poly 1.5g); PROTEIN 6.4g; CARB 29.8g; FIBER 6.1g; CHOL 0mg; IRON 3.5mg; SODIUM 558mg; CALC 117mg

Friends as Family

Set the table for casual company with sophisticated dishes that depart from tradition.

Sweet Vermouth Chicken
(pictured on page 431)

Look for bottled roasted chestnuts at gourmet and specialty markets.

        Cooking spray
    8   (6-ounce) skinless, boneless
        chicken breast halves
    ½   teaspoon salt, divided
    ½   teaspoon freshly ground black
        pepper, divided
    2   cups sliced mushrooms
    1   cup frozen pearl onions
    1   teaspoon minced garlic
    1   tablespoon all-purpose flour
    1   cup sweet vermouth
    1   cup peeled roasted chestnuts
    1   cup fat-free, less-sodium chicken
        broth
    1   tablespoon chopped fresh parsley
    1   teaspoon chopped fresh tarragon
    ¼   cup dried cranberries

1. Preheat oven to 350°.
2. Heat a large nonstick skillet over medium-high heat. Coat pan with cooking spray. Sprinkle chicken with ¼ teaspoon salt and ¼ teaspoon pepper. Add half of chicken to pan; cook 2 minutes on each side or until lightly browned. Place on a jelly-roll pan coated with cooking spray. Repeat procedure with remaining chicken. Bake at 350° for 25 minutes or until chicken is done.
3. Heat a large nonstick skillet over medium-high heat. Coat pan with cooking spray. Add mushrooms, onions, and garlic to pan. Sprinkle flour over mushroom mixture; cook 2 minutes or until flour is lightly browned, stirring constantly. Add vermouth to pan, scraping pan to loosen browned bits; boil 30 seconds. Add chestnuts, broth, parsley, tarragon, remaining ¼ teaspoon salt, and remaining ¼ teaspoon pepper; return to a boil. Reduce heat, and simmer until sauce is reduced to 2 cups (about 10 minutes). Add cranberries to pan; cook 2 minutes. Yield: 8 servings (serving size: 1 chicken breast half and ¼ cup sauce).

CALORIES 315 (7% from fat); FAT 2.7g (sat 0.7g, mono 0.7g, poly 0.7g); PROTEIN 41.2g; CARB 21.4g; FIBER 1.5g; CHOL 99mg; IRON 1.8mg; SODIUM 315mg; CALC 36mg

Smoky Bacon and Vinegar Green Beans

Use mature green beans. Slow cooking allows them to absorb the bacon flavor.

    4   slices (6 ounces) hickory-smoked
        bacon, diced (uncooked)
    1   cup chopped onion
    1   cup fat-free, less-sodium chicken
        broth
    1   cup water
    1   teaspoon salt
    ½   teaspoon freshly ground black
        pepper
    2   pounds green beans, trimmed and
        cut into 2-inch pieces
    ¼   cup cider vinegar

1. Heat a large Dutch oven over medium heat. Add bacon; sauté 3 minutes or until lightly browned. Remove bacon from pan, reserving 2 teaspoons drippings in pan. Add onion to pan; sauté 5 minutes or until tender. Add bacon, broth, water, salt, pepper, and beans; bring to a boil. Cover, reduce heat, and simmer 30 minutes or until beans are very tender. Uncover; cook 5 minutes.
2. Drizzle beans with vinegar; simmer 5 minutes. Serve warm. Yield: 8 servings (serving size: ¾ cup).

CALORIES 75 (31% from fat); FAT 2.6g (sat 1g, mono 0.6g, poly 0.2g); PROTEIN 3.1g; CARB 9.6g; FIBER 4.4g; CHOL 5mg; IRON 0.6mg; SODIUM 380mg; CALC 63mg

Honey-Glazed Carrots

This simple side works with various main meat dishes, such as the Carbonnade à la Flamande (recipe on page 455) and Sweet Vermouth Chicken (recipe on page 452).

1½   quarts water
5   cups thinly sliced carrots
3   tablespoons chopped fresh parsley
2   tablespoons honey
½   teaspoon salt
½   teaspoon grated orange rind
¼   teaspoon freshly ground black
     pepper

1. Bring water to a boil in a medium saucepan. Add carrots; cook 20 minutes or until tender. Drain well. Place carrots and remaining ingredients in a large bowl; toss gently. Yield: 8 servings (serving size: about ½ cup).

CALORIES 51 (4% from fat); FAT 0.2g (sat 0g, mono 0g, poly 0.1g); PROTEIN 0.8g; CARB 12.5g; FIBER 3g; CHOL 0mg; IRON 0.5mg; SODIUM 203mg; CALC 32mg

Smoked Salmon Knishes

FILLING:

3   cups peeled baking potato, cut
     into 1-inch-thick slices (about 2
     large potatoes)
⅓   cup fat-free, less-sodium chicken
     broth
1   tablespoon chopped fresh dill
½   teaspoon salt
½   teaspoon freshly ground black pepper
4   ounces smoked salmon, finely
     chopped
     Cooking spray
1½   cups finely chopped yellow onion
     (about 1 medium)

DOUGH:

2⅓   cups all-purpose flour, sifted
     (about 10½ ounces)
1   teaspoon baking powder
¼   teaspoon salt
½   cup plain fat-free yogurt
5   tablespoons water, divided
2   tablespoons butter, melted
2   large eggs, divided
1   tablespoon all-purpose flour

1. To prepare filling, place potatoes in a saucepan; cover with water. Bring to a boil; reduce heat, and simmer 15 minutes or until tender. Drain. Place potato, broth, dill, ½ teaspoon salt, pepper, and salmon in a large bowl; mash until well combined.

2. Heat a large nonstick skillet over medium-high heat. Coat pan with cooking spray. Add onion; cook 3 minutes or until soft, stirring once. Stir onion into potato mixture. Set aside.

3. To prepare dough, lightly spoon 2⅓ cups flour into dry measuring cups; level with a knife. Combine 2⅓ cups flour, baking powder, and ¼ teaspoon salt in a large bowl. Combine yogurt, ¼ cup water, butter, and 1 egg in a medium bowl, stirring with a whisk. Make a well in center of flour mixture; add yogurt mixture, stirring until dough forms. Turn dough out onto a floured surface. Knead until smooth and elastic (about 10 minutes); add 1 tablespoon flour to prevent dough from sticking to hands (dough will feel sticky). Cover dough; let stand 10 minutes.

4. Preheat oven to 375°.

5. Divide dough into 16 portions. Working with one portion at a time (cover remaining dough to prevent drying), roll each portion into a 5-inch square on a floured surface. Place ¼ cup potato mixture in center of each square. Fold dough over filling, pinching seam and ends to seal. Place knishes, seam sides down, on a baking sheet coated with cooking spray.

6. Make a small cut in center of top of each knish. Combine remaining 1 tablespoon water and 1 egg in a small bowl, stirring with a whisk. Brush egg mixture over knish tops. Bake at 375° for 30 minutes or until golden. Yield: 8 servings (serving size: 2 knishes).

CALORIES 255 (18% from fat); FAT 5.2g (sat 2g, mono 2g, poly 0.6g); PROTEIN 9.9g; CARB 41.9g; FIBER 2.5g; CHOL 64mg; IRON 2.3mg; SODIUM 464mg; CALC 91mg

How to Make a Knish

1. *Place ¼ cup potato mixture in the center of dough.*

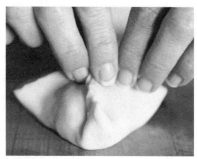

2. *Fold dough over filling, pinching seam and ends to seal.*

3. *Place knishes, seam sides down, on a baking sheet coated with cooking spray.*

Mixed Salad with Vanilla-Pear Vinaigrette and Toasted Walnuts

1 cup vertically sliced red onion
2 (10-ounce) packages Mediterranean-style salad
⅔ cup Vanilla-Pear Vinaigrette
¼ cup chopped walnuts, toasted

1. To prepare salad, combine onion and lettuce mix in a large bowl. Add vinaigrette; toss well. Sprinkle with walnuts. Yield: 8 servings (serving size: 2 cups).

(Totals include Vanilla-Pear Vinaigrette) CALORIES 55 (38% from fat); FAT 2.3g (sat 0.2g, mono 0.5g, poly 1.5g); PROTEIN 1.8g; CARB 8.1g; FIBER 2.9g; CHOL 0mg; IRON 0.4mg; SODIUM 73mg; CALC 20mg

MAKE AHEAD

VANILLA-PEAR VINAIGRETTE:

1 (15-ounce) can pear halves in juice, undrained
⅓ cup white wine vinegar
1 tablespoon honey
¾ teaspoon kosher salt
¼ teaspoon freshly ground black pepper
¼ teaspoon vanilla extract
Dash of ground red pepper

1. To prepare vinaigrette, drain pears, reserving ⅓ cup pear juice. Place pears, juice, vinegar, and remaining ingredients in a blender; process until smooth. Yield: about 2 cups (serving size: about 1½ tablespoons).

CALORIES 14 (0% from fat); FAT 0; PROTEIN 0.1g, CARB 3.7g; FIBER 0.3g; CHOL 0mg; IRON 0.1mg; SODIUM 68mg; CALC 2mg

MAKE AHEAD

Swirled Cranberry Cheesecake

CRUST:

½ cup sugar
⅓ cup unsweetened cocoa
40 chocolate graham cracker sticks (about 3 ounces)
1 tablespoon butter, melted
1 large egg white
Cooking spray

TOPPING:

1½ cups sugar
½ cup orange juice
¼ cup fresh lemon juice
1 (12-ounce) package fresh cranberries
2 teaspoons grated lemon rind
1 teaspoon orange rind
1 large egg white

FILLING:

1 cup sugar
2 (8-ounce) packages ⅓-less-fat cream cheese, softened
1 (3-ounce) package cream cheese, softened
¾ cup fat-free milk
5 large egg whites

1. Preheat oven to 400°.
2. To prepare crust, place first 3 ingredients in a food processor; process until finely ground. Add butter and 1 egg white; pulse just until combined (do not form a ball). Firmly press crust mixture into bottom of a 9-inch springform pan coated with cooking spray. Bake at 400° for 10 minutes; cool on a wire rack.
3. Reduce oven temperature to 350°.
4. To prepare topping, combine 1½ cups sugar and next 3 ingredients in a medium saucepan. Bring to a boil; cook 6 minutes or until cranberries pop and mixture thickens. Cool completely. Stir in rinds. Reserve 1½ cups cranberry mixture. Place 1 cup cranberry mixture in a blender or food processor; process until smooth. Stir in 1 egg white. Set aside.
5. To prepare filling, combine 1 cup sugar and cream cheeses; beat with a mixer at medium speed until smooth. Add milk; beat at low speed until blended. Add 5 egg whites; beat at low speed until blended. Pour filling mixture into prepared pan. Drizzle 1 cup cranberry purée over filling mixture. Swirl mixtures together using a knife. Bake at 350° for 45 minutes or until almost set in center. Turn oven off and partially open oven door; leave cheesecake in oven 30 minutes. Remove from oven; run a knife around outside edge. Cool to room temperature. Cover and chill 8 hours or overnight before serving. Serve with reserved 1½ cups cranberry mixture.

Yield: 16 servings (serving size: 1 wedge and 1½ tablespoons cranberry mixture).

CALORIES 296 (29% from fat); FAT 9.5g (sat 5.6g, mono 2.8g, poly 0.5g); PROTEIN 6.2g; CARB 48.4g; FIBER 1.6g; CHOL 28mg; IRON 0.4mg; SODIUM 69mg; CALC 49mg

---

Entertaining Menu
serves 8

Impress your guests with this Asian-inspired menu. Cook the no-fuss rice and prepare the stir-fry as you roast the tenderloin.

Peppercorn-Crusted Pork Tenderloin with Soy-Caramel Sauce

Asian vegetable stir-fry*

Jasmine rice with green onions

*Heat 1 tablespoon canola oil in a large skillet over medium-high heat. Add 2 teaspoons minced garlic; sauté 30 seconds. Add 2 cups matchstick-cut carrots and 2 cups blanched broccoli florets; sauté 3 minutes or until beginning to soften. Add 1 cup red bell pepper strips, 1 cup sliced shiitake mushrooms, ½ teaspoon salt, and ¼ teaspoon crushed red pepper; sauté 5 minutes or until liquid almost evaporates and vegetables are crisp-tender. Stir in 1½ teaspoons sesame oil.

Peppercorn-Crusted Pork Tenderloin with Soy-Caramel Sauce

Cooking spray
¼ cup minced white onion
1 teaspoon grated peeled fresh ginger
2 garlic cloves, minced
1 cup water
½ cup sugar
¼ cup low-sodium soy sauce
2 tablespoons red wine vinegar
1½ teaspoons Dijon mustard
2 tablespoons butter
2 (1-pound) pork tenderloins, trimmed
1 tablespoon black peppercorns, crushed
1½ teaspoons chopped fresh thyme
¼ teaspoon salt

1. Heat a small saucepan over medium heat. Coat pan with cooking spray. Add onion, ginger, and garlic; sauté 2 minutes. Add water and sugar; bring to a boil. Cook until reduced to ½ cup (about 5 minutes). Remove from heat; carefully stir in soy sauce, vinegar, and mustard. Add butter, stirring with a whisk. Set aside; keep warm.

2. Preheat oven to 350°.

3. Rub tenderloins evenly with pepper, thyme, and salt. Heat a large ovenproof nonstick skillet over medium-high heat. Coat pan with cooking spray. Add tenderloins, browning on all sides (about 5 minutes). Bake at 350° for 23 minutes or until a thermometer registers 160° (slightly pink); let stand 10 minutes. Cut each tenderloin into 12 slices; serve with sauce. Yield: 8 servings (serving size: 3 slices pork and 2 tablespoons sauce).

CALORIES 227 (28% from fat); FAT 7g (sat 2.8g, mono 3g, poly 0.6g); PROTEIN 24.5g; CARB 15.3g; FIBER 0.4g; CHOL 81mg; IRON 1.7mg; SODIUM 441mg; CALC 16mg

Cauliflower and Green Onion Mash

Similar to mashed potatoes, this side dish has a delicate taste.

1 teaspoon olive oil
3 pounds fresh cauliflower, cut into florets (about 8½ cups)
3 garlic cloves, thinly sliced
1 cup chopped green onions
1 cup 1% low-fat milk
2 tablespoons butter
¾ teaspoon ground black pepper
½ teaspoon salt

1. Preheat oven to 500°.

2. Toss oil, cauliflower, and garlic on a jelly-roll pan. Bake at 500° for 20 minutes or until lightly browned, stirring occasionally. Place cauliflower mixture in a large bowl. Add onions and remaining 4 ingredients to cauliflower mixture; mash with a potato masher. Yield: 8 servings (serving size: about ¾ cup).

CALORIES 93 (38% from fat); FAT 3.9g (sat 2.1g, mono 1.3g, poly 0.3g); PROTEIN 4.5g; CARB 12g; FIBER 4.8g; CHOL 9mg; IRON 0.8mg; SODIUM 215mg; CALC 79mg

Hearty Winter Menu
serves 8

Carbonnade à la Flamande

Egg noodles

Angel food cake with hazelnut chocolate sauce*

*Combine ⅓ cup fat-free milk, 3 tablespoons sugar, and 3 tablespoons heavy cream in a microwave-safe bowl. Microwave at HIGH 3 minutes or until sugar dissolves, stirring after every minute. Stir in 1 teaspoon vanilla extract. Pour mixture over 3 ounces semisweet chocolate and 3 ounces bittersweet chocolate, stirring with a whisk until chocolate melts. Stir in 2 tablespoons finely chopped hazelnuts. Pour over cake.

MAKE AHEAD
Carbonnade à la Flamande

¾ cup all-purpose flour (about 3⅓ ounces)
½ teaspoon salt
½ teaspoon black pepper
⅛ teaspoon ground nutmeg
2½ pounds boneless chuck roast, trimmed and cut into 1½-inch cubes
2 strips bacon, diced (uncooked)
2 cups chopped onion (about 2 large onions)
1 tablespoon chopped garlic
1 (14-ounce) can less-sodium beef broth
1 cup water
2 tablespoons brown sugar
2 tablespoons red wine vinegar
2 tablespoons tomato paste
2 tablespoons Dijon mustard
1 teaspoon fresh thyme
2 bay leaves
1 (12-ounce) bottle dark beer
2 tablespoons chopped fresh parsley

1. Combine first 5 ingredients in a large zip-top plastic bag. Seal; shake to coat.

2. Heat a large Dutch oven over medium-high heat. Add bacon to pan; cook 1 minute. Add beef mixture; cook 3 minutes or until browned. Remove beef from pan.

3. Add onion and garlic to pan; sauté 5 minutes or until tender.

4. Return beef to pan. Stir in broth, scraping pan to loosen browned bits. Add water and next 7 ingredients; bring to boil. Cover, reduce heat, and simmer 30 minutes. Uncover and cook 30 minutes or until beef is tender. Discard bay leaves. Garnish with parsley. Yield: 8 servings (serving size: 1 cup).

CALORIES 328 (24% from fat); FAT 8.8g (sat 3.9g, mono 3.2g, poly 0.5g); PROTEIN 41.1g; CARB 19.1g; FIBER 1.2g; CHOL 67mg; IRON 4.2mg; SODIUM 448mg; CALC 46mg

superfast

. . . And Ready in Just About 20 Minutes

More than a week's worth of quick entrées to get dinner on the table in a flash.

QUICK & EASY
Chicken with Sherry-Soy Sauce

Serve with bagged salad greens and quick-cooking rice noodles.

Cooking spray
4 (6-ounce) skinless, boneless chicken breast halves
¼ teaspoon salt
¼ teaspoon freshly ground black pepper
⅓ cup dry sherry
1 tablespoon sugar
2 tablespoons low-sodium soy sauce
2 tablespoons red wine vinegar
⅛ teaspoon crushed red pepper
1 teaspoon sesame oil

1. Heat a large nonstick skillet over medium-high heat. Coat pan with cooking spray. Sprinkle chicken with salt and black pepper. Add chicken to pan; cook 4 minutes on each side or until lightly browned. Remove from pan; keep warm.
Continued

2. Add sherry, sugar, soy sauce, vinegar, and red pepper to pan, scraping pan to loosen brown bits. Bring to a boil; cook 1 minute. Stir in oil. Yield: 4 servings (serving size: 1 chicken breast half and 1 tablespoon sauce.

CALORIES 230 (13% from fat); FAT 3.3g (sat 0.7g, mono 1g, poly 1g); PROTEIN 39.9g; CARB 4.7g; FIBER 0.3g; CHOL 99mg; IRON 1.6mg; SODIUM 528mg; CALC 27mg

Tex-Mex Chipotle Sloppy Joes

Make a quick black bean and corn salad to serve with the sandwiches. The turkey can also be served over rice or as a taco or enchilada filling.

  1 teaspoon olive oil
  ½ cup prechopped onion
  1 tablespoon bottled minced garlic
  2 teaspoons minced seeded jalapeño pepper
  1 teaspoon sugar
  1 teaspoon ground cumin
  1 teaspoon chili powder
  ½ teaspoon ground coriander
  ¼ teaspoon ground chipotle chile powder
  1 pound ground turkey breast
  1½ cups bottled mild salsa
  1 tablespoon chopped fresh cilantro
  4 (2½-ounce) Kaiser rolls, cut in half horizontally

1. Heat oil in a large nonstick skillet over medium-high heat. Add onion, garlic, and jalapeño; sauté 2 minutes or until soft. Add sugar and next 5 ingredients; cook 5 minutes or until turkey is browned, stirring to crumble. Stir in salsa; cook 4 minutes or until slightly thick. Stir in cilantro. Spread about ¾ cup turkey mixture on bottom half of each roll; cover with top half of each roll. Yield: 4 servings (serving size: 1 sandwich).

CALORIES 397 (12% from fat); FAT 5.4g (sat 0.9g, mono 1.9g, poly 1.6g); PROTEIN 35.4g; CARB 44.8g; FIBER 2.5g; CHOL 70mg; IRON 4.1mg; SODIUM 870mg; CALC 92mg

Broiled Tilapia with Tomato-Caper Salsa

  1 cup chopped tomato
  ¼ cup chopped fresh flat-leaf parsley
  1 tablespoon capers, drained
  1 tablespoon white wine vinegar
  ½ teaspoon anchovy paste
  2 garlic cloves, minced
  1½ tablespoons extravirgin olive oil, divided
  ¼ teaspoon salt, divided
  ¼ teaspoon freshly ground black pepper, divided
  4 (6-ounce) tilapia fillets
  Cooking spray

1. Preheat broiler.
2. Combine first 6 ingredients in a medium bowl; stir in 1½ teaspoons oil, ⅛ teaspoon salt, and ⅛ teaspoon pepper.
3. Brush fish with 1 tablespoon oil; sprinkle with ⅛ teaspoon salt and ⅛ teaspoon pepper. Arrange fish in a single layer on a jelly-roll pan coated with cooking spray. Broil 4 minutes or until fish flakes easily when tested with a fork or until desired degree of doneness. Serve with salsa. Yield: 4 servings (serving size: 1 fish fillet and ¼ cup salsa).

CALORIES 206 (29% from fat); FAT 6.6g (sat 1.1g, mono 4.3g, poly 0.8g); PROTEIN 32.2g; CARB 3g; FIBER 0.8g; CHOL 124mg; IRON 2.5mg; SODIUM 392mg; CALC 40mg

Spicy Shrimp and Rice Soup

  4 cups fat-free, less sodium chicken broth
  2 cups water
  1 cup instant long-grain rice (such as Minute brand)
  1 tablespoon canola oil
  1 teaspoon bottled minced garlic
  ½ teaspoon crushed red pepper
  1½ pounds large shrimp, peeled and deveined
  4 lime wedges
  Bean sprouts (optional)
  Sliced green onions (optional)
  Chopped fresh cilantro (optional)
  Sliced jalapeño pepper (optional)

1. Combine broth and water in a large saucepan; bring to a boil. Stir in rice; bring to a boil. Remove from heat; let stand 5 minutes.
2. Heat oil in a large nonstick skillet over medium-high heat. Add garlic, red pepper, and shrimp; sauté 3 minutes or until shrimp are done. Stir shrimp mixture into broth mixture. Ladle soup into each of 4 bowls; serve with lime wedges. Top each serving with sprouts, onions, cilantro, and jalapeño, if desired. Yield: 4 servings (serving size: 1½ cups soup and 1 lime wedge).

CALORIES 315 (20% from fat); FAT 6.9g (sat 1.1g, mono 3.1g, poly 1.6g); PROTEIN 38.8g; CARB 21.1g; FIBER 1.6g; CHOL 259mg; IRON 5.2mg; SODIUM 644mg; CALC 113mg

Chicken Paprikash

Serve this dish with egg noodles tossed with butter, caraway seeds, salt, and pepper.

  1 tablespoon canola oil
  1 pound chicken breast tenders, cut into 1-inch strips
  1 cup prechopped onion
  1 cup thinly sliced red bell pepper (about 1 medium)
  1½ teaspoons bottled minced garlic
  ¼ cup whipping cream
  1 tablespoon paprika
  1 tablespoon tomato paste
  1 teaspoon caraway seeds
  ½ teaspoon salt
  ¼ teaspoon black pepper
  1 (14.5-ounce) can diced tomatoes, undrained

1. Heat oil in a large nonstick skillet over medium heat. Add chicken; cook 5 minutes or until browned, stirring occasionally. Remove from pan; keep warm.
2. Add onion, bell pepper, and garlic to pan; sauté 4 minutes or until tender. Return chicken to pan. Stir in cream and remaining ingredients; cover and simmer 5 minutes or until chicken is done and sauce is slightly thick. Yield: 4 servings (serving size: 1 cup).

CALORIES 241 (31% from fat); FAT 8.2g (sat 2.4g, mono 3.3g, poly 1.7g); PROTEIN 28.4g; CARB 12.9g; FIBER 3.1g; CHOL 76mg; IRON 1.8mg; SODIUM 507mg; CALC 51mg

Menu Index

A topical guide to all the menus that appear in Cooking Light *Annual Recipes 2006.*
See page 479 for the General Recipe Index.

Dinner Tonight

Beans Menu 1 (page 15)
serves 4
White Bean and Sausage
Ragoût with Tomatoes,
Kale, and Zucchini
Garlic-rosemary bruschetta
Green salad with bottled low-fat
vinaigrette

Beans Menu 2 (page 16)
serves 4
Pasta with Chickpeas
and Garlic Sauce
Broccoli rabe with garlic
Chocolate sorbet

Beans Menu 3 (page 16)
serves 4
Southwest Pinto Bean Burgers with
Chipotle Mayonnaise
Stewed onions
Prepared coleslaw tossed with bottled
vinaigrette and queso fresco or goat cheese

High-Flavor Menu 1 (page 70)
serves 4
Pork Tenderloin Medallions with Chinese
Ginger and Lemon Sauce
Stir-fried snow peas and
green onions
Steamed rice

High-Flavor Menu 2 (page 70)
serves 4
Roasted Pork Tenderloin Medallions with
Dried Cranberry Sauce
Quinoa with parsley and
pine nuts
Steamed broccoli

High-Flavor Menu 3 (page 71)
serves 4
Fresh Herb-Coated Beef Tenderloin
Steaks with Mushroom Gravy
Green peas and leeks
Baked potatoes

High-Flavor Menu 4 (page 72)
serves 4
Beef Tenderloin Steaks with
Creole Spice Rub
Corn Maquechoux
Strawberries tossed with brown sugar and
low-fat sour cream

Sausage Menu 1 (page 106)
serves 4
Penne with Sausage, Eggplant,
and Feta
Bitter greens with olive vinaigrette
Lemon sorbet

Sausage Menu 2 (page 106)
serves 4
Chicken Breasts Stuffed with Italian
Sausage and Breadcrumbs
Sautéed zucchini and tomatoes
Mixed greens with bottled
Italian dressing

Sausage Menu 3 (page 107)
serves 4
Jambalaya with Shrimp
and Andouille Sausage
Green beans with rémoulade
Caramel praline crunch frozen yogurt
(such as Edy's/Dreyer's)

Seafood Menu 1 (page 141)
serves 4
Caribbean Grilled Scallop Salad
Grilled baguette
Coconut sorbet

Seafood Menu 2 (page 142)
serves 4
Shellfish and Bacon Spinach Salad
Herb and Parmesan
breadsticks
Oatmeal-raisin cookies

Seafood Menu 3 (page 142)
serves 4
Shrimp and Crab Salad Rolls
Quick corn and potato chowder
Strawberry sorbet

Seafood Menu 4 (page 143)
serves 4
Grilled Tuna Niçoise Salad
Crusty whole wheat rolls
Blueberry-yogurt sundaes

Pasta Salad Menu 1 (page 206)
serves 4
Chicken and Farfalle Salad
with Walnut Pesto
Strawberries in balsamic vinegar
with angel food cake
White wine

Pasta Salad Menu 2 (page 206)
serves 4
Soba and Slaw Salad
with Peanut Dressing
Melon and lime compote
Fortune cookies

Pasta Salad Menu 3 (page 207)
serves 4
Rotini, Summer Squash,
and Prosciutto Salad with
Rosemary Dressing
Tomato bruschetta
Fresh blueberries with low-fat
vanilla yogurt

Pasta Salad Menu 4 (page 207)
serves 4
Mediterranean Orzo Salad
with Feta Vinaigrette
Pita wedges
Mint iced tea

Saté Menu 1 (page 226)
serves 4
Chicken Saté with Ponzu Sauce
Asian slaw
Raspberry sorbet

Saté Menu 2 (page 227)
serves 4
Salmon Saté with Dill Mustard Glaze
Asparagus with tarragon
vinaigrette
Angel hair pasta

Saté Menu 3 (page 227)
serves 4
Shrimp Saté with Pineapple Salsa
Lemony broccoli
White wine

Saté Menu 4 (page 227)
serves 4
Chicken Saté with Peanut Sauce
Spicy cucumber salad
Rice noodles

Weeknight Pizza Menu 1 (page 276)
serves 4
Pizza Olympia
Mixed olives and pepperoncini
Yogurt with honey and walnuts

Weeknight Pizza Menu 2 (page 276)
serves 4
Turkish Turkey Pizza
Minted cucumber and
cherry tomato salad
Iced grapes

Weeknight Pizza Menu 3 (page 277)
serves 4
Garden Tomato and Basil Pesto Pizza
Baby arugula salad with
balsamic vinaigrette
Melon slices

Duck Menu 1 (page 313)
serves 4
Apricot Grilled Duck Breasts
Sautéed green beans with pecans
Israeli couscous

Duck Menu 2 (page 313)
serves 6
Duck Stew
Goat cheese crostini
Spinach salad with low-fat
bottled vinaigrette

High-Flying Menu (page 64)
serves 6
Appetizers
Mini Meatballs with Creamy
Dill Dip
or
Honey-Molasses Chicken Drumsticks
Entrées
Brick Chicken Baguette Sandwiches
or
Roast Beef and
Blue Cheese Wraps
Sides
Farfalle with Zucchini and Prosciutto
or
Olive and Sun-Dried Tomato Tapenade
Potatoes
Salads
Sweet and Sour Slaw
or
Green Bean Salad with Bacon
Dessert
Raspberry Cheesecake Bars

Alfresco Brunch Menu (page 203)
serves 8
Lemon-Buttermilk Scones with
Quick Blackberry Jam
Mixed Greens Salad with
Honey-Orange Dressing
Fresh Mozzarella, Sun-Dried Tomato, and
Prosciutto Strata
Grits Casserole with Pesto Butter
Banana-Chocolate Brunch Cake
Sparkling Fruit Gelées
Sparkling wine and coffee

Lunch Under the Trees Menu
(page 352)
serves 4
Antipasto Plate
Creamy Tomato-Balsamic Soup
Pumpkin-Walnut Focaccia
with Gruyère
Cavatappi Pasta Salad with
Walnut-Sage Pesto
Apple Crumb Croustades

Autumn Picnic Menu (page 354)
serves 4
Creamy Tomato-Balsamic Soup
Marinated Chickpeas
Chicken and Ham Sandwich
with Artichoke-Tomato Spread
Fig and Cream Cheese Bars

Festive Brunch Menu (page 406)
serves 10
Cranberry Mimosa
Blackberry-Mustard Glazed Ham
Sour Cream Muffins
with Poppy Seed Streusel
Mixed fruit salad
Pecan Pie Coffee Cake

**Christmas Morning Breakfast
Menu 1** (page 415)
serves 6
Bacon, Gruyère, and
Ham Strata
Bundt Coffee Cake
Country Sausage Patties
Festive Fruit Punch

**Christmas Morning Breakfast
Menu 2** (page 416)
serves 6
Individual Potato-Bacon Frittatas
Blueberry-Pecan Scones
Fresh Fruit Salad with Nutmeg-Cinnamon
Syrup
Mocha-Spiced Coffee

Casual Entertaining

Chili Party Buffet Menu (page 61)
serves 6
Garlicky Spinach Dip with Hearts of Palm
Southwestern Chili
or
Chunky Two-Bean and Beef Chili
Peanutty Cabbage-Apple Slaw
with Raisins
Savory Two-Cheese Biscotti
or
Sour Cream, Cheddar, and
Green Onion Drop Biscuits
Toffee Blond Brownies
Assorted chili toppings:
sour cream, chopped green onions,
chopped tomato, and shredded cheese
Assorted beers, soft drinks, and red wine

**Casual Get-Together
Menu 1** (page 67)
serves 6
Beet and Leek Salad with Peanut Dressing
Thai Tomato Soup
Sweet Potato and Cashew Korma over
Coconut Rice
Chocolate-Walnut-Cranberry Cake

**Casual Get-Together
Menu 2** (page 68)
serves 6
Romaine Salad with Creamy Dressing
Thai Tomato Soup
Spaghetti Squash with Edamame-Cilantro
Pesto
Sweet Potato Pie

**Simple Entertaining
for Eight Menu** (page 75)
serves 8
Breaded chicken breasts
New Potatoes with Balsamic and Shallot Butter
Steamed green beans

Cocktail Supper Menu (page 85)
serves 12
Eggplant Caponata
Creamy Mushroom Phyllo Triangles
Wrinkled Potatoes with Black Caviar
Marinated Shrimp
Mixed Vegetable Salad
Cognac-Marinated Beef Tenderloin
Sandwiches with Horseradish Cream
Desserts
Coconut Biscotti
Spicy Meringue Kisses
Beverages
Classic Dry Martini
Old-Fashioned
Pineapple Margarita

**Casual Dinner
Party Menu** (page 108)
serves 6
Seared pepper-crusted filets
Roasted Fennel and Ricotta Gratins
with Tarragon
Steamed broccolini
Assorted fruit sorbets

Backyard Barbecue Menu (page 136)
serves 8
Grilled Corn with Mint Butter
Soy and lime-glazed
pork tenderloin
Chilled steamed broccoli with bottled
vinaigrette
Grilled garlic bread

Memorial Day Menu (page 143)
serves 4
Honey-Chipotle
Barbecue Chicken Sandwiches
Marinated Tomatoes
with Lemon and Summer Savory
Green Bean and New
Potato Salad
Frozen Iced Tea
Lemonade or beer

**Soup and Salad
Get-Together Menu** (page 191)
serves 8
Leek and Lima Bean
Soup with Bacon
Crunchy chopped salad
Pumpernickel toast
Lemon sorbet with mixed berries

Picnic Menu (page 265)
serves 4
Papaya-Carrot Slaw
Antipasto Chicken Sandwich
Chewy Chocolate-Coconut Macaroons
Ginger Limeade

Eight Is Enough Menu (page 275)
serves 8
Pork Tenderloin with Onions
and Dried Cranberries
Parmesan spinach
Couscous

**Friday Night Welcome
Menu** (page 287)
serves 8
Fresh Ginger Beer
Turkey Burgers with Goat Cheese
Grilled Pepper Relish
Cabbage and Celery Root Slaw
Oranges and Raspberries with Lavender
Honey and Yogurt

**Saturday Evening
Supper Menu**
(page 289)
serves 8
Striped Bass with Fennel
over Sautéed Spinach
Mixed Bean-Cherry
Tomato Salad
with Basil Vinaigrette
Corn Pudding
Plum Upside-Down Cake

**Veni, Vidi, Vegetarian
Menu** (page 336)
serves 6
Polenta Lasagna
Salad with lemon, garlic, and
Parmesan vinaigrette
Breadsticks

Game-Day Menu (page 345)
serves 8
Grilled Pork Tenderloin Sandwiches
Braised Cranberry-Barbecue Beef
Sandwiches
Roasted Potato Salad
Tabbouleh Salad
Molasses Cookies

Open House Menu (page 406)
serves 8
Vanilla-Scented Mulled Cider
Pumpkin Hummus
Smoked Ham Soup
with White Beans
Mini Corn Muffins with
Currants
Eggnog and Dried Fruit
Bread Pudding

Entertaining Menu (page 454)
serves 8
Peppercorn-Crusted Pork Tenderloin with
Soy-Caramel Sauce
Asian vegetable stir-fry
Jasmine rice with
green onions

Hearty Winter Menu (page 455)
serves 8
Carbonnade à la Flamande
Egg noodles
Angel food cake with hazelnut
chocolate sauce

Special Occasions

Easter Menu (page 74)
serves 8
French-Style Stuffed Eggs
or
Fava Bean Bruschetta
Salmon with Fresh Sorrel Sauce
New Potatoes with Balsamic
and Shallot Butter
or
Spring Risotto
Fresh Peas with Mint
Greek Easter Bread
Chocolate Pots de Crème
or
Strawberry Shortcake Jelly Roll
Sparkling wine and ginger ale

Outdoor Dining Menu (page 101)
serves 4
Pasta with Caramelized Onion Trio,
Arugula, and Mozzarella
Baby Artichokes with Creamy
Horseradish-Dill Dip
Flatbread with Pancetta and Asparagus
Meyer Lemon and Rosemary Brûlées
Pinot grigio or other crisp
white wine

**Romantic Island
Dinner Menu** (page 149)
serves 2
Crab Cocktail with Parmesan Chips
Bistro Bouillabaisse or
"Floribbean" Grouper with
Red Pepper-Papaya Jam
Baby Spinach Salad with
Warm Citrus-Bacon Vinaigrette
Baguette with Homemade Aïoli
Berry-Filled Cinnamon Crepes

Dinner for Two Menu (page 150)
serves 2
"Floribbean" Grouper with
Red Pepper-Papaya Jam
Rice pilaf with green onions
Steamed asparagus

**Summer Steak House
Dinner Menu** (page 195)
serves 6
Spinach and Parmesan
Fallen Soufflé
Potato-artichoke salad
Grilled beef tenderloin steaks

**End-of-Summer Beach
Party Menu** (page 290)
serves 10
Appetizers
Tomato and Parmesan Focaccia with
Caramelized Onions
Smoky Shrimp and Avocado Seviche
Entrées
California Burgers
Cumin-Crusted Pork Soft Tacos
Tex-Mex Pasta Salad
(kids' option)
Sides
End-of-Summer Tomato Salad
Roasted Asparagus with Orange
Vinaigrette
Tuscan White Beans
Desserts
Strawberry-Topped Pavlovas with
Honey-Balsamic Sauce
Lemon-Blueberry Bundt Cake

Holiday Dinner Menu (page 406)
serves 8
Pork Tenderloin with Dried Apricot and
Onion Marmalade
Carrot-Coriander Purée
Seasoned Basmati Rice
White Cheddar and Black Pepper Biscuits
Steamed broccoli
Persimmon Cake

Thanksgiving Feast Menu (page 406)
serves 12
Roasted Beet, Avocado, and
Watercress Salad
Parmesan-Sage Roast Turkey with Sage Gravy
Camembert Mashed Potatoes
Sourdough Stuffing with
Pears and Sausage
Oven-Roasted Green Beans
Flaky Dinner Rolls
Cranberry, Cherry, and Walnut Chutney
Cinnamon Streusel-Topped Pumpkin Pie

Dinner Party Menu (page 406)
serves 6
Roasted Cauliflower Soup
Green salad
Braised Lamb Shanks with
Rosemary Polenta
Baguette
Dark Chocolate Orange Cake

Cocktail Party Menu (page 406)
serves 12
Winter-Spiced Red Wine Sangría
Yogurt Cheese Torte
Baba Ghanoush with
Red Pepper Swirl
Smoked Trout with Apple-Horseradish
Cream on Potato Pancakes
Assorted cheeses and crackers
Italian Anise Cookies

Dessert Buffet Menu (page 408)
serves 12
Popcorn Brittle
Brownie Bourbon Balls
Chocolate Gingersnap Cookies
Chocolate-Speckled Toffee
Key Lime Coconut Snowballs
Bittersweet Chocolate Meringues
Goat Cheese and Chocolate-Stuffed Dates
Assorted beverages

**An Ornamental Supper
Menu** (page 417)
serves 8
Rossini Bellini
Wild Mushroom and Beef Stew
Asiago-Black Pepper Drop Biscuits
Double-Chocolate
Meringue Cookies

**New Year's Eve Buffet
Menu** (page 422)
serves 12
Cherry Chutney Cheese Torte
Salmon Skewers with
Romesco Sauce
Curried Chicken Turnovers
Creamy Corn and Chorizo-Stuffed
Mushrooms
Roast Pork Sandwiches
Hot Artichoke Dip
Pear Gorgonzola Butter
Sweet-and-Sour Red Onions
Chocolate Fondue
Champagne or other
sparkling wine

Hot off the Grill

**Fourth of July
Cookout Menu** (page 224)
serves 8
Grilled Flatbreads with
Tomatoes and Basil
Orzo, Corn, and Roasted
Bell Pepper Salad
Spicy Lamb Kebabs
Polenta Cake with
Late-Summer Berries
Beer or iced tea

Get Grilling Menu (page 253)
serves 6
Pesto turkey tenderloins
Pasta salad with cherry
tomatoes and kalamata olives
Grilled asparagus spears

Vegetarian

Meatless Menu (page 14)
serves 6
Yang Chow Fried Rice
Sesame-soy snow peas
Orange slices

Of All the Crust Menu 1 (page 222)
serves 6
Summer Squash Chowder
Spinach and Gruyère Tart
in a Three-Pepper Crust
Tossed Greens and Beets
with Pistachio Dressing
Strawberries with
Crunchy Almond Topping

Of All the Crust Menu 2 (page 224)
serves 6
Summer Squash Chowder
Roasted Fresh Corn, Poblano,
and Cheddar Pizza
Green Beans with Lemon and Garlic
Fresh Orange Sorbet with
Bittersweet Chocolate

Hearty Dinner Menu (page 255)
serves 4
Creamy Truffle-Scented
White Bean Soup
Fried Green Tomato Salad with
Warm Corn Salsa

Summertime Duo Menu (page 255)
serves 4
Southwestern Falafel with
Avocado Spread
Chickpea and
Hearts of Palm Salad

**Get-Together with Friends
Menu** (page 256)
serves 4
Summer Squash and Pasta Soup
Green Salad with Apples and
Maple-Walnut Dressing
Feta-Basil Sandwiches

**Hot-and-Cold Combo
Menu** (page 257)
serves 4
Asian Cucumber Soup
Monterey Jack and
Jalapeño Sandwiches

**Meatless Thanksgiving
Menu** (page 364)
serves 8
Roasted Pepper and Zucchini Crostini
Beet and Fennel Soup
Butternut-Cheese Pie
Green Beans with Roasted Tomatoes
and Cumin
Parmesan-Buttermilk Biscuits
Caramel, Orange, and Date Sundaes with
Pistachio Brittle
or
Baked Pears with Cranberry-Ginger
Filling and Cider Sauce

Global Kitchen

**Asian Sandwich Night
Menu** (page 119)
serves 4
Asian Catfish Wraps
Sweet-spicy won ton chips
Steamed edamame pods

Asian Vegetarian Menu (page 137)
serves 4
Hot and Sour Soup
Tofu with Red Peppers and
Black Bean Paste
Ginger Fried Rice
Snow Peas with Ginger
Mango sorbet
Jasmine tea or Chinese beer

Try New Things Menu (page 193)
serves 4
Spicy Passion Fruit-
Glazed Shrimp
Jasmine rice pilaf with pistachios
Sautéed yellow squash and red bell peppers

**Scandinavian Tastes
Menu** (page 218)
serves 4
Smoked Salmon with
Mustard and Dill
Creamy cucumber salad
Roasted potato wedges

Tex-Mex Dinner Menu (page 221)
serves 4
Spicy Chicken with Poblano
Peppers and Cheese
Tossed salad with fruit
Chips and salsa

Your Lucky Number Menu 6 (page 230)
serves 6
Five-Spice Pork Lo Mein
Sautéed snow peas
and carrot coins
Jasmine tea

Spanish Nights Menu (page 237)
serves 6
Asparagus Salad with
Piquillo Peppers and Capers
or
Shrimp-Filled Piquillo Peppers
in Sherry Vinaigrette
or
Moorish-Style Salad with
Cumin and Smoked Paprika
or
Steamed Mussels with Lemon, Onion, and
Wine
Chicken with White Wine, Grape Juice,
and Cilantro
or
Dried Plum-Stuffed Pork Loin in Sweet
Sherry Sauce
Baked Rice
Orange Yogurt Cake
or
Spiced Peaches in Crisp Phyllo Pastry
Spanish wine

**Southeast Asian
Supper Menu** (page 244)
serves 4
Pork Strips with Peanut Sauce
and Rice Noodles
Sugar snap pea and carrot sauté
Coconut sorbet

Asian in an Instant Menu (page 285)
serves 4
Seared Sea Scallops on Asian Slaw
Noodle and vegetable toss
Jasmine tea

Indian Inspiration Menu (page 312)
serves 4
Cumin Potatoes
Curried carrot and cauliflower
Grilled lamb loin chops
Flatbreads and mango chutney

A Taste of the Middle East Menu
(page 346)
serves 7
Tabbouleh Salad
Beef and veggie kebabs
Pita bread

Flavor Fiesta Menu (page 449)
serves 6
Chipotle Meat Loaf
Pineapple-pepper salsa
Whipped sweet potatoes

Recipe Title Index

*An alphabetical listing of every recipe title that appeared
in the magazine in 2005. See page 479 for the General Recipe Index.*

Month-by-Month Index

A month-by-month listing of every food story with recipe titles that appeared in the magazine in 2005. See page 479 for the General Recipe Index.

General Recipe Index

*A listing by major ingredient and food category
for every recipe that appeared in the magazine in 2005.*

HOW TO USE IT AND WHY Glance at the end of any *Cooking Light* recipe, and you'll see how committed we are to helping you make the best of today's light cooking. With five chefs, two registered dietitians, four home economists, and a computer system that analyzes every ingredient we use, *Cooking Light* gives you authoritative dietary detail like no other magazine. We go to such lengths so you can see how our recipes fit into your healthful eating plan. If you're trying to lose weight, the calorie and fat figures will probably help most. But if you're keeping a close eye on the sodium, cholesterol, and saturated fat in your diet, we provide those numbers, too. And because many women don't get enough iron or calcium, we can also help there, as well. Finally, there's a fiber analysis for those of us who don't get enough roughage.

Here's a helpful guide to put our nutrition analysis numbers into perspective. Remember, one size doesn't fit all, so take your lifestyle, age, and circumstances into consideration when determining your nutrition needs. For example, women who are pregnant or breast-feeding need more protein, calories, and calcium. And men over 50 need 1,200mg of calcium daily, 200mg more than the amount recommended for younger men.

IN OUR NUTRITIONAL ANALYSIS, WE USE THESE ABBREVIATIONS:

sat	saturated fat	**CHOL**	cholesterol
mono	monounsaturated fat	**CALC**	calcium
poly	polyunsaturated fat	**g**	gram
CARB	carbohydrates	**mg**	milligram

Daily Nutrition Guide

	WOMEN AGES 25 TO 50	WOMEN OVER 50	MEN OVER 24
Calories	2,000	2,000 or less	2,700
Protein	50g	50g or less	63g
Fat	65g or less	65g or less	88g or less
Saturated Fat	20g or less	20g or less	27g or less
Carbohydrates	304g	304g	410g
Fiber	25g to 35g	25g to 35g	25g to 35g
Cholesterol	300mg or less	300mg or less	300mg or less
Iron	18mg	8mg	8mg
Sodium	2,300mg or less	1,500mg or less	2,300mg or less
Calcium	1,000mg	1,200mg	1,000mg

The nutritional values used in our calculations either come from The Food Processor, Version 7.5 (ESHA Research), or are provided by food manufacturers.

Contributing Recipe Developers

Bruce Aidells
Nava Atlas
Mary Corpening Barber
Melanie Barnard
Rick Bayless
Lisabelle Bell
Peter Berley
Monica Bhide
Mark Bittman
David Bonom
Julianna Grimes Bottcher
Brennan's Restaurant
Barbara Seelig Brown
Jennifer Brulé
Maureen Callahan
Viviana Carballo
Floyd Cardoz

Penelope Casas
Andrea Chesman
Judith Choate
Ying Chang Compestine
Maureen Clancy
Martha Condra
Lorrie Hulston Corvin
Isabel Cruz
Nancy Davidson
Cynthia DePersio
Traci Des Jardins
John des Rosiers
Dave DiResta
Paula Disbrowe
Earthbound Farm
Pat Earvolino
Linda Eckhardt
Didi Emmons

Scott Fagan
Judith Fertig
Allison Fishman
Shirley Fong-Torres
Brian Glover
Rozanne Gold
Sandra Gransenth
Jessica B. Harris
Tamar Haspel
Julie Hasson
Lia Huber
Nancy Hughes
Dani Jacobi
Bill Jamison
Cheryl Alters Jamison
Wendy Kalen
Elizabeth Karmel
Jeanne Thiel Kelley
Graham Kerr

John Kirkpatrick
Robin Kline
Aglaia Kremezi
Jean Kressy
Sarah Doyle Lacamoire
Rita LaReau
Barbara Lauterbach
Karen Levin
Alison Lewis
Judy Lockhart
Susan Loomis
Karen MacNeil
Donata Maggipinto
Domenica Marchetti
Gina Martinez
Jennifer Martinkus
Don Mauer
Dana McCauley

James McNair
Jackie Mills
Krista Ackerbloom Montgomery
Diane Morgan
Sean Murphy
Micol Negrin
Cynthia Nicholson
Geoff Norman
Greg Patent
Jean Patterson
Caprial Pence
Marge Perry
Jim Peterson
Michele Powers
David Rosengarten
Julie Sahni
Mark Scarbrough
Andrew Schloss

Steven A. Shaw
Marth Rose Shulman
Marcia Whyte Smart
Lisë Stern
Billy Strynkowski
Sur La Table
Elizabeth Taliaferro
Robin Vitetta-Miller
Lovoni Walker
Robyn Webb
Bruce Weinstein
Joanne Weir
Laura Werlin
Sarah Corpening Whiteford
Chuck Williams
Melissa B. Williams
Joy E. Zacharia
Lisa Zwirn